Jan van Leeuwen Anca Muscholl
David Peleg Jaroslav Pokorný
Bernhard Rumpe (Eds.)

SOFSEM 2010: Theory and Practice of Computer Science

36th Conference on Current Trends
in Theory and Practice of Computer Science
Špindlerův Mlýn, Czech Republic, January 23-29, 2010
Proceedings

Springer

Volume Editors

Jan van Leeuwen
Utrecht University
Department of Information and Computing Sciences
Padualaan 14, 3584 CH Utrecht, The Netherlands
E-mail: j.vanleeuwen@cs.uu.nl

Anca Muscholl
LaBRI, Université Bordeaux 1
351 cours de la Libréation, F-33405 Talence Cedex, France
E-mail: anca@labri.fr

David Peleg
Weizmann Institute
Faculty of Mathematics and Computer Science
Department of Computer Science & Applied Mathematics
Rehovot 76100, Israel
E-mail: david.peleg@weizmann.ac.il

Jaroslav Pokorný
Charles University
Department of Software Engineering
Faculty of Mathematics and Physics
Malostranské nám. 25, 11800 Prague 1, Czech Republic
E-mail: pokorny@ksi.mff.cuni.cz

Bernhard Rumpe
RWTH Aachen University
Software Engineering
Department of Computer Science 3
Ahornstraße 55, D-52074 Aachen, Germany
E-mail: rumpe@se-rwth.de

Library of Congress Control Number: 2009941301

CR Subject Classification (1998): D.2, D.3, H.2, H.2.5, H.2.7, H.2.8, K.8.1

LNCS Sublibrary: SL 1 – Theoretical Computer Science and General Issues

ISSN 0302-9743
ISBN 978-3-642-11265-2 Springer Berlin Heidelberg New York

springer.com

Typesetting: Camera-ready by author, data conversion by Scientific Publishing Services, Chennai, India
Printed on acid-free paper SPIN: 12827305 06/3180 5 4 3 2 1 0

Preface

This volume contains the *invited* and *contributed* papers selected for presentation at SOFSEM 2010, the 36th Conference on Current Trends in Theory and Practice of Computer Science, held January 23–29, 2010 in the Hotel Bedřichov, Špindlerův Mlýn, of the Krkonoše Mountains of the Czech Republic.

SOFSEM (originally: SOFtware SEMinar) is devoted to leading research, and fosters the cooperation among researchers and professionals from academia and industry in all areas of computer science. As a well-established and fully international conference, SOFSEM maintains the best of its original Winter School aspects, such as a high number of invited talks and an in-depth coverage of novel research results in selected areas within computer science. SOFSEM 2010 was organized around the following four tracks:

- *Foundations of Computer Science* (Chairs: David Peleg, Anca Muscholl)
- *Principles of Software Construction* (Chair: Bernhard Rumpe)
- *Data, Knowledge, and Intelligent Systems* (Chair: Jaroslav Pokorný)
- *Web Science* (Chair: Jan van Leeuwen)

With these tracks, SOFSEM 2010 covered the latest advances in research, both theoretical and applied, in leading areas of computer science. The SOFSEM 2010 Program Committee consisted of 78 international experts from 20 different countries, representing the track areas with outstanding expertise.

An integral part of SOFSEM 2010 was the traditional *Student Research Forum* (SRF, Chair: Mária Bieliková), organized with the aim to present student projects in the theory and practice of computer science and to give students feedback on both the originality of their scientific results and on their work in progress. The papers presented at the Student Research Forum were published in the local proceedings.

In response to the call for papers, SOFSEM 2010 received 134 submissions: 76 submissions in Foundations, and 58 in the applied computing tracks. After a detailed reviewing process with four reviewers per paper, a careful electronic selection procedure (using EasyChair) was carried out within each track between September 3 and September 14, 2009. A total of 53 papers were selected for presentation at SOFSEM 2010, following strict criteria of quality and originality: 32 papers in Foundations, 21 in the other tracks.

Of the 53 accepted papers, 15 papers were submitted as student papers. In fact, two student papers, namely, the paper by David Duris and the one by Elisa Pappalardo and Simone Faro, received the highest evaluations of all submissions in their respective tracks.

Furthermore, 12 student papers were selected for the SOFSEM 2010 Student Research Forum, based on the recommendations of the Chair of the SRF, and with the approval of the Track Chairs.

As editors of these proceedings, we are grateful to everyone who contributed to the scientific program of the conference, especially the invited speakers and all authors of contributed papers. We thank all authors for their prompt responses to our editorial requests.

SOFSEM 2010 was the result of a considerable effort by many people. We would like to express our special thanks to:

- The SOFSEM 2010 Program Committees of the four tracks and all additional referees for their precise and detailed reviewing of the submissions
- Jan Oliver Ringert, of the Software Engineering group in the Department of Computer Science at RWTH Aachen University, for his outstanding assistance of the PC for Software Construction
- Mária Bieliková, of the Slovak University of Technology in Bratislava, for her expert preparation and handling of the Student Research Forum
- The SOFSEM Steering Committee headed by Július Štuller, of the Institute of Computer Science (ICS) in Prague, for its excellent guidance and support throughout the preparation of the conference
- Springer-Verlag's LNCS series, for its great support of the SOFSEM conferences.

We are also greatly indebted to:

- The SOFSEM 2010 Organizing Committee consisting of: Roman Špánek (chair), Filip Zavoral, Pavel Tyl, Martin Řimnáč, and Hanka Bílková, for the outstanding support and excellent preparation of all aspects of the conference
- The Action M Agency, in particular Milena Zeithamlová and Pavla Kozáková, for the excellent local arrangements of SOFSEM 2010.

We especially thank Roman Špánek, of the Institute of Computer Science (ICS) in Prague, for his excellent assistance in all duties and responsibilities of the Track Chairs and the General Chair.

Finally, we are very grateful for the financial support of our sponsors, which enabled us to compose a high-quality program of invited speakers and helped us to keep the student fees low. We thank the Institute of Computer Science (ICS) of the Academy of Sciences of the Czech Republic in Prague for its invaluable support of all aspects of SOFSEM 2010.

October 2009

Jan van Leeuwen
Anca Muscholl
David Peleg
Jaroslav Pokorný
Bernhard Rumpe

Organization

SOFSEM 2010 was organized by:

Institute of Computer Science, Academy of Sciences of the Czech Republic, Prague, Czech Republic
Charles University, Faculty of Mathematics and Physics, Prague, Czech Republic
Action M Agency, Prague, Czech Republic

Steering Committee

Július Štuller (Chair)	Institute of Computer Science, Prague, Czech Republic
Mária Bieliková	Slovak University of Technology in Bratislava, Slovak Republic
Bernadette Charron-Bost	Ecole Polytechnique, France
Keith G. Jeffery	CLRC RAL, Chilton, Didcot, Oxon, UK
Antonín Kučera	Masaryk University, Brno, Czech Republic
Jan van Leeuwen	Utrecht University, The Netherlands
Branislav Rovan	Comenius University, Bratislava, Slovak Republic
Petr Tůma	Charles University in Prague, Czech Republic

Program Chairs

Jan van Leeuwen (General Chair)	Utrecht University, The Netherlands
Anca Muscholl	University of Bordeaux, France
David Peleg	Weizmann Institute of Science, Israel
Jaroslav Pokorný	Charles University, Prague, Czech Republic
Bernhard Rumpe	RWTH Aachen University, Germany

Program Committee

Judit Bar-Ilan	Ramat Gan, Israel
Petr Berka	Prague, Czech Republic
Jean Bezivin	Nantes, France
Gregor von Bochmann	Ottawa, Canada
Susanne Boll	Oldenburg, Germany
Manfred Broy	München, Germany
Liliane S. Cabral	Milton Keynes, UK

Barbara Catania	Genova, Italy
Richard Chbeir	Dijon, France
Vassilis Christophides	Heraklion, Greece
Marek Chrobak	Riverside, USA
Philippe Darondeau	Rennes, France
Josep Diaz	Barcelona, Spain
Peter Dolog	Aalborg, Denmark
Guozhu Dong	Dayton, USA
Gregor Engels	Paderborn, Germany
Michal Feldman	Jerusalem, Israel
Piero Fraternali	Milan, Italy
Tim Furche	Munich, Germany
Johann Gamper	Bolzano, Italy
Leszek Gasieniec	Liverpool, UK
Lluis Godo	Bellaterra, Spain
Massimiliano Goldwurm	Milan, Italy
Hele-Mai Haav	Tallinn, Estonia
Lynda Hardman	Amsterdam, The Netherlands
Martin Hepp	Munich, Germany
Holger Hermanns	Aachen, Germany
Geert-Jan Houben	Delft, The Netherlands
Michaela Huhn	Braunschweig, Germany
Hannu Jaakkola	Pori, Finland
Gerti Kappel	Vienna, Austria
Lefteris Kirousis	Patras, Greece
Marc van Kreveld	Utrecht, The Netherlands
Ingolf Krüger	San Diego, USA
Fabian Kuhn	MIT Cambridge, USA
Dietrich Kuske	Leipzig, Germany
Sergei Kuznetcov	Moscow, Russia
Horst Lichter	Aachen, Germany
Karl J. Lieberherr	Zurich, Switzerland
Johan Lilius	Turku, Finland
Rainer Manthey	Bonn, Germany
Alberto Marchetti-Spaccamela	Rome, Italy
Bertrand Meyer	Zurich, Switzerland
Tadeusz Morzy	Poznan, Poland
Madhavan Mukund	Chennai, India
Andrzej Murawski	Oxford, UK
Pavol Navrat	Bratislava, Slovakia
Richard Paige	Heslington, UK
Michal Pěchouček	Prague, Czech Republic

Alberto Pettorossi	Rome, Italy
Klaus Pohl	Duisburg-Essen, Germany
Ivan Porres	Turku, Finland
Christian Prehofer	Helsinki, Finland
Andreas Rausch	Clausthal, Germany
Ralf Reussner	Karlsruhe, Germany
Peter Revesz	Lincoln, USA
Harald Sack	Potsdam, Germany
Philippe Schnoebelen	Paris, France
Helmut Seidl	Munich, Germany
Olivier Serre	Paris, France
Hadas Shachnai	Haifa, Israel
Pawel Sobocinski	Southampton, UK
Friedrich Steimann	Hagen, Germany
Umberto Straccia	Pisa, Italy
Howard Straubing	Boston, USA
Vojtěch Svátek	Prague, Czech Republic
Bernhard Thalheim	Kiel, Germany
Athena Vakali	Thessaloniki, Greece
Laurent Viennot	Inria Paris, France
Tomáš Vojnar	Brno, Czech Republic
Peter Vojtáš	Prague, Czech Republic
Erik Wilde	Berkeley, USA
Ronald de Wolf	Amsterdam, The Netherlands

Organizing Committee

Roman Špánek, *Chair*	Institute of Computer Science, Prague, Czech Republic
Hana Bílková	Institute of Computer Science, Prague, Czech Republic
Pavla Kozáková	Action M Agency, Prague, Czech Republic
Martin Řimnáč	Institute of Computer Science, Prague, Czech Republic
Július Štuller	Institute of Computer Science, Prague, Czech Republic
Pavel Tyl	Institute of Computer Science, Prague, Czech Republic
Filip Zavoral	Charles University in Prague, Czech Republic
Milena Zeithamlová	Action M Agency, Prague, Czech Republic

Sponsors

Supported by

ČSKI – Czech Society for Cybernetics and Informatics

SSCS – Slovak Society for Computer Science

ERCIM – The European Research Consortium for Informatics and Mathematics

Table of Contents

Invited Talks

Regular Papers

Forcing Monotonicity in Parameterized Verification: From Multisets to Words

Parosh Aziz Abdulla

Uppsala University
Department of Information Technology
P.O. Box 337
751 05 Uppsala, Sweden
http://user.it.uu.se/~parosh/

Abstract. We present a tutorial on verification of safety properties for parameterized systems. Such a system consists of an arbitrary number of processes; the aim is to prove correctness of the system regardless of the number of processes inside the system. First, we consider a class of parameterized systems whose behaviours can be captured exactly as Petri nets using *counter abstraction*. This allows analysis using the framework of *monotonic* transition systems introduced in [1]. Then, we consider parameterized systems for which there is no natural ordering which allows monotonicity. We describe the method of *monotonic abstraction* which provides an over-approximation of the transition system. We consider both systems where the over-approximation gives rise to reset Petri nets, and systems where the abstract transition relation is a set of rewriting rules on words over a finite alphabet.

1 Introduction

One of the widely adopted frameworks in the context of infinite-state verification is based on the concept of *monotonic systems wrt. a well-quasi ordering* [1], which provides a scheme for proving the termination of backward reachability analysis. The method was first used for the verification of lossy channel systems [6] and then extended to a general methodology in [1]. Since its introduction in [1], the framework has been extended and used for the design of verification algorithms for various models including Petri nets, cache protocols, timed Petri nets, broadcast protocols, etc. (see, e.g., [2,11,9,10,7]). The idea is to define, for a given class of models, a preorder $\preceq$ on the configuration space such that (1) $\preceq$ is a simulation relation on the considered models, and (2) $\preceq$ is a well-quasi ordering (wqo for short). If such a preorder can be defined, then it can be proved that the reachability problem of an upward-closed set of configurations (w.r.t. $\preceq$) is decidable. Indeed, (1) monotonicity implies that for any upward-closed set, the set of its predecessors is an upward-closed set, and (2) the fact that $\preceq$ is a wqo implies that every upward-closed set can be characterized by a *finite* set of minimal elements. Therefore, starting from an upward-closed set of configurations U, the iterative computation of the backward reachable configurations from U necessarily terminates since only a finite number of steps are needed to capture all

J. van Leeuwen et al. (Eds.): SOFSEM 2010, LNCS 5901, pp. 1–15, 2010.

minimal elements of the set of predecessors of U. Obviously, this requires that upward-closed sets can be effectively represented and manipulated (i.e., there are procedures for, e.g., computing immediate predecessors and unions, and for checking entailment). This general scheme can be applied for the verification of safety properties since this problem can be reduced to checking the reachability of a set of bad configurations which is typically an upward-closed set w.r.t. the considered preorder. (For instance, mutual exclusion is violated as soon as there are (at least) two processes in the critical section.)

Unfortunately, many systems do not fit into this framework, in the sense that there is no nontrivial (useful) wqo for which these systems are monotonic. Nevertheless, a natural approach to overcome this problem is *monotonic abstraction*. Given a preorder $\preceq$, we consider an abstract semantics which *forces* monotonicity for the considered system. In this paper, we introduce the basic ideas through a sequence of simple *parameterized systems*. A parameterized system consists of an arbitrary number of processes. Consequently, it represents an infinite family of systems, namely one for each size of the system. We are interested in *parameterized verification*, i.e., verifying correctness regardless of the number of processes inside the system. The term *parameterized* refers to the fact that the size of the system is (implicitly) a parameter of the verification problem. Examples of parameterized systems include mutual exclusion algorithms, bus protocols, telecommunication protocols, and cache coherence protocols. Parametrized systems do not quite fit into the wqo framework since they induce transition relations which are not monotonic. The main obstacle is that they usually use universal global conditions in which a process may need to check the states of all the other processes inside the system. Universal conditions are inherently non-monotonic, since having larger configurations may lead to the violation of the universal condition. In the case of parametrized systems, monotonic abstraction amounts to killing (deleting) all the processes inside the configuration which violate the universal condition. The abstract transition relation is an over-approximation of the original one. Hence, proving a safety property in the abstract system implies that the property also holds in the original system. For a more technical description of the method and its application to non-trivial examples see, e.g., [4,3,13,5].

2 Parameterized Systems

In this section, we introduce the concept of *parameterized systems*. For this purpose, we use a simple example of a protocol which implements mutual exclusion among an arbitrary number of processes. A *parameterized system* consists of an arbitrary number of components each of which is a finite-state process. In our example, access to the critical section is controlled by a global lock. The system is supposed to satisfy *mutual exclusion*, i.e., at most one process may have access to the global resource at any given time. In each step in the execution of a parameterized system, one process, called the *active* process performs a *local transition* changing its state. The rest of the processes, called the *passive* processes, do not

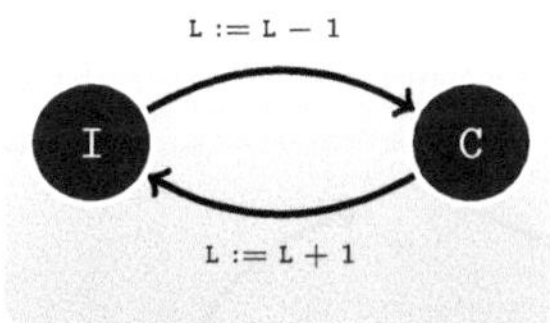

Fig. 1. One process in the simple protocol

Fig. 2. A parameterized system consisting of an arbitrary number of processes

change states. A process (depicted in Figure 1) has two local states, namely I where the process is idle and C where the process is in its critical section. The resource is guarded by a lock L whose value is equal to 1 when the lock is free and 0 otherwise. When a process wants to access the critical section, it must first acquire the lock. This can be done only if no other process has already acquired the lock. Concretely, when the process moves from I to C it checks whether the lock is free, makes the move and at the same time acquires the lock (makes it busy). Acquiring the lock is encoded by decrementing the value of the lock (the value of the lock is not allowed to become negative, and hence the process is blocked in case $\mathtt{L} = 0$). From the critical section, the process eventually releases the lock moving back to the idle state I. We require that the system should never reach a configuration where two or more processes are in the state C. Recall that we are interested in *parameterized verification*, i.e., verifying that this property is satisfied regardless of the number of competing processes.

3 Counter Abstraction

In this section, we describe how to capture the behaviour of certain classes of parameterized systems by Petri nets through the use of *counter abstraction.*

3.1 Petri Nets

A Petri net $\mathcal{N}$ is a tuple (P, T, F), where P is a finite set of *places*, T is a finite set of *transitions*, and $F \subseteq (P \times T) \cup (T \times P)$ is the *flow relation.* If $(p, t) \in F$ then p is said to be an *input* place of t; and if $(t, p) \in F$ then p is said to be an *output* place of t. We use $In\,(t) := \{p|\ (p, t) \in F\}$ and $Out\,(t) := \{p|\ (t, p) \in F\}$ to denote the sets of input places and output places of t respectively.

Figure 3 shows an example of a Petri net with three places (drawn as circles), namely L, W, and C; and two transitions (drawn as rectangles), namely t_1 and t_2. The flow relation is represented by edges from places to transitions, and from transitions to places. For instance, the flow relation in the example includes the pairs $(\mathtt{L}, t_1)$ and $(t_2, \mathtt{W})$, i.e., L is an input place of t_1, and W is an output place of t_2.

The transition system induced by a Petri net is defined by the set of *configurations* together with the *transition relation* defined on them. A *configuration* c

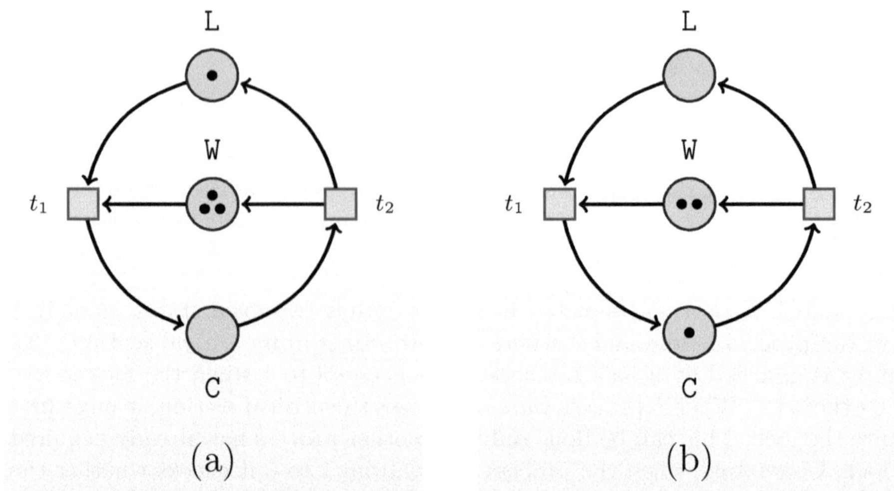

Fig. 3. (a) A simple Petri net. (b) The result of firing t_1.

of a Petri net[1] is a multiset over P. The configuration c defines the number of *tokens* in each place. Figure 3 (a) shows a configuration where there is one token in place L, three tokens in place W, and no token in place C. The configuration corresponds to the multiset $[\mathtt{L}, \mathtt{W}^3]$.

The operational semantics of a Petri net is defined through the notion of *firing* transitions. This gives a transition relation on the set of configurations. More precisely, when a transition t is fired, then a token is removed from each input place, and a token is added to each output place of t. The transition is fired only if each input place has at least one token. Formally, we write $c_1 \longrightarrow c_2$ to denote that there is a transition $t \in T$ such that $c_1 \geq In(t)$ and $c_2 = c_1 - In(t) + Out(t)$ (where $+$ and $-$ are the usual operations defined on multisets). For sets C_1, C_2 of configurations, we write $C_1 \longrightarrow C_2$ to denote that $c_1 \longrightarrow c_2$ for some $c_1 \in C_1$ and $c_2 \in C_2$. We define $\stackrel{*}{\longrightarrow}$ to the reflexive transitive closure of $\longrightarrow$.

3.2 Counter Abstraction

We can use *counter abstraction* to capture the behaviour of the parameterized version of the simple mutual exclusion protocol described in Section 2 as a Petri net (shown in Figure 3). The idea is to *count* the number of processes in each given local state. More precisely, we devote a place in the Petri net for each process state in the protocol. The numbers of tokens in places I and C represent the number of processes in their idle states and critical sections respectively. Absence of tokens in L means that the lock is currently taken by some process. Each transition of the Petri net corresponds to one of the processes performing

[1] A configuration in a Petri net is often called a *marking* in the literature.

a local transition: the transition t_1 corresponds to a process moving from I to C (thus decreasing the number of processes in the state I, increasing the number of processes in C, and taking the lock); and the transition t_2 corresponds to a process moving from C to I (thus increasing the number of processes in the state I, decreasing the number of processes in C, and releasing the lock).

3.3 Safety Properties

We are interested in checking a safety property for the Petri net in Figure 3. In a safety property, we want to show that "nothing bad happens" during the execution of the system. Typically, we define a set *Bad* of configurations, i.e., configurations which we do not want to occur during the execution of the system. In this particular example, we are interested in proving mutual exclusion. The set *Bad* contains those configurations that violate mutual exclusion, i.e., configurations in which at least two processes are in their critical sections. These configurations are of the form $\left[\mathtt{L}^k, \mathtt{W}^m, C^n\right]$ where $n \geq 2$. The set C_{init} of *initial configurations* are those where all processes are idle. Examples of initial configurations are $\left[\mathtt{I}^2\right]$ and $\left[\mathtt{I}^5\right]$, corresponding to instances of the system with two and five processes respectively. Notice that there are infinitely many initial configurations (one for each possible size of the system). Checking the safety property can be carried out by checking whether we can fire a sequence of transitions taking us from an initial configuration to a bad configuration, i.e., we check whether the set *Bad* is reachable (i.e., whether $C_{init} \xrightarrow{*} Bad$).

3.4 Ordering

We define the ordering $\leq$ on configurations to be the standard one on multisets, i.e., $c_1 \leq c_2$ if $c_1(p) \leq c_2(p)$ for each $p \in P$. According to Dickson's lemma [8], the relation $\leq$ is a *well quasi-ordering* (*wqo* for short), i.e., for each infinite sequence $c_0, c_1, c_2, \ldots$ of configurations there are i and j such that $i < j$ and $c_i \leq c_j$.

We will work with sets of configurations which are upward closed with respect to $\leq$. For a configuration c, we define $\widehat{c}$ to be the set of configurations which are larger than c wrt. $\leq$, i.e., $\widehat{c} = \{c' |\ c \leq c'\}$. For a set C, we define $\widehat{C} := \cup_{c \in C} \widehat{c}$. For an upward closed set U, we define the *generator* of U to be the set of minimal elements of U, i.e., the set G such that

- $\widehat{G} = U$, i.e., U can be generated from G by taking the upward closure of G wrt. $\leq$.
- $a \leq b$ implies $a = b$ for all $a, b \in G$. In other words, the set G is canonical in the sense that all its elements are incomparable wrt. $\leq$.

We use $gen(U)$ to denote the set G. Upward closed sets are interesting in our setting for two reasons:

- The set $gen(U)$ is finite; otherwise we would have an infinite set of incomparable elements which contradicts the wqo property. This means that each upward closed set U can be characterized by a *finite* set of configurations, namely its generator $gen(U)$. The set $gen(U) = \{a_1, \ldots, a_n\}$ is a finite characterization of U in the sense that $U = \widehat{a_1} \cup \cdots \cup \widehat{a_n}$.

– Sets of bad configurations are almost always upward closed. For instance, in our example, whenever a configuration contains two processes in their critical sections then any larger configuration will also contain (at least) two processes in their critical sections, so the set *Bad* is upward closed. In this manner, checking the safety property amounts to deciding reachability of an upward closed set.

3.5 Monotonicity

Consider the ordering $\leq$ on the configurations of the Petri net. It follows from the definitions that the transition relation $\longrightarrow$ is *monotonic* wrt. $\leq$. In other words, given configurations c_1, c_2, and c_3, if $c_1 \longrightarrow c_2$ and $c_1 \leq c_3$, then there is a configuration c_4 such that $c_2 \leq c_4$ and $c_3 \longrightarrow c_4$.

3.6 Computing Predecessors

Consider an upward closed set U of configurations. By monotonicity it follows that the set $\{c|\ c \longrightarrow U\}$ is upward closed. For a configuration c and a transition t, we define $Pre(t)(c)$ to be the set $\{c_1, \ldots, c_n\}$ which is the generator of the set of configurations from which we can reach $\widehat{c}$ through a single firing of t.

3.7 Backward Reachability Analysis

As mentioned above, we are interested in checking whether it is the case that the set *Bad* of configurations is reachable. The safety property is violated iff the question has a positive answer. The algorithm, illustrated in Figure 4, starts from the set of bad configurations, and tries to find a path backwards through the transition relation to the set of initial configurations. The algorithm operates on upward closed sets of configurations. An upward closed set is symbolically represented by a finite set of configurations, namely the members of its generator. In the above example, the set $gen\,(Bad)$ is the singleton $\left\{\left[\mathtt{C}^2\right]\right\}$. Therefore, the algorithm starts from the configuration $c_0 = \left[\mathtt{C}^2\right]$, and repeatedly computes predecessors through applying the function *Pre*. From the configuration c_0, we go backwards and derive the generator of the set of configurations from which we can fire a transition and reach a configuration in $Bad = \widehat{c_0}$. Transition t_1 gives the configuration $c_1 = [\mathtt{L}, \mathtt{W}, \mathtt{C}]$, since $\widehat{c_1}$ contains exactly those configurations from which we can fire t_1 and reach a configuration in $\widehat{c_0}$. Analogously, transition t_2 gives the configuration $c_2 = \left[\mathtt{C}^3\right]$, since $\widehat{c_2}$ contains exactly those configurations from which we can fire t_2 and reach a configuration in $\widehat{c_0}$. Since $c_0 \leq c_2$, it follows that $\widehat{c_2} \subseteq \widehat{c_0}$. In such a case, we say that c_2 is *subsumed* by c_0. Since $\widehat{c_2} \subseteq \widehat{c_0}$, we can discard c_2 safely from the analysis without the loss of any information. Now, we repeat the procedure on c_1, and obtain the configurations $c_3 = \left[\mathtt{L}^2, \mathtt{W}^2\right]$ (via t_1), and $c_4 = \left[\mathtt{C}^2\right]$ (via t_2), where c_4 is subsumed by c_0. Finally, from c_3 we obtain the configurations $c_5 = \left[\mathtt{L}^3, \mathtt{W}^3\right]$ (via t_1), and $c_6 = [\mathtt{L}, \mathtt{W}, \mathtt{C}]$ (via t_2). The configurations c_5 and c_6 are subsumed by c_3 and c_1 respectively. The iteration terminates at this point since all the newly generated configurations

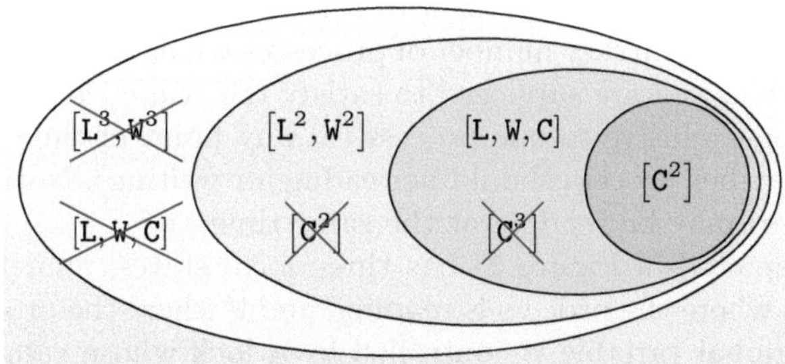

Fig. 4. Running the backward reachability algorithm on the example Petri net. Each ellipse contains the configurations generated during one iteration. The subsumed configurations are crossed over.

were subsumed by existing ones, and hence there are no more new configurations to consider. In fact, the set $B = \{[\mathtt{C}^2], [\mathtt{L}, \mathtt{W}, \mathtt{C}], [\mathtt{L}^2, \mathtt{W}^2]\}$ is the generator of the set of configurations from which we can reach a bad configuration. The three members in B are those configurations which are not discarded in the analysis (they were not subsumed by other configurations). To check whether *Bad* is reachable, we check the intersection $\widehat{B} \cap C_{init}$. Since the intersection is empty, we conclude that *Bad* is not reachable, and hence the safety property is satisfied by the system.

3.8 Sufficient Conditions

We summarize the properties needed in order to derive the above algorithm:

1. *Monotonicity.* This implies that the predecessor set of an upward closed set of configurations is upward closed.
2. $\preceq$ is a wqo. We need this property for two reasons: to represent upward closed sets by a finite set of configurations (a generator of the set); and to guarantee termination of the algorithm.
3. For each c, we can compute the (finite) set $gen(\{c' |\, c' \longrightarrow \widehat{c}\})$. In fact, $Pre(t)(c) = (c \ominus Out(t)) + In(t)$, where $\ominus$ rounds negative values up to 0 (i.e., $y \ominus x = 0$ if $x > y$ and $y \ominus x = y - x$ otherwise).
4. For each c, we can check whether there is a $c' \in C_{init}$ such that $c \preceq c'$. This is needed to check the emptiness of the intersection $\widehat{B} \cap C_{init}$.

4 Monotonic Abstraction

We consider parameterized systems, where the local transitions of a processes may be constrained by global conditions, i.e., the process may have to check the states of all the other processes before proceeding with the transition. To capture such conditions we need a more powerful model than standard Petri nets, namely Petri nets with *inhibitor arcs.* We introduce the concept of *monotonic abstraction* and describe how it transforms inhibitor arcs into *reset* arcs.

We consider a parametrized version of a simple reader-writer protocol. The system consists of an arbitrary number of processes which may read from or write to a global variable, and are supposed to satisfy the *reader-writer* property, i.e., writing should be exclusive to one process (at any point of time, if a process is writing, then no other process should be reading or writing). Notice that several different processes may be reading at the same time.

A process (depicted in Figure 5) has three local states, namely `I` where the process is idle, `R` where the process is reading, and `W` where the process is writing. Writing to the global variable is controlled by a lock whose value is equal to 1 when the lock is free and 0 otherwise. When a process wants to start reading, it checks whether the lock is free. If this is the case, the process moves from `I` to `R` without changing the value of the lock. From `R`, the process eventually moves back to `I`.

When a process wants to start writing, it checks whether there are other processes reading the global variable (encoded by the condition $\#\mathtt{R} = 0?$). It acquires the lock by decreasing the value of `L` by one. If the lock is not free, then $\mathtt{L} = 0$ and the transition is blocked. From `W`, the process eventually moves back to `I` releasing the lock (by increasing the value of `L` by one).

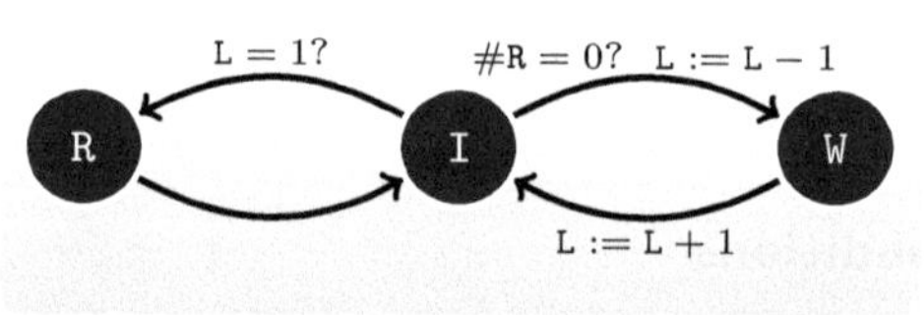

Fig. 5. One process in the reader-writer protocol

4.1 Petri Nets with Inhibitor Arcs

A Petri net with *inhibitor arcs* is a generalization of Petri nets in the sense that an arc form a place p to a transition t may be declared to be an *inhibitor*. In such a case, the transition t may only be fired from configurations in which p is empty (does not contain any tokens). For the arcs which are not inhibitors the standard rules for firing transitions in Petri nets hold.

Figure 6 shows an example of a Petri net with one inhibitor arc (represented by the arrow whose head is a filled circle) between `R` and t_3.

4.2 Counter Abstraction

In a similar manner to Section 3, we can capture the behaviour of the parameterized reader-writer protocol as a Petri net with inhibitor arcs (Figure 6). The numbers of tokens in places `I`, `R`, and `W` represent the number of processes in their idle, read, and write states respectively. Absence of tokens in `L` means that there is currently a process writing to the global variable. The transitions of

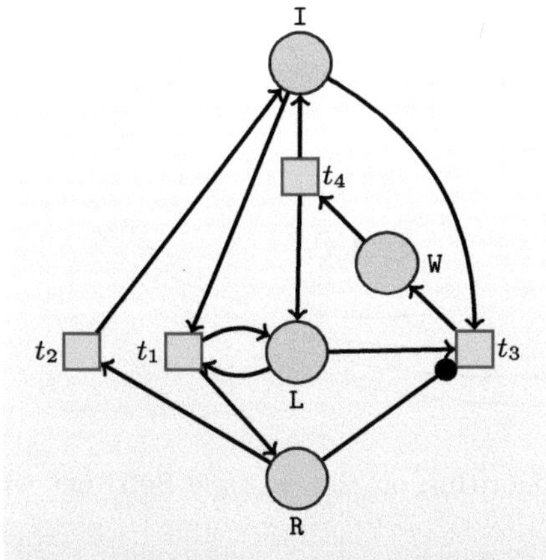

Fig. 6. A Petri net with one inhibitor arc

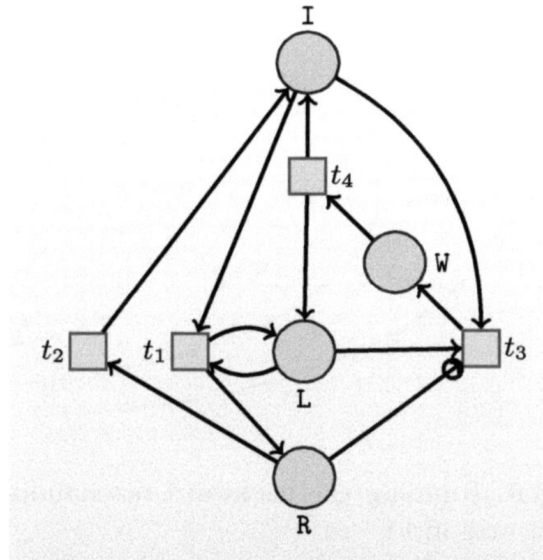

Fig. 7. A Petri net with one reset arc

the Petri net are interpreted as follows. The transition t_1 represents a process moving from I to R. The process checks the state of the lock but does not change its value (this is represented by the two arcs between the place L and t_1). The transition t_2 corresponds to a process moving back from R to I. The transition t_3 means that an idle process becomes a writer. Here, we need an inhibitor arc to encode the condition that there are no processes currently reading the variable. This is done by checking that place R is empty. Finally, transition t_4 represents a process leaving the W state and becoming idle again.

4.3 Forcing Monotonicity

A Petri net with inhibitor arcs is not monotonic. For instance, consider the configurations $c_1 = [\mathtt{L}, \mathtt{I}]$, $c_2 = [\mathtt{W}]$, and $c_3 = [\mathtt{L}, \mathtt{I}, \mathtt{R}]$. Then, we have $c_1 \leq c_3$ and $c_1 \longrightarrow c_2$ (by firing the transition t_3), but there is no c_4 such that $c_3 \longrightarrow c_4$ and $c_2 \leq c_4$. The inhibitor arc does not allow taking t_3 from c_3 since the place R is not empty. In fact, the only transitions enabled from c_3 are t_1 and t_2 leading to the configurations $[\mathtt{L}, \mathtt{R}^2]$ resp. $[\mathtt{L}, \mathtt{I}^2]$ (none of which is larger than $[\mathtt{W}]$).

That Petri nets with inhibitor arcs are not monotonic is not surprising given that they are Turing-powerful. We revert therefore to abstraction, where we compute an over-approximation which is monotonic. The only transitions which violate monotonicity are those with inhibitor arcs. In our abstraction, we change the semantics of the Petri net, by replacing inhibitor arcs with *reset arcs.* A reset arc does not disable the transition. Instead, the reset arc removes all the tokens from the input place thus making it empty. One important property of reset nets is that they are monotonic. Thus we generate an abstraction which is not exact (as in Section 3) but which nevertheless is monotonic.

The existence of tokens in R means that there are processes in the configuration which violate an enabling condition thus blocking the transition t_3. In other

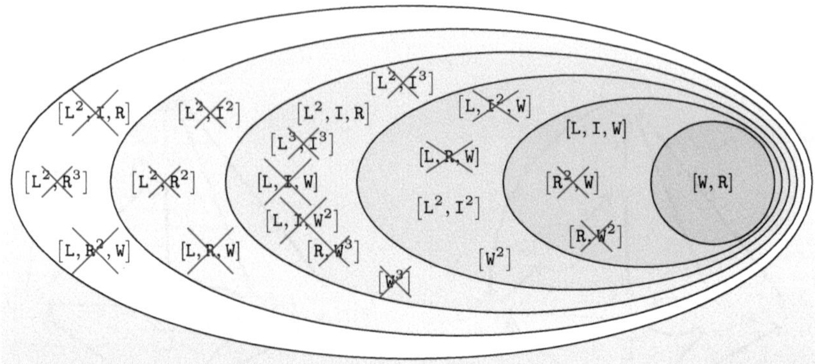

Fig. 8. Running the backward reachability algorithm on the example Petri net with reset arcs in Figure 7

words, the existence of readers prevents a process moving from its idle to its writing state. Our abstraction means that we "kill" all the processes violating the condition, thus enabling the transition again. Since the abstract transition relation is an over-approximation of the original transition relation, it follows that if a safety property holds in the abstract model, then it will also hold in the concrete model.

Figure 7 show the Petri net with reset arcs we get as an abstraction of the Petri net with inhibitor arcs in Figure 6. The inhibitor arc is replaced by a reset arc (with a head which is an empty circle). Figure 8 shows the result of running the backward reachability algorithm on the reset Petri net of Fig 7.

5 Linear Topologies

In many cases, the components of a parameterized systems are organized as a linear array. Configurations of the system can then be represented by *words* over a finite alphabet rather than multisets. Each alphabet symbol inside the word represents the local state of one process. The ordering on the symbols reflects the ordering on the processes. As mentioned earlier, one important (and difficult) feature in the behaviour of parameterized systems is the existence of *global condition* in which a process may have to check the states of the other processes inside the systems before performing a transition. A global transition is either *universally* or *existentially* quantified. An example of a universal condition is that *all* processes in the left context[2] of the active process should be in certain states. In an existential transition we require that *some* (rather than *all*) processes should be in certain states. We have already seen an example of a global condition in the reader-writer protocol of Section 4. A process in the protocol

[2] The left context of the active process contains all the process which are to its left inside the configuration.

changes states from I to W only if the number of reader processes is equal to zero. This is equivalent to the universal condition that all the other processes should be either idle or writing.

5.1 Simple Example

We introduce our method through a simple example of a protocol which implements mutual exclusion among an arbitrary number of processes. Each process (depicted in Figure 9) has four local states, namely the idle (I), requesting (R), waiting (W), and critical (C) states.

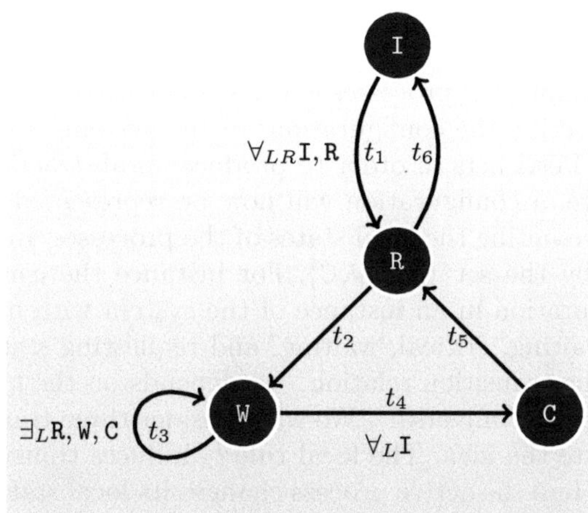

Fig. 9. One process in the mutual exclusion protocol with linear topology

Initially, all the processes are idle (in state I). When a process becomes interested in accessing the critical section (which corresponds to the state C), it declares its interest by moving to the requesting state R.

This is described by the global universal transition rule t_1 in which the move is allowed only if all other processes are in their idle or requesting states. The universal quantifier labeling t_1 encodes the condition that all other processes (whether in the left or the right context – hence the index LR of the quantifier) of the active process should be I or R. In the requesting state, the process may move to the waiting state W through the local transition t_2 (in which the process does not need to check the states of the other processes). Notice that any number of processes may cross from the initial (idle) state to the requesting state. However, once the first process has crossed to the waiting state, it "closes the door" on the processes which are still in their initial states. These processes will no longer be able to leave their initial states until the door is opened again (when no process is in W or C). From the set of processes which have declared interest in accessing the critical section (those which have left their idle states and are now in the requesting or waiting states) the leftmost process has the highest priority. This is encoded by the global universal transition t_4 where a process may move from its waiting state to its critical section only subject to the universal condition that all processes in its left context are idle (the index L of the quantifier stands for "Left"). If the process finds out, through the existential global condition, that there are other processes that are requesting, in their waiting states, or in their critical sections, then it loops back to the waiting state through the existential transition t_3. Once the process leaves the critical section, it will return back to the requesting state through the local transition t_5. In the requesting state, the process chooses either to try to reach the critical section again, or to become idle (through the local transition t_6).

5.2 Abstraction

Since the ordering among the processes in the system is relevant, we can no longer use multisets to describe the configurations of the system. This means that we have to go beyond Petri nets in order to produce an abstraction of the system. As mentioned above, a configuration will now be represented as a word over a finite alphabet representing the local states of the processes. In our example this alphabet is given by the set $\{\mathtt{I}, \mathtt{R}, \mathtt{W}, \mathtt{C}\}$. For instance the configuration IWCWR represents a configuration in an instance of the system with five processes that are in their idle, waiting, critical, waiting, and requesting states in that order. The definition of the transition relation $\longrightarrow$ depends on the type of t (whether it is local, existential, or universal). We will consider three transition rules from Figure 9 to illustrate the idea. The local rule t_2 induces transitions of the form WIRCR $\longrightarrow$ WIWCR. Here the active process changes its local state from requesting to waiting. The existential rule t_3 induces transitions of the form RIWCR $\longrightarrow$ RIWCR. The waiting process can perform the transition since there is a requesting process in its left context. However, the same transition is not enabled from the configuration IIWCR, since there are no critical, waiting, or requesting processes in the left context of the process trying to perform the transition. The universal rule t_4 induces transitions of the form IIWWR $\longrightarrow$ IICWR. The active process (in the waiting state) can perform the transition since all processes in its left context are idle. On the other hand, neither of the waiting processes can perform the transition form the configuration CIWWR since, for each one of them, there is at least one process in its left context which is not idle.

An *initial configuration* is one in which all processes are in their initial states. Examples of initial configurations are II and IIIII, corresponding to instances of the system with two and five processes respectively. As mentioned above, the protocol is intended to guarantee mutual exclusion. In other words, we are interested in verifying a *safety property*. To do this we characterize the set of bad configurations: all configurations which contain at least two processes in their critical sections. Examples of bad configurations are CRC and ICRCWC. Showing the safety property amounts to proving that the protocol, starting from an initial configuration, will never reach a bad configuration.

5.3 Monotonic Abstraction

We define an ordering on configurations where $c_1 \preceq c_2$ if c_1 is a (not necessarily contiguous) subword of c_2. For instance, WC $\preceq$ RWICW. The relation $\preceq$ is a wqo by Higman's lemma [12]. In a similar manner to Section 3 and Section 4, we define an abstraction that generates an over-approximation of the transition system. The abstract transition system is monotonic, thus allowing to work with upward closed sets. In fact, we first show that local and existential transitions are monotonic, and hence need not be approximated. Therefore, we only provide an over-approximation for universal transitions.

Consider the local rule t_2 and the induced transition $c_1 = \texttt{IRC} \longrightarrow \texttt{IWC} = c_2$ in which a process changes state from requesting to waiting. Consider the configuration $c_3 = \texttt{IWIRCR}$ that is larger than c_1. Clearly, c_3 can perform the local transition $c_3 = \texttt{IWIRCR} \xrightarrow{\texttt{I}} \texttt{WIWCR} = c_4$ leading to $c_4 \succeq c_2$. Local transitions are monotonic, since the active process in the small configuration (the requesting process in c_1) also exists in the larger configuration (i.e., c_3). A local transition does not check or change the states of the passive processes; and hence the larger configuration c_3 is also able to perform the transition, while maintaining the ordering $c_2 \preceq c_4$.

Consider the local rule t_3 and the induced transition $c_1 = \texttt{RIWCR} \longrightarrow \texttt{RIWCR} = c_2$. Let us observe that the configuration c_1 can be divided into three parts: the active process in the waiting state, the left context RI, and the right context CR. Furthermore, the left context contains a witness (the process in the requesting state) which enables the transition. Consider the configuration $c_3 = \texttt{IRIWCRC}$ that is larger than c_1. Also, the configuration c_3 can be divided into three parts: the active process in the waiting state, the left context IRI, and the right context CRC. Notice that the left context of c_3 is larger than the left context of c_1, and hence the former will also contain the witness. This means that c_3 can perform the same transition $c_3 = \texttt{IRIWCRC} \longrightarrow \texttt{IRIWCRC} = c_4$ leading to $c_4 \succeq c_2$.

Next, we motivate why universal transitions are not monotonic. Consider the universal rule t_4 and the induced transition $c_1 = \texttt{IIWWR} \longrightarrow \texttt{IICWR} = c_2$. The transition is enabled since all processes in the left context of the active process satisfy the condition of the transition (they are idle). Consider the configuration $c_3 = \texttt{IRICWWR}$. Although $c_1 \preceq c_3$, the universal transition t_4 is not enabled from c_3 since the left context of the active process contains processes that violate the condition of the transition. This implies that universal transitions are not monotonic. In order to deal with non-monotonicity of universal transitions, we will change the semantics of the system using the same idea as the one in Section 4. More precisely, we delete all the processes violating the condition of the universal rule. This means for instance that we have a transition of the form IRICWWR $\longrightarrow$ IICWR since we can first delete the two processes in the requesting and critical states and then perform the transition.

5.4 Computing Predecessors

For a configuration c and a transition rule t, we define $Pre(t)(c)$ to be the set $\{c_1, \ldots, c_n\}$ which is the generator of the set of configurations from which we can reach $\widehat{c}$ through one application of t. We will consider different transition rules in Figure 9 to illustrate how to compute *Pre*. For the local rule t_5 in Figure 9, we have $Pre(t_5)(\texttt{IRW}) = \{\texttt{ICW}\}$. In other words, the predecessor set is characterized by one configuration, namely ICW. Strictly speaking, the set contains also a number of other configurations such as IRCW. However such configurations are subsumed by the original configuration IRW, and therefore we will for simplicity not include them in the set. For existential transitions, there are two cases depending on whether a witness exists or not in the configuration. Consider the existential rule t_3 in Figure 9. We have $Pre(t_3)(\texttt{RWC}) = \{\texttt{RWC}\}$. In this case, there is a witness (a requesting process) in the left context of the active process. On the other hand, we have $Pre(t_3)(\texttt{IWC}) = \{\texttt{RIWC}, \texttt{IRWC}, \texttt{WIWC}, \texttt{IWWC}, \texttt{CIWC}, \texttt{ICWC}\}$. In this case there is no witness available in the left context of the active process. Therefore, we add a witness explicitly in each possible state (requesting, waiting, or critical), at each possible place in the left context of the active process.

Notice that the sizes of the new configurations (four processes) is larger than the size of the original configuration (three processes). This means that the sizes of the configurations generated by the backward algorithm may increase, and hence there is no bound *a priori* on the sizes of the configurations. However, termination is still guaranteed due to the well quasi-ordering of $\preceq$.

For universal conditions, we check whether there are any processes in the configuration violating the condition. Consider the universal rule t_4 in Figure 9. Then $Pre(\texttt{IRICW}) = \emptyset$ since there is a requesting process in the left context of the potential active process (which is in the critical section). On the other hand, $Pre(\texttt{IICW}) = \texttt{IIWW}$ since all processes in the left context of the active process are in their idle states.

5.5 Backward Reachability Algorithm

We show how the backward reachability algorithm runs on our example (Figure 10). We start by the generator of the set of bad configurations, namely $\{\texttt{CC}\}$. The only transition which is enabled backwards from a critical state, is the one induced by the rule t_4. From the two processes in CC only the left one can perform t_4 backwards (the right process cannot perform t_4 backwards since its left context contains a process not satisfying the condition of the quantifier): $Pre(t_4)(\texttt{CC}) = \{\texttt{WC}\}$. From WC, two rules are enabled backwards (both from the waiting process): the local rule t_2: $Pre(t_2)(\texttt{WC}) = \{\texttt{RC}\}$; and the existential rule t_3: $Pre(t_3)(\texttt{WC}) = \{\texttt{RWC}, \texttt{WWC}, \texttt{CWC}\}$. All the three configurations in $Pre(t_3)$ (WC) are subsumed by WC. One rule is enabled backwards from RC, namely the local rule t_5 from the requesting process: Pre_{t_5} (RC) $= \{\texttt{CC}\}$. Notice that the universal transition t_1 is not enabled from the requesting process, since there is another process (the critical process) in the configuration that violates the condition of the quantifier. At this point, the algorithm terminates, since it is not possible to provide any new configurations which are not subsumed by the existing ones.

Since there is no initial configuration (with only idle processes) in $\widehat{\texttt{CC}} \cup \widehat{\texttt{WC}} \cup \widehat{\texttt{RC}}$, the set of bad configurations is not reachable from the set of initial configurations in the abstract semantics. Therefore, the set of bad configurations is not reachable from the set of initial configurations in the concrete semantics, either.

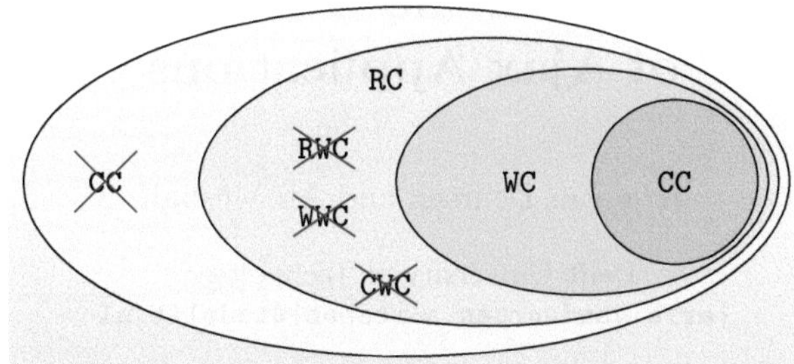

Fig. 10. Running the backward reachability algorithm on the example Protocol

References

1. Abdulla, P.A., Čerāns, K., Jonsson, B., Tsay, Y.-K.: General Decidability Theorems for Infinite-State Systems. In: Proc. LICS 1996, 11th IEEE Int. Symp. on Logic in Computer Science, pp. 313–321 (1996)
2. Abdulla, P.A., Čerāns, K., Jonsson, B., Tsay, Y.-K.: Algorithmic Analysis of Programs with Well Quasi-Ordered Domains. Information and Computation 160, 109–127 (2000)
3. Abdulla, P.A., Delzanno, G., Rezine, A.: Parameterized Verification of Infinite-State Processes with Global Conditions. In: Damm, W., Hermanns, H. (eds.) CAV 2007. LNCS, vol. 4590, pp. 145–157. Springer, Heidelberg (2007)
4. Abdulla, P.A., Henda, N.B., Delzanno, G., Rezine, A.: Regular Model Checking without Transducers (on Efficient Verification of Parameterized Systems). In: Grumberg, O., Huth, M. (eds.) TACAS 2007. LNCS, vol. 4424, pp. 721–736. Springer, Heidelberg (2007)
5. Abdulla, P.A., Henda, N.B., Delzanno, G., Rezine, A.: Handling Parameterized Systems with Non-Atomic Global Conditions. In: Logozzo, F., Peled, D.A., Zuck, L.D. (eds.) VMCAI 2008. LNCS, vol. 4905, pp. 22–36. Springer, Heidelberg (2008)
6. Abdulla, P.A., Jonsson, B.: Verifying Programs with Unreliable Channels. In: Proc. LICS 1993, 8th IEEE Int. Symp. on Logic in Computer Science, pp. 160–170 (1993)
7. Abdulla, P.A., Jonsson, B.: Model Checking of Systems with Many Identical Timed Processes. Theoretical Computer Science 290(1), 241–264 (2003)
8. Dickson, L.E.: Finiteness of the Odd Perfect and Primitive Abundant Numbers with n Distinct Prime Factors. Amer. J. Math. 35, 413–422 (1913)
9. Emerson, E., Namjoshi, K.: On Model Checking for Non-Deterministic Infinite-State Systems. In: Proc. LICS 1998, 13th IEEE Int. Symp. on Logic in Computer Science, pp. 70–80 (1988)
10. Esparza, J., Finkel, A., Mayr, R.: On the Verification of Broadcast Protocols. In: Proc. LICS 1999, 14th IEEE Int. Symp. on Logic in Computer Science (1999)
11. Finkel, A., Schnoebelen, P.: Well-Structured Transition Systems Everywhere! Theoretical Computer Science 256(1-2), 63–92 (2001)
12. Higman, G.: Ordering by Divisibility in Abstract Algebras. Proc. London Math. Soc. (3), 2(7), 326–336 (1952)
13. Yonesaki, N., Katayama, T.: Functional Specification of Synchronized Processes Based on Modal Logic. In: IEEE 6th International Conference on Software Engineering, pp. 208–217 (1982)

Research Issues in the Automated Testing of Ajax Applications

Arie van Deursen and Ali Mesbah

Delft University of Technology
{arie.vandeursen,a.mesbah}@tudelft.nl

Abstract. There is a growing trend to move desktop applications towards the web. This move is made possible through advances in web technologies collectively known as Asynchronous JavaScript and XML (AJAX). With AJAX, the classical model of browsing a series of pages is replaced by a JavaScript engine (running in the browser) taking control of user interaction, exchanging information updates with the web server instead of requesting the complete next page. The benefits of this move include no installation costs, automated upgrading for all users, increased interactivity, reduced user-perceived latency, and universal access, to name a few. AJAX, however, comes at a price: the asynchronous, stateful nature and the use of Javascript make AJAX applications particularly error-prone, causing serious dependability threats. In this paper, we evaluate to what extent automated testing can be used to address these AJAX dependability problems. Based on an analysis of the current challenges in testing AJAX, we formulate directions for future research.

1 Introduction

There is a growing trend to move applications towards the Web. Well-known examples include Google's mail and office applications including spreadsheet, word processing, and calendar applications. The reasons for this move to the web are manifold and include:

- No installation effort for end-users.
- Automatic use of the most recent software version by all users, thus reducing maintenance and support costs.
- Universal access from any browser on any machine with Internet access;
- Possibility to share data and enrich user interaction with information available at the server.
- In-depth insight for software developers in which features are actually used.
- Customization per user, based on, e.g., earlier experience with the application
- Fast innovation cycles, since releasing and deploying a new version is instantaneous.

In an interesting recent blog post [23], McKenzie also argues that the *conversion rate* for web applications is better, i.e., the percentage of site visitors that actually *purchase* a software product is higher for license-based web applications

J. van Leeuwen et al. (Eds.): SOFSEM 2010, LNCS 5901, pp. 16–28, 2010.

than for applications they have to download and install. McKenzie furthermore argues that web applications solve the problem of software piracy, simply by the fact that there is no software anymore that is to be downloaded and (illegally) distributed.

One of the implications of this move to the web, is that *dependability* [3] of web applications is becoming increasingly important [11,29]. Dependability is affected by many factors, including the level of testing, the skills of the developers involved, and the actual software technology used.

For today's web applications, one of the key technologies used is AJAX, an acronym for "Asynchronous JavaScript and XML" [15]. With AJAX, web-browsers not just offer the possibility to navigate through a sequence of HTML pages, but enable rich user interaction via graphical user interface components.

While the use of AJAX technology positively affects user-friendliness and interactiveness of web applications [26], it comes at a price: AJAX applications are notoriously error-prone due to, e.g., the stateful and asynchronous nature as well as the use of (untyped) JavaScript (see Section 3).

In this paper, we will explore how testing can be used to improve the dependability of AJAX applications. In particular, we first provide an abstract view on what exactly is comprised by AJAX. We do this in Section 2, by means of an *architectural style* capturing the essential elements of AJAX applications. Next, in Section 3, we offer a survey of our work on the automated testing of AJAX applications. In particular, we discuss a plugin-based tool infrastructure called ATUSA, which can be used to detect a range of faults typically occurring in AJAX applications. We conclude the paper with an analysis of open issues and research problems in the area of automated testing of AJAX applications.

2 Defining Ajax

AJAX potentially brings an end to the classical *click-and-wait* style of web navigation, providing the responsiveness and interactivity level end users usually expect from desktop applications. In a classical web application, the user has to wait for the entire page to reload to see the response of the server. With AJAX, however, small delta messages are requested from the server, behind the scenes, by the AJAX engine and updated on the current page through modifications to the corresponding DOM-tree. This in sharp contrast to the classical *multi-page* style, in which after each state change a completely new DOM-tree is created from a full page reload.

AJAX gives us a vehicle to build web applications with a *single-page web interface*, in which all interactions take place on one page. Single-page web interfaces can improve complex, non-linear user work-flows [39] by decreasing the number of click trails and the time needed [38] to perform a certain task, when compared to classical multi-page variants.

Another important aspect of AJAX is that of enriching the web user interface with interactive components and widgets. Examples of widgets, which can all co-exist on the single-page web interface, include auto-completion for input fields, in-line editing, slider-based filtering, drag and drop, rich tables with within-page sorting, shiny photo albums and calendars, to name a few. These are all web user interface components that are made possible through extensive DOM programming by means of JavaScript and delta client/server communication.

In most classical web applications, a great deal of identical content is present in page sequences. For each request, the response contains all the redundant content and layout, even for very marginal updates. Using Ajax to update only the relevant parts of the page results, as expected, in a decrease in the bandwidth usage. Experimental results have shown a performance increase of 55 to 73% [35,24,38] for data transferred over the network, when Ajax is used to conduct partial updates.

In our earlier work we have proposed Spiar, an *architectural style* [14,31] for Ajax [26]. Spiar results from a study of different major Ajax frameworks, investigating their salient architectural properties, key elements, and constraints on those elements required to achieve the desired properties. Such a style captures the essence of Ajax frameworks and can be seen as an abstract model of different architectural implementations.

In Spiar three types of architectural elements can be identified: processing (e.g., browser, Ajax engine, server application, service provider, user interface components) , connectors (e.g., events, delta update, push channels), and data (e.g., representation, representational model, delta messages).

Given the processing, data, and connecting elements, we can use different architectural views to describe how the elements work together to form an architecture. Figure 1 depicts the processing view of an Spiar-based architecture based on run-time components rendering as in, e.g., Echo2[1]. The view shows the interaction of the different components some time after the initial page request (the engine is running on the client). User activity on the user interface fires off an event to indicate some kind of component-defined action which is delegated to the Ajax engine. If a listener on a server-side component has registered itself with the event, the engine will make a delta-client message of the current state changes with the corresponding events and send it to the server. On the server, the decoder will convert the message, and identify and notify the relevant components in the component tree. The changed components will ultimately invoke the event listeners of the service provider. The service provider, after handling the actions, will update the corresponding components with the new state which will be rendered by the encoder. The rendered delta-server message is then sent back to the engine which will be used to update the representational model and eventually the interface. The engine has also the ability to update the representational model directly after an event, if no round-trip to the server is required.

Architectural constraints can be used as restrictions on the roles of the architectural elements to induce the architectural properties desired of a system. Table 1 presents an overview of the constraints and induced properties. A "+" marks a direct positive effect, whereas a "–" indicates a direct negative effect.

[1] http://echo.nextapp.com/site/echo2

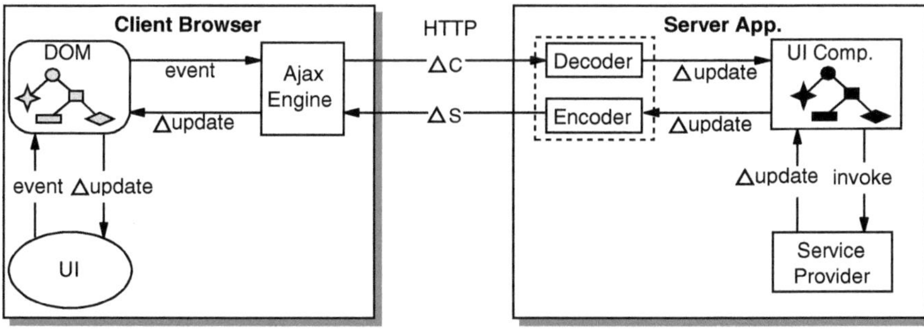

Fig. 1. Processing View of a SPIAR-based architecture

Table 1. Constraints and induced properties in AJAX applications

	User Interactivity	User-perceived Latency	Network Performance	Simplicity	Scalability	Portability	Visibility	Data Coherence	Reliability	Adaptability
Single-page Interface	+									
Asynchronous Interaction	+	+								
Delta Communication	+	+	+		−		−	+		
Client-side processing	+	+	+							
UI Component-based	+			+					+	+
Web standards-based				+		+			+	
Stateful	+	+	+		−		−			
Push-based Publish/Subscribe		+	+		−		−	+		+

SPIAR rests upon these constraints, which are chosen to retain the properties such as user interactivity, data coherence, and scalability.

3 State of the Art in Ajax Testing

For traditional software, analysis and testing is still largely ad hoc [5] and already a notoriously time-consuming and expensive process [4]. Classical web applications present even more challenges [10,2] due to their distributed, heterogeneous nature. In addition, web applications have the ability to generate different user interfaces in response to user inputs and server state.

AJAX-based web applications are not only fundamentally different from classical web applications, but also more error-prone and harder to test. The reasons for this include the stateful as well as asynchronous nature of AJAX programming, the client-side manipulation of the Document Object Model, the use of delta-communication, and the limited possibilities for static (type) checking of

Javascript. In spite of the great success of AJAX, building dependable AJAX applications is a daunting task. Below we will discuss the current state of AJAX testing approaches.

3.1 Current Testing Approaches

The server-side of AJAX applications can be tested with any conventional testing technique. On the client, testing can be performed at different levels. Unit testing tools such as JsUnit[2] can be used to test JAVASCRIPT on a functional level. The most popular AJAX testing tools are currently capture/replay tools such as Selenium,[3] which allow DOM-based testing by capturing events fired by user (tester) interaction. Such tools have access to the DOM, and can assert expected UI behavior defined by the tester and replay the events. Capture/replay tools demand, however, a substantial amount of manual effort on the part of the tester.

Marchetto *et al.* [21] discuss a case study in which they demonstrate the effectiveness of applying traditional web testing techniques (e.g., code coverage testing [33], model-based testing [2], session based testing [12,36]) to AJAX. Their analysis suggests that such traditional techniques have serious limitations in testing modern AJAX-based web applications. They propose [22] an approach for state-based testing of AJAX applications based on traces of the application to construct a finite state machine. Sequences of semantically interacting events in the model are used to generate test cases once the model is refined by the tester. In our recent approach [27], the focus is on automating the testing process by inferring an abstract model of the AJAX application and generating test cases automatically.

3.2 Automatic Testing of Ajax

In order to detect a fault automatically, a testing method should meet the following conditions [28,34]: *reach* the fault-execution, which causes the fault to be executed, *trigger* the error-creation, which causes the fault execution to generate an incorrect intermediate state, and *propagate* the error, which enables the incorrect intermediate state to propagate to the output and cause a detectable output error. In addition, automating the process of assessing the correctness of test case output is a challenging task, known as the oracle problem.

Meeting these reach/trigger/propagate/oracle conditions is more challenging for AJAX applications compared to the classical ones.

One way to *reach* the fault-execution *automatically* for web applications is by adopting a web crawler to crawl through different UI states and infer a model of the navigational paths and states.

3.3 Crawling Ajax

A general approach in testing the client-side of web applications has been to request a response from the server and analyze the resulting HTML page. This

[2] `http://jsunit.net`
[3] `http://selenium.openqa.org`

testing approach based on the page-sequence paradigm has serious limitations when applied to AJAX-based applications. AJAX has a number of properties making it difficult, for e.g., search engines, to crawl. We will briefly outline these challenges below.

Client-side Execution. Any search engine willing to approach such an application must have support for the execution of the scripting language. Equipping a general search crawler with the necessary environment complicates its design and implementation considerably.

Navigation. Ultimately, an AJAX application could consist of a single page with a single URL. This characteristic makes it very difficult for a search engine to index and point to a specific state on an AJAX application. For crawlers, navigating through traditional multi-page web applications has been as easy as extracting and following the hypertext links (or the `src` attribute) on each page.

Dynamic Document Object Model (DOM). The state changes in AJAX applications are dynamically represented through the run-time changes on the DOM. This means that the source code in HTML does not represent the state anymore. Any search engine aimed at crawling and indexing such applications, will need to have access to this run-time dynamic document object model of the application.

Delta-communication. Retrieving and indexing the delta state changes from the server, for instance through a proxy between the client and the server, could have the side-effect of losing the context and actual meaning of the changes. Most of such delta updates become meaningful after they have been processed by the JavaScript engine on the client and injected into the DOM.

Events and Clickables. In AJAX, hypertext links can be replaced by elements with event-listeners, which are handled by the client engine; it is not possible any longer to navigate the application by simply extracting and retrieving the internal hypertext links. DOM Events (e.g., `onClick, onMouseOver`) can be attached to DOM elements at run-time, and as such, even a `div` element can have an `onclick` event attached to it so that it becomes a *clickable* element capable of changing the internal DOM state of the application when clicked. The necessary event handlers can also be programmatically registered in AJAX. Finding these clickables at run-time is another non-trivial task for a crawler.

Despite these challenges, we have proposed [25] a new type of web crawler, called CRAWLJAX, capable of exercising client-side code, detecting and executing doorways (clickables) to various dynamic states of AJAX-based applications within browser's dynamically built DOM. While crawling, CRAWLJAX infers a *state-flow graph* capturing the states of the user interface, and the possible event-based transitions between them, by analyzing the DOM before and after firing an event. CRAWLJAX is open source[4] and based on an embedded browser interface (with different implementations: IE, Firefox) capable of executing JavaScript and the supporting technologies required by AJAX.

[4] `http://spci.st.ewi.tudelft.nl/crawljax/`

3.4 Invariant-Based Testing

Once we are able to derive different dynamic states of an AJAX application, possible faults can be triggered by generating UI events and identifying entry points.

In our recent work [27], we have presented an approach for automatic testing of AJAX user interfaces, called ATUSA. ATUSA is based on the crawling capabilities of CRAWLJAX and provides data-entry point detection and (pre-, in-, and post-crawling) plugin hooks for testing AJAX applications.

To tackle the oracle problem, we have proposed to use generic and application-specific structural *invariants* that serve as oracle to detect faults in and between different DOM states. Such oracles can be defined in various forms such as XPath expressions, Regular expressions, or JavaScript conditions.

3.5 Test-Case Generation

While running ATUSA to derive the state machine can be considered as a first full test pass, the state machine itself can be further used for testing purposes. For example, it can be used to execute different paths to cover the state machine in different ways. To that end, we derive a test suite (implemented in JUnit) automatically from the state machine, which can be used for regression testing of AJAX applications. Figure 2 depicts the processing view of ATUSA, showing a pre-crawling DOM Validator and a post-crawling Test Case Generator as examples of possible plugin implementations.

3.6 Security Testing

AJAX applications can be composed from independent user interface components, often called web *widgets*. As any program code, widgets can be used for

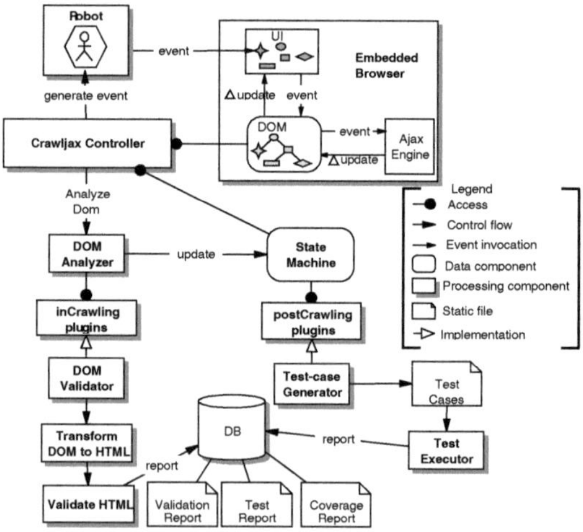

Fig. 2. Processing view of ATUSA

malicious purposes. Example scenarios include when a malicious widget changes the content of another widget to trick the user into releasing sensitive information, or even worse, listens to the account details a user enters in another widget (e.g., PayPal or Email widgets) and sends the data to a malicious site.

Testing modern web applications for security vulnerabilities is far from trivial. Traditional detection-based approaches are generally static analysis-based, which has limitations in revealing faults and violations in the dynamic distributed runtime behavior of modern rich web applications.

In our latest work [6], we propose to extend and use ATUSA for automatically spotting two types of security problems in widget interactions, namely, namely the case in which (1) a malicious widget changes the content (DOM) of another widget, and (2) a widget steals data from another widget and sends it to the server via an HTTP request.

In order to find DOM change violations (1), we first need to automatically detect each widget's boundary in the DOM tree. Once the boundaries are defined, we can analyze the elements receiving events and the actual changes taking place on the DOM tree to decide whether a state change is a violation.

For HTTP request violations (2), the main challenge is in coupling each outgoing request with the corresponding DOM element, from which it originated. Once we know which element is causing the request, we can analyze the behavior and decide whether a violation has occurred.

Our approach, implemented in a number of open source ATUSA plugins, called DIVA, requires no modification of application code, and has few false positives.

4 Open Research Questions

The potential of automatic testing of AJAX applications is high, but there are a number of problems and challenges that need to be addressed, related to the scalability and usability of the proposed approach. In this section, we sketch the main areas of future research we anticipate.

4.1 Invariants in Practice

Testing in ATUSA is based on the notion of *invariants.* This is a fairly weak form of an oracle, which can be used to conduct basic sanity checks on the DOM-tree or transitions in the derived GUI state machine. While initial experiments using DOM-based invariants were successful [27] a number of research questions remain.

1. While in academia the notion of design invariants is well-understood industrial practice has been reluctant to pick up the idea [8]. The premise of ATUSA is that essential design decisions can be captured into invariants. To what extent is this indeed the case? Are developers capable and willing to document these decisions by means of invariants? What is the best notation to express invariants? Are invariants sufficiently stable across different versions of an AJAX application?

2. Another premise in ATUSA is that invariants are effective in finding faults. We anticipate that the more application-specific an invariant is, the likelier it will be that it can reveal a programming fault. Is this indeed the case? How common are violations of generic invariants (concerning, e.g., HTML validity)? What sort of application-specific invariants are likely to reveal faults?
3. Ernst *et al.* have used dynamic analysis to infer "likely invariants" from execution traces [13]. An interesting question is to what extent this would be possible in our setting as well. Can we analyze the DOM in every state, and discover properties on the DOM that must always hold? Can we use the corresponding invariants for testing in subsequent versions of the AJAX application? Can we infer client-side JavaScript invariants automatically through dynamic analysis?

Note that many of these questions are empirical in nature. Therefore, in order to answer them it is necessary to to have access to several AJAX development projects, so that rigorous case studies [40] can be conducted.

4.2 Combinatorial Testing

The combinatorial explosion of the test space is one of the key problems in software testing. A system with N features each having M possibilities, leads to M^N test cases, which rapidly becomes intractable.

To deal with this problem various approaches have been proposed. A well-known method is *Category-Partition*, in which independently testable features and parameter characteristics are identified [30]. In this approach, constraints are used to limit the number of combinations that must be checked.

An alternative is *pairwise* combination testing. In this approach, not all possible combinations, but just all possible *value pairs* between two features are tested (or, more generally, k-tuples for $k < N$) [9]. In this approach, the state space grows logarithmically rather than exponentially. Furthermore, empirical evidence suggests that, in practice, faults are mostly due to two or sometimes three way interactions, making pairwise testing an effective approach [20].

The approach currently used in ATUSA investigates all possibilities, and hence suffers from the combinatorial explosion problem. In order to apply techniques such as category-partition or pairwise combination testing, we need to identify *independent* parts of the DOM-tree. Are annotations provided by developers an effective means to identify such independent parts? To what extent can independent DOM-fragments be found automatically? Are DOM-fragments a good starting point for applying combinatorial testing? To what reductions does this lead in practice?

4.3 State Space Reduction

Related to scalability is the state space explosion problem (see, e.g., [32]). In particular, in the area of *model checking*, a significant body of research has been devoted to reducing state spaces [18].

When deriving state machines from executions, which is what we do in CRAWLJAX, an *abstraction function* is used for mapping concrete program states to abstract GUI states in our state-flow graph. Can we strengthen our abstraction function, and merge more states together? Can we reuse techniques from the area of model checking to manage our state space? Can we involve the software engineering in suggesting states to merge, for example through annotations? Can we reduce the state machine memory footprint by adopting techniques such as hashcode computation, state compression, recursive indexing [17], delta update, or Sweep Line [7]? Is the total running time reducible by using concurrent computation?

4.4 Regression Testing

Regression testing encompasses the selective re-testing of a system to verify that modifications have not caused unintended effects and that the system still complies with its specified requirements [19]. Regression testing of web applications [37] in general and AJAX-based applications in particular is far from trivial due to the high degree of dynamism in such applications. This dynamism is usually caused by various factors such as input data from different users, server-side state, order of event sequences, etc.

In ATUSA for instance, when the generated test suite is run for regression testing, states as seen in the browser are compared with the states in the oracle (the baseline). Imagine a page that displays a date-time that changes after each retrieval. A simple string comparison would result in many false test failures. Even changing the order of followed events can result in a different state than expected according to the baseline. How can we cope with this high level of dynamism in AJAX applications when conducting regression testing? Can we implement or better yet generate intelligent oracle comparators that ignore such state differences so that we can only report real failures?

4.5 Path Seeding

Instead of starting from a single root to explore possible clicks in an AJAX application, a given sequence of clicks can be used as a starting point. From such a click trail, side paths can be explored automatically, for example within a given distance of the original sequence.

This opens various opportunities to refine the way test cases are generated. These initial sequences can be obtained from a first round of manual (acceptance) testing, for example through the use capture-and-playback tools (such as the aforementioned Selenium) or defining pre-conditions on the (e.g., DOM or JavaScript variables) states. Alternatively, the initial trails may be picked to correspond to an operational profile, and thus reflect typical usage scenarios. Subsequently, ATUSA's automated capabilities can be used to expand these initial sequences to a series of closely related sequences.

A particularly intriguing route is to use *failure-inducing* paths as seeds, and then attempt to do automated fault diagnosis [1,16]. Such failing runs can correspond to click trails generated by ATUSA that lead to an invariant violation.

To spot the cause of the failure, ATUSA can then collect trails that are, in one way or another, similar, which do not lead to an invariant violation. Traditional spectrum-based analysis can then be used to identify the differences between these trails in terms of the underlying functionality that gets executed (by instrumenting, e.g., the underlying JavaScript code), which then can be used to localize the root cause of the fault. This amounts to combining click trail similarity with fault diagnosis: a promising direction which, however, requires further research to investigate the feasibility and benefits.

5 Concluding Remarks

As more and more applications are moved to the web, AJAX technology plays an increasingly important role in our society. Unfortunately, the state-based, asynchronous nature of AJAX in combination with the limited possibilities for static analysis of rich Internet applications, pose an increasing threat to dependability.

One way to deal with this threat is the use of automated testing. This requires the use of a crawler that can detect and follow clickable elements introduced by client-side logic. Furthermore, it requires the capability of distinguishing correct from incorrect executions, for which we propose to rely on invariants expressed over the browser's Document Object Model.

While this approach has proven successful in various case studies, a number of questions remain, related in particular to the scaleability of the approach. In order to address these concerns, in this paper we have surveyed a number of research directions and areas of future research, in which techniques from traditional testing are made to work with the specific constraints and opportunities imposed by AJAX applications.

References

1. Abreu, R., Zoeteweij, P., van Gemund, A.J.C.: On the Accuracy of Spectrum-Based Fault Localization. In: TAICPART-MUTATION 2007: Proceedings of the Testing: Academic and Industrial Conference Practice and Research Techniques - MUTATION, Washington, DC, USA, pp. 89–98. IEEE Computer Society, Los Alamitos (2007)
2. Andrews, A., Offutt, J., Alexander, R.: Testing Web Applications by Modeling with FSMs. Software and Systems Modeling 4(3), 326–345 (2005)
3. Avizienis, A., Laprie, J.-C., Randell, B., Landwehr, C.: Basic Concepts and Taxonomy of Dependable and Secure Computing. IEEE Trans. on Dependable and Secure Computing 1(1), 11–33 (2004)
4. Beizer, B.: Software Testing Techniques, 2nd edn. Van Nostrand Reinhold Co. (1990)
5. Bertolino, A.: Software Testing Research: Achievements, Challenges, Dreams. In: ICSE Future of Software Engineering (FOSE 2007), pp. 85–103. IEEE Computer Society, Los Alamitos (2007)

6. Bezemer, C.-P., Mesbah, A., van Deursen, A.: Automated Security Testing of Web Widget Interactions. In: Proceedings of the 7th Joint Meeting of the European Software Engineering Conference and the ACM SIGSOFT Symposium on the Foundations of Software Engineering (ESEC-FSE 2009), pp. 81–91. ACM, New York (2009)
7. Christensen, S., Kristensen, L.M., Mailund, T.: A Sweep-Line Method for State Space Exploration. In: Margaria, T., Yi, W. (eds.) TACAS 2001. LNCS, vol. 2031, pp. 450–464. Springer, Heidelberg (2001)
8. Clarke, L.A., Rosenblum, D.S.: A Historical Perspective on Runtime Assertion Checking in Software Development. ACM SIGSOFT Software Engineering Notes 31(3), 25–37 (2006)
9. Cohen, D.M., Dalal, S.R., Fredman, M.L., Patton, G.C.: The AETG System: An Approach to Testing Based on Combinatiorial Design. IEEE Trans. Software Eng. 23(7), 437–444 (1997)
10. Di Lucca, G.A., Fasolino, A.R.: Testing Web-Based Applications: The State of the Art and Future Trends. Inf. Softw. Technol. 48(12), 1172–1186 (2006)
11. Elbaum, S., Chilakamarri, K.-R., Gopal, B., Rothermel, G.: Helping End-Users 'Engineer' Dependable Web Applications. In: Proceedings of the 16th IEEE International Symposium on Software Reliability Engineering (ISSRE 2005), pp. 31–40. IEEE Computer Society, Los Alamitos (2005)
12. Elbaum, S., Karre, S., Rothermel, G.: Improving Web Application Testing with User Session Data. In: Proc. 25th Int. Conf. on Software Engineering (ICSE 2003), pp. 49–59. IEEE Computer Society, Los Alamitos (2003)
13. Ernst, M.D., Cockrell, J., Griswold, W.G., Notkin, D.: Dynamically Discovering Likely Program Invariants to Support Program Evolution. IEEE Trans. Softw. Eng. 27(2), 99–123 (2001)
14. Fielding, R.: Architectural Styles and the Design of Network-Based Software Architectures. PhD Thesis. UC, Irvine, Information and Computer Science (2000)
15. Garrett, J.: Ajax: A New Approach to Web Applications. Adaptive path (February 2005), `http://www.adaptivepath.com/publications/essays/archives/000385.php`
16. Harrold, M.-J., Rothermel, G., Wu, R., Yi, L.: An Empirical Investigation of Program Spectra. In: PASTE 1998: Proceedings of the 1998 ACM SIGPLAN-SIGSOFT Workshop on Program Analysis for Software Tools and Engineering, pp. 83–90. ACM, New York (1998)
17. Holzmann, G.: State Compression in SPIN: Recursive Indexing and Compression Training Runs. In: Proceedings of Third International SPIN Workshop (1997)
18. Holzmann, G.J.: The Model Checker SPIN. IEEE Transactions on Software Engineering 23(5), 279–295 (1997)
19. IEEE. IEEE Std 610.12-1990: IEEE Standard Glossary of Software Engineering Terminology. IEEE (1990)
20. Kuhn, D.R., Wallace, D.R., Gallo, A.M.: Software Fault Interactions and Implications for Software Testing. IEEE Trans. Software Eng. 30(6), 418–421 (2004)
21. Marchetto, A., Ricca, F., Tonella, P.: A Case Study-Based Comparison of Web Testing Techniques Applied to Ajax Web Applications. Int. Journal on Software Tools for Technology Transfer 10(6), 477–492 (2008)
22. Marchetto, A., Tonella, P., Ricca, F.: State-Based Testing of Ajax Web Applications. In: Proc. 1st IEEE Int. Conference on Sw. Testing Verification and Validation (ICST 2008), pp. 121–130. IEEE Computer Society, Los Alamitos (2008)

23. McKenzie, P.: Why I'm Done Making Desktop Applications. Blog Post on, http://www.kalzumeus.com/2009/09/05/desktop-aps-versus-web-apps/ (Date consulted: 15 September 2009)
24. Merrill, C.L.: Using Ajax to Improve the Bandwidth Performance of Web Applications (2006), http://www.webperformanceinc.com/library/reports/AjaxBandwidth/
25. Mesbah, A., Bozdag, E., van Deursen, A.: Crawling Ajax by Inferring User Interface State Changes. In: Proceedings of the 8th International Conference on Web Engineering (ICWE 2008), pp. 122–134. IEEE Computer Society, Los Alamitos (2008)
26. Mesbah, A., van Deursen, A.: A Component- and Push-Based Architectural Style for Ajax Applications. Journal of Systems and Software 81(12), 2194–2209 (2008)
27. Mesbah, A., van Deursen, A.: Invariant-Based Automatic Testing of Ajax User Interfaces. In: Proceedings of the 31st International Conference on Software Engineering (ICSE 2009), Research Papers, pp. 210–220. IEEE Computer Society, Los Alamitos (2009)
28. Morell, L.: Theoretical Insights into Fault-Based Testing. In: Proc. 2nd Workshop on Software Testing, Verification, and Analysis, pp. 45–62 (1988)
29. Offutt, J.: Quality Attributes of Web Software Applications. IEEE Softw. 19(2), 25–32 (2002)
30. Ostrand, T.J., Balcer, M.J.: The Category-Partition Method for Specifying and Generating Functional Tests. Commun. ACM 31(6), 676–686 (1988)
31. Perry, D.E., Wolf, A.L.: Foundations for the Study of Software Architecture. SIGSOFT Softw. Eng. Notes 17(4), 40–52 (1992)
32. Pezzè, M., Young, M.: Software Testing and Analysis. Wiley, Chichester (2008)
33. Ricca, F., Tonella, P.: Analysis and Testing of Web Applications. In: ICSE 2001: 23rd Int. Conf. on Sw. Eng., pp. 25–34. IEEE Computer Society, Los Alamitos (2001)
34. Richardson, D., Thompson, M.: The RELAY Model of Error Detection and Its Application. In: Proc. 2nd Workshop on Software Testing, Verification, and Analysis, pp. 223–230 (1988)
35. Smullen III, C.V., Smullen, S.A.: An Experimental Study of Ajax Application Performance. Journal of Software 3(3), 30–37 (2008)
36. Sprenkle, S., Gibson, E., Sampath, S., Pollock, L.: Automated Replay and Failure Detection for Web Applications. In: ASE 2005: Proc. 20th IEEE/ACM Int. Conf. on Automated Sw. Eng., pp. 253–262. ACM, New York (2005)
37. Tarhini, A., Ismail, Z., Mansour, N.: Regression Testing Web Applications. In: International Conference on Advanced Computer Theory and Engineering, pp. 902–906. IEEE Computer Society, Los Alamitos (2008)
38. White, A.: Measuring the Benefits of Ajax (2006), http://www.developer.com/java/other/article.php/3554271
39. Willemsen, J.: Improving User Workflows with Single-Page User Interfaces (November 2006), http://www.uxmatters.com/MT/archives/000149.php
40. Yin, R.K.: Case Study Research: Design and Methods, 3rd edn. SAGE Publications Inc., Thousand Oaks (2003)

Essential Performance Drivers in Native XML DBMSs

Theo Härder, Christian Mathis, Sebastian Bächle, Karsten Schmidt, and Andreas M. Weiner

University of Kaiserslautern, Germany
{haerder,mathis,baechle,kschmidt,weiner}@cs.uni-kl.de

Abstract. As a multi-layered XML database management system, we have designed, implemented, and optimized over the recent five years our prototype system XTC, a native XDBMS providing multi-lingual query interfaces (XQuery, XPath, DOM). In particular in higher system layers, we have compared competing concepts and iteratively found salient solutions which drastically improved the overall XDBMS performance. XML query processing is critically affected by the smooth interplay of concepts and methods on all architectural layers: node labeling and mapping options for storage structures; availability of suitable index mechanisms; provision of a spectrum of path processing operators; query language compilation and optimization. Furthermore, effective and efficient locking protocols must be present to guarantee the ACID properties for XML processing and to achieve high transaction throughput.

In this survey, we outline our experiences gained during the implementation and optimization of XTC. We figure out the "key drivers" to maximize throughput while keeping the response times at an acceptable level. Because we have implemented all options and alternatives in XTC, dedicated benchmark runs allow for comparisons in identical environments and illustrate the benefit of all implementation decisions[1].

1 Motivation

In recent years, XML's standardization and, in particular, its flexibility (e. g., data mapping, cardinality variations, optional or non-existing structures, etc.) evolved as driving factors to attract demanding write/read applications, to enable heterogeneous data stores, and to facilitate data integration. Because business models in practically every industry use large and evolving sets of sparsely populated attributes, XML is more and more adopted by those companies which have even now launched consortia to develop XML schemas adjusted to their particular data modeling needs. As an example, world-leading financial companies defined more than a dozen XML schemata and vocabularies to standardize data

[1] This work has been partially supported by the German Research Foundation (DFG) and the Rheinland-Pfalz cluster of excellence "Center of Mathematical and Computational Modelling", Germany (see www.cmcm.de).

J. van Leeuwen et al. (Eds.): SOFSEM 2010, LNCS 5901, pp. 29–46, 2010.

processing and to leverage cooperation and data exchange [43]. For these reasons, XML databases currently get more and more momentum if data flexibility in various forms is a key requirement of the application and they are, therefore, frequently used in collaborative or even competitive environments [26].

Native XML database systems (XDBMSs) promise tailored XML processing, but most of the systems published in the DB literature are primarily designed for efficient document storage and retrieval [22,39]. Furthermore, they are optimized to evaluate complex XQuery statements on large XML documents in single-user mode. Hence, many aspects of proven DBMS functionality and technology are often neglected in these systems, in the first place read/write transaction processing in multi-user mode, but also storage and indexing of dynamic XML documents in flexible formats to best satisfy the needs of specific applications.

As a consequence of the growing demand and the increasing adoption of XDBMSs, enhanced functionality and flexibility is needed in all system layers. At the bottom-most layer of the XDBMS architecture, a spectrum of storage devices, e. g., flash disks and magnetic disks, should be supported to provide for high-performance requirements. In upper layers, tailor-made and automatically chosen storage and index structures should help to approach application-specific needs [38]. These structures should enable complex path processing operations which, in turn, have to be integrated into cost-optimized query plans.

Of course, the original "retrieval-only" focus of XDBMSs – probably caused by the first proposals of XQuery respectively XPath where the update part was left out – is not enough anymore. Due to the growing need of update facilities, XDBMSs should efficiently support fine-grained, concurrent, and transaction-safe document modifications. For example, workloads for *financial application logging*[2] include 10M to 20M inserts in a 24-hour day, with about 500 peak inserts/sec. Because at least a hundred users need to concurrently read the data for troubleshooting and auditing tasks, concurrency control is challenged to provide short-enough response times for interactive operations [26]. Currently, all vendors of XML(-enabled) DBMSs support updates only at document granularity and, thus, cannot manage highly dynamic XML documents, let alone achieve such performance goals. Hence, new concurrency control protocols together with efficient implementations are needed to meet these emerging challenges.

During the last five years, we have addressed – by designing, implementing, analyzing, optimizing, and adjusting an XDBMS prototype system called XTC (XML Transactional Coordinator) – all these issues indispensable for a full-fledged DBMS. To guarantee broad acceptance for our research, we strive for a *general solution* that is even applicable for a spectrum of XML language models (e. g., XPath, XQuery, SAX, or DOM) in a multi-lingual XDBMS environment. In this survey paper, we want to report on our experiences gained and, in particular, focus on the concepts, functionalities, and mechanisms which turned out to be essential performance drivers of XDBMSs.

[2] Another example is monitoring the airline traffic control where legal demands call for collecting and saving huge and rapidly growing volumes of heterogeneous information (formatted data, mail, voice, signal, etc.) for 5 years.

2 Hierarchical DBMS Architecture

As mapping model or reference architecture for relational DBMSs, Andreas Reuter and the first author proposed a hierarchical multi-layer model about 25 years ago [17]. The five layers describe the major steps of dynamic abstraction from the physical storage up to the user interface. At the bottom, the database consists of huge volumes of persistently stored bits interpreted by the DBMS into meaningful information on which the user can operate. With each abstraction level, the objects become more complex, allowing more powerful operations and being constrained by a growing number of integrity rules. The uppermost interface supports a data model using set-oriented and declarative operations.

A key observation made while implementing this model in various projects was that the *invariants in database management determine the mapping steps of the supporting architecture*[13]. Hence, for XML database management, these basic invariants should still hold true: page-oriented mapping to external storage, management of record-oriented data, set-oriented database processing. Therefore, we used the five-layer model shown in Fig. 1 as our reference architecture for XTC. Obviously, both lower layers L1 and L2 keep their essential characteristics and functionality as in the relational world, because neither objects (pages or blocks) nor operations (fix, unfix or read/write) change very much. However, much more adaptations are necessary from L3 upwards[3]. In contrast to handling row sets often based on simple TID access or reference, the performance of handling and manipulating sequences of XML subtrees critically depends on a suitable node labeling scheme. In [19], we have already argued that it is *the key to efficient and fine-grained XML processing.*

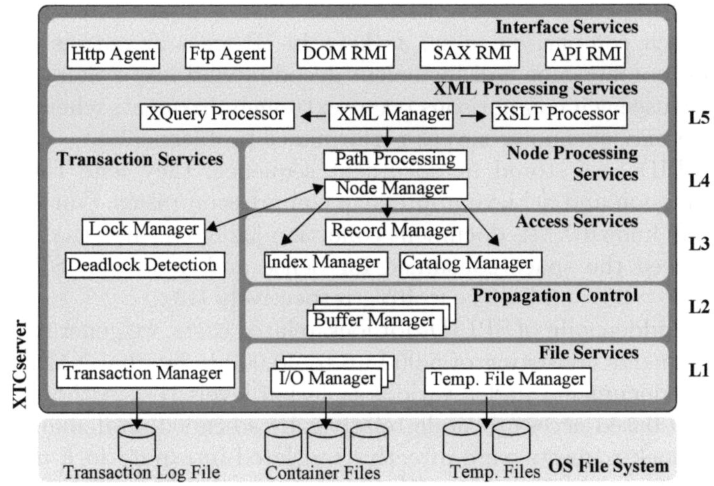

Fig. 1. The five-layer architecture of XTC

[3] For DBMSs, it is especially true: "Performance is not everything, but without performance everything is worth nothing."

3 Node Labeling

In our first XTC version, we started with a simple, but very inefficient solution by choosing a sequential numbering scheme (SEQIDs) which could only guarantee *uniqueness* and *order preservation* of node labels. Exploring fine-grained XML locking as the initial focus of our research, the protocols frequently had to acquire intention locks on all ancestors of the context node *cn*. To find their node labels, overly expensive look-ups in the disk-based document were unavoidable.

Various range-based and prefix-based node labeling schemes [7] were considered the prime candidates for XDBMSs, because their labels directly enable *testing of all XPath axes*. A close comparison and evaluation of those schemes included other XDBMS-specific criteria [14]. While range-based schemes failed to guarantee *immutable labels in dynamic XML documents* (under heavy updates/insertions) and could not directly compute, i. e., without further index access or similar deviation, *all ancestor labels* of *cn*, prefix-based node labeling turned out to be the winner, because they support all desired labeling properties *without the need of document access*. Each label based on the Dewey Decimal Classification, e. g., $d_1 = 1.7.9.5.17$, directly represents the path from the document's root to the related node and the local order w. r. t. the parent node. Some schemes such as OrdPaths [34], DeweyIDs, or DLNs [14] provide immutable labels by supporting an overflow technique for dynamically inserted nodes. Because they are equivalent for all XDBMS tasks, we use the generic name *stable path labeling identifiers* (SPLIDs) for them.

Because SPLIDs tend to be space-consuming, suitable encoding and compression of them in DB pages is a must. Effective encoding of SPLID divisions at the bit level may be accomplished using Huffman codes [14]. It is important that the resulting codes preserve their order when compared at the byte level. Otherwise, each comparison, e. g., as keys in B*-trees or entries in reference lists, requires cumbersome and inefficient decoding and inspection of the bit sequences. Because such comparisons occur extremely frequent, schemes violating this principle may encounter severe performance problems [25].

When SPLIDs are stored in document sequence, they lend themselves to prefix-compression and achieve impressive compression ratios. Our experiments using a widely known XML document collection [32] confirmed that prefix-compression reduced the space consumed for dense and non-dense SPLID orders down to ~15 – ~35% and ~25 – ~40%, respectively [15].

To see the hidden gain of SPLIDs for lock-related costs, we generated a variety of XML documents consisting of 5,000 up to 40,000 individual XML nodes and traversed the documents under various isolation levels [11]. Although we optimized SEQID-based access to node relatives by so-called on-demand indexing, the required lock requests were directly translated into pure lock management overhead as plotted in Fig. 2(a). We have repeated document traversal using SPLID-based lock management (see Fig. 2(b)). Because the difference between *none* and *committed/repeatable* is caused by locking overhead, we see drastic performance gains compared to SEQIDs. While those are responsible for an up to ~600% increase of the reconstruction times in our experiment, SPLIDs keep

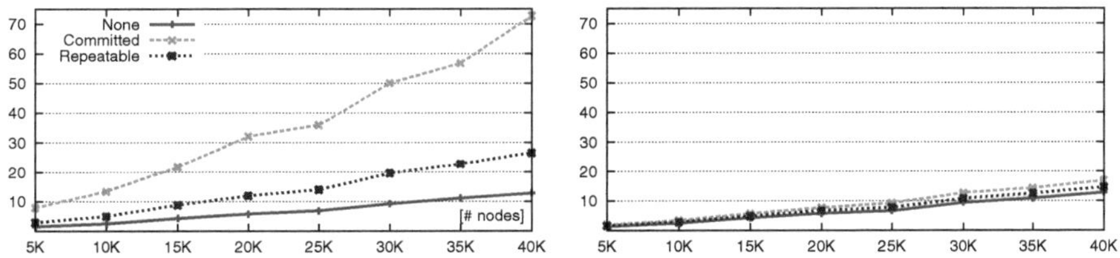

(a) SEQID node labeling (b) SPLID node labeling

Fig. 2. Documents traversal times (sec.)

worst-case locking costs in the range of ~10 – ~20% [3]. SEQIDs have fixed length, whereas SPLIDs require handling of variable-length entries. Coping with variable-length fields adds some complexity to SPLID and B*-tree management. Nevertheless, reconstruction time remained stable when SPLIDs were used – even when locking was turned off (case *none*).

Comparison of document reconstruction in Fig. 2(a) and (b) reveals for identical XML operations that the mere use of SPLIDs improved the response times by a factor of up to 5 and more. This observation confirms that prefix-based node labeling is indispensable for internal XML navigation and set-based query processing, but also for the lock manager's flexibility and performance.

4 Storing and Indexing Documents

Based on specific document characteristics, storage management should provide for automatic selection of appropriate mapping formats and adjusted parameters [38]. Typical methods replace the element/attribute names of the *plain* (external) format by *VocIDs* to save space and need some *Admin* metadata to enable variable-length entries. Inner tree nodes, i. e., the "structure", are stored as records containing $< SPLID, VocID, Admin >$, whereas leaf nodes carry the "content" in $< SPLID, Value, Admin >$ records.

4.1 Storage Formats

Three kinds of mappings are provided in XTC. The document-oriented storage formats keep both content and structure: Using the *naive* format, the VocIDs of all element/attribute and content nodes are directly mapped together with their uncompressed SPLIDs to the underlying storage structure (see Fig. 3), whereas the *pc* format deviates from the *naive* mapping by applying prefix-compression to all SPLIDs. As a novel mapping approach, the path-oriented storage format called *po* virtualizes the entire structure part of the document.

For this reason, an auxiliary, document-related structure called *path synopsis* is needed. It represents for each document path its path class and is enhanced by *path class references* (PCRs) for them (see Fig. 4(a)). Because providing substantial mapping flexibility, effective lock management support, and also considerable

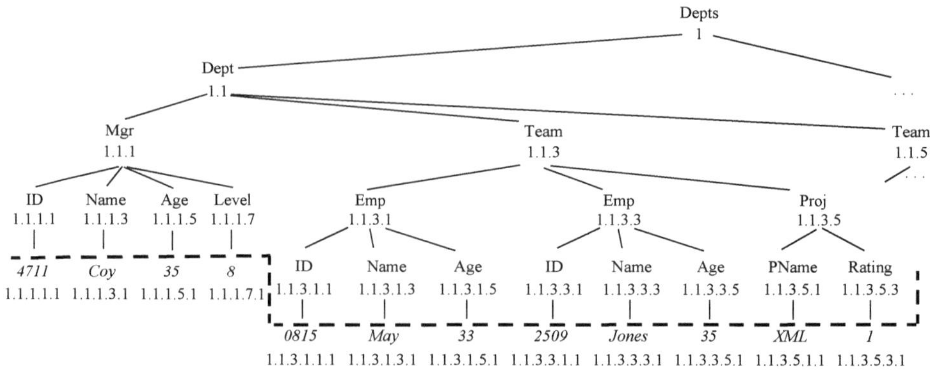

Fig. 3. Document fragment (in the path-oriented storage format, only nodes below the dashed line are physically stored)

speed-up of query evaluation [15], the use of path synopses turned out to be a *key concept* for XTC's processing efficiency.

Only the "content part" is physically stored when the *po* format is used (see Fig. 3). Reference [31] explains the concept of *structure virtualization*, i. e., the *po* mapping, in detail and shows that path reconstruction can be achieved on demand when the SPLID of a node together with its PCR is present. For this reason, leaf records are composed of $< SPLID, Value, PCR, Admin >$ where the SPLIDs are prefix-compressed. All navigational and set-oriented operations can be executed guaranteeing the same semantics as on *naive* or *pc* formats. Fig. 4(b) shows that only the content nodes are stored; using the path synopsis, entry $< 1.1.1.5.1, 6, 35 >$ tells us that the related path to the value 35 is `/Depts/Dept/Mgr/Age` with the ancestor SPLIDs 1, 1.1, 1.1.1, 1.1.1.5.

All documents are physically represented using a B*-tree as base structure, where the records (tree nodes) are consecutively stored in the *document container* thereby preserving the document order. The *document index* is used to provide direct access via SPLIDs. As an example, Fig. 4(b) illustrates the *po* format for the document fragment of Fig. 3.

As compared to the *plain* format, *naive* as the straightforward internal format typically achieves a storage gain of ~10% to ~30%, although the saving from VocID usage is partially compensated by the need for node labels. Extensive empirical (structure-only) tests using our reference document collection [32] have identified a further gain of ~27% to ~43% when using *pc* format and, in turn, a *naive*-to-*po* gain of ~71% to ~83% [15]. Because also exhibiting better mapping and reconstruction times, the *po* format is a substantial performance driver.

Content compression is orthogonal to the storage formats discussed. We have observed [15] that, using simple character-based compression schemes, the content size could be considerably reduced in our rather data-centric reference document collection such that a storage gain of ~22% to ~42% is possible. Even more compression gain could be expected for document-centric XML content.

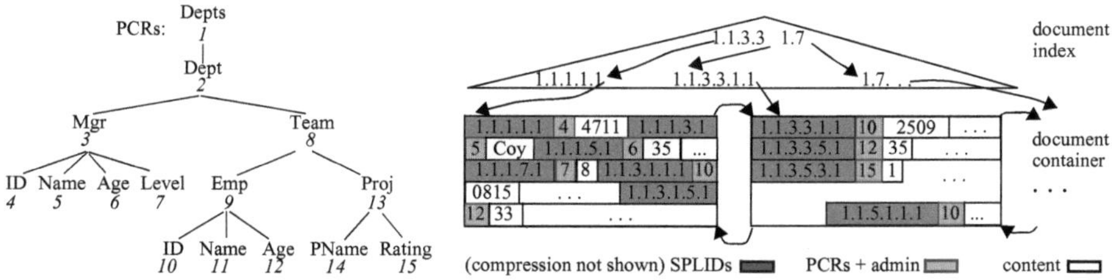

(a) Path synopsis (b) Stored document in *po* format

Fig. 4. Physical storage structures

4.2 Indexing Options

Set-oriented access to the nodes of an XML document is supported by a variety of index types. Similar to the document store including the document index (see Fig. 4(b)), all secondary index types in XTC are implemented using B-tree/B*-tree structures:

- *Element index*: It offers two basic access primitives: *Scan* and *Axis Evaluation*. For this reason, it maintains for each element name a reference list of all its nodes. All element names are organized in a *name directory* where the reference lists are themselves indexed (*node-reference indexes*).
- *Path index*: This structure can index paths qualified by a simple path predicate p, e. g., `//Mgr/Age` or `//Dept//Emp`. Because SPLIDs carry essential path information, they are utilized together with the path synopsis to directly support path queries.
- *Content index*: It maps each content value to the text nodes which stores it.
- *Content-and-Structure (CAS) index*: As a hybrid index combining content and structure information, it supports the evaluation of CAS queries. Each content value is associated with a list of references (SPLID + PCR) to the related document nodes. Such a combined reference enables together with the path synopsis the reconstruction of the entire path without accessing the document.

CAS indexes are particularly powerful, because a large share of matching queries can be evaluated solely on the index structure. Only when additional attributes/elements are requested for output, access to the disk-based document is needed. In a *unique* CAS index, all entries have the same PCR, while in a *homogeneous collective* index, the entries may have varying PCRs, i. e., they may refer to different path classes. For the *heterogeneous collective* CAS index, the index predicate p may be generalized to $p = p_1 \vee ... \vee p_i \vee ... \vee p_n$ where the p_i are simple path predicates. A *generic* CAS index contains all values of a certain type, e. g., $p =$ `//*` [29].

Refined evaluations of XTC's indexing performance can be found in [31]. Furthermore, it is reflected by the query evaluation results reported in Sect. 7.

5 Path Processing Operators

So far, layer L4 of XTC provides about 50 *path processing operators* (PPOs) – exhibiting locking-aware behavior where appropriate [30] – which are tailored to the underlying storage and index structures (L3). They can be considered as part of the physical algebra operations. Here, we can only focus on a prominent PPO generally called *holistic twig join*. A twig query (also called tree-pattern query) contains multiple path branches (twigs) and potentially path and content predicates, e. g. `doc('dept.xml')//Mgr[./Age>=''50'']/Name)` as XPath expression. It can be either decomposed into single paths or processed as a whole. Single paths could be evaluated by structural joins or matched by means of indexes and then joined (or intersected). To avoid joins, special (twig) indexes can answer path pattern queries directly. In contrast to a structural join, a holistic twig join can consume more than two input streams which are combined to match the complex branching path patterns.

As identified in Fig. 5, numerous algorithms were proposed for twig processing, but no algorithm obtains the expressiveness of our (logical) twig operator called

Algorithms for Holistic Twig Joins	**descendant**	**child**	**and**	**or**	**not**	**optional edges**	**projection**	**grouping**	**expressions**	**filters**	**pos. predicates**	**no. of phases**	**element indexes**	**path indexes**
PathStack [2]	+											-		
PathStack ¬ [19]	+				+							-		
TwigStack [2]	+		+									2	+[1]	
TwigStackList [22]	+	+	+									2		
TwigStackList ¬ [38]	+	+	+		+							2		
TJFast [23]	+	+	+									2		+[2]
iTwigJoin [3]	+	+	+									2		+[3]
TSGeneric + [18]	+		+									2	+[4]	
Twig²Stack [4]	+		+			+	+	+				1		
TwigList [29]	+		+				+					1		
TwigOpt. [7]	+		+	+			+					1	+	
Ext. TwigOpt [25]	+	+[5]	+	+	+[5]	+	+	+	+	+[5]	+	1	+	+[6]

1. Skipping in TwigStack only supported by XB-Tree.
2. TJFast requires special embedding of path information into SPLIDs.
3. iTwigJoin supports streams generated by path indexes, but no internal element reconstruction.
4. TSGeneric + relies on the special XR-tree.
5. Matching *child / not / filter* integrated in output generation (and not in matching phase).
6. Index embedding with *ancestor tuple builder* algorithm only possible, when SPLIDs are indexed.

Fig. 5. Survey of twig algorithms

Extended TwigOpt. We consider this operator richness as desirable, because the higher the expressiveness, the more operations can be embedded into the twig algorithm. Hence, the number of operators can be minimized in the final query execution plan (QEP) (see Sect. 6). Therefore, our twig operator includes so many concepts: path pattern supporting axes *child*, *descendant* and *attribute*; logical *and* and *or* conjunctions; optional subtree patterns (i. e., optional edges); projection; positional predicates; output filters; embedded output expressions; grouping.

Depending on the indexes present, it is physically mapped to suitable storage structures during QEP optimization (see Sect. 6). Again, its potential as a performance driver is revealed in Sect. 7.

6 Query Planning and Optimization

For XQuery translation and optimization, we referred to a QGM-based (query graph model [12]) internal structure guiding the entire process of query planning

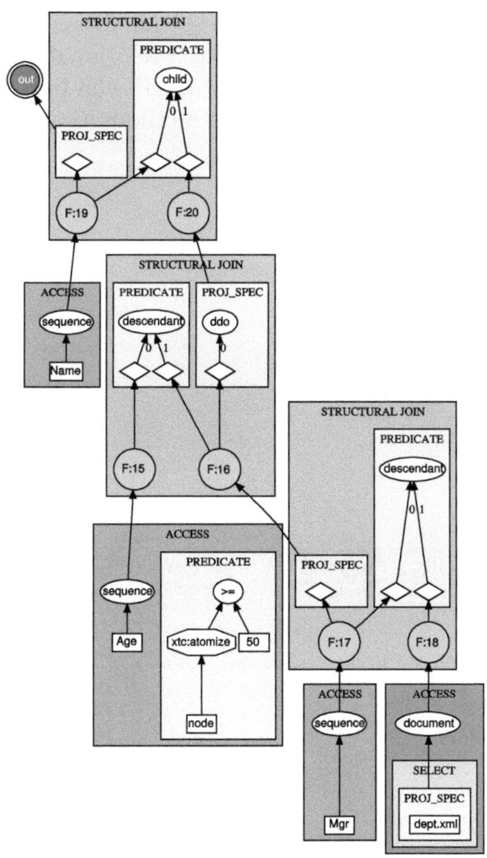

Fig. 6. XQGM instance of the query

and optimization. We substantially extended this model to XQGM [29] to primarily enable *query decorrelation rewrites* [35], i. e., replacing nesting by joins, and to integrate *index support*, i. e., the mapping of XPath/XQuery expressions to our rich collection of index types. With cardinality estimations derived from the related XML documents [1], our cost model can be tailored to the specific XQuery evaluation [42]. In particular, the optimizer tries to apply the more-than-usual expressiveness and functionality of *Extended TwigOpt* combined with CAS index support to minimize operator use and to unlatch XTC's evaluation power.

To only sketch the idea and to limit the explanation needs, the following simple XQuery statement serves as a query planning and optimization example:

```
for $Dept in doc('dept.xml')//Mgr[./Age>=''50''] return $Dept/Name
```

This query returns the department names of managers that are at least 50 years old. As indicated before, the XQGM suits as our logical XML algebra. Fig. 6 shows the XQGM instance that corresponds to the query. Here, the structural predicates (*child* and *descendant* axes) are evaluated using *structural joins* (SJs). The SJs receive their inputs from access operators that work on nested tuple sequences. SJ inputs are connected to so-called *tuple variables* (F:x) having a for-loop semantics, i. e., an SJ is similar to a relational sort-merge join [29].

For the execution of this query, numerous QEPs can be derived. Due to structural join reordering and various indexing methods that can be considered as

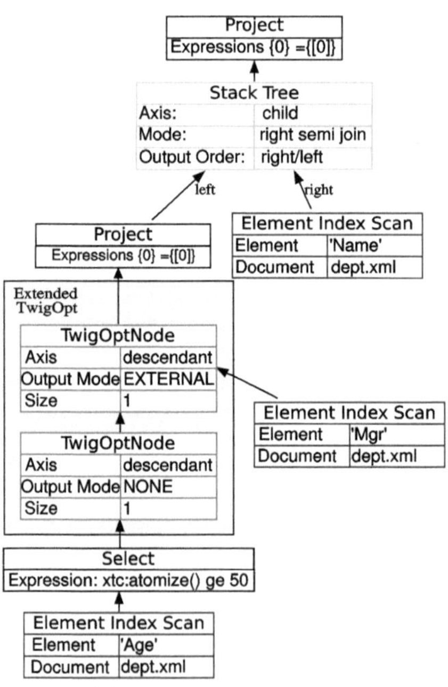

(a) A QEP with PPOs

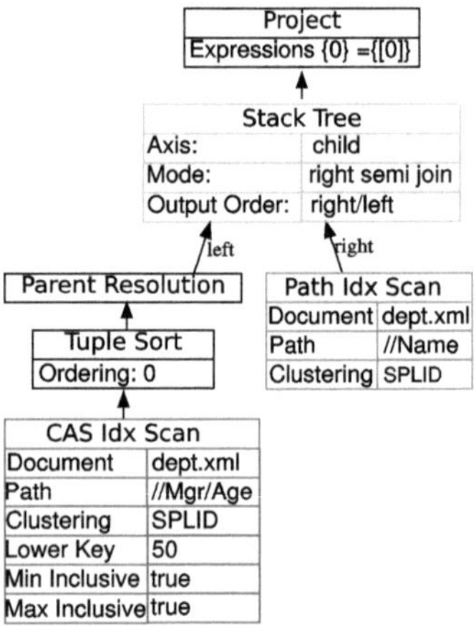

(b) A QEP using CAS and path indexes

Fig. 7. Optimization alternatives

alternatives by our query optimizer [42], the search space quickly becomes very large. Therefore, cost-based query optimization is necessary to wipe out expensive QEPs. Amongst others, Fig. 7(a) and (b) show two possible QEPs. In Fig. 7(a), the structural predicates are evaluated using the PPOs *StackTree* (Structural Join) and *Extended TwigOpt* (Holistic Twig Join). This QEP is gained by performing query rewrite using join fusion [41]. Both operators receive their inputs by accesses to the element index. Even though, a joint application of *StackTree* and *Extended TwigOpt* can outdistance QEPs that only consist of *StackTree* operators [41], Fig. 7(b) shows a more efficient variant. In this case, we assume a CAS index (`//Mgr/Age [Integer]`) and a path index (`//Name`). Instead of filtering all `Age` nodes and costly evaluating the structural predicates for `//Mgr/Age`, the optimizer exploits both types of indexes and connects their results by a *StackTree* operator. On large documents, this alternative is expected to outperform the former one by several orders of magnitude, because CAS indexes and path indexes are similar to materialized views.

7 Query Evaluation Performance

To sketch the interplay and efficiency of PPOs and query optimization, we want to repeat some results of an empircal study [31] and give some speed-up figures illustrating performance gains of index-supported range queries. We used the XMark framework [37] to evaluate in five different cases (C1 – C5) range query `//Asia/Item/[''C'' ≤ Location ≤ ''G'']`, where all tests were carried out on 4 XMark documents of size 10 MB, 50 MB, 100 MB, and 500 MB:

C1: No CAS/content index is available; hence, a holistic twig join operator had to be used.
C2: A content index for all content nodes is present, allowing structure predicate evaluation by the twig join operator. The delivered SPLIDs are not in document order and have to be sorted to serve as input for the twig join.
C3: A generic CAS index (`//*[String]`) enables PCR matching to remove false positives.
C4: A collective CAS index (`//Item/Location [String]`) is more focused than the generic index.
C5: A unique CAS index (`//Asia/Item/Location [String]`) takes care that no false positives can occur.

We refer to case C1 as baseline – no index was present and verification of the content predicate required navigational steps (thus implying expensive random IO) – and illustrate in Fig. 8 that *three orders of magnitude* can be gained by adjusted indexes. While content access support in case C2 achieved some noticeable improvements for the twig join, the real performance boost was observed for cases C3, C4, and C5 exploiting CAS indexes and PCR structure matching such that joins were not needed anymore. Thus, speed-ups in these cases increase with the document sizes by *up to two orders of magnitude.* Note, in cases C1 and C2, missing or insufficient index support caused linear response time growth w.r.t.

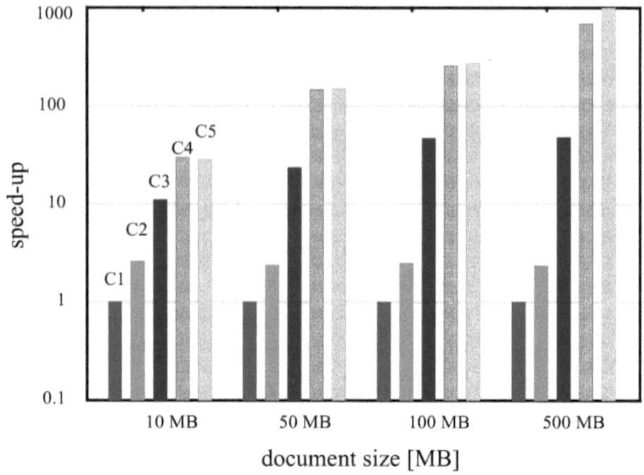

Fig. 8. Index-supported range queries

document sizes, whereas the response times in the remaining cases increased only marginally due to CAS support. This effect enhanced the speed-up factors observed for large document sizes.

Further performance gains and, at the same time, energy savings are possible when flash disks are used. Compared to magnetic disks, these storage devices provide a factor of 100 and more IOPS for random reads (and much lower, but steadily improved random-write performance). Hence, IO-intensive DB applications greatly take advantage of these properties. Initial experiments revealed that XTC in its current version improved its transaction throughput by a factor of ~3 thereby using less energy [16].

8 XML Locking

Multi-granularity lock (MGL) protocols [10,11] have introduced IR, IX, R, U, and X locks to achieve fine-granularity locking on hierarchies. Always locking entire subtrees, they are too strict for XML transactions because writers can sometimes be tolerated in the subtree of a context node *cn* [21].

8.1 Locking Concepts of taDOM

In the context of XTC, we developed a novel approach to XML concurrency control called *taDOM* providing tailor-made modes for fine-grained XML locking [18]. taDOM renames the conventional MGL locks and introduces new lock modes for *single nodes* called NR (node read) and NX (node exclusive), and for *all siblings under a parent* called LR (level read). The novelty of the NR and LR modes is that they allow, in contrast to MGL, to read-lock only a node or all nodes at a level (under the same parent), but not the corresponding subtrees.

To enable transactions to traverse paths in a tree having (levels of) nodes already read-locked by other transactions and to modify subtrees of such nodes,

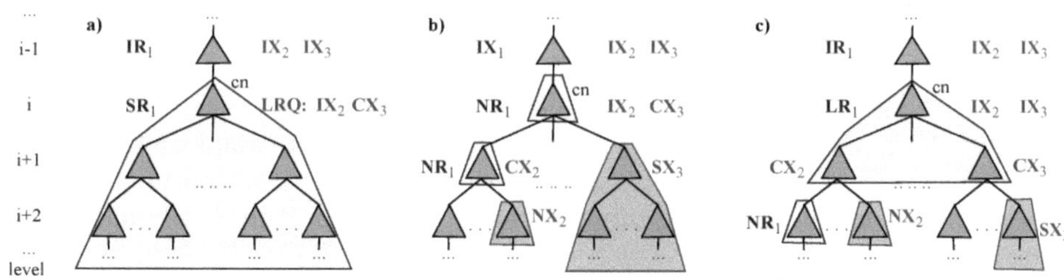

Fig. 9. Examples of locking flexibility and effectivity using taDOM's concepts

a new intention mode CX (child exclusive) had to be defined for a context (parent) node. It indicates the existence of an SX or NX lock on some direct child nodes and prohibits inconsistent locking states by preventing LR and SR locks. It does not prohibit other CX locks on a context node c, because separate child nodes of c may be exclusively locked by other transactions (compatibility is then decided on the child nodes themselves). Altogether these new lock modes enable serializable transaction schedules with read operations on inner tree nodes, while concurrent updates may occur in their subtrees. An important and unique feature (not applicable in MGL or other protocols) is the optional variation of the *lock depth* which can be dynamically controlled by a parameter. Lock depth n determines that, while navigating through the document, individual locks are acquired for existing nodes up to level n. If necessary, all nodes below level n are locked by a subtree lock (SR, SX) at level n.

Let us highlight by three scenarios taDOM's flexibility and tailor-made adaptations to XML documents as compared to competitor approaches. Assume transaction *T1* – after having set appropriate intention locks on the path from the root – wants to read-lock context node *cn*. Independently of whether or not *T1* needs subtree access, MGL only offers a subtree lock on *cn*, which forces concurrent writers (*T2* and *T3* in Fig. 9(a)) to wait for lock release in a lock request queue (LRQ). In the same situation, node locks (NR and NX) would allow greatly enhance permeability in *cn*'s subtree (Fig. 9(b)). As the only lock granule, however, node locks would result in excessive lock management cost and catastrophic performance behavior, especially for subtree deletion [20]. A frequent XML read scenario is scanning of *cn* and all its children, which taDOM enables by a single lock with special mode (LR). As sketched in Fig. 9(c), LR supports write access to deeper levels in the tree. The combined use of node, level, and subtree locks gives taDOM its unique capability to tailor and minimize lock granules. Above these granule choices, additional flexibility comes from lock-depth variations on demand – a powerful option only provided by taDOM.

8.2 The taDOM Protocol Family

Continuous improvement of these basic concepts led to a whole family of lock protocols, the taDOM family, and finally resulted in a highly optimized protocol called taDOM3+ (tailor-made for the operations of the DOM3 standard [8]), which consists of 20 different lock modes and "squeezes transaction parallelism" on XML document trees to the extent possible. Correctness and, especially, serializability of the taDOM protocol family was shown in [21,40].

The concept of *meta-locking* implemented in XTC provides the flexibility to exchange lock protocols at runtime. Hence, such dynamic adaptations of lock management are a prerequisite to achieve workload-dependent optimization of concurrency control and to eventually reach autonomic tuning of multi-user transaction processing [2].

8.3 Enhancing Multi-user Performance

We cross-compared 12 protocols under identical workloads and in the same system environment [20] using meta-locking, i. e., without hardwiring all the different lock protocols in the XTC code. In this lock contest, the taDOM protocols have clearly proven their superiority over all competitors. Protocols only offering *node locks* were beaten roughly by a factor of 2 by MGL protocols which, in addition, provided *subtree locks*. Supplementary to MGL equipped with *level locks*, the taDOM protocol family, in turn, achieved once again a doubling of the transaction throughput [20].

Every improvement of the lock protocol, however, shifts the locking performance a bit more from the level of logical XML trees down to the underlying storage structures. Hence, an efficient and scalable B*-tree implementation in an *adjusted infrastructure* is mandatory. Together with fine-tuning measures to workload characteristics, we added the following drivers for locking performance to our initial XTC version:

- *B*-tree Locking (D1)*: Initial tree traversal locked all visited index pages to rely on stable ancestor paths in case of leaf page split or merges. Provoking high update contentions, we re-implemented our B*-tree to follow the ARIES protocol [33] for index structures, which is completely deadlock-free and can therefore use cheap latches (semaphores) instead of more expensive locks. Contention during tree traversals is reduced by *latch coupling*, where at most a parent page and one of its child pages are latched at the same time.
- *Storage Manager (D2)*: Needing full root-to-leaf traversal, navigation embodies a crucial performance aspect of a B*-tree-based storage manager. We observed high locality in the leaf pages and remembered those pages and their version numbers as a hint for future operations. Each time when re-accessing the B*-tree for navigation, we use this information to first locate the leaf page of the context node. Only if this hint fails, we have to perform a full root-to-leaf traversal of the index to find the correct leaf.
- *Buffer Manager (D3)*: Prefix-compression of SPLIDs is very effective to save storage space and disk IO, but must be paid with higher costs for encoding and decoding of compressed records. To avoid this unnecessary decoding overhead and to speed up record search in a page, we enabled buffer pages to carry a cache for already decoded entries.
- *Dynamic Lock Depth Adjustment(D4)*: Growing lock depth refines lock granules to minimal sizes that do not always pay off, because conflicting oper-

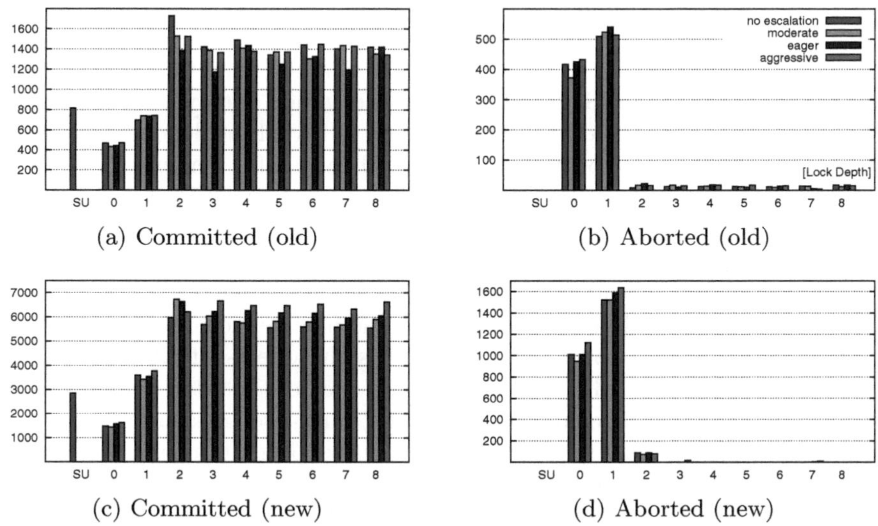

Fig. 10. Effects of lock depth and lock escalation on transaction throughput (tpm)

ations often occur at levels closer to the document root. In turn, it enlarges administration overhead, because the number of locks to be managed increases. Therefore, optimal lock depth depends on document properties, workloads, and other runtime parameters like multiprogramming level, etc., and has to be steadily controlled and adjusted at runtime. For this reason, we leveraged dynamic *lock escalation/deescalation* as the most effective solution. Using empirically proven heuristics for conflict potential in subtrees, the simple formula $threshold = k * 2^{-level}$ delivered escalation thresholds taking into account that typically fanout and conflicts decrease with deeper levels. Parameter k is adjusted to current workload needs.

– *Avoidance of Conversion Deadlocks (D5)*: Typically, deadlocks occurred when two transactions tried to concurrently append new fragments under a node already read-locked by both of them. Conversion to an exclusive lock involved both transactions in a deadlock. Update locks are designed for relational systems to avoid such conversion deadlocks [11], because they allow for a direct upgrade to an exclusive lock, when the transaction decides to modify the current record, or for a downgrade to a shared lock, when the cursor is moved to the next record without any changes. Transactions in XDBMSs do not follow such easy access patterns. Instead, they often perform arbitrary navigation steps, e. g., to check the content of child elements, before modifying a previously visited node. Hence, we carefully enriched our access plans with hints when to use update locks for node or subtree access.

Here, we can only sketch the results of these "performance drivers" which are described in [3]. We created read/write transaction benchmarks with high blocking potential, which access and modify a generated XMark document [37] at varying levels and in different granules. To get insight in the behavior of the lock-depth optimization D4, we measured the throughput of transactions per minute (tpm) and ran the experiments for three escalation thresholds (moderate, eager, aggressive) in single user mode (SU) and in multi-user mode with various initial lock depths (0–8). To draw the complete picture and to reveal the dependencies to our other optimizations, we repeated the tests with two XTC versions: XTC based on the old B*-tree implementation and XTC using the new B*-tree implementation together with the optimizations D2 and D3. To identify the performance gain caused by D1–D3, we focused on transaction throughput, i. e., commit and abort rates, and kept all other system parameters unchanged. Fig. 10 compares the experiment results. In single-user mode, the new version improves throughput by a factor of 3.5, which again highlights the effects of D2 and D3. The absence of deadlocks and the improved concurrency of the latch-coupling protocol in the B*-tree (D1) becomes visible in the multi-user measurements, where throughput speed-up even reaches a factor of 4 (see Fig. 10(a) and (c)) and the abort rates almost disappear for lock depths > 2 (see Fig. 10(b) and (d)).

Deadlocks induced by the old B*-tree protocol were also responsible for the fuzzy results of the dynamic lock depth adjustment (D4). With a deadlock-free B*-tree, throughput directly correlates with lock overhead saved and proves the benefit of escalation heuristics (see Fig. 10(c) and (d)).

9 Conclusions

In this survey, we outlined performance-critical concepts and their implementation in XTC. By observing performance bottlenecks or inappropriate system behavior in early experiments, we could adjust numerous algorithms in XTC. But removing a bottleneck often revealed another one at a higher performance level. Hence, we had to iteratively and repeatedly improve XTC to reach the current system version mature in many aspects. As outlined, we have identified and are still identifying during this maturing process many performance drivers in various architectural layers. So far, we have often gained orders of magnitude in component speed-ups and, as a consequence, dramatic overall performance improvements. Future research will address further enhancements in autonomic system behavior [38] and energy efficiency by using flash disks and implementing energy-aware algorithms in specific XDBMS components.

References

1. Aguiar Moraes Filho, J., Härder, T.: EXsum – An XML Summarization Framework. In: Proc. IDEAS, pp. 139–148 (2008)
2. Bächle, S., Härder, T.: Tailor-Made Lock Protocols and Their DBMS Integration. In: Proc. EDBT 2008 Workshop on Software Engineering for Tailor-made Data Management, pp. 18–23 (2008)
3. Bächle, S., Härder, T.: The Real Performance Drivers Behind XML Lock Protocols. In: Bhowmick, S.S., Küng, J., Wagner, R. (eds.) DEXA 2009. LNCS, vol. 5690, pp. 38–52. Springer, Heidelberg (2009)

4. Bruno, N., Koudas, N., Srivastava, D.: Holistic Twig Joins: Optimal XML Pattern Matching. In: Proc. SIGMOD, pp. 310–321 (2002)
5. Chen, T., Lu, J., Ling, T.W.: On Boosting Holism in XML Twig Pattern Matching Using Structural Indexing Techniques. In: Proc. SIGMOD, pp. 455–466 (2005)
6. Chen, S., Li, H.-G., Tatemura, J., Hsiung, W.-P., Agrawal, D., Candan, K.S.: Twig^{2}Stack: Bottom-Up Processing of Generalized-Tree-Pattern Queries over XML Documents. In: Proc. VLDB, pp. 283–294 (2006)
7. Christophides, W., Plexousakis, D., Scholl, M., Tourtounis, S.: On Labeling Schemes for the Semantic Web. In: Proc.12th Int. WWW Conf., pp. 544–555 (2003)
8. Document Object Model (DOM) Level 2 / Level 3 Core Specification. W3C Recommendation (2004), `http://www.w3.org/TR/DOM-Level-3-Core`
9. Fontoura, M., Josifovski, V., Shekita, E.J., Yang, B.: Optimizing Cursor Movement in Holistic Twig Joins. In: Proc. CIKM, pp. 784–791 (2005)
10. Graefe, G.: Hierarchical Locking in B-Tree Indexes. In: Proc. German National Database Conf. (BTW). LNI, vol. 65, pp. 18–42. Springer, Heidelberg (2007)
11. Gray, J., Reuter, A.: Transaction Processing: Concepts and Techniques. Morgan Kaufmann, San Francisco (1993)
12. Haas, L., Freytag, J.-C., Lohman, G.M., Pirahesh, H.: Extensible Query Processing in Starburst. In: Proc. SIGMOD, pp. 377–388 (1989)
13. Härder, T.: XML Databases and Beyond – Plenty of Architectural Challenges Ahead. In: Eder, J., Haav, H.-M., Kalja, A., Penjam, J. (eds.) ADBIS 2005. LNCS, vol. 3631, pp. 1–16. Springer, Heidelberg (2005)
14. Härder, T., Haustein, M.P., Mathis, C., Wagner, M.: Node Labeling Schemes for Dynamic XML Documents Reconsidered. Data & Knowl. Eng. 60(1), 126–149 (2007)
15. Härder, T., Mathis, C., Schmidt, K.: Comparison of Complete and Elementless Native Storage of XML Documents. In: Proc. IDEAS, pp. 102–113 (2007)
16. Härder, T., Schmidt, K., Ou, Y., Bächle, S.: Towards Flash Disk Use in Databases – Keeping Performance While Saving Energy? In: Proc. German National Database Conf. (BTW). LNI, vol. 144, pp. 167–186. Springer, Heidelberg (2009)
17. Härder, T., Reuter, A.: Concepts for Implementing a Centralized Database Management System. In: Proc. Int. Computing Symposium on Application Systems Development, pp. 28–60. B.G. Teubner-Verlag (1983)
18. Haustein, M.P.: Fine-Granular Transaction Isolation in Native XML Database Management Systems (in German), Ph.D. Thesis, Univ. of Kaiserslautern, Verlag Dr. Hut, München (2006)
19. Haustein, M.P., Härder, T., Mathis, C., Wagner, M.: DeweyIDs – The Key to Fine-Grained Management of XML Documents. In: Proc. SBBD, pp. 85–99 (2005)
20. Haustein, M.P., Härder, T., Luttenberger, K.: Contest of XML Lock Protocols. In: Proc. VLDB, pp. 1069–1080 (2006)
21. Haustein, M.P., Härder, T.: Optimizing Lock Protocols for Native XML Processing. Data & Knowl. Eng. 65(1), 147–173 (2008)
22. Jagadish, H.V., Al-Khalifa, S., Chapman, A.: TIMBER: A Native XML Database. The VLDB Journal 11(4), 274–291 (2002)
23. Jiang, H., Wang, W., Lu, H., Yu, J.X.: Holistic Twig Joins on Indexed XML Documents. In: Proc. VLDB, pp. 273–284 (2003)
24. Jiao, E., Ling, T.W., Chan, C.Y.: *PathStack*¬: A Holistic Path Join Algorithm for Path Query with Not-Predicates on XML Data. In: Zhou, L.-z., Ooi, B.-C., Meng, X. (eds.) DASFAA 2005. LNCS, vol. 3453, pp. 113–124. Springer, Heidelberg (2005)
25. Li, C., Ling, T.W., Hu, M.: Efficient Updates in Dynamic XML Data: from Binary String to Quaternary String. VLDB J. 17(3), 573–601 (2008)

26. Loeser, H., Nicola, M., Fitzgerald, J.: Index Challenges in Native XML Database Systems. In: Proc. German National Database Conf. (BTW). LNI, vol. 144, pp. 508–523. Gesellschaft für Informatik (2009)
27. Lu, J., Chen, T., Ling, T.W.: Efficient Processing of XML Twig Patterns with Parent-Child Edges: a Look-Ahead Approach. In: Proc. CIKM, pp. 533–542 (2004)
28. Lu, J., Chen, T., Ling, T.W.: *TJFast*: Effective Processing of XML Twig Pattern Matching. In: Proc. WWW, pp. 1118–1119 (2005)
29. Mathis, C.: Storing, Indexing, and Querying XML Documents in Native XML Database Management Systems, Ph.D. Thesis, Univ. of Kaiserslautern, Verlag Dr. Hut, München (2009)
30. Mathis, C., Härder, T., Haustein, M.P.: Locking-Aware Structural Join Operators for XML Query Processing. In: Proc. SIGMOD, pp. 467–478 (2006)
31. Mathis, C., Härder, T., Schmidt, K., Bächle, S.: XML Indexing and Storage: Fulfilling the Wish List (submitted, 2009)
32. Miklau, G.: XML Data Repository, `http://www.cs.washington.edu/research/xmldatasets`
33. Mohan, C.: *ARIES/KVL*: A Key-Value Locking Method for Concurrency Control of Multiaction Transactions Operating on B-Tree Indexes. In: Proc. VLDB, pp. 392–405 (1990)
34. O'Neil, P., O'Neil, E., Pal, S., Cseri, I., Schaller, G., Westbury, N.: *OrdPaths*: Insert-Friendly XML Node Labels. In: Proc. SIGMOD, pp. 903–908 (2004)
35. Özcan, F., Seemann, N., Wang, L.: XQuery Rewrite Optimization in IBM DB2 pureXML. Data Engineering Bulletin 31(4), 25–32 (2008)
36. Qin, L., Yu, J.X., Ding, B.: *TwigList*: Make Twig Pattern Matching Fast. In: Kotagiri, R., Radha Krishna, P., Mohania, M., Nantajeewarawat, E. (eds.) DASFAA 2007. LNCS, vol. 4443, pp. 850–862. Springer, Heidelberg (2007)
37. Schmidt, A., Waas, F., Kersten, M.L., Carey, M.J., Manolescu, I., Busse, R.: XMark: A Benchmark for XML Data Management. In: Proc. VLDB, pp. 974–985 (2002)
38. Schmidt, K., Härder, T.: Usage-Driven Storage Structures for Native XML Databases. In: Proc. IDEAS, pp. 169–178 (2008)
39. Schöning, H.: *Tamino*–A DBMS Designed for XML. In: Proc. ICDE, pp. 149–154 (2001)
40. Siirtola, A., Valenta, M.: Verifying Parameterized taDOM+ Lock Managers. In: Geffert, V., Karhumäki, J., Bertoni, A., Preneel, B., Návrat, P., Bieliková, M. (eds.) SOFSEM 2008. LNCS, vol. 4910, pp. 460–472. Springer, Heidelberg (2008)
41. Weiner, A.M., Härder, T.: Using Structural Joins and Holistic Twig Joins for Native XML Query Optimization. In: Grundspenkis, J., Morzy, T., Vossen, G. (eds.) ADBIS 2009. LNCS, vol. 5739, pp. 149–163. Springer, Heidelberg (2009)
42. Weiner, A.M., Härder, T.: A Framework for Cost-Based Query Optimization in Native XML Database Management Systems. In: Li, C., Ling, T.W. (eds.) Advanced Applications and Structures in XML Processing: Label Streams, Semantics Utilization, and Data Query Technologies. IGI Global (2010)
43. XML on Wall Street, Financial XML Projects, `http://lighthouse-partners.com/xml`
44. Yu, J.X., Luo, D., Meng, X., Lu, H.: Dynamically Updating XML Data: Numbering Scheme Revisited. World Wide Web 8(1), 5–26 (2005)
45. Yu, T., Ling, T.W., Lu, J.: *TwigStackList*¬: A Holistic Twig Join Algorithm for Twig Query with Not-Predicates on XML Data. In: Li Lee, M., Tan, K.-L., Wuwongse, V. (eds.) DASFAA 2006. LNCS, vol. 3882, pp. 249–263. Springer, Heidelberg (2006)

Continuous Processing of Preference Queries in Data Streams

Maria Kontaki, Apostolos N. Papadopoulos, and Yannis Manolopoulos

Department of Informatics, Aristotle University
54124 Thessaloniki, Greece
{kontaki,papadopo,manolopo}@csd.auth.gr

Abstract. Preference queries have received considerable attention in the recent past, due to their use in selecting the most preferred objects, especially when the selection criteria are contradictory. Nowadays, a significant number of applications require the manipulation of time evolving data and therefore the study of continuous query processing has recently attracted the interest of the data management community. The goal of continuous query processing is to continuously evaluate long-running queries by using incremental algorithms and thus to avoid query evaluation from scratch, if possible. In this paper, we examine the characteristics of important preference queries, such as skyline, top-k and top-k dominating and we review algorithms proposed for the evaluation of continuous preference queries under the sliding window streaming model.

1 Introduction

Recently, preference queries have significantly attracted the research interest. Preference queries are frequently used in multicriteria decision making applications, where a number of (usually) contradictory criteria are involved to select the most convenient answers to the user.

Assume that a customer is interested in purchasing a PDA device. Assume further, that the customer focuses on two important characteristics of PDAs, namely, price and weight. Unfortunately, these two criteria are frequently contradictory and therefore, the number of candidates should be carefully selected. In this example, each PDA is represented as a tuple containing two attributes (price and weight) and the customer is interested in items that minimize these attributes. Depending on the semantics of each attribute, in other cases the customer may desire the maximization of the attributes in question, or any other combination. For the rest of the discussion, we consider that smaller values are preferable. However, most of the techniques mentioned in this paper are directly applicable to other cases as well.

Preference queries have received considerable attention in the past, due to their use in selecting the most preferred items, especially when the selection criteria are contradictory. Skyline [5,8,29,44] and top-k [3,7,10] queries have been thoroughly studied by the database community. Preferences have been used previously in other disciplines such as Game Theory (e.g., Pareto optimality [34]) and Computational Geometry (e.g., maximal vectors [20]).

J. van Leeuwen et al. (Eds.): SOFSEM 2010, LNCS 5901, pp. 47–60, 2010.

During the last years, we are witnessing a significant interest of the research community towards continuous query processing, due to the fact that many applications deal with data that change frequently with respect to time. In these types of applications, the goal is to continuously evaluate the query and report the result in real time contrary to ad-hoc query executions that are used in traditional applications [1,12,25]. Examples of such emerging applications are network monitoring, financial data analysis, sensor networks to name a few.

The most important property of data streams is that new tuples are continuously appended and, therefore, efficient storage and processing techniques are required to cope with high update rates. More specifically, a stream-oriented algorithm should satisfy the following requirements: (a) fast response time, (b) incremental evaluation, (c) limited number of data access, and (d) in memory storage to avoid expensive disk accesses. Therefore, algorithms proposed for traditional databases are not appropriate and new methods and techniques should be developed to fulfil the requirements posed by the data stream model.

Efficient stream processing algorithms are difficult to be designed, due to the unbounded nature of data streams. Several models have been proposed to reduce and bound the size of the streams. A class of algorithms focuses on the recent past of data streams by applying the *sliding window model* [2,14]. This way, only the most recent tuples (*active* tuples) of the data stream are considered for query processing, whereas older tuples are not taken into account as they are considered obsolete.

There exist two basic forms of sliding windows. In a *count-based* sliding window, the number of active tuples remains constant (i.e., the sliding window contains the last W tuples) and therefore for each new tuple that arrives, the oldest one expires. In a *time-based* sliding window, the number of active tuples may vary. The *expiration time* of a tuple does not depend on the arrival or expiration of other tuples. The set of active tuples is composed of all tuples arrived the last T time instances. Figure 1 illustrates a count-based sliding window.

In this paper, we discuss the state-of-the-art processing techniques of the most important preference queries in data streams under the sliding window model.

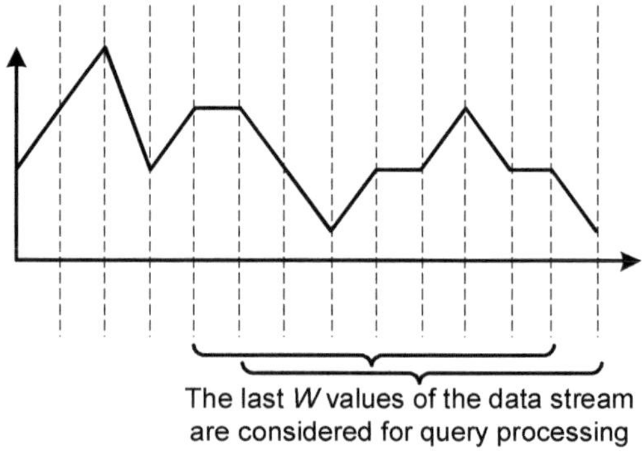

Fig. 1. Example of a count-based sliding window of length W=9

More specifically, we study proposed methods for the continuous evaluation of skyline and top-k queries. Moreover, we examine closely a new type of preference query, the top-k dominating query, that recently has attracted significant researcher interest.

The rest of the paper is organized as follows. Sections 2 and 3 study different processing techniques of skyline and top-k queries respectively and give detailed description for the most important ones. Section 4 presents the top-k dominating query and discusses early related work on this topic. Finally, Section 5 concludes the work and discusses future research directions.

2 Skyline Queries

The skyline query is one of the most widely used preference queries. It is based on the *dominance relationship* between tuples. Assuming that smaller values are preferable in all dimensions, the dominance relationship and the skyline are defined as follows:

Definition 1 (dominant tuple). *A tuple t_i dominates another tuple t_j ($t_i \prec t_j$), if and only if t_i is smaller than or equal to t_j in all dimensions and it is strictly smaller than t_j in at least one of them.*

Definition 2 (skyline). *The skyline consists of the tuples not dominated by any other tuple.*

The key advantage of the skyline query is that it does not require any user-defined information or parameter. Moreover, skyline queries are characterized by the scaling invariance property, which means that if scaling is applied to any dimension values, the result remains unchanged. On the other hand, as the dimensionality increases, the probability for a tuple to dominate another tuple is reduced significantly and, therefore, the number of skyline tuples increases substantially. Overall, the skyline query does not bound the size of the output and therefore in extreme cases it is possible that all the tuples be part of the skyline result.

In the past decade, skyline queries are thoroughly studied for several types of modern applications such as P2P networks [43], MANETs [15] and Web systems [4]. Moreover, methods for different types of data, such as spatial [39] and uncertain data [35], are developed to increase efficiency of skyline query processing. Additionally, several variations of the skyline have been proposed. In [44], the authors study the skyline computation in subspaces. Another variation has been proposed in [29] for selecting skyline tuples according to their domination capabilities. Dominance relationships between different data sets (e.g., products and customers) are examined in [27], where the authors proposed an organization scheme called DADA cube, to support a number of significant query types.

The first attempt to develop an algorithm more suitable for dynamic data was [41], where the authors presented a progressive algorithm for skyline computation. In the sequel, more sophisticated and efficient progressive methods have

Table 1. Continuous skyline algorithms

Method	Query Type	Window Type	Multiple Queries
cnN	skyline	count-based	yes
LookOut	skyline	time-based	no
Lazy and Eager	skyline	both	no
Filter and Sampling	FSQW	time-based	no
CoSMuQ	k-dominant skyline	both	yes

been developed [24,37,38]. These algorithms are not appropriate for continuous evaluation but, instead, they were developed to support online user preferences and data that are not updated frequently and only a small number of insertions/deletions can be handled efficiently. Table 1 contains a brief description of continuous skyline computation algorithms, which are studied in detail in the next subsections.

2.1 cnN

In [28], the authors proposed a novel technique for continuous skyline query processing. First, they provide a pruning technique to reduce the number of elements to be stored for processing. If the data distribution is independent and data values are always distinct, then the average number of elements that are stored is $O(\log^d N)$, where N is the maximum size of the sliding windows and d is the number of dimensions. The survived elements R_N are organized in graphs based on the *critical dominance relationship* between them and these graphs form a forest. Assume two active elements e_1 and e_2. Element e_1 critical dominates e_2, if it is the youngest element that is older than e_2 and dominates it. Each critical dominance relationship is represented by an edge of the forest. The forest is encoded by a set of intervals of 1-dimensional space and then skyline query is evaluated by using stabbing queries.

In addition, a maintenance algorithm of R_N and the encoded scheme of intervals is provided. Then, a trigger-based incremental algorithm *cnN* has been proposed to enable efficient continuous skyline processing. The proposed framework supports multiple n-of-N skyline queries, i.e., skyline queries with different sliding window size n ($n \leq N$). The continuous algorithm updates the result in $O(\delta)$ time per new data element and requires $O(\log s)$ time to update the trigger list per result change, where δ is the number of elements changed in the current result and s is the number of skylines elements. The main disadvantage of the *cnN* algorithm is that it requires the maintenance of several structures, such as graphs, interval tree and R^*-tree used for the survived tuples.

2.2 LookOut

Algorithm *cnN* handles count-based sliding windows, whereas algorithm *LookOut* [33] has been proposed for time-based windows. *LookOut* uses a heap to store the skyline tuples and a R^*-tree to store the active tuples of the window.

The proposed method utilizes some attractive properties of skyline queries, such as the *transitive* property. When a new tuple is inserted, we check if the new tuple is a skyline tuple or not. The algorithm uses a best-first search on the spatial index and discards nodes that their lower left corner does not dominate the new tuple. When a skyline tuple expires, we check the spatial index to find new skyline tuples. The key observation is that new skyline tuples should be part of the skyline of the space dominated by the expired tuple. These tuples are detected by a best-first search and then are checked further to discard tuples that are dominated by other skyline tuples. Notice that the proposed algorithm does not prune tuples (all the active tuples are stored in a R^*-tree), although this is possible as we will see in the next subsection.

2.3 Lazy and Eager

In [42], two algorithms have been presented, called *Lazy* and *Eager*. We begin our description with the first one. When a new tuple t arrives, *Lazy* searches for tuples in the *dominance region* (DR) and the *antidominance region* of t to update the skyline tuples. Region $t.DR$ is the data space that is dominated by t, whereas $t.ADR$ is the area where a tuple dominating t could fall. When a skyline tuple expires, the algorithm deletes all the expired tuples (notice that *Lazy* keep stored tuples even after their expiration) and then tries to find possible skyline tuples in the area dominated *exclusively* by the expired skyline tuple. *Lazy* and *LookOut* methods are similar, since they have same operations.

To improve performance, two attractive properties of "stream skylines" have been presented in [42]: (a) a tuple can be safely discarded if it is dominated by an incoming tuple, and (b) a tuple can be part of skyline for at most a single continuous time interval, which is called *skyline influence time* and denotes the minimum possible time at which the tuple can be part of skyline. Algorithm *Eager* utilizes these properties. Therefore, when a new tuple t is inserted, *Eager* during the skyline update also discards the active tuples belonging to $t.DR$. Then, it computes the skyline influence time of t and forms an event that will be processed in this time. *Eager* compared to *Lazy* reduces the memory consumption by keeping those tuples that may be inserted in the skyline, but requires additional overhead to process the events.

2.4 Filter and Sampling

Continuous skyline queries report the skyline of the active tuples in each update. These types of skylines are called *snapshot skylines*. In [47], the authors state that snapshot skylines are not very meaningful, since in a streaming environment the skyline tuples may change too fast, and thus, it will be more interesting to identify tuples that are consistently part of skyline. Therefore, they introduce a variation of snapshot skylines called *frequent skyline query over a sliding window* (FSQW), which returns the tuples appearing in the skylines of at least μ of the n most recent timestamps. It is proved that an exact algorithm for FSQW requires the exact snapshot skyline computation.

The server-client architecture is considered, where the server continuously maintains the result. Moreover, changes to existing tuples are considered instead of new tuples, i.e., each client transmit a specific tuple and changes of it. Three algorithms have been proposed aiming at minimizing the communication overhead instead of processing cost [47]. The first algorithm, called *Filter*, is an exact algorithm and therefore can be also used for the evaluation of snapshot skylines. *Filter* avoids the transmission of updates to the server if they cannot influence the skyline. Specifically, the server computes a filter for each tuple and an update is transmitted from the client to the server only if (a) the tuple violates its filter, or (b) the server specifically asks the tuple. There are many possible filters for each tuple. The authors propose a model that tries to balance the transmissions due to filter violations and server requests.

Although *Filter* reduces significantly the number of updates transmitted to the server, its performance may degrade for large and frequently updated data sets. Algorithm *Sampling* has been proposed to reduce the communication overhead by computing approximate FSQW outputs. According to *Sampling*, all clients report their current status with some global probability R, which depends on the trade-off between user-defined accuracy and overhead. Finally, an algorithm, called *Hybrid*, has been presented that combines *Filter* and *Sampling*. *Hybrid* exploits the advantages of the two algorithms and avoids their disadvantages by allowing records to switch among different modes.

2.5 CoSMuQ

The number of skyline tuples depends heavily on the dimensionality of the data set and the data distribution. The number of tuples in the skyline increases substantially with increasing dimensionality, leading to difficulties in selecting the best object that satisfy user's preferences. Towards eliminating the huge number of skyline tuples, a novel method has been proposed in [11], which relaxes the dominance definition to increase the probability that a tuple will dominate another. Evidently, by increasing this probability, the number of skyline tuples is reduced. Instead of searching for ordinary skyline tuples in all dimensions, k-dominant skylines are being used. Assuming that the smaller values are preferable, the following definitions explain:

Definition 3 (k-dominant tuple). *A tuple t_i k-dominates another tuple t_j, if and only if t_i is smaller than or equal to t_j in at least k dimensions and it is strictly smaller than t_j in at least one of them.*

Definition 4 (k-dominant skyline). *The k-dominant skyline consists of the tuples not k-dominated by any other tuple.*

The processing techniques reported in [11] are executed in static data sets. In [21] the continuous k-dominant skyline evaluation over sliding windows is studied. The proposed algorithm *CoSMuQ* handles multiple continuous queries. Each query may be defined in a subset of the available dimensions, since different users are usually interested in different attributes. Moreover, the parameter k

set by each query, may be different. The proposed method divides the space in pairs of dimensions. For each pair, a grid is used to compute skyline tuples for these dimensions. Then, the method exploits the discovered skyline tuples to eliminate candidate k-dominant skyline tuples and it combines the partial results to compute the final result. The proposed scheme uses only simple domination checks, which are faster than k-dominant checks. However, in high dimensional spaces, $CoSMuQ$ considers a large number of grids.

3 Top-k Queries

A top-k query uses a user-defined *preference function* to assign scores to tuples and rank them. Assuming that smaller values of the preference function are preferable, the top-k query is defined as follows:

Definition 5 (top-k). *Given a data set and a preference function F, a top-k query returns the k tuples in the data set with the smallest scores according to F.*

Figure 2 depicts a time instance of the sliding window (W=10) of two-dimensional tuples. Assume that the preference function F is the sum of the values in two dimensions, whereas smaller values of F are preferable. A top-3 query (k=3) retrieves tuples t_7, t_8 and t_3, since they have the three smallest score 5, 5 and 5.5 respectively. In this example, the skyline consists of tuples t_3, t_4, t_5, t_7 and t_8, since these tuples are not dominated by any other active tuple.

In contrast to skyline queries, top-k queries bound the output size. If two or more tuples have the same score, then we can either: (a) report all these tuples but we may expect more than k tuples in the result, or (b) use a tie-breaking criterion, e.g., the value of a specific dimension. The major disadvantage of the top-k query is that it requires a user-defined preference function. This means that different preference functions can lead to different score assignments and

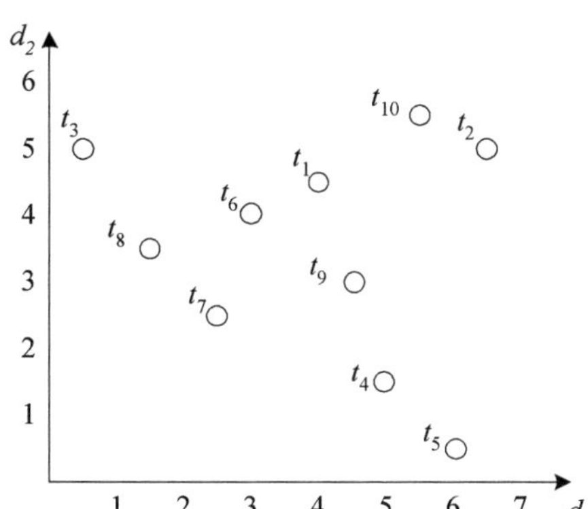

(a) 2-dimensional representation

id	d_1	d_2	$F=d_1+d_2$
t_1	4	4.5	8.5
t_2	6.5	5	7
t_3	0.5	5	5.5
t_4	5	1.5	6.5
t_5	6	0.5	6.5
t_6	3	4	7
t_7	2.5	2.5	5
t_8	1.5	3.5	5
t_9	4.5	3	7.5
t_{10}	5.5	5.5	11

(b) tuples and scores

Fig. 2. Example of preference queries

therefore in different results. Thus, the analysis of the results is not straightforward. Moreover, it is not always easy for a user to specify the appropriate preference function, especially with growing number of dimensions.

The literature is rich in methods proposed for the efficient evaluation of top-k queries [3,7,10,16]. Top-k queries have been studied in the context of several database types, such as relational [3], multimedia [9] and web databases [31]. Algorithms *Onion* [7] and *Prefer* [16] have been proposed for top-k queries in traditional databases. *Onion* uses the convex hulls of the database, whereas *Prefer* uses sorted lists. In [10], the authors presented algorithm *MPro* for the optimization of expensive predicates processing. Views are used in [13] to answer top-k queries. All the aforementioned methods are appropriate for conventional databases. There are many other methods in the bibliography but their description is beyond the scope of this paper. An excellent survey on top-k query processing in relational databases can be found in [18]. We continue with the detailed description of methods proposed for continuous top-k evaluation. A summary of the studied algorithms is given in Table 2.

Table 2. Continuous top-k methods algorithms

Method	Query Type	Window Type	Multiple Queries
TMA and SMA	top-k	both	yes
Distributed top-k	distributed top-k	time-based	no
Compact Set based	top-k on uncertain data	time-based	no
Det and Sam	top-k on uncertain data	time-based	no

3.1 TMA and SMA

Mouratidis et al. [32] proposed two algorithms for continuous top-k query execution in sliding windows. The first one, called *TMA*, is based on simple observations regarding the continuous processing of top-k queries. Each top-k query has an *influence region.* The influence region of a query determines the data space in which a tuple should belong so that it may change the query result. When a new tuple is inserted, *TMA* checks if the new tuple belongs to the influence region of any query and updates its top-k respectively. When a top-k tuple expires, a from scratch computation is performed if the new tuple does not have better score than the expired tuple.

To overcome this disadvantage, the authors proposed the algorithm *SMA*, which is based on the observation that the records appearing in some result of top-k are the ones that belong to the k-skyband [38] in the score-time space. Thus, the proposed algorithm transforms the problem of continuous top-k into k-skyband maintenance. *SMA* restricts the skyband maintenance for a query to tuples falling inside its influence region. It uses a balanced tree to store the arrival time of the k-skyband tuples sorted in descending order. Moreover, it keeps the *dominance counter* for each tuple t stored in balanced tree, which is the number of tuples with better score that arrive after t. However, there may be a scenario where the skyband contains fewer than k tuples. In such a case, the algorithm computes the skyband tuples from scratch.

3.2 Distributed Top-k

Babcock and Olston [6] proposed a distributed algorithm for top-k query processing. The problem considered in [6], assumes a central node and a number of monitor nodes, each one monitoring a data object. The changes of a data object form a data stream and, therefore, multiple data streams should be processed by the central node. The transmission of the entire data stream from a monitor node to the central node is unnecessary. Thus, the authors proposed a scheme in which arithmetic constraints are maintained at monitor nodes and distributed communication happens when constraints are violated. Then, the central node updates the top-k result and assigns new constraint to the monitor node.

The proposed algorithm is exact, i.e., the central node has the correct top-k output in every time instance. Additionally, approximate answers have been studied. Moreover, the algorithm aims at minimizing the network overhead. However, the proposed scheme is not fully distributed, since it uses some sort of "base station" or "coordinator".

3.3 Compact Set-Based Algorithms

In [19], the processing of continuous top-k queries in a sliding window over uncertain data streams is examined. The challenge of processing queries on uncertain data streams lies on high update rates and the exponential growth in the number of possible worlds induced by the uncertain data model. The paper adopts a simple uncertain data model, where each tuple appears with a certain probability independent of other tuples. Also, it defines the $Pk - topk$ query that returns the k most probable tuples of being the top-k among all. Moreover, the paper introduces the concept of *compact set* on which the proposed synopses are based on.

The authors extend the problem of uncertain top-k queries on static data sets to the case of data streams over sliding windows. First, a synopsis is presented that can handle only insertions (i.e., landmark windows). However, handling deletions is much more difficult and requires carefully designed synopses. The paper proposed several space and time efficient synopses with provable bounds to enable continuous top-k evaluation over sliding windows. Overall, the authors proposed and evaluated five algorithms based on the compact set concept.

3.4 Det and Sam

Hua and Pay [17] also examined the continuous evaluation of top-k queries over uncertain data streams. They proposed a novel uncertain data stream model and introduced the continuous probabilistic threshold top-k queries. More specifically, given a probabilistic threshold top-k query, a set of uncertain data streams and a sliding window length, the continuous probabilistic threshold top-k query reports the set of uncertain data streams whose top-k probabilities in the sliding window are at least p, for each time instant t.

The authors proposed four algorithms. The exact algorithm, called *Det*, computes the exact answer of a continuous probabilistic threshold top-k query. Moreover, they proposed a sampling algorithm, called *Sam*, which estimates the probability that an uncertain object being ranked top-k via sampling. Probabilistic guarantees are also provided. Then, *Sam* computes an approximation answer based on the estimated probabilities. Additionally, quantile summary techniques are applied to develop the space efficient versions of both algorithms.

4 Top-*k* Dominating Queries

Recently, an interesting alternative has been proposed [38], which combines the dominance concept with the notion of scoring functions. This new query is called top-k dominating query. The following definitions explain:

Definition 6 (domination power). *The domination power of a tuple is the number of tuples it dominates.*

Definition 7 (top-k dominating query). *A top-k dominating query retrieves the k tuples in the data set with the highest domination power.*

To clarify the definitions above, assume the example of Figure 2. A top-3 (k=3) dominating query retrieves tuples t_7, t_8 and t_6 with domination power 5, 4 and 3 respectively. All the other tuples have smaller domination power than 3. Although preference queries as skyline and top-k, have been studied in a data stream perspective, top-k dominating queries have not received adequate attention for this scenario. However, the top-k dominating query is an important decision support tool. In a sense, it combines skyline and top-k queries, resulting in a more complex one. Practically, it preserves their advantages without sharing their limitations. Top-k dominating queries use the dominant relationship rather than a user defined score function. The determination of the appropriate score function is not obvious, especially when the number of attributes increases. On the other hand, top-k dominating queries use an intuitive score to rank the tuples that can be interpreted easily by a non-expert. Moreover, top-k dominating queries bound the size of the resulting set of tuples, in contrast to skyline queries, where the size of the result is unbounded and increases significantly as the number of attributes grows. Additionally, they preserve the scaling invariance property.

In skylines and top-k queries, we can use the expiration time to prune tuples resulting in more efficient algorithms with respect to the memory requirements and the response time. More specifically, in a skyline query, if a tuple t_i is dominated by another tuple t_j and expires before t_j, then it is safe to prune tuple t_i. Assume the example of Figure 2. Assume further that the pointer of a tuple denotes its arrival time, i.e., $t_1.arr$=1. Tuple t_1 is dominated by t_8 end expires before t_8, thus t_1 can be safely discarded. In a top-k query, if k tuples exist with better scores than the score of a tuple t_i and t_i expires before them, then it is safe to discard tuple t_i. Returning to the example of Figure 2, the score of t_1 is 8.5 and there are more than 3 tuples with score better than 8.5 and expire after t_1 (e.g., t_3, t_4 and t_5), therefore t_1 can be pruned. On the other hand, top-k dominating queries are more complicated. It is not possible to discard tuples, even if we know that it is not possible to be in the result during their lifespan. This is because the existence of a tuple affects the domination power of the other tuples.

Top-k dominating queries have been addressed in [45,46,26]. In [45,46] the authors proposed efficient algorithms to determine the top-k dominating tuples by using an aggregate R-tree index. In [26], the authors studied efficient algorithms for top-k dominating query processing in uncertain databases. A pruning approach has been proposed to reduce the space of a probabilistic top-k dominating query and in addition, approximate queries are examined. The domination power is also used in [36] to rank multidimensional tuples. The concept of dominance score has been used by [40] towards ranking web services.

The literature is limited regarding continuous variants of top-k dominating query processing techniques over data streams. In [23], the authors use a simple grid-based indexing scheme to facilitate efficient search and update operations avoiding expensive reorganization costs of dynamic hierarchical access methods. Three algorithms are proposed. BFA is a naive approach computing all the domination checks in each update and it is simply proposed for comparison reasons. The algorithms EVA and ADA use an event-based approach to reduce both the number of domination checks during an update and the number of exact score computations as well. ADA use two optimizations regarding the event computations achieving the decrease of the number of events processed and, therefore, enhancing the efficiency of EVA. Subspace top-k dominating queries are examined in [22]. A new grid-based indexing scheme is proposed, called adaptive grid, to efficiently process subspace top-k dominating queries. Moreover, several optimizations are proposed to enhance the query processing mechanism. These methods are the first attempt for continuous top-k dominating queries evaluation.

5 Conclusions and Future Work

In this paper, we review various preference queries and we discuss their differences. Moreover, we thoroughly examine the related work on continuous processing of preference queries over sliding windows and we discuss the advantages and the disadvantages of the proposed methods.

Skyline queries have been examined more than other preference queries in the context of data streams. Various methods have been proposed to handle both count-based and time-based sliding windows. However, there are many open issues to be addressed. Subspace skyline queries have not been studied as well as many widely used variations of skylines such as constrained skylines. Recently, a theoretical study of skyline cardinality estimation over sliding windows is presented in [30]. The authors estimate skyline cardinality over uniformly and arbitrary distributed data. The results of this study can be used to optimize the query methodology to improve memory consumption and processing cost or the network overhead.

Although the study of continuous top-k queries has moved onto uncertain data streams, there are many research directions that should be examined, to develop more sophisticated and efficient methods for continuous top-k queries in certain data. Methods, more efficient than the existing ones, are required to handle the expiration of tuples. Distributed top-k evaluation can be enhanced further by developing methods that have as uniformly as possible energy consumption. Methods can exploit various characteristics of data types such as spatial data to improve efficiency in specific modern applications.

Recently, a new alternative preference query, the top-k dominating query, has attracted the research interest. This query is an important tool for decision support since it provides data analysts an intuitive way for finding significant objects. However, the related work is very limited and therefore there are many issues on this topic to be addressed. For example, approximate evaluation is a very promising research direction, since in many cases we are willing to trade accuracy for speed of computation. More complicated scenarios can be also examined, such as distributed environments or multiple queries existence.

References

1. Aggarwal, C.C.: Data Streams: Models and Algorithms. Springer, Heidelberg (2007)
2. Babcock, B., Babu, S., Datar, M., Motwani, R., Widom, J.: Models and Issues in Data Stream Systems. In: Proc. of PODS, pp. 1–16 (2002)
3. Bruno, N., Chaudhuri, S., Gravano, L.: Top-k Selection Queries over Relational Databases: Mapping Strategies and Performance Evaluation. ACM TODS 27(2), 153–187 (2002)
4. Balke, W.-T., Guntzer, U., Zheng, J.X.: Efficient Distributed Skylining for Web Information Systems. In: Bertino, E., Christodoulakis, S., Plexousakis, D., Christophides, V., Koubarakis, M., Böhm, K., Ferrari, E. (eds.) EDBT 2004. LNCS, vol. 2992, pp. 256–273. Springer, Heidelberg (2004)
5. Borzsonyi, S., Kossmann, D., Stocker, K.: The Skyline Operator. In: Proc. of ICDE, pp. 421–430 (2001)
6. Babcock, B., Olston, C.: Distributed Top-k Monitoring. In: Proc. of SIGMOD, pp. 28–39 (2003)
7. Chang, Y.-C., Bergman, L.D., Castelli, V., Li, C.-S., Lo, M.-L., Smith, J.R.: The Onion Technique: Indexing for Linear Optimization Queries. In: Proc. of SIGMOD, pp. 391–402 (2000)
8. Chomicki, J., Godfrey, P., Gryz, J., Liang, D.: Skyline with Presorting. In: Proc. of ICDE, pp. 717–719 (2003)
9. Chaudhuri, S., Gravano, L., Marian, A.: Optimizing Top-k Selection Queries over Multimedia Repositories. IEEE TKDE 16(8), 992–1009 (2004)
10. Chang, K.C.-C., Won Hwang, S.: Minimal Probing: Supporting Expensive Predicates for Top-k Queries. In: Proc. of SIGMOD, pp. 346–357 (2002)

11. Chan, C.Y., Jagadish, H.V., Tan, K.-L., Tung, A.K.H., Zhang, Z.: Finding k-Dominant Skylines in High Dimensional Space. In: Proc. of SIGMOD, pp. 503–514 (2006)
12. Chaudhry, N., Shaw, K., Abdelguerfi, M.: Stream Data Management. Springer, Heidelberg (2006)
13. Das, G., Gunopulos, D., Koudas, N., Tsirogiannis, D.: Answering Top-k Queries Using Views. In: Proc. of VLDB, pp. 451–462 (2006)
14. Gehrke, J., Korn, F., Srivastava, D.: On Computing Correlated Aggregates over Continual Data Stream. ACM SIGMOD Record 30(2), 13–24 (2001)
15. Huang, Z., Jensen, C.S., Lu, H., Ooi, B.C.: Skyline Queries against Mobile Lightweight Devices in MANETs. In: Proc. of ICDE, p. 66 (2006)
16. Hristidis, V., Papakonstantinou, Y.: Algorithms and Applications for Answering Ranked Queries Using Ranked Views. VLDB Journal 13(1), 49–70 (2004)
17. Hua, M., Pei, J.: Continuously Monitoring Top-k Uncertain Data Streams: a Probabilistic Threshold Method. Distrib. Parallel Databases 26, 29–65 (2009)
18. Ilyas, I.F., Beskales, G., Soliman, M.A.: A Survey of Top-k Query Processing Techniques in Relational Database Systems. ACM Comput. Surv. 40(4) (2008)
19. Jin, C., Yi, K., Chen, L., Yu, J.X., Lin, X.: Sliding Window Top-k Queries on Uncertain Streams. In: Proc. of PVLDB, pp. 301–312 (2008)
20. Kung, H.T.: On Finding the Maxima of a Set of Vectors. Journal of the ACM 22(4), 469–476 (1975)
21. Kontaki, M., Papadopoulos, A.N., Manolopoulos, Y.: Continuous k-Dominant Skyline Computation on Multidimensional Data Streams. In: Proc. of SAC, pp. 16–20 (2008)
22. Kontaki, M., Papadopoulos, A.N., Manolopoulos, Y.: Continuous Top-k Dominating Queries in Subspaces. In: Proc. of PCI (2008)
23. Kontaki, M., Papadopoulos, A.N., Manolopoulos, Y.: Continuous Top-k Dominating Queries. Technical Report, Aristotle University of Thessaloniki (2009)
24. Kossmann, D., Ramsak, F., Rost, S.: Shooting Stars in the Sky: an Online Algorithm for Skyline Queries. In: Proc. of VLDB, pp. 275–286 (2002)
25. Koudas, N., Srivastava, D.: Data Stream Query Processing: a Tutorial. In: Proc. of VLDB, p. 1149 (2003)
26. Lian, X., Chen, L.: Top-k Dominating Queries in Uncertain Databases. In: Proc. of EDBT, pp. 660–671 (2009)
27. Li, C., Ooi, B.C., Tung, A.K.H., Wang, S.: DADA: a Data Cube for Dominant Relationship Analysis. In: Proc. of SIGMOD, pp. 659–670 (2006)
28. Lin, X., Yuan, Y., Wang, W., Lu, H.: Stabbing the Sky: Efficient Skyline Computation over Sliding Windows. In: Proc. of ICDE, pp. 502–513 (2005)
29. Lin, X., Yuan, Y., Zhang, Q., Zhang, Y.: Selecting Stars: the k Most Representative Skyline Operator. In: Proc. of ICDE, pp. 86–95 (2007)
30. Lu, Y., Zhao, J., Chen, L., Cui, B., Yang, D.: Effective Skyline Cardinality Estimation on Data Streams. In: Bhowmick, S.S., Küng, J., Wagner, R. (eds.) DEXA 2008. LNCS, vol. 5181, pp. 241–254. Springer, Heidelberg (2008)
31. Marian, A., Bruno, N., Gravano, L.: Evaluating Top-k Queries over Web-Accessible Databases. ACM TODS 29(2), 319–362 (2004)
32. Mouratidis, K., Bakiras, S., Papadias, D.: Continuous Monitoring of Top-k Queries over Sliding Windows. In: Proc. of SIGMOD, pp. 635–646 (2006)
33. Morse, M.D., Patel, J.M., Grosky, W.I.: Efficient Continuous Skyline Computation. In: Proc. of ICDE, p. 108 (2006)
34. Osborne, M.J., Rubenstein, A.: A Course in Game Theory. MIT Press, Cambridge (1994)

35. Pei, J., Jiang, B., Lin, X., Yuan, Y.: Probabilistic Skylines on Uncertain Data. In: Proc. of VLDB, pp. 15–26 (2007)
36. Papadopoulos, A.N., Lyritsis, A., Nanopoulos, A., Manolopoulos, Y.: Domination mining and querying. In: Song, I.-Y., Eder, J., Nguyen, T.M. (eds.) DaWaK 2007. LNCS, vol. 4654, pp. 145–156. Springer, Heidelberg (2007)
37. Papadias, D., Tao, Y., Fu, G., Seeger, B.: An Optimal and Progressive Algorithm for Skyline Queries. In: Proc. of SIGMOD, pp. 467–478 (2003)
38. Papadias, D., Tao, Y., Fu, G., Seeger, B.: Progressive Skyline Computation in Database Systems. ACM TODS 30(1), 41–82 (2005)
39. Sharifzadeh, M., Shahabi, C.: The Spatial Skyline Queries. In: Proc. of VLDB, pp. 751–762 (2006)
40. Skoutas, D., Sacharidis, D., Simitsis, A., Kantere, V., Sellis, T.: Top-k Dominant Web Services Under Multi-Criteria Matching. In: Proc. of EDBT, pp. 898–909 (2009)
41. Tan, K.L., Eng, P.K., Ooi, B.C.: Efficient Progressive Skyline Computation. In: Proc. of VLDB, pp. 301–310 (2001)
42. Tao, Y., Papadias, D.: Maintaining Sliding Window Skylines on Data Streams. IEEE TKDE 18(3), 377–391 (2006)
43. Wang, S., Ooi, B.C., Tung, A.K.H., Xu, L.: Efficient Skyline Query Processing on Peer-to-Peer Networks. In: Proc. of ICDE, pp. 1126–1135 (2007)
44. Xia, T., Zhang, D.: Refreshing the Sky: The Compressed Skycube with Efficient Support for Frequent Updates. In: Proc. of SIGMOD, pp. 491–502 (2006)
45. Yiu, M.L., Mamoulis, N.: Efficient Processing of Top-k Dominating Queries on Multi-Dimensional Data. In: Proc. of VLDB, pp. 483–494 (2007)
46. Yiu, M.L., Mamoulis, N.: Multidimensional Top-k Dominating Queries. VLDB Journal 18(3), 695–718 (2009)
47. Zhang, Z., Cheng, R., Papadias, D., Tung, A.K.H.: Minimizing the Communication Cost for Continuous Skyline Maintenance. In: Proc. of SIGMOD, pp. 495–508 (2009)

Clock Synchronization: Open Problems in Theory and Practice

Christoph Lenzen, Thomas Locher, Philipp Sommer, and Roger Wattenhofer

Computer Engineering and Networks Laboratory TIK
ETH Zurich, 8092 Zurich, Switzerland
{lenzen,lochert,sommer,wattenhofer}@tik.ee.ethz.ch

Abstract. Clock synchronization is one of the most basic building blocks for many applications in computer science and engineering. The purpose of clock synchronization is to provide the constituent parts of a distributed system with a common notion of time. While the problem of synchronizing clocks in distributed systems has already received considerable attention from researchers and practitioners alike, we believe that there are many fascinating problems that remain unsolved. In this paper, we give a brief overview of previous work in this area, followed by a discussion of open clock synchronization problems in theory and practice.

1 Introduction

Although computer science is still a young discipline, certain signs of age are becoming apparent. As the discipline continues to prosper, computer scientists must become experts in some subjects—the days of the universal computer scientist seem to be coming to an end. One of the main dividing lines is between theory and practice (a.k.a. systems). Unfortunately, the gap between theory and practice even seems to be widening as both theory and practice are developing and advancing. One may worry that soon there will be little communication between the two camps because one side often considers questions or answers from the other as "not really relevant". This is unfortunate, since at least new trends, fundamental limits, or open problems should be of interest to the other camp.

In our research group, we try to find synergies between theory and practice, unfortunately with limited success. It is quite rare that the theorists in our group develop algorithms that have enough real-world advantages to justify an implementation. Likewise, building a system hardly ever reveals a beautiful theoretical problem. There are noteworthy exceptions: In the remainder of this invited paper we will discuss *clock synchronization*, a prototypical example that is inspiring from a theoretical as well as a practical point of view.

In clock synchronization, we are given a network of nodes that want to maintain a common notion of time. Having such a notion of time is important for many applications, in the Internet as well as, e.g., in wireless sensor networks. Each node may have its own hardware clock, which is not totally accurate, i.e., it experiences a certain variable clock drift. In order to ensure that the nodes agree more or less on the current time, the nodes must synchronize their drifting hardware clocks

J. van Leeuwen et al. (Eds.): SOFSEM 2010, LNCS 5901, pp. 61–70, 2010.

by perpetually exchanging messages containing information about their current state. It is easy to see that it is impossible to synchronize the clocks perfectly because the nodes never have current information about the other nodes' clock values due to fact that all messages arrive after an unknown and variable delay. Even if the message delays were always the same and the nodes knew this value exactly, they still could not synchronize the clocks perfectly because of the variable hardware clock drifts, i.e., a node cannot determine exactly how much another clock progressed since the last message arrived. This gives rise to a natural question, which is fundamental for many application domains: How well can nodes synchronize their clocks given that the clocks have variable but bounded drift, and given that messages have variable but bounded delay?

Naturally, one objective is to minimize the *clock skew* between any two nodes in the network, regardless of their relative distance in the network. Apart from minimizing this *global* skew, it is essential for several distributed applications that the clock skew between neighboring nodes is as small as possible. One could even think of applications where the global skew is not of great concern, but any node only needs to be well synchronized with its neighbors. Apparently this *local* skew that some neighboring nodes may experience depends on the (maximum) variance of the message delay and also on the (maximum) clock drift rate. Given that locally connected nodes can communicate directly, one may expect that the local skew depends *only* on these parameters. Surprisingly, this is not true! From a worst-case perspective, no matter what clock synchronization protocol is used, it is always possible that two neighboring nodes experience a clock skew that is a function of the network diameter. On the other hand, assuming random delays, there is a high chance that transmitting repeatedly yields better results. These results have an impact on the degree of synchronization that can be achieved in practical distributed systems. In the next section, we give a brief summary of known results, followed by discussions of various open clock synchronization problems in theory and practice.

2 Related Work

There is a large literature on clock synchronization in distributed systems, mostly focusing on (upper and lower) bounding the clock skews that can occur between any two nodes in the system (see, e.g., [19,22,25,27]). A simple technique called *shifting* [19], where the local clock rates and the message delays are adjusted in order to produce indistinguishable executions, is often used to prove lower bounds. Using this technique it can be shown that a worst-case clock skew of $D/2$ cannot be avoided on any graph G of diameter D [2]. A stronger lower bound of $(1+\rho)D$ can be proved for all algorithms that must ensure that the clock values do not drift away from real time faster than the underlying hardware clocks, where ρ denotes the maximum clock drift rate [15].

Not surprisingly, large clock skews may occur between nodes that are far apart in the communicaton network, which means that these nodes experience a significant delay in their communication. An important question is how well the clocks of nodes that are close-by can be synchronized. In their seminal work that introduced the problem of synchronizing clocks of nodes that are close-by as accurately as possible, Fan and Lynch [8] showed that no algorithm can prevent a clock skew of $\Omega(\log_b D)$ between neighboring nodes, where $b \in \mathcal{O}((\log D)/\rho)$. The only constraint is that nodes are required to increase their clock values at a given minimum progress rate. Note that this constraint is quite natural because it ensures that all clocks steadily make progress. Subsequently, the base of the logarithm has been improved to $b \in \Theta(1/\rho)$, i.e., it has been shown that a clock skew of $\Omega(\log_{1/\rho} D)$ between some neighboring nodes cannot be avoided [15]. Moreover, if the progress rate of all clocks must always lie in an interval $[1 - \mathcal{O}(\rho), 1 + \mathcal{O}(\rho)]$, there are indistinguishable executions such that in one of these executions some neighboring nodes experience a clock skew of $\Omega(\log D)$ [15].

The clock synchronization algorithm by Srikanth and Toueg [27] guarantees a bound of $\mathcal{O}(D)$ on the clock skew between any two nodes at all times and is thus asymptotically optimal. The algorithm is further fault-tolerant and achieves an accuracy with respect to real time that is also optimal. However, their algorithm incurs a skew of $\Theta(D)$ between neighboring nodes in the worst case. The first algorithm, which is based on a technique called *blocking*, that guarantees a sublinear bound on the clock skew between neighboring nodes achieves a bound of $\mathcal{O}(\sqrt{\rho D})$ [17,18]. The same technique can also be applied to dynamic settings, where nodes and edges can appear and disappear continuously [13]. In the static scenario, the upper bound has been improved to $\mathcal{O}(\log D)$ [14] and subsequently to $\mathcal{O}(\log_{1/\rho} D)$ [15], which matches the lower bound. The algorithm that achieves this tight bound also guarantees an optimal bound on the clock skew between any two nodes of $(1 + \rho)D$ plus a small term that depends on the frequency of communication. The additional term becomes zero as the frequency of communication tends to infinity.

There has also been a lot of practical work on clock synchronization for specific computing environments. For example, techniques to synchronize the nodes in wireless sensor networks have been studied extensively [7,10,20,23]. It can be argued that in wireless sensor networks message delays are not only bounded, but also distributed (independently) at random. This assumption has a considerable impact on the achievable skew bounds: Under this assumption the skew between any two clocks can be upper bounded by $\tilde{\mathcal{O}}(\sqrt{D})$ w.h.p. [16]. The same work also shows that on most graphs at any point in time there is a constant probability that a clock skew of $\Omega(\sqrt{D})$ can be observed between some nodes. Moreover, some initial practical work on synchronizing nodes that are close-by particularly well has been carried out in the context of wireless sensor networks [26]. Clock synchronization has also been studied in other distributed systems such as the Internet [21] or systems-on-a-chip [9]. In processor design, where one seeks to control signal delays by means of placement and wiring (see, e.g., [12] and references therein), synchronizing devices that are close-by is essential. Furthermore, there has been a considerable amount of work on fault-tolerant clock synchronization for multiprocessor systems where processors communicate among each other via shared memory [5,6,11,24].

3 Model: Worst Case vs. Reality

In theoretical work on clock synchronization, a distributed system is typically modeled as a connected graph $G = (V, E)$, where nodes represent computational devices and edges represent communication links. Communication is usually considered to be bidirectional (i.e., the edges are undirected), but it may also be reasonable to assume unidirectional communication channels. The nodes can communicate directly with their neighboring nodes by exchanging messages, which arrive at their destination after a certain *delay*. In general, a message delay consists of two parts: a constant, known delay and an additional variable delay ("jitter"). A common simplification is to assume that the message delay can be any value in the range $[0, 1]$ and the nodes do not know the normalized upper bound of 1. The second essential aspect of clock synchronization is how *clock drifts* are modeled. Typically, it is assumed that each node has a hardware clock with a bounded drift. A common way to model the clock drift is to define that all hardware clock rates are always in the interval $[1 - \rho, 1 + \rho]$ for a constant $\rho \in (0, 1)$.

Due to the assumption that any node can only read its hardware clock (and not modify it), each node also has a *logical clock* whose value depends on its hardware clock value and the information received from its neighboring nodes. A *clock synchronization algorithm* specifies how the logical clock value is adapted based on the hardware clock and the received information. The main objective of the algorithm is to ensure that the clock skews, both between distant nodes and neighboring nodes, are always as small as possible. Theoretical work typically considers worst-case scenarios, where hardware clock rates and message delays happen in a way that maximizes clock skews.

Ideally, an algorithm that guarantees strong worst-case bounds is also a suitable candidate to maintain tightly synchronized clocks in real-world systems. However, the models employed in theoretical work are often too pessimistic compared to the situations that occur in practice. Clock drift rates change only gradually depending on factors such as the ambient temperature or the supply voltage. Even when operating a system in harsh environments, clock drifts will not change arbitrarily during a single synchronization interval. Similarly, assuming that an adversary takes control of variations in message delays does not reflect reality well. Using sophisticated mechanisms, e.g., timestamping at the MAC layer [20], the effect of variances in the delay can be mitigated up to a few clock ticks. This remaining uncertainty seems to be better captured by a probabilistic rather than a worst-case approach. A more practice-oriented model must take such considerations into account.

4 Dynamic Networks

As briefly outlined in Section 2, it is well understood what the best possible bounds on the worst-case clock skews are that any clock synchronization algorithm can guarantee in static networks. However, in practice distributed systems are often dynamic in the sense that both devices and communication channels can appear and disappear. Thus, the static theoretical model is too simplistic for many practical applications. A more appropriate model must allow for on-going changes to the network topology in order to bridge this chasm between theory and practice.

The necessity of taking network dynamics into account has also been pointed out in [13]. Of course, there are fundamental limits to the degree of synchronization that can be achieved in a completely dynamic setting, where nodes and edges can appear and disappear in an arbitrary manner: According to the lower bound for static networks, a clock skew of roughly D can occur on any graph between some nodes v and w. By adding the edge $\{v, w\}$ between these two nodes, the network suddenly experiences a worst-case clock skew of D between neighboring nodes. Obviously, this situation cannot be avoided. The problem is that a newly added edge may always cause a large clock skew between the two nodes that it connects. However, once the nodes are aware of this situation, they can react to it and reduce the clock skew on this particular edge over time. This means that while we cannot get a sublinear bound on the clock skew between nodes that are connected through a new edge, we can in fact guarantee a better bound for edges that existed for a certain period of time.

It is not known whether the same asymptotic bounds as in the static case can be achieved. The algorithm presented in [13] guarantees an upper bound of $\mathcal{O}(\sqrt{\rho n})$ (where $n := |V|$) on the worst-case clock skew between any two neighboring nodes v and w provided that the edge $\{v, w\}$ has been part of the network for $\Omega(\sqrt{n/\rho})$ time. This bound is exponentially weaker than the bound of $\mathcal{O}(\log_{1/\rho} n)$ in the static setting. It is an interesting open problem whether the same asymptotic bound can be achieved in dynamic networks. Not surprisingly, the proof techniques that are used to prove the bound of $\mathcal{O}(\log_{1/\rho} n)$ cannot be used directly for dynamic graphs. An intriguing aspect of this problem is, however, that these proof techniques cannot even deal with the *removal* of edges. This is quite counterintuitive as one might think that removing edges cannot cause problems because the adjacent nodes are not neighbors anymore and, given the increased distance between these nodes, their clock values are allowed to deviate more. The problem is that the proof relies on the fact that a node v always has a neighbor w that forces v to increase its clock value quickly if v is on the verge of violating the skew bounds. In the dynamic setting, this neighbor w may leave the system at a critical moment. The goal is to show that this is indeed a real problem, by proving a new lower bound, or to prove that the clock skews can nevertheless be kept (asymptotically) as small as in the static case.

This is an open theoretical problem that again considers the skew bounds in the worst case. The dynamics in real-world networks may be benign in comparison and therefore different approaches may be employed. The right choice will likely depend on the nature of the considered distributed system. Coping with dynamics in various (practical) types of distributed systems is another potential direction for future research.

5 Fault-Tolerance

There has been substantial work on fault-tolerant clock synchronization in single-hop networks (see, e.g., references in [28]). A lot of progress has been made over the years on the *digital clock synchronization* problem in shared memory models [1,4,5,6,24], where nodes try to maintain a synchronized counter (digital clock) with certain progress guarantees in spite of crash, Byzantine, or transient failures. In the message passing world, such counters are known as (fault-tolerant) synchronizers, which provide a weaker form of timing information than a "regular" clock, in particular if the diameter of the graph is not constant. Moreover, quite frequently some kind of a priori synchronization of the system is assumed, such as synchronous rounds, bounded message delays, or periodic "beats". Applications for this kind of synchronization algorithms can be found e.g. in fault-tolerant chip design [9] or multiprocessor systems.

To the best of our knowledge, little is known about fault-tolerant clock synchronization in multi-hop environments. From the theory side, it is easy to observe that many protocols assuming full connectivity can be generalized to multi-hop scenarios if the network satisfies certain connectivity constraints in order to handle, e.g., crash or Byzantine failures. This approach might however be unsatisfactory if small local skews are desired, and it gives little information about transient or probabilistic faults. In practice, the problem is mainly tackled in a pragmatic manner. In wireless sensor networks, for example, people may rely on MAC-layer protocols that handle message retransmissions, or they simply accept decreasing synchronization quality in the presence of high message loss rates.

The challenging problem of finding fault-tolerant clock synchronization mechanisms for multi-hop networks merits further attention for various reasons. First, studying fault-tolerant clock synchronization may lead to valuable (theoretical) insights: The problem asks for error detection and error handling techniques that do not interfere with the ability of algorithms to achieve a high precision of clock values, while at the same time the synchronization offered might be helpful in doing so. It is important to understand to what degree synchronization can be maintained given specific failure models and connectivity constraints. There are many interesting open problems that can be addressed: If nodes are faulty with certain probabilities, how dense do carefully crafted graphs have to be to permit reliable synchronization? What degree of resilience to Byzantine faults can be guaranteed on a given graph? In general, which trade-offs exist between achievable accuracy of timing information and resilience to faults? Moreover, since access to a consistent, accurate time is a basic service and nodes in real-world networks are often not fully connected, this topic has a significant practical relevance.

6 Energy Efficiency vs. Accuracy

When developing applications for wireless sensor networks, energy efficiency is an important issue. Sensor nodes should be able to operate unattended for many years, even when running on small batteries. In order to meet the requirements of the application, as much energy as possible has to be conserved by operating the microcontroller and the radio chip in the power-save mode whenever possible. One approach to reduce the energy consumption of sensor nodes is to arrange periodic rendezvous schemes: Neighboring nodes wake up for a short moment to exchange messages and immediately return to sleep afterwards. The better the clock synchronization is between neighboring nodes, the more energy is saved by shortening the necessary guard intervals before and after the designated rendezvous point. However, accurately synchronized clocks can only be achieved by exchanging periodic synchronization messages, which also requires energy.

Furthermore, the synchronization error will grow at least with the square-root of the distance to the reference node due to the jitter in the message delay [16]. To reduce this effect, one can try to reduce the jitter itself. By means of MAC layer timestamping, it can be cut down at best to the hardware clock granularity $1/f$, where f denotes the frequency at which the clock operates. Thus, reducing the jitter means increasing the time resolution, which in turn requires that the hardware clock operates at a higher frequency. The power consumption P of the clock circuits is given by $P \sim C_L V^2 f$, where C_L is the load capacitance, V is the supply voltage, and f is the clock frequency [3]. Therefore, the power consumption will increase linearly with the clock frequency. Taking into account that synchronization quality decreases (at least) linearly when reducing the frequency of message exchange, it might be best to balance the guard time and the time it takes to switch on the radio and send or receive a message, and maximize the time between messages with these parameters fixed.

Another option to abate clock skews is to circumvent the problem that the jitter and thus the inaccuracy of the clock values increases over (long) paths in the network by utilizing the Global Positioning System (GPS). GPS satellites orbiting the earth periodically send their position information together with the current timestamp of their atomic clock down to earth. If a sensor node is equipped with a GPS receiver, it can obtain the high precision timing information included in the GPS messages. This way, the problem of network-wide multi-hop clock synchronization reduces to the single-hop case. Furthermore, external time synchronization using GPS eliminates the need for exchanging synchronization messages over the sensor network. However, this is only a viable solution for applications where a line of sight to the GPS satellites is available.

State-of-the-art GPS devices provide an accuracy within a few nanoseconds. This is a significant improvement compared to the accuracy of common sensor node platforms (e.g., the Mica2 motes), which is in the microsecond range. However, the improved timing accuracy of GPS-based time synchronization solutions comes at the cost of an increased hardware complexity and higher energy consumption. In particular, in order to achieve maximal precision, a hardware clock operating at a sufficiently high frequency to provide the necessary time resolution is mandatory. Even though the size, cost, and energy consumption of modern GPS receivers is continually decreasing, it is often not feasible to equip every node in the network with a GPS receiver. Instead, only one or a few nodes, the so called reference nodes, are equipped with a GPS receiver and synchronized to UTC. Traditional time synchronization protocols for wireless sensor networks must then be used to synchronize the rest of the network to the reference nodes.

It remains an open problem to build a small, cheap, and low-power sensor node that is able to synchronize its clock to the accurate time pulses provided by the GPS satellites. Moreover, it is unknown if the effects considered above determine the minimum energy consumption of sensor nodes. If this is indeed the case, protocol implementations are required that provide an optimal trade-off between energy efficiency and hardware costs.

7 New Applications

Another interesting direction for future future research is finding new applications that put the theoretical knowledge in this field into practice. In light of the ongoing progress of recent years, two ideas for prospective applications came to our mind, both of which particularly aim at exploiting the better understanding of local skew that has been gained in the past few years.

Our first suggestion is to use clock synchronization principles to achieve other forms of coordination, e.g., coordination of movement or formation. There are various coordination tasks where clock synchronization mechanisms may be employed: Maybe some robots intend to move in a line, always maintaining identical distances, or a traffic jam can be avoided if distances between cars are balanced. Other goals might be the coordination of helicopters or, more generally, any kind of swarm trying to maintain a certain formation based only on local distance information. In all these cases the agents may experience *drifts*, because they are not able or willing to control their speeds perfectly, or subject to disturbance by other forces. Furthermore, their information on their neighbors' positions could be outdated and/or inaccurate, which is exactly the effect of *message delays* in clock synchronization. In summary, the underlying model of a coordination problem might be quite similar to the model presented in Section 3, raising the hope that results from clock synchronization could be applicable to such problems.

The second idea refers to chip design. Traditionally, synchronous circuits are controlled by a clock signal dissipated from a single source to all logical gates by means of a clock tree. This clock signal is used to determine when it is safe to advance to the next computational step by guaranteeing sufficient time between clock pulses for gates to switch states and signals to propagate. Therefore, a *local* synchronization guarantee between directly connected gates is needed. Even if the clock tree is well designed, we will observe a stretch in the distance compared to the communication graph of the logical gates. In the worst case, this stretch could be in the order of the diameter. Certainly, the stretch will grow with increasing chip size also in practice because different paths of computations are joined at some point in the chip logic. As a result, weak synchronization guarantees limit the frequency at which a chip can safely operate. We propose to improve this situation by means of a distributed clock generation scheme. Hopefully, by equipping a chip with, e.g., a grid of time sources, running a clock synchronization algorithm with strong local skew bounds on this grid, and dissipating the clock signal only locally by means of clock trees enables the construction of large chips without incurring a decline in the operating frequency. This scheme would come at the expense of additional clocks and chip logic for the synchronization algorithm, which could be compensated for by increasing the area of the chip.

We hope that the presented open problems have stimulated the reader's interest in distributed clock synchronization as a vivid and evolving research area.

References

1. Ben-Or, M., Dolev, D., Hoch, E.N.: Fast Self-Stabilizing Byzantine Tolerant Digital Clock Synchronization. In: Proc. 27th Annual ACM Symposium on Principles of Distributed Computing (PODC), pp. 385–394 (2008)
2. Biaz, S., Lundelius Welch, J.: Closed Form Bounds for Clock Synchronization Under Simple Uncertainty Assumptions. Information Processing Letters 80(3), 151–157 (2001)
3. Chandrakasan, A.P., Sheng, S., Brodersen, R.W.: Low-Power Digital CMOS Design. IEEE Journal of Solid State Circuits 27(4), 473–484 (1992)
4. Dolev, D., Halpern, J.Y., Pinter, S.S., Stark, E.W., Weihl, W.E.: Reaching Approximate Agreement in the Presence of Faults. Journal of the ACM 33(3), 499–516 (1986)
5. Dolev, S.: Possible and Impossible Self-Stabilizing Digital Clock Synchronization in General Graphs. Journal of Real-Time Systems 12(1), 95–107 (1997)
6. Dolev, S., Lundelius Welch, J.: Wait-free Clock Synchronization. Algorithmica 18(4), 486–511 (1997)
7. Elson, J., Girod, L., Estrin, D.: Fine-Grained Network Time Synchronization Using Reference Broadcasts. ACM SIGOPS Operating Systems Review 36, 147–163 (2002)
8. Fan, R., Lynch, N.: Gradient Clock Synchronization. In: Proc. 23rd Annual ACM Symposium on Principles of Distributed Computing (PODC), pp. 320–327 (2004)
9. Függer, M., Schmid, U., Fuchs, G., Kempf, G.: Fault-Tolerant Distributed Clock Generation in VLSI Systems-on-Chip. In: Proc. 6th European Dependable Computing Conference (EDCC-6), pp. 87–96 (2006)
10. Ganeriwal, S., Kumar, R., Srivastava, M.B.: Timing-Sync Protocol for Sensor Networks. In: Proc. 1st ACM Conference on Embedded Networked Sensor Systems (SenSys), pp. 138–149 (2003)
11. Huang, S.T., Liu, T.J.: Four-State Stabilizing Phase Clock for Unidirectional Rings of Odd Size. Information Processing Letters 65(6), 325–329 (1998)
12. Korte, B., Rautenbach, D., Vygen, J.: BonnTools: Mathematical Innovation for Layout and Timing Closure of Systems on a Chip. Proceedings of the IEEE 95(3), 555–572 (2007)
13. Kuhn, F., Locher, T., Oshman, R.: Gradient Clock Synchronization in Dynamic Networks. In: Proc. 21st ACM Symposium on Parallelism in Algorithms and Architectures (SPAA), pp. 270–279 (2009)
14. Lenzen, C., Locher, T., Wattenhofer, R.: Clock Synchronization with Bounded Global and Local Skew. In: Proc. 49th Annual IEEE Symposium on Foundations of Computer Science (FOCS), pp. 500–510 (2008)

15. Lenzen, C., Locher, T., Wattenhofer, R.: Tight Bounds for Clock Synchronization. In: Proc. 28th Annual ACM Symposium on Principles of Distributed Computing (PODC), pp. 46–55 (2009)
16. Lenzen, C., Sommer, P., Wattenhofer, R.: Optimal Clock Synchronization in Networks. In: Proc. 7th ACM Conference on Embedded Networked Sensor Systems, SenSys. (2009)
17. Locher, T.: Foundations of Aggregation and Synchronization in Distributed Systems. PhD Thesis, ETH Zurich (2009)
18. Locher, T., Wattenhofer, R.: Oblivious gradient clock synchronization. In: Dolev, S. (ed.) DISC 2006. LNCS, vol. 4167, pp. 520–533. Springer, Heidelberg (2006)
19. Lundelius Welch, J., Lynch, N.: An Upper and Lower Bound for Clock Synchronization. Information and Control 62(2/3), 190–204 (1984)
20. Maróti, M., Kusy, B., Simon, G., Lédeczi, Á.: The Flooding Time Synchronization Protocol. In: Proc. 2nd ACM Conference on Embedded Networked Sensor Systems (SenSys), pp. 39–49 (2004)
21. Mills, D.: Internet Time Synchronization: the Network Time Protocol. IEEE Transactions on Communications 39, 1482–1493 (1991)
22. Ostrovsky, R., Patt-Shamir, B.: Optimal and Efficient Clock Synchronization under Drifting Clocks. In: Proc. 18th Annual ACM Symposium on Principles of Distributed Computing (PODC), pp. 400–414 (1999)
23. PalChaudhuri, S., Saha, A.K., Johnson, D.B.: Adaptive Clock Synchronization in Sensor Networks. In: Proc. 3rd ACM/IEEE International Symposium on Information Processing in Sensor Networks (IPSN), pp. 340–348 (2004)
24. Papatriantafilou, M., Tsigas, P.: On Self-Stabilizing Wait-free Clock Synchronization. Parallel Processing Letters 7(3), 321–328 (1997)
25. Patt-Shamir, B., Rajsbaum, S.: A Theory of Clock Synchronization. In: Proc. 26th Annual ACM Symposium on Theory of Computing (STOC), pp. 810–819 (1994)
26. Sommer, P., Wattenhofer, R.: Gradient Clock Synchronization in Wireless Sensor Networks. In: Proc. 8th ACM/IEEE International Conference on Information Processing in Sensor Networks (IPSN), pp. 37–48 (2009)
27. Srikanth, T.K., Toueg, S.: Optimal Clock Synchronization. Journal of the ACM 34(3), 626–645 (1987)
28. Sun, K., Ning, P., Wang, C.: Secure and Resilient Time Synchronization in Wireless Sensor Networks. In: Secure Localization and Time Synchronization for Wireless Sensor and Ad Hoc Networks. Springer, US (2007)

Regret Minimization and Job Scheduling

Yishay Mansour*

Blavatnik School of Computer Science
Tel Aviv University, Tel Aviv, Israel
mansour@tau.ac.il

Abstract. Regret minimization has proven to be a very powerful tool in both computational learning theory and online algorithms. Regret minimization algorithms can guarantee, for a single decision maker, a near optimal behavior under fairly adversarial assumptions. I will discuss a recent extensions of the classical regret minimization model, which enable to handle many different settings related to job scheduling, and guarantee the near optimal online behavior.

1 Regret Minimization

Consider a single decision maker attempting to optimize it performance in face of an uncertain environment. This simple online setting has attracted attention from multiple disciplines, including operations research, game theory, and computer science. In computer science, computational learning theory and online algorithms both focus on this task from different perspectives. I will concentrate only on a certain facet of this general issue of decision making, and consider settings related to *regret minimization*, where the performance of the online decision maker is compared to a benchmark based on a class of comparison policies.

Regret minimization has its roots in computational learning theory and game theory. While the motivation for the research in the two fields have been very different, the basic model that both fields has studied have been very similar. They both consider an online setting, where an agent needs to select actions, while having only information about the past performance and having no (or very limited) information regarding the future. Many natural computer science problems give rise to such online settings; typical examples include scheduling problems, paging, routing protocols, and many more. Online regret minimization learning algorithms have been introduced and studied in the computational learning community [27,19,2,13,24] and also in the game theory community [20,17,16,21]. (See [11] for an excellent book on the topic.)

The online model studied has the following general structure. In each time step, the online algorithm needs to select an action, and it can select a specific

* This work was supported in part by the IST Programme of the European Community, under the PASCAL2 Network of Excellence, IST-2007-216886, by a grant from the Israel Science Foundation (grant No. 709/09) and grant No. 2008-321 from the United States-Israel Binational Science Foundation (BSF). This publication reflects the authors' views only.

J. van Leeuwen et al. (Eds.): SOFSEM 2010, LNCS 5901, pp. 71–76, 2010.

action or a convex combination of some of the actions. After the online algorithm performs its action, it observes the loss of all the actions and receives a loss for the action it chose. The aim is to minimize the total cumulative loss. In general, one would like to prove guarantees that hold for arbitrary loss sequences; that is, one imagines there is a powerful adversary that might generates the worse loss sequence for the online learning algorithm.

When evaluating the performance of online algorithms, it is important to select the "right" benchmark. On the one hand we like it to be sufficiently challenging, so that it will encourage innovative algorithms. On the other hand we need to keep the expectation realistic, which will allow to introduce algorithms and not only impossibility results. One way to think about the benchmark is a set of algorithms that we like to match the performance of the *best* of them. In the above online setting it is clear that no online algorithm can hope to compete well against *any* algorithm, simply consider the case of predicting a random coin, any online algorithm will succeed in the prediction only half of the times (in expectation) while someone who first views the coins outcome will be able to predict perfectly. External regret bounds the *difference* between the online algorithm loss and the best algorithm in a comparison class of algorithms, and generally one can achieve a regret bound of the form $O(\sqrt{T \log N})$, where T is the number of time steps, N are the number of algorithms in the comparison class and assuming that the losses are from $[0, 1]$ (see [13,14]). This implies that the per step regret is vanishing at the rate of $O(\sqrt{(\log N)/T})$. From an online algorithm perspective, the external regret can be viewed comparing the online algorithm to the best *static* solution. In the *multi-arm bandit* setting [28,25] the decision maker observes only the payoff of the action it selected (and does not get any information regrading the other actions). In this setting the average regret vanishes at the rate of $O(\sqrt{(N \log N)/T})$ for the adversarial setting [2] and $O((\log T)/T)$ for the stochastic setting [1].[1]

2 Regret Minimization and Job Scheduling

In an online job scheduling setting, at each time step a job arrives and the online algorithm needs to schedule it on one of the machines. At the end of the run, the online algorithm has a certain load on each machine (depending on the jobs it scheduled on it) and the global loss function can be either makespan (the load on the most loaded machine) or some norm of the loads (e.g., the sum of the square of the loads). Such objective functions are very different from the additive objective function usually used in regret minimization.

It is worth first discussing the differences between the regret minimization model, suggested here, and the classical job scheduling model. We have a very different information model, where the decision maker discovers the actions outcome (e.g., in job scheduling this is the load of the job on each machine) only

[1] The O-notation in the stochastic setting hides dependency on the stochastic parameters.

after it selects an action (e.g., a machine where to schedule the job) and not before (e.g., when the job arrives). In contrast, in the classical online job scheduling model, when a job arrives, the decision maker, first observes the load of the job on each machine (the outcome of the actions) and only then selects an action.

Our information model is the "right" abstraction in many applications. For example, consider a *network load balancer* (an *online algorithm*) which has to select an outgoing link for each session (the *action*). The load balancer goal is to minimize the load on the most loaded link (known as *makespan*). When a session arrives, the load balancer needs to be scheduled on an output link before we learn the load of the session. After we scheduled the session we can observe its load, but then we can not change the link on which it is already scheduled.

It is worthwhile to note the difference between our setting and that of online job scheduling in the competitive analysis literature [10]. The main difference is in the *information* that the decision maker observes about the online tasks that arrive. In the online job scheduling setting the "standard" assumption is that the decision maker first observes the "load" of the job on each machine, and only then decides on which machine to schedule it. In our model, much like the regret minimization model, we have a different information model. First the decision maker selects how to schedule the job on the machines, and only then he observes the "load" of the job on each machine. This different information model is a very important distinction between the two models. The other important distinction is regarding the "benchmark class", which in the competitive analysis is the optimal hindsight assignment of jobs to machines, and in our case it is a significantly more limited class. Finally, there is a very significant difference in the results we would like to derive. We are aiming at getting a bounded regret, which is the *difference* between the online cost and the minimal cost policy in the benchmark class, while the competitive analysis is satisfied with bounding the *ratio*.

3 Model and Results

In this section we sketch the model and the results of [15], which would be our main source.

We are interested in studying the following extension of the regret minimization model. For each action we will maintain the cumulative loss of the online algorithm resulting from this action. The online algorithm *global loss function* would be a given (convex) function of the cumulative loss of the actions. (The makespan is a perfect example of such a global loss function.) The online algorithm objective is to minimize the loss of the global loss function. For example, assume that $\ell_i^t \in [0,1]$ is the loss at time t from action i, and let $L_i^T = \sum_{t=1}^T \ell_i^t$ be the cumulative loss of action i. At time t, first, the online algorithm specifies a distribution p_i^t over the actions, and then it observes the losses of the different actions. Its loss from action i at time t is $p_i^t \ell_i^t$, and the cumulative loss of action i is $L_i^{ON,T} = \sum_{t=1}^T p_i^t \ell_i^t$. Unlike the usual regret minimization model, we will not sum the losses of the online algorithm for different action, but consider the global loss function over the $L_i^{ON,T}$. For example, the makespan cost of the online algorithm is $\max_i \{L_i^{ON,T}\}$.

We first need to select an appropriate benchmark, and a reasonable benchmark class is the class of policies that *statically* distributes the weight between actions (and receives the proportional loss in each action). Specifically, given loads $L_1, \ldots, L_N$, for the makespan the best weights are $p_i^* = \frac{L_i^{-1}}{\sum_{j=1}^N L_j^{-1}}$, and the makespan is $\frac{1}{\sum_{j=1}^N L_j^{-1}}$. As before, the regret is the difference between the global loss function (e.g., makespan) of the online algorithm and that of the best set of weights, and the average regret per step is the regret divided by the number of steps.

In the talk we will discuss both an adversarial model (described above) and a stochastic model of losses. For the adversarial mode, the main results appear in [15] and include a general online algorithm whose average regret is vanishing at the rate of $O(\sqrt{N/T})$.

4 Other Extensions of the Regret Minimization Model

Unfortunately, we can not give a comprehensive review of the large body of research on regret minimization algorithm, and we refer the interested reader to [12]. In the following we highlight a few more relevant research directions.

There has been an ongoing interest in extending the basic comparison class for the regret minimization algorithm, for example by introducing *shifting experts* [18], *time selection functions* [5], and *wide range regret* [26]. Still, all those works assume that the loss is additive between time steps.

A different research direction has been to improve the computational complexity of the regret minimization algorithms, especially in the case that the comparison class is exponential in size. General computationally efficient transformation where given by [23], in the case that the cost function is linear and the optimization oracle can be computed in polynomial time, and extended by [22], to the case of an approximate-optimization oracle.

There has been a sequence of works establishing the connection between online competitive algorithms [9] and online learning algorithm [12]. One issue is that online learning algorithms are stateless, while many of the problems address in the competitive analysis literature have a state (see, [6]). For many problems one can use the online learning algorithms and guarantee a near-optimal static solution, however a straightforward application requires both exponential time and space. Computationally efficient solutions have been given to specific problems including, paging [7], data-structures [8], and routing [4,3].

We remark that all the above works concentrate on the case where the global cost function is additive between time steps.

References

1. Auer, P., Cesa-Bianchi, N., Fischer, P.: Finite-Time Analysis of the Multi-Armed Bandit Problem. Machine Learning 47(2-3), 235–256 (2002)
2. Auer, P., Cesa-Bianchi, N., Freund, Y., Schapire, R.E.: The Nonstochastic Multiarmed Bandit Problem. SIAM Journal on Computing 32(1), 48–77 (2002); (A preliminary version appeared in FOCS 1995 as Gambling in a Rigged Casino: The Adversarial Multi-Armed Bandit Problem)

3. Awerbuch, B., Kleinberg, R.: Online Linear Optimization and Adaptive Routing. J. Comput. Syst. Sci. 74(1), 97–114 (2008)
4. Awerbuch, B., Mansour, Y.: Adapting to a Reliable Network Path. In: PODC, pp. 360–367 (2003)
5. Blum, A., Mansour, Y.: From External to Internal Regret. Journal of Machine Learning Research 8, 1307–1324 (2007)
6. Blum, A., Burch, C.: On-Line Learning and the Metrical Task System Problem. In: COLT, pp. 45–53 (1997)
7. Blum, A., Burch, C., Kalai, A.: Finely-Competitive Paging. In: FOCS, pp. 450–458 (1999)
8. Blum, A., Chawla, S., Kalai, A.: Static Optimality and Dynamic Search-Optimality in Lists and Trees. Algorithmica 36(3), 249–260 (2003)
9. Borodin, A., El-Yaniv, R.: Online Computation and Competitive Analysis. Cambridge University Press, Cambridge (1998)
10. Borodin, A., El-Yaniv, R.: Online Computation and Competitive Analysis. Cambridge University Press, Cambridge (1998)
11. Cesa-Bianchi, N., Lugosi, G.: Prediction, Learning and Games. Cambridge University Press, Cambridge (2006)
12. Cesa-Bianchi, N., Lugosi, G.: Prediction, Learning, and Games. Cambridge University Press, New York (2006)
13. Cesa-Bianchi, N., Freund, Y., Helmbold, D.P., Haussler, D., Schapire, R.E., Warmuth, M.K.: How to Use Expert Advice. Journal of the ACM 44(3), 427–485 (1997); (A preliminary version appeared in STOC 1993)
14. Cesa-Bianchi, N., Lugosi, G.: Potential-Based Algorithms in On-Line Prediction and Game Theory. Machine Learning 51(3), 239–261 (2003)
15. Even-Dar, E., Kleinberg, R., Mannor, S., Mansour, Y.: Online Learning for Global Cost Functions. In: COLT (2009)
16. Foster, D., Vohra, R.: Regret in the On-Line Decision Problem. Games and Economic Behavior 21, 40–55 (1997)
17. Foster, D.P., Vohra, R.V.: A Randomization Rule for Selecting Forecasts. Operations Research 41(4), 704–709 (1993)
18. Freund, Y., Schapire, R.E., Singer, Y., Warmuth, M.K.: Using and Combining Predictors that Specialize. In: STOC, pp. 334–343 (1997)
19. Freund, Y., Schapire, R.E.: A Decision-Theoretic Generalization of On-Line Learning and an Application to Boosting. In: Euro-COLT, pp. 23–37. Springer, Heidelberg (1995)
20. Hannan, J.: Approximation to Bayes Risk in Repeated Plays. In: Dresher, M., Tucker, A., Wolfe, P. (eds.) Contributions to the Theory of Games, vol. 3, pp. 97–139. Princeton University Press, Princeton (1957)
21. Hart, S., Mas-Colell, A.: A Simple Adaptive Procedure Leading to Correlated Equilibrium. Econometrica 68, 1127–1150 (2000)
22. Kakade, S.M., Tauman-Kalai, A., Ligett, K.: Playing Games with Approximation Algorithms. In: STOC, pp. 546–555 (2007)
23. Kalai, A., Vempala, S.: Efficient Algorithms for Online Decision Problems. Journal of Computer and System Sciences 71(3), 291–307 (2005); An earlier version appeared in COLT (2003)
24. Kalai, A., Vempala, S.: Efficient Algorithms for On-Line Optimization. J. of Computer Systems and Science (JCSS) 71(3), 291–307 (2005); (A preliminary version appeared in COLT 2003)

25. Lai, T.L., Robbins, H.: Asymptotically Efficient Adaptive Allocations Rules. Advances in Applied Mathmatics 6, 4–22 (1985)
26. Lehrer, E.: A Wide Range No-Regret Theorem. Games and Economic Behavior 42, 101–115 (2003)
27. Littlestone, N., Warmuth, M.K.: The Weighted Majority Algorithm. Information and Computation 108, 212–261 (1994)
28. Robbins, H.: Some Aspects of the Sequential Design of Experiments. Bulletin of the American Mathematical Society 58, 527–535 (1952)

Lessons in Software Evolution Learned by Listening to Smalltalk

Oscar Nierstrasz and Tudor Gîrba

Software Composition Group, University of Bern, Switzerland
http://scg.unibe.ch

Abstract. The biggest challenge facing software developers today is how to gracefully evolve complex software systems in the face of changing requirements. We clearly need software systems to be more dynamic, compositional and model-centric, but instead we continue to build systems that are static, baroque and inflexible. How can we better build *change-enabled* systems in the future? To answer this question, we propose to look back to one of the most successful systems to support change, namely Smalltalk. We briefly introduce Smalltalk with a few simple examples, and draw some lessons for software evolution. Smalltalk's simplicity, its reflective design, and its highly dynamic nature all go a long way towards enabling change in Smalltalk applications. We then illustrate how these lessons work in practice by reviewing a number of research projects that support software evolution by exploiting Smalltalk's design. We conclude by summarizing open issues and challenges for change-enabled systems of the future.

1 Introduction

The conventional view of disciplined software construction is to reason that *correctness* of the final result is paramount, so we must invest carefully in rigorous requirements collection, specification, verification and validation.

Of course these things are important, but the fallacy is to suppose that there *is* a final result. This leads one to the flawed corollary that it is possible to get the requirements right. The truth (as we know) is that in practice *evolution* is paramount [26,32], so the system is never finished, and neither are its requirements [4].

What features are important in a software system to enable graceful software evolution? In previous work we have argued that evolution is enabled by high-level composition of components [2]. We have also argued that such systems should also be dynamic, they should support reflection on-demand, and they should provide mechanisms to manage the scope of change [33]. Change should be represented as a first-class entity, and both static and dynamic models of the running applications should be available at run-time to support continuous monitoring and analysis of evolution [34]. Instead of being merely "model-driven", such systems should be *model-centric*, meaning that models are not only available for analysis, but also to enable and enact change. To control the scope of change, systems need to be *context-aware*, thus allowing selected changes to be

J. van Leeuwen et al. (Eds.): SOFSEM 2010, LNCS 5901, pp. 77–95, 2010.

visible to different parts of the same running system [35]. In a nutshell, change-enabled systems should be (i) compositional, (ii) dynamic, (iii) model-centric, (iv) reflective, (v) self-monitoring, and (vi) context-aware.

But how should we build such change-enabled systems? What are good examples of systems that actively support and enable rather than limit and impede software evolution?

In this paper we take the position that many of these questions can be partially answered by taking a close look at the Smalltalk system. Smalltalk [19,23] was the first programming language and development environment designed to be fully object-oriented from the ground up[1]. Many technical and process innovations arose from Smalltalk, including the first interactive development environments with graphical user interfaces, many virtual machine advances, refactoring tools, unit testing frameworks, and so on. Although it shows its age today, in many ways Smalltalk (like ALGOL [21]) still improves on its successors.

Smalltalk is still interesting today because it offers many features that support graceful software evolution. First of all, at the core it is very simple. Smalltalk is built up from a small set of fully object-oriented principles, starting with the notions that *everything is an object* and *everything happens by sending messages.* The syntax is remarkably simple, and can be read aloud like pidgin English. Second, it is fully reflective, so all features of the Smalltalk system are available at run-time as ... objects. Third, Smalltalk is highly dynamic. While most programming languages are trapped in an edit/compile/run cycle, Smalltalk supports incremental and interactive development of *running applications* by erasing the artificial distinction between "compile-time" and "run-time".

In Section 2 we introduce Smalltalk by means of series of simple examples, and we draw three lessons that illustrate how Smalltalk support software evolution. In Section 3, Section 4, and Section 5 we review a series of research projects that demonstrate how Smalltalk's simplicity, its reflective design, and its dynamic nature enable change. In Section 6 we discuss several shortcomings of Smalltalk and open challenges for change-enabled systems of the future. We conclude with a few closing remarks in Section 7.

2 What Can We Learn from Smalltalk?

Smalltalk was designed to be the programming language and operating system for implementing a new generation of lightweight, interactive computers known as the Dynabook [22,23] (now recognizable as a precursor of today's laptops; see Figure 1). To build such a radically different kind of computer, Kay reasoned that the underlying language and system should be object-oriented from the ground up.

The principle "Everything is an object" pervades Smalltalk's design [19]. As we shall see, this simple starting point inevitably led to a design in which all aspects of Smalltalk are reified and available at run-time.

[1] Simula-67 [6] was earlier, but essentially extended ALGOL with object-oriented constructs, rather than being fully object-oriented.

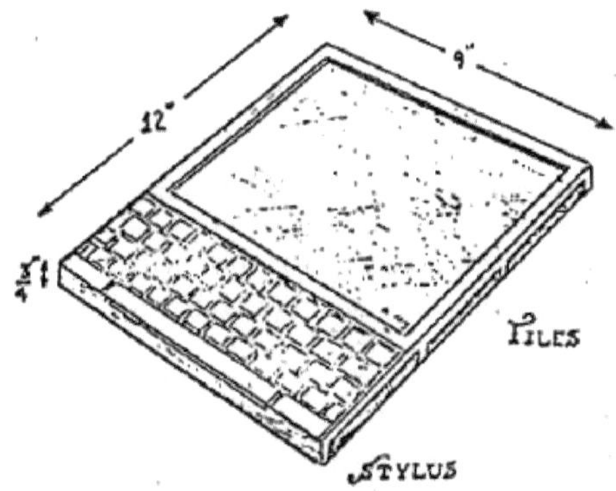

Fig. 1. Dynabook sketch from Kay's 1972 paper [22]

In this section we introduce Smalltalk through a series of simple examples that illustrate surprising aspects of Smalltalk's design principles. We conclude by drawing three lessons for designing change-enabled software systems.

2.1 Simple, Read-Aloud Syntax

Smalltalk as a language is pretty much minimal. It is common to remark that Smalltalk syntax can be learned in an afternoon, while the system itself can take many months to master.

Smalltalk supports three kinds of message syntax, as seen in the following example:

```
2 raisedTo: 1 + 3 factorial    ⟶    128
```

Unary messages, like factorial or new, consist of simple alphabetic identifiers, and are evaluated first. *Binary* messages, like +, are built up of operator symbols (much like in C++), always take a single argument, and are evaluated next. Finally, *keyword* messages, like raisedTo: or ifTrue:ifFalse:, consist of any number of keywords, each of which ends in a colon (:) and takes a single argument.

By exercising some common sense when naming classes, instance variables and methods, this scheme leads to compact code which can be read aloud as though it were a kind of pidgin English.

As a trivial example, try to read the following two roughly equivalent code fragments out loud:

```
for(int n=1; n<=10; n++){
    System.out.println(n);
}
```

```
1 to: 10 do: [:n | Transcript show: n; cr ]
```

By avoiding the need for most declarations, and by adhering to a message syntax that allows verbs and nouns to conveniently alternate, Smalltalk achieves a high level of readability. This is of course important if code is to be largely self-documenting. A large part of continuing development of complex software systems is *reading* of existing code, not just writing of new code.

2.2 Everything Happens by Sending Messages to Objects

Not only the syntax is simple, but also the design and implementation of Smalltalk follow logically from a few basic principles[19]. The most fundamental of these principles are:

1. *Everything is an object.*
2. *Everything happens by sending messages.*

Other important principles state, for instance, that:

3. *Every object is an instance of a class.*
4. *Every class (except the root) has a superclass.*
5. *Method lookup follows the superclass hierarchy.*

Everything is an object, including numbers, so when we compute 3 + 4, we send the message + to the object 3 with argument 4:[2]

```
3 + 4  —→  7
```

Both little numbers and very big numbers are objects:

```
42 factorial  —→
    1405006117752879898543142606244511569936384000000000
```

Since everything is an object, classes and methods are objects too. And since everything happens by sending messages, instantiating objects, defining new classes, and creating methods also happen by sending messages. For example, to define a class, we send a message to its superclass:

```
Object subclass: #Life
    instanceVariableNames: ''
    classVariableNames: ''
    poolDictionaries: ''
    category: 'MyUniverse'
```

We have just asked the root class Object to create a subclass of itself called Life in the category (read "package") called 'MyUniverse'.

To create a new object, we send a message to a class:

```
myLife := Life new
```

[2] To indicate the result of evaluating a Smalltalk expression we use the notation expression —→ result.

To define a method, we can send a message to its class:

```
Life compile: 'answer ↑ 42'
```

This method will be evaluated in response to the message answer, and returns[3] the result 42. Normally, however, we would define methods using the development environment, but it is important to remember that everything a tool does actually happens by sending messages.

Of course we can send messages to plain objects too:

```
myLife answer    ⟶    42
```

(You might have noticed that we just extended the behaviour of a living object.)

What is now more interesting is that we can now easily navigate and query the system as well simply by sending messages:

```
Life superclass                 ⟶    Object
Life methods size               ⟶    1
Life methods first selector     ⟶    #answer
Life methods first class        ⟶    CompiledMethod
```

In this way we can quickly reach the meta-objects that implement the system (such as CompiledMethod). We can also easily explore the system's meta-model:

```
Life class              ⟶    Life class
Life class class        ⟶    Metaclass
Life class class class  ⟶    Metaclass class
```

This tells us that Life is an instance of Life class, that Life class is an instance of Metaclass, and that Metaclass is an instance of Metaclass class.[4]

2.3 Everything Is There, All the Time

In Smalltalk, there is no distinction between the development environment and the runtime environment. They are one and the same.

The fact that all objects of the run-time system are accessible from the running image, and that all the source code is available all the time, leads to a very different style of development from the traditional file-based edit/compile/run life-cycle. Instead, Smalltalk encourages iterative and incremental development in which a single class is created or a single method is compiled at a time. We can change or extend the behaviour of already existing objects (*e.g.*, myLife acquires the answer method at run-time).

As a consequence, Test-Driven Development, in which failing tests are written before the code that makes the test pass, is naturally supported [5]. The surprising fact is that it is possible to add the missing code, using the Smalltalk debugger, *from the context of the failing test.*

---

[3] ↑ is Smalltalk for "return".

[4] The alert reader might be able to conclude how this tale continues.

Perhaps even more surprising is the extent to which it is considered best practice in Smalltalk to make heavy use of the debugger. By contrast, in most programming languages, the debugger is often considered a tool of last resort. In Smalltalk, since the entire system is live, the debugger provides a convenient interface to link source code to live objects. In other words, *the debugger is your friend.* Since code can be evaluated and even changed in the debugger, this leads to an interactive and incremental style of development in which one can modify and test a running application in very tight iterations.

Suppose, for instance, that we try to evaluate the following:

```
myLife meaning
```

Since our Smalltalk environment has never heard of the message "meaning", it asks us to confirm that this is what we intend. When we confirm, the object myLife receives the message meaning, but does not know what to do with it. This causes Smalltalk to send it the message doesNotUnderstand: with the symbol #meaning as its argument. The default behaviour is to launch a pre-debugger window which offers us the possibility of creating the missing method (Figure 2).

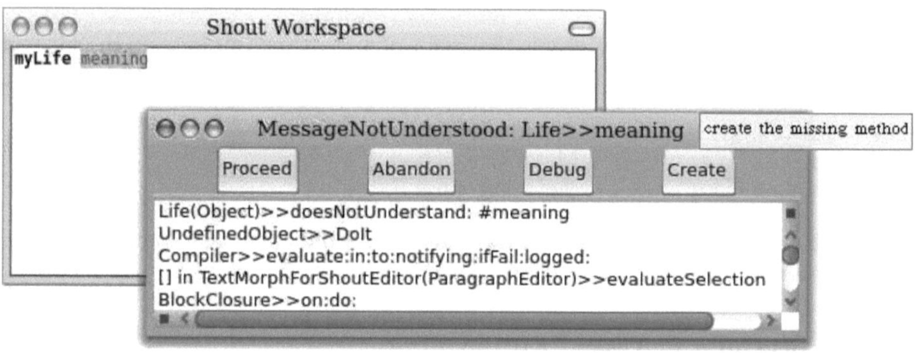

Fig. 2. Not understanding the meaning of life

Smalltalk kindly generates a default implementation within the debugger, which does nothing but send the message shouldBeImplemented to self. From within the debugger we can change this method to something more reasonable (Figure 3).

Now if we ask Smalltalk to *Proceed*, we obtain the result we expect, *without ever having left the running system.*

```
myLife meaning    ⟶    'Try and be nice to people, avoid eating fat, read a good
    book every now and then, get some walking in, and try and live together in
   peace and harmony with people of all creeds and nations'
```

2.4 Lessons in Software Evolution

We have seen how Smalltalk distinguishes itself by its simplicity, its reflective design, and its dynamic nature. These features support software evolution in important ways:

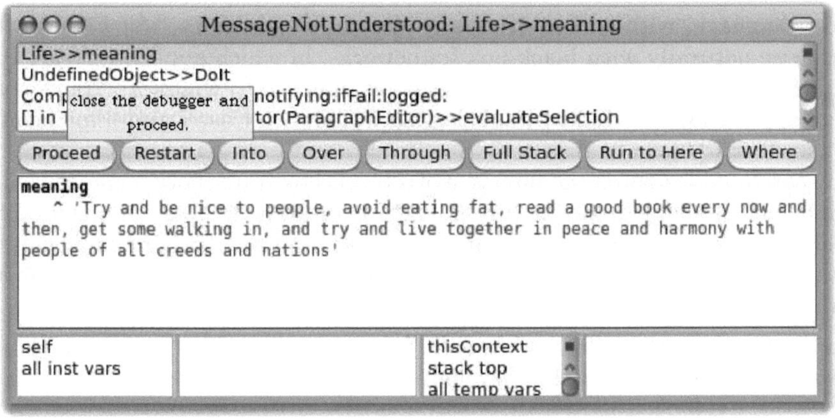

Fig. 3. Redefining the meaning of life

- *Less is more*: Both the model and the syntax of Smalltalk are minimal. The model is extended by introducing new objects, not by changing the language. This minimal syntax allows for fluent interfaces to arise more naturally in Smalltalk than many other languages, thus the code is largely self-documenting — a critical feature for an evolving system.
- *Reify everything*: The design of Smalltalk follows logically from a small set of principles. This makes the system easy to navigate, query and extend.
- *You can change a running system*: Contrary to most other software systems, in Smalltalk you can *only* change a running system. There is no distinction between edit-time, compile-time and run-time. The entire Smalltalk system is described in itself. Essentially all the source code and the entire run-time system is accessible all the time. This makes it a good basis for realizing run-time, model-driven systems.

In the following sections, we will explore these points by reviewing several research projects that exploit Smalltalk to enable change.

Smalltalk also has quite a few wrinkles, grey hairs and creaky joints. For instance, Smalltalk's traditional support for modularity based on "categories" of related classes is primitive at best. We will conclude this paper with a discussion of a number of areas where Smalltalk, and other programming systems, need to better address the needs of software evolution.

3 Less Is More

The simplicity of Smalltalk's syntax makes it easy to learn. But, there is another important aspect that this simple syntax supports well, which is the design of *fluent interfaces* for black-box, component frameworks. A fluent interface resembles a domain specific language (DSL), except that it is entirely embedded in a host language, without requiring any syntactic extensions [18]. Fluent interfaces arise naturally with black-box frameworks, in which applications are built by plugging together existing components, as opposed to white-box frameworks, where applications are built by subclassing framework classes and implementing hook methods [43].

By carefully designing the interface of a black-box framework, compositions of components resemble readable (or "fluent") high-level "scripts" in a DSL. DSLs enable change by raising the level of abstraction, and by offering a more suitable notation for domain experts to express requirements. Let us review a number of examples.

Seaside. Consider the following example from an on-line store programmed using Seaside [15], a web application development framework written in Smalltalk:

```
renderContentOn: html
    html heading: item title.
    html heading level3; with: item subtitle.
    html paragraph: item description.
    html emphasis: item price printStringAsCents.
    html form: [
        html submitButton callback: [self addToCart]; text: 'Add To Cart'.
        html space.
        html submitButton callback: [self answer]; text: 'Done' ]
```

A reader who knows neither the specific application nor Smalltalk, but is familiar with HTML, should be able to read this aloud and make sense of it. The code reads like a script in a DSL, but is actually plain Smalltalk code using Seaside's fluent interface. The result can be seen in the *California Roll* item in Figure 4.

Mondrian. Mondrian [31] is a black-box framework for generating visualizations. The following script generates a simple System Complexity View [25] of a class hierarchy, mapping dimensions and shading of boxes to metrics (see Figure 5):

Fig. 4. Scripting a Seaside component

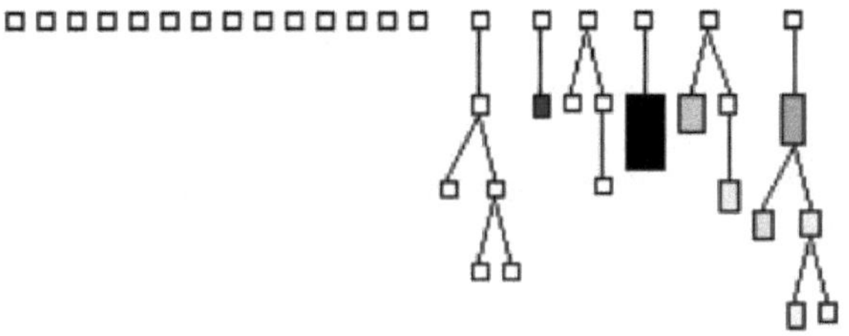

Fig. 5. A Mondrian-scripted System Complexity View

```
view := ViewRenderer new.
view nodeShape rectangle
    width: #NOA; height: #NOM;
    linearColor: #LOC within: model classes.
view nodes: model classes.
view edges: model inheritances from: #superclass to: #subclass.
view treeLayout.
view open.
```

Glamour. Glamour is yet another black-box framework used to develop interactive browsers for diverse information models [8]. As with Seaside and Mondrian, Glamour scripts are compact, readable, and resemble code written in a dedicated DSL, though in fact they simply make use of a fluent interface written in Smalltalk. For example, the following script produces a file browser similar to Windows Explorer (see Figure 6).

```
browser := TableLayoutBrowser new.
browser
    column: #folders;
    column: [ :col | col row: #files span: 2; row: #preview ] span: 2.
browser showOn: #folders; using: [
    browser tree children: [ :folder | folder files select: #isDirectory ] ].
browser showOn: #files; from: #folders; using: [
    browser list display: [ :folder | folder files reject: #isDirectory ] ].
browser showOn: #preview; from: #files; using: [
    browser text display: #contentsOfEntireFile ] ].
```

Black-box frameworks separate what is *stable* (*i.e.*, the components) from what needs to stay *flexible* (*i.e.*, the scripts) [2]. High-level scripts facilitate software evolution by concentrating the *composition* of the system in a readable specification. A fluent interface makes scripts easy to read, and hence easy to modify and test, in contrast to traditional white-box frameworks which can be notoriously difficult to understand, specialize, and configure. Smalltalk's simple syntax and semantics supports both the development of pluggable black-box components and fluent interfaces to compose them.

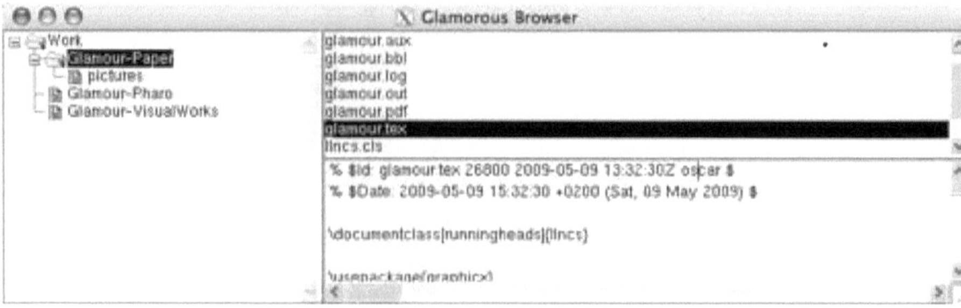

Fig. 6. A Windows Explorer-like browser implemented in Glamour

4 Reify Everything

Smalltalk relies on a simple and explicit meta-model. With a simple meta-model, not only can we easily query our software, we can also extend it. In this section we will review a number of projects that have extended Smalltalk's meta-model to support software evolution.

Traits. Traits [16] extend Smalltalk's meta-model with reusable groups of methods, thus overcoming the limitations of single inheritance, while avoiding fragility problems known to occur with multiple inheritance and mixins. The introduction of traits required changes to the meta-model, the compiler, and the run-time, but no changes to the language or the syntax, since everything happens by sending messages.

Let us define a new trait:

```
Trait named: #TUltimate uses: {} category: 'MyUniverse'.
TUltimate compile: 'question ↑ ''What do you get if you multiply six by nine?'''
```

We change our class to use this trait:

```
Object subclass: #Life
   uses: TUltimate
   instanceVariableNames: ''
   classVariableNames: ''
   poolDictionaries: ''
   category: 'MyUniverse'
```

And now:

```
myLife question   ⟶   'What do you get if you multiply six by nine?'
```

Traits support evolution by simplifying the refactoring of complex hierarchies into finer grained, reusable components [10].

Magritte. Model-driven engineering (MDE) promotes software evolution by raising the level of continuous development to levels that are closer to the problem domain. But conventional MDE makes use of transformations to *generate*

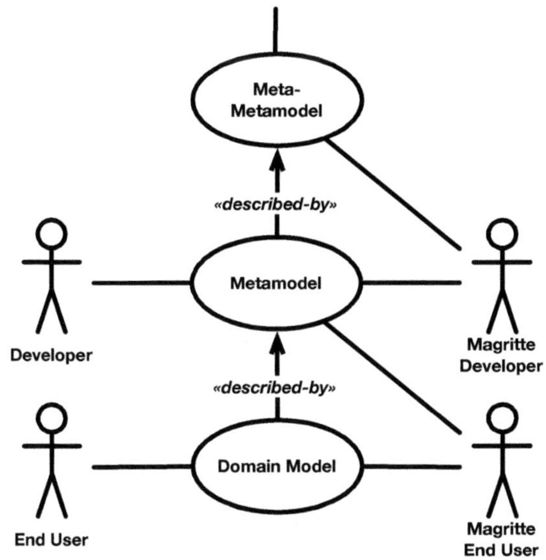

Fig. 7. Magritte enables run-time customization of models and meta-models

platform-specific models (and code) from platform-independent models. The models are not typically available to the run-time system, so further adaptation and evolution are not possible at run-time.

A model-centric system [35] makes high-level, causally-connected models available to the run-time system for analysis and run-time adaptation. Smalltalk offers a good foundation for model-centric systems due to its reflective architecture.

A good example of a model-centric system is *Magritte* [38] a meta-description framework implemented in Smalltalk. Magritte has been used, for example, to meta-describe components of the Pier content management system[5], allowing it to be customized at run-time. Not only users can customize the domain model at run-time, but developers can directly customize many aspects of the meta-model without writing a line of code, since the meta-model is also meta-described and rendered by Pier as web components (Figure 7).

Moose. Moose[6] provides another example of a model-centric system. It offers a platform for capturing, querying, navigating, analyzing and visualizing models of complex software systems [36]. Several analyses have been built on top of it dealing with various aspects of software: static analysis, dynamic analysis, evolution analysis, semantic analysis, code duplication, code ownership analysis and so on.

These analyses require various meta-models. To accommodate them, at its core, Moose has a meta-meta-model in terms of which the various meta-models

[5] `http://www.piercms.com`
[6] `http://moose.unibe.ch`

are defined [14,24]. Based on these descriptions, Moose offers import-export capabilities, it generates user interfaces for navigation, and provides integration mechanisms for extension services that encode specific analyses.

5 You Can Change a Running System

Since in Smalltalk, everything is an object, it follows that the Smalltalk system itself consists of a collection of objects. Since everything happens by sending messages, it follows that all changes to the system are simply consequences of messages being sent. In other words *changes to the system occur within the system*, and are no different than any other events.

The fact that everything is there all the time and can be changed dynamically means that both past and future evolution are accessible to the running system. We will briefly look at three ways this can be exploited.

Object-Flow Analysis. One of the well-known shortcomings of conventional stack-oriented debuggers is that the offending context which may have led to a run-time error may no longer be on the stack. If a method has left an object in an invalid state, this might produce an undesirable side effect at a much later point in time.

A so-called *back-in-time debugger* [29] keeps track of historical execution contexts to allow the developer to debug further back in time. Although appealing, tracking history may generate vast amounts of data, and still it may be difficult to track the actual cause of a defect.

The *object-flow VM* [28] tracks history in a live Smalltalk system by *tracking the flow of objects* with first-class aliases, each of which stores a past state and

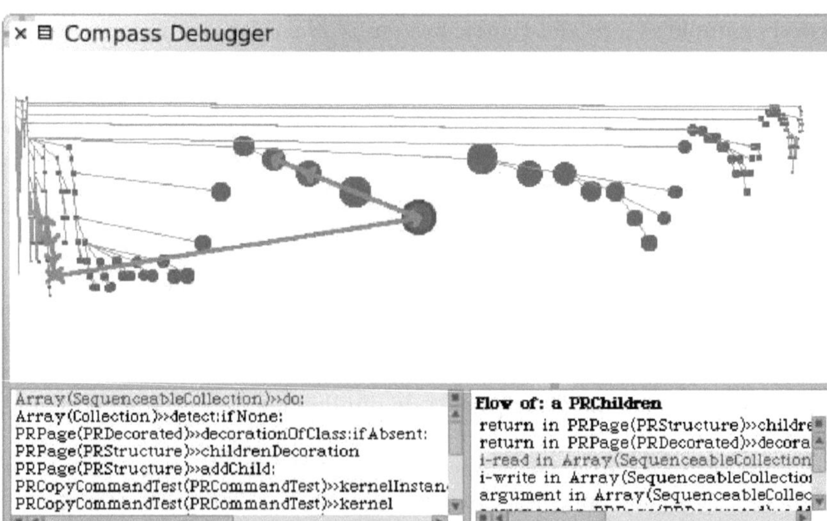

Fig. 8. Tracing object flow with the Compass back-in-time debugger

records the previous alias which led to it. Since aliases are first-class, unreachable aliases are automatically garbage-collected, leading to a simple and elegant saving of space. Since aliases are managed at the VM level, they are invisible to running applications. *Compass* [27] is a back-in-time debugger implemented using the object-flow VM, which exploits object flow to simplify navigation of the tree of past contexts (see Figure 8).

Changeboxes. Change management is an essential task to support software evolution. Smalltalk provides a simple form of change management already within the environment, so it is always possible to roll back changes. All changes are also logged, so it is impossible to lose code.

This form of change management, however, is strictly limited to source code. In a complex and evolving software system, different parts may depend on different versions of the same software base. For a system that cannot afford significant down-time, it may be unrealistic to expect that the entire code base be globally consistent at all times. *Changeboxes* [12] is a prototype of a system supporting change management for running software — deployed and development branches may co-exist in the same running image, and can run different versions of the same software. Branches can be dynamically split and merged without disrupting running clients, since the scope of applicable changes (*i.e.*, a "changebox") is always uniquely defined for any given context. A running web application, for example,

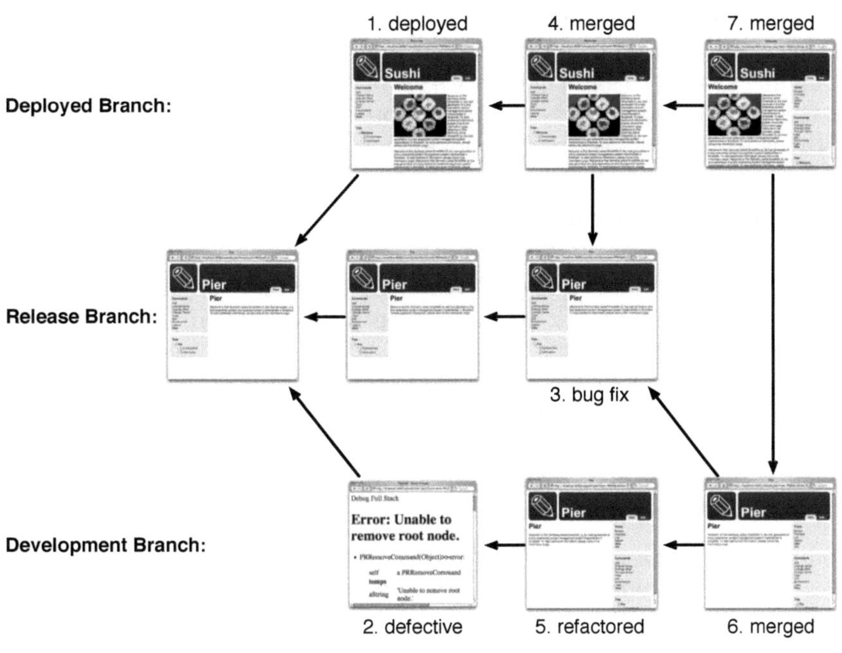

Fig. 9. Multiple versions of the same running system can be dynamically updated, split, and merged

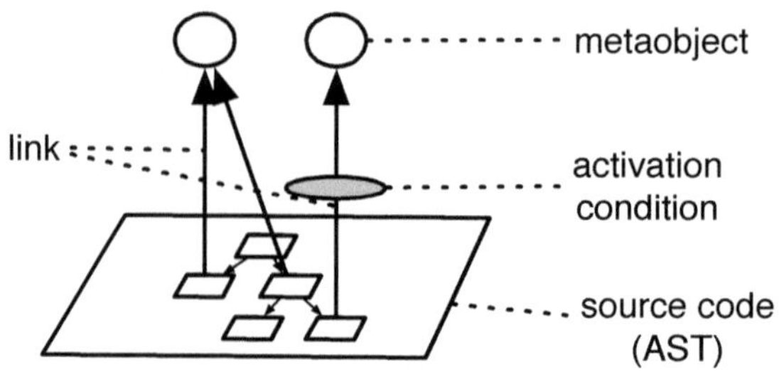

Fig. 10. Links annotate code reified as ASTs to trigger meta-object adaptations

can be modified without impacting clients, and incrementally deployed on the live system by merging branches when they are ready (Figure 9).

The Changeboxes prototype adapted the Smalltalk meta-model by modifying tools to be changebox-aware, and by modifying method lookup to select the right version of a method for the currently active changebox.

Reflectivity. Reflectivity [11] goes a step further in providing a general infrastructure for adapting running code at a fine level of granularity. Code is reified by its abstract syntax tree (AST), and links are installed on this representation as annotations (Figure 10). A compiler plug-in transforms the annotated ASTs before execution to take the links into account. When the annotated code is run, if any optional activation conditions are fulfilled, a message is sent to a designated meta-object to take appropriate action.

A typical application is to dynamically add and remove instrumentation code on a running system to gather statistics for program analysis [40]. Other applications, however, include aspect-oriented adaptation [42] and automatic adaptation of methods to use software transactional memory [39].

6 The Future of Change

Successful software must change to maintain its value. Why is it that the languages and environments we use to develop software inherently *inhibit* change rather than enable it?

We have seen how a simple object model which uniformly reifies all entities of the run-time meta-model supports dynamic change in a system like Smalltalk. Still, there are many aspects of software evolution that are no better handled by Smalltalk than by many other systems, both mainstream and exotic. Let us have a brief look at three of these issues.

Closing the gap between objects and models. Model-driven development (MDD) enables change by generating code from high-level models. When the models change, the corresponding code can be freshly generated. Models, however, are normally absent as artifacts in the running system, so no further changes are possible in a deployed system. Traditionally models, meta-models and meta-meta-models are distinct and their instances do not exist as entities at the same level.

In Smalltalk-like systems, however, everything is an object, so objects, classes and metaclasses (for example) are all objects. They are all causally connected, so a change to a class impacts its instances, just as a change to a metaclass will impact the class.

Ultimately, *programming is modeling*, and a programming language or system is essentially a modeling tool. Object-oriented languages are particularly well-suited for allowing developers to design their own high-level models for a given application domain. An explicit notion of a model, however, is conspicuously missing from programming languages, Smalltalk included.

In the 1950s, FORTRAN was proposed as a high-level language from which computer code would be automatically generated. Nowadays we are used to thinking of programs written in high-level languages as being "the code", and we barely concern ourselves with the machine code that is "generated". By the same token, perhaps we should stop thinking about "generating code from models" and instead target development platforms where models themselves are executable. (Whether models are interpreted or code is generated on the fly should be purely an implementation detail.)

We have argued that change-enabled systems should be model-centric, making models available at run-time [35]. How to achieve this, however, is an open question, though some trends are interesting to watch. Executable UML [30] aims at making UML diagrams executable by means of dedicated compilers (though such models won't be available at run-time). Visual languages come and go [9], but some recent developments, such as Subtext [17], approach the direct manipulation of models. Naked Objects [37] pushes ideas implicit in the model-view-controller paradigm to nearly eliminate the distinction between domain objects, their implementation and their view.

Eliminating the barrier between the image and the VM. Smalltalk objects live in the "image", a persistent representation of object memory. Images are saved as binary files, making it is easy to take multiple snapshots of the state of the system, move images between machines, and share images with other users. The virtual machine abstracts from the underlying hardware, so the same image can run on any hardware or operating system platform.

On the other hand, images are essentially single-user (even if they host web services), and communicating with the outside world (files, servers, other running images) is clumsy at best. Although advanced collaborative tools exist [41,7], objects by and large are "trapped in the image". Little work has been done recently to enable distributed, collaborative development.

Furthermore, although nearly everything is available to the run-time system, objects of the VM are not. There exists a hard barrier between the image and the VM which cannot be overcome. Certain kinds of changes are only possible by implementing a new VM. As we have seen in Section 5, object-flow analysis extended Smalltalks meta-model by introducing first-class aliases, but this was only possible by modifying the Smalltalk VM. Making such functionality available to other users is a non-trivial engineering task, since it is not simply a matter of loading a new package into the image.

To better support such deep changes in the run-time of change-enabled systems, we must either find ways to bridge the boundary between the image and the VM, or we need to erase the boundary completely. Pinocchio[7] [44] is an open language and system whose semantics and implementation is fully bootstrapped, allowing deep changes to be made at run-time. By eliminating the separation between the image and the VM, full control over the run-time semantics is possible. Non-intrusive changes important for software evolution, such as tracking object-flow or monitoring run-time performance can be dynamically enabled without requiring the VM to be replaced.

Putting objects into context. Most languages and systems, including Smalltalk, assume that the world is consistent. We are forced to assume that a name means one thing, that a single version of any piece of software is deployed at a time, that types and interfaces are consistent. The real world is rife with inconsistency, yet we cope with it very well. Why can't our software systems?

We cope with real world inconsistency because we easily keep track of different contexts. How we behave, how we react to events, and how we present ourselves depends on a constantly changing context. Furthermore we generally have little difficulty in managing multiple contexts being active at the same time. (We can deal with family, friends, co-workers and strangers present in the same room.)

The Changebox prototype described in Section 5 managed multiple deployment contexts for software by adapting Smalltalk's method lookup to take a particular kind of context (a "changebox") into account, but this only works for changebox-aware tools. In practice, there are many different kinds of context variables that context-aware applications need to take into account [1,3]. To deal with context in a rigorous and fully general way, we argue that it is necessary to accommodate context deeply in the semantics [13] and the design [20] of programming languages and systems.

7 Conclusion

To sketch out what a change-enabled software system might look like, we have taken a brief look at a classic, dynamic system, Smalltalk, and seen how it supports software evolution in various ways. The single principle, *everything is an object*, can be seen as the driving force behind its simplicity, and its support for change. The key lessons for software evolution that we draw are: (i) *Less is more* — simple syntax and semantics can lead to a system that is easy to understand and change; (ii) *Reify everything* — by making all key entities first-class, they become available for modification and extension; (iii) *You can change a running system* — by causally connecting entities with their meta-descriptions, graceful, incremental change is enabled.

Change is here with us to stay. Increasingly, software systems will need to adapt to change dynamically, which means that software models must be accessible at run-time. Ideally, models will be executable, and different versions of the same models will need to be simultaneously active, and context-aware.

---

[7] `http://scg.unibe.ch/research/pinocchio`

Acknowledgments. We gratefully acknowledge the financial support of the Swiss National Science Foundation for the project "Bringing Models Closer to Code" (SNF Project No. 200020-121594, Oct 1, 2008 - Sept. 30, 2010) and the Hasler project "Enabling the evolution of J2EE applications through reverse engineering and quality assurance" (project no. 2234). We also thank Lukas Renggli, Erwann Wernli, Fabrizio Perin, Bernhard Rumpe and Jan Ringert for their helpful comments and suggestions.

References

1. Abowd, G.D., Dey, A.K.: Towards a Better Understanding of Context and Context-Awareness. In: Proceedings of the CHI 2000 Workshop on the What, Who, Where, When and How of Context-Awareness. ACM Press, New York (2000)
2. Achermann, F., Lumpe, M., Schneider, J.-G., Nierstrasz, O.: Piccola — a Small Composition Language. In: Bowman, H., Derrick, J. (eds.) Formal Methods for Distributed Processing — A Survey of Object-Oriented Approaches, pp. 403–426. Cambridge University Press, Cambridge (2001)
3. Baldauf, M., Dustdar, S., Rosenberg, F.: A Survey on Context-Aware Systems. International Journal of Ad Hoc and Ubiquitous Computing 2(4), 263–277 (2007)
4. Beck, K.: Extreme Programming Explained: Embrace Change. Addison-Wesley, Reading (2000)
5. Beck, K.: Test Driven Development: By Example. Addison-Wesley Longman, Amsterdam (2002)
6. Birtwistle, G., Dahl, O.J., Myhrtag, B., Nygaard, K.: Simula Begin. Auerbach Press, Philadelphia (1973)
7. Bryant, A.: Monticello, `http://www.wiresong.ca/Monticello`
8. Bunge, P.: Scripting Browsers with Glamour. Master's Thesis, University of Bern (April 2009)
9. Burnett, M.M., Goldberg, A.: Visual Object-Oriented Programming. Prentice-Hall, Englewood Cliffs (1995)
10. Cassou, D., Ducasse, S., Wuyts, R.: Traits at Work: the Design of a New Trait-Based Stream Library. Journal of Computer Languages, Systems and Structures 35(1), 2–20 (2009)
11. Denker, M.: Sub-method Structural and Behavioral Reflection. PhD Thesis, University of Bern (May 2008)
12. Denker, M., Gîrba, T., Lienhard, A., Nierstrasz, O., Renggli, L., Zumkehr, P.: Encapsulating and Exploiting Change with Changeboxes. In: Proceedings of the 2007 International Conference on Dynamic Languages (ICDL 2007), pp. 25–49. ACM Digital Library, New York (2007)
13. Dezani-Ciancaglini, M., Giannini, P., Nierstrasz, O.: A Calculus of Evolving Objects. Scientific Annals of Computer Science XVIII, pp. 63–98 (2008)
14. Ducasse, S., Gîrba, T., Kuhn, A., Renggli, L.: Meta-Environment and Executable Meta-Language Using Smalltalk: an Experience Report. Journal of Software and Systems Modeling (SOSYM) 8(1), 5–19 (2009)
15. Ducasse, S., Lienhard, A., Renggli, L.: Seaside: A Flexible Environment for Building Dynamic Web Applications. IEEE Software 24(5), 56–63 (2007)
16. Ducasse, S., Nierstrasz, O., Schärli, N., Wuyts, R., Black, A.: Traits: A Mechanism for Fine-Grained Reuse. ACM Transactions on Programming Languages and Systems (TOPLAS) 28(2), 331–388 (2006)

17. Edwards, J.: Subtext: Uncovering the Simplicity of Programming. In: Johnson, R., Gabriel, R.P. (eds.) Proceedings of the 20th Annual ACM SIGPLAN Conference on Object-Oriented Programming, Systems, Languages, and Applications, OOPSLA 2005, San Diego, CA, USA, October 16-20, pp. 505–518. ACM, New York (2005)
18. Fowler, M.: FluentInterface, on Martin Fowler's Blog (December 2005), `http://www.martinfowler.com/bliki/FluentInterface.html`
19. Goldberg, A., Robson, D.: Smalltalk 80: the Language and Its Implementation. Addison Wesley, Reading (1983)
20. Hirschfeld, R., Costanza, P., Nierstrasz, O.: Context-Oriented Programming. Journal of Object Technology 7(3) (2008)
21. Hoare, C.A.R.: Hints on Programming Language Design. Technical Report CS-TR-73-403, Stanford University (1973)
22. Kay, A.C.: A Personal Computer for Children of All Ages. In: Proceedings of the ACM National Conference. ACM Press, New York (1972)
23. Kay, A.C.: The Early History of Smalltalk. ACM SIGPLAN Notices 28, 69–95 (1993)
24. Kuhn, A., Verwaest, T.: FAME, a Polyglot Library for Metamodeling at Runtime. In: Workshop on Models at Runtime, pp. 57–66 (2008)
25. Lanza, M., Marinescu, R.: Object-Oriented Metrics in Practice. Springer, Heidelberg (2006)
26. Lehman, M., Belady, L.: Program Evolution: Processes of Software Change. London Academic Press, London (1985)
27. Lienhard, A., Fierz, J., Nierstrasz, O.: Flow-Centric, Back-in-Time Debugging. In: Objects, Components, Models and Patterns, Proceedings of TOOLS Europe 2009. LNBIP, vol. 33, pp. 272–288. Springer, Heidelberg (2009)
28. Lienhard, A., Gîrba, T., Nierstrasz, O.: Practical Object-Oriented Back-in-Time Debugging. In: Vitek, J. (ed.) ECOOP 2008. LNCS, vol. 5142, pp. 592–615. Springer, Heidelberg (2008); ECOOP distinguished paper award
29. Maruyama, K., Terada, M.: Debugging with Reverse Watchpoint. In: Proceedings of the Third International Conference on Quality Software (QSIC 2003), Washington, DC, USA, p. 116. IEEE Computer Society, Los Alamitos (2003)
30. Mellor, S.J., Balcer, M.J.: Executable UML: A Foundation for Model-Driven Architecture. Addison-Wesley Professional (2002)
31. Meyer, M., Gîrba, T., Lungu, M.: Mondrian: An Agile Visualization Framework. In: ACM Symposium on Software Visualization (SoftVis 2006), pp. 135–144. ACM Press, New York (2006)
32. Nierstrasz, O.: Software Evolution as the Key to Productivity. In: Wirsing, M., Knapp, A., Balsamo, S. (eds.) RISSEF 2002. LNCS, vol. 2941, pp. 274–282. Springer, Heidelberg (2004)
33. Nierstrasz, O., Bergel, A., Denker, M., Ducasse, S., Gälli, M., Wuyts, R.: On the Revival of Dynamic Languages. In: Gschwind, T., Aßmann, U., Nierstrasz, O. (eds.) SC 2005. LNCS, vol. 3628, pp. 1–13. Springer, Heidelberg (2005)
34. Nierstrasz, O., Denker, M., Gîrba, T., Lienhard, A., Röthlisberger, D.: Change-Enabled Software Systems. In: Wirsing, M., Banâtre, J.-P., Hölzl, M., Rauschmayer, A. (eds.) Soft-Ware Intensive Systems. LNCS, vol. 5380, pp. 64–79. Springer, Heidelberg (2008)
35. Nierstrasz, O., Denker, M., Renggli, L.: Model-Centric, Context-Aware Software Adaptation. In: Cheng, B.H.C., de Lemos, R., Giese, H., Inverardi, P., Magee, J. (eds.) Software Engineering for Self-Adaptive Systems. LNCS, vol. 5525, pp. 128–145. Springer, Heidelberg (2009)

36. Nierstrasz, O., Ducasse, S., Gîrba, T.: The Story of Moose: an Agile Reengineering Environment. In: Proceedings of the European Software Engineering Conference (ESEC/FSE 2005), pp. 1–10. ACM Press, New York (2005); (invited paper)
37. Pawson, R.: Naked Objects. Ph.D. Thesis, Trinity College, Dublin (2004)
38. Renggli, L., Ducasse, S., Kuhn, A.: Magritte – a Meta-Driven Approach to Empower Developers and End Users. In: Engels, G., Opdyke, B., Schmidt, D.C., Weil, F. (eds.) MODELS 2007. LNCS, vol. 4735, pp. 106–120. Springer, Heidelberg (2007)
39. Renggli, L., Nierstrasz, O.: Transactional Memory in a Dynamic Language. Journal of Computer Languages, Systems and Structures 35(1), 21–30 (2009)
40. Röthlisberger, D., Greevy, O., Nierstrasz, O.: Exploiting Runtime Information in the IDE. In: Proceedings of the 16th International Conference on Program Comprehension (ICPC 2008), Los Alamitos, CA, USA, pp. 63–72. IEEE Computer Society (2008)
41. Smith, D.A., Kay, A., Raab, A., Reed, D.P.: Croquet, a Collaboration System Architecture. In: Proceedings of the First Conference on Creating, Connecting and Collaborating through Computing, pp. 2–9 (2003)
42. Strauss, A.: Dynamic Aspects — an AOP Implementation for Squeak. Master's Thesis, University of Bern (November 2008)
43. Szyperski, C.A.: Component Software. Addison-Wesley, Reading (1998)
44. Verwaest, T., Renggli, L.: Safe Reflection through Polymorphism. In: CASTA 2009: Proceedings of the First International Workshop on Context-Aware Software Technology and Applications, pp. 21–24. ACM, New York (2009)

The Web of Things: Extending the Web into the Real World

Dave Raggett

W3C/ERCIM,
2004, route des Lucioles, Sophia Antipolis, 06410 Biot, France
dsr@w3.org
http://www.w3.org/People/Raggett

Abstract. Thanks to Moore's law the incremental cost of adding networking to devices is falling rapidly. This creates opportunities for many new kinds of applications. This paper looks at the potential of Web technologies for reducing the complexity for developing such applications, allowing millions of developers to extend the Web out of the browser and into the real world. This is achieved through mechanisms to provide web run times with access to rich models of users, devices, services, and the environment in which they reside. Privacy and trust are key considerations.

1 Introduction

The World Wide Web is today an essential global infrastructure with a myriad of roles, e.g. news, entertainment, commerce, and education, to name just a few. The Web's origin lay in hypertext, the means to link text-based documents. The Internet has given us the means to follow such links across servers all over the World, continent hopping at a single click. The Web rapidly evolved to include images, forms, and scripting, and soon attracted a new generation of developers, which now vastly outnumber the old school developers for traditional platforms like Microsoft Windows.

Today, the Web is a global platform for information-based applications, but that is about to change. What is driving this is the rapidly dwindling incremental cost of networking for all kinds of devices. This is a happy side-effect of Moore's law which describes the ongoing exponential improvements in integrated circuitry which by now has been happening for more than half a century. It is now easy to integrate radio-frequency components alongside digital circuitry for microcontrollers.

We are in the midst of a proliferation of devices that are largely invisible as they are embedded within everyday objects from toasters to cameras and cars. Microcontrollers are the fastest growing segment of the computer industry, with hundreds in every home. These devices are programmed to serve a single purpose, and today are mostly isolated. Networking them will allow many new kinds of application that add value in ways that the original manufacturer may not have envisaged.

J. van Leeuwen et al. (Eds.): SOFSEM 2010, LNCS 5901, pp. 96–107, 2010.

Barcodes have been part of the everyday environment for many years, and used for tracking library books, identifying items at supermarket checkouts and routing luggage at airports. Two dimensional barcodes contain a lot more information and can be used to link physical objects to their virtual equivalents on the Web. Electronic versions of barcodes, RFID tags, are starting to take over, and appearing in passports, clothing and warehouses. The ability to scan multiple tags at one go, and to be able to write information back to the tag, provide obvious benefits over old fashioned barcodes.

The ability to connect applications running in the Web to devices in the real World has all kinds of benefits. Here are just a few:

- *Reduced energy costs* through management of home/office environments (sensor nets, actuators, ease of configuration, short/long term adaptation to human behaviour patterns)
- *Improved security* through remote monitoring of sensors and actuators (motion, thermal, doors, windows, locks, videocams, energy usage, RFID)
- *Reduced downtime* of household devices through continuous monitoring for signs of wear and proactive scheduling of repairs as part of maintenance contracts (washing machines, air conditioning, plumbing, cars, etc.)
- *Improved standard of care* for the elderly through monitoring patterns of activities as well as explicit health sensors, with the means to alert carers and emergency services

The remainder of this paper will look at some of the challenges in the way of realizing the Web of things, and proposals for how to address them.

2 Challenges

The biggest challenge is the difficulty in developing applications using traditional programming languages such as Java and C++. These involve steep learning curves for the language itself and especially for the complex application programming interfaces needed. This restricts the number of people who can develop applications as well as pushing up the costs.

Another challenge is the rapid pace of change for technologies used for networking devices. Some examples are Ethernet over twisted pair cable, DSL over copper phone lines, Ethernet over building power lines, WiFi and WiMax, BlueTooth, ZigBee, GSM and cellular packet radio, as well as interconnect solutions such as USB and Firewire. This multiplicity of technologies imposes complexity for developers, especially when different devices are using different solutions.

To add further difficulties, devices are likely to have a wide variety of ages, depending on their expected life time and frequency of replacement. Cell phones are replaced in a matter of months, whilst television sets and cars last for many years. The infrastructure built into buildings lasts even longer. How is it possible to create applications that work with a mix of generations of devices and technologies? How can we create applications today that will keep working when next year's devices come along?

Security is clearly important when it comes to controlling real world objects. Imagine a home security system: you wouldn't want a hacker to be able to open your front door and walk right in and take your prized possessions! Security firewalls protect against unwanted access, but also make it hard to configure applications. Few users are prepared to configure their browsers let alone opening ports to allow applications to connect through their firewalls. Usability is a critical factor in ensuring effective security.

If web applications are able to access sensors throughout the environment in public and private spaces, this would enable companies to track your life in immense detail. This calls for strong safeguards on privacy with negotiable obligations on how long personal data is held for, and for what purposes it can be used. You should be provided with a means to access any personal data held on you, to update it and to request its deletion. This means that privacy is not just a bolt on feature, and instead needs to treated as a core component with strong requirements on server middleware.

A final challenge is enabling applications to dynamically adapt to the context which includes user preferences, device capabilities, and the environment in which the application runs. This is especially important for people with sensory or cognitive impairments.

3 Web Run-Time

A Web run-time (WRT) is a component that provides an execution environment for markup languages, style sheets, scripts and related resources. A browser can be implemented as a container for a Web run-time that adds the browser user interface (some times referred to as the browser chrome) and associated components, such as the navigation toolbar, browser history and bookmarks. Widgets are another class of containers for Web run-times, where a single web application runs on its own as a locally installed application, where all of the associated markup, scripts, style sheets and media resources are installed as a package.

Web run-times are not restricted to HTML, and other kinds of markup languages may be appropriate. One example is SVG (Scalable Vector Graphics). Another is VoiceXML, a markup language with similarities to HTML (having forms and links) that is designed for use with telephones, together with speech synthesis and recognition, and is gaining widespread adoption in call centres. Yet another example is SCXML (State Chart XML) which is a markup language for event driven state machines. Whilst most people still think of the Web in terms of graphical user interfaces and HTML browsers, the Web is actually much broader than that.

Web run-times don't need to be associated with a local user interface, and instead user interaction could be mediated through an exchange of events with other devices that act as sensors or actuators. The user could therefore interact with an application using multiple devices and multiple modes (aural, tactile, visual). Users may even be able to control applications through gestures with their hands or by moving objects that lack electronics, and which are sensed by cameras or other devices. The ability to project synthetic images into the user's visual field allows for applications that augment reality.

The means for Web run-times to run remotely allows them to function as agents that act on behalf of their users. Such Web agents could run on computing resources provisioned as part of the cloud. This allows users to run applications 24 by 7. Such applications are always available, something that isn't the case for applications running on devices that may be turned off. When it comes to sharing private information between Web agents, there are challenges for dealing effectively with privacy and trust.

4 Device Coordination

When new devices are added to the environment, they need to obtain an IP address and to advertise their presence. There are a variety of mechanisms available for doing this without the need for manual intervention. These are loosely referred to as "zero configuration networking" or zeroconf, which includes techniques such as UPnP, Bonjour, Avahi, mDNS and SSDP. From the perspective of the Web of Things, these are low level techniques, and local software agents are needed to track devices and to expose the services they offer to Web applications. This involves maintaining live models of the context, something I expand on in a later section. Devices may be shared across multiple applications and users, or may be restricted.

4.1 Virtual Objects as Proxies for Things

Web developers shouldn't be burdened with unnecessary details of lower level transport mechanisms. A way to achieve this is for Web run-times to support virtual objects as proxies for real world things. This allows the application respond to input from a sensor via registering an event handler on the virtual object, and to operate an actuator by targeting an event at the virtual object. The details of how the virtual object communicates with the real world thing are hidden from the developer.

In a markup language, the virtual object could be represented as a markup element. This could name the real world thing with a URI in an attribute, or it could describe the capabilities and the context with markup in the content of the element. The Web run-time invokes a broker to bind the object to the thing. The broker could be implicit in the run-time environment, or it could itself be named with a URI. Successful binding would be signaled by an event (load) with a corresponding event (unload) when the binding is broken, e.g. when the device is removed. An error event would signal a failure in binding and supply some details on why, e.g. unauthorized.

Such objects could also be created from Web page scripts, e.g. using JSON (JavaScript Object Notation) to pass descriptions of the capabilities and the context for the desired service. The virtual object can support properties that can be accessed synchronously by the Web run-time, where the implementation of the object hides the messaging needed to synchronize the object with the real world thing it represents. This allows Web developers to use properties and events for a mix of synchronous and asynchronous control. The implementation of the virtual objects could be provided as part of the run-time environment, or it could be a dynamically loadable extension. This could involve trusted scripts with access to lower level services.

4.2 Composition and Coordination

The virtual object as seen by a Web developer might be realized as a composition of several devices or services, for example, a scanner could be connected to printer to serve as a copier. The process of setting up the binding to the virtual object involves sending commands to the devices/services involved to connect them together, so that communications flow efficiently rather than via a remote server. Coordination may be needed to ensure fair access to a service, or when things have to happen in a particular order or where access control needs to be managed centrally. Strong coordination involves routing all control messages through an agent that controls and coordinates all of the devices/services it manages. Weak coordination is where the controller arranges a contract between the managed devices/services, but thereafter leaves them to communicate directly.

4.3 Distributed Processing

Sensors may perform generic functions, e.g. a microphone captures an audio stream, whilst a camera captures a video stream. This data can be processed for some purpose, e.g. speech recognition on an audio stream, and object and gesture recognition on a video stream. This will often involve some kind of distributed processing model that transforms data and adds metadata. It could also combine data from multiple devices. This could be arranged on behalf of the Web application by the broker as part of a composition of devices and services. This suggests a market for such compositions as something you might pay for.

4.4 Cloud of Things

Web applications will be able to make use of devices you own and control, but with the spreading ubiquity of networked devices, you may want turn to a supplier that provisions sensors and actuators according to your dynamic needs, e.g. electronic advertising hoardings on the side of buildings, and placed throughout the city. The "cloud of things" seems like an appropriate term, drawing upon cloud computing which deals with dynamic provisioning of computing resources.

5 Context Awareness

This involves maintaining a live model of users, things and the environment in which they reside. For example, what devices are present in a given room, what rooms there are in a building, and the location of that building on a map of the city. A device can be modelled in terms of the features it exposes to Web applications, e.g. what properties it has, what events it raises and responds to. The behaviour of some devices depends on the state they are in, and this can be modelled as a declaration of a state machine.

In addition to up to date descriptions (metadata), the context may include live objects as proxies for real world things. This allows applications to sense or interact with the world through the models. The context models allow users to browse through descriptions and to follow links, as well as to carry out searches. Models can be represented in a variety of ways including OWL ontologies and XML. A shared underlying ontology is needed to ensure that different representations share the same models.

Web developers shouldn't normally need to deal with the details of how the context models in the cloud are synchronized with the real world. A variety of mechanisms can be utilized as appropriate.

These models can be used to adapt applications to suit the needs of the particular context in which a Web application is being used. User models can describe general preferences as well as preferences for specific applications. General preferences are especially useful for users with sensory or cognitive impairments, e.g. a hearing impaired user may require captioning with video. User preferences also extend to privacy and trust, see the later section in this paper.

Infrastructure providers will want to ensure that the systems they provide are secure. This is likely to involve automatic means to configure safe communications through firewalls, based upon some form of cryptographic credentials. This will often have to be done on behalf of users. The context models can be likened to ice bergs where the visible part is accompanied by a much larger part hidden below the surface of the sea. The hidden parts of the context models are needed to figure out how to route communications to real world things, how to configure intervening security barriers, and how to keep the models live as the context changes.

6 Authoring Frameworks

In principle, there are many possibilities for authoring applications for the Web of Things, including markup languages, scripts and mixes of the two. Current practices for Web applications emphasise scripting in the web page and in the web server. Developers concentrate on the most popular browsers due to widespread variations in the detailed behaviour of different of browsers from different vendors, and also different versions from the same vendor. The advent of mobile browsers is making this problem even worse with variations in display size and device capabilities.

As a result, most sites pay only lip service to the needs of people with impairments. Browsers offer external APIs for *assistive technology*, such as screen readers, but there are significant challenges for providing a usable interface. A web page designed for a high resolution display will have many parts, but the roles of these aren't identified in a standard way that the assistive technology can rely on. This is bad enough for static web pages, and becomes even worse when the pages make heavy use of scripting. W3C's work on ARIA seeks to rectify this situation by defining ways for developers to annotate markup and scripting objects with roles and states that the assistive technology can exploit.

Current web practices fail to separate application logic, data models and presentation. This contributes to the cost of maintaining websites. A small change made for one web page could break many others. This is also bad news for providing a quality user experience on different devices, and made worse by the wide variability of mobile devices. This motivates taking a step back and looking at what alternatives there could be.

6.1 The Cameleon Reference Framework

Markup and scripting languages can be hand edited in text editors. Syntax colouring helps a bit, but it is still error prone and hand editing involves a fairly steep learning curve. It is still however much easier than languages like Java and C++. This allows beginners to get a considerable way by copying and modifying other people's examples and trying things out. Unfortunately, high level web authoring tools have been slow to evolve, and there is a long way to go.

Rather than designing markup languages for the browser as now, we should instead design them to suit the needs for effective high level authoring tools, and not be concerned about direct human editing of the markup. This allows us to focus on cleanly separating out different concerns without worrying about the resulting complexity of the markup. Yes, it should be simple for computers to deal with, but no, it isn't important to address the concerns voiced by people editing markup directly in text editors.

The Cameleon Reference Framework defines several levels of abstraction:

Application domain and task models: these define data models and task models in a way that is independent of the user interface. Task models describe how tasks decompose into subtasks and partial ordering between them. Richer task models add details on how events trigger actions according to associated conditions, along with pre- and post-conditions.

Abstract User Interface: these describe the user interface, but at a level above that of modalities, for example, a selection from a set of alternatives which might be ordered. There could be integrity constraints across fields as well as dependencies where further details are required depending on prior choices.

Concrete User Interface: this makes commitments to modes of interaction and user interface controls such as radio buttons, and image controls for making selections. There is limited control over layout, but the details are left to the next level down.

Final User Interface: this is normally generated automatically from the concrete user interface guided by rules provided by the developer. You can think of this as skinning the user interface. This approach makes it easy to generate the user interface for different platforms, e.g. HTML, SVG, Java, .Net and Flash.

Each level can be formally treated as graphs, and represented as markup[1]. The relationship between adjacent levels can then be expressed in terms of graph transformations. This applies to the representation of the user interface components, and to the representation of events at each level. The transformations are conditional on the context. This means that developers can control how the application adapts to fulfil user preferences and variations in device capabilities and environmental conditions.

6.2 Mashups and Pluggable Authoring Tools

The authoring tool needs to manage the models for each level as the developer works on the application. Imagine selecting a library of UI controls and then dragging them onto a canvas and performing further operations to link them up and adjust their properties. The authoring tool provides an API for libraries to plug into. Adding a group of radio buttons will also add a selection list at the abstract UI level, and connect this up to the application data model, directly the user makes the appropriate setting.

The authoring tool should allow developers to work top-down, bottom-up or middle-out. This raises challenges for the user interface for developers to relate models at different levels. This can be addressed through a combination of techniques including direct manipulation of graphs, property lists, and browsing mechanisms. An agenda mechanism can be used to guide developers on outstanding design tasks.

The Web of Things will involve an ecosystem with vendors of authoring tools, vendors of extensions for authoring tools, traditional web developers, and end-users. The aim will be to give end-users the means to easily create mashups of different services. This includes the ability to personalize services based upon tracking the user's previous interactions, and also those of others who may be considered to be like the user in some way. Some kinds of application lend themselves to social interaction with peers, for example, leaving virtual post-its on real world objects for your friends to come across later.

7 Privacy and Trust

Modern technology makes it possible for companies and governments to track our lives at a level of detail that would be unimaginable a generation ago. The Web of Things threatens to take this to a whole new level. Imagine your refrigerator tracking your usage of every item and forwarding this onto the supermarket. They already know what you buy from the widespread use of payment cards. The next step would be for them to sell this data onto your health insurance company, and for you to see the effect on your premiums and level of cover. Of course, that scenario is unlikely to be realized so long as there is sufficient pressure from consumers.

[1] The markup can be supplemented with event driven scripts where extra flexibility is needed.

In Europe, there are laws that are intended to safeguard user's privacy by giving them control over what companies can do with personal data. Essentially, users (data subjects) should be able to negotiate their preferences for how long a company (data controller) holds onto personal data, and for what purposes it is put to. This further covers exploitation of personal data by third parties (downstream data controllers). Users should be able to find out what personal data of theirs is being held, to make corrections and to request its deletion. Unfortunately, we are some way from realizing this in practice.

The Web of Things expands the range of personal data that applications have access to. This makes it imperative to consider privacy from the very start when designing the application infrastructure. Protocols are needed for negotiating data handling obligations and for notifying users as part of those obligations. Server-side middleware is needed to track the binding between personal data and the data handling obligations agreed with the data subject.

Privacy goes hand in hand with identity management and access control. The current trend is for websites to identify users via their email address or a web page address (for OpenID). These are globally unique and make it easy to track users across different websites. Privacy has taken a back seat, although most websites do provide a human readable legal disclaimer for their privacy policies, this may be hard to find. Practical deployment of a more flexible approach to privacy will have to wait until better technical solutions are available, and there is sufficient pressure on companies to adopt these.

Researchers are developing cryptographic techniques that minimize the amount of personal data disclosed for a given access control decision. Instead of having to disclose your date of birth, you would instead offer a credential from a trusted third party that you are legally an adult. Another example is where you are required to provide a credential as proof that you are a citizen of a given country, rather than say disclosing your address. Websites will be able to use policy engines to determine what credentials are needed for a given decision, along what data handling policies the site is prepared to implement.

7.1 Call a Friend or Ask the Audience

Users will want to control who can have access to what things under their control. In some cases this is relatively straightforward, for example, in terms of your social network of family, friends and colleagues. In other cases, it is much less clear. Which websites is it reasonable to grant access to your GPS location as determined from your cell phone? Most users don't really know enough to make an informed decision. Public key certificates were proposed as a solution that establishes a chain of trust from certification authorities. Unfortunately, this failed in practice and has been found to be largely unusable.

A likely solution would be to allow users to base their decisions on the advice of friends, trusted authorities, or even the wisdom of crowds (and perhaps based upon a reputation system). This suggests the need for delegation mechanisms where a user agent can consult a trust management service. In one approach, a Web run-time is coupled with a local policy engine that is invoked when an application wants to access a restricted service. The local policies may result in a decision, perhaps by asking the user, or they may invoke a remote trust management service, passing it a description of the security context. The trust management service evaluates the request and returns a policy back to the local engine, which then evaluates it and returns the decision to the Web run-time.

A related problem is when a user needs to authenticate herself with a website, but wishes to minimize any personal data disclosed to that site. Instead of logging in directly with the website, the user signs in with her privacy provider, who in turn passes the relevant credentials to the target website. This is made effortless through HTTP redirection. Users only have to sign on once with their privacy provider and not once per website. The user may further delegate negotiation of privacy preferences to her privacy provider, which becomes a safe place for her to keep her personal data. This raises challenges for how to switch providers, but these should be manageable with the appropriate standards and legal framework.

8 Concluding Remarks

The Web of Things is about exploiting Moore's law to extend the Web out of the browser and into the real world. There are many challenges to overcome, including how to maintain live models of the context, how to simplify authoring, and how to ensure an effective treatment of privacy and trust. Many of the key technologies are becoming available and we can look forward to new opportunities and new businesses.

9 Further Reading

This section provides some pointers to further reading, but is not intended to be comprehensive. You are encouraged to explore further.

9.1 Moore's Law

The doubling of the number of transistors on a chip every 2 years which essentially reflects a steady learning curve and relentless competition:

- `ftp://download.intel.com/research/silicon/moorespaper.pdf`
- `http://en.wikipedia.org/wiki/Moore%27s_law`

9.2 The March of Microcontrollers

These inexpensive single chip computers are appearing everywhere in all kinds of devices. The incremental cost of adding some form of networking is dwindling. This is however a case of chicken and egg. Many of the devices that use microcontrollers often have low profit margins. What's in it for device vendors for adding connectivity if the cost of developing applications is too high? The Web of things alters the economics by reducing costs and providing a vast pool of developers.

- `http://en.wikipedia.org/wiki/Microcontroller`

9.3 The Internet of Things

This is generally used for the widespread use of RFID tags as a way to identify all kinds of everyday objects. It also includes self organizing low power networks of sensors, and the spread of low cost microcontrollers connected via a rapidly evolving pantheon of technologies.

- http://en.wikipedia.org/wiki/Internet_of_Things
- http://en.wikipedia.org/wiki/Wireless_personal_area_network
- http://en.wikipedia.org/wiki/Ambient_network
- http://en.wikipedia.org/wiki/Zero_configuration_networking
- http://en.wikipedia.org/wiki/IEEE_802.15.4

9.4 Semapedia – Hyperlink Your World!

This is one example of an easy way to form links from real world objects to websites. In this case through printing 2D barcodes that link to Wikipedia entries.

- http://en.semapedia.org/

9.5 Privacy and Trust

Everyone should be concerned about privacy in the digital age. How can we safeguard our privacy as our values continue to change? This is an area where privacy enhancing technologies are still in their infancy. The legal principles have been laid down, but we still have to evolve the technologies and practices to

- *The Spy in the Coffee Machine - The End of Privacy as We Know It*, by Kieron O'Hara and Nigel Shadboult, Oneworld Publications, 2008.
- http://www.w3.org/P3P/
- http://ec.europa.eu/dataprotectionofficer/index.cfm?TargetURL=D_INTRO%20EUROPA
- https://www.privacyos.eu/
- https://www.prime-project.eu/
- http://www.primelife.eu/

9.6 Web Widgets

These are web applications that can be installed and executed within HTML-based web pages or as locally installed applications. W3C is developing a suite of specifications for widgets, covering packaging, digital signatures, scripting APIs, and access control.

- http://en.wikipedia.org/wiki/Web_widget
- http://www.w3.org/2008/webapps/wiki/PubStatus
  viz. the Widgets Specifications on this website.

9.7 Context Awareness

This seeks to make computer applications aware of the environment in which they are operating, for instance user preferences, device capabilities, and the environment in which devices are situated, e.g. what devices are present in a particular room, and the location of that room in a building, and that building in the city. The context can play an important role in interpreting input from sensors, including recognizing users' intentions from their actions.

- http://en.wikipedia.org/wiki/Context_awareness

9.8 Model-Based UI Design

This is a field of research on layered architectures for user interface design that seek to separate different design concerns via models at different levels of abstraction. This makes it easier to maintain user interfaces and to adapt to changing contexts.

- http://www.isys.ucl.ac.be/bchi/research/cameleon.htm
- http://www.w3.org/2005/Incubator/model-based-ui/wiki/Main_Page

9.9 Assistive Technology and Designing for Accessibility

- http://en.wikipedia.org/wiki/Assistive_technology
- http://www.w3.org/WAI/

Web Science: The Digital-Heritage Case

Guus Schreiber

VU University Amsterdam, Computer Science
De Boelelaan 1085, 1081 HV Amsterdam, The Netherlands
schreiber@cs.vu.nl
http://wiki.cs.vu.nl/web-media

Abstract. Web Science studies the interpay between web technology and the human behaviour it induces at the micro, meso and macro level. In this extended abstract we examine Web Science research issues by taking a closer look at the area of digital heritage. We discuss engineering, communication and socio-economic aspects.

1 What Is Web Science?

Over the past 15 years the Web has had an increasing impact on the life of people. Web technology has changed the way people operate and communicate, both in their personal and working lives. In many ways the Web is a new phenomenon, for which the principles of the physical world do not always hold. Web science is a new scientific discipline that studies this phenomenon, in particular the interplay between Web technology and the effect it has on human behavior at the personal organizational and societal level.

Good introductions into Web Science can be found in the articles of Berners-Lee *et al.* [1] and Shneiderman [2]. The program and proceeddings of the 1st Web Science Conference in Athens[1] give a good impression of the field. In this extended abstract we illustrate research issues in Web Science by looking at one particular area, namely the digital heritage domain. Digital heritage comprises access to and interaction with large-scale virtual cultural heritage collections. We look at this domain from the experiences gained in a series of digital heritage projects, such as the ongoing work on the Europeana culture portal Europeana[2]. We limit the discussion here to engineering, communication and socio-econmic aspects of digital heritage.

2 Engineering of Digital-Heritage Collections

Cultural heritage is an extremely knowledge-rich domain. Institutions in this field have been gathering knowledge for decades or even centuries. This knowledge is gathered in the form of a multitude of vocabularies, thesauri, classification

[1] http://www.websci09.org/
[2] http://www.europeana.eu

J. van Leeuwen et al. (Eds.): SOFSEM 2010, LNCS 5901, pp. 108–111, 2010.

schemes and other knowledge organization systems, which are used to describe heritage objects, such as paintings, books and archival documents. These knowledge organization systems display a enormous richness, but are seldomly described in the formal way favored by computer scientists. The biggest challenge in digital-heritage ventures, such as Europeana, lies in interoperability. The description of heritage objects inherently shows a large variety of perspectives, caused by differences in type of object, time, place, culture and language.

When constructing a web portal for cultural heritage, such as Europeana or E-Culture [3], we are faced with a number of research questions. Firstly, we have to provide mechanisms for explicating heritage knowledge in a machine-readable web format. SKOS[3] is a recently released web standard for achieving this. The design of SKOS reflects some important principles, in particular the principle of "minimal ontological commitment": schema's for publishing knowledge on the Web need to be restricted to the minimum level of required constructs and semantic constraints for these to be usable across the field. For computer scientists with their formal background this is often counterintuitive. Secondly, to enable collection interoperability we need to provide techniques for *partial alignments* between knowledge organization systems. In other words: unification is infeasible in diverse domains such as cultural heritage; the best we can do is uncover the agreement and overlap that does exist. For this reason vocabulary-alignment techniques have become an active area in web research. Thirdly, due to the fact that cultural-heritage descriptions often partially consist of textual descriptions we also require a range of knowledge-extraction techniques, such as from natural-language processing and machine learning. Finally, we have to deal with large amounts of data, typically billions of statements ("the web of data"). This requires scalable search techniques. Given such amounts of data, the traditional notions of correctness and completeness make no sense. Therefore, alternative approaches to reasoning in a web of data are an active area of research[4].

Engineering web data in other domains, such as health care and biology leads to similar research issues. A pervasive common issue is also the notion of web identity. What should be the URI for Pablo Picasso or for the European union? Despite the many research efforts in this area, this is still an open research problem. It is likely that solutions will require some form of societal consensus.

3 Communication in Digital Heritage

An often-heard opinion in the cultural-heritage field is that the digital experience can never replace the "real thing". In this view digital access is is a surrogate and should ideally be a teaser for the web visitor to come to the museum. This is a lopsided view: the virtual world provides us with alternative and complementary forms of interaction with cultural heritage. An example is the generation of personalized museum tours [4]. Such tours can be first generated for a digital experience and then be downloaded on a mobile device for a physical tour in

[3] `http://www.w3.org/2004/02/skos/`
[4] `http://www.larkc.eu`

a museum. The physical tour has limitation ins time and space; the virtual tour has limitations in freedom of experience. It should also be noted that digital techniques help in accessing objects that would otherwise be inaccessible for conservation reasons (e.g. old manuscripts). Thus the virtual and physical visit both have their own pros and cons.

Social tagging is receiving considerable attention in the museum world (see for example the Steve Museum[5]). Tagging is a way to involve web visitors more actively in the collection. Also, given the large amounts of poorly-described objects the heritage institutions are keen on using web visitors for creating object metadata. This raises two issues. Firstly, institutions have to come up with incentive schemes for web visitors to help annotating the objects. Secondly, quality is seen as a key characteristic of curated metdata and is not yet clear which strategies should be followed in quality control of non-curated metadata. This is now an active area of research.

Central in web communication is the issue of user identity and user profiling. Current practice is that user identity is mostly handled at the level of individual web sites or applications. For web visitors this means they have to recreate their identity and their profile in many different places. The control of users over their own profile is limited, as it is usually stored in application-specific cookies. There are several proposals to "put the web visitor back in the driver seat", such as FOAF[6], OpenID[7] and OpenSocial[8]. We expect these mechanisms to change the scenery significantly over the next few years.

4 Social and Economic Issues in Digital Heritage

Although heritage institutions, at least in Europe, are almost all public institutions funded with public money, this does not mean that open access to cultural-heritage data should be taken for granted. Projects like Europeana face social barriers in it strive for open access. This is understandable: the heritage institutions have built up their knowledge and data over a long time with an eye on quality control, and are anxious to make this available with the risk of it being used or interpreted in the wrong way. For open access to be become the norm instead of the exception leaders in the field have to set the example. In the library world Library of Congress has done this by making their Subject Headings publicly available in a SKOS format[9]. Major European national libraries, musea and archives are now doing the same within Europeana.

Access to object data, such as images of paintings, still gives rise to rights and authority issues. New license schemes are required. Creative Commons[10] is frequently mentioned in this context, but is not really tailored to the type of

[5] `http://www.steve.museum/`
[6] `http://www.foaf-project.org/`
[7] `http://openid.net/`
[8] `http://code.google.com/apis/opensocial/`
[9] `http://id.loc.gov/authorities/`
[10] `http://creativecommons.org/`

heritage field. Similar schemes, but targeted specifically at data collections, have been proposed. Open Data Commons[11] appears to be a promising candidate for deployment in the area.

The business models for digital heritage depend to some extent on the rights issue. A typical web business model would assume that all primary access to the collections is free, including low and medium-resolution images. Secondary services can be profit-based, such as access to high-resolution images, use of objects within a virtual museum shop (e.g., posters, clothing) and integration with tourist services (e.g. combining heritage access with city walks).

5 Outlook

The web should be viewed as a new ecosystem with an ecology that is in various ways different from the systems we know. It deserves scientific attention from a multidisciplinary angle. Universities are already setting up their first Web Science curricula. The researcher in Web Science works in a new playing field, with new types of interplay between technology and society.

Acknowledgements. The ideas in this paper are based on joint work and discussions with many people, in particular colleagues of the VU Semantic Web group, collaborators in research projects, and co-members of the research council of the Web Science Research Initiative[12].

References

1. Berners-Lee, T., Hall, W., Hendler, J.A., O'Hara, K., Shadbolt, N., Weitzner, D.J.: A Framework for Web Science. Foundations and Trends in Web Science 1(1), 1–130 (2006)
2. Shneiderman, B.: Web Science: a Provocative Invitation to Computer Science. Commun. ACM 50(6), 25–27 (2007)
3. Schreiber, G., Amin, A., Aroyo, L., van Assem, M., de Boer, V., Hardman, L., Hildebrand, M., Omelayenko, B., van Ossenbruggen, J., Tordai, A., Wielemaker, J., Wielinga, B.: Semantic Annotation and Search of Cultural-Heritage Collections: The MultimediaN E-Culture Demonstrator. J. Web Semantics 6(4), 243–249 (2008)
4. Wang, Y., Stash, N., Aroyo, L., Gorgels, P., Rutledge, L., Schreiber, G.: Recommendations Based on Semantically Enriched Museum Collections. J. Web Semantics 6(4), 283–290 (2008)

[11] `http://www.opendatacommons.org/`
[12] `http://webscience.org/`

Model-Driven Software Product Line Testing: An Integrated Approach

Andy Schürr[1], Sebastian Oster[1], and Florian Markert[2]

[1] Real-Time Systems Group
{oster,andy.schuerr}@es.tu-darmstadt.de
[2] Computer Systems Group
markert@rs.tu-darmstadt.de
Technische Universität Darmstadt
Merckstr. 25, 64283 Darmstadt, Germany

Abstract. Software Product Line engineering is a popular approach which improves reusability of software in a large number of products that share a common set of features. Feature Models (FMs) are often used to model commonalities and variabilities within a Software Product Line (SPL). Due to their variability, testing SPLs is very challenging and many different approaches exist. Classification Trees (CTs) are a well-known and in practice popular black-box approach for the systematic derivation of a set of test cases of a single software system instance. In this paper, we explore the relations and similarities between FMs and CTs. Our contribution is the introduction of an integrated approach *Feature Model for Testing* (FMT) marrying properties and abilities of CTs and FMs.

1 Introduction

Software Product Line (SPL) engineering is one of the most promising and latest approaches of the Software Engineering community to increase the quality of similar software products, for as well as to reduce costs of development and maintenance [1]. SPL engineering is successfully used in the automotive industry and various other domains. In the automotive sector we are running into a situation, where a single electronic control unit (ECU) may be instantiated in at least 10.000 different ways and the software running on a network of more than 50 ECUs in a single car may exist in millions of different configurations. As a result, we are confronted with a world, where any instance of a certain brand of car possesses a unique configuration of the embedded software of all its ECUs.

In the past each instance of an automotive SPL was tested individually developing a separate suite of integration test cases for each product. Since this is no longer feasible, the automotive industry as well as engineers from other domains are urgently looking for new methods of how to systematically generate sets of software product instances that represent equivalence classes of instances with sufficiently similar behavior from a system integration testing point of view. Furthermore, model-driven as well as black- and white-box testing approaches are adapted in such a way that appropriate test cases for each specific SPL instance are either manually selected or semi-automatically generated.

J. van Leeuwen et al. (Eds.): SOFSEM 2010, LNCS 5901, pp. 112–131, 2010.

1.1 Model-Driven Software Product Line Testing

Examining the state-of-the-art of SPL development and software testing approaches in the automotive industry we experience that on the one hand various kinds of feature modeling concepts and tools are used for the design of SPLs and the derivation of product instances [1,2]. On the other hand, Classification Trees (CTs) and related tools such as CTE [3] are successfully used for black-box testing of single product instances.

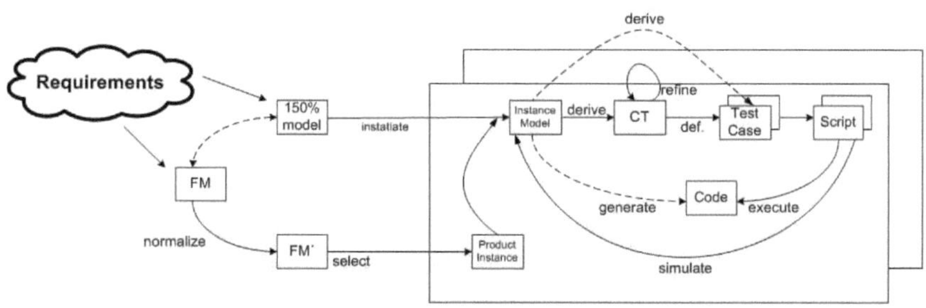

Fig. 1. SPL black-box testing process: state-of-the-art

Fig. 1 depicts a model-driven development and test procedure for SPLs as used in the automotive industry: On the basis of the system requirements an FM is developed that describes commonalities and variability of the SPL as well as a compatible 150% software model containing the functionality of the whole SPL. Often Matlab/Simulink is used to define the 150% model, but an increasing number of projects also adopt the modeling language standards UML/SysML or niche products as the heterogeneous modeling language Ptolemy II.

The selection of a representative set of product instances for testing purposes is then a two step process as described in [4]. First of all a model transformation converts the given FM into a normal form that can be processed more efficiently afterwards. Then a number of heuristics determines the needed set of product instances that are used as "systems under test" (SUT) for all further quality assurance efforts. For each selected SUT a corresponding executable "model under test" (MUT) is derived from the given 150% model. This model is then processed as input for the semi-automatic derivation of a CT, which describes the input parameter domain of the instance model. Afterwards, often a number of semi-automatic refinement steps are applied to the derived CT taking domain-specific knowledge about input parameter values and interactions into account [5]. The refined CT is then used to guide the test case definition process for the regarded MUT. Usually, only CT-based heuristics control the generation of these test cases. The combination of these heuristics with model-based test case generation techniques is still ongoing work. Finally, test scripts are generated that either enact the MUT itself for simulation purposes or a generated code for more realistic SIL/HIL (Software/Hardware-in-the-Loop) testing purposes.

The process as depicted above has one severe disadvantage: for each selected product instance time-consuming manual efforts are needed to define an appropriate set of test cases. Therefore, we are developing a new approach that integrates the FM-based definition of an SPL with the construction of a 150% CT model for the whole SPL. Refinement, normalization, SUT and test case selection process steps are reorganized such that repetitions of manual activities for *each* selected product instance of an SPL are avoided. Furthermore, the new integrated approach has the advantage of using one set of concepts for the definition of SPL feature properties and test case parameter vectors. As a consequence, the same mechanisms are e.g. used to unlock a specific function or to (de-)activate a certain mode of operation of an SPL at compile-, flash- or runtime.

1.2 Related Work

Various approaches for SPL testing have been developed in the past and a summary of methods is e.g. given in [6]. Nevertheless, we are not aware of any SPL testing approach that combines SPL product derivation with parameter value selection strategies for black-box testing as supported by CT. Often FM-modeling tools like pure::variants [7] support the definition of parameters that can be stored as attributes of features. But unfortunately, equivalence classes needed for parameter selection purposes are not introduced with two exceptions: in [8] the authors consider parametrization and use equivalence classes for requirement-based SPL testing. Scenarios are represented as textual use cases and variability is described by using special tags within those use cases. Then, test cases are derived for each product of the SPL instead of intertwining SPL and test case definition activities.

Geppert et al. present the most similar testing method to our approach in [9]. Their approach introduces a decision model to represent the variability of an SPL. Furthermore, it documents the input parameters of the regarded system. However, the decision model is considerably less expressive than the FMT approach presented here. Furthermore, the well-known heuristics for CT-based black-box testing purposes that are adopted by our approach are considerably more elaborate than the selection process introduced in [9].

1.3 Outline

The remainder of this paper is structured as follows: First, we explain the fundamentals relevant for our approach in Section 2. There we also describe the paper's running example, a subset of a car seat SPL. Afterwards, we introduce the current state-of-affairs of our Feature Model for Testing approach (FMT) in Section 3. This introduction relies on the presentation of first ideas how to merge FMs and CTs in a workshop paper [10]. Then, in Section 4 we describe the application of the FMT approach using our running example. Finally, we summarize and conclude our paper and give an overview of future work in Section 5.

2 Fundamentals

In this section we explain the fundamentals relevant for our approach. First of all, we introduce a running example. Afterwards, we explain how variability of

SPLs is modeled by means of feature models and black-box testing of product instances using the CT methodology.

2.1 Running Example

This paper uses a luxory car seat as a running example. Its functional behavior will be specified later on using the heterogenous modeling language Ptolemy II [11]. Our car seat can be moved vertically or horizontally and the angle of its backrest can be changed either manually or electrically. The seat may possess either an air conditioning or a heating system or none of both. The car's speed sensor, the seat belt sensor, and the door sensor have an impact on the behavior of the seat. There is also an optional access support function that moves the seat back, when the driver enters or exits the car, respectively. Table 1 summarizes the equipment and functionality requirements.

Table 1. Excerpts of luxory car seat requirements document

Functionality	Precondition
Motor movement	Only one motor can be active at a time. The priority order is Horizontal-Vertical-Backrest. A motor that moves will not be aborted by a higher priority. Motors can only be active until the speed reaches 15 km/h.
Access Support	Is only active when the car is not moving. Moves the seat back when the door is opened. Moves the seat to the initial position when the door is closed. Is aborted when the user tries to move the seat horizontally.
Heating/Aircon	Is only active when the seatbelt is attached.

2.2 Feature Models

Software Product Lines (SPLs) provide a high level reuse of software in a specific problem domain [1,2]. Feature models (FMs) are frequently used to describe commonalities and variabilities within an SPL. An FM consists of features, each representing a "logical group of requirements" [12] or as defined in [13]: "a system property that is relevant to some stakeholder". The purposes of FMs are summarized in [14] as follows:

- describing feature commonalities and variabilities
- picturing dependencies and constraints between features
- specifying permitted and forbidden combinations of features

For this purpose notations have been defined such that even managers and clients are usually able to read and interprete FMs easily. Of course, feature models are not able to capture *all kinds* of important properties of an SPL; therefore, they are complemented by other development artifacts such as natural languagement descriptions, function network diagrams, executable models, or even code fragments. These artifacts are then mapped to the corresponding features by means of traceability relationships.

FMs were initially introduced by Kang et al. in [15] as part of FODA in 1990. FODA already combines a hierarchical (tree-like) decomposition of features into subfeatures with the definition of mandatory, optional, and alternative features. Different sorts of decomposition relationships (node notations) are used for this purpose. In addition, binary require and exclude constraints describe further cross-tree dependencies between features. The hierarchical structure of FMs, the different node notations, and the additional constraints determine which feature combinations are allowed and which are not.

Since the introduction of FODA, further extensions of FMs were introduced improving precision and expressiveness including amongst others cardinalities, probabilities, and weighting of features. Cardinalities can be employed to formulate how many instances of a feature may be integrated within a product [16]. Probabilities state that a certain feature is more likely to be used than another one [17]. Weights can be used to represent cost factors of features to help the engineers to build products appropriate for a certain budget [18]. For a detailed summary of extensions of FODA feature models the reader is referred to [13].

For the purpose of this paper a very simple FM notation is selected as a starting point. But the proposed incorporation and integration of classification tree elements into the selected FM notation can easily be adapted to other popular FM approaches like the Orthogonal Variability Model (OVM) invented by Pohl et al. [2] or the approach supported by the FM tool pure::variants from pure-systems.

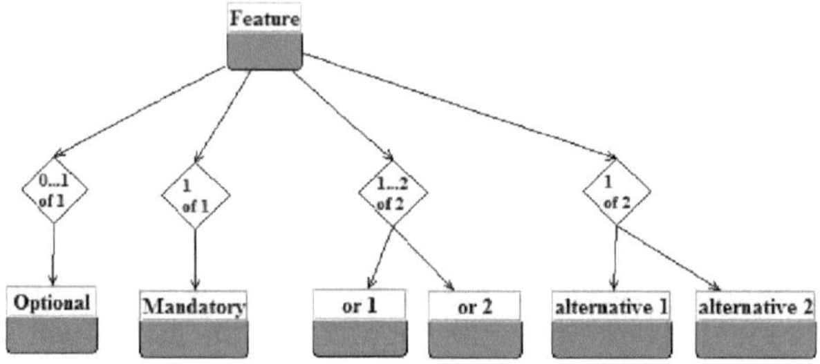

Fig. 2. Used feature model notation

The FM notation used throughout this paper is depicted in Fig. 2. Rectangles represent features and four different kinds of rhombes are used to specify composition relationships between a feature and its subfeatures. The top feature in Fig. 2 has

- an optional subfeature, which may or may not be selected,
- a mandatory subfeature, which is always selected,

– an "or" set of subfeatures, with at least one of them being selected,
– an alternative set of subfeatures, where exactly one of them is selected.

An editor that supports this notation has been implemented using our own meta-modeling tool MOFLON [19] and the Eclipse Graphical Editing Framework GEF. It is used as an experimental platform for rapid prototyping new variants of SPL modeling and test generation approaches. First consolidated results of the joint research project feasiPLe have already been reimplemented as extensions of the above mentioned commercial tool pure::variants.

Fig. 3 shows a drastically simplified feature model of a car seat which serves as our running example. This model has been derived from artefacts generated by requirements elication activities like use case diagrams or function networks that do already distinguish between hardware components (sensors and actuators) on one hand and software control functions on the other hand. Therefore, the root node of the car seat FM is decomposed into the mandatory feature groups `sensors`, `actuators`, and `functions`. For each functionality of the seat—each element beneath the feature group `functions`—corresponding sensors and actuators do exist. First of all, we describe the different sensors and actuators; afterwards, the functionalities are introduced which interact with these hardware elements.

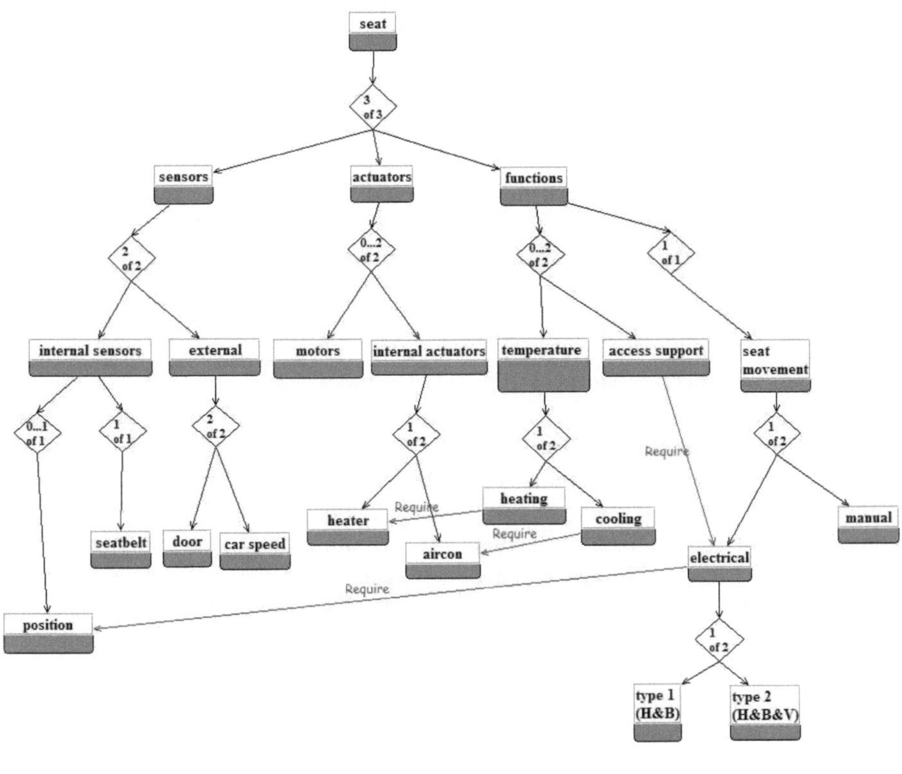

Fig. 3. Simplified feature model screendump of luxory car seat SPL

Each derived product contains the following `external` sensors: `door` and `car speed`. The sensor `door` indicates whether the driver's door is open or not and `car speed` measures the speed of the car. The seat internal sensor `seatbelt` is mandatory for every instance indicating whether the driver has fastened the seat belt, whereas the sensor `position` is optional. The `position` sensors measure the position of the seat horizontally and vertically as well as the inclination angle of the backrest. Two different kinds of actuators may be chosen for a product instance of the car seat SPL and are, therefore, optional: motors which are responsible for the automatic movement of the seat and additional (internal) comfort functions. If `internal actuators` is selected either a heater is included to warm up the seat or an aircon may be placed within the seat to control its temperature precisely. These two actuators exclude each other. Furthermore, high-level functions are introduced that control the heating or air conditioning system, the access control support, and the electrical motors of the seat. There are three different variants of the mandatory `seat movement` feature. First of all the engineers or the customer have to choose whether the seat should be moved manually or electrically. If an electrical interaction is desired two different types of feature packages may be chosen. Both packages exclude each other depicted by the `1..n` notation. `Type 1` realizes horizontal and vertical movements only, whereas `Type 2` supports horizontal, vertical, and backrest movements.

Finally, cross-tree `require` constraints capture existential dependencies between the control functions themselves and their associated optional sensors and actuators. To mention just one example, the optional `access support` function relies on the existance of the optional `electrical` motor control function. Examples of the usage of exclude constraints have been omitted, but could be added easily to prevent e.g. the selection of the optional `motors` actuators and `position` sensors if the seat variant is selected that has to be moved manually. All above listed dependencies and constraints within the FM have to be taken into account when deriving a product.

2.3 Black-Box Testing / CTM

The Classification Tree Method (CTM) was introduced by Grochtmann and Grimm [20] in 1993. The CTM implements a black-box testing technique that uses valid input parameters or input parameter ranges, so-called equivalence classes, to test a system component systematically. A structured approach is vital to handle the complexity of the test case generation and to find a representative set of test cases from the nearly infinite number of possible combination of test parameter values. The equivalence classes are manually selected by an engineer or automatically extracted from a specification such that the regarded System Under Test (SUT) hopefully behaves in a similar way (with respect to an adequately chosen definition of similarity) if the input values of two test cases belong to the same combination of equivalence classes.

A Classification Tree (CT) essentially is an acyclic graph that decomposes a system component into subcomponents, input parameters of (sub-)components, and equivalence classes of parameter values as leaf nodes. Beside equivalence classes a

CT uses two further types of nodes for this purpose. Classifications group related equivalence classes into disjoint subsets. Compositions usually offer a higher level of abstraction by decomposing the regarded SUT and its input domains into a number of subgroups. To extract test cases from a CT, a test case table is built that defines which equivalence classes provide the input values for a specific test case.

The construction of a CT and the generation of test cases is usually performed in a predefined order. First of all the specification needs to be evaluated and the corresponding equivalence classes are extracted. With this information as input an initial version of the CT often can be built automatically and refined manually afterwards [5]. The test case table is then filled either manually by the designer or automatically on the basis of some heuristics and rules that were extracted from the system's specification. When filling the test case table automatically it may happen that some input combinations are invalid or just cannot occur due to the "physical" nature of the system.

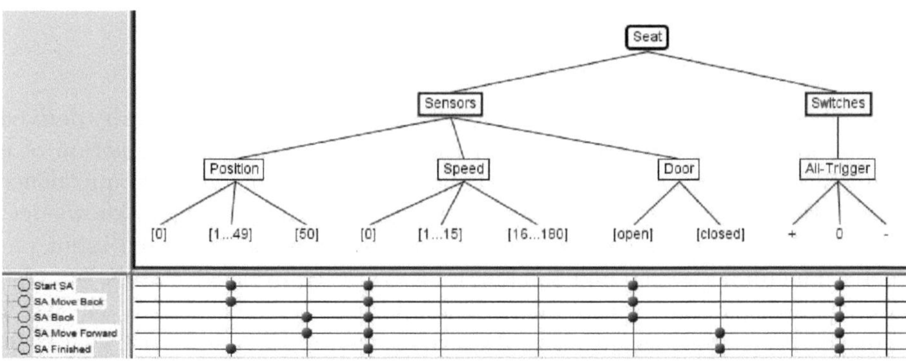

Fig. 4. CT for black-box tests of one seat motor

Today these illegal input combinations are usually identified manually within the test case table and deleted. The resulting table only consists of sequences of valid and representative test cases that need to be performed. Model-based testing approaches that rely e.g. on symbolic model execution or model-checking techniques promise to increase the degree of automation of the test suite definition process.

Fig. 4 shows an example CT, drawn with the CTE tool [3], for the software controller (SUT subcomponent) that moves the seat backward and forward. The compositions are located under the root node and marked with bold lines. The classifications are rectangles with thin lines. The leaf nodes represent the equivalence classes of the CT. The speed node, for instance, divides the corresponding sensor node output (seat control function input parameter) domain into three equivalence classes: `[0]` for not driving (access support function is enabled), `[1..15]` for slowly driving (manually controlled seat movements are enabled), and `[16..180]` for driving faster (all kinds of seat movements are disallowed).

In the test case table (bottom part of Fig. 4) each horizontal line represents a test case. The selected equivalence classes for the test parameter values of each test case are marked with black dots on the corresponding line. The vertical order of the lines defines the temporal order in which the test cases are executed, i.e. the order in which the input parameter values are fed into the SUT. Often, parameter value selection and interpolation functions are provided for actual test script generation purposes that translate the discrete sequence of input parameter equivalence class selections into a needed and physically possible continuously changing graph of values.

The test cases shown in Fig. 4 are used to evaluate the correct behavior of the access support. During the whole test case the car must not be moving and no switch to move the seat is activated. The test case consists of five consecutive steps:

1. The door is opened.
2. The seat moves back due to the automatic entry function.
3. The seat has moved back and the driver can enter the car.
4. The driver has entered the car and closes the door.
5. The seat moves back to its initial position and stops there.

The composition and classification nodes of a CT are often automatically derived from the input interface description of the corresponding system function of a specific SPL instance. The decomposition of classification nodes into equivalence classes is then often a manual process that requires intimate domain knowledge. In our case, the test engineer did not only properly divide the speed input parameter domain between 0 and 180 km/h into three equivalence classes, but also made the decision that speed values below 0 and above 180 km/h will never be considered for testing purposes. As a consequence, FMs and CTs with their associated test cases are only indirectly related to each other via the following sequence of engineering activities (cf. Fig. 1): (1) select a product instance as SUT that fulfills all constraints of the regarded FM, (2) generate the corresponding executable instance model (MUT) using a 150% model as input, (3) derive the upper part of the CT from the generated MUT, (4) refine the generated CT afterwards manually, and (5) finally define all needed test cases for the thus developed CT.

In the following subsection the still missing 150% model for step (2) above will be presented for reasons of completeness. Section 3 afterwards introduces a new approach that integrates FMs and CTs such that steps (4) and (5) above are executed once and for all right after step (1) for a whole SPL instead of repeating these activities again and again for all regarded instances of an SPL.

2.4 Ptolemy II Implementation

Ptolemy II is a modeling and simulation tool developed by the University of Berkeley [11]. It enables the designer to build models of systems that are based on a large variety of different models of computation. This was the main reason for us to select Ptolemy II instead of UML or Matlab/Simulink for modeling purposes. The model of computation defines the way that components called actuators interact with each other. If an actuator fires it emits a token as its output that can then be received by another actuator. The model of computation describes the output and acceptance behavior of an actuator. The most common models of computation are Discrete Events, Continuous Time, Synchronous Data Flow, and Finite State Machine. Different time domains may interact with each other in the same model. A continuous time signal can for instance be sampled by an actuator and converted to the discrete events domain. For our purpose we combined the synchronous data flow domain with the finite state machine domain. To display the resulting system behavior, we use a specialized graphical output domain that just interprets the resulting system behavior.

Ptolemy II, as virtually any other modeling language, can be used to construct a 150% model of our running example. A 150% model incorporates all functionality that may be defined by any product instance derived from the product line. Our model Fig. 5 is based on the three main components test vector input, SUT, and output. Furthermore, we introduce a Boolean configuration parameter for each optional (functional) feature of the regarded SPL. These parameters are displayed in the upper part of Fig. 5 on the right-hand side above the list of "real" runtime parameters.

The conversion of the 150% model into a specific instance Model Under Test (MUT) simply requires the translation of the selection of a specific product instance in the previously introduced FM into a corresponding parameter configuration file. More sophisticated conversion processes can be realized, where model transformation and optimization steps eliminate and simplify an instantiated 150% model if the footprint or runtime of the model itself or its generated code is an issue.

The MUT represents the actual system behavior on the basis of finite state machines. An input controller assures that only one motor can be moved at a time. The FSMs controlling the motor behavior for the backrest and the vertical axis just react on the input buttons, while the motor that moves the seat backward and forward also takes the optional access support function into account. Incorporating optional functionality into the corresponding FSM is realized by using a configuration parameter which enables or disables an FSM for the just regarded

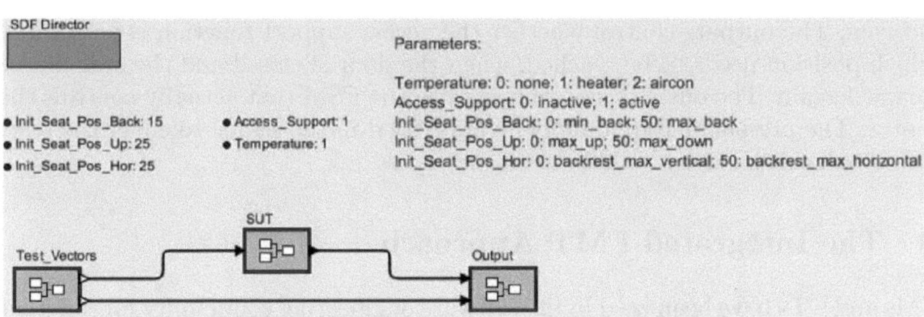

Fig. 5. Ptolemy II model: top level diagram

optional functionality. The configuration parameter also controls a multiplexer that forwards the output of the additional FSM or a constant 0 to the main FSM. An additional FSM controls the optional airconditioning or heating functions.

In the following, the functionality of the FSM for the access support function is described (cf. Fig. 6). It consists of the three states `On` (access support is active), `Off` (access support is inactive) and `Break` (access support was interrupted by the user). An internal signal `Seat_Pos_Req` stores the position of the seat when the access support function is triggered. The stored position is needed later on to move the seat back to its initial position when the driver has entered.

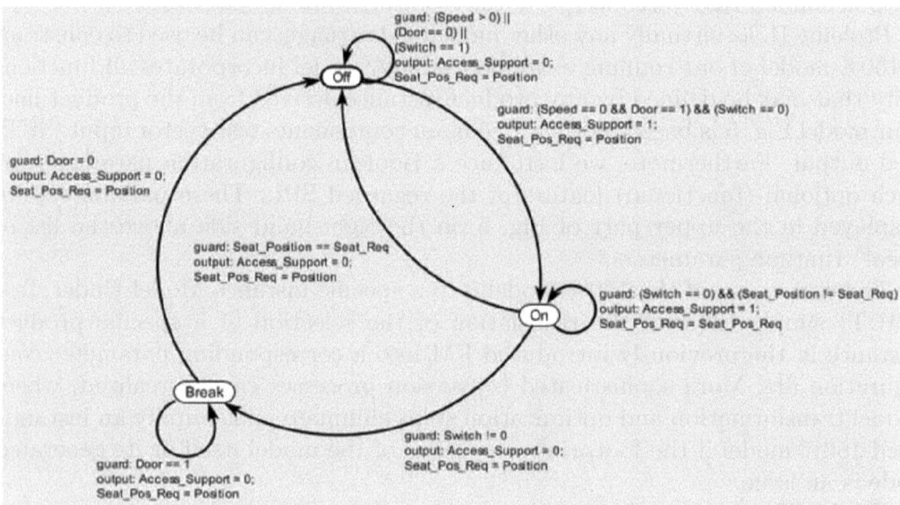

Fig. 6. Ptolemy II model: finite state machine of access support function

The guards of the FSM reference input signals of the actuator, while actions define its outputs. The actuator is embedded into the synchronous data flow model of computation. Therefore, it fires at each iteration of the simulation. The FSM actuator is based on the Mealy FSM model and only fires if a transition is taken. The outputs control whether the access support function is active and which position needs to be reached, when the door is closed and the seat moves forward again. The outputs are connected to the FSM that actually controls the motor. The presented system model will be used in the sequel to enact the tests developed using our new FMT method.

3 The Integrated FMT Approach

FMs and CTs have been used in the software engineering community for different purposes until now, but will be used in the sequel for the integrated definition of an SPL and its database of test cases. On a first glance, an appropriate integration of FM and CT should simply attribute leaves of an FM with CTs for feature parameter description purposes. But when inspecting the modeling constructs of FMs and CTs more closely, we realized that many of their concepts are very similar and can be unified. Furthermore, we made the experience that FM concepts not supported by CT are useful for black-box testing purposes (e.g. introducing optional parameters) as well as that CT concepts not supported by FM should be adopted for SPL development purposes (e.g. adding equivalence classes to feature parameters for test preparation purposes).

3.1 Comparison and Synthesis of FM and CT Language Constructs

The development of the integrated FMT approach started with an in-depth comparison of the FM and CT language constructs. The results of this work is presented in Table 2 as well as a proposal how to merge FM and CT constructs. The resulting FMT modeling language adopted whenever possible the terminology of the feature modeling world due to the fact that its main application area is the definition of SPLs.

The comparison of FM and CT modeling constructs is divided into four parts. The first part of Table 2 deals with all kinds of tree nodes. CTs contain three different sorts of nodes: *composition*, *classification*, and *equivalence class*. *Equivalence classes* are leave nodes, whereas *composition* and *classification* are nodes with child elements. FMs on the other hand do only distinguish two kinds of nodes: *compound features* with child nodes and *atomic features* as leave nodes. FMT in principle adopts the FM distinction between two kinds of nodes only, but adds two subclasses of atomic features: *literal* and *interval* for partitioning parameter value domains into equivalence classes.

The second group of rows of Table 2 deals with the previously explained four sorts of composition relationships of features. As shown, CTs do not support optional elements and the selection of subsets of a set—despite of the fact that both modeling concepts would simplify the handling of optional or set-valued parameters of SUTs.

The CT nodes *composition* and *classification* are always mandatory; *equivalence classes* are always alternatives that exclude each other. FMT simply adopts all FM composition constructs without any modifications (except of choosing more appropriate names). Another difference between the language constructs of FMs and CTs concerns the handling of cross-tree constraints. In CTs cross-tree constraints can only be placed between equivalence classes (due to the fact that all other kinds of nodes are mandatory anyway), whereas FMs permit constraints between any nodes. Again FMT adopts the more general approach of FMs.

The third group of rows of Table 2 deals with FM attributes and types that are used to associate any kind of additional information with features. FMT supports attributes and types, too. Thus we are able to capture data about probabilities, costs, etc. of features as well as to provide users with typing information that may e.g. be used as a guideline for the manual definition of parameter equivalence classes and test cases.

Table 2. Comparison of FM, CT, and FMT language constructs

	FM	CT	FMT
1.	compound feature	composition, classification	feature group
2.	(atomic) feature	—	atomic feature
3.	—	equivalence class	literal, interval
4.	mandatory features (n of n)	composition, classification	mandatory composition (n of n)
5.	optional features (0..1 of 1)	—	optional composition (0..1 of 1)
6.	alternative features(1 of n)	equivalence class	alternative composition (1 of n)
7.	or features (1..n of n)	—	or composition (1..n of n)
8.	cross-tree constraints	only between equivalence classes	cross-tree constraints
9.	feature attributes	—	feature attributes
10.	feature types	—	feature types
11.	—	test case and group	test case and group

The last group of rows of Table 2 simply shows that FMT inherits the capability to define single test cases and groups of test cases from CT. As we will see later on, FMT test cases and test groups do not only specify input parameter values for a given SUT, but are also used for the selection of an SPL instance as a SUT.

3.2 The FMT Modeling Language

Based on the informal description of the synthesis of the new FMT language from FM and CT we are now ready to describe the abstract syntax of FMT precisely. For this purpose a rather generic metamodel has been developed that describes all FMT modeling concepts and their relationships. Please note that the metamodel presented in Fig. 7 introduces just a small subset of the properties of the displayed metamodeling elements.

Furthermore, all kinds of static semantics constraints (defined in OCL), which control the proper usage of binding time constraints, associations of test cases with to be tested features and so forth, have been omitted due to lack of space.

The abstract metaclass `Feature` introduces the most important modeling concept of FMT with its properties like `name` and `bindingTime`. The optional `bindingTime` property is a new FMT modeling element that is neither supported

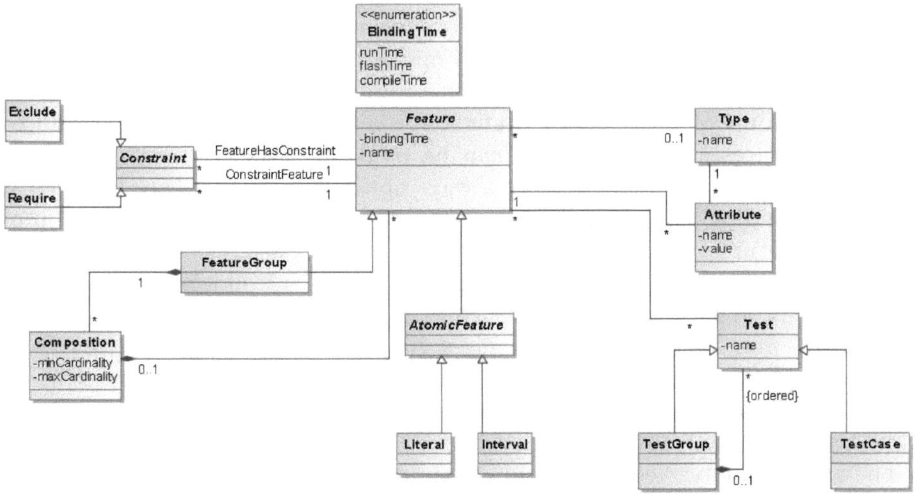

Fig. 7. The FMT language metamodel

by FM nor by CT. It specifies when the variability described by a specific feature is bound in the development process. Right now we distinguish the following binding times: `compileTime`, `flashTime`, and `runTime`. The selection of a feature or parameter value at compile-time corresponds to the traditional selection of a product instance at product design time, whereas the selection at runtime corresponds to the definition of input parameter values within a test script.

For the definition of a hierarchy of features the well-known composite design pattern is used in a slightly modified form: `Feature Group` and `Atomic Feature`, which inherit all properties from the metaclass `Feature`, are not directly associated to each other via a single composition; instead of this an intermediate metaclass `Composition` is introduced that represents an n-ary association with one source element, an arbitrary number of target elements, and lower/upper boundaries for multiplicity constraints. The metaattributes `minCardinality` and `maxCardinality` thus support the definition of all sorts of composition relationships listed in Table 2: `mandatory`, `optional`, `alternative`, and `or` as well as other combinations like choosing between 3 and 5 of n features.

The metaclass `Atomic Feature` has two subclasses `Literal` and `Interval`. Thus, we are not only able to list a finite number of variants of a feature explicitely, but also to specify a range of alternatives in the case, where feature variants are represented as a parameter with an ordered domain as type.

The specification of more complex (sub-)domains of values is supported by combining type annotations with constraints. For this purpose, the abstract metaclass `Constraint` with its two subclasses `Exclude` and `Require` is introduced. `Require` defines a binary directed constraint between two features, which enforces the inclusion of the target feature if the constraint's source feature is part of a product instance. The `Exclude` relationship on the other hand represents a binary undirected constraint. It rules out the existance of any product instance which contains its two associated features simultaneously. The introduction of more general forms of constraints by means of predicate logic formulas is planned for the future. FMT constraints may be used on any level of a feature hierarchy to control the selection of feature combinations as needed.

A third group of metaclasses (`Attribute` and `Type`) of Fig. 7 introduces feature attributes and types which can be used for rather different purposes. Types of features and attributes are always optional; attributes are modeled—as usual—as simple `name/value` pairs without any support for the definition of complex structures.

Last but not least, a fourth group of metaclasses introduces means for the definition of product instances and test cases. Again the composite design pattern is used to define a hierarchy of test cases via the abstract metaclass `Test` and its subclasses `Test Group` and `Test Case`. A `Test Group` is composed of an ordered sequence of tests, whereas a single `Test Case` represents one test call in a test script for the regarded SUT.

The association between `Test` and `Feature` is used for two different purposes. First of all a test group associates itself with a set of required features and defines thereby a subset of all product instances that can be evaluated using the just regarded test group. Furthermore, atomic test cases use this assocation for the definition of a specific product instance together with the needed vector of input parameter values.

The binding time attributes of the selected features determine whether parameter instantiation takes place at compile-, flash-, or runtime. In practice, design guidelines are needed that require, e.g., that high level test groups select all compile-time features of an SPL, lower level test subgroups then add data about the selection of flash-time features, whereas low level test groups and single test cases within one group may only differ with respect to their runtime parameter/feature selection values.

A more detailed description of how all the above introduced FMT modeling concepts are applied in practice is presented in the following Section 4. This section introduces a number of modeling guidelines (pragmatics) for the design of FMT hierarchies for a specific application domain. We are planning to refine the rather generic FMT abstract syntax description introduced here in various ways thereby creating a family of domain-specific versions for automotive, automation, ... SPL development and testing purposes. These specific FMT variants will introduce among other things subclasses like `System`, `Sensor`, `Function`, `Parameter`, etc. of the metaclass `Feature Group` together with a number of constraints for their places in an FMT hierarchy.

4 Application of the FMT Approach

In the following we describe the application of the FMT approach for Software Product Line testing purposes in a step-by-step manner. We use our running example to explain the procedure which is summarized in Fig. 8. The variability of our SPL is defined as an FMT in a so-called preparation phase. Afterwards,

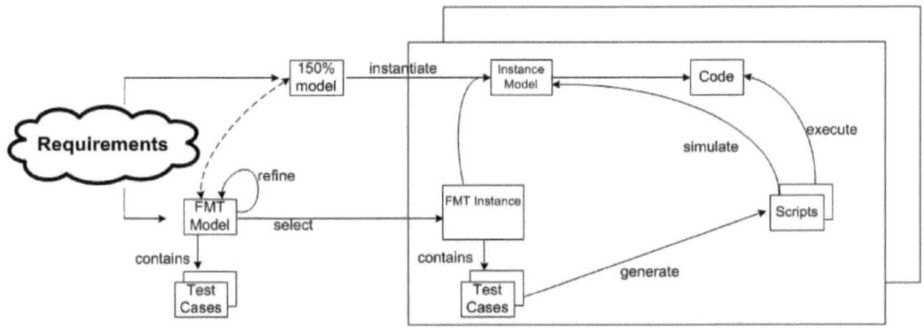

Fig. 8. New FMT-based SPL testing approach

a database of test cases is added as an integral part of the constructed FMT. The resulting FMT may be refined using similar heuristics as suggested in [5]. Afterwards, a representative set of product instances is selected as SUTs. Each instance is associated with the subset of all previously defined test cases that are compatible with the just regarded SUT. Then the description of a selected SUT is used to instantiate an executable 150% model. Finally, this model or generated code is executed using the just selected test cases as input.

4.1 FMT Preparation Phase

The first step towards using the FMT approach for testing SPLs is an exhaustive analysis of its requirements specification. This specification may already comprise a first version of an executable 150% model. An already existing "traditional" feature model as presented in Section 2 can be used as a starting point to set up the FMT. Afterwards, missing data about input parameters of the regarded system functions (derived from the accompanying 150% model) are added together with a decomposition of their value domains into appropriate equivalence classes. Furthermore, the binding time of each feature has to be determined

A small excerpt of the FMT of the car seat is shown in the upper half of Fig. 9. It has been developed as follows using the FM of Fig. 3 as a starting point:

First of all missing features, components, and devices relevant for testing purposes are added. In case of our running example this concerns the buttons that control all functions of the seat. These missing UI elements are added as subfeatures of a new feature group `ui`: the subfeature `switch-up` controls vertical movements of the seat, `switch-climate` controls the airconditioning system, ...

Afterwards, a new layer of subfeatures is added to the FMT tree that exactly corresponds to the input parameters of our 150% model introduced in Subsection 2.4. Considering the Ptolemy II model of our running example, we introduce parameters together with their trivial equivalence classes for the `door`, `seatbelt`, the button and the lever controlling the `seat aircon`, and the vertical `seat movement`. The features `door` and `seatbelt` have a single parameter

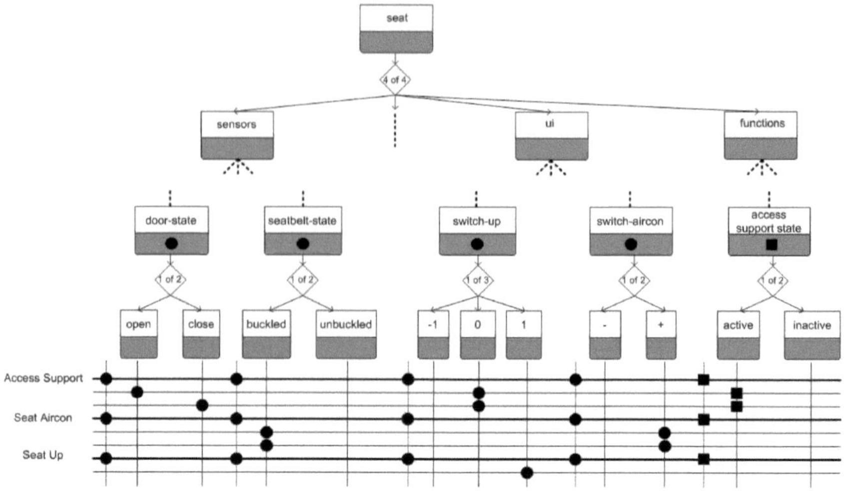

Fig. 9. Excerpt of the FMT with Test Cases

`status` describing its state. Both parameters possess two possible values which are added as `Literal`. The state of the door can either be open or closed and the seatbelt can either be buckled or unbuckled.

The lever for the seat position has a parameter `switch-up` with the values `-1, 0, 1` for "move down" (`-1`), "move up" (`1`) or "stop" (`0`). Analogously, the button for the seat aircon possesses a single parameter `switch-climate` with two values for increasing (`+`) or decreasing (`-`) its operating level. The optional feature `access support` has a parameter `access support state` with the two states `active` and `inactive`. These states control whether the optional feature is part of a regarded product instance or not.

Finally, binding time information is added where appropriate. All features labeled with a square are selected at compile-time (or beforehand), all features labeled with a triangle are selected at flash-time, and features labeled with a circle are (de-)activated at runtime. Subfeatures inherit the binding property of its parent, but may overwrite it if needed.

4.2 FMT Test Case Definition Phase

Having defined our SPL with all its features and input parameters as an FMT model we are now prepared to select a representative set of product instances as well as their corresponding test cases. Heuristics like pair-wise testing [4] provide us with guidelines for the selection process. Furthermore, the finite state machines of the executable 150% model as well as additional requirements engineering artefacts like UML Use Case diagrams may also be used to define a representative set of product instances and test cases as explained in [21]. The bottom part of Fig. 9 shows some results of our test case definition efforts. Bold lines separate groups of test cases (test sequences) from each other.

Each group of test cases starts with the definition of a specific product instance and the selection of the regarded subset of parameters. The first group of test cases, called `Access Support`, requires that the selected SUT offers the `access support state` feature. This is expressed by the fact that the parameter `access support state` has the value `active` which is already determined at compile-time (squares denote compile-time selections).

Furthermore, the test group selects values for the parameters `door-state` and `switch-up` as input which are determined at runtime (circles denote runtime selections): in the first test case the car's door is open, in the second case it is closed. The `switch-up` parameter has the value `0` in both cases.

The inputs of the other parameters `seatbelt-state` and `switch-climate` are available, but irrelevant for the execution of the two test cases of the regarded test group. Therefore, the bold line of the `Access Support` test group selects these runtime parameters, but the following two thin lines do not pick a specific value. The remaining two test groups displayed in Fig. 9 test the functionality of aircondition and the vertical seat movements.

To summarize, the basic principles for the definition of test cases with FMT have been adopted from CTM. Important extensions allow us to distinguish between different parameter value binding times and to use the same mechanism for the selection of product instances of an SPL as well as for the definition of runtime parameter values. An FMT editor, which can be used in practice, obviously has to support folding and unfolding of feature subtrees as well as of test groups. Therefore, we are just experimenting with different user interface designs including the reuse of the front-end of a matrix browser tool which has originally been developed for the manipulation of traceability relationships between two hierarchically structured software engineering artefacts.

4.3 Product Instance Selection and Test Execution Phase

Having defined and refined our FMT for the car seat SPL we can now generate a suite of test scripts as follows: first of all the compile- and flash-time parameters of each test group are evaluated and a corresponding parameter configuration file is generated which transforms our 150% model into the specified concrete MUT/SUT. Afterwards a test script is generated which provides the just selected MUT with the needed sequence of input parameters. For this purpose parameter value generators compute (sequences of) concrete parameter values which belong to the previously determined equivalence classes. These test scripts may only be used for regression testing purposes as long as FMT does not yet support the definition of expected output parameter values.

5 Conclusion and Future Work

The development of effective and efficient new SPL testing approaches is of vital importance in many engineering domains due to the rapidly increasing complexity of embedded system SPLs. In this paper we have used the running example of an automotive SPL to present the state-of-the-art of model-driven SPL development and testing processes and discuss their deficiencies. Afterwards, we have introduced a new methodology together with an integrated modeling language called FMT that combines the capabilities of "classical" feature modeling and classification-tree-based test case description languages. The resulting SPL testing approach has the following advantages compared to the state-of-the-art, where the selection of a set of product instances as SUTs and the selection of test cases for each SUT are separate activities:

- test parameter value creating heuristics can easily be adapted to the new task of computing a set of SPL instances as SUTs
- integrated algorithms can be developed for the computation and optimization of cost-effective sets of SUTs and their associated sets of test cases
- manual activities can be reduced to a minimum that are nowadays performed for each selected SUT in a product-by-product SPL testing approach

The presented FMT language is still under development as well as the accompanying new SPL modeling and testing process. A first version of an FMT tool prototype has been implemented using the metamodeling tool MOFLON [19]. Right now we are busy to refine and automatize various steps of the development process presented in the previous section. For this purpose, we

- use our tool integration framework TiE for the creation and maintenance of traceability relationships between requirements documents and FMTs,
- redesign the product instance generating approach, which has been developed in the BMBF project feasiPLe [4], to FMT
- specify bidirectional transformations in MOFLON that keep a 150% model and its related FMT in a consistent state,
- explore the usefulness of model-checking techniques for the derivation of test case sequences from executable FSM models as suggested in [22].

References

1. Clements, P., Northrop, L.: Software Product Lines: Practices and Patterns. Addison-Wesley Longman Publishing Co., Inc., Boston (2001)
2. Pohl, K., Böckle, G., Linden, F.J.v.d.: Software Product Line Engineering: Foundations, Principles and Techniques. Springer, New York (2005)
3. Alekseev, S., Tiede, R., Tollkühn, P.: Systematic Approach for Using the Classification Tree Method for Testing Complex Software-Systems. In: SE 2007: Proceedings of the 25th Conference on IASTED, Anaheim, CA, USA, pp. 261–266. ACTA Press (2007)
4. Oster, S., Schürr, A.: Architekturgetriebenes Pairwise-Testing für Software-Produktlinien. In: Workshop Software Engineering 2009: PVLZ 2009 (2009)
5. Conrad, M., Dörr, H., Schürr, A.: Graph Transformations for Model-Based Testing. In: Glinz, M., Müller-Luschnat, G. (eds.) Proc. Modellierung 2002. GI-Edition Lecture Notes in Informatics, vol. P-12, Bonn, GI, pp. 39–50 (2002)
6. Tevanlinna, A., Taina, J., Kauppinen, R.: Product Family Testing: a Survey. ACM SIGSOFT Software Engineering Notes 29, 12 (2004)

7. Beuche, D.: Modeling and Building Software Product Lines with Pure: Variants. In: Proceeding of the SPLC, p. 358 (2008)
8. Bertolino, A., Gnesi, S.: Use Case-Based Testing of Product Lines. SIGSOFT Softw. Eng. Notes 28, 355–358 (2003)
9. Geppert, B., Li, J.J., Rößler, F., Weiss, D.M.: Towards Generating Acceptance Tests for Product Lines. In: ICSR, pp. 35–48 (2004)
10. Oster, S., Markert, F., Schürr, A.: Integrated Modeling of Software Product Lines with Feature Models and Classification Trees. In: Proceedings of the SPLC 2009 - Workshop MAPLE, pp. 75–82 (2009)
11. Eker, J., Janneck, J.W., Lee, E.A., Liu, J., Liu, X., Ludvig, J., Neuendorffer, S., Sachs, S., Xiong, Y.: Taming Heterogeneity - the Ptolemy Approach. Proceedings of the IEEE, 127–144 (2003)
12. Bosch, J.: Design and Use of Software Architectures - Adopting and Evolving a Product Line Approach. Addison-Wesley, Reading (2000)
13. Czarnecki, K., Helsen, S., Eisenecker, U.: Staged Configuration through Specialization and Multilevel Configuration of Feature Models. Software Process: Improvement and Practice 10(2), 143–169 (2005)
14. Heymans, P., Schobbens, P.Y., Trigaux, J.C., Bontemps, Y., Matulevicius, R., Classen, A.: Evaluating Formal Properties of Feature Diagram Languages. Software, IET 2(3), 281–302 (2008)
15. Kang, K.C., Cohen, S.G., Hess, J.A., Novak, W.E., Peterson, A.S.: Feature-Oriented Domain Analysis (FODA) Feasibility Study. Technical Report, Carnegie-Mellon University Software Engineering Institute (November 1990)
16. Czarnecki, K., Helsen, S., Eisenecker, U.: Formalizing Cardinality-Based Feature Models and Their Specialization. In: Soft. Process: Improv. and Pract., pp. 7–29 (2005)
17. Czarnecki, K., She, S., Wasowski, A.: Sample Spaces and Feature Models: There and Back Again. In: SPLC 2008, Washington, DC, USA, pp. 22–31. IEEE CS, Los Alamitos (2008)
18. Jules White, B.D., Schmidt, D.C.: Selecting Highly Optimal Architectural Feature Sets with Filtered Cartesian Flattening. Journal of Systems and Software
19. Amelunxen, C., Königs, A., Rötschke, T., Schürr, A.: MOFLON: A Standard-Compliant Metamodeling Framework with Graph Transformations. In: Rensink, A., Warmer, J. (eds.) ECMDA-FA 2006. LNCS, vol. 4066, pp. 361–375. Springer, Heidelberg (2006)
20. Grochtmann, M., Grimm, K., Wegener, J., Daimler-Benz, A.G.: Tool-Supported Test Case Design for Black-Box Testing by Means of the Classification-Tree Editor. In: Proc. of EuroSTAR 1993, pp. 169–176 (1993)
21. Bertolino, A., Fantechi, A., Gnesi, S., Lami, G.: Product Line Use Cases: Scenario-Based Specification and Ttesting of Requirements. In: Software Product Lines – Research Issues in Engineering and Management, pp. 425–445. Springer, Heidelberg (2006)
22. Weißleder, S., Sokenou, D., Schlinglo, B.H.: Reusing State Machines for Automatic Test Generation in Product Lines. In: 1st Workshop on Model-based Testing in Practice MoTiP 2008 (June 2008)

Taming the Complexity of Inductive Logic Programming

Filip Železný and Ondřej Kuželka

Czech Technical University in Prague
Faculty of Electrical Engineering, Department of Cybernetics
Technická 2, 16627 Prague 6, Czech Republic
{zelezny,kuzelon2}@fel.cvut.cz

1 Introduction

Inductive logic programming (ILP) [12] is concerned with the induction of *theories* from specific *examples* and *background knowledge*, using first-order logic representations for all the three ingredients. In its early days some twenty years ago, ILP was perceived as a means for automatic synthesis of logic programs, i.e. Horn clausal theories. Current research views ILP algorithms mainly in the context of machine learning [14] and data mining [1]. ILP has enriched both of the two fieds significantly by providing them with formalisms and algorithms for learning (or 'mining') complex pieces of knowledge from non-trivially structured data such as relational databases.

Two significant streams of fruitful research have shaped up in ILP in the last few years. One of them, motivated by the data mining need to capture uncertainty in real-world data, blends the crisp logic foundations of ILP with instruments for representing probability [15]. The other one also responds to a call from the application world, this time for algorithms that are scalable. This is to say that their runtimes do not skyrocket as the size of the learning problems approaches real-world standards. In this paper we review our contributions to this latter research.

We consider our contributions significant to the general fields of relational machine learning and relational data mining. This may appear overambitious to state. Indeed, ILP is only one of the plethora of approaches investigated in the two domains of which a significant portion is based on graphical, rather than logical representations. However, these approaches typically use knowledge and data representations strictly subsumed by the first-order logic formalism of ILP. Thus, in principle, they inherit any finding relevant to ILP. And indeed, this argument applies to our results reviewed below.

2 Two Battlefronts of ILP Complexity

In the most popular instantiation of the general ILP framework, one works with a set of *positive examples* E^+ and a set of *negative examples* E^- such that the two sets are disjoint. Examples are usually first-order clauses although other

J. van Leeuwen et al. (Eds.): SOFSEM 2010, LNCS 5901, pp. 132–140, 2010.

representations of examples have been considered, such as first-order theories or Herbrand interpretations [13]. A first-order clausal theory B called *background knowledge* is also supplied although it may be empty. In this setting, called *normal ILP*, the goal is to construct a first-order clausal theory H called the *hypothesis* that explains the examples in the presence of background knowledge. That is, $H \cup B \models e$ must hold for all (or as many as possible) $e \in E^+$ and for no (or as few as possible) $e \in E^-$, where $\models$ denotes the relation of logical entailment. Further assumptions are usually installed to prevent trivial solutions such as $H = E^+$.

Example. Given $E^+ = \{man(sokrates) \rightarrow mortal(sokrates), man(aristotle) \rightarrow mortal(aristotle)\}$, $E^- = \{mortal(zeus)\}$, and $B = \{\}$, we acomplish the ILP task by finding (i.e. inducing, learning) the hypothesis $H = \{\forall x\ man(x) \rightarrow mortal(x)\}$. H is also a solution to an alternate formulation of the exemplary task that uses only ground facts and non-empty background knowledge; here $E'^+ = \{mortal(sokrates)\}$, $E'^- = \{mortal(zeus)\}$ and $B' = \{man(sokrates), man(aristotle)\}$.

In the general formulation above, the normal ILP problem is undecidable since the very testing of $H \cup B \models e$ is undecidable [11] even in the simplistic case when H and e are single Horn clauses and B is empty. Therefore the entailment relation is usually approximated by the decidable θ-subsumption relation $\preceq_\theta$; $C \preceq_\theta D$ for two clauses C and D whenever there is a substitution θ such that $C\theta$ contains all literals of D. Thus e.g. $\forall x\ mortal(x) \preceq_\theta man(sokrates) \rightarrow mortal(sokrates)$, here in agreement with logical entailment.

Using subsumption in place of entailment, we trade off at least three assets. First, we loose completeness in the sense that entailment does not imply subsumption. The two relations can however be made equivalent if one avoids clauses that are self-resolvable [3]. Second, since subsumption is only defined for clauses (rather than entire clausal theories), we are instantly constrained to learning single-clause theories. This is less of a problem than may seem, because clausal theories can be ultimately induced clause by clause. This is done in a greedy (i.e., suboptimal) manner well known as the *covering strategy* in machine learning [14]. Third, subsumption does not account for background knowlege B, that is, there is 'no place' for B in checking $H \preceq_\theta e$ between two clauses H and e. Although the concept of *subsumption relative to B* has been well defined [12], algorithms for its calculation are known only for the very special case when B consists of ground facts. In this situation, B can be in fact fully avoided by reformulating the ILP task. Roughly speaking, such a reformulation corresponds to obtaining $E^+, E^-, B = \{\}$ from E'^+, E'^-, B' in the above Example.

In summary, adopting subsumption introduces syntactic constraints on the representation of hypotheses and examples (non-self-resolving single clauses in both cases) as well as background knowledge (ground facts). The question remains, how difficult it is to solve the ILP problem under such bias. Gottlob et al. [4] considered this question, assuming further that hypotheses H are function-free and Horn (i.e., containing at most one positive literal), and examples are ground and Horn. Morever, H may contain no more than k literals, where k defines the size of the problem instance. It turned out that the problem is not only NP-hard but resides in Σ_2^P, i.e. at the second level of the polynomial hierarchy of problem complexity.

Less formally, Gottlob et al. showed that two sources of exponential complexity are intrinsic to the ILP problem.

1. One rests in the size of the search space that must be explored to find a clause the solves the ILP problem.
2. Another one is incurred by the subsumption test which is NP-complete and which must be conducted for each clause explored.

Whereas Gottlob et al.'s results on the complexity of the ILP problem are pessimistic in terms of *worst-case expectations*, we wanted to model the *average-case* performance of ILP algorithms. That is because we had assumed that reliable performance models are a prerequsite if one wishes to systematically improve the performance. We reasoned that the methods for modeling average case behavior must rely on methods different from deductive analysis of algorithms in the classical complexity framework, and more aking to statistical analysis of empirical runtime measurements.

3 Front One: Clause Search

We first embarked to attack the first complexity source, i.e. the problem of searching in the space of first-order clauses. We sourced general inspiration from the breakthrough work [6] on complexity modeling in the phase transition framework, and – of even more relevance – from the vigorous line of research of Gomes et al, represented e.g. by the paper [2]. These studies investigated properties of large search spaces corresponding to difficult combinatorial problems under controled randomized generation of problem instances. Some intriguing properties have been identified, such as the high irregularity of the search spaces and "heavy-tailedness" of the cost distributions of search algorithms used. Such properties manifest themselves in a large collection of real-world problems and have been the inspiration for the design of randomized restarted search procedures. The basic idea of these procedures is simple: if each search trial has a small, but fixed probability of finding a good clause, then the probability of finding a good clause in a sequence of such trials can be made quite high very rapidly. Put differently, the cost distribution from the sequence has an exponential decay.

In our preliminary study [17], we demonstrated on two experimental domains that heavy-tailed phenomena can be observed also in ILP, namely in the search for a clause in an organized search space known as the subsumption lattice [12]. We also reformulated the technique of randomized rapid restarts to make it applicable in ILP and showed that it can reduce the average search-time. Cheered by these findings, we commenced the study [18] in which a massive number of ILP processes were conducted on a high-performance distributed computing platform. They provided an extensive statistical performance sample of five kinds of ILP search algorithms operating on two principally different classes of ILP problems, one represented by an artificially generated graph problem and the other by three traditional benchmarks. These concern the induction of theories for predicting mutagenicity and carcinogenicity of chemical molecules, and lastly for the prediction of optimal decomposition of shapes in the context of finite element mesh design. The collected sample allowed us to

1. estimate the conditional expected value of the search cost (measured by the total number of clauses explored in the search) given the minimum clause score (difference between the number of positive and negative examples subsumed by the clause) required and a cutoff value (the number of clauses examined before the search is restarted),
2. estimate the conditional expected clause score given the cutoff value and the invested search cost, and
3. compare the performance of randomized restarted search strategies to a deterministic non-restarted search.

Our findings indicated striking similarities across the five search algorithms and the four domains, in terms of the basic trends of both the statistics (1) and (2).

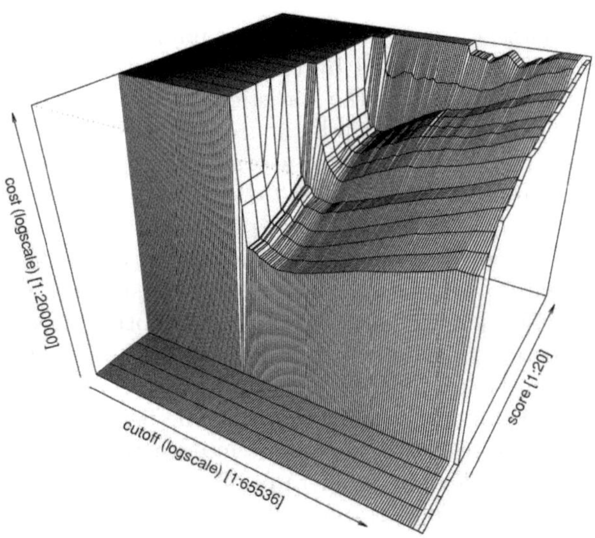

Fig. 1. A statistical model of the performance of a randomized restarted ILP algorithm resulting from a mass computation experiment (originally published in [18]). It shows the mean cost (corresponding to runtime) of search conducted by the algorithm before a clause with desired quality (score) is found. The cost also critically depends on the cutoff value that is inversely proportional to the frequency with which the randomized ILP algorithm is restarted. The flat area on top corresponds to cost values exceeding a prescribed runtime threshold. Note that the cost is shown in logarithmic scale so mild variations in the cutoff incur abrupt changes in search cost.

Also, we observed that the cutoff value is critical for the performance of the search algorithm, and using its optimal value in a randomized restarted search may decrease the mean search cost *by several orders of magnitude* or increase the mean achieved score significantly with respect to that obtained magnitude) or increase the mean achieved score significantly with respect to that obtained. Figure 1 provides a graphical insight into our main statistical findings.

The general and most important lesson learned from the study [18] was that a miniscule change in an auxiliary parameter of an ILP algorithm (namely the restart cutoff value) incurs an abrupt change in its statistically expected runtime, resembling phase transition effects described in [6]. This is all the more important since the parameter indeed only tunes the working of the *algorithm* but it does not reduce the size of the *problem*. Put informally, one can boost the performance by orders of magnitude "free of charge" by randomizing and restarting the ILP algoritm and carefuly choosing the restart cutoff value. While our work [18] was not concerned with strategies for finding the optimal cutoff, these can be translated from studies such as [5].

4 Front Two: Subsumption

In [18], the term *runtime* corresponded to the number of clauses explored in the combinatorial search conducted by the ILP algorithm. While our findings showed a way to drastically reduce the statistical mean of this quantity, runtime profiles measured in seconds may still be unacceptable. This is because the ILP algorithm may be overwhelmed by the second source of complexity, that is, by computing the fitness of each explored clause with respect to the data by checking, for each example, whether or not it is subsumed by the clause.

Triggered by the observed effects of randomized restarts on the average complexity of clause search, we reasoned that a restart strategy could be a way to achieve similar effects in the problem of subsumption checking. In [9] we thus studied runtime distributions of the subsumption test. Subsumption is an NP-complete problem that is readily analogical to the graph homomorphism problem. The latter bears crucial importance in the field of *graph mining*. Our intention was to produce results of immediate interest to the wide graph mining community. Therefore we devised a generator of subsumption problem instances that are directly interpretable in graph terminology. In particular, all generated clauses represented graphs, that in turn were randomly sampled from two well-known generative models known as Erdos-Renyi and scale-free ("small-world" graphs). In both cases, we observed heavy-tailed distributions when checking subsumption between pairs of clauses corresponding to such graphs. The heavy tails were then straightforwardly avoided by designing a correct and complete randomized restarted subsumption testing algorithm RESUMER. Figure 2 shows the distribution both before and after our modification. We next subjected RESUMER to comparative testing against the algorithm Django [10] which relies on strong heuristics inspired from the constraint satisfaction domain and which had then been known as the fastest state-of-the-art subsumption tester. RESUMER

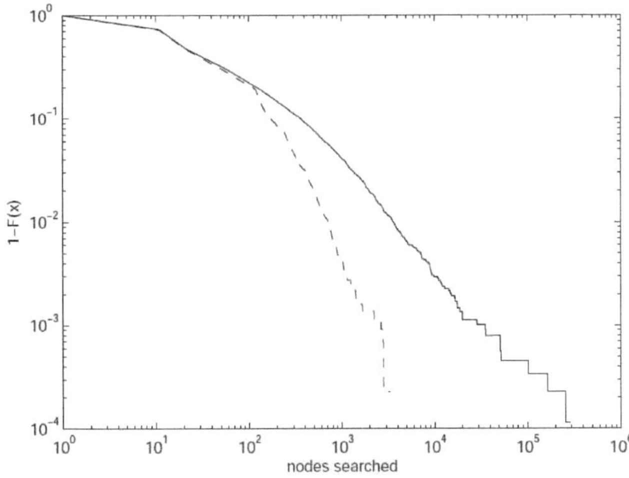

Fig. 2. Runtime distributions of two subsumption checking algorithms (originally published in [9]). The vertical axis shows the estimated probability that the algorithm will not finish before exploring the number of search nodes shown on the horizontal axis. The number of search nodes is directly proportional to runtime. The full line corresponds to a deterministic heuristic algorithm and exhibits a heavy tail; i.e. a non-negligible probability of extremly high runtimes. The dotted line pertains to a randomized restarted (though still complete and correct) version of the algorithm, effectively avoiding the heavy tail.

performed comparably with Django for relatively small examples (tens to hundreds of literals), while for further growing example sizes, RESUMER became vastly superior.

We furthermore explored the idea of allowing certain communication of between individual restarts of RESUMER, propagating some hints that proved useful. We namely considered guiding the heuristic selection of the variable to be first instantiated by the substitution θ. In particular we decided to choose the variable which caused the last backtrack in the previous restart, since this variable is more likely to be highly constrained than a randomly chosen variable. As such it is a good candidate to start the search with. The dotted line in Fig. 3 shows that this modification is significantly beneficial in terms of the runtime profile. The modification has the consequence that pairs of restarts are no longer statistically independent trials. In general, this might represent a problem. A restarted strategy exhibits the desirable property of an exponentially decaying runtime only if individual restarts are independent. For this reason we also tried to only allow the above described transfer of knowledge from odd restarts into the subsequent even restarts, resulting in a series of restart pairs, which are mutually independent. Thus we maintained the exponential decay guarantee while not sacrificing much of the performance improvement as illustrated by the dash line in Fig. 3.

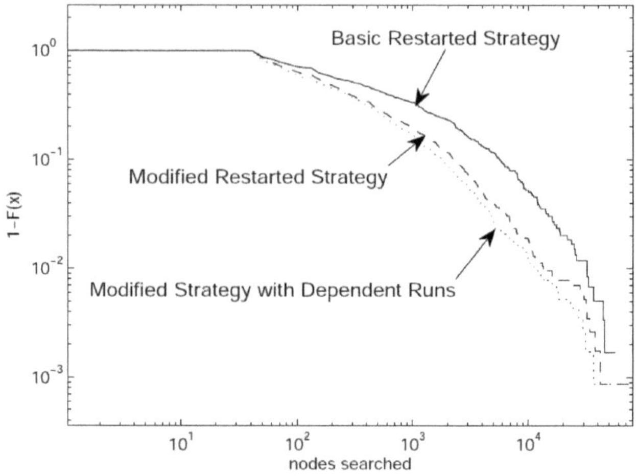

Fig. 3. Runtime distributions of restarted subsumption testing (originally published in [9]). The diagram displays distributions in the same setting as in Fig. 2. Here, the restarted algorithm from Fig. 2 is compared to its two modifications that involve a transfer of information among individual runs. See main text for details.

Up to this point, all runtime improvements, both in clause search and subsumption, have been achieved through rather straightforward adoptions of existing restarting strategies known in the context of constraint satisfaction problems, such as those investigated in [2]. At first sight, there is not much else to do, at least in the case of subsumption. Indeed, subsumption and constraint satisfaction are both NP-complete and thus mutually reducible. However, subsumption employed in the working of an ILP algorithm has a principal distinguishing point. Each hypothesised clause is checked against a usually large number of examples, which often have a very similar structure. This corresponds to solving a series of subsumption instances, all sharing the same subsumer and only slightly differing in the subsumee. Viewed dually, each example is tested against a large number of hypothesized clauses, and a series of subsumption tests may thus as well be considered that differs only on the subsumer part. In any case, the tantalizing question was whether this mode of operation, special to the ILP setting, can be exploited for further efficiency improvements.

In the work [8], we developed a strategy that exploits the scenario of numerous repetitions of similar subsumption checks that is characteristic to ILP. A crucial point that further motivates the strategy is as follows. The reason why one conducts subsumption checking in ILP is ultimately to evaluate the quality of a candidate clause. For this purpose, however, one does not neccessarily need to find out which particular examples are subsumed. One in fact only cares about the total number of subsumed examples. In [8], we developed a probabilistic algorithm that estimates this quantity without having to decide subsumption for all examples. The intuition behind its design can be explained as follows.

We are given a clause C, an example set E, and we would like to estimate $n = |\{e \in E | C \preceq_\theta e\}|$. Let us run the above described algorithm RESUMER on C and e, successively for all $e \in E$. For each e, we however stop the algorithm if no decision has been made in some prescribed number of steps. Let $\mathcal{E} \subseteq E$ be the subset of examples proven to be subsumed by C in this experiment. Denote $s_1 = |E|$. We now remove all examples in $\mathcal{E}$ from E and repeat this experiment, obtaining an analogical number s_2. Further such iterations generate numbers s_3, s_4, etc. Clearly, for the desired value n, we have that $n = \lim_{j \to \infty} S_j$ where $S_j = \sum_{i=1}^{j} s_i$. Under a certain assumption that is elaborated in [8], the series S_j is geometrical rather than arbitrary. The main idea is that the limit of S_j for $j \to \infty$ can thus be estimated by extrapolating the series from its first few elements S_1, S_2. On both generated graph data and real-world datasets, we showed that this algorithm provides reasonably accurate estimates while achieving dramatic runtime improvements.

5 Conclusions and Ongoing Work

Affording a bit of inflated language, we have presented our victories on the two battlefields of ILP complexity, which are represented by the combinatorial search for a good clause and the subsumption test needed to evaluate a clause. A lateral goal of this review was to demonstrate that significant improvements can be achieved by translating performance-boosting tricks from one domain to another. In fact, many of the improvements we have achieved in the performance of ILP algorithms were a result of a suitable translation of strategies designed in the field of constraint satisfaction problems (CSP). We are currently continuing this line of exploration, trying to merge the two problems (clause search and clause evaluation) into a single problem reducible to a series of CSP instances. These can in turn be tackled by advanced heuristic strategies that undergo perpetual development in the CSP field. In our latest study [7], we have been able to progress along this line under a strong syntactic bias in the ILP framework known as propositionalization [16]. Using the approach of [7], we are now able to effectively learn conjunctions of tens to hundreds of first-order literals, far beyond the reach of traditional propositionalization or ILP systems.

Acknowledgements. FŽ acknowledges the support from the Czech Ministry of Education through project MSM6840770038 and from the Czech Science Foundation through project 201/09/1665. OK is supported by the Czech Academy of Sciences through project 1ET101210513 and by the Czech Science Foundation through project 201/08/0509.

References

1. Džeroski, S., Lavrač, N. (eds.): Relational Data Mining. Springer, Heidelberg (2001)
2. Gomes, C., Selman, B., Crato, N., Kautz, H.: Heavy-Tailed Phenomena in Satisfiability and Constraint Satisfaction Problems. Journal of Automated Reasoning 24, 67–100 (2000)

3. Gottlob, G.: Subsumption and Implication. Information Processing Letters 24, 109–111 (1987)
4. Gottlob, G., Leone, N., Scarcello, F.: On the Complexity of Some Inductive Logic Programming Problems. New Generation Computing 17, 53–75 (1999)
5. Kautz, H., Horvitz, E., Ruan, Y., Gomes, C., Selman, B.: Dynamic Restart Policies. In: AAAI 2002, Association for the Advancement of Artificial Intelligence Symposium (2002)
6. Kirkpatrick, S., Selman, B.: Critical Behavior in the Satisfiability of Random Boolean Expressions. Science 264, 1297–1301 (1994)
7. Kuželka, O., Železný, F.: Block-Wise Construction of Acyclic Relational Features with Monotone Irreducibility and Relevancy Properties. In: ICML 2009, the 26th Int. Conf. on Machine Learning (2009)
8. Kuželka, O., Železný, F.: Fast Estimation of First-Order Clause Coverage through Randomization and Maximum Likelihood. In: ICML 2008, the 25th Int. Conf. on Machine Learning (2008)
9. Kuželka, O., Železný, F.: A Restarted Strategy for Efficient Subsumption Testing. Fundamenta Informaticae 89, 95–109 (2008)
10. Maloberti, J., Sebag, M.: Fast Theta-Subsumption with Constraint Satisfaction Algorithms. Machine Learning 55(2), 137–174 (2004)
11. Marcinkowski, J., Pacholski, L.: Undecidability of the Horn-Clause Implication Problem. In: FOCS 2002, the 33rd Ann. Sympos. on Foundations of Computer Science (2002)
12. Nienhuys-Cheng, S.H., de Wolf, R.: Foundations of Inductive Logic Programming. Springer, Heidelberg (1997)
13. Raedt, L.D.: Logical Settings for Concept Learning. Artificial Intelligence 95, 187–201 (1997)
14. Raedt, L.D.: Logical and Relational Learning. Springer, Heidelberg (2008)
15. Raedt, L.D., Frasconi, P., Kersting, K., Muggleton, S. (eds.): Probabilistic Inductive Logic Programming. Springer, Heidelberg (2008)
16. Železný, F., Lavrač, N.: Propositionalization-Based Relational Subgroup Discovery with RSD. Machine Learning 62, 33–63 (2006)
17. Železný, F., Srinivasan, A., Page, D.: Lattice Search Runtime Distributions May Be Heavy Tailed. In: Matwin, S., Sammut, C. (eds.) ILP 2002. LNCS (LNAI), vol. 2583, pp. 333–345. Springer, Heidelberg (2003)
18. Železný, F., Srinivasan, A., Page, D.: Randomized Restarted Search in ILP. Machine Learning 64, 183–208 (2006)

A Rule Format for Unit Elements*

Luca Aceto[1], Anna Ingolfsdottir[1],
MohammadReza Mousavi[2], and Michel A. Reniers[2]

[1] ICE-TCS, School of Computer Science, Reykjavik University
Kringlan 1, IS-103 Reykjavik, Iceland
[2] Department of Computer Science, Eindhoven University of Technology
P.O. Box 513, NL-5600 MB Eindhoven, The Netherlands

Abstract. This paper offers a meta-theorem for languages with a Structural Operational Semantics (SOS) in the style of Plotkin. Namely, it proposes a generic rule format for SOS guaranteeing that certain constants act as left- or right-unit elements for a set of binary operators. We show the generality of our format by applying it to a wide range of operators from the literature on process calculi.

1 Introduction

In many process algebras and specification languages, one encounters constructs that are unit elements for certain composition operators. The concept of (left) unit element for a binary operator f can be concisely summarized in the following algebraic equation, where $\mathbf{0}$ is the left-unit element for f: $f(\mathbf{0}, x) = x$.

In this paper, we propose a generic rule format guaranteeing that certain constants are left- or right-unit elements for a set of binary operators, whose semantics is defined using Plotkin's style of Structural Operational Semantics (SOS) [2,12,13]. The notions of left and right unit are defined with respect to a notion of behavioural equivalence. There are various notions of behavioural equivalence presented in the literature (see, e.g., [7]), which are, by and large, weaker than bisimilarity. Thus, to be as general as possible, we prove our main result for all equivalences that contain, i.e., are weaker than, bisimilarity.

This paper is part of our ongoing line of research on capturing basic properties of composition operators in terms of syntactic rule formats, exemplified by rule formats for commutativity [11], associativity [6], determinism and idempotence [1].

This line of research serves multiple purposes. Firstly, it paves the way for a tool-set that can mechanically prove such properties without involving user interaction. Secondly, it provides us with an insight as to the semantic nature of such properties and its link to the syntax of SOS deduction rules. In other words, our rule formats may serve as a guideline for language designers who want to

* The work of Aceto and Ingolfsdottir has been partially supported by the projects "The Equational Logic of Parallel Processes" (nr. 060013021), and "New Developments in Operational Semantics" (nr. 080039021) of the Icelandic Research Fund.
The first author dedicates the paper to the memory of his mother, Imelde Diomede Aceto, who passed away a year ago.

J. van Leeuwen et al. (Eds.): SOFSEM 2010, LNCS 5901, pp. 141–152, 2010.

ensure, a priori, that the constructs under design enjoy certain basic algebraic properties. There is value in determining what conditions on the SOS description of the semantics of operators guarantee that certain elements are left or right units. The fact that the constraints imposed by our general format are non-trivial indicates that the isolation of a widely applicable syntactic characterization of the semantic properties that underlie the existence of unit elements is, perhaps surprisingly, difficult.

The rest of this paper is organized as follows. In Section 2, we define some basic notions that are required for the technical developments in the rest of the paper. In Section 3, we present our rule format and prove that it guarantees the unit element property. In Section 4, we apply the rule format to various examples from the literature. In order to ease the application of our rule format to operators whose operational semantics is specified using predicates, we extend the format to that setting in Section 4.2. Section 5 concludes the paper and discusses directions for future work. Proofs can be found in [3].

2 Preliminaries

We begin by recalling the basic notions from the theory of SOS that are needed in the remainder of this study. We refer the interested readers to, e.g., [2,12] for more information and background.

Definition 1 (Signatures, Terms and Substitutions). *We let V represent an infinite set of variables and use $x, x', x_i, y, y', y_i, \ldots$ to range over elements of V. A* signature *Σ is a set of function symbols, each with a fixed arity. We call these symbols* operators *and usually represent them by $f, g, \ldots$. An operator with arity zero is called a* constant*. We define the set $\mathbb{T}(\Sigma)$ of* terms *over Σ as the smallest set satisfying the following conditions.*

- *A variable $x \in V$ is a term.*
- *If $f \in \Sigma$ has arity n and $t_1, \ldots, t_n$ are terms, then $f(t_1, \ldots, t_n)$ is a term.*

We use s, t, possibly subscripted and/or superscripted, to range over terms. We write $t_1 \equiv t_2$ if t_1 and t_2 are syntactically equal. The function $vars : \mathbb{T}(\Sigma) \to 2^V$ gives the set of variables appearing in a term. The set $\mathbb{C}(\Sigma) \subseteq \mathbb{T}(\Sigma)$ is the set of closed terms, *i.e., terms that contain no variables. We use $p, q, p', p_i, \ldots$ to range over closed terms. A* substitution *σ is a function of type $V \to \mathbb{T}(\Sigma)$. We extend the domain of substitutions to terms homomorphically and write $\sigma(t)$ for the result of applying the substitution σ to the term t. If the range of a substitution lies in $\mathbb{C}(\Sigma)$, we say that it is a* closed substitution*. An explicit substitution $[x \mapsto t]$ maps x to t and is the identity function on all variables but x.*

Definition 2 (Transition System Specifications). *A* transition system specification *(TSS) is a triple $(\Sigma, \mathcal{L}, D)$ where:*

- *Σ is a signature.*
- *$\mathcal{L}$ is a set of labels (or actions) ranged over by a, b, l. If $l \in \mathcal{L}$, and $t, t' \in \mathbb{T}(\Sigma)$ we say that $t \xrightarrow{l} t'$ is a* positive transition formula *and $t \stackrel{l}{\nrightarrow}$ is a* negative

transition formula. *A transition formula (or just formula), typically denoted by ϕ or ψ, is either a negative transition formula or a positive one.*
- *D is a set of* deduction rules, *i.e., pairs of the form (Φ, ϕ) where Φ is a set of formulae and ϕ is a positive formula. We call the formulae contained in Φ the* premises *of the rule and ϕ the* conclusion.

We write vars(r) to denote the set of variables appearing in a deduction rule r. We say that a formula is closed *if all of its terms are closed. Substitutions are also extended to formulae and sets of formulae in the natural way. For a rule r and a substitution σ, the rule $\sigma(r)$ is called a substitution instance of r. A set of positive closed formulae is called a* transition relation.

We often refer to a positive transition formula $t \xrightarrow{l} t'$ as a *transition* with t being its *source*, l its *label*, and t' its *target*. A deduction rule (Φ, ϕ) is typically written as $\frac{\Phi}{\phi}$. An *axiom* is a deduction rule with an empty set of premises. We call a deduction rule *f-defining* when the outermost function symbol appearing in the source of its conclusion is f.

In this paper, for each constant c, we assume that each c-defining deduction rule is an axiom of the form $c \xrightarrow{l} p$ for some label l and closed term p.

The meaning of a TSS is defined by the following notion of least three-valued stable model. To define this notion, we need two auxiliary definitions, namely provable transition rules and contradiction, which are given below.

Definition 3 (Provable Transition Rules). *A deduction rule is called a* transition rule *when it is of the form $\frac{N}{\phi}$ with N a set of* negative formulae. *A TSS $\mathcal{T}$ proves $\frac{N}{\phi}$, denoted by $\mathcal{T} \vdash \frac{N}{\phi}$, when there is a well-founded upwardly branching tree with formulae as nodes and of which*
- *the root is labelled by ϕ;*
- *if a node is labelled by ψ and the labels of the nodes above it form the set K then:*
  - *ψ is a negative formula and $\psi \in N$, or*
  - *ψ is a positive formula and $\frac{K}{\psi}$ is a substitution instance of a deduction rule in $\mathcal{T}$.*

Definition 4 (Contradiction and Entailment). *The formula $t \xrightarrow{l} t'$ is said to* contradict *$t \overset{l}{\nrightarrow}$, and vice versa. For a set Φ of formulae and a formula ψ, Φ* contradicts *ψ, denoted by $\Phi \nvDash \psi$, when there is a $\phi \in \Phi$ that contradicts ψ. We write $\Phi \vDash \Psi$ if Φ does not contradict any $\psi \in \Psi$. A formula ϕ* entails *ψ when there is a substitution σ such that $\sigma(\phi) \equiv \psi$. A set Φ entails a set Ψ of formulae, when there exists a substitution σ such that, for each $\psi \in \Psi$, there exists a $\phi \in \Phi$ such that $\sigma(\phi) \equiv \psi$.*

It immediately follows from the above definition that contradiction is a symmetric relation on (sets of) formulae. We now have all the necessary ingredients to define the semantics of TSSs in terms of three-valued stable models.

Definition 5 (Least Three-Valued Stable Model). *A pair (C, U) of disjoint sets of positive closed transition formulae is called a* three-valued stable model *for a TSS $\mathcal{T}$ when the following conditions hold:*

– *for each* $\phi \in C$, $\mathcal{T} \vdash \frac{N}{\phi}$ *for a set* N *of negative formulae such that* $C \cup U \models N$,
– *for each* $\phi \in U$, $\mathcal{T} \vdash \frac{N}{\phi}$ *for a set* N *of negative formulae such that* $C \models N$.

C *stands for* Certainly *and* U *for* Unknown; *the third value is determined by the formulae not in* $C \cup U$. *The* least *three-valued stable model is a three-valued stable model that is the least one with respect to the ordering on pairs of sets of formulae defined as* $(C, U) \leq (C', U')$ *iff* $C \subseteq C'$ *and* $U' \subseteq U$. *We say that* $\mathcal{T}$ *is* complete *when for its least three-valued stable model it holds that* $U = \emptyset$. *In a complete TSS, we say that a closed substitution* σ *satisfies a set of formulae* Φ *if* $\sigma(\phi) \in C$, *for each positive formula* $\phi \in \Phi$, *and* $C \models \sigma(\phi)$, *for each negative formula* $\phi \in \Phi$.

Definition 6 (Bisimulation and Bisimilarity). *Let* $\mathcal{T}$ *be a TSS with signature* Σ *and label set* $\mathcal{L}$. *A relation* $\mathcal{R} \subseteq \mathbb{C}(\Sigma) \times \mathbb{C}(\Sigma)$ *is a* bisimulation relation *if* $\mathcal{R}$ *is symmetric and, for all* $p_0, p_1, p_0' \in \mathbb{C}(\Sigma)$ *and* $l \in \mathcal{L}$,

$$(p_0 \,\mathcal{R}\, p_1 \wedge \mathcal{T} \vdash p_0 \xrightarrow{l} p_0') \Rightarrow \exists_{p_1' \in \mathbb{C}(\Sigma)} (\mathcal{T} \vdash p_1 \xrightarrow{l} p_1' \wedge p_0' \,\mathcal{R}\, p_1').$$

Two terms $p_0, p_1 \in \mathbb{C}(\Sigma)$ *are called* bisimilar, *denoted by* $p_0 \leftrightarroweq p_1$, *when there exists a bisimulation relation* $\mathcal{R}$ *such that* $p_0 \,\mathcal{R}\, p_1$.

Bisimilarity is extended to open terms by requiring that $s, t \in \mathbb{T}(\Sigma)$ are bisimilar when $\sigma(s) \leftrightarroweq \sigma(t)$ for each closed substitution $\sigma : V \to \mathbb{C}(\Sigma)$.

3 Rule Format

We now proceed to define our rule format guaranteeing that certain constants in the language under consideration are left or right units for some binary operators. In the definition of the format proposed in the remainder of this section, we make use of a syntactic characterization of equivalence of terms up to their composition with unit elements; we call such terms *unit-context equivalent*. Intuitively, if s is unit-context equivalent to t, then s and t are bisimilar because one can be obtained from the other by applying axioms stating that some constant is a left or right unit for some binary operator. For instance, if c_1 is a left unit for a binary operator f and c_2 is a right unit for a binary operator g, then the terms $f(c_1, g(t, c_2))$ and $g(f(c_1, t), c_2)$ are both unit-context equivalent to t and also unit-context equivalent to each other.

The following definition formalizes this intuition. (While reading the technical definition, our readers may find it useful to bear in mind that $(f, c) \in L$ means that c is a left unit for a binary operator f and $(f, c) \in R$ means that c is a right unit for f.)

Definition 7 (Unit-Context Equivalent Terms). *Given sets* $L, R \subseteq \Sigma \times \Sigma$ *of pairs of binary function symbols and constants,* $\overset{L,R}{\cong}$ *is the smallest equivalence relation satisfying the following conditions, for each* $s \in \mathbb{T}(\Sigma)$:

1. $\forall_{(f,c)\in L}\ s \overset{L,R}{\cong} f(c,s)$, *and*
2. $\forall_{(g,c)\in R}\ s \overset{L,R}{\cong} g(s,c)$.

We say that two terms $s,t \in \mathbb{T}(\Sigma)$ *are* unit-context equivalent, *if* $s \overset{L,R}{\cong} t$.

In what follows, we abbreviate $\overset{L,R}{\cong}$ to $\cong$ since the sets L and R are always clear from the context.

Lemma 8. *For all* $s,t \in \mathbb{T}(\Sigma)$, *if* $s \cong t$ *then* $vars(s) = vars(t)$ *and* $\sigma(s) \cong \sigma(t)$, *for each substitution* σ.

We are now ready to define our promised rule format for unit elements.

Definition 9 (Left- and Right-Aligned Pairs). *Given a TSS, the sets* L *and* R *of pairs of binary function symbols and constants are the largest sets satisfying the following conditions.*

1. *For each* $(f,c) \in L$, *the following conditions hold:*
   (a) *For each action* $a \in \mathcal{L}$, *there exists at least one deduction rule of the following form:*

$$\frac{\{x_0 \xrightarrow{a_i} y_i \mid i \in I\} \cup \{x_0 \overset{a_j}{\nrightarrow} \mid j \in J\} \cup \{x_1 \xrightarrow{a} z_1\}}{f(x_0,x_1) \xrightarrow{a} t'},$$

   where

   i. *the variables* y_i, z_1, x_0 *and* x_1 *are all pairwise distinct,*
   ii. *for each* $j \in J$, *there is no* c*-defining axiom with* a_j *as label, and*
   iii. *there exists a collection* $\{c \xrightarrow{a_i} q_i \mid i \in I\}$ *of* c*-defining axioms such that* $\sigma(t') \cong z_1$, *where* σ *is the substitution mapping* x_0 *to* c, *each* y_i *to* q_i, $i \in I$, *and is the identity on all the other variables.*

   (b) *Each* f*-defining deduction rule has the following form:*

$$\frac{\Phi}{f(t_0,t_1) \xrightarrow{a} t'}$$

   where $a \in \mathcal{L}$ *and, for each closed substitution* σ *such that* $\sigma(t_0) \equiv c$,

   i. *either there exists some* $t_1 \xrightarrow{a} t'' \in \Phi$ *with* $\sigma(t') \cong \sigma(t'')$, *or*
   ii. *there exists a premise* $\phi \in \Phi$ *with* t_0 *as its source such that*

      A. *either* ϕ *is a positive formula and the collection of conclusions of* c*-defining deduction rules does not entail* $\sigma(\phi)$, *or*
      B. ϕ *is a negative formula and the collection of conclusions of* c*-defining axioms contradicts* $\sigma(\phi)$.

2. *The definition of right-aligned pairs of operators and constant symbols – that is, those such that $(f, c) \in R$ – is symmetric and is not repeated here.*

For a function symbol f and a constant c, we call (f, c) left aligned *(respectively,* right aligned*) if $(f, c) \in L$ (respectively, $(f, c) \in R$).*

Condition 1a in the above definition ensures that, whenever (f, c) is in L, each transition of the form $p \xrightarrow{a} p'$, for some closed terms p and p' and action a, can be used to infer a transition $f(c, p) \xrightarrow{a} q'$ for some q' that is bisimilar to p'. This means that if (f, c) is in L then, in the context of the constant c, f does not "prune away" any of the behaviour of its second argument.

Condition 1(b)i, on the other hand, ensures that, whenever (f, c) is in L, each transition $f(c, p) \xrightarrow{a} q'$ is due to a transition $p \xrightarrow{a} p'$ for some p' that is bisimilar to q'. Thus, if (f, c) is in L then, in the context of the constant c, a term of the form $f(c, p)$ can only mimic the behaviour of p. As will become clear from the examples to follow, condition 1(b)ii ensures that the f-defining rule cannot be used to derive a transition for $f(c, p)$ and hence it is exempted from further conditions; the presence of this condition enhances the generality of our format and allows us to handle common examples of unit constants from the literature (see, e.g., Example 3). A slightly more technical discussion of the conditions is given in [3].

Remark 1. Note that the requirement that $\sigma(t') \cong z_1$ in condition 1a of the above definition implies that $vars(\sigma(t')) = \{z_1\}$. Therefore x_1, z_1 and the y_i, $i \in I$, are the only variables that may possibly occur in t'.

Note that, since the sets L and R are defined as the *largest* sets of pairs satisfying the conditions from Definition 9, in order to show that (f, c) is a left-aligned pair, say, it suffices only to exhibit two sets L and R satisfying these conditions, such that (f, c) is contained in L.

The following two examples illustrate that it is in general advantageous to consider sets of left- and/or right-aligned operators instead of just a single one.

Example 1. Assume that a is the only action and consider the binary operators f_i, $i \geq 0$, with rules

$$\frac{x_1 \xrightarrow{a} y_1}{f_i(x_0, x_1) \xrightarrow{a} f_{i+1}(x_0, y_1)} .$$

Let $\mathbf{0}$ be a constant with no rules. Then each of the pairs $(f_i, \mathbf{0})$ is left aligned because the sets $L = \{(f_i, \mathbf{0}) \mid i \geq 0\}$ and $R = \emptyset$ meet the conditions from Definition 9. In particular, note that $f_{i+1}(x_0, y_1)[x_0 \mapsto \mathbf{0}] \equiv f_{i+1}(\mathbf{0}, y_1) \cong y_1$, for each $i \geq 0$. Note that, for each $i \geq 0$, the equations $f_i(\mathbf{0}, x) = x$ hold modulo bisimilarity. This fact can be checked directly by showing that the symmetric closure of the relation $\mathcal{R} = \{(f_i(\mathbf{0}, p), p) \mid p \text{ a closed term}\}$ is a bisimulation, and is also a consequence of Theorem 10 to follow, which states the correctness of the rule format we described in Definition 9.

Example 2. Consider the following TSS, which is defined for a signature with $\mathbf{0}$ and a as constants and f and g as binary function symbols.

$$\frac{}{a \xrightarrow{a} \mathbf{0}} \qquad \frac{y \xrightarrow{a} y'}{f(x,y) \xrightarrow{a} g(y',x)} \qquad \frac{x \xrightarrow{a} x'}{g(x,y) \xrightarrow{a} f(y,x')}$$

The TSS fits our rule format with $L = \{(f,\mathbf{0})\}$ and $R = \{(g,\mathbf{0})\}$. Note that it is essential for the above example to consider both L and R simultaneously.

Theorem 10. *Let $\mathcal{T}$ be a complete TSS in which each rule is f-defining for some function symbol f. Assume that L and R are the sets of left- and right-aligned function symbols according to Definition 9. For each $(f,c) \in L$, it holds that $f(c,x) \leftrightarrow x$. Symmetrically, for each $(f,c) \in R$, it holds that $f(x,c) \leftrightarrow x$.*

Note that Theorem 10 trivially extends to any notion of behavioural equivalence weaker than bisimilarity.

4 Applications and Extensions

Apart from its correctness, the acid test for the usefulness of a rule format is that it be expressive enough to cover examples from the literature that afford the property they were designed to ensure. Our order of business in this section will be to offer examples of applications of the format for unit elements we introduced in Definition 9 and to show how the format can be extended to deal with operators whose semantic definition involves the use of predicates.

4.1 Applications of the Basic Rule Format

We start by presenting examples of applications of the format for unit elements we introduced in Definition 9.

Example 3 (Nondeterministic Choice). Consider the nondeterministic choice operator from Milner's CCS [10] specified by the rules below, where $a \in \mathcal{L}$.

$$\frac{x \xrightarrow{a} x'}{x + y \xrightarrow{a} x'} \qquad \frac{y \xrightarrow{a} y'}{x + y \xrightarrow{a} y'}$$

The sets $R = L = \{(+,\mathbf{0})\}$ meet the conditions in Definition 9. Indeed, condition 1a and its symmetric version are trivially satisfied by the right-hand and the left-hand rule schemas, respectively. (Note that the substitution σ associated with the empty collection of axioms in condition 1(a)iii is the identity function over the set of variables.) To see that condition 1b is also met, let σ be a closed substitution such that $\sigma(x) = \mathbf{0}$. Observe that

- each instance of the right-hand rule schema meets condition 1(b)i and
- each instance of the left-hand rule schema meets condition 1(b)iiA because the set of rules for $\mathbf{0}$ is empty and therefore does not entail $\sigma(x) = \mathbf{0} \xrightarrow{a} \sigma(x')$.

The reasoning for condition 2 is symmetric. Therefore, Theorem 10 yields the soundness of the well known equations [8]: $\mathbf{0} + x = x = x + \mathbf{0}$.

Example 4 (Synchronous Parallel Composition). Assume, for the sake of simplicity, that a is the only action. Consider a constant RUN_a and the synchronous parallel composition from CSP [9][1] specified by the rules

$$\frac{}{\mathrm{RUN}_a \xrightarrow{a} \mathrm{RUN}_a} \qquad \frac{x \xrightarrow{a} x' \quad y \xrightarrow{a} y'}{x \parallel_a y \xrightarrow{a} x' \parallel_a y'} \,.$$

Take $L = R = \{(\parallel_a, \mathrm{RUN}_a)\}$. These sets L and R meet the conditions in Definition 9. To see that condition 1a and its symmetric version are satisfied by the above rule for $\parallel_a$, observe that the substitution σ associated with the singleton set containing the only axiom for RUN_a in condition 1(a)iii maps both the variables x and x' to RUN_a and is the identity function over the other variables. For such a σ, $\sigma(x' \parallel_a y') = \mathrm{RUN}_a \parallel_a y' \cong y'$.

To see that condition 1b is also met, let σ be a closed substitution mapping x to RUN_a, and assume that $\mathrm{RUN}_a \xrightarrow{a} \mathrm{RUN}_a$ entails $\mathrm{RUN}_a \xrightarrow{a} \sigma(x')$. It follows that $\sigma(x') = \mathrm{RUN}_a$. Therefore,

$$\sigma(x' \parallel_a y') = \mathrm{RUN}_a \parallel_a \sigma(y') \cong \sigma(y')$$

and condition 1(b)i is met. Theorem 10 thus yields the soundness of the well known equations $\mathrm{RUN}_a \parallel_a x = x = x \parallel_a \mathrm{RUN}_a$. These are just equation L3B from [9, page 69] and its symmetric counterpart.

Example 5 (Left Merge and Interleaving Parallel Composition). The following rules describe the operational semantics of the classic left merge and interleaving parallel composition operators [5,10].

$$\frac{x \xrightarrow{a} x'}{x \mathbin{\|\!\!\lfloor} y \xrightarrow{a} x' \parallel y} \qquad \frac{x \xrightarrow{a} x'}{x \parallel y \xrightarrow{a} x' \parallel y} \qquad \frac{y \xrightarrow{a} y'}{x \parallel y \xrightarrow{a} x \parallel y'}$$

Take $L = \{(\parallel, \mathbf{0})\}$ and $R = \{(\parallel, \mathbf{0}), (\mathbin{\|\!\!\lfloor}, \mathbf{0})\}$. It is easy to see that these sets L and R meet the condition in Definition 9. Therefore, Theorem 10 yields the well known equalities $\mathbf{0} \parallel x = x$, $x \parallel \mathbf{0} = x$, and $x \mathbin{\|\!\!\lfloor} \mathbf{0} = x$.

Note that the pair $(\mathbin{\|\!\!\lfloor}, \mathbf{0})$ cannot be added to L while preserving condition 1a in Definition 9. Indeed, $\mathbf{0}$ is not a left unit for the left merge operator $\mathbin{\|\!\!\lfloor}$.

Example 6 (Disrupt). Consider the following disrupt operator $\blacktriangleright$ [4] with rules

$$\frac{x \xrightarrow{a} x'}{x \blacktriangleright y \xrightarrow{a} x' \blacktriangleright y} \qquad \frac{y \xrightarrow{a} y'}{x \blacktriangleright y \xrightarrow{a} y'} \,.$$

[1] In [9], Hoare uses the symbol $\parallel$ to denote the synchronous parallel composition operator. Here we will use that symbol for parallel composition.

Note that the equation $\mathbf{0} \blacktriangleright x = x$ holds modulo bisimilarity. We now argue that its soundness is a consequence of Theorem 10. Indeed, take $L = \{(\blacktriangleright, \mathbf{0})\}$ and $R = \emptyset$. It is easy to see that these sets L and R meet the conditions in Definition 9. In particular, to see that condition 1b is met by the first rule, observe that the set of rules for $\mathbf{0}$ is empty and therefore does not entail $\mathbf{0} \xrightarrow{a} p$ for any closed term p. A symmetric reasoning shows that the valid equation $x \blacktriangleright \mathbf{0} = x$ is also a consequence of Theorem 10.

Example 7 (Timed Nondeterministic Choice). Consider nondeterministic choice in a timed setting. It is defined by means of the deduction rules from Example 3 and additionally the deduction rules

$$\frac{x \xrightarrow{1} x' \quad y \xrightarrow{1} y'}{x + y \xrightarrow{1} x' + y'} \qquad \frac{x \xrightarrow{1} x' \quad y \stackrel{1}{\nrightarrow}}{x + y \xrightarrow{1} x'} \qquad \frac{x \stackrel{1}{\nrightarrow} \quad y \xrightarrow{1} y'}{x + y \xrightarrow{1} y'} .$$

The equations $\mathbf{0} + x = x$ and $x + \mathbf{0} = x$ hold modulo bisimilarity. This is a consequence of Theorem 10 by taking $L = R = \{(+, \mathbf{0})\}$. For label 1, condition 1a is met by the third deduction rule. The first deduction rule satisfies condition 1(b)iiA, the second deduction rule satisfies condition 1(b)iiB, and the third deduction rule satisfies condition 1(b)i trivially.

4.2 Predicates

In the literature concerning the theory of rule formats for SOS (especially, the work devoted to congruence formats for various notions of bisimilarity), most of the time predicates are neglected at first and are only added to the considerations at a later stage. The reason is that one can encode predicates quite easily by means of transition relations. One can find a number of such encodings in the literature – see, for instance, [6,15]. In each of these encodings, a predicate P is represented as a transition relation $\xrightarrow{P}$ (assuming that P is a fresh label) with some fixed target. However, choosing the "right" target term to cope with the examples in the literature (and the new ones appearing in the future) within our format is extremely intricate, if not impossible. That is why we introduce an extension of our rule format that handles predicates as first-class objects, rather than coding them as transitions with dummy targets. To this end, we extend the basic notions presented in Section 2 to a setting with predicates.

Definition 11 (Predicates). *Given a set $\mathcal{P}$ of predicate symbols, Pt is a* positive predicate formula *and $\neg Pt$ is a* negative predicate formula, *for each $P \in \mathcal{P}$ and $t \in \mathbb{T}(\Sigma)$. We call t the* source *of both predicate formulae. In the extended setting, a (positive, negative)* formula *is either a (positive, negative) transition formula or (positive, negative) predicate formula. The notions of deduction rule, TSS, provable transition rules and three-valued stable models are then naturally extended by adopting the more general notion of formulae. The label of a deduction rule is either the label of the transition formula or of the predicate formula in its conclusion.*

Next, we define the extension of our rule format to cater for predicates. As we did in the earlier developments, in this section we assume that, for each constant c, each c-defining deduction rule for predicates is an axiom of the form $P\ c$.

Definition 12 (Extended Left- and Right-Aligned Pairs). *Given a TSS, the sets L and R of pairs of binary function symbols and constants are the largest sets satisfying the following conditions.*

1. *For each $(f, c) \in L$, the following conditions hold:*
   (a) *For each action $a \in \mathcal{L}$, there exists a deduction rule of the following form:*

$$\frac{\{x_0 \xrightarrow{a_i} y_i \mid i \in I\} \cup \{P_k\ x_0 \mid k \in K\} \cup \{x_0 \overset{a_j}{\nrightarrow} \text{ or } \neg P_j\ x_0 \mid j \in J\} \cup \{x_1 \xrightarrow{a} z_1\}}{f(x_0, x_1) \xrightarrow{a} t'}$$

   where

   i. *the variables y_i, z_1, x_0 and x_1 are all pairwise distinct,*
   ii. *for each $j \in J$, there is no c-defining deduction rule with a_j or P_j as label (depending on whether the formula with index j is a transition or a predicate formula),*
   iii. *there exists a collection $\{P_k\ c \mid k \in K\}$ of c-defining axioms, and*
   iv. *there exists a collection $\{c \xrightarrow{a_i} q_i \mid i \in I\}$ of c-defining axioms such that $\sigma(t') \cong z_1$, where σ is the substitution mapping x_0 to c, each y_i to q_i, $i \in I$, and is the identity on all the other variables.*

   (b) *For each predicate $P \in \mathcal{P}$, there exists a deduction rule, of the following form:*

$$\frac{\{P_i\ x_0 \mid i \in I\} \cup \{\neg P_j\ x_0 \mid j \in J\} \cup \{P\, x_1\}}{P\ f(x_0, x_1)}$$

   where

   i. *for each $j \in J$, there is no c-defining axiom with P_j as label, and*
   ii. *there exists a collection $\{P_i\ c \mid i \in I\}$ of c-defining axioms.*

   (c) *Each f-defining deduction rule has one of the following forms:*

$$\frac{\Phi}{f(t_0, t_1) \xrightarrow{a} t'} \quad \text{or} \quad \frac{\Phi}{P\ f(t_0, t_1)}$$

   where $a \in \mathcal{L}$, $P \in \mathcal{P}$ and for each closed substitution σ with $\sigma(t_0) \equiv c$,

   i. *either there exists some $t_1 \xrightarrow{a} t'' \in \Phi$ with $\sigma(t') \cong \sigma(t'')$ (if the conclusion is a transition formula), or $P\ t_1 \in \Phi$ (if the conclusion is a predicate formula), or*
   ii. *there exists a premise $\phi \in \Phi$ with t_0 as its source such that*

A. either ϕ is a positive formula and the collection of conclusions of c-defining deduction rules does not entail $\sigma(\phi)$, or

B. ϕ is a negative formula and the collection of conclusions of c-defining axioms contradicts $\sigma(\phi)$.

2. *The definition of right-aligned pairs of operators and constant symbols – that is, those such that $(f, c) \in R$ – is symmetric and is not repeated here.*

The definition of bisimulation is extended to a setting with predicates in the standard fashion. In particular, bisimilar terms must satisfy the same predicates.

We are now ready to state the counterpart of Theorem 10 in a setting with predicates.

Theorem 13. *Let $\mathcal{T}$ be a complete TSS in which each rule is f-defining for some function symbol f. Assume that L and R are the sets of extended left- and right-aligned function symbols according to Definition 12. For each $(f, c) \in L$, it holds that $f(c, x) \leftrightarrow x$. Symmetrically, for each $(f, c) \in R$, it holds that $f(x, c) \leftrightarrow x$.*

We now provide an example of the application of the rule format. In [3], we give two additional examples involving the use of predicates.

Example 8 (Sequential Composition). A standard operator whose operational semantics can be given using predicates is that of sequential composition. Consider the following deduction rules, where $p \downarrow$ means that "p can terminate successfully". (As usual in the literature, we write the termination predicate $\downarrow$ in postfix notation.)

$$\frac{}{1 \downarrow} \qquad \frac{x \downarrow \quad y \downarrow}{x \cdot y \downarrow} \qquad \frac{x \xrightarrow{a} x'}{x \cdot y \xrightarrow{a} x' \cdot y} \qquad \frac{x \downarrow \quad y \xrightarrow{a} y'}{x \cdot y \xrightarrow{a} y'}$$

Take $L = R = \{(\cdot, 1)\}$. The TSS conforms to our extended rule format. The second deduction rule matches criteria 1b and 1c of Definition 12 (and the symmetric ones omitted for the right-aligned operators). The third deduction rule satisfies criterion 1(c)iiA of Definition 12 (and the omitted 2(a) and 2(c) conditions). The rightmost deduction rule satisfies conditions 1a and 1(c)i of Definition 12, as well as the omitted condition 2(c)iiA because 1 has no transitions.

5 Conclusions

In this paper, we proposed a rule format for Structural Operational Semantics, guaranteeing constants to be left- or right-unit elements of certain operators. The rule format encompasses advanced features such as negative premises and complex terms appearing nearly anywhere in the deduction rules. We further extended the proposed format to accommodate predicates, which are among the common ingredients in the SOS of many contemporary process description languages. The rule format is applied to a number of examples from the literature, motivating its applicability.

A straightforward extension of our rule format allows one to deal with unit elements that are complex closed terms (instead of constants). We are not aware of many practical examples in which such unit elements are present. Another algebraic property, which can be captured using the same technique, is the existence of a (left or right) zero element, i.e., a constant $\mathbf{0}$ such that $f(\mathbf{0}, x) = f(x, \mathbf{0}) = \mathbf{0}$. Mechanizing the existing rule formats for algebraic properties in a tool-set is another direction for future work.

For many contemporary process algebras the SOS framework as used in this paper is still too restricted. Indeed, the SOS semantics of those languages involves more advanced features such as configurations that consist of more than only a process term, i.e., SOS with data, or the presence of structural congruences as an addendum to the SOS. Future work will show whether our format can be generalized to deal with such additions.

References

1. Aceto, L., Birgisson, A., Ingolfsdottir, A., Mousavi, M.R., Reniers, M.A.: Rule Formats for Determinism and Idempotence. In: FSEN 2009. LNCS, vol. 5961. Springer, Heidelberg (to appear, 2010)
2. Aceto, L., Fokkink, W.J., Verhoef, C.: Structural Operational Semantics. In: Handbook of Process Algebra, ch. 3, pp. 197–292. Elsevier, Amsterdam (2001)
3. Aceto, L., Ingolfsdottir, A., Mousavi, M.R., Reniers, M.A.: A Rule Format for Unit Elements. Tech. Rep. CSR-0913, Eindhoven University of Technology (2009)
4. Baeten, J.C.M., Bergstra, J.: Mode Transfer in Process Algebra. Tech. Rep. CSR-0001, Eindhoven University of Technology (2000)
5. Bergstra, J.A., Klop, J.W.: Fixedpoint Semantics in Process Algebra. Tech. Rep. IW 206/82, Center for Mathematics, Amsterdam (1982)
6. Cranen, S., Mousavi, M.R., Reniers, M.A.: A Rule Format for Associativity. In: van Breugel, F., Chechik, M. (eds.) CONCUR 2008. LNCS, vol. 5201, pp. 447–461. Springer, Heidelberg (2008)
7. van Glabbeek, R.J.: The Linear Time - Branching Time Apectrum I. In: Handbook of Process Algebra, ch. 1, pp. 3–100. Elsevier, Amsterdam (2001)
8. Hennessy, M., Milner, R.: Algebraic Laws for Non-Determinism and Concurrency. J. ACM 32(1), 137–161 (1985)
9. Hoare, C.A.R.: Communicating Sequential Processes. Prentice-Hall, Englewood Cliffs (1985)
10. Milner, R.: Communication and Concurrency. Prentice-Hall, Englewood Cliffs (1989)
11. Mousavi, M.R., Reniers, M.A., Groote, J.F.: A Syntactic Commutativity Format for SOS. IPL 93, 217–223 (2005)
12. Mousavi, M.R., Reniers, M.A., Groote, J.F.: SOS Formats and Meta-Theory: 20 Years after. TCS 373(3), 238–272 (2007)
13. Plotkin, G.D.: A Structural Approach to Operational Semantics. JLAP 60-61, 17–140 (2004)
14. Plotkin, G.D.: A Powerdomain for Countable Non-Determinism (extended abstract). In: Nielsen, M., Schmidt, E.M. (eds.) ICALP 1982. LNCS, vol. 140, pp. 418–428. Springer, Heidelberg (1982)
15. Verhoef, C.: A Congruence Theorem for Structured Operational Semantics with Predicates and Negative Premises. Nordic Journal of Computing 2(2), 274–302 (1995)

Approximability of Edge Matching Puzzles

Antonios Antoniadis[1] and Andrzej Lingas[2]

[1] Institut für Informatik, Humboldt-Universität zu Berlin, 10099 Berlin, Germany
antoniad@informatik.hu-berlin.de
[2] Department of Computer Science, Lund University, S-22100 Lund, Sweden
Andrzej.Lingas@cs.lth.se

Abstract. This paper deals with the (in)approximability of *Edge Matching Puzzles*. The interest in EdgeMatching Puzzles has been raised in the last few years with the release of the *Eternity II*™ puzzle, with a $2 million prize for the first submitted correct solution. It is known [1] that it is NP-hard to obtain an exact solution to Edge Matching Puzzles. We extend on that result by showing an approximation-preserving reduction from Max-3DM-B and thus proving that Edge Matching Puzzles do not admit polynomial-time approximation schemes unless P=NP. We then show that the problem is APX-complete, and study the difficulty of finding an approximate solution for several other optimisation variants of the problem.

1 Introduction

Informally, an *Edge Matching Puzzle* is a puzzle where the goal is to arrange a given set of square tiles with coloured edges into a given rectangle so that colours match along the edges of adjacent tiles. Edge Matching Puzzles first appeared in the 1890s. They are more challenging than the classical jigsaw puzzles we are all familiar with; mainly because there is no global image that can provide guidance. Additionally, there are usually more pieces that match together, but one cannot be sure they should be placed next to each other before attaining

Fig. 1. A solved Edge Matching Puzzle instance with no edges broken

J. van Leeuwen et al. (Eds.): SOFSEM 2010, LNCS 5901, pp. 153–164, 2010.

the complete solution. In other words, a local solution does not generally lead to a global solution.

The computational problem of filling plane areas with rectangular tiles has been extensively studied. Berger [2] has shown that a generalisation of our problem where an infinite number of copies for each tile is given and the goal is to fill the entire plane, is undecidable. The problem of wether a bounded area can be filled by a subset of the given tiles is NP-complete [3]. Additionally, it has been shown that bounded-tiling (having infinite copies of each tile and filling a bounded area) is a viable alternative to the satisfiability problem as a foundation of NP-completeness [4]. The complexity of the game variant of the problem has also been studied: It is PSPACE-complete and EXPTIME-complete when the tiles are to be placed into a square and a rectangle respectively [5]. Unlike the variant we study, all the above do not allow rotations of the tiles given.

Demaine and Demaine [1] established the NP-completeness of edge matching puzzles and some of its variants (a species of jigsaw puzzles, signed edge matching puzzles, and polyonimo packing puzzles) by a reduction from *3-partition*. Their result confirmed the difficulties that people have had in trying to solve this puzzle, and justified the exhaustive search that seemed necessary for the puzzle to be solved by a computer. Benoist and Bourreau [6] studied Edge Matching Puzzles using constraint programming, and Ansótegui et al. [7] worked on the generation of EMP instances of varied hardness, and the application of SAT/CSP solving techniques to the problem.

We show that the maximisation version of a variant of the problem is APX-complete by presenting an approximation-preserving reduction from a problem that is known to be APX-complete (namely Max-3DM-B, defined later) to our problem, and providing a constant-factor approximation algorithm for the problem. The APX-hardness result is then used to show some equivalent results for some other optimisation variants of Edge Matching Puzzles.

1.1 Outline

In the next section some definitions that will be used later on are presented. In Sect. 3, we present and analyse the actual reduction. Finally, Sect. 4 adds some results regarding the minimisation version.

2 Preliminaries

We adhere to the definitions of *approximation ratio*, *relative error* and *absolute error* from [8].

Definition 1. APX *is the complexity class of all optimisation problems Q such that the decission version of Q is in NP, and for some $r \geq 1$ there exists a polynomial-time r-approximation algorithm for Q.*

Definition 2. *A* Polynomial-Time Approximation Scheme *(PTAS) [8] for a problem is a set of algorithms A such that for each $\epsilon > 0$, there is an approximation algorithm in A with ratio $1 + \epsilon$ for the problem, running in polynomial time (under the assumption that ϵ is fixed).*

Note 1. Since under the P $\neq$ NP conjecture, there exist problems in *APX* that do not admit a PTAS, if P$\neq$NP then no *APX-hard* problem can admit a PTAS.

Definition 3. *An* L-reduction *[9] with constant parameters $\alpha, \beta > 0$, from a problem A to a problem B, with cost functions c_A and c_B respectively (where $c_X(v, w)$ denotes the cost of solution w to a problem X on instance v), is a pair of polynomial time computable functions f and g such that the following hold.*

- *f transforms instances of A to instances of B.*
- *If y is a solution to $f(x)$, then $g(y)$ is a solution to x.*
- *For every instance x of A: $OPT_B(f(x)) \leq \alpha OPT_A(x)$.*
- *For every solution y to $f(x)$: $|OPT_A(x) - c_A(x, g(y))| \leq \beta |OPT_B(f(x)) - c_B(f(x), y)|$.*

Theorem 1. *([9]) If there is an L-reduction with parameters α and β, from a problem A to a problem B, and there exists a polynomial-time approximation algorithm for B with relative error c, then there also exists a polynomial-time approximation algorithm for A with relative error $\delta = \alpha\beta c$.*

Definition 4. *Formally, an* Edge Matching Puzzle (EMP) *is a puzzle where the goal is to arrange a given collection of n square-shaped and edge-coloured tiles (of area a each), into a given rectangle of area $n \cdot a$ such that adjacent tiles are coloured identically along their common edge.*

We say that an edge e in a solution of an EMP is broken *if the two adjacent tiles in that solution sharing e have different colours along it. In the* maximisation version *of EMP, which we consider in the following section, we are looking for a solution maximizing the number of edges that match (are not broken).*

Definition 5. *In* Maximum Three-Dimensional Matching (Max-3DM) *we are given a set of triples $T \subseteq X \times Y \times Z$ from pairwise disjoint sets X, Y and Z, and we are looking for a subset M of the triples T of maximum size, such that no two triples of M agree on any coordinate.*

In the bounded version of Max-3DM, *Maximum Bounded 3-Dimensional Matching* (Max-3DM-B) the number of occurrences of every element in X, Y or Z is bounded by the constant B. Kann showed in 1991 [10] that Max-3DM-B is *APX-complete* for $B \geq 3$. More recently, Chlebìk and Chlebìkovà [11] improved that result by showing that Max-3DM-B is *APX-complete* for $B \geq 2$. Specifically, it is NP-hard to approximate the solution within $\frac{141}{140}$ even on instances with exactly two occurrences of each element. They later improved that bound to $\frac{95}{94}$ [12].

3 The Reduction and Its Analysis

Here we present an L-reduction of Max-3DM-B (with every element appearing exactly twice) to EMP. Whenever an edge of a tile has colour u it should be interpreted as a unique colour, thus it does not match to any other edge, including other u's. All other symbols that appear on edges of tiles represent a specific colour, and can be matched with edges of other tiles where the same symbol occurs.

3.1 Constructing the EMP Instance

This subsection describes how given a Max-3DM-B instance, a corresponding EMP instance is produced. An informal description on why the EMP instance is produced this way and what the purpose of every tile is, is provided in Subsect. 3.2; followed by a formal proof in Subsect. 3.3 and 3.4.

We define f as the function that given any instance of the Max-3DM-B problem with every element occuring exactly two times, will produce an instance of EMP as follows:

1. For each triple (x, y, z) with $x \in X$, $y \in Y$ and $z \in Z$, f produces the tiles seen in Fig. 2(a). We can call these tiles of *Type 1*, *Type 2* and *Type 3* respectively (from the lowest to the highest).
2. For each element $x \in X$, f produces the tiles seen in Fig. 2(b).
3. For each element $z \in Z$, f produces the tiles seen in Fig. 2(c).
4. For each element $y \in Y$, f produces the tiles seen in Fig. 2(d).
5. We are given a rectangle in which we want to arrange the tiles with the fewest possible edges being broken. The rectangle has height 2 and length half the number of tiles produced.

3.2 Informal Description

The purpose of this subsection is to provide an insight on the reduction and this way make the material and the proofs in the rest of this section easier to follow.

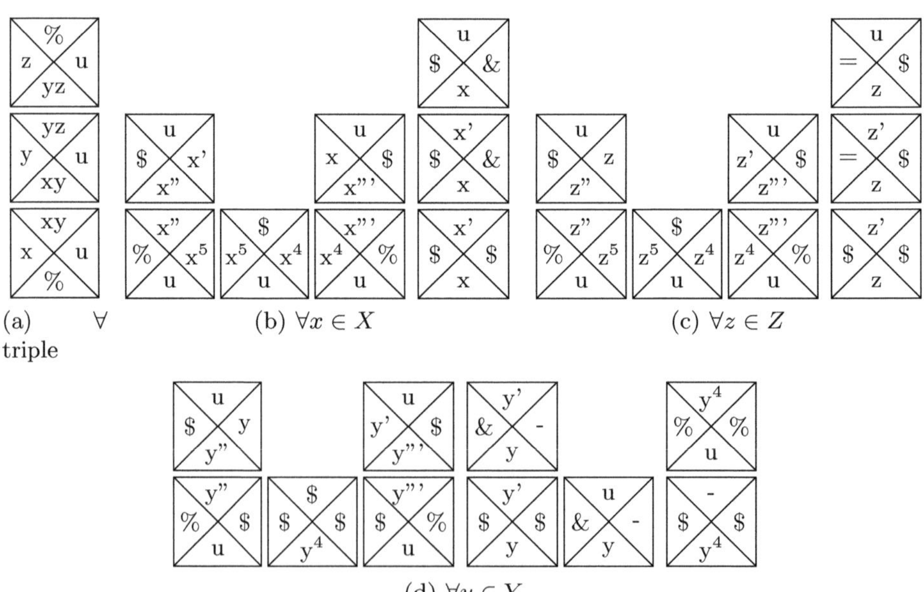

Fig. 2. The tiles constructed in Subsect. 3.1

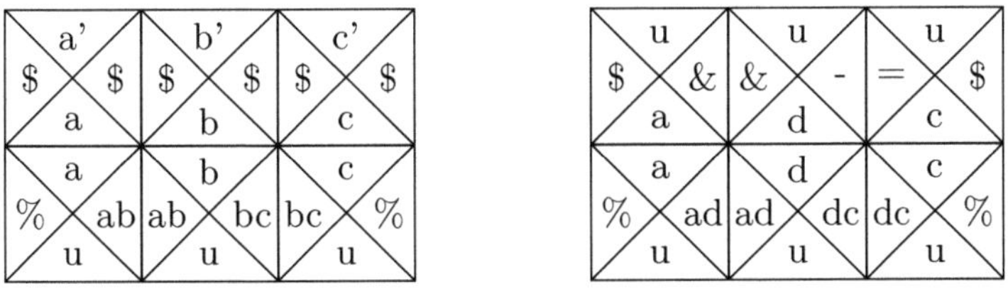

(a) a set corresponding to a picked triple, with no edges broken

(b) a set corresponding to an not picked triple, with exactly one edge broken

Fig. 3. A "good" and a non "good" set

Suppose that we have the two triples (a, b, c) and (a, d, c) among others in our given Max-3DM-B instance. Clearly in an optimal solution to that instance at most one of these triples can be picked, assume that it is (a, b, c). The main idea is that after the construction of the EMP instance in the way described in Subsect. 3.1, its optimal solution will contain the two sets of tiles seen in Fig. 3.

This way whenever a triple is picked we have no broken edge in the corresponding set, and whenever one is not picked we have exactly one edge that is broken in the corresponding set. Also note that no two triples that have a common element can be picked. To make the two sets of Fig. 3 always possible we have additionally produced some excess tiles. These, are not being discarded (the EMP definition does not allow this) but will be placed somewhere else in the rectangle. We are aware that from the first three tiles made for each element exactly one tile will be excess. Taking as an example a tile corresponding to an element $x \in X$, out of the tiles

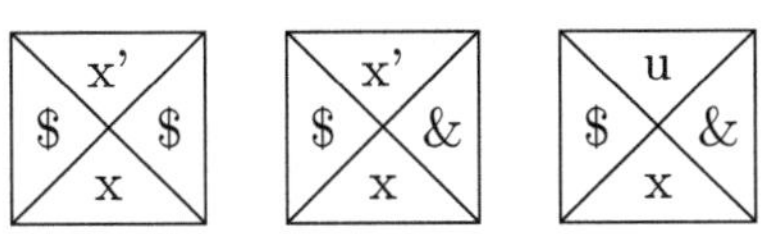

two will be used, and one will be excess. By the pigeonhole principle either the second or the third tile **has** to be used, and when used these tiles are equivalent because of differing only in the colour placed on the border. Thus we may assume that always the third tile is used and either the first or the second tile are unused. Less formally, an element can either appear in two not picked triples (the second and the third tile are used), or in one picked and one not picked triple (the first and third tile are used). Note here that no matter which of the first two tiles is the excess one it can be matched with the other tiles constructed for that element, producing a set (call it "dumping set"), with cost 0. For a detailed example of an arrangement, including the placement of excess tiles, see Fig. 4.

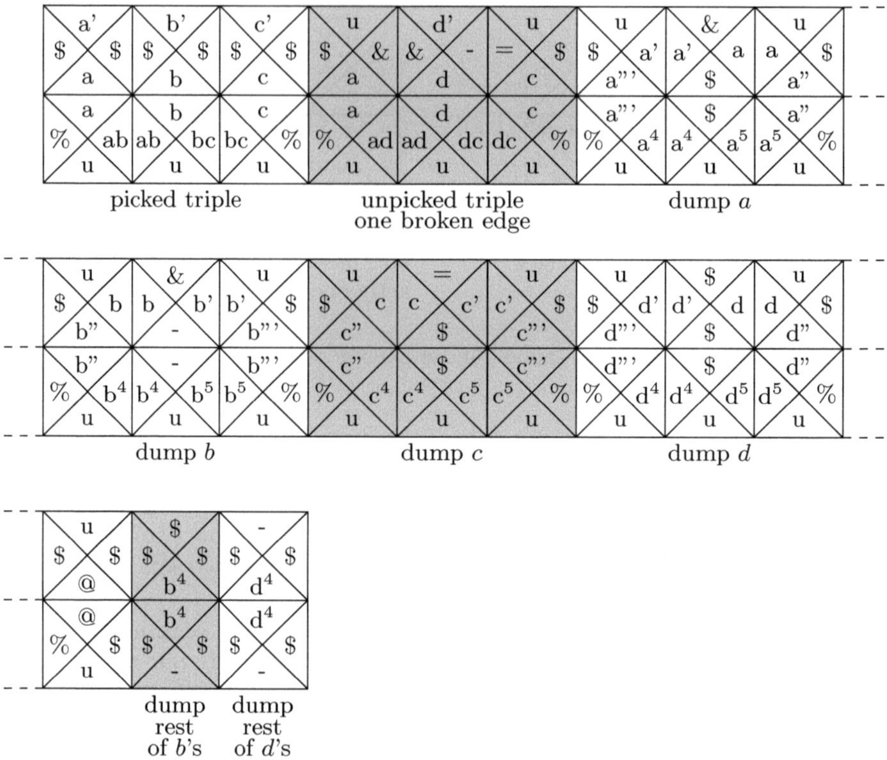

Fig. 4. A solution of the EMP instance, split into three pieces, corresponding to the Max-3DM-B instance consisting of choosing triple (a,b,c) but not (a,d,c)

3.3 Some Useful Lemmas

We say that a *good set* is a formation of six tiles arranged as seen in Fig. 3(a). Such a set in a solution of our instance of EMP always corresponds to a triple (a, b, c) that we want to pick in the Max-3DM-B instance.

A transformation of a solution to the EMP instance to a solution to the Max-3DM-B instance can easily be done in polynomial time by selecting the good sets, and picking the corresponding triples. By the construction of the instance of EMP there is a solution to it of the form seen in Fig. 4, which corresponds to the optimal solution of the initial Max 3-DM-B instance.

Lemma 1. *Given an instance C of Max-3DM-B containing n triples, an instance D of EMP can be constructed as described above. Any solution to D that breaks k edges yields a solution to C consisting of at least $n - k$ triples.*

Proof. *The core idea of this proof is to show that if k edges are broken in the solution to D, then this solution must contain at least $n - k$ good sets.*

Assume that our instance D has at least k_1 tiles of Type 2 *that are adjacent to a broken edge in the solution (note that $k_1 \leq k$). This means that the form of set seen in Fig. 5(a) will appear $n - k_1$ times.*

The symbol '?' in Fig. 5 is a placeholder indicating that the colour of that edge is still unknown. Assume now that out of these $n - k_1$ sets, k_2 have the upper edge of the bottom right tile broken, or the right edge of the top tile broken. This means that there are at least $n - k_1 - k_2$ sets where these edges are not broken. The only way for this to be the case, is when the sets look like in Fig. 5(b).

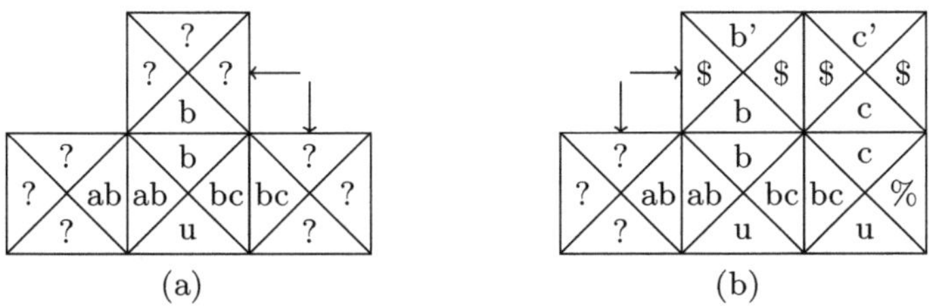

Fig. 5.

Finally, out of these $n - k_1 - k_2$ sets, let k_3 have the top edge of the bottom left tile broken, or the leftmost edge of the top row broken. It follows that we have at least $n - k_1 - k_2 - k_3$ good sets. As $k_1 + k_2 + k_3 \leq k$ (the total number of broken edges is at most k), we conclude that we have at least $n - k$ good sets, and thus select $n - k$ triples in our solution of the Max 3DM-B instance. □

As a natural consequence of the way the EMP instance is constructed and Lemma 1, we get the following Lemma.

Lemma 2. *Given an instance x of Max-3DM-B, let $f(x)$ denote the corresponding instance produced as described in Sect. 3.1. Given an optimal solution to $f(x)$, by picking the triples that correspond to good sets in the optimal solution of $f(x)$, an optimal solution to x is produced.*

3.4 The Reduction Preserves Approximability

Lemma 3. *The function f defined in Sect. 3.1 transforms instances of Max-3DM-B to instances of EMP, and can be computed in polynomial time.*

Lemma 4. *There is a polynomial-time computable function g, such that if y is a solution to $f(x)$, $g(y)$ is a solution to x.*

Proof. The function g takes as input a solution to an instance $f(x)$ of EMP, and produces a solution to instance x of Max-3DM-B. This is done by selecting the triples corresponding to the good sets. Clearly also g can be computed in polynomial time. □

Lemma 5. *Let x be a given instance to problem Max-3DM-B, with $B = 2$, $|E|$ representing the number of elements in instance x (that is $|E| = |X|+|Y|+|Z|$) and the number of triples in that instance being n. Then the following hold:*

- $OPT_{\text{Max-3DM-B}}(x) \geq \frac{1}{4}n$
- $OPT_{\text{Max-3DM-B}}(x) \geq \frac{1}{9}|E|$

Proof. Every element can appear at most 2 times, and in at most 2 triples. Thus, for every selected triple there can be **at most** 6 elements that never get used in another selected triple (2 for every variable that is used in the selected one).

To make this more clear, if triple (a, b, c) is selected then a can appear in one more triple (two occurrences in total), with two new, unique elements. For example $(a, 1, 2)$. The same is the case for elements b and c. We also notice that for a we can have up to one more triple that is unselected, the same for b and c. Thus, if we select (a, b, c) in the worst case we may not select 3 more triples which in the worst case again, would contain 6 more unique elements.

As an example, consider having the following 4 triples that use 9 elements and only 1 triple can get selected: $\{(a, b, c), (a, 1, 2), (3, b, 4), (5, 6, c)\}$. □

Lemma 6. *Let $\alpha = 150$. For every instance x of Max-3DM-B with $B = 2$ of size $n \geq n_0$ for some constant $n_0 > 0$:*

$$\text{OPT}_{\text{EMP}}(f(x)) \leq \alpha \text{OPT}_{\text{Max-3DM-B}}(x) \ .$$

Proof. Assume that the optimum of the Max-3DM-B (with $B = 2$) instance has k non-selected triples. Then $OPT_{\text{Max-3DM-B}}(x) \geq n - k$. Now, $f(x)$ will consist of 3 tiles for every triple, and less than or equal to 10 tiles for every element. The most tiles will be produced if the element is in set Y, when we produce $7 + (\lambda + 1)$ tiles given that it appears λ times in total (here, $\lambda = 2$). Thus, the number of tiles is $|T| \leq 3n + 10|E|$. If we consider the optimum of the corresponding EMP instance to be the number of edges in a solution that are not adjacent to the border, and assume that the optimal solution has again k broken edges (we can always achieve this by placing the tiles as seen in Fig. 4), then the optimal solution is at most the number of edges that are not adjacent to the border:

$$\begin{aligned}
OPT_{\text{EMP}}(f(x)) \leq |T|/2 + |T| - 2 - k = 1.5|T| - 2 - k \leq \\
1.5 \cdot (3n + 10|E|) - 2 - k = 4.5n + 15|E| - 2 - k = 4.5n - k + 15|E| - 2 \leq \\
3.5n + OPT_{\text{Max-3DM-B}}(x) + 15 \cdot 9 \cdot OPT_{\text{Max-3DM-B}}(x) - 2 \leq \\
3.5 \cdot 4 OPT_{\text{Max-3DM-B}}(x) + 136 \cdot OPT_{\text{Max-3DM-B}}(x) - 2 = \\
150 OPT_{\text{Max-3DM-B}}(x) - 2 \ .
\end{aligned}$$ □

Lemma 7. *For $\beta = 1$, and for every solution y to $f(x)$ the following inequality holds:*

$$\begin{aligned}
|OPT_{\text{Max-3DM-B}}(x) - c_{\text{Max-3DM-B}}(x, g(y))| \leq \\
\beta |OPT_{\text{EMP}}(f(x)) - c_{\text{EMP}}(f(x), y)| \ .
\end{aligned}$$

Proof. $OPT_{\text{EMP}}(f(x)) = \left(\frac{3}{2}|T| - 2\right) - k$ *that is, the optimal solution to problem EMP on instance* $f(x)$ *breaks* k *edges, and a solution* y *to* $f(x)$ *breaks* k' *edges (thus* $c_{\text{EMP}}(f(x), y) = \left(\frac{3}{2}|T| - 2\right) - k'$ *(Note that our instance has dimensions* $2 \times \frac{|T|}{2}$*). Because of Lemma 2,* $OPT_{\text{Max-3DM-B}}(x) = n - k$*. Also, obviously* $c_{\text{Max-3DM-B}}(x, g(y)) = n - k'$*. The above means that there is a positive constant* $\beta = 1$*, such that for every solution* y *to* $f(x)$*,* $n - k - (n - k') \leq \beta\left(\frac{3}{2}|T| - k - 2 - \left(\frac{3}{2}|T| - k' - 2\right)\right) \Rightarrow k' - k \leq \beta(k' - k)$*,* □

As a natural consequence of the definition of the L-reduction, and Lemmas 2, 3, 4, 6 and 7,

Lemma 8. *The reduction described above, is an L-reduction from Max-3DM-B to EMP with* $\alpha = 150$ *and* $\beta = 1$*.*

The following theorem follows naturally,

Theorem 2. *Edge Matching Puzzle is APX-hard, and thus under the P≠NP assumption it does not admit a PTAS.*

3.5 APX-Completeness

Theorem 3. *Edge Matching Puzzle is in APX.*

Proof. Suppose that the optimal solution to a given EMP instance is known and has cost OPT*. We then can construct a graph* G *by representing each tile as a node, and for every matched edge in the optimal solution draw an edge between the corresponding tiles/nodes. Then one can proceed from this graph:*

Initialise an empty list M. While there are edges left in G pick one of them, push it into M, and remove both its endpoints and their adjacent edges from G.

As every tile has 4 *edges, the degree of every node in* G *has to be at most* 4*, so there are at most* 8 *edges removed in every step of the algorithm, and* M *has size at least* $OPT/8$*. Now, the following is a constant factor approximation algorithm for EMP:*

Construct a graph G' by creating a node for every tile, and connecting with edges all the pairs of nodes corresponding to two tiles with at least one edge with the same colour. Find a maximum matching M' of G' using a polynomial time algorithm [13]. Now, for every edge uv in M' match the tiles corresponding to vertices u and v into a pair of tiles. Place the pairs of tiles into the given rectange in a snake fashion: fill in row by row, and if the rows have odd size place the last tile so that it takes one place in the current row and one in the next one. If there are single tiles left over place them arbitrarily in the free space of the rectangle.

The algorithm described above is running in polynomial time. As the matching M' *is maximum,* $|M'| \geq |M|$*, the solution returned by the algorithm has cost at least* $1/8$ *times* OPT*, and it is an* $\Theta(1)$*-approximation algorithm for EMP.* □

As a natural consequence of Theorems 2 and 3,

Theorem 4. *Edge Matching Puzzle is APX-complete.*

3.6 Approximation Lower Bound

This subsection, copes with finding an approximation lower bound for the EMP problem using the following approximation lower bound for Max-3DM-B:

Theorem 5 ([12]). *It is NP-hard to approximate the solution of Max-3DM-B, with exactly two occurrences of every element, to within any constant smaller than* $\delta' = \frac{95}{94}$.

An approximation lower bound for EMP can now be easily derived:

Theorem 6. *It is NP-hard to approximate the solution of EMP to within any constant smaller than* $c' = \frac{14250}{14249}$.

Proof. *It easily follows from Theorems 1 and 5 by using* $\alpha = 150$ *and* $\beta = 1$*:*

$$c' = \frac{1}{1 - \frac{1-(1/\delta')}{\alpha\beta}} = \frac{14250}{14249}$$

□

4 The Corresponding Minimisation Problem

In this section we study two other optimisation variants of the problem: the absolute error for both the minimisation and the maximisation version, and the approximation ratio of the minimisation version. For the latter, as the optimum solution could have cost 0, to make the problem interesting we introduce an assumption that changes the problem a bit; namely that the optimum solution has exactly k edges broken.

We define a minimisation and a maximisation problem to be *corresponding* when the following holds: For every instance with a fixed rectangle, the sum of the costs of the maximisation and the minimisation version is constant. Formally, there exists some $M(x)$ such that $c_{\max}(x,y) = M(x) - c_{\min}(x,y)$, and $OPT_{P_{\min}} = M(x) - OPT_{P_{\max}}$. In the EMP case, $M(x)$ is the number of edges that instance x has in total (either broken or non-broken).

4.1 Absolute Error

It has been shown that EMP does not admit a PTAS. Here it will also be shown that it cannot be approximated within an absolute error of size $o(n)$ if P≠NP.

Theorem 7. *Any maximisation problem* $P_{\max}$ *with an optimal solution* $OPT_{P_{\max}} = \Omega(n)$*, which can be approximated within an absolute error of* $o(n)$*, admits a PTAS for large enough instances.*

Proof. *Let* $OPT_{P_{\max}} = \Omega(n)$*, and* $f(n) = o(n)$ *be an absolute error within which we can approximate the problem and* $\epsilon = \frac{f(n)}{OPT_{P_{\max}}}$*. Then, by definition, for* *the feasible solution y returned by the approximation algorithm when run on instance x,*

$$c(x,y) \geq OPT_{P_{\max}} - f(n) = OPT_{P_{\max}} \left(1 - \frac{f(n)}{OPT_{P_{\max}}}\right)$$

$$\Rightarrow c(x,y) \geq OPT_{P_{\max}}(1-\epsilon) \overset{\forall \epsilon \leq \frac{1}{2}}{\geq} \frac{OPT_{P_{\max}}}{1+2\epsilon} \Rightarrow 1+2\epsilon \geq \frac{OPT_{P_{\max}}}{c(x,y)}$$

which – as ϵ can be made arbitrarily small for large enough instances – implies a PTAS for $P_{\max}$. □

Note 2. For $P_{\max}$ to have a PTAS, $f \in o(g)$ would be enough.

Theorem 8. *If a minimisation problem $P_{\min}$ can be approximated within an absolute error of $o(n)$ and it has a corresponding maximisation problem with $OPT_{P_{\max}} = \Omega(n)$ then $P_{\max}$ admits a PTAS for large enough instances.*

Proof. Let again $OPT_{P_{\max}} = \Omega(n)$, and $f(n) = o(n)$ be an absolute error within which we can approximate the problem. By definition, we have that

$$c_{\min}(x,y) \leq (M(x) - OPT_{P_{\max}}) + f(n) \Rightarrow M(x) - c_{\min}(x,y) \geq OPT_{P_{\max}} - f(n)$$
$$\Rightarrow c_{\max}(x,y) \geq OPT_{P_{\max}} - f(n)$$

and the rest of the proof is identical with the proof of Theorem 7. □

Theorem 9. *EMP cannot be approximated within an absolute error of size $o(n)$, neither in the minimisation, nor in the maximisation version.*

Proof. That the maximisation version cannot be approximated within an absolute error of size $o(n)$ directly follows from Theorem 7, as it admits no PTAS and has an optimum of size $\Omega(n)$. Now clearly, because of Theorem 8 the corresponding minimimisation version of EMP also cannot be approximated within an absolute error of $o(n)$. □

4.2 Approximation Ratio

In this subsection a result on the approximation ratio of the minimisation version is presented, namely, the minimisation version cannot be approximated within an approximation ratio of $o(n)$.

Theorem 10. *If a minimisation problem $P_{\min}$ with $OPT_{P_{\min}} = \Omega(1)$, can be approximated within an approximation ratio of $o(n)$, then it also can be approximated within an absolute error of $o(n)$.*

Proof. Assume that $P_{\min}$ is a minimisation problem with $OPT_{P_{\min}} = \Omega(1)$ and that A is an approximation algorithm that can approximate it within an approximation ratio of $o(n)$. Then for some $h(n) = o(n)$ being the approximation ratio,

$$\forall x, c_{\min}(x, A(x)) \leq OPT_{P_{\min}} h(n) \Rightarrow c_{\min}(x, A(x)) \leq o(n)$$
$$\Rightarrow c_{\min}(x, A(x)) \leq OPT_{P_{\min}} + f(n)$$

for some function $f = o(n)$. Naturally that $P_{\min}$ can be approximated within an absolute error of $o(n)$. □

Theorem 11. *The minimisation version of EMP cannot be approximated within an approximation ratio of $o(n)$, assuming that $OPT_{\mathrm{EMP}_{\min}} \neq 0$.*

Proof. *For EMP when $OPT_{\mathrm{EMP}_{\min}} \neq 0$ it holds that $OPT_{\mathrm{EMP}_{\min}} = \Omega(1)$. Thus applying Theorems 9 and 10 we get that the minimisation version of EMP cannot be approximated within an approximation ratio of $o(n)$.* □

References

1. Demaine, E.D., Demaine, M.L.: Jigsaw Puzzles, Edge Matching, and Polyonymo Packing: Connections and Complexity. Graphs and Combinatorics 23, 195–208 (2007)
2. Berger, R.: The Undecidability of the Domino Problem. Memoirs of the American Mathematical Society 66 (1966)
3. Garey, M.R., Johnson, D.S., Papadimitriou, C.H.: Computers and Intractability: A Guide to the Theory of NP-completeness, p. 257. W.H. Freeman & Co., New York (1979)
4. Savelsberg, M.P.W., van Emde Boas, P.: BOUNDED TILING, an Alternative to SATISFIABILITY? In: Proceedings 2nd Frege Conference, vol. 20, pp. 354–363. Akademie Verlag, Schwerin (1984)
5. Chlebus, B.S.: Domino-Tiling Games. Journal of Computer and System Sciences 32, 374–392 (1986)
6. Benoist, T., Bourreau, E.: Fast Global Filtering for Eternity II. Constraint Programming Letters 3, 36–49 (2008)
7. Ansótegui, C., Béjar, R., Fernández, C., Mateau, C.: Edge Matching Puzzles as Hard SAT/CSP Benchmarks. In: Stuckey, P.J. (ed.) CP 2008. LNCS, vol. 5202, pp. 560–565. Springer, Heidelberg (2008)
8. Ausiello, G., Crescenzi, P., Gambosi, G., Kann, V., Marchetti-Spaccamela, A., Protasi, M.: Complexity and Approximation: Combinatorial Optimization Problems and their Approximability Properties. Springer, Heidelberg (1999)
9. Papadimitriou, C.H., Yannakakis, M.: Optimization, Approximation, and Complexity Classes. Journal of Computer and System Sciences 43, 425–440 (1991)
10. Kann, V.: Maximum Bounded 3-Dimensional Matching is MAX SNP-Complete. Information Processing Letters 37, 27–35 (1991)
11. Chlebìk, M., Chlebìkovà, J.: Approximation Hardness for Small Occurrence Instances of NP-hard Problems. In: Petreschi, R., Persiano, G., Silvestri, R. (eds.) CIAC 2003. LNCS, vol. 2653. Springer, Heidelberg (2003); (also ECCC Report) (2002)
12. Chlebìk, M., Chlebìkovà, J.: Inapproximability Results for Bounded Variants of Optimization Problems. In: Proocedings of FCT 2003: the 14th International Symposium on Fundamentals of Computation Theory (2003)
13. Cormen, T., Leiserson, C., Rivest, R., Stein, C.: Introduction to Algorithms, 2nd edn. MIT Press, Cambridge (2001)

A Linear Time Algorithm for Finding Three Edge-Disjoint Paths in Eulerian Networks

Maxim A. Babenko*, Ignat I. Kolesnichenko, and Ilya P. Razenshteyn

Moscow State University
max@adde.math.msu.su, {ignat1990,ilyaraz}@gmail.com

Abstract. Consider an undirected graph $G = (VG, EG)$ and a set of six *terminals* $T = \{s_1, s_2, s_3, t_1, t_2, t_3\} \subseteq VG$. The goal is to find a collection $\mathcal{P}$ of three edge-disjoint paths P_1, P_2, and P_3, where P_i connects nodes s_i and t_i $(i = 1, 2, 3)$.

Results obtained by Robertson and Seymour by graph minor techniques imply a polynomial time solvability of this problem. The time bound of their algorithm is $O(m^3)$ (hereinafter we assume $n := |VG|$, $m := |EG|$, $n = O(m)$).

In this paper we consider a special, *Eulerian* case of G and T. Namely, construct the *demand graph* $H = (VG, \{s_1t_1, s_2t_2, s_3t_3\})$. The edges of H correspond to the desired paths in $\mathcal{P}$. In the Eulerian case the degrees of all nodes in the (multi-) graph $G + H$ $(= (VG, EG \cup EH))$ are even.

Schrijver showed that, under the assumption of Eulerianess, cut conditions provide a criterion for the existence of $\mathcal{P}$. This, in particular, implies that checking for existence of $\mathcal{P}$ can be done in $O(m)$ time. Our result is a combinatorial $O(m)$-time algorithm that constructs $\mathcal{P}$ (if the latter exists).

1 Introduction

We shall use some standard graph-theoretic notation through the paper. For an undirected graph G, we denote its sets of nodes and edges by VG and EG, respectively. For a directed graph, we speak of arcs rather than edges and denote the arc set of G by AG. A similar notation is used for paths, trees, and etc. We allow parallel edges and arcs but not loops in graphs.

For an undirected graph G and $U \subseteq VG$, we write $\delta_G(U)$ to denote the set of edges with exactly one endpoint in U. If G is a digraph then the set of arcs entering (resp. leaving) U is denoted by $\delta_G^{\text{in}}(U)$ and $\delta_G^{\text{out}}(U)$. For a graph G and a subset $U \subseteq VG$, we write $G[U]$ to denote the subgraph of G induced by U.

Let G be an undirected graph. Consider six nodes $s_1, s_2, s_3, t_1, t_2, t_3$ in G. These nodes need not be distinct and will be called *terminals*. Our main problem is as follows:

* Supported by RFBR grant 09-01-00709-a.

J. van Leeuwen et al. (Eds.): SOFSEM 2010, LNCS 5901, pp. 165–175, 2010.

(1) Find a collection of three edge-disjoint paths P_1, P_2, P_3, where P_i goes from s_i to t_i (for $i = 1, 2, 3$).

Robertson and Seymour [4] developed sophisticated graph minor techniques that, in particular, imply a polynomial time solvability of the above problem. More specifically, they deal with the general case where k pairs of terminals $\{s_1, t_1\}, \ldots, \{s_k, t_k\}$ are given and are requested to be connected by paths. These paths are required to be *node-disjoint*. The edge-disjoint case, however, can be easily simulated by considering the line graph of G. For fixed k, the running time of the algorithm of Robertson and Seymour is cubic in the number of nodes (with a constant heavily depending on k). Since after reducing the edge-disjoint case to the node-disjoint one the number of nodes becomes $\Theta(m)$, one gets an algorithm of time complexity $O(m^3)$ (where, throughout the paper, $n := |VG|$, $m := |EG|$; moreover, it is assumed that $n = O(m)$). If k is a part of input, then it was shown by Marx [3] that finding k edge-disjoint paths is NP-complete even in the Eulerian case.

We may also consider a general *integer multiflow problem*. To this aim, consider an arbitrary (multi-)graph G and also an arbitrary (multi-)graph H obeying $VH = VG$. The latter graph H is called the *demand graph*. The task is to find a function f assigning each edge $uv \in EH$ a u–v path $f(uv)$ in G such that the resulting paths $\{f(e) \mid e \in EH\}$ are edge-disjoint. Hence, the edges of H correspond to the paths in the desired solution. By a *problem instance* we mean the pair (G, H). An instance is *feasible* if the desired collection of edge-disjoint paths exists; *infeasible* otherwise.

In case of three terminal pairs one has $H = (VG, \{s_1t_1, s_2t_2, s_3t_3\})$. We can simplify the problem and get better complexity results by introducing some additional assumptions regarding the degrees of nodes in G. Put $G + H := (VG, EG \cup EH)$. Suppose the degrees of all nodes in $G + H$ are even; the corresponding instances are called *Eulerian.*

As observed by Schrijver, for the Eulerian case there exists a simple feasibility criterion. For a subset $U \subseteq VG$ let $d_G(U)$ (resp. $d_H(U)$) denote $|\delta_G(U)|$ (resp. $|\delta_H(U)|$).

Theorem 1 ([5], Theorem 72.3). *An Eulerian instance (G, H) with three pairs of terminals is feasible if and only if $d_G(U) \geq d_H(U)$ holds for each $U \subseteq VG$.*

The inequalities figured in the above theorem are called *cut conditions.* In a general problem (where demand graph H is arbitrary) these inequalities provide necessary (but not always sufficient) feasibility requirements.

For the Eulerian case, the problem is essentially equivalent to constructing two paths (out of three requested by the demand graph). Indeed, if edge-disjoint paths P_1 and P_2 (where, as earlier, P_i connects s_i and t_i, $i = 1, 2$) are found, the remaining path P_3 always exists. Indeed, remove the edges of P_1 and P_2 from G. Assuming $s_3 \neq t_3$, the remaining graph has exactly two odd vertices, namely s_3 and t_3. Hence, these vertices are in the same connected component. However, once we no longer regard s_3 and t_3 as terminals and try to solve the four terminal instance, we lose the Eulerianess property. There are some efficient algorithms (e.g. [7,6,8,9]) for the case of two pairs of terminals (without Eulerianess assumption) but no linear time bound seems to be known.

The proof of Theorem 1 presented in [5] is rather simple but non-constructive. Our main result is as follows:

Theorem 2. *An Eulerian instance of the problem (1) can be checked for feasibility in $O(m)$ time. If the check turns out positive, the desired path collection can be constructed in $O(m)$ time.*

2 The Algorithm

2.1 Preliminaries

This subsection describes some basic techniques for working with edge-disjoint paths. If the reader is familiar with network flow theory, this subsection may be omitted.

Suppose we are given an undirected graph G and a pair of distinct nodes s (*source*) and t (*sink*) from VG. An *s–t cut* is a subset $U \subseteq VG$ such that $s \in U$, $t \notin U$.

Edge-disjoint path collections can be described in flow-like terms as follows. Let $\overrightarrow{G}$ denote the digraph obtained from G by replacing each edge with a pair of oppositely directed arcs. A subset $F \subseteq A\overrightarrow{G}$ is called *balanced* if $\left|F \cap \delta^{\text{in}}(v)\right| = \left|F \cap \delta^{\text{out}}(v)\right|$ holds for each $v \in VG - \{s, t\}$. Consider the *value* of F defined as follows:

$$\text{val}(F) := \left|F \cap \delta^{\text{out}}(s)\right| - \left|F \cap \delta^{\text{in}}(s)\right|.$$

Proofs of upcoming Lemma 1, Lemma 2, and Lemma 3 are quite standard and hence omitted (see, e.g. [2,1]).

Lemma 1. *Each balanced arc set decomposes into a collection arc-disjoint s–t paths $\mathcal{P}_{st}$, a collection of t–s paths $\mathcal{P}_{ts}$, and a collection of cycles $\mathcal{C}$. Each such decomposition obeys $|\mathcal{P}_{st}| - |\mathcal{P}_{ts}| = \text{val}(F)$. Also, such a decomposition can be carried out in $O(m)$ time.*

Obviously, for each collection $\mathcal{P}$ of edge-disjoint s–t paths in G there exists a balanced arc set of value $|\mathcal{P}|$. Vice versa, each balanced arc set F in $\overrightarrow{G}$ generates at least $\text{val}(F)$ edge-disjoint s–t paths in G. Hence, finding a maximum cardinality collection of edge-disjoint s–t paths in G amounts to maximizing the value of a balanced arc set.

Given a balanced set F, consider the *residual digraph* $\overrightarrow{G}_F := (VG, (A\overrightarrow{G} - F) \cup F^{-1})$, where $F^{-1} := \left\{a^{-1} \mid a \in F\right\}$ and a^{-1} denotes the arc reverse to a.

Lemma 2. *Let P be an arc-simple s–t path in $\overrightarrow{G}_F$. Construct the arc set F' as follows: (i) take set F; (ii) add all arcs $a \in AP$ such that $a^{-1} \notin F$; (iii) remove all arcs $a \in F$ such that $a^{-1} \in AP$. Then, F' is balanced and obeys* $\text{val}(F') = \text{val}(F) + 1$.

Lemma 3. *Suppose there is no s–t path in* $\overrightarrow{G}_F$. *Then F is of maximum value. Moreover, the set U of nodes that are reachable from s in* $\overrightarrow{G}_F$ *obeys* $d_G(U) = \mathrm{val}(F)$. *Additionally, U is an inclusion-wise minimum such set.*

Hence, to find a collection of r edge-disjoint s–t paths one needs to run a reachability algorithm in a digraph at most r times. Totally, this takes $O(rm)$ time and is known as the *method of Ford and Fulkerson* [2].

2.2 Checking for Feasibility

We start with a number of easy observations. Firstly, there are some simpler versions of (1). Suppose only one pair of terminals is given, i.e. $H = (VG, \{s_1t_1\})$. Then the problem consists in checking if s_1 and t_1 are in the same connected component of G. Note that if the instance (G, H) is Eulerian then it is always feasible since a connected component cannot contain a single odd vertex. An s_1–t_1 path P_1 can be found in $O(m)$ time.

Next, consider the case of two pairs of terminals, i.e. $H = (VG, \{s_1t_1, s_2t_2\})$. Connected components of G not containing any of the terminals may be ignored. Hence, one may assume that G is connected since otherwise the problem reduces to a pair of instances each having a single pair of terminals.

Lemma 4. *Let* (G, H) *be an Eulerian instance with two pairs of terminals. If G is connected then* (G, H) *is feasible. Also, the desired path collection* $\{P_1, P_2\}$ *can be found in* $O(m)$ *time.*

Proof
The argument is the same as in Section 1. Consider an arbitrary s_1–t_1 path P_1 and remove it from G. The resulting graph G' may lose connectivity, however, s_2 and t_2 are the only odd vertices in it (assuming $s_2 \neq t_2$). Hence, s_2 and t_2 are in the same connected component of G', we can trace an s_2–t_2 path P_2 and, hence, solve the problem. The time complexity of this procedure is obviously $O(m)$. □

Now we explain how the feasibility of an Eulerian instance (G, H) having three pairs of terminals can be checked in linear time. Put $T := \{s_1, s_2, s_3, t_1, t_2, t_3\}$. There are exponentially many subsets $U \subseteq VG$. For each subset U consider its *signature* $U^* := U \cap T$. Fix an arbitrary signature $U^* \subseteq T$ and assume w.l.o.g. that $\delta_H(U^*) = \{s_1t_1, \ldots, s_kt_k\}$. Construct a new undirected graph $G(U^*)$ as follows: add source s^*, sink t^*, and $2k$ auxiliary edges $s^*s_1, \ldots, s^*s_k, t_1t^*, \ldots, t_kt^*$ to G.

Let $\nu(U^*)$ be the maximum cardinality of a collection of edge-disjoint s^*–t^* paths in $G(U^*)$. We restate Theorem 1 as follows:

Lemma 5. *An Eulerian instance* (G, H) *with three pairs of terminals is feasible if and only if* $\nu(U^*) \geq d_H(U^*)$ *for each* $U^* \subseteq T$,

Proof

Necessity being obvious, we show sufficiency. Let (G, H) be infeasible, then by Theorem 1 $d_G(U) < d_H(U)$ for some $U \subseteq VG$. Consider the corresponding signature $U^* := U \cap T$. One has $d_H(U) = d_H(U^*)$, hence there is a collection of $d_H(U)$ edge-disjoint s^*–t^* paths in $G(U^*)$. Each of these paths crosses the cut $\delta_G(U)$ by a unique edge, hence $d_G(U) \geq d_H(U)$ — a contradiction. □

By the above lemma, to check (G, H) for feasibility one has to validate the inequalities $\nu(U^*) \geq d_H(U^*)$ for all $U^* \subseteq T$. For each fixed signature U^* we consider graph $G(U^*)$, start with an empty balanced arc set and perform up to three augmentations, as explained in Subsection 2.1. Therefore, the corresponding inequality is checked in $O(m)$ time. The number of signatures is $O(1)$, which gives the linear time for the whole feasibility check.

We now present our first $O(m^2)$ time algorithm for finding the required path collection. It will not be used in the sequel but gives some initial insight on the problem. Consider an instance (G, H) and let $s_1, t_1 \in T$ be a pair of terminals ($s_1 t_1 \in EH$). If $s_1 = t_1$ then the problem reduces to four terminals and is solvable in linear time, as discussed earlier. Otherwise, let e be an edge incident to s_1, and put s_1' to be the other endpoint of e. We construct a new problem instance (G_e, H_e), where $G_e = G - e$, $H_e = H - s_1 t_1 + s_1' t_1$ (i.e. we remove edge e and choose s_1' instead of s_1 as a terminal). Switching from (G, H) to (G_e, H_e) is called *a local move*. Local moves preserve Eulerianess. If a local move generates a feasible instance then it is called *feasible*, *infeasible* otherwise.

If (G_e, H_e) is feasible (say, $\mathcal{P}_e$ is a solution) then so is (G, H) as we can append the edge e to the s_1'–t_1 path in $\mathcal{P}_e$ and obtain a solution $\mathcal{P}$ to (G, H).

Since (G, H) is feasible, there must be a feasible local move (e.g. along the first edge of an s_1–t_1 path in a solution). We find this move by enumerating all edges e incident to s_1 and checking (G_e, H_e) for feasibility. Once e is found, we recurse to the instance (G_e, H_e) having one less edge. This way, a solution to the initial problem is constructed.

To estimate the time complexity, note that if a move along some edge e is discovered to be infeasible at some stage then it remains infeasible for the rest of the algorithm (since the edge set of G can only decrease). Hence, each edge in G can be checked for feasibility at most once. Each such check costs $O(m)$ time, thus yielding the total bound of $O(m^2)$. This is already an improvement over the algorithm of Robertson and Seymour. However, we can do much better.

2.3 Reduction to a Critical Instance

To solve an Eulerian instance of (1) in linear time we start by constructing an arbitrary node-simple s_1–t_1 path P_1. Let $e_1, \ldots, e_k$ be the sequence of edges of P_1. For each $i = 0, \ldots, k$ let (G_i, H_i) be the instance obtained from the initial one (G, H) by a sequence of local moves along the edges $e_1, \ldots, e_i$. In particular, $(G_0, H_0) = (G, H)$.

If (G_k, H_k) is feasible (which can be checked in $O(m)$ time) then the problem reduces to four terminals and can be solved in linear time by Lemma 4. Otherwise we find an index j such that (G_j, H_j) is a feasible instance whereas (G_{j+1}, H_{j+1}) is not feasible.

This is done by walking in the reverse direction along P_1 and considering the sequence of instances (G_k, H_k), ..., (G_0, H_0). Fix an arbitrary signature U^* in (G_k, H_k). As we go back along P_1, terminal s_1 is moving. We apply these moves to U^* and construct a sequence of signatures U_i^* in (G_i, H_i). ($i = 1, \ldots, k$; in particular, $U_k^* = U^*$). Let $\nu_i(U^*)$ be the maximum cardinality of an edge-disjoint collection of s^*–t^* paths in $G_i(U_i^*)$.

Consider a consequent pair $G_{i+1}(U_{i+1}^*)$ and $G_i(U_i^*)$. When s_1 is moved from node v back to v', edge s^*v is removed and edges s^*v' and $v'v$ are inserted. Note, that this cannot decrease the maximum cardinality of an edge-disjoint s^*–t^* paths collection (if the dropped edge s^*v was used by some path in a collection, then we may replace it by a sequence of edges s^*v' and $v'v$). Hence,

$$\nu_0(U_0^*) \geq \nu_1(U_1^*) \geq \ldots \geq \nu_k(U_k^*).$$

Our goal is to find, for each choice of U^*, the largest index i (denote it by $j(U^*)$) such that

$$\nu_i(U_i^*) \geq d_H(U_i^*).$$

Then, taking

$$j := \min_{U^* \subseteq T} j(U^*)$$

we get the desired feasible instance (G_j, H_j) such that (G_{j+1}, H_{j+1}) is infeasible.

To compute the values $\nu_i(U_i^*)$ consider the following dynamic problem. Suppose one is given an undirected graph Γ with distinguished source s and sink t, and also an integer $r \geq 1$. We need the following operations:

> Query: Report $\min(r, c)$, where c is the maximum cardinality of a collection of edge-disjoint s–t paths in Γ.
>
> Move(v, v'): Let v, v' be a pair nodes in VG, $v \neq s$, $v' \neq s$, $sv \in E\Gamma$. Remove the edge sv from Γ and add edges sv' and $v'v$ to Γ.

Lemma 6. *There exists a data structure that can execute any sequence of* Query *and* Move *requests in $O(rm)$ time.*

Proof
We use a version of a folklore incremental reachability data structure. When graph Γ is given to us, we start computing a balanced arc set F in $\overrightarrow{\Gamma}$ of maximum value $\mathrm{val}(F)$ but stop if $\mathrm{val}(F)$ becomes equal to r. This takes $O(rm)$ time. During the usage of the required data structure, the number of edge-disjoint s–t paths (hence, $\mathrm{val}(F)$) cannot decrease (it can be shown using arguments similar to the described earlier). Therefore, if $\mathrm{val}(F) = r$ we may stop any maintenance and report the value of r on each Query.

Otherwise, as $\mathrm{val}(F)$ is maximum, there is no s–t path in $\overrightarrow{\Gamma}_F$ by Lemma 3. As long as no r edge-disjoint s–t paths in Γ exist, the following objects are maintained:

- a balanced subset $F \subseteq A\Gamma$ of maximum value $\mathrm{val}(F)$ (which is less than r);
- an inclusionwise maximal directed tree $\mathcal{T}$ rooted at t and consisting of arcs from $\overrightarrow{\Gamma}_F$ (oriented towards to t).

In particular, $\mathcal{T}$ covers exactly the set of nodes that can reach t by a path in $\overrightarrow{\Gamma}_F$. Hence, s is not covered by $\mathcal{T}$ (by Lemma 2).

Consider a MOVE(v, v') request. We update F as follows. If $sv \notin F$, then no change is necessary. Otherwise, we remove sv from F and also add arcs sv' and $v'v$ to F. This way, F remains balanced and $\mathrm{val}(F)$ is preserved.

Next, we describe the maintenance of $\mathcal{T}$. Adding an arbitrary edge e to Γ is simple. Recall that each edge in Γ generates a pair of oppositely directed arcs in $\overrightarrow{\Gamma}$. Let $a = pq$ be one of these two arcs generated by e. Suppose a is present in $\overrightarrow{\Gamma}_F$. If $a \in \delta^{\mathrm{in}}(V\mathcal{T})$ (i.e., p is not reachable and q is reachable) then add a to $\mathcal{T}$. Next, continue growing $\mathcal{T}$ incrementally from p by executing a depth-first search and stopping at nodes already covered by $\mathcal{T}$. This way, $\mathcal{T}$ is extended to a maximum directed tree rooted at t. In other cases ($a \notin \delta^{\mathrm{in}}(V\mathcal{T})$) arc a is ignored.

Next consider deleting edge sv from G. We argue that its removal cannot invalidate $\mathcal{T}$, that is, sv does not generate an arc from $\mathcal{T}$. This is true since t is not reachable from s and, hence, arcs incident to s may not appear in $\mathcal{T}$.

Note that a *breakthrough* may occur during the above incremental procedure, i.e. node t may become reachable from s at some point. When this happens, we trace the corresponding s–t path in $\mathcal{T}$, augment F according to Lemma 2, and recompute $\mathcal{T}$ from scratch. Again, any further activity stops once $\mathrm{val}(F)$ reaches r.

To estimate the complexity, note that between breakthroughs we are actually dealing with a single suspendable depth-first traversal of $\overrightarrow{\Gamma}_F$. Each such traversal costs $O(m)$ time and there are at most r breakthroughs. Hence, the total bound of $O(rm)$ follows. □

We apply the above data structure to graph $G_k(U_k^*)$ for $r = d_H(U^*)$ and make the moves in the reverse order, as explained earlier. Once QUERY reports the existence of r edge-disjoint s^*–t^* paths in $G_i(U_i^*)$, put $j(U^*) := i$ and proceed to the next signature. This way, each value $j(U^*)$ can be computed in $O(m)$ time. There are $O(1)$ signatures and $r = O(1)$, hence computing j takes linear time as well.

2.4 Dealing with a Critical Instance

The final stage deals with problem instance (G_j, H_j). For brevity, we reset $G := G_j$, $H := H_j$ and also denote $G' := G_{j+1}$, $H' := H_{j+1}$. Consider the connected components of G. Components not containing any terminals may be dropped. If G contains at least two components with terminals, the problem reduces to simpler cases described in Subsection 2.2. Hence, one can assume that G is connected. We prove that (G, H) is, in a sense, *critical*, that is, it admits a cut of a very special structure.

Lemma 7. *There exists a subset $U \subseteq VG$ such that $d_G(U) = d_H(U) = 2$, $G[U]$ is connected and $|U \cap T| = 2$ (see Fig. 1(b)).*

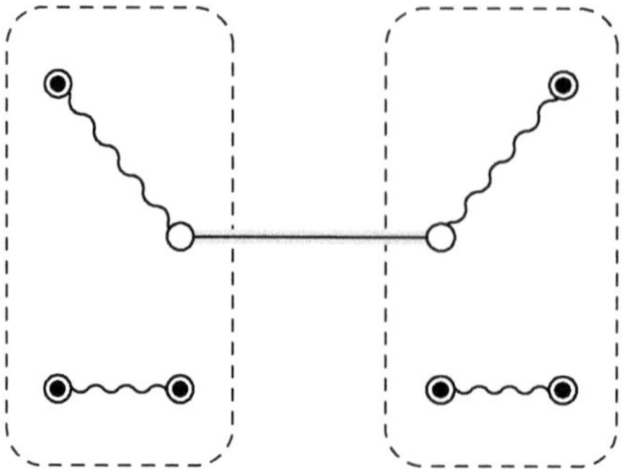

(a) Case 1: $d_G(U) = d_H(U) = 1$.

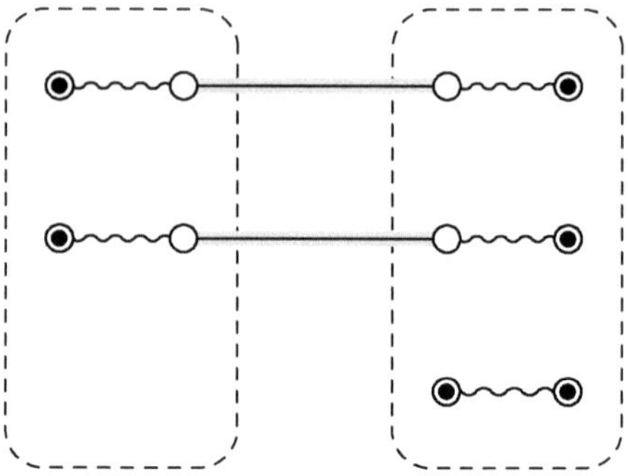

(b) Case 2: $d_G(U) = d_H(U) = 2$.

Fig. 1. A critical instance (G, H). Terminals are marked with dots and renumbered. Wavy lines indicate parts of paths in the desired collection $\mathcal{P}$.

Proof
The following is true:

(2) For problem instances (G, H) and (G', H')
  (i) (G, H) is feasible,
  (ii) (G', H') is obtained from (G, H) by a single local move,
  (iii) (G', H') is infeasible,
  (iv) let $s \in VG'$ be the new location of the moved terminal, $st \in EH'$, then s and t are in the same connected component of G'.

Properties (i)–(iii) are ensured by the choice of j. Property (iv) holds since there exists a remaining (untraversed) part of the initial s_1–t_1 path in the original graph G.

We apply a number of contractions to (G, H) and (G', H') that preserve condition (2). Suppose the following:

(3) there is a subset $U \subseteq VG$ such that $d_G(U) = d_H(U) = 1$ and $|U \cap T| = 1$.

In other words, there is a *bridge* $e = uv \in EG$, $u \in U$, $v \in VG - U$ (an edge whose removal increases the number of connected components) that separates G into parts $G[U]$ and $G[VG - U]$ and the former part contains a single terminal, say s.

We argue that the local move, which produced (G', H'), was carried out in the subgraph $G[VG - U]$ (but not in $G[U]$ or along the edge e).

Firstly, the move could not have been applied to s. Suppose the contrary. Terminal s is connected to node v by some path in $G[U \cup \{v\}]$ and this property remains true even if apply a local move to s. (Nodes v and s are the only odd vertices in $G[U \cup \{v\}]$, hence, these nodes cannot fall into distinct connected components after the move.) Therefore, (G, H) and (G', H') are simultaneously feasible or infeasible.

Next, suppose that v is a terminal and the move is carried out along the bridge e. Then, $vs \notin EH'$ (otherwise, (G', H') remains feasible). Therefore,

$vw \in EH'$ for some $w \in VG - U$. Then v and w belong to different connected components of G' after the move, which is impossible by (2)(iv).

Contract the set $U \cup \{v\}$ in instances (G, H) and (G', H') thus producing instances $(\overline{G}, \overline{H})$ and $(\overline{G}', \overline{H}')$, respectively. The above contraction preserves feasibility, hence $(\overline{G}, \overline{H})$ is feasible and $(\overline{G}', \overline{H}')$ is infeasible. Moreover, the latter instance is obtained from the former one by a local move. Property (2) is preserved.

We proceed with these contractions until no subset U obeying (3) remains. Next, since (G', H') is infeasible by Theorem 1 there exists a subset $U \subseteq VG$ such that $d_{G'}(U) < d_{H'}(U)$. Eulerianess of $G' + H'$ implies that each cut in $G' + H'$ is crossed by an even number of edges, hence $d_{G'}(U) \equiv d_{H'}(U) \pmod 2$. Therefore,

$$d_{G'}(U) \leq d_{H'}(U) - 2. \tag{4}$$

At the same time, (G, H) is feasible and hence

$$d_G(U) \geq d_H(U). \tag{5}$$

Graph G' is obtained from G by removing a single edge. Similarly, H' is obtained from H by one edge removal and one edge insertion. Hence, $d_G(U)$ and $d_H(U)$ differ from $d_{G'}(U)$ and $d_{H'}(U)$ (respectively) by at most 1. Combining this with (4) and (5), one has

$$d_{G'}(U) + 1 = d_G(U) = d_H(U) = d_{H'}(U) - 1.$$

So $d_H(U) \in \{1, 2\}$.

Suppose $d_H(U) = 1$. Subgraphs $G[U]$ and $G[VG - U]$ are connected (since otherwise G is not connected). Also, $|U \cap T| = 3$ (otherwise, $|U \cap T| = 1$ or $|(VG - U) \cap T| = 1$ and (3) still holds). Therefore, Case 1 from Fig. 1(a) applies (note that terminals s_i and t_i depicted there are appropriately renumbered). Let us explain, why this case is impossible. Graph G' is obtained from G by removing edge uv. Let, as in (2)(iv), s denote the terminal in (G, H) that is being moved and t denote its "mate" terminal (i.e. $st \in EH$). We can assume by symmetry that $u = s$. Hence, v is the new location of s in (G', H'). By (2)(iv), v and t are in the same connected component of G'. The latter is only possible if $s = u = s_1$ and $t = t_1$. But then feasibility of (G, H) implies that of (G', H').

Finally, let $d_H(U) = 2$. Replacing U by $VG - U$, if necessary, we may assume that $|U \cap T| = 2$, see Fig. 1(b). It remains to prove that $G[U]$ is connected. Let us assume the contrary. Then, $U = U_1 \cup U_2$, $U_1 \cap U_2 = \emptyset$, $d_G(U_1) = d_H(U_1) = 1$, $d_G(U_2) = d_H(U_2) = 1$ (due to feasibility of (G, H) and connectivity of G). Therefore, (3) still holds (both for $U := U_1$ and $U := U_2$) — a contradiction.

Once set U is found, we undo the contractions described in the beginning and obtain a set U for the original instance (G, H). Clearly, these uncontractions preserve the required properties of U. □

Lemma 8. *Set U figured in Lemma 7 can be constructed in $O(m)$ time.*

Proof
We enumerate pairs of terminals $p, q \in T$ that might qualify for $U^* := U \cap T = \{p, q\}$. Take all such pairs $U^* = \{p, q\}$ except those forming an edge in H ($pq \in EH$). Contract U^* and $T - U^*$ into s^* and t^*, respectively, in the graphs G and H. The resulting graphs are denoted by G^* and H^*. If a subset obeying Lemma 7 and having the signature U^* exists then there must be an s^*–t^* cut U in G^* such that $d_{G^*}(U) = 2$.

We try to construct U by applying three iterations of the max-flow algorithm of Ford and Fulkerson, see Subsection 2.1. If the third iteration succeeds, i.e. three edge-disjoint s^*–t^* paths are found, then no desired cut U having signature U^* exists; we continue with the next choice of U^*. Otherwise, a subset $U \subseteq VG^*$ obeying $d_{G^*}(U) \leq 2$ is constructed. Case $d_{G^*}(U) < 2 = d_{H^*}(U)$ is not possible due to feasibility of (G, H).

Set U is constructed for graph G^* but may also be regarded as a subset of VG. We keep notation U when referring to this subset.

Connectivity of $G[U]$ is the only remaining property we need to ensure. This is achieved by selecting an inclusion-wise maximal set U among minimum-capacity cuts that separate $\{p, q\}$ and $T - \{p, q\}$. Such maximality can achieved in a standard way, i.e. by traversing the residual network in backward direction from the sink t^*, see Lemma 3.

To see that $G[U]$ is connected suppose the contrary. Then, as in the proof of Lemma 7, let U_1 and U_2 be the node sets of the connected components of $G[U]$. Edges in $\delta_G(U) = \{e_1, e_2\}$ are bridges connecting $G[U_i]$ to the remaining part of graph G (for $i = 1, 2$). Also, $|U_1 \cap T| = |U_2 \cap T| = 1$ (recall that G is connected). Denote $U_1 \cap T = \{q_1\}$ and $U_2 \cap T = \{q_2\}$. Terminals q_1 and q_2 are not connected in $G[U]$. Since set U is inclusion-wise maximal, any subset U' satisfying Lemma 7 also obeys $U' \subseteq U$. But then q_1 and q_2 are also disconnected in $G[U']$, which is a contradiction. Therefore, no valid subset U of signature U^* obeying Lemma 7 exists.

In the algorithm, we check $G[U]$ for connectivity in $O(m)$ time. If the graph is not connected, then we proceed with the next signature U^*. □

Now everything is in place to complete the proof of Theorem 2. By Lemma 8, finding set U takes $O(m)$ time. It remains to construct a solution to (G, H). Put $\delta_G(U) = \{e_1, e_2\}$, $e_i = u_i v_i$, $u_i \in U$, $v_i \in VG - U$, $i = 1, 2$. Again, after renaming some terminals we may assume that $s_1, s_2 \in U$, $t_1, t_2, s_3, t_3 \in VG - U$. Augment G by adding two new nodes s^* and t^* and *auxiliary* edges $s^* u_1$, $s^* u_2$, $t_1 t^*$, and $t_2 t^*$. Due to feasibility of (G, H), there exists (and can be constructed in $O(m)$ time) a collection of two edge-disjoint s^*–t^* paths. After removing auxiliary edges we either obtain a u_1–t_1 path and a u_2–t_2 path (Case A) or a u_1–t_2 path and a u_2–t_1 path (Case B). To extend these paths to an s_1–t_1 path and an s_2–t_2 path we consider a four terminal instance in the subgraph $G[U]$. The demand graph is $(U, \{s_1 u_1, s_2 u_2\})$ in Case A and $(U, \{s_1 u_2, s_2 u_1\})$ in Case B. As $G[U]$ is connected, the latter instance is feasible by Lemma 4. Therefore, we obtain edge-disjoint s_1–t_1 and s_2–t_2 paths P_1 and P_2, respectively. As explained earlier in Section 1, the remaining path P_3 always exists and can be found in $O(m)$ time. Therefore, the proof of Theorem 2 is complete.

References

1. Cormen, T., Stein, C., Rivest, R., Leiserson, C.: Introduction to Algorithms. McGraw-Hill Higher Education, New York (2001)
2. Ford, L., Fulkerson, D.: Flows in Networks. Princeton University Press, Princeton (1962)
3. Marx, D.: Eulerian Disjoint Paths Problem in Grid Graphs is NP-Complete. Discrete Applied Mathematics 143, 336–341 (2004)
4. Robertson, N., Seymour, P.D.: Graph Minors XIII. The Disjoint Paths Problem. Journal of Combinatorial Theory (Series B) 63, 65–110 (1995)
5. Schrijver, A.: Combinatorial Optimization. Springer, Berlin (2003)
6. Shiloach, Y.: A Polynomial Solution to the Undirected Two Paths Problem. J. ACM 27(3), 445–456 (1980)
7. Shiloach, Y., Perl, Y.: Finding Two Disjoint Paths between Two Pairs of Vertices in a Graph. J. ACM 25(1), 1–9 (1978)
8. Tholey, T.: Solving the 2-Disjoint Paths Problem in Nearly Linear Time. In: Diekert, V., Habib, M. (eds.) STACS 2004. LNCS, vol. 2996, pp. 350–361. Springer, Heidelberg (2004)
9. Tholey, T.: Improved Algorithms for the 2-Vertex Disjoint Paths Problem. In: Nielsen, M., Kucera, A., Miltersen, P.B., Palamidessi, C., Tuma, P., Valencia, F.D. (eds.) SOFSEM 2009. LNCS, vol. 5404, pp. 546–557. Springer, Heidelberg (2009)

R-Programs: A Framework for Distributing XML Structural Joins across Function Calls

David Bednárek*

Department of Software Engineering, Faculty of Mathematics and Physics
Charles University in Prague
bednarek@ksi.mff.cuni.cz

Abstract. Structural joins and, in particular, twig joins are essential operations in XML query processing. Algorithms presented so far treat a twig join as a single operator with multiple inputs. However, in XQuery and XSLT, a twig pattern may be scattered across several functions (templates); thus, function integration is required before the application of a twig join operator. This paper presents R-programs – a novel evaluation framework based on an expanding network of operators. In this environment, a function may repeatedly and bidirectionally interact with its caller; consequently, a structural join algorithm may be distributed across the boundary of a function. Given this ability, function integration is no longer required and twig join algorithms become applicable even in the presence of recursive functions.

1 Introduction

The most successful XML query-processing methods are based on the architecture inherited from relational database systems [1]. The XML-specific part of query processing is concentrated mainly in various versions of structural join operators. A number of methods that process more than one structural relationship at a time were developed; both theory and experiments show that such *holistic* approach is advantageous because it avoids unnecessary intermediate results. In the query, *twig patterns* are detected [2], containing ancestor-descendant or parent-child relationships, OR operators, and, in the most advanced methods, negation. For example, a twig pattern, corresponding to the XPath expression `a/b[c]/d/e` is shown in Fig. 2a.

In the physical plan, a holistic *twig join* is represented by an n-ary operator that consumes n streams assigned to the nodes of the twig pattern, as shown in Fig. 2b. Each stream carries XML elements that meet the local condition of the corresponding twig node (in our example, the condition on their element names).

This approach works well when a twig pattern is located inside an XPath expression. However, functions may be defined in XQuery and, thus, a twig

* Supported by the Project GA201/09/0983 – Agile systems and service-oriented software of the Czech Science Foundation.

J. van Leeuwen et al. (Eds.): SOFSEM 2010, LNCS 5901, pp. 176–187, 2010.

```
for $X in a               declare function f($X)   declare function g($Y)
  return f($X)            { for $Y in $X/b[c]/d     { $Y/e
                              return g($Y)          };
                          };
```

Fig. 1. A twig pattern scattered across functions

pattern may be scattered across function boundaries. An example, containing the same pattern as in Fig. 2b, is shown in Fig. 1.

In such a case, integration of the bodies of the functions into the main expression is required because the twig-join algorithm is represented as an atomic physical operator that can not be spanned across function calls. Such integration is expensive (as it may lead to exponential expansion of the program size) and generally impossible in the presence of recursive functions.

In this paper, we suggest that centralized implementations of twig joins be replaced by distributed versions as shown in the example in Fig. 2c. Note that the word *distributed* does not necessarily mean that the algorithm is run on more than one computing node; nevertheless, the original centralized algorithm is divided into smaller blocks that run conceptually in parallel, communicating using pipes.

Our approach allows a twig algorithm to run on the whole twig pattern scattered across several functions, even though there is no inter-procedural detection of twig patterns. Each function may be compiled independently, producing a partial network; at run-time, the connected networks will behave exactly like a twig join algorithm.

Although this idea is quite simple, it requires significant changes in the architecture of the query evaluation system. At run time, function evaluation may no longer follow the usual call-return scheme. Instead, function bodies must run in parallel with their callers and they must be able to exchange data in both directions.

In this paper, we present a mathematical model of such a system, named *R-program*. R-programs may be used as an intermediate language for both logical and physical plans, depending on the set of operators used.

An R-program is conceptually a network of computing nodes, connected by pipes carrying relations (more exactly, sequences of tuples). Each node performs a relational or XML-specific operation. Instead of calling, functions are *expanded*, i.e. added to the existing network at run-time so that they can run in parallel with their callers, exchanging data in both directions. While there is one-to-one correspondence between R-program functions and XQuery functions, a single expansion of an R-program function corresponds to multiple calls to the corresponding XQuery function. This fact ensures that the cost of the expansion is relatively small with respect to the amount of data processed.

The rest of this paper is organized as follows: The principle of twig join and the common skeleton found in most existing twig join algorithms is reviewed in Sect. 2. In Sect. 3 we will show how a twig-join algorithm may be rewritten in

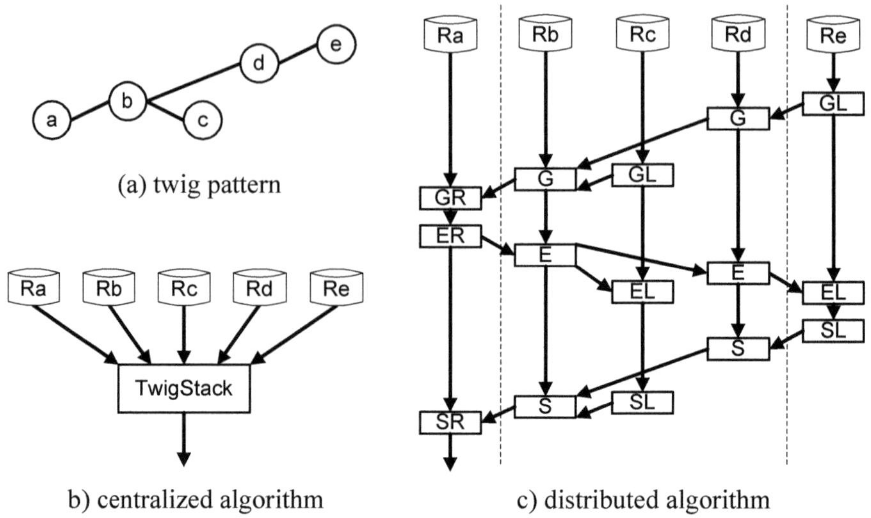

Fig. 2. Centralized vs. distributed processing of a twig pattern

distributed manner; we will also discuss which twig-join algorithms can fit into our schema. In Sect. 4, we will define the mathematical model of R-programs, we will explain their evaluation and show the principles of the translation from XQuery. In the last section, we will summarize the contribution of this paper and compare our approach to the most important related work.

2 Preliminaries

In XML databases, especially in schema-oblivious systems, structural relationship is usually represented using node *numbering* – a scheme that allows decoding the position of a XML node from its identification (*number*). Structural-join algorithms are traditionally presented using *region encoding* (also called *Dietz numbering*) [3]. In region encoding, nodes are identified using a pair of pre-order and post-order ranks L and R, usually augmented with the depth D of the node. In this encoding, XPath axes are represented using a combination of comparisons, like $L_1 < L_2 \wedge R_2 < R_1$ for the `descendant` axis.

Holistic twig joins were developed from binary structural joins, through path-joins. Later, ability to handle OR operators and negation [5] were added. Many current algorithms are still presented using the same skeleton, shown in Alg. 1, which was presented already in the *TwigStack* algorithm [4].

Twig-join algorithms have two phases; the first phase scans the inputs, producing a stream of *path solutions* that are merged in the second phase (by the routine mergeAllPathSolutions). Except of negation-enabled algorithms, the first

Algorithm 1. Skeleton of the *TwigStack* algorithm, adapted from [4]

```
1: while ¬end(q_root) do
2:    q := getNext(q_root)
3:    cleanStack(S_q, next(C_q))
4:    cleanStack(S_parent(q), next(C_q))
5:    if isRoot(q) ∨
          ¬empty(S_parent(q)) then
6:       pushToStack(S_q, next(C_q),
            linkToTop(S_parent(q)))
7:       if isLeaf(q) then
8:          showSolutions(q)
9:          popStack(S_q)
10:   advance(C_q)
11: mergeAllPathSolutions()

function getNext(q)
12: if isLeaf(q) then
13:    return q
14: for q_i ∈ children(q) do
15:    n_i := getNext(q_i)
16:    if n_i ≠ q_i then
17:       return n_i
18: L_max := getLMax(C_q1, ..., C_qk)
19: while nextR(C_q) < L_max do
20:    advance(C_q)
21: n_min := minarg_{n_i} nextL(C_{n_i})
22: if nextL(C_q) < nextL(C_{n_min}) then
23:    return q
24: else
25:    return n_min
```

phase requires time linear with respect to the size of the inputs, while the second phase is linear with respect to the size of the output.

In the first phase, the elements from all inputs C_q are read in the document order. The getNext function retrieves the nearest element across all inputs that has a *lower extension*, i.e. there is a match in the corresponding twig sub-tree. When processing OR-predicates, the function getLMax (line 18) is altered to produce minimal instead of maximal positions. Negated predicates require additional processing placed usually before the final test at line 22.

The main algorithm (lines 1–10) maintains a stack S_q in each twig-pattern node q to hold the corresponding elements that intersect with the current position. Elements returned by the function getNext are pushed on the stack of the corresponding twig node only if the stack of the parent twig node is not empty, which ensures the existence of an *upper extension*. Therefore, whenever the area of non-empty stacks reaches a leaf node, the elements in the stacks form at least one match of the whole twig pattern. In this moment, the function showSolutions generates a set of path solutions combining the information from the stacks along the path to the leaf q.

The presented version reads the input elements one-by-one, by the advance statements at the lines 20 and 10. Advanced versions like [6] replace these calls by *skip* commands, employing indexes on the inputs similarly to zig-zag joins.

3 Distributed Twig-Join Algorithm

In this section, we present a distributed version of the twig-join algorithm shown in Sect. 2. Since the main purpose of this section is to show the motivation for the introduction of R-programs, we describe only the basic version of the algorithm and we will omit some technical details. Figure 2c shows the three levels that form the twig-join algorithm:

The G-level corresponds to the getNext function (the GL and GR-boxes are specialized for twig pattern leaves and the root, respectively). Each G-box receives the corresponding input stream C_q and a vector of GG_{q_i} streams from its children. Each G-box produces a GG_q stream to the parent (if any) and a GE_q stream leading to the corresponding E-box.

The E-level implements the lines 3–6 of Alg. 1 which maintain the stacks and propagate information down in the twig pattern tree. Each E-box receives the GE_q stream from the corresponding G-box and an EE_q stream from the parent (if any). Each E-box produces a vector of EE_{q_i} streams to its children and an ES_q stream to the S-level.

The S-level replicates the stacks maintained by the E-level and implements the routine showSolutions which collects path solutions in the leaf-to-root direction. Additionally, in nodes with more than one children, it performs the joins required to merge path solutions in the second phase of the original algorithm. An S-box receives the ES_q stream from the E-level and several SS_{q_i} streams from the children. Each S-box produces the SS_q stream; the GR-box produces the final result of the twig join.

The internal streams carry the following information: Each GG_q stream carries a copy of those elements from the input C_q stream that have lower extension. It corresponds to the executions of the line 23 of Alg. 1.

The outgoing GE_q stream merges all the incoming GG_{q_i} streams (line 25) with a copy of the output stream GG_q. The merged elements are document ordered (line 22) and augmented with an identification i of their origin (child index or zero).

Each EE_q stream is a copy of the corresponding GG_q stream in the opposite direction, with the results of empty($S_{\text{parent}(q)}$) and linkToTop($S_{\text{parent}(q)}$) added to each element.

ES_q streams merely replicate their respective GE_q streams.

SS_q streams carry the tuples of partial solutions corresponding to the twig sub-tree q, each tuple is augmented with a link to the stack $S_{\text{parent}(q)}$. For synchronization, the partial solutions are interleaved with elements copied from the ES_q stream.

The life cycles of the G and E-boxes are shown in Alg. 2; the GR/GL as well as ER/EL-boxes are derived from these algorithms. The S/SL/SR-boxes implement the showSolutions and mergeAllPathSolutions routines from the original algorithm.

As illustrated in Fig. 2c which shows the function boundaries using dashed lines, if the twig pattern is spanned across a function call, the three layers of the distributed twig algorithm require three communication channels between the function body and its caller. In the first layer, data are sent from the function to the caller and the caller responds back in the second layer – during the processing in the caller, internal state of the called must be preserved. This is the motivation for the introduction of the R-programs in the following section.

Algorithm 2. Life cycles of the G and E-boxes

```
procedure G-box(q)
  L_max := getLMax(GG_{q1}, ..., GG_{qk})
  while nextR(C_q) < L_max do
     advance(C_q)
  i_min := minarg_i nextL(GG_i)
  if nextL(C_q) < nextL(GG_{i_min}) then
     send(GG_q, next(C_q))
     send(GE_q, next(C_q), 0)
     advance(C_q)
  else
     send(GE_q, next(GG_{i_min}), i_min)
     advance(GG_{i_min})

procedure E-box(q)
  cleanStack(S_q, next(GE_q))
  if nextI(GE_q) ≠ 0 then
     send(EE_{nextI(GE_q)}, next(GE_q),
        empty(S_q), linkToTop(S_q))
     if ¬empty(S_q) then
        send(ES_q, next(GE_q))
  else
     if ¬nextEmpty(EE_q) then
        pushToStack(S_q, next(EE_q))
        send(ES_q, next(EE_q), 0)
     advance(EE_q)
  advance(GE_q)
```

4 R-Programs

An *R-program* consists of a set of *R-functions*. The interior of each R-function is described by a directed graph of operators and R-function calls. Each R-function receives one or more relations as its input arguments and produces one or more relations at its output.

The notion of R-net forms the core of our formalism, representing a directed graph of operations. Besides physical operators, function calls are allowed. Note that, unlike in classical relational algebra, we allow an operator to have more than one output.

Note that the definition of R-net does not require that the directed graph be acyclic. Acyclicity will be studied on the complete R-program, allowing a kind of cycle around a function call. Such a cycle does not necessarily paralyze the evaluation of the program; it may just require multiple entry and exit to the same function. This approach to acyclicity is crucial as it allows distributed computations like the one described in the previous section.

Definition 1 (R-net). *Let* RelOp *be a set of* operators, ArcNm *be a* vocabulary of arc names, *and* Fncs *be a set of function names.* R-net over Fncs *is a tuple*

$$N = (\mathsf{Plcs}, \mathsf{Ops}, \mathsf{In}, \mathsf{Out}, \mathsf{op}, \mathsf{ini}, \mathsf{fin})$$

where Plcs *is a finite set of* places, Ops *is a finite set of* operations, $\mathsf{ini}, \mathsf{fin} \in \mathsf{Ops}$ *are* initial *and* final operations. $\mathsf{In} : (\mathsf{Ops} \setminus \{\mathsf{ini}\}) \times \mathsf{ArcNm} \rightarrow \mathsf{Plcs}$ *and* $\mathsf{Out} : (\mathsf{Ops} \setminus \{\mathsf{fin}\}) \times \mathsf{ArcNm} \rightarrow \mathsf{Plcs}$ *are finite partial mappings that define the* input *and* output arcs. *The* Out *mapping must be a projection, i.e.* $\mathrm{rng}(\mathsf{Out}) = \mathsf{Plcs}$. *An R-net is called* non-redundant *if the mapping* Out *is an injection.*

$$\mathsf{op} : (\mathsf{Ops} \setminus \{\mathsf{ini}, \mathsf{fin}\}) \rightarrow (\ \mathsf{RelOp} \cup \{\ \mathsf{trigger}\} \cup \{\ \mathsf{call}[f] \mid f \in \mathsf{Fncs}\ \}\ )$$

is a mapping that assigns operators to operations. The number of input/output arcs for an operation t, as well as their arc names, must correspond to the number of input/output arguments of the operator $\mathsf{op}(t)$*, except for call operations.*

We will use the notation
$p \xrightarrow[N]{a} t$ as an abbreviation for $p = \mathsf{In}_N(t, a)$ and $t \xrightarrow[N]{a} p$ for $p = \mathsf{Out}_N(t, a)$.

Definition 2 (R-program). R-program *is a tuple*

$$M = (\mathsf{Fncs}, \mathsf{Plcs}, \mathsf{Ops}, \mathsf{In}, \mathsf{Out}, \mathsf{op}, \mathsf{ini}, \mathsf{fin}, \mathsf{owner}^P, \mathsf{owner}^T, \mathsf{main})$$

where Fncs *is a finite set of* function names. $\mathsf{owner}^P : \mathsf{Plcs} \rightarrow \mathsf{Fncs}$ *and* $\mathsf{owner}^T : \mathsf{Ops} \rightarrow \mathsf{Fncs}$ *are total functions that divide* Plcs *and* Ops *into partitions* P_f, T_f *for each* $f \in \mathsf{Fncs}$. *The partitioning of places and transitions then induces partitioning of the remaining elements such that the following tuple*

$$N(f) = (P_f, T_f, \mathsf{In}_f, \mathsf{Out}_f, \mathsf{op}_f, \mathsf{ini}_f, \mathsf{fin}_f)$$

is a correct R-net. $\mathsf{main} \in \mathsf{Fncs}$ *is called the* main function. *Finally, for each* $t \in \mathsf{Ops}$ *such that* $\mathsf{op}(t) = \mathsf{call}[f]$, *the following conditions must be met for each* a*:*

$$\left\{a \mid p_1 \xrightarrow[M]{a} t\right\} = \left\{a \mid \mathsf{ini}(f) \xrightarrow[M]{a} p_2\right\} \quad \wedge \quad \left\{a \mid p_3 \xrightarrow[M]{a} \mathsf{fin}(f)\right\} = \left\{a \mid t \xrightarrow[M]{a} p_4\right\}$$

4.1 Dependency Closure and Acyclicity

The following definitions form the condition of acyclicity.

Definition 3 (Dependency closure). *Let* d *be a binary relation on the places of an R-program* M *such that*

$$d \subseteq \{\ \langle p_1, p_2 \rangle \in \mathsf{Plcs}_M \times \mathsf{Plcs}_M \mid \mathsf{owner}^P_M(p_1) = \mathsf{owner}^P_M(p_2)\ \}$$

The dependency closure *of* d *is the smallest relation* $\overline{d} \subseteq \mathsf{Plcs}_M \times \mathsf{Plcs}_M$ *such that* $d \subseteq \overline{d}$,

$$\langle p_1, p_2 \rangle \in \overline{d} \wedge \langle p_2, p_3 \rangle \in \overline{d} \Rightarrow \langle p_1, p_3 \rangle \in \overline{d}$$

and

$$\begin{pmatrix} \mathsf{op}_M(t) = \mathsf{call}[f] \wedge p_1 \xrightarrow[M]{a} t \wedge \mathsf{ini}_M(f) \xrightarrow[M]{a} p_2 \\ \wedge \langle p_2, p_3 \rangle \in \overline{d} \wedge p_3 \xrightarrow[M]{b} \mathsf{fin}_M(f) \wedge t \xrightarrow[M]{b} p_4 \end{pmatrix} \Rightarrow \langle p_1, p_4 \rangle \in \overline{d}$$

for each $p_1, p_2, p_3, p_4 \in \mathsf{Plcs}_M$, $a, b \in \mathsf{ArcNm}$, $t \in \mathsf{Ops}_M$, *and* $f \in \mathsf{Fncs}_M$

Note that all conditions in the definition of dependency closure are implications with conjunctive positive premises. Therefore, the set of relations $\overline{d}$ that satisfy these conditions is closed under intersection. Consequently, a single minimum with respect to inclusion exists.

Definition 4 (Acyclic R-program). *Let* D *be the relation (called* primitive dependency relation*) induced by the primitive operators in an R-program* M, *i.e.*

$$D = \left\{ \langle p_1, p_2 \rangle \;\middle|\; \begin{array}{l} (\exists t \in \mathsf{Ops}, a_1, a_2 \in \mathsf{ArcNm}) \\ (p_1 \xrightarrow[M]{a} t \wedge t \xrightarrow[M]{b} p_2 \wedge \mathsf{op}_M(t) \in \mathsf{RelOp}) \end{array} \right\}$$

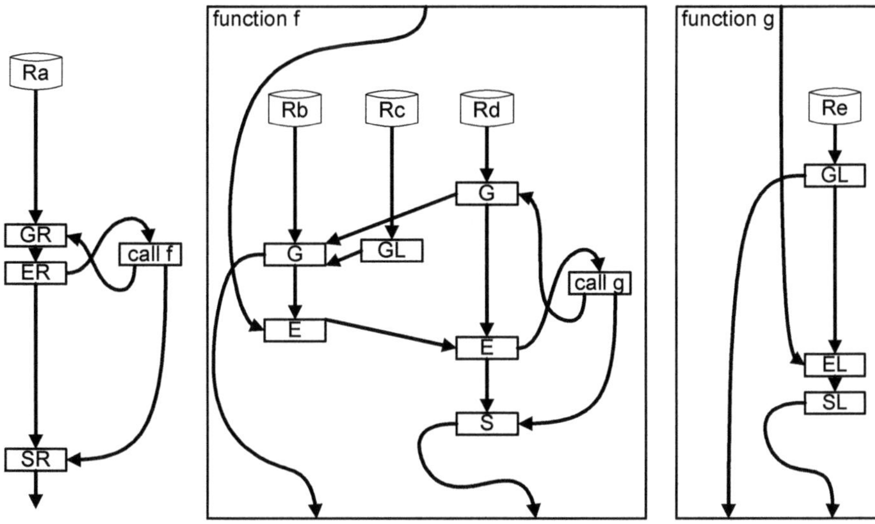

Fig. 3. The R-program corresponding to the query from Fig. 1

The R-program M is called acyclic *if the dependency closure* $\overline{D}$ *of the primitive dependency relation is antisymmetric and irreflexive, i.e.*

$$\langle p_1, p_2 \rangle \in \overline{D} \Rightarrow \langle p_2, p_1 \rangle \notin \overline{D}$$

An R-program is displayed in Fig. 3, corresponding to the XQuery program from Fig. 1. Although the graphs are cyclic in the usual graph-theoretical sense, the R-program is acyclic in the sense of Def. 4.

For acyclic R-programs, evaluation is possible. However, the evaluation may not follow the classical call-return scheme; instead, the R-program functions must be gradually instantiated and integrated into the main function.

4.2 Semantics of R-Programs

The execution of an R-program is based on instantiation of R-functions and merging them into one R-net. A call tree corresponds to a (partial) expansion of the R-program. The expansion creates copies of the instantiated function bodies and glues them together using identity operators on their input and output arguments.

In this section, we will present a simplified definition of R-program semantics, based on complete expansion of the program code. For recursive programs, more elaborate definition is required, based on partial expansion driven by *triggers*; partial expansion is also used to avoid unnecessary expansion of function calls that do not contribute to the result. The full definition of the semantics is presented in the thesis [7].

Definition 5 (Call tree). Call tree *of an R-program M is any finite tree whose nodes are mapped to functions, the root is mapped to* main_M*, and edges are labelled with call operations that exist in the function associated to the parent. We will represent a call tree using the language (over the alphabet formed by call operations) of label strings collected over all the paths (starting at the root) in the call tree.*

Definition 6 (Complete expansion). *Let c be a* call tree *of an R-program M The* expansion of M associated to c *is the R-net N whose elements are defined using the following auxiliary definitions:*

$$C = \{ \langle s,t,f \rangle \mid t \in \mathsf{Ops}_M \wedge f \in \mathsf{Fncs}_M \wedge \mathsf{op}_M(t) = \mathsf{call}[f] \}$$
$$K = \{ \langle \lambda, \mathsf{main}_M \rangle \} \cup \{ \langle s.t, f \rangle \mid \langle s,t,f \rangle \in C \}$$

(C is the set of function calls and K is the set of function expansions.)

The expansion N is composed of copies of places, operations (except of function calls and initial/final operations), and arcs from the functions of the R-program M – for each $\langle s,f \rangle \in K$, the function f is copied.

In addition, there are identity operations corresponding to passing input arguments to R-functions and returning output arguments, for each expanded function call $\langle s,t,f \rangle \in C$, connecting the actual argument places in the expansion $\langle s,f \rangle$ with the corresponding formal argument places in the expansion $\langle s.t,f \rangle$.

Lemma 1 (Acyclicity of expansion)
Let M be an acyclic R-program, c_1 be a call tree of M, N be the complete expansion of M associated to c. Then the R-net N is a directed acyclic graph.

The proof of this lemma follows directly from the definitions of expansion and R-program acyclicity.

The following definition defines the *computation* of an R-net with no function calls.

Definition 7 (Computation of R-net). *Let N be an R-net and $\mathcal{U}$ be a universe of values (relations).* Computation of N *is any mapping $\kappa : \mathsf{Plcs}_N \to \mathcal{U}$ that satisfies the condition $\kappa(q_j) = \odot_j(\kappa(p_1), \ldots, \kappa(p_n))$ for each $t \in \mathsf{Ops}_N$ and each j such that $t \xrightarrow[N]{j} q_j$, where $p_i \xrightarrow[N]{i} t$ for $i \in \{1, \ldots, n\}$ and $\odot_j$ is the implementation of the operator $\mathsf{op}_N(t)$ with respect to its j-th output argument.*

4.3 Evaluation of R-Programs

R-programs require pipelined evaluation in the architecture shown in Fig. 4. The R-program is gradually expanded by the *expander* into an R-net. The expansion is controlled by *triggers* inserted into the expanded R-net in all places where an unexpanded R-function is called. When a trigger encounters the first tuple of data arriving in the actual arguments of the R-function, a further expansion step is invoked, consisting of integration of the R-function body into the expanded R-program.

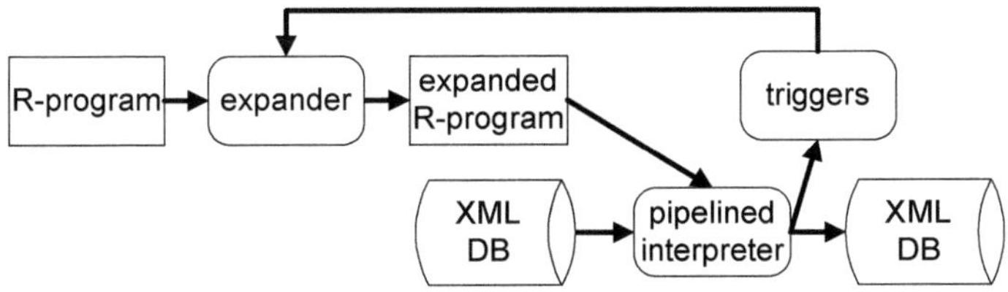

Fig. 4. Pipelined R-program run-time

4.4 Translation from XQuery to R-Programs

The R-program representation is created from the XQuery program during a process called *transcription*. Before the transcription, a *mode selection* phase analyzes the XQuery program and determines the *evaluation mode* assigned to each variable, expression, and operation in the source program. Each mode consists of a set of relations that hold the value of a variable or expression and transcription rules for each XQuery operator or statement. Some transcription rules form a bridge between different modes.

Our distributed twig-join algorithm is represented as a pair of modes, applied to the control variables and return values of the FLWOR statements that participate in the twig pattern. Besides these twig-specific modes, there are modes designed to handle output trees, Boolean values, unordered context etc. [7]. Most of the modes are not general; therefore the main goal of the mode selection phase is determining the applicability of the modes at various places in the source program. Where no alternate mode applies, the evaluation fails back to the *canonical mode* [8] which follows the W3C definition of XQuery semantics (but still employs bulk-evaluation based on relational representation).

Each mode is essentially a group of pipes carrying relational data; in the terminology of R-programs, the pipes correspond to places. To bind transcription rules together, these places are identified using the common dictionary ArcNm of arc names.

Employing the flexibility of R-programs, transcription rules may reverse the flow of information partially; in the case of distributed twig join algorithms, the G-layer propagates information against the original data flow associated to the control variables.

A static analysis algorithm for rule-based selection of the transcription mode was presented in [8]; the ability to handle reversed flow was added in the thesis [7]. The time complexity of the algorithm is $O(n \cdot m^4)$ while the space complexity is $O(n \cdot m^2)$ where n is the size of the XQuery program and m is the maximal number of local variables visible at any place in the program.

5 Conclusion and Related Work

Twig join algorithm form an important branch in research of XML data bases; nevertheless, little is known about the application of a twig join algorithm in a fully-featured XQuery system. One of the obstacles that an implementation must overcome is the presence of functions. This paper contributes to the solution of this problem with the following ideas:

First, we have shown in Sect. 3 that holistic twig join algorithms may be rewritten in a distributed way, using a set of binary operators instead a single n-way join. In this arrangement, a twig pattern scattered across several functions does not require compile-time detection and integration; consequently, independent compilation of functions is possible.

Second, we have presented a mathematical model, called R-programs, as an intermediate representation into which XQuery programs are translated. R-programs are based on the same principle of bulk evaluation as the majority of XQuery systems based on a relational-like algebra (see, for instance, the *loop-lifting* technique in MonetDB [1]). On the other hand, R-programs offer the ability of data-flow reversal which is required in the distributed version of twig join.

Consequently, R-programs allow application of twig join algorithms across function boundaries, a feature that would not be possible in purely algebraic systems. Systems like Pathfinder [2] can achieve this goal using function integration; thus, at the cost of code expansion.

Twig-join algorithms extended to OR and NOT predicates [5] may be transformed to distributed versions similarly. On the other hand, skipping versions like [6] cannot be transformed to R-programs because of the mutual dependency between input cursors which violates the acyclicity requirement. Some twig-join algorithms replace the path-solution streams by lists [9,10] – such algorithms do not fit to the scheme shown in Sect. 2; it is not yet known whether these algorithms may be rewritten in distributed manner suitable for R-programs. Finally, since there is no twig-pattern detection, our system can not make use of extended labeling schemes like TJFast [11] or DataGuide trees [12].

Besides the ability to handle twig joins across function calls, the R-program model naturally allows distributed evaluation over several computing nodes on cluster or grid architectures. The proposed architecture may also be useful outside the area of XML data bases, whenever a complex transformation of streams is required.

References

1. Grust, T., Rittinger, J.: Jump through Hoops to Grok the Loops Pathfinder's Purely Relational Account of XQuery-Style Iteration Semantics. In: Proceedings of the ACM SIGMOD/PODS 5th International Workshop on XQuery Implementation, Experience and Perspectives, XIME-P 2008 (2008)
2. Grust, T., Mayr, M., Rittinger, J.: XQuery Join Graph Isolation: Celebrating 30+ Years of XQuery Processing Technology. In: ICDE 2009, Proceedings of the 2009 IEEE International Conference on Data Engineering, Washington, DC, USA, pp. 1167–1170. IEEE Computer Society, Los Alamitos (2009)
3. Haw, S.C., Lee, C.S.: Extending Path Summary and Region Encoding for Efficient Structural Query Processing in Native XML Databases. Journal of Systems and Software 82(6), 1025–1035 (2009)

4. Bruno, N., Koudas, N., Srivastava, D.: Holistic Twig Joins: Optimal XML Pattern Matching. In: SIGMOD 2002, Proceedings of the 2002 ACM SIGMOD International Conference on Management of Data, pp. 310–321. ACM, New York (2002)
5. Che, D.: Holistically Processing XML Twig Queries with AND, OR, and NOT Predicates. In: InfoScale 2007, Proceedings of the 2nd International Conference on Scalable Information Systems, ICST, Brussels, Belgium, pp. 1–4. ICST (Institute for Computer Sciences, Social-Informatics and Telecommunications Engineering) (2007)
6. Fontoura, M., Josifovski, V., Shekita, E., Yang, B.: Optimizing Cursor Movement in Holistic Twig Joins. In: CIKM 2005, Proceedings of the 14th ACM International Conference on Information and Knowledge Management, pp. 784–791. ACM, New York (2005)
7. Bednárek, D.: Bulk Evaluation of User-Defined Functions in XQuery. PhD Thesis, Department of Software Engineering, Charles University, Prague, the Czech Republic (2009)
8. Bednárek, D.: Reducing Temporary Trees in XQuery. In: Atzeni, P., Caplinskas, A., Jaakkola, H. (eds.) ADBIS 2008. LNCS, vol. 5207, pp. 30–45. Springer, Heidelberg (2008)
9. Qin, L., Yu, J.X., Ding, B.: TwigList: Make Twig Pattern Matching Fast. In: Kotagiri, R., Radha Krishna, P., Mohania, M., Nantajeewarawat, E. (eds.) DASFAA 2007. LNCS, vol. 4443, pp. 850–862. Springer, Heidelberg (2007)
10. Li, J., Wang, J.: TwigBuffer: Avoiding Useless Intermediate Solutions Completely in Twig Joins. In: Haritsa, J.R., Kotagiri, R., Pudi, V. (eds.) DASFAA 2008. LNCS, vol. 4947, pp. 554–561. Springer, Heidelberg (2008)
11. Lu, J., Chen, T., Ling, T.W.: TJFast: Effective Processing of XML Twig Pattern Matching. In: Ellis, A., Hagino, T. (eds.) WWW (Special Interest Tracks and Posters), pp. 1118–1119. ACM, New York (2005)
12. Bača, R., Krátký, M., Snášel, V.: On the Efficient Search of an XML Twig Query in Large DataGuide Trees. In: IDEAS 2008, Proceedings of the 2008 International Symposium on Database Engineering and Applications, pp. 149–158. ACM, New York (2008)

Fast Arc-Annotated Subsequence Matching in Linear Space

Philip Bille and Inge Li Gørtz

Technical University of Denmark
{phbi,ilg}@imm.dtu.dk

Abstract. An arc-annotated string is a string of characters, called bases, augmented with a set of pairs, called arcs, each connecting two bases. Given arc-annotated strings P and Q the arc-preserving subsequence problem is to determine if P can be obtained from Q by deleting bases from Q. Whenever a base is deleted any arc with an endpoint in that base is also deleted. Arc-annotated strings where the arcs are "nested" are a natural model of RNA molecules that captures both the primary and secondary structure of these. The arc-preserving subsequence problem for nested arc-annotated strings is basic primitive for investigating the function of RNA molecules. Gramm et al. [ACM Trans. Algorithms 2006] gave an algorithm for this problem using $O(nm)$ time and space, where m and n are the lengths of P and Q, respectively. In this paper we present a new algorithm using $O(nm)$ time and $O(n+m)$ space, thereby matching the previous time bound while significantly reducing the space from a quadratic term to linear. This is essential to process large RNA molecules where the space is a likely to be a bottleneck. To obtain our result we introduce several novel ideas which may be of independent interest for related problems on arc-annotated strings.

1 Introduction

An *arc-annotated string* S is a string augmented with an *arc set* A_S. Each character in S is called a *base* and the arc set A_S is a set of pairs of positions in S connecting two distinct bases. We say that S is a *nested arc-annotated string* if no two arcs in A_S share an endpoint and no two arcs cross each other, i.e., for all $(i_l, i_r), (i'_l, i'_r) \in A_S$ we have that $i_l < i'_l < i_r$ iff $i_l < i'_r < i_r$. Given arc-annotated strings P and Q we say that P is a *arc-preserving subsequence* (APS) of Q, denoted $P \sqsubseteq Q$, if P can be obtained from Q by deleting 0 or more bases from Q. Whenever a base is deleted any arc with an endpoint in that base is also deleted. The *arc-preserving subsequence problem* (APS) is to determine if $P \sqsubseteq Q$. If P and Q are both nested arc-annotated strings we refer to the problem as the *nested arc-preserving subsequence problem* (NAPS). Fig. 1(a) shows an example of nested arc-annotated strings.

Ribonucleic acid (RNA) molecules are often modeled as nested arc-annotated strings. Here, the string consists of bases from the 4-letter alphabet $\{\mathrm{A}, \mathrm{U}, \mathrm{C}, \mathrm{G}\}$, called the *primary structure*, and an arc set consisting of pairings between bases,

J. van Leeuwen et al. (Eds.): SOFSEM 2010, LNCS 5901, pp. 188–199, 2010.

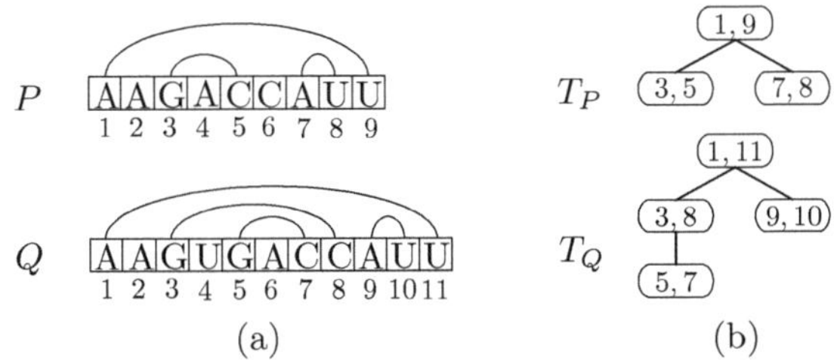

Fig. 1. (a) Nested arc-annotated strings P and Q. Here, P and Q contain arcs connecting their first and last bases. (b) The corresponding trees T_P and T_Q induced by the arcs.

called the *secondary structure*. RNA molecules are central for many biological functions and NAPS is a basic primitive for investigating the precise functionality of RNA molecules. The key idea is to model a specific function of RNA molecules as an arc-annotated string F. Given a RNA molecule R we can then determine (to some extent) if R performs the same function by computing if $F \sqsubseteq R$.

Building on earlier work in a related model of RNA molecules by Vialette [16], Gramm et al. [10] introduced and gave an algorithm for NAPS using $O(nm)$ time and space, where m and n are the lengths of P and Q, respectively. Kida [12] presented an experimental study of this algorithm and Damaschke [8] considered a special restricted case of the problem.

Results. We assume a standard unit-cost RAM model with word size $\Theta(\log n)$ and a standard instruction set including arithmetic operations, bitwise boolean operations, and shifts. The space complexity is the number of words used by the algorithm. All of the previous results are in same model of computation. Throughout the paper P and Q are nested arc-annotated strings of lengths m and n, respectively. In this paper we present a new algorithm with the following complexities.

Theorem 1. *Given nested arc-annotated strings P and Q of lengths m and n, respectively, we can solve the nested arc-preserving subsequence problem in time $O(nm)$ and space $O(n + m)$.*

Hence, we match the running time of the currently fastest known algorithm and at the same time we improve the space from $O(nm)$ to $O(n + m)$. This space improvement is critical for processing large RNA molecules. In particular, an algorithm using $O(nm)$ space quickly becomes infeasible, even for moderate sizes of RNA molecules, due to costly accesses to external memory. An algorithm using $O(m+n)$ space is much more scalable and allows us to handle significantly larger RNA molecules. Furthermore, we note that obtaining an algorithm using $O(nm)$ time and $o(nm)$ space is mentioned as an open problem in Gramm et al. [10].

Compared to the previous work by Gramm et al. [10] our algorithm is not only more space-efficient but also simpler. Our algorithm is based on a single unified dynamic programming recurrence, whereas the algorithm by Gramm et al. requires computing and tabulating auxiliary information in multiple phases mixed with dynamic programming. Our approach allows us to better expose the features of NAPS and is essential for obtaining a linear space algorithm.

Techniques. As mentioned above, our algorithm is based on a new dynamic programming recurrence. Essentially, the recursion expresses for any pair of substrings P' and Q' of P and Q, respectively, the longest prefix of P' which is an arc-preserving subsequence of Q' in term of smaller substrings of P' and Q'. We combine several new ideas with well-known techniques to convert our recurrence into an efficient algorithm.

First, we organize the dynamic programming recurrence into Γ *sequences*. A Γ sequence for a given substring Q' of Q is a simple $O(m)$ space representation of the longest arc-preserving subsequences of each prefix of P in Q'. We show how to efficiently manipulate Γ sequences to get new Γ sequences using a small set of simple operations, called the *primitive operations*. Secondly, we organize the computation of Γ sequences using a recursive algorithm that traverses the tree structure of the arcs in Q. The algorithm computes the Γ sequence for each arc in Q using the primitive operations. To avoid storing too many Γ sequences during the traversal we direct the computation according to the well-known *heavy-path decomposition* of the tree. This leads to an algorithm that stores at most $O(\log |A_Q|)$ Γ sequences. Since each Γ sequence uses $O(m)$ space the total space becomes $O(m \log |A_Q| + n)$.

Finally, to achieve linear space we exploit a structural property of Γ sequences to compress them efficiently. We obtain a new representation of Γ sequences that only requires $O(m)$ *bits*. Plugging in the new representation into our algorithm the total space becomes $O(n + m)$ as desired. However, the resulting algorithm requires many costly compressions and decompressions of Γ sequences at each arc in the traversal. As a practical and more elegant solution we show how to augment the compressed representation of Γ sequences using standard *rank/select indices* to obtain constant time random access to elements in Γ sequences. This allows us to compress each Γ sequence only once and avoid decompression entirely without affecting the complexity of the algorithm.

Related Work. Arc-annotated strings are a natural model of RNA molecules that captures both the primary and secondary structure of these. Consequently, a wide range of pattern matching problems for them have been studied, see e.g., [1–3, 6, 9, 10, 14]. Among these, NAPS is one of the most basic and fundamental problems.

The NAPS problem generalizes the *tree inclusion problem* for ordered trees [4, 7, 13]. Here, the goal is to determine if a tree can be obtained from another tree by deleting nodes. This is equivalent to NAPS where all bases in both strings have an incident arc. The authors have shown how to solve the tree inclusion problem in time $O(nm/\log n + n \log n)$ and space $O(n + m)$ [4]. Compared to our current result for NAPS the space complexity is the same but the time complexity for tree inclusion is a factor $O(\log n)$ better for most values of m and n. Though our obtained complexities for the tree inclusion problem and NAPS are very similar, the ideas and techniques behind the results differ significantly. While the definition of the two problems seems very similar it appears that the more general NAPS is significantly more complicated. We leave it as an interesting research direction to determine the precise relationship between NAPS and the tree inclusion problem.

Several generalizations of NAPS have also been studied relaxing the requirement that arcs should be nested [5, 9, 10]. In nearly all cases the resulting problem becomes NP-complete.

Due to lack of space some of the proof are omitted from this extended abstract. They can be found in the full version of the paper.

2 Preliminaries and Notation

Let S be an arc-annotated string with arc set A_S. The length of S is the number of bases in S and is denoted $|S|$. We will assume that our input strings P and Q have the arcs $(1, |P|)$ and $(1, |Q|)$, respectively. If this is not the case we may always add additional connected bases to the start and end of P and Q without affecting the solution or complexity of the problem. We do this only to ensure that the nesting of the arcs form a tree (rather than a forest) which simplifies the presentation of our algorithm.

The *arc-annotated substring* $S[i_1, i_2]$, $1 \leq i_1, i_2 \leq |S|$, is the string of bases starting at i_1 and ending at i_2. The arc set associated with $S[i_1, i_2]$ is the subset of A_S of arcs with both endpoints in $[i_1, i_2]$. We define $S[i_1] = S[i_1, i_1]$ and $S[i_1, i_2] = \epsilon$ (the empty string) if $i_1 > i_2$. Note the arc set of an arc-annotated string of length ≤ 1 is also empty. A *split* of S is a partition of S into two substrings $S[1, i]$ and $S[i+1, |S|]$, for some i, $0 \leq i \leq |S|$. The split is an *arc-preserving split* if no arcs in A_S cross i, i.e., all arcs either have both endpoints in $S[1, i]$ or $S[i+1, |S|]$. We say that the index i *induces* a (arc-preserving) split of S.

An *embedding* of P in Q is an injective function $f : \{1, \ldots, m\} \rightarrow \{1, \ldots, n\}$ such that

1. for all $j \in \{1, \ldots, m\}$, $P[j] = Q[f(j)]$. (base match condition)
2. for all indices $j_l, j_r \in \{1, \ldots, m\}$, $(j_l, j_r) \in A_P \Leftrightarrow (f(j_l), f(j_r)) \in A_Q$. (arc match condition)
3. for all $j \in \{1, \ldots, m\}$, $i < j \Leftrightarrow f(i) < f(j)$. (order condition)

If $f(j) = i$ we say that j is *matched* to i in the embedding. From the definition of arc-preserving subsequences we have that $P \sqsubseteq Q$ iff there is an embedding of P in Q.

3 The Dynamic Programming Recurrence

In this section we give our dynamic programming recurrence for the NAPS problem. Essentially, the recursion expresses for any pair of substrings P' and Q' of P and Q, respectively, the longest prefix of P' which is an arc-preserving subsequence of Q' in terms of smaller substrings of P' and Q'.

We show the following key properties of arc-preserving splits.

Lemma 1 (Splitting Lemma). *Let P' and Q' be arc-annotated substrings of P and Q, respectively, and let (Q_1, Q_2) be any arc-preserving split of Q'.*

(i) If $P' \sqsubseteq Q'$ then there exists an arc-preserving split (P_1, P_2) of P' such that $P_1 \sqsubseteq Q_1$ and $P_2 \sqsubseteq Q_2$.
(ii) Let (P_1, P_2) be an arc-preserving split of P'. Then $P_1 \sqsubseteq Q_1$ and $P_2 \sqsubseteq Q_2 \Rightarrow P' \sqsubseteq Q'$.

For $1 \leq j_l \leq m$, $l \in \{1, 2\}$ and $1 \leq i_1 \leq i_2 \leq n$ define $\gamma(j_1, j_2, i_1, i_2)$ to be the largest integer k such that $P[j_1, k] \sqsubseteq Q[i_1, i_2]$ and k induces an arc-preserving split of $P[j_1, j_2]$. It follows that $\gamma(1, m, 1, n) = m$ if and only if $P \sqsubseteq Q$.

The Splitting Lemma gives us a very useful property of γ: The requirement that k induces an arc-preserving split of $P[j_1, j_2]$ in the definition of γ implies that if there exists an embedding f of $P[k+1, j_2]$ in $Q[i_2, i]$ for some i then by the Splitting Lemma the embedding of $P[j_1, k]$ in $Q[i_1, i_2]$ (which exists by the definition of γ) can be extended with f to get an embedding of $P[j_1, j_2]$ in $Q[i_1, i]$. This would not be true if we dropped the requirement that k induces an arc-preserving split of $P[j_1, j_2]$. Formally,

Corollary 1. *Let i be an index inducing an arc-preserving split of $Q[i_1, i_2]$. Then, $\gamma(j_1, j_2, i_1, i_2) = \gamma(\gamma(j_1, j_2, i_1, i) + 1, j_2, i + 1, i_2)$.*

Intuitively, the corollary says that to compute the largest prefix of P that can be embedded in Q we can greedily match the bases and right endpoints of arcs of P as much to the left in Q as possible. The dynamic programming recurrence for γ is as follows.

Base cases. $\gamma(j_1, j_2, i_1, i_2)$ is equal to

$$\begin{cases} j_1 - 1 & \text{if } j_1 > j_2, \quad (1) \\ j_1 & \text{if } i_1 = i_2 \text{ and } P[j_1] = Q[i_1] \text{ and} \\ & \quad (j_1, j_r) \notin A_P \text{ for all } j_r \leq j_2, \quad (2a) \\ j_1 - 1 & \text{if } i_1 = i_2 \text{ and } (P[j_1] \neq Q[i_1] \text{ or} \\ & \quad (j_1, j_r) \in A_P \text{ for some } j_r \leq j_2). \quad (2b) \end{cases}$$

Recursive cases. $i_1 < i_2$ and $j_1 \leq j_2$.

If $(i_1, i_r) \notin A_Q$ for all $i_r \leq i_2$ then $\gamma(j_1, j_2, i_1, i_2)$ is equal to

$$\begin{cases} \gamma(j_1 + 1, j_2, i_1 + 1, i_2) & \text{if } (j_1, j_r) \notin A_P \text{ for all } j_r \leq j_2 \text{ and } P[j_1] = Q[i_1], \quad (3) \\ \gamma(j_1, j_2, i_1 + 1, i_2) & \text{if } (j_1, j_r) \in A_P \text{ for some } j_r \leq j_2 \text{ or } P[j_1] \neq Q[i_1], \quad (4) \end{cases}$$

If $(i_1, i_r) \in A_Q$ for some $i_r < i_2$, then $\gamma(j_1, j_2, i_1, i_2)$ is equal to

$$\gamma(\gamma(j_1, j_2, i_1, i_r) + 1, j_2, i_r + 1, i_2) \quad (5)$$

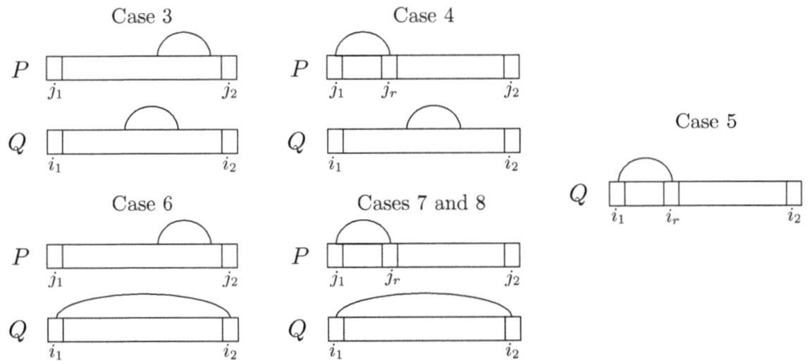

Fig. 2. The main cases from the recurrence relation. Case (3): Neither P or Q starts with an arc. Case (4): P starts with an arc, Q does not. Case (5): Q starts with an arc not spanning Q. We split Q after the arc and compute γ first in the first half and then continue the computation in the other. Case (6): Q starts with an arc, P does not. Case (7)-(8): Both P and Q starts with an arc.

If $(i_1, i_2) \in A_Q$ then $\gamma(j_1, j_2, i_1, i_2)$ is equal to

$$\begin{cases} \max\{\gamma(j_1, j_2, i_1 + 1, i_2), \\ \qquad \gamma(j_1, j_2, i_1, i_2 - 1)\} & \text{if } (j_1, j_r) \notin A_P \text{ for all } j_r \leq j_2, & (6) \\ \gamma(j_1, j_2, i_1 + 1, i_2) & \text{if } (j_1, j_r) \in A_P \text{ for some } j_r \leq j_2, & (7) \\ & \quad \text{and } P[j_1] \neq Q[i_1] \text{ or } P[j_r] \neq Q[i_2], \\ \max\{\phi, \gamma(j_1, j_2, i_1 + 1, i_2)\} & \text{if } (j_1, j_r) \in A_P \text{ for some } j_r \leq j_2, & (8) \\ & \quad P[j_1] = Q[i_1] \text{ and } P[j_r] = Q[i_2], \end{cases}$$

where

$$\phi = \begin{cases} j_r & \text{if } \gamma(j_1 + 1, j_r - 1, i_1 + 1, i_2 - 1) = j_r - 1 \\ j_1 - 1 & \text{otherwise.} \end{cases}$$

The cases are visualized in Fig. 2.

The base cases (1) – (2) cover the cases where $P[j_1, j_2]$ is the empty string ($j_2 > j_1$) or $Q[i_1, i_2]$ is a single base ($i_1 = i_2$). Let $k = \gamma(j_1, j_2, i_1, i_2)$. Case (3) and (5) follows directly from Corollary 1. In case (4) and (7) the base $Q[i_1]$ cannot be part of an embedding of $P[j_1, k]$ in $Q[i_1, i_2]$ and thus $\gamma(j_1, j_2, i_1, i_2) = \gamma(j_1, j_2, i_1+1, i_2)$. In case (6) either $Q[i_1]$ or $Q[i_2]$, but not both, can be part of an embedding of $P[j_1, k]$ in $Q[i_1, i_2]$. Thus, $\gamma(j_1, j_2, i_1, i_2) = \max\{\gamma(j_1, j_2, i_1, i_2-1), \gamma(j_1, j_2, i_1 + 1, i_2)\}$. Case (8) is the most complicated one. Both $Q[i_1, i_2]$ and $P[j_1, j_2]$ starts with an arc and the bases of the arcs match. An embedding of $P[j_1, k]$ into $Q[i_1, i_2]$ either (i) matches the two arcs, (ii) matches the arc (j_1, j_r) and the rest of $P[j_1, k]$ in $Q[i_1 + 1, i_2]$ or (iii) matches nothing ($k = j_1 - 1$). In case (ii) $\gamma(j_1, j_2, i_1, i_2) = \gamma(j_1, j_2, i_1 + 1, i_2)$. Case (i) requires that $P[j_1 + 1, j_r - 1] \sqsubseteq Q[i_1 + 1, i_2 - 1]$. We express this in the recurrence by using an auxiliary function ϕ which is j_r if $\gamma(j_1 + 1, j_r - 1, i_1 + 1, i_2 - 1) = j_r - 1$ and

$j_1 - 1$ otherwise, since in the last case the arc (j_1, j_r) cannot be matched to the arc (i_1, i_2). Since we want the largest match we take the maximum of the two cases (i) and (ii) (case (iii) is covered by these two).

In the next sections we show how to transform the recurrence into a space efficient algorithm for NAPS.

4 The Algorithm

We now present an algorithm to solve NAPS in $O(nm)$ time and $O(m \log |A_Q| + n)$ space. In the next section we show how to further reduce the space to $O(n+m)$ to get Theorem 1. The result relies on a well-known path decomposition for trees applied to arc-annotated strings combined with a new idea to organize the dynamic programming recurrence computation.

Heavy-Path Decomposition of Arc-Annotated Sequences. Let S be a nested arc-annotated string containing the arc $(1, |S|)$ (recall that we assume that both P and Q have this arc). The arcs in A_S induce a rooted and ordered tree T_S rooted at the arc $(1, |S|)$ as shown in Fig. 1(b). We use standard tree terminology for the relationship between arcs in T_S. Let (i_l, i_r) be an arc in A_S. The *depth* of (i_l, i_r) is the number of edges on the path from (i_l, i_r) to the root in T_S. An arc with no children is a leaf arc and otherwise an internal arc. Define $T_S(i_l, i_r)$ to be the subtree of T_S rooted at (i_l, i_r) and let $\text{size}(i_l, i_r)$ be the number of arcs in $T_S(i_l, i_r)$. Note that $\text{size}(1, |S|) = |A_S|$. If (i'_l, i'_r) is an arc in $T_S(i_l, i_r)$ then (i_l, i_r) is an ancestor of (i'_l, i'_r) and if also $(i'_l, i'_r) \neq (i_l, i_r)$ then (i_l, i_r) is a proper ancestor of (i'_l, i'_r). If (i_l, i_r) is a (proper) ancestor of (i'_l, i'_r) then (i'_l, i'_r) is a (proper) descendant of (i_l, i_r).

As in [11] we partition T_S into disjoint paths. We classify each arc as either *heavy* or *light*. The root is light. For each internal arc (i_l, i_r) we pick a child (i^h_l, i^h_r) of maximum size and classify it as heavy. The remaining children are light. An edge to a light child is a *light edge* and an edge to a heavy child is a *heavy edge*. Let $\text{lightdepth}(i_l, i_r)$ denote the number of light edges on the path from (i_l, i_r) to the root of T_S. We use the following well-known bound for trees restated for nested arc-annotated sequences.

Lemma 2 (Harel and Tarjan [11]). *Let S be a nested arc-annotated string containing the arc $(1, |S|)$. For any arc $(i_l, i_r) \in A_S$,* $\text{lightdepth}(i_l, i_r) \leq \log |A_S| + O(1)$.

Removing the light edges we partition T_S into *heavy paths.*

Manipulating Γ Sequences. For positions i_1 and i_2 in Q, $i_1 \leq i_2$, define the *Γ sequence* for i_1 and i_2 as

$$\Gamma(i_1, i_2) = \gamma(m, m, i_1, i_2), \gamma(m-1, m, i_1, i_2), \ldots, \gamma(1, m, i_1, i_2).$$

Thus, $\Gamma(i_1, i_2)$ is the sequence of endpoints of the longest prefixes of each suffix of P that is an arc-preserving subsequence of $Q[i_1, i_2]$. We can efficiently manipulate Γ sequences as suggested by the following lemma.

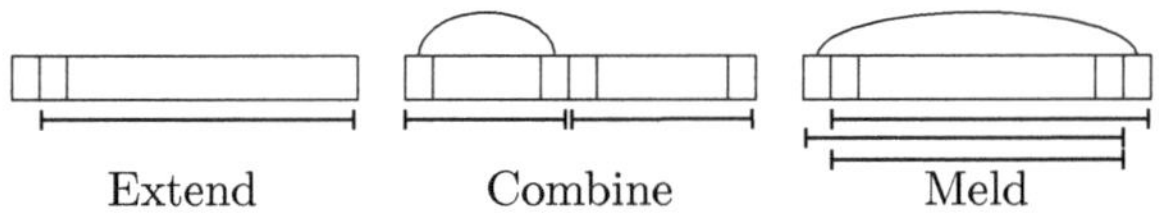

Fig. 3. The extend, combine, and meld operations, respectively. For each operation the substring range(s) below the string indicate the endpoints of the input Γ sequence(s) needed in the operation to compute the Γ sequence for the entire string.

Lemma 3. *For any positions i_1 and i_2 in Q, $i_1 \leq i_2$, we can compute in $O(m)$ time*

(i) $\Gamma(i_2, i_2)$.
(ii) $\Gamma(i_1, i_2)$ *from* $\Gamma(i_1 + 1, i_2)$ *if* $(i_1, i_r) \notin A_Q$ *for any* $i_r \leq i_2$.
(iii) $\Gamma(i_1, i_2)$ *from* $\Gamma(i_1, i_r)$ *and* $\Gamma(i_r + 1, i_2)$ *if* $(i_1, i_r) \in A_Q$ *for some* $i_r < i_2$.
(iv) $\Gamma(i_1, i_2)$ *from* $\Gamma(i_1, i_2 - 1)$, $\Gamma(i_1 + 1, i_2)$, *and* $\Gamma(i_1 + 1, i_2 - 1)$ *if* $(i_1, i_2) \in A_Q$.

Proof. All the cases follow directly from the dynamic programming recurrence. Case (i) follows from case (2) of the recurrence, Case (ii) from case (3) and (4) of the recurrence, Case (iii) from case (5) of the recurrence and Case (iv) from case (6)–(8) of the recurrence. □

We will use each of 4 cases in Lemma 3 as primitive operations in our algorithm and we refer to (i), (ii), (iii), and (iv) as an *initialize*, an *extend*, a *combine*, and a *meld* operation, respectively. Fig. 3 illustrates the extend, combine, and meld operations. An extend operation from $\Gamma(i_1 + k, i_2)$ to $\Gamma(i_1, i_2)$, for some $k > 1$, is defined to be the sequence of k extend operations needed to compute $\Gamma(i_1, i_2)$ from $\Gamma(i_1 + k, i_2)$.

The Algorithm. We now present our main algorithm. Initially, we construct T_Q with a heavy path decomposition in $O(n)$ time and space. Then, we recursively compute Γ sequences for each arc $(i_l, i_r) \in A_Q$ in a top-down traversal of T_Q. The Γ sequence for the root contains the value $\gamma(1, m, 1, n)$ and hence this suffices to solve NAPS. At an arc $(i_l, i_r) \in A_Q$ in the traversal there are two cases to consider:

Case 1: (i_l, i_r) is a leaf arc. We compute $\Gamma(i_l, i_r)$ as follows.

1. Initialize $\Gamma(i_r, i_r)$ and $\Gamma(i_r - 1, i_r - 1)$.
2. Extend $\Gamma(i_r, i_r)$ and $\Gamma(i_r - 1, i_r - 1)$ to get $\Gamma(i_l + 1, i_r)$, $\Gamma(i_l, i_r - 1)$, and $\Gamma(i_l + 1, i_r - 1)$.
3. Meld $\Gamma(i_l + 1, i_r)$, $\Gamma(i_l, i_r - 1)$, and $\Gamma(i_l + 1, i_r - 1)$ to get $\Gamma(i_l, i_r)$.

Case 2: (i_l, i_r) is an internal arc. Let $(i_l^1, i_r^1), \ldots, (i_l^s, i_r^s)$ be the childen arcs of (i_l, i_r) in left-to-right order. To simplify the algorithm we set $i_r^0 = i_l$. We compute $\Gamma(i_l, i_r)$ as follows.

1. Recursively compute $R_h := \Gamma(i_l^h, i_r^h)$, where (i_l^h, i_r^h) is the heavy child arc of (i_l, i_r).

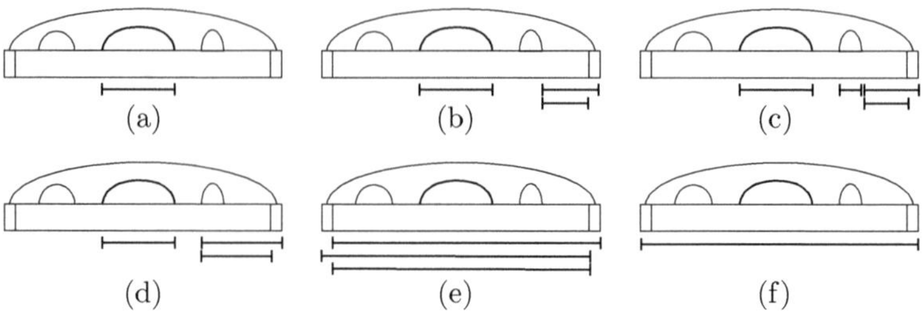

Fig. 4. Snapshot of the Γ sequences computed at an internal arc. The ranges below the arc-annotated sequences represent Γ sequence endpoints. (a) After the recursive call to the heavy child in line 1. (b) After the extend operations in line 3. (c) After the recursive call in line 4(a) (d) After the combine operations in line 4(b). (e) Before the meld operation in line 6. (f) After the meld operation.

2. Initialize $\Gamma(i_r, i_r)$ and $\Gamma(i_r - 1, i_r - 1)$.
3. Extend $\Gamma(i_r, i_r)$ and $\Gamma(i_r - 1, i_r - 1)$ to get $\Gamma(i_r^s + 1, i_r)$ and $\Gamma(i_r^s + 1, i_r - 1)$.
4. For $k := s$ down to 1 do:
   (a) If $k \neq h$ recursively compute $R_k := \Gamma(i_l^k, i_r^k)$.
   (b) Combine R_k with $\Gamma(i_r^k + 1, i_r)$ and with $\Gamma(i_r^k + 1, i_r - 1)$ to get $\Gamma(i_l^k, i_r)$ and $\Gamma(i_l^k, i_r - 1)$.
   (c) Extend $\Gamma(i_l^k, i_r)$ and $\Gamma(i_l^k, i_r - 1)$ to get $\Gamma(i_r^{k-1} + 1, i_r)$ and $\Gamma(i_r^{k-1} + 1, i_r - 1)$.
5. Extend $\Gamma(i_l + 1, i_r - 1)$ to get $\Gamma(i_l, i_r - 1)$.
6. Meld $\Gamma(i_l + 1, i_r)$, $\Gamma(i_l, i_r - 1)$, and $\Gamma(i_l + 1, i_r - 1)$ to get $\Gamma(i_l, i_r)$.

The computation in case 2 is illustrated in Fig. 4. Note that when $k = 1$ in the loop in line 4, line 4(c) computes $\Gamma(i_r^0+1, i_r) = \Gamma(i_l+1, i_r)$ and $\Gamma(i_r^0+1, i_r-1) = \Gamma(i_l + 1, i_r - 1)$. In both cases above the algorithm computes several *local Γ sequences* of the form $\Gamma(i, i_r)$ and $\Gamma(i, i_r - 1)$, for some $i \leq i_r$. These sequences are computed in order of decreasing values of i and each sequence only depends on the previous one and recursively computed Γ sequences. Hence, we only need to store a constant number of local sequences during the computation at (i_l, i_r).

Analysis. We first consider the time complexity of the algorithm. To do so we bound the total number of primitive operations. For each arc in A_Q there is 1 initialize and 1 meld operation and for each internal arc there is 1 combine operation. Hence, the total number of initialize, meld, and combine operations is $O(|A_Q|)$. To count the number of extend operations we first define for any arc $(i_l, i_r) \in A_Q$ the set spaces(i_l, i_r) as the set of positions inside (i_l, i_r) but not inside any child arc of (i_l, i_r), that is,

$$\text{spaces}(i_l, i_r) = \{i \mid i_l \leq i \leq i_r \text{ but not } i_l^k \leq i \leq i_r^k \text{ for any child } (i_l^k, i_r^k) \text{ of } (i_l, i_r)\}.$$

For example, spaces$(1, 11)$ for Q in Fig. 1(a) is $\{1, 2, 11\}$. The spaces sets for all arcs is a partition of the positions in Q and thus $\sum_{(i_l, i_r) \in A_Q} \text{spaces}(i_l, i_r) = n$.

At an arc (i_l, i_r) the algorithm performs $O(\text{spaces}(i_l, i_r))$ extend operations and hence the total number of extend operations is $O(n)$. By Lemma 3 each primitive operation takes $O(m)$ time and therefore the total running time of the algorithm is $O(|A_Q|m + nm) = O(nm)$.

For the space complexity we bound the number of Γ sequences stored by the algorithm. When the algorithm visits an arc (i_l, i_r) we are currently processing a nested sequence of recursive calls corresponding to a path p in T_Q from the root to (i_l, i_r). The number of Γ sequences stored at each of these recursive calls is the total number of Γ sequences stored. Consider an edge e in p from a parent (i'_l, i'_r) to a child (i''_l, i''_r). If e is heavy the recursive call to (i''_l, i''_r) is done in line 1 of case 2 in the algorithm immediately at the start of the visit to (i'_l, i'_r). Therefore, no Γ sequence at (i'_l, i'_r) is stored. If e is light the recursive call to (i''_l, i''_r) is done in line 4(a). The algorithm stores at most 3 Γ sequences, namely $\Gamma(i''_r+1, i'_r)$, $\Gamma(i''_r+1, i'_r-1)$, and $\Gamma(i^{h'}_l, i^{h'}_r)$, where $(i^{h'}_l, i^{h'}_r)$ is the heavy child of (i'_l, i'_r). By Lemma 2 there are at most $\log|A_Q| + O(1)$ light ancestors of (i_l, i_r) in T_Q and therefore the total space for stored Γ sequences is $O(m \log |A_Q|)$. The additional space used by the algorithm is $O(n)$. We have,

Lemma 4. *Given nested arc-annotated strings P and Q of lengths m and n, respectively, we can solve the nested arc-preserving subsequence problem in time $O(nm)$ and space $O(m \log |A_Q| + n)$.*

5 Squeezing into Linear Space

We now show how to compress Γ sequence into a compact representation using $O(m)$ *bits*. Plugging the new representation into our algorithm the total space becomes $O(n + m)$ as desired for Theorem 1.

Our compression scheme for Γ sequences relies on the following key property of the values of γ.

Lemma 5. *For any integers j_1, j_2, i_1, i_2, $1 \leq j_1 \leq j_2 \leq m$, $1 \leq i_1 \leq i_2 \leq n$,*

$$j_1 - 1 \leq \gamma(j_1, j_2, i_1, i_2) \leq \gamma(j_1 + 1, j_2, i_1, i_2) \leq m$$

Proof. Adding another base in front of the substring $P[j_1+1, j_2]$ cannot increase the endpoint of an embedding of $P[j_1+1, j_2]$ in Q and therefore $\gamma(j_1, j_2, i_1, i_2) \leq \gamma(j_1+1, j_2, i_1, i_2)$. Furthermore, for any substring $P[j_1, j_2]$ we can embed at most $j_1 - j_2$ bases and at least 0 bases in Q implying the remaining inequalities. □

Let i_1, i_2 be indices in Q such that $i_1 \leq i_2$ and consider the sequence

$$\Gamma(i_1, i_2) = \gamma(m, m, i_1, i_2), \ldots, \gamma(1, m, i_1, i_2) = \gamma_m, \ldots, \gamma_1$$

By Lemma 5 we have that $\gamma_m, \ldots, \gamma_1$ is a non-increasing and non-negative sequence where γ_m is either m or $m - 1$. We encode the sequence efficiently using two bit strings V and U defined as follows. The string V is formed by the concatenation of m bit strings $s_m, \ldots, s_1$, that is, $V = s_m \cdot s_{m-1} \cdots s_1$, where $\cdot$ denotes concatenation. The string s_m is the single bit $s_m = m - \gamma_m$ and s_k, $1 \leq k < m$, is given by

$$s_k = \begin{cases} 0 & \text{if } \gamma_{k+1} - \gamma_k = 0 \\ \underbrace{1 \cdots 1}_{\gamma_{k+1} - \gamma_k \text{ times}} & \text{if } \gamma_{k+1} - \gamma_k > 0 \end{cases}$$

Let D_k denote the sum of bits in string $s_m \cdots s_k$. We have that $m - D_m = m - s_m = \gamma_m$ and inductively $m - D_k = \gamma_k$. The string U is the bit string of length $|V|$ consisting of a 1 in each position where a substring in V ends. Given V and U we can therefore uniquely recover $\gamma_m, \ldots, \gamma_1$. Since $\gamma_m, \ldots, \gamma_1$ can decrease by at most $m + 1$ the total number of 1s in V is at most $m + 1$. The total number of 0s is at most m and therefore $|V| \leq 2m + 1$. Hence, our representation uses $O(m)$ bits. We can compress $\gamma_m, \ldots, \gamma_1$ into V and U in a single scan in $O(m)$ time. Reversing the process we can also decompress in $O(m)$ time. Hence, we have the following result.

Lemma 6. *We represent any Γ sequence using $O(m)$ bits. Compression and decompression takes $O(m)$ time.*

We modify our algorithm from Section 4 to take advantage of Lemma 6. Let (i_l, i_r) be an internal arc in A_Q. Immediately before a recursive call to a light child (i_l^k, i_r^k) of (i_l, i_r) we compress the at most 3 Γ sequences maintained at (i_l, i_r), namely $\Gamma(i_l^h, i_r^h)$, where (i_l^h, i_r^h) is the heavy child, $\Gamma(i_r^k + 1, i_r)$, and $\Gamma(i_r^k + 1, i_r - 1))$. Immediately after returning from the recursive call we decompress the sequences again.

The total number of compressions and decompressions is $O(n)$. Hence, by Lemma 6 the additional time used is $O(nm)$ and therefore the total running time of the algorithm remains $O(nm)$. The space for storing the $O(\log |A_Q|)$ Γ sequences becomes $O(m \log |A_Q|) = O(m \log n)$ *bits*. Hence, the total space is $O(n + m)$. In conclusion, we have shown Theorem 1.

Avoiding Decompression. The above algorithm requires $O(n)$ decompressions. We briefly describe how one can these by augmenting the representation of Γ sequences slightly. A *rank/select index* for a bit string B supports the operations $\text{RANK}(B, k)$ that returns the number of 1 in $B[1, k]$ and $\text{SELECT}(B, k)$ that returns the position of the kth 1 in S. We can construct a rank/select index in $O(|B|)$ time that uses $o(|B|)$ bits and supports both operations in constant time [15]. We add a rank/select index to the bit strings V and U in our compressed representation. Since these use $o(m)$ bits this does not affect the space complexity. Let $\gamma_m, \ldots, \gamma_1$ be a Γ sequence compressed into bit strings V and U augmented with a rank/select index. For any k, $1 \leq k \leq m$ we can compute the element γ_k in constant time as

$$m - \text{RANK}(V, \text{SELECT}(U, m + 1 - k))$$

To see the correctness, first note that $\text{SELECT}(U, m + 1 - k)$ is end position of the $m + 1 - k$th substring in V. Therefore, $\text{RANK}(V, \text{SELECT}(U, m + 1 - k))$ is the sum of the bits in the first $m+1-k$ substrings of V. This is D_k and since $\gamma_k = m - D_k$ the computation returns γ_k. In summary, we have the following result.

Lemma 7. *We can represent any Γ sequence in $O(m)$ bits while allowing constant time access to any element.*

The algorithm now only needs to compress Γ sequences once. Whenever, we need an element of a compressed Γ sequence we extract it in constant time as above. Hence, the asymptotic complexities of the algorithm remains the same.

References

1. Alber, J., Gramm, J., Guo, J., Niedermeier, R.: Computing the Similarity of Two Sequences with Nested Arc Annotations. Theor. Comput. Sci. 312(2-3), 337–358 (2004)
2. Backofen, R., Landau, G.M., Möhl, M., Tsur, D., Weimann, O.: Fast RNA Structure Alignment for Crossing Input Structures. In: Proc. 20th CPM (2009)
3. Bafna, V., Muthukrishnan, S., Ravi, R.: Computing Similarity between RNA Strings. In: Galil, Z., Ukkonen, E. (eds.) CPM 1995. LNCS, vol. 937, pp. 1–16. Springer, Heidelberg (1995)
4. Bille, P., Gørtz, I.L.: The Tree Inclusion Problem: In Optimal Space and Faster. In: Caires, L., Italiano, G.F., Monteiro, L., Palamidessi, C., Yung, M. (eds.) ICALP 2005. LNCS, vol. 3580, pp. 66–77. Springer, Heidelberg (2005)
5. Blin, G., Fertin, G., Rizzi, R., Vialette, S.: What Makes the Arc-Preserving Subsequence Problem Hard? In: Proc. 5th ICCS, pp. 860–868 (2005)
6. Blin, G., Touzet, H.: How to Compare Arc-Annotated Sequences: The Alignment Hierarchy. In: Crestani, F., Ferragina, P., Sanderson, M. (eds.) SPIRE 2006. LNCS, vol. 4209, pp. 291–303. Springer, Heidelberg (2006)
7. Chen, W.: More Efficient Algorithm for Ordered Tree Inclusion. J. Algorithms 26, 370–385 (1998)
8. Damaschke, P.: A Remark on the Subsequence Problem for Arc-Annotated Sequences with Pairwise Nested Arcs. Inf. Process. Lett. 100(2), 64–68 (2006)
9. Evans, P.: Algorithms and Complexity for Annotated Sequence Analysis. PhD Thesis, University of Victoria (1999)
10. Gramm, J., Guo, J., Niedermeier, R.: Pattern Matching for Arc-Annotated Sequences. ACM Trans. Algorithms 2(1), 44–65 (2006); Announced at: Agrawal, M., Seth, A.K. (eds.) FSTTCS 2002. LNCS, vol. 2556, pp. 182–193. Springer, Heidelberg (2002)
11. Harel, D., Tarjan, R.E.: Fast Algorithms for Finding Nearest Common Ancestors. SIAM J. Comput. 13(2), 338–355 (1984)
12. Kida, T.: Faster Pattern Matching Algorithm for Arc-Annotated Sequences. In: Jantke, K.P., Lunzer, A., Spyratos, N., Tanaka, Y. (eds.) Federation over the Web. LNCS (LNAI), vol. 3847, pp. 25–39. Springer, Heidelberg (2006)
13. Kilpeläinen, P., Mannila, H.: Ordered and Unordered Tree Inclusion. SIAM J. Comput. 24, 340–356 (1995)
14. Lin, G., Chen, Z.-Z., Jiang, T., Wen, J.: The Longest Common Subsequence Problem for Sequences with Nested Arc Annotations. J. Comput. Syst. Sci. 65(3), 465–480 (2002)
15. Munro, I.: Tables. In: Chandru, V., Vinay, V. (eds.) FSTTCS 1996. LNCS, vol. 1180, pp. 37–42. Springer, Heidelberg (1996)
16. Vialette, S.: On the Computational Complexity of 2-Interval Pattern Matching Problems. Theor. Comput. Sci. 312(2-3), 223–249 (2004); Announced at CPM 2002

Automated Deadlock Detection in Synchronized Reentrant Multithreaded Call-Graphs*

Frank S. de Boer[1] and Immo Grabe[1,2]

[1] CWI, Amsterdam, The Netherlands
[2] Christian-Albrechts-University Kiel, Germany

Abstract. In this paper we investigate the synchronization of multi-threaded call graphs with reentrance similar to call graphs in Java programs. We model the individual threads as Visibly Pushdown Automata (VPA) and analyse the reachability of a state in the product automaton by means of a Context Free Language (CFL) which captures the synchronized interleaving of threads. We apply this CFL-reachability analysis to detect deadlock.

1 Introduction

Due to the behavioural complexity formal methods are needed when it comes to reasoning about a program. This is particularly true for concurrent (or multi-threaded) programs. Such programs in general involve the synchronization of different processes (or threads) which may lead to undesirable deadlock situations.

A group of activities competing for a number of resources can block each other if each of them holds resources another one needs. A typical example of such a resource is exclusive access to a part of the system, i.e. a class or object, guarded by a lock. Modern programming languages like Java opt for an implicit lock handling, i.e. instead of explicitly grabbing a lock a region is declared to be subject to a lock and the lock handling is done by the execution platform rather than the programmer.

These languages also allow for reentrance, i.e. a thread is allowed to enter each region guarded by a lock several times if it holds the lock. In such a setting the number of times a thread has entered a lock-guarded region has to be counted to decide when to release the lock again. Though there are some techniques to avoid this problem (preemption, global lock orders) on the programming level most concurrent programming languages have to deal with this problem.

The combination of multithreading, implicit lock handling and reentrance makes the detection of deadlocks hard. This explains the need for methods and tools to do automatic deadlock analysis.

---

* This work has been supported by the EU-project IST-33826 *Credo: Modelling and analysis of evolutionary structures for distributed services*. For more information, see `http://credo.cwi.nl`

J. van Leeuwen et al. (Eds.): SOFSEM 2010, LNCS 5901, pp. 200–211, 2010.

Contribution. In order to develop an automated method for deadlock detection applicable to Java-like languages we abstract from data and focus on the control flow of method calls and returns. The unsynchronized interleaving of a finite number of reentrant (abstract) threads is naturally modelled as a multi-stack Visibly Pushdown Automaton [2]. In order to analyse the synchronization between threads we apply Context-Free-Language(CFL)-reachability as introduced in [11] to the underlying finite state automaton. Information about the ownership of the locks is included in the CFL to model synchronized sequences of calls and returns and to identify deadlock states.

In general however CFLs are not closed under arbitrary interleavings. We resolve this lack of expressive power of CFL languages in this particular setting by showing that for every (synchronized) interleaving there exists a *rescheduling* which does not affect the synchronization and is included in the CFL language. In fact, the CFL language only restricts the scheduling of the returns and we can anticipate returns of synchronised method calls without affecting the synchronization.

To the best of our knowledge this is the first automata based approach tailored to deadlock detection of the abstract control flow of method calls and returns of multithreaded reentrant programs. A sketch of an implementation is described in the concluding section. In this implementation the programmer only needs to indicate a finite number of threads, i.e., for each thread class the number of threads involved in the deadlock analysis.

Related Work. In [12] Rinard gives an overview of recent techniques to analyse multithreaded programs. Deadlock detection is only covered for languages communicating via pairwise rendezvous. Ramalingam (see [10]) has shown that the analysis of synchronization problems is not decidable even for only two threads if a CCS-style pairwise rendezvous is used to synchronize among the threads.

In [7] Kahlon et al. give a compositional method to reason about programs synchronizing via locks based on Visibly Pushdown Automata. Visibly Pushdown Automata are a kind of pushdown automata tailored to the generation of nested words reflecting the structure of traces generated by languages with nested call and return structures. The languages generated by these automata are closed under intersection. The result from [10] is generalized by showing that the reachability problem is not decidable for two threads communicating via non-nested locks. The language presented is non-reentrant and uses explicit acquire and release primitives. The automata are extended by so called acquisition histories to record relevant locking information to synchronize the threads. These acquisition histories can be used together with the explicit acquire primitives to identify deadlock situations. As soon as reentrance is allowed the setting gets more complicated. Due to reentrance the number of calls to synchronised methods has to be counted to decide whether or not to release a lock. Note that Java provides a nested call and return structure (with respect to one thread) which implies a nested acquire and release of locks.

Kidd et al. [8] introduce a technique called language strength reduction to reduce reentrant locks to non-reentrant locks in the context of Visibly Pushdown

Languages. They check for atomic-set serializability violations, i.e. an illegal data access pattern. Due to this goal they take data into consideration. They create a CFL for each thread and for each lock. These languages are approximated by regular languages. Additionally a language describing a violation of a data access pattern is defined and the intersection of all languages is checked for emptiness. Up to our understanding there is no natural way to express a deadlock in this setting.

Lammich and Müller–Olm [9] present a model that can deal with thread creation and reentrant monitors. Their analysis is also focused on atomic-set serializability violations. Their approach is based on a fixpoint construction. They also use acquisition histories but only for synchronization purposes again. To reduce the number of executions to analyse they reduce the executions to a restricted subset involving the notion of a macrostep, i.e. a number of steps by one thread such that the stack only grows that is there are at most new locks taken after a macrostep but none are freed. In general, their analysis answers whether a given program location and a stack of method calls can be reached by a computation. However solutions to this reachability problem do not solve the more abstract problem of checking the reachability of a deadlock configuration.

In [5] Carotenuto et al. introduce Visibly Pushdown Automata with a finite number of stacks. The languages generated by these automata are also closed under intersection. However the emptiness problem is not decidable for these automata.

A variety of other synchronization and communication mechanisms in concurrent programs with recursion have been studied (we only mention here [3,6]). In [4] Bouajjani et al. present a formalism to compute abstractions of multithreaded call-graphs.

Outline. This paper is organized as follows. We start with a section on the syntax and semantics of synchronised multithreaded programs. In section 3 we introduce Thread Automata to model the individual threads. Based on Thread Automata we introduce a technique based on CFL-reachability for the analysis of the product automaton in section 4. In section 5 we prove soundness and completeness of our method. We conclude in section 6.

2 Synchronized Multithreaded Programs

We abstract from data which includes object identities. In our setting locks are bound to classes. A system consists of a finite number of given classes and a finite number of given threads synchronizing via locks.

2.1 Syntax

We assume a given set of method names M with typical element m. Methods are specified by the following regular expressions.

$$r ::= \tau \mid m \mid r;r \mid r+r \mid r^*$$

Here τ denotes an internal step and m denotes a call.

We denote by M_s the synchronised methods and by M_u the unsynchronised ones. Every method is either synchronised or not:

$$M = M_s \cup M_u \text{ and } M_s \cap M_u = \emptyset$$

We assume a given set D of method definitions. A method definition consists of a method name m and a method body given by a regular expression $m ::= r$. Furthermore we assume a finite partitioning C of the method names into classes with typical element c.

For every class c, we denote by

- M^c its methods,
- M_s^c its synchronised methods,
- M_u^c its unsynchronised methods.

We assume that every method belongs to exactly one class.

The set of method definitions D and the set of classes C define a program P. The behaviour of a program is defined in terms of a given set of threads T with typical element t. Each thread t has an initial (run) method denoted by run(t).

2.2 Operational Semantics

The operational semantics of a multithreaded program is described by a labelled transition relation between configurations Θ which consist of pairs (t, θ), where θ is a stack of labelled expressions $m@r$. We require that Θ contains for each thread $t \in T$ at most one such pair. The label $m@r$ indicates that r is the continuation of the execution of the body of method m. We record the name of the method to formalize synchronization as described below. The label at the top of the stack represents the method currently executed by the thread. By $\theta \cdot m@r$ we denote the result of pushing the label $m@r$ unto the stack θ.

In order to describe operationally the return of a method we extend the syntax of expressions by return expression *ret*. We identify the method body r in a declaration $m ::= r$ with $r; ret$.

Method Calls. We have the following transition for unsynchronised methods:

$$\Theta \cup \{(t, \theta \cdot m@m'; r)\} \to \Theta \cup \{(t, \theta \cdot m@r \cdot m'@r')\}$$

with $m' ::= r' \in D$ and $m' \in M_u^c$ for some class c. A call of the method m' thus pushes the corresponding label on the stack. Note that upon return of m' the execution of m continues with r.

For synchronised methods we additionally require that no other thread is executing a synchronised method subject to the same lock:

$$\Theta \cup \{(t, \theta \cdot m@m'; r)\} \to \Theta \cup \{(t, \theta \cdot m@r \cdot m'@r')\}$$

with $m' ::= r' \in D$, $m' \in M_s^c$ for some class c, and there does not exist $(t', \theta') \in \Theta$ such that $t \neq t'$ and θ' contains a continuation $m''@r''$ of method $m'' \in M_s^c$.

Return. Returning from a method is described by

$$\Theta \cup \{(t, \theta \cdot m@ret)\} \rightarrow \Theta \cup \{(t, \theta)\}$$

The top of the stack thus is simply popped upon return.

The rules for the choice and iteration operators are obtained by a straightforward lifting of the corresponding transitions for regular expressions as described in the next section.

The above transition relation maintains the following synchronization invariant:

Corollary 1. *For every class c there is at most one $(t, \theta) \in \Theta$ such that θ contains a continuation $m@r$ of a synchronised method $m \in M_s^c$.*

This characterization of threads and locks can be modelled in a straightforward manner as a multistack pushdown automaton with counters for each class. Reachability is not decidable in this general setting. Therefore we model the system differently. Each thread is modelled as a Visibly Pushdown Automata (VPA, for short). We show that the product of these automata are amenable to analysis via a technique based on CFL-reachability. We give a grammar to steer this analysis.

3 Thread Automata

In this section we model and analyse the operational semantics of multithreaded programs described above in terms of thread automata. For each thread t a Thread Automaton TA(t) is defined as a VPA, in terms of a *call* alphabet $\Sigma^t_{\text{call}} = \{t_m \mid m \in M\}$ and a *return* alphabet $\Sigma^t_{ret} = \{t_{ret}\}$. By Σ^t we denote the visible alphabet $\Sigma^t_{\text{call}} \cup \Sigma^t_{ret}$ of thread t. A call of method m by thread t is indicated by t_m. The return of thread t from a method call is indicated by t_{ret}. The idea is that the call alphabet generates push operations, whereas the return alphabet generates pop operations. For each thread t its local alphabet is defined by $\{\tau\}$, used to describe internal steps.

States

The set of states of TA(t) is the set R_t of regular expressions reachable from the run method run(t). Here reachability is defined in terms of the following standard transition relation describing the behaviour of (regular) expressions:

- $m; r \rightarrow r$
- $r_1 + r_2; r \rightarrow r_i; r$ for $i \in \{1, 2\}$
- $r^*; r' \rightarrow r; r^*; r'$
- $r^*; r' \rightarrow r'$

Transitions

The external transitions of TA(t) are of the form (r, a, r', s), where r and r' are states as introduced above, a is an action of the visible alphabet of t, and s

a stack symbol. The stack alphabet Γ^t of a Thread Automaton TA(t) is given by the set $\{t_r \mid t \in T,\ r \in R_t\}$, where the regular expression r denotes the return "address" of t. Method calls push a stack symbol upon the stack. This symbol encodes the location to return to later. Method returns pop a symbol from the stack. The location to return to can be derived from this symbol.

Internal transitions are of the form (r, τ, r') with r and r' states in terms of regular expressions, and τ to denote the internal step.

Method call. For every state $m; r'$ we have the transition $(m; r', t_m, r, t_{r'})$, where $m ::= r \in D$. This transition models a move of control from state $m; r'$ to state r and a push of token $t_{r'}$ on the stack when reading t_m . The states encode the actual code to execute whereas the stack symbol encodes the location to return to when the method call terminates, i.e. a return is received.

Return. For every state r, returning from a method is described by the transition (ret, t_{ret}, r, t_r) which models a move of control from state ret to state r and a pop of token t_r from the stack when reading t_{ret}. For each caller of the method a *return* transition exists. The location of return to is determinate by the token popped of the stack. Because the return location being determined by the stack symbol an unspecific return action t_{ret} is sufficient.

Internal transitions. The choice construct is described by the transitions $(r_1 + r_2; r, \tau, r_i; r)$ for $i \in \{1, 2\}$ and iteration is described by a transition modelling looping $(r^*; r', \tau, r; r^*; r')$ and a transition modelling termination $(r^*; r', \tau, r')$. Note that internal transitions do not involve an operation on the stack.

Unsynchronised Product

We model the whole system by the product of the above automata for the individual threads. This automaton does not take synchronization between the individual threads into account. We add this synchronization by means of a grammar in section 4.

Let $T = \{t^1, \ldots, t^n\}$. By TA(T) we denote the *unsynchronised* product of the automata TA(t^i). This product is described by a multistack VPA with call alphabet $\Sigma_{\text{call}} = \{t_m \mid t \in T,\ m \in M\}$, return alphabet $\Sigma_{\text{return}} = \{t_{ret} \mid t \in T\}$ and for each thread t a stack over the alphabet Γ^t. We denote by q_0 the initial state $q_0 = \langle \text{run}(t_1), \ldots, \text{run}(t_n) \rangle$.

States. The states of the product automaton are of the form $\langle r_1, \ldots, r_n \rangle$ where r_i denotes the state of t^i.

Transitions. We lift the transitions of the individual threads to transitions of the product in the obvious manner. Note that this lifting still does not provide any synchronization between the threads.

Reachability. Similar to the operational semantics for the definition of reachability in TA(T) we give a declarative characterization of the synchronization between threads in terms of arbitrary sequences of calls and returns.

This characterization involves the following language theoretic properties:

- Calls and returns in a sequence are *matched* according to formal language theory, i.e. a bracketed grammar.
- A call without a matching return is called *pending*.
- A return without a matching call is called *pending*.
- A sequence is *well-formed* if it does not contain any pending returns.

Note 1. The words generated by the unsynchronised product are already well-formed.

Now we define synchronised sequences of calls and returns:
A sequence is called *synchronised* if for each call t_m to a synchronised method m ($m \in M_s^c$) by thread t there exists no pending call $t'_{m'}$ to a synchronised method m' of c by a thread $t' \neq t$ in the prefix of the sequence up to t_m.

We conclude this section with the definition of reachability and a definition of deadlock freedom in TA(T).

A state $q = \langle r_1, \ldots, r_n \rangle$ of TA(T) is *reachable* in TA(T) if there exists a computation in TA(T)

$$(q_0, \{\perp\}^n) \xrightarrow{W} (q, \bar{\theta})$$

for a synchronised sequence of calls and returns W and a tuple of stacks $\bar{\theta} = \langle \theta_1, \ldots, \theta_n \rangle$. Where $\perp$ denotes the empty stack.

This notion of reachability of a state does not provide enough information for deadlock detection. Therefore we extend the definition in the obvious manner to configurations: A configuration $(q, \bar{\theta})$ of TA(T) is *reachable* in TA(T) if there exists a computation in TA(T)

$$(q_0, \{\perp\}^n) \xrightarrow{W} (q, \bar{\theta})$$

for a synchronised sequence. Furthermore a configuration $(q, \bar{\theta})$ is a deadlock configuration iff $(q, \bar{\theta}) \not\rightarrow$, which indicates there is no transition possible, and at least one thread is not yet terminated, i.e. there exists an i such that $r_i \neq ret$ or $\theta_i \neq \perp$.

Finally we define the automaton TA(T) to be deadlock free iff there does not exist a reachable deadlock configuration.

4 CFL-Reachability

For the proof of the decidability of the reachability problem and deadlock freedom we apply CFL-reachability to the finite state automaton FA(T) embodied in TA(T). We first focus on the unsynchronised product and introduce synchronization later.

CFL-Modelling of Unsynchronised Interleavings

The the finite state automaton FA(T) contains all internal transitions (q, τ, q') of TA(T). To model the push and pop transitions of TA(T) we introduce the set of actions

$$\Sigma = \{t_r^m, t_r \mid t \in T,\ m \in M,\ r \in R\}$$

where t_r^m denotes a call of m by t with return expression r and t_r indicates that t returns to the regular expression r. We then model the transitions (q, t_m, q', t_r) and (q, t_{ret}, q', t_r) in TA(T) by (q, t_r^m, q') and (q, t_r, q'), respectively.

In order to compensate for the loss of information we introduce next for each thread t the following context free grammar which describes the structure of recursive call/return sequences.

$$\begin{array}{ll} S^t & ::= \epsilon \mid B^t \mid t_r^m S^t \mid S^t S^t \\ B^t & ::= \epsilon \mid t_r^m r^t \mid B^t B^t \\ r^t & ::= B^t t_r \end{array}$$

Sequences generated by the non-terminal S^t can contain pending calls, whereas sequences generated by B^t do not contain pending calls. Sequences generated by the non-terminal r^t ($r \in R_t$) describe a return from a method call to the expression r. In these sequences the call itself does not appear, e.g., these sequences contain a return t_r without a matching call. Note that the non-terminal r^t should be distinguished from the corresponding terminal t_r.

Starting with S^t or B^t the grammar produces well-formed sequences.

We lift this grammar to the definition of another CFL grammar describing the *unsynchronised* interleavings of the individual threads. The non-terminals of this grammar are sets G, where G contains for each thread t one of its non-terminals S^t, B^t, and r^t. The above rules are lifted to this grammar as follows.

$$\begin{array}{lll} G & ::= \epsilon & (G \subseteq \{S^t, B^t \mid t \in T\}) \\ G \cup \{S^t\} & ::= G \cup \{B^t\} \mid t_r^m\ G \cup \{S^t\} & \\ G \cup \{B^t\} & ::= t_r^m\ G \cup \{r^t\} & \\ G \cup \{r^t\} & ::= G \cup \{B^t\}\ t_r & \\ G_1 \circ G_2 & ::= G_1\ G_2 & \end{array}$$

where the composition $G_1 \circ G_2$ contains for every thread a non-terminal U^t for which there exist a rule $U^t ::= V_1^t V_2^t$, with V_1^t in G_1 and V_2^t in G_2. Note that only sets G which contain for each thread t either S^t or B^t can be split (in other words, the non-terminal r^t cannot be split). Note also that the non-terminal r^t cannot be generated by a split.

We denote by $G_0 = \{S^t \mid t \in T\}$ the initial configuration of a derivation.

Note 2. Not all possible interleavings can be derived by this grammar (see the following example). But for any possible interleaving an equivalent one (with respect to synchronization) exists which can be derived by the grammar. Since the non-terminal r^t can not be split the location of a method return is restricted. This does not affect the reachability or deadlock analysis. The method returns can be shuffled within certain limits (a return can be brought forward ignoring steps of other threads and can be delayed by steps of other threads on other locks). This holds also for the synchronised case as we show later. In the synchronized case this property is ensured by the requirements with respect to the lock sets.

Example 1. We give an example of a sequence that can not be derived directly. The sequence $t^m_r, t'^{m'}_{r'}, t_r, t'^m_{r''}, t'_{r''}, t'_{r'}$ with $m \in M^c_s$ and $m' \in M^{c' \neq c}_s$. It is not possible to find a direct derivation for $G_0 \Rightarrow^* t^m_r, t'^{m'}_{r'}, t_r, t'^m_{r''}, t'_{r''}, t'_{r'}$. Since the projection on t resp. t' contains a matching return for every call it can only be derived by a rule starting from B^t resp. $B^{t'}$. We have to start with B^t to get the t^m_r in the front position of the sequence. The next step has to be a $B^{t'}$ step to get $t'^{m'}_{r'}$ to the second position. Now $G = \{r^t\} \cup \{r'^{t'}\}$. The next step has to be a $r'^{t'}$ to get $t'_{r'}$ to the end of the sequence. Now we get $G = \{r^t\} \cup \{B^{t'}\}$. Here we are stuck. To get the t_r in front of the $t'^m_{r''}, t'_{r''}$ we could only use the composition rule but this one is forbidden for Gs containing a r^t. Instead we can derive $t^m_r, t_r, t'^{m'}_{r'}, t'^m_{r''}, t'_{r''}, t'_{r'}$. By reordering the returns we can get the original sequence.

According to the technique of CFL-reachability we define inductively transitions of the form (q, G, q'), where q and q' are states of FA(T) and G is a set of non-terminals. Such a transition indicates that q' is reachable from q by a sequence generated by G.

- For every rule $G ::= \epsilon$ and state q we add a transition (q, G, q).
- For transitions (q, τ, q') and (q', G, q'') we add a transition (q, G, q''). Similarly, for transitions (q, G, q') and (q', τ, q'') we add a transition (q, G, q'').
- Given a transition (q, G, q'), an application of a rule $G' ::= G$ generates a transition (q, G', q).
- Given transitions (q_0, t^m_r, q) and (q, G, q_1), an application of a rule $G' ::= t^m_r\ G$ generates a transition (q_0, G', q_1).
- Given transitions (q_0, G, q) and (q, t_r, q_1), an application of a rule $G' ::= G\ t_r$ generates a transition (q_0, G', q_1).
- Given transitions (q_0, G_1, q) and (q, G_2, q_1), an application of rule $G_1 \circ G_2 ::= G_1 G_2$ generates a transition $(q_0, G_1 \circ G_2, q_1)$.

Reachability of a state q in FA(T) from the initial state q_0 by a word $G_0 \Rightarrow^* W$ then can be decided by checking the existence of a transition (q_0, G_0, q).

CFL-Modelling of Synchronised Interleavings

We now extend the above grammar for unsynchronised interleavings of threads with input/output information about the locks. This information is represented by pairs (I, L), where $I, L \subseteq T \times C$. The set of locks I are taken by some threads at the beginning of a derivation (step), whereas L is the set of locks that are taken by some threads at the end of a derivation (step). We denote an element of $T \times C$ by t_c which indicates that t holds the lock of class c. We implicitly restrict to subsets of $T \times C$ where for each class c at most one thread holds its lock. The non-terminals of this new grammar are annotated sets $(I, L) : G$, where $I \subseteq L$ and G contains for each thread t one of its non-terminals S^t, B^t, and r^t.

We have the following rules (here $I_c = \{t \in T \mid t_c \in I\}$ and $L_c = \{t \in T \mid t_c \in L\}$).

$$
\begin{array}{llll}
(I,I) : G & ::= \epsilon & & (G \subseteq \{S^t, B^t \mid t \in T\}) \\
(I,L) : G \cup \{S^t\} & ::= (I,L) : G \cup \{B^t\} & & \\
& \mid \quad t_r^m \ (I,L) : G \cup \{S^t\} & & (m \notin M_s^c \text{ or } t_c \in I \cap L) \\
& \mid \quad t_r^m \ (I \cup \{t_c\}, L) : G \cup \{S^t\} & & (m \in M_s^c,\ I_c = \emptyset,\ t_c \in L) \\
(I,L) : G \cup \{B^t\} & ::= t_r^m \ (I,L) : G \cup \{r^t\} & & (m \notin M_s^c \text{ or } t_c \in I \cap L) \\
& \mid \quad t_r^m \ (I \cup \{t_c\}, L \cup \{t_c\}) : G \cup \{r^t\} & & (m \in M_s^c,\ I_c = L_c = \emptyset) \\
(I,L) : G \cup \{r^t\} & ::= (I,L) : G \cup \{B^t\}\ t_r & & \\
(I,L) : G_1 \circ G_2 & ::= (I,L') : G_1\ (L',L) : G_2 & &
\end{array}
$$

The above grammar generates synchronised sequences. The conditions of the rules reflect in a natural manner the locking mechanism. To characterize the language generated by the above grammar we denote for a sequence of calls and returns W the set of locks still taken at the end of W by Lock(W): $t_c \in \text{Lock}(W)$ iff there exists a pending call to a method m by thread t with $m \in M_s^c$.

Theorem 1. *For every sequence W generated by $(I,L) : G$ we have the following properties:*

- *W is synchronised*
- *$t_c \in L$ iff $t_c \in I \cup \text{Lock}(W)$.*

Proof. The theorem is proven by induction on the length of the derivation of W. Details of the proof can be found in the appendix.

To check reachability we add inductively transitions $(q, \alpha : G, q')$ to FA(T) analogous to the unsynchronised case above.

5 Soundness and Completeness of CFL-Reachability

Soundness and completeness of our method follows from the general technique of CFL-reachability and the following properties of our specific grammars together with the properties for sequences generated by the grammar established in theorem 1.

We define an equivalence relation $W' \approx W$ as follows: For every thread t

- the projection of W' on t equals that of W on t
- $\text{Lock}(W') = \text{Lock}(W)$.

Lemma 1. *For every well-formed synchronised sequence W there exists a well-formed synchronised sequence W' such that $G_0 \Rightarrow^* W'$ with $G_0 = \{S^t \mid t \in T\}$ and $W' \approx W$.*

Proof. The lemma is proven by induction on the length of the word W. Details of the proof can be found in the appendix.

We extend the notion of a synchronised sequence to a sequence synchronised with respect to a lock set I. A sequence W is synchronised with respect to I if for each $t_c \in I$ W does not contain any calls or returns of a thread $t' \neq t$ to a synchronised method of class c.

Lemma 2. *If* $G_0 \Rightarrow^* W$ *with* W *synchronised then* $(\emptyset, \mathrm{Lock}(W)) : G_0 \Rightarrow^* W$.

Proof. Instead of proving the lemma directly we prove a more general statement: If $G_0 \Rightarrow^* W$ with W synchronised with respect to I, then $(I, I \cup \mathrm{Lock}(W)) : G_0 \Rightarrow^* W$.

The statement is proven by induction on the length of the derivation $G_0 \Rightarrow^* W$. Details of the proof can be found in the appendix.

Theorem 2. *The reachability problem of* $\mathrm{TA}(T)$ *is decidable.*

Our method for checking reachability of a state q in $\mathrm{TA}(T)$ consists of checking the existence of a transition $(q_0, (\emptyset, L) : G_0, q)$ in $\mathrm{FA}(T)$.

Decidability follows from soundness and completeness proven above.

Theorem 3. *The problem of deadlock freedom of* $\mathrm{TA}(T)$ *is decidable.*

In this case our method consists of checking reachability of $(q_0, (\emptyset, L) : G_0, q)$ for some state q for which there exists a subset of threads $T' \subseteq T$ such that in q each thread $t \in T'$ is about to execute a synchronised method $m \in M_s^c$ of a class c the lock of which is already held by a different thread $t' \in T'$, i.e., $t'_c \in L$.

Note 3. This notion of deadlock is a refinement of the notion presented in section 3. With this notion we do not only cover a deadlock of the whole system but also of parts of the system.

6 Conclusion

We generalized the technique of CFL-reachability to the analysis of the synchronized interleavings of multithreaded Java programs. By means of this technique we can decide whether a state in the finite state automaton underlying the product of the individual thread automata is reachable by a synchronized interleaving. We also can decide deadlock freedom.

Future Work. We are working on an implementation of our approach using the Meta Environment tools (see [13]). This work first involves the development of a suitable ASF specification to rewrite the parse tree of a Java program to the call graphs which form the basis of our analysis. The next step will be to provide a Meta Environment tool to perform the actual CFL-reachability analysis. Once this implementation for Java is finished it will be interesting to extend the method with further static analysis of the control flow graphs and dataflow in Java programs.

References

1. Alpuente, M., Vidal, G. (eds.): SAS 2008. LNCS, vol. 5079. Springer, Heidelberg (2008)
2. Alur, R., Madhusudan, P.: Visibly Pushdown Languages. In: Babai, L. (ed.) STOC, pp. 202–211. ACM, New York (2004)
3. Bouajjani, A., Esparza, J., Schwoon, S., Strejcek, J.: Reachability Analysis of Multithreaded Software with Asynchronous Communication. In: Sarukkai, S., Sen, S. (eds.) FSTTCS 2005. LNCS, vol. 3821, pp. 348–359. Springer, Heidelberg (2005)
4. Bouajjani, A., Esparza, J., Touili, T.: A Generic Approach to the Static Analysis of Concurrent Programs with Procedures. Int. J. Found. Comput. Sci. 14(4), 551 (2003)
5. Carotenuto, D., Murano, A., Peron, A.: 2-Visibly Pushdown Automata. In: Harju, T., Karhumäki, J., Lepistö, A. (eds.) DLT 2007. LNCS, vol. 4588, pp. 132–144. Springer, Heidelberg (2007)
6. Chaki, S., Clarke, E.M., Kidd, N., Reps, T.W., Touili, T.: Verifying Concurrent Message-Passing C Programs with Recursive Calls. In: Hermanns, H., Palsberg, J. (eds.) TACAS 2006. LNCS, vol. 3920, pp. 334–349. Springer, Heidelberg (2006)
7. Kahlon, V., Ivancic, F., Gupta, A.: Reasoning About Threads Communicating via Locks. In: Etessami, K., Rajamani, S.K. (eds.) CAV 2005. LNCS, vol. 3576, pp. 505–518. Springer, Heidelberg (2005)
8. Kidd, N., Lal, A., Reps, T.W.: Language Strength Reduction. In: Alpuente, Vidal [1], pp. 283–298
9. Lammich, P., Müller-Olm, M.: Conflict Analysis of Programs with Procedures, Dynamic Thread Creation, and Monitors. In: Alpuente, Vidal [1], pp. 205–220
10. Ramalingam, G.: Context-Sensitive Synchronization-Sensitive Analysis is Undecidable. ACM Transactions on Programming Languages and Systems 22 (2000)
11. Reps, T.W.: Program Analysis via Graph Reachability. Information & Software Technology 40(11-12), 701–726 (1998)
12. Rinard, M.C.: Analysis of Multithreaded Programs. In: Cousot, P. (ed.) SAS 2001. LNCS, vol. 2126, pp. 1–19. Springer, Heidelberg (2001)
13. van den Brand, M., van Deursen, A., Heering, J., de Jong, H., de Jonge, M., Kuipers, T., Klint, P., Moonen, L., Olivier, P., Scheerder, J., Vinju, J., Visser, E., Visser, J.: The asf+sdf Meta-Environment: A Component-Based Language Development Environment. Electronic Notes in Theoretical Computer Science 44(2), 3–8 (2001); LDTA 2001, First Workshop on Language Descriptions, Tools and Applications (a Satellite Event of ETAPS 2001)

A Kernel for Convex Recoloring of Weighted Forests

Hans L. Bodlaender[1] and Marc Comas[2]

[1] Department of Information and Computing Sciences
Utrecht University, Utrecht, The Netherlands
[2] Departament de Llenguatges i Sistemes Informàtics
Universitat Politècnica de Catalunya, Barcelona, Spain

Abstract. In this paper, we show that the following problem has a kernel of quadratic size: given is a tree T whose vertices have been assigned colors and a non-negative integer weight, and given is an integer k. In a recoloring, the color of some vertices is changed. We are looking for a recoloring such that each color class induces a subtree of T and such that the total weight of all recolored vertices is at most k. Our result generalizes a result by Bodlaender et al. [3] who give quadratic size kernel for the case that all vertices have unit weight.

1 Introduction

In this paper, we consider the following problem. Given is a tree T with for each vertex a color from some given set of colors, and a non-negative integer weight. In a recoloring of T, the color of some vertices is changed. The cost of a recoloring is the total weight of all vertices with a changed color. A coloring is convex, if for each color, the set of vertices with that color forms a (connected) subtree of T. We consider the decision version of the problem: given an integer k, we ask if there is a convex recoloring with cost at most k.

In this paper, w1e look at the parameterized variant of the problem, and show that the problem has a quadratic kernel, i.e., we give a polynomial time algorithm, that given an instance of the problem, transforms it to an equivalent instance with $O(k^2)$ vertices and edges. Our result generalizes an earlier result by Bodlaender et al. [3] who give a quadratic kernel for the unweighted version of the problem, i.e., for the case that all vertices have unit weight. We call the problem Weighted Convex Tree Recoloring. A generalization with only positive weights appears to be relatively simple, by reducing it to the unweighted case; allowing zero weight vertices asks for a different set of rules and analysis. These zero weight vertices are interesting, also from application point of view, as they also model vertices that initially do not have a color assigned to them.

The convex recoloring problem for trees is motivated from applications in phylogenetic and other areas from bio-informatics and linguistics. We refer the reader to [6,8,9] for more background and motivation of the problem.

Finding kernels of small size for combinatorial problems is a topic of much current research, and an important topic in the area of parameterized complexity and

J. van Leeuwen et al. (Eds.): SOFSEM 2010, LNCS 5901, pp. 212–223, 2010.

algorithms. We assume the reader to be familiar with standard notions from parameterized complexity and kernelization; for an introduction, see e.g., [7], [5], [4] or [10].

In [8], Moran and Snir showed that the Convex Tree Recoloring problem is NP-complete. Also, several special cases remain NP-complete, even when the tree is restricted to be a path. Improving some of the previous results in [8,9,12], Bar-Yehuda et al. [2] gave a polynomial $(2+\epsilon)$-approximation algorithm and an exact algorithm whose parameterized complexity, parameterized by the number of recolorings k, is $O(n^2 + nk2^k)$. Further improvements on the running time for an exact algorithm can be found in [11].

In [8,9], different variants of the problem are presented. In [1], an algorithm with a running time of $O(4^k n)$ is given for the case that only the leafs are colored, and the problem asks if it is possible to recolor the leafs in such a way that the resulting coloring can be extended to a convex one. In [3], a quadratic kernel is given for the unweighted version of the problem. One step of the algorithm in [3] is to generalize the problem to the case where some vertices can have a fixed color, and to forests instead of trees. Two final steps can transform the problem back to an instance without fixed color vertices and with a tree instead of a forest. In [3], it is asked as an open problem if it is possible to find small kernels for other convex recoloring variants. In this paper, we extend the result of [3] by allowing zero weights (thus allowing leaf and other partial colorings) and positive weights to the vertices (which generalizes the case when we allow vertices with a fixed color), and we show that indeed, in this situation we are also able to obtain a quadratic kernel.

2 Convex Recoloring Problem

We denote the set of non-negative integers by $\mathbb{N}_0$. Let $F = (V, E, \mu)$ be a weighted forest, with $\mu : V \to \mathbb{N}_0$ and let $\mathcal{C}$ be a set of colors. A *coloring* of F is a function defined from the set of vertices V to the set of colors $\mathcal{C}$. Given a coloring Γ, any different coloring will be called a *recoloring* of Γ. We define the *cost* of a recoloring Γ' of Γ, denoted $cost_\Gamma(\Gamma')$, to be the sum of the weights of recolored vertices:

$$cost_\Gamma(\Gamma') = \sum_{v \in V, \Gamma(v) \neq \Gamma'(v)} \mu(v)$$

For any forest F' contained in F, we denote by $\mu_{\Gamma,c}(F')$, the sum of $\mu(v)$ over all vertices v in F' colored c by Γ. We also use the previous notation for any subset of vertices of V, i.e., for $W \subseteq V$, $\mu_{\Gamma,c}(W) = \sum_{v \in \Gamma^{-1}(c) \cap W} \mu(v)$, where $\Gamma^{-1}(c) = \{v \mid \Gamma(v) = c\}$.

We say that a coloring Γ is *convex* if for every color c, $\Gamma^{-1}(c)$ induces a connected component. In this paper, we deal with the following parameterized problem.

Convex recoloring of a Weighted Colored Forest (CRP)
Instance: A weighted forest $F = (V, E, \mu)$, a set of colors $\mathcal{C}$, a coloring Γ of F and a positive integer k.

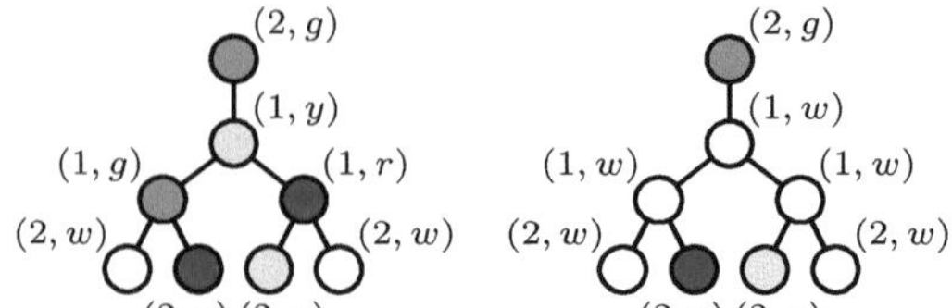

Fig. 1. Γ' is the only recoloring of Γ with cost at most 3 and convex. In every node we represent the pair *weight-color*.

Parameter: k
Question: Is there a convex recoloring Γ' of Γ with $cost_\Gamma(\Gamma') \leq k$?

While the case that F is a tree is most interesting from an application point of view, the version with forests helps to design our algorithms. As in [3], an instance with a forest can be transformed to an instance with a tree by adding one new vertex with cost $k + 1$ and making it incident to a vertex in each tree in the forest.

In Figure 1, we can see a coloring Γ in a tree T and a convex recoloring with cost at most 3. In fact, it is not difficult to check that Γ' is the only convex recoloring with cost at most three, all other convex recolorings have larger cost.

We use the consideration introduced in [9], of adding a set of new special colors. Formally, for each vertex v, we add a new color c_v, and we allow that a vertex v can be recolored to this color c_v. Using the previous consideration, we are going to assume that any instance with a vertex v such that $\mu(v) = 0$, has v colored with $\Gamma(v) = c_v$. The motivation of such assumption, comes from the fact that any convex recoloring Γ' of Γ will have $cost_\Gamma(\Gamma') = cost_{\Gamma_{v=c_v}}(\Gamma')$ for the coloring $\Gamma_{v=c_v}$ obtained from Γ by changing the color of v to c_v. We make this assumption for each vertex v with $\mu(v) = 0$.

3 Definitions

Given a forest $F = (V_F, E_F)$ and a coloring Γ, we denote by $sub_\Gamma(F, c)$ the set of vertices in V_F colored c by Γ, i.e., $sub_\Gamma(F, c) = V_F \cap \Gamma^{-1}(c)$. For a forest F and a color c, $Bag_c(F)$ is defined as the subset $sub_\Gamma(T^*, c)$ for a component T^* of F with maximum $\mu_{\Gamma,c}(T^*)$. In other words, $Bag_c(F)$ is the set of vertices of color c in the connected component of F in which the total weight of such vertices is maximum.

Consider a path s between two vertices with color c, and consider the forest $F - s$ obtained after removing s from F. Let $Tag(s)$ be the set consisting of all vertices with color c' different from c not belonging to a $Bag_{c'}(F - s)$, i.e.,

$$Tag(s) = \bigcup_{c' \in \mathcal{C} \setminus \{c\}} sub_\Gamma(F - Bag_{c'}(F - s), c'). \tag{1}$$

Let

$$tag(s) = \sum_{v \in Tag(s)} \mu(v). \tag{2}$$

From (1), it is not difficult to see that (2) can also be written as

$$tag(s) = \sum_{c' \in \mathcal{C} \setminus \{c\}} \mu_{\Gamma,c'}(F) - \mu_{\Gamma,c'}(Bag_{c'}(F - s)).$$

Proposition 1. *Let s be a path between two vertices with color c. For any convex recoloring Γ' such that for all vertices v in s, $\Gamma'(v) = c$,*

$$tag(s) \leq cost_\Gamma(\Gamma').$$

Proof. If all vertices in s receive color c, then for any color $c' \neq c$, at most one component of $F - s$ can have vertices of color c'. So, we need to recolor all vertices with color c' in all except maybe one component of $F - s$. Because for any component T in $F - s$ we have $\mu_{\Gamma,c'}(T) \leq \mu_{\Gamma,c'}(Bag_{c'}(F - s))$, the cost for recoloring vertices with color c' is at least $\mu_{\Gamma,c'}(F) - \mu_{\Gamma,c}(Bag_{c'}(F - s))$. Summation over all $c' \neq c$ gives:

$$\sum_{c' \in \mathcal{C} \setminus \{c\}} \mu_{\Gamma,c'}(F) - \mu_{\Gamma,c'}(Bag_{c'}(F - s)).$$ □

The previous proposition is the motivation for the following definitions. A *k-string* of color c is a path s consisting of two vertices u and v with color c and positive weight, called endpoints, and *interior* vertices (vertices different of u and v in s) with color different of c, in such a way that $tag(s) \leq k$. Note that we allow $u = v$. In this case, we denote the path with only the vertex v indistinctly by s_v or $\{v\}$. Let $\mathcal{S}tr_k$ be the set of all k-strings of any color and let $\mathcal{S}tr_k^c$ be the set with all k-strings of color c. If $\mathcal{S}$ is a subset of $\mathcal{S}tr_k$, we denote by $F_\mathcal{S}$ the forest obtained by the union of all k-strings contained in $\mathcal{S}$.

Note that from Proposition 1, if two vertices with the same color are not forming a k-string, one of them have to be recolored. Concretely, if for a vertex v $\{v\}$ is not a k-string, in a convex recoloring v is recolored.

Similar to [2,3], for every vertex v, we define a subset of $\mathcal{C}$, defined by

$$S_k(v) = \{c \in \mathcal{C} \mid v \in s \text{ for some } s \in \mathcal{S}tr_k^c\}.$$

Let $S_k^*(v) = S_k(v) \cup \{c_v\}$. A recoloring Γ' of Γ is *k-normalized* if for every vertex v, $\Gamma'(v) \in S_k^*(v)$. This means, that in a k-normalized recoloring, any vertex v receives a color of some k-strings containing it or a color c_v.

Lemma 1. *If there is a convex recoloring Γ' of Γ with $cost_\Gamma(\Gamma') \leq k$, there is a convex recoloring Γ'' of Γ with $cost_\Gamma(\Gamma'') \leq k$ which is k-normalized.*

Proof. Consider a convex recoloring Γ' of Γ with $cost_\Gamma(\Gamma') \leq k$. Moreover, assume Γ' has the maximum number of vertices colored c_v. Under the last assumption (being maximum in the number of vertices colored c_v), we claim that the recoloring Γ' is exactly the recoloring Γ'' of Γ defined by

$$\Gamma''(v) = \begin{cases} \Gamma'(v) & \text{if } \Gamma'(v) \in S_k(v) \\ c_v & \text{if } \Gamma'(v) \notin S_k(v), \end{cases}$$

which is clearly k-normalized. Suppose not, this is $\Gamma'' \neq \Gamma'$. Then, there is a vertex v with $\Gamma'(v) \notin S_k(v)$ such that $\Gamma'(v) \neq c_v$. By definition, in this situation, $\Gamma''(v) = c_v$. Also note that $\Gamma(v) \neq \Gamma'(v)$, this is because if v maintain the color, then v is forming a k-string of color $\Gamma(v)$ and therefore $\Gamma(v) \in S_k(v)$. So, let $\Gamma'(v) = c \ (\neq \Gamma(v))$ and let T_c be the tree induced by all the vertices colored c by Γ'. Let x and y be two leaves in T_c having v in the path joining them. If such a vertices don't exists, it means that v is a leaf in T_c and therefore can be recolored to c_v maintaining the convexity and contradicting the optimality of Γ' on the number of vertices colored c_v. At last, note that $\Gamma(x) = \Gamma(y) = c$, otherwise, if one of them (for example x) has $\Gamma(x) \neq c$, then we can recolor x to c_v maintaining again the convexity and contradicting the optimality. Finally, rest to point out that if x and y have $\Gamma(x) = \Gamma(y) = \Gamma'(x) = \Gamma'(y) = c$, the path between x and y is forming a k-string and therefore, $c \in S_k(v)$ which contradicts the first assumption. □

4 Kernelization Rules and Analysis

The next two rules allow us to have an instance holding some desirable properties, by recoloring some vertices or eliminating some edges in the instance.

Rule 1. *Consider a vertex v such that $\{s\}$ is not a k-string, i.e., $tag(\{v\}) > k$. Suppose $|S_k(v)| \leq 1$. Then,*

- *if $S_k(v) = \emptyset$, return NO,*
- *if $S_k(v) = \{c\}$, recolor vertex v to c and reduce k by $\mu(v)$.*

Rule 2. *If Rule 1 cannot be applied, set $F = F_{\mathcal{S}tr_k}$.*

Lemma 2. *In any instance reduced with respect to Rule 1 and Rule 2, the forest*

$$F - \bigcup_{c' \in \mathcal{C} \setminus c} F_{\mathcal{S}tr_k^{c'}}$$

contains only vertices v with color c and c_v.

Proof. By Rule 2, we have that $F = F_{\mathcal{S}tr_k}$ and then,

$$F_c = F - \bigcup_{c' \in \mathcal{C} \setminus c} F_{\mathcal{S}tr_k^{c'}}$$

only contains vertices belonging to k-strings of color c. If there exists a vertex v in F_c with color c' different from c and c_v, then s_v is not a k-string and $S_k(v) = \{c\}$. So, vertex v is recolored to c by Rule 1. □

From now on, we assume that Rule 1 and Rule 2 cannot be applied.

4.1 Pieces of a Color

Consider the forest $F_c = F - \bigcup_{c' \in \mathcal{C} \setminus \{c\}} F_{\mathcal{S}tr_k^{c'}}$. Every component of F_c is called a *piece of color* c. By Lemma 2, F_c contains only vertices v with color c or c_v, and moreover, by Lemma 1, we can assume that the vertices in F_c can only receive color c or c_v. We have the following lemma,

Lemma 3. *There is always an optimum recoloring such that for each piece of color c, every vertex v in the piece is colored c or c_v.*

Proof. Clearly, if a piece of color c has some vertex v recolored to c_v (c_v or c are the only colors in $S_k(v)$) by a recoloring Γ', then the recoloring Γ'' with all vertices in the pieces colored c has at most the same cost as Γ', and it is not difficult to see that this recoloring is still convex. □

Suppose that a piece W of color c has at least half of the total weight of the sum of vertices of color c. Then, by Lemma 3, if a recoloring Γ' recolors some vertex in W from c to c_v, the recoloring Γ'' not recoloring any vertex in W from c to c_v has at most the same cost as Γ'. So we can assume that the piece of color is not recolored in an optimum recoloring. This argument and Lemma 3 are captured by the following rule.

Rule 3. *For every piece W of color c, contract W to a single vertex w with color c and $\mu(w)$ defined as follows,*

- *if $\mu_{\Gamma,c}(W) > \mu_{\Gamma,c}(F - W)$, set $\mu(w) = k + 1$,*
- *otherwise set $\mu(w) = \mu_{\Gamma,c}(W)$.*

4.2 Irrelevant Colors

We say that a color c is *irrelevant*, if all the vertices of color c are contained in some piece of color c, and for any vertex v with color different of c and c_v, $c \notin S_k(v)$. The *cost of removing* an irrelevant color c is defined by

$$\Delta_c = \mu_{\Gamma,c}(F_{\mathcal{S}tr_k^c}) - \mu_{\Gamma,c}(Bag_c(F_{\mathcal{S}tr_k^c})).$$

Intuitively, when a color c is irrelevant, forests $F_{\mathcal{S}tr_k^c}$ and $\bigcup_{c' \in \mathcal{C} \setminus \{c\}} F_{\mathcal{S}tr_k^{c'}}$ are disjoint. Moreover, by Lemma 2, all the colors in one forest do not appear in the other one. So, we can solve both forests separately. Because $F_{\mathcal{S}tr_k^c}$ is easy to solve (it only contains color c and c_v), we can solve $F_{\mathcal{S}tr_k^c}$ and reduce F to $\bigcup_{c' \in \mathcal{C} \setminus \{c\}} F_{\mathcal{S}tr_k^{c'}}$ and decrease k by Δ_c which is the cost of making $F_{\mathcal{S}tr_k^c}$ convex. We have the following rule,

Rule 4. *Suppose c is an irrelevant color in F. Then, set $F = \bigcup_{c' \in \mathcal{C} \setminus \{c\}} F_{\mathcal{S}tr_k^{c'}}$ and decrease k by Δ_c.*

Suppose a vertex v with color c has weight greater than k, then in any recoloring with cost at most k, v cannot be recolored. In this situation, the vertices recolored in one component of $F - v$ do not affect the vertices recolored in another component of $F - v$. In other words, there are no k-strings, containing v, with color different from v's color. So, we can study the problem with respect to v and each component in $F - v$ independently. These independencies can be carried out by splitting v into a number of copies: as many as there are components in $F - v$ and recolor all vertices with color c in each of these components by a new color, unique for the component.

Rule 5. *Suppose there is a vertex v with color c and $\mu(v) > k$. Let T_v be the component containing v in F, let $F_0 = F - T_v$ and let $T_1, \ldots, T_\ell$ be the components in $T_v - v$ with $w_1, \ldots, w_\ell$ the neighbors of v in $T_1, \ldots, T_\ell$ respectively. Then, remove the vertex v from F, connect every w_i to a new vertex v_i with a new color c_i and weight $\mu_{\Gamma,c}(T_i)$, and recolor all vertices in T_i with color c to c_i (for each i, $1 \leq i \leq \ell$), add an isolated vertex v_0 with a new color c_0 and weight $\mu_{\Gamma,c}(F_0)$, and recolor all vertices in F_0 with color c to c_0.*

Lemma 4. *When Rules 1-5 cannot be applied, the total weight of vertices with a color c is at least two times the total weight of vertices in any piece of color c. I.e., for any piece W of color c,*

$$2\mu_{\Gamma,c}(W) \leq \mu_{\Gamma,c}(F).$$

Proof. When Rule 3 cannot be applied, for any piece W of color c, either $\mu_{\Gamma,c}(W) \leq \mu_{\Gamma,c}(F - W)$ or W consists of a single vertex w with $\mu_{\Gamma,c}(w) = k+1$. In the first case, we get directly that $2\mu_{\Gamma,c}(W) \leq \mu_{\Gamma,c}(F)$. In the second case, Rule 5 applies, which gives again that $\mu_{\Gamma,c}(w) \leq \mu_{\Gamma,c}(F - w)$ □

At this point, the kernelization is almost completed. In the rest of this section, we assume that the next rule (Rule 6) is safe. Its safeness will be proved in the next section.

Rule 6. *If Rules 1-5 cannot be applied and $\sum_{c \in C} \mu_{\Gamma,c}(F) > 6k^2$, return NO.*

From Rule 6, we know that there are at most $6k^2$ vertices with positive weight. It remains to show that the number of vertices with zero weight are also bounded. The following rules are clearly safe.

Rule 7. *If a vertex v has $\mu(v) = 0$ and $deg(v) \leq 1$, remove v.*

Rule 8. *If a vertex v has $\mu(v) = 0$ and $deg(v) = 2$, add an edge between its neighbors and remove v.*

It is well known that the number of vertices of degree greater than two in a tree is bounded by the number of leaves. So, because every vertex with zero weight has degree greater than 2 and every leaf has positive weight, the next result follows.

Theorem 1. *In a reduced instance, there are at most $12k^2$ vertices and the sum of its weights is at most $6k^2$.*

4.3 Removing k-Strings and Counting Them

A *skeleton* of $\mathcal{S}tr_k$ is a subset $\mathcal{R}$ of $\mathcal{S}tr_k$ containing a minimal number of k-strings of $\mathcal{S}tr_k$ in such a way that, if we denote the k-strings in $\mathcal{R}$ of color c by $\mathcal{R}^c$, for every $c \in \mathcal{C}$, $F_{\mathcal{R}^c} = F_{\mathcal{S}tr_k^c}$. A possible procedure for generating a skeleton of $\mathcal{S}tr_k$ can be the following: Initially, let $\mathcal{R} = \mathcal{S}tr_k$ and then, apply the following operation while possible, remove from $\mathcal{R}$ a k-string s of color c if it is contained in the rest of k-strings of color c in $\mathcal{R}$. Clearly, when the procedure ends, we have $F_{\mathcal{R}^c} = F_{\mathcal{S}tr_k^c}$ for every $c \in \mathcal{C}$. Let $Tag_{\mathcal{R}} = \bigcup_{s \in \mathcal{R}} Tag(s)$. We say that a vertex v is *tagged* by $\mathcal{R}$ if it is contained in $Tag_{\mathcal{R}}$.

Lemma 5. *In an instance reduced by Rule 1-5, for any color c in $\mathcal{C}$ and a skeleton $\mathcal{R}$ of $\mathcal{S}tr_k$,*

$$\mu_{\Gamma,c}(F - Tag_{\mathcal{R}}) \leq \mu_{\Gamma,c}(Tag_{\mathcal{R}}).$$

Proof. First, we prove that all the vertices of color c not belonging to $Tag_{\mathcal{R}}$ are contained in *one* piece of color c.

Note that a vertex of color c not belonging to $Tag_{\mathcal{R}}$ has to be in some piece of color c. Suppose two vertices x and y of color c are in different components of

$$F_c = F_{\mathcal{S}tr_k^c} - \bigcup_{c' \in \mathcal{C} \setminus \{c\}} F_{\mathcal{S}tr_k^{c'}} = F_{\mathcal{R}^c} - \bigcup_{c' \in \mathcal{C} \setminus \{c\}} F_{\mathcal{R}^{c'}}.$$

To be in different components of F_c, either there is a k-string s' in $\mathcal{R}^{c'}$ between them or x and y are in different components of $F_{\mathcal{S}tr_k^c} = F_{\mathcal{R}^c}$. In the first case, $Tag(s')$ contains x or y. In the second case, because by Rule 2, $F = F_{\mathcal{S}tr_k} = F_{\mathcal{R}}$, and therefore, either x and y have a k-string in $\mathcal{R}^{c'}$ for some c' different of c between them like in the first case or they are in different component of F. In such a case, any k-string with color different from c tags x or y. In any case, there is always a k-string in $\mathcal{R}$ tagging x or y and then, x and y must be in the same piece of color c.

Because all vertices with color c in $F - Tag(\mathcal{R})$ are contained in a piece of color c, by Lemma 4,

$$2\mu_{\Gamma,c}(F - Tag_{\mathcal{R}}) \leq \mu_{\Gamma,c}(F).$$

Using that

$$\mu_{\Gamma,c}(F) = \mu_{\Gamma,c}(F - Tag_{\mathcal{R}}) + \mu_{\Gamma,c}(Tag_{\mathcal{R}}),$$

we get

$$\mu_{\Gamma,c}(F - Tag_{\mathcal{R}}) \leq \mu_{\Gamma,c}(Tag_{\mathcal{R}}).$$ □

Lemma 6. *Rule 6 is safe.*

Proof. Suppose Γ' is a convex recoloring with $cost_{\Gamma}(\Gamma') \leq k$, we want to show that in this situation $\sum_{c \in \mathcal{C}} \mu_{\Gamma,c}(F) \leq 6k^2$. For this, we construct a skeleton $\mathcal{R}_{\Gamma'}$ of $\mathcal{S}tr_k$ in the following way, let $W_c = \{v \mid \Gamma(v) = \Gamma'(v) = c\}$:

- For every color c, add to $\mathcal{R}_{\Gamma'}$ a minimal number of k-strings of color c in such a way that the vertices in W_c are connected in $F_{\mathcal{R}_{\Gamma'}}$.
- For every color c, add to $\mathcal{R}_{\Gamma'}$ a minimal number of k-strings of color c in such a way that $F_{\mathcal{R}^c_{\Gamma'}} = F_{\mathcal{S}tr^c_k}$.

We separate the set $\mathcal{R}_{\Gamma'}$ into two parts: a subset $\mathcal{R}^{\mathcal{N}}_{\Gamma'}$ containing all the k-strings added in the first step and a subset $\mathcal{R}^{\mathcal{Y}}_{\Gamma'}$ containing the vertices added in the second step. In other words, $\mathcal{R}^{\mathcal{N}}_{\Gamma'}$ contains k-strings whose endpoints are not recolored, and $\mathcal{R}^{\mathcal{Y}}_{\Gamma'}$ contains k-strings with some endpoint recolored.

Claim. For every convex recoloring Γ' with $cost_\Gamma(\Gamma') \leq k$,

$$\sum_{c \in \mathcal{C}} \mu_{\Gamma,c}(Tag_{\mathcal{R}^{\mathcal{Y}}_{\Gamma'}}) \leq k^2$$

Proof of claim. In the way $Tag_{\mathcal{R}^{\mathcal{Y}}_{\Gamma'}}$ is constructed, for every recolored vertex at most one k-string is added to $Tag_{\mathcal{R}^{\mathcal{Y}}_{\Gamma'}}$. Because, $cost_\Gamma(\Gamma') \leq k$, in the second step we add at most k k-strings to $\mathcal{R}^{\mathcal{Y}}_{\Gamma'}$, i.e., $|\mathcal{R}^{\mathcal{Y}}_{\Gamma'}| \leq k$. From k-string definition we have $\sum_{c \in \mathcal{C}} \mu_{\Gamma,c}(Tag(s)) \leq k$. Putting all together,

$$\begin{aligned}
\sum_{c \in \mathcal{C}} \mu_{\Gamma,c}(Tag_{\mathcal{R}^{\mathcal{Y}}_{\Gamma'}}) &= \sum_{c \in \mathcal{C}} \mu_{\Gamma,c}\Big(\bigcup_{s \in \mathcal{R}^{\mathcal{Y}}_{\Gamma'}} Tag(s)\Big) \\
&\leq \sum_{c \in \mathcal{C}} \sum_{s \in \mathcal{R}^{\mathcal{Y}}_{\Gamma'}} \mu_{\Gamma,c}(Tag(s)) \\
&= \sum_{s \in \mathcal{R}^{\mathcal{Y}}_{\Gamma'}} \sum_{c \in \mathcal{C}} \mu_{\Gamma,c}(Tag(s)) \\
&\leq |\mathcal{R}^{\mathcal{Y}}_{\Gamma'}| k \leq k^2.
\end{aligned}$$

□

Claim. For every convex recoloring Γ' with $cost_\Gamma(\Gamma') \leq k$,

$$\sum_{c \in \mathcal{C}} \mu_{\Gamma,c}(Tag_{\mathcal{R}^{\mathcal{N}}_{\Gamma'}}) \leq 2k^2$$

Proof of claim. To prove the claim, we first reduce the set $\mathcal{R}^{\mathcal{N}}$ to a subset $\mathcal{R}^*$ of $\mathcal{R}^{\mathcal{N}}$ in the following way: Initially, let $\mathcal{R}^* = \mathcal{R}^{\mathcal{N}}$ and while possible, remove from $\mathcal{R}^*$ any k-string s such that $Tag(s) \subseteq \bigcup_{s' \in \mathcal{R}^* \setminus \{s\}} Tag(s')$. After the procedure is applied, the following two properties are held by $\mathcal{R}^*$, (1) $Tag_{\mathcal{R}^{\mathcal{N}}_{\Gamma'}} = Tag_{\mathcal{R}^*}$, and (2) for every k-string s in $\mathcal{R}^*$ there is a vertex ν_s such that $\nu_s \in Tag(s)$ and for any $s' \in \mathcal{R}^*$ different of s, $\nu_s \notin Tag(s')$. From the last property, we can associate to every string s of $\mathcal{R}^*$ a vertex ν_s not tagged by any other k-string in $\mathcal{R}^*$.

Let $\mathcal{C}^+ = \{c \in \mathcal{C} \mid \exists s \in \mathcal{R}^*, \Gamma(\nu_s) = c\}$. Note if c is the color of a vertex ν_s associated to a k-string s, at least one vertex of color c should be recolored, otherwise s (that is a k-string not recolored) is separating ν_s from $Bag_c(F - s)$

and then, Γ' cannot be convex. From previous argument, $\mathcal{C}^+$ has at most k colors, i.e., $|\mathcal{C}^+| \leq k$.

Let n_c be the number of k-strings in $\mathcal{R}^*$ with an associated vertex of color c. We show that at least $n_c - 1$ vertices of color c are recolored by Γ'. Suppose not. Then, there are two vertices ν_{s_1} and ν_{s_2} with color c for two k-strings s_1 and s_2 in $\mathcal{R}^*$. Because Γ' maintains ν_{s_1} and ν_{s_2} with color c, ν_{s_1} and ν_{s_2} are in the same component of $F_{\mathcal{S}tr_k^c}$. An then, the only way s_1 tags ν_{s_1} but not tag ν_{s_2} is because ν_{s_2} is in $Bag_c(F - s_1)$. Implying that s_1 and $p(\nu_{s_1}, \nu_{s_2})$, the path going from ν_{s_1} to ν_{s_2}, intersect in some vertex, contradicting the convexity of Γ'. Consequently, at least $n_c - 1$ vertices of color c are recolored by Γ'. So, $\sum_{c \in \mathcal{C}^+} n_c - 1 \leq k$. Because $|\mathcal{C}^+| \leq k$, we get $|\mathcal{R}^*| = \sum_{c \in \mathcal{C}^+} n_c \leq 2k$. Finally, putting all together,

$$\begin{aligned}
\sum_{c \in \mathcal{C}} \mu_{\Gamma,c}(Tag_{\mathcal{R}^{\mathcal{N}}_{\Gamma'}}) &= \sum_{c \in \mathcal{C}} \mu_{\Gamma,c}(Tag_{\mathcal{R}^*}) \\
&= \sum_{c \in \mathcal{C}} \mu_{\Gamma,c}(\bigcup_{s \in \mathcal{R}^*} Tag(s)) \\
&\leq \sum_{c \in \mathcal{C}} \sum_{s \in \mathcal{R}^*} \mu_{\Gamma,c}(Tag(s)) \\
&\leq \sum_{s \in \mathcal{R}^*} \sum_{c \in \mathcal{C}} \mu_{\Gamma,c}(Tag(s)) \\
&\leq |\mathcal{R}^*| k \leq 2k^2.
\end{aligned}$$ □

Using Lemma 5 with the skeleton $\mathcal{R}_{\Gamma'}$, we have that

$$\mu_{\Gamma,c}(F) = \mu_{\Gamma,c}(Tag_{\mathcal{R}_{\Gamma'}}) + \mu_{\Gamma,c}(F - Tag_{\mathcal{R}_{\Gamma'}}) \leq 2\mu_{\Gamma,c}(Tag_{\mathcal{R}_{\Gamma'}}).$$

Finally, by the previous claims,

$$\mu_{\Gamma,c}(F) \leq 2(\sum_{c \in \mathcal{C}} \mu_{\Gamma,c}(Tag_{\mathcal{R}^{\mathcal{Y}}_{\Gamma'}}) + \sum_{c \in \mathcal{C}} \mu_{\Gamma,c}(Tag_{\mathcal{R}^{\mathcal{N}}_{\Gamma'}})) \leq 6k^2.$$ □

We have shown that all rules are safe, and thus, by Theorem 1 and the fact that we can test in polynomial time if a rule can be carried out, and if so, apply it, we obtain:

Theorem 2. *There is a polynomial time kernelization algorithm for* Weighted Convex Tree Recoloring *that yields a kernel with at most* $12k^2$ *vertices whose total weight is at most* $6k^2$.

5 Conclusions

In this paper, we gave a kernel of quadratic size for the Weighted Convex Tree Recoloring problem. As we also allow weights that are zero, our result also implies a kernel for the case where we have initially some uncolored vertices. We have fewer rules than the result that we generalize from [3]. In particular,

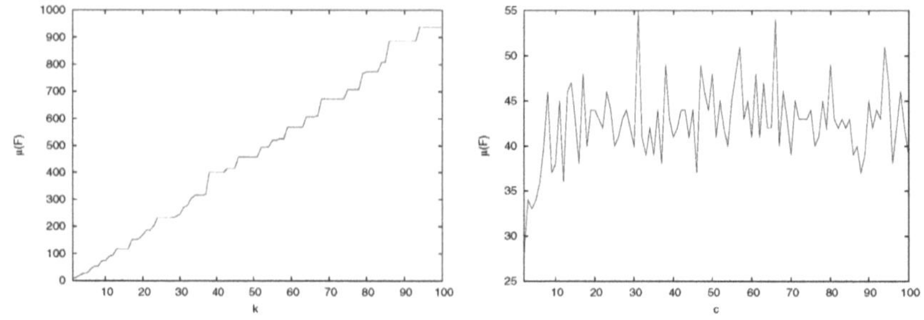

Fig. 2. On the left, we represent the maximum over 100 simulations, taking k until 100 and $n = 10k^2$. On the right, fixed $k = 5$ and $n = 500$, the maximum after 1000 simulations modifying c between 2 and 100.

we did not need most of the rules that we used in [3] to ensure that each color is given to a linear number of vertices. In a practical setting, it is not hard to generalize these rules from [3] to the weighted case, and add these as additional preprocessing heuristics to our rules. An intriguing open problem is whether a linear kernel exists for our problem, or, at least, for the unweighted case.

We implemented Rules 1-4 and applied these to randomly generated instances; in each case, we took a randomly generated tree and then recolored k randomly chosen vertices. The results of this experiment are shown in Figure 2. In these random instances, it seems that in a practically point of view, the size of the kernel is linear. Although, it is not difficult to construct instances such that its reduced instance grows quadratically on k. We leave such an analysis (or a different set of rules with a linear kernel) as open problem for further research.

References

1. Bachoore, E.H., Bodlaender, H.L.: Convex recoloring of leaf-colored trees. Technical Report UU-CS-2006-010, Department of Information and Computing Sciences, Utrecht University (2006)
2. Bar-Yehuda, R., Feldman, I., Rawitz, D.: Improved Approximation Algorithm for Convex Recoloring of Trees. Theory Comput. Syst. 43(1), 3–18 (2008)
3. Bodlaender, H.L., Fellows, M.R., Langston, M.A., Ragan, M.A., Rosamond, F.A., Weyer, M.: Quadratic Kernelization for Convex Recoloring of Trees. In: Lin, G. (ed.) COCOON 2007. LNCS, vol. 4598, pp. 86–96. Springer, Heidelberg (2007)
4. Downey, R.G., Fellows, M.R.: Parameterized Complexity. Springer, Heidelberg (1999)
5. Flum, J., Grohe, M.: Parameterized Complexity Theory. Springer, Secaucus (2006)
6. Gramm, J., Nickelsen, A., Tantau, T.: Fixed-Parameter Algorithms in Phylogenetics. The Computer Journal 51(1), 79–101 (2008)
7. Guo, J., Niedermeier, R.: Invitation to Data Reduction and Problem Kernelization. SIGACT News 38(1), 31–45 (2007)
8. Moran, S., Snir, S.: Efficient Approximation of Convex Recolorings. Journal of Computer and System Sciences 73(7), 1078–1089 (2007)

9. Moran, S., Snir, S.: Convex Recolorings of Strings and Trees: Definitions, Hardness Results and Algorithms. Journal of Computer and System Sciences 74(5), 850–869 (2008)
10. Niedermeier, R.: Invitation to Fixed Parameter Algorithms. Oxford Lecture Series in Mathematics and Its Applications. Oxford University Press, USA (2006)
11. Ponta, O., Hüffner, F., Niedermeier, R.: Speeding up Dynamic Programming for Some NP-Hard Graph Recoloring Problems. In: Agrawal, M., Du, D.-Z., Duan, Z., Li, A. (eds.) TAMC 2008. LNCS, vol. 4978, pp. 490–501. Springer, Heidelberg (2008)
12. Razgon, I.: A $2^{O(k)}\text{Poly}(n)$ Algorithm for the Parameterized Convex Recoloring Problem. Information Processing Letters 104(2), 53–58 (2007)

Symbolic OBDD-Based Reachability Analysis Needs Exponential Space

Beate Bollig

LS2 Informatik, TU Dortmund
44221 Dortmund, Germany

Abstract. Ordered binary decision diagrams (OBDDs) are one of the most common dynamic data structures for Boolean functions. Nevertheless, many basic graph problems are known to be PSPACE-hard if their input graphs are represented by OBDDs. Despite the hardness results there are not many concrete nontrivial lower bounds known for the complexity of problems on OBDD-represented graph instances. Computing the set of vertices that are reachable from some predefined vertex $s \in V$ in a directed graph $G = (V, E)$ is an important problem in computer-aided design, hardware verification, and model checking. Until now only exponential lower bounds on the space complexity of a restricted class of OBDD-based algorithms for the reachability problem have been known. Here, the result is extended by presenting an exponential lower bound on the space complexity of an arbitrary OBDD-based algorithm for the reachability problem. As a by-product a general exponential lower bound is obtained for the computation of OBDDs representing all connected node pairs in a graph, the transitive closure.

Keywords: Computational complexity, lower bounds, ordered binary decision diagrams, reachability analysis, transitive closure.

1 Introduction

1.1 Motivation

When working with Boolean functions as in circuit verification, synthesis, and model checking, ordered binary decision diagrams, denoted OBDDs, introduced by Bryant [5], are one of the most often used data structures supporting all fundamental operations on Boolean functions.

Some modern applications require huge graphs so that explicit representations by adjacency matrices or adjacency lists are not any longer possible, e.g., in hardware verification and in the process of synthesis of sequential circuits state transition graphs that consist of 10^{27} vertices and 10^{36} edges are not uncommon. Since time and space do not suffice to consider individual vertices, one way out seems to be to deal with sets of vertices and edges represented by their characteristic functions. Since OBDDs are well suited for the representation and manipulation of Boolean functions, in the last years a research branch has emerged which is concerned with the theoretical design and analysis of so-called

J. van Leeuwen et al. (Eds.): SOFSEM 2010, LNCS 5901, pp. 224–234, 2010.

symbolic algorithms for classical graph problems on OBDD-represented graph instances (see, e.g., [11,12], [17,18], and [23]). Symbolic algorithms have to solve problems on a given graph instance by efficient functional operations offered by the OBDD data structure. At the beginning the OBDD-based algorithms have been justified by analyzing the number of executed OBDD operations (see, e.g., [11,12]). Since the number of OBDD operations is not directly proportional to the running time of an algorithm, as the running time for one OBDD operation depends on the sizes of the OBDDs on which the operations are performed, newer research tries to analyze the overall running time of symbolic methods including the analysis of all OBDD sizes occurring during such an algorithm (see, e.g., [23]).

In reachability analysis the task is to compute the set of states of a state-transition system that are reachable from a set of initial states. Besides explicit methods for traversing states one by one and SAT-based techniques for deciding distance-bounded reachability between pairs of state sets, symbolic methods are one of the most commonly used approaches to this problem (see, e.g., [7,8]). In the OBDD-based setting our aim is to compute a representation for the characteristic function $\mathcal{X}_R$ of the solution set $R \subseteq V$. I.e., the input consists of an OBDD representing the characteristic function of the edge set of a graph $G = (V, E)$ and a predefined vertex $s \in V$ and the output is an OBDD representing the characteristic function of the vertex set R which contains all vertices reachable from the vertex s via a directed path in G. BFS-like approaches using $O(|V|)$ OBDD operations [13] and iterative squaring methods using $O(\log^2 |V|)$ operations [17] are known. In [20] Sawitzki has proved that algorithms that solve the reachability problem by computing intermediate sets of vertices reachable from the vertex s via directed paths of length at most 2^p, $p \in \{1, \ldots, \lfloor \log |V| \rfloor\}$, need exponential space if the variable ordering is not changed during the algorithms. For this result he has proved the first exponential lower bound on the size of OBDDs representing the most significant bit of integer multiplication for a predefined variable ordering. Afterwards, he has defined inputs for the reachability problem such that during the computation of the investigated restricted class of algorithms representations for the most significant bit of integer multiplication are necessary. In [4] his result has been improved by presenting a larger lower bound on the OBDD size of the most significant bit for the variable ordering considered in [20]. Lower bounds on the size of OBDDs for a predefined variable ordering do not rule out the possibility that there are other variable orderings leading to OBDDs of small size. Since Sawitzki's assumption that the variable ordering is not changed during the computation is not realistic because in application reordering heuristics are used in order to minimize the OBDD size for intermediate OBDD results, in [2,3] the result has been improved by presenting general exponential lower bounds on the OBDD size of the most significant bit of integer multiplication. Here, we generalize Sawitzki's result and show that the reachability problem for graphs represented by OBDDs needs exponential space for all possible OBDD-based algorithms.

1.2 Results and Organization of the Paper

Our main result can be summarized as follows.

Theorem 1. *The reachability problem on* OBDD*-represented graphs needs exponential space.*

In Section 2 we define some notation and present some basics concerning OBDDs. Section 3 contains the results of the paper. We prove that OBDD-based reachability analysis needs exponential space. As a by-product a general exponential lower bound is obtained for the computation of OBDDs representing all connected node pairs in a graph, the transitive closure.

2 Preliminaries

2.1 Ordered Binary Decision Diagrams

Boolean circuits, formulae, and binary decision diagrams (BDDs), sometimes called branching programs, are standard representations for Boolean functions. (For a history of results on binary decision diagrams see, e.g., the monograph of Wegener [22]). Besides the complexity theoretical viewpoint people have used restricted binary decision diagrams in applications. Bryant [5] has introduced ordered binary decision diagrams (OBDDs) which have become one of the most popular data structures for Boolean functions. Among the many areas of application are verification, model checking, computer-aided design, relational algebra, and symbolic graph algorithms.

Definition 1. *Let $X_n = \{x_1, \ldots, x_n\}$ be a set of Boolean variables. A variable ordering π on X_n is a permutation on $\{1, \ldots, n\}$ leading to the ordered list $x_{\pi(1)}, \ldots, x_{\pi(n)}$ of the variables.*

In the following a variable ordering π is sometimes identified with the corresponding ordering $x_{\pi(1)}, \ldots, x_{\pi(n)}$ of the variables if the meaning is clear from the context.

Definition 2. *A π-*OBDD *on X_n is a directed acyclic graph $G = (V, E)$ whose sinks are labeled by Boolean constants and whose non-sink (or inner) nodes are labeled by Boolean variables from X_n. Each inner node has two outgoing edges one labeled by* 0 *and the other by* 1*. The edges between inner nodes have to respect the variable ordering π, i.e., if an edge leads from an x_i-node to an x_j-node, then $\pi^{-1}(i) \leq \pi^{-1}(j)$ (x_i precedes x_j in $x_{\pi(1)}, \ldots, x_{\pi(n)}$). Each node v represents a Boolean function $f_v \in B_n$, i.e., $f_v : \{0,1\}^n \rightarrow \{0,1\}$, defined in the following way. In order to evaluate $f_v(b)$, $b \in \{0,1\}^n$, start at v. After reaching an x_i-node choose the outgoing edge with label b_i until a sink is reached. The label of this sink defines $f_v(b)$. The width of an* OBDD *is the maximum number of nodes labeled by the same variable. The size of a π-*OBDD *G is equal to the number of its nodes and the π-*OBDD *size of a function f, denoted by π-*OBDD*(f), is the size of the minimal π-*OBDD *representing f.*

The size of the reduced π-OBDD representing f is described by the following structure theorem [21].

Theorem 2. *The number of $x_{\pi(i)}$-nodes of the π-OBDD for f is the number s_i of different subfunctions $f_{|x_{\pi(1)}=a_1,\ldots,x_{\pi(i-1)}=a_{i-1}}$, $a_1,\ldots,a_{i-1} \in \{0,1\}$, that essentially depend on $x_{\pi(i)}$ (a function g depends essentially on a Boolean variable z if $g_{|z=0} \neq g_{|z=1}$).*

Theorem 2 implies the following simple observation which is helpful in order to prove lower bounds. Given an arbitrary variable ordering π the number of nodes labeled by a variable x in the reduced π-OBDD representing a given function f is not smaller than the number of x-nodes in a reduced π-OBDD representing any subfunction of f.

It is well known that the size of an OBDD representing a function f, that is defined on n Boolean variables and depends essentially on all of them, depends on the chosen variable ordering and may vary between linear and exponential size. Since in applications the variable ordering π is not given in advance we have the freedom (and the problem) to choose a good ordering for the representation of f.

Definition 3. *The* OBDD *size or* OBDD *complexity of f is the minimum of all π-OBDD(f).*

2.2 Graph Representations by OBDDs

In the following for $z = (z_{n-1},\ldots,z_0) \in \{0,1\}^n$ let $|z| := \sum_{i=0}^{n-1} z_i 2^i$. Let $G = (V,E)$ be a graph with N vertices $v_0,\ldots v_{N-1}$. The edge set E can be represented by an OBDD for its characteristic function, where $\mathcal{X}_E(x,y) = 1 \Leftrightarrow (|x|,|y| < N) \wedge (v_{|x|}, v_{|y|}) \in E$, $x,y \in \{0,1\}^n$ and $n = \lceil \log N \rceil$. Undirected edges are represented by symmetric directed ones. In the rest of the paper we assume that N is a power of 2 since it has no bearing on the essence of our results.

Figure 1 shows an example of a directed graph $G = (V,E)$, where $|V| = N = 2^3$, and the OBDD representation for the characteristic function of its edge set E (with respect to the variable ordering x_0,y_0,x_1,y_1,x_2,y_2). (Note, that the represented graph G is only a toy example so that the difference in the representation size is only small.)

3 OBDD-Based Reachability Analysis Needs Exponential Space

In this section we prove Theorem 1 and show that OBDD-based reachability analysis needs exponential space. The proof structure is the following one. First, we define a sequence G_n of pathological graph instances. G_n is an input for the reachability problem. We show that the size of the corresponding OBDD representation for the characteristic function of its edge set is polynomial with respect to the number of Boolean variables. Furthermore, we choose the vertex s which

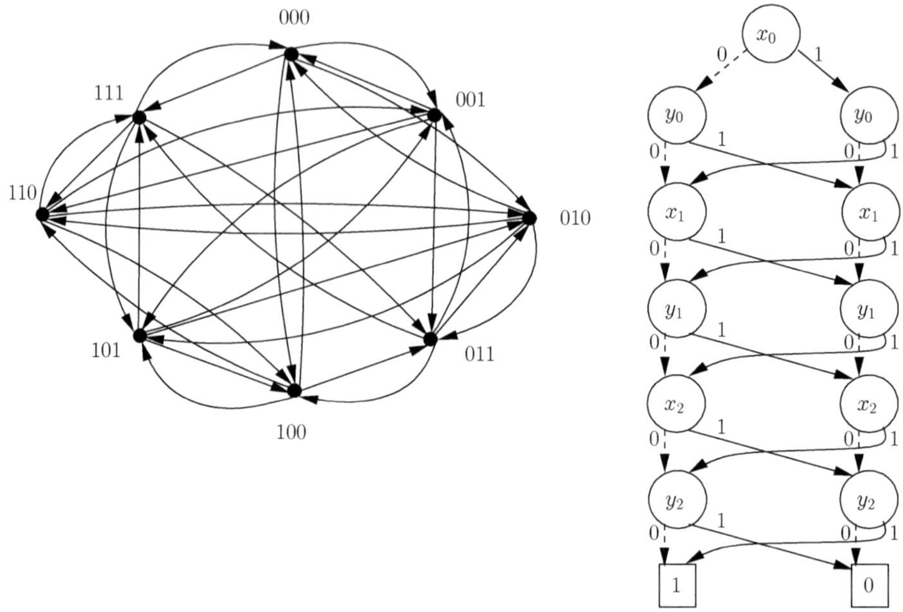

Fig. 1. A directed graph $G = (V, E)$ together with an encoding of its vertices and the corresponding OBDD representation of its edge set E

is also a part of the input in a clever way so that the characteristic function of the vertex set R, that consists of all vertices reachable from the vertex s via directed paths in G_n, is equal to a Boolean function called permutation test function PERM_n. The OBDD complexity of PERM_n is known to be exponential [14,15]. Therefore, every OBDD-based algorithm that solves the reachability problem needs exponential space with respect to its input size. Note, that this result is independent of the chosen variable ordering for the output OBDD. Now, we make our ideas more precise.

1. The definition of the input graph G_n:
   The graph G_n consists of 2^{n^2} vertices $v_{i_1,\dots,i_n}$, $i_j \in \{0,\dots,2^n-1\}$ and $j \in \{1,\dots,n\}$. All vertices $v_{i_1,\dots,i_n}$ for which there exists an index i_j where i_j is not a power of 2, $j \in \{1,\dots,n\}$, are isolated vertices with no incoming or outgoing edges. A vertex $v_{i_1,\dots,i_n}$, where i_j is a power of 2 for all $j \in \{1,\dots,n\}$, has $n-1$ directed outgoing edges. There exists an edge $(v_{i_1,\dots,i_n}, v_{l_1,\dots,l_n})$ in E iff there exists $k \in \{1,\dots n-1\}$ such that $i_1 = l_1, \dots, i_{k-1} = l_{k-1}, i_k = l_{k+1}, i_{k+1} = l_k, i_{k+2} = l_{k+2}, \dots, i_n = l_n$. The vertex s is equal to $v_{i_1,\dots,i_n}$, where $i_1,\dots,i_n$ are different powers of 2, i.e., $i_j := 2^{n-j}$.
   The graph G_n can be described in the following way. If we write the binary representation of the indices i_j, $1 \le j \le n$, in a rowwise manner one below the other such that the indices are represented by a Boolean matrix of dimension $n \times n$, the vertices that correspond to matrices where there

is not exactly one 1-entry in each row are isolated vertices. For the other vertices there exists a directed edge from one vertex to another iff the binary matrix representing the indices of one vertex can be obtained by exchanging two neighbored rows in the matrix corresponding to the other vertex. The vertex s corresponds to a matrix where there exists exactly one 1-entry in each row and in each column. Such a matrix can be seen as an encoding of a permutation π in S_n. For our construction this property is sufficient for the definition of the distinguished vertex s. For a unique definition we define s is such a way that the binary representation of s corresponds to the permutation $1\ 2\ \ldots n$.

2. The polynomial upper bound on the size of the OBDD representation for the characteristic function of the edge set of G_n:

   The characteristic function $\mathcal{X}_E$ of the edge set depends on $2n^2$ Boolean variables. Our aim is to prove that $\mathcal{X}_E$ can be represented by OBDDs of size $O(n^4)$ according to the variable ordering

$$x_{11}, y_{11}, x_{12}, y_{12}, \ldots, x_{nn}, y_{nn},$$

   where $x_{j1}, \ldots, x_{jn}$ is the Boolean representation of the index i_j and x_{jn} the least significant bit.

   Theorem 2 tells us that it is sufficient to prove that there are only $O(n^2)$ different subfunctions obtained by replacements of the first i variables with respect to the considered variable ordering, $i \in \{0, \ldots, 2n^2 - 1\}$. Then we can conclude that the OBDD size is at most $O(n^4)$ since there are only $2n^2$ variables altogether. Different subfunctions represent in a certian sence different information about partial assignments to some of the variables. Let $x^\ell = (x_{\ell 1}, \ldots, x_{\ell n})$, $\ell \in \{1, \ldots, n\}$, and y^ℓ analogously defined. The OBDD for $\mathcal{X}_E$ checks whether $x^\ell = y^\ell$ and $x_{\ell 1} + \cdots + x_{\ell n} = 1$. This can be done by a part of the OBDD of width 3. (Figure 2 shows an OBDD with respect to the variable ordering $x_{\ell 1}, y_{\ell 1}, \ldots, x_{\ell n}, y_{\ell n}$ which represents the function $x^\ell = y^\ell$.)

   If $x^j = y^j$ and $x_{j1} + \cdots + x_{jn} = 1$ for $j < \ell$, $x^\ell \neq y^\ell$ but $x_{\ell 1} + \cdots + x_{\ell n} = 1$ and $y_{\ell 1} + \cdots + y_{\ell n} = 1$, the values for x^ℓ and y^ℓ are stored, afterwards it is checked whether $x^{\ell+1} = y^\ell$, $x^\ell = y^{\ell+1}$, $x^i = y^i$, and $x_{i1} + \cdots + x_{in} = 1$ for $i > \ell + 1$. The values are stored in the sense that partial assignments corresponding to different values for x^ℓ and y^ℓ lead to different nodes in the OBDD for $\mathcal{X}_E$. (The reason is that in this case different values for x^ℓ and y^ℓ correspond to different subfunctions.) If all requirements are fulfilled, the function value of $\mathcal{X}_E$ is 1, otherwise it is 0. Since x^ℓ and y^ℓ are binary representations of powers of 2, there are only $\binom{n}{2}$ possibilities for different values for x^ℓ and y^ℓ. (If one of them is not a power of 2 the function value is 0 and we do not have to store anything.) Therefore, the different values for x^ℓ and y^ℓ can be stored by a part of the OBDD with width $\binom{n}{2}$. Altogether the width of the OBDD for $\mathcal{X}_E$ is bounded above by $O(n^2)$. (Figure 3 shows the first part of an OBDD for $\mathcal{X}_E$ with respect to the considered variable ordering and $n = 3$.)

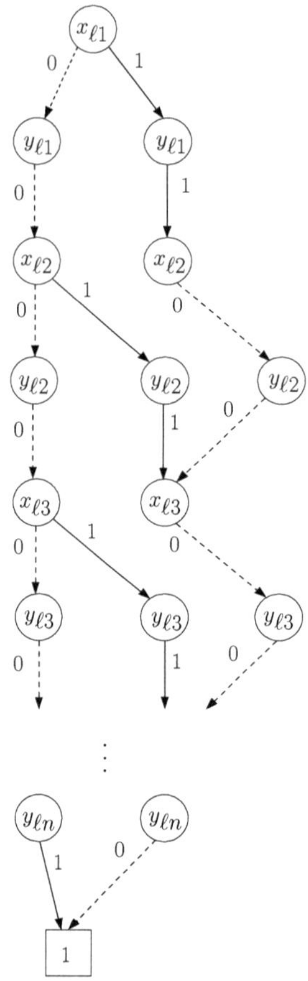

Fig. 2. An OBDD that checks whether $x^\ell = y^\ell$ and $x_{\ell 1} + \cdots + x_{\ell n} = 1$. Missing edges are leading to the 0-sink.

Since there are altogether $2n^2$ Boolean variables, the OBDD for the function $\mathcal{X}_E$ has size at most $O(n^4)$.

3. The exponential lower bound on the size of the OBDD representation for the characteristic function of the vertex set R:

   It remains to show that the output $\mathcal{X}_R$ has exponential OBDD complexity. In [14,15] exponential lower bounds of $\Omega(n^{-1/2}2^n)$ on the size of so-called nondeterministic read-once branching programs representing the function PERM_n, the test whether a Boolean matrix contains exactly one 1-entry in each row and in each column, have been presented. It is not difficult to see that the characteristic function of the set R of reachable vertices from s in G_n is equal to the function PERM_n. The reasoning is the following. Since the number of 1-entries in a column of a Boolean matrix does not change if rows

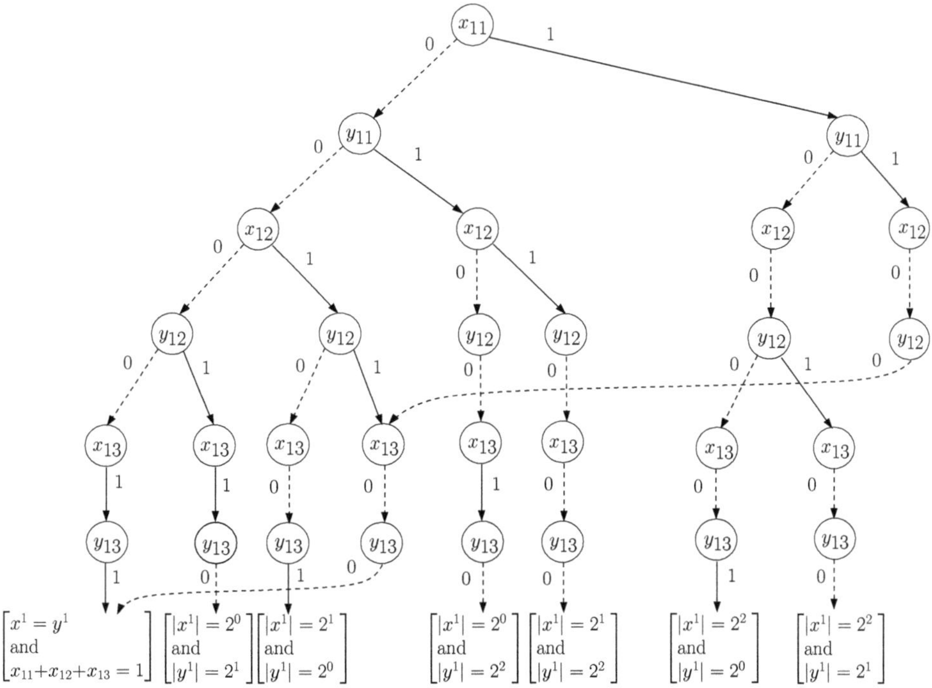

Fig. 3. The first part of an OBDD for the characteristic function of the edge set $\mathcal{X}_E$, where $n = 3$ and the variable ordering $x_{11}, y_{11}, x_{12}, y_{12}, x_{13}, y_{13} \ldots$. Missing edges are leading to the 0-sink. [...] contains the necessary and sufficient information about the partial assignments to the variables $x_{11}, \ldots, y_{13}$. Different information lead to different subfunctions.

are exchanged, in G_n there are only directed paths from s to vertices whose binary representations correspond to Boolean matrices with exactly one 1-entry in each row and in each column, i.e., the binary encodings correspond to permutations in S_n. Moreover, each permutation π in S_n can be obtained from $1\ 2\ \ldots\ n$ by using only swaps between two neighbored integers. As a result we can conclude that there exists a directed path from s to a vertex $v_{i_1,\ldots,i_n}$ iff the binary representation of $i_1, \ldots, i_n$ corresponds to a Boolean matrix with exactly one 1-entry in each row and in each column. Summarizing $\mathcal{X}_R$ is equal to PERM_n. Since read-once branching programs are even a more general model than OBDDs, we obtain the desired exponential lower bound on the size of our output OBDD.

By simple variable replacements the reachability problem can be reduced to the computation of an OBDD for all connected node pairs, the so-called transitive closure. The problem is an important submodule in many OBDD-based graph algorithms (see, e.g., [13,17,23]).

Corollary 1. *Let transitive closure be the problem to compute an* OBDD *representing all connected node pairs for a graph symbolically represented by an* OBDD. *The problem transitive closure is not computable in polynomial space.*

If we replace the x-variables by the binary representation of the vertex s in an OBDD for the characteristic function of the transitive closure of G_n, we obtain an OBDD for PERM_n. As we have mentioned before, Theorem 2 implies that the OBDD size for a subfunction of a Boolean function f cannot be larger than the OBDD size of f. Therefore, we are done.

Sawitzki [19] has commented that it is easy to show that the computation of (strong) connected components in a (directed) graph is a problem which is not computable in polynomial space for OBDD-based algorithms by looking at graphs without any edges since then the number of (strong) connected components is exponential with respect to the number of Boolean variables. Nevertheless, it would be nice to have an example for a graph where the OBDD-representation is small but for which at least one connected component has exponential OBDD-size. Obviously, our graphs fulfills the required properties. Let a connected component be non-trivial if it contains more than a single vertex. Our graph G_n has 2^{n-1} non-trivial connected components.

4 Concluding Remarks

Representing graphs with regularities by means of data structures smaller than adjacency matrices or adjacency lists seems to be a natural idea. But problems typically get harder when their input is represented implicitly. For circuit representations this has been shown in [1,10,16]. These results do not directly carry over to problems on OBDD-represented inputs since there are Boolean functions like some output bits of integer multiplication whose OBDD complexity is exponentially larger than its circuit size [6]. In [9] it has been shown that even the very basic problem of deciding whether two vertices s and t are connected in a directed graph G, the so-called graph accessibility problem GAP, is PSPACE-complete on OBDD-represented graphs. Despite the hardness results there are not many nontrivial lower bounds known for the complexity of problems on OBDD-represented graph instances. The challenge is to prove small upper bounds on the OBDD size of input graphs and simultaneously large lower bounds on the size of OBDDs occuring during the computation. In [20] exponential lower bounds on OBDD-based algorithms for the single-source shortest paths problem, the maximum flow problem, and a restricted class of algorithms for the reachability problem have been presented. We have extended these results by presenting a concrete exponential lower bound on the space complexity of general OBDD-based algorithms for the reachability problem and the transitive closure, where the input and the output OBDD can be ordered according to different variable orderings.

Moreover, since the exponential lower bound on the representation size for the permutation test function PERM_n has been shown for so-called nondeterministic read-once branching programs [14,15], our results do also carry over to a more general model than OBDDs.

Acknowledgment. The author would like to thank the anonymous referees for their helpful comments.

References

1. Balcázar, J.L., Lozano, A.: The Complexity of Graph Problems for Succinctly Represented Graphs. In: Nagl, M. (ed.) WG 1989. LNCS, vol. 411, pp. 277–285. Springer, Heidelberg (1990)
2. Bollig, B.: On the OBDD Complexity of the Most Significant Bit of Integer Multiplication. In: Agrawal, M., Du, D.-Z., Duan, Z., Li, A. (eds.) TAMC 2008. LNCS, vol. 4978, pp. 306–317. Springer, Heidelberg (2008)
3. Bollig, B.: Larger Lower Bounds on the OBDD Complexity of Integer Multiplication. In: Dediu, A.H., Ionescu, A.M., Martín-Vide, C. (eds.) LATA 2009. LNCS, vol. 5457, pp. 212–223. Springer, Heidelberg (2009)
4. Bollig, B., Klump, J.: New Results on the Most Significant Bit of Integer Multiplication. In: Hong, S.-H., Nagamochi, H., Fukunaga, T. (eds.) ISAAC 2008. LNCS, vol. 5369, pp. 883–894. Springer, Heidelberg (2008)
5. Bryant, R.E.: Graph-Based Algorithms for Boolean Function Manipulation. IEEE Trans. on Computers 35, 677–691 (1986)
6. Bryant, R.E.: On the Complexity of VLSI Implementations and Graph Representations of Boolean Functions with Application to Integer Multiplication. IEEE Trans. on Computers 40, 205–213 (1991)
7. Burch, J.R., Clarke, E.M., Long, D.E., Mc Millan, K.L., Dill, D.L., Hwang, L.J.: Symbolic Model Checking: 10^{20} States and Beyond. In: Proc. of Symposium on Logic in Computer Science, pp. 428–439 (1990)
8. Coudert, O., Berthet, C., Madre, J.C.: Verification of Synchronous Sequential Machines Based on Symbolic Execution. In: Sifakis, J. (ed.) CAV 1989. LNCS, vol. 407, pp. 365–373. Springer, Heidelberg (1990)
9. Feigenbaum, J., Kannan, S., Vardi, M.V., Viswanathan, M.: Complexity of Problems on Graphs Represented as OBDDs. In: Meinel, C., Morvan, M. (eds.) STACS 1998. LNCS, vol. 1373, pp. 216–226. Springer, Heidelberg (1998)
10. Galperin, H., Wigderson, A.: Succinct Representations of Graphs. Information and Control 56, 183–198 (1983)
11. Gentilini, R., Piazza, C., Policriti, A.: Computing Strongly Connected Components in a Linear Number of Symbolic Steps. In: Proc. of SODA, pp. 573–582. ACM Press, New York (2003)
12. Gentilini, R., Piazza, C., Policriti, A.: Symbolic Graphs: Linear Solutions to Connectivity Related Problems. Algorithmica 50, 120–158 (2008)
13. Hachtel, G.D., Somenzi, F.: A Symbolic Algorithm for Maximum Flow in $0-1$ Networks. Formal Methods in System Design 10, 207–219 (1997)
14. Jukna, S.: The Effect of Null-Chains on the Complexity of Contact Schemes. In: Csirik, J.A., Demetrovics, J., Gecseg, F. (eds.) FCT 1989. LNCS, vol. 380, pp. 246–256. Springer, Heidelberg (1989)
15. Krause, M., Meinel, C., Waack, S.: Separating the Eraser Turing Machine Classes L_e, NL_e, co-NL_e and P_e. Theoretical Computer Science 86, 267–275 (1991)

16. Papadimitriou, C.H., Yannakakis, M.: A Note on Succinct Representations of Graphs. Information and Control 71, 181–185 (1986)
17. Sawitzki, D.: Implicit Flow Maximization by Iterative Squaring. In: Van Emde Boas, P., Pokorný, J., Bieliková, M., Štuller, J. (eds.) SOFSEM 2004. LNCS, vol. 2932, pp. 301–313. Springer, Heidelberg (2004)
18. Sawitzki, D.: Lower Bounds on the OBDD Size of Graphs of Some Popular Functions. In: Vojtáš, P., Bieliková, M., Charron-Bost, B., Sýkora, O. (eds.) SOFSEM 2005. LNCS, vol. 3381, pp. 298–309. Springer, Heidelberg (2005)
19. Sawitzki, D.: Algorithmik und Komplexität OBDD-repräsentierter Graphen. PhD Thesis, University of Dortmund, in German (2006)
20. Sawitzki, D.: Exponential Lower Bounds on the Space Complexity of OBDD-Based Graph Algorithms. In: Correa, J.R., Hevia, A., Kiwi, M. (eds.) LATIN 2006. LNCS, vol. 3887, pp. 781–792. Springer, Heidelberg (2006)
21. Sieling, D., Wegener, I.: NC-Algorithms for Operations on Binary Decision Diagrams. Parallel Processing Letters 48, 139–144 (1993)
22. Wegener, I.: Branching Programs and Binary Decision Diagrams – Theory and Applications. SIAM Monographs on Discrete Mathematics and Applications (2000)
23. Woelfel, P.: Symbolic Topological Sorting with OBDDs. Journal of Discrete Algorithms 4(1), 51–71 (2006)

A Social Vision of Knowledge Representation and Reasoning

François Bry and Jakub Kotowski

Institute for Informatics, University of Munich
Oettingenstr. 67, 80538 München, Germany
`http://pms.ifi.lmu.de`

Abstract. Knowledge representation and reasoning so far have focused on the ideal ultimate goal, thus stressing logical consistency and semantic homogeneity. On the way to consistent and homogenous knowledge representation and reasoning, inconsistencies and divergent opinions often have to be dealt with. In this article, a social vision of knoweldge representation is proposed which accomodates conflicting views that possibly even result in logical inconsistencies; reasoning is used to track divergent, possibly incompatible viewpoints. This approach to knowledge repsresentation and reasoning has been developped for a social software, a social semantic wiki.

1 Introduction

Traditionally knowledge representation and reasoning focuses on processing of consistent data curated by experts in advance to conform to predfined schemes. This paper explores the needs of social semantic software, such as semantic Wikis, with respect to reasoning and knowledge representation. The phrase "Semantic Wiki" can have two basic meanings [1]: "Wiki enhanced with semantic technologies" and "Wiki for ontology engineers". This paper is focused primarily on the first sense. Several semantic Wikis were developed, e.g. [2,3,4,5], this paper presents a part of work developed in the project KiWi – Knowledge in a Wiki[1] – which develops a social semantic platform inspired by Wikis and the main application of which is a Wiki. In social software, knowledge representation is usually restricted to keyword tagging. Traditional keyword tagging can be extended in a number of ways, some of which have been investigated previously [6,7,8]. We are proposing a generalization of tagging which we call structured tagging (section 3) to provide expressive power to casual users while maintaining the simplicity of traditional tagging. Section 4 outlines how this formalism can be used together with an inconsistency-tolerant rule-based language to "emerge semantics" from user specified annotations with the help of rules. Finally, section 5 shows how a rule-language about annotations can be extended to provide further support of user-annotation and explanation by means of rule scopes and tracking of origins of newly derived annotations. This work is related to CSCW[2]

[1] `http://www.kiwi-project.eu/`
[2] Computer-supported collaborative learning.

J. van Leeuwen et al. (Eds.): SOFSEM 2010, LNCS 5901, pp. 235–246, 2010.

but is more flexible, does not rely on complex prescribed knowledge and process models. It is also closely related to work on collaborative learning with a shared knowledge artifact ("trialogical learning"), as e.g. in [9], but the focus is more specifically on supporting collaboration through automated reasoning. The concept of shared understanding is found to be very important for collaborative learning (both in synchronous learning e.g. for educational purposes and in asynchronous settings where information exchange is the main goal), see for example [10,11] for more details. In this paper we use a similar in spirit but more technical, annotation-based notion of shared understanding which is also close to a kind of social provenance information that [12] calls for. To the best of our knowledge there is currently little or no research on rule-based languages for *social* semantic environment.

2 Motivation

KiWi is an enterprise social platform that should support knowledge workers in their varied, creative work which does not adhere to predefined schemes (e.g. ontologies) and involves inadvertent transient inconsistencies. Inconsistencies are even desirable in creative process. An enterprise social semantic application should support such work and should not hinder it by enforcing unnecessary constraints. Concepts and schemes should emerge, inconsistencies should be tolerated, and users should be supported in discovering them and resolving them.

Knowledge representation and reasoning the Wiki way. Traditionally, knowledge is represented in complex formalisms by experts cooperating with domain experts. Such an approach is neither possible nor desirable in social software. Casual users should be able to semantically enrich content. The approach we suggest is to provide users with a means of creating annotations which can be made gradually more formal and precise and which can accomodate inconsistencies and incompatible viewpoints.

Emergent semantics: from informal to formal knowledge representation. Traditional approaches to knowledge representation impose a rigid prior structure on information. In contrast, collaborative tagging leads to emergence of folksonomies[3] advantages of which over predefined taxonomies have been discussed before. We argue that, given proper tools, user collaboration can gradually lead to semantically rich structures. We suggest that the right tools are structured tags and inconsistency-tolerant rule-based reasoning which can accomodate both formal (e.g. RDF/S) and informal (e.g. simple tags and structured tags) annotations.

Negative information. In real life, people are used to working with negative information. We suggest *negative tagging* as a way to express negative information in KiWi. For example someone can tag a page as "*–risky*" to express that in his

[3] We use the word *folksonomy* to mean a user-generated taxonomy. Folksonomy is implicitly present in the bag of all tags but can also be extracted and represented the way traditional taxonomies are represented.

or her opinion that the project described on the page is not risky. A manager could be interested in finding all projects that are not risky and have not been reviewed yet. This query refers to explicitly assigned negative tag "*–risky*" (explicit negation) and to a missing tag "*reviewed*" (negation as failure). We argue that users will benefit from both kinds of negations as they increase expressivity of the knowledge representation formalism.

3 Conceptual Model

This section shortly reviews the basic concepts a user will interact with within the KiWi system, focus is on concepts most relevant to reasoning. It is based on work published in [13], refer there for a detailed discussion of the conceptual model.

Content Items. Content items, the primary unit of information in the KiWi wiki, are composable, non-overlapping documents. Every content item has a unique URI and can be addressed and accessed individually. As a consequence, there is by default no inherent distinction between Wiki pages and content items.

Annotations. Annotations are meta-data that can be attached to content items and which convey information about their meaning or properties. Annotations can be assigned by the user, either manually or via rules. Content items and tag assignments also have system meta-data such as their creation date and their author(s). There are three kinds of annotations: simple tags, structured tags, and RDF triples whereas simple tags can be seen as a special case of structured tags. Tags allow to express knowledge informally, that is, without having to use a pre-defined vocabulary. RDF triples are used for formal knowledge representation, possibly using a pre-defined vocabulary. Structured tags can serve as a step in-between: they are structured but not yet formal.

RDF. The KiWi system chooses the RDF/S language [14,15] to specify its ontologies [16] because it is in many ways simpler than OWL [17] and yet it is sufficient for most purposes in KiWi. Simple and structured tags are represented in RDF using a predefined vocabulary in order to make them accessible to semantic querying and reasoning.

Tags. For the purpose of this paper we identify a tag with the content item that (optionally) describes it. Therefore each tag has a unique URI and can be referred to by its name (label) which can be disambiguated by cooperation of the user with the system.

Tagging. The assignment of a tag, a tagging, means the association of a content item with a tag and a user (who assigned the tag). The assignment additionally includes maintenance information. A tagging is thus a tuple consisting of a tag, a user, the tagged page, and maintenance information needed for a processing of taggings such as information about the origin of the tagging, the date when the tagging was created, a marker which allows to distinguish between explicit, derived, and system taggings. Tagging can be either positive or negative. This is distinguished by a *polarity property.* Negative taggings are displayed with a minus ("–") sign directly in front of their tag label.

Negative taggings. Although negative tagging could be seen as classical negation, it in fact is only a very weak form of classical negation because only pure taggings can be negated, not general formulae (or sets of taggings), and the only way to interpret this kind of negation is by introducing a rule which says that from tagging "t" and tagging "–t" a contradiction symbol should be derived.

Structured tags. Structured tags can be used as an intermediate step between simple tags and formal RDF annotations. Two basic operations lie at the core of structured tagging: grouping and characterization. Grouping, denoted "()", allows to relate several (complex or simple) tags using the grouping operator. The group can then be used for annotation. Example: a Wiki page describes a meeting that took place in Warwick, UK and involved a New York customer. Using atomic tags, this page can be tagged as "*Warwick*", "*New York*", "*UK*" leaving an observer in doubts whether "*Warwick*" refers to the city in UK or to a town near New York. Grouping can be used in this case to make the tagging more precise: "*(Warwick, UK), New York*". Note that, if Warwick was already defined in RDF, it could be disambiguated using its URI. Structured tags help when concepts are undefined and thus have no URI yet.

Characterization enables the classification or, in a sense, naming of a tag. The characterization operator, denoted ":", can be used to make the tagging even more precise. For example, if we wanted to tag the meeting Wiki page with a geo-location of the city Warwick, we could tag it as "*(52.272135, -1.595764)*" using the grouping operator. This, however, would not be sufficient as the group is unordered. Therefore we could use the characterization operator to specify which number refers to latitude and which to longitude: "*(lat:52.272135, lon:-1.595764)*" and later perhaps specify that the whole group refers to a geo-location: "*geo:(lat:52.272135, lon:-1.595764)*".

An important feature of structured tagging is that it allows users to work with concepts which are not fully clear. Users can begin with only a set of tags, later group them and only then realize that they, in fact, are describing a specific concept. In contrast, a formalism such as RDF/S makes its users to think in terms of concepts or classes from the very beginning and therefore constrains them in cases when the concepts are not yet clear.

The meaning of a structured tagging rests, for the most part, on the user who specified it. Structured tags do not impose strict rules on their use or purpose, they only allow users to introduce structure into taggings. It can be seen as a Wiki-like approach to annotation which enables a gradual, bottom-up refinement process during which meaning emerges as the user's work and understanding develop.

Minimal rules are, however, necessary in order to ensure a flexible, useful order and to avoid unfruitful chaos. Grouping can be applied on positive and negative simple tags and groups. Groups are unordered, cannot contain two identical members (e.g. "*(Bob, Bob, Anna)*" is not allowed), can be nested, are equal to a tag when the tag is the only one in the group, i.e. "*(Anna)*" is equal to "*Anna*".

Characterization can be used on positive and negative atomic tags and groups. Characterization is not commutative, i.e. "*geo:x*" is not the same as "*x:geo*". Structured tags have to be syntactically correct, e.g. "*Bob:190cm,90kg*" is not a valid structured tag.

The above described way of structuring geo-location is only one of several. Other may include: "*geo:(x:y):(1,23:2,34)*" or "*geo:1,23:2,34*", and many more. This heterogeneity is an advantage. It provides users with freedom and it can be beneficial for different communities to encode similar kinds of information differently as the precise meaning of a similar concept may differ. Consider e.g. geo-tagging using different coordinate systems in different communities – different geo-tagging encoding would facilitate automatic translation of structured tags to formal annotations because it would allow to distinguish the two concepts structurally.

4 A Social Approach to Knowledge Representation – Emergent Semantics

Structured tags allow users to enrich ordinary tags by structuring them in order to clarify their context or qualify the thought statement that the tag is supposed to express. These structural hints can then be used to translate structured tags to formal RDF annotations via rules that specify their mapping to a predefined ontology. The advantage is that the simplicity of tagging is preserved: users can first tag and make the tagging more precise only later and eventually map it to a formal annotation. The approach could thus be summarized as "Tag, Think, Qualify, Map" – a cycle consisting of four steps. Let us take a look at an example.

Consider an enterprise Wiki in which each employee has a profile page. Alice, a junior assistant from the HR department of a company, has just hired a new employee, Bob. She creates a new page in the Wiki for Bob and decides to tag it with a few pieces of information about him. She assigns two tags to the page: "*manager*" and "*programmer*" because it is what came to her mind first. Later she realizes that the tagging can be confusing. Therefore she qualifies the tags to make it apparent that Bob is a manager with a programming background: "*position:manager*", "*experience:programmer*". Claire, a more experienced colleague of Alice, notices Alice's tags and lets her know about a new Wiki feature that their IT team is about to introduce. It is an org-chart widget that, given a name of an employee, displays the name of his or her manager and employees which report to him or her. The widget would be a nice addition to profile pages, so Alice and Claire talk to a contact from the IT department to ask how to include it. It turns out to be rather easy. The Wiki will automatically display the org-chart on any user page. User page is a page with type ucont:Employee defined in the company's UCONT[4] RDF/S ontology. Therefore all it takes to use the widget is to create a new rule in the Wiki: $position : manager \rightarrow rdf : type\ ucont : Employee$. It translates each structured

[4] UCONT stands for "use-case ontology."

tag "*position:manager*" to a formal RDF annotation "*rdf:type ucont:Employee*". Alice and Claire don not have to learn anything about ontologies and RDF/S and they still can indirectly enrich the Wiki content with formal annotations. Maybe, in the future, another widget will be able to summarize skills of an employee in which case Alice and Claire will benefit from their distinguishing between e.g. "*experience:programmer*" and "*position:programmer*".

This admittedly simplified example indicates how knowledge can emerge from initial tagging and user collaboration inside and outside a Wiki environment by taking advantage of structured tags and rules.[5] Rules could of course be more sophisticated. In the above scenario users could add the rule: "$type : \$TypeName \rightarrow ucont : \$TypeName$" and use simple structured tags of the form "type:typeName" to specify RDF/S types from the company's predefined ontology. Using similar rules, user taggings could be enriched with information from e.g. a SKOS[6] thesaurus.

5 A Social Approach to Automated Reasoning

Reasoning suitable for social software such as Wikis should be in line with their main defining traits: simplicity and collaboration. This section proposes an approach to automated reasoning which supports users collaboration and facilitates user understanding of reasoning.

5.1 Shared Understanding

During collaborative work it is important that every member knows what other members think about a subject in question. In a Wiki-like environment, collaboration takes place in and around content items. Users' understanding of a content item in KiWi can be expressed via annotations. Therefore the set of annotations of an item could be seen as the *shared understanding* of the item of all users who annotated it. Inconsistencies found within a shared understanding may be indicative of disagreements or misunderstandings of the item between the users. Such inconsistencies can be important for the future success and efficiency of the collaborative effort. The reasoning we propose is able to work in presence of inconsistencies and to point them out to users. Note that inconsistencies can emerge through constraint rules, are treated as special symbols that can be derived but cannot be matched in rule bodies and thus the classical principle "ex falso quodlibet" (anything can be inferred from a contradiction) is avoided (see [18] for details).

Often it is also important to know who worked on what topic, who approved which content item or who agreed with something. The reasoning system we

[5] Note that structured tags are only an unrestrictive formalism. The actual implementation is likely to provide a more convenient UI metaphor for them than textual which should also allow for easy continuous development of existing annotations.

[6] SKOS stands for Simple Knowledge Organization System – a data model to support the use of thesauri and other classification schemes, see http://www.w3.org/2004/02/skos/

propose will keep track of how which annotation originated – depending on which users and which content-items. Therefore the system is capable of answering questions such as: "What are the inconsistencies stemming from annotations originating in content items X, Y, and Z?" and "What follows from information entered by Alice, Bob, and Claire?"

Authorship of derived annotations. The author of a derived annotation is defined as the author of the rule by which the annotation was derived. An annotation may be derived based on annotations by multiple users – this kind of information is called the user-origin of the annotation. Similarly, the content-item origin of an annotation contains information about which content-items the derived annotation depends on.

5.2 Rule Scope

In professional context the quality and source of information is often very important. For collaborative work it means that it can be effective only when people know with whom they collaborate. Consider the example from the previous section again. It could be the case that only the marketing department is allowed to decide which bugs must be fixed. Rule R_2 should therefore apply only to tags by users who work in the marketing department; the rule's *scope* should be limited only to marketing users.

Limiting the rule scope with respect to users is only one of several options. Rule scope restricts a rule to only certain data. Data in a Wiki are usually created by *users* and divided into *pages*. Therefore, content items are another candidate for a rule scope.

User scope and content item scope. Users and content items are the most important candidates for rule scope in KiWi. After all, almost everything in KiWi is represented by a content item, including users. However, a distinction has to be made between users and content items with respect to scope. Restricting a rule to a set of users understood as a set of content items would restrict them to the actual content items and not to the tags entered by these users.

Other notions of scope. There could be other candidates for a rule scope, notably time – to restrict a rule to only a certain period of time. There is, however, a significant difference between time as scope and users or content items as scope. Users and content items are a kind of provenance data of derived annotations meaning that they change according to who and where created the annotations used in the rule antecedent. Time, in contrast, does not propagate via rules. This means that while a rule with a time scope can easily be rewritten to an equivalent rule without time scope, it is not as simple in the case of rules with a user or content item scope. Such rules still could possibly be rewritten but they would necessarily have to "walk the tag dependency tree" and gather all the (user and content item) information on the way. This would have to be done before each rule application for each tag. So, at the very least, it would be inefficient. Therefore a further support from the rule language and reasoning is necessary for efficient evaluation of rules with user and/or content item scopes.

The focus in the following is therefore on user and content item scopes as they are more than a mere syntactic sugar.

Extensional vs. intensional scope. So far, it was silently assumed that the user and content item scope is defined extensionally, i.e. that it consist of an explicit list of users and an explicit list of content items. The groups could also be defined *intensionally*: a rule could be meant to be applied only to tags by managers who have worked for the company for at least three years. The KiWi system will support extensional scopes. Intensional groups remain as a possible future extension because they can increase the amount of interdependencies between rules and in a language with negation as failure lead even to reasoning loops. In the following text, the words *group* and *scope* refer to the extensional meaning unless stated otherwise.

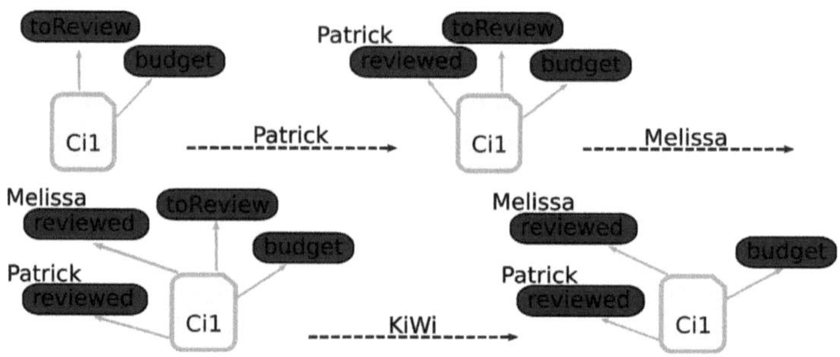

Fig. 1. A scenario illustrating how rule scope affects negation as failure. The applied rule is "$(not\ reviewed \rightarrow toReview) WithScopeMarketing$", where $Marketing = \{Melissa, John\}$.

Rule scope and negation as failure. Rule scope limits rule application to only certain data. Negation as failure in a rule is also subject to this limitation. See Figure 1. If a rule, such as rule R_1, with negation as failure has scope consisting of two users, Melissa and John, then a negated tag in the rule body will be satisfied even if there exists this tag but is assigned by someone else than Melissa or John. In the scenario in Figure 1, Patrick tags content item "Ci1" as "*reviewed*" which does not lead to removal of the tag "*toReview*" because Patrick is not in the scope of rule R_1. The "*toReview*" tag is removed only after Melissa tags the content item as "*reviewed*". Rule scope in combination with negation as failure therefore leads to a concept similar to Axel Polleres's scoped negation as failure [19].

5.3 Computing Shared Understanding

Shared understanding of a group of users of a group of content items is the set of all tags of these content items assigned by these users. Knowing what a shared understanding looks like may help users to assess the influence a group of users or a group of content items has on the overall state of knowledge. Thus, shared understandings can play the role of additional explanation of the system behaviour. This section outlines how shared understandings can be computed in an efficient fashion. For space reasons, only user-origin of annotations is discussed in detail, for content-item-origins analogical analysis can be made.

Definition 1. *Author of an explicit annotation is the user who assigned the annotation. Author of an implicit annotation is the user who created the rule by which the annotation was derived.*

User-origin of an annotation consists of all the users based on whose annotations the annotation was derived. As there can be multiple ways to derive a certain annotation, the user-origin can consist of multiple sets of users.

Definition 2. *User-origin of an annotation is a set of sets of users. User-origin of an explicit annotation t, denoted $UO(t)$, is a set containing a singleton set containing the author of the annotation. User-origin of an implicit annotation t, $UO(t)$, derived via rule $B \to t$, where $t_1, ..., t_n$ are all annotations in the rule body B, is*

$$UO(t) = \left\{ \bigcup_{i=1}^{n} s_i | s_1 \in UO(t_1) \text{ and } \ldots \text{ and } s_n \in UO(t_n) \right\} .$$

Consider the following example: $UO(bug) = \{\{Melissa\}\}$, $UO(-processed) = \{\{John\}\}$. The user-origin of the "*todo*" tag derived by rule $bug \wedge -processed \to todo$ is then $UO(todo) = \{\{Melissa, John\}\}$. If, in addition, it was possible to derive the tags "*bug*" and "*-processed*" by other rules and taggings by John's and Melissa's colleagues Alice and Bob and the user-origins were $UO(bug) = \{\{Melissa\}, \{Alice, Bob\}\}$ and $UO(-processed) = \{\{John\}, \{Alice\}\}$ then the origin of "*todo*" would be

$$UO(todo) = \{\{Mel., John\}, \{Mel., Alice\}, \{Alice, Bob, John\}, \{Alice, Bob\}\} .$$

$UO(t)$ intuitively consists of such "groups" of users where each group "agrees on / supports" the annotation t. Or in other words: the distributed knowledge[7] of each group of users from $UO(t)$ implies the annotation t.

Definition 3. *Shared understanding of a set of users U of a set of content items C, designated $SU(U, C)$, is*

$$SU(U, C) = \{ t \mid t \in A(C) \text{ and } (\exists s \in UO(t)) s \subseteq U \} ,$$

where $A(C)$ is a set of annotations assigned to content items C. It is a set of annotations where the user-origin set of each annotation contains a set which is a subset of U.

User-scope of a rule is a set of users. Each rule has a user-scope. The default user-scope is the set of all users.

[7] In the modal logic sense.

Looking at the above example (by Definition 2), it is easy to see that tracking origins can lead to a combinatorial explosion if all possible combinations users and all possible combination of content items are tracked. For n users there are $n!$ possible user-origin sets. On the one hand, users can ask a question about any of these user-origin sets, on the other hand, it is likely that they are interested mainly in the sets that correspond for example to teams of their company. A team is basically a group of employees, in our case that would be a group of users. It is likely that teams would be defined as groups of users in an enterprise Wiki. Therefore, it is reasonable to focus on tracking origin-sets with respect to predefined groups of users and content items. This way the combinatorial explosion can be avoided while providing the same functionality to users.

User-origin sets with groups. When tracking user-origin sets using groups, the way of computing the origin sets is basically the same, only each origin set is replaced by the smallest predefined "group" which subsumes the origin set[8]. The user-origin set is then a set of predefined groups. For this to work correctly and as expected, a number of groups (from the full lattice of groups) has to be added. First, a group containing all users has to be added to the predefined groups so as to ensure that there always is a smallest encompassing group. Also, a group for each single user needs to be added as it is natural to require that user-scopes are possible to define for single users too.

With groups, the shared understanding of a set of users U can be computed the same way as in Definition 3 as long as the set of users U is one of the predefined groups. If the set of users is not one of the predefined groups then:

$$SU(U, C) = \bigcup_{i \in I} SU(G_i, C) \restriction (G_i \cap U), \tag{1}$$

where $|G_i \cap U| \geq 1$ for all $i \in I$, G_i are all the predefined groups, and $A \restriction G$ filters out all annotations from the set of annotations A the user origin-set of which does not contain a set which is a subset of G, and $A \restriction \emptyset = \emptyset$. Equation 1 is correct under the assumption that each rule has one of the predefined groups as a user-scope (because then if U has a subset U' which is not subset of any G_i then there are no derivations dependent on tags by users U'). A consequence of this assumption is that the administrator of the system can influence what gets precomputed by creating predefined groups. The assumption could be generalized to allow the scope to be a set of groups. This would allow the user to restrict a rule to a combination of teams (resp. teams and employees) instead of restricting it to a single group.

Content-item origins with groups. Content-item origins can be adapted in a similar way to allow to work with groups of content-items. A group of content items could be imagined as a working space of a group of users which is separate from other content items with respect to annotations and other users. In this sense, each group of content items could be seen as a "knowledge space" - a closed group of content items "generating knowledge" which is self-contained: depends

[8] This is correct if each rule scope is one of the predefined groups.

only on these and no other content items. If the KiWi system included a mechanism for dividing pages into strictly separate groups (e.g. with different access rights, etc.), the mechanism of content-items groups as rule scope would allow to ensure this separation at the level of reasoning too.

5.4 Explanation

Explanation is a desirable feature of a user-friendly system enhanced with reasoning. The approach to explanation and user-friendliness in KiWi is manifold and inherent in the general approach. Zacharias [20] points out four principles for building tool support for the creation of rule bases: interactivity, visibility (users should be informed about possible rule interactions), declarativity (all aspects or rule-base development should be declarative, i.e. including "debugging"), modularization (prevention of unintended interaction by providing means to modularize the rule base). The KiWi reasoning and explanation system tries to build on these principles. For example rule scope helps to modularize the rule base by limiting possible rule interactions. There are plans to support true modularization – of the rule base and of the knowledge base. Modularization of knowledge base is one step towards providing higher efficiency and therefore responsiveness and interactivity of the system as a set of rules will operate only on a specific, relevant part of the whole knowledge base (determined by the author of the rules). Of course, this is complemented by an explanation system which presents an interactive, pre-processed derivation tree of any derived annotation or inconsistency. In addition to a derivation tree, origins of derived facts are displayed too so that users can spot possible culprits of conflicts and inconsistencies more easily.

6 Conclusion

In this paper we presented a rule-based language about annotations suitable for a social semantic environment such as semantic Wikis. The approach stresses the importance of user-friendliness and lenience of both the formalism and reasoning by tolerating inconsistencies, allowing rules about not fully specified semi-formal annotations (structured tags) and we also show how simple explanations can be enhanced and enriched.

Acknowledgements. The research leading to these results is part of the project "KiWi - Knowledge in a Wiki" and has received funding from the European Community's Seventh Framework Programme (FP7/2007-2013) under grant agreement No. 211932.

References

1. Krötzsch, M., Schaffert, S., Vrandecic, D.: Reasoning in Semantic Wikis. In: Reasoning Web Summer School 2007, pp. 310–329 (2007)
2. Auer, S., Dietzold, S., Riechert, T.: Ontowiki - a Tool for Social, Semantic Collaboration. In: Cruz, I., Decker, S., Allemang, D., Preist, C., Schwabe, D., Mika, P., Uschold, M., Aroyo, L.M. (eds.) ISWC 2006. LNCS, vol. 4273, pp. 736–749. Springer, Heidelberg (2006)

3. Oren, E.: Semperwiki: a Semantic Personal Wiki. In: Proceedings of 1st Workshop on The Semantic Desktop - Next Generation Personal Information Management and Collaboration Infrastructure, Galway, Ireland (2005)
4. Schaffert, S., Westenthaler, R., Gruber, A.: Ikewiki: A User-Friendly Semantic Wiki. In: Sure, Y., Domingue, J. (eds.) ESWC 2006. LNCS, vol. 4011. Springer, Heidelberg (2006)
5. Popitsch, N., Schandl, B., Amiri, A., Leitich, S., Jochum, W.: Ylvi - Multimedia-izing the Semantic Wiki. In: Proceedings of the 1st Workshop SemWiki 2006 - From Wiki to Semantics, Budva, Montenegro (2006)
6. Bar-Ilan, J., Shoham, S., Idan, A., Miller, Y., Shachak, A.: Structured vs. Unstructured Tagging a Case Study. In: Proceedings of the WWW 2006 Collaborative Web Tagging Workshop (2006)
7. Sereno, B., Shum, B., Motta, E.: Formalization, User Strategy and Interaction Design: Users' Behaviour with Discourse Tagging Semantics. In: Proceedings of the Workshop on Social and Collaborative Construction of Structured Knowledge, WWW 2007 (2007)
8. Yang, J., Matsuo, Y., Ishizuka, M.: Triple Tagging: Toward Bridging Folksonomy and Semantic Web. In: ISWC 2007, p. 14 (2007)
9. Tzitzikas, Y., Christophides, V., Flouris, G., Kotzinos, D., Plexousakis, D., Spyratos, N.: Emergent Knowledge Artifacts for Supporting Trialogical E-Learning. International Journal of Web-based Learning and Teaching Technologies 3, 19–41 (2007)
10. Mulder, I., Swaak, J., Kessels, J.: Assessing Group Learning and Shared Understanding in Technology-Mediated Interaction. Educational Technology & Society 1, 35–47 (2002)
11. Hinds, P., Weisband, S.: 2. Virtual Teams that Work: Creating Conditions for Virtual Team Effectiveness. Jossey-Bass (2003)
12. Harth, A., Polleres, A., Decker, S.: Towards a Social Provenance Model for the Web. In: Workshop on Principles of Provenance (PrOPr), Edinburgh, Scotland (2007)
13. Bry, F., Eckert, M., Kotowski, J., Weiand, K.: What the User Interacts with: Reflections on Conceptual Models for Sematic Wikis. In: Proceedings of the Fourth Semantic Wiki Workshop (SemWiki 2009), ESWC 2009 (2009)
14. Manola, F., Miller, E.: Rdf Primer (2004)
15. Brickley, D., Guha, R.: Rdf Vocabulary Description Language 1.0: Rdf Sschema (2004)
16. Gruber, T., et al.: A Translation Approach to Portable Ontology Specifications. Knowledge Acquisition, p. 199 (1993)
17. McGuinness, D.L., van Harmelen, F.: Owl Web Ontology Language Overview (2004)
18. Bry, F., Kotowski, J.: Towards Reasoning and Explanations for Social Tagging. In: Proc. of ExaCt 2008 - ECAI 2008 Workshop on Explanation-Aware Computing. Patras, Greece (2008)
19. Polleres, A., Feier, C., Harth, A.: Rules with contextually scoped negation. In: Sure, Y., Domingue, J. (eds.) ESWC 2006. LNCS, vol. 4011, pp. 332–347. Springer, Heidelberg (2006)
20. Zacharias, V.: Tackling the Debugging Challenge of Rule Based Systems. In: Filipe, J., Cordeiro, J. (eds.) ICEIS 2008. LNBIP, vol. 19, pp. 144–154. Springer, Heidelberg (2009)

Flavors of KWQL, a Keyword Query Language for a Semantic Wiki

François Bry and Klara Weiand

Institute for Informatics, University of Munich
Oettingenstr. 67, 80538 München, Germany
http://pms.ifi.lmu.de

Abstract. This article introduces KWQL, spoken "quickel", a rule-based query language for a semantic wiki based on the label-keyword query paradigm. KWQL allows for rich combined queries of full text, document structure, and informal to formal semantic annotations. It offers support for continuous queries, that is, queries re-evaluated upon updates to the wiki. KWQL is not restricted to data selection, but also offers database-like views, enabling "construction", the re-shaping of the selected (meta-)data into new (meta-)data. Such views amount to rules that provide a convenient basis for an admittedly simple, yet remarkably powerful form of reasoning.

KWQL queries range from simple lists of keywords or label-keyword pairs to conjunctions, disjunctions, or negations of queries. Thus, queries range from elementary and relatively unspecific to complex and fully specified (meta-)data selections. Consequently, in keeping with the "wiki way", KWQL has a low entry barrier, allowing casual users to easily locate and retrieve relevant data, while letting advanced users make use of its full power.

1 Introduction

Wikis are a popular tool for managing personal and professional knowledge. Wiki content usually consists of simple hypertext documents, that is, web pages which are connected through simple hyperlinks.

In traditional wikis, knowledge is expressed mostly as natural language text and is not directly amenable to automated semantic processing. Therefore, knowledge in wikis can be located only through full-text keyword search or simple (mostly user-generated) structures like tables of content and inter-page links. More sophisticated functionalities such as querying, reasoning and semantic browsing, highly desirable in knowledge intensive, professional contexts such as software development and project management, are not provided.

Semantic wikis promise to provide at least some of these enhancements by relying on so-called semantic technologies, that is knowledge representation formalisms and automated reasoning methods. Semantic wikis add to conventional

J. van Leeuwen et al. (Eds.): SOFSEM 2010, LNCS 5901, pp. 247–258, 2010.

wikis informal tags and –more or less sophisticated– formal languages for expressing knowledge as annotations to (textual as well as multimedia) wiki pages that are machine processable. These annotations can range from informal, freely chosen tags to semi-formal tags selected from a pre-defined vocabulary to formal concepts and relationships from an ontology. Thus, semantic wikis are often referred to as "wikis enhanced with semantic technologies" or, after [19], "semantics for wikis". Semantic wikis have also been called "Semantic Web in the small" [7]. On the other hand, semantic wikis are also used as wikis for knowledge engineering, that is, ontology editors of some kind, or after [19], "wikis for semantics". This article uses the term "semantic wiki" in the first sense.

If the data include not only text but also informal and formal semantic annotations, then querying necessarily becomes a difficult task – so at least a conventional wisdom. Conventional web query languages [3] [13] are tools for precise data selection and processing by informed users. As such, they are no candidate query languages for a wiki which is a social application where users should be able to locate content without investing much time or effort.

In line with this reasoning, easier to use query language for semi-structured data aimed at casual users have been developed, often using keywords to express queries. Queries in these languages are usually very simple and imprecise, information retrieval techniques such as fuzzy matching and ranking are consequently used to find documents relevant to the query. While this practice is suitable and convenient for helping casual users retrieve content, the expressive power of such languages is limited. This means that the exact selection of data according to complex criteria is not possible.

KWQL aims to fill the gap between these two kinds of query languages that becomes evident in the social semantic web where selecting data (and being able to do so with precision) is an essential task but where not all users can be expected to be querying experts.

In this article, we introduce KWQL, a query language under development for the semantic wiki KiWi [1]. KWQL refutes the above-mentioned conventional wisdom by relying on the label-keyword query paradigm to allow for selections from full text, from semantic annotations and structure-based selection. Furthermore, following the concept of database views, KWQL offers means not only for selections, but also for "constructions", that is the re-shaping of the selected (meta-)data into new (meta-)data.

The contributions of this article are: (1) Requirements for a wiki query language (2) The syntax of a versatile rule-based label-keyword query language fulfilling these requirements.

The remainder of this article is organized as follows: Section 2 gives and overview over the conceptual model of the KiWi wiki. Section 3 outlines the requirements for a Semantic wiki query language. Section 4 uses example queries to introduce KWQL, Section 5 gives an outlook on query evaluation and functionality to be added in the future. Section 6 presents related work and gives a conclusion.

---

[1] http://kiwi-project.eu

2 Conceptual Model

In the KiWi wiki, information is represented in the form of content items, links between content items, annotations, meta-data and the structure of content items and fragments.

Content items. Content items, the primary unit of information in the KiWi wiki, are composable documents. A content item may consist of a sequence of (included) content items, for example a chapter may consist of a sequence of paragraphs. For reasons of simplicity, content item composition precludes any form of overlapping or of cycles. Thus, content item composition provides a conventional structuring of documents and a content item can be seen as a tree (of content items). Atomic content items may consist of either text or multimedia. A content item is directly addressable by a unique URI. There is no inherent distinction between wiki pages and content items, or rather, by default, all content items are wiki pages. Root nodes, that is, content items that are not embedded in another content items, then have a special status in that they encompass all content that forms a cohesive unit. In this, they can be seen as being alike to a wiki page in a regular wiki.

Fragments. Text Fragments are continuous portions of text that can be annotated. Text fragments are useful for –especially collaborative– document editing for adding annotations like "improve transition", "style to be polished" or "is this correct?". For the purpose of this article, it is assumed that fragments can be nested but do not overlap and do not span over content items. Fragments of this kind are generally desirable, but are problematic with respect to query evaluation.

Links. Links, that is simple hypertext links as in HTML, can be used for relating content items to each other. Links have a single origin, which is a content item, an anchor in this origin, and a single target, which is also a content item. Links can be annotated.

Annotations. Annotations are meta-data that can be attached to content items and links. Two kinds of annotations are available: tags and RDF triples. Tags allow to express knowledge informally, that is, without having to use a pre-defined vocabulary, while RDF triples are used for formal knowledge representation, possibly using an ontology or other application-dependent vocabulary.

Tag syntax and normalization are of significant practical concern but irrelevant to the present paper, thus not addressed in the following.

In the KiWi wiki, annotations can be in the form of –simple or complex– free tags or RDF, but regular users are generally not confronted with RDF, which is considered an enhancement for experienced users. However, querying RDF annotations will be supported in KWQL at a later point.

System meta-data. Finally, content items and tag assignments have system meta-data. These meta-data are automatically generated by the system and cannot be edited by the user. System meta-data represent for example the creation and last edit date and the author(s) of a content item or tagging.

In the following, *resources* refers to the basic concepts in the data model – content items, links, fragments and tag assignments (referred to as "tag")– and *qualifiers* refers to properties of resources like their meta-data and tags.

3 Requirements for a Wiki Query Language

Low Entry Barrier. A wiki query language should reflect the "wiki way" [21], that is, have a low entry barrier, enabling users to find the information they need without forcing them to undergo extensive training. Searching for wiki pages containing a string, say "query language", should be expressible as this very keyword query, "query language". A more complex syntax might become necessary as more complex selections are expressed – but only in such cases. The transition between simple and complex queries should be smooth and flexible. Conventional web query languages [3] [13] are no candidate query languages for a wiki: With such languages, for example XPath [9] and XQuery [8], even elementary keywords selections turn out to be complex and demanding.

Full Awareness of the Conceptual Model. The query language can help express more or less complex selections using any concept of the wiki or combinations thereof. Thus, a content item selection should be possible that refers not only to its textual content but also to the structuring of the content items it includes, to the links from or to the content item, and to its atomic or structured annotations. In short, the query language should be fully aware of the conceptual model.

Answer-closedness. The data queried and the query results should adhere to the same data model [26]. That means that query answers are amenable to further queries. This is desirable because no new concept needs to be introduced to represent query answers – the consistency and simplicity of the conceptual model are maintained – and because answer-closedness means that rule chaining can be realized naturally without transformations between different data formats.

Monotonicity. As a query gets more complex, it should become more selective. This property, which we call "monotonicity", ensures the intuitiveness of a query language. Monotonicity has limits, of course, primarily when negation is concerned: If "Q" is a query, then the answers to "NOT Q" cannot be expected to be a subset of the answers to "Q".

Construction. In a wiki, views are desirable. "View" is understood here in the database sense of pre-defined queries used for making implicit data explicit. If wiki pages contain management information on a project, it might be convenient to generate a wiki page listing the persons contributing to the project from mentions of personal wiki pages within the project pages. Views require more than selection. They require *construction*, that is, the capability to specify how the selected data are re-organized in a new wiki page, a "view".

Continuous Queries. As wikis are tools for work in progress, furthermore in a collaborative setting, tracking wiki data is an essential activity of a wiki user. KQWL's *continuous* queries are a means for the automation of this activity. We call queries continuous that are posed once, and, as the data evolve, are automatically evaluated again and again. For efficiency reasons, continuous queries call for incremental evaluation.

Ranking and Grouping. Ranking and grouping are convenient ways to deliver query answers. Inexperienced users tend to pose short, simple queries that may not be very precise and yield many results; grouping enables facetted browsing of query results which helps the user locate the information she is looking for, while the ranking mechanism makes sure that the most relevant results are at the top of the result list.

No Striving for Completeness. Completeness is often a desirable property of a query language. Relational completeness ensures that no data can remain unfound in a relational database. We suggest that completeness, however it might be defined, might not be an essential property of the query language of a wiki. Language simplicity is more important and browsing remains an option.

4 KWQL Query Examples

Keywords for full-text search. In KWQL, query terms consist of resources which are associated with lists of qualifiers –functioning as labels– and their values, that is, keywords.

```
ci(text:Java title:XML)
```

This query selects content items whose text contains "Java" and which have "XML" in their title. *ci* is the resource, a content item, and text and title are the qualifiers. KWQL has an implicit conjunctive semantics, i.e., if no operator is given, conjunction is assumed. The two qualifier-value pairs here need to separated only by whitespace to indicate that both conditions must be met.

The query `ci(fragment(text:Java))` selects fragments which contain "Java". Since links, fragments and tags are always anchored or contained in a content item, they are considered to be sub-resources of a content item. A query can refer to sub-resources by nesting one resource term inside another, as shown above. Not only content items, but also fragments and links have sub-resources, namely tags and, in the case of fragments, links. Table 1 lists the possible sub-resources for the different resource types.

Query answers in KWQL are always (sets of) content items, ensuring answer-closedness. When no construction is specified, matching content items or fragments are returned. Links and tags are never returned as query answers since they cannot be easily displayed or understood outside of the context of their associated content item or fragment and to maintain answer-closedness.

The list of matching content items is itself displayed as a content item. The content items returned as answers are either wiki pages or Lowest Common Ancestor (LCA) [15] content items. Wiki pages are defined as content items not embedded in any other content item. Wiki pages are the units of informations visible while browsing, which makes it natural to return them as query answers. On the other hand, the user might only be interested in the parts of a wiki page

Table 1. KWQL resources and qualifiers

Resource	content item	fragment	link	tag
Qualifiers	URI	URI	target	URI
	author	author	anchorText	author
	created	created		created
	lastEdited	descendant		name
	title	child		
	text			
	numberEdits			
	descendant			
	child			
Subresources	fragment			
	link	link		
	tag	tag	tag	

relevant to his query. In this case, he can select to return only the content item that is an ancestor to all content items in the wiki page that match the query.

Keywords for system meta-data and tags. Meta-data are qualifiers (see the list given in table 1). The following query selects content items authored by the user Mary: `ci(author:Mary)`

If both a resource and qualifier are given in the query, the description is assumed to be complete, i.e. sub-resources not stated in the query are not matched when they fulfill the criterion given in the qualifier-value pair.

This strictness of interpretation is required in order to be able to explicitly refer to e.g. a content item's author (`ci(author:Mary)`) but not the author of one of its tags (`ci(tag(author:Mary))`).

Both resources and qualifiers are optional and do not have to be specified in the query, extending the query to all resources or qualifiers respectively. If no qualifier is specified, the query is matched against all qualifier values of the given resource type. "Child", "descendant" and "target" are excluded from this to unintended avoid link traversals. On the other hand, if no resource is given but a qualifier is present, the query matches all resources with the given qualifier(s) and value(s), regardless of resource type.

If only a value but no qualifier or resource are stated, the query is matched on all qualifier values (except those of "child", "descendant" and "target") of all types of resources.

The fact that everything in a KWQL query apart from keywords, that is, qualifier values, is optional, enables more general queries that, at the same time, are easier to construct than fully specified queries.

```
author:Mary
```

This query, not stating a resource, returns content items of which Mary is the author or that contain tag assignments by Mary.

```
tag(Mary)
```

Here, no qualifier is given, but the matching is restricted to tag assignments where "Mary" occurs as a qualifier value.

Finally, the most simple KWQL query consists of only a single value, a keyword matched over all qualifiers of content items. It returns all content items where Mary occurs anywhere in the qualifier values of the content items or a contained sub-resource: `Mary`.

"tag" is used to query the tags of content items, links and fragments. The following query selects content items which have a tag containing "Java".

```
ci(tag(name:Java))
```

Values do not have to be singular but can also be sets as in this query which matches content items that have a tag in whose name both Java and XML occur:

```
ci(tag(name:(Java XML)))
```

The same type of resource can occur several times within another resource, e.g. a content items can contain several links or can be tagged with multiple tags. To specify criteria that two or more distinct instances of a resource should fulfill, the resource and its respective selection criteria have to be given the appropriate number of times. For example, to match a content item tagged with two distinct tags, "Java" and "XML", the query is `ci(tag(name:Java) tag(name:XML))`.

Keywords for Structure. KWQL allows for the selection of data based on the structure of documents, that is, content items and fragments using the "child" and "descendant" qualifiers. KWQL does not offer qualifiers for parent and ancestors so to avoid navigational queries, this keeping the language simple. [22] has shown that queries using qualifiers ancestor and/or parent can be expressed without the qualifiers.

KWQL structure qualifiers give rise to recursive data retrieval through a wiki page structure. For example, the following query selects content items which have a tag "Java" and a child content item which has a tag "XML".

```
ci(tag(name:Java) child:ci(tag:XML))
```

Structure qualifiers can thus be seen as links to other content items or fragments and recursive querying as a kind of graph traversal.

Link traversal can be expressed similarly:

```
ci(tag(name:Java) link(target:ci(title:XML)))
```

Here, content items which have a tag "Java" and include a link that points to a content item that has XML in its title are matched: Note that, although numerous structural queries or link traversals can be nested, no infinite loops can occur. This is because the query is always finite and KWQL does not support Kleene closure.

Connectives and Negation. To support more expressive queries, KWQL allows for the combination of several query terms through not only conjunction (which can be explicitly stated as "AND") but also disjunction, expressed as "OR". The following query matches resources authored by Mary or tagged with Java.

```
author:Mary OR tag(name:Java)
```

Query operators are evaluated in order, parentheses are used to specify precedence.

```
ci(text:Java) OR (ci(text:XML) AND ci(title:Java))
```

The unary operator "NOT" is used to express the negation of a query or query term. The following query selects content items which contain "Java" but not "XML" in their text.

```
ci(text:Java AND NOT XML)
```

Variables and Construction. Variables and a construction specification enable a fine-grained customization of query results.

```
ci(author:$A title:$T)
```

In this query, the variables $TandA$ are bound to the titles of content items and their authors respectively. Variable assignments are qualifier-value-like terms where the qualifier specifies the value that the variable name, given in place of a value, is bound to. qualifier-value pairs thus express selection constraints, while qualifier-variable pairs indicate variable assignments.

There are cases where the need to use a qualifier both with a selection constraint and a variable binding arises, for example in conjunction with partial matchings. When all content item tags labels that contain "Java" are to be retrieved and bound to a variable, there is a constraint on the tag labels, but at the same time, the tag labels are to be assigned to a variable.

```
ci(tag(name:(Java -> $X)))
```

"OPTIONAL" is a unary operator used in connection with variables. In the query below, the authors of content items that have "Java" in their text are bound to the variable X. Only if the content items has been assigned at least one tag, additionally the tag name(s) are bound to the variable Y. In the construction, Y can then be used where present, otherwise a value which must be specified by the user (e.g. "no tags assigned") is inserted. The functionality of OPTIONAL could be replicated using two queries, one with the selection of tags and one without, and fusing the results. However, this would be inconvenient for the user and more costly in terms of evaluation.

```
ci(text:Java author:$X OPTIONAL tag(name:$Y))
```

The construction part of a rule creates new data or meta-data from the variables bound in the query part of the rule. There is thus a clear separation between constraining results and selecting data and processing them for display - the construction part of a rule never selects data, while the query part is not concerned with the presentation of the results.

To maintain answer-closedness, constructions always specify at least one content item. Content items can be created explicitly in the construction, in resource(qualifier:value) syntax. If no content item is specified, the result of the construction is wrapped into a content item automatically.

Given a query that binds titles of content items to T and authors to A, the construct term below creates a list which for an author gives the content items he helped create, presented in a content item with the title "Contents".

```
ci(title:"Contents" text:$A "-" ALL($T,","))
```

The "ALL" construct serves to collect all possible bindings for the given variable returned by the query. It takes a variable or nesting of variables and construct terms as a parameter. A second, optional parameter indicates the string that is to be used as a separator between the individual variable bindings. The construction below thus yields a name of an author, followed by a dash and a comma separated list of content item titles. "SOME N" can be used in the similarly as "ALL", collecting at most N variable binding instances. N is given as a second parameter.

In addition to re-shaping data, new information can be computed in the construction through the aggregation of data, for example in the form of counting, or determining minima, maxima and averages.

```
ci(title:"Number of Content items" text:$A "-" COUNT($T))
```

Putting it all together: Rules The query part and the construction part are fused together to form a complete rule.

```
ci(title:"Content" text:$A"-"ALL($T,","))@ci(title:$T author:$A)
```

Rules in KWQL as presented here are limited to selecting, reshaping and aggregating data into views. By allowing for a broader functionality in the construction part, for example by allowing for the assignment of new tags to existing content items, a simple but powerful language for reasoning could easily be derived.

5 Outlook

Ranking and grouping. Ranking should leverage properties specific to semantic wikis to determine a document's relevance such as the number and extent of edits, the approval rating and the author's equity value or relation to the user posing the query. Since a semantic wiki may contain big amounts of data, it is desirable to be able to generate the top-k answers without having to compute query results exhaustively.

The grouping, or clustering, and ranking of results complement each other in helping the user navigate the query results. Facetted browsing of query results, enabled by result clusters, helps the user find the query results most relevant to him by grouping results under several aspects. In the semantic wiki context, these could be for example tags assigned, but also explicit or implicit social relations between users.

Evaluation of Selections. The restrictions imposed on content item and tag composition –cycles in content item structure and in tag orderings are precluded– make an evaluation without memoing possible; however, memoing is necessary in evaluating some RDF/S selections which may be supported in the future. The extent of the RDF query facilities KWQL should offer is still is an open issue.

Evaluation of Rules. Both forward and backward rule processing might make sense in a wiki context. Forward rule processing amounts to materializing all views so far specified, thus improving the efficiency of querying and browsing. Functionalities of a wiki such as personalization services might however rely on too large a number of views for full materialization. In such a case, backward rule processing would be necessary.

We currently investigate how rules are used for wiki functionalities, e.g. personalization, aiming at finding a clear-cut separation between rule sets to be evaluated by forward and by backward processing. An evaluation relying on forward processed "system" or "meta rules" implementing a backward processing of application, or "object rules" a la "backward fix-point procedure" [6] or relying on the "magic set rewriting" [4] seems promising.

Evaluation of Continuous Queries. Continuous queries are rules that are re-evaluated after each update of the wiki so as to deliver to the user – or service – subscribing to the query an "incremental answer", that is a difference to the previously returned answer(s). The key to computing incremental answers is finite differencing [24]. Finite differencing of a KWQL rule can be pre-computed, resulting in an "incremental" version of the original rule.

The presentation of incremental answers to the user is an issue requiring more research. Both novel answers caused by the last update and invalidated answers "destroyed" by the last update have to be presented to the user. It is an open issue whether simple listings, or more sophisticated presentations are desirable in a wiki context.

6 Related Work and Conclusion

6.1 Related Work

In recent years, research has been undertaken towards keyword querying of structured data, both in databases [17,16] and for XML and RDF data [31]. Unlike KWQL, the keyword query languages suggested usually do not allow for the creation of views and combined queries over heterogeneous data, although efforts have been made towards combining RDF and XML querying [5,12]. Further, many of the keyword query languages do not offer a rich syntax, being limited to simple keywords or label-keyword pairs and an implicit conjunctive semantics.

While the need for simple but powerful retrieval of semantic information in semantic wikis has been pointed out [25], current semantic wikis use either simple full-text search [18,10,1,20], allow querying of annotations using a traditional query language like SPARQL, or both [11,29,28,23,2,27]; however in the latter case, the two are not integrated but used separately. Embedded queries, a form of views, are possible in several semantic wikis [25].

Semantic Media Wiki [30] uses a query language using a syntax based on a property:value pairs which offers limited capabilities for construction, querying over non-annotation elements of the wiki.

[14] use queries consisting of multiple simple keywords that are translated into conjunctive SPARQL queries to query SMW. Their query language has no connectives, variables or possibilities for customizing views and is limited to querying annotations.

6.2 Conclusion

In this article, we outlined the requirements for querying in a semantic wiki. We presented KWQL, a rule-based query language that is versatile with respect to the expressiveness and, at the same time, simplicity, of queries, and versatile in the respect that it can be used to combine queries over textual data, annotations and structure.

Building on these principles, KWQL enables querying, re-shaping and aggregation of semantic wiki content. An implementation of the core of KWQL as described here is currently underway, while further research is being undertaken to enable the querying of versions and RDF triples and ranking and grouping mechanisms.

Acknowledgements. The research leading to these results is part of the project "KiWi - Knowledge in a Wiki" and has received funding from the European Community's Seventh Framework Programme (FP7/2007-2013) under grant agreement No. 211932.

References

1. Auer, S., Dietzold, S., Riechert, T.: OntoWiki – a Tool for Social, Semantic Collaboration. In: Cruz, I., Decker, S., Allemang, D., Preist, C., Schwabe, D., Mika, P., Uschold, M., Aroyo, L.M. (eds.) ISWC 2006. LNCS, vol. 4273, pp. 736–749. Springer, Heidelberg (2006)
2. Aumueller, D., Auer, S.: Towards a Semantic Wiki Experience – Desktop Integration and Interactivity in WikSAR. In: 1st Workshop on the Semantic Desktop (2005)
3. Bailey, J., Bry, F., Furche, T., Schaffert, S.: Web and Semantic Web Query Languages: A Survey. In: Eisinger, N., Małuszyński, J. (eds.) Reasoning Web 2005. LNCS, vol. 3564, pp. 35–133. Springer, Heidelberg (2005)
4. Bancilhon, F., Ramakrishnan, R.: An Amateur's Introduction to Recursive Query Processing Strategies. SIGMOD Record 15(2) (1986)
5. Battle, S.: Round-Tripping between XML and RDF. In: Intern. Semantic Web Conf. (2004)
6. Bry, F.: Query Evaluation in Deductive Databases: Bottom-up and Top-down Reconciled. Data & Knowledge Engineering 5(4) (1990)
7. Bry, F., Baumeister, J., Kiesel, M.: Semantic Wikis. IEEE Software 25(4) (2008)
8. Chamberlin, D.: XQuery: A Query Language for XML. In: ACM SIGMOD Int. Conf. on Management of Data (2003)
9. Clark, J., DeRose, S.: XML Path Language (XPath) Version 1.0. W3C (1999)
10. El Ghali, A., Tifous, A., Buffa, M., Giboin, A., Dieng-Kuntz, R.: Using a Semantic Wiki in Communities of Practice. In: 2nd Intern. Workshop on Building Technology Enhanced Learning Solutions for Communities of Practice (2007)

11. Fischer, J., Gantner, Z., Rendle, S., Stritt, M., Schmidt-Thieme, L.: Ideas and Improvements for Semantic Wikis. In: Sure, Y., Domingue, J. (eds.) ESWC 2006. LNCS, vol. 4011, pp. 650–663. Springer, Heidelberg (2006)
12. Furche, T., Bry, F., Bolzer, O.: XML Perspectives on RDF Querying: Towards Integrated Access to Data and Metadata on the Web. In: Grundlagen von Datenbanken (2005)
13. Furche, T., Linse, B., Bry, F., Plexousakis, D., Gottlob, G.: RDF Querying: Language Constructs and Evaluation Methods Compared. In: Barahona, P., Bry, F., Franconi, E., Henze, N., Sattler, U. (eds.) Reasoning Web 2006. LNCS, vol. 4126, pp. 1–52. Springer, Heidelberg (2006)
14. Haase, P., Herzig, D., Musen, M., Tran, T.: Semantic Wiki Search. In: European Semantic Web Conf. (2009)
15. Harel, D., Tarjan, R.: Fast Algorithms for Finding Nearest Common Ancestors. SIAM Journal on Computing 13(2) (1984)
16. Hristidis, V., Papakonstantinou, Y.: DISCOVER: Keyword Search in Relational Databases. In: 28th Intern. Conf. on Very Large Data Bases (2002)
17. Hulgeri, A., Nakhe, C.: Keyword Searching and Browsing in Databases Using BANKS. In: 18th Intern. Conf. on Data Engineering (2002)
18. Kiesel, M.: Kaukolu: Hub of the Semantic Corporate Intranet. In: First Workshop on Semantic Wikis: From Wiki to Semantics (2006)
19. Krötzsch, M., Schaffert, S., Vrandecic, D.: Reasoning in Semantic Wikis. In: Antoniou, G., Aßmann, U., Baroglio, C., Decker, S., Henze, N., Patranjan, P.-L., Tolksdorf, R. (eds.) Reasoning Web 2007. LNCS, vol. 4636, pp. 310–329. Springer, Heidelberg (2007)
20. Kuhn, T.: Acewiki: A Natural and Expressive Semantic Wiki. In: Semantic Web User Interaction (2008)
21. Leuf, B., Cunningham, W.: The Wiki Way: Quick Collaboration on the Web. Addison-Wesley, Reading (2001)
22. Olteanu, D., Meuss, H., Furche, T., Bry, F.: XPath: Looking forward. In: Chaudhri, A.B., Unland, R., Djeraba, C., Lindner, W. (eds.) EDBT 2002. LNCS, vol. 2490, pp. 109–127. Springer, Heidelberg (2002)
23. Oren, E.: SemperWiki: a Semantic Personal Wiki. In: 1st Workshop on the Semantic Desktop (2005)
24. Paige, R.: Symbolic Finite Differencing - Part I. In: Jones, N.D. (ed.) ESOP 1990. LNCS, vol. 432, pp. 36–56. Springer, Heidelberg (1990)
25. Panagiotou, D., Mentzas, G.: A Comparison of Semantic Wiki Engines. In: 22nd European Conf. on Operational Research (2007)
26. Schaffert, S., Bry, F.: Querying the Web Reconsidered: A Practical Introduction to Xcerpt. In: Extreme Markup Languages (2004)
27. Schaffert, S., Westenthaler, R., Gruber, A.: Ikewiki: A User-Friendly Semantic Wiki. In: 3rd European Semantic Web Conf. (2006)
28. Souzis, A.: Building a Semantic Wiki. IEEE Intelligent Systems 20(5) (2005)
29. Tazzoli, R., Castagna, P., Campanini, S.: Towards a Semantic Wiki Wiki Web. In: 3rd Intern. Semantic Web Conf. (2004)
30. Völkel, M., Krötzsch, M., Vrandecic, D., Haller, H., Studer, R.: Semantic Wikipedia. In: 15th Intern. Conf. on World Wide Web (2006)
31. Weiand, K., Furche, T., Bry, F.: Quo Vadis, Web Queries. In: Intern. Workshop on Semantic Web Technologies (2008)

On Pattern Density and Sliding Block Code Behavior for the Besicovitch and Weyl Pseudo-distances

Silvio Capobianco

Institute of Cybernetics at Tallinn University of Technology
Akadeemia tee 21, 12618 Tallinn, Estonia
silvio@cs.ioc.ee

Abstract. Initially proposed by Formenti et al. for bi-infinite sequences, the Besicovitch and Weyl pseudo-distances express the viewpoint of an observer moving infinitely far from the grid, rather than staying close as in the product topology. We extend their definition to a more general setting, which includes the usual infinite hypercubic grids, and highlight some noteworthy properties. We use them to measure the "frequency" of occurrences of patterns in configurations, and consider the behavior of sliding block codes when configurations at pseudo-distance zero are identified. One of our aims is to get an alternative characterization of surjectivity for sliding block codes.

Keywords: Pattern, pseudo-distance, sliding block code.

Mathematics Subject Classification 2000: 37B15, 68Q80.

1 Introduction

The Besicovitch and Weyl pseudo-distances [1] were defined in the context of one-dimensional cellular automata (CA) as a way to overcome several unwanted properties of the ordinary product topology. One of the requirements for such distances was to be invariant by translations; which is impossible for any distance that induces the product topology. The basic idea is to take a "window" of the form $X_n = [-n, \dots, n]$, and evaluate the *density* of the set of points under the window where two configurations take different values.

- For the Besicovitch pseudo-distance, the window is *kept in place*, progressively enlarged, and the upper limit d_B of the density computed.
- For the Weyl pseudo-distance, the window is *moved all around* between enlargements, and the upper limit d_W of the *maximum density* computed.

In the case of bi-infinite words, these pseudo-distances show remarkable properties, such as the requested invariance by translations. When two configurations

J. van Leeuwen et al. (Eds.): SOFSEM 2010, LNCS 5901, pp. 259–270, 2010.

are identified if and only if their pseudo-distance is zero, a quotient space is obtained whose topology is very different from the product one. Interestingly, CA are well-defined *on equivalence classes*, and the properties of the transformations induced by CA can provide information on those of the original CA.

In this respect, one of the most renowned properties possessed by CA regards the characterization of surjectivity. Namely, there is a *configuration* which is not reachable via the *global law* of a CA, if and only if there is a *pattern* which has no predecessor according to the *local law* of the CA.

In this paper, which is ideally a continuation of both [1] and our previous work [5], we look for a similar characterization of global behavior in local terms which may hold for the Besicovitch and Weyl spaces. By doing so, the first difficulty is encountered: in fact, it follows from the definitions that both pseudo-distances *make finite differences vanish*, *i.e.*, identify configurations that only differ on finitely many points. However, while single occurrences cannot make any difference, *the set of all occurrences* might. This leads to the problem of having a *measure* of sets which is compatible with the given pseudo-distance. To this aim, we re-use the idea of enlarging windows.

To make our results more general, we consider a definition of d_B and d_W that holds for arbitrary *finitely generated groups* [7], which includes all of the usual d-dimensional grids. The role of expanding windows is taken by *exhaustive sequences* of finite sets growing up to cover the whole group. Moreover, we consider *sliding block codes* (briefly, SBC) which respect local constraints such as CA do, but operate between space of configurations with possibly different alphabets. Under suitable conditions, which hold in the 1D case considered in [1] as well as its straightforward generalization to arbitrary dimension d, SBC induce transformations of the Besicovitch (resp., Weyl) quotient spaces.

In parallel with these pseudo-distances, we consider two *densities* on subsets of the groups, which in a certain sense provide *similar information in different context.* In particular, we consider the Besicovitch (resp., Weyl) density of (the set of occurrences of) a given pattern in a given configuration. These quantities are shown to be *equivalence class invariants*, *i.e.*, the Besicovitch (resp., Weyl) density of a given pattern is the same for any two configurations having Besicovitch (resp., Weyl) distance zero. It is then meaningful to define the density of a pattern in a point of the Besicovitch or Weyl space.

One could now ask whether such density can give any information about the behavior of the induced map. Our main result is that—provided that certain conditions on the group and the windows are satisfied—a transformation between Besicovitch (resp., Weyl) spaces induced by a SBC is surjective if and only if, given any pattern p, there is a configuration c such that p occurs in $F(c)$ with positive Besicovitch (resp., Weyl) density. This is parallel to the previously stated characterization of surjective SBC in the product topology. Most important, said conditions are also verified in the rather common case when the group is $\mathbb{Z}^d$ and the windows are d-dimensional hypercubes. As a concluding remark, we show that—again, under suitable conditions—injective CA induce injective transformations of these quotient spaces.

2 Background

Let $f, g : \mathbb{N} \to [0, +\infty)$. We write $f(n) \preccurlyeq g(n)$ if there exist $n_0 \in \mathbb{N}$ and $C, \beta > 0$ such that $f(n) \leq C \cdot g(\beta n)$ for all $n \geq n_0$; we write $f(n) \approx g(n)$ if $f(n) \preccurlyeq g(n)$ and $g(n) \preccurlyeq f(n)$. Observe that, if either f or g is a polynomial, the choice $\beta = 1$ is always allowed.

Let G be a group. Call 1_G the identity of the group G. Product and inverse are extended to subsets of G element-wise. If $E \subseteq G$ is finite and nonempty, the **closure** and **boundary** of $X \subseteq G$ w.r.t. E are the sets $X^{+E} = \{g \in G \mid gE \cap X \neq \emptyset\} = XE^{-1}$ and $\partial_E X = X^{+E} \setminus X$, respectively. In general, $X \not\subseteq X^{+E}$ unless $1_G \in E$. $V \subseteq G$ is a **set of generators** if every $g \in G$ can be obtained as a word on $V \cup V^{-1}$. A group is **finitely generated** (briefly, f.g.) if it has a finite set of generators (briefly, FSOG). The **length** of $g \in G$ w.r.t. V is the minimal length of a word on $V \cup V^{-1}$ that equals g; the **distance** between g and h w.r.t. V is the length of $g^{-1}h$. The **disk** of center g and radius r w.r.t. the FSOG V will be indicated by $D_{r,V}(g)$; we will omit g if equal to 1_G, and V if irrelevant or clear from the context. Observe that $D_r(g) = gD_r$ and $(D_{n,V})^{+D_{r,V}} = D_{n+r,V}$. For the rest of the paper, we will only consider f.g. infinite groups.

The **growth function** of G w.r.t. V is $\gamma_V(n) = |D_{n,V}|$. It is well-known [6] that $\gamma_V(n) \approx \gamma_{V'}(n)$ for any two FSOG V, V'. G is of **sub-exponential growth** if $\gamma_V(n) \preccurlyeq \lambda^n$ for all $\lambda > 1$; G is of **polynomial growth** if $\gamma_V(n) \approx n^k$ for some $k \in \mathbb{N}$. Observe that, if $G = \mathbb{Z}^d$, then $\gamma_V(n) \approx n^d$.

A sequence $\{X_n\}$ of *finite* subsets of G is **exhaustive** if $X_n \subseteq X_{n+1}$ for every $n \in \mathbb{N}$ and $\bigcup_{n\in\mathbb{N}} X_n = G$. $\{D_n\}$ is an exhaustive sequence. An exhaustive sequence is **amenable** [6,7,9] if $\lim_{n\to\infty} |\partial_E X_n|/|X_n| = 0$ for every finite $E \subseteq G$; a finitely generated group is amenable if it has an amenable sequence. If G is of sub-exponential growth, then $\{D_n\}$ contains an amenable subsequence, and is itself an amenable sequence if G is of polynomial growth (cf. [6]).

An **alphabet** is a set S s.t. $2 \leq |S| < \infty$. If S is an alphabet and G is a f.g. group, the space S^G of **configurations** on G over S, endowed with the product topology, is homeomorphic to the *Cantor set*. In this topology, $\lim_{k\to\infty} c_k = c$ if and only if, for all $g \in G$, $|\{k \in \mathbb{N} \mid c_k(g) \neq c(g)\}| < \infty$.

If S is a set and G is a group, the transformation $c \mapsto c^g$ of S^G defined by $c^g(h) = c(gh)$ for all $h \in G$, is called a **translation**. For $S = \{0, 1\}$, $G = \mathbb{Z}$ and $g = +1$, the translation $c \mapsto c^{+1}$ is the shift map.

If $E \subseteq G$ is finite, a **pattern** over S with **support** E is a map $p : E \to S$. An **occurrence** of a pattern p with support E in a configuration $c \in S^G$ is a point $g \in G$ such that $c^g|_E = p$; we indicate by $\mathrm{occ}(p, c)$ the set of occurrences of p in c.

A **sliding block code** (briefly, SBC) over G is a quadruple $\mathcal{K} = \langle S, T, \mathcal{N}, f \rangle$, where S and T are the **source** and **target** alphabets, the **neighborhood index** $\mathcal{N} \subseteq G$ is finite and nonempty, and the **local function** f maps $S^{\mathcal{N}}$ into T. The map $F_{\mathcal{K}} : S^G \to T^G$ defined by

$$(F_{\mathcal{K}}(c))(g) = f\left(c^g|_{\mathcal{N}}\right) \tag{1}$$

is the **global function** of $\mathcal{K}$. Observe that $F_{\mathcal{K}}$ is continuous in the product topology and commutes with translations; **Hedlund's theorem** (cf. [8, Proposition 1.5.8]) states that any $F : S^G \to T^G$ with these two properties is the global function of some SBC. A SBC where $S = T$ is usually called a **cellular automaton** (briefly, CA). $\mathcal{K}$ is injective, surjective, and so on, if $F_{\mathcal{K}}$ is.

Let $\mathcal{K} = \langle S, T, \mathcal{N}, f \rangle$ be a SBC on G. A configuration $c \in T^G \setminus F_{\mathcal{K}}(S^G)$ is a **Garden of Eden** (briefly, GoE) for $\mathcal{K}$. A pattern p on T with support E is an **orphan** for $\mathcal{K}$ if it has no occurrence in $F_{\mathcal{K}}(c)$ for every $c \in S^G$. It is well-known (cf. [10, Lemma 2]) that a SBC has a GoE configuration (*i.e.*, it is non-surjective) iff it has an orphan pattern.

A **pseudo-distance** on a set X is a symmetric map $d : X \times X \to [0, +\infty)$ that satisfies the triangle inequality and such that $d(x, x) = 0$ for all $x \in X$. If d is a pseudo-distance on X, then $x_1 \sim x_2$ iff $d(x_1, x_2) = 0$ is an equivalence relation, and $d(\kappa_1, \kappa_2) = d(x_1, x_2)$ with $x_i \in \kappa_i$ is a distance on $X/\sim$.

Let $U, W \subseteq G$ be nonempty. A **(U, W)-net** is a set $N \subseteq G$ such that the sets xU, $x \in N$, are pairwise disjoint, and $NW = G$. Any subgroup is a (U, U)-net for any set U of representatives of its right cosets. By Zorn's lemma, for every nonempty $U \subseteq G$ there exists a (U, UU^{-1})-net.

3 The Besicovitch and Weyl Distances

If $X \subseteq G$ is finite, call $H_X(c_1, c_2) = |\{g \in X \mid c_1(g) \neq c_2(g)\}|$ the *Hamming distance* of $c_1, c_2 \in S^G$ relative to X. If $X = D_{n,V}$ for some FSOG V and $n \in \mathbb{N}$, we may write $H_{n,V}$ instead of $H_{D_{n,V}}$.

If $\mathcal{X} = \{X_n\}$ is an exhaustive sequence for G, then

$$d_{B,\mathcal{X}}(c_1, c_2) = \limsup_{n \in \mathbb{N}} \frac{H_{X_n}(c_1, c_2)}{|X_n|} \tag{2}$$

and

$$d_{W,\mathcal{X}}(c_1, c_2) = \limsup_{n \in \mathbb{N}} \sup_{g \in G} \frac{H_{gX_n}(c_1, c_2)}{|X_n|} \tag{3}$$

are pseudo-distances on S^G, and are distances if and only if G is finite. In the latter case, they coincide with the discrete distance; otherwise, they are not continuous in the product topology.

Example 1. Suppose $c_k(g) = c(g)$ if and only if $g \in X_k$. Then $c_k \to c$ in the product topology, but $d_B(c_k, c) = d_W(c_k, c) = 1$ for all k.

Definition 1. *The quantity (2) is the* Besicovitch distance *of c_1 and c_2 w.r.t. $\mathcal{X}$. The quotient space $\mathrm{Bes}_{\mathcal{X}}^{S,G} = S^G/\sim$ where $c_1 \sim c_2$ iff $d_{B,\mathcal{X}}(c_1, c_2) = 0$, is the* Besicovitch space *on S^G induced by $\mathcal{X}$. The* Weyl distance *and the* Weyl space *$\mathrm{Wey}_{\mathcal{X}}^{S,G}$ are similarly defined according to (3).*

Since c_1 and c_2 differ on $y = gx \in gX$ if and only if c_1^g and c_2^g differ on $x \in X$, we get for free

$$d_{W,\mathcal{X}}(c_1, c_2) = \limsup_{n \in \mathbb{N}} \sup_{g \in G} \frac{H_{X_n}(c_1^g, c_2^g)}{|X_n|} . \tag{4}$$

Observe that $d_{W,\mathcal{X}}(c_1, c_2) \geq d_{B,\mathcal{X}}(c_1, c_2)$. $\mathrm{Wey}_{\mathcal{X}}^{S,G}$ is thus *finer-grained* than $\mathrm{Bes}_{\mathcal{X}}^{S,G}$, *i.e.*, every class of Besicovitch equivalence is union of classes of Weyl equivalence.

Example 2. Let $S = \{0, 1\}$, $G = \mathbb{Z}$, $V = \{+1\}$, $X_n = D_{n,V} = \{-n, \ldots, n\}$. (We shall call this the *standard case* in the rest of the paper.) Let $c_1(x) = 0$ for all x, and let $c_2(x) = 1$ if and only if $|x| \in \{2^k, \ldots, 2^k + k\}$ for some k. Then $d_{B,\mathcal{X}}(c_1, c_2) = 0$ but $d_{W,\mathcal{X}}(c_1, c_2) = 1$.

Similarly to d_B and d_W, one can define for a set U the *Besicovitch upper density*

$$\mathrm{dens\,sup}_{B,\mathcal{X}} U = \limsup_{n \in \mathbb{N}} \frac{|U \cap X_n|}{|X_n|} \tag{5}$$

and the *Weyl upper density*

$$\mathrm{dens\,sup}_{W,\mathcal{X}} U = \limsup_{n \in \mathbb{N}} \sup_{g \in G} \frac{|U \cap gX_n|}{|X_n|} = \limsup_{n \in \mathbb{N}} \sup_{g \in G} \frac{|gU \cap X_n|}{|X_n|} . \tag{6}$$

Symmetrically, we can consider the corresponding *lower densities* $\mathrm{dens\,inf}_{B,\mathcal{X}} U$ and $\mathrm{dens\,inf}_{W,\mathcal{X}} U$, defined as the lower limits of the corresponding quantities.

Observe that $d_{B,\mathcal{X}}(c_1, c_2) = \mathrm{dens\,sup}_{B,\mathcal{X}}(\{g \in G \mid c_1(g) \neq c_2(g)\})$. Also observe that $\mathrm{dens\,sup}_{B,\mathcal{X}}(U) = d_{B,\mathcal{X}}(\chi_U, \chi_\emptyset)$, where $\chi_U(x)$ is s_1 if $x \in U$ and $s_0 \neq s_1$ if $x \notin U$. A similar "dualism" occurs between $d_{W,\mathcal{X}}$ and $\mathrm{dens\,sup}_{W,\mathcal{X}}$.

The properties of the Besicovitch and Weyl distances usually depend on the choice of the exhaustive sequence $\mathcal{X}$. In [1] it is shown that $d_{B,\mathcal{X}}$ is invariant by translations—*i.e.*, $d_{B,\mathcal{X}}(c_1^g, c_2^g) = d_{B,\mathcal{X}}(c_1, c_2)$ for any c_1, c_2 and g—in the standard case. On the other hand, in [5] an example is given where the Besicovitch distance is not invariant by translations (the other one is immune to this flaw) and a sufficient condition is provided for translational invariance. The latter holds in particular for $G = \mathbb{Z}^d$ and $X_n = \{-n, \ldots, n\}^d$. Observe that such X_n is the disk of radius n with respect to the *d-dimensional Moore neighborhood*

$$\mathcal{M}_d = \{x \in \mathbb{Z}^d \mid |x_i| \leq 1 \, \forall i \leq d\} ; \tag{7}$$

in this case, $d_{W,\mathcal{X}}$ is actually a limit because of Fekete's lemma (cf. [2]).

Since there are several neighborhoods of choice, each being a FSOG for $\mathbb{Z}^d$, one could ask what happens to the quotient space when one or another of those is chosen. In the case of $\mathbb{Z}^d$, things are remarkably tame, making the choice as free as possible.

Lemma 1. *Let S be an alphabet. Let G be a group of polynomial growth of order d. Let V, V' be* FSOG *for G. There exist $C, \beta, n_0 > 0$ such that for any $n > n_0$, $c_1, c_2 \in S^G$*

$$\frac{H_{n,V'}(c_1, c_2)}{\gamma_{V'}(n)} \leq C \cdot \frac{H_{\beta n,V}(c_1, c_2)}{\gamma_V(\beta n)} . \tag{8}$$

One can, for instance, choose $C = \alpha_1 \beta^d / \alpha_2$, where $D_{1,V'} \subseteq D_{\beta,V}$ and $\gamma_V(n) \leq \alpha_1 n^d$, $\gamma_{V'}(n) \geq \alpha_2 n^d$ are satisfied for all $n > n_0$.

From Lemma 1 and the arbitrariness of c_1, c_2, V and V' follows

Theorem 1. *Let G be a group of polynomial growth. Let $\mathcal{I}$ be the family of exhaustive sequences $\mathcal{X}$ of the form $X_n = D_{n,V}$ for some* FSOG *V. The Besicovitch distances $d_{B,\mathcal{X}}$ for $\mathcal{X} \in \mathcal{I}$ are pairwise metrically equivalent; in particular, they all induce the same notion of convergence, and the same equivalence classes.*

The above remain true if $d_{B,V}$ is replaced with $d_{W,V}$.

Topologically, $\text{Bes}_{\mathcal{X}}^{S,G}$ and $\text{Wey}_{\mathcal{X}}^{S,G}$ are rather different from S^G. For instance, in the standard case, $\text{Bes}_{\mathcal{X}}^{S,G}$ is not compact and $(\text{Wey}_{\mathcal{X}}^{S,G}, d_{W,\mathcal{X}})$ is not complete [1]. Moreover, as we have seen before and will see later on, some of their properties depend on those of $\mathcal{X}$. It is thus remarkable that the following result extends immediately from the standard to the general case.

Theorem 2. $(\text{Bes}_{\mathcal{X}}^{S,G}, d_{B,\mathcal{X}})$ *is a complete metric space.*

Theorem 2 generalizes [1, Proposition 2] from $G = \mathbb{Z}$ and $\mathcal{X} = \{[-n, \ldots, n]\}_{n \in \mathbb{N}}$ to arbitrary G and $\mathcal{X}$: indeed, the key ideas are the same both in the standard [1] and general case. First, being "near" in the Besicovitch pseudo-distance means being equal outside a "sparse" set. Next, a Cauchy sequence has at most one limit point, so that it is convergent if it has a convergent subsequence. Finally, G is infinite and $\mathcal{X}$ is exhaustive, so that $|X_n|$ is unbounded: which allows, given an arbitrary Cauchy sequence, to construct a convergent sub-sequence.

A detailed proof of Theorem 2 is given in [4].

4 Patterns in Besicovitch and Weyl Spaces

Consider a pattern p and a configuration c. The set $\text{occ}(p, c)$ of the occurrences of p in c has Besicovitch and Weyl upper and lower densities. What kind of information do these quantities provide?

Suppose $\text{dens sup}_{B,\mathcal{X}} \text{occ}(p, c) = 0$. Can we infer that there exists c' such that $d_{B,\mathcal{X}}(c, c') = 0$ and p does not occur in c'? The answer is negative.

Example 3. In the standard case, let $c \in S^{\mathbb{Z}}$ such that $c(i) = 1$ iff $i \geq 0$. Choose $E = \{0, 1\}$ and define $p : E \to S$ as $p(i) = i$: then $\text{dens sup}_{B,\mathcal{X}}(p, c) = 0$. However, any c' s.t. $d_{B,\mathcal{X}}(c, c') = 0$ must have at least one occurrence of p. Indeed, if $\text{occ}(p, c') = \emptyset$, then either $c'(x) = 0$ for all $x \in \mathbb{Z}$, or $c'(x) = 1$ for all $x \in \mathbb{Z}$, or there exists $y \in \mathbb{Z}$ such that $c'(x) = 0$ iff $x \geq y$. In the first two cases, $d_{B,\mathcal{X}}(c, c') = \frac{1}{2}$; in the third one, $c'(x) \neq c(x)$ for all x such that $|x| > |y|$, so that $d_{B,\mathcal{X}}(c, c') = 1$.

Suppose now $d_{B,\mathcal{X}}(c_1, c_2) = 0$. Suppose that $\text{dens sup}_{B,\mathcal{X}} \text{occ}(p, c_1) = D$. What can we infer from this about $\text{dens sup}_{B,\mathcal{X}} \text{occ}(p, c_2)$? The answer is welcome.

Theorem 3. *Let $d_{B,\mathcal{X}}(c_1, c_2) = 0$. For every pattern p, $\text{dens sup}_{B,\mathcal{X}} \text{occ}(p, c_1) = \text{dens sup}_{B,\mathcal{X}} \text{occ}(p, c_2)$ and $\text{dens inf}_{B,\mathcal{X}} \text{occ}(p, c_1) = \text{dens inf}_{B,\mathcal{X}} \text{occ}(p, c_2)$. These hold for Weyl pseudo-distance and densities as well.*

Proof. Let $D_i = \operatorname{dens\,sup}_{B,\mathcal{X}} \operatorname{occ}(p, c_i)$. Suppose, for the sake of contradiction, $D_1 > D_2$. Let $\delta > 0$ and let $\{n_k\} \subseteq \mathbb{N}$ be a strictly increasing sequence such that $|\operatorname{occ}(p, c_1) \cap X_{n_k}| \geq (D_2 + \delta)\,|X_{n_k}|$ for all $k \in \mathbb{N}$. On the other hand, for all k large enough,

$$|\operatorname{occ}(p, c_2) \cap X_{n_k}| < \left(D_2 + \frac{\delta}{2}\right) |X_{n_k}| \,. \tag{9}$$

Let E be the support of p. There are at least $\left\lfloor \frac{1}{2}\delta |X_{n_k}| \right\rfloor$ points $g \in G$ such that $gE \subseteq X_{n_k}$, $c_1^g|_E = p$, and $c_2^g|_E \neq p$: hence, $H_{X_{n_k}}(c_1, c_2) \geq \left\lfloor \frac{1}{2|E|}\delta |X_{n_k}| \right\rfloor$ for every $k \in \mathbb{N}$. This implies $d_{B,\mathcal{X}}(c_1, c_2) \geq \frac{\delta}{2|E|}$, against the hypothesis that $d_{B,\mathcal{X}}(c_1, c_2) = 0$. The case $D_1 < D_2$ is analogous, as is the proof for lower densities.

The proof in the Weyl case is similar, replacing (9) with

$$|\operatorname{occ}(p, c_2) \cap g_k X_{n_k}| < \left(D_2 + \frac{\delta}{2}\right) |X_{n_k}| \tag{10}$$

for suitable $g_k \in G$ s.t. $|\operatorname{occ}(p, c_1) \cap g_k X_{n_k}| \geq (D_2 + \delta)\,|X_{n_k}|$ for every $k \in \mathbb{N}$.

Theorem 3 states that the Besicovitch upper and lower densities of the occurrences of a pattern in a configuration are preserved by the Besicovitch equivalence, and similarly for the Weyl case. We can then speak, for example, of the Besicovitch upper density of a pattern p in a point $x \in \mathrm{Bes}_{\mathcal{X}}^{S,G}$.

The condition of Theorem 3 is sufficient, but not necessary.

Example 4. In the standard case, let $c_1(x) = 1$ iff $x \geq 0$, $c_2(x) = 1$ iff $x < 0$. It is straightforward to check that any density of any pattern is the same for c_1 and c_2. However, $d_{B,V}(c_1, c_2) = 1$.

As another application of our tools, we consider a generalization of *higher block codes*, a common construct of one-dimensional symbolic dynamics.

Definition 2. *Let $E \subseteq G$ s.t. $|E| < \infty$ and $1_G \in E$. The E-*shaped block transform *(briefly, E-SBT) of $c : G \to S$ is the configuration $c^{[E]} : G \to S^E$ defined as $c^{[E]}(g) = c^g|_E$, that is,*

$$(c^{[E]}(g))(e) = c(ge)\ \forall g \in G, e \in E \,. \tag{11}$$

The value of $c^{[E]}$ at g is the set of values of c on a set shaped as E and based on g. This is what is done in the 1D case, where the N-th higher block code is obtained by taking $E = \{0, \ldots, N-1\}$ (cf. [8, Section 1.4]).

The construction of higher block transforms commutes with translations. In fact, let $g \in G$: then for every $h \in G$, $e \in E$

$$\left((c^{[E]})^g(h)\right)(e) = (c^{[E]}(gh))(e) = c(ghe) = c^g(he) = ((c^g)^{[E]}(h))(e) \,,$$

so that $\left(c^{[E]}\right)^g = (c^g)^{[E]}$. This commutation property is satisfied even on non-commutative groups, because translations operate via *left* multiplication, while E-SBT operate via *right* multiplication.

Neither the Besicovitch nor the Weyl distance are preserved in the passage to E-shaped block transform.

Example 5. In the standard case, let $N = 2$ (*i.e.*, $E = \{0, 1\}$), $c_1(x) = 0$ for all x, $c_2(x) = x \mod 2$. Then $d_{B,\mathcal{X}}(c_1, c_2) = \frac{1}{2}$ but $d_{B,\mathcal{X}}(c_1^{[E]}, c_2^{[E]}) = 1$.

Again, what is preserved is the equivalence class. This time, however, an additional hypothesis is needed.

Theorem 4. *Let $\mathcal{X}$ be an amenable sequence for G. Let $c_1, c_2 \in S^G$. For each finite $E \subseteq G$ s.t. $1_G \in E$,*

$$d_{B,\mathcal{X}}(c_1, c_2) \leq d_{B,\mathcal{X}}\left(c_1^{[E]}, c_2^{[E]}\right) \leq |E| \cdot d_{B,\mathcal{X}}(c_1, c_2) \,. \qquad (12)$$

In particular, the following are equivalent:

1. $d_{B,\mathcal{X}}(c_1, c_2) = 0$.
2. $d_{B,\mathcal{X}}\left(c_1^{[E]}, c_2^{[E]}\right) = 0$ *for some finite E s.t. $1_G \in E$.*
3. $d_{B,\mathcal{X}}\left(c_1^{[E]}, c_2^{[E]}\right) = 0$ *for all finite E s.t. $1_G \in E$.*

The same hold with $d_{W,\mathcal{X}}$ in place of $d_{B,\mathcal{X}}$.

Proof. If $c_1(x) \neq c_2(x)$ then $c_1^{[E]}(x) \neq c_2^{[E]}(x)$ as well, from which the first inequality in (12) follows easily.

For the second one, given $U \subseteq G$, to each $x \in U$ s.t. $c_1^{[E]}(x) \neq c_2^{[E]}(x)$ correspond no more than $|E|$ points $y \in UE$ s.t. $c_1(y) \neq c_2(y)$, *i.e.*,

$$H_U(c_1^{[E]}, c_2^{[E]}) \leq |E| \cdot H_{UE}(c_1, c_2) \,. \qquad (13)$$

But $UE = U^{+E^{-1}} = U \sqcup \partial_{E^{-1}} U$ because $1_G \in E$, hence $H_{UE}(c_1, c_2) \leq H_U (c_1, c_2) + |\partial_{E^{-1}} U|$. From this, (13), and the fact that $\{X_n\}$ is amenable follows the thesis.

The corresponding statements for $d_{W,\mathcal{X}}$ can be proved similarly.

5 Sliding Block Codes in Besicovitch and Weyl Spaces

We have seen what happens to configuration spaces if, instead of staying near the grid, we move infinitely far from them. We are then interested in understanding what happens to sliding block codes, which are a very noteworthy family of transformations between configuration spaces. In particular, there are two questions that we ask ourselves.

1. Do SBC preserve Besicovitch and/or Weyl equivalence?
2. In this case, are properties of SBC linked to those of the maps they induce on Besicovitch and Weyl spaces?

The first question might have a positive answer if SBC were, at least under certain conditions, continuous w.r.t. the Besicovitch and/or Weyl distance. This is not immediate, because SBC are ensured to be continuous only w.r.t. the product topology; and we have seen that the notions of convergence in these spaces are completely uncorrelated.

If the choice of the sequence $\mathcal{X}$ is "good", something more than continuity actually happens. Recall that $F : X \to Y$ is *Lipschitz continuous* w.r.t. the pair of (pseudo-)distances (d_X, d_Y) if there exists $L > 0$ such that

$$d_Y(F(x_1), F(x_2)) \leq L \cdot d_X(x_1, x_2) \; \forall x_1, x_2 \in X \, . \tag{14}$$

In [5, Theorem 3.7] we prove that any CA is Lipschitz continuous w.r.t. the pair $(d_{B,\mathcal{X}}, d_{B,\mathcal{X}})$, provided $\{X_n\}$ is either amenable or a sequence of disks. Since SBC commute with translations, the argument in the proof of [5, Theorem 3.7] can be adapted to prove

Theorem 5. *Let G be a f.g. group and let $\mathcal{K} = \langle S, T, \mathcal{N}, f \rangle$ be a* SBC *over G.*

1. *If $\mathcal{X}$ is amenable, then $F_\mathcal{K}$ satisfies (14) w.r.t. $(d_{B,\mathcal{X}}, d_{B,\mathcal{X}})$ and $(d_{W,\mathcal{X}}, d_{W,\mathcal{X}})$, with $L = |\mathcal{N} \cup \{1_G\}|$.*
2. *If $X_n = D_{n,V}$ for all n for some* FSOG *V, and $\mathcal{N} \subseteq D_{r,V}$, then $F_\mathcal{K}$ satisfies (14) w.r.t. $(d_{B,\mathcal{X}}, d_{B,\mathcal{X}})$ and $(d_{W,\mathcal{X}}, d_{W,\mathcal{X}})$, with $L = (\gamma_V(r))^2$.*

Theorem 5 is not completely surprising. In fact, if V is a FSOG for G, then

$$d_V(c_1, c_2) = 2^{-\inf\{r \geq 0 \mid \exists g \in D_{r,V} \mid c_1(g) \neq c_2(g)\}} \tag{15}$$

with the conventions $\inf \emptyset = +\infty$, $2^{-\infty} = 0$, is a distance that induces the product topology on S^G. Thus, if $\mathcal{K} = \langle S, T, \mathcal{N}, f \rangle$ is a SBC, and $\mathcal{N} \subseteq D_{r,V}$, then $d_V(F_\mathcal{K}(c_1), F_\mathcal{K}(c_2)) \leq 2^r d_V(c_1, c_2)$. However, Lipschitz continuity is a property of the (pseudo-)distances, rather than the topologies.

The converse of Theorem 5 does not hold, *i.e.*, commutation with translations and Lipschitz continuity w.r.t. (d_B, d_B) (resp., (d_W, d_W)) are not sufficient to ensure that $F : \mathrm{Bes}_\mathcal{X}^{S,G} \to \mathrm{Bes}_\mathcal{X}^{T,G}$ (resp., $F : \mathrm{Wey}_\mathcal{X}^{S,G} \to \mathrm{Wey}_\mathcal{X}^{T,G}$) is the global function of some SBC.

Example 6 (Taken from [1], Example 7). In the standard case, let $T = \{0, 1, \tau\} = S \cup \{\tau\}$. Consider the function $F : T^\mathbb{Z} \to T^\mathbb{Z}$ defined as follows:

- If $c(x) = \tau$ then $(F(c))(x) = \tau$.
- If $c(x) \in S$, let $l = \sup\{z \leq x - 1 \mid c(z) \in S\}$, $r = \inf\{z \geq x + 1 \mid c(z) \in S\}$, with the conventions $\sup \emptyset = -\infty$, $\inf \emptyset = +\infty$, and let $\mathcal{I} = \{x, l, r\} \cap \mathbb{Z}$. Then $(F(c))(x) = \sum_{i \in \mathcal{I}} c(i) \mod 2$.

F is clearly translation-commuting. Moreover, the value of c at a point can influence the value of $F(c)$ at no more than three points: consequently, F satisfies (14) w.r.t. $(d_{B,\mathcal{X}}, d_{B,\mathcal{X}})$ and $(d_{W,\mathcal{X}}, d_{W,\mathcal{X}})$, with $L = 3$. However, F is not continuous in the product topology, and thus not a CA global function. (Intuitively, F needs an *unbounded* neighborhood.) Indeed, let $c(0) = 0$ and $c(x) = \tau$ if $x \neq 0$; let $c_k(x) = c(x)$ if $x \neq k$, $c_k(k) = 1$. Then $d_V(c_k, c) = 2^{-k}$ but $d_V(F(c_k), F(c)) = 1$.

From Theorem 5 follows that, for any group G and sequence $\mathcal{X}$ "good enough" and any SBC $\mathcal{K} = \langle S, T, \mathcal{N}, f \rangle$ on G two Lipschitz continuous transformations $F_B : \mathrm{Bes}_{\mathcal{X}}^{S,G} \to \mathrm{Bes}_{\mathcal{X}}^{T,G}$ and $F_W : \mathrm{Wey}_{\mathcal{X}}^{S,G} \to \mathrm{Wey}_{\mathcal{X}}^{T,G}$ are well-defined, respectively, as $F_B([c]_B) = [F_{\mathcal{K}}(c)]_B$ and $F_W([c]_W) = [F_{\mathcal{K}}(c)]_W$.

At this point we have what we need to make an attempt towards a characterization akin to [10, Lemma 2]. Instead of linking surjectivity to single occurrences of patterns (which are meaningless in our quotient topologies) we take into account the *density* of the set of occurrences of given patterns—which, by Theorem 3, is a property of *the equivalence class* of a configuration.

To make our ground more solid, we observe that the argument for point 1 of [5, Theorem 3.11] can be adapted to establish, at least under "good" conditions, a link between the surjectivity of a SBC and that of the induced maps.

Theorem 6. *Let G be an amenable f.g. group and let $\mathcal{K} = \langle S, T, \mathcal{N}, f \rangle$ be a* SBC *on G. If $\mathcal{X}$ contains an amenable sub-sequence, then the following are equivalent.*

1. *$F_{\mathcal{K}}$ is surjective.*
2. *For every $c_T \in T^G$ there exists $c_S \in S^G$ such that $d_{B,\mathcal{X}}(F_{\mathcal{K}}(c_S), c_T) = 0$.*
3. *For every $c_T \in T^G$ there exists $c_S \in S^G$ such that $d_{W,\mathcal{X}}(F_{\mathcal{K}}(c_S), c_T) = 0$.*

Theorem 6 can be proved via [5, Lemma 3.10], which we restate as we are going to need it again: if $\mathcal{X}$ is amenable and N is a (U, W)-net with $|U|, |W| < \infty$, then $\operatorname{dens\,inf}_{B,\mathcal{X}} N \geq 1/|W|$ and $\operatorname{dens\,sup}_{B,\mathcal{X}} N \leq 1/|U|$.

Theorem 7. *Let G be an amenable f.g. group and let $\mathcal{K} = \langle S, T, \mathcal{N}, f \rangle$ be a* SBC *on G. If $\mathcal{X}$ contains an amenable sub-sequence, then the following are equivalent.*

1. *For every $c_T \in T^G$ there exists $c_S \in S^G$ such that $d_{B,\mathcal{X}}(c_T, F_{\mathcal{K}}(c_S)) = 0$. (Thus, $F_{\mathcal{K}}$ is surjective by Theorem 6.)*
2. *For every finite $E \subseteq G$ and every $p : E \to T$ there exists $c_S \in S^G$ such that* $\operatorname{dens\,sup}_{B,\mathcal{X}} \operatorname{occ}(p, F_{\mathcal{K}}(c_S)) > 0$.

The same hold with d_W and $\operatorname{dens\,sup}_W$ *in place of d_B and* $\operatorname{dens\,sup}_B$.

Proof. Let $p : E \to T$. Suppose $D_R \supseteq E$. Let N be a (D_R, D_{2R})-net. Define $c_T \in T^G$ as

$$c_T(g) = \begin{cases} p(x^{-1}g) & \text{if } \exists x \in N \mid x^{-1}g \in E\,, \\ \text{arbitrary otherwise}\,. \end{cases} \tag{16}$$

Then each $x \in N$ is an occurrence of p in c, so that $\operatorname{dens\,sup}_{W,\mathcal{X}} \operatorname{occ}(p, c_T) \geq \operatorname{dens\,sup}_{B,\mathcal{X}} \operatorname{occ}(p, c_T) \geq \operatorname{dens\,sup}_{B,\mathcal{X}} N \geq 1/\gamma(2R)$. If $d_{B,\mathcal{X}}(c_T, F_{\mathcal{K}}(c_S)) = 0$ for some $c_S \in S^G$, then $\operatorname{dens\,sup}_{B,\mathcal{X}} \operatorname{occ}(p, F(c_S)) \geq 1/\gamma(2R)$ as well. The previous statement holds if d_B and $\operatorname{dens\,sup}_B$ are replaced by d_W and $\operatorname{dens\,sup}_W$. The thesis then follows by Theorem 6.

We stress that the hypotheses of Theorems 6 and 7 do not, as far as we know, ensure that F_B and F_W are well-defined. They are if G is of sub-exponential growth (*e.g.*, $\mathbb{Z}^d$) and $\mathcal{X}$ is a sequence of disks (*e.g.*, $X_n = \{-n, \ldots, n\}^d$).

We conclude with a short note about injectivity.

Definition 3. *A group G is* surjunctive *if, for every alphabet S, every injective continuous map $F : S^G \to S^G$ which commutes with translations is surjective.*

We stress that Definition 3 does not require the group to be finitely generated. Amenable groups (*e.g.*, $\mathbb{Z}^d$) are surjunctive. Currently, no example of a non-surjunctive group is known [11].

Let G be a f.g. group: by Hedlund's theorem, G is surjunctive if and only if every injective CA on G is surjective. This cannot be extended to arbitrary SBC, for if S is a proper subset of T, then embedding S^G into T^G yields an injective, non-surjective SBC. The last theorem of this paper thus holds only for CA.

Theorem 8. *Let $\mathcal{A}$ be a CA and let F be its global map. Suppose G is surjunctive and $\{X_n\}$ is either amenable or a sequence of disks. If F is injective then F_B and F_W are injective.*

Proof. Since F is injective and G is surjunctive, F is a bijection. As a consequence of Hedlund's theorem (cf. [3, Corollary 3.11]) $P = F^{-1}$ is the global map of some CA, and it is Lipschitz continuous w.r.t. $(d_{B,\mathcal{X}}, d_{B,\mathcal{X}})$ and $(d_{W,\mathcal{X}}, d_{W,\mathcal{X}})$ by Theorem 5.

Suppose then $[c_1]_B \neq [c_2]_B$. Put $\chi_i = F(c_i)$: then $P_B([\chi_1]_B) = [P(\chi_1)]_B \neq [P(\chi_2)]_B = P_B([\chi_2]_B)$. Since P_B is a function by Theorem 5, $F_B([c_1]_B) = [\chi_1]_B \neq [\chi_2]_B = F_B([c_2]_B)$. A similar argument holds for F_W.

6 Conclusions

The Besicovitch and Weyl distances and densities represent points of view radically different from that of the usual product topology. Nonetheless, several of their features have been shown to be relevant and useful in the study of symbolic dynamics and the properties of SBC global functions. The main result of this paper, that SBC surjectivity can be checked through an application of these concepts, belongs to this thread of research.

Many more questions arise about these spaces. It is of interest, for instance, to describe in detail the topologies of these quotient spaces; we specifically address compactness and connectedness, which in the 1D case are known to be very different from those of the product topology. Other research topics are related to finding suitable dense subspaces that may be "handy" in the study of both spaces and SBC properties; this is especially important since periodic configurations are not dense in the Besicovitch and Weyl spaces. For the former, an option (suggested in [1]) is provided by *Toeplitz configurations*, which are not necessarily periodic, but where every pattern occurs periodically.

In our hopes, the small compendium of results presented in this paper shall raise interest in the subject and attract more researchers towards this field.

Acknowledgements. The author was supported partially by the Estonian Centre of Excellence in Theoretical Computer Science (EXCS) mainly funded by European Regional Development Fund (ERDF). The author wishes to thank

Tommaso Toffoli, Patrizia Mentrasti, and Tarmo Uustalu for their suggestions and encouragements. The author also thanks the anonymous referees for their thorough reviews and helpful suggestions.

References

1. Blanchard, F., Formenti, E., Kůrka, P.: Cellular Automata in Cantor, Besicovitch, and Weyl Topological Spaces. Complex Systems 11(2), 107–123 (1999)
2. Capobianco, S.: Multidimensional Cellular Automata and Generalization of Fekete's Lemma. Disc. Math. Theor. Comp. Sci. 10(3), 95–104 (2008)
3. Capobianco, S.: On the Induction Operation for Shift Subspaces and Cellular Automata as Presentations of Dynamical Systems. Inform. Comput. 207(11), 1169–1180 (2009)
4. Capobianco, S.: Some Notes on Besicovitch and Weyl Distances over Higher-Dimensional Configurations. In: de Oliveira, P.P.B., Kari, J. (Eds.): Proceedings of Automata 2009: 15th International Workshop on Cellular Automata and Discrete Complex Systems, Universidade Presbiteriana Mackenzie, São Paulo, SP, Brazil, Section 2: Short Papers, pp. 300–308 (2009)
5. Capobianco, S.: Surjunctivity for Cellular Automata in Besicovitch Spaces. J. Cell. Autom. 4(2), 89–98 (2009)
6. de la Harpe, P.: Topics in Geometric Group Theory. The University of Chicago Press (2000)
7. Fiorenzi, F.: Cellular Automata and Strongly Irreducible Shifts of Finite Type. Theor. Comp. Sci. 299, 477–493 (2003)
8. Lind, D., Marcus, B.: An Introduction to Symbolic Dynamics and Coding. Cambridge University Press, Cambridge (1995)
9. Namioka, I.: Følner's Condition for Amenable Semi Groups. Math. Scand. 15, 18–28 (1962)
10. Toffoli, T., Capobianco, S., Mentrasti, P.: When—and How—Can a Cellular Automaton be Rewritten as a Lattice Gas? Theor. Comp. Sci. 403, 71–88 (2008)
11. Weiss, B.: Sofic Groups and Dynamical Systems. Sankhyā: Indian J. Stat. 62, 350–359 (2000)

On a Labeled Vehicle Routing Problem

Hatem Chatti, Laurent Gourvès, and Jérôme Monnot

LAMSADE, CNRS FRE 3234 & Université de Paris-Dauphine
{hatem.chatti,laurent.gourves,monnot}@lamsade.dauphine.fr

Abstract. In this paper, we study the complexity and (in)approximability of the *minimum label vehicle routing* problem. Given a simple complete graph $G = (V, E)$ containing a special vertex 0 called the depot and where the edges are colored (labeled), the minimum label k-vehicle routing problem consists in finding a k-vehicle routing E', i.e. a collection of cycles of size at most $k + 1$ which all contain the depot 0, and such that every customer $v \in V \setminus \{0\}$ is visited once, minimizing the number of colors used.

1 Introduction

In many graph connectivity problems each edge is associated with a numerical attribute, which may represent length, weight or cost, depending on the related real-life context, and the task is to identify a minimum cost subgraph satisfying given connectivity requirements. In contrast with this standard framework, *labeled optimization* supposes that the set of available edges is partitioned into classes, each of which can be purchased in its entirety or not at all. A convenient representation of such a model couples each edge with a *label*, or color, that specifies its class, and a subset of labels forms a feasible solution when the edges whose labels belong to this subset induce a subgraph satisfying the given connectivity requirements. The objective is to find a solution that optimizes the number of picked labels.

The main fundamental labeled connectivity problems, namely spanning tree, s-t-path, matching, traveling salesman problems have been studied in the literature from a complexity and approximation theories point of view, see for instance [2,3,4,8,10]. In all these labeled problems, if for example every color represents a technology consulted by a different vendor, then we wish to use as few colors as possible, so as to diminish incompatibilities among different technologies.

We are interested in studying the complexity and approximability of a *vehicle routing* problem. Vehicle routing problems that involve the periodic collection and delivery of goods and services such as mail delivery or trash collection are of great practical importance. Usually there is a constraint on the number of customers visited by a vehicle. This constraint reflects the assumption that the vehicle has a finite capacity and that it *collects* from the customers (or *distributes* among them) a commodity.

Simple variants of these real problems can be modeled naturally with graphs. Unfortunately even simple variants of vehicle routing problems are **NP**-hard [1].

J. van Leeuwen et al. (Eds.): SOFSEM 2010, LNCS 5901, pp. 271–282, 2010.

For the well known metric k-vehicle routing problem (METRIC kVRP in short), we are given a complete graph K_{n+1} of $(n+1)$ vertices $\{0,\ldots,n\}$ containing a special vertex 0 (the depot), an integer $k \geq 1$ and a distance d between pair of vertices satisfying the triangular inequality. The objective is to find a collection of cycles $C_1,\ldots,C_p$ of K_{n+1} minimizing $\sum_{i=1}^{k}\sum_{e\in C_i} d(e)$ where vertices of $\{1,\ldots,n\}$ are visited once by the collection of cycles, each cycle C_i is of size at most $k+1$ and contains the depot. It is easy to see that 2VRP is polynomial time solvable. For $k \geq 3$, METRIC kVRP was proved **NP**-hard in [6]. In [7], the authors gave a $(\frac{5}{2}-\frac{3}{2k})$-approximation for METRIC kVRP. In [1], an improvement to $\frac{197}{99}$ is proposed for METRIC 3VRP and some other approximation bounds are presented using the differential measure. To the best of our knowledge, these performance ratios are the best known for any fixed $k \geq 3$.

This paper deals with a labeled version of kVRP. In the *minimum label vehicle routing* problem, n *customers* have to be served by *vehicles* of limited capacity from a common *depot*. A solution consists of a set of routes, where each starts at the depot and returns there after visiting a subset of customers, such that each customer is visited exactly once. In the model studied in this paper, each route has a label and we seek solutions which use a minimum number of distinct labels.

The problem arises in *multimodal transportation networks* [12]. In such problems, it is desirable to provide a complete service using the minimum number of companies. The multimodal transportation network is represented by a graph where each edge is assigned a label, denoting a different company managing that edge. Another example is the following. Suppose that the customers are distributed over an area (e.g. a map). This area is partitioned into zones which are owned by some entities (e.g. countries). An entity can own several zones. To enter a zone, one needs to get an authorization from its owner. It is assumed that an authorization concerns all zones owned by an entity and not only a subset. One can model the situation as a labeled vehicle routing problem where there are as many labels as entities. A trip between two points (two customers or the depot and a customer) has label ℓ_e if one needs to enter a zone owned by entity e. If each authorization induces a cost or a delay, the goal is to minimize their number. In other words, a routing which minimizes the number of labels is sought. In this paper, we consider that all authorizations have the same cost and every trip has a unique label but natural extensions can be investigated as a future work.

Contribution and organization of the paper. In Section 2 we formally define the labeled vehicle routing problem and give some properties that are often used in the proofs. Some simple polynomially solvable cases are identified in Section 3. Section 4 and 5 are devoted to hardness and inapproximability results which draw a rather complete picture of the complexity of the labeled vehicle routing problem. Before we conclude and list future directions in Section 7, some approximation results are given Section 6.

2 Definitions, Notations and Some Properties

Given a simple graph $G = (V, E)$ where $V = \{v_1, \ldots, v_n\}$, a *path* P of G is a sequence $P = (v_{r_1}, \ldots, v_{r_{k+1}})$ where $[v_{r_i}, v_{r_{i+1}}] \in E$ for $i = 1, \ldots, k$ and $v_{r_i} \neq v_{r_j}$ for $i \neq j$. A *cycle* C of G is a sequence $P = (v_{r_1}, \ldots, v_{r_{k+1}}, v_{r_1})$ where $[v_{r_i}, v_{r_{i+1}}] \in E$ for $i = 1, \ldots, k$, $[v_{r_{k+1}}, v_{r_1}] \in E$ and $v_{r_i} \neq v_{r_j}$ for $1 \leq i < j \leq k+1$. For a path P or cycle C, $V(P)$ and $V(C)$ denote the set of the vertices of P and C respectively. The *length* of a path P or cycle C (denoted by $|P|$ and $|C|$ respectively) is the number of its edges. So, with the previous notations, we get $V(P) = V(C) = \{v_{r_1}, \ldots, v_{r_{k+1}}\}$, $|P| = k = |V(P)| - 1$ and $|C| = k + 1 = |V(C)|$.

Given a complete graph K_{n+1} of $(n+1)$ vertices $\{0, \ldots, n\}$ containing a special vertex 0 (the depot) and an integer $k \geq 1$, a k-vehicle routing E' of K_{n+1} is a collection of cycles $C_1, \ldots, C_p$ of K_{n+1} such that

(*a*) $\forall i = 1, \ldots, p$, $0 \in V(C_i)$,
(*b*) $\cup_{i=1}^{p} V(C_i) = \{0, \ldots, n\}$,
(*c*) $V(C_i) \cap V(C_j) = \{0\}$ for $1 \leq i < j \leq p$,
(*d*) $\forall i = 1, \ldots, p$, $|V(C_i)| \leq k + 1$.

The vertices of $V(K_{n+1}) \setminus \{0\}$ will be called *the customers*. In other words, each vehicle starts at the depot 0, visits at most k customers and returns to the depot. Each customer is visited exactly once. The specific solution $E_0 = \{C_1, \ldots, C_n\}$ where $C_i = (0, i, 0)$ will be called the *star* of K_{n+1} and it will be extensively studied in this paper (see Figure 1). When $C_i = (0, i, 0)$ is used, the edge $[0, i]$ and its color will be counted once.

In the *minimum label k-vehicle routing* problem for $k \geq 1$ (LVRP(k) in short), we are given a complete graph K_{n+1} of $(n+1)$ vertices $\{0, \ldots, n\}$ containing a special vertex 0 (the depot) and an edge-labeling function $\mathcal{L} : E(K_{n+1}) \rightarrow L = \{\ell_1, \ldots, \ell_q\}$. The objective is to find a k-vehicle routing E' of K_{n+1} minimizing the number of colors used by E', i.e., $|\mathcal{L}(E')|$, where $\mathcal{L}(E') = \{\mathcal{L}(e) : e \in E'\}$. The *minimum label vehicle routing* problem (LVRP in short) is the restriction of the minimum label k-vehicle routing problem when $k \geq n$.

Given $I = (K_{n+1}, \mathcal{L})$ instance of LVRP(k), the *frequency* of color ℓ_i, denoted by $f(\ell_i)$, is the number of times that color ℓ_i appears in I. For $L' \subseteq L = \{\ell_1, \ldots, \ell_q\}$, the *frequency* of L', denoted by $f(L')$ is the maximum frequency of colors in L',

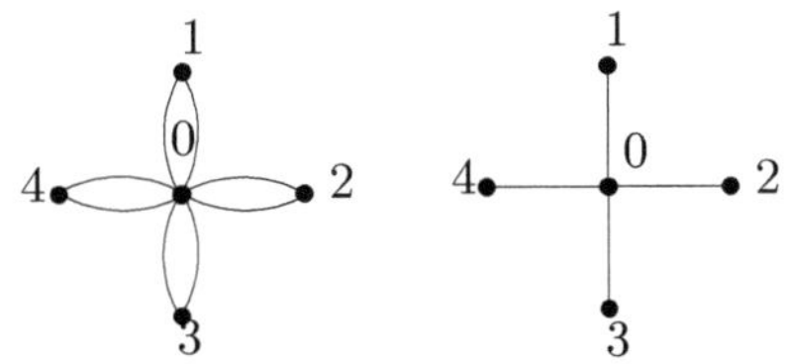

Fig. 1. Two equivalent representations of the star E_0

i.e., $f(L') = \max\{f(\ell) : \ell \in L'\}$. The *frequency* of I is the maximum number of times that a color appears in I, i.e., $f(L)$. Using abusive notations, the frequency of a set E' of edges, denoted by $f(E')$, is the maximum frequency of colors used by E', i.e., $f(E') = f(\mathcal{L}(E'))$. The restriction of LVRP(k) to instances where the frequency is upper bounded by f is denoted by LVRP(k, f).

Given an instance $I = (K_{n+1}, \mathcal{L})$ of LVRP(k) and a feasible (resp., optimal) k-vehicle routing $E' = \{C_i : i = 1, \ldots, p\}$ (resp., $E^* = \{C_i^* : i = 1, \ldots, p^*\}$) of I, s'_i (resp., s^*_i) for $i = 2, \ldots, k+1$ denotes the number of cycles of E' (resp., E^*) of size exactly i. We have the following properties:

Property 1. We can always assume that:

(*i*) $s'_3 = 0$.
(*ii*) For each cycle $C_i = (0, x_1, x_2, \ldots, x_{p-1}, x_p, 0)$ of size $p + 1 \geq 4$ of E', the color(s) $\mathcal{L}([x_1, x_2])$ and $\mathcal{L}([x_{p-1}, x_p])$ appears at least twice in E'.
(*iii*) $s'_2 + \sum_{i=4}^{k+1}(i-1)s'_i = n$.

Obviously Property 1 also holds if we consider the optimal solution E^*.

3 Polynomial Cases

We present some simple polynomial cases of LVRP(k, f). In each case, the star E_0 will be an optimal solution.

Theorem 1. *The following cases are polynomial:*

- LVRP(k, f) *if* $f = 1$ *or* $k = 1, 2$.
- LVRP($3, 2$) *if* $f(E_0) = 1$.

4 Hardness Results

All the hardness results presented here will be done from the k-path partition problem (denoted by k-PPP). In k-PPP, we are given a simple graph $G = (V, E)$ with $|V| = kq$ and we want to decide whether a collection of q vertex-disjoint paths, each of length exactly $k - 1$, exists.

This problem is **NP**-complete for any $k \geq 3$, and polynomial otherwise, [5,9]. More recently, k-PPP has been proved **NP**-complete in bipartite graphs of maximum degree 3 for any $k \geq 3$, [11].

4.1 When $f(E_0) = 1$

From Theorem 1, we know that LVRP($3, 2$) when $f(E_0) = 1$ is polynomial (we recall $f(E_0) = 1$ means that for each edge $[0, x]$, the color $\mathcal{L}([0, x])$ appears exactly once in the instance). Now, we prove that it is not the case for LVRP($3, 3$).

Theorem 2. LVRP$(3,3)$ *with* $f(E_0)=1$ *is* ***NP*****-hard.**

When we deal with LVRP(k) with $k \geq 4$, we can obtain stronger hardness results since similar results hold with a frequency equal to 2.

Theorem 3. *For any* $k \geq 4$, LVRP$(k,2)$ *with* $f(E_0)=1$ *is* ***NP*****-hard.**

Proof. The proof is very similar to Theorem 2, except that we start from k-PPP and we duplicate the graph twice instead of 3 times. Formally, fix $k \geq 4$ and let $G=(V,E)$ with $|V|=kq$ be an instance of k-PPP. We build an instance $I=(K_{2kq+1},\mathcal{L})$ of LVRP$(k,2)$ as follows:

- Color each edge of G with a unique color.
- Make two copies of G, denoted by $G_i=(V_i,E_i)$ for $i=1,2$.
- Add a depot 0 and complete the graph into K_{2kq+1} by adding a unique color per missing edge.

Obviously, I is an instance of LVRP$(k,2)$ with $f(E_0)=1$.

We claim that G admits a collection $\mathcal{P}=\{P_1,\dots,P_q\}$ of q vertex-disjoint paths with $|P_i|=k-1$ iff there is a k-vehicle routing E' of I with $|\mathcal{L}(E')| \leq q(k+3)$.

Let $\mathcal{P}=\{P_1,\dots,P_q\}$ be a collection of paths of G, vertex-disjoint and such that $|P_i|=k-1$. Consider $E'=\{C_i : i=1,\dots,2q\}$ where $C_{i+(j-1)q}$ is the cycle in the j-th copy G_j for $=1,2$, isomorphic to $(0,P_i,0)$. E' is a feasible solution of I and since $f(E_0)=1$, $|\mathcal{L}(E')|=|\mathcal{L}(E'\cap E_0)|+|\mathcal{L}(E'\setminus E_0)|=4q+(k-1)q=q(k+3)$.

Conversely, let $E'=\{C_1,\dots,C_r\}$ be a k-vehicle routing of I such that $|\mathcal{L}(E')| \leq q(k+3)$. Since the frequency of I is 2 and the problem studied is LVRP(k), we deduce that $|\mathcal{L}(E'\setminus E_0)| \geq (\sum_{i=4}^{k+1}(i-2)s'_i)/2$. On the other hand, by hypothesis, we have $f(E_0)=1$; so, $|\mathcal{L}(E'\cap E_0)|=s'_2+2\sum_{i=4}^{k+1}s'_i$. Finally, using arguments similar to those given in Theorem 2 (in this case, equality (*iii*) of Property 1 gives $s'_2=2qk-\sum_{i=4}^{k+1}(i-1)s'_i)$, we obtain:

$$|\mathcal{L}(E')|=|\mathcal{L}(E'\setminus E_0)|+|\mathcal{L}(E'\cap E_0)| \geq 2kq-\frac{\sum_{i=4}^{k+1}(i-4)s'_i}{2} \quad (1)$$

Using inequality (1) and $|\mathcal{L}(E')| \leq q(k+3)$, we obtain:

$$\sum_{i=4}^{k+1}(i-4)s'_i \geq 2q(k-3) \quad (2)$$

Since $(i-4) \leq k-3$ for $i \in \{4,\dots,k+1\}$, we deduce from inequality (2), the bound

$$\sum_{i=4}^{k+1} s'_i \geq 2q \quad (3)$$

On the other hand, since $\sum_{i=4}^{k+1}(i-4)s'_i = \sum_{i=4}^{k+1}(i-1)s'_i - 3\sum_{i=4}^{k+1} s'_i$, by using equality (iii) of Property 1, i.e. $\sum_{i=4}^{k+1}(i-1)s'_i = 2qk - s'_2$, we obtain:

$$\sum_{i=4}^{k+1}(i-4)s'_i = 2kq - s'_2 - 3\sum_{i=4}^{k+1} s'_i \tag{4}$$

Using inequalities (2) and (4), we deduce:

$$6q \geq s'_2 + 3\sum_{i=4}^{k+1} s'_i \tag{5}$$

From inequalities (3) and (5), we obtain $s'_2 \leq 0$, that is $s'_2 = 0$. Then, we also deduce that $\sum_{i=4}^{k+1} s'_i = 2q$. Using this last equality and $2qk = \sum_{i=4}^{k+1}(i-1)s'_i$ (given by (iii) of Property 1) we obtain $\sum_{i=4}^{k+1}(i-1)s'_i = 2qk = k\sum_{i=4}^{k+1} s'_i$ or equivalently $\sum_{i=4}^{k+1}(k+1-i)s'_i$. This implies that $s'_i = 0$ for $i = 4, \ldots, k$ and then in conclusion, we get:

$$s'_{k+1} = 2q \tag{6}$$

Hence, from equality (6), we deduce that $|\mathcal{L}(E')| = q(k+3)$. This means that the edges of $E' \setminus E_0$ corresponds to edges of G and in particular $E' \cap E_1$ (the edges of E' in the first copy G_1) is a collection of q vertex-disjoint paths, each of length exactly $k-1$ in G_1 and then in G. □

4.2 LVRP(3) with Frequency 2

We conclude this section by studying the complexity of LVRP(3) with frequency 2. Hence, we will get a complete description of the complexity of LVRP(k) following the parameters k, $f(E_0)$ and the frequency.

Theorem 4. *LVRP(3, 2) is **NP**-hard.*

Proof. We polynomially reduce 3-PPP to LVRP(3, 2). Let $G = (V, E)$ with $|V| = 3q$ and $E = \{e_1, \ldots, e_m\}$ be an instance of 3-PPP. We build an instance $I = (K_{3q+m+1}, \mathcal{L})$ of LVRP(3, 2) as follows:

- Color each edge e_i of G with a unique color $\mathcal{L}(e_i)$.
- Add m new vertices $3q + i$ for $i = 1, \ldots, m$ and set $\mathcal{L}([0, 3q + i]) = \mathcal{L}(e_i)$
- Add a depot 0 and complete the graph into K_{3q+m+1} by adding a unique color per missing edge.

Obviously, I is an instance of LVRP(3, 2).

We claim that G admits a collection $\mathcal{P} = \{P_1, \ldots, P_q\}$ of q vertex-disjoint paths with $|P_i| = 2$ iff there is a 3-vehicle routing E' of I with $|\mathcal{L}(E')| \leq 2q + m$.

Let $\mathcal{P} = \{P_1, \ldots, P_q\}$ be a collection of vertex-disjoint paths of G such that $|P_i| = 2$. Consider $E' = \{C_i : i = 1, \ldots, q + m\}$ where for $i \leq q$, $C_i = (0, P_i, 0)$ while for $i = q + 1, \ldots, q + m$, $C_i = (0, 3q + i, 0)$. E' is a 3-vehicle routing of I and $|\mathcal{L}(E')| = 2q + m$.

Conversely, let $E' = \{C_1, \ldots, C_r\}$ be a 3-vehicle routing of I such that $|\mathcal{L}(E')| \leq 2q + m$. Let us prove that the following property holds:

Property 2. We can always assume that $\{(0, 3q+i, 0) : i = q+1, \ldots, q+m\} \subset E'$.

Proof. By contradiction, assume that some vertex $3q+i$ is contained in a cycle C_i of E' with $|C_i| > 2$. Using (i) of Property 1 and the fact that E' is a 3-vehicle routing, we get $|C_i| = 4$. Since the color of every edge incident to $3q+i$, except $\mathcal{L}([0, 3q+i])$ appears once, we obtain a contradiction with (ii) of Property 1. □

Now, since $|\mathcal{L}(E' \cap E_0)| \leq |\mathcal{L}(E')| \leq 2q + m$ and $|\mathcal{L}((E' \cap E_0) \setminus E)| = m$ (from Property 2 where we recall that E is the edge set of G), we deduce that $|\mathcal{L}(E' \cap E_0 \cap E)| \leq 2q$ because $f(E_0 \cap E) = 1$. On the other hand, $|\mathcal{L}(E' \cap E_0 \cap E)| \geq 2|V|/3 = 2q$ since E' is a 3-vehicle routing. Thus, $|\mathcal{L}(E' \cap E_0 \cap E)| = 2q$, and then every cycle of E' which is in the complete subgraph induced by $V \cup \{0\}$, has a length 4. We also deduce that $|\mathcal{L}(E' \setminus E_0)| = |\mathcal{L}(E' \cap E)| = m$. Thus $E' \setminus E_0$ are edges of G. In conclusion, G admits a collection of q vertex-disjoint paths, each of length exactly 2. □

5 Inapproximation Results

We now present for some value of k, some inapproximation results of LVRP(k), that is, we produce some lower bounds that the performance ratio of any approximation algorithms can not reach unless **P**=**NP**. For this, we will apply a gap-reduction from MAX$\mathbf{P}_k$PACKING. This problem consists, given a simple graph $G = (V, E)$, of finding a maximum number of vertex-disjoint paths of length $k - 1$. In [11], it is proved that MAX$\mathbf{P}_k$PACKING, for $k \geq 3$, admits a constant $\varepsilon_k > 0$, such that for every bipartite graph $G = (V, E)$ of maximum degree 3, it is **NP**-hard to decide between $opt(G) = \frac{|V|}{k}$ and $opt(G) \leq (1-\varepsilon_k)\frac{|V|}{k}$. Here $opt(G)$ is the value of a maximum $\mathbf{P}_k$-Packing on G. All these results hold if $|V|$ is assumed to be even.

Theorem 5. *There is a constant $\varepsilon_3 > 0$, such that for all $\varepsilon > 0$,* LVRP(3, 2) *is not $(\frac{13+2\varepsilon_3}{13} - \varepsilon)$-approximable unless **P**=**NP**.*

The same kind of result holds if we consider LVRP(4).

Theorem 6. *There is a constant $\varepsilon_4 > 0$, such that for all $\varepsilon > 0$,* LVRP(4, 2) *is not $(\frac{7+\varepsilon_4}{7} - \varepsilon)$-approximable unless **P**=**NP**.*

If we study LVRP(k) where k depends on the number of customers, we can obtain stronger results. For instance, for the labeled vehicle routing problem LVRP, i.e. without any constraint on the length of each cycle, we prove that LVRP is not $n^{1-\varepsilon}$-approximable, for all $\varepsilon \in (0; 1)$. On the other hand, any Hamiltonian cycle of K_{n+1}, which is a feasible solution of $I = (K_{n+1}, \mathcal{L})$, guarantees the performance ratio $n+1$. Indeed the Hamiltonian cycle uses at most $n+1$ colors while $opt(I) \geq 1$.

Theorem 7. *For all $\varepsilon \in (0; 1)$, for any $k \geq n^{\varepsilon}$,* LVRP(k) *is not $n^{1-\varepsilon}$-approximable unless **P**=**NP**, where n is the number of customers.*

Proof. Let $\varepsilon > 0$ and let $G = (V, E)$ be an instance of the Hamiltonian s-t-path problem on a graph with two specified vertices $s, t \in V$ having degree 1 in G. The Hamiltonian s-t-path problem is defined as follows: given a graph $G = (V, E)$ with two specified vertices $s, t \in V$, decide whether G has an Hamiltonian path from s to t (see [5]). The restriction of the Hamiltonian s-t-path problem on graphs where vertices s, t are of degree 1 remains **NP**-complete.

Let $p = \lceil \frac{1}{\varepsilon} \rceil - 1$. We construct the following instance I of LVRP(k) where $k \geq q^{\varepsilon}$, q is the number of customers of the resulting instance: take a graph consisting of n^p copies of G and add a depot 0, where the i-th copy is denoted by $G_i = (V_i, E_i)$ and s_i, t_i are the corresponding copies of vertices s and t. Set $\mathcal{L}(e) = c_0$ for every $e \in \cup_{i=1}^{n^p} E_i$, $\mathcal{L}([s_i, 0]) = c_0$ and $\mathcal{L}([t_i, 0]) = c_0$ for all $i = 1, \ldots, n^p$. Complete this graph by taking a new color per remaining edge. This construction can obviously be done in polynomial time, and the resulting graph has $n^{p+1}+1$ vertices. Moreover since $q = n^{p+1}$, then $k \geq n$. Let $I = (K_{n^{p+1}+1}, \mathcal{L})$ be the resulting instance of LVRP(k) and let E^* be an optimal k-vehicle routing of I with value $opt(I) = |\mathcal{L}(E^*)|$.

- If G has an Hamiltonian s-t-path P, then let P_i be the Hamiltonian s-t-path in G_i. By setting $E^* = \{(0, P_i, 0) : i = 1, \ldots, n^p\}$, we get $opt(I) = 1$.
- Otherwise, G (and then, each copy G_i) has no Hamiltonian path for any pair of vertices since vertices $s, t \in V$ have a degree 1 in G. Hence $OPT(I) \geq n^p$, because on the one hand, for each copy G_i, there is at least one vertex v_i which is incident to an edge $e_i \in E^*$ with $\mathcal{L}(e_i) \neq c_0$, and on the other hand there are n^p copies.

We deduce that it is **NP**-complete to distinguish between $OPT(I) = 1$ and $OPT(I) \geq |V(K_{n^{p+1}+1}) \setminus \{0\}|^{1-\frac{1}{p+1}} \geq |V(K_{n^{p+1}+1}) \setminus \{0\}|^{1-\varepsilon}$. □

6 A Simple Approximation

We first analyze how far the star E_0, i.e. the solution where every customer is covered by a cycle of length 2, is from an optimal k-vehicle routing. We provide tight bounds on the approximation ratio. Next we show that local improvements made on the star E_0 lead to better worst case performances.

Theorem 8. *For all $f \geq 2$ and $k \geq 3$, The star E_0 is a $\frac{f(k-2)+1}{k-1}$-approximation for* LVRP(k, f) *when $f \leq \frac{k+1}{2}$ and it is a $\frac{f(k-2)+k+1}{k+1}$-approximation for* LVRP(k, f) *when $f \geq \frac{k+1}{2}$.*

The following proposition shows the upper bounds on the approximation ratio of the star are tight.

Proposition 1. *Given $f \geq 2$ and $k \geq 4$, the star E_0 is at most a $\frac{f(k-2)+1}{k-1}$-approximation of the optimum when $f \leq \frac{k+1}{2}$ and at most a $\frac{f(k-2)+k+1}{k+1}$-approximation of the optimum when $f \geq \frac{k+1}{2}$.*

We recall that the surplus of any k-vehicle routing E'' is defined as $R(E'') = |E'' \cap E_0| - |\mathcal{L}(E'' \cap E_0)|$ where $E_0 = \{(0,v,0) : v \in V(K_{n+1}) \setminus \{0\}\}$ is the star of I (see Theorem 8). For instance, if $f = 2$, then for any $A \subseteq E(K_{n+1})$, $R(A)$ counts the number of colors ℓ which appears twice in A and such that the two edges of color ℓ are incident to the depot. One can see that the following property holds:

Property 3. For any couple of sets A, B of E, we have:

$$A \subseteq B \Rightarrow R(A) = R(A \cap E_0) \leq R(B \cap E_0) = R(B) \tag{7}$$

Proof. Actually, if $e \notin E_0$ (or $e \in E_0$ and $\mathcal{L}(e) \notin \mathcal{L}(A \cap E_0)$) then $R(A) = R(A \cup \{e\})$; otherwise, $R(A \cup \{e\}) = R(A) + 1$. □

Now, we focus on a restriction of LVRP$(3,f)$ for $f \geq 2$ where no two edges incident to the depot have the same color. In other words, there are n colors incident to the depot, or equivalently we assume $R(E_0) = 0$. In the light of Theorems 3 and 4, this restriction remains **NP**-hard for any $f \geq 2$ and for instance, the star E_0 is exactly a $\frac{3}{2}$-approximation for LVRP$(3,2)$ when $R(E_0) = 0$ (see the tightness in Proposition 1). More generally, one can prove that the star E_0 is, in this case (i.e., $R(E_0) = 0$), a $\frac{3}{2}$-approximation of the optimum for LVRP$(3,f)$ for every $f \geq 2$. Below we analyze an algorithm which, starting from E_0, resorts to local improvements to try to reduce the number of labels. A simple (informal) description of the algorithm (called here Loc Improv) is the following: Start with $L' := \mathcal{L}(E_0)$. While there exists $\ell \in L'$ such that the set of edges having a color in $L' \setminus \{\ell\}$ contains a 3-vehicle routing, do $L' := L' \setminus \{\ell\}$. Return a 3-vehicle routing E' such that $\mathcal{L}(E') = L'$. Formally, the algorithm maintains a feasible 3-vehicle routing E' which is initialized to E_0. While it is possible, a label is removed from $\mathcal{L}(E')$ by replacing three cycles of length two by one cycle of length four: Take three nodes u, v and w which are all covered by a cycle of length 2 in E', then do $E' \leftarrow E' \cup \{[u,v],[v,w]\} \setminus \{[0,v]\}$ if $\mathcal{L}(E') \supset \mathcal{L}(E' \cup \{[u,v],\ [v,w]\} \setminus \{[0,v]\})$. At the end, the algorithm returns a 3-vehicle routing E', a local minimum, which uses $|\mathcal{L}(E')|$ labels. Loc Improv is clearly polynomial and it provides a $\left(1 + \frac{f+3}{2f+8}\right)$-approximation of the optimum for LVRP$(3,f)$ when $R(E_0) = 0$ which is always better than $\frac{3}{2}$.

Theorem 9. *For every $f \geq 2$,* Loc Improv *is a $\left(1 + \frac{f+3}{2f+8}\right)$-approximation for* LVRP$(3,f)$ *when $R(E_0) = 0$.*

Proof. Let $f \geq 2$ and let $I = (K_{n+1}, \mathcal{L})$ be an instance of LVRP$(3,f)$ such that $R(E_0) = 0$. Let $E' = \mathcal{C}'_2 \cup \mathcal{C}'_4$ and $E^* = \mathcal{C}^*_2 \cup \mathcal{C}^*_4$ be the approximate and an optimal solutions respectively where $\mathcal{C}'_i$ and $\mathcal{C}^*_i$ for $i = 2,4$ are the cycles of size i of E' and E^* respectively (using (i) of Property 1, we know that $\mathcal{C}^*_3 = \mathcal{C}'_3 = \emptyset$). Moreover, using the previous notations, we have $s'_i = |\mathcal{C}'_i|$ and $s^*_i = |\mathcal{C}^*_i|$ for $i = 2,4$. By construction, the algorithm may only delete some colors which appear once in the star E_0; hence, we get $|\mathcal{L}(E')| = |\mathcal{L}(E' \cap E_0)|$. Since, by hypothesis, $R(E_0) = 0$, inequality (7) of Property 3 leads to the conclusion that $R(E'') = 0$ for every $E'' \subseteq E(K_{n+1})$. In particular, $R(E') = R(E^*) = 0$. Thus, $|\mathcal{L}(E' \cap E_0)| = |E' \cap E_0| = n - s'_4$ and we obtain:

$$apx(I) = |\mathcal{L}(E' \cap E_0)| = n - s'_4 \tag{8}$$

Concerning the optimal solution E^*, let $\mathcal{C}^*_{4,0} = \{C \in \mathcal{C}^*_4 : \mathcal{L}(C) \subseteq \mathcal{L}(E_0)\}$ and $\mathcal{C}^*_{4,1} = \mathcal{C}^*_4 \setminus \mathcal{C}^*_{4,0}$. This means that for each cycle $C = (0, x, y, z, 0) \in \mathcal{C}^*_{4,1}$, we have $\mathcal{L}([x, y]) \notin \mathcal{L}(E_0)$ or $\mathcal{L}([y, z]) \notin \mathcal{L}(E_0)$ or both. Let $s^*_{4,i} = |\mathcal{C}^*_{4,i}|$ for $i = 0, 1$; by construction, $s^*_4 = s^*_{4,0} + s^*_{4,1}$. We have the following inequality:

$$|\mathcal{L}(E^*) \setminus \mathcal{L}(E_0)| \geq \frac{s^*_{4,1}}{f} \tag{9}$$

Actually, $|\mathcal{L}(E^*) \setminus \mathcal{L}(E_0)|$ is the number of colors of the cycles of $\mathcal{C}^*_4$ which do not belong to $\mathcal{L}(E_0)$. By construction, these cycles are in $\mathcal{C}^*_{4,1}$ and each one has at least one edge with a color in $\mathcal{L}(E^*) \setminus \mathcal{L}(E_0)$. Finally, since each color appears at most f times, the result follows.

On the other hand, we also have $|\mathcal{L}(E^*) \cap \mathcal{L}(E_0)| \geq |\mathcal{L}(E^* \cap E_0)| = |E^* \cap E_0| = n - s^*_4$. Hence, using this latter inequality, inequality (9) and $opt(I) = |\mathcal{L}(E^*) \setminus \mathcal{L}(E_0)| + |\mathcal{L}(E^*) \cap \mathcal{L}(E_0)|$, we obtain:

$$opt(I) \geq n - s^*_4 + \frac{1}{f} s^*_{4,1} \tag{10}$$

Since $R(E_0) = 0$, we also deduce for every $f \geq 2$:

$$\frac{1}{2} opt(I) \geq s^*_4 = (s^*_{4,0} + s^*_{4,1}) \tag{11}$$

Actually, the edges of E^* incident to the depot have distinct colors because $R(E_0) = 0$. Hence, since E^* contains s^*_4 cycles of cycles 4, we get $opt(I) \geq 2s^*_4$.

Now, we prove the main inequality:

Property 4. The following inequality holds:

$$s^*_{4,0} \leq (f + 4) s'_4 \tag{12}$$

Using equality (8) and inequalities (10), (11), (12), we obtain:

$$\begin{aligned} apx(I) &= n - s'_4 \\ &\leq n - \tfrac{s^*_{4,0}}{f+4} \\ &\leq \left(n - s^*_{4,0} + \tfrac{1}{f} s^*_{4,1}\right) + \tfrac{(f+3)}{f+4} s^*_{4,0} + \tfrac{(f-1)}{f} s^*_{4,1} \\ &\leq opt(I) + \tfrac{f+3}{f+4}(s^*_{4,0} + s^*_{4,1}) \\ &\leq opt(I) + \tfrac{1}{2} \times \tfrac{f+3}{f+4} opt(I) \\ &\leq (1 + \tfrac{f+3}{2f+8}) opt(I) \end{aligned}$$

The result follows. □

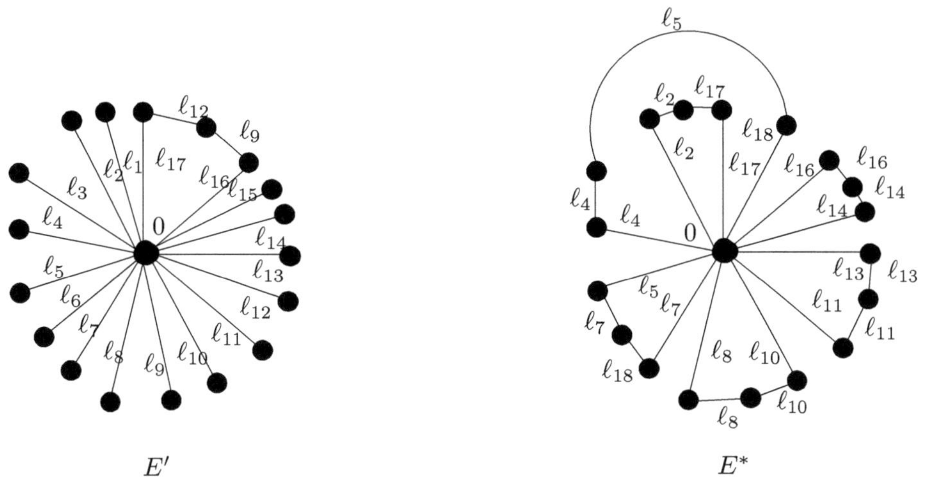

Fig. 2. An instance of LVRP$(3,2)$ with $R(E_0) = 0$ where E' is a $\frac{17}{12}$-approximation of the optimum. The value of approximate solution E' is $apx = |\mathcal{L}(E')| = 17$ where $\mathcal{L}(E') = \{\ell_1, \ldots, \ell_{17}\}$ while the value of optimal solution E^* is $opt = |\mathcal{L}(E^*)| = 12$ where $\mathcal{L}(E^*) = \{\ell_2, \ell_4, \ell_5, \ell_7, \ell_8, \ell_{10}, , \ell_{11}, \ell_{13}, \ell_{14}, \ell_{16}, \ell_{17}, \ell_{18}\}$.

Below, an instance proving that E' is exactly a $\left(1 + \frac{f+3}{2f+8}\right)$-approximation for LVRP$(3, f)$ when $R(E_0) = 0$ for $f = 2$. In Figure 2, only the edges of $E' \cup E^*$ are indicated. We complete the graph by adding a new color for each missing edge.

7 Conclusion

The results presented in this article give a good picture of the computational complexity of the problem. Indeed LVRP(k, f) is polynomial when $k = 1, 2$ or $f = 1$. LVRP$(3, 2)$ is polynomial if $f(E_0) = 1$ and **NP**-hard otherwise. In addition LVRP$(k, 2)$ for $k > 3$ and LVRP$(3, f)$ for $f > 2$ are **NP**-hard, even if $f(E_0) = 1$. Without any bound on f, the problem is - from an approximability point of view - closed since the approximation guarantee of any Hamiltonian cycle is almost the best we can expect.

In this paper we provide a non trivial analysis of simple approximation solutions like the star (or minimal solutions with respect to the colors used in some particular cases) but it would be interesting to investigate more elaborate approximation algorithms.

As a future work, it would be interesting to study the case when every label has a weight. The goal is to minimize the total weight of the labels used by a feasible solution, not the cardinality.

In another related problem, there is a known positive cost $c_{i,j}$, called *reload cost*, associated with every change from label i to label j. The goal is not the minimization of the number of labels but to minimize the sum of reload costs induced by the k-vehicle routing. Reload costs captures situations where the travel time crucially depends on the number of times the transportation mode is changed.

References

1. Bazgan, C., Hassin, R., Monnot, J.: Approximation Algorithms for Some Routing Problems. Discrete Applied Mathematics 146, 3–26 (2005)
2. Broersma, H., Li, X.: Spanning Trees with Many or Few Colors in Edge-Colored Graphs. Discussiones Mathematicae Graph Theory 17(2), 259–269 (1997)
3. Chang, R.-S., Leu, S.-J.: The Minimum Labeling Spanning Trees. Information Processing Letters 63(5), 277–282 (1997)
4. Couetoux, B., Gourvès, L., Monnot, J., Telelis, O.: On Labeled Traveling Salesman Problems. In: Hong, S.-H., Nagamochi, H., Fukunaga, T. (eds.) ISAAC 2008. LNCS, vol. 5369, pp. 776–787. Springer, Heidelberg (2008)
5. Garey, M.R., Johnson, D.S.: Computers and Intractability. A Guide to the Theory of NP-Completeness. Freeman, CA (1979)
6. Haimovich, M., Rinnooy Kan, A.H.G.: Bounds and Heuristics for Capacitated Routing Problems. Mathematics of Operations Research 10, 527–542 (1985)
7. Haimovich, M., Rinnooy Kan, A.H.G., Stougie, L.: Vehicle Routing Methods and Studies. In: Golden, A. (ed.) Analysis of Heuristics for Vehicle Routing Problems, pp. 47–61. Elsevier, Amsterdam (1988)
8. Hassin, R., Monnot, J., Segev, D.: Approximation Algorithms and Hardness Results for Labeled Connectivity Problems. J. of Combinatorial Optimization 14(4), 437–453 (2007)
9. Kirkpatrick, D.G., Hell, P.: On the Completeness of a Generalized Matching Problem. In: Proceedings of STOC 1978, pp. 240–245 (1978)
10. Monnot, J.: The Labeled Perfect Matching in Bipartite Graphs. Information Processing Letters 96, 81–88 (2005)
11. Monnot, J., Toulouse, S.: The Path Partition Problem and Related Problems in Bipartite Graphs. Operations Research Letters 35, 677–684 (2007)
12. Van-Nes, R.: Design of Multimodal Transport Networks: A Hierarchical Approach. PhD Thesis. Delft University Press (2002)

Improved Matrix Interpretation*

Pierre Courtieu, Gladys Gbedo, and Olivier Pons

Cédric – CNAM, Paris, France

Abstract. We present a new technique to prove termination of Term Rewriting Systems, with full automation. A crucial task in this context is to find suitable well-founded orderings. A popular approach consists in interpreting terms into a domain equipped with an adequate well-founded ordering. In addition to the usual interpretations: natural numbers or polynomials over integer/rational numbers, the recently introduced matrix based interpretations have proved to be very efficient regarding termination of string rewriting and of term rewriting. In this spirit we propose to interpret terms as polynomials over integer matrices. Designed for term rewriting, our generalisation subsumes previous approaches allowing for more orderings without increasing the search space. Thus it performs better than the original version. Another advantage is that, interpreting terms to actual polynomials of matrices, it opens the way to matrix non linear interpretations. This result is implemented in the CiME3 rewriting toolkit.

1 Introduction

The property of termination, well-known to be undecidable, is fundamental in many aspects of computer science and logic. It is crucial in the proof of programs correctness, it underlies induction proofs, etc. Despite its non-decidability, many heuristics have been proposed to provide automation for termination proofs. In particular, many heuristics have been defined in the framework of term rewriting systems (TRS). All of them require, possibly after several transformations of the initial termination problem, to search a well-founded ordering satisfying some properties. Among the different kinds of orderings, polynomial interpretations [19,4,6] and recursive path ordering [8] are the most used.

More recently matrix interpretation introduced in the context of string rewriting [16] and adapted to term rewriting system by Endrullis et al. in [11] has proved to be very efficient. They interpret term into vectors associating to each symbol a linear mapping with matrix coefficients. We propose a generalization of this method interpreting term into matrix and associating to each symbol an actual matrix polynomial. Our generalization subsumes the previous methods and allows for more matrices and more orderings. In particular it allows for more systems to be proved to be terminating without increasing the bounds for coefficients or the size of matrices.

* Work partially supported by A3PAT project of the French ANR (ANR-05-BLAN-0146-01).

J. van Leeuwen et al. (Eds.): SOFSEM 2010, LNCS 5901, pp. 283–295, 2010.

Due to the monotonicity requirement for interpretations, the original matrix interpretations are restricted to matrices with a strictly positive upper left coefficient, and the associated strict ordering only considers the upper coefficient on vectors. We propose weaker limitation still preserving monotonicity. We require for each matrices to have a fixed sub-matrix with no null columns. The strict ordering only consider coefficients corresponding to this sub-matrix. In this framework the original matrix interpretation is a particular case where the sub-matrix is reduced to the upper left coefficients.

Section 2 recalls preliminary notions on term rewriting systems, termination criteria, usual orderings and presents the matrix interpretation. It also introduces our model of presentation of termination proof as an inference tree [5]. Section 3 presents the extension we propose and the proof of its correctness. Section 4 describes the proof search and Section 5 presents severals examples. Section 6 illustrate the efficiency of our method on the *termination problems database (TPDB)* and show how it improves previous methods. Finally we present future work and conclude in Section 7.

2 Preliminaries

2.1 Term Rewriting Systems

We assume that the reader is familiar with basic concepts of term rewriting [9,3] and termination. We recall the usual notions, and give our notations.

Terms. A *signature* Σ is a finite set of *symbols* with fixed arities. Let X be a countable set of *variables*; $T(\Sigma, X)$ denotes the set of finite *terms* on Σ and X. $\Lambda(t)$ is the symbol at the root position in term t. We write $t|_p$ for the subterm of t at position p and $t[u]_p$ for term t where $t|_p$ is replaced by u. *Substitutions* are mappings from variables to terms and $t\sigma$ denotes the application of a substitution σ to a term t.

Monotonicity. A function $f : D^n \to D$ on a domain D is *monotonic* with respect to a relation R on D iff $\forall d_1, d_2 \in D$, $\forall 1 \leq i \leq n : \forall a_1, \ldots a_{i-1}, a_{i+1}, \ldots, a_n \in D, d_1 \; R \; d_2 \Rightarrow f(a_1, \ldots, a_{i-1}, d_1, a_{i+1}, \ldots, a_n) R \; f(a_1, \ldots, a_{i-1}, d_2, a_{i+1}, \ldots, a_n)$. We say that a *relation on terms* R is monotonic if all function symbols are monotonic with respect to R.

Rewriting. A *term rewriting system* (TRS for short) over a signature Σ is a set S of *rewrite rules* $l \to r$ with $l, r \in T(\Sigma, X)$. In this work we only consider *finite* systems. A TRS S defines a monotonic relation $\to_S$ closed under substitution (aka a *rewrite relation*) in the following way: $s \to_S t$ (s *reduces to* t) if there is a position p such that $s|_p = l\sigma$ and $t = s[r\sigma]_p$ for a rule $l \to r \in S$ and a substitution σ. We shall omit systems and positions that are clear from the context. We denote the reflexive-transitive closure of a relation $\to$ by $\to^\star$. Symbols occurring at root position in the left-hand sides of rules in S are said to be *defined*, the others are said to be *constructors*. We denote $\to_1 . \to_2$ the relation defined by $x \to_1 . \to_2 y$ iff $\exists z, x \to_1 z \to_2 y$ where $\to_1$ and $\to_2$ are two relations.

Ordering. Termination proofs usually make use of orderings and *ordering pairs* [18]. We use a slightly restricted definition of ordering pair but it does not interfere with the topic of this work. An ordering pair is a pair $(\geq, >)$ of relations over $T(\mathcal{F}, X)$ such that: 1) $\geq$ is a quasi-ordering, i.e. reflexive and transitive, 2) $>$ is a strict ordering, i.e. irreflexive and transitive, and 3) $\geq \cdot > = >$.

An ordering $>$ is *well-founded* (denoted by $\mathsf{WF}(>)$) if there is no infinite strictly decreasing sequence $t_1 > t_2 > \ldots$. An ordering pair $(\geq, >)$ is *well-founded* (denoted by $\mathsf{WF}(\geq, >)$ if its strict ordering is well-founded. An ordering $<$ is stable by substitution if $\forall \sigma \forall t \forall u, t < u \Rightarrow t\sigma < u\sigma$. An ordering pair is *stable* if $>$ and $\geq$ are stable by substitution. If a strict ordering $>$ is monotonic we call it *strictly monotonic* (denoted $\mathsf{SM}(>)$). An ordering pair $(\geq, >)$ is *weakly monotonic* (denoted by $\mathsf{WM}(\geq, >)$ if $\geq$ is monotonic and *strictly monotonic*(denoted by $\mathsf{SM}(\geq, >)$) if $>$ is monotonic.

Termination. A term is *S-strongly normalizable* if it cannot reduce infinitely many times for $\rightarrow_S$. A rewrite relation $\rightarrow_S$ *terminates* if any term is S-strongly normalizable, which we denote $\mathsf{SN}(\rightarrow_S)$. In such case we may say that S terminates. A termination criterion due to Manna and Ness [3] states that it is sufficient to find a stable and well-founded strictly monotonic ordering $>$ such that for all rule $l \rightarrow r \in S$, $l > r$. This is stated in the rule MN below.

Moreover, it is also well known that the lexicographic combination of two well-founded relations is well-founded. This is stated in the rule LEX below. An effective termination criterion using this property is described in [13]. It allows to prove the so-called *relative* termination of a relation of the form $\rightarrow^*_{S_1} \cdot \rightarrow_{S_2}$ by finding a strictly monotonic, stable and well-founded ordering pair $(\geq, >)$ for which all rules of S_1 decrease for $\geq$ and all rules of S_2 decrease for $>$. This is stated in the rule LEX_{AX} below.

Dependency pairs. The set of *unmarked* dependency pairs [2] of a TRS S, denoted $\mathsf{DP}(S)$ is defined as $\{\langle u, v\rangle \mid u \rightarrow t \in S \text{ and } t|_p = v \text{ and } \Lambda(v) \text{ is defined}\}$. Let $\mathscr{D}$ be a set of dependency pairs, a dependency chain in $\mathscr{D}$ is a *sequence* of dependency pairs $\langle u_i, v_i\rangle$ with a substitution σ such that $\forall i,\ v_i\sigma \xrightarrow[S]{\neq\Lambda\ \star} u_{i+1}\sigma$. Remark that to enhance this technique, implementations may distinguish the root symbols of dependency pairs (by means of marks). We will omit the details of this technique as it is not crucial in this work. Given a TRS S and a set of dependency pairs $\mathscr{D}$, $s \xrightarrow[S]{\neq\Lambda\ \star} u\sigma \xrightarrow[\langle u,v\rangle \in \mathscr{D}]{\Lambda} v\sigma \equiv t$ is denoted by $s \twoheadrightarrow_{\mathscr{D},S} t$. The main theorem of dependency pairs of [2] is the following: Let S be a TRS, $\twoheadrightarrow_{\mathsf{DP}(S),S}$ terminates if and only if $\rightarrow_S$ terminates. This is stated in the inference rule DP below. An effective technique for proving that $\twoheadrightarrow_{\mathscr{D},S}$ terminates consists in discovering a stable and well-founded *weakly monotonic* ordering pair $(\geq, >)$ for which $S \subseteq \geq$ and $\mathscr{D} \subseteq >$. This is stated in the rule DP_{AX} below.

Termination proofs. The algorithms of an automated termination prover is usually presented as popularised by the APROVE *processors* [15]. It transforms recursively problems into equivalent sets of sub-problems until each sub-problem can be directly solved by a suitable well-founded ordering (pair). We call *crite-*

rion a transformation of a well-foundation problem p into a set of new problems $p_1 \dots p_n$ such that p is well-founded iff $p_1 \dots p_n$ are. Following the idea introduced in [5,7] we model a termination proof by an inference tree where inference rules are criteria possibly guarded by a parameter (an ordering) and conditions. Guard conditions are properties that are not proved by inference trees but must be checked when applying rules. The termination criteria described above are summarized by the rules below[1]. Rules MN, Lex_{AX} and DP_{AX} are axioms of the inference system. In automated termination provers, these orderings are typically found by constraint solvers. In particular, term interpretation is a well-known method to define such orderings.

$$\text{MN}(>)\ \frac{}{\mathsf{SN}(\rightarrow_S)}\ \begin{array}{l}\text{WF}(>) \wedge \text{SM}(>)\\ \wedge \forall l \rightarrow r \in S, l > r\end{array}$$

$$\text{Lex}\ \frac{\mathsf{SN}(\rightarrow_{S_1})\quad \mathsf{SN}(\overset{*}{\rightarrow}_{S_1} \cdot \rightarrow_{S_2})}{\mathsf{SN}(\rightarrow_{S_1 \cup S_2})} \qquad \text{Lex}_{\text{AX}}(\geq,>)\ \frac{}{\mathsf{SN}(\overset{*}{\rightarrow}_{S_1} \cdot \rightarrow_{S_2})}\ \begin{array}{l}\text{WF}(\geq,>)\ \text{SM}(\geq,>)\\ \forall l \rightarrow r \in S_2, l > r\\ \forall l \rightarrow r \in S_1, l \geq r\end{array}$$

$$\text{DP}\ \frac{\mathsf{SN}(\twoheadrightarrow_{DP(S),S})}{\mathsf{SN}(\rightarrow_S)} \qquad \text{DP}_{\text{AX}}(\geq,>)\ \frac{}{\mathsf{SN}(\twoheadrightarrow_{\mathcal{D},S})}\ \begin{array}{l}\text{WF}(\geq,>)\ \text{WM}(\geq,>)\\ \forall \langle l,r\rangle \in \mathcal{D}, l > r\\ \forall l \rightarrow r \in S, r \geq l\end{array}$$

2.2 Orderings by Interpretation

As explained in section above, a crucial task in termination proofs is to find *strictly* or *weakly monotonic* ordering pairs. In this section we describe the general framework of homomorphic interpretations which allows for both. All the following results are well known and can be found in [14,8,3]. In the sequel we suppose a non empty set D (domain), a quasi-ordering $\geq_D$ on D, and $>_D = \geq_D - \leq_D$. Therefore $(\geq_D, >_D)$ is an ordering pair. The following definitions and results are well known:

Definition 2.2.1. *A* valuation function *is a function $v : X \rightarrow D$ from variables to D.*

Definition 2.2.2. *A* homomorphic interpretation *φ is a function that takes a symbol f and returns a function $[f]_\varphi : D^n \rightarrow D$, where n is the arity of f. We define the homomorphic interpretation $\varphi(t)$ of a (possibly non-closed) term t as a function from valuation functions to D by induction on t as follows: $\varphi(x)(v) = v(x)$ and $\varphi(f(t_1, \dots, t_n))(v) = [f]_\varphi(\varphi(t_1)(v), \dots, \varphi(t_n)(v))$.*

Definition 2.2.3. *We define the ordering pair $(\succeq_\varphi, \succ_\varphi)$ on terms by: $s \succeq_\varphi t$ iff $\forall v \in (X \rightarrow D)$, $\varphi(s)(v) \geq_D \varphi(t)(v)$ and $s \succ_\varphi t$ iff $\forall v \in (X \rightarrow D)$, $\varphi(s)(v) >_D \varphi(t)(v)$.*

Theorem 2.2.1. *$(\succeq_\varphi, \succ_\varphi)$ is stable, and well-founded if $(\geq_D, >_D)$ is.*

Theorem 2.2.2. *If $[f]_\varphi$ is monotonic with respect to $>_D$ (respectively $\geq_D$), then $(\succeq_\varphi, \succ_\varphi)$ is* strictly monotonic *(respectively weakly monotonic).*

[1] Refer to [7] for a detailed presentation of more criteria in a similar framework.

2.3 Matrix Interpretation

The main idea of matrix interpretation of [11] is to define homomorphic interpretations suitable to apply rules MN, Lex_{AX}(strictly monotonic), and DP_{AX} (weakly monotonic) by interpreting terms as vectors ($D = \mathbb{N}^d$) using linear mappings represented by polynomials with matrix coefficients. The ordering pair on $\mathbb{N}^d$, that we note $(\geq_{\mathbb{N}^d}, >_{\mathbb{N}^d})$ is defined as follows: $(u_i) \geq_{\mathbb{N}^d} (v_i)$ iff $\forall i,\ u_i \geq_{\mathbb{N}} v_i$ and $(u_i) >_{\mathbb{N}^d} (v_i)$ iff $\forall i,\ u_i \geq_{\mathbb{N}} v_i$ and $u_1 >_{\mathbb{N}} v_1$. As homomorphic interpretations defined by matrix polynomials may not be monotonic, Endrullis et alf [11] propose a restriction on the form of vectors and matrices to ensure strict monotonicity: the upper-left coefficient of vectors and matrices must be strictly positive.

In the following we define a family of interpretations parmetrized by the set of coefficients considered by the strict ordering. We adapt the restriction accordingly.

3 Generalized Matrix Interpretation

We use polynomials with *matrix* constants instead of vectors ($D = \mathbb{N}^{d \times d}$). This corresponds to the usual notion of polynomials where constants and coefficients have the same type. However all the following results and proofs are applicable to interpretations as defined in [11].

We define in the following matrix interpretation as homomorphic interpretations as defined in Section 2.2. First we define the ordering (family) $(\geq_{\mathbb{N}^{d\times d}}, >^E_{\mathbb{N}^{d\times d}})$ on the domain, then we define the form of an interpretation, finally we prove in which cases interpretations are weakly and strictly monotonic.

3.1 The Ordering

We define a family of orderings $(\geq_{\mathbb{N}^{d\times d}}, >^E_{\mathbb{N}^{d\times d}})$ parametrized by the set $E \subset \mathbb{N}$ of column and line numbers that can be considered for strict comparison between matrices (the large comparison being on all coefficients).

Definition 3.1.1. *We define the orderings $\geq_{\mathbb{N}^{d\times d}}$ and $>^E_{\mathbb{N}^{d\times d}}$ on $\mathbb{N}^{d\times d}$ as follows: Let $m, m' \in \mathbb{N}^{d\times d}$ and $E \subseteq \{1, ..., d\}$, $m \geq_{\mathbb{N}^{d\times d}} m' \iff \forall i,k \in [1..d], m_{ik} \geq_{\mathbb{N}} m'_{ik}$ and $m >^E_{\mathbb{N}^{d\times d}} m' \iff \forall i,k \in [1..d], m_{ik} \geq_{\mathbb{N}} m'_{ik} \wedge \exists i,j \in E, m_{ij} >_{\mathbb{N}} m'_{ij}$*

Remark 1. By definition, if $E \subset E'$ then $>^E_{\mathbb{N}^{d\times d}} \subset >^{E'}_{\mathbb{N}^{d\times d}}$.

Lemma 3.1.1. *For any E, $(\geq_{\mathbb{N}^{d\times d}}, >^E_{\mathbb{N}^{d\times d}})$ is a well-founded ordering pair.*

Proof. $>^E_{\mathbb{N}^{d\times d}}$ is well-founded because it is included in the ordering $>^{\Sigma}$ defined by $m >^{\Sigma} m' \iff \sum_{1 \leq i,j \leq d} m_{ik} >_{\mathbb{N}} \sum_{1 \leq ik \leq d} m_{ik}$ which is well-founded. Moreover $\geq_{\mathbb{N}^{d\times d}} . >^E_{\mathbb{N}^{d\times d}} \subseteq >^E_{\mathbb{N}^{d\times d}}$ follows from $\geq_{\mathbb{N}} . >_{\mathbb{N}} = >_{\mathbb{N}}$ on each coefficient. □

3.2 The Interpretation

We now define the homomorphic interpretation of a symbol $f \in \Sigma$ by a matrix linear polynomial, as explained in definition 2.2.2.

Definition 3.2.1 (matrix interpretation). *Given a signature Σ and a dimension $d \in \mathbb{N}$, a* matrix interpretation *φ is a homomorphic interpretation that takes a symbol f of arity n and returns a function of the form: $[f]_\varphi(m_1,\ldots,m_n) = F_1 m_1 + \cdots + F_n m_n + F_{n+1}$ where $F_i \in \mathbb{N}^{d \times d}$ and $m_1,\ldots,m_n$ take their values in $\mathbb{N}^{d \times d}$.*

Definition 3.2.2 (E-interpretation). *An E-interpretation is a matrix interpretation where the ordering pair used on matrices is $(\geq_{\mathbb{N}^{d\times d}}, >^E_{\mathbb{N}^{d\times d}})$.*

Definition 3.2.3. *The ordering pair $(\succeq_\varphi, \succ^E_\varphi)$ is defined from $(\geq_{\mathbb{N}^{d\times d}}, >^E_{\mathbb{N}^{d\times d}})$ as explained in definitions 2.2.3 (with $D = \mathbb{N}^{d\times d}$).*

Lemma 3.2.1. *Given an interpretation φ, The ordering pair $(\succeq_\varphi, \succ^E_\varphi)$ is (1) stable by substitution and (2) well-founded.*

Proof. (1) is proved by theorem 2.2.1 and (2) by theorems 2.2.1 and 3.1.1. □

The following lemma shows that homomorphic interpretations are weakly monotonic with respect to $(\succeq_\varphi, \succ^E_\varphi)$.

Lemma 3.2.2. *Let φ be a matrix interpretation. Then $(\succeq_\varphi, \succ^E_\varphi)$ is weakly monotonic.*

Proof. By lemma 2.2.2 it is sufficient to prove that for all symbol f, $[f]_\varphi$ is monotonic with respect to $\geq_{\mathbb{N}^{d\times d}}$. Let $f \in \Sigma$ of arity n and $1 \leq k \leq n$. Let x, y, $a_1 \ldots a_n \in \mathbb{N}^{d\times d}$ s.t. $x \geq_{\mathbb{N}^{d\times d}} y$, let us show that $[f]_\varphi(a_1,\ldots,a_{k-1},x,\ldots,a_n) \geq_{\mathbb{N}^{d\times d}} [f]_\varphi(a_1,\ldots,a_{k-1},y,\ldots,a_n)$. By definition there exists $n+1$ matrices F_i such that:

$$\begin{aligned}
[f]_\varphi(a_1,\ldots,a_{k-1},x,\ldots,a_n) &= F_1 a_1 + \ldots + F_k x + \ldots + F_n a_n + F_{n+1} \\
&= [f]_\varphi(\ldots,0,\ldots) + F_k x \\
[f]_\varphi(a_1,\ldots,a_{k-1},y,\ldots,a_n) &= F_1 a_1 + \ldots + F_k y + \ldots + F_n a_n + F_{n+1} \\
&= [f]_\varphi(\ldots,0,\ldots) + F_k y
\end{aligned}$$

Since the (matrix $\times$ matrix) product is monotonic with respect to $\geq_{\mathbb{N}^{d\times d}}$, $F_k x \geq_{\mathbb{N}^{d\times d}} F_k y$ and thus $[f]_\varphi(a_1,\ldots,a_{k-1},x,\ldots,a_n) \geq_{\mathbb{N}^{d\times d}} [f]_\varphi(a_1,\ldots,a_{k-1},y,\ldots,a_n)$. □

Remark 2. The corollary of this lemma is that all matrix interpretations are suitable to define weakly monotonic orderings on terms, whatever E is. Therefore according to remark 1 we will always chose the maximal $E = \{1,\ldots,d\}$ when searching weakly monotonic ordering pairs.

Remark 3. Since the (matrix $\times$ matrix) product is *not* monotonic with respect to $>^E_{\mathbb{N}^{d\times d}}$, there exists some E-interpretation such that $(\succeq_\varphi, \succ^E_\varphi)$ is not strictly monotonic.

Therefore we define the set of *E-compatible* matrices, parametrized by E, on which (matrix $\times$ matrix) product is monotonic with respect to $>^E_{\mathbb{N}^{d\times d}}$.

Definition 3.2.4. *Let $E \subseteq \{1, ..., d\}$, we call an E-position in a matrix $m \in \mathbb{N}^{d \times d}$ a position m_{ij} where $i \in E$ and $j \in E$. We also call E-columns and E-lines the sub-columns and sub-lines of E-positions.*

Definition 3.2.5 (E-compatible matrices). *Let $E \subseteq \{1, ..., d\}$, we say that a matrix $m \in \mathbb{N}^{d \times d}$ is* E-compatible *if and only if each E-column is non null, that is at least one E-position on each E-column is non null.*

For example the matrix $\begin{pmatrix} \underline{\mathbf{0}} & 1 & \underline{\mathbf{0}} & 0 \\ 0 & 0 & 0 & 0 \\ \underline{\mathbf{2}} & 3 & \underline{\mathbf{1}} & 0 \\ 0 & 2 & 1 & 0 \end{pmatrix}$ is $\{1, 3\}$-compatible whereas $\begin{pmatrix} \underline{\mathbf{1}} & 1 & \underline{\mathbf{0}} & 0 \\ 0 & 0 & 0 & 0 \\ \underline{\mathbf{2}} & 3 & \underline{\mathbf{0}} & 0 \\ 0 & 2 & 1 & 0 \end{pmatrix}$ is not.

Definition 3.2.6 (E-compatible interpretation). *Let φ be a matrix interpretation. We say that φ is E-compatible if for all symbol f s. t. $[f]_\varphi(m_1, \ldots, m_n) = F_1 m_1 + \cdots + F_n m_n + F_{n+1}$, the matrices $F_1 \ldots F_n$ are E-compatible. Notice that F_{n+1} does not need to be E-compatible.*

The following lemma shows that E-compatible homomorphic interpretations are strictly monotonic with respect to $(\succeq_\varphi, \succ_\varphi^E)$.

Lemma 3.2.3. *Let φ be an E-compatible interpretation. Then $(\succeq_\varphi, \succ_\varphi^E)$ is strictly monotonic.*

Proof. We proceed as above: By lemma 2.2.2 it is sufficient to prove that the following property holds for all symbol f (of arity n):

$$\forall 1 \leq k \leq n, \forall a_1 \ldots a_{i-1}, a_{i+1} \ldots a_n \in \mathbb{N}^{d \times d}, \forall x, y \in \mathbb{N}^{d \times d}, x >_{\mathbb{N}^{d \times d}}^E y \rightarrow$$
$$[f](a_1, \ldots, a_{k-1}, x, a_{k+1}, \ldots, a_n) >_{\mathbb{N}^{d \times d}}^E [f](a_1, \ldots, a_{k-1}, y, a_{k+1}, \ldots, a_n)$$

By definition there exists n E-compatible matrices $F_1 \ldots F_n$ and a matrix F_{n+1} s.t.:

$$[f](a_1 ..., x, ...a_n) = F_1 m_1 + ... + F_k x + ... + F_n m_n + F_{n+1} = [f](..., 0, ...) + F_k x$$
$$[f](a_1 ..., y, ...a_n) = F_1 m_1 + ... + F_k y + ... + F_n m_n + F_{n+1} = [f](..., 0, ...) + F_k y$$

Therefore it is sufficient to prove that $\forall 1 \leq k \leq n, \forall x, y \in \mathbb{N}^{d \times d}, x >_{\mathbb{N}^{d \times d}}^E y \Longrightarrow F_k x >_{\mathbb{N}^{d \times d}}^E F_k y$. Since the product ($E$ compatible matrix) $\times$ (matrix) is monotonic with respect to $>_{\mathbb{N}^{d \times d}}^E$, the statement of the lemma follows. □

The corollary of this lemma is that when an E-interpretation is E-compatible, it can be used to build a strictly monotonic ordering pair on terms.

3.3 Proving Termination

To prove termination of a given TRS R using rules MN, LEX$_{\text{AX}}$ or DP$_{\text{AX}}$, we need to compare matrix interpretations of the left hand side and the right hand side of rules with $\succ_\varphi$. These interpretations can be computed by developing polynomials, as stated by the two following lemmas:

Lemma 3.3.1. *Let φ be a matrix interpretation and t, a term with n free variables $x_1 \dots x_n$. There exists $n+1$ matrices $M_1 \dots M_{n+1}$ such that $\varphi(t)(v) = M_1 v(x_1) + \dots + M_n v(x_n) + M_{n+1}$.*

Proof. By induction on t. If t is a variable x, then by definition 2.2.2 the property holds: $\varphi(x)(v) = v(x)$. If $t = f(t_1, \dots, t_m)$ then by definition 2.2.2: $\varphi(t)(v) = [f]_\varphi(\varphi(t_1)(v), \dots, \varphi(t_m)(v)) = F_1(\varphi(t_1)(v)) + \dots + F_m(\varphi(t_m)(v)) + F_{m+1}$ where by induction hypothesis each $\varphi(t_i)(v)$ is itself a linear polynomial of the form $\sum_j M_{i_j} v(x_j) + M_{i_{n+1}}$. Thus $\varphi(t)(v)$ is equal to $(\sum_k F_k M_{k_1}) v(x_1) + \dots + (\sum_k F_k M_{k_n}) v(x_n) + (\sum_k F_k M_{k_{n+1}}) + F_{m+1}$. □

Lemma 3.3.2. *Let φ be an E-compatible homomorphic interpretation and t a term containing n variables $x_1 \dots x_n$. There exists a set of n E-compatible matrices $M_1 \dots M_n$ and a matrix M_{n+1} such that $\varphi(t)(v) = M_1 v(x_1) + \dots + M_n v(x_n) + M_{n+1}$.*

Proof. We proceed by the same induction as above and in equation above $F_1 \dots F_n$ are E-compatible matrices by hypothesis, and $M_{k_1} \dots M_{k_n}$ are E-compatible matrices by induction hypothesis. Since matrix addition and product are stable on E-compatible matrices we can conclude that the $\sum_k F_k M_{k_i}$ are E-compatible matrices in equation above. □

Therefore in order to check that rules or dependency pairs are decreasing, we must compare matrix linear polynomials, which is decidable:

Lemma 3.3.3. *Let t and u be terms such that $\varphi(t)(v) = L_1 v(x_1) + \dots + L_k v(x_k) + L_{k+1}$ and $\varphi(u)(v) = R_1 v(x_1) + \dots + R_k v(x_k) + R_{k+1}$. If $\forall 1 \leq i \leq k+1, L_i \geq_{\mathbb{N}^{d \times d}} R_i$ then $\varphi(t)(v) \geq_{\mathbb{N}^{d \times d}} \varphi(u)(v)$ for any valuation $v : \mathbb{N}^k \to \mathbb{N}$. If moreover $L_{k+1} >^E_{\mathbb{N}^{d \times d}} R_{k+1}$, then $\varphi(t)(v) >^E_{\mathbb{N}^{d \times d}} \varphi(u)(v)$ for any valuation $v : \mathbb{N}^k \to \mathbb{N}$.*

Proof. Let v be a valuation. Since $\forall 1 \leq i \leq k+1, L_i \geq_{\mathbb{N}^{d \times d}} R_i$, the matrix $m = \varphi(t)(v) - \varphi(u)(v)$ is such that $m = \sum_{i=1}^k ((L_i - R_i) v(x_i)) + L_{k+1} - R_{k+1} \geq_{\mathbb{N}^{d \times d}} 0$ which proves the first property. If $L_{k+1} >^E_{\mathbb{N}^{d \times d}} R_{k+1}$ then moreover we have $m \geq_{\mathbb{N}^{d \times d}} L_{k+1} - R_{k+1} >^E_{\mathbb{N}^{d \times d}} 0$. □

4 Proof Search

In this section we describe the adaptation of the method of [11] for generating termination proofs. The main differences are the choice of an E, the treatment of E-compatibility and the ordering constraints using E.

Due to the symmetrical shape of our orderings with respect to matrices, it is clear that for E and E' having the same cardinality, if there exists an E-interpretation satisfying conditions of lemma 3.3.3, then there exists an E'-interpretation satisfying the same conditions, obtained by applying to all matrices the same column and line permutation. Therefore it is enough to try each E of the form $\{1, \dots, n\}$ where $2 \leq n \leq d$.

4.1 Manna and Ness Criterion

In order to prove the termination of a given TRS S using Rule MN, we need to find an E and an E-compatible matrix interpretation φ such that $\forall l \to r \in S$, $\varphi(l) \succ_\varphi^E \varphi(r)$. This amounts to solving constraints on matrix coefficients. More precisely, for each rule $l \to r \in S$, where $\varphi(l) = \sum_1^n L_i x_i + L_{n+1}$ and $\varphi(r) = \sum_1^n R_i x_i + R_{n+1}$ (If r has less variables than l, the corresponding R_i are null matrices), we have the following constraint: $\forall 1 \leq i \leq n$, $L_i \geq_{\mathbb{N}^{d \times d}} R_i$ and $L_{n+1} >_{\mathbb{N}^{d \times d}}^E R_{n+1}$. The E-compatibility of interpretation are also expressed as constraints on E-positions.

We try to solve these constraints using a SAT solver, which is common practice [12,1],[11]. In order to call the SAT solver once, we encode the constraints corresponding to all desired sizes of E in one disjunctive formula.

4.2 Lexicographic Composition Criterion

In order to use the lexicographic criteria we need to split the TRS S into two systems S_1 and S_2, such that we can apply rule Lex_{AX} to prove $\mathsf{SN}(\to_1^* \cdot \to_2)$. Then we are left with the property $\mathsf{SN}(S_1)$ that can be proved by any other criterion recursively.

$$\text{Lex}\ \dfrac{\dfrac{\vdots}{\mathsf{SN}(\to_{S_1})} \qquad \text{Lex}_{\text{AX}}(\succeq_\varphi, \succ_\varphi^E)\ \dfrac{}{\mathsf{SN}(\to_{S_1}^* \cdot \to_{S_2})}\ \begin{array}{l} \text{WF}(\succeq_\varphi, \succ_\varphi^E)\ \text{SM}(\succeq_\varphi, \succ_\varphi^E) \\ \forall l \to r \in S_2, l \succ_\varphi^E r \\ \forall l \to r \in S_1, l \succeq_\varphi r \end{array}}{\mathsf{SN}(\to_{S_1 \cup S_2})}$$

In order to find φ we first fix E then we solve the following constraint: $\forall l \to r \in S, l \succeq_\varphi r \wedge \exists l \to r \in S, l \succ_\varphi^E r$. The existential part of this property may be expressed by a disjunction on rules of S. If a solution is found, then S_2 is the set of strictly decreasing rules and S_1 the remaining ones. As previously we can try several E.

4.3 Dependency Pairs Criterion

In order to use the dependency pair criterion, we first need to apply DP then find an matrix interpretation φ satisfying the condition of Rule DP_{AX}. This is done by similar techniques than above taking the maximal E as explained in remark 2.

4.4 Comparison with Previous Notions of Matrix Interpretation

The interpretation defined in [11] almost corresponds to one member of our family of interpretations, namely $\{1\}$-interpretations. To be precise it corresponds to $\{1\}$-interpretations where constant coefficients of polynomials are vectors instead of matrices. In the following we analyze the differences between $\{1\}$-interpretations and E-interpretations where $|E| > 1$ in the case of each criterion. For the symmetry reasons given in Section 4, we focus on $\{1, \ldots, k\}$-interpretations.

MN and LEX$_{\text{AX}}$—. In the strict monotonic setting, when $E \neq \{1\}$ matrix interpretations do not solve the same sets of problems. This is due to several facts. On one hand a greater E makes more matrices comparable. For instance $\begin{pmatrix} 1 & 0 \\ 1 & 1 \end{pmatrix}$ and $\begin{pmatrix} 1 & 0 \\ 0 & 1 \end{pmatrix}$ are comparable with $>^{\{1,2\}}_{\mathbb{N}^{2\times2}}$ but not with $>^{\{1\}}_{\mathbb{N}^{2\times2}}$. Therefore the comparison of *constant* coefficient of polynomials is more powerful when E is greater.

On the other hand strict monotonicity constraints (for non constant coefficients) are such that the sets of allowed matrices are different when E changes. More precisely there is no inclusion relation between them. For example if f is a unary symbol, then $[f](m) = \begin{pmatrix} \underline{\mathbf{0}} & 0 \\ 1 & 1 \end{pmatrix} m + \begin{pmatrix} 1 & 0 \\ 1 & 0 \end{pmatrix}$ is $\{1,2\}$-compatible and not $\{1\}$-compatible, whereas $[f](m) = \begin{pmatrix} 1 & \underline{\mathbf{0}} \\ 1 & \underline{\mathbf{0}} \end{pmatrix} m + \begin{pmatrix} 1 & 0 \\ 1 & 0 \end{pmatrix}$ is $\{1\}$-compatible and not $\{1,2\}$-compatible. Therefore the set of ordering problems solved by different sizes of E are usually different. For this reason an implementation should try all possible size for E. In practice in our prototype C*i*ME3 this is configurable.

DP$_{\text{AX}}$— In the weak monotonic setting, there is no monotonicity constraint on matrices, therefore the set of allowed matrices is the same whatever E is. Therefore the maximal $E = \{1, \ldots, n\}$ is always more powerful because, as said above, it allows for more matrices to be compared strictly.

However this statement is not true anymore when trying to remove *only one* pair $\langle l, r\rangle$ of a set of dependency pairs $\mathscr{D}$. This is done (for example in the graph refinement) by finding a weakly monotonic well-founded ordering pair $(\geq, >)$ such that: $l > r$ and $\forall\langle t, u\rangle \in \mathscr{D}, t \geq u$ and $\forall t \to u \in \mathscr{D}, t \geq u$. In that case, the fact that only one pair needs to be ordered strictly implies that if a solution exists with any non empty E, then by the adequate permutation of columns and lines, we can obtain an interpretation which also works for $E = \{1\}$. Therefore for example *the choice of E is not critical anymore* when using the graph refinement, as shown in the results of section 6. However, a greater E may lead to shorter proofs, which is interesting in the framework of termination *certificate* (see Section 7).

As a conclusion, we see that the best strategy is to try all possible sizes of E for MN and LEX, and only the maximal E for DP.

5 Examples

In this section we show examples of rewrite systems where $\{1,2\}$-interpretations are used to prove termination, whereas $\{1\}$-interpretations cannot. In all these examples, matrix coefficients are forced to be 0 or 1. It is worth noticing that some of these examples can be solved by $\{1\}$-interpretations if the bound on matrix coefficients is higher, but at a price of a greater search space.

LEX and LEX$_{\text{AX}}$— Consider the following rewrite system: $\{(1) plus(plus(x, y), z) \to plus(x, plus(y, z)); (2)\ times(x, s(y)) \to plus(x, times(y, x))\}$. Rule (2) can be removed as explained in section 4.2 by the following interpretation:

$$[plus]_\varphi(x,y) = \begin{pmatrix}1&0\\0&1\end{pmatrix}x + \begin{pmatrix}1&0\\0&1\end{pmatrix}y + \begin{pmatrix}1&0\\0&0\end{pmatrix} \quad [s]_\varphi(x) = \begin{pmatrix}1&1\\1&1\end{pmatrix}x + \begin{pmatrix}1&1\\1&1\end{pmatrix}$$

$$[times]_\varphi(x,y) = \begin{pmatrix}1&1\\1&1\end{pmatrix}x + \begin{pmatrix}0&1\\1&0\end{pmatrix}y$$

and rule (1) by: $$[plus]_\varphi(x,y) = \begin{pmatrix}1&0\\0&1\end{pmatrix}y + \begin{pmatrix}1&1\\0&1\end{pmatrix}x + \begin{pmatrix}0&1\\1&1\end{pmatrix}$$

DP— Consider the system: $f(0,x) \to f(s(x),x)$; $f(x,s(z)) \to s(f(0,z))$ which leads to the following dependency pairs: $\langle f(x,s(z)), f(0,z)\rangle$ and $\langle f(0,x), f(s(x),x)\rangle$. There is no matrix $\{1\}$-interpretation (with coefficients bound ≤ 1) such that all pairs are strictly decreasing and all rule weakly decreasing. However there is a $\{1,2\}$-interpretation (DP_{AX}):

$$[f]_\varphi(x,y) = \begin{pmatrix}0&0\\0&1\end{pmatrix}x + \begin{pmatrix}1&0\\1&0\end{pmatrix}y \quad [s]_\varphi(x) = \begin{pmatrix}1&0\\0&0\end{pmatrix}x + \begin{pmatrix}0&1\\0&0\end{pmatrix} \quad [0]_\varphi() = \begin{pmatrix}1&1\\0&1\end{pmatrix}$$

6 Results

The benchmarks were made with a prototype of C*i*ME on the 1436 problems of the termination problems database (TPDB) (category *standard TRS termination*, 2008-11-04 termination competition). Ordering constraints are solved by giving an upper bound b to matrix coefficients and then by translation to the SAT solver `minisat2` [10]. Each call to the SAT solver is limited to 100s and the overall timeout is 300s for each problem. The first table compares the number of problems solved using *matrix 2×2 interpretations only* with different E and b. The tested criteria are: MN, LEX, DP, DPG (graph refinement of dependency pairs), LGST (LEX *then* graph and subterm refinements). The latter being close to the best heuristic of C*i*ME. The second table shows the results using the strategy LGST and the usual combination of orderings of C*i*ME (linear polynomial, RPO, simple polynomial) followed by matrix interpretations (2×2 and 3×3). This shows how our matrix interpretations increase the power of the full system[2].

Ordering = Matrix interpretation only, matrix size = 2									
Criterion	MN			LEX			DP		
Bounds	1	2	3	1	2	3	1	2	3
$E=\{1\}$	88	167	186	230	278	285	266	345	358
$E=\{1,2\}$	+41,-0	+14,-0	+6,-6	+26,-0	+39,-2	+36,-3	+63,-0	+11,-1	+3,-2

Ordering = Matrix interpretation only, matrix size = 2						
Criterion	DPG			LGST		
Bounds	1	2	3	1	2	3
$E=\{1\}$	433	448	452	466	479	482
$E=\{1,2\}$	+0,-0	+0,-6	+0,-12	+14,-0	+30,-11	+30,-7

Ordering = usual+Matrix interpretation						
Criterion	LGST (mat. 2×2)			LGST (mat. 3×3)		
Bounds	1	2	3	1	2	3
$E=\{1\}$	576	583	586	592	588	587
$E=\{1,2\}$	+5,-0	+12,-0	+16,-1	+3,-0	+7,-10	+10,-10
$E=\{1,2,3\}$	N/A	N/A	N/A	+7,-3	+13,-19	+10,-17

[2] C*i*ME is devoted to certification of termination proofs, it only implements criteria that it can certify and it is not multi-threaded. Therefore it performs lower than state of the art provers such as APROVE.

A cell containing $+n, -m$ sums up the comparison with $E = \{1\}$: n new problems solved, m problems not solved anymore because of timeouts. Timeouts are caused by larger E leading to more complex constraints, despite the search space is the same. Our benchmarks showed an average overhead time of 20 to 30%. This explains why the current state of our implementation does not always reflect the expected improvement of our interpretations, in particular with 3×3 matrices. Except those timeouts, larger E is, as expected, always more powerful excepted in the DPG column (see section 4.4).

7 Conclusion and Future Work

Our approach generalizes the original matrix interpretations. It should naturally extend to other refinement of matrix interpretations such as arctic interpretations (where the usual plus/times operations are generalized to an arbitrary semi-ring [17]). Our approach using true polynomials over matrices, instead of mixing matrices and vectors, may allow for *matrix non linear polynomials*. Another point is that when discovering a solution our implementation (an early prototype of C*i*ME-3) *produces a proof trace* which we translate into a *proof certificate*[5] for verification. We are currently working on adapting our proofs to our matrix interpretations.

References

1. Annov, E., Codish, M., Giesl, J., Schneider-Kamp, P., Thiemann, R.: A Sat-Based Implementation for rpo Termination. In: International Conference on Logic for Programming, Artificial Intelligence and Reasoning (Short Paper) (November 2006)
2. Arts, T., Giesl, J.: Termination of Term Rewriting Using Dependency Pairs. Theoretical Computer Science 236, 133–178 (2000)
3. Baader, F., Nipkow, T.: Term Rewriting and All That. Cambridge University Press, Cambridge (1998)
4. Cherifa, A.B., Lescanne, P.: Termination of Rewriting Systems by Polynomial Interpretations and Its Implementation. Science of Computer Programming 9(2), 137–159 (1987)
5. Contejean, E., Courtieu, P., Forest, J., Pons, O., Urbain, X.: Certification of Automated Termination Proofs. In: Konev, B., Wolter, F. (eds.) FroCos 2007. LNCS (LNAI), vol. 4720, pp. 148–162. Springer, Heidelberg (2007)
6. Contejean, É., Marché, C., Tomás, A.P., Urbain, X.: Mechanically Proving Termination Using Polynomial Interpretations. Journal of Automated Reasoning 34(4), 325–363 (2005)
7. Courtieu, P., Forest, J., Urbain, X.: Certifying a Termination Criterion Based on Graphs, without Graphs. In: Mohamed, O.A., Muñoz, C., Tahar, S. (eds.) TPHOLs 2008. LNCS, vol. 5170, pp. 183–198. Springer, Heidelberg (2008)
8. Dershowitz, N.: Orderings for Term Rewriting Systems. Theoretical Computer Science 17(3), 279–301 (1982)
9. Dershowitz, N., Jouannaud, J.-P.: Rewrite Systems. In: van Leeuwen, J. (ed.) Handbook of Theoretical Computer Science, vol. B, pp. 243–320. North-Holland, Amsterdam (1990)

10. Eén, N., Biere, A.: Effective Preprocessing in SAT Through Variable and Clause Elimination. In: Bacchus, F., Walsh, T. (eds.) SAT 2005. LNCS, vol. 3569, pp. 61–75. Springer, Heidelberg (2005)
11. Endrullis, J., Waldmann, J., Zantema, H.: Matrix Interpretations for Proving Termination of Term Rewriting. Jar 40(2-3), 195–220 (2008)
12. Fuhs, C., Middeldorp, A., Schneider-Kamp, P., Zankl, H.: Sat Solving for Termination Analysis with Polynomial Interpretations. In: Marques-Silva, J., Sakallah, K.A. (eds.) SAT 2007. LNCS, vol. 4501, pp. 340–354. Springer, Heidelberg (2007)
13. Geser, A.: Relative Termination. Dissertation, Fakultät für Mathematik und Informatik, Universität Passau, Germany (1990) 105 pages. Also available as: Report 91-03, Ulmer Informatik-Berichte, Universität Ulm (1991)
14. Giesl, J. (ed.): RTA 2005. LNCS, vol. 3467. Springer, Heidelberg (2005)
15. Giesl, J., Thiemann, R., Schneider-Kamp, P., Falke, S.: Mechanizing and Improving Dependency Pairs. Journal of Automated Reasoning 37(3), 155–203 (2006)
16. Hofbauer, D., Waldmann, J.: Termination of String Rewriting with Matrix Interpretations. In: Pfenning, F. (ed.) RTA 2006. LNCS, vol. 4098, pp. 328–342. Springer, Heidelberg (2006)
17. Koprowski, A., Waldmann, J.: Arctic Termination..Below Zero. In: Voronkov, A. (ed.) RTA 2008. LNCS, vol. 5117, pp. 202–216. Springer, Heidelberg (2008)
18. Kusakari, K., Nakamura, M., Toyama, Y.: Argument Filtering Transformation. In: Nadathur, G. (ed.) PPDP 1999. LNCS, vol. 1702, pp. 47–61. Springer, Heidelberg (1999)
19. Lankford, D.S.: On Proving Term Rewriting Systems Are Noetherian. Technical Report MTP-3, Mathematics Department, Louisiana Tech. Univ. (1979), `http://perso.ens-lyon.fr/pierre.lescanne/not_accessible.html`

Efficient Algorithms for Two Extensions of LPF Table: The Power of Suffix Arrays*

Maxime Crochemore[1,3], Costas S. Iliopoulos[1,4],
Marcin Kubica[2], Wojciech Rytter[2,5,**], and Tomasz Waleń[2]

[1] Dept. of Computer Science, King's College London, London WC2R 2LS, UK
[2] Institute of Informatics, University of Warsaw, Warsaw, Poland
[3] Université Paris-Est, France
[4] Digital Ecosystems & Business Intelligence Institute, Curtin University of Technology, Perth WA 6845, Australia
[5] Faculty of Math. and Informatics, Copernicus University, Torun, Poland

Abstract. Suffix arrays provide a powerful data structure to solve several questions related to the structure of all the factors of a string. We show how they can be used to compute efficiently two new tables storing different types of previous factors (past segments) of a string. The concept of a longest previous factor is inherent to Ziv-Lempel factorization of strings in text compression, as well as in statistics of repetitions and symmetries. The longest previous reverse factor for a given position i is the longest factor starting at i, such that its reverse copy occurs before, while the longest previous non-overlapping factor is the longest factor v starting at i which has an exact copy occurring before. The previous copies of the factors are required to occur in the prefix ending at position $i-1$. We design algorithms computing the table of longest previous reverse factors (LPrF table) and the table of longest previous non-overlapping factors (LPnF table). The latter table is useful to compute repetitions while the former is a useful tool for extracting symmetries. These tables are computed, using two previously computed read-only arrays (SUF and LCP) composing the suffix array, in linear time on any integer alphabet. The tables have not been explicitly considered before, but they have several applications and they are natural extensions of the LPF table which has been studied thoroughly before. Our results improve on the previous ones in several ways. The running time of the computation no longer depends on the size of the alphabet, which drops a log factor. Moreover the newly introduced tables store additional information on the structure of the string, helpful to improve, for example, gapped palindrome detection and text compression using reverse factors.

Keywords: Longest previous reverse factor, longest previous non-overlapping factor, longest previous factor, palindrome, runs, Suffix Array, text compression.

---

* Research supported in part by the Royal Society, UK.
** Supported by grant N206 004 32/0806 of the Polish Ministry of Science and Higher Education.

J. van Leeuwen et al. (Eds.): SOFSEM 2010, LNCS 5901, pp. 296–307, 2010.

1 Introduction

In this paper we show new algorithmic results which exploit the power of suffix arrays [5]. Two useful new tables related to the structure of a string are computed in linear time using additionally the power of data structures for Range Minimum Queries (RMQ, in short) [7]. We assume throughout the paper we have an integer alphabet, sortable in linear time. This assumption implies we can compute the suffix array in linear time, with constant coefficient independent of the alphabet size.

The first problem is to compute efficiently, for a given string y, the LPrF table, that stores at each index i the maximal length of factors (substrings) that both start at position i in y and occur reverse at a smaller position.

The LPrF table is a concept close to the LPF table for which the previous occurrence is not reverse (see [6] and references therein). The latter table extends the Ziv-Lempel factorization of a text [17] intensively used for conservative text compression (known as LZ77 method, see [1]). In the sense of the definition the LPnF table differs very slightly from LPF (because the latter allows overlaps between the considered occurrences while the former does not), but the LPF table is a permutation of the LCP array, while LPnF usually is not, and the algorithms for LPnF differ much from those for LPF.

The LPrF table generalises a factorization of strings used by Kolpakov and Kucherov [13] to extract certain types of palindromes in molecular sequences. These palindromes are of the form uvw where v is a short string and w is the complemented reverse of u (complement consists in exchanging letters A and U, as well as C and G, the Watson-Crick pairs of nucleotides). These palindromes play an important role in RNA secondary structure prediction because they signal potential hair-pin loops in RNA folding (see [3]). In addition the reverse complement of a factor has to be considered up to some degree of approximation.

An additional motivation for considering the LPrF table is text compression. Indeed, it may be used, in connection with the LPF table, to improve the Ziv-Lempel factorization (basis of several popular compression software) by considering occurrences of reverse factors as well as usual factors. The feature has already been implemented in [10] but without LPrF and LPF tables, and our algorithm provides a more efficient technique to compress DNA sequences under the scheme.

As far as we know, the LPrF table of a string has never been considered before. Our source of inspiration was the notion of LPF table and the optimal methods for computing it in [6]. It is shown there that the LPF table can be derived from the Suffix Array of the input string both in linear time and with only a constant amount of additional space.

Our second problem, the computation of the LPnF table of non-overlapping previous factors, emerged from a version of Ziv-Lempel factorization. An alternative algorithm solving this problem was given in [16]. The factorization it leads to plays an important role in string algorithms because the work done on an element of the factorization is skipped since already done on one of its previous occurrences. A typical application of this idea resides in algorithms to compute repetitions in strings (see [4,14,12]). It happens that the algorithm for the LPnF table computation is a simple adaptation of the algorithm for LPrF. It may be surprising, because in one case we deal with exact copies of factors and in the second with reverse copies.

In this article we show that the computation of the LPrF and LPnF tables of a string can be done in linear time from its Suffix Array. So, we get the same running time as the algorithm described in [13] for the corresponding factorization although our algorithm produces more information stored in the table and ready to be used. Based on it, the factorizations of strings used for designing string algorithms may be further optimised.

In addition to the Suffix Array of the input string, the algorithm makes use of the RMQ data structure that yields constant-time queries answers. The question of whether for integer alphabets a direct linear-time algorithm not using all this machinery exists is open.

2 Preliminaries

Let us consider a string $y = y[0\,..\,n-1]$ of length n. By y^R we denote the reverse of y, that is $y^R = y[n-1]y[n-2]\ldots y[0]$. The LPF table (see [6] and references therein), and the two other tables we consider, LPrF and LPnF, are defined (for $0 \leq i < n$) as follows (see Figure 2):

$$\begin{aligned}
\mathsf{LPF}[i] &= \max\{j : \exists_{0\leq k<i} : y[k\,..\,k+j-1] = y[i\,..\,i+j-1]\}\\
\mathsf{LPrF}[i] &= \max\{j : \exists_{0\leq k\leq i-j} : y[k\,..\,k+j-1]^R = y[i\,..\,i+j-1]\}\\
\mathsf{LPnF}[i] &= \max\{j : \exists_{0\leq k\leq i-j} : y[k\,..\,k+j-1] = y[i\,..\,i+j-1]\}
\end{aligned}$$

It can be noted that in the definition of the LPF table the occurrences of $y[k\,..\,k+j-1]$ and $y[i\,..\,i+j-1]$ may overlap, while it is not the case with the other above concepts. For example, the string $y =$ abbabbaba has the following tables:

position i	0	1	2	3	4	5	6	7	8
$y[i]$	a	b	b	a	b	b	a	b	a
LPF$[i]$	0	0	1	5	4	3	2	2	1
LPrF$[i]$	0	0	2	1	3	3	2	2	1
LPnF$[i]$	0	0	1	3	3	3	2	2	1

We start the computation of these arrays with computation of the Suffix Array for the text y. It is a data structure used for indexing the text. It comprises two

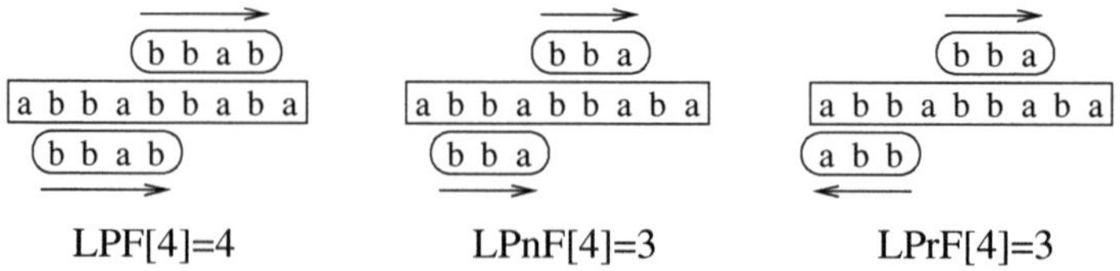

Fig. 1. Illustration of LPF[4], LPnF[4] and LPrF[4] for the string abbabbaba

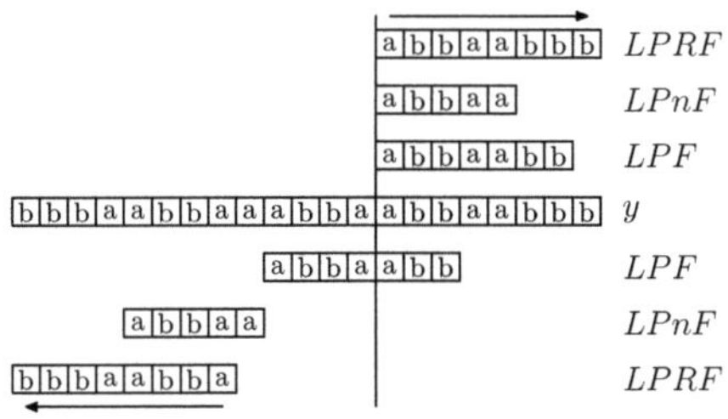

Fig. 2. Comparison of LPF, LPrF and LPnF notions; it shows differences between LPF and LPnF

tables denoted by SUF and LCP, and defined as follows. The SUF array stores the list of positions in y sorted according to the increasing lexicographic order of suffixes starting at these positions. That is, the SUF table is such that:

$$y[\mathsf{SUF}[0]\,..\,n-1] < y[\mathsf{SUF}[1]\,..\,n-1] < \ldots < y[\mathsf{SUF}[n-1]\,..\,n-1]$$

Thus, indices of SUF are ranks of the respective suffixes in the increasing lexicographic order. The Suffix Array can be built in time $O(n)$ (see [5]). The LCP array is also indexed by the ranks of the suffixes, and stores the lengths of the longest common prefixes of consecutive suffixes in SUF. Let us denote by $\mathsf{lcp}(i, j)$ the length of the longest common prefix of $y[i\,..\,n-1]$ and $y[j\,..\,n-1]$ (for $0 \le i, j < n$). Then, we set $\mathsf{LCP}[0] = 0$ and, for $0 < r < n$, we have:

$$\mathsf{LCP}[r] = \mathsf{lcp}(\mathsf{SUF}[r-1], \mathsf{SUF}[r])$$

For example, the Suffix Array of the text $y =$ abbabbaba is:

rank r	0	1	2	3	4	5	6	7	8
$\mathsf{SUF}[r]$	8	6	3	0	7	5	2	4	1
$\mathsf{LCP}[r]$	0	1	2	5	0	2	3	1	4

In the algorithms presented in this paper we use the Minimum (Maximum) Range Query data-structure (RMQ, in short). Let us assume, that we are given an array $A[0\,..\,n-1]$ of numbers. This array is preprocessed to answer the following form of queries: given an interval $[\ell\,..\,r]$ (for $0 \le \ell \le r < n$), find the minimum (maximum) value $A[k]$ for $\ell \le k \le r$.

The problem RMQ has received much attention in the literature. Bender and Farach-Colton [2] presented an algorithm with $O(n)$ preprocessing complexity and $O(1)$ query time, using $O(n \log n)$-bits of space. The same result was previously achieved in [9], albeit with a more complex data structure. Sadakane [15], and recently Fischer and Heun [8] presented a succinct data structures, which achieve the same time complexity using only $O(n)$ bits of space.

3 The Technique of Alternating Search

At the heart of our algorithms for computing the LPrF and LPnF tables, there is a special search in a given interval of the table SUF for a position k (the best candidate) which gives the next value of the table (LPrF or LPnF). This search is composed of two simple alternating functions, so we call it here the *alternating search.*

Assume we have an integer function $Val(k)$ which is non-increasing for $k \geq i$. Our goal is to find any position k in the given range $[i\,..\,j]$, which maximises $Val(k)$ and satisfies some given property $Candidate(k)$ (we call values satisfying $Candidate(k)$ simply *candidates*). We assume, that $Val(k)$ and $Candidate(k)$ can be computed in $O(1)$ time. Let us also assume, that the following two functions are computable in $O(1)$ time:

- $FirstMin(i, j)$ — returns the first position k in $[i\,..\,j]$ with the minimum value of $Val(k)$,
- $NextCand(i, j)$ — returns any candidate k from $[i\,..\,j)$ if there are any, otherwise it returns some arbitrary value not satisfying $Candidate(k)$.

Without loss of generality, we can assume that j is a candidate — otherwise, we can narrow our search to the range $[i\,..\,NextCand(i, j)]$. Please, observe, that:

$$Val(k) > Val(j) \text{ for } i \leq k < FirstMin(i, j)$$

Hence, if $FirstMin(i, j) > i$ and $NextCand(i, FirstMin(i, j))$ is a candidate, then we can narrow our search to the interval $[i\,..\,NextCand(i, FirstMin(i, j))]$. Otherwise, j is the position we are looking for.

Consequently, we can iterate $FirstMin$ and $NextCand(i, k)$ queries, increasing with each step the value of $Val(j)$ by at least one unit. This observation is crucial for the complexity analysis of our algorithms.

Algorithm 1. Alternating-Search(i, j)

```
k := initial candidate in the range [i..j], satisfying Candidate;
while Candidate(k) do
    j := k;  k := NextCand(i, FirstMin(i, j));
return j;
```

Lemma 1. *Let k = Alternating-Search(i, j). The execution time of Alternating-Search(i, j) is $O(Val(k) - Val(j) + 1)$.*

Proof. Observe, that each iteration of the while loop, except the last one, increases $Val(k)$ by at least one. The last iteration assigns the value of k to j, which is then returned as a result. Hence, the number of iterations performed by the while loop is not greater than $Val(k) - Val(j) + 1$. Each iteration requires $O(1)$ time, what concludes the proof. □

In the following two sections, we apply the Alternating-Search algorithm to compute the LPrF and LPnF tables. Our strategy is to design the algorithm in which, in each invocation of the Alternating-Search algorithm, the initial value of $Val(k)$ is smaller than the previously computed element of the LPrF/LPnF table by at most 1. In other words, we start with a reasonably good candidate, and the cost of a single invocation of the Alternating-Search algorithm can be charged to the difference between two consecutive values. The linear time follows from a simple amortisation argument. The details are in the following sections.

4 Computation of the LPrF Table

This section presents how to calculate the LPrF table, for a given string y of size n, in $O(n)$ time. First, let us create a string $x = y\#y^R$ of size $N = 2n + 1$ (where $\#$ is a character not appearing in y). For the sake of simplicity, we set that $y[n] = \#$ and $y[-1] = x[-1] = x[N]$ are defined and smaller than any character in $x[0\,..\,N-1]$.

Let SUF be the suffix array related to x, RANK be the inverse of SUF (that is $\mathsf{SUF}[\mathsf{RANK}[i]] = i$, for $0 \le i < N$), and LCP be the longest common prefix table related to x. Let i and j, $0 \le i, j < N$ be two different positions in x, and let $i' = \mathsf{RANK}[i]$ and $j' = \mathsf{RANK}[j]$. Observe, that:

$$\mathsf{lcp}(i,j) = \min\{\mathsf{LCP}[\min(i',j') + 1\,..\,\max(i',j')]\}$$
$$\mathsf{LPrF}[i] = \max\{\mathsf{lcp}(i,j) : j \ge N - i\}$$

Let us define two arrays: $\mathsf{LPrF}_>$ and $\mathsf{LPrF}_<$, which are variants of the LPrF array restricted to the case, where the first mismatch character in the reversed suffix is greater (smaller) than the corresponding character in the suffix. More formally, using x:

$$\mathsf{LPrF}_>[i] = \max\left\{\begin{array}{r} j : \exists_{N-i \le k \le N-j} : x[k\,..\,k+j-1] = x[i\,..\,i+j-1] \\ \text{and} \;\; x[k+j] > x[i+j] \end{array}\right\}$$
$$\mathsf{LPrF}_<[i] = \max\left\{\begin{array}{r} j : \exists_{N-i \le k \le N-j} : x[k\,..\,k+j-1] = x[i\,..\,i+j-1] \\ \text{and} \;\; x[k+j] < x[i+j] \end{array}\right\}$$

The following lemma, formulates an important property of the LPrF array, which is extensively used in the presented algorithm.

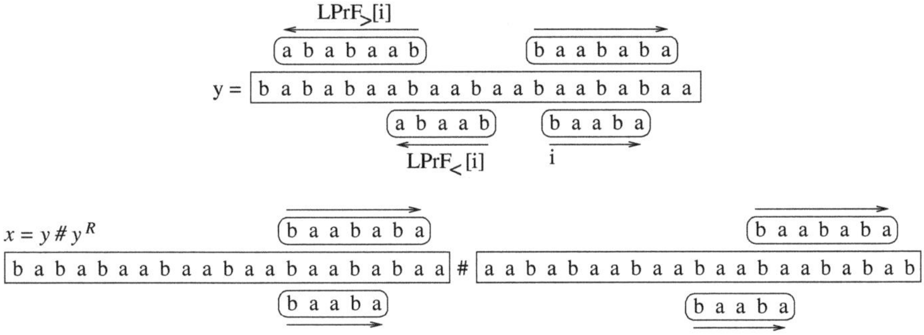

Fig. 3. Examples of $\mathsf{LPrF}_>$ and $\mathsf{LPrF}_<$ values, in the text y and in $x = y\#y^R$

Lemma 2. *For $0 < i < n$, we have $\mathsf{LPrF}_>[i] \geq \mathsf{LPrF}_>[i-1]-1$ and $\mathsf{LPrF}_<[i] \geq \mathsf{LPrF}_<[i-1]-1$.*

Proof. Without loss of generality, we can limit the proof to the first property. Let $\mathsf{LPrF}_>[i-1] = j$. So, there exists some $k < i-1$, such that: $y[k-j+1\,..\,k]^R = y[i-1\,..\,i+j-2]$ and $y[k-j] > y[i+j-1]$. Omitting the first character, we obtain: $y[k-j+1\,..\,k-1]^R = y[i\,..\,i+j-2]$ and $y[k-j] > y[i+j-1]$ and hence $\mathsf{LPrF}_>[i] \geq j-1 = \mathsf{LPrF}_>[i-1]-1$. □

In the algorithm computing the LPrF array, we use two data structures for RMQ queries. They are used to answer, in constant time, two types of queries:

- $\mathsf{FirstMinPos}(p, q, \mathsf{LCP})$ returns the first (from the left) position in the range $[p\,..\,q]$ with minimum value of LCP,
- $\mathsf{MaxValue}(p, q, \mathsf{SUF})$ returns the maximal value from $\mathsf{SUF}[p\,..\,q]$.

Lemma 3. *The $\mathsf{MaxValue}(p, q, \mathsf{SUF})$ and $\mathsf{FirstMinPos}(p, q, \mathsf{LCP})$ queries require $O(n)$ preprocessing time, and then can be answered in constant time.*

Proof. Clearly, the SUF and LCP arrays can be constructed in $O(n)$ time (see [5]). The $\mathsf{MaxValue}(p, q, \mathsf{SUF})$ and $\mathsf{FirstMinPos}(p, q, \mathsf{LCP})$ queries are applied to the sequence of $O(n)$ length. Hence they require $O(n)$ preprocessing time and then can be answered using Range Minimum Queries in constant time (see [7]). Note that, in the $\mathsf{FirstMinPos}$ query we need slightly modified range queries, that return the first (from the left) minimal value, but the algorithms solving RMQ problem can be modified to accommodate this fact. □

Algorithm 2. Compute-$\mathrm{LPrF}_>$

```
initialization: LPrF>[0] := 0; k0 := 0 ;
for i = 1 to n − 1 do
    r_i := RANK(i) { start Alternating Search } ;
    k := InitialCandidate(k_{i−1}, LPrF>[i − 1]) ;
    while k ≥ N − i do
        k_i := k;  r_k := RANK(k) ;
        r'_k := FirstMinPos(r_i + 1, r_k, LCP);  LPrF>[i] := LCP[r'_k] ;
        if r_i + 1 < r'_k then k := MaxValue(r_i + 1, r'_k − 1, SUF) else break;
return LPrF>;
```

Function `InitialCandidate` (k, l)

```
if l > 0 then return k + 1 else return N;
```

Algorithm 2 computes the $\mathsf{LPrF}_>$ array from left to right. In each iteration it also computes the value k_i, which is the position of the substring (in the second half of x), that maximizes $\mathsf{LPrF}_>[i]$. Namely, if $\mathsf{LPrF}_>[i] = j$, then:

$$y[i\,..\,i+j-1] = x[k_i\,..\,k_i+j-1] = y[N-k_i-j+1\,..\,N-k_i]^R$$

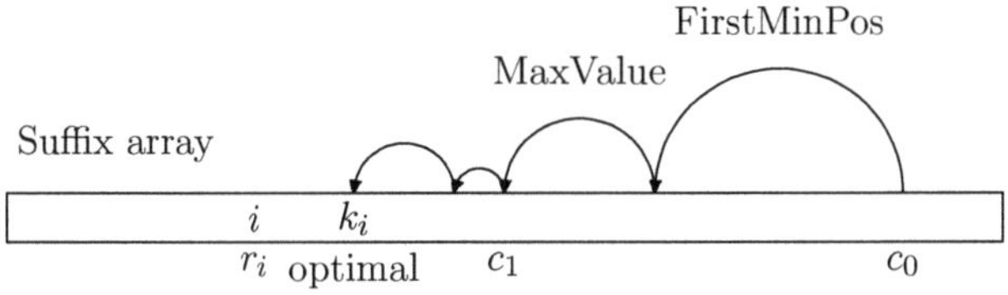

Fig. 4. Iterations of the while loop of Algorithm 2

Lemma 4. *Algorithm 2 works in $O(n)$ time.*

Proof. We prove this lemma using amortized cost analysis. The amortization function equals $\mathsf{LPrF}_>[i]$. Initially we have $\mathsf{LPrF}_>[0] = 0$.
Observe, that the body of the for loop is an instance of the Algorithm 1, with:

$$\begin{aligned} \mathit{Val}(k) = \mathsf{lcp}(i,k), \quad \mathit{Candidate}(k) \equiv k \geq N - i \\ \mathit{FirstMin}(i,k) = \mathsf{FirstMinPos}(\mathsf{RANK}[i]+1, \mathsf{RANK}[k], \mathsf{LCP}) \\ \mathit{NextCand}(i,j) = \mathsf{MaxValue}(\mathsf{RANK}[i]+1, j-1, \mathsf{SUF}) \end{aligned}$$

Hence, by Lemmas 1 and 2, each iteration of the for loop takes $O(\mathsf{LPrF}_>[i] - \mathsf{LPrF}_>[i-1]+2)$ time, and the overall time complexity of Algorithm 2 is $O(n + \mathsf{LPrF}[n-1] - \mathsf{LPrF}[0]) = O(n)$.

The correctness of the algorithm follows from the fact that (for each i) the body of the while loop is executed at least once (as a consequence of Lemma 2). □

Theorem 1. *The LPrF array can be computed in $O(n)$ time. For (polynomially bounded) integer alphabets the complexity does not depend on the size of the alphabet.*

Proof. The table $\mathsf{LPrF}_<$ can be computed using similar approach in $O(n)$ time. Then, $\mathsf{LPrF}[i] = \max(\mathsf{LPrF}_<[i], \mathsf{LPrF}_>[i])$. □

5 Longest Previous Non-overlapping Factor

This section presents how to calculate the LPnF table in $O(n)$ time. First, let us investigate the values of the LPnF array. For the sake of simplicity, we set that $y[n]$ is defined and smaller than any character in $y[0\,..\,n-1]$. For each value $j = \mathsf{LPnF}[i]$, let us have a look at the characters following the respective factors of length j. Let $0 \leq k < i$ be such that $y[k\,..\,k+j-1] = y[i\,..\,i+j-1]$. There are two possible reasons, why these factors cannot be extended:

- either the following characters do not match (that is, $y[k+j] \neq y[i+j]$), or
- they match, but if the factors are extended, then they would overlap (that is, $y[k+j] = y[i+j]$ and $k+j = i$).

We divide the LPnF problem into two subproblems, and (for $0 \le i < n$) define:

$$\mathsf{LPnF}^M[i] = \max\left\{ \begin{array}{r} j : \exists_{k<j} : y[k \mathinner{..} k+j-1] = y[i \mathinner{..} i+j-1], \\ y[k+j] \neq y[i+j] \text{ and } k+j \le i \end{array} \right\}$$

$$\mathsf{LPnF}^O[i] = \max\{j : \exists_{k<j} : y[k \mathinner{..} k+j-1] = y[i \mathinner{..} i+j-1] \text{ and } k+j = i\}$$

It is easy to see that $\mathsf{LPnF}[i] = \max\{\mathsf{LPnF}^M[i], \mathsf{LPnF}^O[i]\}$. The $\mathsf{LPnF}^O[i]$ is, in fact, the maximum radius of a square that has its center between positions $i-1$ and i. Such array can be easily computed in linear time from runs, using approach proposed in [12]. The LPnF^O array can also be computed without using runs, however we leave it for the full version of the paper.

We have to show how to compute the LPnF^M array. Following the same scheme we have used for the LPrF problem, we reduce this problem to the computation of two tables, namely $\mathsf{LPnF}^M_>$ and $\mathsf{LPnF}^M_<$, defined as LPnF^M with the restriction that the mismatch character in the previous factor $y[k+j]$ is greater (smaller) than $y[i+j]$. More formally:

$$\mathsf{LPnF}^M_>[i] = \max\left\{ \begin{array}{r} j : \exists_{0 \le k \le i-j} : y[k \mathinner{..} k+j-1] = y[i \mathinner{..} i+j-1] \\ \text{and } \; y[k+j] > y[i+j] \end{array} \right\}$$

$$\mathsf{LPnF}^M_<[i] = \max\left\{ \begin{array}{r} j : \exists_{0 \le k \le i-j} : y[k \mathinner{..} k+j-1] = y[i \mathinner{..} i+j-1] \\ \text{and } \; y[k+j] < y[i+j] \end{array} \right\}$$

Clearly, $\mathsf{LPnF}^M[i] = \max(\mathsf{LPnF}^M_>[i], \mathsf{LPnF}^M_<[i])$. Without loss of generality, we can limit our considerations to computing $\mathsf{LPnF}^M_>$. Just like LPrF, the $\mathsf{LPnF}^M_>$ array has the property, that for any i, $1 < i \le n$, $\mathsf{LPnF}^M_>[i] \ge \mathsf{LPnF}^M_>[i-1] - 1$.

Algorithm 4. Compute-$\mathsf{LPnF}_>$

```
initialization: LPnF^M_>[0] := 0; k_0 = 0 ;
for i = 1 to n − 1 do
    r_i := RANK[i];  (k, l) = InitialCandidate(k_{i−1}, LPnF^M_>[i − 1]) ;
    while l = 0 or k + l ≤ i do
        k_i = k;  r_k := RANK[k];  r'_k := FirstMinPos(r_i + 1, r_k, LCP) ;
        LPnF^M_>[i] := l ;
        if [r_i + 1 ≤ r'_k − 1] ≠ ∅ then
            k := MinValue(r_i + 1, r'_k − 1, SUF);  l := lcp(r_i, RANK[k]) ;
        else break;
return LPnF^M_>;
```

Function `InitialCandidate`(k, l)

```
if l > 0 then return (k + 1, l − 1) else return (n, 0);
```

Lemma 5. *For $0 < i < n$, we have $\mathsf{LPnF}^M_>[i] \ge \mathsf{LPnF}^M_>[i-1] - 1$.*

Proof. Let $\mathsf{LPnF}^M_>[i-1] = j$. So, there exists some $0 \le k \le i-j-1$, such that $y[k \mathinner{..} k+j-1] = y[i-1 \mathinner{..} i+j-2]$ and $y[k+j] > y[i+j-1]$. If we omit the first characters, then we obtain $y[k+1\,..\,k+j-1] = y[i\,..\,i+j-2]$ and $y[k+j] > y[i+j-1]$, and hence $\mathsf{LPnF}^M_>[i] \geq j-1 = \mathsf{LPnF}^M_>[i-1]-1$. □

In the algorithm computing the $\mathsf{LPnF}^M_>$ array, we use two data structures for RMQ queries. They are used to answer, in constant time, two types of queries:

- $\mathsf{FirstMinPos}(p, q, \mathsf{LCP})$ returns the first (from the left) position in the range $[p\,..\,q]$ with minimum value of LCP,
- $\mathsf{MinValue}(p, q, \mathsf{SUF})$ returns the minimal value from $\mathsf{SUF}[p\,..\,q]$.

Lemma 6. *Algorithm 4 works in $O(n)$ time.*

Proof. We prove this lemma using amortized cost analysis. The amortization function equals $\mathsf{LPnF}^M_>[i]$. Initially we have $\mathsf{LPnF}^M_>[0] = 0$. Please observe, that the body of the for loop is an instance of the Algorithm 1, with:

$$Val(k) = \mathsf{lcp}(i,k), \quad Candidate(k) \equiv k+l \leq i \text{ or } l = 0$$
$$FirstMin(i,k) = \mathsf{FirstMinPos}(\mathsf{RANK}[i]+1, \mathsf{RANK}[k], \mathsf{LCP})$$
$$NextCand(i,j) = \mathsf{MinValue}(\mathsf{RANK}[i]+1, j-1, \mathsf{SUF})$$

Hence, by Lemmata 1 and 5, each iteration of the for loop takes $O(\mathsf{LPnF}^M_>[i] - \mathsf{LPnF}^M_>[i-1]+2)$ time, and the overall time complexity of Algorithm 4 is $O(n + \mathsf{LPnF}^M_>[n-1] - \mathsf{LPnF}^M_>[0]) = O(n)$.

The correctness of the algorithm follows from the fact that (for each i) the body of the while loop is executed at least once (as a consequence of 5). □

Theorem 2. *The LPnF array can be computed in $O(n)$ time (without using the suffix trees). For (polynomially bounded) integer alphabets the complexity does not depend on the size of the alphabet.*

Proof. The table $\mathsf{LPnF}^M_<$ can be computed using similar approach in $O(n)$ time. As already mentioned, the LPnF^O array can also be computed in $O(n)$ time. Then, $\mathsf{LPnF}[i] = \max(\mathsf{LPnF}^M_<[i], \mathsf{LPnF}^M_>[i], \mathsf{LPnF}^O[i])$. □

6 Applications to Text Compression

Several text compression algorithms and many related software are based on factorizations of input text in which each element is a factor of the text occurring at a previous position possibly extended by one character (see [1] for variants of the scheme). We assume, to simplify the description, that the current element occurs before as it is done in LZ77 parsing [17], which is related a notion of complexity of strings.

An improvement on the scheme, called optimal parsing, has been proposed in [11]. It optimises the parsing by utilising a semi-greedy algorithm. The algorithm reduces the number of elements of the factorization. Algorithm 6 is an abstract semi-greedy algorithm for computing factorization of the word w. At a given step, instead of choosing the longest factor starting at position i and

Algorithm 6. AbstractSemiGreedyfactorization(w)

```
i = 1; j = 0; n = |w| ;
while i ≤ n do
    j = j + 1 ;
    if w[i] doesn't appear in w[1..(i − 1)] then f_j = w[i];
    else
        f_j = u such that uv is the longest prefix of w[i..n] for which u appears
        before position i and v appears before position i + |u|.
    i = i + |f_j| ;
return (f_1 ... f_j)
```

occurring before, which is the greedy technique, the algorithm chooses the factor whose next factor goes to the furthest position. The semi-greedy scheme is simple to implement with the LPF table. We should also note, that LPrF array can be used to construct reverse Lempel-Ziv factorization described in [13] in $O(n)$ time, while in [13] authors present $O(n \log \Sigma)$ algorithm.

Combining reverse and non-reverse types of factorization is a mere application of the LPF (or LPnF) and LPrF tables as shown in Algorithm 7. We get the next statement as a conclusion of the section.

Theorem 3. *The optimal parsing using factors and reverse factors can be computed in linear time independently of the alphabet size.*

Algorithm 7. LinearTimeSemiGreedyfactorization(w)

```
i = 1; j = 0; n = |w| ;
compute LPF and LPrF arrays for word w ;
let MAXF[i] = max{LPF[i], LPrF[i]} ;
let MAXF+[i] = MAXF[i] + i ;
prepare MAXF+ for range maximum queries ;
while i ≤ n do
    j = j + 1 ;
    if w[i] doesn't appear in w[1..(i − 1)] then f_j = w[i];
    else
        let k = MAXF[i] ;
        find i ≤ q < i + k such that MAXF+[q] is maximal ;
        f_j = w[i..q] ;
return (f_1..f_j)
```

References

1. Bell, T.C., Clearly, J.G., Witten, I.H.: Text Compression. Prentice Hall Inc., New Jersey (1990)
2. Bender, M.A., Farach-Colton, M.: The LCA Problem Revisited. In: Gonnet, G.H., Viola, A. (eds.) LATIN 2000. LNCS, vol. 1776, pp. 88–94. Springer, Heidelberg (2000)

3. Böckenhauer, H.-J., Bongartz, D.: Algorithmic Aspects of Bioinformatics. Springer, Berlin (2007)
4. Crochemore, M.: Transducers and Repetitions. Theoretical Computer Science 45(1), 63–86 (1986)
5. Crochemore, M., Hancart, C., Lecroq, T.: Algorithms on Strings. Cambridge University Press, Cambridge (2007)
6. Crochemore, M., Ilie, L., Iliopoulos, C., Kubica, M., Rytter, W., Waleń, T.: LPF Computation Revisited. In: Fiala, J., Kratochvíl, J., Miller, M. (eds.) IWOCA 2009. LNCS, vol. 5874, pp. 158–169. Springer, Heidelberg (2009)
7. Fischer, J., Heun, V.: Theoretical and Practical Improvements on the RMQ-Problem, with Applications to LCA and LCE. In: Lewenstein, M., Valiente, G. (eds.) CPM 2006. LNCS, vol. 4009, pp. 36–48. Springer, Heidelberg (2006)
8. Fischer, J., Heun, V.: A New Succinct Representation of RMQ-Information and Improvements in the Enhanced Suffix Array. In: Chen, B., Paterson, M., Zhang, G. (eds.) ESCAPE 2007. LNCS, vol. 4614, pp. 459–470. Springer, Heidelberg (2007)
9. Gabow, H., Bentley, J., Tarjan, R.: Scaling and Related Techniques for Geometry Problems. In: Symposium on the Theory of Computing (STOC), pp. 135–143 (1984)
10. Grumbach, S., Tahi, F.: Compression of DNA Sequences. In: Data Compression Conference, pp. 340–350 (1993)
11. Hartman, A., Rodeh, M.: Optimal Parsing of Strings. In: Apostolico, A., Galil, Z. (eds.) Combinatorial Algorithms on Words, Computer and System Sciences, vol. 12, pp. 155–167. Springer, Berlin (1985)
12. Kolpakov, R.M., Kucherov, G.: Finding Maximal Repetitions in a Word in Linear Time. In: FOCS, pp. 596–604 (1999)
13. Kolpakov, R.M., Kucherov, G.: Searching for Gapped Palindromes. In: Ferragina, P., Landau, G.M. (eds.) CPM 2008. LNCS, vol. 5029, pp. 18–30. Springer, Heidelberg (2008)
14. Main, M.G.: Detecting Leftmost Maximal Periodicities. Discret. Appl. Math. 25, 145–153 (1989)
15. Sadakane, K.: Succinct Data Structures for Flexible Text Retrieval Systems. Journal of Discrete Algorithms 5(1), 12–22 (2007)
16. Tischler, G.: Personal communication
17. Ziv, J., Lempel, A.: A Universal Algorithm for Sequential Data Compression. IEEE Transactions on Information Theory, 337–343 (1977)

Query Optimization through Cached Queries for Object-Oriented Query Language SBQL

Piotr Cybula[1] and Kazimierz Subieta[2,3]

[1] Institute of Mathematics and Computer Science, University of Lodz, Lodz, Poland
cybula@math.uni.lodz.pl
[2] Institute of Computer Science, Polish Academy of Sciences, Warsaw, Poland
subieta@ipipan.waw.pl
[3] Polish-Japanese Institute of Information Technology, Warsaw, Poland

Abstract. We present a new approach to optimization of query languages using cached results of previously evaluated queries. It is based on the stack-based approach (SBA) and object-oriented query language SBQL, which assume description of semantics in the form of abstract implementation of query/ programming language constructs. Pragmatic universality of SBQL and its precise, formal operational semantics make it possible to investigate various crucial issues related to this kind of optimization, in particular, organization of the cache enabling fast retrieval of cached queries, decomposition of complex queries into smaller ones and query normalization enabling higher reuse of cached queries, development of fast method to recognize consistency of queries after database updates and development of methods of incremental altering of cached query results after database updates. This paper is focused on the issues concerning optimal and fast utilization of the result cache and on the elimination method devoted to detecting cached queries that become inconsistent after a database update.

1 Introduction

Caching results of previously evaluated queries seems to be an obvious method of query optimization. It assumes that there is a relatively high probability that the same query will be issued again by the same or another application, thus instead of evaluating the query the cached result can be reused. There are many cases when such an optimization strategy makes a sense. This concerns the environments where data are not updated or are updated not frequently. Examples are data warehouses (OLAP applications), various kinds of archives, legal regulations databases, knowledge bases, decision support systems, etc. Some operational databases, where the frequency of updates is small in comparison to the frequency of retrieval (say, one update for 100 retrieval operations) are also candidates for application caching queries methods.

Besides the frequency of database updates, which is critical to such methods, another critical factor concerns the probability of caching query reuse. For some environments this probability is very high. For instance, in a typical internet shop we can estimate that 90% of requests concerns some 10% of products, hence queries addressing these 10% products are worth to be cached. Such caching (in the form of HTML pages or XML files) is assumed in many commercial Web applications, in particular,

J. van Leeuwen et al. (Eds.): SOFSEM 2010, LNCS 5901, pp. 308–320, 2010.

in projects that we were involved in. For databases where the probability of cached query reuse is low such methods are of course inefficient. For instance, a database on current mobile phone connections gives a little chance to reuse a cached query before it will be invalid due to a database change.

Cached queries remind materialized views, which are also snapshots on database states and are used for enhancing information retrieval. There are, however, two essential differences. The first one concerns the scale. One can expect that there will be at most dozens of materialized views, but the number of cached queries could be thousands or millions. Such a scale difference implies the conceptual difference. The second difference concerns transparency: while materialized views are explicit for the users, cached queries are an internal feature that is fully transparent for the users. Our research is just about how this transparent mechanism can be used to query optimization, assuming no changes in syntax, semantics and pragmatics of the query language itself.

Cached queries are also similar to database indices. Both cached queries and indices are server-side auxiliary structures that are used for fast retrieval. For instance, an item of a dense index having a key value "designer" from the *Job* attribute of the *Person* table can be perceived as a cached SBQL query <*Person* where *Job* = "designer", collection of OIDs>, where the 'collection of OIDs' is a non-key index value (object identifiers returned by the query) associated with the key value "designer" in the index. This observation suggests implementation of cached queries in the form of data structures, where a collection of similar cached queries is represented by a query with a parameter, augmented by a two-column table. Its first column contains the value of the parameter (key value) and the second column contains the query result for this parameter (non-key value). For fast retrieval such a structure can be implemented e.g. as a hash table or B-tree, similarly to the methods of organizing indices. However cached queries are conceptually different from indices. Indices usually materialize very simple queries, while in general we can cache arbitrarily complex queries if they are promising to be reused. For instance, we can consider caching queries containing multi-parameterized selections, aggregations, long path expressions, grouping, etc. Indices are also made in advance, while cached queries are a side effect of previous query evaluations. Indices contain items for all database values of the given attribute (e.g. for all values of the *Job* attribute), while cached queries usually contain only a subset of them. There is also a difference in updating: indices are usually automatically updated after altering a database, while for cached queries the updating problem is a research issue (that we will try to discuss in this paper). For these reasons cached queries imply quite new research and implementation problems.

In the following we assume a special server-side data structure recording all cached queries; we call it *query cache registry* or simply *cache*. Conceptually, the cache can be understood as a two-column table, where one column contains queries in some internal format (e.g. normalized syntactic query trees), and the second column contains query results. A query result can be stored as a collection of OIDs, but for special purposes can also be stored e.g. as an XML file enabling further quick reuse in Web applications. There are several strategies of dealing with cached queries and a lot of combinations of these strategies. A cached query can be created as a side effect of normal evaluation of user query or by the database administrator in advance. It is also possible that not all queries are to be cached, but only some of them that are promising for reuse. There are also several strategies of removing cached queries from the cache (providing limits of the cache size or limited maintenance cost). The choice of a combination of particular strategies can be predefined, or alternatively can be the subject of more complex strategy involving some query evaluation cost model. The model must involve at least the following costs:

- The cost of creating cached query. As suggested by the above strategies, the cost is less significant concerning creation of the cached query itself (creation is a side effect), but can be increased if putting a query into the cache requires additional actions, e.g. checking the query if it is promising to be reused, if it should be decomposed to subqueries, etc.
- The cost of an extra RAM and/or disk space. Nowadays this is a minor problem.
- The cost of using the cache. If the cache would be very large, searching for a given query may be a time-consuming process, in many cases unsuccessful (the input query is not cached).
- The cost of cache maintenance. After a database update some cached queries are no more consistent thus should be removed, altered or re-calculated. The issue is the bottleneck of the whole affair and therefore in this paper we devote to it more attention.

In this paper we deal mainly with the methods of fast retrieval of cached queries and the method allowing fast recognition which cached queries are affected by a database update (thus must be removed, altered or re-calculated). Our concept of cached queries follows the work presented in [17] and [21], devoted to a kind of a network database model. In comparison, object-oriented and XML-oriented data models and their query languages present new qualities, thus the methods that we discuss and propose are significantly different. Our research is done within the Stack-Based Approach (SBA) to object-oriented query/programming languages. SBA is a formal theory and a universal conceptual frame addressing this kind of languages, thus it allows precise reasoning concerning various aspects of caching queries, in particular, query semantics, query decomposition, query indexing in the cache, and so on. The caching query methods we have implemented as a part of the optimizer developed for the query language SBQL (Stack-Based Query Language) in our last project ODRA (Object Database for Rapid Application development) devoted to Web and grid applications [15]. In [7] we have described how query caching can be used to enhance performance of applications operating on grids. We based our consideration on grid architecture where the key element is the mechanism of updatable views. We showed where in this architecture caching can be implemented and how query rewriting techniques can use these cached results.

The database literature contains few papers devoted to cached queries. A relevant, but rather obsolete work [12] (oriented towards the relational algebra) concerns usability of a set of cached queries in the query optimization processes. The approach of maintaining cached queries assumed in the paper resembles the idea presented in [2], but the relationship between the number of database updates and the data units to maintain is in the case of cached queries opposite to that of materialized views case described in the paper. There are many papers concerning maintenance of relational materialized views, for instance see [3,4]. The papers assume some restrictions on a query language expressions and cached structures. Such materialized views are currently implemented in popular relational database systems as DB2 and Oracle [10,16]. Materialization of query results in object-oriented algebras in the form of materialized views is considered in [1] and [11]. In [5] and [19] a solution for XML query processing using materialized XQuery views is proposed. The authors of these papers present an algebraic approach for incremental maintenance of such views.

New Oracle 11g database system [16] offers also caching of SQL and PL/SQL results. The cached results of SQL queries and PL/SQL functions are automatically reused while subsequent invocation and updated after database modifications. On the other hand, in opposition to our proposal, materialization of the results is not fully transparent. Query results are cached only when query code contains a comment with a special parameter 'result_cache', so the evaluation of old codes without the parameter is not optimized. Cache update is also supported with dedicated syntactic clause 'relies_on' in stored function declaration with a list of tables, modification of which extorts the invalidation of the results while next call of the function.

Query cache is also implemented into MySQL database [14], where only full SELECT query texts together with the corresponding results are stored in the cache. In the solution caching does not work for subselects and stored procedure calls (even if it simply performs select query). Queries must be absolutely the same - they have to match byte by byte for cache utilization, because of matching of not normalized query texts (e.g. the use of different letter case causes insertion of different queries into the query cache). MySQL maintains table level granularity for invalidation – if a table changes, all cached queries that use the table become invalid and are removed from the cache. There is no incremental update mechanism.

The paper is organized as follows. In section 2 we briefly present the Stack-Based Approach. Section 3 describes the architecture of query optimization using cached queries, main problems concerning it and our suggestions for solving them. Section 4 contains the description of the cache update strategies, in particular the elimination method proposed for recognizing of cached query independence of database update. Section 5 presents experimental results and Section 6 concludes.

2 Overview of the Stack-Based Approach (SBA)

The *Stack-Based Approach* (SBA) along with its query language SBQL (*Stack-Based Query Language*) is the result of investigations into a uniform conceptual and semantic platform for integrated query and programming languages for object-oriented databases. SBA assumes that query languages are a special case of programming languages. The approach is abstract and universal, which makes it relevant to a general object model. SBA makes it possible to precisely determine the semantics of query languages, their relationships with object-oriented concepts, with imperative programming constructs, and with programming abstractions, including procedures, functional procedures, views, modules, etc. SBA respects the naming-scoping-binding principle, which means that each name occurring in a query is bound to the appropriate run-time entity (an object, attribute, method parameter, etc) according to the scope of this name. One of its basic mechanisms is an environment stack (ES), which is responsible for scope control and for binding names. In contrast to classical stacks, it does not store objects, but some structures built upon object identifiers, names, and values. SBA assumes the principles of semantic relativity, orthogonal persistence and full internal identification.

Stack-Based Query Language (SBQL) is in details described in [19,20]. The language has several implementations - for the XML DOM model, for OODBMS Objectivity/DB, and recently for the object-oriented ODRA system [15]. SBQL is based on an abstract syntax and the principle of *compositionality*: it avoids syntactic sugar and syntactically separates as far as possible query operators. In contrast to SQL and OQL, SBQL queries have the useful property: they can be easily decomposed into subqueries, down to atomic ones, connected by unary or binary operators. The property simplifies implementation and greatly supports query optimization. The syntax of SBQL is as follows:

- A single name or a single literal is an (atomic) query. For instance, *Student*, *name*, *year*, *x*, *y*, "Smith", 2, 2500, etc, are queries.
- If q is a query, and σ is a unary operator (e.g. sum, count, distinct, sin, sqrt), then $\sigma(q)$ is a query.
- If q_1 and q_2 are queries, and θ is a binary operator (e.g. **where**, dot, **join**, +, =, **and**), then $q_1\ \theta\ q_2$ is a query.

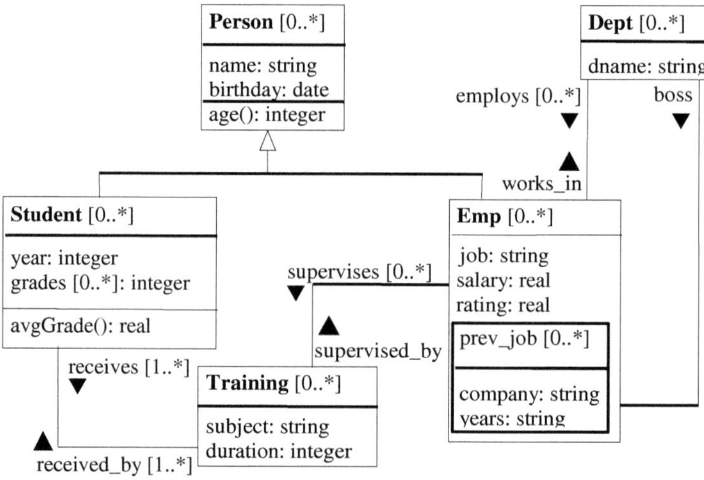

Fig. 1. Class diagram of the example database

To present an example SBA object store we assume the class diagram in Fig.1. The schema defines five classes (i.e. five collections of objects): *Training*, *Student*, *Emp*, *Person*, and *Dept*. The classes *Training*, *Student*, *Emp* and *Dept* model students receiving trainings, which are supervised by employees of departments organizing these trainings. *Person* is the superclass of the classes *Student* and *Emp*. An *Emp* objects can contain multiple complex *prev_job* subobjects (previous jobs). Names of classes (as well as names of attributes and links) are followed by cardinality numbers, unless the cardinality is 1.

3 Optimization Using Cached Queries

Cache registry organization. Since the amount of cached queries may be very large, structures used to implement the query registry must ensure very fast access and search capabilities. We propose the linear hashing table [13] with a single, primary key as fast and efficient search data structure for cached results. The single key retrieval is very simple to implement and independent of the query type - the response time is short and always the same regardless of the complexity of request. There are several candidate solutions for the search key. The simplest one is simply a query text (normalized using some sophisticated techniques) considered as a character string. Taking into account the equivalence of text of a query and its syntactic tree, instead of difficult searching within the set of syntactic trees of cached queries, we can search in the efficient and proved linear hashing index structure containing texts. Non-key values of the index are references to the metabase nodes containing meta-information concerning cached queries, i.e. a signature of cached results for type-checking purposes and a reference to the data store node containing compiled cached query (for further reevaluation), cached results, statistic data and auxiliary structures for efficient update of the results after database change (maintained in the next section). Queries are cached both in the physical object store (persistent memory cache guarantying maintenance of the cache after database restart) and in virtual object store (volatile main memory cache guarantying fast access).

Query optimization steps. Query optimization using cached results involves main subsystems of query evaluation environment, such query optimizer, query interpreter and query cache registry placed in the object store and a metabase. We propose the following algorithm of the optimization using cached queries in query evaluation environment for SBA:

1. A user sends a query to a database system.
2. The parser receives it and transforms to form of a syntactic tree.
3. This tree is sent to the cache optimizer being one of many optimizers, which rewrites it. To prevent from placing in the cache queries with different text forms but the same semantic meanings we introduce several query text normalization methods. Most of these methods can be easily applied in a way of reconstructing a query text from early generated query syntactic tree. The main methods are: alphabetical ordering of operands for operators, which for a succession of operands is not substantial, ordering of operators (e.g. putting sum operations before subtractions), object name and auxiliary name unification. The normalization methods are thoroughly presented in [8].
4. Additionally the optimizer analyses the query as a candidate for caching. Too simple queries (without object names or non-algebraic operators) are omitted. If possible, it is virtually decomposed into one or many simpler candidate subqueries. Query decomposition is a useful mechanism to speed up evaluating a greater number of new queries. If we materialize a small independent subquery instead of a whole complex query, then the probability of reusing of its results is risen. In addition, a simple semantic of the decomposed query reduces the costs of its updating. We use such decomposition techniques (widely described in [8])

such factoring out independent subqueries, removing path expressions finalizing query evaluation and transforming queries into equivalent forms using operations on Boolean expressions and on sets of query results (bags). Finally the modified query evaluation plan is produced.

5. The optimizer analyses the query in context of the set of cached queries defined in the query cache registry. Query is converted to the text form and the optimizer performs search process using query index stored in the cache registry. Each (sub)tree of found cached (sub)query is replaced with call of an appropriate special cache function defined in the registry for the chosen cached query (parameterized with references to its nodes in the metabase and object store). Each not yet cached candidate (sub)query is also replaced with call of the cache function – new cached query is placed into query index. In this case query node in object store doesn't contain query results – it is marked as not fully cached and will be populated with its results while the first need of use. Finally the modified query syntactic tree is compiled into query evaluation plan and analyzed by the type-checker.
6. The plan is executed by the query interpreter. Call of the special cache function causes returning materialized results of used cached query from the query cache registry. Not yet cached or marked for update queries are evaluated and their results are stored and utilized immediately. If a cached query is used, the system updates its use counter. Use counters are used to generate global cache statistics implemented as priority lists of use levels in form of MRU lists. The system controls the cache by deleting unprofitable, rarely used cached queries (by count of use cases or last use time stamp) or queries dependent on too often updates. Such cache adaptability property is performed under the control of the administrator, who configures cache system parameters. For each new cached query system generates additional structures, which describe a subset of involved objects for maintenance purposes. The system updates cached results after changes in the database accordingly to the algorithm presented in the next section.
7. After the evaluation of whole query plan interpreter sends its results to the user.

Taking into account the client/server architecture the above scenario is valid when all the query processing is performed on the server (c.f. SQL). In the ODRA system majority of query processing is shifted to the client side, to avoid server overloading. In such a case the method of cached queries needs to be changed. Firstly, similarly to indices, the cached query registry is stored at the server. Hence the client-side query optimizer should look up in this registry before starts optimization and processing a given query. Secondly, the storing of the query result should also be processed differently. Because only the client knows the form of the query and its result, the client is responsible to send the pair <query, result> to the server in order to include it within the caching query registry.

4 Update of Cached Results

The main problem of the cache maintenance concerns an aspect of synchronization of the cache with the database state. If a database is updated then some of cached queries may not be up to date - their results may be wrong, therefore some synchronization steps are required. On the other hand, reevaluating all of the queries materialized in the cache may spend too much time, at the expense of a cost necessary to answer for other queries. It is necessary to recognizing the possibly small group of cached queries which could be affected by the changes in a database. We have chosen for this purpose an elimination method introduced for first time in the context of the NETUL query language, which was constructed for network databases [17], [21].

The elimination method. The elimination method aims at removing from consideration those queries that are certainly not influenced by a database update. Since in the modified database they still remain valid, their cached results can be eliminated from the synchronization process, and in consequence the process will proceed much faster. To facilitate this task the method based on the concept of "subschema" is used. A subschema sufficient for a query is a part of the database schema necessary to process the query. Similarly, a subschema sufficient for an update contains that part of the database schema, instances of which have been altered, removed or inserted. The subschema for a cached query is generated by a special function when the query is cached and is stored together with cached query results. The subschema for an update is generated by another function, which analyses the transaction registry and the metabase.

Recognizing if a query result is affected by a database update requires comparing the sufficient subschemas for the query and the update. If these subschemas are disjoint (in a proper sense) then the update cannot influence the cached query. Thus the query is eliminated from the updating process. Such comparison must be done for all cached queries. The comparison can be much fasten by a properly organized index (presented in the next subsection) which makes it possible fast retrieval of all the queries that can be affected by an update.

The efficiency of elimination may depend on the applied subschema language and in consequence on the data structures and algorithms used for storing the subschemas and comparing them. Subschema languages with better precision (which better approximate necessary parts of the database schema) allow to eliminate more cached queries. More precise languages, however, may cause performance difficulties when generating sufficient subschemas and testing whether they are disjoint. Note that the considered subschema language is an internal feature, transparent for the users. Hence we have a lot of freedom concerning how it has to be constructed.

For SBA we propose subschema function definitions based on the database schema graph. Each node of the graph describing a database object has an internal unique identifier being a reference to the node. We use these identifiers as basic building blocks of our subschema language. According to the SBA assumptions, during the static analysis of a query each name occurring in it is associated with a database schema node. The node identifiers are fixed-length integer values, so proposed subschemas are light-weight structures which can be easy compared and maintained. Then, the algorithm of subschema extracting is as follows:

- Query subschema function *subQ* returns for a query q the set of the schema graph node references of all object names N_q occurring in the query syntactic tree. The set contains therefore references of names of root objects, their native and derived properties and methods, which are involved within the query.

- Update subschema function *subU* returns for each update u the set of the references of all names N_u of objects influenced by the update. If some complex objects were removed, altered or inserted, then the references of all their native or inherited subobjects names are also in the set. If a name reference of objects of a subclass is in the set, the references of names of all its superclasses are also included.

To compare the subschemas we should only check, whether there are common elements in the generated subschemas using the above functions for a query and an update. If there are no such elements, the subschemas are disjoint. Below we present an example of the elimination method activity, which utilizes proposed subschema definitions. To simplify examples we use object names instead of references to schema graph nodes.

For the example we use the database schema presented in Fig.1. For query q:

```
(Emp where salary > 1200).(name, works_in.Dept.dname)
```

we obtain the set of involved names *subQ*(q) = {*Emp*, *salary*, *name*, *works_in*, *Dept*, *dname*}. The name *name* is an example of inherited subname - objects named *Emp* inherit all subobjects and methods from class *Person*. Example updates are:

```
u1: (Emp where works_in.Dept.dname = "Trade").salary :=
1300

u2: delete Emp where name = "Brown"

u3: (Student where name = "Smith").(grades as g where g
= 3) := 4
```

After the update u_1 only objects named *salary* are changed, hence *subU*(u_1) = {*salary*} and *subQ*(q) $\cap$ *subU*(u_1) $\neq \emptyset$, therefore after the update u_1 cached q should be removed or the result of q has to be corrected. After that decision query should be marked in the cache registry as update needed. Identifiers of changed, inserted or deleted objects (in the case identifiers of changed *salary* objects) are stored for possibly incremental update presented later in the section. The cached query will be updated immediately after the commitment of the update (or multi-update within a database transaction) or while next use of its cached results (deferred update).

The update u_2 deletes from the database entire objects of class *Emp* together with all their subobjects (with inherited from class *Person*), thus *subU*(u_2) = {*Emp*, *Person*, *name*, *birthday*, *job*, *salary*, *rating*, *works_in*, *prev_job*, *company*, *years*, *employs*}. By constructing the subschema we have assumed that at least one of the deleted (by update u_2) *Emp* objects has contained the *prev_job* subobject. Name *Person* is included in the set, because of the inheritance relation between *Emp* and *Person* objects. The subschema contains also name *employs,* which represents the subobject of objects named *Dept* not included in the set. Object named *employs* was deleted by the update, because of the deletion of its twin pointer object named *works_in*. On the other hand we have assumed that before the update all of the deleted *Emp* objects didn't have got subobjects named *supervises* nor *manages*, so the subschema omits them and their twin pointer object names *supervised_by* and *boss*. We obtain *subQ*(q) $\cap$ *subU*(u_2) $\neq \emptyset$, thus, like after the update u_1, after the update u_2 query q should be corrected.

The update u_3 modifies objects named *grades*, thus $subU(u_3) = \{grades\}$, $subQ(q) \cap subU(u_3) = \emptyset$, so this update does not influence the results of the query q, which in the situation may be omitted by updating process.

Subschema index for efficient elimination. As we have mentioned earlier, efficiency of elimination may depend on the applied subschema language and in consequence on the data structures and algorithms used for storing the subschemas and comparing them. The subschema language proposed in previous subsection is set-based, therefore, to compare the subschemas, one has to check, whether there are common elements in the subschemas sufficient for a query and an update. After a database update, the database system generates the subschema sufficient for the update and, according to the elimination method, compares the subschema with subschemas of all cached queries to recognize which of them were not influenced by the update. If the database is updated quite often, this check process may be very expensive. Some optimization mechanisms have to be introduced for subschema comparison implementation.

Firstly, set-based subschema organization allows for very simple way for reduction of the comparison process frequency by accumulation of a few successive updates into one update. After each single update system caches its subschema and waits for another database update. After several such operations, the number of which is system specific and may depend on time since the first update subschema was cached, system generates the subschema sufficient for a group of the updates. This new global subschema is realized as a sum of the particular cached subschemas, which is simply the sum of sets. This optimization step may cause temporarily, that the results of some cached queries will not comply with current database state.

Second way to speed up the comparison of subschemas is to introduce special index for a set of cached query subschemas. The number of subschemas to traverse is significant, thus the index must be very fast. Searched elements are sets, which the common elements occurrence is to be checked for. In our approach we can assume that the schema of the database is fixed or at least changes very rarely. Taking into account this assumption we recognize, that a set of all object name references being elements of the searched sets is also fixed. For set-valued index elements, the inverted file organization supposes to be very convenient, as recognized in [9].

Our data structure for efficient query elimination, called subschema index, consists therefore of a directory containing all distinct values that can be searched for (identifiers of schema graph nodes) and a list for each value containing all references to data items in which the corresponding value appears (identifiers of cached queries which subschemas contain the object name identifier). We place the search values of the directory in a B-tree [6] for quick access. The first bytes of a node in the B-tree directory are used to store the offset of the first free byte on a page. In leaf nodes we have search-keys along with the references to the corresponding list of data item references. In inner nodes we store references to child nodes which are separated by search keys. The occurrence lists are sorted and compressed by storing the gaps between values instead of proper values (indexed query identifiers). The technique decreases the size of them significantly and in effect increases the performance of the index structure.

Performing elimination, we search all occurrence lists for all elements occurring in the subschema generated for an database update (using *subU* function) and then we sum all the lists. The resultant list contains identifiers of all cached queries that should be deleted or corrected after the update – other queries are eliminated from synchronization process. In case of insertion of new cached query its identifier is added to the occurrence lists for all values appearing in the subschema produced for that query by *subQ* function. Deletion of a cached query deletes its identifier from all corresponding occurrence lists (based on the subschema stored within the cached query node in the cache registry). So implementing the subschema comparison using the inverted-file, we index the subschemas sufficient for cached queries as indexed sets. Having a given set being the subschema for an update of the database, it is very quick to recognize such group of cached queries, subschemas of which overlap (have common elements) with the given set.

Incremental update. Queries influenced by an update (not eliminated using the elimination method) should be updated in order to comply with the database state. The full reevaluation of such queries may be very expensive, so some optimization is required. Changes in the database are usually local, that means concern relatively small part of the database. Therefore, the majority of cached query results remain wholly or partly valid for the new database state. Instead of results reevaluation, it is preferred to correct them. The correction means deleting from materialized results of the query all the uncertain elements and completing the remainder with the appropriate missing elements. Such correction is often called an incremental updating and our proposals for the method are explained in detail in [8].

5 Experimental Results

We have tested the performance of the optimizer by calculating a response times for 100 subsequent requests using a set of the same queries retrieving data from database containing over 100000 objects, comparing four optimization strategies: without optimization (NoCache), caching in volatile memory (TMP), caching in persistent memory (DB) and mixed caching (TMP+DB). Results presented in Fig.2 show that in case of TMP strategy average response time is more than 10 times shorter than response without using of the cache. In many cases, specially for more complex queries, responses were 100 times faster.

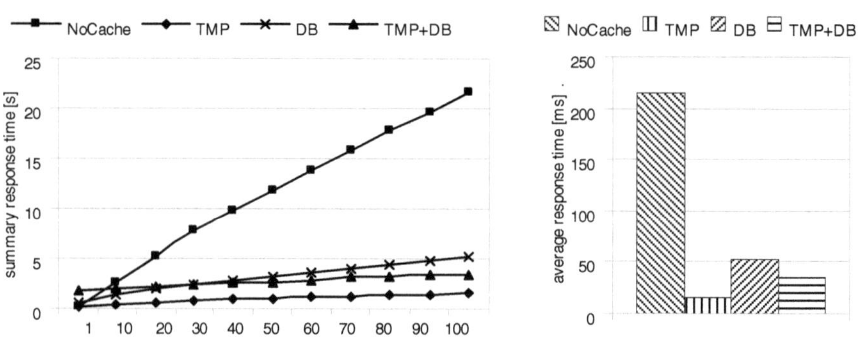

Fig. 2. Efficiency of optimization using cached queries

6 Conclusions and Future Work

We have presented a new approach to optimization of query languages using caching of results of previously answered queries. Our solution addresses the stack-based approach (SBA) to object-oriented query languages, which is a new and powerful concept in the database systems research. The cached queries as a tool for the optimization ensure short and scalable response time to any user request types. Proper structures for fast retrieval of cached queries results were proposed. Important problem of this optimization method is the high cost of updating results of cached queries after a database state modification. The elimination method, based on the concept of subschemas, reduces the cost of maintenance of the cache up to date by estimating and removing from consideration after a database update those queries that are for sure not influenced by the update. The subschemas generated by sets of object names were proposed and the data structures aiding fast comparison of the subschemas sufficient for queries and updates are also introduced.

The work on cached queries is continued. There are many open research areas concerning the optimization method. The main areas concern some additional features of SBA and SBQL not mentioned in this paper. In general, the problem is practical rather than theoretical, hence much effort should be devoted to experiments with different strategies of caching queries and keeping in sync their stored results.

References

1. Ali, M.A., Fernandes, A.A.A., Paton, N.W.: MOVIE: An Incremental Maintenance System for Materialized Object Views. In: Proc. of Data & Knowledge Engineering, vol. 47, pp. 131–166 (2003)
2. Blakeley, J.A., Larson, P., Tompa, W.M.: Efficiently Updating Materialized Views. In: Proc. of ACM SIGMOD, pp. 61–71 (1986)
3. Chaudhuri, S., Krishnamurthy, R., Potamianos, S., Shim, K.: Optimizing Queries with Materialized Views. In: Proc. of Intl. Conf. on Data Engineering, pp. 190–200 (1995)
4. Chen, C.M., Roussopoulos, N.: The Implementation and Performance Evaluation of the ADMS Query Optimizer: Integrating Query Result Caching and Matching. In: Jarke, M., Bubenko, J., Jeffery, K. (eds.) EDBT 1994. LNCS, vol. 779. Springer, Heidelberg (1994)
5. Chen, L., Rundensteiner, E.A.: ACE-XQ: A CachE-ware XQuery Answering System. In: Proc. of WebDB, pp. 31–36 (2002)
6. Comer, D.: The Ubiquitous B-Tree. Computing Surveys 11(2), 121–137 (1979)
7. Cybula, P., Kozankiewicz, H., Stencel, K., Subieta, K.: Optimization of Distributed Queries in Grid via Caching. In: Meersman, R., Tari, Z., Herrero, P. (eds.) OTM-WS 2005. LNCS, vol. 3762, pp. 387–396. Springer, Heidelberg (2005)
8. Cybula, P., Subieta, K.: Cached Queries in the Stack-Based Approach. Institute of Computer Science, Polish Academy of Sciences, Report 985, Warsaw (2005)
9. Helmer, S., Moerkotte, G.: A Study of Four Index Structures for Set-Valued Attributes of Low Cardinality. Technical Report 2/99, Universität Mannheim (1999)
10. IBM DB2 Universal Database SQL Reference, 2, Version 8 (2002); Faster Federated Queries with MQTs, DB2 Magazine 8(3) (2003)
11. Kemper, A., Moerkotte, G.: Access Support in Object Bases. In: Proc. of ACM SIGMOD, pp. 364–376 (1990)

12. Larson, P., Yang, H.: Computing Queries from Derived Relations. In: Proc. of VLDB, pp. 259–269 (1985)
13. Litwin, W.: Linear Hashing: A New Tool for File and Table Addressing. In: Proc. of 6th VLDB, pp. 212–223 (1980)
14. MySQL 5.4 Reference Manual, Ch. 7.5.5: The MySQL Query Cache (2009)
15. ODRA (Object Database for Rapid Application Development), Description and Programmer Manual, http://sbql.pl/various/ODRA/ODRA_manual.html
16. Oracle 9i Materialized Views, An Oracle White Paper (May 2001); On Oracle Database 11g, Oracle Magazine, vol. XXI(5)(2007)
17. Rzeczkowski, W., Subieta, K.: Stored Queries – a Data Organization for Query Optimization. In: Proc. of Data & Knowledge Engineering, vol. 3, pp. 29–48 (1988)
18. EL-Sayed, M., Wang, L., Ding, L., Rundensteiner, E.A.: An Algebraic Approach for Incremental Maintenance of Materialized XQuery Views. In: Proc. of WIDM (2002)
19. Subieta, K.: Theory and Practice of Object Query Languages. Polish-Japanese Institute of Information Technology (2004) (in Polish)
20. Subieta, K., Beeri, C., Matthes, F., Schmidt, J.W.: A Stack Based Approach to Query Languages. In: Proc. of 2nd Springer Workshops in Computing (1995)
21. Subieta, K., Rzeczkowski, W.: Query Optimization by Stored Queries. In: Proc. of VLDB, pp. 369–380 (1987)

Perfect Matching for Biconnected Cubic Graphs in $O(n \log^2 n)$ Time

Krzysztof Diks and Piotr Stanczyk

Institute of Informatics, University of Warsaw
Banacha 2, 02-097 Warsaw, Poland
{diks,stanczyk}@mimuw.edu.pl

Abstract. The main result of this paper is a new perfect matching algorithm for biconnected cubic graphs. The algorithm runs in time $O(n \log^2 n)$. It is also possible, by applying randomized data structures, to get $O(n \log n \log\log^3 n)$ average time. Our solution improves the one given by T. Biedl et al. [3]. The algorithm of Biedl et al. runs in time $O(n \log^4 n)$. We use a similar approach. However, thanks to exploring some properties of biconnected cubic graphs we are able to replace complex fully-dynamic biconnectivity data structure with much simpler, dynamic graph connectivity and dynamic tree data structures. Moreover, we present a significant modification of the new algorithm which makes application of a decremental dynamic graph connectivity data structure possible, instead of one supporting the fully dynamic graph connectivity. It gives hope for further improvements.

Let $G = (V, E)$ be a graph and let n denote the number of vertices and m the number of edges of the graph. In this paper by a graph we mean an undirected multigraph. A matching of G is a subset $M \subset E$ of the edges such that no two edges in M have a common vertex. A maximum matching is a matching of maximum cardinality. Any matching of cardinality $\frac{|V|}{2}$ is called a perfect matching. An alternating cycle is a cycle of even length with edges alternately belonging and not belonging to the matching.

A graph G is connected if there is a path in G between any two of its vertices. Every maximal connected subgraph of a graph is called a connected component. Two vertices belonging to the same connected component are called connected. A connected graph is called vertex (edge) biconnected if removal of any vertex (edge) leaves the graph connected. A bridge is an edge which removal increases the number of connected components of the graph. Graph is bridgeless if it does not contain any bridge. Graph G is cubic if every vertex in G has degree 3. Observe that every vertex biconnected cubic graph is also edge biconnected and vice versa.

In this paper we present a new algorithm for computing perfect matching in cubic biconnected graphs running in time $O(n \log^2 n)$. Moreover, we prove that if there exists a decremental dynamic graph connectivity data structure for sparse graphs, with query/update time $O(f(n))$, then our algorithm can be implemented in time $O(n\, f(n))$.

J. van Leeuwen et al. (Eds.): SOFSEM 2010, LNCS 5901, pp. 321–333, 2010.

The history of matchings in graphs goes back to the end of the nineteenth century when Petersen published a pioneering paper on matchings [9]. Finding a maximum matching is one of the most fundamental problems both in the classic and in the algorithmic graph theory [7,10,11]. The fastest known algorithm for computing maximum matching in general graphs proposed by M. Mucha and P. Sankowski [17] runs in $O(n^{\omega})$ time[1], but it is very complicated and impractical. Although N. J. A. Harvey [18] managed to greatly simplify the algorithm, because of utilization of complex fast matrix multiplication algorithm, this approach does not turn into practical solution of the matching problem. By applying classical techniques it is possible to construct a maximum matching in $O(\sqrt{n}\,m)$ time [8]. A maximum matching in a bipartite graph can be computed faster, i.e. in time $O(n^{1.5}\sqrt{m\log n})$ [1]. In 2001 Therese Biedl showed a linear reduction from the maximum matching problem in general graphs to the maximum matching problem in 3-regular (cubic) graphs [2]. Her result implies that any $O(f(m))$ algorithm for maximum matching in 3-regular graphs yields an $O(f(m)+m)$ algorithm for maximum matching in arbitrary graphs. R. Greenlaw and R. Petreschi in [19] survey algorithms for the different classes of cubic graphs giving motivation for further exploration.

This paper goes back to the pioneering work of Petersen from 1891. Petersen proved that every cubic graph without bridges (actually two bridges are allowed) has a perfect matching. It is interesting from the algorithmic point of view how quickly such a perfect matching can be computed. In 2001 Biedl at al. [3] showed an algorithm for computing a perfect matching in a bridgeless cubic graph running in time $O(n\log^4 n)$. Our paper contains a significant modification of the previous algorithm leading to a time complexity of $O(n\log^2 n)$. Moreover, we show what is needed to get time complexity of $O(n\log n)$. There are linear time complexity algorithms for computing perfect matching in some classes of cubic biconnected graphs. Biedl at al. [3] showed that it is possible for planar graphs and Schrijver [12] did the same for bipartite graphs. This gives hope for a linear time algorithm for computing a perfect matching in cubic biconnected graph as well.

The paper is organized into 3 sections. The first section introduces Frink's quadratic time algorithm and its implementation proposed by T. Biedl et al. leading to $O(n\log^4 n)$ time complexity. The second section presents a new algorithm with $O(n\log^2 n)$ time complexity. A randomized implementation runs in $O(n\log n\log\log^3 n)$ average time. The third section presents possible improvements and introduces a modification of the algorithm which requires only edge deletions from the dynamic graph connectivity data structure. This makes possible to utilize only decremental counterpart of this data structure.

1 Frink's Algorithm

The keys to Frink's algorithm are Petersen's Theorem and Frink's Theorem.

[1] $O(n^{\omega})$ is an optimal matrix multiplication time. It is known that $\omega < 2.38$.

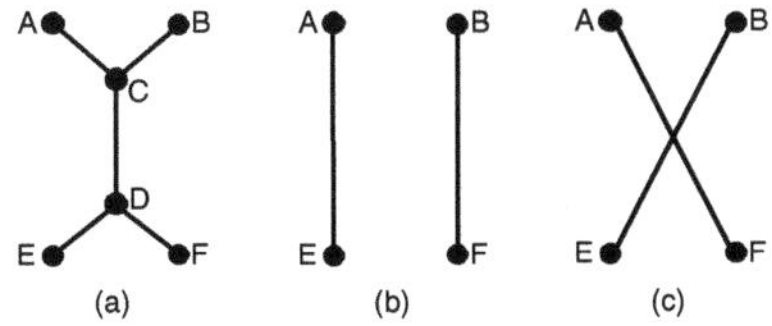

Fig. 1. (a) Vertices C and D are to be removed from the graph. (b) The first type of reduction — vertex A is connected with E, vertex B is connected with F. (c) The second type of reduction — vertex A is connected with F, vertex B is connected with E.

Petersen's Theorem [9]: If a cubic graph does not contain a perfect matching, it contains at least three bridges.

It follows that every biconnected cubic graph has a perfect matching.

Frink's Theorem [4]: Let G be a biconnected cubic graph with at least 4 vertices. Consider a single edge $e = (C, D)$. Let A and B be the neighbors of vertex C in G different from D. Let E and F be the neighbors of D different from C (see Figure 1).

At least one of two reductions of graph G consisting of removing vertices C and D and reconnecting vertices A, B, E and F in one of two ways — by adding edges (A, E) and (B, F) or (A, F) and (B, E) (cases (b) and (c) in Figure 1), leads to a biconnected cubic graph.

The above observation allows to perform a sequence of reductions of graph G (preserving biconnectivity) until it consists of only 2 vertices. Testing which of the two possible reductions leads to a biconnected graph can be performed by applying a fully-dynamic data structure for 2-edge connectivity problem. The best known algorithm for solving this problem runs in $O(\log^4 n)$ time per query or update. It is then possible to match one of the edges in the final 2-vertices graph (constructing initial perfect matching) and extend it by reverting the sequence of reductions. Any single reversion can lead to one of four possible cases presented in Figure 2. The only problematic case is when both edges being reverted belong to the perfect matching. In such a situation it is required to find an alternating

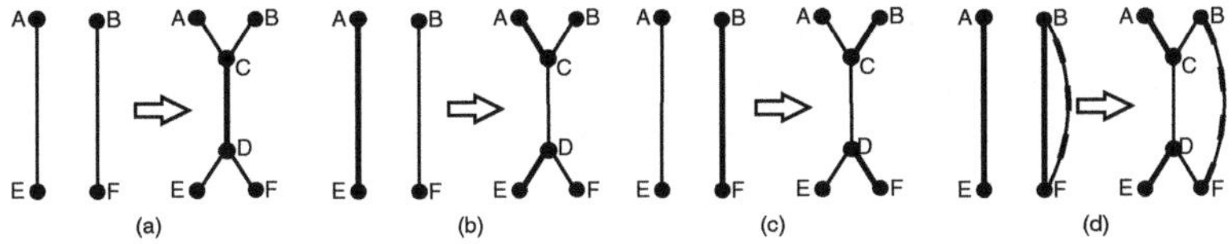

Fig. 2. (a) None of the edges being reverted are matched — add edge (C, D) to the matching. (b) Edge (A, E) is in the matching — remove (A, E) from the matching and add (A, C) and (D, E) to the matching. (c) Edge (B, F) is in the matching — remove (B, F) from the matching and add (B, C) and (D, F) to the matching. (d) Both edges (A, E) and (B, F) are in the matching — find an alternating cycle containing at least one of these two edges ((B, F) in the example) and switch the matching on the cycle. This way case (d) is reduced to one of cases (a), (b) or (c).

cycle containing at least one of these edges, which takes time $O(n)$ [3,14]. The total execution time of the algorithm is $O(n^2)$.

T. Biedl et al. proposed a clever implementation of Frink's algorithm [3]. An invariant of their algorithm guaranties that at most one edge being reverted is matched. For an arbitrary edge e of a biconnected cubic graph there always exists a perfect matching not containing e [9]. The Biedl's algorithm first selects an arbitrary edge $e = (A, C)$ (we will refer to this edge as excluded — the algorithm constructs a perfect matching not containing e). Then reduction step against an edge $f = (C, D)$ incident to e is performed — let $g = (A, E)$ be the added edge incident to A. The reduced graph G' is biconnected and cubic, so it is possible to find a perfect matching M' in G' not containing g (using the same approach). Matching M' can be easily extended to a perfect matching M in G not containing e, without the need of finding an alternating cycle (since the case when both edges being reverted are in the matching does not occur). This leads to the $O(n \log^4 n)$ time complexity.

2 New Algorithm

It turns out that it is possible to perform biconnectivity testing for each reduction performed by Frink's algorithm without utilizing complex dynamic biconnectivity data structure. By taking into account some biconnected cubic graphs' properties and by applying a fully-dynamic connectivity data structure and the Sleator/Tarjan's dynamic trees, it is possible to solve the problem faster.

For fully-dynamic graph connectivity problem we apply the data structure presented in [6]. This data structure supports the following operations:

- edge insertion,
- edge deletion,
- answering a question whether two given vertices of a graph are connected.

Each of the above operations is performed in $O(\log^2 n)$ amortized time. M. Thorup introduced another dynamic data structure for solving the same problem which supports the same set of operations in $O(\log n \log\log^3 n)$ expected time per operation [15]. Choosing one of these data structures leads to a perfect matching algorithm for biconnected cubic graphs running in $O(n \log^2 n)$ time or $O(n \log n \log\log^3 n)$ expected time.

The second data structure to be used are dynamic trees of Sleator and Tarjan [13]. It maintains a dynamic forest and supports edge deletion and insertion in $O(\log n)$ time per operation. It also supports computation of the nearest common ancestor of any two vertices of a rooted tree in $O(\log n)$ time per query.

Both dynamic connectivity data structures from [6] and [15] maintain a spanning forest of graph G. A newly added edge $e = (X, Y)$ becomes the forest edge if X and Y were not connected in G prior to insertion of e. No other edge of G changes its status (is removed or added to the spanning forest). In case of removal of a spanning forest edge $e = (X, Y)$, the algorithm tries to find a replacement edge reconnecting components of X and Y in the spanning forest. Any operation over dynamic connectivity data structure results in $O(1)$ inserted/removed edges in the maintained spanning forest. Our algorithm during execution needs to know the lowest common ancestor of some pairs of vertices in the arbitrary rooted spanning tree of G. To answer these questions we represent trees of the forest (after being rooted) using Tarjan's dynamic trees.

Our algorithm works in the following way:

- Initialize dynamic connectivity data structure $\mathcal{D}$ by adding all edges of an input biconnected cubic graph G.
- Initialize dynamic tree data structure $\mathcal{T}$ by adding all spanning tree edges of $\mathcal{D}$.
- Perform Frink/Biedl algorithm but instead of using dynamic biconnectivity data structure for verifying which reduction is correct, use the new approach described below.

We already know that one of two possible reductions performed in each step of Frink's algorithm leads to a biconnected graph. Searching for the correct reduction might be hard sometimes. However, if we find out that one connection does not preserve biconnectivity then Frink's theorem implies that the other reduction is the one of our interest. In order to find the correct reduction we first need to update data structure $\mathcal{D}$ by removing edges (A, C), (B, C), (C, D), (D, E) and (D, F), leading to graph G'. Two different scenarios are now possible — graph G' stays connected or not (this can be verified using data structure $\mathcal{D}$ by querying if A is connected with B, E and F).

2.1 Case 1: G' Is Unconnected

Since graph G is biconnected, each of the removed edges ((A, C), (B, C), (C, D), (D, E) and (D, F)) lies on some cycle in G. As G has a cycle containing (C, D), there has to be at least one of the following paths in G':

- between A and E
- between A and F
- between B and E
- between B and F

Assume (without loss of generality) that G' contains a path connecting A and E (see Figure 3). There has to be another cycle (or cycles) in G containing edges

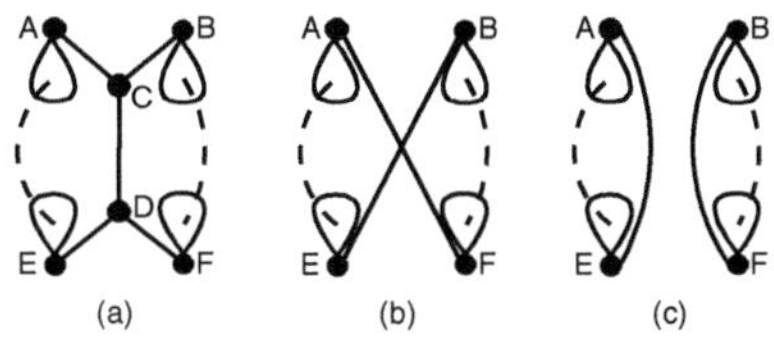

Fig. 3. (a) The structure of G prior to edge deletions (every edge to be removed lies on some cycle). (b) Reduction leading to a biconnected graph. (c) Reduction leading to unconnected graph.

(B, C) and (D, F). Since G' is unconnected but A and E are connected, there has to be a path between B and F in G'. In order to maintain biconnectivity of the reduced graph it is required to connect A with F and B with E (the second type of connection leads to unconnected graph and Frink's theorem implies that the first connection is the one we are looking for).

2.2 Case 2: G' Is Connected

As G' is connected, it is possible to use Tarjan's trees to compute the lowest common ancestor for any pair of vertices of G' in a rooted spanning tree T being maintained. Consider the subtree T' of the spanning tree T consisting of all edges lying on paths connecting vertices A, B, E and F in T. We need to select one of the two possible connections of vertices A, B, E and F using new edges u and v such that every edge of T' lies on some cycle in $T' \cup \{u, v\}$. As we prove later, such a connection guarantees biconnectivity of the reduced graph.

If we connected A with E and B with F, edges lying on paths connecting A with E and B with F would be included in cycles of $T' \cup \{u, v\}$. The only edges in question are located between the lowest common ancestor $LCA(A, E)$ of A and E and the lowest common ancestor $LCA(B, F)$ of B and F. There are three possible cases depending on the relative position of $LCA(A, E)$ and $LCA(B, F)$ in T':

- $LCA(A, E) = G$, $LCA(B, F) = H$, $LCA(G, H) = I$, $I \neq G, H$ (parts (a), (b) of Figure 4) — after connecting A with F and B with E ($LCA(A, F) = LCA(B, E) = I$), every edge of T' lies on some cycle in $T' \cup \{u, v\}$.
- $LCA(A, E) = I$, $LCA(B, F) = I$ (parts (c), (d) of Figure 4) — after connecting A with E and B with F, every edge of T' lies on some cycle in $T' \cup \{u, v\}$.
- $LCA(A, E) = G$, $LCA(B, F) = I$, $LCA(G, I) = I$ (parts (e), (f) of Figure 4, $LCA(G, I) = G$ is the symmetric case) — it is required to add such edges which generate cycles containing all edges between vertices G and I in T', so edge w connecting G with its parent in T' has to be a part of the added cycles

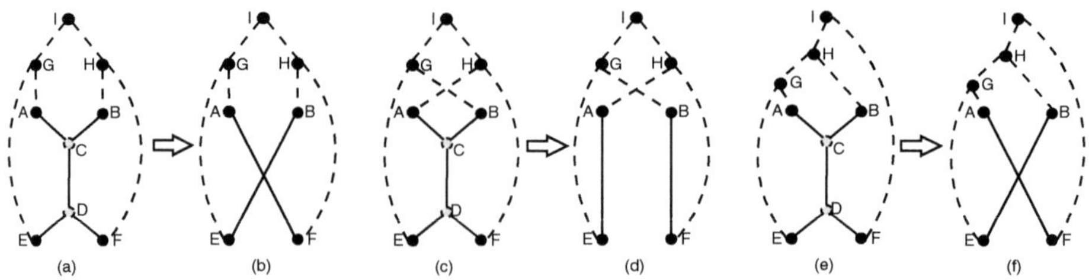

Fig. 4. (a) Example graph G with $LCA(A, E) = G$, $LCA(B, F) = H$ and $LCA(G, H) = I$. (b) Graph G' obtained from (a) after reduction. (c) Example graph G with $LCA(A, E) = I = LCA(B, F)$. (d) Graph G' obtained from (c) after reduction. (e) Example graph G with $LCA(A, E) = G$, $LCA(B, F) = I$. (f) Graph G' obtained from (e) after reduction.

as well. If a cycle obtained by connecting B and F contains w (which can be tested by checking if $LCA(B, G) = G$ or $LCA(F, G) = G$) then connection of A with E and B with F is the correct reduction. Otherwise, we have a situation presented in case (e) — edges between G and H are not included in any cycle. However, by taking the second possibility — connection of A with F and B with E — the edges are included in both cycles.

What remains is to prove that if every edge of T' is included in some cycle in $T' \cup \{u, v\}$, the graph resulting from the reduction is biconnected. In order to prove this fact it is sufficient to show that every edge of reduced graph G' lies on some cycle (as all bridgeless cubic graphs are biconnected).

It has been already shown that it is possible to perform reduction in such a way that every edge of $T' \cup \{u, v\}$ lies on some cycle. The proof of this fact remains for the rest of the edges. Let's consider such an edge $e \in G'/(T' \cup \{u, v\})$. As G is biconnected, there is a cycle c in G containing e. Assume (without loss of generality) that when performing the reduction we have connected A with E and B with F. A few cases have to be considered:

- Cycle c does not contain any of removed edges — c is also a cycle in the reduced graph, so e stays on a cycle.
- Cycle c contains three removed edges (A, C), (C, D) and (D, E) (symmetrically (B, C), (C, D) and (D, F)) — replacing those edges in c with (A, E) (symmetrically (B, F)) leads to a cycle containing e in the reduced graph.
- c contains two edges (A, C) and (B, C) (symmetrically (D, E) and (D, F)) — T' is a tree, so there exists a path d connecting A and B in T' (symmetrically E and F). Symmetric difference of c and $d \cup \{(A, C), (B, C)\}$ is a collection of cycles and one of them contains e.
- c contains three edges (A, C), (C, D) and (D, F) (symmetrically (B, C), (C, D) and (D, E)) — T' is a tree, so there exists a path d connecting A and F in T' (symmetrically B and E). Symmetric difference of c and d is a collection of cycles and one of them contains e.
- c contains four removed edges (A, C), (B, C), (E, D) and (D, F) — by replacing those edges with (A, E) and (B, F) we obtain a cycle (possibly two cycles) containing e.

The above completes the proof that reduced graph stays biconnected.

The proposed implementation requires $O(n)$ operations on both dynamic connectivity and dynamic tree data structures, so its total execution time is $O(n \log^2 n)$ in case of applying dynamic connectivity algorithm from [6] and $O(n \log n \log \log^3 n)$ expected time in case of the data structure from [15].

3 Further Improvements

In this section we present a sketch of a modification of our algorithm which makes it possible to replace dynamic connectivity data structure with its decremental counterpart. If we did not need to insert new edges to the graph G we could have applied a decremental dynamic connectivity data structure. It may turn out to be more efficient than fully-dynamic one as it does not have to support edge insertions. M. Thorup proposed such a data structure [16]. It starts from an n-vertex graph with m edges and maintains a spanning forest of the graph and allows to perform m deletion operations in $O(min\{n^2, m\,n\log n\} + \sqrt{n\,m}\,\log^{2.5} n)$ expected time. In case of graphs with $\Omega(n\,\log^6 n)$ edges the time reduces to $O(\log n)$ per operation, while for graphs with $\Omega(n^2)$ to $O(1)$ per operation. This data structure does not help in our case as the graphs under consideration are very sparse. However, there is a chance that one may design a more efficient decremental algorithm for biconnected cubic graphs in the future.

In order to utilize a decremental dynamic connectivity data structure, apart from original graph G we maintain a modified representation of that graph — graph G'. At the beginning each vertex X of G is represented in G' with two vertices X_1 and X_2 connected by an edge (X_1, X_2). Each edge (X, Y) of G is replaced with four edges (X_1, Y_1), (X_1, Y_2), (X_2, Y_1), (X_2, Y_2). The representation of edge (X, Y) from graph G in graph G' is presented in Figure 5(a). As it is not possible to add edges to G' (we want to use only a decremental data structure) we represent new edges of G by utilizing parts of already removed edges.

Figure 6 presents the change of graph G' by the process of performing a single reduction – in G five edges are removed and two edges are added. Every added edge is represented in a special way as a subgraph of G'. Such an edge is called *disallowed* as it is not possible to perform further reductions against it. A general representation of a *disallowed* edge is given in Figure 5(c). In course of the algorithm it may turn out that it is required to perform reduction against a *disallowed* edge. In such a case a reverse process is applied to the decremental dynamic connectivity data structure (described later in this section) leading to appearance of another type of edges presented in Figure 5(b). We refer to them as *allowed* as the reductions against them are possible.

The decremental dynamic connectivity data structure is used to maintain a spanning tree T of G' (just like in the algorithm from the previous section). If all edges that represent vertices (all edges (X_1, X_2) for $X \in V(G)$) are included

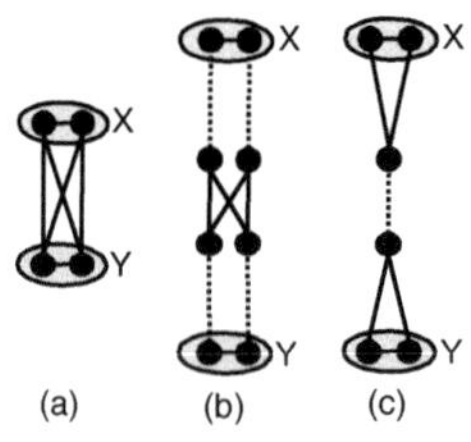

Fig. 5. (a) Initial representation of two vertices X and Y connected by an edge. (b) General representation of an *allowed* edge — X_1 is connected by a path with Y_1, X_2 with Y_2. In addition the paths are joined by a „crossing". (c) General representation of a *disallowed* edge.

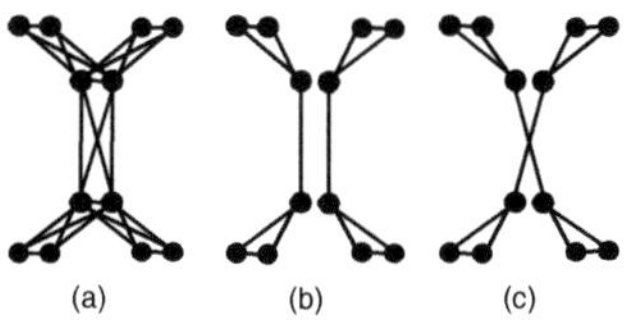

Fig. 6. (a) Set of 5 edges with the *allowed* center edge to be reduced. (b) First type of reduction — the representations of added *disallowed* edges are obtained from the representations of the removed edges. (c) Second type of reduction.

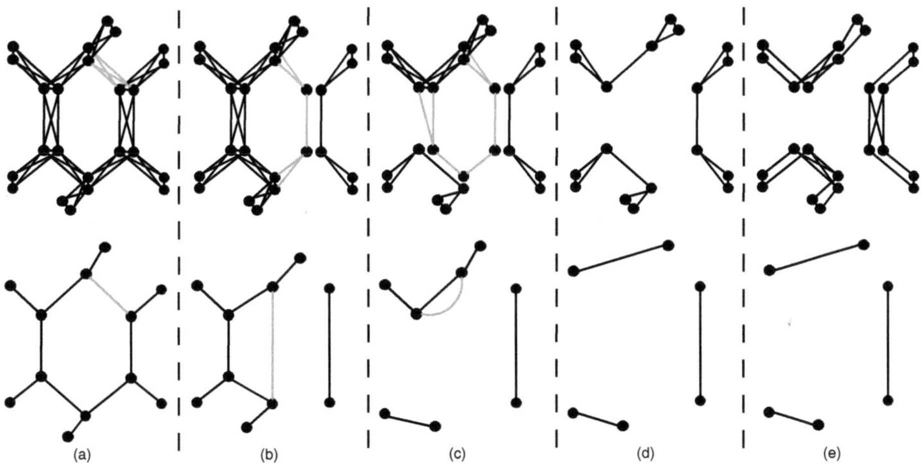

Fig. 7. The process of performing reductions along an even cycle. The lower row presents changes in graph G, while the upper row contains corresponding graph G'. Light edges represent edge e which is excluded from the matching. (a) Initial graph G and its corresponding graph G'. (b) G and G' after the first reduction along the cycle. (c) G and G' after the second reduction along the cycle. This reduction introduces a double edge which has to be reduced in the way depicted in Figure 8. (d) State of G and G' after reduction of the double edge. (e) State of the data structure after executing a restoration point and fixing representation of all *disallowed* edges in G'.

in T[2] it is easy to derive a spanning tree of G from T — edge (X, Y) is a spanning edge of G if edges from T representing (X, Y) form a path in T connecting X with Y. This way it is possible to verify in a constant time if a given edge of G is a tree edge (it is sufficient to maintain a counter of the number of tree-edges of T representing an edge under consideration).

The algorithm starts by selecting a single edge e from G which is not to be included in the perfect matching. A sequence of reductions is then performed

[2] It can be easily fulfilled in case of the data structures used in our algorithm from the previous section by adding vertex-edges to G' before edges that represent edges of G.

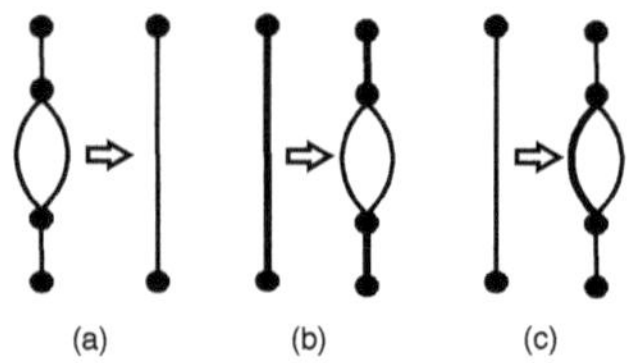

Fig. 8. (a) Reduction of a double edge maintaining graph biconnectivity. (b) The case of extending perfect matching when an edge that had replaced double edge is included in the matching. (c) The case of extending perfect matching when an edge that had replaced double edge is not included in the matching.

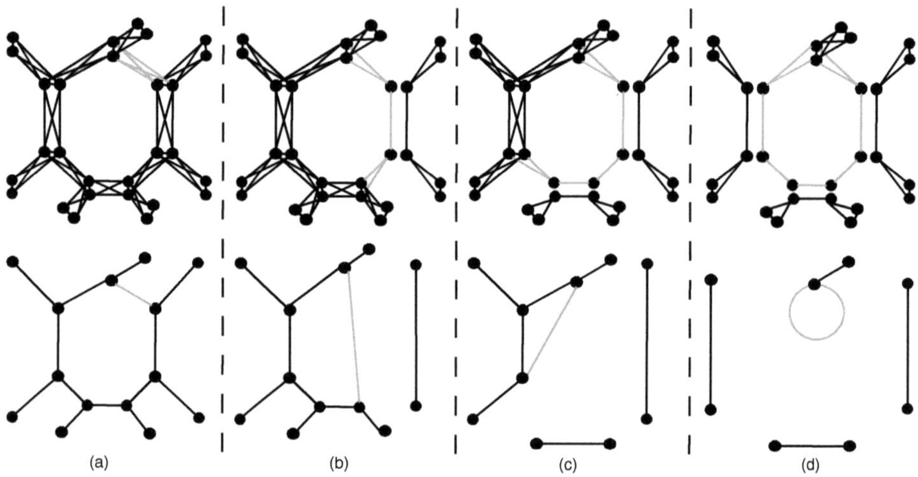

Fig. 9. The process of performing reductions along an odd cycle. The lower row presents changes in graph G while the upper row contains corresponding graph G'. Light edges represent edge e which is excluded from the matching. (a) Initial graph G and its corresponding graph G'. (b) G and G' after the first reduction along the cycle. (c) G and G' after the second reduction along the cycle. (d) The last reduction along the cycle leads to not biconnected graph (edge e is connected with the rest of the graph by a bridge), so this reduction cannot be performed by the algorithm.

— each of them against one of 4 edges incident to edge e. Apart from the way of detecting tree edges of G there are yet no differences in comparison with the algorithm utilizing fully-dynamic connectivity data structure. The only problem shows up when it turns out that a reduction is about to be performed against *disallowed* edge. In such a situation it is not possible to update G' to reflect changes in G. In order to go around this problem we extend the decremental dynamic data structure with the possibility of creating restoration points. Any restoration point allows to restore the state of the data structure to the moment when restoration point was created. Restoration points can be easily realized by recording all modifications to the data structure and reverting them upon

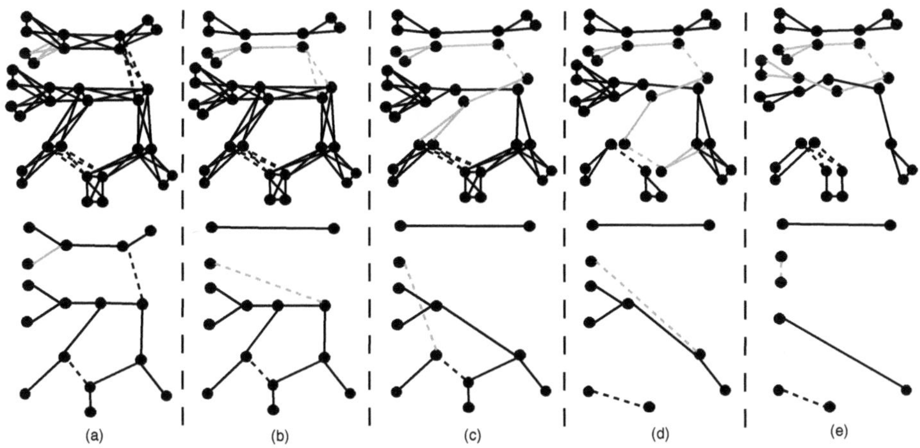

Fig. 10. The process of reductions in case of encountering *disallowed* edge f, different from e. The lower row presents changes in graph G while the upper row contains corresponding graph G'. Light edges represent edge e which is excluded from the matching. (a) Initial graph G and its corresponding graph G'. (b) The first sequence of reductions. (c) Reduction r_m which makes edge f *disallowed.* (d) The second sequence of reductions. (e) Reduction to be performed is against *disallowed* edge f which is different from e. In order to make this reduction possible, it is required to execute restoration point created before stage (c). This way, all *disallowed* edges introduced into G after stage (b) can be turned into *allowed* representation, while the reduction is also possible.

restoration point execution. There is no additional performance cost (by means of asymptotic time complexity) to record changes made to the data structure. Time required to execute a restoration point is amortized by the process of performing operations on the data structure. Before performing a single reduction a restoration point needs to be created. This way it is possible to restore the state of the data structure before any reduction.

Two situations are possible when it turns out that the next reduction is to remove *disallowed* edge f — f can be edge e, i.e. the edge where the reduction process has started from (see Figure 7, 9), or not (see Figure 10).

If f turns out to be e it means that a sequence of reductions performed since the last selection of the excluded edge e has lead to creation of a cycle. If the cycle was of even length we would not be able to meet e on our way — first we would have encountered a double edge case (see Figure 7) and the algorithm would have done a reduction from Figure 8. Representation of removed edge e can be used to fix all *disallowed* edges introduced by the sequence of reductions performed for e. To do so restoration point created prior to the first reduction with excluded edge e has to be executed (see Figure 7).

If the cycle was of odd length the reduction performed prior to encountering excluded edge would have generated a bridge in the graph (see Figure 9) which is not possible as algorithm maintains biconnectivity of the graph.

If f is not e it must have been added to the graph as a result of one of not reverted reductions. Denote by $r_1, r_2, \ldots, r_k$ a sequence of reductions that has not yet been reverted (each of these reductions has a restoration point). Let r_m be the reduction which made edge f *disallowed.* Reduction r_{k+1} is to be executed against f, so f has been encountered twice by a sequence of reductions (see Figure 10). Reduction r_m splits representation of an excluded edge e into two parts — the part obtained prior to execution of r_m and the part generated after r_m. By executing a restoration point for r_m it is possible to use reverted edges of G' (the once that were removed from the graph by reductions $r_{m+1} \ldots r_k$) to make all *disallowed* edges added to the graph after r_m *allowed.* Edge f is one of those edges, so it is possible to reduce it.

Once the graph G consists of only two vertices it is possible to extend the perfect matching to the initial graph, as it was done in the algorithm from the previous section. Each reduction step executes $O(1)$ restoration points (the cost of such an operation is amortized by all operations being reverted by the restoration point) and $O(1)$ edge deletions. Hence the total execution time of the algorithm is bounded by $O(n \log n + nf(n))$ where $f(n)$ is the cost of a single operation over the decremental dynamic connectivity data structure. If one designs an algorithm running in $O(\log n)$ time per operation for sparse graphs it is possible to find perfect matching in biconnected cubic graphs in time $O(n \log n)$.

References

1. Alt, H., Blum, N., Mehlhorn, K., Paul, M.: Computing a Maximum Cardinality Matching in a Bipartite Graph in Time $O(n^{1.5}\sqrt{m/\log n})$. Information Processing Letters 37, 237–240 (1991)
2. Biedl, T.C.: Linear Reductions of Maximum Matching. In: SODA 2001, pp. 825–826 (2001)
3. Biedl, T., Bose, P., Demaine, E., Lubiw, A.: Efficient Algorithms for Petersen's Matching Theorem. Journal of Algorithms 38, 110–134 (2001)
4. Frink, O.: A Proof of Petersen's Theorem. The Annals of Mathematics, Series 2 27(4), 491–493 (1926)
5. Henzinger, M., King, V.: Fully Dynamic 2-Edge Connectivity Algorithm in Polylogarithmic Time per Operation. Technical Note, Digital Equipment Corp., Systems Research Ctr. (June 12, 1997)
6. Holm, J., De Lichtenserg, K., Thorup, M.: Poly-Logarithmic Deterministic Fully-Dynamic Algorithms for Connectivity, Minimum Spanning Tree, 2-Edge and Biconnectivity. Journal of the ACM (JACM) 48, 723–760 (2001)
7. Lovasz, L., Plummer, M.D.: Matching Theory. North-Holland Publishing Co., Amsterdam (1986)
8. Micali, S., Vazirani, V.V.: An $O(\sqrt{n}m)$ Algorithm for Finding Maximum Matching in General Graphs. In: Proceedings of FOCS 1980, pp. 17–27. IEEE, Los Alamitos (1980)
9. Petersen, J.: Die Theorie der regulären Graphs. Acta Mathematica 15, 193–220 (1891)
10. Karpiński, M., Rytter, W.: Fast Parallel Algorithms for Graph Matching Problem. Oxford University Press, Oxford (1998)

11. Schrijver, A.: Combinatorial Optimization – Polyhedra and Efficiency. Parts II and III. Springer, Berlin (2003)
12. Schrijver, A.: Bipartite Edge Coloring in $O(\Delta m)$ Time. SIAM Journal on Computing 28(3), 841–846 (1999)
13. Sleator, D.D., Tarjan, R.E.: A Data Structure for Dynamic Trees. In: Proceedings of the Thirteenth Annual ACM Symposium on Theory of Computing, pp. 114–122 (1981)
14. Tarjan, R.E.: Data Structures and Network Algorithms. Society for Industrial and Applied Mathematics (SIAM), Philadelphia (1983)
15. Thorup, M.: Near-Optimal Fully-Dynamic Graph Connectivity. In: Proceedings of the Thirty-Second Annual ACM Symposium on Theory of Computing, pp. 343–350 (2000)
16. Thorup, M.: Decremental Dynamic Connectivity. In: Proceedings of the 8th ACM Symposium on Discrete Algorithms (SODA), pp. 305–313 (1997)
17. Mucha, M.: Finding Maximum Matchings via Gaussian Elimination. PhD Thesis, Warsaw University, Faculty of Mathematics, Informatics and Mechanics
18. Harvey, N.J.A.: Algebraic Algorithms for Matching and Matroid Problems. Computer Science and Artificial Intelligence Laboratory, Massachusetts Institute of Technology
19. Greenlaw, R., Petreschi, R.: Cubic Graphs. ACM Computing Surveys (CSUR) 27(4), 471–495 (1995)

Destructive Rule-Based Properties and First-Order Logic

David Duris

Equipe de Logique Mathématique - Université Paris 7
duris@logique.jussieu.fr

Abstract. We study properties characterized by applying successively a "destructive" rule expressed in first-order logic. The rule says that points $a_1, \ldots, a_k$ of a structure can be removed if they satisfy a certain first-order formula $\varphi(a_1, \ldots, a_k)$. The property defined this way by the formula is the set of finite structures such that we are able to obtain the empty structure when applying the rule repeatedly. Many classical properties can be formulated by means of a "destructive" rule. We do a systematic study of the computational complexity of these properties according to the fragment of first-order logic in which the rule is expressed. We give the list of minimal fragments able to define **NP**-complete properties and maximal fragments that define only **PTIME** properties (unless **PTIME** = **NP**), depending on the number k of free variables and the quantifier symbols used in the formula. We also study more specifically the case where the formula has one free variable and is universal.

Keywords: Finite model theory, definability, complexity, model checking, destructive rule.

1 Introduction

Checking a property by eliminating successively elements of a finite structure satisfying a certain condition is quite natural in algorithmics. A good illustrating example is graph acyclicity: removing one by one elements of degree at most one will yield the empty graph if and only if the graph does not contain a cycle. From a logical point of view, defining a property amounts to giving a formula which describes the condition for an element to be eliminated. In the example of graph acyclicity, this formula says "x is a vertex of degree at most 1". In this paper, we do a systematic study of the expressive power of first-order logic in this framework. We will consider properties defined by means of a "destructive" rule expressed in first-order logic on finite relational structures. We call a rule "destructive" if it is in the following form: if elements $a_1, \ldots, a_k$ satisfy a first-order formula $\varphi(a_1, \ldots, a_k)$ then we can remove $a_1, \ldots, a_k$ from the structure. The structure satisfies the property defined by the rule if applying the rule successively can lead to the empty structure. There are many classes of structures that can be naturally expressed this way. For instance, we can define many

J. van Leeuwen et al. (Eds.): SOFSEM 2010, LNCS 5901, pp. 334–345, 2010.

first-order properties like partial and linear orders and, more generally, every universal first-order property. We can also define properties that cannot be expressed in first-order logic like acyclic graphs, directed paths, function graphs, connected graphs, γ-, β- and α-acyclic hypergraphs (cf. [4]), graphs having a perfect matching and even **NP**-complete properties like collections of 3-sets having an exact cover. In this study, we are concerned with algorithmic issues depending on the syntax of the formula $\varphi(x_1, \ldots, x_k)$. We consider fragments of first-order logic defined by the quantifier symbols and the number of free variables used in the formula and we evaluate the influence of these fragments to the computational complexity of the properties they can define. As a main result, we give a complete classification of the fragments that contain **NP**-complete properties and those included in **PTIME**.

This destructive rule framework can be seen as a particular case of graph rewriting with first-order preconditions (see [10]). It is also connected to deflationary fixed point inductions (a concept dual to inflationary fixed points) that are studied in [6].

2 Preliminaries

The structures we consider are finite and relational. More precisely, they are in the form $\mathcal{A} = (A, \{R^{\mathcal{A}} \mid R \in \sigma\})$, where A is a finite set, σ is a signature containing only relation symbols and $R^{\mathcal{A}}$ is the interpretation of R in $\mathcal{A}$. A *substructure* of a structure $\mathcal{A}$ is a substructure $\mathcal{B}$ of $\mathcal{A}$ induced by some B included in A, i.e. $\mathcal{B} = (B, \{R^{\mathcal{A}} \cap B^r : R \in \sigma\})$ (with r the arity of R). For convenience, the notation $\mathcal{A} \setminus B$ will designate the substructure of $\mathcal{A}$ induced by $A \setminus B$. An *extension* of $\mathcal{A}$ is a structure $\mathcal{E}$ such that $\mathcal{A}$ is a substructure of $\mathcal{E}$.

A *property* is a set of structures closed under isomorphisms. A property $\mathcal{P}$ is *preserved under substructures* (resp. *preserved under extensions*) if every substructure (resp. extension) of a structure in $\mathcal{P}$ is in $\mathcal{P}$.

The interpretation of first-order formulas (**FO**) on σ is standard (see for instance [3]). For quantifier symbols Q_1, ..., Q_n in $\{\forall, \exists\}$, the fragment of first-order logic $Q_1 \ldots Q_n\mathbf{FO}$ consists of the formulas of the form $Q_1x_1 \ldots Q_nx_n\psi$ where ψ is quantifier free. The use of the symbol $*$ after a quantifier means that it can be repeated any finite number of times. More precisely, for every i, $Q_1 \ldots Q_i^* \ldots Q_n\mathbf{FO}$ is the union of every fragment $Q_1 \ldots Q_i^1 \ldots Q_i^k \ldots Q_n\mathbf{FO}$ (for $k \geq 0$) where, for every l, $Q_i^l = Q_i$. *Universal* and *existential* formulas are respectively the formulas in $\forall^*\mathbf{FO}$ and $\exists^*\mathbf{FO}$.

3 General Case

Definition 1 (Destructive rule-based properties). *Let $\varphi(x_1, \ldots, x_k)$ be a first-order formula with k free variables x_1, ..., x_k and let $\mathcal{A}$ be a finite relational structure. Let $\mathcal{R}_{\varphi(x_1,\ldots,x_k)}$ be the following rule: if there exist elements a_1, ..., a_k of A such that $\mathcal{A} \models \varphi(a_1, \ldots, a_k)$ then remove a_1, ..., a_k from $\mathcal{A}$, i.e. replace $\mathcal{A}$ with the substructure $\mathcal{A} \setminus \{a_1, \ldots, a_k\}$. The set* $\mathbf{DR}(\varphi(x_1, \ldots, x_k))$

is the property containing every structure $\mathcal{A}$ such that there is a way to apply the rule $\mathcal{R}_{\varphi(x_1,\ldots,x_k)}$ to $\mathcal{A}$ successively until we obtain the empty structure. More precisely, $\mathcal{A} \in \mathbf{DR}(\varphi(x_1,\ldots,x_k))$ if there exist pairwise disjoint subsets of A $\{a_1^1,\ldots,a_k^1\}$, ..., $\{a_1^n,\ldots,a_k^n\}$ such that:

- $\bigcup_{l=1}^n \{a_1^l,\ldots,a_k^l\} = A$, *and*
- *for every $i < n$, $\mathcal{A} \setminus \bigcup_{l=1}^i \{a_1^l,\ldots,a_k^l\} \models \varphi(a_1^{i+1},\ldots,a_k^{i+1})$.*

The class $\mathbf{DR}^k$ is the set of properties that can be written $\mathbf{DR}(\varphi(x_1,\ldots,x_k))$ for some $\varphi(x_1,\ldots,x_k)$. The class $\mathbf{DR}$ is the union of every $\mathbf{DR}^k$ for $k \geq 1$.

(Note that the sets $\{a_1^l,\ldots,a_k^l\}$ are not necessarily of size k.) We give some examples of classical properties that belong to **DR**.

Example 1

- $\mathbf{DR}((\forall u \forall v(\neg Euu \wedge (Euv \Rightarrow Evu))) \wedge (\exists u Exu \vee \forall u\ x = u))$ is the set of connected graphs. Indeed, if a graph is connected, we can remove every element one after another so that the successive obtained subgraphs are always connected (so there is always some vertex a connected to another). And if there are at least two connected components, there will always remain at least two disconnected vertices.
- $\mathbf{DR}(x \neq y) =$ EVEN the class of structures of even size.
- $\mathbf{DR}(Exy)$ is the class of digraphs having a perfect matching, i.e. a set M of disjoint edges such that every vertex is an endpoint of some edge of M.
- On the signature $\{T\}$ (with T of arity 3), $\mathbf{DR}(Txyz) =$ X3C the set of collections of 3-sets (sets of size 3) having an exact cover. (An exact cover for a collection $\mathcal{B} = \{B_1,\ldots,B_n\}$ of 3-sets is a subcollection $\{B_{i_1},\ldots,B_{i_k}\}$ such that the B_{i_l} are pairwise disjoint and their union is equal to $\cup\mathcal{B}$.)
- In the case of hypergraphs, we consider the signature $\{\in\}$. We have $a \in b$ if a is a vertex, b is a hyperedge and a belongs to b. In order to have models that actually represent hypergraphs, we add to each rule the condition $\forall u \forall v \forall w \neg(u \in v \wedge v \in w)$. The following formula $\varphi_\alpha(x)$ (which says "x is an isolated vertex or x is a hyperedge included in some other hyperedge") is such that $\mathbf{DR}(\varphi_\alpha(x))$ is the set of α-acyclic hypergraphs (see for instance [4]). This is usually called the GYO-reduction (for Graham-Yu-Ozsoyoglu).

  $$\varphi_\alpha(x) = \forall u \forall v((x \in u \wedge x \in v) \Rightarrow u = v) \vee \exists w(w \neq x \wedge \forall t(t \in x \Rightarrow t \in w)).$$

  There also exist a $\varphi_\beta(x)$ and a $\varphi_\gamma(x)$ such that $\mathbf{DR}(\varphi_\beta(x))$ and $\mathbf{DR}(\varphi_\gamma(x))$ are respectively the sets of β- and γ-acyclic hypergraphs (cf. [2]):

  $$\begin{aligned} \varphi_\beta(x) = {} & \forall u \forall v((x \in u \wedge x \in v) \Rightarrow (\forall t(t \in u \Rightarrow t \in v) \\ & \vee \forall t(t \in v \Rightarrow t \in u))) \ \vee \ \forall t \neg(t \in x) \\ \text{and } \varphi_\gamma(x) = {} & \forall u \forall v((x \in u \wedge x \in v) \Rightarrow \forall t(t \in u \Leftrightarrow t \in v)) \vee \\ & \forall u(\forall t(t \in x \Rightarrow t \in u) \vee \forall t(t \in x \Rightarrow \neg(t \in u))). \end{aligned}$$

  Note that $\varphi_\beta(x)$ and $\varphi_\gamma(x)$ are universal. There is no universal formula for α-acyclicity because this notion is not preserved under substructures and, as we will see, every $\mathbf{DR}(\varphi(x))$ with $\varphi(x)$ universal is preserved under substructures.

- It is not hard to see that, if $\psi(x) = \forall u \neg Eux \wedge \forall v \forall w((Exv \wedge Exw) \Rightarrow v = w)$, then $\mathbf{DR}(\psi(x) \wedge \forall t(\psi(t) \Rightarrow t = x))$ is the set of directed paths.

There are formulas $\varphi(x_1, \ldots, x_k)$ such that the property $\mathbf{DR}(\varphi(x_1, \ldots, x_k))$ is **NP**-complete (X3C for example). We will see more precisely which fragments of **FO** contain such formulas and which ones are such that $\mathbf{DR}(\varphi(x_1, \ldots, x_k))$ is always in **PTIME**.

Definition 2. *Let $Q_1, \ldots, Q_n$ be quantifier symbols (i.e. $Q_i \in \{\forall, \exists\}$), possibly followed by a $*$ symbol. For every integer k, $Q_1 \ldots Q_n\mathbf{DR}^k$ is the class of properties in the form $\mathbf{DR}(\varphi(x_1, \ldots, x_k))$ where $\varphi(x_1, \ldots, x_k)$ is a formula of $Q_1 \ldots Q_n\mathbf{FO}$ with k free variables. Quantifier free $\mathbf{DR}^k$ denotes the class of properties $\mathbf{DR}(\varphi(x_1, \ldots, x_k))$ where $\varphi(x_1, \ldots, x_k)$ is quantifier free.*

The next sections contain the proof of the following theorem.

Theorem 1. *We have the following classification.*

Contain **NP**-*complete properties:*	*Included in* **PTIME**:
$\exists\forall\mathbf{DR}^1$	$\exists^*\mathbf{DR}^1$
$\forall\exists\mathbf{DR}^1$	$\forall^*\mathbf{DR}^1$
$\exists\mathbf{DR}^2$	*Quantifier free* $\mathbf{DR}^2$
$\forall\mathbf{DR}^2$	
Quantifier free $\mathbf{DR}^3$	

Unless **PTIME** = **NP**, *these are precisely the minimal fragments containing* **NP**-*complete properties and the maximal fragments containing only* **PTIME** *properties.*

Note that this classification enables us to know for each fragment $Q_1 \ldots Q_n\mathbf{DR}^k$ if it contains **NP**-complete properties or if it is included in **PTIME**.

We finish this section with a remark concerning confluent properties.

Since in many cases it is hard to find an execution of the rule such that we obtain the empty structure, it would be convenient for instance to detect the *confluent* formulas. These are the formulas such that, for every finite structure, the fact of obtaining the empty structure does not depend on the order we successively apply the rule. More formally, a formula $\varphi(x_1, \ldots, x_k)$ is confluent for $\mathbf{DR}^k$ if, for every $\mathcal{A} \in \mathbf{DR}(\varphi(x_1, \ldots, x_k))$, there are no pairwise disjoint subsets of A $\{a_1^1, \ldots, a_k^1\}, \ldots, \{a_1^n, \ldots, a_k^n\}$ such that:

- for every $i < n$, $\mathcal{A} \setminus \bigcup_{l=1}^{i}\{a_1^l, \ldots, a_k^l\} \models \varphi(a_1^{i+1}, \ldots, a_k^{i+1})$,
- $\bigcup_{l=1}^{n}\{a_1^l, \ldots, a_k^l\} \neq A$, and
- $\mathcal{A} \setminus \bigcup_{l=1}^{n}\{a_1^l, \ldots, a_k^l\} \models \forall x_1 \ldots \forall x_k \neg\varphi(x_1, \ldots, x_k)$.

In particular, it is not hard to see that this condition for a formula $\varphi(x_1, \ldots, x_k)$ ensures that the property $\mathbf{DR}(\varphi(x_1, \ldots, x_k))$ is in **PTIME**. However, not surprisingly, detecting confluent formulas is an undecidable problem, even for $\mathbf{DR}^1$.

Proposition 1. *The following problem is undecidable:*

INPUT: a first-order formula $\varphi(x)$.
OUTPUT: is $\varphi(x)$ *confluent for* $\mathbf{DR}^1$*?*

Proof. According to Theorem 20 from [1], the following two sets F_0 and F_1 are recursively inseparable (i.e. there is no recursive set E such that $F_0 \subset E$ and $F_1 \cap E = \emptyset$):

- F_0 is the set of first-order sentences which have no model.
- F_1 is the set of first-order sentences with exactly one finite model (and this model has size at least 2).

Let *not* be the (recursive) function that maps each sentence ψ to $\neg\psi \wedge x = x$ (so that x appears as a free variable). Let C be the set of confluent formulas. If ψ is in F_0, every structure is a model of $\neg\psi$. Thus for every finite structure $\mathcal{A}$ and every a in A, we have $\mathcal{A} \models \neg\psi \wedge a = a$. So, when removing elements satisfying the rule $\mathcal{R}_{\neg\psi\wedge x=x}$, we will necessarily obtain the empty structure, which means that $not(\psi)$ is confluent. If ψ is in F_1, there is only one finite structure, say $\mathcal{S}$, which does not satisfy $\neg\psi$, and this structure has size at least 2. As $|S| \geq 2$, there is a structure $\mathcal{A}$ such that the substructures of $\mathcal{A}$ of size $|S|$ are not all isomorphic to $\mathcal{S}$ and at least one of these substructures is isomorphic to $\mathcal{S}$. Moreover, for every finite structure $\mathcal{B}$ not isomorphic to $\mathcal{S}$ and for every $b \in B$, we have $\mathcal{B} \models \neg\psi \wedge b = b$. So we have the choice: either we decide to remove elements b successively until we obtain $\mathcal{S}$ (and in this case we cannot apply $\mathcal{R}_{\neg\psi\wedge x=x}$ anymore) or we avoid obtaining an $\mathcal{S}$ (i.e. we fix some substructure of size $|S|$ that is not isomorphic to $\mathcal{S}$ and remove all other elements one by one) and we will be able to continue until we obtain the empty structure. This shows that $not(\psi)$ is not confluent. Consequently, if C was recursive, $not^{-1}(C)$ would recursively separate F_0 and F_1, which is a contradiction.

Corollary 1. *The confluence problem is not recursively enumerable.*

Proof. This is because it is co-recursively enumerable. Indeed, we can enumerate finite relational structures and linear orders on them until we find a structure and two orders on it (corresponding to applications of the rule) such that one of them yields the empty structure and the other does not.

4 NP-Complete Properties

In this section, we give examples of **NP**-complete properties in the following classes: $\exists\forall\mathbf{DR}^1$, $\forall\exists\mathbf{DR}^1$, $\exists\mathbf{DR}^2$, $\forall\mathbf{DR}^2$ and quantifier free $\mathbf{DR}^3$. This is the list of minimal fragments of **DR** containing **NP**-complete properties. They are minimal because we will see in Section 5 that every strictly smaller fragment (those contained in $\exists^*\mathbf{DR}^1$, $\forall^*\mathbf{DR}^1$ or quantifier free $\mathbf{DR}^2$) is included in **PTIME**.

The fact that **DR** is included in **NP** is clear by definition. An **NP** algorithm for deciding if a structure $\mathcal{A}$ belongs to $\mathbf{DR}(\varphi(x_1,\dots,x_k))$ consists in guessing the subsets $\{a_1^1,\dots,a_k^1\}$, ..., $\{a_1^n,\dots,a_k^n\}$, checking that they form a partition of A and that, for every $i < n$, $\mathcal{A} \setminus \bigcup_{l=1}^{i}\{a_1^l,\dots,a_k^l\} \models \varphi(a_1^{i+1},\dots,a_k^{i+1})$.

The latter is polynomial in the size of $\mathcal{A}$ because computing the substructure $\mathcal{A} \setminus \bigcup_{l=1}^{i}\{a_1^l, \dots, a_k^l\}$ takes polynomial time and the model checking for **FO** is polynomial in the size of the structure. As a result, it remains to prove **NP**-hardness.

In each case (except the last one), we give a polynomial time reduction of the SAT problem to some $\mathbf{DR}(\varphi(x_1, \dots, x_k))$ with $\varphi(x_1, \dots, x_k)$ in the appropriate fragment of **FO**. An instance of SAT is a formula of propositional logic $f := \wedge_{i\in[1,n]}C_i$. For every i, C_i is a clause $\vee_{j\in[1,n_i]}B_j$, where B_j is a propositional variable (A_j) or the negation of a propositional variable ($\neg A_j$). The question is to know if there is a truth value assignment for the variables such that f is true. For every fragment of **FO** under consideration, we describe a transformation which associates to each instance f of SAT a structure $m(f)$ (a digraph) on the signature $\{E\}$ with E binary. Then we define a formula $\varphi(x_1, \dots, x_k)$ in this fragment such that f is satisfiable if and only if $m(f) \in \mathbf{DR}(\varphi(x_1, \dots, x_k))$. Each case is illustrated with an example in Figure 1.

<u>$\exists\forall\mathbf{DR}^1$:</u> For each propositional variable A appearing in f, there are two points 0_A and 1_A in $m(f)$. They represent the two possible truth value assignments for the variable A. For each clause C, there is a point p_C. Each p_C is connected to every 0_A or 1_A such that the assignment 0 or 1 to the variable A makes C true. More precisely, $m(f)$ contains the edge $(1_A, p_C)$ if A appears positively in C (C contains A) and the edge $(0_A, p_C)$ if A appears negatively in C (C contains $\neg A$).

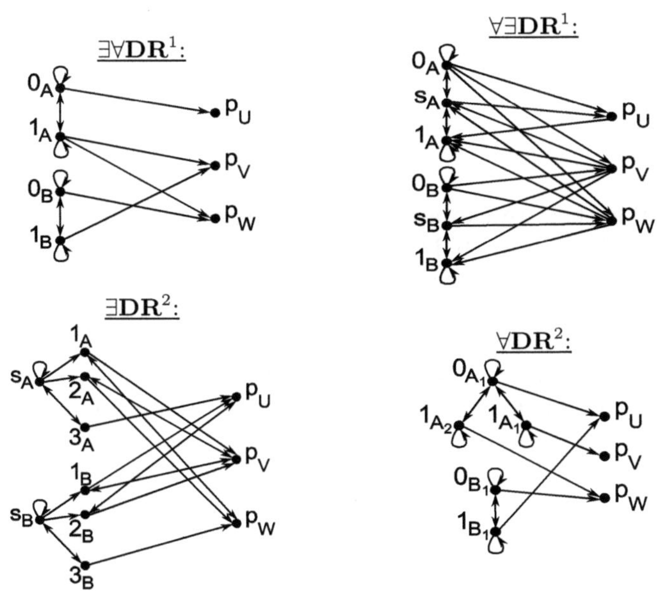

Fig. 1. Examples of structures $m(U \wedge V \wedge W)$ for the SAT-reductions of Section 4. In each case, $U = \neg A$, $V = A \vee B$ and $W = A \vee \neg B$, except for the $\exists\mathbf{DR}^2$ case where $U = \neg A \vee B$.

Moreover $m(f)$ contains the edges $(0_A, 0_A)$, $(1_A, 1_A)$, $(0_A, 1_A)$ and $(1_A, 0_A)$ for every variable A. We set

$$\varphi(x) := \exists u \forall v((Eux \wedge ((Euv \wedge Evu) \Rightarrow v = u)) \vee Exx).$$

Applying successively $\mathcal{R}_{\varphi(x)}$ to $m(f)$ consists of choosing a truth value assignment (by removing a point a satisfying Eaa) or removing a clause satisfied by this assignment (i.e. a clause containing an A such that 1_A is still in $m(f)$ or a $\neg A$ such that 0_A is still in $m(f)$). We cannot remove a clause before the assignment is done (i.e. when 0_A and 1_A are both still here) because the subformula $(Euv \wedge Evu) \Rightarrow v = u$ ensures that 0_A or 1_A has been removed. After every satisfiable clause is removed from $m(f)$, we can remove every remaining 0_A or 1_A by applying Exx. Thus, the only elements left in $m(f)$ will be the unsatisfiable clauses of f. This proves that f is satisfiable if and only if $m(f) \in \mathbf{DR}(\varphi(x))$.

<u>$\forall\exists$**DR**^{1}:</u> For each propositional variable A of f, there are three points 0_A, 1_A and s_A in $m(f)$. Again, $m(f)$ contains a point p_C for each clause C. For every variable A and every C containing an occurrence of A (A or $\neg A$), the following edges are in $m(f)$:

- $(s_A, 0_A)$, $(0_A, s_A)$, $(s_A, 1_A)$, $(1_A, s_A)$, $(0_A, 0_A)$, $(1_A, 1_A)$,
- $(0_A, p_C)$, $(p_C, 1_A)$,
- (s_A, p_C) if $\neg A$ belongs to C and
- (p_C, s_A) if A belongs to C.

We set

$$\begin{aligned}\varphi(x) := \quad & \forall u \exists v(((\neg Evv \wedge (Evx \vee Exv)) \\ & \wedge((Euu \wedge Eux) \Rightarrow (Evx \wedge Euv \wedge Evu)) \\ & \wedge((Euu \wedge Exu) \Rightarrow (Exv \wedge Euv \wedge Evu))) \\ & \vee(Exv \wedge Evx)).\end{aligned}$$

If f is satisfiable then we can apply the rule repeatedly and obtain the empty structure. Indeed, let $a \in \{0,1\}^{\mathrm{vars}(f)}$ be an assignment of the variables of f making f true. Then, for every A, we choose to remove the point ε_A (with $\varepsilon \in \{0,1\}$) such that $a(A) = 1 - \varepsilon_A$ (i.e. we keep the 0_A or 1_A that has been assigned to A by the assignment a). The point ε_A can be removed because there is a v (ε_A itself) such that $E\varepsilon_A v \wedge Ev\varepsilon_A$ holds. Then every p_C can be removed because now for every u there is a v (any s_A such that $a(A)$ makes the clause p_C true) such that the only point connected to s_A and p_C corresponds to the assignment (either $a(A) = 0$ and we have Eup_C and Evp_C or $a(A) = 1$ and we have Ep_Cu and Ep_Cv). After removing every p_C, we can remove the remaining points $a(A)_A$ and s_A for every A by removing first s_A (applying the subformula saying that there exists a v ($= a(A)_A$) such that $Exv \wedge Evx$ holds) and then $a(A)_A$ (again by applying this subformula).

Conversely, suppose we can obtain the empty structure and consider one of the execution of the rule giving the empty structure. In particular, every p_C will be removed. Let C be a clause and consider the step where p_C is actually removed. There is no point s_A still in $m(f)$ such that 0_A and 1_A are not in $m(f)$ anymore because in this case s_A will never be removed (the only way to remove s_A is to apply the formula saying that there exists a v such that $Exv \wedge Evx$) which contradicts the fact that we consider an execution giving the empty structure. There is necessarily at least one s_A connected to p_C (there is a v such that $\neg Evv \wedge (Evx \vee Exv)$). The points 0_A and 1_A cannot be both connected to p_C. Indeed, suppose for instance that A appears positively in C (the case where $\neg A$ is in C is symmetric). Let v be the point associated to $u = 0_A$ in the formula $\varphi(x)$. We have $E0_A0_A$ and $E0_Ap_C$, so we must have $Evp_C \wedge E0_Av \wedge Ev0_A$. The only v satisfying $E0_Av \wedge Ev0_A$ is s_A, but we have not Es_Ap_C because A appears positively in C. So we have the contradiction that $\varphi(p_C)$ does not hold. We have proved that either 0_A or 1_A remains at this step but not both. The corresponding value 0 or 1 is an assignment of A satisfying C. Indeed, if for instance 1_A is the remaining point then, since $E1_A1_A \wedge Ep_C1_A$ holds, we have Ep_Cs_A which means that A appears positively in C ; so assigning the value 1 to A makes the clause C true. Let $\varepsilon^{C,A}$ be the element of $\{0,1\}$ such that $\varepsilon_A^{C,A}$ is the remaining point between 0_A and 1_A. Let a be any assignment in $\{0,1\}^{\text{vars}(f)}$ such that, for every C, $a(A) = \varepsilon^{C,A}$. This assignment clearly satisfies f.

$\underline{\exists\mathbf{DR}^2}$: For this case, we assume that each variable appears in exactly three clauses and at least one time positively and one time negatively. This is still an **NP**-complete instance of SAT (cf. [11] proof of Theorem 2.1). We can even assume that A appears two times positively and one time negatively (by replacing A by $\neg A$ if necessary). For every variable A, there are four points s_A, 1_A, 2_A, 3_A in $m(f)$ and edges (s_A, s_A), $(s_A, 1_A)$, $(s_A, 2_A)$, $(s_A, 3_A)$ and $(3_A, s_A)$. For every A, let C_1, C_2 and C_3 be the clauses containing A, where A appears positively in C_1 and C_2 and negatively in C_3. Then $m(f)$ contains the edges

$$(1_A, p_{C_1}),\ (2_A, p_{C_2}),\ (1_A, p_{C_2}),\ (p_{C_2}, 1_A),\ (2_A, p_{C_1}),\ (p_{C_1}, 2_A) \text{ and } (3_A, p_{C_3}).$$

We set

$$\begin{aligned}\varphi(x,y) := \exists t((&Exx \wedge Exy \wedge \neg Eyx \wedge Eyt \wedge Ety)\\ &\vee(Ett \wedge x \neq t \wedge Etx \wedge Exy \wedge \neg Eyx)\\ &\vee(Ett \wedge Etx \wedge x \neq t \wedge x = y)\\ &\vee(Exx \wedge Exy \wedge Eyx \wedge x \neq y)).\end{aligned}$$

Note that the only two ways to remove s_A are by

a. removing $\{s_A, 3_A\}$ (via the fourth line of $\varphi(x,y)$) or
b. removing a $\{s_A, \varepsilon_A\}$ with $\varepsilon \in \{1,2\}$ (via the first line of $\varphi(x,y)$).

In the former case, the point 3_A becomes unavailable to remove p_{C_3} via line 2 with $x = 3_A$. In the latter case, suppose that $\varepsilon = 1$ (without loss of generality because the case $\varepsilon = 2$ is symmetric). Then p_{C_1} could not be removed by applying line 2 with $x = 1_A$ (the presence of 1_A is required to remove $\{s_A, 1_A\}$. And p_{C_2} could not be removed via line 2 with $x = 2_A$, because either p_{C_2} is removed before $\{s_A, 1_A\}$ and then line 1 could not remove $\{s_A, 1_A\}$ anymore (p_{C_2} is required in the role of t), or $\{s_A, 1_A\}$ is removed before p_{C_2} and then s_A is not available anymore to use line 2 with $x = 2_A$. Thus, in a sense, the case a. corresponds to the case where we choose the value 1 for the variable A and the case b. is the choice of the value 0. When this choice is made (resp. a. or b.) but not yet applied (s_A is still in $m(f)$), we can either use a point ε_A (resp. with $\varepsilon \in \{1,2\}$ or $\varepsilon = 3$) to remove p_{C_ε} via line 2 with $x = \varepsilon_A$ or just remove ε_A via line 3 if p_{C_ε} is already removed with some χ_B where $B \neq A$ and $\chi \in \{1,2,3\}$. There is a choice a. or b. for each variable A that allows to remove every p_C (and obtain the empty structure) if and only if f is satisfiable.

$\forall$**DR**^{2}: Let A be a variable of f with k negative occurrences and l positive occurrences in f. The digraph $m(f)$ contains the points $0_{A_1}, \ldots, 0_{A_k}$ and $1_{A_1}, \ldots, 1_{A_l}$ and the edges $(0_{A_i}, 0_{A_i})$, $(1_{A_j}, 1_{A_j})$, $(0_{A_i}, 1_{A_j})$ and $(1_{A_j}, 0_{A_i})$ for every $i \in [1,k]$ and $j \in [1,l]$. Moreover, for every i and j, there is an edge $(0_{A_i}, p_D)$ where D contains the i-th negative occurrence of A and an edge $(1_{A_j}, p_E)$ where E contains the j-th positive occurrence of A. We set

$$\varphi(x,y) := \forall u((Exy \wedge \neg(u \neq x \wedge Eux \wedge Exu)) \vee (Exy \wedge x = y)).$$

Each point p_C can only be removed with an ε_{A_i} connected to it and when there is no point $u = (1-\varepsilon)_{A_j}$ remaining in $m(f)$. In this case, it means that we have chosen the assignment ε for A. We can remove every p_C (and every other point using the subformula $Exy \wedge x = y$) if and only if f is satisfiable.

Quantifier free **DR**^{3}: An example of an **NP**-complete property on the signature $\{E\}$ is the set of digraphs having a partition into triangles (cf. [5] p. 68). It is equal to **DR**$(Exy \wedge Eyz \wedge Ezx)$.

5 Polynomial Time Fragments

In this section, we investigate $\forall^*$**DR**^{1}, $\exists^*$**DR**^{1} and quantifier free **DR**^{2}, the maximal fragments of **DR** containing only properties in **PTIME**.

We begin with $\exists^*$**DR**^{1} and quantifier free **DR**^{2}. To illustrate the former case, we can notice for example that **DR**$(\exists u(Exu \vee Eux))$ is the set of digraphs such that every connected component contains a loop.

Proposition 2. $\exists^*$**DR**$^1 \subset$ **PTIME**.

Proof. Suppose we have a finite structure $\mathcal{A}$ and an existential formula $\varphi(x)$ and we want to check if $\mathcal{A} \in$ **DR**$(\varphi(x))$. In this proof, the notation $\mathcal{A}(e_0, \ldots, e_m)$ designates the substructure of $\mathcal{A}$ induced by $\{e_0, \ldots, e_m\}$.

First we take any element a_0 of A such that $\mathcal{A}(a_0) \models \varphi(a_0)$. If there is no such a_0, then we already know that $\mathcal{A} \notin$ **DR**$(\varphi(x))$ because, before obtaining the empty structure, we need to find a point satisfying the rule in a substructure with one element. Then we take any a_1 different from a_0 such that $\mathcal{A}(a_0, a_1) \models \varphi(a_1)$. We continue to take points (a_2, a_3, etc.) as long as possible. At step i, we choose a_i different from $a_0, \ldots, a_{i-1}$ such that $\mathcal{A}(a_0, \ldots, a_i) \models \varphi(a_i)$. It is not hard to see that this process can be done in polynomial time. Indeed, we choose at most $|A|$ points a_i, and choosing a point consists in doing at most $|A|$ **FO** model checkings (which take $O(|A|^k)$ time for some k). So the whole process takes $O(|A|^{k+2})$ time.

Let a_n be the last point we choose. To complete the proof, we prove that $\mathcal{A}$ is in $\mathbf{DR}(\varphi(x))$ if and only if $\{a_0, \ldots, a_n\} = A$. Clearly, by definition of the points a_i, if $\{a_0, \ldots, a_n\} = A$, then the sequence $(a_n, a_{n-1}, \ldots, a_0)$ is such that we can remove every point of A according to the rule in this order and obtain the empty structure. Conversely, suppose that $\mathcal{A} \in \mathbf{DR}(\varphi(x))$, i.e. there exists a sequence $(b_0, \ldots, b_m)$ such that $\{b_0, \ldots, b_m\} = A$ and $\mathcal{A}(b_0, \ldots, b_i) \models \varphi(b_i)$ for every i. Suppose that $\{b_0, \ldots, b_m\} \neq \{a_0, \ldots, a_n\}$. Let b_l be the first element different from $a_0, \ldots, a_n$ in the sequence $(b_0, \ldots, b_m)$. In particular, we have $\{b_0, \ldots, b_{l-1}\} \subset \{a_0, \ldots, a_n\}$. It is well-known that existential formulas are preserved under extensions. In particular, since $\mathcal{A}(b_0, \ldots, b_l) \models \varphi(b_l)$, we also have $\mathcal{A}(b_l, a_0, \ldots, a_n) \models \varphi(b_l)$. This means that the point b_l could be chosen as point a_{n+1} in our preceding construction. This is a contradiction. So $\{a_0, \ldots, a_n\} = A$.

The second case is quantifier free $\mathbf{DR}^2$. In a sense, every property in this fragment is a particular instance of the PerfectMatching problem.

Proposition 3. *Quantifier free* $\mathbf{DR}^2$ *is included in* **PTIME**.

Proof. Let $\mathcal{A}$ be a finite structure and let $\varphi(x, y)$ be a quantifier free formula. We define the graph $G := (A, \{\{a, b\} \mid \mathcal{A} \models \varphi(a, b)\})$. The graph G has a perfect matching $\{\{a_1, b_1\}, \ldots, \{a_n, b_n\}\}$ if and only if there is a partition $\{a_1, b_1\}, \ldots, \{a_n, b_n\}$ of A such that, for every $i < n$, $\mathcal{A} \setminus \bigcup_{l=1}^{i} \{a_l, b_l\} \models \varphi(a_{i+1}, b_{i+1})$. This is because quantifier free formulas are preserved under substructures and extension (i.e. for every substructure $\mathcal{B}$ of $\mathcal{A}$ containing a and b, $\mathcal{A} \models \varphi(a, b)$ if and only if $\mathcal{B} \models \varphi(a, b)$). Thus, deciding if $\mathcal{A}$ is in $\mathbf{DR}(\varphi(x, y))$ takes polynomial time because PerfectMatching is in **PTIME** (see for instance [8]).

We now consider the $\forall^*\mathbf{DR}^1$ fragment. We have seen that for instance the sets of directed paths, acyclic graphs, γ- and β-acyclic hypergraphs belong to $\forall^*\mathbf{DR}^1$. For this fragment, we can prove a little more than **PTIME** recognition.

Proposition 4. $\forall^*\mathbf{FO} \subsetneq \forall^*\mathbf{DR}^1$.

Proof. Let φ be a universal first-order sentence. We have $\mathcal{A} \models \varphi$ if and only if $\mathcal{A} \in \mathbf{DR}(\varphi \wedge x = x)$. Indeed, if $\mathcal{A} \not\models \varphi$, then the rule $\mathcal{R}_{\varphi \wedge x = x}$ will not remove any element. If $\mathcal{A} \models \varphi$, then we remove any element and so on until all elements are removed (because φ is preserved under substructures). This shows the inclusion. The equality does not hold because graph acyclicity is in $\forall^*\mathbf{DR}^1$ and this is well-known that it is not in **FO**.

Notation. We call **PS** the class of properties preserved under substructures (this notation is not standard).

Proposition 5. $\forall^*\mathbf{DR}^1 \subsetneq \mathbf{PS} \cap \mathbf{PTIME}$.

Proof. $\forall^*\mathbf{DR}^1 \subset \mathbf{PS}$: Suppose $\varphi(x)$ is universal, $\mathcal{A} \in \mathbf{DR}(\varphi(x))$ and $\mathcal{B}$ is a substructure of $\mathcal{A}$. Let $(a_1, \ldots, a_n)$ be a sequence such that we can remove these elements from $\mathcal{A}$ by $\mathcal{R}_{\varphi(x)}$ in this order, i.e. a_i is the i-th element we remove.

In particular $\{a_1, \ldots, a_n\} = A$. Let $(a_{i_k})_{k\in[1,m]}$ be the subsequence containing the elements of B, i.e. $\{a_{i_k} \mid k \in [1,m]\} = B$. For every $l \in [1,m]$, we have $\mathcal{B} \setminus \{a_{i_k} \mid k \in [1,l-1]\} \models \varphi(a_{i_l})$ because $B \setminus \{a_{i_k} \mid k \in [1,l-1]\}$ is included in $A \setminus \{a_i \mid i \in [1,i_l-1]\}$, $\mathcal{A} \setminus \{a_i \mid i \in [1,i_l-1]\} \models \varphi(a_{i_l})$ and $\varphi(x)$ is preserved under substructures. So $(a_{i_k})_{k\in[1,m]}$ is a sequence such that the elements of B can be removed in this order by $\mathcal{R}_{\varphi(x)}$. Thus $\mathcal{B} \in \mathbf{DR}(\varphi(x))$.

<u>$\forall^*\mathbf{DR}^1 \subset \mathbf{PTIME}$:</u> When $\varphi(x)$ is universal, it is preserved under substructures. So, if an element a could be removed according to $\mathcal{R}_{\varphi(x)}$, it will be removed anyway (possibly later). This implies that $\varphi(x)$ is confluent for $\mathbf{DR}^1$. At each step, we can remove any a satisfying $\varphi(a)$ without changing the result (obtaining the empty structure or not). Testing if an element a satisfies $\varphi(a)$ takes polynomial time ($O(|A|^k)$ where k is the number of quantified variables in $\varphi(x)$). Updating the structure (replacing $\mathcal{A}$ with $\mathcal{A} \setminus \{a\}$) takes linear time. Checking $\mathcal{A} \in \mathbf{DR}(\varphi(x))$ consists in doing not more than $|A|^2$ tests of the rule and at most $|A|$ updates, so it takes $O(|A|^{k+2})$ time.

<u>$\forall^*\mathbf{DR}^1 \neq \mathbf{PS} \cap \mathbf{PTIME}$:</u> GRAPH PLANARITY is preserved under substructures and it is in **PTIME** (there even exists a linear time algorithm). But it is not in $\forall^*\mathbf{DR}^1$. In fact, it is not even in **DR**. Indeed, suppose GRAPH PLANARITY=$\mathbf{DR}(\varphi(x_1, \ldots, x_k))$ and let q be the quantifier rank of $\varphi(x_1, \ldots, x_k)$. There exist two graphs $\mathcal{A}$ and $\mathcal{B}$ equivalent under $\equiv_{q+k}$ (i.e. they satisfy the same sentences of quantifier rank at most $q+k$) such that $\mathcal{B}$ is planar and $\mathcal{A}$ is not and such that every proper subgraph of $\mathcal{A}$ is planar (cf. Figure 2). They are equivalent under $\equiv_{q+k}$ because they have the same neighborhoods. More precisely, by Hanf-locality of first-order logic (see for instance [9] Chap. 4), there is an integer N_{q+k} such that, if two structures have the same neighborhoods of radius N_{q+k} then they are equivalent under $\equiv_{q+k}$. Thus, if each dotted line in Figure 2 has length greater than N_{q+k}, then $\mathcal{A}$ and $\mathcal{B}$ have the same neighborhoods of radius N_{q+k} and so $\mathcal{A} \equiv_{q+k} \mathcal{B}$. As $\mathcal{B}$ is planar there are elements b_1, $\ldots$, b_k in B which can be removed by $\mathcal{R}_{\varphi(x_1,\ldots,x_k)}$. But $\mathcal{A} \equiv_{q+k} \mathcal{B}$, so $\mathcal{A}$ satisfies also $\exists x_1 \ldots \exists x_k \varphi(x_1, \ldots, x_k)$ and so there are also elements a_1, $\ldots$, a_k in A that can be removed by $\mathcal{R}_{\varphi(x_1,\ldots,x_k)}$. But since $A \setminus \{a_1, \ldots, a_k\}$ is planar and GRAPH PLANARITY=$\mathbf{DR}(\varphi(x_1, \ldots, x_k))$, then $\mathcal{A} \in \mathbf{DR}(\varphi(x_1, \ldots, x_k))$. This is a contradiction.

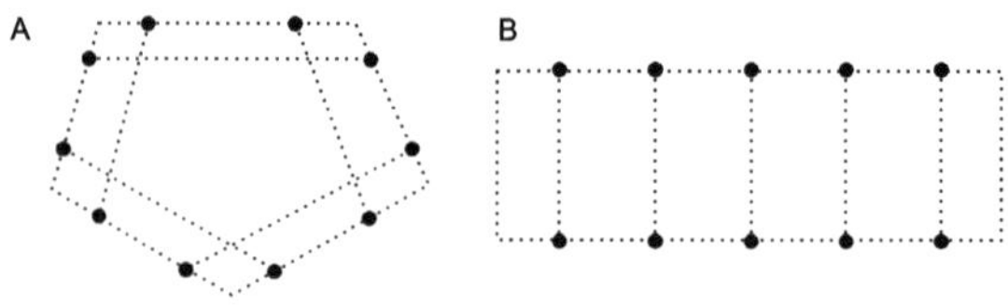

Fig. 2. The dotted lines represent long (enough) paths. We have $\mathcal{A} \equiv_{q+k} \mathcal{B}$. $\mathcal{A}$ is not planar but its proper subgraphs are planar and $\mathcal{B}$ is planar.

6 Concluding Remarks

A possible objective would be to detect more **PTIME** properties defined in the framework of destructive rules. We could find semantical conditions that are easy to check or other syntactical conditions. We can notice that, when we remove a point via a rule, we do not keep information about the original structure. So, we could add the possibility of remembering the removed points or marking certain remaining points each time we apply a rule.

The classification of Theorem 1 is concerned with the class of all digraphs and the presence of loops and directed edges seems to be important in the SAT-reductions of Section 4. Thus, it is possible that there is another classification of polynomial fragments in the case of undirected graphs. We can remark that such a distinction plays a crucial role in [7]. The classification is maybe also different on the class of hypergraphs seen as structures over $\{\in\}$ without elements a, b and c such that $a \in b \in c$. In particular, it would be interesting if α-acyclicity of hypergraphs belonged to a polynomial fragment of **DR** in this particular case.

Acknowledgements. I am grateful to Arnaud Durand for his help and his precious advice. I also want to thank the anonymous referees for their comments and suggestions.

References

1. Alechina, N., Gurevich, Y.: Syntax vs Semantics on Finite Structures. In: Mycielski, J., Rozenberg, G., Salomaa, A. (eds.) Structures in Logic and Computer Science. LNCS, vol. 1261, pp. 14–33. Springer, Heidelberg (1997)
2. Duris, D.: Some Characterizations of γ and β-Acyclicity of Hypergraphs (2008), `http://hal.archives-ouvertes.fr/hal-00360321/fr/`
3. Ebbinghaus, H.-D., Flum, J., Thomas, W.: Mathematical Logic. Springer, Heidelberg (1994)
4. Fagin, R.: Degrees of Acyclicity for Hypergraphs and Relational Database Schemes. J. of the ACM 30(3), 514–550 (1983)
5. Garey, M.R., Johnson, D.S.: Computers and Intractability: A Guide to the Theory of NP-Completeness. W.H. Freeman, New York (1979)
6. Grädel, E., Kreutzer, S.: Will Deflation Lead to Depletion? on Non-Monotone Fixed Point Inductions. In: Proceedings of the 18th Annual IEEE Symposium on Logic in Computer Science (LICS 2003), pp. 158–167 (2003)
7. Gottlob, G., Kolaitis, G., Schwentick, T.: Existential Second-Order Logic over Graphs: Charting the Tractability Frontier. J. of the ACM 51, 664–674 (2000)
8. Jungnickel, D.: Graphs, Networks and Algorithms. Springer, Heidelberg (2005)
9. Libkin, L.: Elements of Finite Model Theory. Springer, Heidelberg (2004)
10. Nagl, M.: Graph-Grammatiken: Theorie, Anwendungen, Implementierung. Vieweg (1979)
11. Tovey, C.A.: A Simplified NP-Complete Satisfiability Problem. Discrete Applied Mathematics 8(1), 85–90 (1984)

Learning User Preferences for 2CP-Regression for a Recommender System

Alan Eckhardt[1,2] and Peter Vojtáš[1,2]

[1] Department of Software Engineering, Charles University
[2] Institute of Computer Science, Czech Academy of Science
Prague, Czech Republic
{eckhardt,vojtas}@ksi.mff.cuni.cz,

Abstract. In this paper we deal with a task to learn a general user model from user ratings of a small set of objects. This general model is used to recommend top-k objects to the user. We consider several (also some new) alternatives of learning local preferences and several alternatives of aggregation (with or without 2CP-regression). The main contributions are evaluation of experiments on our prototype tool Pref-Work with respect to several satisfaction measures and the proposal of method Peak for normalisation of numerical attributes. Our main objective is to keep the number of sample data which the user has to rate reasonable small.

1 Introduction

The problem studied in this paper is based on the idea of automating to help the user in making right decisions when selecting an object from a large number of objects. The main motivation lies in e-commerce, where user might benefit from a recommendation of top-k objects that might interest her without needing to process all the objects manually. This recommendation should be rather automatic and transparent, because user typically does not want to fill in any complicated forms and she is annoyed when spending too much time on her search.

When user is buying, for example, a notebook, she is considering such attributes as price, producer, size of RAM, hard disk and display. In traditional e-shop environment, it is possible to make some restrictions on these attributes and thus lower the number of notebooks the user has to process manually. But these restrictions are inflexible - when the user selects the price under 2000\$, any notebook with price 2001\$ would not appear in the result set although it might be very interesting for the user. This is the reason for a flexible search, based on scoring (fuzzy) user preferences.

In this paper we deal with preference learning - user is assumed to rate a small set S of notebooks according to her preference. Recommender system constructs her preference model from these ratings; the model allows evaluation of all notebooks in database. The process of preference learning is in Figure 1.

J. van Leeuwen et al. (Eds.): SOFSEM 2010, LNCS 5901, pp. 346–357, 2010.

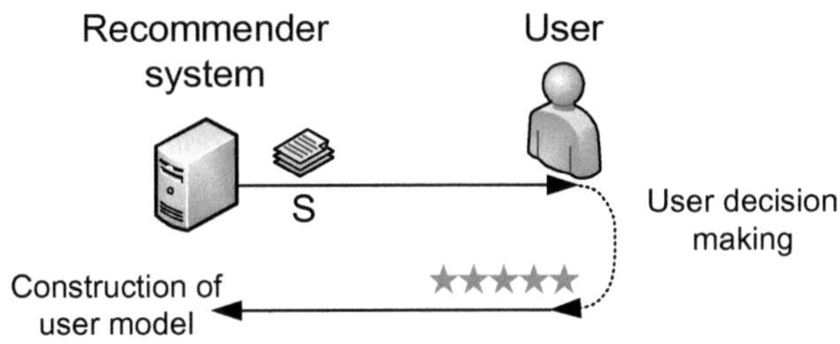

Fig. 1. Interaction between user and recommender system

Main contributions of this paper are:

- Proposal of method Peak for normalisation of numerical attributes for 2CP regression
- Comparison of proposed approach with other approaches
- Introducing several measures of satisfaction of user

Related work is studied in Section 2. Our particular model is described in Section 3. It is based on two steps - the first step is the learning of degree of preference for each attribute, which acts as normalisation of attribute values. E.g. value 15,4" is transformed to its preference degree 0.7, which was learnt from the ratings of notebooks. The second step is to learn the combination of these preference degrees into the overall rating of the notebook (it is expected that the user would assign this rating to the notebook if she was asked to). This paper is focused on the first step and particularly on the normalisation of numerical domains such as price.

In Section 4 are described several methods for local preference learning. Then the new approach Peak is tested in Section 5, we use several error measures and provide comparison using our prototype tool PrefWork [1] for the evaluation of quality of preference learning method. We end with conclusion and future work in Section 6.

2 Related Work

User preferences are a wide field so there is a plenty of research areas. For automated decision process, the user preference learning is the most important one.

We focus on content based learning, which means that the preferences are based on the attributes of objects. This approach corresponds well to how users decide in the real world in our view. The difficulty is that users are often inconsistent or they take into account attributes that are not known or impossible to quantify, such as the design of a notebook.

In this area, the main focus was on the search of documents in the past [2,3]. This is a specific area, because the features of documents are of little structure.

We are interested more in the recommendation of more complicated objects like notebooks, with clear attribute structure.

Following works [4,5,6,7] deal with general, more structured, objects. One of our main inspirations were also CP-nets [8]. This model captures complex user preferences in graph representation, in which a preference over one attribute may depend on the values of other attributes. There are many papers dealing with CP-nets, but there is very few which describes a way to construct a CP-net automatically, by learning from a simple user input (user ratings, in our case). First, paper [9] propose a method for learning CP-nets but only those without preferential dependencies, which degrades the CP-net to the set of isolated vertices. Second, and the last paper currently available, is [10], which use preference elicitation - it poses questions directly about her preferences. This approach requires a lot of effort from the user, so we do not consider it. Finally, in [11] is an extensive inspection of CP-nets learning from a given set of object comparisons. In this work, theoretical limits of learning are studied, no particular algorithm is presented.

Because preferences over attribute A_1 may depend on another attribute A_2, user has to specify her preferences not only for all values of A_1 but she has to do it for every possible value of A_2. This means very much work and insight for user, work that probably few people will undergo (according to [12], as little as 9 out of 260 people provided a more complex feedback to their system). That is why learning of CP-nets is important for us.

Another different approach for representing user preferences are preference relations, or especially fuzzy preference relations [13]. Studying of preference relations often concerns of detecting and removing cycles in preferences. However, preference relations without cycles can be easily mapped to the approach using ratings commonly used in recommender systems. We do not consider this model; we rather follow approach identified by R.Fagin in [14] and consider user ratings as fuzzy sets.

The relation to decision theory (e.g. [15]) is very close, except the terminology. Our local preferences are objectives (Chapter 15 in [15]) in decision theory, with exactly the same meaning, except that in our view, every user can have different objectives – one wants small display, another wants large display. Utility function (Chapter 16 in [15]) corresponds to our aggregation with again the same meaning – to resolve the possible conflict between attributes (incompatible objects on the Pareto front). On the other hand, decision support theory is focused more on the case with few alternatives and very complex decision process. Decision support then tries to help the user to orient himself in the structure of objectives. Our approach focuses on recommender systems, with a large number of objects, changing objectives, utility and very small amount of user ratings.

3 Two Step Monotone User Model

We describe the same model as in [16,17]. To be self contained we describe it briefly. Experiments compare this model to the adapted one, which uses the CP-net learning, which is described in Section 4.4.

3.1 Notation

We will work with a set of objects X, which is a set of notebooks in our experiment. User's overall rating of a small sample of objects S is a fuzzy subset of X, i.e. a function $r(o) : S \to [0,1]$, where 0 means the least preferred and 1 means the most preferred. In practical applications this can be $\{1 =$ the worst,...,5 $=$ the best$\}$. Every object has attributes $A_1, ..., A_N$ with domains $D_{A_1}, ..., D_{A_N}$. Let $X \subseteq \prod_{i=1}^{N} D_{A_i}$. We will use $X(A_1 = a)$ when denoting a set of objects with a as the value of attribute A_1.

User model, in our view, is a method for representing user decision process when considering user's preference of an object $o \in X$ that is an extension of r to $\widehat{r} : X \to [0,1]$, preserving some criteria. Our user model consists of two steps.

Local Preferences. In the first step, which we call local preferences, every attribute value of object o is normalised using a fuzzy set $f_i : D_{A_i} \to [0,1]$. These fuzzy sets are also called objectives or preferences over attributes. With this transformation, the original space of objects' attributes $X \subset \prod_{i=1}^{N} D_{A_i}$ is transformed into $X' \subset [0,1]^N$. Moreover, we know that the object with transformed attribute values equal to $[1, ..., 1]$ is the most preferred object. It probably does not exist in the real world, though. On the other side, the object with values $[0, ..., 0]$ is the least preferred, which is more probable to be found in reality.

Global Preferences. In the second step, called global preferences, the normalised attributes are aggregated into the overall score of the object using an aggregation function $@ : X' \to [0,1]$. Aggregation functions are also often called utility functions ([15]).

Aggregation function may have different forms; one of the most common is a weighted average, as in the following formula:

$$@(o) = (2 * f_{Price}(o) + 1 * f_{Display}(o) + 3 * f_{HDD}(o) + 1 * f_{RAM}(o))/7,$$

where f_A is a fuzzy set for normalisation of attribute A.

For 2CP model, we use a slightly adapted model, see Section 4.4 for details.

3.2 Aggregation Function Learning

We focus on the learning of user model. User is expected to rate a small sample $S \subseteq X$ of objects ($r : S \to \{0, 0.25, 0.5, 0.75, 1\}$), where $|S| \ll |X|$. The size of the training set is expected to be very small. Our model consist of $f_1, ..., f_N$ and @, so we expect to construct these functions from user ratings of S. Learning of aggregation function is described in following section. This paper focuses on the learning of local preferences, which is described in Section 4.

In this section we describe some methods of aggregation of local preferences given by f_i.

Statistical. Aggregation function serves to combine preferences over attributes into a single rating that represents the preference of the object as a whole. There are many ways to aggregate local preferences; we are currently using a weighted average with weights learnt from user ratings. Method called "Statistical" was described in [17,18].

The distributions of ratings for attribute values $a_i \in A$ are considered when determining the weight of attribute A. In Figure 2 is an example of distribution of ratings across the domain of attribute Producer. If there is a lot of ratings near one value as in Figure 2 for HP or Asus, the attribute value is considered as decisive when doing the overall rating. However, if the distribution is rather uniform such as in Figure 2 for Dell, then attribute value a_i does not play an important role in the overall rating. The measure of importance of an attribute value is computed with formula

$$imp(a_i) = 1/\sum_{o \in X(A=a_i)} |r(o) - avg_{o \in X(A=a_i)} r(o)|/|X(A = a_i)|$$

where $X(A = a_i)$ denotes the set of objects o with a_i as the value of attribute A. Then the importance of attribute A is computed as

$$W(A) = 1/(\textstyle\sum_{a_i \in A} imp(a_i/|A|).$$

Instances. Another possible aggregation function uses objects from the training set as delimiters for the rating of objects from testing set. This method is called "Instances" and was proposed in [17]. It is based on the idea of Pareto dominance – if an object o_1 is better in all attributes than object o_2, than $r(o_1) \geq r(o_2)$. When given an object o to evaluation, Instances search the training set for objects that are dominated by o and uses maximum of their rating as an estimate of rating of o.

There is an example how the training set can be used for rating estimation in Figure 3. White circles S_i^j are objects from the training set with rating j and id i. Black circles x and y are objects from testing set - in our case, x gets rating 0.9 and y gets 1.0. The distance from objects from the training set also plays role and can be taken into account. Interested reader may see [17].

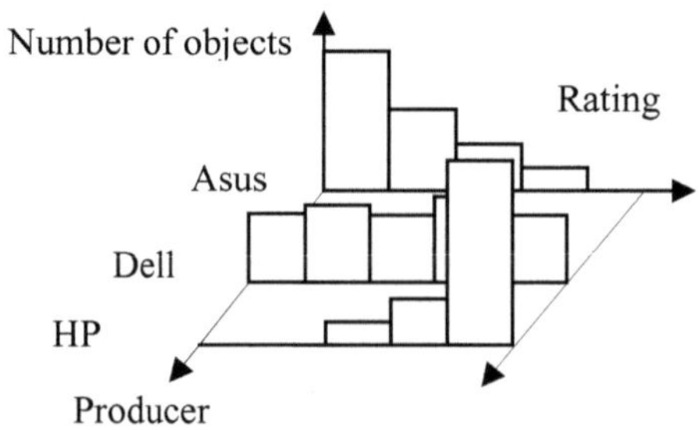

Fig. 2. Uniform and expressive distributions of ratings over an categorical attribute

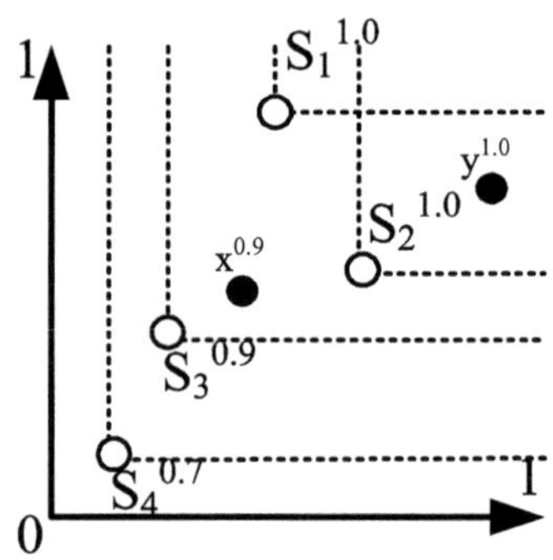

Fig. 3. Instances

Other Possible Approaches. Our approach is certainly not the only one – any data mining technique can be used here, e.g. SVM, multilayer perceptron etc. This means a method that given a function $S \rightarrow [0,1]$ constructs a globally defined function $X \rightarrow [0,1]$.

Reader can easily imagine training e.g. a multilayer perceptron with normalised attribute values. This will make use of normalisation that should help these data mining methods for better learning. However, we did not do any experiment with this approach yet.

4 Local Preferences Learning

As mentioned in Section 3, our user model is divided into two steps.

The first step is used for normalisation of every attribute value to interval $[0,1]$, so that the best object would have coordinates $[1,...,1]$. This can be viewed also as monotonisation of data - if the normalised attribute values of object o_1 are all lower than those of object o_2, then o_2 is surely preferred to o_1 (if the normalisation is determined correctly). In the following section, the main task is to find the normalisation of attribute A_i, i.e. to find a function $f_i : D_{A_i} \rightarrow [0,1]$.

4.1 Linear Regression

Linear regression is very useful method that serves to find a relation in a set of data in form of a linear function. It can be used for finding the preference of attribute values for numerical attributes, e.g. price. When given a set of prices and ratings of notebooks, linear regression creates a linear function $f_{price}(price) = \alpha * price + \beta$. Then we can normalise all values of price using this function.

Linear regression is based on minimising squares of errors. It typically uses the mean squared error as the error function, which has the form of $MSE(f_i) = \sum_{o \in X} (f_i(o) - r(o))^2$.

4.2 Quadratic Regression

Quadratic regression is an extension of linear regression (see 4.1). It also uses a set of ratings and prices, but the output is a quadratic function $f_{price}(price) = \alpha * price * price + \beta * price + \gamma$. The obvious fact is that quadratic function is more complex than linear function but also more costly to find. Again, quadratic regression minimises $MSE(f_i)$.

Another, maybe not so obvious, disadvantage of quadratic regression is that it requires more points for its construction. Linear regression requires at least two points, quadratic requires three. We did not succeed to find any comparison of linear and quadratic regressions with respect to the size of the training set and to the accuracy in literature. It is possible that the linear regression may perform better on small training sets, but we did not made any experiment to confirm this idea.

4.3 Peak – A Method for Finding Triangular Fuzzy Functions

Because it is natural for user to have the most preferred value of an attribute, we created a new method for finding triangular fuzzy functions. We made a simplifying assumption that triangular function is composed of only two linear functions (often fuzzy triangular function consists of two linear functions and two intervals on both extremes of the domain, where the value is 0). This method is called Peak, but the functions do not have to share the common point at the top.

Peak works on any numerical domain. It traverses values of the domain present in the training set and the value a is tried if it is a good "peak". We construct two linear functions, one is defined on numbers lower than a and the other defined on higher numbers. Then the error is measured using $MSE(f_i)$. After traversing all the domain, we choose the best peak (that with minimal $MSE(f_i)$) for that attribute.

An illustrative example of such a peak in attribute price is in Figure 4. White circles represent objects with given price and rating forming the training set. Note that the peak needs not to be at the top - this method would also learn the most unpreferred value. In that case, the peak would be at the bottom of axis y forming a shape more similar to a "valley".

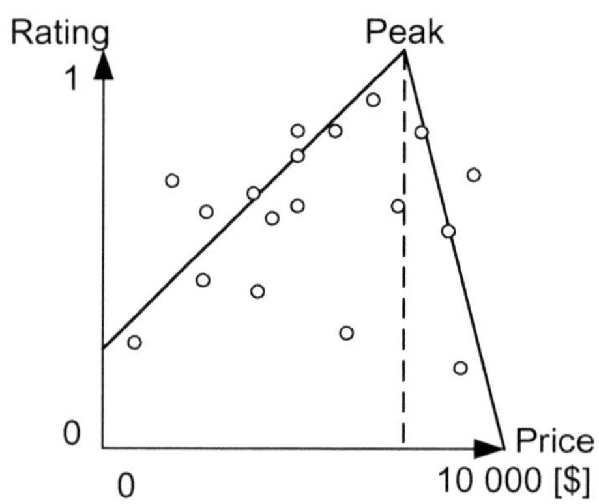

Fig. 4. Example of a peak in price

The obvious argument against Peak is that it is not a very efficient method. That is surely true, but we expect to work with small sets of ratings, up to 50 objects in the training set. Also some values may repeat in the set, e.g. sizes of hard disk or display whose domains are rather limited. These factors reduce the work needed to find the right peak.

4.4 2CP-Regression

In our previous work we proposed a method 2CP for finding relations between attributes that allowed us to construct a very simple CP-net in [16]. For more details about CP-nets see [8].

In brief, 2CP serves as normalisation of a numerical attribute A_1. It tries to find a relation between A_1 and another nominal attribute A_2. The motivation for this is that e.g. the preferred price of a notebook may depend on the producer. For producers HP, IBM, Lenovo, Toshiba and Sony the best price may be 2200\$, because these producers are renowned. But for Fujitsu-Siemens, Acer, Asus and MSI the best price is 750\$ because user is not willing to pay more money for these producers. After having found this relation, a method such as linear regression is used to normalise the numerical attribute that is split by values of A_2.

Using 2CP changes slightly the user model - instead of having $f_1 : D_{A_1} \rightarrow [0,1]$, the normalisation is rather $f_1 : D_{A_1} \times D_{A_2} \rightarrow [0,1]$. This fact also affect the monotonicity of the user model - it is no longer monotone with regard to particular attributes. The training set S is split into subsets $S_{a_1}, ..., S_{a_k}, k = |A_2|$ with the same value of attribute A_2 (each of S_a is monotone). 2CP constructs a function $f_1^a : D_{A_1} \rightarrow [0,1]$ for each value $a \in A_2$ using only corresponding S_a. For better learning, a clustering on the values of A_2 can be performed - see more the future work in Section 6.1.

2CP is not a regression technique by itself - it has to be combined with one of the methods presented above (linear, quadratic or Peak regressions).

5 Experiments

5.1 Experiment Settings

We used the same dataset as in [16], so the description of experiment setting remains the same: Our experiment was done on a set of 200 notebooks crawled from a web shop. There are five attributes: hard disk, display, price, producer and ram. We have created an artificial user U with preferences on the scale {1,2,3,4,5} for every notebook. Preferences were generated using a set of fuzzy sets f_i and an aggregation function @.

The user preferences on price were dependent on the actual value of the producer of the notebook. As it was mentioned in Section 4.4, for producers HP, IBM, Lenovo, Toshiba and Sony the best price was set to 2200\$ and for Fujitsu-Siemens, Acer, Asus and MSI the best price was set to 750\$. Hence the same price would produce different degree of preference for different producers.

Testing was performed with an altered cross-validation method. Because we are dealing with user ratings, it can not be expected that the user rates many objects. That is why we limited the training set size (TSS in following text) up to 60 ratings at maximum. Methods were tested on the rest of the set. When the user model is constructed from the first 10 notebooks, it is tested on the remaining 190 notebooks. Then the next 10 notebooks are taken as the training set and the model is tested on the remaining 190. For TSS = 20 the model is tested on the remaining 180 notebooks. Resulting errors are averaged for every TSS so that the results are reliable.

We have tested various methods with following parameters:

- Local preferences learning : Linear, Quadratic or Peak
- Use of 2CP procedure: it is indicated by presence or absence of "2CP" at the end of the name of the method.
- Aggregation function learning : Statistical (see [18,17] and 3.2) and Instances (see [17] and 3.2).

We also tested methods Mean and Support Vector Machine. Method Mean returns the average rating from the training set. Mean serves as indicator, whether a method is useful or not. Finally, Support Vector Machine, a traditional data mining method, was tested, using default implementation from Weka [19].

No tuning of any method was performed - these methods are supposed to work on arbitrary data automatically without the need of adjusting any parameters.

Methods in following figures were divided into two groups - in the first group, only methods that use 2CP are compared; in the second group, non-2CP methods are compared to Statistical with Peak and with 2CP.

5.2 Experiment Results

We studied three types of error measures. The first and most commonly used is RMSE - root mean squared error. RMSE captures the average error across the whole testing set. The second, Weighted RMSE, adds weight to each contribution to the error. The weight associated is the same as the real rating, because good objects are of greater concern than objects that are not preferred. In other words, it is worse if a good notebook does not appear on the first page of results than if a bad notebook does. Finally, the third is Kendall tau rank coefficient. Kendall tau rank coefficient is a measure of correspondence between two ordered lists : objects from the testing set ordered by the real user preferences are in the first list. The second list consists of the same objects, ordered by preferences

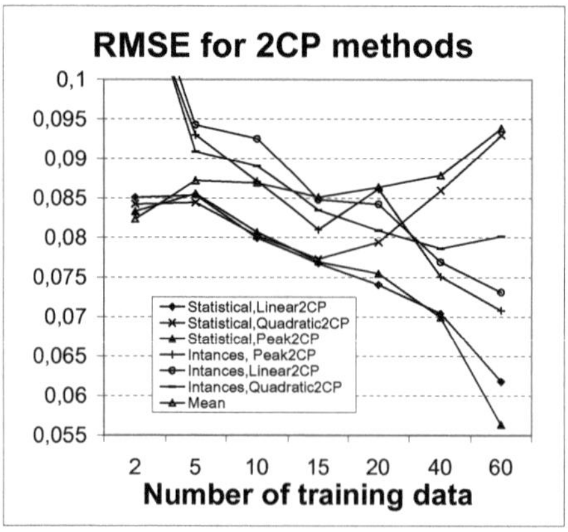

Fig. 5. RMSE for 2CP methods

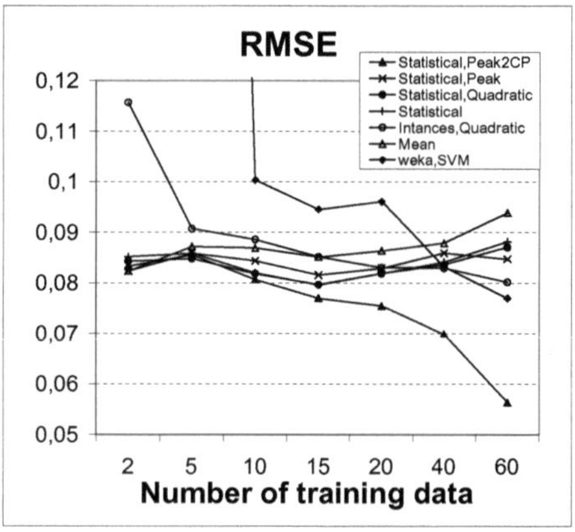

Fig. 6. RMSE for various methods

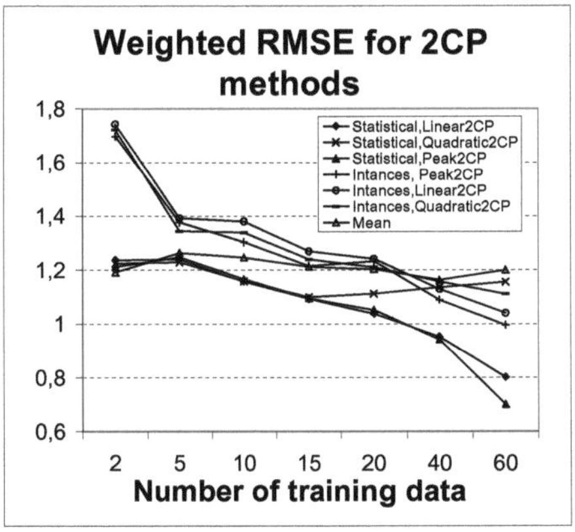

Fig. 7. Weighted RMSE for 2CP methods

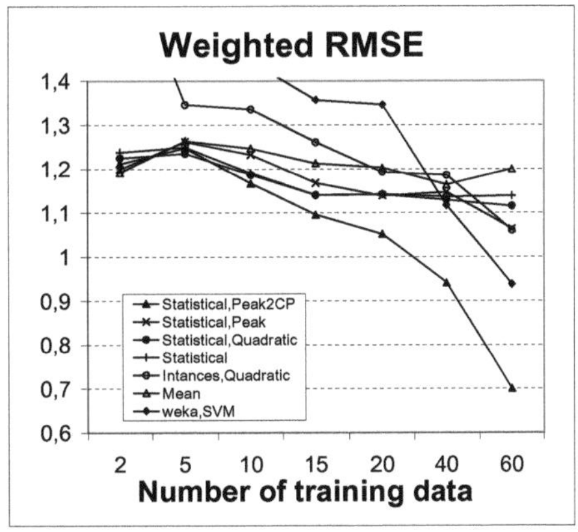

Fig. 8. Weighted RMSE for various methods

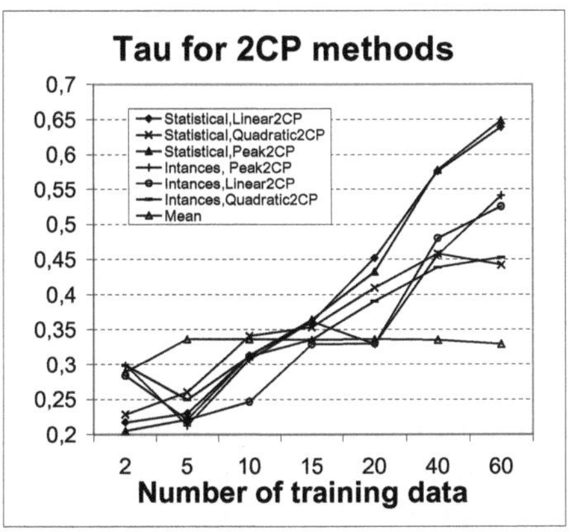

Fig. 9. Tau coefficient for 2CP methods

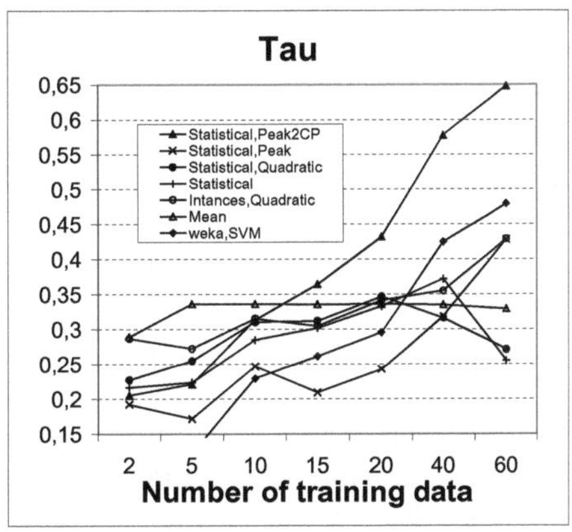

Fig. 10. Tau coefficient for various methods

proposed by the tested method. In this way, we can estimate the similarity of the ordering given by the method and the ordering given by the real user. Tau coefficient ranges from -1 to 1; 1 means the absolute correlation, i.e. the same lists, and -1 means the opposite correlation, i.e. the reversed lists. Tau coefficient of 0 means that there is no correlation between the two lists.

In Figures 5 and 6 are results for RMSE. Clearly, Statistical with Linear or Peak normalisation are the best, with Peak having a small advantage. Strange is that Statistical with Quadratic normalisation is the worst from Statisticals. Instances were overall worse than Statistical. Mean is worst for larger TSS but not as bad as Instances for smaller TSS. The most surprising was the very bad performance of SVM - for smaller training sets of size 5,10,15 and 20, it performed even worse than Mean. It begins to improve from 20.

When looking to Weighted RMSE (Figure 7,8), the phenomenon is even clearer. Instances are on average worse than Statisticals.

The results for Tau coefficient, are mixed (Figure 9,10). The only exception is again Statistical with Peak2CP, which is the clear winner. Instances are on the average worse than Statisticals again, and SVM is good only for the two largest training sets.

6 Conclusions

Several possibilities for finding normalisation of numerical domain have been studied in this paper. They have been tested with a method for the learning of simple CP-nets and have been tested thoroughly.

We have also proposed a method for finding the preference dependence between two attributes, which was demonstrated on the example of a user for whom the ideal price depends on the producer of the notebook. We are aware that our model does not correspond to CP-nets completely, but the proposed part of our fuzzy model can be considered as a simple CP-net. This method proved itself to be very efficient in case when ceteris paribus phenomenon occurs. Method Peak for finding the triangular fuzzy sets was also tested with good results.

6.1 Future Work

We would like to extend 2CP to finding relations between more than two attributes, making a more general nCP-regression. However, this will be strongly influenced by the small size of the training set.

The other important issue is to be able to find if there is a relation between the preference of two attributes, and to be able to measure the strength of the relation. This will enable to detect, whether to use 2CP regression or not. In the current settings, we are always looking for the dependence. To solve this, we can either use the information about the correctness of the normalisation or we can measure the degree of the preference dependence between the two attributes.

Finally, a clustering on f_i^a can be performed to allow a more robust regression on similar values. E.g. in our example, we have learnt the regression for each producer separately. Clustering would enable to have only two functions for the two clusters of producers.

Acknowledgment. The work on this paper was supported by Czech projects MSM 0021620838, 1ET 100300517 and GACR 201/09/H057.

References

1. Eckhardt, A.: Prefwork – a Framework for User Preference Learning Methods Testing. In: Vojtas, P. (ed.) Proceedings of ITAT 2009 Information Technologies - Applications and Theory, Slovakia, CEUR-WS.org (to appear, 2009)

2. Joachims, T.: Optimizing Search Engines Using Clickthrough Data. In: KDD 2002: Proceedings of the Eighth ACM SIGKDD International Conference on Knowledge Discovery and Data Mining, pp. 133–142. ACM Press, New York (2002)
3. Joachims, T., Granka, L., Pan, B., Hembrooke, H., Gay, G.: Accurately Interpreting Clickthrough Data as Implicit Feedback. In: SIGIR 2005: Proceedings of the 28th Annual International ACM SIGIR Conference on Research and Development in Information Retrieval, pp. 154–161. ACM, New York (2005)
4. Cao-Van, K.: Supervised Ranking, from Semantics to Algorithms. Ph.D. Dissertation, Ghent University (2003)
5. Apolloni, B., Zamponi, G., Zanaboni, A.M.: Learning Fuzzy Decision Trees. Neural Networks 11(5), 885–895 (1998)
6. Holland, S., Ester, M., Kiessling, W.: Preference Mining: A Novel Approach on Mining User Preferences for Personalized Applications. In: Lavrač, N., Gamberger, D., Todorovski, L., Blockeel, H. (eds.) PKDD 2003. LNCS (LNAI), vol. 2838, pp. 204–216. Springer, Heidelberg (2003)
7. Jung, S.Y., Hong, J.H., Kim, T.S.: A Statistical Model for User Preference. Knowledge and Data Engineering. IEEE Transactions on Knowledge and Data Engineering 17(6), 834–843 (2005)
8. Boutilier, C., Brafman, R.I., Hoos, H.H., Poole, D.: Cp-Nets: A Tool for Representing and Reasoning with Conditional Ceteris Paribus Preference Statements. Journal of Artificial Intelligence Research 21 (2004)
9. Lang, J., Mengin, J.: The Complexity of Learning Separable Ceteris Paribus Preferences. In: International Joint Conference on Artificial Intelligence (2009)
10. Koriche, F., Zanuttini, B.: Learning Conditional Preference Networks with Queries. In: Boutilier, C. (ed.) Proc. 21st International Joint Conference on Artificial Intelligence (IJCAI 2009), pp. 1930–1935 (2009)
11. Chevaleyre, Y., Koriche, F., Lang, J., Mengin, J., Zanuttini, B.: Learning Ordinal Preferences on Multiattribute Domains: the Case of Cp-Nets. In: Fürnkranz, J., Hüllermeier, E. (eds.) To appear in the Book Preference Learning. Springer, Heidelberg
12. Middleton, S.E., Shadbolt, N., Roure, D.D.: Capturing Interest through Inference and Visualization: Ontological User Profiling in Recommender Systems. In: K-CAP 2003 (2003)
13. de Baets, B., Fodor, J.C.: Twenty Years of Fuzzy Preference Structures (1978–1997). Decisions in Economics and Finance 20, 45–66 (1997)
14. Fagin, R., Lotem, A., Naor, M.: Optimal Aggregation Algorithms for Middleware. In: Proceedings of Twentieth ACM Symposium on Principles of Database Systems (PODS 2001), pp. 102–113. ACM, New York (2001)
15. Clemen, R.T.: Making Hard Decisions: an Introduction to Decision Analysis. Duxbury Press, Belmont (1996)
16. Eckhardt, A., Vojtáš, P.: How to Learn Fuzzy User Preferences with Variable Objectives. In: Proceedings of 2009 IFSA World Congress/EUSFLAT Conference, Lisbon, Portugal, July 2009, pp. 938–943 (2009)
17. Eckhardt, A., Vojtáš, P.: Considering Data-Mining Techniques in User Preference Learning. In: 2008 International Workshop on Web Information Retrieval Support Systems, pp. 33–36 (2008)
18. Eckhardt, A.: Inductive Models of User Preferences for Semantic Web. In: Pokorný, J., Snášel, V., Richta, K. (eds.) DATESO 2007. CEUR Workshop Proceedings, vol. 235, pp. 108–119. Matfyz Press, Praha (2007)
19. Witten, I.H., Frank, E.: Data Mining: Practical Machine Learning Tools and Techniques, 2nd edn. Morgan Kaufmann, San Francisco (2005)

Parallel Randomized Load Balancing: A Lower Bound for a More General Model

Guy Even and Moti Medina

School of Electrical Engineering, Tel-Aviv Univ., Tel-Aviv 69978, Israel
{guy,medinamo}@eng.tau.ac.il

Abstract. We extend the lower bound of Adler et. al [1] and Berenbrink [2] for parallel randomized load balancing algorithms.

The setting in these asynchronous and distributed algorithms is of n balls and n bins. The algorithms begin by each ball choosing d bins independently and uniformly at random. The balls and bins communicate to determine the assignment of each ball to a bin. The goal is to minimize the maximum load, i.e., the number of balls that are assigned to the same bin. In [1,2], a lower bound of $\Omega(\sqrt[r]{\log n/\log\log n})$ is proved if the communication is limited to r rounds.

Three assumptions appear in the proofs in [1,2]: the topological assumption, random choices of confused balls, and symmetry. We extend the proof of the lower bound so that it holds without these three assumptions. This lower bound applies to every parallel randomized load balancing algorithm we are aware of [1,2,3,4].

Keywords: Static randomized parallel allocation, load balancing, balls and bins, lower bounds.

1 Introduction

We consider randomized parallel distributed algorithms for the following distributed load balancing problem. We are given a set of N terminals and n servers, for $N \gg n$. Suppose a random subset of n terminals, called the set of clients, is selected. Assume that clients do not know of each other. Each client must choose a server, and the goal is to minimize the maximum number of clients that choose the same server. We consider algorithms in which the number of communication rounds is limited as well as the number of messages each client can send in each communication round.

This load balancing problem was studied in a sequential setting by Azar et al. [5]. They regarded the clients as balls and the servers and bins. If each ball selects a bin uniformly and independently at random, then with high probability (w.h.p.)[1] the maximum load of a bin is $\Theta(\ln n/\ln\ln n)$ [6,7]. Azar et al. proved that, if each ball chooses two random bins and each ball is sequentially placed in a bin that is less loaded among the two, then w.h.p. the maximum load is only $\ln\ln n/\ln 2 + \Theta(1)$.

[1] We say that an event X occurs *with high probability* if $\Pr(X) \geq 1 - O\left(\frac{1}{n}\right)$.

J. van Leeuwen et al. (Eds.): SOFSEM 2010, LNCS 5901, pp. 358–369, 2010.

This surprising improvement of the maximum load has spurred a lot of interest in randomized load balancing in various settings. Adler et al. [1] studied randomized load-balancing algorithms in a parallel, distributed, asynchronous setting. They presented asymptotic bounds for the maximum load using r rounds of communication. The upper and lower bounds match and equal $\Theta(\sqrt[r]{\ln n / \ln \ln n})$. This lower bound holds for constant number of rounds and constant number of bin choices. Another parallel algorithm with the same asymptotic bounds was presented by Stemann [3] with a single synchronization point. Berenbrink et al. [2] generalized to $r \leq \log \log n$ communication rounds and to weighted balls.

In this paper we extend the proof of lower bounds so that they hold without assumptions on the algorithms that appear in [1,2]. The proof of the lower bound applies to every parallel randomized load balancing algorithms we are aware of [1,2,3,4] (these algorithms are described in the full version).

2 Preliminaries

2.1 The Model for Parallel Randomized Load Balancing Algorithms

We briefly describe the model for parallel randomized load balancing algorithms used in [1,2].

There are n balls and n bins. Each ball and each bin has a unique name called its identifier (ID). In the beginning, each ball chooses a constant number of bins independently and uniformly at random (i.u.r). The number of bins chosen by each ball is denoted by d.

The *communication graph* is a bipartite graph over the balls and the bins. Each ball is connected to each of the d bins it has chosen. Messages are sent only along edges in the communication graph. Communication proceeds in *rounds*. There is a bound on the number of rounds. This bound is denoted by r. Each round consists of messages from balls to bins and responses from bins to balls. We assume that each node (i.e., ball or bin) may simultaneously send messages to all its neighbors in the communication graph. In the last round, each ball decides which bin to be assigned to, and sends a commitment message to one of the d bins that it has chosen initially. Thus the last round is, in effect, "half" a round whose sole purpose is the transmission of the commitment messages. In this model, no limitation is imposed over the length of messages.

We are interested in asynchronous parallel algorithms. Each ball and bin runs its own program without a central clock. Messages are delayed arbitrarily, and a bin or a ball may wait for a message only if it is guaranteed to be sent to it. In particular, arrival of messages may be delayed so that messages from later rounds may precede messages from earlier rounds.

2.2 The Access Graph

Consider the case that each ball chooses two bins, i.e., $d = 2$. Following [1,2] we associate a random graph with these choices. The random graph has n vertices that correspond to the bins and n edges that correspond to the balls. If ball b choose bins u_0 and u_1, then the edge corresponding to b is (u_0, u_1). This random graph is called the *access graph*. Extensions for $d = O(1)$ are discussed in Sect. 3.4 (Case (III)).

We consider two versions of the access graph: the labeled version and the unlabeled version. In the labeled version, the "name" of each vertex is the ID of the corresponding bin and the "name" of each edge is the ID of the corresponding ball.

In the unlabeled version, the ID's of the ball and bins are hidden. Namely, we do not know which ball corresponds to which edge and which bin corresponds to which vertex.

The notation we use to distinguish between the labeled and unlabeled access graphs is as follows. The labeled access graph is denoted by G. The vertices are ID's of bins and are denoted by u_0, u_1, etc. The edges are ID's of balls and are denoted by b. The endpoints of a labeled edge b are denoted by $u_0(b)$ and $u_1(b)$.

The unlabeled access graph is denoted by G'. An unlabeled edge is denoted by e. We denote by $e(b)$ the unlabeled edge in G' whose label in G is b.

Neighborhoods. The r-neighborhood of a vertex v is the set of all vertices and edges reachable from v by a path containing r edges. We denote the r-neighborhood of v by $N_r(v)$. For example, $N_0(v) = \{v\}$ and $N_1(v)$ is the star whose center is v.

The r-neighborhood of an edge $e = (v_1, v_2)$ is the set $N_r(e) \triangleq N_r(v_1) \cup N_r(v_2)$.

Let v_j denote an endpoint of an edge e. The r-endpoint-neighborhood of v_j with respect to e is the r-neighborhood of v_j in the graph $G' - \{e\}$. We denote it by $N_{r,e}(v_j)$.

2.3 The Witness Tree

Following [1,2,8], the lower bound is proved by showing that a high load is obtained with at least constant probability conditioned on the existence of a witness tree, defined below.

We denote a complete rooted unlabeled tree of degree T and height r by a (T, r)-tree (see Fig. 1).

The Witness Tree Event. We say there exists a witness tree if there exists a copy of a (T, r)-tree in the unlabeled access graph [2]. We refer to such a copy of a (T, r)-tree as the *witness tree* [3].

The following theorems state that a witness tree exists with constant probability.

Theorem 1 ([8,1]). *Let* $r \leq \log\log n$, $d = 2$, *and* $T = O(\sqrt[r]{\ln n / \ln\ln n})$. *The unlabeled access graph* G' *contains a copy of a* (T, r)*-tree with probability at least* $1/2$.

[2] The (T, r)-tree need not be isolated as in [1,2] since we consider a synchronous oblivious adversary (see Sect. 3.1).

[3] If there is more than one copy, then select one arbitrarily.

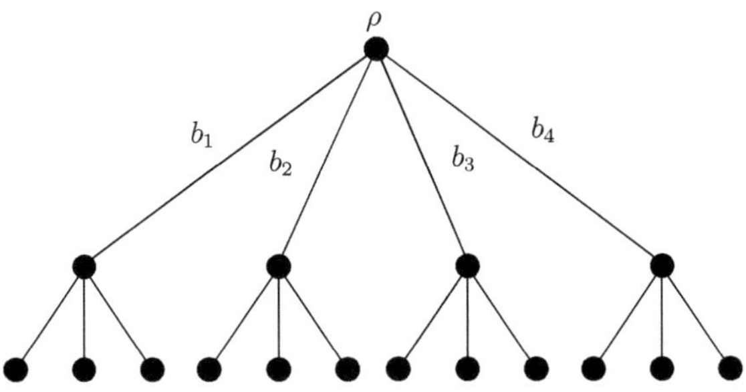

Fig. 1. A $(4,2)$-tree. For every ball b_i, the two endpoint-neighborhoods of radius 1 are isomorphic, e.g., stars of 3 edges.

Theorem 2 ([1]). *Let* $r = O(1)$, $d = O(1)$, *and* $T = O(\sqrt[r]{\ln n / \ln\ln n})$. *The unlabeled access hypergraph* G' *contains a copy of a* (T, r)*-tree with constant probability.*

2.4 Previous Lower Bounds and Gaps in Their Application

In [1,2], a lower bound of $\Omega(\sqrt[r]{\ln n / \ln\ln n})$ was proved for the maximum load obtained by parallel randomized load balancing algorithms, where r denotes the number of rounds and n denotes the number of bins and balls. These lower bounds hold for $d = 2$ and $r \leq \log\log n$ [2], or for a constant d and a constant r [1]. The proof is based on Theorems 1 and 2 that prove that a witness tree exists in the unlabeled access graph with constant probability. In addition, the proof of the lower bound relies on the assumptions described below.

The Topological Assumption. The topological assumption [1,2] states that each ball's decision is based only on collisions between choices of balls, as formalized below.

Assumption 1 [Topological Assumption]. *The decision of a ball* b *in round* r *is a randomized function*[4] *of the subgraph* $N_{r-1}(e(b))$ *in the unlabeled access graph.*

We emphasize that topology in the unlabeled graph does not include ID's of balls and bins, and therefore ID's do not affect the decisions. In fact, the topological assumption as stated in [1,2], requires a deterministic decision except for the case of a confused ball defined below. Note that, in an asynchronous setting, after $r-1$ rounds, a ball b may be aware of a subgraph of the access graph that strictly contains $N_{r-1}(e(b))$ (see also Sect. 3.2).

The Confused Ball Assumption. Under the confused ball assumption [1,2], if the topology of both $(r-1)$-endpoint-neighborhoods of a ball in the unlabeled

[4] Let $\mu : \Omega \to [0,1]$ denote a probability measure over a finite set Ω. A randomized function is a function $f : X \to Y^{\Omega}$. Therefore, for every $x \in X$, $f(x)$ is a random variable attaining values in Y whose distribution over Y is determined by μ.

access graph are isomorphic, then the ball commits to one of the chosen bins by flipping a fair coin. Such balls are referred to in [1] as *confused balls.*

A *rooted subgraph* is a subgraph with a special vertex called the root. We regard each endpoint-neighborhood $N_{r-1,e}(u_j)$ as a rooted subgraph in which the root is u_j. An isomorphism between rooted subgraphs is an isomorphism of subgraphs that maps a root to a root.

Assumption 2 [Confused Ball Assumption]. *If $N_{r-1,e(b)}(u_0(b))$ and $N_{r-1,e(b)}(u_1(b))$ are isomorphic rooted subgraphs of the unlabeled access graph, then the ball b commits to an endpoint of $e(b)$ by flipping a fair coin.*

The Symmetry Assumption. Under the symmetry assumption [2], all balls and bins perform the same underlying algorithm, as formalized below.

Assumption 3 [Symmetry Assumption]. *For every execution σ of the algorithm, and for any permutation π of the balls and bins (i.e., renaming), the corresponding execution $\pi(\sigma)$ is a valid execution of the algorithm.*

The symmetry assumption captures the notion of identical algorithms in each ball and bin. Moreover, these algorithms are *insensitive* to ID's of balls and bins.

Gaps in the Application of the Lower Bounds. Even et al. [4]. showed that the topological assumption and the confused ball assumption do not hold for algorithms PGREEDY and THRESHOLD presented in [1]. The reason these assumptions do not hold is that the commitment is based on nontopological information such as heights and round numbers. Since the proof of the lower bound in [1,2] is based on the topological assumption and the confused ball assumption, and since it is natural to design algorithms that violate these assumptions, the question of proving general lower bounds for the maximum load in parallel randomized load balancing algorithms was reopened. In Even et al. [4] specific proofs of the lower bounds were given for PGREEDY ($d = 2$ and $r = 2$) and THRESHOLD algorithms. In this paper we prove the lower bound without requiring Assumptions 1-3.

3 The Lower Bound

We prove a lower bound for the maximum load of randomized parallel algorithms (see Theorems 3, 4 and 5). The lower bound holds with respect to algorithms with r rounds of communication in which each ball chooses i.u.r. a constant number of d bins. For n balls and n bins, the maximum load is $\Omega(\sqrt[r]{\ln n/\ln\ln n})$.

We prove this lower bound conditioned on the event that a witness tree exists (see Sect. 2.3). Recall that, by Theorems 1 and 2, a witness tree exists with constant probability. We begin by assuming that $d = 2$ and $r = 2$, and close this sect. with extensions to other cases.

3.1 The Adversary

In this sect. we describe the adversary for the lower bound. Recall that in proving a lower bound, the weaker the adversary, the stronger the lower bound.

An *oblivious adversary* in our model is unaware of the random choices made by the algorithm. A concrete specification of a rather limited oblivious adversary is simply a sequence of delays $\{d_i\}_{i \in \mathbb{N}}$. Suppose the messages are sorted according to their transmission times. Then the time it takes the i'th message to arrive to its destination is d_i, and this is the only influence the adversary has over the execution of the algorithm. Moreover, we also use the convention that the delay of a message also includes the time it took to compute it, thus computation of the messages incurs no extra delay.

We refer to an oblivious adversary that assigns the same delay to all messages as a *synchronous adversary.* Indeed, all messages of the same "half" round are transmitted simultaneously and received simultaneously. Messages transmitted or received simultaneously are ordered uniformly at random by the adversary (namely, every permutation is equally likely).

Note that an oblivious synchronous adversary is not aware of traffic congestion, sources or destinations of messages, or contents of messages. Moreover, the adversary may not drop or corrupt messages.

3.2 Propagation of Information in Rounds

Recall that we do not have any limitation over the length of the messages. For the sake of the lower bound proof, we assume that, in each round, each ball or bin forwards all the information it has to its neighbors. Thus, in the beginning of round r, all the information that a ball has is included in the last two messages that the ball received from its two chosen bins in round $r-1$.

The following lemma captures the notion of locality of information after $r-1$ rounds of communication. It states that after ℓ rounds, each ball or bin gathers information only from its ℓ-neighborhood in the labeled access graph.

Lemma 1. *Under a synchronous oblivious adversary, after ℓ rounds of communication, each ball b gatherers information only from $N_\ell(b)$, and each bin u gathers information only from $N_r(u)$.*

Proof. The proof is by induction on the number of rounds. The base of the induction for $\ell = 1$ holds since every bin u has been accessed by the balls that have chosen it. Every bin forwards this information to the balls that have chosen it. We assume the lemma holds for $\ell' < \ell$. By the induction hypothesis, the information gathered by a bin u after round ℓ is gathered from $\cup_{b \in N_1(u)} N_{\ell-1}(b)$. Indeed, $N_\ell(u) = \cup_{b \in N_1(u)} N_{\ell-1}(b)$. Now the information gathered by a ball b after ℓ rounds is gathered from $\cup_{j \in \{0,1\}} N_\ell(u_j(b))$. Indeed, $N_\ell(b) = \cup_{j \in \{0,1\}} N_\ell(u_j(b))$, and the lemma follows.

3.3 The Probability Space

We give a nonformal description of the probability space $\mathcal{S}$ over the possible executions of the algorithm. Each execution is influenced by the following events: (i) Random choices made by the balls (i.e., the d chosen bins of each ball) as well as additional random bits used by the balls and bins. (ii) The ordering in each round of incoming messages to each ball or bin. (iii) The final decisions of the balls.

3.4 The Lower Bound Proof

Since all information held by balls and bins is forwarded in each message, the decision of each ball b is based on the last messages that it received from the two bins $u_0(b)$ and $u_1(b)$. Let $\mathcal{I}$ denote the set of possible pairs of data that a ball receives from the bins in round $r-1$ before making its decision.

Let $\{I_0(b), I_1(b)\} \in \mathcal{I}$ denote the pair of messages sent to b by its chosen bins, $u_0(b)$ and $u_1(b)$, in round $r-1$. The accumulation of data described above implies the following fact.

Fact 1. *The final decision of a ball b can be modeled by a decision function f_b: $\mathcal{I} \to [0,1]$. Namely, $f_b(\{I_0(b), I_1(b)\})$ equals the probability that ball b chooses bin $u_0(b)$.*

Note that in contrary to the symmetry assumption in [1] (see Assumption 3), we allow different balls to use different decision functions f_b.

(I) The Case $d = 2$, $r = 2$.

Notation. In the sequel we assume that a $(T,2)$-tree exists in the unlabeled access graph (see Sect. 2.3). Let τ denote this $(T,2)$-tree. The root ρ of τ is unlabeled as well as the edges incident to it. Since the tree τ is unlabeled, the ID of each edge (i.e., ball) is not determined, and hence the ID of each edge is a random variable. We denote by b_i the random variable that equals the ID of the ball corresponding to the i'th edge incident to the root ρ. Let $load(\rho)$ denote the random variable that equals the load of the root ρ. Let χ_i be a random variable defined by: $\chi_i = 1$ if b_i chooses the root ρ, and $\chi_i = 0$ otherwise. The load of the root $load(\rho)$ equals $\sum_{i=1}^{T} \chi_i$.

We now analyze the expected value of each χ_i. It is important to note that the random variables $\{\chi_i\}_{i=1}^{T}$ are *not* independent. Indeed, the analysis shows that they are equally distributed and uses linearity of expectation but not independence. Let us fix an edge incident to the root ρ. Consider the i'th edge and the random variable b_i. Fix two ID's u_0 and u_1 and assume that b_i chose u_0 and u_1. Let $\{I_0, I_1\} \in \mathcal{I}$ denote a specific pair of data.

Definition 1. *Let A denote the event that: (i) Ball b_i chooses bins whose ID's are u_0 and u_1 and (ii) b_i gathers information I_j from u_j, for $j \in \{0,1\}$.*

Note that while b_i is a random variable, the ID's u_0 and u_1 and the data I_0 and I_1 are not random variables. Namely, A is a set of executions characterized by (i, u_0, u_1, I_0, I_1). For simplicity we write A instead of $A(i, u_0, u_1, I_0, I_1)$.

Definition 2. *Let $j \in \{0,1\}$. Let A_j denote the event $A \cap \{\rho = u_j\}$ (i.e., ball b_i gathers information I_0, I_1 from bins u_0, u_1, respectively, and the root ρ is labeled by u_j).*

We emphasize that in this setting the ball b_i has no way of distinguishing between the events A_0 and A_1.

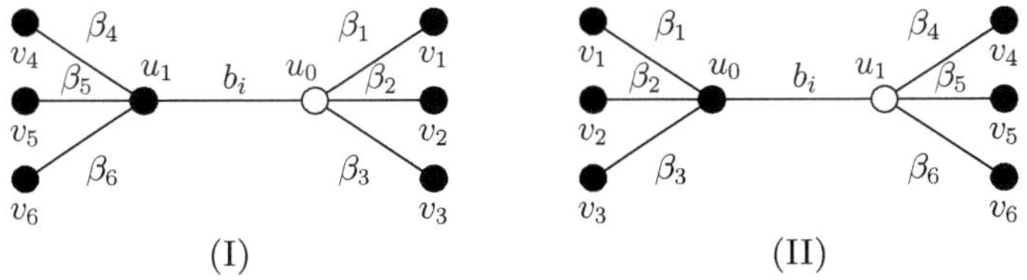

Fig. 2. (I) An execution in A_0 from the "point of view" of ball b_i. Ball b_i chooses bins u_0 and u_1. Bin u_0 is also chosen by balls $\beta_1, \beta_2, \beta_3$. Bin u_1 is also chosen by balls $\beta_4, \beta_5, \beta_6$. The root ρ of the witness tree is u_0 and is depicted by an unfilled circle. (II) The mirror execution of (I). This mirror execution is in A_1. The mirror permutation swaps u_0 and u_1, etc. Since ball b_i cannot distinguish between executions (I) and (II), it follows that if ball b_i chooses u_0 in (I) then it also chooses u_0 in (II).

Lemma 2. $\Pr[A_0 \mid A] = \Pr[A_1 \mid A]$.

Proof. The proof is based on the fact that the labeling of vertices and edges in the witness tree τ is a random permutation. Hence, given an execution in A, we can apply a "mirror" automorphism with respect to b_i, as depicted in Fig. 2. Note that this mirror automorphism is applied only to $N_2(b_i)$; all other edges and vertices are fixed. We claim that this automorphism is a one-to-one measure preserving mapping between executions in A_0 and executions in A_1.

The automorphism "mirrors" ID's of balls and bins labels in $N_2(b_i)$, and each element inherits the random bits tossed by its pre-image. Indeed, if vertex u is mapped to vertex v, then v inherits the label of u and all its random bits.

As for the ordering of messages. The bins u_0 and u_1 have the same labeled neighbors before and after the automorphism. Hence, the adversary orders their incoming messages in the same way. All other bins might change their neighbors as a result of the automorphism (e.g., v_4 may be a leaf in (I) but is a nonleaf in (II)). Therefore, the order of messages incoming to a bin $v \notin \{u_0, u_1\}$ is inherited from its unlabeled vertex in the access graph G'.

Note that the root is not affected by the mirror automorphism. This is depicted in Fig. 2 by the fixed unfilled circle. From the point of view of u_0, u_1, and b_i the executions before and after the automorphism are identical. Hence, the automorphism maps executions in A_0 to executions in A_1.

Therefore, the probability of an execution in A_0 equals the probability of the image of this execution under the mirror permutation. Finally, the mirror automorphism is one-to-one since differences between two executions in A_0 are not "erased" by the automorphism.

Lemma 3. *For every* $1 \leq i \leq T$, $\Pr[\chi_i = 1] = 1/2$.

Proof. Lemma 2 and Fact 1 imply that:

$$\Pr[\chi_i = 1 \mid A] = \frac{1}{2} \cdot \Pr[\chi_i = 1 \mid A_0] + \frac{1}{2} \cdot \Pr[\chi_i = 1 \mid A_1] \quad (1)$$

$$= \frac{1}{2} \cdot f_{b_i}(\{I_0, I_1\}) + \frac{1}{2} \cdot (1 - f_{b_i}(\{I_0, I_1\}))$$
$$= \frac{1}{2} .$$

Since Equation 2 holds for every A (i.e., choice of (i, u_0, u_1, I_0, I_1)), it follows that $\Pr[\chi_i = 1] = 1/2$.

Theorem 3. *If $d = 2$ and $r = 2$, then the maximum load obtained by any load balancing algorithm in the model is $\Omega(\sqrt{\lg n / \lg\lg n})$ with constant probability.*

Proof. By linearity of expectation and by Lemma 3:

$$\mathrm{E}[load(\rho) \mid \exists \text{witness tree}] = \mathrm{E}[\sum_{i=1}^{T} \chi_i] = T \cdot \mathrm{E}[\chi_i] = T/2 .$$

By applying Markov's inequality to $T - load(\rho)$, we conclude that

$$\Pr[load(\rho) > T/4 \mid \exists \text{witness tree}] \geq 1/3.$$

The theorem follows from Theorem 1.

(II) The Case $d = 2$, $r \leq \lg\lg n$. The same arguments prove the next theorem.

Theorem 4. *If $d = 2$ and $r \leq \lg\lg n$, then the maximum load obtained by any load balancing algorithm in the model is $\Omega(\sqrt[r]{\lg n / \lg\lg n})$ with constant probability.*

(III) The Case $d = O(1)$, $r = O(1)$. In this sect. we outline the differences between this case and Case (I). Proofs similar to the case $d = 2$ are omitted.

An *access hypergraph* G over the bins is associated with the d random choices of each ball [1]. For each ball b, the hyperedge $e(b)$ equals the d bins $(u_0(b), \ldots, u_{d-1}(b))$ chosen[5] by b.

Let $\{I_0(b), \ldots, I_{d-1}(b)\} \in \mathcal{I}$ denote the information that is gathered by a ball b from its d chosen bins, $u_0(b), \ldots, u_{d-1}(b)$, in round $r - 1$.

Fact 2. *The final decision of a ball b can be modeled by a decision function $f_b \colon \mathcal{I} \to [0,1]^d$ i.e., $f_b(\{I_0(b), \ldots, I_{d-1}(b)\})$ equals to a probability vector $\mathbf{p} = \langle p_0, p_2, \ldots, p_{d-1}\rangle$ where p_j is the probability that ball b chooses bin $u_j(b)$.*

Notation. In the sequel we assume that a (T, r)-hypertree exists (see Fig. 3) in the unlabeled access hypergraph (see Sect. 2.3). Let τ denote this (T, r)-hypertree. The root ρ of τ is unlabeled as well as the hyperedges incident to it. We denote by b_i the random variable that equals the ID of the ball corresponding

[5] For simplicity, we assume here that the d choices are distinct. Otherwise, we would need to consider hyperedges with repetitions.

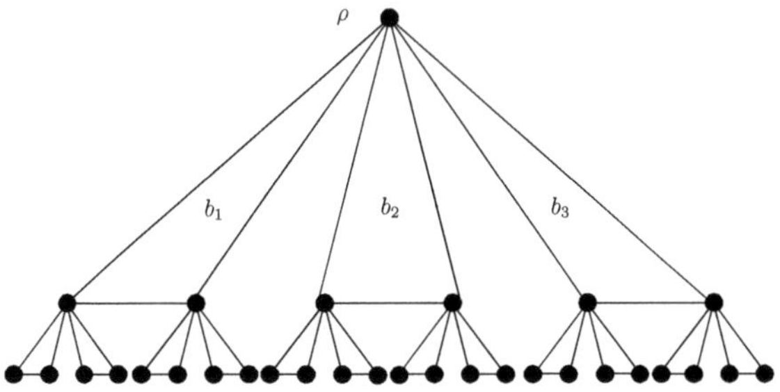

Fig. 3. A $(3, 2)$-tree is the witness hypertree for the case of $r = 2$ and $d = 3$

to the i'th hyperedge incident to the root ρ. We denote the load of the root ρ by $load(\rho)$. Let χ_i be a random variable defined by: $\chi_i = 1$ if b_i chooses the root ρ, and $\chi_i = 0$ otherwise. The load of the root $load(\rho)$ equals $\sum_{i=1}^{T} \chi_i$.

We now analyze the expected value of each χ_i. As in the case $d = 2$, it is important to note that the random variables $\{\chi_i\}_{i=1}^{T}$ are *not* independent. Let us fix an hyperedge incident to the root ρ. Consider the i'th hyperedge and the random variable b_i. Fix d ID's $u_0, \ldots, u_{d-1}$ and assume that b_i chose $u_0, \ldots, u_{d-1}$. Let $\{I_0, I_1, \ldots, I_{d-1}\}$ denote a specific d-tuple of data.

Definition 3. *Let A denote the event that: (i) Ball b_i chooses bins whose ID's are $u_0, u_1, \ldots, u_{d-1}$ and (ii) b_i gathers information I_j from u_j, for $j \in \{0, 1, \ldots, d-1\}$.*

Definition 4. *For $j \in \{0, 1, \ldots, d-1\}$, let A_j denote the event $A \cap \{\rho = u_j\}$ (i.e., ball b_i gathers information $I_0, I_1, \ldots, I_{d-1}$ from bins $u_0, u_1, \ldots, u_{d-1}$, respectively, and the root ρ is labeled by u_j).*

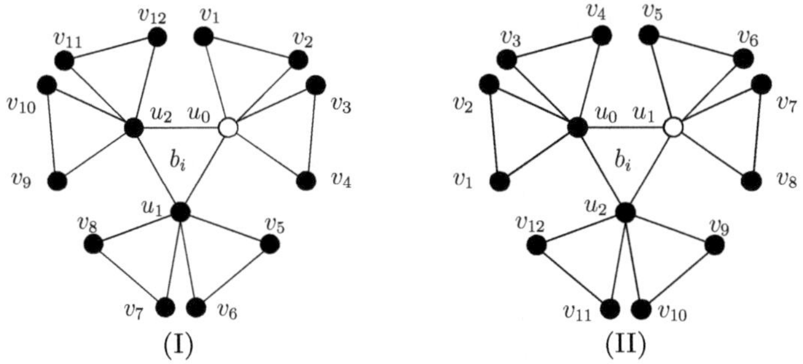

Fig. 4. (I) An execution in A_0 from the "point of view" of ball b_i. Ball b_i chooses bins u_0, u_1 and u_2. The root ρ of the witness tree is u_0 and is depicted by an unfilled circle. (II) The rotated execution of (I). This rotated execution is in A_1. The rotation permutation rotates the bins in b_i in a counter-clockwise manner. Since ball b_i cannot distinguish between executions (I) and (II), it follows that if ball b_i chooses u_0 in (I) then it also chooses u_0 in (II).

Lemma 4. *For every* $\ell \in \{0, 1, \ldots, d-1\}$, $\Pr[A_\ell \mid A] = \Pr[A_{\ell+1 \pmod d} \mid A]$, *and therefore* $\Pr[A_\ell] = \frac{1}{d} \cdot \Pr[A]$.

Proof sketch: As in Lemma 2, we apply a one-to-one measure preserving mapping from A_ℓ to $A_{\ell+1 \pmod d}$. The mapping is a "rotation" mapping. An example for $d = 3$ and $r = 2$ is depicted in Fig. 4. □

Lemma 5. *For every* $1 \leq i \leq T$, $\Pr[\chi_i = 1] = 1/d$.

Proof. Lemma 4 and Fact 2 imply that:

$$\Pr[\chi_i \mid A] = \frac{1}{d} \cdot \sum_{\ell=0}^{d-1} \Pr[\chi_i \mid A_\ell] = \frac{1}{d} \cdot \sum_{\ell=0}^{d-1} p_\ell = \frac{1}{d} .$$

Since Equation 2 holds for every A, it follows that $\Pr[\chi_i = 1] = 1/d$.

Based on Theorem 2 we conclude with the following theorem.

Theorem 5. *For* $d = O(1)$ *and* $r = O(1)$, *the maximum load obtained by any load balancing algorithm in the model is* $\Omega(\sqrt[r]{\lg n / \lg\lg n})$ *with constant probability.*

4 Discussion

We prove the lower bounds from [1,2] without relying on Assumptions 1-3. The proof applies to parallel load balancing algorithms in which each ball selects d bins independently and uniformly at random. The proof allows each ball and bin to run a completely different randomized program that depends on its ID. The proof does not limit the message length; hence, all local information can be gathered by the balls via messages.

In [4], we presented a heuristic, H-RETRY, and simulations that matched the loads obtained by the best known sequential load balancing algorithms [5,9] for 1-8 million balls and bins. The proof presented here shows that such heuristics do not obtain better asymptotic loads.

A key technical issue in our proof is the distinction between a labeled and unlabeled access graph. In the labeled access graph, each node is labeled by an ID of a bin and each edge is labeled by an ID of a ball. In the unlabeled graph, ID's are "hidden". The proofs that a witness tree exists with constant probability hold, in fact, with respect to the unlabeled access graph. Given the existence of an "unlabeled" witness tree, we show that a constant fraction of the labelings of the tree incur a high load in the root.

The adversary we consider in the proof is very limited. It assigns identical delays to all messages, and orders simultaneous messages uniformly at random.

It is possible to extend the lower bound also for constant d provided that $r \leq \log\log n/(1 + \log d)$. In this case, the lower bound on the maximum load is $\Omega(\sqrt[r]{\frac{\log n}{\frac{1}{r}\log\log n + \log\frac{1}{d}}})$.

References

1. Adler, M., Chakrabarti, S., Mitzenmacher, M., Rasmussen, L.E.: Parallel Randomized Load Balancing. Random Struct. Algorithms 13(2), 159–188 (1998)
2. Berenbrink, P., auf der Heide, F.M., Schröder, K.: Allocating Weighted Jobs in Parallel. Theory of Computing Systems 32(3), 281–300 (1999)
3. Stemann, V.: Parallel Balanced Allocations. In: SPAA 1996, pp. 261–269. ACM, New York (1996)
4. Even, G., Medina, M.: Revisiting Randomized Parallel Load Balancing Algorithms. In: SIROCCO 2009 (2009)
5. Azar, Y., Broder, A., Karlin, A., Upfal, E.: Balanced Allocations. SIAM Journal on Computing 29(1), 180–200 (2000)
6. Raab, M., Steger, A.: "Balls into Bins" - A Simple and Tight Analysis. In: Rolim, J.D.P., Serna, M., Luby, M. (eds.) RANDOM 1998. LNCS, vol. 1518, pp. 159–170. Springer, Heidelberg (1998)
7. Kolchin, V., Sevastyanov, B., Chistyakov, V.: Random Allocations. John Wiley & Sons, Chichester (1978)
8. Czumaj, A., auf der Heide, F., Stemann, V.: Contention Resolution in Hashing Based Shared Memory Simulations. SIAM Journal On Computing 29(5), 1703–1739 (2000)
9. Voecking, B.: How Asymmetry Helps Load Balancing. Journal of the ACM 50(4), 568–589 (2003)

Ant-CSP: An Ant Colony Optimization Algorithm for the Closest String Problem

Simone Faro and Elisa Pappalardo

Università di Catania, Dipartimento di Matematica e Informatica
Viale Andrea Doria 6, I-95125 Catania, Italy
{faro,epappalardo}@dmi.unict.it

Abstract. Algorithms for sequence analysis are of central importance in computational molecular biology and coding theory. A very interesting problem in this field is the Closest String Problem (CSP) which consists in finding a string t with minimum Hamming distance from all strings in a given finite set. To overcome the NP-hardness of the CSP problem, we propose a new algorithm, called ANT-CSP, based on the Ant Colony Optimization metaheuristic. To assess its effectiveness and robustness, we compared it with two state-of-the-art algorithms for the CSP problem, respectively based on the simulated annealing and the genetic algorithm approaches. Experimental results show that ANT-CSP outperforms both of them in terms of quality of solutions and convergence speed.

Keywords: Closest string problem, string comparison problems, metaheuristic algorithms, ant colony optimization, NP-hard problems.

1 Introduction

The task of finding a string that is close to each of the strings in a given finite set is a combinatorial optimization problem particularly important in computational biology and coding theory. In molecular biology, one of the main issues related to DNA or protein sequences comparison is to find similar regions. Such problem finds applications, for instance, in genetic drug target and genetic probes design [16], in locating binding sites [25,11], and in coding theory [6,5], where one is interested in determining the best way to encode a set of messages [24].

A precise definition of the Closest String Problem (CSP, for short) is given next. To begin with, for a string s over a finite alphabet Σ, we denote by $|s|$ and $s[i]$ the length of s and the i-th character of s, respectively. The *Hamming distance* $H(s,t)$ between two strings s and t, of equal length, is the number of positions in which s and t differ.

Definition 1 (CSP problem). *Let* $S = \{s_1, s_2, \ldots, s_n\}$ *be a finite set of* n *strings, over an alphabet* Σ*, each of length* m*. The Closest String Problem for* S *is to find a string* t *over* Σ*, of length* m*, that minimizes the Hamming distance* $H(t,S) =_{Def} \max_{s \in S} H(t,s)$.

J. van Leeuwen et al. (Eds.): SOFSEM 2010, LNCS 5901, pp. 370–381, 2010.

Recently, the CSP problem has received much attention. Frances and Litman [5] have proved the NP-hardness of the problem for binary codes. Gramm *et al.* [9,10] provided a fixed-parameter algorithm for the CSP problem with running time $O(nm + nd^{d+1})$, where d is the parameter. Plainly, for large values of d, such approach becomes prohibitive.

Several approximation algorithms have been proposed for the CSP problem: Gasieniec *et al.* [6] and Lanctot *et al.* [16] developed two $(4/3 + \epsilon)$-polynomial time approximation algorithms. Then, based on such results, Li *et al.* [17] and Ma and Sun [20] presented two new polynomial-time approximation algorithms. However, the running time of these algorithms make them of theoretical importance only. We mention also an approach based on the integer-programming formulation proposed by Meneses, Pardalos *et al.* in [21]: the CSP is reduced to an integer-programming problem, and then using a branch-and-bound algorithm to solve it. Despite the high quality of solutions, such algorithm is not always efficient and has an exponential time complexity. Moreover, the branch-and-bound tecnique leads easily to memory explosion.

Another approach to NP-hard problems consists in using heuristics. In 2005, Liu *et al.* [18] proposed to apply two heuristic algorithms to solve the CSP problem, based on the simulated annealing and the genetic algorithm approaches; then in [19], Liu and Holger presented a hybrid algorithm which combines both the genetic and the simulated annealing approaches, though limited only to binary alphabets. We mention also the approach in [8], based on a combination of a 2-approximation algorithm with local search strategies, consisting in taking a string s and modifying it until a local optimal solution is found. However, approximation algorithms sacrifice solution quality for speed [12].

In this paper we propose a new heuristic solution, Ant-CSP, based on the Ant Colony Optimization (ACO) metaheuristic, and we compare it to those proposed by Liu *et al.* [18], which are to date the fastest algorithms for the CSP problem. The ACO metaheuristic is inspired by the foraging behaviour of ant colonies [3]. Artificial ants implemented in ACO are stochastic procedures that, taking into account heuristic information and artificial pheromone trails, probabilistically construct solutions by iteratively adding new components to partial solutions.

The paper is organized as follows. In Sections 2 and 3, we present in some detail the two heuristic algorithms by Liu *et al.* [18] for the CSP problem, respectively based on the simulated annealing and the genetic algorithm approaches. Then, in Section 4, after describing the Ant Colony Optimization metaheuristic, we illustrate our proposed solution, Ant-CSP. In Section 5, we discuss the results of an extensive experimental comparison of our algorithm with the ones by Liu *et al.* [18]. Finally, we report our conclusions in Section 6.

2 A Simulated Annealing Algorithm for the CSP Problem

Simulated Annealing (SA) is a generalization of Monte Carlo methods, originally proposed by Metropolis and Ulam [23,22] as a means of finding the equilibrium configuration of a collection of atoms at a given temperature. The basic idea of SA was taken from an analogy with the annealing process used in metallurgy, a technique involving heating and controlled cooling of a material to increase the size of its crystals and reduce their defects. In the original Metropolis scheme, an initial state of a thermodynamic system is chosen, having energy E and temperature T. Keeping T constant, the initial configuration is perturbed, and the energy change ΔE is computed. If ΔE is negative, the new configuration is always accepted, otherwise it is accepted with a probability given by the Boltzmann factor $e^{-(\Delta E/T)}$. This process is repeated L times for the current temperature, then the temperature is decremented and the entire process is repeated until a frozen state is reached at $T = 0$. Due to such characteristics, methods based on the SA may accept not only transitions that lead to better solutions, but also transitions that lead to worse ones, though with probabilities which tend to 0: at the beginning of the search, when temperatures are high, the algorithm behaves as a random search and therefore bad solutions can be accepted; whereas for lower values of T, solutions are located in promising regions of the search space.

Kirkpatrick [15] first proposed to apply SA to solve combinatorial optimization problems. The SA algorithm for the CSP problem by Liu *et al.* [18] works much along the same lines as Kirkpatrick's algorithm. Initially, the temperature T is set to $m/2$, where m is the common string length. For each temperature value, a block of L iterations is performed. At each iteration, a new string u' of length m, over Σ, is constructed in the following way: the current string u is split around a random point and the two substrings are interchanged. Then the energy change $\Delta E = H(u', S) - H(u, S)$ is evaluated, where S is the input set of strings. If $\Delta E \leq 0$, u' becomes the new current solution, otherwise u' is choosen as current solution with probability $e^{-(\Delta E/T)}$ only. At the end of each block of iterations, the temperature value is multiplied by a reduction factor γ. Liu *et al.* [18] report experiments with the parameters $L = 100$ and $\gamma = 0.9$. The algorithm stops when a suitable termination criterion is met.

The pseudo-code of the algorithm SA for the CSP problem (SA-CSP) is shown below.

3 A Genetic Algorithm for the CSP Problem

Genetic algorithms were first proposed by John Holland [13,7,14,1] as an abstraction of the biological evolution of living organisms. Genetic algorithms are based on natural selection and sexual reproduction processes. The first mechanism determines which members of a population survive and are able to reproduce, the second one assures genic recombination among individuals of a same population. The principle of selection is based on a function, called *fitness*, that measures "how good is an individual": individuals with better fitness have higher probability to reproduce and survive.

In the genetic algorithm for the CSP problem (GA-CSP, for short) proposed by Liu *et al.* [18], an initial population P of random candidate solutions $ind_0, \ldots,$

Algorithm 1. SA-CSP(S)

```
randomly generate an initial string u
set an initial T = T_max
set the number of iterations L
set γ
while not (TERMINATION_CRITERION) do
    for 0 ≤ I < L do
        u' ← mutate(u);
        Δ = evaluate_energy(u', S) − evaluate_energy(u, S);
        if ((Δ ≤ 0) or ((Δ > 0) and (e^{−Δ/T} > random(0, 1)))) then
            u ← u';
        end if
    end for
    T ← γ · T;
end while
```

$ind_{popsize-1}$ is generated. An individual/solution is a string of length m over the alphabet Σ of the input string set S. The fitness function f is evaluated for each string in the current population, where $f = m - H_{\max}$ and $H_{\max}$ is the maximum Hamming distance of s from all strings in S: therefore the larger is f, the better will be the solution represented by the string. A crossover step allows to generate new individuals from members of the current population. More specifically, firstly two "parental" individual ind_x and ind_y, are randomly selected according to their crossover probability p_c, which is proportional to the fitness value of each individual. Then the crossover operator simply exchanges a randomly selected segment in the pair of "parents" so that two new strings are generated, each inheriting a part from each of the parents. At this intermediate stage, there are two populations, namely, parents and offsprings. To create the next generation, an elitist strategy is applied, i.e., the best individuals from both populations are selected, based on their fitness. Finally, a mutation operator is applied to each individual, depending on a probability p_m: this consists in exchanging two random positions in the string. Reproduction and mutation steps are repeated until a termination criterion is met. We report the pseudo-code of GA-CSP as Algorithm 2 below.

4 Ant Colony Optimization

We present now a new algorithm for the CSP problem based on the Ant Colony Optimization (ACO) metaheuristic.

ACO is a multi-agent metaheuristic approach particularly suited for hard combinatorial optimization problems. ACO was firstly proposed by Dorigo [3] as an innovative approach to the Traveling Salesman problem. It has been inspired by the real behaviour of ant colonies, where the behaviour of single ants is directed to the survival of the whole colony. In particular, in his analysis Dorigo observed the foraging behaviour of colonies: when a new food source is found,

Algorithm 2. GA-CSP(S)

```
t ← 0
initialize P(t) = {ind_i ∈ P(t), i = 0, 1, ...popSize − 1}
evaluate P(t) to get the fitness of each individual in S
calculate the probability of each individual, p_i ∝ ind_i.fitness
currentBest = best_ind(P(t));
bestInd = ind_currBest;
while t < TERMINATION_CRITERION do
    i = 0;
    while i < popSize/2 do
        select (ind_x ind_y) from P(t) according to their p_ind
        {chd_(2i), chd_(2i+1)} = crossover(ind_x, ind_y);
    end while
    i = 0;
    while i < popSize do
        r ← random(0, 1);
        if (r < p_m) then
            mutate(chd_i);
        end if
        P(t + 1) ← P(t + 1) ⋃ chd_i
    end while
    evaluate P(t + 1) to get the fitness of each individual in S
    calculate the probability of each individual, p_i ∝ ind_i.fitness
    worst = worst_ind(P(t + 1));
    ind_worst ← bestInd;
    currBest = best_ind(P(t + 1));
    if (ind_currBest.fitness > bestInd.fitness) then
        bestInd = ind_currBest;
    end if
    t ← t + 1;
end while
```

ants search the shortest and easiest way to return to nest. While walking from food sources to the nest, and vice versa, ants deposit on the ground a substance called pheromone [4]. Ants can smell pheromones and, when choosing their way, they select, with higher probability, paths marked by strong pheromone concentrations. It has been proved that pheromone trails make shortest paths to emerge over other paths [2], due to the fact that pheromone density tends to be higher on shortest paths.

In analogy with the real behaviour of ant colonies, ACO applies pheromone trails and social behaviour concepts to solve hard optimization problems. In short, ACO algorithms work as follows: a set of asynchronous and concurrent agents, a colony of ants, moves through the states of the problem. To determine the next state, ants apply stochastic local decisions based on pheromone trails. Ants can release (additional) pheromone into a state, while building a solution, and/or after a solution has been built, by moving back to all visited states.

In an elitist strategy, only the ant that has produced the best solution is allowed to update pheromone trails. In general, the amount of pheromone deposited is proportional to the quality of the solution built.

To avoid a too rapid convergence towards suboptimal regions, ACO algorithms include another mechanism for the updating of pheromone trails, namely, pheromone evaporation. This consists in decreasing over time the intensity of the components of pheromone trails, as pheromone density tends to increase on shortest paths. Thus, the evaporation mechanism limits premature stagnation, namely situations in which all ants repeatedly construct the same solutions, which would prevent further explorations of the search space.

The ACO metaheuristic has two main application fields: NP-hard problems, whose best known solutions have exponential time worst-case complexity, and shortest path problems, in which the properties of the problem's graph representation can change over time, concurrently with the optimization process. As the CSP problem is NP-hard, and searching a closest string can be viewed as finding a minimum path into the graph of all feasible solutions, it is natural to apply the ACO heuristic to the CSP problem. This is what we do next.

4.1 The Ant-CSP Algorithm

We describe now our proposed ACO algorithm for the CSP problem, called Ant-CSP. Given an input set S of n strings of length m, over an alphabet Σ, at each iteration of the Ant-CSP algorithm, a $COLONY$ consisting of u ants is generated. Each of the artificial ant, say $COLONY_i$, searches for a solution by means of the $find\_solution$ procedure, by building a string while it moves character by character on a table T, represented as a $|\Sigma| \times m$ matrix. The location $T[i,j]$, with $1 \leq i \leq |\Sigma|$ and $0 \leq j \leq m-1$, mantains the pheromone trail for the i-th character at the j-th position of the string.

Ants choose "their way" probabilistically, using a probability depending on the value $T[i,j]$ of the local pheromone trail: the normalized probability for each character is computed, depending on the pheromone value deposited on it. So, the algorithm probabilistically chooses a character. Initially, $T[i,j] = 1/|\Sigma|$; when each ant has built and evaluated its own solution, respectively by means of the $find\_solution()$ and $evaluate\_solution()$ procedures, pheromone trails are updated. We adopted an elitist strategy, so that only the ant that has found the best solution, say $COLONY_{best}$, updates the pheromone trails, by depositing on the characters that appear in the best solution an amount of pheromone proportional to the quality of the solution itself. In particular:

$$T^{(t+1)}[i,j] = T^{(t)}[i,j] + \left(1 - \frac{HD}{m}\right),$$

where HD is the maximum Hamming distance of the current string from all strings in S. Thus, the larger is the pheromone trail for the i-th character, the higher will be the probability that this character will be chosen in the next iteration.

Pheromone values are normalized and are used as probabilities. After additional pheromone trail on the best string has been released, the evaporation procedure is applied: this consists in decrementing each value $T[i, j]$ by a constant factor ρ; in our experiments, we put $\rho = 0.03$.

The pseudo-code of the Ant-CSP algorithm is shown as Algorithm 3 below.

Algorithm 3. Ant-CSP(S)

```
initialize table T
for i ← 1 to m do
    for j ← 1 to |Σ| do
        T_ij ← 1/|Σ|
    end for
end for
initialize COLONY
while not (TERMINATION_CRITERION) do
    for i ← 1 to u do
        COLONY_i ← new_ant()
        COLONY_i.find_solution()
        COLONY_i.evaluate_solution()
    end for
    for i ← 1 to m do                        ▷ start pheromone evaporation
        for j ← 1 to |Σ| do
            T_ij ← (1 − ρ) · T_ij;
        end for
    end for                                  ▷ end pheromone evaporation
    COLONY_best.update_trails()
end while
```

5 Experimental Results

We have tested the SA-CSP, the GA-CSP, and the ACO-CSP algorithms using the azotated compounds alphabet $\Sigma = \{A, C, G, T\}$ of the fundamental components of nucleic acids.

In our test platform, we considered a number of input strings $n \in \{10, 20, 30, 40, 50\}$, and string length $m \in \{10, 20, ..., 50\} \cup \{100, 200, \ldots, 1000\}$. For each of a randomly generated problem instances, all algorithms were run 20 times.

The total colony size for the Ant-CSP algorithm as well as the population size for the GA-CSP algorithm have been set to 10, whereas the number of generations has been set to 1500. In the case of the SA-CSP algorithm, we fixed the number of function evaluations in 15,000, making the number of function evaluations comparable to the computational work performed by the former two algorithms.

Our tests have been performed on an Intel Pentium M 750, 1.86 GHz, 1 GB RAM, running Ubuntu Linux.

We report the results of our tests in the five tables below: *HD* indicates the Hamming distance value, that we want to minimize, *Time* is the running

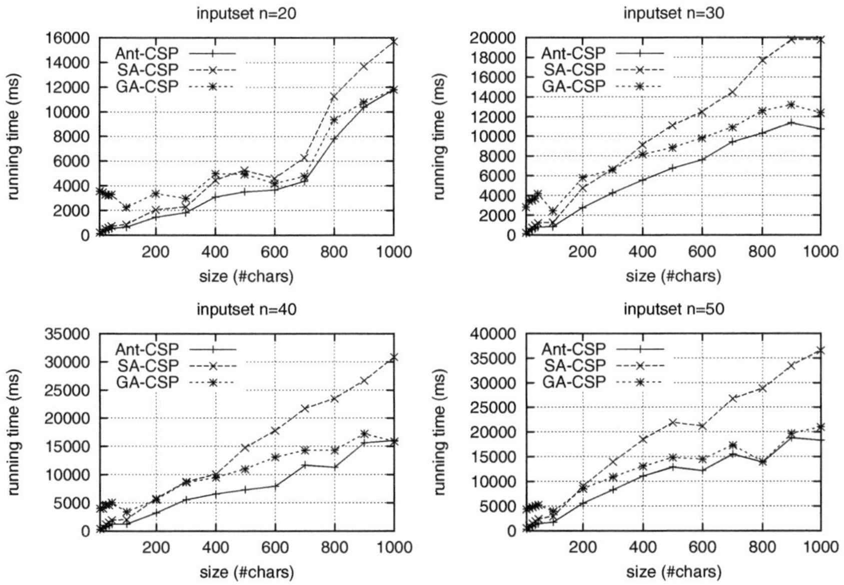

Fig. 1. Running times plot for $n = 20, 30, 40, 50$. Notice that, as n increases, the gap between Ant-CSP and the other two algorithms becomes more noticeable.

time in milliseconds. For each length, we computed the average (AVG) of the closest string scores found in the 20 runs and the standard deviation σ. Also, we computed the average of the running time over the 20 runs (AVG). Best results are reported in bold.

Experimental results show that almost always the Ant-CSP outperforms both the GA-CSP and the SA-CSP algorithms both in terms of solution quality and

Table 1. Results for inputset of 10 strings of length m

	SA-CSP			GA-CSP			Ant-CSP		
Size (m)	HD		Time	HD		Time	HD		Time
	AVG	σ	AVG	AVG	σ	AVG	AVG	σ	AVG
10	8.45	0.497	67.5	**6.9**	0.3	1840	7.05	0.218	50.5
20	15.9	0.384	112	13.3	0.714	1860	**13.1**	0.589	97
30	23.6	0.663	216	19.6	0.583	2700	**19.3**	0.557	200
40	31.4	0.589	313	25.3	0.714	3040	**25.1**	0.654	281
50	38.8	0.678	428	31.8	0.994	3220	**31.6**	0.805	386
100	75.9	0.943	465	63.4	1.31	2060	**62.2**	0.766	433
200	151	1.04	901	129	1.43	2290	**124**	1.58	855
300	226	1.18	1350	195	2.19	2540	**188**	1.57	1290
400	301	2.01	1780	262	2.52	2720	**252**	1.68	1700
500	375	2.05	2190	330	2.52	2940	**317**	2.15	2110
600	450	1.87	2740	400	3.71	3800	**385**	2.5	2920
700	525	1.68	3980	470	3.43	4860	**451**	2.95	4270
800	600	1.51	3720	540	4.04	4370	**517**	2.11	3860
900	675	1.19	5670	610	4.01	6110	**585**	4.05	5690
1000	750	1.53	7720	680	4.12	7850	**652**	3.72	7850

efficiency. As a matter of fact, the tables below show that our algorithm is much faster than both the GA-CSP and SA-CSP algorithms. In particular, in the case of short instances, i.e. for $10 \leq m \leq 50$, the Ant-CSP algorithm is from 5 to 36 times faster than GA-CSP.

Furthermore, it turns out that as n increases, the gap between the running time of the Ant-CSP and the SA-CSP algorithms becomes considerable. In Figure 1 we report the running times of the algorithms for some sets of strings.

We also remark that the Ant-CSP provides results of a better quality than the other two algorithms in terms of Hamming distance. In fact, the cooperation among the colony ants and the pheromone trails tend to orient the search towards optimal solutions, allowing to explore and modify local optima. On the other hand, the SA-CSP algorithm behaves as a random search, as it simply modifies a string without considering local promising solutions. Likewise,

Table 2. Results for inputset of 20 strings of length m

Size (m)	SA-CSP			GA-CSP			Ant-CSP		
	HD		Time	HD		Time	HD		Time
	AVG	σ	AVG	AVG	σ	AVG	AVG	σ	AVG
10	8.95	0.384	211	**7.95**	0.218	3560	**7.95**	0.218	132
20	17.1	0.589	342	**14.8**	0.4	3460	**14.8**	0.4	258
30	24.8	0.536	502	21.6	0.497	3300	**21.4**	0.49	370
40	32.5	0.497	602	28.1	0.477	3220	**28**	0.632	452
50	40.1	0.726	735	35	0.589	3300	**34.8**	0.536	546
100	78.4	0.663	874	69.5	0.921	2250	**67.7**	0.853	646
200	154	0.917	2070	140	1.74	3370	**135**	0.963	1460
300	229	1.16	2300	210	2.09	2970	**203**	1.95	1810
400	305	1.18	4460	281	1.95	4980	**272**	1.56	3090
500	380	1.25	5270	353	2.52	4930	**341**	1.65	3510
600	456	1.46	4610	426	1.89	4180	**411**	1.68	3660
700	531	1.16	6280	499	3.51	4770	**482**	1.95	4350
800	607	1.32	11300	572	1.88	9370	**553**	2.84	7780
900	682	1.49	13700	645	2.58	10800	**623**	2.51	10400
1000	757	1.69	15700	720	2.79	11800	**695**	2.49	11800

Table 3. Results for inputset of 30 strings of length m

Size (m)	SA-CSP			GA-CSP			Ant-CSP		
	HD		Time	HD		Time	HD		Time
	AVG	σ	AVG	AVG	σ	AVG	AVG	σ	AVG
10	9	0	245	8.25	0.433	2830	**8.15**	0.357	148
20	17.3	0.458	518	15.3	0.458	3460	**15.2**	0.4	341
30	25.1	0.357	772	22.7	0.458	3520	**22.4**	0.477	508
40	33	0.316	985	29.5	0.5	3720	**29.1**	0.357	638
50	40.9	0.539	1230	36.9	0.357	4180	**36.1**	0.436	814
100	79.3	0.557	1280	72.2	0.726	2450	**70.8**	0.536	850
200	156	0.829	4760	144	1.08	5800	**140**	0.975	2750
300	232	0.831	6640	216	1.77	6610	**209**	1.27	4260
400	308	0.829	9160	290	2.93	8160	**280**	1.28	5550
500	383	0.963	11110	362	1.66	8830	**351**	1.79	6760
600	459	1.24	12500	436	2.14	9800	**423**	1.95	7610
700	534	1.03	14500	510	2.57	10900	**495**	2.01	9430
800	610	1.14	17700	583	2.57	12600	**568**	2.36	10300
900	686	1.69	19800	658	3.42	13200	**640**	2.09	11400
1000	760	2.24	19800	731	2.97	12400	**713**	2.29	10700

Table 4. Results for inputset of 40 strings of length m

Size (m)	SA-CSP			GA-CSP			Ant-CSP		
	HD		Time	HD		Time	HD		Time
	AVG	σ	AVG	AVG	σ	AVG	AVG	σ	AVG
10	9.4	0.49	428	8.9	0.3	4000	**8.55**	0.497	252
20	17.6	0.477	742	15.9	0.218	3990	**15.8**	0.433	471
30	25.6	0.49	1210	23.1	0.384	4690	**22.9**	0.384	754
40	33.3	0.458	1540	30.4	0.572	4640	**30.1**	0.218	962
50	41.2	0.433	1940	37.5	0.497	5070	**37**	0.589	1220
100	80	0.669	2080	73.6	0.663	3420	**71.7**	0.477	1260
200	157	0.889	5740	146	1.24	5570	**142**	0.669	3230
300	233	0.889	8760	219	0.954	8640	**214**	1.05	5550
400	309	0.831	10090	293	1.87	9510	**285**	1.16	6560
500	385	0.748	14800	368	2.07	11000	**358**	1.24	7330
600	461	1.01	17800	441	1.69	13100	**431**	1.91	7940
700	536	1.05	21700	515	2.1	14300	**503**	1.01	11700
800	612	1.1	23500	590	2.34	14300	**577**	1.93	11300
900	688	1.34	26700	664	2.52	17200	**649**	2.31	15600
1000	763	1.43	30900	738	2.62	15900	**722**	1.91	16000

Table 5. Results for inputset of 50 strings of length m

Size (m)	SA-CSP			GA-CSP			Ant-CSP		
	HD		Time	HD		Time	HD		Time
	AVG	σ	AVG	AVG	σ	AVG	AVG	σ	AVG
10	9.45	0.497	574	9	0	4390	**8.85**	0.357	334
20	17.8	0.433	1030	16.2	0.4	4620	**16.1**	0.218	620
30	25.9	0.3	1490	23.5	0.5	4820	**23.2**	0.4	899
40	33.5	0.497	1960	30.9	0.357	5070	**30.6**	0.497	1180
50	41.7	0.458	2410	38.2	0.433	5270	**37.8**	0.433	1450
100	80.6	0.49	2970	74.7	0.64	3970	**73.3**	0.64	1750
200	158	0.671	9090	148	0.91	8530	**144**	0.698	5550
300	234	0.678	14000	222	0.91	10900	**216**	0.889	8320
400	310	0.792	18500	297	1.65	13100	**289**	1.41	11100
500	386	1.16	21900	369	1.69	14800	**362**	1.24	12900
600	462	1.13	21200	444	1.5	14500	**434**	1.74	12200
700	538	1.14	26800	519	1.9	17300	**508**	1.7	15500
800	614	1.43	28900	594	2.9	14000	**582**	2.29	13900
900	689	1.1	33500	667	1.64	19700	**656**	2.11	18800
1000	765	1.19	36600	742	3.09	21000	**729**	1.68	18300

the GA-CSP algorithm performs random mutations and crossovers, whereas the Ant-CSP probabilistically selects each character for the solution.

We note also that the Ant-CSP algorithm is quite robust, as its standard deviation σ remains low.

The above considerations show that our algorithm represents a valid and innovative alternative to the SA-CSP and GA-CSP algorithms.

6 Conclusions

In this paper, we proposed a new promising method for the CSP problem and we presented and commented some experimental results.

We compared our approach, Ant-CSP, to two heuristic algorithms proposed by Liu *et al.* [18]: the SA-CSP algorithm, based on the simulated annealing approach, and the GA-CSP algorithm, based on the genetic algorithm approach. Experimental results show that our algorithm computes almost always better solutions and is much faster than the GA-CSP and SA-CSP algorithms, regardless the number and the length of input strings.

Future works will be focused on two fronts: performance improvements and search for heuristic information to improve quality of solutions and convergence speeds. Additionally, we plan to extend our algorithm to the Closest Substring Problem.

Acknowledgments. The authors thank the referees for their helpful comments.

References

1. Booker, L.B., Goldberg, D.E., Holland, J.H.: Classifier Systems and Genetic Algorithms. Artif. Intell. 40(1-3), 235–282 (1989)
2. Deneubourg, J.L., Aron, S., Goss, S., Pasteels, J.M.: The Self-Organizing Exploratory Pattern of the Argentine Ant. Journal of Insect Behavior 3(2), 159–168 (1990)
3. Dorigo, M.: Optimization, Learning and Natural Algorithms. PhD Thesis, Dipartimento di Elettronica, Politecnico di Milano, Italy (1992)
4. Dorigo, M., Caro, G.D., Gambardella, L.M.: Ant Algorithms for Discrete Optimization. Artificial Life 5(2), 137–172 (1999)
5. Frances, M., Litman, A.: On Covering Problems of Codes. Theory of Computing Systems 30(2), 113–119 (1997)
6. Gasieniec, L., Jansson, J., Lingas, A.: Efficient Approximation Algorithms for the Hamming Center Problem. In: Proceedings of the 10th Annual ACM-SIAM Symposium on Discrete Algorithms, pp. 905–906. Society for Industrial and Applied Mathematics, Philadelphia (1999)
7. Goldberg, D.E., Holland, J.H.: Genetic Algorithms and Machine Learning. Machine Learning 3(2), 95–99 (1988)
8. Gomes, F.C., Meneses, C.N., Pardalos, P.M., Viana, G.V.R.: A Parallel Multistart Algorithm for the Closest String Problem. Computers and Operations Research 35(11), 3636–3643 (2008)
9. Gramm, J., Niedermeier, R., Rossmanith, P.: Exact Solutions for Closest String and Related Problems. In: Eades, P., Takaoka, T. (eds.) ISAAC 2001. LNCS, vol. 2223, pp. 441–453. Springer, Heidelberg (2001)
10. Gramm, J., Niedermeier, R., Rossmanith, P.: Fixed-Parameter Algorithms for Closest String and Related Problems. Algorithmica 37(1), 25–42 (2003)
11. Hertz, G.Z., Hartzell, G.W., Stormo, G.D.: Identification of Consensus Patterns in Unaligned DNA Sequences Known to Be Functionally Related. Bioinformatics 6(2), 81–92 (1990)
12. Hochba, D.S.: Approximation algorithms for NP-hard problems, vol. 28. ACM, New York (1997)
13. Holland, J.H.: Adaptation in Natural and Artificial Systems. MIT Press, Cambridge (1992)

14. Holland, J.H.: Genetic Algorithms Computer Programs that "Evolve" in Ways that Resemble Natural Selection Can Solve Complex Problems even Their Creators Do not Fully Understand. Scientific American 267, 62–72 (1992)
15. Kirkpatrick, S., Gelatt, C.D., Vecchi, M.P.: Optimization by Simulated Annealing. Science 220(4598), 671–680 (1983)
16. Lanctot, J.K., Li, M., Ma, B., Wang, S., Zhang, L.: Distinguishing String Selection Problems. In: Proceedings of the 10th Annual ACM-SIAM Symposium on Discrete Algorithms, pp. 633–642. Society for Industrial and Applied Mathematics, Philadelphia (1999)
17. Li, M., Ma, B., Wang, L.: On the Closest String and Substring Problems. Journal of the ACM 49(2), 157–171 (2002)
18. Liu, X., He, H., Sykora, O.: Parallel Genetic Algorithm and Parallel Simulated Annealing Algorithm for the Closest String Problem. In: Li, X., Wang, S., Dong, Z.Y. (eds.) ADMA 2005. LNCS (LNAI), vol. 3584, pp. 591–597. Springer, Heidelberg (2005)
19. Liu, X., Holger, M., Hao, Z., Wu, G.: A Compounded Genetic and Simulated Annealing Algorithm for the Closest String Problem. In: 2nd International Conference on Bioinformatics and Biomedical Engineering, ICBBE 2008, pp. 702–705 (2008)
20. Ma, B., Sun, X.: More Efficient Algorithms for Closest String and Substring Problems. In: Vingron, M., Wong, L. (eds.) RECOMB 2008. LNCS (LNBI), vol. 4955, pp. 396–409. Springer, Heidelberg (2008)
21. Meneses, C.N., Lu, Z., Oliveira, C.A.S., Pardalos, P.M.: Optimal Solutions for the Closest-String Problem via Integer Programming. Informs Journal on Computing 16(4), 419–429 (2004)
22. Metropolis, N., Rosenbluth, A.E., Rosenbluth, M.N., Teller, A.H., Teller, E.: Perspective on Equation of State Calculations by Fast Computing Machines. J. Chem. Phys. 21, 1087–1092 (1953)
23. Metropolis, N., Ulam, S.: The Monte Carlo Method. Journal of the American Statistical Association 44(247), 335–341 (1949)
24. Roman, S.: Coding and information theory. Springer, Heidelberg (1992)
25. Stormo, G.D., Hartzell, G.W.: Identifying Protein-Binding Sites from Unaligned DNA Fragments. Proc. Natl. Acad. Sci. USA 86, 1183–1187 (1989)

Linear Complementarity Algorithms for Infinite Games*

John Fearnley[1], Marcin Jurdziński[1], and Rahul Savani[2]

[1] Department of Computer Science, University of Warwick, UK
[2] Department of Computer Science, University of Liverpool, UK

Abstract. The performance of two pivoting algorithms, due to Lemke and Cottle and Dantzig, is studied on linear complementarity problems (LCPs) that arise from infinite games, such as parity, average-reward, and discounted games. The algorithms have not been previously studied in the context of infinite games, and they offer alternatives to the classical strategy-improvement algorithms. The two algorithms are described purely in terms of discounted games, thus bypassing the reduction from the games to LCPs, and hence facilitating a better understanding of the algorithms when applied to games. A family of parity games is given, on which both algorithms run in exponential time, indicating that in the worst case they perform no better for parity, average-reward, or discounted games than they do for general P-matrix LCPs.

1 Introduction

In this paper we consider infinite-duration zero-sum games played on finite graphs, such as parity, average-reward, and discounted games. Parity games are important in the theory of algorithmic formal verification because they provide a combinatorial characterization of the meaning of nested inductive and co-inductive definitions, as formalized in the modal μ-calculus and other fixpoint logics [12]. In particular, deciding the winner in parity games is polynomial-time equivalent to checking non-emptiness of non-deterministic parity tree automata, and to the modal μ-calculus model checking, two fundamental algorithmic problems in automata theory, logic, and verification [7,18,12]. Discounted and average-reward games have been introduced by Shapley [17] and Gillette [11] in the 1950s, and they have been extensively studied in the game theory, mathematical programming, algorithms, and AI communities [21,8]. Parity, average-reward, and discounted games have an intriguing complexity-theoretic status. The problems of deciding the winner in these games are some of the few known combinatorial problems in NP $\cap$ co-NP (and even UP $\cap$ co-UP [13]) that are not known to be solvable in polynomial time.

The linear complementarity problem (LCP) is a fundamental problem in mathematical programming. It naturally captures equilibrium problems, as well as the complementary slackness and Karush-Kuhn-Tucker conditions of linear

* An extended version of this paper with full proofs is available as `arXiv:0909.5653`.

J. van Leeuwen et al. (Eds.): SOFSEM 2010, LNCS 5901, pp. 382–393, 2010.

and quadratic programming, respectively. The monograph of Cottle *et. al.* [6] is the authoritative source on the LCP. In general, deciding if an LCP has a solution is NP-complete [3]. If, however, the matrix (which is a part of the LCP input) is a P-matrix (i.e., if all its principal minors are positive) then the problem is arguably easier computationally. Every P-matrix LCP (P-LCP) has a unique solution and computing it is in PLS $\cap$ PPAD. A significant amount of effort has been invested by the mathematical programming community towards finding an efficient algorithm for the P-LCP, which has led to a wide body of literature in this area. Polynomial-time reductions from simple stochastic games [10,19] and discounted games [14] to the P-LCP have been recently proposed, however the techniques commonly used to solve P-LCPs remain largely unknown in the infinite games community. It is possible that these techniques could shed new light on the computational complexity of solving infinite games.

In this paper we consider two classical pivoting algorithms for the P-LCP, Lemke's algorithm and the Cottle-Dantzig principal pivoting algorithm, and we study their performance on P-LCPs obtained from discounted games by the reduction of Jurdziński and Savani [14]. Our first main contribution is to describe both algorithms purely as a process that works on the original discounted game, bypassing the reduction from games to the P-LCP, and hence we facilitate their analysis without the need to consider or understand concepts of the LCP theory. We present the algorithms for discounted games because they have technical advantages that make the exposition particularly transparent [14]. We argue, however, that this is done without loss of generality: the algorithms can be readily applied to parity games and average-reward games because there are transparent polynomial-time reductions from parity games to average-reward games [16,13], and from average-reward games to discounted games [21].

It has long been known that the two algorithms can take exponential time when applied to P-LCPs. However, it is not known whether these lower bounds hold for the LCPs that arise from infinite games. Our second main contribution is to prove that there is a family of discounted games on which the algorithms of Lemke, and Cottle and Dantzig run in exponential time, and hence we indicate limitations of the classical LCP theory in the context of infinite games. Our family of examples are derived from those given by Björklund and Vorobyov [2] for their strategy improvement algorithm for average-reward games. For technical convenience and without loss of generality, we present these families of hard examples as discounted games; it is easy to construct parity and average-reward games from which those discounted games are obtained via the standard reductions [16,13,21].

We stress that these lower bounds are not fatal. The lower bound for Lemke's algorithm requires a specific covering vector and the lower bound for the Cottle-Dantzig algorithm relies on a specific choice of ordering on the vertices. The covering vector and the ordering are free choices left up to the user of the algorithm. This situation can be compared to the classical strategy improvement algorithms for infinite games [5,20,2]. It has long been known that these algorithms can be made to run in exponential time by choosing sufficiently bad vertices to switch [15]. However, it has only recently been shown that reasonable switching policies can be made to run in exponential time [9]. The complexity of our algorithms when equipped with reasonable covering vectors and reasonable orderings remains open. The literature on LCPs contains exciting complexity results for special cases. For example Adler and Megiddo [1] studied the performance of Lemke's algorithm for the LCPs arising from linear programming problems. They showed that for randomly chosen linear programs and a carefully selected covering vector, the expected number of pivots performed by the algorithm is quadratic. Our results open the door to extending such analyses to infinite games.

2 Preliminaries

A binary discounted game is given by a tuple $G = (V, V_{\text{Max}}, V_{\text{Min}}, \lambda, \rho, r^{\lambda}, r^{\rho}, \beta)$, where V is a set of vertices and V_{Max} and V_{Min} partition V into the set of vertices of player Max and the set of vertices of player Min, respectively. Each vertex has exactly two outgoing edges which are given by the left and right successor functions $\lambda, \rho : V \to V$. Each edge has a reward associated with it given by the functions $r^{\lambda}, r^{\rho} : V \to \mathbb{R}$. Finally, the discount factor β is such that $0 \leq \beta < 1$.

The game begins with a token on a starting vertex v_0. In each round, the player who owns the vertex on which the token is placed chooses one of the two successors of that vertex and moves the token to that successor. In this fashion the two players form an infinite path $\pi = \langle v_0, v_1, v_2, \dots \rangle$ where v_{i+1} is equal to either $\lambda(v_i)$ or $\rho(v_i)$. The path yields the infinite sequence of rewards $\langle r_0, r_1, r_2, \dots \rangle$, where $r_i = r^{\lambda}(v_i)$ if $\lambda(v_i) = v_{i+1}$, and $r_i = r^{\rho}(v_i)$ otherwise. The payoff of an infinite path is denoted by $\mathcal{D}(\pi) = \sum_{i=0}^{\infty} \beta^i r^i$. Since the game is zero-sum, player Max wins $\mathcal{D}(\pi)$ and player Min loses an equal amount.

A positional strategy for player Max is a function that, for each vertex belonging to player Max, chooses one of the two successors of the vertex. The strategy is denoted by $\chi : V_{\text{Max}} \to V$ with the condition that, for every vertex v in V_{Max}, the function $\chi(v)$ is equal to either $\lambda(v)$ or $\rho(v)$. Positional strategies for player Min are defined analogously. The sets of pure positional strategies for Max and Min are denoted by Π_{Max} and Π_{Min}, respectively. Given a pair of positional strategies, χ and μ for Max and Min respectively, and an initial vertex v_0, there is a unique infinite path $\langle v_0, v_1, v_2 \dots \rangle$, where $\chi(v_i) = v_{i+1}$ if v_i is in V_{Max} and $\mu(v_i) = v_{i+1}$ if v_i is in V_{Min}. This path, referred to as the play induced by the two strategies, will be denoted by $\text{Play}(\chi, \mu, v_0)$.

For all v in V, we define $\text{Val}^*(v) = \min_{\mu \in \Pi_{\text{Min}}} \max_{\chi \in \Pi_{\text{Max}}} \mathcal{D}(\text{Play}(\chi, \mu, v))$, and $\text{Val}_*(v) = \max_{\chi \in \Pi_{\text{Max}}} \min_{\mu \in \Pi_{\text{Min}}} \mathcal{D}(\text{Play}(\chi, \mu, v))$. These will be known as the lower and upper values of v, respectively. It is always true that $\text{Val}_*(v) \leq \text{Val}^*(v)$. It is well known that for discounted games the two values are equal, a property known as determinacy.

Theorem 1 ([17]). *For every discounted game G and every vertex $v \in V$, we have* $\text{Val}_*(v) = \text{Val}^*(v)$.

The value of the game starting at a vertex v, equal to both $\mathrm{Val}_*(v)$ and $\mathrm{Val}^*(v)$, is denoted by $\mathrm{Val}(v)$. The computational task associated with discounted games is to compute $\mathrm{Val}(v)$. Moreover, we want to find optimal strategies, i.e., a strategy χ that achieves the upper value and a strategy μ that achieves the lower value.

For convenience, we introduce the concept of a joint strategy $\sigma : V \to V$ that specifies moves for both players. The notation $\sigma \upharpoonright \mathrm{Max}$ and $\sigma \upharpoonright \mathrm{Min}$ will be used to refer to the individual strategies of Max and Min that constitute the joint strategy. For a vertex v, the function $\overline{\sigma}(v)$ gives the successor of v not chosen by σ. The functions r^σ and $r^{\overline{\sigma}}$ give the reward on the edge chosen by σ and the reward on the edge not chosen by σ, respectively. The path denoted by $\mathrm{Play}(\sigma, v)$ is equal to the path $\mathrm{Play}(\sigma \upharpoonright \mathrm{Max}, \sigma \upharpoonright \mathrm{Min}, v)$. The joint strategy is optimal if both $\sigma \upharpoonright \mathrm{Max}$ and $\sigma \upharpoonright \mathrm{Min}$ are optimal. For a given joint strategy σ, the value of a vertex v when σ is played will be denoted by $\mathrm{Val}^\sigma(v) = \mathcal{D}(\mathrm{Play}(\sigma, v))$.

Given a joint strategy σ and a vertex v, the *balance* of v is the difference between the value of v and the value of the play that starts at v, moves to $\overline{\sigma}(v)$ in the first step, and then follows σ,

$$\mathrm{Bal}^\sigma(v) = \begin{cases} \mathrm{Val}^\sigma(v) - (r^{\overline{\sigma}}(v) + \beta \cdot \mathrm{Val}^\sigma(\overline{\sigma}(v))) & \text{if } v \in V_{\mathrm{Max}}, \\ (r^{\overline{\sigma}}(v) + \beta \cdot \mathrm{Val}^\sigma(\overline{\sigma}(v))) - \mathrm{Val}^\sigma(v) & \text{if } v \in V_{\mathrm{Min}}. \end{cases} \tag{1}$$

A vertex v is said to be switchable under σ if $\mathrm{Bal}^\sigma(v) < 0$. If $\mathrm{Bal}^\sigma(v) = 0$ for some vertex then that vertex is said to be indifferent. There is a simple characterisation of optimality in terms of switchable vertices.

Theorem 2 ([17]). *If no vertex is switchable in a joint strategy σ then it is an optimal strategy for every choice of starting vertex.*

The two algorithms that we will present use only positional joint strategies. From now on, all joint strategies that we refer to can be assumed to be positional joint strategies. If a play begins at a vertex v and follows a positional joint strategy σ then the resulting infinite path can be represented by a simple path followed by an infinitely repeated cycle. Let $\mathrm{Play}(\sigma, v) = \langle v_0, v_1, \ldots, v_{k-1}, \langle c_0, c_1, \ldots, c_{l-1} \rangle^\omega \rangle$. It is then easy to see that

$$\mathrm{Val}^\sigma(v) = \sum_{i=0}^{k-1} \beta^i \cdot r^\sigma(v_i) + \sum_{i=0}^{l-1} \frac{\beta^{k+i}}{1 - \beta^l} \cdot r^\sigma(c_i).$$

Therefore, the amount that the reward on the outgoing edge of a vertex u contributes towards the value of v can be defined as follows.

Definition 1 (Contribution Coefficient). *For vertices v and u, and for a positional joint strategy σ, we define:*

$$\mathrm{D}^v_\sigma(u) = \begin{cases} \beta^i & \text{if } u = v_i \text{ for some } 0 \le i < k, \\ \frac{\beta^{k+i}}{1-\beta^l} & \text{if } u = c_i \text{ for some } 0 \le i < l, \\ 0 & \text{otherwise.} \end{cases}$$

3 Lemke's Algorithm for Discounted Games

Lemke's algorithm is a classical algorithm for solving the linear complementarity problem [6]. We can apply Lemke's algorithm to a discounted game by utilising the reduction of Jurdziński and Savani [14], however this yields little insight into how the algorithm works on a discounted game. In this section we bypass the reduction, and give a description of Lemke's algorithm entirely in terms of discounted games.

Lemke's algorithm begins with the joint strategy $\sigma_0 = \rho$ that selects the right successor for every vertex in the game. This is actually a free choice since the left and right successors can be swapped to obtain an arbitrary starting strategy. The algorithm will then move through a sequence of strategies until it arrives at the optimal strategy. The algorithm will also construct a modified game for each strategy that it considers. The modified games will take the following form.

Definition 2 (Modified Game for Lemke's Algorithm). *For a real number z, we define the game G_z to be the same as G but with a modified left-edge reward function, denoted by r_z^λ, and defined, for every vertex v, by:*

$$r_z^\lambda(v) = \begin{cases} r^\lambda(v) - z & v \in V_{Max}, \\ r^\lambda(v) + z & v \in V_{Min}. \end{cases} \tag{2}$$

For a modified game G_z, the function r_z^σ will give the rewards on the edges chosen by σ. The notations Val_z^σ and Bal_z^σ will give the values the balances of the vertices in the game G_z, respectively. For every strategy σ_i that is considered, the algorithm must choose an appropriate value z_i so that σ_i is optimal in G_{z_i}. Moreover, we want to choose the minimum value z_i for which this property holds. The next proposition shows how to compute this for the initial strategy σ_0.

Proposition 1. *Let $z_0 = \max\{-\mathrm{Bal}^{\sigma_0}(v) : v \in V\}$. The strategy σ_0 is optimal in G_{z_0} and the vertex v in V that maximizes $-\mathrm{Bal}^{\sigma_0}(v)$ is indifferent. Moreover, there is no value $y < z_0$ for which σ_0 is optimal in G_y.*

Proposition 1 gives an initial value for the parameter z. The principal idea behind the algorithm is to drive z down from its initial value to 0, while maintaining optimality of the current strategy in G_z. Unfortunately, Proposition 1 implies that we cannot drive z down further without losing the optimality of σ_0 in G_z. We do however know that there is some vertex v that is indifferent under σ_0 in G_{z_0}. We define $\sigma_1 = \sigma_0[\overline{\sigma}_0(v)/v]$, i.e., $\sigma_1(u) = \overline{\sigma}_0(u)$ if $u = v$, and $\sigma_1(u) = \sigma_0(u)$ otherwise. The operation of modifying a strategy by changing the successor of a vertex v will be referred to as switching v.

The value of no vertex changes when switching an indifferent vertex in a strategy. Since σ_0 was optimal in G_{z_0} and v was indifferent we therefore have that σ_1 is optimal in G_{z_0}. There is one important difference however, whereas z could not be decreased without σ_0 losing its optimality, the parameter z can be decreased further whilst maintaining the optimality of σ_1. The task now is to find z_1, the minimum value of z for which σ_1 is still optimal.

At a high level, when the algorithm arrives at a strategy σ_i its task is to find z_i, the minimum value of z for which σ_i is optimal in G_z. As we shall show, for this minimum value of z there will always be at least one vertex that is indifferent under σ_i played in G_z. The algorithm then switches this indifferent vertex to create σ_{i+1} and the process is repeated. The remainder of this section is dedicated to showing how z_i can be computed.

Each step begins with a strategy σ_i and the value z_{i-1}, which was the minimum value of z for which σ_{i-1} was optimal in G_z. We now wish to know how much further z can be decreased before σ_i ceases to be optimal. From Theorem 2 we know that a strategy is optimal as long as no vertex is switchable and that a vertex is switchable only when it has a negative balance. It is for this reason that we want to know how the balance of each vertex changes as z is decreased. In order to understand this, we must first know how the value of each vertex changes as z is decreased. We will use the notation $\partial_{-z} \operatorname{Val}_z^\sigma(v)$ to denote the rate of change of the value of v as z decreases, i.e., $-\partial_z \operatorname{Val}_z^\sigma(v)$. This notation will be used frequently throughout the rest of the paper to denote the rate of change of various expressions. For a proposition p, we define $[p]$ to be equal to 1 if p is true, and 0 otherwise. We can now give an explicit formula for $\partial_{-z} \operatorname{Val}_z^\sigma(v)$, which is based on the left edges that are passed through after visiting the vertex v while playing the strategy σ, and the contribution coefficient of those edges to the value of v.

Proposition 2. *For a vertex v and a joint strategy σ, let L be the set of vertices for which σ picks the left successor, $L = \{v \in V \ : \ \sigma(v) = \lambda(v)\}$. The rate of change of the value of v is*

$$\partial_{-z} \operatorname{Val}_z^\sigma(v) = \sum_{u \in L} ([u \in V_{Max}] - [u \in V_{Min}]) \cdot \mathrm{D}_\sigma^v(u).$$

From equation (1) we know that the balance of a vertex is computed as a difference of the values of two vertices. We now show how the rate of change of the balance can be derived by substituting the rate of change of the values into equation (1).

Proposition 3. *For a vertex v and a joint strategy σ we have*

$$\partial_{-z} \operatorname{Bal}_z^\sigma(v) = \begin{cases} \partial_{-z}\operatorname{Val}_z^\sigma(v) - ([\overline{\sigma}(v) = \lambda(v)] + \beta \cdot \partial_{-z}\operatorname{Val}_z^\sigma(\overline{\sigma}(v))) & \text{if } v \in V_{Max}, \\ -[\overline{\sigma}(v) = \lambda(v)] + \beta \cdot \partial_{-z}\operatorname{Val}_z^\sigma(\overline{\sigma}(v)) - \partial_{-z}\operatorname{Val}_z^\sigma(v) & \text{if } v \in V_{Min}. \end{cases}$$

Now that we have an expression for the rate of change of the balance of a vertex, we can compute how far z can be decreased from z_{i-1} before some vertex gets a negative balance. For each vertex v, the expression $\operatorname{Bal}_{z_{i-1}}^{\sigma_i}(v)/\partial_{-z} \operatorname{Bal}_z^{\sigma_i}(v)$ gives the amount that z can be decreased before v gets a negative balance, and so the minimum over all these ratios gives the amount that z can be decreased before some vertex gets a negative balance. It should also be clear that a vertex that achieves this minimum will be indifferent in the modified game when z is decreased by this amount. We can also show that this is the minimum value of z for which σ_i is optimal in G_z.

Proposition 4. *Let a joint strategy σ_i be optimal in the modified game $G_{z_{i-1}}$, and*

$$z_i = z_{i-1} - \min \left\{ \frac{\mathrm{Bal}^{\sigma}_{z_{i-1}}(v)}{\partial_{-z} \mathrm{Bal}^{\sigma}_{z}(v)} \ : \ v \in V \text{ and } \partial_{-z} \mathrm{Bal}^{\sigma}_{z}(v) < 0 \right\}. \quad (3)$$

Then strategy σ is optimal in G_{z_i}, and it is not optimal in G_x for all $x < z_i$.

Until now, we have ignored the possibility of reaching a strategy σ in which there is more than one indifferent vertex. In LCP algorithms this is known as a degenerate step. In this case, the task is to find a strategy in which every indifferent vertex v satisfies $\partial_{-z} \mathrm{Bal}^{\sigma}_{z}(v) > 0$, so that z can be decreased further. It is not difficult to prove that such a strategy can be reached by switching only the indifferent vertices. One method for degeneracy resolution is Bland's rule, which uses the least index method to break ties, and another is to use lexicographic perturbations; both methods are well-known, and are also used with the simplex method for linear programming [4].

Algorithm 1. Lemke(G)

$i := 0$; $\sigma_0 := \rho$; $z_0 := \max\{-\mathrm{Bal}^{\sigma_0}(v) \ : \ v \in V\}$
while $z_i > 0$ **do**
  $\sigma_{i+1} := \sigma_i[\overline{\sigma}_i(v)/v]$ for some vertex v with $\mathrm{Bal}^{\sigma_i}_{z_i}(v) = 0$
  $z_{i+1} := z_i - \min\{\frac{\mathrm{Bal}^{\sigma_{i+1}}_{z_i}(v)}{\partial_{-z} \mathrm{Bal}^{\sigma_{i+1}}_{z}(v)} \ : \ v \in V$ and $\partial_{-z} \mathrm{Bal}^{\sigma_{i+1}}_{z}(v) < 0\}$
  $i := i + 1$
end while

Lemke's algorithm is shown as Algorithm 1. Since in each step we know that there is no value of $z < z_i$ for which σ_i is optimal in G_z and we decrease z in every step it follows that we can never visit the same strategy twice without violating the condition that the current strategy should be optimal in the modified game. Therefore the algorithm must terminate after at most $2^{|V|}$ steps, which corresponds to the total number of joint strategies. The algorithm can only terminate when z has reached 0, and G_0 is the same game as G. It follows that whatever strategy the algorithm terminates with must be optimal in the original game.

Theorem 3. *Algorithm 1 terminates, with a joint strategy σ that is optimal for G after at most $2^{|V|}$ iterations.*

Lemke's algorithm for LCPs allows a free choice of *covering vector*, and in our description we used a unit covering vector. This can be generalised by giving a positive covering value to every vertex. If each vertex v has a covering value d_v then the modification of the left edges in Definition 2 becomes:

$$r^{\lambda}_{z}(v) = \begin{cases} r^{\lambda}(v) - d_v \cdot z & v \in V_{\mathrm{Max}}, \\ r^{\lambda}(v) + d_v \cdot z & v \in V_{\mathrm{Min}}. \end{cases}$$

The algorithm can then easily be modified to account for this altered definition.

4 The Cottle-Dantzig Algorithm for Discounted Games

The principle idea behind the Cottle-Dantzig algorithm is to maintain a set of vertices whose balance is non-negative. The algorithm begins with an arbitrary strategy, and it goes through a series of major iterations, where in each iteration one vertex is brought into the set of vertices with non-negative balances, while maintaining the non-negative balances of the vertices that are already in that set. It is clear that if such a task can be accomplished, then the algorithm will terminate after $|V|$ major iterations.

We require a method for bringing some distinguished vertex v into the set of vertices with a non-negative balance without the vertices currently in the set getting a negative balance in the process. To accomplish this we will modify the game by adding a bonus to the edge that the strategy currently chooses at v. We will then drive the bonus up from 0 while maintaining an optimal strategy for the modified game. Eventually the balance of v will become 0 in the modified game, at which point the strategy at v can be switched away from the edge with the bonus attached to it, and the bonus can be removed. We will prove that after this procedure v will have a positive balance.

In this section we will override many of the notations that were used to describe Lemke's algorithm.

Definition 3 (Modified Game for the Cottle-Dantzig Algorithm). *For a real number w, a joint strategy σ, and a distinguished vertex v, we define the game G_w to be the same as G but with a different reward on the edge chosen by σ at v. If σ chooses the left successor at v then the left reward function is defined, for every u in V, by:*

$$r^{\lambda}_{w}(u) = \begin{cases} r^{\lambda}(u) + w & \text{if } u = v \text{ and } u \in V_{Max}, \\ r^{\lambda}(u) - w & \text{if } u = v \text{ and } u \in V_{Min}, \\ r^{\lambda}(u) & \text{otherwise.} \end{cases}$$

If σ chooses the right successor at v then r^{ρ} modified in a similar manner.

We begin the major iteration with a strategy σ_0, a value $w_0 = 0$, and a set of vertices with non-negative balances P. The task is to raise w from 0 until $\mathrm{Bal}^{\sigma}_{w}(v) = 0$, while maintaining the invariant that every vertex in P has a non-negative balance. This can be accomplished using methods that are similar to those used in Lemke's algorithm. For every vertex in P we must compute how the balance of that vertex changes as w is increased. The following propositions are analogues of Propositions 2, 3, and 4.

Proposition 5. *Consider a vertex u and a joint strategy σ. Suppose that v is the distinguished vertex. The rate of change $\partial_w \mathrm{Val}^{\sigma}_{w}(u)$ is $\mathrm{D}^{u}_{\sigma}(v)$.*

Proposition 6. *Consider a vertex u and a joint strategy σ in the game G_w. The rate of change $\partial_w \mathrm{Bal}^{\sigma}_{w}(u)$ is:*

$$\partial_w \mathrm{Bal}^{\sigma}_{w}(u) = \begin{cases} \partial_w \mathrm{Val}^{\sigma}_{w}(u) - \beta \cdot \partial_w \mathrm{Val}^{\sigma}_{w}(\overline{\sigma}(u)) & \text{if } u \in V_{Max}, \\ \beta \cdot \partial_w \mathrm{Val}^{\sigma}_{w}(\overline{\sigma}(u)) - \partial_w \mathrm{Val}^{\sigma}_{w}(u) & \text{if } u \in V_{Min}. \end{cases}$$

Algorithm 2. Cottle-Dantzig(G, σ)

$P := \emptyset$
while $P \neq V$ **do**
  $i := 0$; $w_0 := 0$; $v :=$ Some vertex in $V \setminus P$
  while $\mathrm{Bal}^{\sigma}_{w_i}(v) < 0$ **do**
    $w_{i+1} := w_i + \min\{-\frac{\mathrm{Bal}^{\sigma}_{w_i}(u)}{\partial_w \mathrm{Bal}^{\sigma}_{w}(u)} \ : \ u \in P \cup \{v\} \text{ and } \partial_w \mathrm{Bal}^{\sigma}_{w}(u) < 0\}$
    $\sigma := \sigma[\overline{\sigma}(u)/u]$ for some vertex u with $\mathrm{Bal}^{\sigma}_{w_i}(v) = 0$
    $i := i + 1$
  end while
  $\sigma := \sigma[\overline{\sigma}(v)/v]$; $P := P \cup \{v\}$
end while

Proposition 7. *Consider a modified game G_w, a joint strategy σ, and a set of vertices P which must not have negative balances. Let*

$$y = w + \min\{-\frac{\mathrm{Bal}^{\sigma}_{w}(u)}{\partial_w \mathrm{Bal}^{\sigma}_{w}(u)} \ : \ u \in P \cup \{v\} \text{ and } \partial_w \mathrm{Bal}^{\sigma}_{w}(u) < 0\}.$$

No vertex in P has a negative balance in G_y. Moreover, one vertex in $P \cup \{v\}$ is indifferent, and for all values $x > y$ that vertex has a negative balance in G_x.

The process of raising w up from 0 until the balance of v is 0 in the modified game is the same as the process of decreasing z in Lemke's algorithm, only using the different definitions from Propositions 5, 6, and 7. Once the balance of v has reached 0 we can stop increasing w. Since v is now indifferent we can switch it away from the edge that has the bonus attached to it. Once this has been done, the values of all vertices are no longer affected by w, since the edge to which it is attached is no longer chosen by the current strategy. Therefore we can remove the bonus and recover the original game. The major iteration then terminates with a strategy in which every vertex in $P \cup \{v\}$ has a non-negative balance, and the next major iteration can begin.

Theorem 4. *Algorithm 2 terminates, with the optimal joint strategy, after at most $2^{|V|}$ iterations.*

5 Exponential Lower Bounds

We show that both Lemke's and the Cottle-Dantzig algorithms take exponentially many steps on the family of games shown in Figure 1. Max vertices are depicted as squares and Min vertices are depicted as circles. For every vertex, we define the right successor to be the vertex with the same owner as the vertex itself, and the left successor to be the vertex that belongs to the other player. Recall that the initial strategy for Lemke's algorithm is the one that chooses the right successor for every vertex. When speaking about vertices in the game we often refer to either the leftmost or the rightmost vertex with a certain property.

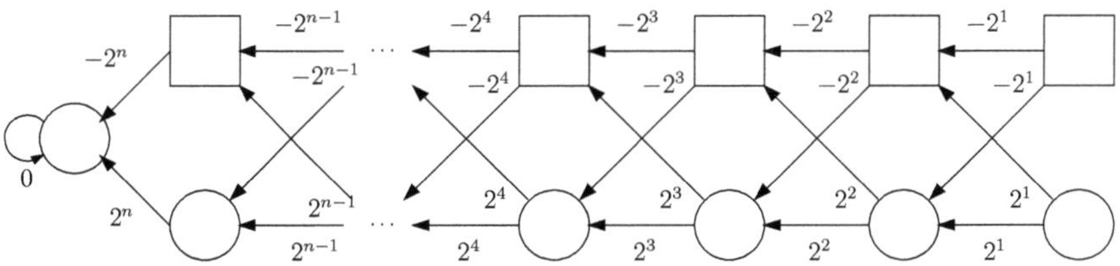

Fig. 1. The game $\mathcal{G}_n$

In this context, the vertex being referred to is the one that is furthest to the right or to the left in Figure 1.

For ease of exposition, we will describe the steps of the algorithm as if the discount factor was 1. Although this is forbidden by the definition of a discounted game, since the game contains one cycle, whose value is zero, the value of every vertex under every strategy will be finite. As long as the discount factor is chosen sufficiently close to 1, the algorithm will behave as we describe.

Note that the game graph is symmetric with respect to the line that separates the vertices of the two players. We frequently refer to a vertex and the vertex that it is opposite to, and hence we introduce the concept of vertex reflections. For a vertex v that is not the sink, we write $\overline{v}$ to denote the reflection of v, that is the vertex belonging to the other player that is shown directly opposite v in Figure 1. We say that a joint strategy σ is symmetric if for all vertices v, the strategy σ chooses the right successor of v if and only if it chooses the right successor of $\overline{v}$. The initial strategy for Lemke's algorithm is a symmetric strategy. Lemke's algorithm always switches v directly before or after $\overline{v}$ and so it can be seen as traversing through symmetric strategies.

Before discussing the modified games that Lemke's algorithm constructs, we give a simple characterisation of when a vertex is switchable in the original game.

Proposition 8. *If σ is a symmetric joint strategy, then a vertex v is switchable if and only if the path from v has an even number of left edges.*

We now use this characterisation to give a simple formula for $\partial_{-z} \operatorname{Bal}^{\sigma}_{z}(v)$ for every vertex v under every symmetric joint strategy σ.

Proposition 9. *If σ is a symmetric joint strategy, then $\partial_{-z} \operatorname{Bal}^{\sigma}_{z}(v)$, the rate of change of the balance of a vertex v, is 1 if v is switchable, and -1 otherwise.*

Together, Propositions 8 and 9 imply that the parameter z can be set to the largest balance of a switchable vertex. We show that the largest balance will always belong to the rightmost switchable vertex.

Proposition 10. *Let σ be a symmetric joint strategy, v be the rightmost switchable Max vertex, and $z = -\operatorname{Bal}^{\sigma}(v)$. Then no vertex in G_z is switchable, both v and the reflection of v are indifferent, and for every real number $y < z$, there is a switchable vertex in G_y.*

Proposition 10 implies that whenever Lemke's algorithm is considering a symmetric joint strategy, it must choose a z so that the rightmost switchable vertex is indifferent. We show that this leads to an exponential number of switches.

Theorem 5. *Lemke's algorithm performs* $2^{n+1} - 2$ *iterations on the game* $\mathcal{G}_n$.

The Cottle-Dantzig algorithm is sensitive to the order in which to bring the vertices into the non-negative set. We prove that there is an order that causes exponential-time behaviour for this algorithm. The sequence of strategies is similar to the sequence that Lemke's algorithm follows.

Theorem 6. *Consider an order in which all Min vertices precede Max vertices, and Max vertices are ordered from right to left. The Cottle-Dantzig algorithm performs* $2^{n+1} - 1$ *iterations.*

We have shown that both algorithms can take an exponential number of steps on the discounted game $\mathcal{G}_n$. We argue that this also implies an exponential lower bound for parity and average-reward games. From the game $\mathcal{G}_n$ we can obtain a parity game by replacing the reward $\pm 2^c$ with the priority c. The standard reductions [16,21,13] convert this parity game into average-reward and discounted games where priority c is replaced with reward $(-n)^c$, and the discount factor is chosen to be very close to 1. All arguments used to prove Theorems 5 and 6 continue to hold if rewards of magnitude 2^c are replaced with rewards of magnitude n^c, which implies the exponential lower bounds also hold for parity games and average-reward games.

6 Future Work

Our adaptation of Lemke's algorithm for solving discounted games corresponds to its implementation in which the unit covering vector is used [6], and our lower bounds are specific to this choice. Similarly our lower bounds for the Cottle-Dantzig algorithm require a specific choice of ordering over the vertices. Randomizing these choices may exhibit better performance and should be considered.

Adler and Megiddo [1] studied the performance of Lemke's algorithm for the LCPs arising from linear programming problems. They showed that, for randomly chosen linear programs and a carefully selected covering vector, the expected number of pivots performed by the algorithm is quadratic. A similar analysis for randomly chosen discounted games should be considered.

References

1. Adler, I., Megiddo, N.: A Simplex Algorithm whose Average Number of Steps is Bounded between Two Quadratic Functions of the Smaller Dimension. Journal of the ACM 32(4), 871–895 (1985)
2. Björklund, H., Vorobyov, S.: A Combinatorial Strongly Subexponential Strategy Improvement Algorithm for Mean Payoff Games. Discrete Applied Mathematics 155(2), 210–229 (2007)

3. Chung, S.J.: NP-Completeness of the Linear Complementarity Problem. Journal of Optimization Theory and Applications 60(3), 393–399 (1989)
4. Chvátal, V.: Linear Programming. Freeman, New York (1983)
5. Condon, A.: On Algorithms for Simple Stochastic Games. In: Advances in Computational Complexity Theory. DIMACS Series in Discrete Mathematics and Theoretical Computer Science, vol. 13, pp. 51–73. American Mathematical Society (1993)
6. Cottle, R.W., Pang, J.-S., Stone, R.E.: The Linear Complementarity Problem. Academic Press, London (1992)
7. Emerson, E.A., Jutla, C.S., Sistla, A.P.: On Model-Checking for Fragments of μ-Calculus. In: Courcoubetis, C. (ed.) CAV 1993. LNCS, vol. 697, pp. 385–396. Springer, Heidelberg (1993)
8. Filar, J., Vrieze, K.: Competitive Markov Decision Processes. Springer, Heidelberg (1997)
9. Friedman, O.: A Super-Polynomial Lower Bound for the Parity Game Strategy Improvement Algorithm as We Know It. In: Logic in Computer Science (LICS). IEEE, Los Alamitos (to appear, 2009)
10. Gärtner, B., Rüst, L.: Simple Stochastic Games and P-Matrix Generalized Linear Complementarity Problems. In: Liśkiewicz, M., Reischuk, R. (eds.) FCT 2005. LNCS, vol. 3623, pp. 209–220. Springer, Heidelberg (2005)
11. Gillette, D.: Stochastic Games with Zero Stop Probabilities. In: Contributions to the Theory of Games, pp. 179–187. Princeton University Press, Princeton (1957)
12. Grädel, E., Thomas, W., Wilke, T. (eds.): Automata, Logics, and Infinite Games. A Guide to Current Research. LNCS, vol. 2500. Springer, Heidelberg (2002)
13. Jurdziński, M.: Deciding the Winner in Parity Games Is in UP $\cap$ co-UP. Information Processing Letters 68(3), 119–124 (1998)
14. Jurdziński, M., Savani, R.: A Simple P-Matrix Linear Complementarity Problem for Discounted Games. In: Beckmann, A., Dimitracopoulos, C., Löwe, B. (eds.) CiE 2008. LNCS, vol. 5028, pp. 283–293. Springer, Heidelberg (2008)
15. Melekopoglou, M., Condon, A.: On the Complexity of the Policy Improvement Algorithm for Markov Decision Processes. ORSA Journal on Computing 6, 188–192 (1994)
16. Puri, A.: Theory of Hybrid Systems and Discrete Event Systems. PhD Thesis, University of California, Berkeley (1995)
17. Shapley, L.S.: Stochastic Games. Proceedings of the National Academy of Sciences of the United States of America 39(10), 1095–1100 (1953)
18. Stirling, C.: Local Model Checking Games (Extended abstract). In: Lee, I., Smolka, S.A. (eds.) CONCUR 1995. LNCS, vol. 962, pp. 1–11. Springer, Heidelberg (1995)
19. Svensson, O., Vorobyov, S.: Linear Complementarity and P-Matrices for Stochastic Games. In: Virbitskaite, I., Voronkov, A. (eds.) PSI 2006. LNCS, vol. 4378, pp. 409–423. Springer, Heidelberg (2007)
20. Vöge, J., Jurdziński, M.: A Discrete Strategy Improvement Algorithm for Solving Parity Games (Extended abstract). In: Emerson, E.A., Sistla, A.P. (eds.) CAV 2000. LNCS, vol. 1855, pp. 202–215. Springer, Heidelberg (2000)
21. Zwick, U., Paterson, M.: The Complexity of Mean Payoff Games on Graphs. Theoretical Computer Science 158, 343–359 (1996)

Mixing Coverability and Reachability to Analyze VASS with One Zero-Test

Alain Finkel[1,⋆] and Arnaud Sangnier[2,⋆⋆]

[1] LSV, ENS Cachan & CNRS, France
finkel@lsv.ens-cachan.fr
[2] Dipartimento di Informatica, Università di Torino, Italy
sangnier@di.unito.it

Abstract. We study Vector Addition Systems with States (VASS) extended in such a way that one of the manipulated integer variables can be tested to zero. For this class of system, it has been proved that the reachability problem is decidable. We prove here that boundedness, termination and reversal-boundedness are decidable for VASS with one zero-test. To decide reversal-boundedness, we provide an original method which mixes both the construction of the coverability graph for VASS and the computation of the reachability set of reversal-bounded counter machines. The same construction can be slightly adapted to decide boundedness and hence termination.

1 Introduction

Vector Addition Systems with States (VASS), which are equivalent to Petri nets, are a model which has received a lot of attention and thousands of papers exist on this subject [17]. Whereas many problems are decidable for VASS [4], it is well-known that VASS with the ability for testing to zero (or with inhibitor arcs) have the power of Turing machines. Hence all the non-trivial problems are undecidable for this class of models.

Recently in [18], Reinhardt proved that the reachability problem for VASS with an unique integer variable (or counter) tested to zero is decidable in reducing this problem to the reachability problem for Petri nets, which is decidable (see the papers of Kosaraju [12] and Mayr [14] and Leroux [13] for a conceptual decidability proof of reachability). For VASS, many problems like zero reachability, coverability (is it possible to reach a configuration larger than a given configuration?), boundedness (whether the reachability set is finite?) and termination (is there an infinite execution?) can be reduced to reachability and this is still true for extended (well-structured) Petri nets [3,9] (polynomial reductions of reachability for well-structured Petri nets extensions are given in [2]). For VASS with one zero-test, coverability reduces (as usual) to reachability but it is less clear for the other properties like boundedness whether the known reductions

⋆ Partly supported by project AVERISS (ANR-06-SETIN-001).
⋆⋆ Supported by a post-doctoral scolarship from DGA/ENS Cachan.

J. van Leeuwen et al. (Eds.): SOFSEM 2010, LNCS 5901, pp. 394–406, 2010.

can be adapted. Note that in [1], Abdulla and Mayr proposes a method to decide coverability for VASS with one zero-test without using the Reinhardt's result.

In many verification problems, it is convenient not only to have an algorithm for the reachability problem, but also to be able to compute effectively the reachability set. In [10], the class of reversal-bounded counter machines is introduced as follows: each counter can only perform a bounded number of alternations between increasing and decreasing mode. Ibarra shows that reversal-bounded counter machines enjoy the following nice property: their reachability set is a semi-linear set which can be effectively computed. In a recent work [7], we have proved that reversal-boundedness is decidable for VASS, whereas for VASS extended with two counters which can be tested to zero this property is undecidable.

Our contribution. We investigate here the three following problems: given a VASS with one zero-test, can we decide whether it is bounded, whether it is reversal-bounded and whether it terminates. We first consider the most difficult problem, which is the reversal-boundedness problem and from the algorithm for solving it, we deduce another algorithm for solving boundedness. The decidability of termination is then obtained by a classical reduction into boundedness. The algorithm we propose mix the classical construction of the coverability graph for VASS [11] and the computing of the reachability set of reversal-bounded counter machines.

Due to lack of space, some details are omitted and can be found in [8].

2 VASS with One Zero-Test and Reversal-Bounded Property

2.1 Useful Notions

Let $\mathbb{N}$ (resp. $\mathbb{Z}$) denotes the set of nonnegative integers (resp. integers). The usual total order over $\mathbb{Z}$ is written $\leq$. By $\mathbb{N}_\omega$, we denote the set $\mathbb{N} \cup \{\omega\}$ where ω is a new symbol such that $\omega \notin \mathbb{N}$ and for all $k \in \mathbb{N}_\omega$, $k \leq \omega$. We extend the binary operation $+$ and $-$ to $\mathbb{N}_\omega$ as follows : for all $k \in \mathbb{N}$, $k + \omega = \omega$ and $\omega - k = \omega$. For $k, l \in \mathbb{N}_\omega$ with $k \leq l$, we write $[k..l]$ for the interval of integers $\{i \in \mathbb{N} \mid k \leq i \leq l\}$.

Given a set X and $n \in \mathbb{N}$, X^n is the set of n-dim vectors with values in X. For any index $i \in [1..n]$, we denote by $\mathbf{v}(i)$ the ith component of a n-dim vector $\mathbf{v}$. We write $\mathbf{0}$ the vector such that $\mathbf{0}(i) = 0$ for all $i \in [1..n]$. The classical order on $\mathbb{Z}^n$ is also denoted $\leq$ and is defined by $\mathbf{v} \leq \mathbf{w}$ if and only if for all $i \in [1..n]$, we have $\mathbf{v}(i) \leq \mathbf{w}(i)$. We also define the operation $+$ over n-dim vectors of integers in the classical way (ie for $\mathbf{v}$, $\mathbf{v}' \in \mathbb{Z}^n$, $\mathbf{v} + \mathbf{v}'$ is defined by $(\mathbf{v} + \mathbf{v}')(i) = \mathbf{v}(i) + \mathbf{v}'(i)$ for all $i \in [1..n]$).

Let $n \in \mathbb{N}$. A subset $S \subseteq \mathbb{N}^n$ is *linear* if there exist $k+1$ vectors $\mathbf{v}_0, \mathbf{v}_1, \ldots, \mathbf{v}_k$ in $\mathbb{N}^n$ such that $S = \{\mathbf{v} \mid \mathbf{v} = \mathbf{v}_0 + \lambda_1.\mathbf{v}_1 + \ldots + \lambda_k.\mathbf{v}_k$ with $\lambda_i \in \mathbb{N}$ for all $i \in [1..k]\}$. A *semi-linear set* is any finite union of linear sets. We extend the notion of semi-linearity to subsets of $Q \times \mathbb{N}^n$ where Q is a finite (non-empty) set. This can be easily done assuming Q is for instance a finite subset of $\mathbb{N}$. For an alphabet Σ, we denote by Σ^* the set of finite words over Σ and ϵ represents the empty word.

2.2 Counter Machines

We call a *n-dim guarded translation* (shortly a translation) any function $t : \mathbb{N}^n \to \mathbb{N}^n$ characterized by $\# \in \{=, \leq, \geq\}^n$, $\mu \in \mathbb{N}^n$ and $\delta \in \mathbb{Z}^n$ such that $dom(t) = \{\mathbf{v} \in \mathbb{N}^n \mid \mathbf{v}\#\mu \text{ and } \mathbf{v} + \delta \in \mathbb{N}^n\}$ and for all $\mathbf{v} \in dom(t)$, $t(\mathbf{v}) = \mathbf{v} + \delta$. We will sometimes use the encoding $(\#, \mu, \delta)$ to represent a translation. With this notation $\#$ and μ encode a test and δ an update. In the following, T_n will denote the set of the n-dim guarded translations.

Definition 1. *A* n-dim counter machine *(shortly* counter machine*) is a tuple* $S = \langle Q, E \rangle$ *where* Q *is a finite set of control states and* E *is a finite relation* $E \subseteq Q \times T_n \times Q$.

The semantics of a counter machine $S = \langle Q, E \rangle$ is given by its associated transition system $TS(S) = \langle Q \times \mathbb{N}^n, \to \rangle$ where $\to \subseteq (Q \times \mathbb{N}^n) \times T_n \times (Q \times \mathbb{N}^n)$ is a relation defined as follows: $(q, \mathbf{v}) \xrightarrow{t} (q', \mathbf{v}')$ iff $\exists\, (q, t, q') \in E$ such that $\mathbf{v} \in dom(t)$ and $\mathbf{v}' = t(\mathbf{v})$. We write $(q, \mathbf{v}) \to (q', \mathbf{v}')$ if there exists $t \in T_n$ such that $(q, \mathbf{v}) \xrightarrow{t} (q', \mathbf{v}')$. The relation $\to^*$ represents the reflexive and transitive closure of $\to$. Given a configuration $(q, \mathbf{v})$ of $TS(S)$, $\mathtt{Reach}(S, (q, \mathbf{v})) = \{(q', \mathbf{v}') \mid (q, \mathbf{v}) \to^* (q', \mathbf{v}')\}$. Given a counter machine $S = \langle Q, E \rangle$ and an initial configuration $c_0 \in Q \times \mathbb{N}^n$, the pair (S, c_0) is an intialized counter machine. Since, the notations are explicit, in the following we shall write counter machine for both (S, c_0) and S.

Definition 2. *A counter machine* (S, c_0) *is bounded if there exists* $k \in \mathbb{N}$ *such that for all* $(q, \boldsymbol{v}) \in \mathtt{Reach}(S, c_0)$ *and for all* $i \in [1..n]$, *we have* $\boldsymbol{v}(i) \leq k$.

Note that a counter machine has a finite number of reachable configurations if and only if it is bounded. It is well-known [15] that many verification problems, such as the reachability of a control state or the boundedness, are undecidable for 2-dim counter machines. We present in the sequel some restricted classes of counter machines for which these problems become decidable.

2.3 VASS with One Zero-Test

Definition 3. *A* n*-dim counter machine*$\langle Q, E \rangle$ *is a* Vector Addition System with States *(shortly VASS) if for all transitions* $(q, t, q') \in E$, t *is a guarded translation* $(\#, \mu, \delta)$ *such that* $\# = (\geq, \ldots, \geq)$,

Hence in VASS, it is not possible to test if a counter value is equal to a constant but only if it is greater than a constant. In opposite to general counter machines, many problems are decidable for VASS, for instance the problem of the reachability of a configuration or the boundedness [11,12,14]. We finally present here another class of counter machine, which extends the VASS.

Definition 4. *A n-dim counter machine $S = \langle Q, E\rangle$ is a* VASS with one zero-test *if $Q = Q' \uplus \{q_{?0}, q_{=0}\}$, $E = E_{\geq} \uplus \{(q_{?0}, g_{=0?}, q_{=0})\}$ where $g_{=0?}$ is the guarded translation $((=, \geq, \ldots, \geq), \mathbf{0}, \mathbf{0})$ and $S_{\geq} = \langle Q' \uplus \{q_{?0}\}, E_{\geq}\rangle$ is a VASS.*

Without loss of generality we will impose that the transition $(q_{?0}, g_{=0?}, q_{=0})$ is the only transition leading to $q_{=0}$ in S. We see that in a VASS with one zero-test, the transition $(q_{?0}, g_{=0?}, q_{=0})$ has the ability to test if the value of the first counter is 0. Even if this class of counter machines has been less studied than VASS, it has been proved in [18] that the problem of reachability of a configuration is decidable for it. Note that we restrict this class of machines to use only one transition with an equality test over the first counter, but this is only to improve the readability of our work. In fact, our results still hold for any VASS with more than one zero-test on the first counter.

If we define the $\leq_1$ in $\mathbb{N}^n \times \mathbb{N}^n$ as follows, $\mathbf{v} \leq_1 \mathbf{v}'$ if and only if $\mathbf{v} \leq \mathbf{v}'$ and $\mathbf{v}(1) = \mathbf{v}'(1)$, then VASS with one zero-test enjoy the following property:

Lemma 5. *Let $S = \langle Q, E\rangle$ be a n-dim VASS with one zero-test and $TS(S) = \langle Q \times \mathbb{N}^n, \rightarrow\rangle$ its associated transition system. We consider $(q, \boldsymbol{v}), (q, \boldsymbol{w})$ in $Q \times \mathbb{N}^n$, if $\boldsymbol{v} \leq_1 \boldsymbol{w}$ and if there exists $(q', \boldsymbol{v}') \in Q \times \mathbb{N}^n$ such that $(q, \boldsymbol{v}) \rightarrow (q', \boldsymbol{v}')$ then there exists $(q', \boldsymbol{w}') \in Q \times \mathbb{N}^n$ such that $(q, \boldsymbol{w}) \rightarrow (q', \boldsymbol{w}')$ and $\boldsymbol{v}' \leq_1 \boldsymbol{w}'$.*

In the following, we will propose a new method to analyze VASS with one zero-test.

2.4 Reversal-Bounded Counter Machines

In [10], the class of reversal-bounded counter machines has been introduced as follows: each counter can only perform a bounded number of alternations between increasing and decreasing mode. This class of counter machines is interesting because it has been shown that these machines have a semi-linear reachability set which can be effectively computed. We recall here their formal definition.

Let $S = \langle Q, E\rangle$ be a n-dim counter machine and $TS(S) = \langle Q \times \mathbb{N}^n, \rightarrow\rangle$ its associated transition system . From it, we define another transition system $TS_{rb}(S) = \langle Q \times \mathbb{N}^n \times \{\downarrow, \uparrow\}^n \times \mathbb{N}^n, \rightarrow_{rb}\rangle$. For a configuration $(q, \mathbf{v}, \mathbf{m}, \mathbf{r}) \in Q \times \mathbb{N}^n \times \{\downarrow, \uparrow\}^n \times \mathbb{N}^n$, the vector $\mathbf{v}$ contains the values of each counter, the vector $\mathbf{m}$ is used to store the current mode of each counter -increasing ($\uparrow$) or decreasing ($\downarrow$)- and the vector $\mathbf{r}$ the numbers of alternations performed by each counter. A formal definition of $TS_{rb}(S)$ is given in [8].

We denote by $\rightarrow_{rb}^*$ the reflexive and transitive closure of $\rightarrow_{rb}$. Given a configuration $(q, \mathbf{v}, \mathbf{r}, \mathbf{m})$ of $TS_{rb}(S)$, $\mathtt{Reach}_{rb}(S, (q, \mathbf{v}, \mathbf{m}, \mathbf{r})) = \{(q', \mathbf{v}', \mathbf{m}', \mathbf{r}') \mid (q, \mathbf{v}, \mathbf{m}, \mathbf{r}) \rightarrow_{rb}^* (q', \mathbf{v}', \mathbf{m}', \mathbf{r}')\}$. We extend this last notation to the configurations of $TS(S)$, saying that if $(q, \mathbf{v}) \in Q \times \mathbb{N}^n$ is a configuration of $TS(S)$, then $\mathtt{Reach}_{rb}(S, (q, \mathbf{v}))$ is equal to the set $\mathtt{Reach}_{rb}(S, (q, \mathbf{v}, \uparrow, \mathbf{0}))$ where $\uparrow$ denotes here the vector with all components equal to $\uparrow$.

Definition 6. *A counter machine (S, c_0) is* reversal-bounded *if and only if there exists $k \in \mathbb{N}$ such that for all $(q, \boldsymbol{v}, \boldsymbol{m}, \boldsymbol{r}) \in \mathtt{Reach}_{rb}(S, c_0)$ and for all $i \in [1..n]$, we have $\boldsymbol{r}(i) \leq k$.*

Using a translation into a finite automaton and the fact that the Parikh map of a regular language is a semi-linear set [16], Ibarra proved in [10] the following result:

Theorem 7. *[10] The reachability set of a reversal-bounded counter machine is an effectively computable semi-linear set.*

3 Computing Coverability

3.1 Coverability Graph of a VASS

In [11], Karp and Miller provide an algorithm to build from a VASS a labeled tree, the *Karp and Miller tree*. We recall here the construction of this tree. We first define a function $\texttt{Acceleration}: \mathbb{N}^n_\omega \times \mathbb{N}^n_\omega \rightarrow \mathbb{N}^n_\omega$ as follows, for $\mathbf{w}, \mathbf{w}' \in \mathbb{N}^n_\omega$ such that $\mathbf{w} \leq \mathbf{w}'$, we have $\mathbf{w}'' = \texttt{Acceleration}(\mathbf{w}, \mathbf{w}')$ if and only if for all $i \in [1..n]$:

- if $\mathbf{w}(i) = \mathbf{w}'(i)$ then $\mathbf{w}''(i) = \mathbf{w}(i)$,
- if $\mathbf{w}(i) < \mathbf{w}'(i)$ then $\mathbf{w}''(i) = \omega$.

The Karp and Miller tree is a labeled tree (P, δ, r, l) where P is a finite set of nodes, $\delta \subseteq P \times T_n \times P$ is the transition relation, $r \in P$ is the root of the tree, and $l : P \rightarrow Q \times \mathbb{N}^n_\omega$ is a labeling function. To represent a node p with the label $l(p) = (q, \mathbf{w})$, we will sometimes directly write $p[q, \mathbf{w}]$. The Algorithm 1 shows how the Karp and Miller tree is obtained from an initialized VASS.

The main idea of this tree is to cover in a finite way the reachable configurations using the symbol ω, when a counter is not bounded. It has been proved that the Algorithm 1 always terminates and that the produced tree enjoys some good properties. In particular, this tree can be used to decide the boundedness of a VASS. In [19], Vack and Vidal-Naquet have proposed a further construction based on the Karp and Miller tree in order to test the regularity of the language of the unlabeled traces of a VASS. This last construction is known as the *coverability graph.* To obtain it, the nodes of the Karp and Miller tree with the same label are gathered in an unique node. If (S, c_0) is a n-dim VASS, we denote by $\texttt{KMG}(S, c_0)$ its coverability graph.

For a vector $\mathbf{w} \in \mathbb{N}^n_\omega$, we denote by $\texttt{Inf}(\mathbf{w})$ the set $\{i \in [1..n] \mid \mathbf{w}(i) = \omega\}$ and $\texttt{Fin}(\mathbf{w}) = [1..n] \setminus \texttt{Inf}(\mathbf{w})$. Using these notions, it has been proved that the coverability graph satisfies the following properties.

Theorem 8. *[11,19] Let (S, c_0) be a n-dim VASS with $S = \langle Q, E\rangle$, $TS(S) = \langle Q \times \mathbb{N}^n, \rightarrow\rangle$ its associated transition system and $\texttt{KMG}(S, c) = \langle P, \delta, r, l\rangle$ its coverability graph.*

1. *If $p[q, \boldsymbol{w}]$ is a node in $\texttt{KMG}(S, c_0)$, then for all $k \in \mathbb{N}$, there exists $(q, \boldsymbol{v}) \in \texttt{Reach}(S, c_0)$ such that for all $i \in \texttt{Inf}(\boldsymbol{w})$, $k \leq \boldsymbol{v}(i)$ and for all $i \in \texttt{Fin}(\boldsymbol{w})$, $\boldsymbol{w}(i) = \boldsymbol{v}(i)$.*
2. *For $\sigma \in T_n^*$, if $c \xrightarrow{\sigma} (q, \boldsymbol{v})$ then there is a unique path in $\texttt{KMG}(S, c_0)$ labeled by σ and leading from r to a node $p[q, \boldsymbol{w}]$ and for all $i \in \texttt{Fin}(\boldsymbol{w})$, $\boldsymbol{v}(i) = \boldsymbol{w}(i)$.*

Algorithm 1. $T = \mathtt{KMT}(\langle Q, E\rangle, c_0)$

Input : $(\langle Q, E\rangle, c_0)$ an initialized VASS;
Output : $T = \langle P, \delta, r, l\rangle$ the Karp and Miller tree;

```
P = {r}, δ = ∅, l(r) = c0
ToBeTreated = {r}
while ToBeTreated ≠ ∅ do
   Choose p[q, w] ∈ ToBeTreated
   if there does not exist a predecessor p'[q, w] of p in T then
      for each (q, (#, μ, δ), q') ∈ E do
         if μ ≤ w then
            let w' = w + δ
            if there exists a predecessor p'[q', w''] of p in T
            such that w'' < w' then
               let w' = Acceleration(w'', w')
            end if
            Add a new node p' to P such that l(p') = (q', w')
            Add (p, (#, μ, δ), p') to δ
            Add p' to ToBeTreated
         end if
      end for
   end if
   Remove p of ToBeTreated
end while
```

3.2 Minimal Covering Set

We present here the notion of minimal covering set of a set, notion that we will use later to build the coverability graph of a reversal-bounded VASS with one zero-test. The minimal covering set of a possibly infinite set of vectors is the smallest set of vectors which cover all the vectors belonging to the considered set. Before giving its definition, we introduce some notations.

If $V \subseteq \mathbb{N}^n$, we denote by $\mathtt{Inc}(V)$, the set of the increasing sequences of elements of V. Each $(v_n)_{n\in\mathbb{N}} \in \mathtt{Inc}(V)$ has a least upper bound in $\mathbb{N}^n_\omega$ denoted $\mathtt{lub}((v_n)_{n\in\mathbb{N}})$. We then define the set $\mathtt{Lub}(V)$ of elements of $\mathbb{N}^n_\omega$ as the set $\{\mathtt{lub}(v_n)_{n\in\mathbb{N}} \mid (v_n)_{n\in\mathbb{N}} \in \mathtt{Inc}(V)\}$. Note that in [6], this last set is defined using the least upper bound of the directed subsets of V, but in the case of vectors of integers, it is equivalent to use the set of increasing sequences. If we consider the maximal elements of $\mathtt{Lub}(V)$ under the classical order over $\mathbb{N}^n_\omega$, we obtain what is called the minimal covering set of V.

Definition 9. *[5,6] Let $n \in \mathbb{N} \setminus \{0\}$ and $V \subseteq \mathbb{N}^n$. The* minimal covering set *of V, denoted by $\mathtt{MinCover}(V)$, is the set* $\mathtt{Max}(\mathtt{Lub}(V))$.

Using the definition of $\mathtt{MinCover}(V)$ and the fact that $(\mathbb{N}^n_\omega, \leq)$ is a well-quasi-order, we have the following proposition.

Proposition 10. *[5] Let $V \subseteq \mathbb{N}^n$. We have then:*

- *$\mathtt{MinCover}(V)$ is finite, and,*
- *for all $\boldsymbol{u} \in \mathtt{MinCover}(V)$, $\forall k \in \mathbb{N}$, there exists $\boldsymbol{v} \in V$ such that $\forall i \in \mathtt{Fin}(\boldsymbol{u})$, $\boldsymbol{v}(i) = \boldsymbol{u}(i)$ and $\forall i \in \mathtt{Inf}(v)$, $k \leq \boldsymbol{v}(i)$ and,*
- *for all $\boldsymbol{v} \in V$, there exists $\boldsymbol{u} \in \mathtt{MinCover}(V)$ such that $\boldsymbol{v} \leq \boldsymbol{u}$.*

Furthermore, for what concerns the minimal covering set of a semi-linear set, we have the following result.

Lemma 11. *Given a semi-linear set L, the set $\mathtt{MinCover}(L)$ can effectively be computed.*

Note that this last result can not be extended to any recursive set V. In fact if we were able to compute the minimal covering set of a recursive set V, we would be able to deduce if it is finite or not, which is known as an undecidable problem (this being a consequence of Rice's theorem).

4 Decidability Results for VASS with One Zero-Test

4.1 Counting the Number of Alternations in a VASS

In [10], it has been proved that the problem to decide whether a counter machine is reversal-bounded or not is undecidable, but this problem becomes decidable when considering VASS [7]. We recall here how this last result is obtained.

Let $S = \langle Q, E \rangle$ be a n-dim counter machine. We build a $2n$-dim counter machine $\widetilde{S} = \langle Q \times \{\uparrow, \downarrow\}^n, E' \rangle$ in which the n-th last counters count the alternations between increasing and decreasing modes of the n-th first counters. A formal definition of E' is is given in [8]. Note that by construction, since we never test the values of the added counters, if S is a VASS then $\widetilde{S}$ is a VASS too. For an initial configuration $c_0 = (q_0, \mathbf{v}_0)$, if we denote by $\widetilde{c}_0$ the pair $((q_0, \uparrow), (\mathbf{v}_0, \mathbf{0}))$, we have the following proposition:

Proposition 12. *A n-dim counter machine (S, c_0) is reversal-bounded if and only if there exists $k \in \mathbb{N}$ such that for all $((q, \boldsymbol{m}), \boldsymbol{v}) \in \mathtt{Reach}(\widetilde{S}, \widetilde{c}_0)$ and for all $i \in [1..n]$, $\boldsymbol{v}(n+i) \leq k$.*

Using the result of Theorem 8, we deduce that a VASS (S, c_0) is reversal-bounded if and only if for all nodes $p[q, \mathbf{w}]$ of the coverability graph of $(\widetilde{S}, \widetilde{c}_0)$ and for all $i \in [1..n]$, $\mathbf{w}(n+i) \neq \omega$. Hence:

Theorem 13. *[7] Reversal-boundedness is decidable for VASS.*

In the sequel, we will see how this method can be adapted to the case of VASS with one zero-test, which will allow us to extend the result of the previous theorem.

4.2 Mixing the Coverability Graph and Reachability Analysis

In this section, we will give an algorithm to build a labeled graph which will provide us a necessary and sufficient condition to decide whether a VASS with one zero-test is reversal-bounded. The classical construction of the Karp and Miller Tree cannot be used in the case of VASS with one zero-test, because when we introduce the symbol ω for the counter which might be tested to zero, we do not know for which values this ω stands for, and hence it is not possible to evaluate the test to zero when it occurs.

Let (S, c_0) be a n-dim counter machine with $S = \langle Q, E \rangle$. We define a (S, c_0)-labeled graph G as a tuple $\langle P, \delta, r, l \rangle$ where P is a set of nodes, $\delta \subseteq P \times T_n \times P$ is a set of edges labeled with guarded commands, $r \in P$ is the initial node and $l : P \to Q \times N_\omega^n$ is a labeling function such that $l(r) = c_0$. If $G = \langle P, \delta, r, l \rangle$ is a (S, c_0)-labeled graph, then $\langle P, \delta \rangle$ defines a counter machine we will denote by S_G. Furthermore to S_G we associate the initial configuration $r_0 = (r, \mathbf{v}_0)$ where $\mathbf{v}_0$ is the valuation function associated to c_0.

In the sequel we will consider a n-dim VASS with one zero-test (S, c_0) and its associated $2n$-dim counter machine $(\widetilde{S}, \widetilde{c}_0)$ in which we count the alternations between increasing and decreasing mode. Note that since when we build $\widetilde{S}$ we only introduce counters which never decrease, we have that (S, c_0) is reversal-bounded if and only if $(\widetilde{S}, \widetilde{c}_0)$ is reversal-bounded. As for S, we denote by $\widetilde{S}_{\geq}$ the $2n$-dim VASS obtained from $\widetilde{S}$ removing all the transitions of the form $(q, g_{=0?}, q')$.

We propose the Algorithm 2 to build a partial coverability graph of $(\widetilde{S}, \widetilde{c}_0)$. We will then use this graph to decide whether the input VASS with one zero-test is reversal-bounded or not. Our algorithm builds a $(\widetilde{S}, \widetilde{c}_0)$-labeled graph G as follows:

- First, we build the coverability graph of $(\widetilde{S}_{\geq}, \widetilde{c}_0)$ and test if $(\widetilde{S}_{\geq}, \widetilde{c}_0)$ is reversal-bounded. The predicate `ConditionRB`(G) will ensure that.
- If $(\widetilde{S}_{\geq}, \widetilde{c}_0)$ is not reversal-bounded, we can already deduce that $(\widetilde{S}, \widetilde{c}_0)$ is not reversal-bounded and we stop our construction.
- If $(\widetilde{S}_{\geq}, \widetilde{c}_0)$ is reversal-bounded, so is (S_G, r_0). We then compute the reachability set of (S_G, r_0) to know which test to zero will be accepted and we compute the minimal covering set of the vectors we obtain after realizing one test to zero (Lines 8-9 of Algorithm 2).
- From this covering set, we obtain a new set of labeled nodes from which we build again the coverability graph of $\widetilde{S}_{\geq}$. Doing so we complete the graph G. We then again test if (S_G, r_0) is reversal-bounded and if it is the case we proceed as previous considering again all the nodes from which a zero-test is done.
- Finally, in order to ensure termination (in case `ConditionRB`(G) is always evaluated to $True$) we insert ω when computing the reachability set for the

[1] p' is a predecessor of p if there exists a path in G of length greater than or equal to 1 from p' to p.

[2] p'' is a one step successor of p if there exists t such that $(p, t, p'') \in \delta$.

Algorithm 2. $G =$ `CoverGraph`(S, c_0)

Input : (S, c_0) VASS with one zero-test
Output : $G = \langle P, \delta, r, l\rangle$ a graph
1: $HasChanged = True$ /**This boolean becomes True when G is changed**/
2: Compute $(\widetilde{S}, \widetilde{c}_0)$ /**See the definition on the previous page**/
3: $\langle P, \delta, r, l\rangle =$ `KMG`$(\widetilde{S}_{\geq}, \widetilde{c}_0)$ /*$\widetilde{S}_{\geq}$ *is a VASS obtained from* $\widetilde{S}$ *deleting the zero-tests**/
4: $G = \langle P, \delta, r, l\rangle$
5: **while** $HasChanged = True$ and `ConditionRB`$(G) = True$ **do**
6:   $HasChanged = False$
7:   **for** each $p[(q_{?0}, \mathbf{m}), \mathbf{u}] \in P$ **do**
8:     $V_p = \{\mathbf{v} \mid (p, \mathbf{v}) \in$ `Reach`$(S_G, r_0) \wedge \mathbf{v}(1) = 0\}$
/*(S_G, r_0) *is the counter machine obtained from G* */
9:     Compute `MinCover`(V_p)
10:     **for** each $\mathbf{u} \in$ `MinCover`(V_p) **do**
11:       **if** there exists a predecessor[1] $p'[(q_{=0}, \mathbf{m}), \mathbf{u}']$of p such that $\mathbf{u}' \leq_1 \mathbf{u}$ **then**
12:         $\mathbf{u} =$ `Acceleration`$(\mathbf{u}', \mathbf{u})$
13:       **end if**
14:       **if** there is no one-step successor[2] $p''[(q_{=0}, \mathbf{m}), \mathbf{u}'']$of p such that $\mathbf{u} \leq \mathbf{u}''$ **then**
15:         $HasChanged = True$
16:         Let $t \in T_{2n}$ with $dom(t) = \{\mathbf{v} \mid \forall i \in \mathtt{Fin}(\mathbf{u}).\ \mathbf{v}(i) \leq \mathbf{u}(i)\}$ and $\forall \mathbf{v}.t(\mathbf{v}) = \mathbf{v}$
17:         **if** there exists a predecessor $p'''[(q_{=0}, \mathbf{m}), \mathbf{u}]$of p **then**
18:           Add (p, t, p''') to δ
19:         **else**
20:           Add a new node $newp[(q_{=0}, \mathbf{m}), \mathbf{u}]$ to P
21:           Add $(p, t, newp)$ to δ
22:           $G' =$ `KMG`$(\widetilde{S}_{\geq}, ((q_{=0}, \mathbf{m}), \mathbf{u}))$
23:           Add G' to G merging the root node of G' and $newp$
24:         **end if**
25:       **end if**
26:     **end for**
27:   **end for**
28: **end while**

zero-test we encounter a covering vector bigger than a preceding one (Line 11-12 of Algorithm 2).

An example of the result of the computation of Algorithm 2 is provided in [8].

We will now analyze more formally the Algorithms 2. First, we define the condition `ConditionRB`(G) for a $(\widetilde{S}, \widetilde{c}_0)$-labeled graph G as follows: `ConditionRB`$(G) = True$ if and only if for all nodes $p[q, \mathbf{u}]$ of G, for all $i \in [1..n]$, we have $\mathbf{u}(n+i) \neq \omega$.

Note that the first graph we compute being the coverability graph of $(\widetilde{S}_{\geq}, \widetilde{c}_0)$, according to Proposition 12, we have that $(\widetilde{S}_{\geq}, \widetilde{c}_0)$ is reversal-bounded if and only if the predicate `ConditionRB`(G) is true.

In order to prove that our algorithm is correct, we need to prove the following points:

1. If G is a $(\widetilde{S}, \widetilde{c}_0)$-labeled graph computed during the execution of the Algorithm 2 and if $\texttt{ConditionRB}(G) = True$ then (S_G, r_0) is reversal-bounded,
2. For any VASS with one zero-test (S, c_0), the algorithm $\texttt{CoverGraph}(S, c_0)$ terminates.

The first point is a sufficient condition which allows us to compute effectively the set V_p at Line 8 of the Algorithm 2 and also the set $\texttt{MinCover}(V_p)$. In fact, if (S_G, r_0) is reversal-bounded, according to Theorem 7, the set $\texttt{Reach}(S_G, r_0)$ is an effectively computable semi-linear set and consequently so is the corresponding set $V_p = \{\mathbf{v} \mid (p, \mathbf{v}) \in \texttt{Reach}(S_{G_i}, r_0) \wedge \mathbf{v}(1) = 0\}$, and hence from Lemmas 10 and 11, we also deduce that $\texttt{MinCover}(V_p)$ is finite and can be effectively computed.

Let (S, c_0) be a n-dim VASS with one zero-test and let $G = (P, \delta, r, l)$ be a $(\widetilde{S}, \widetilde{c}_0)$-labeled graph obtained at Line 4 after some iterations of the loop of Algorithm 2. We recall that by construction, $l(r) = \widetilde{c}_0$ and that the initial configuration r_0 of the counter machine S_G associated to the graph G is the pair $(r, \mathbf{v}_0)$ where $\mathbf{v}_0$ is the vector associated to the configuration $\widetilde{c}_0$. We have then the following lemma:

Lemma 14. *For all $(p, \boldsymbol{v}) \in \texttt{Reach}(S_G, r_0)$, if $l(p) = (q, \boldsymbol{u})$, then for all $i \in [1..2n]$, we have $\boldsymbol{v}(i) \leq \boldsymbol{u}(i)$.*

Since by construction in the counter machine S_G the n-th last counters count the numbers of alternations of the n-th first counters and since the graph G has a finite number of nodes we deduce that if $\texttt{ConditionRB}(G) = True$ then there exists a constant k which bounds the number of alternations for each counter in (S_G, r_0), consequently:

Proposition 15. *If $\texttt{ConditionRB}(G) = True$ then (S_G, r_0) is reversal-bounded.*

At Line 8 of Algorithm 2, when we compute the reachability set $\texttt{Reach}(S_G, r_0)$, we are hence sure that the counter machine (S_G, r_0) is effectively reversal-bounded and according to Theorem 7 and Lemma 11 we can effectively compute this set and also its minimal covering set. Finally, we have the following proposition:

Proposition 16. *The Algorithm 2 always terminates when its input is a VASS with one zero-test.*

Idea of proof: This is ensured by the fact that if the algorithm does not terminate we can extract an infinite sequence of vectors $(\mathbf{u}_i)_{i \in \mathbb{N}}$ such that for all $i \in \mathbb{N}$, $\mathbf{u}_i(1) = 0$ and $\mathbf{u}_i$ belongs to a node predecessor of the node containing $\mathbf{u}_{i+1}$ and for all $i, j \in \mathbb{N}$, $\mathbf{u}_i \neq \mathbf{u}_j$. Using that $\{\mathbf{u} \in \mathbb{N}_\omega^{2n} \mid \mathbf{u}(1) = 0\}$ together with the order $\leq_1$ is a well-quasi order, we deduce that we can extract from this sequence an infinite strictly increasing sequence of vectors, but this is not possible because if $\mathbf{u}$ preceeds $\mathbf{u}'$ in this sequence then there are strictly more components equal to ω in $\mathbf{u}'$ than in $\mathbf{u}$ (thanks to the function $\texttt{Acceleration}$) and so this sequence cannot be infinite. □

4.3 Reversal-Boundedness

In this last section, we will show how to use the $(\widetilde{S}, \widetilde{c}_0)$-labeled graph produced in output of the Algorithm 2 to decide whether the VASS with one zero-test (S, c_0) is reversal-bounded or not. First, we will show that if the graph $G = \texttt{CoverGraph}(S, c_0)$ is such that $\texttt{ConditionRB}(G) = False$, i.e. there exists a node $p[q, \mathbf{u}]$ and $i \in [1..n]$ such that $\mathbf{u}(n+i) = \omega$ then the counter machine $(\widetilde{S}, \widetilde{c}_0)$ is not reversal-bounded. This is due to the following lemma:

Lemma 17. *If $p[q, \mathbf{u}]$ is a node of $\texttt{CoverGraph}(S, c_0)$ and if $i \in \texttt{Inf}(\mathbf{u})$ then for all $k \in \mathbb{N}$, there exists a configuration $(q, \mathbf{v}) \in \texttt{Reach}(\widetilde{S}, \widetilde{c}_0)$ such that $\mathbf{v}(i) > k$.*

We then prove that if $G = \texttt{CoverGraph}(S, c_0)$ is such that $\texttt{ConditionRB}(G) = True$ then $(\widetilde{S}, \widetilde{c}_0)$ and hence (S, c_0) are reversal-bounded. To prove this, we have to prove that for each reachable configuration $(q, \mathbf{v})$ of $(\widetilde{S}, \widetilde{c}_0)$ there is a node of G which "covers" this configuration. This point can be proved by induction on the length of any execution of $\texttt{Reach}(\widetilde{S}, \widetilde{c}_0)$ and leads to the following lemma:

Lemma 18. *If $G = \texttt{CoverGraph}(S, c_0)$ is such that $\texttt{ConditionRB}(G) = True$ then for all configurations $(q, \mathbf{v}) \in \texttt{Reach}(\widetilde{S}, \widetilde{c}_0)$, there exists a node $p[q', \mathbf{u}]$ in G such that $q = q'$ and for all $i \in [1..2n]$, $\mathbf{v}(i) \leq \mathbf{u}(i)$.*

Using the two previous lemma and the result of Proposition 12, we deduce the following theorem:

Theorem 19. *A n-dim VASS with one zero-test (S, c_0) is reversal-bounded if and only if for all nodes $p[q, \mathbf{u}]$ in $\texttt{CoverGraph}(S, c_0)$, for all $i \in [1..n]$, $\mathbf{u}(n+i) \neq \omega$.*

Proof: Assume there exists a node $p[q, \mathbf{u}]$ in $\texttt{CoverGraph}(S, c_0)$ and $i \in [1..n]$, such that $\mathbf{u}(n+i) = \omega$. Then according to Lemma 17 for all $k \in \mathbb{N}$, there exists a configuration $(q, \mathbf{v}) \in \texttt{Reach}(\widetilde{S}, \widetilde{c}_0)$ such that $\mathbf{v}(n+i) > k$, hence using Proposition 12, we deduce that (S, c_0) is not reversal-bounded. If for all nodes $p[q, \mathbf{u}]$ in $\texttt{CoverGraph}(S, c_0)$, for all $i \in [1..n]$, $\mathbf{u}(n+i) \neq \omega$, since the number of nodes in $\texttt{CoverGraph}(S, c_0)$ is finite, we can find a $k \in \mathbb{N}$ such that for all nodes $p[q, \mathbf{u}]$ in $\texttt{CoverGraph}(S, c_0)$, for all $i \in [1..n]$, $\mathbf{u}(n+i) \leq k$. Using lemma 18, we deduce that for all configurations $(q, \mathbf{v}) \in \texttt{Reach}(\widetilde{S}, \widetilde{c}_0)$, for all $i \in [1..n]$, we have $\mathbf{v}(n+i) \leq k$, hence according to Proposition 12 (S, c_0) is reversal-bounded. □

Consequently, we obtain that:

Corollary 20. *Reversal-boundedness is decidable for VASS with one zero-test.*

4.4 Boundedness and Termination

We can adapt the reasoning we have performed to decide reversal-boundedness in order to decide boundedness for VASS with one zero-test. In fact, we still use the Algorithm 2 but instead of building the coverability graph of $(\widetilde{S}, \widetilde{c}_0)$, we build directly the one of (S, c_0) and instead of using condition `ConditionRB`, we use the following condition on a (S, c_0)-labeled graph G:

- for all $i \in [1..n]$, for all nodes $p[q, \mathbf{u}]$ of G, we have $\mathbf{u}(i) \neq \omega$.

The idea here is exactly the same as for reversal-boundedness. In fact, at the first step of the Algorithm 2, the coverability graph of $(S_{\geq}, c_0)$ is computed and it can be directly tested if this VASS is bounded or not. If it is not bounded, the algorithm stops, because all the executions in $(S_{\geq}, c_0)$, are also executions in (S, c_0) and hence if $(S_{\geq}, c_0)$ is not bounded, then (S, c_0) is also not bounded. In the other case, if $(S_{\geq}, c_0)$ is bounded, then its coverability graph corresponds exactly to its reachability graph. The algorithm can then proceed its computation exactly as for deciding reversal-boundedness. This consideration allows us to deduce the following result:

Theorem 21. *Boundedness is decidable for VASS with one zero-test.*

Note that this implies also the decidability of the termination problem for VASS with one zero-test. In fact, the termination problem for counter machines, which consists in deciding whether the counter machine has an infinite execution or not, can be reduced easily to the boundedness. This is due to the following consideration: if a counter machine is not bounded, then it has an infinite execution and if it is bounded, then it is possible to build its reachability graph and hence to decide whether there exists an infinite execution or not.

Corollary 22. *Termination is decidable for VASS with one zero-test.*

5 Conclusion

In this paper, we have provided an original method to decide whether a VASS extended with one-zero test is reversal-bounded (resp. bounded) or not. The main idea consists in mixing the construction of the classical coverability graph for VASS and the computing of the reachability set of reversal-bounded VASS. In the future, we would like to continue our investigation on methods to analyze this class of system and our aim would be to find a construction of a complete coverability graph for VASS with one-zero test. This would in particular gives us a way to decide the problem of place-boundedness which consists in deciding whether a set of counters has bounded values or not. In fact, the method we present in this paper does not allow us to solve this problem, because the graph we build is partial and the construction stops whenever it encounters a non reversal-bounded (resp. non bounded) behavior.

References

1. Abdulla, P.A., Mayr, R.: Minimal Cost Reachability/Coverability in Priced Timed Petri Nets. In: de Alfaro, L. (ed.) FOSSACS 2009. LNCS, vol. 5504, pp. 348–363. Springer, Heidelberg (2009)

2. Dufourd, C.: Réseaux de Petri avec Reset/Transfert: décidabilité et indécidabilité. Thèse de doctorat, Laboratoire Spécification et Vérification, ENS Cachan, France (1998)
3. Dufourd, C., Finkel, A.: Polynomial-Time Many-One Reductions for Petri Nets. In: Ramesh, S., Sivakumar, G. (eds.) FST TCS 1997. LNCS, vol. 1346, pp. 312–326. Springer, Heidelberg (1997)
4. Esparza, J.: Petri Nets, Commutative Context-Free Grammars, and Basic Parallel Processes. Fundam. Inform. 31(1), 13–25 (1997)
5. Finkel, A.: The Minimal Coverability Graph for Petri Nets. In: Rozenberg, G. (ed.) APN 1993. LNCS, vol. 674, pp. 210–243. Springer, Heidelberg (1993)
6. Finkel, A., Goubault-Larrecq, J.: Forward Analysis for WSTS, Part II: Complete WSTS. In: Albers, S., et al. (eds.) ICALP 2009, Part II. LNCS, vol. 5556, pp. 188–199. Springer, Heidelberg (2009)
7. Finkel, A., Sangnier, A.: Reversal-Bounded Counter Machines Revisited. In: Ochmański, E., Tyszkiewicz, J. (eds.) MFCS 2008. LNCS, vol. 5162, pp. 323–334. Springer, Heidelberg (2008)
8. Finkel, A., Sangnier, A.: Mixing Coverability and Reachability to Analyze VASS with One Zero-Test. Research Report, Laboratoire Spécification et Vérification, ENS Cachan (2009)
9. Hack, M.: Petri Net Language. Technical Report, Massachusetts Institute of Technology (1976)
10. Ibarra, O.H.: Reversal-Bounded Multicounter Machines and Their Decision Problems. J. ACM 25(1), 116–133 (1978)
11. Karp, R.M., Miller, R.E.: Parallel Program Schemata: A Mathematical Model for Parallel Computation. In: FOCS 1967, pp. 55–61. IEEE, Los Alamitos (1967)
12. Kosaraju, S.R.: Decidability of Reachability in Vector Addition Systems (preliminary version). In: STOC 1982, pp. 267–281. ACM, New York (1982)
13. Leroux, J.: The General Vector Addition System Reachability Problem by Presburger Inductive Invariants. In: LICS 2009, pp. 4–13. IEEE Computer Society Press, Los Alamitos (2009)
14. Mayr, E.W.: An Algorithm for the General Petri Net Reachability Problem. SIAM J. Comput. 13(3), 441–460 (1984)
15. Minsky, M.L.: Computation: Finite and Infinite Machines. Prentice-Hall, Inc., Upper Saddle River (1967)
16. Parikh, R.: On Context-Free Languages. Journal of the ACM 13(4), 570–581 (1966)
17. `http://www.informatik.uni-hamburg.de/TGI/PetriNets/`
18. Reinhardt, K.: Reachability in Petri Nets with Inhibitor Arcs. ENTCS 223, 239–264 (2008)
19. Valk, R., Vidal-Naquet, G.: Petri Nets and Regular Languages. J. Comput. Syst. Sci. 23(3), 299–325 (1981)

Practically Applicable Formal Methods

Jędrzej Fulara and Krzysztof Jakubczyk

Institute of Informatics, University of Warsaw
ul. Banacha 2, 02-097 Warsaw, Poland

Abstract. Formal methods are considered to be highly expensive. Therefore, they are currently applied almost only in high risk software development. In this paper, we show that formal techniques can be also efficiently used in standard large-scale applications. We focus on the generation of specifications which state the termination condition of `for` loops in Java code (expressed as so called Java Modeling Language *decreases* clauses). We demonstrate that with help of relatively simple techniques it is possible to successfully generate the clauses for almost 80% of the loops in a number of widely deployed applications. Moreover, it turns out that the remaining 20% cases contain loops which should be carefully reviewed by software quality assurance personnel. The results show that our technique might be helpful in spreading the usage of formal methods onto typical business software.

Keywords: Formal methods, annotation generation, Java, termination.

1 Introduction

Commercial applications often do not make use of specification and verification techniques, because people believe that such theoretical solutions are not applicable to software created for the real market. Business managers know that employing formal methods would increase quality of produced software, but these methods are considered to be very expensive and impractical. Therefore program specification and verification methods are used only in critical components or high risk software, e.g. avionics [10] or in nuclear power plants control software [23], places where correctness and reliability is crucial. It is considered to be not profitable to apply these techniques to standard code.

In standard program production unit tests [4] are used to assure clients that created code meets their requirements and to assure code producers that the code is faultless. The structure of the majority of specifications languages, such as JML [19] for Java or Microsoft Code Contracts for .NET platform [3] follows the structure of programming languages, so it seems that specifications should be written by the same team that has developed the code. Since the most expensive resource in the code production is programmers' time, letting them write annotations along with the code would increase overall costs, making company not competitive on the market. To reduce costs of verification techniques, one can generate annotations automatically. They can be used later by static analysis tools (e.g. ESC/Java2 [9]). Automatic generation of annotations has already

J. van Leeuwen et al. (Eds.): SOFSEM 2010, LNCS 5901, pp. 407–418, 2010.

been explored and several generators were presented, e.g. CANAPA [8] for JML, Houdini [15] for ESC/Java or Daikon [14] for various programming languages.

In this paper, we present an approach to develop formal techniques which may be useful in typical code. This approach relies on existing tools that check if the code realises given specifications, like ESC/Java2 or JmlRAC [7] but it broadens their applicability by automatic generation of specifications based on the existing code. If the code is mature and its functionality was well tested using common testing techniques, generated specifications may still be helpful, when someone wants to turn the code into a library or may act as documentation for maintenance. If the code is immature, automatic generation of specifications describing correctness properties of the program (such as loop termination, absence of NullPointerExceptions and ArrayIndexOutOfBoundsExceptions, etc.) combined with static checking can give feedback on what errors are present in the code. With these scenarios in mind we have developed a tool which helps to build annotations generators and reveals code fragments that are not obvious and should be reviewed by a human. In addition we have conducted an experiment which shows that our approach, using even very basic techniques, can give promising results on real, large-scale code.

Applicability of formal methods has been discussed in [5], but the considerations are mostly limited to safety-critical systems. A great number of examples of formal method applications can be found in [12]. There exist also tools that analyse various source code properties. For example, Eclipse Metrics plugin [22] helps to find unnecessarily complex places in the code. Semmle, a more powerful, commercial code analyser, comes with its own Query Language [21]. It allows to create and run your checks to enforce specific architecture rules and coding standards. FindBugs [17] detects code instances that are likely to be errors. Our *CodeStatistics* is designed to find any user defined patterns and is able to insert annotations into the code. In [2], statistics collected on Java libraries are used as a motivation to focus on particular aspect of the code in termination analysis. In our approach statistics are used to estimate coverage of a given formal method.

1.1 JML

The Java Modelling Language is a behavioural specification language for Java programs [18]. It allows to write specifications in the design-by-contract fashion, introduced by B. Meyer for Eiffel [20]. JML includes annotations which make possible to describe the invariant properties that are maintained by objects, method specifications (pre- and postconditions) and some lower level properties of the code (e.g. loop invariants). JML annotations are written in Java comments, so they do not disturb standard Java compilers. JML already has very rich tool support [6].

In our research presented in Section 3 we focus on generation of *decreases* clauses to prove loop termination. These clauses consist of the *decreases* JML keyword followed by expression whose value is decreased in each loop iteration (and cannot be smaller than 0). Figure 1 shows a simple loop together with a valid *decreases* formula.

```
//@ decreases 15 - i;
for (int i = 0; i < 15; i++) {
    // Loop body that does not change i
}
```

Fig. 1. Simple for loop with *decreases* formula

1.2 Formal Methods

This work is an attempt to answer the question what does it mean to create specification-based formal methods suitable for typical large-scale business applications, where code correctness is not considered to be critical. A formal method designed for the real market cannot increase development costs too much. The "80/20" rule applies to the development process: 20% of work produces 80% of a project — big parts of systems can even be generated automatically from requirements or specifications [16], so business managers may expect the same from formal methods. Thus we should provide them solutions that cover automatically at least 80% of the code and leave the remaining 20% (often unclear, messy and unnecessarily complicated) to be reviewed by the programmers.

If we could show that a formal method gives acceptable results on various, existing projects, then the code producers might expect that this method would be applicable also to their software. Thus, to rate the created formal method, a large set of well known projects should be used.

Modern programming languages offer developers big flexibility in creating the code. This may lead to some inconsistencies in the code that can result in errors which are hard to find. Using tests we can check, if the code meets functional requirements, but to find programming errors (such as null pointer dereferences, not terminating loops etc.) that occur in rare, but sometimes critical situations, we should employ other techniques. This is especially important when the code changes its original context of use, what often happens in case it is turned to a library or is subject to maintenance tasks. Generating logical conditions assuring absence of such inconsistencies may be the first step in introducing formal methods in real, large-scale code. Such conditions can be safely generated automatically. However specifications that describe program semantics (for example method pre- or postconditions) might be generated only for mature and well tested code. When they would be generated from incorrect code, they could be even misleading.

We suggest building simple verification methods iteratively. This process involves following steps:

1. Select code constructions you want to handle — e.g. for loops
2. Execute created method on the selected set of projects.
3. Find cases that are not handled yet.
4. From these cases pick up one for which you are able to provide generic solution.
5. Mark as solved cases covered by the solution.

6. Generate statistics and calculate effectiveness.
7. If effectiveness does not meet the selected threshold, go to step 2.

To apply this strategy in practice, one has to identify interesting constructions and their frequencies in the real code. Collecting frequencies should be done automatically, based on a big, representative sample of software. In our work we have developed a flexible tool to compute necessary statistics on the code and estimate how effective given annotation generation (and verification) method is.

For example let us classify Java `for` loops in the context of generating termination condition. First step will be to identify all interesting code constructions – that is all `for` loops that appear in the code. Next we need to take a look at all loops and try to find patterns, for which we could easily generate the termination condition. The simplest pattern is a `for` loop which increments a counter up to some constant, see Figure 1. Termination condition for this case is trivial.

Now we should generate statistics — how many loops matching this pattern are present in the code and discover what part of all `for` loops is covered by this case. After this we know for how many loops we can generate termination condition. If this coverage does not meet the selected threshold, we should do another iteration — look at the `for` loops that are not covered and produce new patterns.

Each iteration of the presented methodology can take advantage of different strategy and technique as far as the goal — achieving desired threshold, is accomplished. The main advantage of the presented procedure is a possibility to use different verification techniques, each applied where it performs the best.

A formal method created using this approach will give satisfying results on a large and representative set of projects. It should convince managers and developers that such solution can be successfully applied in their work.

In our research we have checked if it is possible to achieve, using simple methods, the expected by the market 80% coverage for a practical problem. We have applied the above described methodology to generate annotations for loop termination in Java programs. Our results are described in Section 3.

2 The *CodeStatistics* Tool

To make the above described approach applicable in practice, a tool that helps to rate the effectiveness of a verification method for different programming languages, is necessary. In our work we have developed *CodeStatistics* [1], a tool for Java. It can recognize patterns specified by the user, count their frequencies in given Java projects and output all matching code fragments, together with their locations in the project. Patterns are defined in XPath and correspond to nodes from the Abstract Syntax Tree (AST) of the processed project.

[1] Available at `http://www.mimuw.edu.pl/~fulara/CodeStatistics`

2.1 Source Code Representation

Source code can be represented as an AST [1]. Each node in AST denotes a construct occurring in the source code. Figure 2 contains an example of AST representation for a small code fragment. Patterns that *CodeStatistics* finds, can be expressed as structural conditions for the AST. Our tool is generic. The patterns are not hardcoded, but supplied by the user as a part of the system configuration. They should be written in a simple and expressive language. We have decided to adapt XML as an AST text representation format and XPath as a query language (described in Section 2.2).

```
while (x>y) {
        a = a + 1;
}
```

(a) Source code

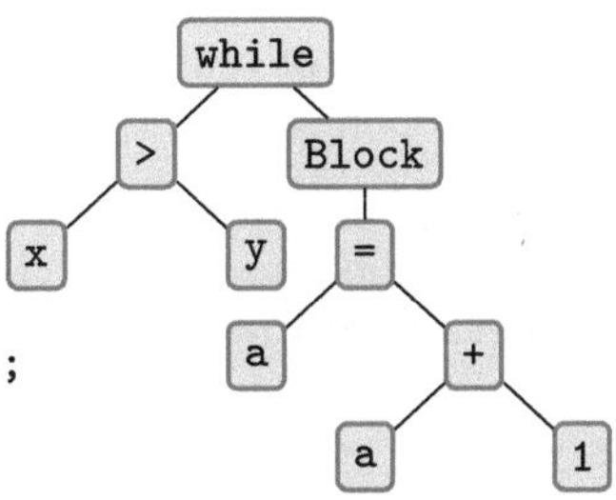

(b) Abstract Syntax Tree

```
<While>
  <Cond> ... <Cond>
  <Block>
    <Assignment>
      <Left>
         <Var name="a"/>
      </Left>
      <Right>...</Right>
    </Assignment>
  </Block>
</While>
```

(c) XML representation

Fig. 2. Sample AST representation

2.2 XML and XPath

The Extensible Markup Language (XML) is a general-purpose specification for creating custom markup languages recommended by the World Wide Web Consortium (W3C). It is used in our tool to represent the AST.

In *CodeStatistics* user defines queries in XPath. XPath is a language for finding information in an XML document and provides the ability to navigate around the tree, selecting nodes by a variety of criteria. A path notation is used to navigate over the hierarchical XML structure.

An XPath query that finds all `while` loops that assign something to variable `a` (such as the loop in Figure 2) is presented in Figure 3. It finds all `<While>` elements that have `<Block>` child that has `Assignment` descendant (but maybe not direct child) that has `<Left>` child that has `<Var>` child which has attribute `name` set to `a`.

```
//While[Block//Assignment/Left/Var/attribute::name="a"]
```

Fig. 3. XPath query example

2.3 *CodeStatistics* in Eclipse

CodeStatistics works as an Eclipse plugin. One can generate statistics for any part of a Java project (for any subtree of the project tree in Eclipse) or print out the XML representation of the AST for a selected class.

User specifies path to his configuration file in *CodeStatistics* submenu available from *Preferences* in *Window* menu. One can choose there also output file location and the desired logging level.

3 Experiment

In our experiment we have developed a generator of termination conditions of `for` loops in Java programs. According to the approach described in this paper, we have analysed structural properties of real, productional code. We have categorized `for` loops in the following open source applications:

- **Apache Hadoop**[2] is a software platform that lets one easily write and run applications that process vast amounts of data. It implements MapReduce [13], using the Hadoop Distributed File System. Hadoop was tested on clusters with 2000 nodes.
- **Google App Engine**[3] lets you run your web applications on Google's infrastructure. App Engine applications are easy to build, easy to maintain, and easy to scale as your traffic and data storage needs grow. With App Engine, there are no servers to maintain: You just upload your application, and it's ready to serve your users.
- **JEdit**[4] is a cross platform programmer's text editor that is customizable with plugins. JEdit provides syntax highlighting for more than 130 programming languages and supports the most important character encodings.
- **Hibernate**[5] is a powerful, high performance object/relational persistence and query service. Hibernate lets you develop persistent classes following object-oriented idiom — including polymorphism, association, inheritance, composition and collections. Hibernate allows you to express queries in its own portable SQL extension (HQL), as well as in native SQL, or with an object-oriented Criteria and Example API.
- **Oracle Berkeley DB**[6] is an open source, fast, embeddable database that eliminates the overhead of SQL. It stores arbitrary key/value pairs as byte arrays. Berkeley DB can handle multiple threads or concurrent processes accessing the database.
- **Tomcat**[7] is a servlet container developed by the Apache Software Foundation. It implements the Java Servlet and Java Server Pages specifications and it provides a web server for Java code to run.

---

[2] `http://hadoop.apache.org/`
[3] `http://code.google.com/appengine/`
[4] `http://www.jedit.org/`
[5] `http://www.hibernate.org/`
[6] `http://www.oracle.com/technology/products/berkeley-db/index.html`
[7] `http://tomcat.apache.org/`

Details of these projects are presented in Figure 4.

Project	Size	No. of `for` loops
Apache Hadoop	221	1817
Google App Engine	184	1048
JEdit	108	974
Hibernate	247	720
Oracle Berkeley DB	154	1191
Tomcat	181	1452

Fig. 4. Details of analysed projects (sizes are given in Kilo Lines of Code)

Our goal was to prove automatically termination property of at least 80% of `for` loops in the code. The ideas used in this research are very basic. The main advantage of our approach is that we are showing the effectiveness of such methods in practical, large-scale applications.

Literal. Let us start with the simplest category of `for` loops. It can be classified as loops, where the control variable (which is not modified in the loop body) is compared to a literal.

For loops that match this pattern, we can automatically generate the appropriate JML *decreases* formula (Figure 5a presents such loop together with valid decreases formula). Using *CodeStatistics* one can find out that this kind of loops covers 2% of all `for` loops (in the set of projects used in this experiment).

Constant. In the next step we focus on loops that use in the comparison a constant defined in the code and do not modify the control variable in the loop body (an example is shown in Figure 5b). Also for loops that match this pattern, the *decreases* formula can be generated automatically. These two categories cover together 8,4% of `for` loops.

Local expression. Another simple case that can be easily solved automatically is when the control variable is compared to an arithmetic expression composed of local variables that are not modified in the loop body.

The automatically generated *decreases* formula for the loop from Figure 6, would be $n + m - 7 - i$. 18,6% of all `for` loops are recognized using the "local expression pattern". Together 27% are solved now.

```
int j = 0;
//@ decreases 5 - i;
for (int i = 0; i < 5; i += 1){
  j += i;
}
```

(a) For to a literal

```
public final static int CONST = 5;
...
//@ decreases i - CONST;
for (int i = 15; i > CONST; i--){
  ...
}
```

(b) For to a constant

Fig. 5. Examples of loops that match the basic patterns

```
int j = 0, m = 9, n = 12;
//@ decreases n + m - 7 - i;
for (int i = 0; i < n + m - 7; i++)
  j += i;
```

Fig. 6. For to a non-modified local variable

```
int[] tab = new int[17];
//@ decreases tab.length - i;
for (int i = 0; i < tab.length; i++)
  tab[i] = i * i;
```

Fig. 7. For to a final field

Final field. Often programmers iterate over a table. This case can be generalized as iterating to a final field in an object (Figure 7). We have chosen a very restrictive "alias safe" approach. If the guard (in our simple example `tab.length`) was of form $o_1.o_2.o_3...o_n$, then

- o_1 must either be declared as final or be a local variable that is not assigned in the loop body,
- all o_2, o_3, ... o_n must be declared as final.

In this case, the well-known problem of modification using aliases (when the same object is referenced by multiple variables and modifications to one of them induces changes of the others) is eliminated. Using *CodeStatistics* it occurs that 47,7% of all `for` loops match this pattern. All the above described categories cover 74,7% of all `for` in the code.

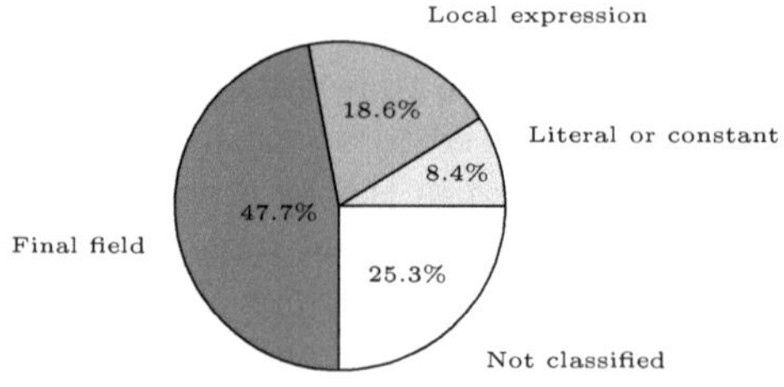

Fig. 8. Contribution of each loop type

All the above described categories can be expressed by pure syntactic criteria. In order to verify that the obtained results should also apply to other projects, we have checked our method against a fresh set of applications:

- **AspectJ**[8] is a seamless aspect-oriented extension to the Java programming language that enables clean modularization of these 'crosscutting concerns'.

[8] `http://www.eclipse.org/aspectj/`

- **Spring**[9] is an application framework for Java platform. It includes Inversion of Control container that manages object lifecycles.
- **Vuze**[10] is an application to exchange and distribute data over the Internet, currently the most popular BitTorrent client.

On these projects the recognized loop types cover 71% of `for` loops.

3.1 Bad Loops Found

Using *CodeStatistics*, we were also able to find non-trivial loops. They were sometimes written improperly, sometimes could be simplified, may contain bugs, or cause errors after the maintenance. Our tool provides them (their code, location in the project etc.) so that a programmer can handle them manually. Using output generated by *CodeStatistics* it was very easy to select examples for this section. We have just taken random examples from the code snippets that were marked as "not classified" and were short enough to be included in this paper.

```
for (int i=nSamples - 1; i < nSamples - nRemove; i--)
  deltas.remove(i);
```

Fig. 9. Vuze: NetworkAdminSpeedTesterBTImpl.java, lines 644-645

In the code fragment from Figure 9 it is not obvious why the loop should be terminating. At first it seems correct but one can notice that the inequality direction in termination condition is against intuition. The loop will terminate only if `nSamples - nRemove` gets smaller than `i`, but this can be done only inside the `deltas.remove` method.

In the next example (Figure 10) the termination depends on data stored in some array (`data`). If it contained only negative numbers, the loop would not terminate (and would probably cause an `ArrayIndexOutOfBoundsException`).

```
for (int shift=0; ; shift+=15) {
  long s=data[index++];
  if (s < 0) {
    val+=(-1 - s) << shift;
  } else {
    val+=s << shift;
    break;
  }
}
```

Fig. 10. BerkeleyDB: PackedOffsets.java, lines 120-128

---

[9] `http://www.springsource.org/`

[10] `http://www.vuze.com`

In the example from Figure 11 the control variable j is decreased in the loop body. Since in some iterations j does not change, and count is not modified in the loop body, it is not clear why should this loop terminate (in fact it terminates, because count is decreased inside removeHeader(j−−) function call).

```
for (int j=i + 1; j < count; j++)
  if (headers[j].getName().equalsIgnoreCase(name))
    removeHeader(j--);
```

Fig. 11. Tomcat: MimeHeaders.java, lines 268-272

In all examples presented in this section, it is not obvious why the loops are eventually terminating. It should be at least documented why it is working correctly. It should be explained in the loop and in the place which is responsible for the termination (e.g. in example from Figure 9, in the deltas.remove() function it should be marked that termination of some loop depends on changes made here to the nremove field). Finding such error prone code fragments is crucial also for maintenance.

3.2 Verification

We have used ESC/Java2 tool to verify loop termination property of for loops enriched with *decreases* annotations inserted by *CodeStatistics* tool. ESC/Java2 provides -LoopSafe option that can be used to verify these annotations. Since ESC/Java2 accepts only Java 1.4 source code and selected projects use features introduced in Java 1.5 (generics and enums), we had to adapt source code to older Java version. We have done this successfully to jEdit project. Unfortunately ESC/Java2 did not manage to verify all files containing for loops — there were some fatal errors caused by missing or invalid standard library specifications (most of them caused by java.awt package). All files that were successfully processed by ESC/Java2 did not return any errors or warnings concerning *decreases* formulae.

4 Summary

We have presented a simple approach for creating verification methods and described the *CodeStatistics* tool that supports this methodology. We have also applied the approach in an experiment — simple loop termination prover for Java for loops. The received results show that basic verification techniques can be successfully used in real, productional code. Tools similar to ours can be really helpful in Quality Assurance process. Code reviewers can pay less attention to simple cases, hence they can focus on difficult aspects that are usually more error prone. Such methods can even guarantee correctness of some aspect of the code (in our case that for loops terminate). They can be used as a first step in introducing formal methods into business applications.

5 Future Work

We plan to employ the described way of creating verification methods, *CodeStatistics* and Abstract Interpretation techniques [11] to prove that no incorrect array accesses may occur during program execution (or find places where such errors could possibly occur).

Acknowledgements. This work was partly supported by Polish government grant 177/6.PR UE/2006/7 and Information Society Technologies programme of the European Commission FET project IST-2005-015905 MOBIUS. This paper reflects only authors' views and the Community is not liable for any use that may be made of the information contained therein.

References

1. Aho, A.V., Lam, M.S., Sethi, R., Ullman, J.D.: Compilers: Principles, Techniques, and Tools, 2nd edn. Addison Wesley, Reading (2006)
2. Albert, E., Arenas, P., Genaim, S., Puebla, G.: Dealing with Numeric Fields in Termination Analysis of Java-Like Languages. In: FTfJP, pp. 77–87 (2008)
3. Andersen, M., Barnett, M., FÄhndrich, M., Grunkemeyer, B., King, K., Logozzo, F.: Code Contracts User Manual
4. Beck, K.: Test Driven Development: By Example. Addison-Wesley Professional, Reading (2002)
5. Bowen, J.P., Hinchey, M.G.: The Use of Industrial-Strength Formal Methods. In: Proceedings of 21st International Computer Software and Application Conference (COMPSAC 1997), pp. 332–337. IEEE Computer Society Press, Los Alamitos (1997)
6. Burdy, L., Cheon, Y., Cok, D.R., Ernst, M.D., Kiniry, J.R., Leavens, G.T., Leino, K.R.M., Poll, E.: An Overview of JML Tools and Applications. Int. J. Softw. Tools Technol. Transf. 7(3), 212–232 (2005)
7. Chalin, P., Rioux, F.: JML Runtime Assertion Checking: Improved Error Reporting and Efficiency Using Strong Validity. In: Cuellar, J., Maibaum, T., Sere, K. (eds.) FM 2008. LNCS, vol. 5014, pp. 246–261. Springer, Heidelberg (2008)
8. Cielecki, M., Fulara, J., Jakubczyk, K., Jancewicz, L.: Propagation of JML Non-Null Annotations in Java Programs. PPPJ, 135–140 (2006)
9. Cok, D.R., Kiniry, J.R.: ESC/Java2: Uniting ESC/Java and JML: Progress and Issues in Building and Using ESC/Java2 and a Report on a Case Study Involving the Use of ESC/Java2 to Verify Portions of an Internet Voting Tally System. In: Barthe, G., Burdy, L., Huisman, M., Lanet, J.-L., Muntean, T. (eds.) CASSIS 2004. LNCS, vol. 3362, pp. 108–128. Springer, Heidelberg (2005)
10. Cousot, P.: Avionic Software Verification by Abstract Interpretation. In: 2007 ISoLA Workshop On Leveraging Applications of Formal Methods, Verification and Validation. Special Workshop Theme: Formal Methods in Avionics, Space and Transport, Poitiers, France, December 12-14 (2007)
11. Cousot, P., Cousot, R.: Abstract Interpretation: a Unified Lattice Model for Static Analysis of Programs by Construction or Approximation of Fixpoints. In: Conference Record of the Fourth Annual ACM SIGPLAN-SIGACT Symposium on Principles of Programming Languages, Los Angeles, California, pp. 238–252. ACM Press, New York (1977)

12. Craigen, D., Craigen, D., Canada, O., Canada, O., Gerhart, S., Gerhart, S., Ralston, T., Brown, R.H.: An International Survey of Industrial Applications of Formal Methods, vol. 2 Case studies (1993)
13. Dean, J., Ghemawat, S.: Mapreduce: Simplified Data Processing on Large Clusters. Commun. ACM 51(1), 107–113 (2008)
14. Ernst, M.D., Perkins, J.H., Guo, P.J., McCamant, S., Pacheco, C., Tschantz, M.S., Xiao, C.: The Daikon System for Dynamic Detection of Likely Invariants. Science of Computer Programming 69(1-3), 35–45 (2007)
15. Flanagan, C., Rustan, K., Leino, M.: Houdini, an Annotation Assistant for ESC/Java. In: Oliveira, J.N., Zave, P. (eds.) FME 2001. LNCS, vol. 2021, pp. 500–517. Springer, Heidelberg (2001)
16. Harel, D., Marelly, R.: Specifying and Executing Behavioral Requirements: the Play-in/Play-out Approach. Software and System Modeling 2(2), 82–107 (2003)
17. Hovemeyer, D., Pugh, W.: Finding Bugs is Easy. SIGPLAN Not. 39(12), 92–106 (2004)
18. Leavens, G., Cheon, Y.: Design by Contract with JML (2003)
19. Leavens, G.T., Poll, E., Clifton, C., Cheon, Y., Ruby, C., Cok, D., Kiniry, J.: JML Reference Manual
20. Meyer, B.: Object-Oriented Software Construction. Prentice Hall PTR, Englewood Cliffs (1997)
21. Moor, O., Sereni, D., Verbaere, M., Hajiyev, E., Avgustinov, P., Ekman, T., Ongkingco, N., Tibble, J.: QL: Object-Oriented Queries Made Easy. In: Generative and Transformational Techniques in Software Engineering II: International Summer School, GTTSE 2007, Braga, Portugal, Revised Papers, July 2-7, pp. 78–133 (2008)
22. Walton, L.: Eclipse Metrics Plugin, `http://metrics.sourceforge.net/`
23. Yoo, J., Cha, S., Jee, E.: A Verification Framework for fbd Based Software in Nuclear Power Plants. In: APSEC 2008: Proceedings of the 2008 15th Asia-Pacific Software Engineering Conference, Washington, DC, USA, pp. 385–392. IEEE Computer Society, Los Alamitos (2008)

Fast and Compact Prefix Codes*

Travis Gagie[1,2], Gonzalo Navarro[2], and Yakov Nekrich[3]

[1] Research Group in Genome Informatics, Bielefeld University
travis.gagie@gmail.com
[2] Department of Computer Science, University of Chile
gnavarro@dcc.uchile.cl
[3] Department of Computer Science, University of Bonn
yasha@cs.uni-bonn.de

Abstract. It is well-known that, given a probability distribution over n characters, in the worst case it takes $\Theta(n \log n)$ bits to store a prefix code with minimum expected codeword length. However, in this paper we first show that, for any ϵ with $0 < \epsilon < 1/2$ and $1/\epsilon = \mathcal{O}(\mathrm{polylog}(n))$, it takes $\mathcal{O}(n \log\log(1/\epsilon))$ bits to store a prefix code with expected codeword length within an additive ϵ of the minimum. We then show that, for any constant $c > 1$, it takes $\mathcal{O}\left(n^{1/c} \log n\right)$ bits to store a prefix code with expected codeword length at most c times the minimum. In both cases, our data structures allow us to encode and decode any character in $\mathcal{O}(1)$ time.

1 Introduction

Compression is most important when space is in short supply, so popular compressors are usually heavily engineered to reduce their space usage. Theory has lagged behind practice in this area, however, and there remain basic open questions about the space needed for even the simplest kinds of compression. For example, while compression *with* prefix codes is familiar to any student of information theory, very little has been proven about compression *of* prefix codes. Suppose we are given a probability distribution P over an alphabet of n characters. Until fairly recently, the only general bounds known seem to have been, first, that it takes $\Theta(n \log n)$ bits in the worst case to store a prefix code with minimum expected codeword length and, second, that $\mathcal{O}(n)$ bit suffice to store a prefix code with expected codeword length within 1 of the minimum.

In 1998 Adler and Maggs [1] showed it generally takes more than $(9/40)n^{1/(20c)} \log n$ bits to store a prefix code with expected codeword length at most $cH(P)$, where $H(P)$ is P's entropy and a lower bound on the expected codeword length. (In this paper we consider only binary codes, and by log we always mean $\log_2$.) In 2006 Gagie [6,7] (see also [8]) showed that, for any constant $c \geq 1$, it takes $\mathcal{O}(n^{1/c} \log n)$ bits to store a prefix code with expected codeword length at most

* Funded in part by Millennium Institute for Cell Dynamics and Biotechnology (ICDB), Grant ICM P05-001-F, Mideplan, Chile.

J. van Leeuwen et al. (Eds.): SOFSEM 2010, LNCS 5901, pp. 419–427, 2010.

$cH(P) + 2$. He also showed his upper bound is nearly optimal because, for any positive constant ϵ, we cannot always store a prefix code with expected codeword length at most $cH(P)+o(\log n)$ in $\mathcal{O}(n^{1/c-\epsilon})$ bits. Gagie proved his upper bound by describing a data structure that stores a prefix code with the prescribed expected codeword length in the prescribed space and allows us to encode and decode any character in time at most proportional to its codeword's length. This data structure has three obvious defects: when $c = 1$, it is as big as a Huffman tree, whereas its redundancy guarantee can be obtained with just $\mathcal{O}(n)$ bits [10]; when $H(P)$ is small, a possible additive increase of 2 in the expected codeword length may be prohibitive; and it is slower than the state of the art.

In this paper we answer several open questions related to efficient representation of codes. First, in Section 3 we show that, for any ϵ with $0 < \epsilon < 1/2$ and $1/\epsilon = \mathcal{O}(\text{polylog}(n))$, it takes $\mathcal{O}(n \log\log(1/\epsilon))$ bits to store a prefix code with expected codeword length within an additive ϵ of the minimum. Thus, if we can tolerate an additive increase of, say, 0.01 in the expected codeword length, then we can store a prefix code using only $\mathcal{O}(1)$ bits per character. Second, in Section 4 we show that, for any constant $c > 1$, it takes $\mathcal{O}(n^{1/c} \log n)$ bits to store a prefix code with expected codeword length at most c times the minimum, with no extra additive increase. Thus, if we can tolerate a multiplicative increase of, say, 2.01, then we can store a prefix code in $\mathcal{O}(\sqrt{n})$ bits. In both cases, our data structures allow us to encode and decode any character in $\mathcal{O}(1)$ time on a unit-cost word RAM.

2 Related Work

A simple pointer-based implementation of a Huffman tree takes $\mathcal{O}(n \log n)$ bits and it is not difficult to show this is an optimal upper bound for storing a prefix code with minimum expected codeword length. For example, suppose we are given a permutation π over n characters. Let P be the probability distribution that assigns probability $1/2^i$ to the $\pi(i)$th character, for $1 \leq i < n$, and probability $1/2^{n-1}$ to the $\pi(n)$th character. Since P is dyadic, every prefix code with minimum expected codeword length assigns a codeword of length i to the $\pi(i)$th character, for $1 \leq i < n$, and a codeword of length $n - 1$ to the $\pi(n)$th character. Therefore, given any prefix code with minimum expected codeword length and a bit indicating whether $\pi(n-1) < \pi(n)$, we can find π. Since there are $n!$ choices for π, in the worst case it takes $\Omega(\log n!) = \Omega(n \log n)$ bits to store a prefix code with minimum expected codeword length.

Considering the argument above, it is natural to ask whether the same lower bound holds for probability distributions that are not so skewed, and the answer is 'no'. A prefix code is *canonical* [19] if the first codeword is a string of 0s and any other codeword can be obtained from its predecessor by adding 1, viewing its predecessor as a binary number, and appending some number of 0s. (See, e.g., [16,14] for more recent work on canonical codes.) Given any prefix code, without changing the length of the codeword assigned to any character, we can put the code into canonical form by just exchanging left and right siblings in the code-tree. Moreover, we can reassign the codewords such that, if a character is lexicographically the jth with a codeword of length ℓ, then it is assigned the jth consecutive codeword of length ℓ. It is clear that it is sufficient to store the codeword length of each character to be able to reconstruct such a code, and thus the code can be represented in $\mathcal{O}(n \log L)$ bits, where L is the length of the longest codeword.

The above gives us a finer upper bound. For example, Katona and Nemetz [13] showed that, if a character has probability p, then any Huffman code assigns it a codeword of length at most about $\log(1/p)/\log\phi$, where $\phi \approx 1.618$ is the golden ratio, and thus L is at most about $1.44\log(1/p_{\min})$, where $p_{\min}$ is the smallest probability in P. Alternatively, one can enforce a value for L and pay a price in terms of expected codeword length. Milidiú and Laber [15] showed how, for any $L > \lceil \log n \rceil$, we can build a prefix code with maximum codeword length at most L and expected codeword length within $1/\phi^{L-\lceil \log(n+\lceil \log n \rceil - L)\rceil - 1}$ of the minimum. Their algorithm works by building a Huffman tree T_1; removing all the subtrees rooted at depth greater than L; building a complete binary tree T_2 of height h whose leaves are those removed from T_1; finding the node v at depth $L-h-1$ in T_1 whose subtree T_3's leaves are labelled by characters with minimum total probability (which they showed is at most $1/\phi^{L-\lceil \log(n+\lceil \log n \rceil - L)\rceil - 1}$); and replacing v by a new node whose subtrees are T_2 and T_3.

A simple upper bound for storing a prefix code with expected codeword length within a constant of the minimum, follows from Gilbert and Moore's proof [10] that we can build an alphabetic prefix code with expected codeword length less than $H(P) + 2$ and, thus, within 2 of the minimum. Moreover, in an optimal alphabetic prefix code, the expected codeword length is within 1 of the minimum [18,20] which, in turn, is within 1 of the entropy $H(P)$. In an alphabetic prefix code, the lexicographic order of the codewords is the same as that of the characters, so we need store only the code-tree and not the assignment of codewords to characters. If we store the code-tree in a succinct data structure due to Munro and Raman [17], then it takes $\mathcal{O}(n)$ bits and encoding and decoding any character takes time at most proportional to its codeword length. This can be improved to $\mathcal{O}(1)$ by using table lookup, but doing so may worsen the space bound unless we also restrict the maximum codeword length, which may in turn increase the expected codeword length.

The code-tree of a canonical code can be stored in just $\mathcal{O}(L^2)$ bits: By its definition, we can reconstruct the whole canonical tree given only the first codeword of each length. Unfortunately, Gagie's lower bound [7] suggests we generally cannot combine results concerning canonical codes with those concerning alphabetic prefix codes.

Constant-time encoding and decoding using canonical code-trees is simple. Notice that if two codewords have the same length, then the difference between their ranks in the code is the same as the difference between the codewords themselves, viewed as binary numbers. Suppose we build an $\mathcal{O}(L^2)$-bit array A and a dictionary D supporting predecessor queries, each storing the first codeword of each length. Given the length of a character's codeword and its rank among codewords of the same length (henceforth called its offset), we can find the actual codeword by retrieving the first codeword of that length from A and then, viewing that first codeword as a binary number, adding the offset minus 1. Given a binary string starting with a codeword, we can find that codeword's length and offset by retrieving the string's predecessor in D, which is the first codeword of the same length; truncating the string to the same length in order to obtain the actual codeword; and subtracting the first codeword from the actual codeword, viewing both as binary numbers, to obtain the offset minus 1. (If D supports numeric predecessor queries instead of lexicographic predecessor queries, then we store the first codewords with enough 0s appended to each that they are all the same length, and store their original lengths as auxiliary information.) Assuming it takes $\mathcal{O}(1)$ time to compute the length and offset of any character's codeword given that character's index in the alphabet, encoding any character takes $\mathcal{O}(1)$ time. Assuming it takes $\mathcal{O}(1)$ time to compute any character's index in the alphabet given its codeword's length and offset, decoding takes within a constant factor of the time needed to perform a predecessor query on D. For simplicity, in this paper we consider the number used to represent a character in the machine's memory to be that character's index in the alphabet, so finding the index is the same as finding the character itself.

In a recent paper on adaptive prefix coding, Gagie and Nekrich [9] (see also [12]) pointed out that if $L = \mathcal{O}(w)$, where w is the length of a machine word, then we can implement D as an $\mathcal{O}(w^2)$-bit dictionary data structure due to Fredman and Willard [5] such that predecessor queries take $\mathcal{O}(1)$ time. (We note that Beame and Fich's well-known lower bound [2] on predecessor queries does not apply when the size of the dictionary is proportional to the length of a word.) This seems a reasonable assumption since, for any string of length m with $\log m = \mathcal{O}(w)$, if P is the probability distribution that assigns to each character probability proportional to its frequency in the string, then the smallest positive probability in P is at least $1/m$; therefore, the maximum codeword length in either a Huffman code or a Shannon code for P is $\mathcal{O}(w)$. Gagie and Nekrich used $\mathcal{O}(n \log n)$-bit arrays to compute the length and offset of any character's codeword given that character's index in the alphabet, and vice versa, and thus achieved $\mathcal{O}(1)$ time for both encoding and decoding.

A technique we will use to obtain our first result, presented in section 3, is the *wavelet tree* of Grossi et al. [11], and more precisely the multiary variant due to Ferragina et al. [3]. The latter represents a sequence $S[1, n]$ over an alphabet Σ of size σ such that the following operations can be carried out in $\mathcal{O}\left(\frac{\log \sigma}{\log \log n}\right)$ time on the RAM model with a computer word of length $\Omega(\log n)$: (1) Given i, retrieve $S[i]$; (2) given i and $a \in \Sigma$, compute $rank_a(S, i)$, the number of occurrences of a in $S[1, i]$; (3) given j and $a \in \Sigma$, compute $select_a(S, j)$, the position in S of the j-th occurrence of a. The wavelet tree requires $nH_0(S) + \mathcal{O}\left(\frac{n \log \log n}{\log_\sigma n}\right)$ bits of space, where $H_0(S) \le \log \sigma$ is the *empirical zero-order entropy* of S, defined as $H_0(S) = H(\{\mathrm{occ}(a, S)/n\}_{a \in \sigma})$, where $\mathrm{occ}(a, S)$ is the number of occurrences of a in S. Thus $nH_0(S)$ is a lower bound to the output size of any zero-order compressor applied to S. It will be useful to write $H_0(S) = \sum_{a\in\sigma} \frac{occ(a,S)}{n} \log \frac{n}{occ(a,S)}$.

Our second result is based on constructing a length-restricted canonical code with maximum codeword length L. We divide all symbols into "probable" symbols that are assigned codewords of length at most $L/c+2$ and "improbable" symbols that are assigned codewords of length greater than $L/c+2$. It will be shown in section 4 that all "probable" symbols can be encoded and decoded in $O(1)$ time using $O(n^{1/c}\log n)$ bits. We replace all codewords of length at least $L/c+3$ with codewords of length L, so that the "improbable" symbols can be encoded and decoded in constant time but we do not have to store the new codewords explicitly.

3 Additive Increase in Expected Codeword Length

In this section we exchange a small additive penalty over the optimal prefix code for a space-efficient representation of the encoding, which in addition enables encode/decode operations in constant time.

It follows from Milidiú and Laber's bound [15] that, for any ϵ with $0 < \epsilon < 1/2$, there is always a prefix code with maximum codeword length $L = \lceil \log n \rceil + \lceil \log_\phi(1/\epsilon) \rceil + 1$ and expected codeword length within an additive

$$\frac{1}{\phi^{L-\lceil \log(n+\lceil \log n \rceil - L) \rceil - 1}} \leq \frac{1}{\phi^{L-\lceil \log n \rceil - 1}} \leq \frac{1}{\phi^{\log_\phi(1/\epsilon)}} = \epsilon$$

of the minimum. The techniques described in the previous section give a way to store such a code in $\mathcal{O}\big(L^2 + n\log L\big)$ bits, yet it is not immediately obvious how to do constant-time encoding and decoding. Alternatively, we can achieve constant-time encoding and decoding using $\mathcal{O}\big(w^2 + n\log n\big)$ bits for the code-tree, if $L = \mathcal{O}(w)$.

To achieve constant encoding and decoding times without ruining the space, we use multiary wavelet trees. We use a canonical code, and sort the characters (i.e., leaves) alphabetically within each depth, as described in the previous section. Let $S[1,n]$ be the sequence of depths in the canonical code-tree, so that $S[a]$ $(1 \leq a \leq n)$ is the depth of the character a. Now, the depth and offset of any $a \in \Sigma$ is easily computed from the wavelet tree of S: the depth is just $S[a]$, while the offset is $rank_{S[a]}(S,a)$. Inversely, given a depth d and an offset o, the corresponding character is $select_d(S,o)$. The $\mathcal{O}(w^2)$-bit data structure of Gagie and Nekrich [9] converts in constant time pairs *(depth, offset)* into codes and vice versa (if $L = \mathcal{O}(w)$), whereas the multiary wavelet tree on S requires $n\log L + \mathcal{O}\Big(\frac{n\log\log n}{\log_L n}\Big)$ bits of space and completes encoding/decoding in time $\mathcal{O}\Big(\frac{\log L}{\log\log n}\Big)$. Under the restriction $1/\epsilon = \mathcal{O}(\text{polylog}(n))$, the space is $\mathcal{O}\big(w^2\big) + n\log L + o(n)$ and the time is $\mathcal{O}(1)$. This is the key to the result of this section.

Theorem 1. *For any ϵ with $0 < \epsilon < 1/2$ and $1/\epsilon = \mathcal{O}(\text{polylog}(n))$, and under the RAM model with computer word size w, so that the text to encode is of* *length $2^{\mathcal{O}(w)}$, we can store a prefix code with expected codeword length within an additive term ϵ of the minimum, using $\mathcal{O}(w^2 + n \log\log(1/\epsilon))$ bits, such that encoding and decoding any character takes $\mathcal{O}(1)$ time.*

Proof. The data structure we have described achieves the given time bounds if we assume the text to encode is of length $m = 2^{\mathcal{O}(w)}$, as usual under the RAM model of computation, and thus $L = \mathcal{O}(w)$ enables constant-time encoding and decoding [9].

As for the space, we have shown it is $\mathcal{O}(w^2) + n \log L + o(n)$. To achieve the claim of the theorem we show that $H_0(S)$ is at most $\log(L - \lceil \log n \rceil + 1) + \mathcal{O}(1)$, so we can store S in $\mathcal{O}(n \log(L - \log n + 1) + n) = \mathcal{O}(n \log\log(1/\epsilon))$ bits.

To see this, consider S as two interleaved subsequences, S_1 and S_2, of length n_1 and n_2, with S_1 containing those lengths less than or equal to $\lceil \log n \rceil$ and S_2 containing those greater. Thus $nH_0(S) \le n_1 H_0(S_1) + n_2 H_0(S_2) + n$.

Since there are at most 2^ℓ codewords of length ℓ, assume we complete S_1 with spurious symbols so that it has exactly 2^ℓ occurrences of symbol ℓ. This completion cannot decrease $n_1 H_0(S_1) = \sum_{1 \le \ell \le \lceil \log n \rceil} \mathrm{occ}(\ell, S_1) \log \frac{n_1}{\mathrm{occ}(\ell, S_1)}$, as increasing some $\mathrm{occ}(\ell, S_1)$ to $\mathrm{occ}(\ell, S_1) + 1$ produces a difference of $f(n_1) - f(\mathrm{occ}(\ell, S_1)) \ge 0$, where $f(x) = (x+1)\log(x+1) - x \log x$ is increasing. Hence we can assume S_1 contains exactly 2^ℓ occurrences of symbol $1 \le \ell \le \lceil \log n \rceil$; straightforward calculation then shows that $n_1 H_0(S_1) = \mathcal{O}(n_1)$.

On the other hand, S_2 contains at most $L - \lceil \log n \rceil$ distinct values, so $H_0(S_2) \le \log(L - \lceil \log n \rceil)$, unless $L = \lceil \log n \rceil$, in which case S_2 is empty and $n_2 H_0(S_2) = 0$. Thus $n_2 H_0(S_2) \le n_2 \log(\lceil \log_\phi (1/\epsilon) \rceil + 1) = \mathcal{O}(n_2 \log\log(1/\epsilon))$.

Combining both bounds, we get $H_0(S) = \mathcal{O}(1 + \log\log(1/\epsilon))$ and the theorem holds. □

In other words, under mild assumptions, we can store a code using $\mathcal{O}(n \log\log(1/\epsilon))$ bits at the price of increasing the average codeword length by ϵ, and in addition have constant-time encoding and decoding. For constant ϵ, this means that the code uses just $\mathcal{O}(n)$ bits at the price of an arbitrarily small constant additive penalty over the shortest possible prefix code.

4 Multiplicative Increase in Expected Codeword Length

In this section we focus on a multiplicative rather than an additive penalty over the optimal prefix code, in order to achieve a sublinear-sized representation of the encoding, which still enables constant-time encoding and decoding.

Our main idea is to divide the alphabet into probable and improbable characters and to store information about only the probable ones. Given a constant $c > 1$, we use Milidiú and Laber's algorithm [15] to build a prefix code with maximum codeword length $L = \lceil \log n \rceil + \lceil 1/(c-1) \rceil + 1$. We call a character's codeword *short* if it has length at most $L/c + 2$, and *long* otherwise. Notice there are at most $2^{L/c+3} - 1 = \mathcal{O}(n^{1/c})$ characters with short codewords. Also, although applying Milidiú and Laber's algorithm may cause some exceptions, characters with short codewords are usually more probable than characters with long ones. We will hereafter call *infrequent characters* those encoded with long codewords in the code of Milidiú and Laber.

We transform this length-restricted prefix code into a canonical code as described in Section 2; specifically, we sort the characters lexicographically within each depth. We use a dictionary data structure F due to Fredman, Komlós and Szemerédi [4] to store the indices of the characters with short codewords. This data structure takes $\mathcal{O}(n^{1/c} \log n)$ bits and supports membership queries in $\mathcal{O}(1)$ time, with successful queries returning the target character's codeword. We also build $\lfloor L/c \rfloor + 2$ arrays that together store the indices of all the characters with short codewords; for $1 \leq \ell \leq \lfloor L/c \rfloor + 2$, the ℓth array stores the indices of the characters with codewords of length ℓ, in lexicographic order by codeword. Again, we store the first codeword of each length in $\mathcal{O}(w^2)$ bits overall, following Gagie and Nekrich [9], such that it takes $\mathcal{O}(1)$ time to compute any codeword given its length and offset, and vice versa. With these data structures, we can encode and decode any character with a short codeword in $\mathcal{O}(1)$ time. To encode, we perform a membership query on the dictionary to check whether the character has a short codeword; if it does, we receive the codeword itself as satellite information returned by the query. To decode, we first find the codeword's length ℓ and offset j in $\mathcal{O}(1)$ time as described in Section 2. Since the codeword is short, $\ell \leq \lfloor L/c \rfloor + 2$ and the character's index is stored in the jth cell of the ℓth array. These data structures use a total of $\mathcal{O}(w^2 + n^{1/c} \log n)$ bits of space.

We replace each long codeword with *new* codewords: instead of a long codeword α of length ℓ, we insert $2^{L+1-\ell}$ new codewords $\alpha \cdot s$, where $\cdot$ denotes concatenation and s is an arbitrary binary string of length $L + 1 - \ell$. Figure 1 shows an example. Since $c > 1$, we have $n^{1/c} < n/2$ for sufficiently large n, so we can assume without loss of generality that there are fewer than $n/2$ short codewords; hence, the number of long codewords is at least $n/2$. Since every long codeword is replaced by at least two new codewords, the total number of new codewords is at least n. Since new codewords are obtained by extending all codewords of length $\ell > L/c + 1$ in a canonical code, all new codewords are binary representations of consecutive integers. Therefore the i-th new codeword equals to $\alpha_f + i - 1$, where α_f is the first new codeword. If a is an infrequent character, we encode it with the a-th new codeword, $\alpha_f + a - 1$. To encode a character a, we check whether a belongs to the dictionary F. If $a \in F$, then we output the codeword for a. Otherwise we encode a as $\alpha_f + a - 1$. To decode a codeword α, we read its prefix bitstring s_α of length $L + 1$ and compare s_α with α_f. If $s_\alpha \geq \alpha_f$, then $\alpha = s_\alpha$ is the codeword for $s_\alpha - \alpha_f + 1$. Otherwise, the codeword length of the next codeword α is at most $L/c+1$ and α can be decoded as described in the previous paragraph. Notice we do not need to store the new codewords we just described, so the total space used is still $\mathcal{O}(w^2 + n^{1/c} \log n)$ bits.

Theorem 2. *For any constant $c > 1$, under the RAM model with computer word size w, so that the text to encode is of length $2^{\mathcal{O}(w)}$, we can store a prefix code with expected codeword length within c times the minimum in $\mathcal{O}(w^2 + n^{1/c} \log n)$ bits, such that encoding and decoding any character takes $\mathcal{O}(1)$ time.*

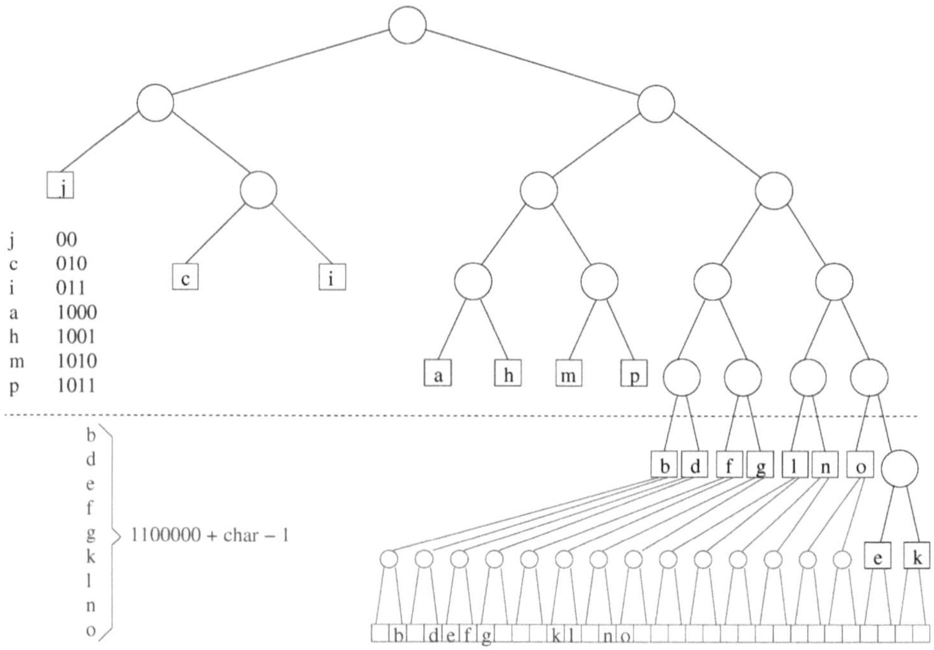

Fig. 1. An example with $n = 16$ and $c = 3$. The tree consisting of the nodes drawn as large circles and squares (in black) is the result of applying the algorithm of Milidiú and Laber on the original prefix code. Now, we set $L = 6$ according to our formula, and declare short the codeword lengths up to $\lfloor L/c \rfloor + 2 = 4$. Short codewords — i.e., those above the dashed line — are stored unaltered in a dictionary (in blue). Longer codewords — i.e., those below the dashed line — are changed: All are extended up to length $L+1 = 7$ and reassigned a code according to their values in the contiguous slots of length 7 (in red).

Proof. The structure described throughout the section achieves the promised time and space bounds. We analyze now the expected codeword length.

By analysis of the algorithm by Milidiú and Laber [15] we can see that the codeword length of a character in their length-restricted code exceeds the codeword length of the same character in an optimal code by at most 1, and only when the codeword length in the optimal code is at least $L - \lceil \log n \rceil - 1 = \lceil 1/(c-1) \rceil$. Hence, the codeword length of a character encoded with a short codeword exceeds the codeword length of the same character in an optimal code by a factor of at most $\frac{\lceil 1/(c-1) \rceil + 1}{\lceil 1/(c-1) \rceil} \leq c$. Every infrequent character is encoded with a codeword of length $L + 1$. Since the codeword length of an infrequent character in the length-restricted code is more than $L/c + 2$, its length in an optimal code is more than $L/c + 1$. Hence, the codeword length of a long character in our code is at most $\frac{L+1}{L/c+1} < c$ times greater than the codeword length of the same character in an optimal code. Hence, the average codeword length for our code is less than c times the optimal one. □

Again, under mild assumptions, this means that we can store a code with expected length within c times the optimum, in $\mathcal{O}(n^{1/c} \log n)$ bits and allowing constant-time encoding and decoding.

References

1. Adler, M., Maggs, B.M.: Protocols for Asymmetric Communication Channels. Journal of Computer and System Sciences 63(4), 573–596 (2001)
2. Beame, P., Fich, F.E.: Optimal Bounds for the Predecessor Problem and Related Problems. Journal of Computer and System Sciences 65(1), 38–72 (2002)
3. Ferragina, P., Manzini, G., Mäkinen, V., Navarro, G.: Compressed Representations of Sequences and Full-Text Indexes. ACM Transactions on Algorithms 3(2), Article 20 (2007)
4. Fredman, M.L., Komlós, J., Szemerédi, E.: Storing a Sparse Table with $\mathcal{O}(1)$ Worst Case Access Time. Journal of the ACM 31(3), 538–544 (1984)
5. Fredman, M.L., Willard, D.E.: Surpassing the Information Theoretic Bound with Fusion Trees. Journal of Computer and System Sciences 47(3), 424–436 (1993)
6. Gagie, T.: Compressing Probability Distributions. Information Processing Letters 97(4), 133–137 (2006)
7. Gagie, T.: Large alphabets and incompressibility. Information Processing Letters 99(6), 246–251 (2006)
8. Gagie, T.: Dynamic asymmetric communication. Information Processing Letters 108(6), 352–355 (2008)
9. Gagie, T., Nekrich, Y.: Worst-Case Optimal Adaptive Prefix Coding. In: Proceedings of the Algorithms and Data Structures Symposium (WADS), pp. 315–326 (2009)
10. Gilbert, E.N., Moore, E.F.: Variable-Length Binary Encodings. Bell System Technical Journal 38, 933–967 (1959)
11. Grossi, R., Gupta, A., Vitter, J.: High-Order Entropy-Compressed Text Indexes. In: Proceedings of the 14th Symposium on Discrete Algorithms (SODA), pp. 841–850 (2003)
12. Karpinski, M., Nekrich, Y.: A Fast Algorithm for Adaptive Prefix Coding. Algorithmica 55(1), 29–41 (2009)
13. Katona, G.O.H., Nemetz, T.O.H.: Huffman Codes and Self-Information. IEEE Transactions on Information Theory 22(3), 337–340 (1976)
14. Klein, S.T.: Skeleton Trees for the Efficient Decoding of Huffman Encoded Texts. Information Retrieval 3(4), 315–328 (2000)
15. Milidiú, R.L., Laber, E.S.: Bounding the Inefficiency of Length-Restricted Prefix Codes. Algorithmica 31(4), 513–529 (2001)
16. Moffat, A., Turpin, A.: On the Implementation of Minimum-Redundancy Prefix Codes. IEEE Transactions on Communications 45(10), 1200–1207 (1997)
17. Munro, J.I., Raman, V.: Succinct Representation of Balanced Parentheses and Static Trees. SIAM Journal on Computing 31(3), 762–776 (2001)
18. Nakatsu, N.: Bounds on the Redundancy of Binary Alphabetical Codes. IEEE Transactions on Information Theory 37(4), 1225–1229 (1991)
19. Schwarz, E.S., Kallick, B.: Generating a Canonical Prefix Encoding. Communications of the ACM 7(3), 166–169 (1964)
20. Sheinwald, D.: On Binary Alphabetic Codes. In: Proceedings of the Data Compression Conference (DCC), pp. 112–121 (1992)

New Results on the Complexity of Oriented Colouring on Restricted Digraph Classes

Robert Ganian and Petr Hliněný*

Faculty of Informatics, Masaryk University
Botanická 68a, Brno, Czech Republic
{xganian1,hlineny}@fi.muni.cz

Abstract. Oriented colouring is a quite intuitive generalization of undirected colouring, yet the problem remains NP-hard even on digraph classes with bounded usual directed width measures. In light of this fact, one might ask whether new width measures are required for efficient dealing with this problem or whether further restriction of traditional directed width measures such as DAG-width would suffice. The K-width and DAG-depth measures (introduced by [Ganian et al, IWPEC'09]) are ideal candidates for tackling this question: They are both closely tied to the cops-and-robber games which inspire and characterize the most renowned directed width measures, while at the same time being much more restrictive.

In this paper, we look at the oriented colouring problem on digraphs of bounded K-width and of bounded DAG-depth. We provide new polynomial algorithms for solving the problem on "small" instances as well as new strong hardness results showing that the input restrictions required by our algorithms are in fact "tight".

Keywords: Directed graph, complexity, oriented colouring, DAG-depth.

1 Preliminaries

1.1 Introduction

The study of ordinary colourings of graphs has become the focus of many authors and lead to a number of interesting results. However, only in the last decade has this been extended to directed graphs. The notion of oriented colouring was first introduced by Courcelle [2], see Definition 1. Briefly, while an ordinary colouring is a homomorhpism into a complete graph, an oriented colouring is a homomorhpism into an orientation of a complete graph.

Properties of oriented colouring have been studied by several authors, see e.g. the work of Nešetřil and Raspaud [11] or the survey by Sopena [14]. Similarly

* This research has been supported by the Czech research grants GAČR 201/-08/0308 (P. Hliněný) and 201/09/J021 (R. Ganian), and by the research intent MSM0021622419 of the Czech Ministry of Education.

J. van Leeuwen et al. (Eds.): SOFSEM 2010, LNCS 5901, pp. 428–439, 2010.

to undirected colouring, computing the oriented chromatic number (further referred to as OCN) and deciding oriented colourability of digraphs are both NP-hard problems. However, while undirected colouring becomes easy if we restrict the input to the graph class of trees, deciding oriented colourability already by 4 colours (OCN_4) remains NP-hard even on on acyclic digraphs (DAGs) [3]. Apart from being an interesting notion from a theoretical point of view, oriented colouring also has practical applications, e.g. in mobile networks.

There exists a wide range of width parameters for digraphs: directed tree-width [8], DAG-width [1,12], Kelly-width [7], and cycle rank [4] perhaps being the best known. A shared feature of all these width parameters is that they assume their minimum values on DAGs. Thus, it is impossible to use a bound on any of these width parameters to efficiently decide oriented colourability at all — there will always be instances in which deciding OCN_4 remains NP-hard.

One way to interpret this finding is to ask whether there exist stronger, more restrictive digraph width parameters which could help with computing OCN.

Very recently, a possible lead to answering this question has been given in [6]. Two new directed width measures have been introduced in that article, both related to cops-and-robber games (and thus to the classical directed width measures) and both very restrictive. The first one is K-width (Def. 2) which restricts the maximum number of directed paths between pairs of vertices, and the second one is DAG-depth (Def. 3) which on the other hand restricts the maximum number of moves in a cops-and-robber game.

These parameters have been successfully used in [6] to design some new FPT algorithms, e.g. for the Hamiltonian Path and c-Paths problems. We analyse the relationship of these new measures to OCN. The first results of this paper (Section 2) are two new polynomial algorithms for computing OCN on digraphs of DAG-depth 2, and on digraphs of K-width 1 with a "single reachable fragment". Then we show that, although our algorithms do seem relatively simple and one would expect there to be more involved variants for (at least slightly) more general cases, the bounds in these algorithms are in fact "tight". To this end we introduce a new reduction proving that the OCN_4 problem is NP-complete already for digraphs with K-width 1 and DAG-depth 3 (Theorem 5).

1.2 Definitions

We assume that the reader is familiar with all basic definitions related to undirected and directed graphs. Keep in mind that digraph stands for directed graph and DAG stands for acyclic digraph. Our digraphs are simple; they have no parallel arcs or loops, but can have two arcs in opposite directions.

Let G, H be digraphs. A *homomorphism* of G to H is a mapping $f : V(G) \to V(H)$ such that for all $(a, b) \in E(G)$, it holds $(f(a), f(b)) \in E(H)$.

Definition 1 ([2]). The *k-oriented chromatic number* (OCN_k) problem is defined as follows: Given a digraph G, is there a homomorphism from G to H_k, where H_k is some (irreflexive antisymmetric) orientation of edges of the complete graph on k vertices?

There is also the natural optimization variant (OCN) — to find the minimum k such that OCN_k is true.

For simplicity, we will sometimes say that a set of vertices of G have the same colour — meaning that they all map into the same vertex of H. Notice that each colour class is an independent set in G, and that if there is an arc from a vertex coloured a to a vertex coloured b, then there can never be an arc from a vertex coloured b to a vertex coloured a. This is a useful and intuitive way of looking at oriented colouring.

Next, we introduce the first of the two aforementioned width parameters:

Definition 2 ([6]). A digraph G has *K-width* k if k is the lowest integer such that, for any pair of vertices $s, t \in V(G)$, the number of distinct directed paths from s to t is at most k. Note that these paths need not be pairwise disjoint.

K-width is related to the better-known DAG-width [1,12] in the sense that bounded K-width implies bounded DAG-width. More precisely, the K-width of a G is greater or equal to the DAG-width of G minus one [6]. On the other hand, DAGs (which have DAG-width 0) can have arbitrarily high K-width.

The last part of the definitions introduces DAG-depth, an interesting directed counterpart to the better known tree-depth [10]. First, we need to formalize the notion of *reachable fragments*. For a digraph G and any $v \in V(G)$, let G_v denote the subdigraph of G induced by the vertices reachable from v. The maximal elements of the poset $\{\, G_v : v \in V(G) \,\}$ in the digraph-inclusion order are then called *reachable fragments* of G (further referred to as $\mathcal{RF}(G)$). Notice that reachable fragments in the undirected case coincide with connected components.

Definition 3 ([6]). The *DAG-depth* $ddp(G)$ of a digraph G is inductively defined as follows: If $|V(G)| = 1$, then $ddp(G) = 1$. If G has a single reachable fragment, then $ddp(G) = 1 + \min\{ddp(G - v) : v \in V(G)\}$. Otherwise, $ddp(G) = \max\{ddp(F) : F \in \mathcal{RF}(G)\}$.

DAG-width has a beautiful characterization [12] via a "cops and robber" game: In this game, on a digraph G, the robber can move between the vertices of G along cop-free directed paths at great speed, while cops move to vertices of G in a helicopter which the robber can see and escape. The DAG-width of G then equals the minimum number t of cops sufficient to catch the robber in G (by landing at him when he has no escape route). Similarly:

Theorem 1 ([6]). *The DAG-depth of a digraph G is at most t if, and only if, the cop player has a "lift-free" winning strategy in the t-cops and robber game on G, i.e. a strategy that never moves a cop from a vertex once he has landed.*

Based on the game characterization, it is easy to see that DAG-depth may never be higher than DAG-width. However, DAG-depth is in fact much more restrictive than DAG-width: [6] The number of vertices on the longest directed path in a digraph G is at most $2^t - 1$ where $t = ddp(G)$. Theorem 1 will be useful for determining the DAG-depth of some digraphs in the next sections.

2 The Algorithms

First of all, we remark that the problems OCN_2 and OCN_3 are trivially solvable, see e.g.[3]. We present our results for solving OCN_4 on digraphs of K-width 1 consisting of a single reachable fragment, and of DAG-depth 2.

2.1 Digraphs of K-Width 1

We begin by proving a few structural properties of digraphs G with K-width 1 consisting of a single reachable fragment (i.e. having $|\mathcal{RF}(G)| = 1$). First, choose any vertex such that the whole digraph G is reachable from that vertex. This will be the unique *source* of G, or s. Then perform a Depth-First search of G from s to create a Depth-First search tree; the paths from s to the leaves of this Depth-First search tree will be called *branches*, and the (x, y) arcs where y is a predecessor of x in some branch will be called *back-arcs*.

Proposition 1. *For any two branches $X = (x_0, x_1, \dots x_a)$ and $Y = (y_0, y_1, \dots y_b)$ starting in $s = x_0 = y_0$, the following holds:*

1) For any two vertices $x \in V(X) \setminus V(Y)$ and $y \in V(Y) \setminus V(X)$, there is no (x, y) arc in G.
2) X and Y intersect in a single path starting in s.
3) For any back-arc (x_i, x_j), $i > j$, it holds that no x_k, $i \geq k > j$ can be the start point of a back-arc, and no x_l, $i > l \geq j$ can be the endpoint of a back-arc.
4) If $x_i = y_i$ is the last vertex in common of X and Y, and there is a back-arc $(x_m, x_n), m > i > n$, then there can be no back-arc $(y_p, y_q), p > i > q$.

Proof. Points 1) and 2) follow trivially from the digraph having K-width 1.

For point 3), if x_k, $i \geq k > j$ were the starting point of a back-arc in G, then there would be two paths from x_k to x_{k-1}: One would use the back-arc starting at x_k and then follow down the branch, the other would follow down the branch, use the back-arc (x_i, x_j) and then follow down the branch to x_{k-1}. On the other hand, if x_l, $i > l \geq j$ were the endpoint of a back-arc in G, again there would be

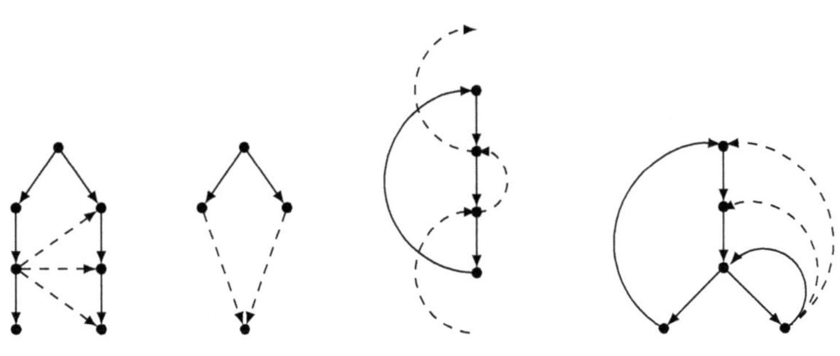

Fig. 1. Forbidden situations by 1), 2), 3) and 4) respectively

two paths from x_{l+1} to x_l: One would go down the branch and use the back-arc ending at x_l, the other would go down to x_i, use the back-arc (x_i, x_j) and then follow down to x_l.

As for point 4), if there was a back-arc $(y_p, y_q), p \geq i > q$, there would be two paths from x_i to x_{i-1}: One going through X and using (x_m, x_n), the other going through Y and using (y_p, y_q). □

This means that our digraph is formed by a set of (non-disjoint) branches from a common source, which at some point disconnect from one another and each end up at separate leaves. Cycles only occur when a back-edge is present, and each back-edge corresponds to precisely one cycle, since there is only one path from the endpoint of the back-edge to its start. And, finally, any two cycles can only intersect in at most one vertex. From these facts, we get:

Theorem 2. *A digraph G with K-width 1 consisting of a single reachable fragment either contains a directed cycle of length 2 or 5, or can be orientedly coloured by 4 colours in polynomial time.*

Proof. It is a trivial observation that directed cycles of length 5 require 5 colours for oriented colouring. Cycles of length 2 can not be orientedly coloured at all. We prove the oriented colourability of digraphs without such cycles by providing an algorithm for colouring them using 4 colours:

We start by giving the following orientation of arcs in the target 4-vertex digraph H_4 (cf. Def. 1).

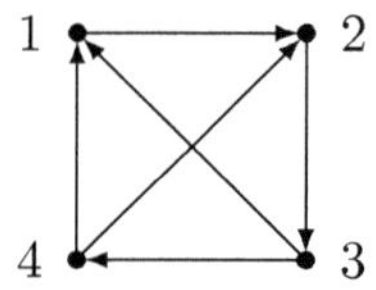

Notice that, given any cycle (of length other than 2 and 5) with fixed colouring at one single vertex, such a cycle always remains colourable by using H. For cycles of length 3 and 4, one can fill in the colours by using the 3-cycles and 4-cycle in H, and any number above 5 can be decomposed into a sum of threes and fours – which provides a suitable colouring for such cycles.

Our algorithm works as follows:

- First, find a source s of the reachable fragment by performing a reversed Depth-First search on G.
- Then, start a Depth-First search from s. The only reason for this Depth-First search is to identify back-arcs (we remember whether every arc is *normal* or a back-arc).
- Next, start a new, slightly modified Depth-First search from s. During the search, colour every traversed vertex in accordance with H until an incoming back-arc b is reached. The arc b corresponds to a cycle, and we must ensure that the colouring respects this cycle. So, go to the vertex x starting the back-arc $b = (x, y)$ and then backtrack via normal arcs all the way up to the end y of b. If we had not avoided back-arcs, we could have ended up

backtracking further down the Depth-First search tree. While backtracking, we record the length of the cycle so that we can colour accordingly. Note that even if this means that vertices can be visited more often than in an ordinary Depth-First search, in fact the number of visits only goes up by at most two. Once we reach the end y of the back-arc b (where we had originally started backtracking), start colouring in a manner respecting the length of the cycle and always choose the branch leading to the start of the back-arc.
- If we ever find a 2-cycle or 5-cycle, return false. Otherwise, using Proposition 1, we are left with a valid oriented 4-colouring when the algorithm ends. □

We remark that the previous algorithm can be trivially adjusted to find an oriented 5-colouring for any digraph of K-width 1 consisting of a single reachable fragment, unless a directed 2-cycle is present.

Corollary 1. *There is a polynomial algorithm that, given a digraph G of K-width 1 consisting of a single reachable fragment, determines the oriented chromatic number of G.*

Proof. (sketch) First check for directed cycles of length 2. If any are present, the digraph is not orientedly colourable. Otherwise run the algorithms for OCN_2, OCN_3 (always polynomial) and the introduced algorithms for OCN_4 and OCN_5. One of them must suceed. □

2.2 Digraphs of DAG-Depth 2

Again, we start by introducing a few structural remarks about digraphs of DAG-depth 2. We then use these remarks to prove that all digraphs of DAG-depth 2 are either orientedly 3-colourable or contain a 2-cycle by providing an algorithm for computing a valid 3-colouring.

Remark 1. Digraphs of DAG-depth 2 contain none of the following subgraphs:

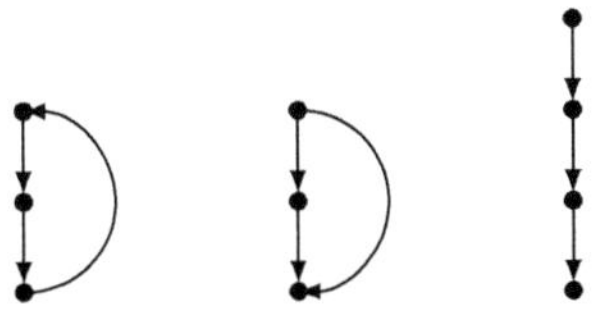

Proposition 2. *In a digraph of DAG-depth 2, for any two paths of length 2 $P = (a_1, a_2, a_3)$, $Q = (b_1, b_2, b_3)$, and any $v \in V(P) \cap V(Q)$, it holds $v = a_i = b_i$ for some $1 \leq i \leq 3$. Also, an arc (a_i, b_j) can only exist if $j > i$.*

Proof. (sketch) It is easy to check that all other possibilities result in a path of length 3, which is forbidden by Remark 1. □

Theorem 3. *Digraphs of DAG-depth 2 without 2-cycles are always orientedly 3-colourable. Furthermore, there exists a simple polynomial algorithm computing a 3-colouring for such digraphs.*

Proof. We utilize the fact that DAG-depth 2 implies no path of length higher than 2. $H = (V, E)$ will be defined as follows: $V = \{1, 2, 3\}$, $E = \{(1, 2),\ (1, 3),\ (2, 3)\}$. Start by colouring all paths of length 2 by colours 1, 2, 3 for the first, second and third vertices respectively. If a 2-cycle is found, return "false" and terminate. If there are no 2-cycles then this is a valid partial oriented colouring by H – paths will remain properly coloured even when they intersect or have arcs between them thanks to Proposition 2.

Now, iteratively run through all arcs with at least one endpoint in an uncoloured vertex. Note that all arcs from uncoloured vertices must start at sources and all arcs into uncoloured vertices must end at sinks, since otherwise an uncoloured 2-path would be present. Simply colour all the sinks by 3 and sources by 1, and the remaining disconnected vertices can be coloured arbitrarily. We end up with a valid oriented 3-colouring, assuming the digraph had DAG-depth 2 and no 2-cycles. □

3 Hardness Proofs

3.1 Acyclic Digraphs

The first NP-hardness proof in this article is for OCN_4 on the class of DAGs. Although the same result was claimed true already by the authors of [3], their paper only sketched a reduction gadget with a picture, and the sketch missed a key point — which would require further work and proving to ensure that no cycles are present in the resulting digraph. So, we decided to include our own reduction here, which is more straightforward and avoids the aforementioned problem. Another reason for proving the acyclic case first is that it serves as a motivation for the DAG-depth and K-width reduction (Theorem 5), and allows us to introduce tools which are useful for both of these cases. Please note that the target homomorphism digraph for our reduction is necessarily H of Fig. 3; the reasons will be made clear in the proof of Theorem 4.

Lemma 1. *Consider the gadget S from Fig. 2 and the target H from Fig. 3.*

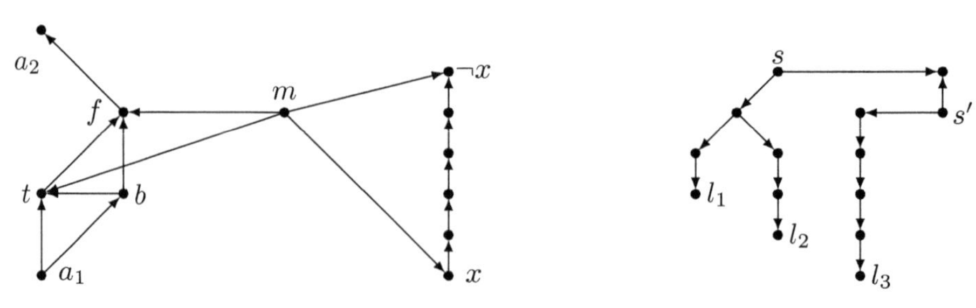

Fig. 2. Gadgets L to the left and S to the right

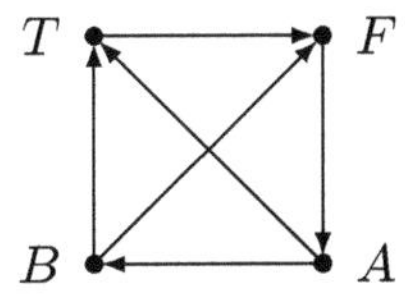

Fig. 3. The unique target colouring digraph H for our reductions

1. *For any precolouring* $(l_1, l_2, l_3) \mapsto \{T, F\}^3$ *of* S *with the exception of* (F, F, F)*, there is a homomorphism* $S \to H$ *extending it.*
2. *No homomorphism* $S \to H$ *maps* (l_1, l_2, l_3) *to* (F, F, F)*.*

Proof. To explain one issue in advance, we remark that the same statement holds also for a "simpler" gadget S' which results from S by identifying s with s'. It is, however, that this S' has DAG-depth 4 while S has only 3, cf. Theorem 5.

1. As the proof, we show a table containing instructions on how to colour S for all combinations of T and F at l_1, l_2, l_3 (except for triple-F). For each l_i, the table contains the colours to be used in the sequence of vertices from s to l_i.

(l_1, l_2, l_3) Evaluation	l_1-branch	l_2-branch	l_3-branch
T,T,T	BFAT	BFABT	BFBTFABT
T,T,F	BFAT	BFABT	BFBTFABF
T,F,T	BFAT	BFABF	BFBTFABT
T,F,F	BFAT	BFABF	BFBTFABF
F,T,T	ABTF	ABFAT	ABABFABT
F,T,F	ABTF	ABFAT	ABABFABF
F,F,T	FABF	FABTF	FAFABFAT

2. Here we show another table, this time describing the relationship between the colour of s and possible l_i colourings. As one can see, all combinations are possible except for triple-F, thus concluding our proof.

Colour at s	Admissible l_1 col.	Admissible l_2 col.	Admissible l_3 col.
A	F	T	T,F
B	T	T,F	T,F
T	T	T,F	T,F
F	T,F	F	T

□

Theorem 4. *The OCN*$_4$ *problem is NP-complete even on the class of DAGs.*

Proof. We reduce 3-SAT to OCN$_4$ with the use of two gadgets, S for clauses and L for literals – see Fig. 2.

The reduction works as follows: Given a 3-SAT formula, for every literal we construct a copy of the gadget L consisting of vertices $\{a_1, f, b, t, a_2, m\}$ as depicted by the figure. For every clause we then construct a copy of the gadget S, where l_1, l_2 and l_3 are identified with the vertices we have created for the appropriate literals or their negations which appear in that particular clause.

Assume we have a 3-SAT evaluation. Then we must show that it is possible to provide a valid oriented 4-colouring of this digraph. Let us name the colours A, B, F, T (Fig. 3). The vertices a_1, a_2, b, t, f will be coloured in accordance to their names, m will be coloured by B and every x and $\neg x$ will be coloured by T and F depending on whether the literal is true or false in the 3-SAT evaluation — if it is true, then the vertex marked x in the figure will be coloured by T and $\neg x$ by F, and otherwise the colours will be switched. The T–F and F–T paths of length 5 are 4-colourable by the sequences (T, A, F, T, A, F) and (F, T, A, B, F, T) respectively. All that remains now is to orientedly colour all S gadgets. Notice that the arcs between colours allow us to use H as the orientation of edges for the colouring. So, the colourability of S is certified by Lemma 1(1).

On the other hand, assume we are given an oriented 4-colouring of such a digraph and want to find a valid 3-SAT evaluation. Vertices a_1, t, b, f all need to have distinct colours, and without loss of generality we can again name these colours A, T, B, F. The arcs between these four vertices in L, and the existence of an arc (f, a_2) easily leave the homomorphism image H from Fig 3 as the only admissible variant of colouring. Notice that a_2 and m must then be coloured by A, B respectively.

Now all the vertices x and $\neg x$ have to be coloured by either T or F. Our goal is to have T represent "true" and F represent "false", but for that to make sense x and $\neg x$ may not be both coloured by the same colour — that is where the interconnecting 5-path is used. It is easy to verify that a 5-path starting with T (or F) can not end with T (or F). So right now, we are given an evaluation of literals in the 3-SAT formula by the colouring: If the appropriate literal is coloured by T in x, evaluate it as "true", otherwise evaluate it as "false".

But what certifies that such an evaluation of all literals satisfies the 3-SAT formula? Here the specifics of S come into play. As proved in Lemma 1(2), S allows any combination of the colours T, F at l_1, l_2, l_3 except for F, F, F.

So, to recapitulate, it is possible to straightforwardly translate an oriented 4-colouring of such a digraph to the evaluation of the 3-SAT formula. The digraph structure guarantees that the evaluation will be sound (i.e. every literal is "true" iff its negation is "false") and that the evaluation will satisfy the formula. This concludes our proof. □

Remark 2. The digraph instances of the OCN_4 problem in Theorem 4 are of K-width 3 and DAG-depth 5.

3.2 Digraphs of DAG-Depth 3 and K-Width 1

Here we prove NP-hardness of the OCN_4 problem on another very restricted (c.f. Remark 2) digraph class — those that have simultaneously K-width 1 and DAG-depth 3. Although the constructed instances are not acyclic, all the values of traditional directed width parameters such as directed tree-width [8], DAG-width [1,12], Kelly-width [7] and cycle rank [4] remain bounded and very small. To recapitulate, these bounds on K-width and DAG-depth mean that there exists at most one path between any two vertices and that the robber can always be caught by cops in 3 moves in the cops-and-robber game of Theorem 1. This is just a little less restrictive than in Theorems 2 and 3.

Theorem 5. *The OCN_4 problem is NP-complete even on the class of digraphs with K-width 1 and DAG-depth 3.*

Proof. We prove the theorem by a reduction very similar to the case of Theorem 4. Notice that if the gadget S is applied on literals which are sinks in the graph, then the conditions on DAG-depth and K-width hold. We will however use a different variable gadget L_1 (Fig. 4) of smaller K-width and DAG-depth.

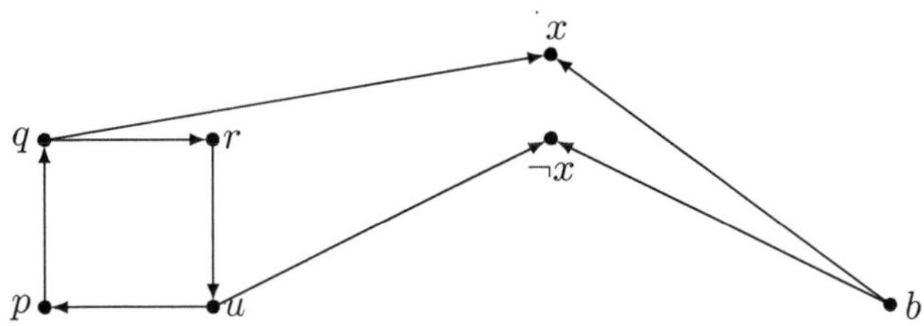

Fig. 4. Gadget L_1

Then, for every literal in the 3-SAT formula we create a separate copy of L_1, for each clause a separate copy of S and merge the copies of vertices x and $\neg x$ with l_1, l_2, l_3 of S in accordance with clauses of the formula. It is easy to verify that such a digraph will have K-width 1 and DAG-depth 3: Since the gadget S only intersects with other gadgets in copies of l_i and all l_i are sinks, K-width can only be increased above 1 by L_1. However, the K-width of L_1 is also 1. As for DAG-depth, the robber can be caught in 3 moves regardless of his starting point in S or L_1. Specifically, if the robber is in L_1 and starts in n, x or $\neg x$, then he can be caught trivially. Otherwise, place cops on q, u and then he is caught by the third one. Catching the robber in S is also simple and we leave the details to the reader as an exercise.

So, assume we have a 3-SAT evaluation. We will use the same H as in the previous reduction. If the literal is true in the evaluation, then we colour (p, q, r, u, b) as (F, A, B, T, B) and $x, \neg x$ as T and F. If it is false, we colour (p, q, r, u, b) as (B, T, F, A, B) and $x, \neg x$ as F and T. Finally, colour S by Lemma 1(1).

On the other hand, assume we have a valid oriented 4-colouring of such a digraph. Choose any 4-cycle C in a copy of L_1. C must be coloured by 4 distinct colours, without loss of generality let's say p, q, r, u are coloured by some colours P, Q, R, U respectively. This forces a 4-cycle in H and at this moment the only two orientations of arcs which remain undetermined in H are $\{P, R\}$ and $\{Q, U\}$.

If x and $\neg x$ were to be coloured by R and P (i.e. without using a "cross arc" in the cycle), we would not be able to assign any colour to B. So, only two possibilities can occur:

Fig. 5. The colour digraphs H_1 and H_2 respectively

1. $\neg x$ coloured by P and x coloured by U. Then b must be coloured by R and we obtain $H = H_1$ (Fig. 5 and 3). By identifying $(R, U, P, Q) = (B, T, F, A)$ we see that this is isomorhpic to H as before.
2. $\neg x$ coloured by Q and x coloured by R. Then b must be coloured by P and we obtain $H = H_2$ (Fig. 5 and 3). By identifying $(R, U, P, Q) = (F, A, B, T)$ we again see that this is isomorhpic to H.

So both admissible cases lead to the same (up to isomorphism) and only possible orientation of arcs in H. Since the aforementioned holds separately for every copy of L_1, each copy of x and $\neg x$ must be coloured only by T or F and never by the same colour as the other. Lemma 1(2) already certifies that under these conditions S forces every clause in the 3-SAT formula to hold true, concluding our proof. □

4 Conclusions

There are two possible interpretations of the results of the article. One is optimistic: there are some positive results and the problem can be algorithmically solved for DAG-depth 2 and special cases of K-width 1. This is a step forward, since no such positive results exist for traditional directed width parameters. It also remains an open question whether the algorithm for K-width 1 could be extended to a parameterized FPT algorithm with respect to the number of sources in the digraph.

In light of OCN_4 remaining NP-hard even after such severe restriction of the class of input graphs, we believe that new width parameters are needed for tackling this and perhaps other hard problems on digraphs. The recently introduced bi-rank-width measure [9], a natural directed extension of rank-width, could be a promising candidate. However, bi-rank-width is conceptually quite far away from the aforementioned width measures—these are mostly inspired by cops-and-robber games and undirected tree-width (see e.g. [13])—while bi-rank-width is close to the undirected clique-width and rank-width measures.

A strong positive aspect of bi-rank-width is that it performs much better [6] than the other aforementioned directed width measures with respect to an existence of polynomial algorithms for hard problems on digraphs (such as Directed Steiner Tree or Directed Feedback Vertex Set). Particularly, the OCN_c problem can be solved in FPT time on digraphs of bounded bi-rank-width for every fixed c [6].

There still are many unanswered questions though. One such question is the parameterized complexity of computing the oriented chromatic number (the optimization variant OCN) on digraphs of bounded bi-rank-width, as the algorithm used for computing the ordinary chromatic number on graphs of bounded rank-width [5] can not be straightforwardly extended to oriented colourings.

The major question in this context seems to be the following: Can one find a more restrictive directed width measure which is conceptually related to tree-width (and to cops and robber games), and which at the same time allows to solve the OCN_c problem efficiently?

References

1. Berwanger, D., Dawar, A., Hunter, P., Kreutzer, S.: DAG-Width and Parity Games. In: Durand, B., Thomas, W. (eds.) STACS 2006. LNCS, vol. 3884, pp. 524–536. Springer, Heidelberg (2006)
2. Courcelle, B.: The Monadic Second Order-Logic of Graphs VI: on Several Representations of Graphs by Relational Structures. Discrete Appl. Math. 54, 117–149 (1994)
3. Culus, J.-F., Demange, M.: Oriented Coloring: Complexity and Approximation. In: Wiedermann, J., Tel, G., Pokorný, J., Bieliková, M., Štuller, J. (eds.) SOFSEM 2006. LNCS, vol. 3831, pp. 226–236. Springer, Heidelberg (2006)
4. Eggan, L.: Transition Graphs and the Star-Height of Regular Events. Michigan Mathematical Journal 10(4), 385–397 (1963)
5. Ganian, R., Hliněný, P.: Better Polynomial Algorithms on Graphs of Bounded Rank-Width. In: IWOCA 2009, Extended Abstract. LNCS. Springer, Heidelberg (to appear, 2009)
6. Ganian, R., Hliněný, P., Kneis, J., Langer, A., Obdržálek, J., Rossmanith, P.: On Digraph Width Measures in Parameterized Algorithmics. In: Chen, J., Fomin, F.V. (eds.) IWPEC 2009. LNCS, vol. 5917, pp. 185–197. Springer, Heidelberg (2009)
7. Hunter, P., Kreutzer, S.: Digraph Measures: Kelly Decompositions, Games, and Orderings. Theor. Comput. Sci. 399(3), 206–219 (2008)
8. Johnson, T., Robertson, N., Seymour, P.D., Thomas, R.: Directed Treewidth. J. Combin. Theory Ser. B 82(1), 138–154 (2001)
9. Kanté, M.: The Rank-Width of Directed Graphs. arXiv:0709.1433v3 (2008)
10. Nešetřil, J., Ossona de Mendez, P.: Tree-Depth, Subgraph Coloring and Homomorphism Bounds. European J. Combin. 27(6), 1024–1041 (2006)
11. Nešetřil, J., Raspaud, A.: Colored Homomorphisms of Colored Mixed Graphs. J. Combin. Theory Ser. B 80(1), 147–155 (2000)
12. Obdržálek, J.: DAG-Width: Connectivity Measure for Directed Graphs. In: SODA 2006, pp. 814–821. ACM-SIAM (2006)
13. Robertson, N., Seymour, P.: Graph Minors X. Obstructions to Tree-Decomposition. J. Combin. Theory Ser. B 52(2), 153–190 (1991)
14. Sopena, É.: Oriented Graph Coloring. Discrete Math. 229, 359–369 (2001)

Smooth Optimal Decision Strategies for Static Team Optimization Problems and Their Approximations

Giorgio Gnecco[1,2] and Marcello Sanguineti[2]

[1] Department of Computer and Information Science (DISI), University of Genova
Via Dodecaneso, 35, 16146 Genova, Italy
[2] Department of Communications, Computer, and System Sciences (DIST)
University of Genova
Via Opera Pia 13, 16145 Genova, Italy
giorgio.gnecco@dist.unige.it, marcello@dist.unige.it

Abstract. Sufficient conditions for the existence and uniqueness of smooth optimal decision strategies for static team optimization problems with statistical information structure are derived. Approximation methods and algorithms to derive suboptimal solutions based on the obtained results are investigated. The application to network team optimization problems is discussed.

Keywords: Team utility function, value of a team, statistical information structure, approximation schemes, suboptimal solutions, network optimization.

1 Introduction

Decision makers (*DMs*) cooperating to achieve a common goal, expressed via a *team utility function*, model a variety of problems in engineering, economic systems, management science and operations research, in which centralization is not feasible and so distributed optimization processes have to be performed. Each DM has at disposal various possibilities of *decisions* generated via *strategies*, on the basis of the available *information* that it has about a random variable, called *state of the world*. In the model that we adopt, the information is expressed via a probability density function, so we have a *statistical information structure* [13, Chapter 3].

In general, one centralized DM that, relying on the whole available information, maximizes the common goal, provides a better performance than a set of decentralized DMs, each of them having partial information. However, centralization is not always feasible. For example, each DM may have access only to local information that cannot be instantaneously exchanged. Alternatively, the cost of making the whole information available to one single DM may be too high with respect to having several DMs with different information. This is often the case, e.g., in communication and computer networks extending in large

J. van Leeuwen et al. (Eds.): SOFSEM 2010, LNCS 5901, pp. 440–451, 2010.

geographical areas, production plants, energy distribution systems, and traffic systems in large metropolitan areas divided into sectors.

In the team optimization problems that we address in this paper, the information of each DM depends on the state of the world but is independent of the decisions of the other DMs. These are called *static teams*, in contrast to *dynamic teams*, for which each DM's information can be affected by the decisions of the other members. However, many dynamic team optimization problems can be reformulated in terms of equivalent static ones [28].

Static teams were first investigated by Marschak and Radner [22,23,24], who derived closed-form solutions for some cases of interest. Then, dynamic teams were studied [5]. Unfortunately, closed-form solutions to team optimization problems can be derived only under quite strong assumptions on the team utility function and the way in which each DM's information is influenced by the state of the world (and, in the case of dynamic teams, by the decisions previously taken by the other DMs). In particular, most available results hold under the so-called *LQG hypotheses* (i.e., linear information structure, concave quadratic team utility, and Gaussian random variables) and with *partially nested information*, i.e, when each DM can reconstruct all the information available to the DMs that affect its own information [7,12]. However, as remarked in [9], these assumptions are often too simplified or unrealistic. For more general problems, closed-form solutions are usually not available, so one has to search for suboptimal solutions.

In this paper, we derive sufficient conditions for the existence and uniqueness of *smooth* optimal decision strategies, for static team optimization problems with statistical information structure. Then, we show that a sufficiently high degree of smoothness of the optimal decision strategies is a useful property when searching for suboptimal solutions.

The paper is organized as follows. Section 2 introduces definitions and assumptions and formulates the family of static team optimization problems under consideration. Section 3 investigates existence and uniqueness of smooth optimal strategies for such problems. Section 4 examines some consequences of the obtained results in developing approximation methods and algorithms to derive suboptimal solutions. Section 5 discusses the application of our results to static network team optimization problems.

2 Problem Formulation

The context in which we shall formalize the optimization problem and derive our results is the following.

- *Static team* of n *decision makers* (*DMs*), $i = 1, \dots, n$.
- $x \in X \subseteq \mathbb{R}^{d_0}$: vector-valued random variable, called *state of the world*, describing a stochastic environment. The vector x models the uncertainties in the external world, which are not controlled by the DMs.
- $y_i \in Y_i \subseteq \mathbb{R}^{d_i}$: vector-valued random variable, which represents the *information* that the DM i has about x.

- $s_i : Y_i \to A_i \subseteq \mathbb{R}$: measurable *strategy* of the i-th DM.
- $a_i = s_i(y_i)$: *decision* that the DM i chooses on the basis of the information y_i.
- $u : X \times \Pi_{i=1}^n Y_i \times \Pi_{i=1}^n A_i \subseteq \mathbb{R}^N \to \mathbb{R}$, where $N = \sum_{i=0}^n d_i + n$: real-valued *team utility* function.
- The information that the n DMs have on the state of the world x is modelled by an n-tuple of random variables $y_1, \ldots, y_n$, i.e., by a *statistical information structure* [6] represented by a joint probability density $\rho(x, y_1, \ldots, y_n)$ on the set $X \times \Pi_{i=1}^n Y_i$.

We shall address the following family of static team optimization problems.

Problem STO (Static Team Optimization with Statistical Information). *Given the statistical information structure $\rho(x, y_1, \ldots, y_n)$ and the team utility function $u(x, y_1, \ldots, y_n, a_1, \ldots, a_n)$, find*

$$\sup_{s_1, \ldots s_n} v(s_1, \ldots, s_n),$$

where

$$v(s_1, \ldots, s_n) = \mathbb{E}_{x, y_1, \ldots, y_n} \{u(x, \{y_i\}_{i=1}^n, \{s_i(y_i)\}_{i=1}^n)\}.$$

The quantity $\sup_{s_1, \ldots s_n} v(s_1, \ldots, s_n)$ is called the *value of the team.*

Throughout the paper, we make the following three assumptions. For $\Omega \subseteq \mathbb{R}^d$, by $\mathcal{C}(\Omega)$ we denote the space of continuous functions on Ω; for a positive integer $m > 0$, by $\mathcal{C}^m(\Omega)$ we denote the spaces of functions on Ω, which are continuous together with their partial derivatives up to the order m.

A1. *The sets $X, Y_1, \ldots, Y_n$ are compact, and $A_1, \ldots, A_n$ are bounded closed intervals. For an integer $m \geq 2$, the team utility u is of class $\mathcal{C}^m$ on an open set containing $X \times \Pi_{i=1}^n Y_i \times \Pi_{i=1}^n A_i$, and ρ a (strictly) positive probability density on $X \times \Pi_{i=1}^n Y_i$, which can be extended to a function of class $\mathcal{C}^m$ on an open set containing $X \times \Pi_{i=1}^n Y_i$.*

A concave function f defined on a convex set Ω has *concavity at least* $\tau > 0$ if for all $u, v \in \Omega$ and every supergradient[1] p_u of f at u one has $f(v) - f(u) \leq p_u \cdot (v - u) - \tau \|v - u\|^2$. If f is of class $\mathcal{C}^2(\Omega)$, then a necessary condition for its concavity at least τ is $\sup_{u \in \Omega} \lambda_{\max}(\nabla^2 f(u)) \leq -\tau$, where $\lambda_{\max}(\nabla^2 f(u))$ is the maximum eigenvalue of the Hessian $\nabla^2 f(u)$.

A2. *There exists $\tau > 0$ such that the team utility function $u : X \times \Pi_{i=1}^n Y_i \times \Pi_{i=1}^n A_i$ is separately concave in each of the decision variables, with concavity at least τ (i.e., if all the arguments of u are fixed except the decision variable a_i, then the resulting function of a_i has concavity at least τ).*

Assumption A2 is motivated by tractability reasons and encountered in practice. For example, in economic problems it can be motivated by the "law of diminishing returns", i.e., the fact that the marginal productivity of an input usually diminishes as the amount of output increases [23, p. 99 and p. 110].

[1] For $\Omega \subseteq \mathbb{R}^d$ convex and $f : \Omega \to \mathbb{R}$ concave, $p_u \in \mathbb{R}^d$ is a *supergradient* of f at $u \in \Omega$ if for every $v \in \Omega$ it satisfies $f(v) - f(u) \leq p_u \cdot (v - u)$.

A3. *For every n-tuple $\{s_1, \dots, s_n\}$ of strategies, the strategies defined as*

$$\hat{s}_1(y_1) = \operatorname*{argmax}_{a_1 \in A_1} \mathbb{E}_{x,y_2,\dots,y_n|y_1}\{u(x, \{y_i\}_{i=1}^n, a_1, \{s_i(y_i)\}_{i=2}^n)\} \,\forall y_1 \in Y_1 \,,$$

$$\dots$$

$$\hat{s}_n(y_n) = \operatorname*{argmax}_{a_n \in A_n} \mathbb{E}_{x,y_1,\dots,y_{n-1}|y_n}\{u(x, \{y_i\}_{i=1}^n, \{s_i(y_i)\}_{i=1}^{n-1}, a_n)\} \,\forall y_n \in Y_n$$

do not lie on the boundaries of $A_1, \dots, A_n$, respectively.

The interiority condition in Assumption A3 can be imposed *a-priori*, by strongly penalizing the team utility function on the boundary. Simple examples of problems for which Assumptions A1, A2 and A3 hold simultaneously can be constructed by starting from a problem in which there is no interaction among the DMs (i.e., $u(x, y_1, \dots, y_n, s_1(y_1), \dots, s_n(y_n)) = \sum_{i=1}^n u_i(x, y_1, \dots, y_n, s_i(y_i))$, so that the assumptions are easy to impose), then adding to the team utility function a sufficiently small smooth interaction term.

3 Existence and Uniqueness of Smooth Optimal Strategies

The next theorem (which takes the hint from [13, Theorem 11, p. 162], and extends it to a higher degree of smoothness) gives conditions guaranteeing that Problem STO has a solution made of an n-tuple of strategies that are Lipschitz continuous together with their partial derivatives up to a certain order. For limitations of space, we only sketch the proof for $n = 2$; details can be found in [8, Chapter 5].

Theorem 1. *Let Assumptions A1, A2 and A3 hold. Then Problem STO admits an n-tuple $(s_1^o, \dots, s_n^o)$ of $\mathcal{C}^{m-2}$ optimal strategies with partial derivatives that are Lipschitz up to the order $m-2$.*

Sketch of proof. Let $n = 2$. Consider a sequence $\{s_1^j, s_2^j\}$ of pairs of strategies, indexed by $j \in \mathbb{N}_+$, such that $\lim_{j\to\infty} v(s_1^j, s_2^j) = \sup_{s_1,s_2} v(s_1, s_2)$ (such a sequence exists by the definition of supremum). From the sequence $\{s_1^j, s_2^j\}$, we generate another sequence $\{\hat{s}_1^j, \hat{s}_2^j\}$ defined by

$$\hat{s}_1^j(y_1) = \operatorname*{argmax}_{a_1 \in A_1} M_1^j(y_1, a_1) \,\forall y_1 \in Y_1 \,,$$

$$\hat{s}_2^j(y_2) = \operatorname*{argmax}_{a_2 \in A_2} M_2^j(y_2, a_2) \,\forall y_2 \in Y_2 \,,$$

where for every $(y_1, a_1) \in Y_1 \times A_1$ and $(y_2, a_2) \in Y_2 \times A_2$, we let

$$M_1^j(y_1, a_1) = \mathbb{E}_{x,y_2|y_1}\{u(x, y_1, y_2, a_1, s_2^j(y_2))\} \,,$$
$$M_2^j(y_2, a_2) = \mathbb{E}_{x,y_1|y_2}\{u(x, y_1, y_2, \hat{s}_1^j(y_1), a_2)\} \,.$$

Since the probability density $\rho(x, y_1, y_2)$ is of class $\mathcal{C}^m$ and strictly positive on an open set containing $X \times Y_1 \times Y_2$, we obtain that the conditional density $\rho(x, y_2|y_1)$

is of class $\mathcal{C}^m$ on the compact set $X \times Y_1 \times Y_2$ and the team utility function u is of class $\mathcal{C}^m$ on the compact set $X \times Y_1 \times Y_2 \times A_1 \times A_2$. So M_1^j, as an integral dependent on parameters, is of class $\mathcal{C}^m$ on the compact set $Y_1 \times A_1$, with upper bounds on the sizes of its partial derivatives up to the order m independent of y_1, a_1, and j. In particular, it is easy to show that M_1^j has concavity at least τ in a_1. By such continuity and concavity properties of M_1^j with respect to a_1, for all $y_1 \in Y_1$ the set $\operatorname{argmax}_{a_1 \in A_1} M_1^j(y_1, a_1)$ consists of exactly one element. An analogous conclusion holds for $\operatorname{argmax}_{a_2 \in A_2} M_2^j(y_2, a_2)$. So $\hat{s}_1^j$ and $\hat{s}_2^j$ are well-defined.

Let $y'_1, y''_1 \in Y_1$. By the definition of $\hat{s}_1^j$, exploiting the concavity τ of M_1^j with respect to a_1 and taking the supergradient 0 of M_1^j with respect to the second variable at $(y'_1, \hat{s}_1^j(y'_1))$ and $(y''_1, \hat{s}_1^j(y''_1))$, respectively, we get

$$M_1^j(y'_1, \hat{s}_1^j(y''_1)) - M_1^j(y'_1, \hat{s}_1^j(y'_1)) \leq -\tau |\hat{s}_1^j(y''_1) - \hat{s}_1^j(y'_1)|^2 \tag{1}$$

and

$$M_1^j(y''_1, \hat{s}_1^j(y'_1)) - M_1^j(y''_1, \hat{s}_1^j(y''_1)) \leq -\tau |\hat{s}_1^j(y'_1) - \hat{s}_1^j(y''_1)|^2 . \tag{2}$$

By (1) and (2) we obtain

$$|M_1^j(y'_1, \hat{s}_1^j(y''_1)) - M_1^j(y'_1, \hat{s}_1^j(y'_1))| + |M_1^j(y''_1, \hat{s}_1^j(y'_1)) - M_1^j(y''_1, \hat{s}_1^j(y''_1))|$$

$$\geq 2\tau |\hat{s}_1^j(y''_1) - \hat{s}_1^j(y'_1)|^2 . \tag{3}$$

Let $L_1 > 0$ (which can be chosen independently of j) be an upper bound on the Lipschitz constant of M_1^j. Then by (3) we obtain $2L_1 \|y''_1 - y'_1\| \geq 2\tau |\hat{s}_1^j(y''_1) - \hat{s}_1^j(y'_1)|^2$, i.e.,

$$|\hat{s}_1^j(y''_1) - \hat{s}_1^j(y'_1)| \leq \sqrt{\frac{L_1}{\tau}} \sqrt{\|y''_1 - y'_1\|} , \tag{4}$$

which proves the Hölder continuity of $\hat{s}_1^j$, hence its continuity and measurability. Continuity and measurability of $\hat{s}_2^j$ can be proved in the same way. Then it makes sense to evaluate $v(\hat{s}_1^j, \hat{s}_2^j)$, and by construction we have $v(\hat{s}_1^j, \hat{s}_2^j) \geq v(s_1^j, s_2^j))$.

Let us focus on the strategies of the first DM. The next step consists in showing that there exists a subsequence of $\{\hat{s}_1^j\}$ that converges uniformly to a strategy $s_1^o \in \mathcal{C}^{m-2}(Y_1)$ with Lipschitz $(m-2)$-order partial derivatives. By Assumption A3, for every $y_1 \in Y_1$ $\hat{s}_1^j(y_1)$ is interior, so $\left.\frac{\partial M_1^j}{\partial a_1}\right|_{a_1 = \hat{s}_1^j(y_1)} = 0$. Then, by the Implicit Function Theorem, for every $k = 1, \ldots, d_1$ we get $\frac{\partial \hat{s}_1^j}{\partial y_{1,k}} = -\left(\frac{\partial^2 M_1^j}{\partial {\hat{s}_1^j}^2}\right)^{-1} \frac{\partial^2 M_1^j}{\partial \hat{s}_1^j \partial y_{1,k}}$, where $\left(\frac{\partial^2 M_1^j}{\partial {\hat{s}_1^j}^2}\right) \leq -\tau < 0$ by the concavity at least τ of M_1^j in a_1 and its smoothness.

As M_1^j is of class $\mathcal{C}^m$, by taking higher-order partial derivatives we conclude that $\hat{s}_1^j(y_1)$ is locally of class $\mathcal{C}^{m-1}$. As this holds for every $y_1 \in Y_1$, it is of class $\mathcal{C}^{m-1}$ on all Y_1. Since M_1^j has upper bounds on the sizes of its partial derivatives up to the order m that are independent of y_1, a_1, and j, then for every $(i_1, \ldots, i_{d_1})$ such that $i_1 + \ldots + i_{d_1} = m-1$, there exists a finite upper bound on $\left| \frac{\partial^{m-1} \hat{s}_1^j}{\partial y_{1,1}^{i_1}, \ldots, \partial y_{1,d_1}^{i_{d_1}}} \right|$, which is independent of y_1 and j. So, one can easily show that for every $(i_1, \ldots, i_{d_1})$ such that $i_1 + \ldots + i_{d_1} = m-2$, the functions of the sequence $\left\{ \frac{\partial^{m-2} \hat{s}_1^j}{\partial y_{1,1}^{i_1}, \ldots, \partial y_{1,d_1}^{i_{d_1}}} \right\}$ are equibounded and have the same upper bound on their Lipschitz constants, so they are uniformly equicontinuous on Y_1. Hence, by Ascoli-Arzelà's Theorem [1, Theorem 1.30, p. 10], such sequence admits a subsequence that converges uniformly to a function defined on Y_1, which is also Lipschitz, with the same upper bound on its Lipschitz constant as above.

By integrating $m-2$ times, we conclude that also the integrals of these subsequences converge uniformly to the integrals of the limit functions. Therefore, there exists a subsequence of $\{\hat{s}_1^j\}$ that converges uniformly to a strategy $s_1^o \in \mathcal{C}^{m-2}(Y_1)$ with Lipschitz $(m-2)$-order partial derivatives. Similarly, one proves that there exists a subsequence of $\{\hat{s}_2^j\}$ that converges uniformly to $s_2^o \in \mathcal{C}^{m-2}(Y_1)$ with Lipschitz $(m-2)$-order partial derivatives.

By the continuity of the functional $v(s_1, s_2)$ on $\mathcal{C}(Y_1) \times \mathcal{C}(Y_2)$ with the respective sup-norms, finally we obtain $v(s_1^o, s_2^o) = \lim_{j \to \infty} v(\hat{s}_1^j, \hat{s}_2^j) = \sup_{s_1, s_2} v(s_1, s_2)$. □

The next theorem show that, under additional conditions, the optimal n-tuple of smooth strategies is unique. We denote by $\mathcal{C}(Y_i, A_i)$ the set of continuous functions from Y_i to A_i with the sup-norm. Without loss of generality, we restrict the spaces of admissible strategies to $\mathcal{C}(Y_i, A_i)$, as one can show that under the assumptions of Theorem 1 any optimal strategy coincides almost everywhere with a continuous function. To simplify the statement, in Theorem 2 we consider the case of $n = 2$ DMs, but it can be extended to $n \geq 2$ DMs.

Theorem 2. *Let the assumptions of Theorem 1 hold with $m \geq 3$ and $n = 2$, and let also $\frac{\beta_{1,2}}{\tau} < 1$, where $\beta_{1,2} = \max_{(a_1,a_2) \in A_1 \times A_2} \left| \frac{\partial^2}{\partial a_1 \partial a_2} u(x, y_1, y_2, a_1, a_2) \right|$. Then (s_1^o, s_2^o) given in Theorem 1 is the unique optimal pair of strategies in $\mathcal{C}(Y_1, A_1) \times \mathcal{C}(Y_2, A_2)$.*

Sketch of proof. Inspection of the first part of the proof of Theorem 1 shows that there exists a (possibly nonlinear) operator $\mathcal{T} : \mathcal{C}(Y_1, A_1) \times \mathcal{C}(Y_2, A_2) \to \mathcal{C}(Y_1, A_1) \times \mathcal{C}(Y_2, A_2)$ such that

$$\mathcal{T}_1(s_1, s_2)(y_1) = \operatorname*{argmax}_{a_1 \in A_1} \mathbb{E}_{x, y_2 \mid y_1} \{u(x, y_1, y_2, a_1, s_2(y_2))\} \, \forall y_1 \in Y_1,$$

$$\mathcal{T}_2(s_1, s_2)(y_2) = \operatorname*{argmax}_{a_2 \in A_2} \mathbb{E}_{x, y_1 \mid y_2} \{u(x, y_1, y_2, \mathcal{T}_1(s_1, s_2)(y_1), a_2)\} \, \forall y_2 \in Y_2.$$

Let $(s_1^{o'}, s_2^{o'}) \in \mathcal{C}(Y_1, A_1) \times \mathcal{C}(Y_2, A_2)$ be an optimal pair of strategies. Then it is easy to see that $(s_1^{o'}, s_2^{o'}) = \mathcal{T}(s_1^{o'}, s_2^{o'})$ is a necessary condition for its optimality. By Assumption A3 and the compactness of Y_1 and Y_2, for any $(s_1, s_2) \in \mathcal{C}(Y_1, A_1) \times \mathcal{C}(Y_2, A_2)$ the strategies $\mathcal{T}_1(s_1, s_2)$ and $\mathcal{T}_2(s_1, s_2)$ belong respectively to the interiors of $\mathcal{C}(Y_1, A_1)$ and $\mathcal{C}(Y_2, A_2)$. So, Problem STO is reduced to an unconstrained infinite-dimensional game theory problem, for which one can apply the techniques developed in [17] to study the stability of Nash equilibria. This can be done since every pair of optimal strategies for Problem STO constitutes a Nash equilibrium for a two-player game, for which the individual utilities J^1 and J^2 are the same and are equal to $v(s_1, s_2)$. By using the norm $\sqrt{\mathbb{E}_{y_i}\{(s_i(y_i))^2\}}$ on $\mathcal{C}(Y_1, A_1)$ and $\mathcal{C}(Y_2, A_2)$ (instead of the usual sup-norms), computing the Frechét derivatives of the integral functional v up to the second order and applying [17, Theorem 1, formula (1)], one can show that, for $m \geq 3$, $\mathcal{T}$ is a contraction operator with contraction constant bounded from above by $\frac{\beta_{1,2}^2}{\tau^2} < 1$. So, $\mathcal{T}$ has at most a unique fixed point $(s_1^{o'}, s_2^{o'}) \in \mathcal{C}(Y_1, A_1) \times \mathcal{C}(Y_2, A_2)$, which by Theorem 1 coincides with (s_1^o, s_2^o). □

4 Approximation Methods and Algorithms

In this section, we discuss how the existence and uniqueness of an optimal n-tuple of strategies with a sufficiently high degree of smoothness can be exploited when searching for suboptimal solutions to Problem STO.

4.1 Estimates of the Accuracy of Suboptimal Solutions by Nonlinear Approximation Schemes

In [10, Propositions 4.2 and 4.3] we have shown that, for a degree of smoothness m in Assumption A1 that is linear in $\max_i\{d_i\}$ (i.e., the maximum dimension of the information vectors y_i), the smooth optimal strategies $s_1^o, \ldots, s_n^o$ (whose existence is guaranteed by Theorem 1), can be approximated by suitable nonlinear approximation schemes modelling one-hidden-layer neural networks [11] with Gaussian and trigonometric computational units, with upper bounds on the approximation errors of order $k^{-1/2}$, where k is the number of computational units used in such schemes. This is an instance of the so-called *blessing of smoothness* [21]. We are currently investigating the extension of such results to other nonlinear approximation schemes with sigmoidal and spline computational units. The numerical results in [2,3,4] show that often these approximation schemes (which belong to the wider family of *variable-basis approximation schemes* [15,16]) are able to find accurate suboptimal solutions to team optimization problems with high-dimensional states, using a small number of parameters to be optimized. Variable-basis approximation schemes have been successfully exploited also in other optimization tasks (see the references in [30,31]).

4.2 Application of Quasi-Monte Carlo Methods

Another consequence of a sufficiently high degree of smoothness of the optimal strategies is that it allows the application of quasi-Monte Carlo methods [20] and related ones (such as Korobov's method; see [29] and [14, Chapter 6]) for the approximate computation of the multidimensional integrals $v(s_1^o, \ldots, s_n^o)$ and $v(\tilde{s}_1, \ldots, \tilde{s}_n)$, where $\tilde{s}_1, \ldots, \tilde{s}_n$ are smooth approximations of $s_1^o, \ldots, s_n^o$. For example, upper bounds on the error in the approximate evaluation of a multidimensional integral by quasi-Monte Carlo methods can be obtained via Koksma-Hlawka's inequality [20, p. 20], which requires that the integrand has a finite variation in the sense of Hardy and Krause [20, p. 19]. Considering, e.g., the case of an integrand f defined on a r-dimensional unit-cube $[0,1]^r$, the most common formula [20, p. 19, formula (2.5)] used to prove that f has a finite variation in the sense of Hardy and Krause requires that $f \in \mathcal{C}^r([0,1]^r)$ (i.e., its degree of smoothness has to be at least equal to the number of variables). With the obvious changes in notation, Theorem 1 provides such a degree of smoothness, for $m \geq \sum_{i=0}^n d_i + 2$.

4.3 Algorithms for Suboptimal Solutions

Finally, we investigate some implications of our results in the development of algorithms to find suboptimal solutions to Problem STO. For simplicity of exposition, we consider the case of $n = 2$ agents.

Recall that under the assumptions of Theorem 2, the operator $\mathcal{T}$ defined in the proof of such theorem is a contraction operator. Then, given any initial pair of smooth suboptimal strategies $(\tilde{s}_1^0, \tilde{s}_2^0)$ and the unique (and a-priori unknown) optimal one (s_1^o, s_2^o), for every positive integer M one has

$$\max\left\{\max_{y_1 \in Y_1} |s_1^o(y_1) - \tilde{s}_1^M(y_1)|, \max_{y_2 \in Y_2} |s_2^o(y_2) - \tilde{s}_2^M(y_2)|\right\}$$
$$\leq \left(\frac{\beta_{1,2}^2}{\tau^2}\right)^M \max\left\{\max_{y_1 \in Y_1} |s_1^o(y_1) - \tilde{s}_1^0(y_1)|, \max_{y_2 \in Y_2} |s_2^o(y_2) - \tilde{s}_2^0(y_2)|\right\}, \quad (5)$$

where

$$(\tilde{s}_1^M, \tilde{s}_2^M) = \mathcal{T}^M(\tilde{s}_1^0, \tilde{s}_2^0) \quad (6)$$

and $\frac{\beta_{1,2}^2}{\tau^2} < 1$. So, for the algorithm (6), the upper bound (5) shows that the rate of convergence to the optimal pair of strategies is exponential in M.

In practice, however, the operator $\mathcal{T}$ itself has to be replaced by a finite-dimensional approximating operator. Consider, e.g., an approximation scheme in which one searches for suboptimal strategies of the form

$$\tilde{s}_1 = \sum_{j=1}^h c_{j,1}\phi_{j,1} \quad \text{and} \quad \tilde{s}_2 = \sum_{j=1}^h c_{j,2}\phi_{j,2},$$

where the positive integer h and the basis functions $\{\phi_{j,1}\}_{j=1}^h$ and $\{\phi_{j,2}\}_{j=1}^h$ are fixed, and $\{c_{j,1}\}_{j=1}^h$, $\{c_{j,2}\}_{j=1}^h$ are real coefficients to be optimized. Let

$$\tilde{u}(x, y_1, y_2, \{c_{j,1}\}, \{c_{j,2}\}) = u(x, y_1, y_2, \tilde{s}_1(y_1), \tilde{s}_2(y_2)).$$

Then, one can replace (6) by

$$(\{c_{j,1}^M\},\{c_{j,2}^M\}) = \tilde{\mathcal{T}}_h^M\left(\{c_{j,1}^0\},\{c_{j,2}^0\}\right), \tag{7}$$

where one chooses the approximating operator $\tilde{\mathcal{T}}_h$ such that

$$\tilde{\mathcal{T}}_{h,1}(\{c_{j,1}\},\{c_{j,2}\}) = \underset{\{\hat{c}_{j,1}\}}{\operatorname{argmax}}\, \mathbb{E}_{x,y_1,y_2}\{\tilde{u}(x,y_1,y_2,\{\hat{c}_{j,1}\},\{c_{j,2}\})\}, \tag{8}$$

$$\tilde{\mathcal{T}}_{h,2}(\{c_{j,1}\},\{c_{j,2}\}) = \underset{\{\hat{c}_{j,2}\}}{\operatorname{argmax}}\, \mathbb{E}_{x,y_1,y_2}\{\tilde{u}(x,y_1,y_2,\mathcal{T}_{h,1}(\{c_{j,1}\},\{c_{j,2}\}),\{\hat{c}_{j,2}\})\} \tag{9}$$

(for simplicity, we are assuming that there exist unique maxima). Exploiting Assumption A2, one can show that finding the argmax in (8) and (9) for fixed $\{c_{j,1}^M\},\{c_{j,2}^M\}$ requires one to solve two stochastic finite-dimensional concave optimization problems, to which the information-based-complexity results [27] and the efficient algorithms described in [19, Chapter 14] may be applied.

Subjects of future research include studying the properties of the above-defined operator $\tilde{\mathcal{T}}_h$ and of other approximating operators. In particular, it is of interest finding conditions under which

- the operator $\tilde{\mathcal{T}}_h$ is a contraction operator (like $\mathcal{T}$);
- the minimum positive integer h and the minimum number of elementary operations of the algorithms described in [19, Chapter 14], required to find a suboptimal solution to Problem STO with an error at most $\varepsilon > 0$, grow "slowly" with respect to $1/\varepsilon$.

5 Network Team Optimization

For static network team optimization problems [10], our smoothness results take on a simplified form. For these problems, the team utility function u can be written as the sum of a finite number of individual utility functions u_i, each one associated with a single DM (e.g., a router) or with a shared resource in the network (e.g., a communication link). In addition, each u_i depends only on a subset of the DMs. This situation can be described by a multigraph, where the DMs are the nodes and there is an edge between two DMs if and only if both appear in a same individual utility function.

Figure 1 gives an idea of a network team optimization problem modeling a store-and-forward packet-switching telecommunication network (see [2,4]). Suppose that the DMs are n routers acting as members of a same team (i.e., they aim to maximize a common objective, decomposable into the sum of several individual objectives related, e.g., to the congestion of the links). Each router has at its disposal some private information (e.g., the total lengths of its incoming packet queues). Assume also that the traffic flows can be described by continuous variables. Then, on the basis of its private information, each router decides how to split the incoming traffic flows into its output links. The network team optimization problem consists in finding optimal (or nearly optimal) n-tuples of

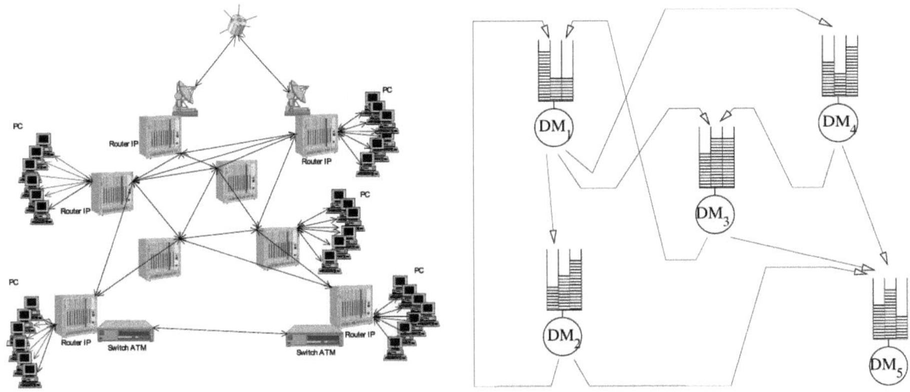

Fig. 1. An example of store-and-forward packet-switching telecommunication network (left). An example of graph model with buffers at the nodes (right).

strategies according to some given optimality criterion (for simplicity we ignore any dynamics in the problem, and we model it as a static one).

Compared with a general instance of Problem STO, the particular structure of a static network team optimization allows various simplifications:

- For any n-tuple of strategies, the integral $v(s_1, \dots, s_n)$ can be decomposed into the sum of a finite number of integrals, each usually dependent on less than $\sum_{i=0}^{n} d_i$ real variables. So, the minimum degree m of smoothness required to apply [20, p. 19, formula (2.5)] is usually less than $\sum_{i=0}^{n} d_i + 2$ (compare with the general case in Section 4).
- Since the strategy of each DM is influenced only by those of its neighbors in the network, Assumption A3 may be easier to impose.
- One can show that an extension of Theorem 2 to $n > 2$ DMs can be formulated in terms of interaction terms $\beta_{i,j}$, where (i, j) are pairs of different DMs in the team. For a static network team optimization problem, usually most of the $\beta_{i,j}$ are equal to 0 (since the interaction of each DM is limited to its neighbors in the graph), so such extension takes a simplified form.

As to specific applications to static network team optimization problems, our smoothness results may be applied, e.g., to stochastic versions of the congestion, routing, and bandwidth allocation problems considered in [18, Lectures 3 and 4], which are stated in terms of smooth and concave individual utility functions.

Acknowledgement. The authors were partially supported by a grant "Progetti di Ricerca di Ateneo 2008" of the University of Genova, project "Solution of Functional Optimization Problems by Nonlinear Approximators and Learning from Data".

References

1. Adams, R.A.: Sobolev Spaces. Academic Press, New York (1975)
2. Baglietto, M., Parisini, T., Zoppoli, R.: Distributed-Information Neural Control: The Case of Dynamic Routing in Traffic Networks. IEEE Trans. on Neural Networks 12, 485–502 (2001)
3. Baglietto, M., Parisini, T., Zoppoli, R.: Numerical Solutions to the Witsenhausen Counterexample by Approximating Networks. IEEE Trans. on Automatic Control 46, 1471–1477 (2001)
4. Baglietto, M., Sanguineti, M., Zoppoli, R.: The Extended Ritz Method for Functional Optimization: Overview and Applications to Single-Person and Team Optimal Decision Problems. Optimization Methods and Software 24, 15–43 (2009)
5. Basar, T., Bansal, R.: The Theory of Teams: A Selective Annotated Bibliography. Lecture Notes in Control and Information Sciences, vol. 119. Springer, Heidelberg (1989)
6. Blackwell, D.: Equivalent Comparison of Experiments. Annals of Mathematical Statistics 24, 265–272 (1953)
7. Chu, K.C.: Team Decision Theory and Information Structures in Optimal Control Problems – Part II. IEEE Trans. on Automatic Control 17, 22–28 (1972)
8. Gnecco, G.: Functional Optimization by Variable-Basis Approximation Schemes. PhD Thesis in Mathematics and Applications, Dept. of Mathematics, University of Genova (2009)
9. Hess, J., Ider, Z., Kagiwada, H., Kalaba, R.: Team Decision Theory and Integral Equations. J. of Optimization Theory and Applications 22, 251–264 (1977)
10. Gnecco, G., Sanguineti, M.: Suboptimal Solutions to Network Team Optimization Problems. In: CD-Proc. of the Int. Network Optimization Conf. 2009 (INOC 2009), Pisa, Italy (April 2009)
11. Haykin, S.: Neural Networks. A Comprehensive Foundation. MacMillan, New York (1994)
12. Ho, Y.C., Chu, K.C.: Team Decision Theory and Information Structures in Optimal Control Problems - Part I. IEEE Trans. on Automatic Control 17, 15–22 (1972)
13. Kim, K.H., Roush, F.W.: Team Theory. Ellis Horwood, Chichester (1987)
14. Krommer, A.R., Ueberhuber, C.W.: Computational Integration. SIAM, Philadelphia (1998)
15. Kůrková, V., Sanguineti, M.: Error Estimates for Approximate Optimization by the Extended Ritz Method. SIAM J. of Optimization 18, 461–487 (2005)
16. Kůrková, V., Sanguineti, M.: Geometric upper Bounds on Rates of Variable-Basis Approximation. IEEE Trans. on Information Theory 54, 5681–5688 (2008)
17. Li, S., Basar, T.: Distributed Algorithms for the Computation of Noncooperative Equilibria. Automatica 23, 523–533 (1987)
18. Mansour, Y.: Computational Game Theory. Tel Aviv University, Israel (2006), `http://www.cs.tau.ac.il/~mansour/course_games/2006/course_games_05_06.htm`
19. Nemirovski, A.: Efficient Methods in Convex Programming. Technion, Haifa, Israel (1994), `http://www2.isye.gatech.edu/~nemirovs/Lect_EMCO.pdf`
20. Niederreiter, H.: Random Number Generation and Quasi-Monte Carlo Methods. SIAM, Philadelphia (1992)
21. Poggio, T., Smale, S.: The Mathematics of Learning: Dealing with Data. Notices of the American Mathematical Society 50, 537–544 (2003)

22. Marschak, J.: Elements for a Theory of Teams. Management Science 1, 127–137 (1955)
23. Marschak, J., Radner, R.: Economic Theory of Teams. Yale University Press, New Haven (1972)
24. Radner, R.: Team Decision Problems. Annals of Mathematical Statistics 33, 857–881 (1962)
25. Rantzer, A.: Using Game Theory for Distributed Control Engineering. In: 3rd World Congress of the Game Theory Society Games (2008); (Tech. Rep. ISRN LUTFD2/TFRT--7620–SE, Dept. of Aut. Contr., Lund Univ., Sweden) (July 2008)
26. Segall, A.: The Modeling of Adaptive Routing in Data–Communication Networks. IEEE Trans. on Communications 25, 85–95 (1977)
27. Traub, J.F., Wasilkowski, G.W., Woźniakowski, H.: Information Based Complexity. Academic Press, New York (1988)
28. Witsenhausen, H.S.: Equivalent Stochastic Control Problems. Mathematics of Control, Signals, and Systems 1, 3–11 (1988)
29. Zinterhof, T.: High Dimensional Integration: New Weapons Fighting the Curse of Dimensionality. Physics of Particles and Nuclei Letters 5, 145–149 (2008)
30. Zoppoli, R., Parisini, T., Baglietto, M., Sanguineti, M.: Neural Approximations for Optimal Control and Decision. Springer, London (in preparation)
31. Zoppoli, R., Sanguineti, M., Parisini, T.: Approximating Networks and Extended Ritz Method for the Solution of Functional Optimization Problems. J. of Optimization Theory and Applications 112, 403–439 (2002)

Algorithms for the Minimum Edge Cover of H-Subgraphs of a Graph

Alexander Grigoriev, Bert Marchal, and Natalya Usotskaya

School of Business and Economics
Department of Quantitative Economics, Maastricht University
PO Box 616, 6200 MD Maastricht, The Netherlands
{a.grigoriev,b.marchal,n.usotskaya}@maastrichtuniversity.nl

Abstract. We consider the following problem: given graph G and a set of graphs $H = \{H_1, \ldots, H_t\}$, what is the smallest subset S of edges in G such that all subgraphs of G that are isomorphic to one of the graphs from H contain at least one edge from S? Equivalently, we aim to find the minimum number of edges that needs to be removed from G to make it H-free. We concentrate on the case where all graphs H_i are connected and have fixed size. Several algorithmic results are presented. First, we derive a polynomial time dynamic program for the problem on graphs of bounded treewidth and bounded maximum vertex degree. Then, if H contains only a clique, we adjust the dynamic program to solve the problem on graphs of bounded treewidth having arbitrary maximum vertex degree. Using the constructed dynamic programs, we design a Baker's type approximation scheme for the problem on planar graphs. Finally, we observe that our results hold also if we cover only induced H-subgraphs.

Keywords: Minimum edge deletion, H-free graph, bounded treewidth, Baker's approximation scheme, planar graph.

1 Introduction

In the field of combinatorial graph theory, lately there has been an increased interest in graphs that do not contain some specified graph as a subgraph or as an induced subgraph. An apparent reason for this is that many combinatorial problems on graphs become easier when restricted to graphs that exclude certain subgraphs. For some examples of such problems, we refer to [1,8,11]. In this paper, we present methods for turning an arbitrary input graph into a graph that excludes certain subgraphs. This will be done by removing edges from the input graph. Given input graph G and a finite set of graphs $H = \{H_1, \ldots, H_t\}$, we call a subgraph of G an H-subgraph of G if it is isomorphic to one of the graphs in set H. In this context, graph G is usually referred to as the *text* and H as the set of *patterns*. Graph G is called H*-free* if there are no H-subgraphs in G. The set of edges that needs to be removed from G to make it H-free obviously covers all occurrences of an H-subgraph in G. The problem that is addressed in this paper can therefore be formulated in the following two ways:

J. van Leeuwen et al. (Eds.): SOFSEM 2010, LNCS 5901, pp. 452–464, 2010.

PROBLEM: *H-Free Edge Deletion*
Input: Text graph G and finite set of patterns $H = \{H_1, \ldots, H_t\}$
Question: What is the minimum number of edges that needs to be deleted from G to make it H-free?

PROBLEM: *H-Subgraph Edge Cover*
Input: Text graph G and finite set of patterns $H = \{H_1, \ldots, H_t\}$
Question: What is the cardinality of a smallest set of edges of G covering all H-subgraphs of G?

From here on, we will stick to the problem *H-Subgraph Edge Cover* and by default, we intent to find a minimum edge cover of the set of all H-subgraphs of G. By making some small adjustments in the dynamic program that is described later, we can also deal with the problem of covering the set of all *induced* H-subgraphs of G. We leave the details to the full journal version of the paper.

The decision version of the problem *H-Subgraph Edge Cover* (given integer k, is it possible to cover all H-subgraphs of G with at most k edges?) is NP-complete, since the case where G is planar and has maximum degree 7 and $H = \{K_3\}$ was shown to be NP-complete by Brügmann, Komusiewicz and Moser, see [7].

Several papers in the field deal with constructing graphs that are H-free for a set H that often contains just one pattern, see [6,10]. Only a very limited amount of papers deal with turning graphs into H-free graphs. In [7], the problem is considered of making graphs K_3-free by minimum number of edge deletions. We consider the more general problem where H is a finite set of connected patterns of constant size.

The paper is organized in the following way: in Section 2, some preliminaries and definitions are introduced. In Section 3, a polynomial time dynamic program is derived for *H-Subgraph Edge Cover* for the case where text graph G has bounded treewidth and bounded degree and H is one fixed connected graph. In Section 4, we consider the case where H is a fixed clique and we present a polynomial time algorithm for the problem on text graphs G that have bounded treewidth and arbitrary maximum vertex degree. In Section 5, we describe a Baker's type approximation scheme (see [2]) for *H-Subgraph Edge Cover* for the case where G is planar. In the last section, we briefly show how the methods in Sections 3, 4 and 5 can be extended to deal with a finite set $H = \{H_1, \ldots, H_t\}$ of fixed connected patterns instead of with one such pattern.

2 Preliminaries and Definitions

A *planar graph* is a graph that can be drawn in the plane in such a way that its edges intersect only at their endpoints. Such a drawing is called a *planar embedding* of the graph. A planar embedding in which all vertices are on the exterior face is called a 1-outerplanar embedding. For $k \geq 1$, a planar embedding is *k-outerplanar* if removing the vertices that are on the exterior face results in a $(k-1)$-outerplanar embedding. A graph is called k-outerplanar if it has a k-outerplanar embedding. The *outerplanarity index* of a planar graph is the smallest value k for which G is k-outerplanar. The following lemma is due to Kammer, see [9]:

Lemma 1. *Given a planar graph G, the outerplanarity index k of G and a k-outerplanar embedding of G can be found in $O(n^2)$ time.*

Given a planar embedding of planar graph $G = (V, E)$, vertex v is of *level* 1 if it is on the exterior face of the embedding. Let V_i be the set of all vertices of level i or lower than i, then vertex w is in level $i+1$ if it is on the exterior face of the embedding induced by $G[V \setminus V_i]$. We say that edge $e = (v, w) \in E$ is in level i of the embedding if both vertices v and w are in level i. We assume throughout the rest of the paper, that a planar embedding is represented by an appropriate data structure such that levels of vertices can be computed in linear time.

A *tree decomposition* of G is a pair (X, T), where T is a tree and X is a family of bags. The bags X_i are identified with the nodes of the tree. Every bag X_i contains a subset of V such that:

- $\forall\, v \in V\ \exists\, X_i \in X\ :\ v \in X_i$.
- $\forall\, (u, v) \in E\ \exists\, X_i \in X\ :\ \{u, v\} \subseteq X_i$.
- $\forall\, v \in V$ the collection of bags containing v forms a connected subtree of T.

The *width* w of tree decomposition (X, T) of G is equal to the size of its largest bag minus one. The *treewidth* $tw(G)$ of G is the minimum width over all tree decompositions of G. The following lemma is due to Bodlaender, see [4]:

Lemma 2. *The treewidth of a k-outerplanar graph is at most $3k-1$.*

A lot of research has been dedicated to the fixed parameter case for treewidth, i.e. check whether the treewidth of a graph is at most some constant w and if so, return a tree decomposition of width at most w. For an overview of this work we refer to [5]. Finally, in [3] the following result was obtained:

Lemma 3. *Given a graph of treewidth at most w, a tree decomposition of width at most w can be obtained in linear time.*

From a practical viewpoint the algorithm is only useful for low values of w because of a big hidden constant in the $'O'$-notation in the running time of the linear algorithm.

3 Dynamic Program for G with Bounded $\Delta(G)$, $tw(G)$

In this section, we consider *H-Subgraph Edge Cover* on text graph G that has bounded degree and bounded treewidth and arbitrary fixed pattern H. We construct a dynamic programming algorithm for this setting that solves *H-Subgraph Edge Cover* in time that is exponential only in the maximum degree of G, in the width of a tree decomposition of G and in some fixed parameters of H. As we believe that *H-Subgraph Edge Cover* can be formulated in Monadic Second Order Logic, the restriction of bounded degree is likely to be superfluous. We hope to present an algorithm for the unrestricted case in a journal version of the paper. Our algorithms run on so called nice tree decompositions of G, which we define as follows:

Definition 1. *We call a tree decomposition (X, T) of G* nice *when:*

- *all bags corresponding to leaves of T contain exactly one vertex,*
- *for all pairs of adjacent bags X_1 and X_2 in T there is a vertex $v \in V$ such that either $X_1 = X_2 \cup \{v\}$ or $X_2 = X_1 \cup \{v\}$,*
- *for any bag X no two neighbors bags of X contain the same vertex set.*

Note that our definition of a nice tree decomposition differs from the one that is very commonly used in the literature. We now make a simple observation concerning nice tree decompositions of G.

Observation 1. *The maximum degree in the tree of a nice tree decomposition (X, T) of G is at most n.*

Proof. Consider any bag X in T. It has no neighbors with the same vertex set, so if X contains k vertices, then in at most k neighbor bags of X a vertex is deleted compared to X and in at most $n - k$ neighbor bags of X a vertex is introduced compared to X. Hence bag X has at most n neighbor bags in (X, T). □

It is not difficult to show that any 'reasonable' tree decomposition of G, like one that is obtained using the algorithm from Lemma 3, can be turned into a nice tree decomposition of the same width in linear time. From now on, we assume that a nice tree decomposition (X, T) of G is given that is rooted in some arbitrary bag X_r. By w, we denote the *width* of (X, T). The *maximum degree* in G will be denoted by $\Delta(G)$ and by h and d we denote respectively the *size* and the *diameter* of pattern H. Since G has bounded degree and bounded treewidth and H is a fixed pattern, the values $\Delta(G)$, w, h and d are constants.

Given bag X in tree decomposition (X, T), we let T_X be a subtree of T that is rooted in X and we let $G[T_X]$ be the subgraph of G that is induced by all vertices from the bags in T_X. By $\mathcal{E}_X$ we denote the set of all edges of G for which both end points are present in bag X and by E_X, we denote a subset of $\mathcal{E}_X$, i.e. $E_X \in 2^{\mathcal{E}_X}$. For bag X, by V_X we denote the set of vertices of G that are in bag X. For subtree T_X, by V_{T_X} we denote the set of vertices of G that are present in some bag of T_X. Finally for vertex set S, by $\mathcal{H}_S$ we denote the set of different H-subgraphs in G that are incident to some vertex in S and by H_S, we denote a subset of $\mathcal{H}_S$.

Lemma 4. *Given $Q = h!\binom{\Delta(G)^{d+1}}{h}$,*

- *For vertex v, $|\mathcal{H}_{\{v\}}|$ is bounded from above by Q,*
- *For bag X, the value $|\mathcal{H}_{V_X}|$ is bounded from above by $(w + 1)Q$,*

Proof. Given that v corresponds to some vertex of an H-subgraph in G it is clear that all h vertices in this H-subgraph have distance at most d to v in this H-subgraph and thus also in G. Since the maximum degree in G is $\Delta(G) > 1$, there are at most $\sum_{i=0}^{d} \Delta(G)^i = \frac{\Delta(G)^{d+1}-1}{\Delta(G)-1} \leq \Delta(G)^{d+1}$ vertices in G that have distance at most d to v. Since $\binom{\Delta(G)^{d+1}}{h}$ different sets of h vertices can be chosen among $\Delta(G)^{d+1}$ vertices and each such set can contain at most $h!$ different H-subgraphs, the result follows. The second statement is a straightforward corollary of the first one, since $|X| \leq w+1$. □

We now present the main theorem of this section.

Theorem 2. *Given G of bounded maximum degree $\Delta(G)$, fixed connected pattern H and a nice tree decomposition (X,T) of G of bounded width w, the problem H-*Subgraph Edge Cover *on G can be solved in time $O(n^2 2^{2w^2+3(w+1)Q} w^4 Q^2)$, where $Q = h!\binom{\Delta(G)^{d+1}}{h}$.*

Proof. Given subtree T_X of T, we define:

- $F(E_X, T_X, H_{V_X})$ is the minimum cardinality of a set S of edges from $G[T_X]$ that covers all H-subgraphs from $(\mathcal{H}_{V_{T_X}} \setminus \mathcal{H}_{V_X}) \cup H_{V_X}$ in G, given that $S \cap \mathcal{E}_X = E_X$
- $F(E_X, T_X, H_{V_X}) = \infty$ if H-subgraphs from $(\mathcal{H}_{V_{T_X}} \setminus \mathcal{H}_{V_X}) \cup H_{V_X}$ can *not* be covered by E_X plus some set of edges from $E(G[T_X]) \setminus \mathcal{E}_X$.

For each bag X in (X,T), we compute a table of such $F-$values for several subtrees rooted in X, one value for each combination of a subset from $\mathcal{E}_X$ and a subset from $\mathcal{H}_{V_X}$. One such table thus contains $2^{|\mathcal{E}_X|+|\mathcal{H}_{V_X}|}$ values. To be more specific, we compute a table for the following three types of subtrees:

(1) For each bag X in T, except for root bag X_r, we compute the table for the subtree consisting of the parent X^+ of X, X and all descendants of X in T. The root bag of this subtree is X^+. Such subtree will be denoted by T_{X^+}.
(2) For each non-leaf bag X: if X has m children $X_1, \ldots, X_m$ then for each j, $1 \leq j \leq m$ we compute a table for the subtree consisting of X, $X_1, \ldots, X_j$ and all descendants of $X_1, \ldots, X_j$ in T. Such a subtree will be denoted by $T_{\{X,j\}}$. Bag X is thus the root bag of subtree $T_{\{X,j\}}$.
(3) For each leaf bag X we compute the table for the unique subtree $T_{\{X,0\}}$ that is rooted in X.

Since in a nice tree decomposition leaf bag X contains only one vertex and thus $\mathcal{E}_X = \emptyset$, computing the table for the unique subtree $T_{\{X,0\}}$ that is rooted in X is trivial (note that for leaf bag X it holds that $V_{T_{\{X,0\}}} = V_X$):

Lemma 5. *The table for subtree $T_{\{X,0\}}$ rooted in leaf bag X contains the following $|\mathcal{H}_{V_X}| \leq Q$ values:*

$$F(\emptyset, T_{\{X,0\}}, H_{V_X}) = \begin{cases} 0 & , \textit{if } H_{V_X} = \emptyset \\ \infty & , \textit{otherwise.} \end{cases}$$

The following lemmas give recursive formulations that show how to compute the tables for subtrees that are rooted in a non-leaf bag of (X,T). First we show how to update the table when we combine two subtrees that are rooted in the same bag and have only this bag in common.

Lemma 6. *Let T'_X and T''_X be two subtrees rooted in X that only share bag X. Let T_X be the subtree that is obtained by combining T'_X and T''_X and let H_{V_X}, I_{V_X}, $J_{V_X} \in 2^{\mathcal{H}_{V_X}}$. Then*

$$F(E_X, T_X, H_{V_X}) = \min_{I_{V_X}, J_{V_X} : H_{V_X} \subseteq I_{V_X} \cup J_{V_X}} F(E_X, T'_X, I_{V_X}) + F(E_X, T''_X, J_{V_X}) - |E_X|$$

The next two lemmas show how to update the values for a subtree when we extend it by the parent bag of its root.

Lemma 7. *Let T_Y be a subtree rooted in Y and let $X = Y \cup \{v\}$ be the parent bag of Y. Furthermore let $T_X = T_{Y^+}$ and let $E_Y = E_X \cap \mathcal{E}_Y$. Then:*

$$F(E_X, T_X, H_{V_X}) = \min_{H_{V_Y}:\ E_X \setminus E_Y \text{ covers } H_{V_X} \setminus H_{V_Y} \text{ in } G} F(E_Y, T_Y, H_{V_Y}) + |E_X \setminus E_Y|$$

and $F(E_X, T_X, H_{V_X}) = \infty$ if there is no such H_{V_Y}.

Lemma 8. *Let T_Y be a subtree rooted in Y and let $X = Y \setminus \{v\}$ be the parent bag of Y. Furthermore, let $T_X = T_{Y^+}$. Then:*

$$F(E_X, T_X, H_{V_X}) = \min_{E_Y, H_{V_Y}:\ H_{V_X} \cup (\mathcal{H}_{\{v\}} \setminus \mathcal{H}_{V_X}) \subseteq H_{V_Y},\ E_Y \cap \mathcal{E}_X = E_X} F(E_Y, T_Y, H_{V_Y})$$

The following lemma gives an upper bound on the time to compute one F-value.

Lemma 9. *The time needed to determine an F-value by one of the Lemmas 5, 6, 7 or 8 is bounded from above by $O(2^{w^2+2(w+1)Q} w^4 Q^2)$.*

Proof. By Lemma 5, determining the F-values for subtrees rooted in leaf bags is a constant time operation.

To determine a value using Lemma 6 takes $O(4^{|\mathcal{H}_{V_X}|} |\mathcal{H}_{V_X}|^2)$ time. Using Lemma 4, this is bounded from above by $O(4^{(w+1)Q} w^2 Q^2)$.

To determine a value using Lemma 7, for all subsets H_{V_Y} we have to check whether all elements from $H_{V_X} \setminus H_{V_Y}$ contain an edge from $E_X \setminus E_Y$. This takes less than $2^{|\mathcal{H}_{V_Y}|} |H_{V_X}| |E_X|$ time and by using Lemma 4 and the observation that $|E_X| \leq w^2$, this is bounded from above by $O(2^{(w+1)Q} w^3 Q)$.

To determine a value using Lemma 8, for all combinations of E_Y and H_{V_Y} we have to check whether $H_{V_X} \subseteq H_{V_Y}$, whether $\mathcal{H}_{\{v\}} \setminus \mathcal{H}_{V_X} \subseteq H_{V_Y}$ and whether $E_Y \cap \mathcal{E}_X = E_X$. This takes less than $2^{|\mathcal{E}_Y| + |\mathcal{H}_{V_Y}|} (|H_{V_X}| + |\mathcal{H}_{V_X}|^2 + |E_X|^2)$ time and as before this can be bounded from above by $O(2^{w^2+(w+1)Q} w^4 Q^2)$.

Clearly, all these running times are smaller than $O(2^{w^2+2(w+1)Q} w^4 Q^2)$. □

Using Lemmas 5, 6, 7 and 8, we can compute all tables. For all bags in the tree, in post order, we can compute the tables for the necessary subtrees rooted in this bag. By Lemma 5, computing the table for a leaf bag X is trivial. If X is not a leaf bag, suppose X has m children $X_1, \ldots, X_m$, then for all j, $1 \leq j \leq m$, we compute the tables for all subtrees $T_{\{X,j\}}$. We note that $T_{\{X,1\}}$ is the same subtree as $T_{X_1^+}$. Thus using Lemma 7 or 8 we can compute the table for subtree $T_{\{X,1\}}$ from the already earlier computed table for subtree T_{X_1}. For $2 \leq j \leq m$, we note that $T_{\{X,j\}}$ is the union of $T_{\{X,j-1\}}$ and $T_{X_j^+}$. Thus we first use Lemma 7 or 8 to compute the table for subtree $T_{X_j^+}$ using the table for subtree T_{X_j}. Then we use Lemma 6 to compute the table for subtree $T_{\{X,j\}}$ from the tables for subtrees $T_{\{X,j-1\}}$ and $T_{X_j^+}$. If root bag X_r has m children in T, then subtree $T_{\{X_r,m\}}$ is equal to T. The answer to *H-Subgraph Edge Cover* can be found in the table of $T_{\{X_r,m\}}$. To be more precise, the solution is:

$$\min_{E_{X_r}} F(E_{X_r}, T_{\{X_r,m\}}, \mathcal{H}_{V_{X_r}}) \ .$$

Using the optimal set E_{X_r}, we can do a backward search in the tree to determine a minimum set of edges covering all H-subgraphs in G. To estimate the running time of the dynamic program, in the following lemma we determine an upper bound on the number of individual F-values that will be computed:

Lemma 10. *During a run of the dynamic program, at most* $O(n^2 2^{w^2+(w+1)Q})$ *F-values need to be determined.*

Proof. Consider arbitrary bag X in (X,T). By Observation 1, X has at most n child bags Y, so we compute tables for at most n subtrees T_{Y^+} of type 1 rooted in X. Moreover, since X has at most n child bags we compute tables for at most n subtrees of type 2 that are rooted in X. Finally, it is obvious that we compute tables for at most 1 subtree of type 3 that is rooted in X. Hence we compute tables for at most $O(n)$ subtrees of T rooted in X.

Since a nice tree decomposition of G has $O(n)$ bags, we compute at most $O(n^2)$ tables in total. Since the width of tree decomposition (X,T) is w, there are at most $w+1$ vertices in bag X and therefore $|\mathcal{E}_X|$ is bounded from above by $\frac{w^2+w}{2} \leq w^2$ for $w \geq 1$. Furthermore, by Lemma 4, $|\mathcal{H}_{V_X}|$ is bounded from above by $(w+1)Q$. The latter two observations imply that the number of values in one table is bounded from above by $2^{w^2+(w+1)Q}$, from which the result follows. □

By Lemma 10, we need to compute at most $O(n^2 2^{w^2+(w+1)Q})$ F-values and by Lemma 9, it takes at most $O(2^{w^2+2(w+1)Q} w^4 Q^2)$ time to compute one such value. The total time needed is thus bounded by $O(n^2 2^{2w^2+3(w+1)Q} w^4 Q^2)$. □

4 Dynamic Program for Clique *H* and Bounded *tw*(*G*)

In this section, we consider *H-Subgraph Edge Cover* for the special case where H is a clique and G has bounded treewidth, i.e. compared to Section 3 we drop the constraint that G should have bounded vertex degree. We exploit the fact that every tree decomposition contains a bag with all vertices from the clique and we find a polynomial time algorithm that again acts on a nice tree decomposition of the text graph G. It is important to notice that in this section we consider H-subgraphs of G that are induced by the vertex set of $G[T_X]$, not the vertex set of G. The main theorem of this section is the following:

Theorem 3. *Given arbitrary text graph G, clique pattern H of size h and a nice tree decomposition (X,T) of G of bounded width w. Then* H-Subgraph Edge Cover *on graph G can be solved in $O(n^2 2^{2w^2} w^4 \binom{w}{h-1} h^2)$ time.*

Proof. For subtree T_X of T rooted in bag X, we define:

- $F(E_X, T_X)$ is the minimum cardinality of a set S of edges from $G[T_X]$ that covers all H-subgraphs of $G[T_X]$, given that $S \cap \mathcal{E}_X = E_X$.
- $F(E_X, T_X) = \infty$, if **not** all H-subgraphs of $G[T_X]$ can be covered by E_X plus some set of edges from $E(G[T_X]) \setminus \mathcal{E}_X$.

We compute tables for the same subtrees as in the previous section. Note that one table for a subtree rooted in bag X now consists of $2^{|\mathcal{E}_X|}$ F-values. Using similar arguments as those used in the previous section, it is easy to show that:

Lemma 11. *During a run of the dynamic program, at most $O(n^2 2^{w^2})$ individual F-values have to be determined.*

The table for a leaf bag X contains only one value: $F(\emptyset, T_{\{X,0\}}) = 0$. The following lemmas give recursive formulations that show how to compute the tables for subtrees that are rooted in a non-leaf bag of T. The first lemma shows how we can combine subtrees that are rooted in the same bag and have only this bag in common.

Lemma 12. *Let T_X be obtained by taking the union of subtrees T'_X and T''_X such that the root X of T'_X and T''_X is the only bag that belongs to both subtrees. Then*

$$F(E_X, T_X) \;=\; F(E_X, T'_X) + F(E_X, T''_X) - |E_X|.$$

The next two lemmas show how to update the values for a subtree when we extend it by the parent bag of its root.

Lemma 13. *Let T_Y be a subtree of T rooted in bag Y, let $X = Y \cup \{v\}$ be the parent bag of Y in T. Furthermore let $T_X = T_{Y^+}$ and let $E_Y = E_X \cap \mathcal{E}_Y$. Then:*

$$F(E_X, T_X) = \begin{cases} F(E_Y, T_Y) + |E_X \setminus E_Y| & \text{, if } E_X \text{ covers all } H\text{-subgraphs of } G[T_X] \text{ that are incident to vertex } v. \\ \infty & \text{, otherwise.} \end{cases}$$

Indeed, since X is the only bag containing v in T_X, it also contains all neighbors of v in $G[T_X]$. Therefore, all edges of an H-subgraph of $G[T_X]$ that is incident to v are part of $\mathcal{E}_X$ and thus if such an H-subgraph is not covered by E_X then it is not covered at all.

Lemma 14. *Let T_Y be a subtree of T rooted in bag Y, let $X = Y \setminus \{v\}$ be the parent bag of Y in T and let $T_X = T_{Y^+}$. Then*

$$F(E_X, T_X) = \min_{E_Y \,:\, E_Y \cap \mathcal{E}_X = E_X} F(E_Y, T_Y).$$

In the previous section, it is explained how Lemmas 12, 13 and 14 can be used to determine the tables for all necessary subtrees. If root bag X_r has m children, then the minimum value in the table of subtree $T_{\{X_r,m\}}$ is the solution to *Triangle Free Edge Deletion.*

Lemma 15. *The time needed to determine an F-value in the algorithm is bounded from above by $O(2^{w^2}w^4\binom{w}{h-1}h^2)$.*

Proof. Determining the value for a subtree rooted in a leaf bag or by using Lemma 12 takes constant time. When using Lemma 13, we check whether E_X covers all H-subgraphs of $G[T_X]$ that are incident to v. Vertex v has at most w neighbors in $G[T_X]$, so we have to check for each of the at most $\binom{w}{h-1}$ different combinations of $(h-1)$ such neighbors whether they form an h-clique with v in $G[T_X]$ for which all $\frac{h^2-h}{2}$ edges are in $\mathcal{E}_X \setminus E_X$. Since $|\mathcal{E}_X|$ is bounded by $O(w^2)$, this takes at most $O(w^2\binom{w}{h-1}h^2)$ time.

When using Lemma 14 to determine an F-value, for all E_Y we have to check whether $E_Y \cap \mathcal{E}_X = E_X$, which can be done in time $O(2^{w^2}w^4)$. Clearly, all these algorithmic time complexities are bounded from above by $O(2^{w^2}w^4\binom{w}{h-1}h^2)$.

By Lemma 11, we need to compute at most $O(n^2 2^{w^2})$ F-values and by Lemma 15, it takes at most $O(2^{w^2}w^4\binom{w}{h-1}h^2)$ time to compute one such value. Therefore, the dynamic program runs in $O(n^2 2^{2w^2}w^4\binom{w}{h-1}h^2)$ time. □

5 Baker's Approximation Scheme for Planar Graphs

In this final section, we consider *H-Subgraph Edge Cover* for planar text graphs and patterns. By using the dynamic programs from Section 3 and 4, we construct a Baker's approximation scheme for the two cases where respectively G has bounded degree and where H is a 3-clique or 4-clique.

Lemma 16. *Given planar text graph G of bounded maximum degree $\Delta(G)$ and bounded outerplanarity index l and a fixed connected pattern H. Then an optimal solution for* H-Subgraph Edge Cover *can be obtained in time $O(n^2 2^{18l^2+9lQ} l^4 Q^2)$, where $Q = h!\binom{\Delta(G)^{d+1}}{h}$.*

Proof. By Lemma 1, the outerplanarity index l of G can be determined in $O(n^2)$ time. By Lemma 2, $tw(G) \leq 3l-1$ and by Lemma 3, a tree decomposition of G of width $w \leq 3l-1$ can be obtained in linear time that can be turned into a nice tree decomposition in linear time. By Theorem 2 we can use this nice tree decomposition to solve *H-Subgraph Edge Cover* on G in time $O(n^2 2^{2w^2+3(w+1)Q} w^4 Q^2)$. Since $w \leq 3l-1$, the result follows. □

A similar result can be obtained for *H-Subgraph Edge Cover* on planar graphs when H is a 3-clique or 4-clique.

Lemma 17. *Given planar text graph G of bounded outerplanarity index l and pattern H that is either a K_3 or K_4, an optimal solution for* H-Subgraph Edge Cover *on G can be obtained in time $O(n^2 2^{18l^2} l^4 \binom{3l-1}{h-1} h^2)$.*

Proof. Similar as proof of Lemma 16. By Theorem 3, *H-Subgraph Edge Cover* on G can be solved in $O(n^2 2^{2w^2} w^4 \binom{w}{h-1} h^2)$. Since $w \leq 3l - 1$, the result follows. □

H-Subgraph Edge Cover on planar graphs of bounded degree with fixed pattern and *H-Subgraph Edge Cover* on planar graphs with clique pattern are thus both fixed parameter tractable, since they are tractable when parameterized by outerplanarity index l of G. We now use this property to construct a Baker's approximation scheme that can be applied to both problems. In the following theorem and its proof, we denote by E_{opt} a minimum set of edges from G covering all H-subgraphs of G and by OPT we denote the size of E_{opt}.

Theorem 4. *For planar text graph G of bounded degree, fixed connected pattern H and any positive s, there is an $O(n^3 2^{18l^2+9lQ} l^4 Q^2)$-time algorithm for* H-Subgraph Edge Cover *on G that finds a solution of size at most $(\frac{s+1}{s})OPT$.*

Proof. First, we use Lemma 1 to determine G's outerplanarity index k and a k-outerplanar embedding of G in $O(n^2)$ time. I.e, each vertex of G belongs to one of the k levels. Similarly, we determine H's outerplanarity index k' in $O(h^2)$ time. Now for some fixed $2k' \leq l \leq k$ and for each $i \in I = \{mk'+1 \mid 0 \leq m \leq \lfloor \frac{l}{k'} - 2 \rfloor\}$ we construct a set G^i of induced subgraphs of G, consisting of the l-outerplanar subgraphs of G:

- induced by levels 1 to $i + k' - 1$.
- induced by levels $j(l - k') + i$ to $j(l - k') + i + l - 1$, $0 \leq j \leq \lfloor \frac{k-i-l+1}{l-k'} \rfloor$.
- induced by levels $\lfloor \frac{k-i-l+1}{l-k'} \rfloor (l - k') + i + l - k'$ to k.

See Figure 1 for an illustration. Note that $i + k' - 1 \leq \lfloor \frac{l}{k'} - 2 \rfloor k' + 1 + k' - 1 \leq l - k' < l$ and also that $k - (\lfloor \frac{k-i-l+1}{l-k'} \rfloor (l - k') + i + l - k') + 1 \leq k - (k - i - 2l + 1 + k' + i + l - k') + 1 = l$, so both the subgraph induced by the first bullet and the one induced by the third bullet are l-outerplanar. Clearly, also the subgraphs under the second bullet are l-outerplanar. Since $|I| = \lfloor \frac{l}{k'} - 1 \rfloor$ and for each i we construct $\lfloor \frac{k-i-l+1}{l-k'} + 3 \rfloor$ subgraphs, in total we construct less than $(\frac{l-k'}{k'})(\frac{k+2l+1}{l-k'}) = \frac{k+2l+1}{k'} \leq 3k \leq 3n = O(n)$ induced subgraphs of G for fixed value of l.

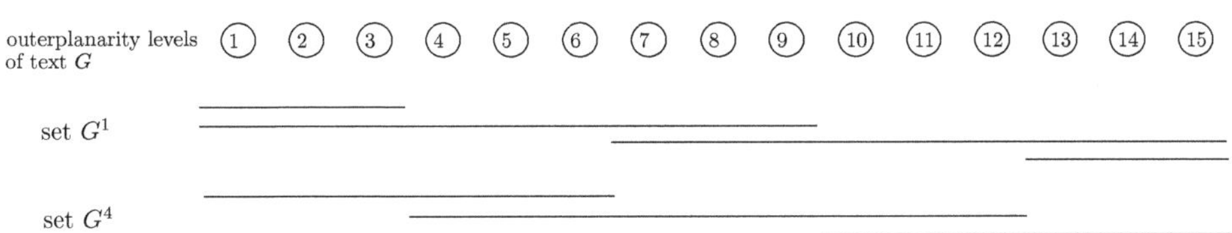

Fig. 1. Suppose text G has 15 outerplanarity levels and pattern H is 3-outerplanar. For $l = 9$, we construct two sets (G^1 and G^4) of 9-outerplanar subgraphs of G. For example, the first graph in G^1 is induced by all vertices in G's first three levels.

Observation 5. *For every $i \in I$, the vertices in the following set of levels are the only vertices that are part of more than one graph from G^i:*

- *levels $j(l-k')+i,\ldots,j(l-k')+i+k'-1,\ 0 \leq j \leq \lfloor \frac{k-i-l+1}{l-k'} \rfloor$ and*
- *levels $\lfloor \frac{k-i-l+1}{l-k'} \rfloor (l-k')+i+l-k'$ to $\lfloor \frac{k-i-l+1}{l-k'} \rfloor (l-k')+i+l-1$*

Observation 6. *For at least one $i \in I$ the set of levels from Observation 5 contain at most $\frac{k'}{l-2k'}OPT$ edges from E_{opt}.*

Proof. For any two different values of i from I, the two sets of levels from Observation 5 are disjoint. Thus if for all $i \in I$, the sets of levels would contain strictly more than $\frac{k'}{l-2k'}OPT$ edges from E_{opt}, then all these levels would contain strictly more than

$$\sum_{m=0}^{\lfloor \frac{l}{k'}-2 \rfloor} \frac{k'}{l-2k'}OPT = \lfloor \frac{l}{k'} - 1 \rfloor \frac{k'}{l-2k'}OPT \geq \left(\frac{l-k'}{k'} - 1\right)\frac{k'}{l-2k'}OPT = OPT$$

edges from E_{opt}, a contradiction. □

Now for each $i \in I$, we use Lemma 16 to compute optimal solutions to *H-Subgraph Edge Cover* for all l-outerplanar subgraphs. Since for all values of i together, the number of l-outerplanar subgraphs is bounded by $O(n)$, this can be done in time $O(n^3 2^{18l^2+9lQ} l^4 Q^2)$. We note that for each i, any H-subgraph of G is present in at least one of the subgraphs of G induced by this i. Therefore, for each i, the union of the optimal solutions for its induced subgraphs is a set of edges that covers all H-subgraphs in G. The algorithm picks the best of these unions as an approximation to the optimal solution. To see that this approximation is at most $(\frac{s+1}{s})OPT$, consider again an optimal solution E_{opt} for G. We pick the value i that by Observations 5 and 6 has not more than $\frac{k'}{l-2k'}OPT$ edges from E_{opt} in intersecting levels of graphs from G^i. For each element $S \in G^i$ we let E_S be the set of edges in E_{opt} in subgraph S. Furthermore, we let E'_S be the edges in an optimal solution of *H-Subgraph Edge Cover* for S. For this choice of i, we thus have a solution of *H-Subgraph Edge Cover* for G of size no larger than the sum of the $|E'_S|$'s. Clearly for each S it holds that $|E'_S| \leq |E_S|$. Moreover, since at most $\frac{k'}{l-2k'}OPT$ edges are counted twice while summing the $|E_S|$'s, we conclude that $\sum_{S \in G^i} |E'_S| \leq \sum_{S \in G^i} |E_S| \leq \frac{k'}{l-2k'}OPT + OPT = \frac{l-k'}{l-2k'}OPT$. Thus in total time $O(n^2) + O(h^2) + O(n^3 2^{18l^2+9lQ} l^4 Q^2)$ we constructed a solution of size at most $\frac{l-k'}{l-2k'}OPT$. By choosing $l = (s+2)k' \geq 2k'\ \forall s > 0$, we obtain the $(\frac{s+1}{s})$-approximation to OPT. □

Theorem 7. *For planar text graph G, pattern H that is either a K_3 or K_4 and any positive s, there is a $O(n^3 2^{18l^2} l^4 \binom{3l-1}{h-1} h^2)$-time algorithm for* H-Subgraph Edge Cover *on G that finds a solution of size at most $(\frac{s+1}{s})OPT$.*

Proof. Same as proof of Theorem 4, with the only difference that Lemma 17 is used instead of Lemma 16. □

6 Generalization to Finite Sets of Patterns

In this section we generalize the results from the previous sections for a finite set $H = \{H_1, \ldots, H_t\}$, $t > 1$ of fixed connected patterns. If H_i is a subgraph of H_j, $j \neq i$, then H_j is not relevant, as any edge cover of all occurrences of H_i as a subgraph would also cover all occurrences of H_j. For the set of cliques this means that only the smallest clique is significant and hence there is no need to generalize the result from Section 4. Thus we consider graph G of bounded maximum degree and a finite set H of fixed connected patterns such that for each $1 \leq i \neq j \leq t$, H_i is not isomorphic to a subgraph of H_j. By h_i, d_i and k_i we denote respectively the size, the diameter and the outerplanarity index of pattern H_i. The following theorem generalizes the result of Theorem 2:

Theorem 8. *Given text graph G of bounded maximum degree $\Delta(G)$, finite set of fixed connected patterns H and a nice tree decomposition (X, T) of G of bounded width w, the problem H-*Subgraph Edge Cover *on G can be solved in time $O(n^2 2^{2w^2+3(w+1)Q} w^4 Q^2)$, where $Q = \sum_{i=1}^{t} h_i! \binom{\Delta(G)^{d_i+1}}{h_i}$.*

Proof. We repeat the proof of Theorem 2, taking $Q = \sum_{i=1}^{t} h_i! \binom{\Delta(G)^{d_i+1}}{h_i}$ as a new upper bound on the number of the considered subgraphs of G. □

Theorem 9. *For planar text graph G of bounded degree, finite set of fixed connected patterns H and any positive s, there is a $O(n^3 2^{18l^2+9lQ} l^4 Q^2)$-time algorithm for* H-Subgraph Edge Cover *on G that finds a solution of size at most $(\frac{s+1}{s})OPT$.*

Proof. The proof is similar to the proof of Theorem 4, with Q as defined in Theorem 8 and $k' = \max_{1 \leq i \leq t} k_i$. □

References

1. Alon, N., Krivelevich, M., Sudakov, B.: Maxcut in H-Free Graphs. Comb. Probab. Comput. 14(5-6), 629–647 (2005)
2. Baker, B.S.: Approximation Algorithms for NP-Complete Problems on Planar Graphs. J. ACM 41(1), 153–180 (1994)
3. Bodlaender, H.L.: A Linear-Time Algorithm for Finding Tree-Decompositions of Small Treewidth. SIAM J. Comput. 25(6), 1305–1317 (1996)
4. Bodlaender, H.L.: A Partial k-Arboretum of Graphs with Bounded Treewidth. Theor. Comput. Sci. 209(1-2), 1–45 (1998)
5. Bodlaender, H.L.: Discovering Treewidth. In: Vojtáš, P., Bieliková, M., Charron-Bost, B., Sýkora, O. (eds.) SOFSEM 2005. LNCS, vol. 3381, pp. 1–16. Springer, Heidelberg (2005)
6. Bohman, T.: The Triangle-Free Process. Advances in Math. 221(5), 1653–1677 (2009)
7. Brügmann, D., Komusiewicz, C., Moser, H.: On Generating Triangle-Free Graphs. Electronic Notes in Discrete Mathematics 32, 51–58 (2009)

8. Dunbar, J.E., Frick, M.: The Path Partition Conjecture is True for Claw-Free Graphs. Discrete Math. 307(11-12), 1285–1290 (2007)
9. Kammer, F.: Determining the Smallest k Such That G Is k-Outerplanar. In: Arge, L., Hoffmann, M., Welzl, E. (eds.) ESA 2007. LNCS, vol. 4698, pp. 359–370. Springer, Heidelberg (2007)
10. Osthus, D., Taraz, A.: Random Maximal H-Free Graphs. Random Struct. Algorithms 18(1), 61–82 (2001)
11. Robertson, N., Seymour, P.D., Thomas, R.: Hadwiger's Conjecture for K_6-Free Graphs. Combinatorica 13(3), 279–361 (1993)

On the Complexity of the Highway Pricing Problem

Alexander Grigoriev[1], Joyce van Loon[1,⋆], and Marc Uetz[2]

[1] Maastricht University, Quantitative Economics,
P.O. Box 616, NL–6200 MD Maastricht, The Netherlands
{a.grigoriev,j.vanloon}@ke.unimaas.nl
[2] University of Twente, Applied Mathematics,
P.O. Box 217, NL–7500 AE Enschede, The Netherlands
m.uetz@utwente.nl

Abstract. The highway pricing problem asks for prices to be determined for segments of a single highway such as to maximize the revenue obtainable from a given set of customers with known valuations. The problem is NP-hard and a recent quasi-PTAS suggests that a PTAS might be in reach. Yet, so far it has resisted any attempt for constant-factor approximation algorithms. We relate the tractability of the problem to structural properties of customers' valuations. We show that the problem becomes NP-hard as soon as the average valuations of customers are not homogeneous, even under further restrictions such as monotonicity. Moreover, we derive an efficient approximation algorithm, parameterized along the inhomogeneity of customers' valuations. Finally, we discuss extensions of our results that go beyond the highway pricing problem.

Keywords: Pricing problems, highway pricing problem, computational complexity, approximation algorithm.

1 Introduction

We consider the *highway pricing problem*, introduced by Guruswami et al. [9]. The problem is motivated by determining revenue-maximizing tolls to be charged for segments of a highway. The highway is thought of as a simple path, and capacity is considered unlimited. There are potential customers, each of them requesting to travel a sub-path of the highway, and the maximal valuation for utilizing the requested sub-path is considered public knowledge. The objective is to find prices to be charged for the segments of the highway so as to maximize the total revenue obtained by the customers.

More formally, let $I = \{1, \ldots, m\}$ represent the highway segments, and regard them as consecutive edges on a simple path. Let $J = \{1, \ldots, n\}$ denote the set of potential customers. Every customer $j \in J$ requests a sub-path of the highway,

⋆ Supported by METEOR, the Maastricht Research School of Economics of Technology and Organizations.

J. van Leeuwen et al. (Eds.): SOFSEM 2010, LNCS 5901, pp. 465–476, 2010.

denoted $I_j \subseteq I$, and we assume that each I_j is of the form $I_j = \{k, k+1, \dots, \ell\}$, $k \leq \ell$. The valuation v_j for traveling sub-path I_j is publicly known. This is quite reasonable when assuming that the valuation is a monetary expression for the time saving that can be realized by using the highway instead of the next-fastest alternative route. We assume $v_j > 0$, for otherwise that customer can be deleted from the instance. Given a vector of prices $p = (p_1, \dots, p_m)$, containing one price for each highway segment, denote by $W = \{j \in J \mid \sum_{i \in I_j} p_i \leq v_j\}$ the set of *winners*.

Definition 1. *The highway pricing problem asks for a vector of prices* $(p_1, \dots, p_m)$, *one for each segment of the highway, such that the total revenue* $\sum_{j \in W} \sum_{i \in I_j} p_i$ *extracted from the set* W *of winners is maximal.*

1.1 Related Work

The complexity of the highway problem was left open in [9], but it was shown weakly NP-hard by Briest and Krysta [2]. A more recent paper claims strong NP-hardness [4]. Guruswami et al. [9] propose a polynomial time dynamic programming algorithm when the valuations are bounded by a constant, and a pseudo-polynomial time dynamic programming algorithm when the lengths of the sub-paths are bounded by a constant. Note that the problem can be interpreted as a bilevel linear program, and if either the price vector or the set of winners is known, the problem is polynomially solvable [7,9], even under the requirement of integral prices. Balcan and Blum [1] derive an $O(\log m)$-approximation algorithm for the highway problem, improving upon the previous $O(\log m + \log n)$-approximation of Guruswami et al. [9], where m is the number of highway segments and n is the number of customers. Under the monotonicity condition that the total price of any given path is no more than the total price of a longer path, Grigoriev et al. [8] show that a $O(\log B)$-approximation exists, where B is an upper bound on the valuations. Furthermore, Grigoriev et al. [7] derive an FPTAS, assuming that the maximum capacity of any segment of the highway is bounded by a constant. Finally, Elbassioni et al. [5] present a quasi-polynomial time approximation scheme for both the capacitated and uncapacitated version of the problem, thereby suggesting that a PTAS is likely to exist.

1.2 Motivation and Results

Intrigued by the gap between NP-hardness on the one hand, and only logarithmic polynomial-time approximation algorithms on the other hand, in this paper we interpret customers' valuations in such a way that we come a step closer towards understanding this complexity gap. To start with, let us make the following definition, illustrated also by Example 1 below.

Definition 2 (Inhomogeneity of valuations). *For any instance of the highway pricing problem, define* $\bar{v}_j = v_j / |I_j|$ *as the average (per segment) valuation of customer* j*, and define the inhomogeneity of valuations as*

$$\alpha = \max_{j,k \in J} \left\{ \frac{\bar{v}_j}{\bar{v}_k} \right\} .$$

Example 1. Figure 1 shows an example with three segments, $I = \{1, 2, 3\}$, and six customer requests $J = \{1, \ldots, 6\}$. The left part of this figure shows the underlying highway with its alternative roads and distances, and the right part shows the corresponding instance of the highway problem. The valuation for traveling from the start of segment k until the end of segment ℓ is denoted $v_{k,\ell}$. This instance has inhomogeneity $\alpha = 2$; comparing the valuations for $\{1, 2, 3\}$ and $\{2\}$.

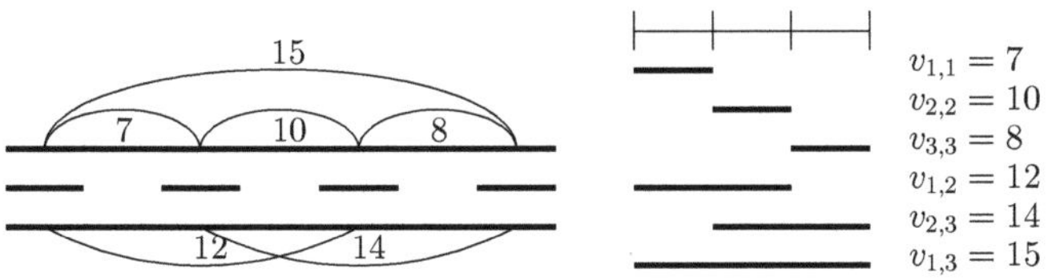

Fig. 1. An instance of the highway pricing problem

Notice that $\alpha \geq 1$, and that the problem becomes trivial as soon as the valuations are *homogeneous* (that is, $\alpha = 1$), since this corresponds to the case where all customers' valuations per segment are identical; see Section 2.

Our first result is to show that, in contrast to the trivially solvable homogeneous case, the problem with inhomogeneity of valuations is (weakly) NP-hard. While this does not sound very surprising, the main point is that this NP-hardness result holds even if the inhomogeneity α is bounded from above by any constant $1 + \varepsilon$. In some sense, we thereby delineate the borderline between triviality and NP-hardness for the highway pricing problem.

Furthermore, the NP-hardness result remains true even if we impose further restrictions on customers' valuations, such as monotonicity, that is,

$$v_j \leq v_k \qquad \text{for all } I_j \subseteq I_k \,,$$

and monotonicity of average valuations, that is,

$$\frac{v_j}{|I_j|} \geq (\leq, \text{resp.}) \, \frac{v_k}{|I_k|} \qquad \text{for all } I_j \subseteq I_k \,.$$

Our second result is a parametric approximation algorithm for the highway pricing problem that complements the NP-hardness result. The proposed algorithm has performance guarantee $O(\log \alpha)$ and computation time $O(n(\log n + m))$, where the constant hidden in the O-notation of the performance bound is not more than e. More specifically, it is easy to see that an α-approximation exists, and for large values of α we show how to improve this bound to $1 + \ln \alpha + \varepsilon$ for any $\varepsilon > 0$. Notice that this is a constant-factor approximation algorithm as soon as the inhomogeneity α of customers' valuations is bounded by some constant. We believe that such a constant bound is not unreasonable in practical applications, and note that $\alpha \leq m$ for the case of monotone and decreasing average valuations.

Finally, we briefly comment on the fact that the $O(\log \alpha)$ approximation result even holds for the more general bundle pricing problem where customers are interested in arbitrary bundles instead of sub-paths only. In this context, notice that if there exists any constant upper bound on the inhomogeneity α then the semi-logarithmic inapproximability result of Demaine et al. [3] for that problem is not longer valid. For that problem we also derive a (strong) NP-hardness result, again for any constant upper bound on the inhomogeneity of the valuations.

2 Complexity of the Highway Problem with Inhomogeneous Valuations

We start with the short argument that the highway problem with homogeneous average valuations is trivially solvable: consider the average valuation $\bar{v}$, which is, by homogeneity, the same for each customer, and define the price $p_i = \bar{v}$ for every segment $i \in I$. Clearly, each customer contributes her entire valuation to the revenue, and the obtained solution is optimal.

Surprisingly enough, even if we allow only arbitrarily small deviations of homogeneous valuations, the highway problem becomes intractable. The following theorem shows that the problem with inhomogeneous valuations remains NP-hard even in further restricted settings.

Theorem 1. *The highway problem is NP-hard even when restricted to the instances satisfying the following conditions:*

1. *the inhomogeneity $\alpha \leq 1 + \varepsilon$ where ε is an arbitrary positive constant;*
2. *customers valuations are monotone, i.e., $v_j \leq v_k$ for any $j, k \in J$ such that $I_j \subseteq I_k$;*
3. *customers average valuations are monotone decreasing, i.e., $\bar{v}_k \leq \bar{v}_j$ for any $j, k \in J$ such that $I_j \subseteq I_k$.*

Proof. The reduction is from the Partition problem, and extends an idea by Briest and Krysta [2]. Partition: Given integers $a_1, \ldots, a_{2L}$ and A, does there exist a set $S \subseteq \{1, \ldots, 2L\}$ such that $\sum_{\ell \in S} a_\ell = \sum_{\ell \notin S} a_\ell = A$? This problem is known to be NP-hard, even under the additional restriction that $|S| = L$; see [6]. We may assume that $L > 3/\varepsilon$, for otherwise Partition is solvable in polynomial time. Without loss of generality, we also assume that $0 \leq a_1 \leq \ldots \leq a_{2L}$ and $a_\ell \leq A$ for all $\ell = 1, \ldots, 2L$. Let $a'_\ell = a_\ell + (4L + 2)A$ for all $\ell = 1, \ldots, 2L$, and $A' = (4L^2 + 2L + 1)A$. Note that $\sum_{\ell=1}^{2L} a'_\ell = 2A'$.

We now create an instance $\mathcal{H}$ of the highway problem with $7L + 3$ segments combined in *gadgets*. Gadget $\ell = 1, \ldots, 2L$ contains two segments, $i = 2\ell - 1$ and $i = 2\ell$. Each of these two segments are requested by $2L - 1$ customers with valuation a'_ℓ. The combination of two segments, $2\ell - 1$ and 2ℓ, is requested by one customer with valuation $(2 - \frac{1}{L})a'_\ell$. Finally, gadget $2L + 1$ contains $3L + 3$ segments, where the first three segments, $4L+1, 4L+2, 4L+3$, are requested by one customer with valuation $\frac{12}{4L+3}A'$ and the last $3L$ segments, $4L+4, \ldots, 7L+3$, are requested by 3 customers with valuation $\frac{12L}{4L+3}A'$. All segments in gadget

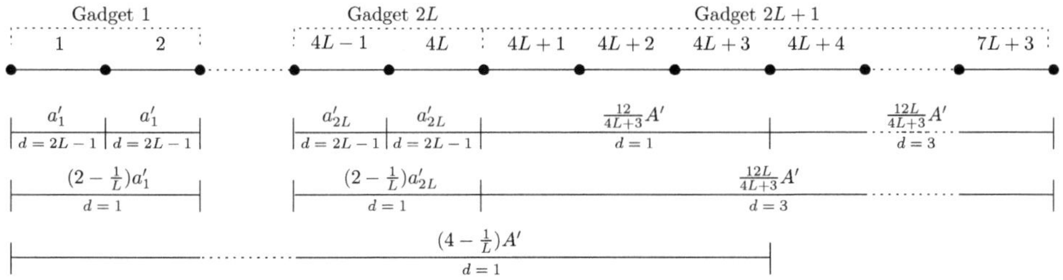

Fig. 2. Instance $\mathcal{H}$

$2L+1$ are also requested by 3 customers with valuation $\frac{12L}{4L+3}A'$. There is one *big* customer, who requests the first $4L+3$ items with valuation $(4-\frac{1}{L})A'$. Instance $\mathcal{H}$ is displayed in Figure 2, where the number of customers interested in a sub-path is presented by d.

Though it requires a quite extensive case study, one can straightforwardly verify that conditions (1)-(3) of Theorem 1 are satisfied. For the first condition, we have that $\alpha = 1 + O(1/L)$ implying that it can be upper bounded by $1+\varepsilon$ where ε is any positive constant.

Now we claim that there exists a feasible solution to PARTITION if and only if there is a feasible solution to instance $\mathcal{H}$ of the highway problem with a total revenue of at least $\left(8L + \frac{72L}{4L+3} - \frac{1}{L}\right)A'$.

($\Rightarrow$) Given a set $S \subseteq \{1,\dots,2L\}$ such that $\sum_{\ell\in S} a_\ell = \sum_{\ell\notin S} a_\ell = A$ and $|S| = L$. For all $\ell \in \{1,\dots,2L\}$, let $p_{2\ell-1} = p_{2\ell} = a'_\ell$ if $\ell \in S$ and $p_{2\ell-1} = p_{2\ell} = (1-\frac{1}{2L})a'_\ell$ if $\ell \notin S$. Furthermore, we set $p_{4L+1} = \dots = p_{7L+2} = 0$ and $p_{7L+3} = \frac{12L}{4L+3}A'$. Applying this price vector, the revenue without contribution of the big customer is equal to $(4L-2)a'_\ell$ in each gadget $\ell = 1,\dots,2L$. The big customer contributes her entire valuation $(4-\frac{1}{L})A'$. In gadget $2L+1$, the customer requesting segments $4L+1, 4L+2, 4L+3$ gets this path for free. The other customers in this gadget contribute their respective valuations. The total revenue generated with this pricing vector equals

$$(4L-2)\sum_{\ell=1}^{2L} a'_\ell + \left(4 - \frac{1}{L}\right)A' + 6\cdot\frac{12L}{4L+3}A' = \left(8L + \frac{72L}{4L+3} - \frac{1}{L}\right)A'.$$

($\Leftarrow$) Given is an optimal solution to instance $\mathcal{H}$ with a total revenue at least $(8L + \frac{72L}{4L+3} - \frac{1}{L})A'$. First, we observe that in such optimal solution, segments $4L+1, 4L+2, 4L+3$ are necessarily priced to 0 and the total price of the remaining segments in gadget $2L+1$ is $\frac{12L}{4L+3}A'$, yielding revenue $\frac{72L}{4L+3}A'$. To see this, we notice that the total demand on the first three segments in this gadget is 5 and on the latter $3L$ segments the demand is 6. Therefore, if the total price on the first three segments of gadget $2L+1$ is $0 < x \leq \frac{12}{4L+3}A'$, the total revenue obtained in the gadget is at most $\frac{72L}{4L+3} - x$, that is, we receive x from the big customer and at most $x + 3(\frac{12L}{4L+3}A' - x) + 3(\frac{12L}{4L+3}A')$ from the customers in gadget $2L+1$. The above suggested pricing does not decrease revenue generated in gadgets $1, \ldots, 2L$, and generates the total revenue in gadget $2L+1$ equal to $\frac{72L}{4L+3}$.

Second, in the optimal solution to the highway problem, there could be only two alternative pricing strategies in gadgets $\ell = 1, \ldots, 2L$: either $p_{2\ell-1} = p_{2\ell} = a'_\ell$ or $p_{2\ell-1} + p_{2\ell} = (2 - \frac{1}{L})a'_\ell$, where both prices do not exceed a'_ℓ. In both realizations, the contribution of the gadget (without big customer) to the total revenue is $(4L-2)a'_\ell$. Therefore, in the optimal solution to instance $\mathcal{H}$ with revenue at least $(8L + \frac{72L}{4L+3} - \frac{1}{L})A'$, the big customer must contribute her entire valuation. This amount is to be spent in the first $4L$ segments as the price of segments $4L+1, 4L+2$ and $4L+3$ is set to 0.

Define set $S = \{\ell \in \{1, \ldots, 2L\} : p_{2\ell-1} = p_{2\ell} = a'_\ell\}$. The payment of the big customer is $\sum_{\ell \in S} 2a'_\ell + \sum_{\ell \notin S}(2 - 1/L)a'_\ell$. As this must be equal to the valuation of the big customer, we have $\sum_{\ell \in S} a'_\ell = \sum_{\ell \notin S} a'_\ell = A'$ and consequently, $\sum_{\ell \in S} a_\ell = \sum_{\ell \notin S} a_\ell = A$. □

3 $O(\log \alpha)$-Approximation Algorithm

The idea for the approximation algorithm is as follows. We partition the set of customers J into $O(\ln \alpha)$ subsets $S_1, \ldots, S_K$, such that in each subset any two customers have average valuations different from each other by at most a constant factor $\delta > 1$. Denote by Π_k the maximum revenue for the highway problem restricted to the set of customers S_k (referred to as *S_k-restricted problem*). Then $\sum_{k=1}^{K} \Pi_k$ is clearly an upper bound for the optimum Π of the original problem. Therefore, the highest maximum revenue $\max_{k=1,\ldots,K} \Pi_k$ over all restricted problems is at least Π/K. Next, from the fact that the inhomogeneity of the average valuations in S_k is bounded by at most factor of δ, we derive that for the S_k-restricted problem there exists a price vector generating revenue at least Π_k/δ. Thus, taking the pricing vector yielding the highest revenue over all restricted problems, we generate a total revenue at least $\Pi/\delta K$. Finally, we optimize the performance guarantee over parameters K and δ.

To partition the set of customers J into subsets $S_1, \ldots, S_K$, we use the following recursive procedure running in K steps. At step $k = 1, \ldots, K$, we construct subset S_k. Consider the set of customers J_k not yet assigned to any of the subsets $S_1, \ldots, S_{k-1}$, assuming $J_1 = J$. Add all customers $j \in J_k$ to S_k for which $\bar{v}_j \leq \delta^k \bar{v}_{\min}$, where $\bar{v}_{\min} = \min_{j \in J}\{\bar{v}_j\}$ and $\delta > 1$ to be defined later. Set $J_{k+1} = J_k \setminus S_k$ and recurse on this set.

By definition of the inhomogeneity α, we have $\bar{v}_k \leq \alpha \bar{v}_j$ for every pair of customers $k, j \in J$. Then, by straightforward induction on k, one can prove that the ratio between the highest and the lowest average valuations in J_k is at most α/δ^{k-1}, yielding $K \leq 1 + \log_\delta \alpha = 1 + \ln \alpha / \ln \delta$. Thus, we derived the first ingredient of the approximation algorithm, formulated in the following lemma.

Lemma 1. *For any $\delta > 1$ the number of subsets K is at most $1 + \ln \alpha / \ln \delta$.*

Second, we show that there is a solution to the S_k-restricted problem such that (i) the set of winners $W = S_k$; and (ii) the revenue generated in this solution is at least Π_k/δ. Consider the pricing vector $p^k = (p_1^k, \ldots, p_m^k)$ where price p_i^k of segment $i \in I$ is determined as follows. Let $S_{ik} \subseteq S_k$ be the set of customers requesting segment i. If $S_{ik} = \emptyset$, then price p_i^k can be chosen arbitrarily. If $S_{ik} \neq \emptyset$, define $p_i^k = \min\{\bar{v}_j |\ j \in S_{ik}\}$. Now, consider a customer $j \in S_k$. By definition of price vector p^k, the price of sub-path I_j is $\sum_{i \in I_j} p_i^k \leq \sum_{i \in I_j} \bar{v}_j = v_j$, and therefore $j \in W$. By definition of set S_k, $\max_{j \in S_k} \bar{v}_j / \min_{j \in S_k} \bar{v}_j \leq \delta$, that yields the revenue of the solution is at least Π_k/δ. Thus, we proved the following lemma.

Lemma 2. *In the S_k-restricted problem, price vector p^k yields a revenue at least Π_k/δ.*

Clearly, the combination of Lemma 1 and Lemma 2 immediately implies that the total revenue generated by the best price vector p^* from $\{p^k |\ k = 1, \ldots, K\}$ is at least $\Pi/\delta(1 + \frac{\ln \alpha}{\ln \delta})$, which is maximized for $\delta = e^{\left(\frac{1}{2}+\sqrt{\frac{1}{4}+\frac{1}{\ln \alpha}}\right)^{-1}}$. Notice that for big α the value of δ is close to e. Therefore, we have the following result.

Theorem 2. *Price vector p^* yields a total revenue at least $\Pi/(e \ln \alpha + e)$ for the highway problem, where Π is the maximal revenue, and it can be computed in $O(n(\log n + m))$ time.*

We arrive at the computation time as follows. First, we order the customers according to their average valuation (increasingly), which takes $O(n \log n)$ time. Then, for all $k = 1, \ldots, K$, we use binary search to create set S_k in $O(\log n)$ time, and for all items $i = 1, \ldots, m$ we determine the set of customers that request the item in $O(n)$ time, and the item price and the revenue in constant time. So, the total runtime is $O(n \log n + K(\log n + nm))$, which is in $O(n(\log n + m))$, as K is a constant.

There are several directions for improvement of the obtained approximate solution to the highway problem. First, instead of the constructed price vectors p^k, $k = 1, \ldots, K$, we can use price vectors maximizing the revenue in the S_k-restricted problems, with given set of winners $W = S_k$. Notice that, for any set of winners $W \subseteq J$, the price vector maximizing the revenue obtained from W can be found in polynomial time by solving a simple linear program; see [7,9]. Unfortunately, this approach does not necessarily lead to any provable improvement of the performance guarantee.

The second approach allows us to improve the performance guarantee, and is based on more careful analysis of the revenue generated by price vector p^* when applied to the entire set J instead of S_k only. By construction of the partition of J, for any two subsets S_k and $S_{k'}$, $k \leq k'$, the average valuation of any customer from S_k is at most the average valuation of a customer from $S_{k'}$. Therefore, for any $k = 1, \ldots, K$, and for all $k' \geq k$, if $S_k \subseteq W$, then $S_{k'} \subseteq W$ as well. By definition of the subsets, the maximum average valuation in set S_{k+1} is at most δ times the maximum average valuation in set S_k. Thus, we have that the revenue generated by price vector p^k applied to the set of customers J is at least

$$R_k = \frac{1}{\delta}\Pi_k + \frac{1}{\delta^2}\Pi_{k+1} + \ldots + \frac{1}{\delta^{K-k+1}}\Pi_K, \quad \forall k = 1, \ldots, K.$$

These equalities can be equivalently represented by the following recurrent formulas

$$R_k = \frac{1}{\delta}\Pi_k + \frac{1}{\delta}R_{k+1}, \quad \forall k = 1, \ldots, K-1, \tag{1}$$

with an additional equality

$$R_K = \frac{1}{\delta}\Pi_K. \tag{2}$$

Summing up all Equations (1) and (2) and dividing both sides by K, we derive

$$\bar{R} = \frac{1}{K}\sum_{k=1}^{K} R_k = \frac{1}{K\delta}\sum_{k=1}^{K}\Pi_k + \frac{1}{K\delta}\sum_{k=1}^{K} R_k - \frac{1}{K\delta}R_1.$$

Let $R_1 = \phi\bar{R}$. Since $\sum_{k=1}^{K}\Pi_k \geq \Pi$, we derive

$$\bar{R} \geq \frac{\Pi}{K(\delta-1)+\phi}.$$

Taking the maximum revenue over all price vectors $p^k, k = 1, \ldots, K$, we obtain

$$\max_{k=1,\ldots,K} R_k \geq \max\{R_1, \bar{R}\} \geq \max\left\{\frac{\phi\Pi}{K(\delta-1)+\phi}, \frac{\Pi}{K(\delta-1)+\phi}\right\},$$

that is minimized with $\phi = 1$, yielding

$$\max_{k=1,\ldots,K} R_k \geq \frac{\Pi}{\delta(1+\frac{\ln\alpha}{\ln\delta}) - \frac{\ln\alpha}{\ln\delta}}.$$

Clearly, price vector p^* yields a total revenue at least $\Pi/(\delta(1+\frac{\ln\alpha}{\ln\delta}) - \frac{\ln\alpha}{\ln\delta})$. Note that $\delta(1+\frac{\ln\alpha}{\ln\delta}) - \frac{\ln\alpha}{\ln\delta} < \delta\ln\alpha + \delta$. Given $\varepsilon > 0$, let $\delta = 1 + \varepsilon/(\ln\alpha + 1)$. Then,

$$\delta\ln\alpha + \delta = \left(1 + \frac{\varepsilon}{\ln\alpha+1}\right)\ln\alpha + \left(1 + \frac{\varepsilon}{\ln\alpha+1}\right) = 1 + \ln\alpha + \varepsilon,$$

and we arrive at the following theorem.

Theorem 3 (Improved Bound). *Price vector p^* yields a total revenue at least $\Pi/(1+\ln\alpha+\varepsilon)$ for the highway problem for any $\varepsilon > 0$, and it can be computed in $O(n(\log n + m))$ time.*

4 General Bundle Pricing

As a matter of fact, in all arguments developed in the previous sections, we did not make use of the fact that the subsets I_j requested by customers are sub-paths of a path. Hence, the results hold for the more general bundle pricing problem where customers request arbitrary subsets of a given set of items, each of which available in unlimited supply (digital goods, for example). This problem is in general known to be inapproximable by a semi-logarithmic factor in the number of customers n [3]. This inapproximablity result is no longer valid as soon as the inhomogeneity is bounded by a constant, since we have:

Corollary 1. *Given $\varepsilon > 0$, the bundle pricing problem admits an approximation algorithm that yields a revenue at least $(1+\ln\alpha+\varepsilon)^{-1}$ times the optimal revenue, with computation time $O(n(\log n + m))$.*

For this problem, we can even derive a stronger negative result than for the more restrictive highway pricing problem.

Theorem 4. *The bundle pricing problem is strongly NP-hard, even when restricted to the instances satisfying the following conditions:*

1. *the inhomogeneity $\alpha \leq 1+\varepsilon$ where ε is an arbitrary positive constant;*
2. *customers valuations are monotone, i.e., $v_j \leq v_k$ for any $j,k \in J$ such that $I_j \subseteq I_k$;*
3. *customers average valuations are monotone decreasing, i.e., $\bar{v}_k \leq \bar{v}_j$ for any $j,k \in J$ such that $I_j \subseteq I_k$.*

Proof. We show that the bundle pricing problem is strongly NP-hard by using a reduction from the strongly NP-hard problem IndependentSet [6]. Given a graph $G = (V,E)$ and integer $s \leq |V|$. Does there exist a set of vertices that are pairwise non-adjacent with cardinality at least s. We define an instance $\mathcal{I}$ of the pricing problem as follows. Given an $\varepsilon > 0$, let $M > \max\{1/\varepsilon, s+1/2\}$. For every vertex $v \in V$ we create two *vertex-items*, v^1 and v^2, and for every edge $e \in E$ we introduce two *edge-items*, e^1 and e^2. Every vertex- and edge-item is requested by $2M^2+2M-1$ customers with valuation $M+1$. For every vertex $v \in V$, there is one customer interested in bundle $\{v^1,v^2\}$ and similarly, for every edge $e \in E$, there is one customer interested in bundle $\{e^1,e^2\}$. These customers have valuation $2M+2-1/M$. There is one customer interested in item x with valuation $M+1$, and there are 2 customers interested in bundle y of size M with valuation M^2. Also, there are two customers requesting bundle $\{x,y\}$ (of size $M+1$) with valuation M^2+M. Then, for every edge $e=\{u,v\} \in E$, there is one customer interested in bundle $\{u^1,u^2,v^1,v^2,e^1,e^2\} \cup \{x\}$ with valuation $7M+6-2/M$. One customer requests all vertex items and item x, that is, bundle $\{v^1,v^2 : v \in V\} \cup \{x\}$, with valuation $(2M+2-1/M)|V| + M + (1/M)s$. The instance is displayed in Figure 3.

Let us give a short intuition as to why we need these particular bundles. The bundles on the vertex- and edge-items determine which vertices are in the independent set of G and bundles $\{u^1,u^2,v^1,v^2,e^1,e^2\} \cup \{x\}$ assure later that a feasible solution to the general bundle pricing problem corresponds to an independent set in G. Bundle $\{v^1,v^2 : v \in V\} \cup \{x\}$ assures that a feasible solution to the pricing problem corresponds to an independent set of cardinality s. Finally, bundles $\{x\}$, $\{y\}$ and $\{x,y\}$ are present to fulfill the conditions required in this theorem.

The single-item bundles have the largest average valuation of $M+1$, and bundles $\{y\}$ and $\{x,y\}$ have the smallest average valuation of M, thus $\alpha = 1+1/M < 1+\varepsilon$. Though it requires an extensive case study, one can straightforwardly verify that conditions (2) and (3) are also satisfied.

We define π_i as the revenue obtained from the customers requesting a bundle from set $\{i^1,i^2,\{i^1,i^2\}\}$ for all $i \in I = V \cup E$. We define π_e as the revenue from

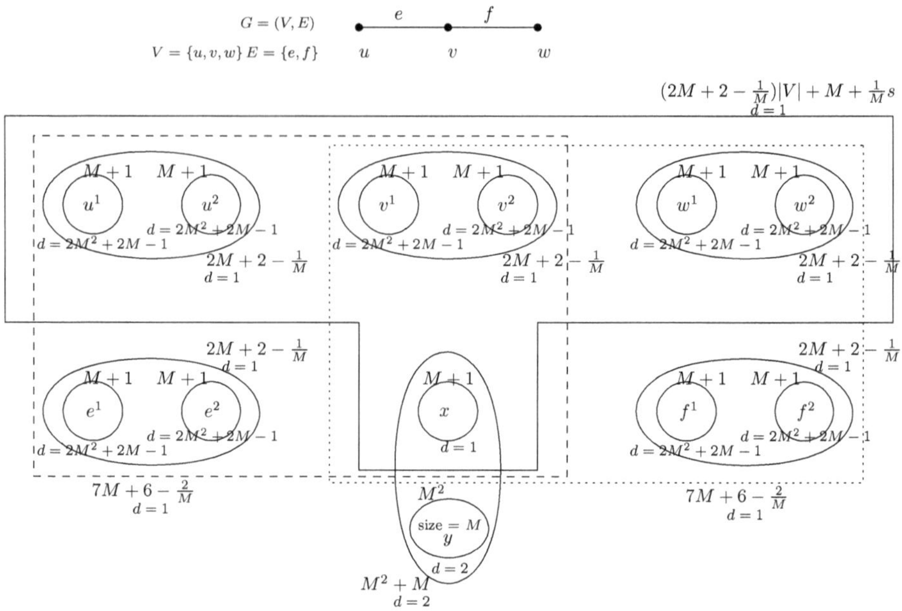

Fig. 3. An instance of the bundle pricing problem created from original graph G above

the customers requesting $\{u^1, u^2, v^1, v^2, e^1, e^2\} \cup \{x\}$ for some $e = \{u, v\} \in E$. We define π_{xy} as the revenue received from customers requesting a bundle from set $\{x, y, \{x, y\}\}$, and finally, π_V represents the revenue obtained from the customer requesting $\{v^1, v^2 : v \in V\} \cup \{x\}$. Obviously, the total revenue is $\pi = \sum_{i\in I} \pi_i + \sum_{e\in E} \pi_e + \pi_{xy} + \pi_V$. Also, let C be a constant equal to $(|V| + |E|)(4M^3 + 8M^2 + 2M - 2)| + |E|(7M + 6 - 2/M) + 4M^2 + 4M$. We claim that there exists an independent set in G of size s if and only if there exists a solution to the general bundle pricing problem with revenue at least $C + s/M$.

Given an independent set $V' \subseteq V$ of size $|V'| = s$. Define $E_0 = \{e = \{u, v\} \in E : u, v \notin V'\}$. Let $p_i = (p_{i^1}, p_{i^2})$ be defined by $p_i = (M + 1, M + 1)$ if $i \in V \cap V'$ or $i \in E \cap E_0$ and $p_i = (M + 1 - \frac{1}{2M}, M + 1 - \frac{1}{2M})$ if $i \in V \setminus V'$ or $i \in E \setminus E_0$. Also, let $p_x = M$ and $p_y = M^2$, where p_y denotes the sum of all M item prices in bundle $\{y\}$. Under this pricing strategy, we see that $\pi_i = 4M^3 + 8M^2 + 2M - 2$ for all $i \in I = V \cup E$, irrespective of which pricing is used for item i. Then, every edge $e = \{u, v\} \in E$ contains one item priced at $(M + 1, M + 1)$ and two at $(M + 1 - \frac{1}{2M}, M + 1 - \frac{1}{2M})$ by definition of the pricing and set E_0. As $p_x = M$, we have $\pi_e = 2(M + 1) + 4(M + 1 - \frac{1}{2M}) + M = 7M + 6 - 2/M$. The customer requesting all vertex-items and item x spends $(2M+2-1/M)|V \setminus V'| + (2M+2)|V'| + p_x = (2M+2-1/M)|V| + M + (1/M)s$. Then, the total revenue is $\pi = (|V| + |E|)\pi_i + |E|\pi_e + \pi_{xy} + \pi_V = C + (1/M)s$.

For the converse, we are given a solution to instance $\mathcal{I}$ with revenue at least $C + (1/M)s$. First, we consider π_{xy}. If the customer requesting bundle $\{x, y\}$ is not a winner, the maximum revenue is $M + 1 + 2M^2$. Otherwise, let p_x be the price for item x. Then, the maximum revenue is $p_x + 2(M^2 + M - p_x) + (M^2 + M)$, where $p_x \in [M, M+1]$ such that all customers are winners. Then, $\pi_{xy} \leq 4M^2 + 3M$ (attained when $p_x = M$). For every item $i \in I$, we have $\pi_i = \max\{2(2M^2+2M-1)(M+1), (2M^2+2M-1+1)(2M+2-1/M)\}$. Both values are equal and therefore, $\pi_i = 4M^3 + 8M^2 + 2M - 2$. Clearly, for every $e \in E$, the revenue π_e is at most the valuation $7M + 6 - 2/M$. Now, we know that the revenue from the customer requesting bundle $\{v^1, v^2 : v \in V\} \cup \{x\}$ is

$$\pi_V = \pi - (|V| + |E|)\pi_i - |E|\pi_e - \pi_{xy} \geq (2M + 2 - 1/M)|V| + M + (1/M)s.$$

Thus, the minimum revenue is at least equal to the valuation. As this customer cannot contribute more than the valuation, it should be equality throughout. This also means that all other revenues described above attain their maximum, thus $p_x = M$ and $p_y = M^2$. Now, let $V' = \{v \in V : p_v = (M+1, M+1)\}$ and $E_0 = \{e \in E : p_e = (M+1, M+1)\}$. As $\pi_e = 7M+6-2/M$ and $p_x = M$ for all $e = \{u, v\} \in E$, we know that either $u \in V'$ and $v \notin V'$, $e \notin E_0$, or $v \in V'$ and $u \notin V'$, $e \notin E_0$, or $e \in E_0$ and $u, v \notin V'$. Thus, for each edge, either one vertex is in V' or both are not in. Hence, V' is an independent set. Furthermore, the customer requesting bundle $\{v^1, v^2 : v \in V\} \cup \{x\}$ pays

$$(2M+2-1/M)|V \setminus V'| + (2M+2)|V'| + p_x = (2M+2-1/M)|V| + M + (1/M)|V'|.$$

As this payment is equal to the revenue, which in turn has to be equal to the valuation, we know that $|V'| = s$. □

5 Conclusions

Clearly, the existence of a quasi-PTAS for the highway pricing problem suggests that a PTAS might be in reach [4,5]. Yet, we leave it as an open problem to derive a PTAS, even for bounded inhomogeneity of valuations.

References

1. Balcan, M.F., Blum, A.: Approximation Algorithms and Online Mechanisms for Item Pricing. In: Proceedings of the 7th ACM Conference on Electronic Commerce, pp. 29–35. ACM, New York (2006)
2. Briest, P., Krysta, P.: Single-Minded Unlimited Supply Pricing on Sparse Instances. In: Proceedings of the 17th Annual ACM-SIAM Symposium on Discrete Algorithms, pp. 1093–1102. ACM-SIAM (2006)
3. Demaine, E.D., Feige, U., Hajiaghayi, M.T., Salavatipour, M.R.: Combination Can Be Hard: Approximability of the Unique Coverage Problem. In: Proceedings of the 17th Annual ACM-SIAM Symposium on Discrete Algorithms, pp. 162–171. ACM-SIAM (2006)
4. Elbassioni, K., Raman, R., Ray, S., Sitters, R.: On Profit-Maximizing Pricing for the Highway and Tollbooth Problems. Retrieved from arXiv:0901.1140v3 (June 2009)
5. Elbassioni, K., Sitters, R., Zhang, Y.: A Quasi-PTAS for Profit-Maximizing Pricing on Line Graphs. In: Arge, L., Hoffmann, M., Welzl, E. (eds.) ESA 2007. LNCS, vol. 4698, pp. 451–462. Springer, Heidelberg (2007)

6. Garey, M.R., Johnson, D.S.: Computers and Intractability: a Quide to the Theory of NP-Completeness. W.H. Freeman, New York (1979)
7. Grigoriev, A., van Loon, J., Sitters, R., Uetz, M.: Optimal Pricing of Capacitated Networks. Networks 53(1), 79–87 (2009)
8. Grigoriev, A., van Loon, J., Sviridenko, M., Uetz, M., Vredeveld, T.: Bundle Pricing with Comparable Items. In: Arge, L., Hoffmann, M., Welzl, E. (eds.) ESA 2007. LNCS, vol. 4698, pp. 475–486. Springer, Heidelberg (2007)
9. Guruswami, V., Hartline, J.D., Karlin, A.R., Kempe, D., Kenyon, C., McSherry, F.: On Profit-Maximizing Envy-Free Pricing. In: Proceedings of the 16th Annual ACM-SIAM Symposium on Discrete Algorithms, pp. 1164–1173. ACM-SIAM (2005)

Accelerating Smart Play-Out*

David Harel[1], Hillel Kugler[2], Shahar Maoz[1], and Itai Segall[1]

[1] The Weizmann Institute of Science, Israel
{dharel,shahar.maoz,itai.segall}@weizmann.ac.il
[2] Microsoft Research, Cambridge, UK
hkugler@microsoft.com

Abstract. Smart play-out is a method for executing declarative scenario-based specifications, which utilizes powerful computation methods to compute safe supersteps, thus helping to avoid violations that may be caused by naïve execution. Major challenges for smart play-out are performance and scalability. In this work we show how to accelerate smart play-out by adapting and applying ideas inspired by formal verification and compiler optimization. Specifically, we present an algorithm that can reduce the size of the specification considered for smart play-out, while maintaining soundness and completeness. Experimental results show significant performance improvements and thus open the way to the application of smart play-out to large scenario-based programs.

1 Introduction

Scenario-based modeling using various variants of sequence diagrams has attracted intensive research efforts in recent years (see, e.g., [1,2,3,4,5]). In this paper, we focus on the language of *live sequence charts* (LSC), which has been suggested in [3] as a highly expressive extension of message sequence charts (MSCs) [6]. LSC has been endowed with an operational semantics termed *play-out*, where a specification consisting of a set of charts is executed directly [4]. In the original play-out algorithm, non-determinism is solved ad-hoc without considering the future effects of its choices. To help alleviate this, *smart play-out* was proposed in [7], where formal reasoning (originally, model-checking) is used to compute safe execution paths. In [8] we prove smart play-out to be PSPACE-hard for the general case, and NP-hard if multiple copies of the same chart are not allowed.

In this paper we introduce an algorithm that accelerates smart play-out of scenario-based specifications. The algorithm exploits special syntactic and semantic properties of the language in order to reduce the size of the specification

* This research was partially supported by the John von Neumann Minerva Center for the Development of Reactive Systems at the Weizmann Institute of Science, and by an Advanced Research Grant from the European Research Council (ERC) under the European Community's 7th Framework Programme (FP7/2007-2013).

J. van Leeuwen et al. (Eds.): SOFSEM 2010, LNCS 5901, pp. 477–488, 2010.

before smart play-out is computed. It consists of several steps, each aimed at identifying different types of constructs that may be temporarily removed from the specification without affecting correctness. First, entire charts are removed in a cone-of-influence-like iterative fixpoint algorithm [9], computing a safe approximation (an over approximation) of the set of charts that may influence the current computation. Second, constructs within the remaining LSCs are precomputed or eliminated using an approach inspired by compiler optimization methods, such as constant propagation and early evaluation. All these result in an overall smaller specification that is then used as the input for the smart play-out computation.

The algorithm takes advantage of the following typical features of LSC specifications. First, the breakdown of the specification into user-friendly intuitive scenarios often creates redundancies that can be removed without affecting the execution. Second, intentional under-specification can sometimes be abstracted away from the smart play-out mechanism and be left for the naïve implementation. Third, the execution paths we are looking for are typically rather short and local, involving only a subset of the specification, especially in large systems. Finally, the specification may be exponentially more succinct than the state space of the model it induces; we benefit from attacking the problem already at the level of the specification, before the input model for smart play-out is constructed.

Our work can be viewed as an adaptation and application of well-known program analysis and abstraction techniques from the domains of compiler optimization and formal verification to our specific need, which is the acceleration of smart execution of scenario-based specifications.

A technical report with additional details and proofs is available [10].

2 Preliminaries

LSC [3] is an extension of message sequence charts (MSC) [6]. Both contain vertical lines, termed *lifelines*, which denote objects, and *events*, which involve one or more of these objects. The most basic construct of the language are messages: a message is denoted by an arrow between two lifelines (or from a lifeline to itself), representing the event of the source object sending a message to the target object. More advanced constructs, like conditions, `if-then-else`, loops, etc., can also be expressed. A typical LSC consists of a prechart (denoted by a blue dashed hexagon), and a main chart (denoted by a solid frame). Roughly, the intended semantics is that whenever the prechart is satisfied in a run of the system, eventually the main chart must also be satisfied (see Fig. 1).

LSCs are multi-modal; almost any construct in the language can be either *cold* (usually denoted by the color blue) or *hot* (denoted by red), with a semantics of "may happen" or "must happen", respectively. If a cold element is violated (say a condition that is not true when reached), this is considered a legal behavior and some appropriate action is taken. Violation of a hot element, however, is considered a violation of the specification and is not allowed to happen in an execution.

2.1 An Example

An example specification, consisting of six LSCs, is given in Fig. 1. It describes a simple telephone system with three objects – a phone, an operator, and a logger. The operator may wish to force low-priority calls to disconnect (e.g., due to a system overload). The LSC `HangupAllLowPri`, in Fig. 1(a), refers to the operator notifying the phone that a low-priority hangup is called for. Specifically, the LSC states that if the phone sends the message `InCall` to the operator, and the operator sends `HangupLowPri` to itself, then the operator sends `HangupLowPri` to the phone.

Fig. 1(b) shows LSC `CheckPri`, where the phone checks whether it is in a low-priority mode. The LSC uses an if-then-else construct, represented by two sequential boxes, with a condition at the beginning of the first box. It states that if the message `HangupLowPri` is sent from the operator to the phone (note that this is the same message sent in the main chart of the previous LSC; the process of deciding at runtime that the messages are the same is termed *unification*), then if the property *LowPri* of the telephone is true, it should send `hangup` to itself. Otherwise, it sends `NoLowPri` to the operator, and the operator replies with an `Ack`.

Fig. 1(c) shows LSC `Hangup`, which describes the hangup process. It states that whenever the phone sends `Hangup` to itself, it sends `StartHangup` to the logger, then sends `InCall(False)` to itself, and `CallTime(0)` to itself. The logger also sends `LogHangup` to itself. Finally, the phone sends `EndHangup` to the logger. Two features worth noting in this LSC are the following: (1) The partial order of an LSC is defined by the lifelines (from top to bottom) and the messages (and other multi-lifeline constructs) that synchronize between lifelines. Therefore, in this example, no explicit order is defined between the `LogHangup` message and the two messages `InCall(False)` and `CallTime(0)`, while these two must be executed in this order. The message `EndHangup`, appearing on both lifelines, is executed last. (2) Some messages change object properties. For example, `InCall(False)` changes the property *InCall* of the phone to be false. Similarly, `CallTime(0)` sets $Tel1.CallTime$ to be 0.

The LSC `Logger`, in Fig. 1(d), specifies how the logger replies to the telephone: If the phone sends `StartHangup` to the logger, the *Logger.On* condition is checked. If it is true, the execution continues, and the logger sends `Ack` to the phone. If the *Logger.On* is false, then being a cold condition, the chart exits gracefully and the `Ack` is not sent. The LSC `NotifyHangup`, in Fig. 1(e), specifies the notification to the operator that the hangup has completed. Finally, the LSC `CorrectLogging`, given in Fig. 1(f), is an anti-scenario; it states that the scenario in which the three messages, `StartHangup` from the phone to the logger, `EndHangup` from the phone to the logger, and `Ack` from the logger to the phone, are sent in this order is forbidden.

Throughout the paper, we consider a generalization of this example specification, for n phones, in which the six LSCs are replicated n times. In replica i, the object Tel1 is replaced by Tel$i$. Note that LSCs, in general, support symbolic instances (lifelines that represent entire classes rather than concrete objects), with

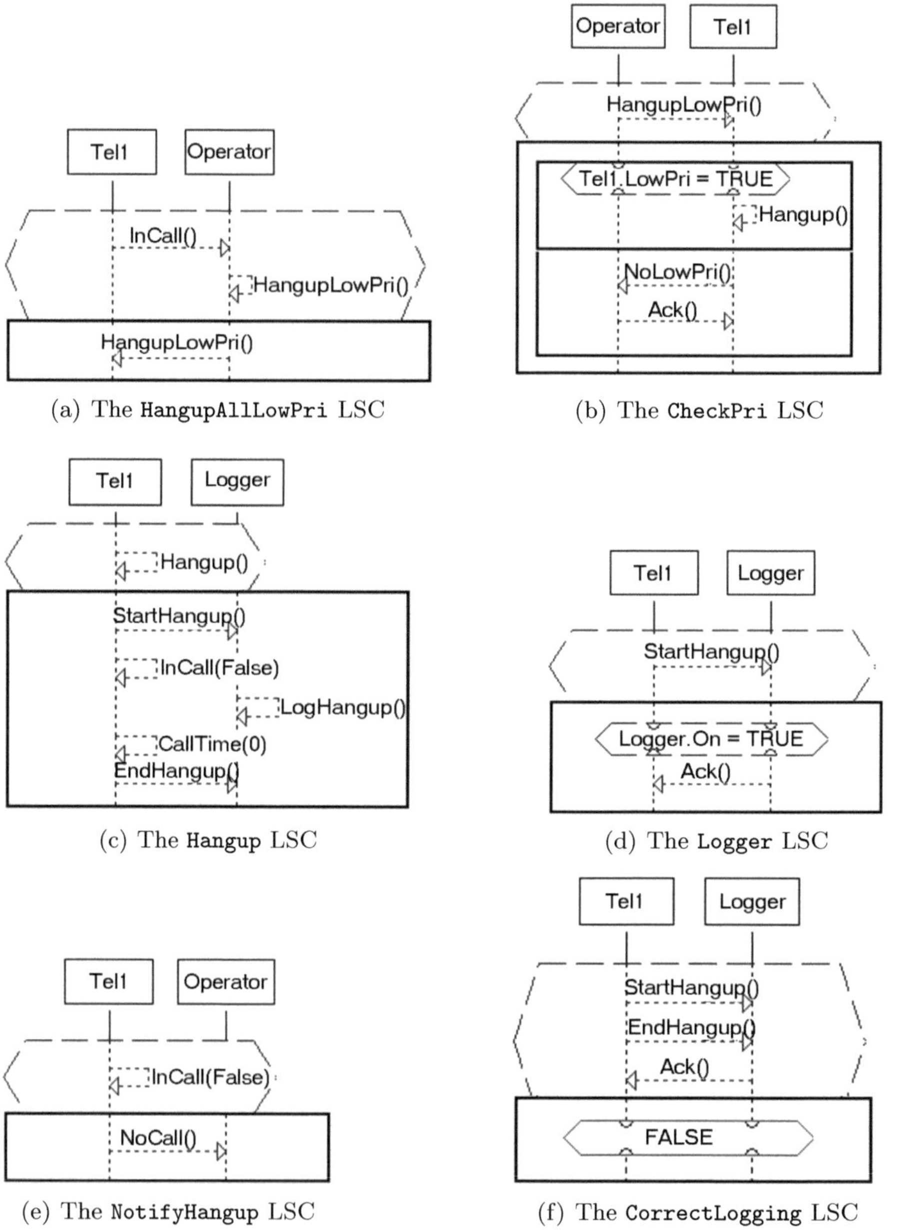

(a) The `HangupAllLowPri` LSC

(b) The `CheckPri` LSC

(c) The `Hangup` LSC

(d) The `Logger` LSC

(e) The `NotifyHangup` LSC

(f) The `CorrectLogging` LSC

Fig. 1. A 6-LSC specification for a simple phone system in which the operator may decide to hang up low priority calls which this replication could have been avoided [4]. However, since as of now none of the currently known smart play-out implementations supports symbolic instances, we avoid using them in this paper.

2.2 Play-Out

An operational semantics and an execution technique termed *play-out* were defined for the LSC language in [4]. Play-out remembers at each point in time the set of *active* LSCs (those for which the prechart has already completed, but the main chart hasn't), and for each such LSC it holds the current *cut* (listing what has already happened, and what has not). At each step, the play-out mechanism chooses one message that is *enabled* in some LSC (i.e., it appears directly after the current cut), and does not violate any other chart (a message is violating if it appears in an active chart but is not enabled in it), and executes it.

The original play-out mechanism of [4] is naïve, in the sense that there is no look-ahead when selecting the action to be executed. Thus, non-determinism is solved ad-hoc without considering the long-term consequences of the choice. Two "smart" techniques have been suggested thus far to partly address this issue: (1) model-checking based play-out, termed *smart play-out* [7], and (2) AI planning-based play-out, termed *planned play-out* [11]. In this paper we use the term *smart play-out* to refer to the general idea of smart look-ahead execution of scenario-based programs, and not only to the specific model-checking based implementation thereof.

While naïve play-out chooses its steps one by one, smart play-out reacts to an external event by seeking a sequence of system events that drive the specification to completion. The problem of smart play-out can be defined as follows: given a specification and a current configuration (the set of current cuts, together with the current state of all objects and variables), find a sequence of legal steps that lead the system to a stable state, i.e., one in which no main charts remain active. This sequence of steps is termed a *superstep*. Both known smart play-out implementations solve this by reduction: they translate a given specification and configuration into a model, and then use powerful computational methods (model-checking or planning) in order to find an appropriate path in this model. When found, such a path is translated back into a superstep in the original specification. The model created by both algorithms is proportional in size to that of the LSC specification, which refers to the number of lifeline locations in it. Thus, any reduction in the size of the LSC specification fed to a smart play-out algorithm will yield a smaller model created by them, which in turn may result in better running time.

3 Accelerating Smart Play-Out

We now show how to reduce the size of the specification before smart play-out is computed, by exploiting the special structure of LSCs, and details of its operational semantics. Our algorithm identifies constructs that are either irrelevant to the current superstep, or are unnecessary input for smart play-out.

These constructs are then temporarily removed from the specification.

The algorithm consists of four steps. The first three are performed iteratively, until a fixpoint is reached, and then the last one is applied; see Fig. 2. Intuitively, *Activation Closure* detects charts that cannot participate in the superstep, *Early Evaluation* pre-evaluates conditions and assignments whenever possible, *Unreachable Elimination* removes superfluous unreachable constructs, and finally *Construct Elimination* eliminates constructs for which no reasoning is needed to order them correctly during execution of the superstep. Note that each step acts on the result of the previous steps, which will, in general, be a smaller specification. Thus, for example, a construct that is reachable in the original specification may become unreachable by some early evaluation, and will be removed by later steps.

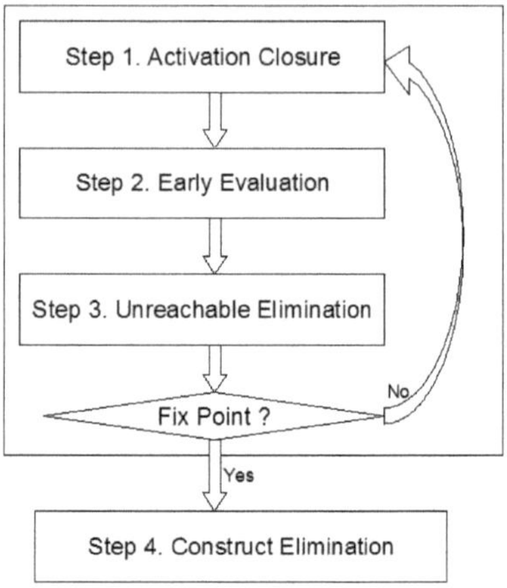

Fig. 2. An overview of the acceleration algorithm

3.1 The Example

We refer here to the example from Fig. 1, expanded to support three phones by replicating all six LSCs three times, and replacing the Tel1 object with Tel1, Tel2, and Tel3 in each replica. We denote the copy number of each LSC by a subscript (e.g., $\texttt{Hangup}_1$ denotes the Tel1 copy of LSC `Hangup`). Also, we denote the event of object o_1 sending message `msg` to object o_2 by $o_1 \xrightarrow{\texttt{msg}} o_2$.

We consider the following initial configuration: Phone 1 is in a low priority call (i.e., the message `InCall` was sent from Tel1 to Operator, and $Tel1.LowPri$ is true). Phone 2 is in a high priority call (i.e., the message `InCall` was sent from Tel2 to Operator, and $Tel2.LowPri$ is false). Phone 3 is not in a call (i.e., the message `InCall` was never sent from Tel3 to the Operator).

Now, suppose the operator decides it must hang up all low priority calls, i.e., the message `HangupLowPri` is sent from the operator to itself. At this point some main charts become active, and smart play-out starts. The initial configuration is as follows: two main charts are active – $\texttt{HangupAllLowPri}_1$ and $\texttt{HangupAllLowPri}_2$ – and all other charts are closed. Recall that $Tel1.LowPri$ is true and $Tel2.LowPri$ is false. Also assume that *Logger.on* is true.

3.2 Activation Closure

Consider the message $Operator \xrightarrow{\texttt{HangupLowPri}} Operator$ in the example. It does not appear in any main chart, and therefore will never be sent again throughout the superstep. Since LSC $\texttt{HangupAllLowPri}_3$ is not active, we can conclude that it will never become active in the superstep (as one of its prechart messages will not be sent). Therefore this LSC can be safely removed from the specification. Now we know that *Operator* $\xrightarrow{\texttt{HangupLowPri}}$ *Tel*3 will not be sent, since it appears in no main chart of the remaining specification, and hence $\texttt{CheckPri}_3$ can be removed.

The *Activation Closure* step removes from the specification LSCs that can not become active in the superstep by computing the least fixpoint of LSCs, such that for every LSC in the activation closure, each message in its prechart appears in some main chart in the closure (regardless of their order in the prechart).

We ignore here the case where advanced constructs such as `if-then-else`, appear in the prechart. To adapt the method to the more general case, one needs to add an LSC to the activation closure not only if its entire prechart is contained in the set of possible messages, but even if some set of messages that could satisfy the prechart is contained in it.

3.3 Early Evaluation

Now consider phones 1 and 2. Their value of *LowPri* cannot change throughout the superstep (there is no main chart message that changes them in the specification). Therefore, the condition of the `if-then-else` construct in $\texttt{CheckPri}_1$ and $\texttt{CheckPri}_2$ can be evaluated in advance. This will be carried out by the *Early Evaluation* step.

More generally, the *Early Evaluation* step locates properties that will not be changed during any superstep, and pre-evaluates all conditions and assignments that use their value. This step does not affect the set of legal supersteps.

3.4 Unreachable Elimination

Following the early evaluation of conditions, some parts of the LSC may become unreachable. In our example, the “else” part in $\texttt{CheckPri}_1$ and the “if” part in $\texttt{CheckPri}_2$ are both unreachable now, and can be removed. This will be done by the *Unreachable Elimination* step.

Note that even if a message is unreachable in one LSC, it may be executed by another chart, so that unreachable messages can still cause chart violations if executed when not enabled, and one needs to take extra care when eliminating messages. Therefore, we eliminate a message only if all its appearances in main charts are unreachable. To avoid changing the partial order of the LSC, eliminated constructs are replaced by an appropriate synchronization construct (a constant true condition covering the relevant lifelines). The *Unreachable Elimination* step does not affect the set of legal supersteps.

3.5 Repeating Steps 1-3

Applying the steps on the example as above may lead to the conclusion that *Tel*2 $\xrightarrow{\texttt{Hangup}}$ *Tel*2 will not be sent. Therefore by rerunning *Activation Closure* we can conclude that $\texttt{Hangup}_2$, for example, can now also be removed. This illustrates why the first three steps are executed repeatedly until a fixpoint is reached.

In general, the set of messages appearing in main charts of the *Activation Closure* dictates which properties may be modified in the superstep, thus affecting the *Early Evaluation* and *Unreachable Elimination* steps. In turn, those steps affect the *Activation Closure* computation, by removing messages from the charts. Therefore, the three steps need to be computed iteratively until a (greatest) fixpoint is reached.

Since each step removes only elements (or entire LSCs) that will never take part in any superstep and does not change the set of legal supersteps, the same applies to the repeated execution.

Note that in our example, *Activation Closure* is exact; all LSCs in the final specification will take part in the superstep. In the general case, this is not necessarily true. *Activation Closure* calculates a safe approximation of the set of LSCs that may participate in the execution, and not necessarily the exact set.

3.6 Construct Elimination

All steps mentioned so far eliminate constructs that cannot participate in the superstep. The purpose of the *Construct Elimination* step is to identify (and eliminate) constructs that may participate in the superstep, but for which the exact timing is not important.

For example, consider the message $Logger \xrightarrow{\texttt{LogHangup}} Logger$. It appears in one main chart only, $\texttt{Hangup}_1$ (we have already removed $\texttt{Hangup}_2$ and $\texttt{Hangup}_3$), and does not change any object property. Therefore, there is no real need for smart evaluation in determining when to send it; sending it whenever it is enabled is fine. This is the purpose of the last step, *Construct Elimination*, which identifies constructs for which no smart evaluation is needed and removes them.

The most important part of this step is identifying constructs that are redundant in terms of the smart play-out computation. For example, a message that changes no properties and appears only once in the (already reduced) specification can be sent whenever it is enabled, without the need for any smart ordering. These messages are removed by the *Construct Elimination* step. Similarly, this step identifies redundant conditions, subcharts and entire LSCs, and removes them.

3.7 Superstep Reconstruction

The output of our algorithm is a new specification and initial configuration, which can then be given as input to any smart play-out method. However, in general, a superstep found by this combined method, though legal in the modified specification, is not necessarily legal in the original one.

Consider the result of applying the algorithm to the example, as shown in Section 3.1. As we saw, the *Activation Closure* step removed the LSCs related to phone 3. These LSCs will never become active in this superstep, therefore there is nothing to do regarding them in the superstep reconstruction. Similarly, the modifications performed by *Early Evaluation* and *Unreachable Elimination* do not affect the set of legal supersteps, and their modifications need not be taken into account in the superstep reconstruction.

However, the last step, *Construct Elimination*, does affect the set of supersteps and we must take its modifications into account when constructing a legal superstep for the original specification. In the example above we saw that $Logger \xrightarrow{\texttt{LogHangup}} Logger$ is removed from the specification by this step. As opposed to previous steps, this is not because it will not participate in any superstep but because it is easy to decide when to execute it: it can be executed whenever enabled. For example, consider the LSC $\texttt{Hangup}_1$, and suppose the message $Logger \xrightarrow{\texttt{LogHangup}} Logger$ is the only one removed from it. Now consider a superstep found by applying smart play-out to the modified specification. This superstep may activate this LSC and then send the message $Tel1 \xrightarrow{\texttt{StartHangup}} Logger$. As a result, the message $Logger \xrightarrow{\texttt{LogHangup}} Logger$ becomes enabled (in the original specification); since it was removed by *Construct Elimination*, we know it should be executed (naïvely) whenever enabled, therefore we should now execute it and advance the cut accordingly.

This example is representative of the general rule that constructs removed by *Construct Elimination* should be executed whenever enabled. Therefore, in order to reconstruct a legal superstep in the original specification, one merely needs to start executing the superstep found for the new one. Following each step, the list of eliminated constructs should be checked. Any construct that was eliminated and is now enabled can, and should, be safely executed.

3.8 Complexity

It is easy to see that all steps of our algorithm take time polynomial in the size of their input (the LSC specification). Moreover, the number of times they are performed is linear in the size of the specification (each iteration must remove at least one construct in order for a fixpoint not to be reached). Therefore, the entire algorithm is in PTIME.

Clearly, the algorithm is heuristic. On some specifications it may work very well, while on others it might not change the specification at all. Section 4 shows cases for which the algorithm yields a significant improvement in running time, as well as a case for which no improvement is achieved.

4 Experimental Results

Consider a parameterized generalization of the example introduced in Section 2, containing n phones, and an initial configuration where half of the phones are in call, and half of those are low priority. Fig. 3 plots the running time (log scale) of model-checking-based smart play-out on a standard PC, as a function of n, for four different specifications: (1) The original specification with no acceleration,

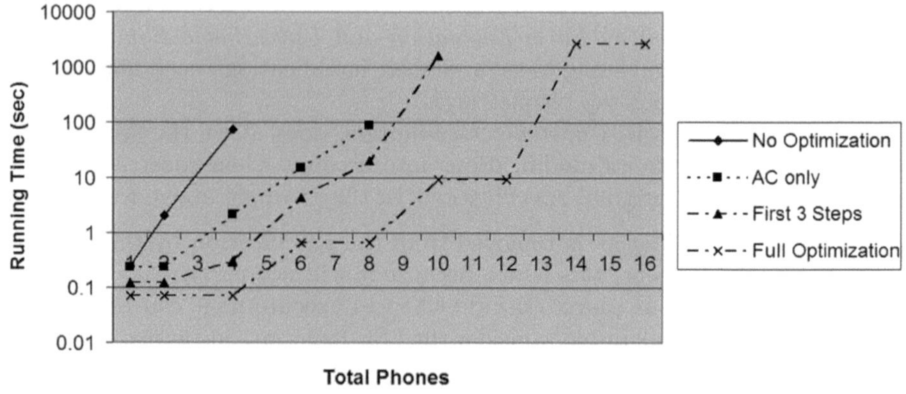

Fig. 3. Running time as a function of the number of phones, for different setups. Smart play-out runs that did not terminate within one hour were aborted, thus the maximum number of phones that could be handled within this time frame are 4 (no optimization), 8 (*Activation Closure* only), 10 (first 3 steps) and 16 (full optimization).

(2) the specification after applying *Activation Closure* only, (3) the specification with the first three steps applied iteratively until a fixpoint is reached, and (4) the specification with the complete acceleration algorithm applied. It is evident from the figure that each step adds a significant improvement to the running time, and allows a better scale-up of the size of the specification.

Interestingly, by a slight modification of the initial configuration, in which we set *logger.On* to be false (instead of true as in the previous run), the acceleration algorithm ends up with an empty specification: it removes all constructs, as it finds that non of them is crucial for the smart play-out algorithm. This means that all supersteps from the initial state are correct, and any naive play-out would succeed in this case. We are thus able to completely avoid running the model-checker; smart play-out computation time reduces to zero.

We have also applied our algorithm to two previously published specifications: (1) The Depannage telecommunication system described in [12]. Two subsets of the specification were executed. For the first, the acceleration saved 36% of the running time (21 seconds instead of 33), and for the second, the algorithm ended with an empty specification (smart play-out computation time reduces to zero). (2) The elevator example presented in [11]. The algorithm made no changes to the specification, thus no improvement was achieved in running time.

In all experiments, the running time of the algorithm itself was negligible.

5 Related and Future Work

In model-checking, the cone of influence method [9] attempts to locate only those variables that affect variables referred to in the specification, and remove all other variables. Thus, parts of our method may be viewed as a variant of the cone of influence method.

The *Early Evaluation* step can be viewed as a special case of constant propagation [13], which is used in compiler optimization to pre-evaluate expressions for which the value is known in advance.

Our work may also be viewed as a mix of static and dynamic forward program slicing [14], but applied to models rather than to code. In this sense, the reduced specification represents a safe approximation of the minimal forward model slice required for a correct superstep computation.

In this paper we focus on execution of LSCs, an extension of MSC. We believe some of the ideas presented here may be adapted to accelerate execution and simulation of other variants of MSCs, see, e.g., [1,15].

Our algorithm uses ideas from static analysis of code, such as early evaluation of conditions [16]. Additional ideas could probably be adapted to our needs. For example, we could probably conduct better data-flow and control-flow analysis to identify which messages are dependent on which others, and thus gain better knowledge for the acceleration process. Clearly, there is a trade-off between the power of the acceleration method and its own running time. The goal is to find the best possible approximation of the minimal specification needed for the smart play-out method. The better the approximation, the less running time will be needed for the smart play-out itself.

Some limitations of our approach are worth noting. In the *Activation Closure* step we do not consider the order of messages but only whether they are included in the LSCs or not. This results in an over approximation; in the worst case the fixpoint may include all LSCs in the specification, even though only a small subset of them may participate in one of the possible supersteps. Other limitations relate to data; e.g., we ignore the value assigned in property set messages so we may fail to identify some conditions that can be evaluated early.

In model-checking, partial order reduction [9] reduces the state-space to be explored by identifying transitions that result in the same state when executed in different orders. Similarly, some steps of scenario-based specifications, when executed in different order, may result in the same global system state. Therefore, methods and ideas similar to those used in partial order reduction may help in improving smart play-out as well. Note that our *Construct Elimination* step may have the effect of a partial order reduction.

Our method reduces the size of the LSC specification, which in turn reduces the size of the model given to the smart play-out techniques. However, smart play-out efficiency may be improved also by adding constraints, such as anti-scenarios or forbidden elements. This would make the LSC specification larger but could induce a smaller state-space for applying smart play-out.

As mentioned above, our algorithm computes a safe approximation of the minimal forward model slice required for a correct superstep computation, for the purpose of smart play-out acceleration. However, this model slice can also be used for model comprehension, since presenting it to the user may aid in focusing on the more important LSCs, modulo a given configuration. Developing techniques for presenting scenario-based model slices to the user, textually or visually, is an interesting direction for future work.

Acknowledgments. We thank Moshe Vardi for his advice on this work. We thank Andrew Phillips for comments on a draft of this paper.

References

1. Alur, R., Etessami, K., Yannakakis, M.: Inference of Message Sequence Charts. IEEE Trans. Software Eng. 29(7), 623–633 (2003)
2. Broy, M.: A Semantic and Methodological Essence of Message Sequence Charts. Sci. Comput. Program. 54(2-3), 213–256 (2005)
3. Damm, W., Harel, D.: LSCs: Breathing Life into Message Sequence Charts. J. on Form. Meth. in Sys. Design 19(1), 45–80 (2001)
4. Harel, D., Marelly, R.: Come Let's Play: Scenario-Based Programming Using LSCs and the Play-Engine. Springer, Heidelberg (2003)
5. Uchitel, S., Kramer, J., Magee, J.: Synthesis of Behavioral Models from Scenarios. IEEE Trans. Software Eng. 29(2), 99–115 (2003)
6. ITU: International Telecommunication Union Recommendation Z.120: Message Sequence Charts. Technical report (1996)
7. Harel, D., Kugler, H., Marelly, R., Pnueli, A.: Smart Play-out of Behavioral Requirements. In: Aagaard, M.D., O'Leary, J.W. (eds.) FMCAD 2002. LNCS, vol. 2517, pp. 378–398. Springer, Heidelberg (2002)
8. Harel, D., Kugler, H., Maoz, S., Segall, I.: How Hard is Smart Play-Out? On the Complexity of Verification-Driven Execution. In: Perspectives in Concurrency Theory (Festschrift for P.S. Thiagarajan), pp. 208–230. University Press, India (2009)
9. Clarke, E.M., Grumberg, O., Peled, D.: Model Checking. MIT Press, Cambridge (1999)
10. Harel, D., Kugler, H., Maoz, S., Segall, I.: Accelerating Smart Play-Out. Technical Report, Weizmann Institute of Science (2009)
11. Harel, D., Segall, I.: Planned and Traversable Play-Out: A Flexible Method for Executing Scenario-Based Programs. In: Grumberg, O., Huth, M. (eds.) TACAS 2007. LNCS, vol. 4424, pp. 485–499. Springer, Heidelberg (2007)
12. Combes, P., Harel, D., Kugler, H.: Modeling and Verification of a Telecommunication Application Using Live Sequence Charts and the Play-Engine Tool. Int. J. Soft. Sys. Mod (SoSyM) 7(2), 157–175 (2008)
13. Callahan, D., Cooper, K.D., Kennedy, K., Torczon, L.: Interprocedural Constant Propagation. In: Proc. SIGPLAN Symp. on Compiler Construction (CC 1986), pp. 152–161. ACM, New York (1986)
14. Korel, B., Yalamanchili, S.: Forward Computation of Dynamic Program Slices. In: Proc. ACM SIGSOFT Int. Symp. on Software Testing and Analysis (ISSTA 1994), pp. 66–79. ACM, New York (1994)
15. Krüger, I.: Capturing Overlapping, Triggered, and Preemptive Collaborations Using MSCs. In: Pezzé, M. (ed.) FASE 2003. LNCS, vol. 2621, pp. 387–402. Springer, Heidelberg (2003)
16. Pezzé, M., Young, M.: Software Testing and Analysis: Process, Principles and Techniques. John Wiley & Sons, Chichester (2008)

Optimum Broadcasting in Complete Weighted-Vertex Graphs

Hovhannes Harutyunyan[1] and Shahin Kamali[2]

[1] Department of Computer Science and Software Engineering
Concordia University, Montreal, QC, H3G 1M8, Canada
haruty@cs.concordia.ca
[2] David R. Cheriton School of Computer Science
University of Waterloo, Waterloo, ON, N2L 3G1, Canada
s3kamali@cs.uwaterloo.ca

Abstract. The weighted-vertex broadcast model is an extension of the original model of broadcasting to the graphs with weighted vertices. A vertex of weight ω is supposed to wait for ω time rounds before sending data to its neighbors; after this delay, in each round, it can inform one of its neighbors with no additional delay. We consider the problem in complete weighted-vertex graphs, and introduce a set of properties which describe a class of optimum solutions. Based on these, we present an algorithm which gives optimum broadcast schemes in polynomial time.

1 Introduction

The classical *broadcasting problem* is defined as follows: Given a graph G and an *originator* vertex $r \in V(G)$ containing a message, find a scheme that broadcast the message to all vertices in the minimum number of time steps. The communication is assumed to be synchronous, i.e., occurs in discrete rounds, and in every round an informed vertex is allowed to send the message to at most one of its neighbors. For some results and surveys on the classical model see [5,6,11,12,13].

In [9], the classical model is enhanced to the graphs with weighted vertices. The weights on the vertices may have different meanings. In parallel computers they reflect an internal process a machine needs to perform before informing its uninformed neighbors (sometimes we refer to the weights as *internal process* or *internal delay*). In modelling large networks, a node may represent a smaller network (cluster) and the weight of a vertex is an upper bound for the broadcast time of the network it represents. The weights on the vertices can also represent the delay involved in receiving the message due to the input device limitations. Another application of weighted-vertex model is in Satellite-Terrestrial networks where each vertex is either a satellite or a terrestrial station [1]. Since the delay and cost of communication through satellite nodes is higher than terrestrial nodes, these networks are modelled by weighted-vertex graphs with positive weights for satellite nodes and weight 0 for terrestrial nodes [1,17,14].

Broadcasting in weighted-vertex model is defined as follows [9]: Let $G=(V,E)$ be an undirected graph and $r \in V$ be the originator node. Each node v has a non-negative integer weight $\omega(v)$. Suppose v 'receives' the message at time t from

J. van Leeuwen et al. (Eds.): SOFSEM 2010, LNCS 5901, pp. 489–502, 2010.

one of its neighbors. Then, v should wait for $\omega(v)$ rounds before it can inform any uninformed neighbors; this is the time in which v 'completes' handling its delay. After v completes, in each round it can inform at most one neighbor. In this way, the ith neighbor of v receives at time $t(v) + \omega(v) + i$. Note that there is distinction between *receive time* in which a vertex gets informed and *complete time* in which the vertex completes its delay. The *broadcast time* of a scheme T, denoted by $b(T)$, is the maximum complete time of all vertices.

There is another model for broadcasting in weighted-vertex graphs defined in [15]. In this model, a vertex of weight ω is busy for ω rounds for informing *any* of its neighbors; hence two consecutive neighbors receive the message with a delay of ω rounds. Such model is in close connection with LogP model [4] where ω represents the gap (g) for transmitting successive messages. In the model we concern, a vertex of weight ω needs to wait *once* for ω rounds and after completing this delay, in each round, it can inform an uninformed neighbor with no additional delay. Regardless of some similarities in the definition, two models have totally different characteristics. In particular, in the mentioned model, broadcasting problem remains NP-hard for complete graphs [15]; however we show this is not the case for the weighted-vertex model.

In unweighted graphs, any broadcast scheme can be described by a directed spanning tree of the graph rooted at the originator [16]. In [9], this result is extended to the weighted-vertex graphs and a linear algorithm for broadcasting in weighted-vertex trees is provided. Consequently, in this paper we present any broadcast scheme with a tree in which the children of a node receive from left to right. Note that the root and the leaves of such *broadcast trees* have also weights that are a part of the broadcast time, i.e., when a leaf x receives, the broadcasting is not complete before additional $\omega(x)$ time units.

The weights on the vertices are non-negative integers. When all weights are 0, the model is equivalent to the classical model. Since it is NP-hard to perform broadcasting in minimum time in the classical model [8], it is also NP-hard to find an optimum broadcast time in he more generalized weighted-vertex graphs. In [9] some approximation results are provided for broadcasting in general weighted-vertex graphs, and in [10] some heuristics are suggested to the problem.

In this paper we present a polynomial algorithm for finding an optimum broadcast scheme in complete weighted-vertex graphs. Besides being simple and fast for message dissemination, complete graphs are important in modeling networks in which the exact underlying structure is unknown [2]. It is not obvious that the optimum schemes for broadcasting in weighted-vertex complete graphs can be found in polynomial time. The broadcasting problem in complete graphs with weights on the edges (instead of vertices) is NP-hard [3]. Also there are communication models for which the broadcasting problem and its variants remain NP-hard even in unweighted complete graphs (see [7] for some results on the difficulty of broadcasting and gossiping under *telegraph model* in unweighted complete graphs). Consequently, it makes sense to consider the broadcasting problem in complete weighted-vertex graphs as a separate, nontrivial problem.

In Section 2 of the paper, the problem is formulated and the structure of optimum solutions is described. In Section 3 an algorithm is introduced which provides an optimum solution in polynomial time. Section 4 concludes the paper.

2 Weighted Broadcasting in Complete Graphs

The broadcasting problem asks for a scheme to inform all vertices in minimum number of rounds. The problem is easy in unweighted complete graphs as in each round an informed vertex can send the message to any of the uninformed vertices. In complete weighted-vertex graphs the problem is not that easy as the weights are not uniform and in each round, an informed vertex should look at the weights of the uninformed vertices and choose one to send the message to.

It is good to inform lighter vertices sooner as they can perform their internal process faster and participate in informing other nodes. However, this approach does not always create the optimum broadcast scheme. Figure 1 shows two broadcast schemes for the same complete graph. In the first scheme, where the vertices with lower receive sooner, the broadcasting completes in 11 units; while the second scheme depicts the optimum broadcast scheme with broadcast time equal to 7. This example shows an optimum scheme may switch the priority between light and heavy vertices for several times; as at time $t = 1$ the heaviest vertex (K) is informed, then at $t = 2$ the lightest vertex is informed (B), and at $t = 3$ again the heaviest uninformed vertices (I, J) are informed.

We propose a set of properties that describe a certain class of optimum schemes for broadcasting in complete weighted-vertex graph. We show that any optimum scheme informs the vertices in almost the same order as these schemes. The presence of all edges in a complete graph gives freedom to manipulate a broadcast tree to achieve better broadcast schemes. In fact any tree rooted at r containing all vertices is an eligible broadcast scheme. We present some methods for modifying an arbitrary scheme to get better schemes with certain properties.

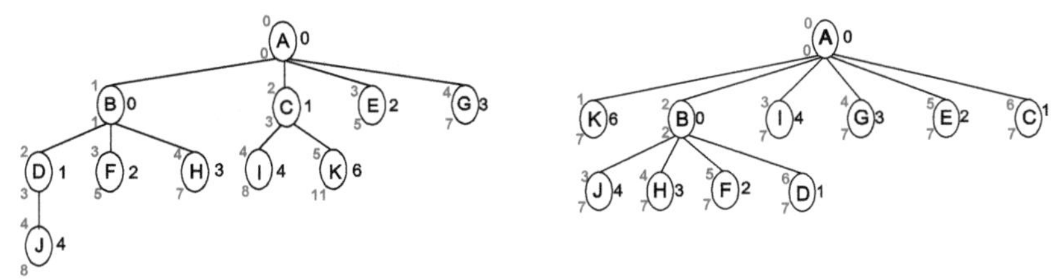

(a) A scheme in which the vertices with smaller weights receive first

(b) An optimum scheme

Fig. 1. Two broadcast schemes for the same complete graph. The numbers on the right of vertices are the weights, while the numbers on the left are the time in which vertices receive the message (top) and complete their delay (bottom).

Lemma 1. *Any broadcast tree T_0 with $b(T_0) = \tau$ can be modified to a broadcast tree T_1 with $b(T_1) \leq \tau$ in which the weight of any internal node is not greater than the weight of (any of) its children (η_0 property).*

To see the proof, suppose there is an internal node u in T_0 with a child x such that $\omega(u) > \omega(x)$; swapping u and x gives a tree with broadcast time at most equal to that of T_0. Here, swapping u and x is an *atomic modification* involving two nodes of the tree. In general, to achieve a new broadcast tree which holds a specific property, we sort the vertices by their receive time and apply the appropriate atomic modification on the first pair violating the desired property. Suppose (u, x) be such a pair and $t(u) < t(x)$, the atomic modification does not change the previously checked vertices, i.e., the receive time of a node v with $t(v) < t(u)$ would not be affected by the modification on (u, x).

Next we consider *non-laziness* of broadcast schemes. A non-lazy scheme is a scheme in which every vertex, in each round after it completes, informs exactly one neighbor until all neighbors receive the message. In complete graphs, this term can be redefined more explicitly: A non-lazy broadcast scheme is a scheme in which for any two nodes u and v we have $t(u) + \omega(u) + deg(u) + 1 \geq t(v)$.

Lemma 2. *For any complete weighted-vertex graph, a lazy broadcast tree T_1 with $b(T_1) = \tau$ can be modified to a non-lazy tree T_2 with $b(T_2) \leq \tau$.*

Proof. Let T_1 be such a lazy tree, so there is an internal node u which is idle at time t after it completes while another node v receives at time $t' > t$. A better broadcast tree can be achieved by placing the subtree rooted at v as the rightmost subtree of u.

Lemma 3. *If a broadcast tree T_1 with $b(T_1) = \tau$ has η_0 property, it can be modified to a broadcast tree T_2 with $b(T_2) \leq b(T_1)$ in which for any two internal nodes (excluding the root) the one with smaller weight receives sooner (η_1 property).*

Proof. Let u and v be two internal nodes in T_1 which violate the property, i.e., $\omega(u) < \omega(v)$ and $t(u) > t(v)$. To simplify notation let $\omega(u) = \omega$, $\omega(v) = \omega + z$, $t(u) = t + k$, and $t(v) = t$ (for some positive z,k). Also let d and d' respectively denote the number of children of u and v. Suppose the children of u and v are labeled as $u_1, u_2, \ldots u_d$ and $v_1, v_2, \ldots v_{d'}$ from left to right; so v_i receives at time $t+\omega+z+i$ and u_i receives at $t+k+\omega+i$ [Figure 2(a)]. To create the new tree T_2 consider two cases: If $k \leq d'$, swap the subtree rooted at u with the one rooted at v [Figure 2(b)]; so u receives at time t and v receives at $t+k$. Also remove the first k children of v and attach them to u. Consider an ordering of the children of u in the new tree in which the recently added children $(v_1, v_2, \ldots v_k)$ receive before the old children $(v_1, v_2, \ldots v_d)$; so u_i receives at time $t+\omega+k+i$ which is the same time prescribed by T_1. Similarly a node v_i $(i > k)$ receives in the same time it receives in T_1. Moreover any node $v_i (i \leq k)$ receives at $t + \omega + i$, which is an improvement comparing to $t + \omega + i + z$ prescribed by T_1. Now consider the other case in which $k > d$; replace u with v and set u as the parent of v, $\{v_1 \ldots v_{d'}\}$, and $\{u_1..u_d\}$ [Figure 2(c)]. Informing children of v in the same order

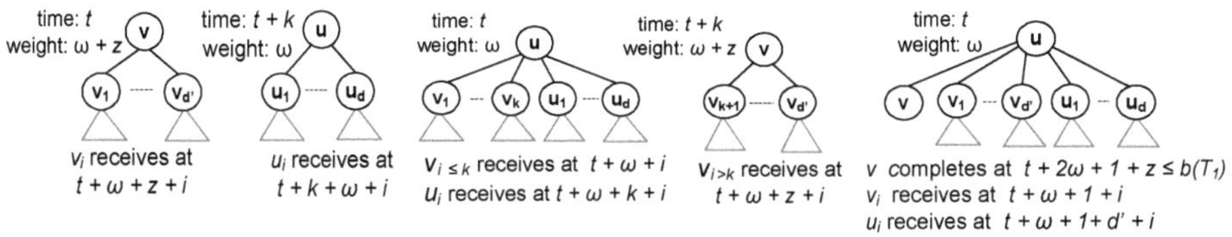

(a) A broadcast tree T_1 (b) T_2 when $d' \geq k$ (c) T_2 when $d' < k$

Fig. 2. The original tree T_1 can be modified to a tree T_2 with improved (or same) broadcast time in which internal nodes with smaller weights receive sooner

gives a broadcast scheme for the new tree which is not worst than T_1. Note that $\tau \geq t+\omega+z+1+\omega(v_1)$; since T_1 satisfies η_0 property, we gives $\omega \leq \omega(v_1)$ which implies $b(T_1) \geq t+\omega+1+\omega+z$. The last term is the time in which v completes in T_2, which means attaching v to u does not increase the broadcast time of T_2 comparing to T_1. Also, note that v_is receive at $t+\omega+1+i$, which is not worst than $t+\omega+z+i$ by T_1 (since $z \geq 1$). Similarly, u_i receives at $t+\omega+1+d+i$ which is not worst than $t+k+\omega+i$.

Lemma 4. *If a broadcast tree T_1 with $b(T_1) = \tau$ has η_0 property, it can be modified to a broadcast tree T_2 with $b(T_2) \leq \tau$ in which the weight of any internal node is not greater than the weight of any of the leaves.*

The proof of this lemma is almost the same as the previous one. Figure 3 illustrates how to apply the modification for a pair (u, x) violating the desired property. Based on the properties described above, we define *normal* trees as a kind standard broadcasting schemes for complete graphs:

Definition 1. *A broadcast tree T_η is normal iff the followings hold:*

- *T_η is non-lazy*
- *for any two internal nodes $u, v \neq r, \omega(u) \leq \omega(v) \Leftrightarrow t(u) \leq t(v)$ [η_1 property]*
- *for any internal node $u(\neq r)$ and leaf x, $\omega(u) \leq \omega(x)$ [η_2 property]*

Theorem 1. *A broadcast tree T with $b(T) = \tau$ can be modified to a normal tree T_η with $b(T_\eta) \leq \tau$.*

(a) A broadcast tree T_β (b) The modified tree T_γ

Fig. 3. The original tree T_β can be modified to a tree T_γ with improved (or same) broadcast time such that internal nodes have smaller weights than leaves

Proof. The proof is a direct result of Lemma 1,2,3,4. We just need to be careful as the set of atomic modifications applied for achieving one property may disrupt other properties. So instead of applying a set of modifications to tackle a property and then going to the next one, we walk on the original tree in the order of the receive time of vertices. For any node that receives at time t, we look at future vertices to set the first pair which violates a property and apply the appropriate atomic modification. It is easy to see the modifications does not affect previously checked vertices (those which receive before t). Hence, after a limited number of modifications, we achieve the broadcast tree holding all desired properties.

An optimum scheme is not necessarily normal; also a normal scheme is not necessarily optimum. The following definition introduces two more properties which connect broadcast trees to a candidate broadcast time br.

Definition 2. *A broadcast tree T with $b(T) = \tau$ 'respects' a candidate broadcast time br if $b(T) \leq br$ and for any internal node u and leaf x the followings hold:*

- $t(x) < t(u) \Rightarrow t(u) + \omega(x) > br$ *(ρ_1 property)*
- $t(x) < t(u) \Rightarrow t(x) + \omega(u) + 1 + \omega(x) > br$ *(ρ_2 property)*

In fact, in a scheme that respects a candidate solution, the leaves are informed as late as possible, with the restriction that the broadcast time should not exceed the candidate broadcast time. By property ρ_1 if we swap a leaf x with an internal node u informed after x, the broadcast time exceeds the candidate time br; similarly property ρ_2 implies x cannot be informed as a descendant of u. The proof of the following lemma gives a more clear understanding of these properties.

Lemma 5. *Let T_η be a broadcast tree with $b(T_\eta) = \tau$. For any candidate time $br \geq \tau$, T_η can be modified to a broadcast tree T_ρ which respects br.*

Proof. We modify T_η to get a new tree T_ρ with broadcast time not more than br (Figure 4). Let x and u respectively represent a leaf and an internal node in T_η with $t(x) < t(u)$. If $t(u) + \omega(x) \leq br$, swap the subtree rooted at u with x [Figure 4(b)]. So u completes at $t(u)+\omega(x)$ which is not greater than br while the broadcast time of the subtree rooted at u improves. If $t(x) + \omega(u) + 1 + \omega(x) \leq br$, swap x and u and let x be the leftmost child of u [Figure 4(c)]. One can see x completes within br , while receive time of other children of u is also improved.

The construction in this lemma may result in broadcast trees with higher broadcast time; but this is not a problem as the broadcast time is enough to be smaller or equal to the candidate time br. When br is large, the schemes converge to a naive scheme in which the vertices with smaller weights receive sooner [Figure 1(a)]. In fact we are interested in a normal schemes that respect the smallest value of br (this will be more discussed in the next section).

Theorem 2. *Let T_η be a broadcast tree with $b(T_\eta) = \tau$. For any candidate time $br \geq \tau$, T_η can be modified to a normal broadcast tree which respects br.*

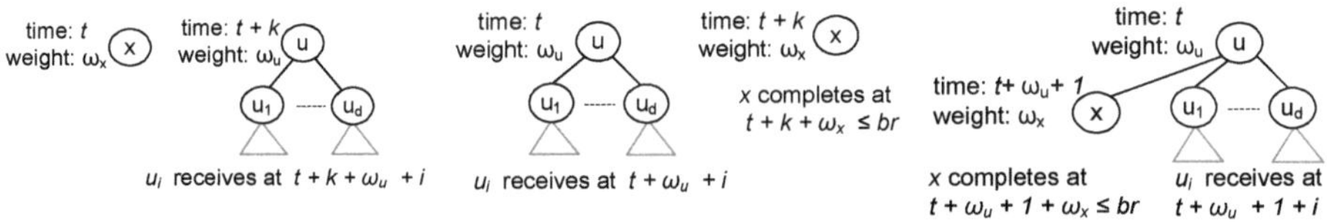

(a) A broadcast tree T_η (b) T_ρ when $t_\eta(u)+\omega(x) \leq br$ (c) T_ρ when $t_\eta(x)+\omega(u)+1+\omega(x) \leq br$

Fig. 4. Broadcast tree T_η which completes within br can be modified to another tree T_ρ which respects br

This theorem is a direct result from the Theorem 1 and Lemma 5. Like before, the modifications applied in the proof of Lemma 5 may disrupt normality of the tree. We use the same idea as presented in the proof of Theorem 1 to address this problem. So instead of constructing a normal tree and modifying it to a tree which respects br, we tackle all desired properties with one walk on the tree.

Next, we present an important theorem which informally states all normal schemes which respect a candidate time are the same. We are mainly concerned with internal nodes as they define the structure of the tree. It is shown the set of internal nodes informed in any round are the same in all broadcast trees which are normal and respect a candidate broadcast time br. When the equivalence of vertices is concerned, it is assumed they are labeled by their weights.

Theorem 3. *Let T_0, T_1 be two normal broadcast trees which respect a broadcast time br, and $I_0(t), I_1(t)$ be the set of internal nodes informed at time t by these two schemes respectively. Then, for each round $t \leq br$, $I_0(t) = I_1(t)$.*

Proof. Let t' denote the first round when $I_0(t') \neq I_1(t')$; so both schemes inform the same set of internal nodes in same times in previous rounds. Adding this to non-laziness of schemes, both schemes inform exactly k nodes at time t'. Consider T_0 informs k_0 internal nodes in round t'. Properties η_1, η_2 imply that these are k_0 uninformed nodes with minimum weights. Similarly, T_1 informs k_1 uniformed nodes with minimum weights. So $k_0 = k_1$ implies $I_0(t') = I_1(t')$ (contradiction).

Now let $k_0 < k_1$, i.e., there is an internal node v informed at time t' by T_1 which is not informed by T_0. Since both schemes inform k nodes at t', there should be a leaf x where $x \in I_1(t')$ and $x \notin I_0(t')$. To summarize, v is an internal node in T_0 and x is a leaf in T_1 while $t' = t_0(x) = t_1(v)$. Let I' denote the set of informed vertices before time t' (would be same for both trees). Consider those vertices informed by T_0 at period $[t', t''-1]$ where $t'' = t_0(v)$. Denote with B the members of this set except those internal nodes informed at t'. Note that members of B are all leaves in T_0, since if there is an internal node v' among them, by property η_1 for T_0 we get $\omega(v') < \omega(v)$, which contradicts property η_1 for T_1 as v is informed before v' in T_1. We claim not all members of B can receive at $[t', t''-1]$ in T_1. The reason is that by ρ_2 property, for any $z \in B$ we have $t'+\omega(v)+1+\omega(z) > br$ which implies those members of B informed at $[t', t''-1]$

should find their parents in I'. By non-laziness of T_1, members of I' can exactly inform $b = |B|$ nodes in this time period. Since $v \notin B$ is already one of these b vertices, there should be another node $y \in B$ which is informed either in $[0, t']$ or $[t'', br]$. We show that none of these can happen. If y receives in period $[0, t'-1]$ then it should be a leaf in T_1 (internal nodes of both schemes are the same in this period). Property $\rho 1$ for T_1 implies that $t' + \omega(v) > br$. Also T_0 completes within br which means $t_0(y) + \omega(y) \leq br$; adding this to $t' < t_0(y)$ we come to contradiction. If y receives in $[t'', br]$, property ρ_1 for T_0 implies $t'' + \omega(y) > br$. Also T_1 completes in br time which means $t_1(y) + \omega(y) \leq br$; adding this to $t' < t_1(y)$ we come to contradiction. As a result, there is no round t' such that $I_0(t') \neq I_1(t')$ which completes the proof.

3 An Algorithm for Finding Optimum Schemes

We design an algorithm named *BroadGuess* which gets as input a weighted complete graph G, an originator vertex r, and a guess value br as the candidate broadcast time. If br is not greater than the optimum broadcast time, the algorithm returns a scheme which completes within br; otherwise, it returns *Bad_Guess*. Note that an upper bound for the broadcast time is $n-1+W$, where n is the number of vertices and W is the total weight of the graph [9]. Provided by this, we conduct a binary search to find the smallest value of br for which the algorithm returns a scheme. Such scheme would be the optimum scheme.

Any broadcast scheme is represented with a spanning tree directed from the originator to the leaves. The algorithm is based on the following construction: It starts with the originator r as the broadcast tree and repeatedly *stick*s new vertices to it until all the vertices gets attached. During this process the algorithm may fail and return *Bad_Guess*.

In each round of the algorithm, the vertex set $V(G)$ is partitioned into *Tree Vertices* denoted by T and *Uninformed Vertices* denoted by U. Tree vertices are those which are already attached to the tree, while uninformed vertices are waiting to be attached. At the beginning of the algorithm these sets are respectively initiated by $\{r\}$ and $V(G) - \{r\}$. The algorithm ends when all vertices are moved from U to T. The following notations are used in the algorithm: For any $u \in T$: $par(u)$ is the parent of u in the tree, $ch_i(u)$ is the child of u at index i (initialized by $NULL$), and $avi(u)$ is the smallest index of u such that $ch_{avi(u)} = NULL$ (initialized by 1). Also, $max, min \in U$ are two uninformed vertices with the maximum and minimum weights. These variables get updated when a new node sticks to the tree. Algorithm 1 illustrates these updates.

In each round of the algorithm a member of U with either minimum or maximum weight (min or max) is selected to be attached to the tree. Note that after attaching a new vertex the broadcast time of the tree should remain smaller or equal to the guess value br. Let y be a node of the tree which minimizes $t(y) + \omega(y) + avi(y)$. Define α as $t(y) + \omega(y) + avi(y)$, which means the uninformed vertices cannot receive the message sooner than α. If the weight of min is small enough that attaching it to y guarantees that max can be attached later

---

Algorithm 1. Stick

Input: A vertex $x \in U$, a vertex $p \in T$, an integer i as the index of x among children of p { Updating control values when new node x sticks to node p }

$t(x) \leftarrow t(p) + \omega(p) + i$

$par(x) \leftarrow v \;\; ch_i(p) \leftarrow x$

if $i = avi(v)$ **then**

  $avi(v) \leftarrow$ the smallest $j > i$ having $ch_j(v) = Null$

end if

$U = U - \{x\}, \;\; T = T \cup \{x\}$

---

as a descendant of min, then we stick min to y. More formally, we stick min to y if $\alpha + \omega(min) + 1 + \omega(max) \leq br$. If max cannot be informed through min, it should stick max somewhere in the current tree; but we try to inform it as late as possible. The reason is max cannot inform other vertices [otherwise min could be its parent], and just needs to receive in a time to complete within br.

If we cannot attach max anywhere in the tree in a way that it completes within br, the algorithm returns *Bad_Guess*. It happens when min is heavy and in the last consecutive rounds just maxs have been attached to the tree. In this case, the tree does not have an available index for the current max and the algorithm fails to create a scheme which completes within time br.

Algorithm 2 illustrates *BroadGuess* in more details. Note that all nodes stick to the tree in Lines 7 and 14 of the algorithm, while in Lines 6 and 9 it is checked the broadcast time of the tree not exceed br after attaching new nodes. Consequently, if the algorithm returns a broadcast scheme, it completes within the candidate time br. Hence, to prove the correctness of the algorithm it suffices to show if the output is *Bad_Guess* for a candidate time br, there is no scheme which completes in br time.

Let T^* be the tree created by the algorithm just before returning *Bad_Guess*, and t^* be the time unit in which the last vertex receives in this tree. We describe a set of properties for tree T^* to show this tree has all properties of a normal broadcast tree which respects candidate time br.

Lemma 6. *If a vertex v sticks to T^* as a max node (Line 14 of the algorithm), then v is a leaf of the tree.*

Proof. Suppose v has a child x; so in the iteration in which v sticks to the tree we have $\alpha + \omega(v) + 1 + \omega(x) \leq br$. Note that x is a feature vertex, so $\omega(x) \geq \omega(min)$ which gives $\alpha + \omega(v) + 1 + \omega(min) \leq br$. But v has been added as a max vertex in this iterations; so $\alpha + \omega(min) + 1 + \omega(v) > br$ which is a contradiction.

Lemma 7. *A vertex is added as min if and only if it is an internal node in T^*.*

Proof. By Lemma 6 any vertex added as max is a leaf which implies all internal nodes are added as min. For the other side, we need to show any vertex v added as min is internal in T^*. Since v is added as min in some iteration i, we get $t(v) + \omega(v) + 1 + \omega(max) \leq br$ (since max is the heaviest uninformed vertex in

Algorithm 2. BroadGuess

Input: A weighted complete graph G, the originator r, and candidate time br
Output: A broadcast tree T which completes within br or *Bad_Guess*

Initialize the sets T and U with $\{r\}$, $V - \{r\}$ respectively
while $U \neq \Phi$ **do** {main loop}
  Set $max, min \in U$ as the vertices with extreme weights
  Find $y \in T$ which minimizes $t(y) + \omega(y) + avi(y)$
  Set $\alpha = t(y) + \omega(y) + avi(y)$
  if $\alpha + \omega(min) + 1 + \omega(max) \leq br$ **then**
    call $Stick(min, y, avi(y))$ {Stick min to y at index $avi(y)$ }
  else
    Set $P = \{v \in T | t(v) + \omega(v) + avi(v) + \omega(max) \leq br\}$ {feasible parents of max}
    if $P = \Phi$ **then**
      return *Bad_Guess*
    else
      Find a pair (v, k) where $v \in P$ and $ch_k(v) = Null$ with maximum $t(v) + \omega(v) + k$ such that $t(v) + \omega(v) + k + \omega(max) \leq br$ {inform max as late as possible}
      call $Stick(max, v, k)$ {Stick max to v at index k}
    end if
  end if
end while

the iteration i). Since the vertex z which failed to stick is uniformed in iteration i we have $\omega(z) \leq \omega(max)$ which implies $t(v) + \omega(v) + 1 + \omega(z) \leq br$. So if v has no children, it can be the parent of z, which is not true as z failed to stick to T^*.

The following theorem states T^* is a normal broadcast tree and respects the candidate time br (for which the algorithm returned *Bad_Guess*). We show T^* is *partially non-lazy*, i.e., the completed vertices are not idle at any time $t \leq t^*$. Since the uninformed vertices are missing in T^*, they are considered as a separate class of vertices along with the internal nodes and leaves of T^*:

Theorem 4. *The tree T^* has the following properties:*

- *it is partially non-lazy*
- *for any internal node $u \in T^*(u \neq r)$:* [η_1 property]
  - *for any internal node $v \in T^*(v \neq r), \omega(u) \leq \omega(v) \Leftrightarrow t(u) \leq t(v)$*
- *for any internal node $u \in T^*(u \neq r)$:* [η_2 property]
  - *for any leaf $x \in T^*$, $\omega(u) \leq \omega(x)$*
  - *for any vertex $z \in U$, $\omega(u) \leq \omega(z)$*
- *for any leaf $x \in T^*$:* [ρ_1 property]
  - *for any internal node $u \in T^*$, $t(x) < t(u) \Rightarrow t(u) + \omega(x) > br$*
- *for any leaf $x \in T^*$:* [ρ_2 property]
  - *for any internal node $u \in T^*$, $t(x) < t(u) \Rightarrow t(x) + \omega(u) + 1 + w(x) > br$*
  - *for any vertex $z \in U$, $t(x) + w(z) + 1 + w(x) > br$*

The proof of this theorem can be found in the appendix. As this theorem implicitly guaranties T^* is a normal broadcast tree which respects the candidate time br, we can extend previous results to this tree. In particular we can state the following theorem which is an extension of Theorem 3:

Theorem 5. *Given T^* as the created tree just before returning Bad_Guess for candidate time br, and t^* be the latest time a vertex receives in T^*, for each round $t < t^*$ we have $I_{T^*}(t) = I_{\aleph}(t)$ where $\aleph$ is a normal scheme respecting br and $I(t)$ is the set of internal nodes informed at time t.*

Note that $\aleph$ represents all normal schemes that respect br since all these schemes inform the same set of internal nodes in all rounds (Theorem 3). Theorem 5 states that any internal node informed by these schemes before round t^* is present in T^* and is informed at the same time unit. The proof of the theorem is similar to that of Theorem 3. It is just needed to consider more scenarios as T^* does not contain all vertices of $\aleph$. A detailed proof is presented in the appendix.

Theorem 6. *If the output of the algorithm BroadGuess is Bad_Guess for a candidate broadcast time br, then $b(G) > br$.*

Proof. Suppose there is a scheme which completes within br. By Theorem 2 this scheme can be modified to a normal scheme $\aleph$ which respects br. Let T^* be the constructed tree before returning Bad_Guess and M be the set of internal nodes of T^*. We can apply Theorem 5 to state any member of M receives at the same time in $\aleph$ as in T^*. Now consider the leaves of T^* which are k nodes with maximum weights (the algorithm picks the vertices with maximum weight). All these nodes should find their parents (in $\aleph$) among the members of M; otherwise their missing parents in T^* should have been attached to T^* by η_2 property. Similarly, the vertex z which failed to attach to T^* has its parent (in $\aleph$) among the members of M. Consequently vertices of M in $\aleph$ are parents of at least $k+1$ nodes with weights not less than $\omega(z)$. This contradicts the fact that the same vertices with same broadcast time failed to inform these $k+1$ nodes in T^*.

With a rough implementation, *BroadGuess* algorithm needs $O(n^2)$ time to complete. Recall that $n+W+1$ is an upper bound for broadcasting in any weighted graph where W is the sum of all weights of vertices; so we need to run *Broad Guess* $O(\log(n+W))$ times. Consequently, the total time complexity would be $O(n^2 \log(n+W))$, which is polynomial even if W be exponential with respect to n.

4 Conclusion

We investigated the problem of broadcasting in complete weighted-vertex graphs, discussed why the problem is not trivial, and provided a set of properties an optimum solution may have. Based on these, we presented an algorithm which gives an optimum solution for an instance of the problem in time $O(n^2 \log(n+W))$ time, where n is the size and W is the total weight of the graph.

References

1. Asaka, T., Miyoshi, T., Tanaka, Y.: Multicast Routing in Satellite-Terrestrial Networks. In: Fifth Asia-Pacific Conference on Communications and Fourth Optoelectronics and Communications Conference, vol. 1, pp. 768–771 (1999)
2. Bar-Noy, A., Kipnis, S.: Designing Broadcasting Algorithms in the Postal Model for Message-Passing Systems. In: ACM Symposium on Parallel Algorithms and Architectures, pp. 13–22 (1992)
3. Bar-Noy, A., Nir, U.: The Generalized Postal Model-Broadcasting in a System with Non-Homogeneous Delays. In: Electrotechnical Conference, 1998. MELECON 1998, 9th Mediterranean, May 18-20, vol. 2, pp. 1323–1327 (1998)
4. Culler, D., Karp, R., Patterson, D., Sahay, A., Schauser, K.E., Santos, E., Subramonian, R., Von Eicken, T.: Logp: Towards a Realistic Model of Parallel Computation. SIGPLAN Not. 28(7), 1–12 (1993)
5. Elkin, M., Kortsarz, G.: Sublogarithmic Approximation for Telephone Multicast: Path Out of Jungle (extended abstract). In: SODA 2003, Proceedings of the Fourteenth Annual ACM-SIAM Symposium on Discrete Algorithms, pp. 76–85 (2003)
6. Fraigniaud, P., Lazard, E.: Methods and Problems of Communication in Usual Networks. Discrete Appl. Math. 53(1-3), 79–133 (1994)
7. Fraigniaud, P., Vial, S.: Approximation Algorithms for Information Dissemination Problems. In: IEEE Second International Conference on Algorithms and Architectures for Parallel Processing (ICAPP), pp. 155–162 (1996)
8. Garey, M.R., Johnson, D.S.: Computers and Intractability; A Guide to the Theory of NP-Completeness. W.H. Freeman & Co., New York (1990)
9. Harutyunyan, H., Kamali, S.: Broadcasting in Weighted-Vertex Graphs. In: ISPA Intl Symposium on Parallel and Distributed Processing with Applications, pp. 301–307 (2008)
10. Harutyunyan, H., Kamali, S.: Efficient Broadcasting in Networks with Weighted Nodes. In: ICPADS Intl Conference on Parallel and Distributed Systems, pp. 879–884 (2008)
11. Hedetniemi, S.M., Hedetniemi, S.T., Liestman, A.L.: A Survey of Gossiping and Broadcasting in Communication Networks. Networks 18(4), 319–359 (1998)
12. Hromkovic, J., Klasing, R., Monien, B., Peine, R.: Dissemination of Information in Interconnection Networks (Broadcasting & Gossiping). Combinatorial Network Theory, 125–212 (1996)
13. Hromkovič, J., Klasing, R., Pelc, A., Ružička, P., Unger, W.: Dissemination of Information in Communication Networks: Broadcasting, Gossiping, Leader Election, and Fault-Tolerance. Springer Monograph. Springer, Heidelberg (2005)
14. hsu Chang, C., Wu, E.H.: An Intelligent Multicast Protocol for Satellite-Terrestrial Broadband Network, 138–143 (October 2002)
15. Khuller, S., Kim, Y.-A.: Broadcasting in Heterogeneous Networks. Algorithmica 48(1), 1–21 (2007)
16. Slater, P.J., Cockayne, E.J., Hedetniemi, S.T.: Information Dissemination in Ttrees. SIAM Journal on Computing 10(4), 692–701 (1981)
17. Wu, E.H.-k., Chang, C.: Adaptive Multicast Routing for Satellite-Terrestrial Network. In: Global Telecommunications Conference, GLOBECOM 2001, vol. 3, pp. 1440–1444. IEEE, Los Alamitos (2001)

Appendix

Proof (Theorem 4)
non-laziness: Let x be a vertex which receives at time t^* [such a vertex exists by definition of t^*]; so we have $t^* + \omega(x) \leq br$. Since x is the last node that receives in T^*, it is a leaf and sticks to the tree as max (Lemma 7). Now consider a vertex z fails to stick to the tree; since it is uninformed in the iteration in which x sticks, we get $\omega(z) \leq \omega(x)$ which implies $t^* + \omega(z) \leq br$. So if a node is idle at any round $t \leq t^*$, it can be the parent of z to inform it in this round; this contradicts the fact z failed to stick to the tree.

η_1*:* Let u and v be two internal nodes with $\omega(u) \leq \omega(v)$. Both u and v stick to the tree as min (Lemma 7). Since u is lighter than v, it sticks to the tree in an iteration in which v is still among uninformed vertices. In this iteration, the algorithm finds a node y to inform u as soon as possible [Line 4 of the algorithm]. So u receives sooner than all uninformed vertices in this iteration including v.

η_2*:* Suppose a leaf x sticks to T^* before an internal node u. By Lemma 7, x has the maximum weight among all uninformed vertices including u in the iteration in which it sticks to T^*, i.e., $\omega(u) \leq \omega(x)$. Similarly, if u sticks to T^* before x (uninformed vertex z), it has the minimum weight among all uninformed vertices in the iteration it sticks to T^*; x (and z) are among these uninformed vertices which implies $\omega(u) \leq \omega(x)$ (and $\omega(u) \leq \omega(z)$).

ρ_1*:* Consider an internal node u receives after a leaf x, so $t(x) < t(u)$; we need to show $t(u) + \omega(x) > br$. Note that u and x stick to the tree as min and max respectively. Also u sticks to T^* after x since u sticks as min and receives not later than any uninformed vertex. Suppose ρ_1 does not hold, i.e., $t(u) + \omega(x) \leq br$. Consider the iteration in which x sticks to T^*; if the parent of u ($par(u)$) is already in the tree in this iteration, we can stick x in the appropriate index of $par(u)$ to inform it at time $t(u)(> t(x))$; this contradicts x being informed as late as possible [Line 13]. If $par(u)$ is not in the tree, $t(u) + \omega(x) \leq br$ implies $t(par(u)) + \omega(par(u)) + 1 + \omega(x) \leq br$. Note the algorithm could attach the vertex with minimum weight (min) with $t(min) \leq t(par(u))$ [min receives sooner than any other uninformed node] and $\omega(min) \leq \omega(par(u))$. Consequently, we get $t(min) + \omega(min) + 1 + \omega(x) \leq br$ which contradicts x being stick as max in the iteration [Line 6].

ρ_2*:* Let u be an internal node and x be a leaf such that $t(u) > t(x)$; so u is uninformed in the iteration in which x sticks to the tree. Having α as the earliest time a vertex can be informed [Line 5], we get $t(x) \geq \alpha$; also x is the uninformed vertex with the maximum weight, i.e., $\omega(u)$ is not smaller than min. So if we assume $t(x) + \omega(u) + 1 + \omega(x) \leq br$ then $\alpha + \omega(\min) + 1 + \omega(\max) \leq br$, which contradicts x being stick as max. Similarly, any $z \notin T^*$ is uninformed at the iteration in which x sticks, and $\omega(z)$ is not smaller than min. Consequently, assuming $t(x) + \omega(z) + 1 + \omega(x) \leq br$ implies $\alpha + \omega(\min) + 1 + \omega(\max) \leq br$ which is a contradiction.

Proof (Theorem 5)
We start with the observation that the weight of any leaf in T^* is not smaller than the weight of vertices in U. The reason is that the leaves of T^* stick as *max*, which implies they have been the heaviest uninformed vertices when added to the tree. We refer to this property as μ *property*.

Let $t' \leq t^*$ be the first round such that $I_{\aleph}(t') \neq I_T(t')$. Both schemes inform exactly k nodes at time t' as both are non-lazy (in period $[0, t^*]$) and have informed the same set of internal nodes in the same times in previous rounds. Also properties η_1 and η_2 guaranty the internal nodes informed at t' are the same; so there is an internal node v informed at t' by one of the schemes which is replaced by a leaf x in the other scheme. We discuss different cases and come to contradiction in all:

Consider the case in which T^* and $\aleph$ respectively inform x and v at time t' while v is not missing in T^*; then we can apply the same reasoning as in the proof of Theorem 3; just replace T_0 and T_1 with T^* and $\aleph$ in the proof.

Consider the case in which T^* and $\aleph$ respectively inform x and v at t' while v is missing in T^* (v is uninformed). Let B denote the set of vertices of T^* that received in time period $[t', t^*]$. All members of B are leaves, since by η_1 and η_2 properties v is the first internal node which receives after t' in T^*. Since v is missing, there is no internal node informed after t' in T^*. Also property ρ_2 for T^* along with non-laziness of schemes imply there is a vertex $y \in B$ that receives out of the period $[t', t^*]$ in $\aleph$. By property ρ_1 for $\aleph$, y cannot receive in $[0, t']$, hence it receives in $[t^* + 1, br]$. Since the output has been *Bad_Guess*, there is a vertex $z \in U$ such that $t^* + 1 + \omega(z) > br$. Moreover, μ property for T^* implies $\omega(y) > \omega(z)$ which means $t^* + \omega(y) > br$. Applying $t_{\aleph}(y) + \omega(y) \leq br$ we get $t^* > t_{\aleph}(y)$ which contradicts informing y in $[t^* + 1, br]$.

Consider the case in which T^* and $\aleph$ respectively inform v and x. Let t'' denote the time in which v receives in $\aleph$, i.e., $t'' = t_{\aleph}(v)$. First we show $t'' < t^*$: define S as the set of leaves of T^*, included to it the single vertex z failed to attach to T^* ($t^* + 1 + \omega(z) > br$). By μ property, the weights of members of S cannot be smaller than z. Having $t'' \geq t^*$ requires the leaves of $\aleph$ informed within t^* receive through members I'. Adding to this the non-laziness of T^* (before t^*), there should be a member s of S informed after t^* in $\aleph$, i.e., $t^* + 1 + \omega(s) \leq br$. Since $\omega(s) \geq \omega(c)$, we get $t^* + 1 + \omega(z) \leq br$ which is a contradiction. Now consider $t'' \leq t^*$; let B denote the set of leaves informed by $\aleph$ in period $[t', t'' - 1]$. By ρ_2 property for $\aleph$, members of B should find their parents in I'. Since T^* and $\aleph$ are both non-lazy in period $[t', t'' - 1]$, and v is one of the vertices informed by I' in this period, there exists a vertex $y \in B$ which is not informed by T^* in $[t', t'' - 1]$. We discuss y should be a node of T^*: ρ_2 property for $\aleph$ implies $t'' + \omega(w) > br$. Moreover, t^* is defined as the latest time in which a leaf c receives which implies $t^* + \omega(c) \leq br$. Applying $t'' < t^*$, we conclude $\omega(c) < \omega(y)$; by μ property, y should be a node of T^*. Now we can use similar techniques as previous parts; y receives in T^* either in $[0, t']$ or $[t'', t^*]$. Applying ρ_1 property for T^* and $\aleph$ respectively, none of these two cases can happen.

On Contracting Graphs to Fixed Pattern Graphs

Pim van 't Hof[1,⋆], Marcin Kamiński[2], Daniël Paulusma[1,⋆], Stefan Szeider[1], and Dimitrios M. Thilikos[3,⋆⋆]

[1] School of Engineering and Computing Sciences, University of Durham
Science Laboratories, South Road
Durham DH1 3LE, England
{pim.vanthof,daniel.paulusma,stefan.szeider}@durham.ac.uk
[2] Computer Science Department, Université Libre de Bruxelles
Boulevard du Triomphe CP212, B-1050 Brussels, Belgium
marcin.kaminski@ulb.ac.be
[3] Department of Mathematics, National and Kapodistrian University of Athens
Panepistimioupolis, GR15784 Athens, Greece
sedthilk@math.uoa.gr

Abstract. For a fixed graph H, the H-CONTRACTIBILITY problem asks if a graph is H-contractible, i.e., can be transformed into H via a series of edge contractions. The computational complexity classification of this problem is still open. So far, H has a dominating vertex in all cases known to be polynomially solvable, whereas H does not have such a vertex in all cases known to be NP-complete. Here, we present a class of graphs H with a dominating vertex for which H-CONTRACTIBILITY is NP-complete. We also present a new class of graphs H for which H-CONTRACTIBILITY is polynomially solvable. Furthermore, we study the (H,v)-CONTRACTIBILITY problem, where v is a vertex of H. The input of this problem is a graph G and an integer k. The question is whether G is H-contractible such that the "bag" of G corresponding to v contains at least k vertices. We show that this problem is NP-complete whenever H is connected and v is not a dominating vertex of H.

1 Introduction

There are several natural and elementary algorithmic problems that check if the structure of some fixed graph H shows up as a *pattern* within the structure of some input graph G. This paper studies the computational complexity of one such problem, namely the problem of deciding if a given graph G can be transformed into a fixed pattern graph H by performing a sequence of edge contractions. Theoretical motivation for this research, which started in [2] and was continued in [11,12], comes from hamiltonian graph theory [9] and graph minor theory [13], as we will explain below. Practical applications include surface simplification in computer graphics [1,3] and cluster analysis of large data

⋆ Supported by EPSRC (EP/D053633/1).
⋆⋆ Supported by the project "Kapodistrias" (AΠ 02839/28.07.2008) of the National and Kapodistrian University of Athens (project code: 70/4/8757).

J. van Leeuwen et al. (Eds.): SOFSEM 2010, LNCS 5901, pp. 503–514, 2010.

sets [4,8,10]. In the first practical application, graphic objects are represented using (triangulated) graphs and these graphs need to be simplified. One of the techniques to do this is by using edge contractions. In the second application, graphs are coarsened by means of edge contractions.

Basic Terminology. All graphs in this paper are undirected, finite, and have neither loops nor multiple edges. Let G and H be two graphs. The *edge contraction* of edge $e = uv$ in G removes u and v from G, and replaces them by a new vertex adjacent to precisely those vertices to which u or v were adjacent. If H can be obtained from G by a sequence of edge contractions, vertex deletions and edge deletions, then G contains H as a *minor*. If H can be obtained from G by a sequence of edge contractions and vertex deletions, then G contains H as an *induced minor*. If H can be obtained from G by a sequence of edge contractions, then G is said to be *contractible to* H and G is called H-*contractible*. This is equivalent to saying that G has a so-called H-*witness structure* $\mathcal{W}$, which is a partition of V_G into $|V_H|$ sets $W(h)$, called H-*witness sets*, such that each $W(h)$ induces a connected subgraph of G and for every two $h_i, h_j \in V_H$, witness sets $W(h_i)$ and $W(h_j)$ are adjacent in G if and only if h_i and h_j are adjacent in H. Here, two subsets A, B of V_G are called *adjacent* if there is an edge $ab \in E_G$ with $a \in A$ and $b \in B$. Clearly, by contracting the vertices in the witness sets $W(h)$ to a single vertex for every $h \in V_H$, we obtain the graph H. See Figure 1 for an example that shows that in general the witness sets $W(h)$ are not uniquely defined.

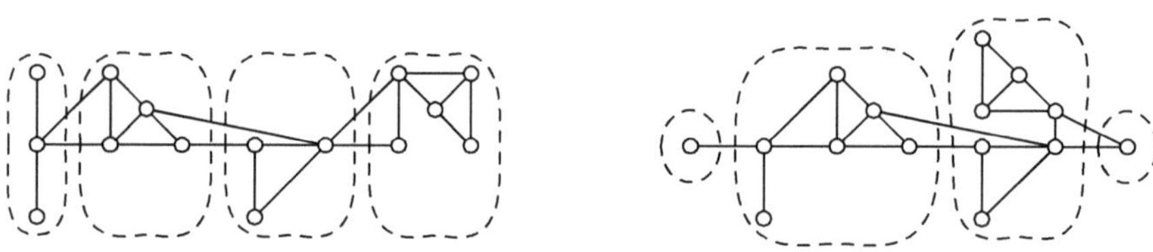

Fig. 1. Two P_4-witness structures of a graph

Known Results. The problems H-Minor Containment, H-Induced Minor Containment and H-Contractibility ask if a graph has H as an induced minor, has H as a minor or is H-contractible, respectively. A celebrated result by Robertson and Seymour [13] states that H-Minor Containment can be solved in polynomial time for every fixed graph H. The complexity classification of the other two problems is still open. Fellows et al. [6] give both polynomially solvable and NP-complete cases for the the H-Induced Minor Containment problem. Their main result is that, for every fixed H, the H-Induced Minor Containment problem is polynomially solvable for planar input graphs. Brouwer and Veldman [2] initiated the research on the H-Contractibility problem. Their main result is stated below. A *dominating* vertex is a vertex adjacent to all other vertices.

Theorem 1 ([2]). *Let H be a connected triangle-free graph. The H-Contractibility problem is in* P *if H has a dominating vertex, and is* NP-*complete otherwise.*

Note that a connected triangle-free graph with a dominating vertex is a star and that $H = P_4$ (path on four vertices) and $H = C_4$ (cycle on four vertices) are the smallest graphs H for which H-Contractibility is NP-complete. Levin et al. [11,12] continued the research of [2].

Theorem 2 ([11,12]). *Let H be a connected graph with $|V_H| \leq 5$. The H-Contractibility problem is in P if H has a dominating vertex, and is NP-complete otherwise.*

The NP-completeness results in Theorem 1 and 2 can be extended using the notion of degree-two covers. Let $d_G(x)$ denote the degree of a vertex x in a graph G. A graph H' with an induced subgraph H is called a *degree-two cover* of H if the following two conditions both hold. First, for all $x \in V_H$, if $d_H(x) = 1$ then $d_{H'}(x) \geq 2$, and if $d_H(x) = 2$ and its two neighbors in H are adjacent then $d_{H'}(x) \geq 3$. Second, for all $x' \in V_{H'} \setminus V_H$, either x' has one neighbor and this neighbor is in H, or x' has two neighbors and these two neighbors form an edge in H.

Theorem 3 ([11]). *Let H' be a degree-two cover of a connected graph H. If H-Contractibility is NP-complete, then so is H'-Contractibility.*

In [2,11] a number of other results are shown. To discuss these we need some extra terminology (which we will use later in the paper as well). For two graphs $G_1 = (V_1, E_1)$ and $G_2 = (V_2, E_2)$ with $V_1 \cap V_2 = \emptyset$, we denote their *join* by $G_1 \bowtie G_2 = (V_1 \cup V_2, E_1 \cup E_2 \cup \{uv \mid u \in V_1, v \in V_2\})$, and their *disjoint union* by $G_1 \cup G_2 = (V_1 \cup V_2, E_1 \cup E_2)$. For the disjoint union $G \cup G \cup \cdots \cup G$ of k copies of the graph G, we write kG; for $k = 0$ this yields the empty graph $(\emptyset, \emptyset)$. For integers $a_1, a_2, \ldots, a_k \geq 0$, we let $H_i^*(a_1, a_2, \ldots, a_k)$ be the graph $K_i \bowtie (a_1 P_1 \cup a_2 P_2 \cup \cdots \cup a_k P_k)$, where K_i is the complete graph on i vertices and P_i is the path on i vertices. Note that $H_1^*(a_1)$ denotes a star on a_1+1 vertices. Brouwer and Veldman show that H-Contractibility is polynomially solvable for $H = H_1^*(a_1)$ or $H = H_1^*(a_1, a_2)$ for any $a_1, a_2 \geq 0$. Observe that $H_i^*(0) = K_i$ and that K_i-Contractibility is equivalent to K_i-Minor Containment, and consequently, polynomially solvable. These results have been generalized in [11] leading to the following theorem.

Theorem 4 ([11]). *The H-Contractibility problem is in P for:*

1. $H = H_1^*(a_1, a_2, \ldots, a_k)$ *for any* $k \geq 1$ *and* $a_1, a_2, \ldots, a_k \geq 0$
2. $H = H_2^*(a_1, a_2)$ *for any* $a_1, a_2 \geq 0$
3. $H = H_3^*(a_1)$ *for any* $a_1 \geq 0$
4. $H = H_i^*(0)$, *for any* $i \geq 1$.

So far, in all polynomially solvable cases of the H-Contractibility problem the pattern graph H has a dominating vertex, and in all NP-complete cases H does not have such a vertex.

Our Results and Paper Organization. The presence of a dominating vertex seems to play an interesting role in the complexity classification of the H-Contractibility problem. However, in Section 2.1 we present a class of graphs

H with a dominating vertex for which H-CONTRACTIBILITY is NP-complete. In Section 2.2 we extend Theorem 4 by showing that $H_4^*(a_1)$ is polynomially solvable for all $a_1 \geq 0$. In Section 3 we study the following problem.

(H, v)-CONTRACTIBILITY
Instance: A graph G and a positive integer k.
Question: Does G have an H-witness structure $\mathcal{W}$ with $|W(v)| \geq k$?

We show that (H, v)-CONTRACTIBILITY is NP-complete whenever H is connected and v is not a dominating vertex of H. For example, let $P_3 = p_1p_2p_3$. Then the (P_3, p_3)-CONTRACTIBILITY problem is NP-complete (whereas P_3-CONTRACTIBILITY is polynomially solvable). Section 4 contains the conclusions and mentions a number of open problems.

2 The H-Contractibility Problem

2.1 NP-Complete Cases with a Dominating Vertex

We show the existence of a class of graphs H with a dominating vertex such that H-CONTRACTIBILITY is NP-complete. To do this we need the following.

Proposition 1. *Let H be a graph. If H-*INDUCED MINOR CONTAINMENT *is* NP-*complete, then so are* $(K_1 \bowtie H)$-CONTRACTIBILITY *and* $(K_1 \bowtie H)$-INDUCED MINOR CONTAINMENT.

Proof. Let H and G be two graphs. Write $K_1 = (\{x\}, \emptyset)$. We claim that the following three statements are equivalent.

(i) G has H as an induced minor;
(ii) $K_1 \bowtie G$ is $(K_1 \bowtie H)$-contractible;
(iii) $K_1 \bowtie G$ has $K_1 \bowtie H$ as an induced minor.

"*(i)* $\Rightarrow$ *(ii)*" Suppose G has H as an induced minor. Then, by definition, G contains an induced subgraph G' that is H-contractible. We extend an H-witness structure $\mathcal{W}$ of G' to a $(K_1 \bowtie H)$-witness structure of $K_1 \bowtie G$ by putting x and all vertices in $V_G \setminus V_{G'}$ in $W(x)$. This shows that $K_1 \bowtie G$ is $(K_1 \bowtie H)$-contractible.

"*(ii)* $\Rightarrow$ *(iii)*" Suppose $K_1 \bowtie G$ is $(K_1 \bowtie H)$-contractible. By definition, $K_1 \bowtie G$ contains $K_1 \bowtie H$ as an induced minor.

"*(iii)* $\Rightarrow$ *(i)*" Suppose $K_1 \bowtie G$ has $K_1 \bowtie H$ as an induced minor. Then $K_1 \bowtie G$ contains an induced subgraph G^* that is $K_1 \bowtie H$-contractible. Let $\mathcal{W}$ be a $(K_1 \bowtie H)$-witness structure of G^*. If $x \in V_{G^*}$, then we may assume without loss of generality that $x \in W(x)$. We delete $W(x)$ and obtain an H-witness structure of the remaining subgraph of G^*. This subgraph is an induced subgraph of G. Hence, G contains H as an induced minor. □

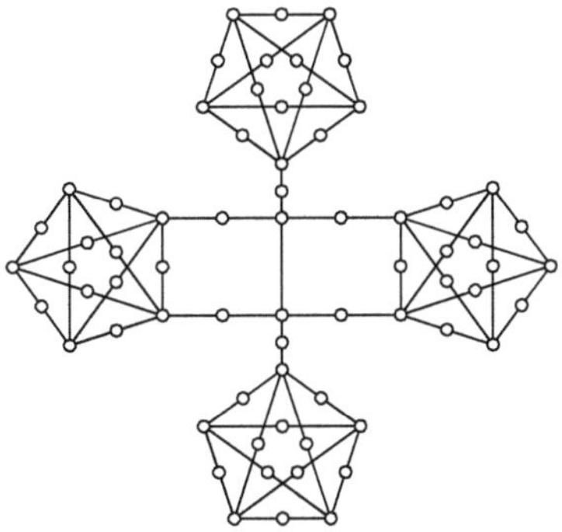

Fig. 2. The graph $\bar{H}$

Fellows et al. [6] showed that there exists a graph $\bar{H}$ on 68 vertices such that $\bar{H}$-Induced Minor Containment is NP-complete; this graph is depicted in Figure 2. Combining their result with Proposition 1 (applied repeatedly) leads to the following corollary.

Corollary 1. *For any $i \geq 1$, $(K_i \bowtie \bar{H})$-*Contractibility *is* NP*-complete.*

2.2 Polynomial Cases With Four Dominating Vertices

In this section, we extend Theorem 4 by showing that H-Contractibility is polynomially solvable for $H = H_4^*(a_1)$ for any integer $a_1 \geq 0$.

Let H and G be graphs such that G is H-contractible. Let $\mathcal{W}$ be an H-witness structure of G. We call the subset of vertices in a witness set $W(h_i)$ that are adjacent to vertices in some other witness set $W(h_j)$ a *connector* $C_{\mathcal{W}}(h_i, h_j)$. We use the notion of connectors to simplify the witness structure of an $H_4^*(a_1)$-contractible graph. Let $G[U]$ denote the subgraph of G induced by $U \subseteq V_G$. Let $y_1, \ldots, y_4$ denote the four dominating vertices of $H_4^*(a_1)$ and let $x_1, \ldots, x_{a_1}$ denote the remaining vertices of $H_4^*(a_1)$.

Lemma 1. *Let $a_1 \geq 0$. Every $H_4^*(a_1)$-contractible graph has an $H_4^*(a_1)$-witness structure $\mathcal{W}'$ such that $1 \leq |C_{\mathcal{W}'}(x_i, y_j)| \leq 2$ for all $1 \leq i \leq a_1$ and for all $1 \leq j \leq 4$.*

Proof. Let $\mathcal{W}$ be an $H_4^*(a_1)$-witness structure of an $H_4^*(a_1)$-contractible graph G. Below we transform $\mathcal{W}$ into a witness structure $\mathcal{W}'$ that satisfies the statement of the lemma.

From each $W(x_i)$ we move as many vertices as possible to $W(y_1) \cup \cdots \cup W(y_4)$ in a greedy way and without destroying the witness structure. This way we obtain an $H_4^*(a_1)$-witness structure $\mathcal{W}'$ of G. We claim that $1 \leq |C_{\mathcal{W}'}(x_i, y_j)| \leq 2$ for all $1 \leq i \leq a_1$ and for all $1 \leq j \leq 4$.

Suppose, for contradiction, that $|C_{\mathcal{W}'}(x_i, y_j)| \geq 3$ for some x_i and y_j. Let u_1, u_2, u_3 be three vertices in $C_{\mathcal{W}'}(x_i, y_j)$. Then $G[W'(x_i) \setminus \{u_1\}]$ has at least one component that contains a vertex of $C_{\mathcal{W}'}(x_i, y_1) \cup \cdots \cup C_{\mathcal{W}'}(x_i, y_4)$. Let $L_1, \ldots, L_p$ denote the vertex sets of these components. Observe that each L_q must be adjacent to at least two witness sets from $\{W'(y_1), \ldots, W'(y_4)\}$ that are not adjacent to $W'(x_i) \setminus L_q$, since otherwise we would have moved L_q to $W'(y_1) \cup \cdots \cup W'(y_4)$. Since u_1 is adjacent to at least one witness set, we deduce that $p = 1$. The fact that $p = 1$ implies that u_1 must even be adjacent to at least two unique witness sets from $\{W'(y_1), \ldots, W'(y_4)\}$, i.e., that are not adjacent to $W'(x_i) \setminus \{u_1\}$; otherwise we would have moved u_1 and all components of $G[W'(x_i) \setminus \{u_1\}]$ not equal to L_1 to $W'(y_1) \cup \cdots \cup W'(y_4)$. By the same arguments, exactly the same fact holds for u_2 and u_3. This is not possible, as three vertices cannot be adjacent to two unique sets out of four. □

We need one additional result, which can be found in [11] but follows directly from the polynomial time result on minors in [13].

Lemma 2 ([11]). *Let G be a graph and let $Z_1, \ldots, Z_p \subseteq V_G$ be p specified non-empty pairwise disjoint sets such that $\sum_{i=1}^{p} |Z_i| \leq k$ for some fixed integer k. The problem of deciding whether G is K_p-contractible with K_p-witness sets $U_1, \ldots U_p$ such that $Z_i \subseteq U_i$ for $i = 1, \ldots, p$ is polynomially solvable.*

We are now ready to state the main result of this section.

Theorem 5. *The $H_4^*(a_1)$-Contractibility problem is solvable in polynomial time for any fixed non-negative integer a_1.*

Proof. Let $G = (V, E)$ be a connected graph. We guess a set $\mathcal{S} = \{C_{\mathcal{W}}(x_i, y_j) \mid 1 \leq i \leq a_1, 1 \leq j \leq 4\}$ of connectors of size at most two. For each vertex u in each connector $C_{\mathcal{W}}(x_i, y_j) \in \mathcal{S}$ we pick a neighbor of u that is not in $\mathcal{S}$ and place it in a set Z_j. This leads to four sets $Z_1, \ldots, Z_4$. We remove $\mathcal{S}$ from G and call the resulting graph G'. We check the following. First, we determine in polynomial time whether $Z_1 \cup \cdots \cup Z_4$ is contained in one component T of G'. If so, we check whether T is K_4-contractible with K_4-witness sets $U_1, \ldots, U_4$ such that $Z_i \subseteq U_i$ for $i = 1, \ldots, 4$. This can be done in polynomial time due to Lemma 2. We then check whether the remaining components of G' together with the connectors $C_{\mathcal{W}}(x_i, y_j) \in \mathcal{S}$ form witness sets $W(x_i)$ for $i = 1, \ldots, a_1$. Also, this can be done in polynomial time; there is only one unique way to do this because witness sets $W(x_i)$ are not adjacent to each other. If somewhere in the whole process we get stuck, we check another set $\mathcal{S}$ of connectors and start all over. Due to Lemma 1, it indeed suffices to consider only sets of connectors that have size at most two. Hence, the total number of different 5-tuples $(\mathcal{S}, Z_1, \ldots, Z_4)$ is bounded by a polynomial in a_1, and consequently, the polynomial time result follows. □

3 The (H, v)-Contractibility Problem

We start with an observation. A *star* is a complete bipartite graph in which one of the partition classes has size one. The unique vertex in this class is called the *center* of the star. We denote the star on $k+1$ vertices with center c and leaves $b_1, \ldots, b_p$ by $K_{p,1}$.

Observation 1. *The* $(K_{p,1}, c)$-CONTRACTIBILITY *problem is polynomially solvable for all* $p \geq 1$.

Proof. Let graph $G = (V, E)$ and integer k form an instance of the $(K_{p,1}, c)$-CONTRACTIBILITY problem. We may without loss of generality assume that $|V| \geq k+p$. If G is $K_{p,1}$-contractible, then there exists a $K_{p,1}$-witness structure $\mathcal{W}$ of G such that $|W(b_i)| = 1$ for all $1 \leq i \leq k$. This can be seen as follows. As long as $|W(b_i)| \geq 2$ we can move vertices from $W(b_i)$ to $W(c)$ without destroying the witness structure. Our algorithm would just guess the witness sets $W(b_i)$ and check whether $V \setminus (W(b_1) \cup \cdots W(b_p))$ induces a connected subgraph. As the total number of guesses is bounded by a polynomial in p, this algorithm runs in polynomial time. □

We expect that there are relatively few pairs (H, v) for which (H, v)-CONTRACTIBILITY is in P (under the assumption P $\neq$ NP). This is due to the following observation and the main result in this section that shows that (H, v)-CONTRACTIBILITY is NP-complete whenever v is not a dominating vertex of H.

Observation 2. *Let H be a graph. If H-*CONTRACTIBILITY *is* NP*-complete, then (H, v)-*CONTRACTIBILITY *is* NP*-complete for every vertex $v \in V_H$.*

Theorem 6. *Let H be a connected graph and let $v \in V_H$. The (H, v)-*CONTRACTIBILITY *problem is* NP*-complete if v does not dominate H.*

Proof. Let H be a connected graph, and let v be a vertex of H that does not dominate H. Let $N_H(v)$ denote the neighborhood of v in H. We partition $V_H \setminus \{v\}$ into three sets $V_3 := V_H \setminus (N_H(v) \cup \{v\})$, $V_2 := \{w \in N_H(v) \mid w \text{ is not adjacent to } V_3\}$ and $V_1 := \{w \in N_H(v) \mid w \text{ is adjacent to } V_3\}$. Note that neither V_1 nor V_3 is empty because H is connected and v does not dominate H; V_2 might be empty.

Clearly, (H, v)-CONTRACTIBILITY is in NP, because we can verify in polynomial time whether a given partition of the vertex set of a graph G forms an H-witness structure of G with $|W(v)| \geq k$. In order to show that (H, v)-CONTRACTIBILITY is NP-complete, we use a reduction from 3-SAT, which is well-known to be NP-complete (cf. [7]). Let $X = \{x_1, \ldots, x_n\}$ be a set of variables and $C = \{c_1, \ldots, c_m\}$ be a set of clauses making up an instance of 3-SAT. Let $\overline{X} := \{\overline{x} \mid x \in X\}$. We introduce two additional literals s and t, as well as $2n$ additional clauses $s_i := (x_i \vee \overline{x}_i \vee s)$ and $t_i := (x_i \vee \overline{x}_i \vee t)$ for $i = 1, \ldots, n$. Let $S := \{s_1, \ldots, s_n\}$ and $T := \{t_1, \ldots, t_n\}$. Note that all $2n$ clauses in $S \cup T$ are satisfied for any satisfying truth assignment for C. For every vertex $w \in V_1$ we create a copy X^w of the set X, and we write $X^w := \{x_1^w, \ldots, x_n^w\}$. The literals s^w, t^w and the sets $\overline{X}^w$, C^w, S^w and T^w are defined similarly for every $w \in V_1$.

We construct a graph G such that C is satisfiable if and only if G has an H-witness structure $\mathcal{W}$ with $|W(v)| \geq k$. In order to do this, we first construct a subgraph G^w of G for every $w \in V_1$ in the following way:

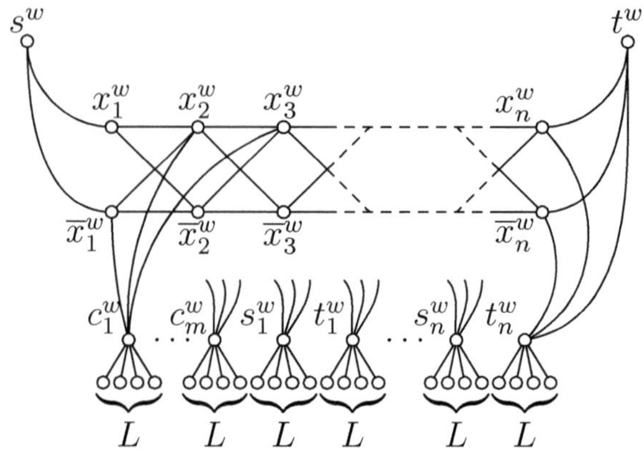

Fig. 3. A subgraph G^w, where $c_1^w = (\overline{x}_1^w \vee x_2^w \vee x_3^w)$

- every literal in $X^w \cup \overline{X}^w \cup \{s^w, t^w\}$ and every clause in $C^w \cup S^w \cup T^w$ is represented by a vertex in G^w
- we add an edge between $x \in X^w \cup \overline{X}^w \cup \{s^w, t^w\}$ and $c \in C^w \cup S^w \cup T^w$ if and only if x appears in c;
- for every $i = 1, \ldots, n-1$, we add edges $x_i^w x_{i+1}^w$, $x_i^w \overline{x}_{i+1}^w$, $\overline{x}_i^w x_{i+1}^w$, and $\overline{x}_i^w \overline{x}_{i+1}^w$
- we add edges $s^w x_1^w$, $s^w \overline{x}_1^w$, $t^w x_n^w$, and $t^w \overline{x}_n^w$
- for every $c \in C^w \cup S^w \cup T^w$, we add L vertices whose only neighbor is c; we determine the value of L later and refer to the L vertices as the *pendant vertices.*

See Figure 3 for a depiction of subgraph G^w. For clarity, most of the edges between the clause vertices and the literal vertices have not been drawn. We connect these subgraphs to each other as follows. For every $w, x \in V_1$, we add an edge between s^w and s^x in G if and only if w is adjacent to x in H. Let v^* be some fixed vertex in V_1. We add an edge between $s_1^{v^*}$ and s_1^w for every $w \in V_1 \setminus \{v^*\}$. No other edges are added between vertices of two different subgraphs G^w and G^x.

We add a copy of $H[V_2 \cup V_3]$ to G as follows. Vertex $x \in V_2$ is adjacent to s^w in G if and only if x is adjacent to w in H. Vertex $x \in V_3$ is adjacent to both s^w and t^w in G if and only if x is adjacent to w in H. Finally, we connect every vertex $x \in V_2$ to $s_1^{v^*}$. See Figure 4 for an example.

We define $L := (2 + 2n)|V_1| + |V_2| + |V_3| + 1$ and $k := (L + 1)(m + 2n)|V_1|$. We prove that G has an H-witness structure $\mathcal{W}$ with $|W(v)| \geq k$ if and only if C is satisfiable.

Suppose $t : X \to \{T, F\}$ is a satisfying truth assignment for C. Let X_T (respectively X_F) be the variables that are set to true (respectively false) by t. For every $w \in V_1$, we define $X_T^w := \{x_i^w \mid x_i \in X_T\}$ and $\overline{X}_T^w := \{\overline{x} \mid x \in X_T^w\}$; the sets X_F^w and $\overline{X}_F^w$ are defined similarly. We define the H-witness sets of G as follows. Let $W(w) := \{w\}$ for every $w \in V_2 \cup V_3$, and let $W(w) := \{s^w, t^w\} \cup X_F^w \cup \overline{X}_T^w$ for every $w \in V_1$. Finally, let $W(v) := V_G \setminus (\bigcup_{w \in V_1 \cup V_2 \cup V_3} W(w))$. Note

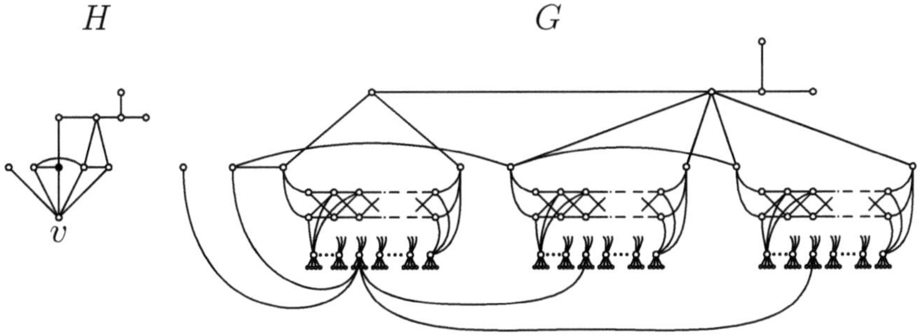

Fig. 4. A graph H, where v^* is the black vertex, and the corresponding graph G

that for every $w \in V_1$ and for every $i = 1, \ldots, n$, exactly one of $x_i^w, \overline{x}_i^w$ belongs to $X_F^w \cup \overline{X}_T^w$. Hence, $G[W(w)]$ is connected for every $w \in V_1$.

Since t is a satisfying truth assignment for C, every c_i^w is adjacent to at least one vertex of $X_T^w \cup \overline{X}_F^w$ for every $w \in V_1$; by definition, this also holds for every s_i^w and t_i^w. This together with the edges between $s_1^{v^*}$ and s_1^w for every $w \in V_1 \setminus \{v^*\}$ assures that $G[W(v)]$ is connected. So the witness set $G[W(w)]$ is connected for every $w \in V_H$. By construction, two witness sets $W(w)$ and $W(x)$ are adjacent if and only if w and x are adjacent in H. Hence $\mathcal{W} := \{W(w) \mid w \in V_H\}$ is an H-witness structure of G. Witness set $W(v)$ contains $n|V_1|$ literal vertices, $(m+2n)|V_1|$ clause vertices and L pendant vertices per clause vertex, i.e., $|W(v)| = (L+1)(m+2n)|V_1| + n|V_1| \geq k$.

Suppose G has an H-witness structure $\mathcal{W}$ with $|W(v)| \geq k$. We first show that all of the $(m+2n)|V_1|$ clause vertices must belong to $W(v)$. Note that for every $w \in V_1$, the subgraph G^w contains $2 + 2n + (L+1)(m+2n)$ vertices: the vertices s^w and t^w, the $2n$ literal vertices in $X^w \cup \overline{X}^w$, the $m+2n$ clause vertices and the $L(m+2n)$ pendant vertices. Hence we have

$$|V_G| = (2 + 2n + (L+1)(m+2n))|V_1| + |V_2| + |V_3|.$$

Suppose there exists a clause vertex c that does not belong to $W(v)$. Then the L pendant vertices adjacent to c cannot belong to $W(v)$ either, as $W(v)$ is connected and the pendant vertices are only adjacent to c. This means that $W(v)$ can contain at most $|V_G| - (L+1) = (L+1)(m+2n)|V_1| - 1$ vertices, contradicting the assumption that $W(v)$ contains at least $k = (L+1)(m+2n)|V_1|$ vertices. So all of the $(m+2n)|V_1|$ clause vertices, as well as all the pendant vertices, must belong to $W(v)$.

We define $W_i := \bigcup_{w \in V_i} W(w)$ for $i = 1, 2, 3$ and prove four claims.

Claim 1: $V_3 = W_3$.

The only vertices of G that are not adjacent to any of the clause vertices or pendant vertices in $W(v)$ are the vertices of V_3. As W_3 contains at least $|V_3|$ vertices, this proves Claim 1.

Claim 2: For any $w \in V_1$, both s^w and t^w belong to W_1.

Let w be a vertex in V_1, and let $w' \in V_3$ be a neighbor of w in H. Recall that both s^w and t^w are adjacent to w' in G. Suppose that s^w or t^w belongs to $W(v) \cup W_2$. By Claim 1, $w' \in W_3$. Then $W(v) \cup W_2$ and W_3 are adjacent. By construction, this is not possible. Suppose that s^w or t^w belongs to W_3. Then W_3 and $W(v)$ are adjacent, as s^w and t^w are adjacent to at least one clause vertex, which belongs to $W(v)$. This is not possible.

Claim 3: For any $w \in V_1$, at least one of each pair $x_i^w, \overline{x}_i^w$ of literal vertices belongs to $W(v)$.

Let $w \in V_1$. Suppose there exists a pair of literal vertices $x_i^w, \overline{x}_i^w$ both of which do not belong to $W(v)$. Apart from its L pendant vertices, the vertex t_i^w is only adjacent to x_i^w, $\overline{x}_i^w$ and t^w. The latter vertex belongs to W_1 due to Claim 2. Hence t_i^w and its L pendant vertices induce a component of $G[W(v)]$. Since $G[W(v)]$ contains other vertices as well, this contradicts the fact that $G[W(v)]$ is connected.

Claim 4: There exists a $w \in V_1$ for which at least one of each pair $x_i^w, \overline{x}_i^w$ of literal vertices belongs to W_1.

Let $S' := \{s^w \mid w \in V_1\}$ and $T' := \{t^w \mid w \in V_1\}$. By Claim 2, $S' \cup T' \subseteq W_1$. Suppose, for contradiction, that for every $w \in V_1$ there exists a pair $x_i^w, \overline{x}_i^w$ of literal vertices, both of which do not belong to W_1. Then for any $x \in V_1$, the witness set containing t^x does not contain any other vertex of $S' \cup T'$, as there is no path in $G[W_1]$ from t^x to any other vertex of $S' \cup T'$. But that means W_1 contains at least $|V_1| + 1$ witness sets, namely $|V_1|$ witness sets containing one vertex from T', and at least one more witness set containing vertices of S'. This contradiction to the fact that W_1, by definition, contains exactly $|V_1|$ witness sets finishes the proof of Claim 4.

Let $w \in V_1$ be a vertex for which of each pair $x_i^w, \overline{x}_i^w$ of literal vertices exactly one vertex belongs to W_1 and the other vertex belongs to $W(v)$; such a vertex w exists as a result of Claim 3 and Claim 4. Let t be the truth assignment that sets all the literals of $X^w \cup \overline{X}^w$ that belong to $W(v)$ to true and all other literals to false. Note that the vertices in C^w form an independent set in $W(v)$. Since $G[W(v)]$ is connected, each vertex $c_i^w \in C^w$ is adjacent to at least one of the literal vertices set to true by t. Hence t is a satisfying truth assignment for C. □

4 Conclusions and Open Problems

The main open problem is to finish the computational complexity classification of the H-Contractibility problem. All previous evidence suggested some working conjecture stating that this problem is polynomially solvable if H contains a dominating vertex and NP-complete otherwise. However, in this paper we presented an infinite family of graphs H *with* a dominating vertex for which H-Contractibility is NP-complete. As such, it sheds a new light on this problem and raises a whole range of new questions.

*1. What is the smallest graph H that contains a dominating vertex for which H-*CONTRACTIBILITY *is* NP*-complete?*

The smallest graph known so far is the graph $K_1 \bowtie \bar{H}$, where $\bar{H}$ is the graph on 68 vertices depicted in Figure 2. By Observation 2, we deduce that $(K_1 \bowtie \bar{H}, v)$-CONTRACTIBILITY is NP-complete for all $v \in V_{K_1 \bowtie \bar{H}}$. The following question might be easier to answer.

*2. What is the smallest graph H that contains a dominating vertex v for which (H, v)-*CONTRACTIBILITY *is* NP*-complete?*

We showed that (H, v)-CONTRACTIBILITY is NP-complete if H is connected and v does not dominate H. We still expect a similar result for H-CONTRACTIBILITY.

*3. Is the H-*CONTRACTIBILITY *problem* NP*-complete if H does not have a dominating vertex?*

Lemma 1 plays a crucial role in the proof of Theorem 5 that shows that $H_4^*(a_1)$-CONTRACTIBILITY is polynomially solvable. This lemma cannot be generalized such that it holds for the $H_i^*(a_1)$-CONTRACTIBILITY problem for $i \geq 5$ and $a_1 \geq 2$. Hence, new techniques are required to attack the $H_i^*(a_1)$-CONTRACTIBILITY problem for $i \geq 5$ and $a_1 \geq 2$.

*4. Is $H_5^*(a_1)$-*CONTRACTIBILITY *in* P *for all $a_1 \geq 0$?*

We expect that the (H, v)-CONTRACTIBILITY problem is in P for only a few target pairs (H, v). One such class of pairs might be (K_p, v), where v is an arbitrary vertex of K_p. Using similar techniques as before (i.e., simplifying the witness structure), one can easily show that (K_p, v)-CONTRACTIBILITY is polynomially solvable for $p \leq 3$.

*5. Is (K_p, v)-*CONTRACTIBILITY *in* P *for all $p \geq 4$?*

We finish this section with some remarks on fixing the parameter k in an instance (G, k) of the (H, v)-CONTRACTIBILITY problem. The complexity class XP is defined in the framework of parameterized complexity as developed by Downey and Fellows [5]. It consists of parameterized decision problems Π such that for each instance (I, k) it can be decided in $\mathcal{O}(f(k)|I|^{g(k)})$ time whether $(I, k) \in \Pi$, where f and g are computable functions depending only on k. That is, XP consists of parameterized decision problems which can be solved in polynomial time if the parameter is considered as a constant.

Proposition 2. *The (P_3, p_3)-*CONTRACTIBILITY *problem is in* XP.

Proof. We first observe that any graph G that is a yes-instance of this problem has a P_3-witness structure $\mathcal{W}$ with $|W(p_1)| = 1$. This is so, as we can move all but one vertex from $W(p_1)$ to $W(p_2)$ without destroying the witness structure. Moreover, such a graph G contains a set $W^* \subseteq W(p_3)$ such that $|W^*| = k$ and $G[W^*]$ is connected. Hence we act as follows.

Let G be a graph. We guess a vertex v and a set V^* of size k. We put all neighbors of v in a set W_2. We check if $G[V^*]$ is connected. If so, we check for each $y \in V_G \setminus (V^* \cup N(v) \cup \{v\})$ whether it is separated from $N(v)$ by V^* or not. If so, we put y in V^*. If not, we put y in W_2. In the end we check if $G[W_2]$ and $G[V^*]$ are connected. If so, G is a yes-instance of (P_3, p_3)-CONTRACTIBILITY, as $W(p_1) = \{v\}$, $W(p_2) = W_2$ and $W(p_3) = V^*$ form a P_3-witness structure of G with $|W(p_3)| \geq k$. If not, we guess another pair (v, V^*) and repeat the steps above. Since these steps can be performed in polynomial time and the total number of guesses is bounded by a polynomial in k, the result follows. □

6. Is (H, v)-CONTRACTIBILITY in XP whenever H-CONTRACTIBILITY is in P?

References

1. Andersson, M., Gudmundsson, J., Levcopoulos, C.: Restricted Mesh Simplification Using Edge Contraction. In: Chen, D.Z., Lee, D.T. (eds.) COCOON 2006. LNCS, vol. 4112, pp. 196–204. Springer, Heidelberg (2006)
2. Brouwer, A.E., Veldman, H.J.: Contractibility and NP-Completeness. Journal of Graph Theory 11, 71–79 (1987)
3. Cheng, S., Dey, T., Poon, S.: Hierarchy of Surface Models and Irreducible Triangulations. Computational Geometry Theory and Applications 27, 135–150 (2004)
4. Cong, J., Lim, S.K.: Edge Separability-Based Circuit Clustering with Application to Multilevel Circuit Partitioning. IEEE Transactions on Computer-Aided Design of Integrated Circuits and Systems 23, 346–357 (2004)
5. Downey, R.G., Fellows, M.R.: Parameterized Complexity. Monographs in Computer Science. Springer, Heidelberg (1999)
6. Fellows, M.R., Kratochvíl, J., Middendorf, M., Pfeiffer, F.: The Complexity of Induced Minors and Related Problems. Algorithmica 13, 266–282 (1995)
7. Garey, M.R., Johnson, D.S.: Computers and Intractability. W.H. Freeman and Co., New York (1979)
8. Harel, D., Koren, Y.: On Clustering Using Random Walks. In: Hariharan, R., Mukund, M., Vinay, V. (eds.) FSTTCS 2001. LNCS, vol. 2245, pp. 18–41. Springer, Heidelberg (2001)
9. Hoede, C., Veldman, H.J.: Contraction Theorems in Hamiltonian Graph Theory. Discrete Mathematics 34, 61–67 (1981)
10. Karypis, G., Kumar, V.: A Fast and High Quality Multilevel Scheme for Partitioning Irregular Graphs. SIAM Journal on Scientific Computing 20, 359–392 (1999)
11. Levin, A., Paulusma, D., Woeginger, G.J.: The Computational Complexity of Graph Contractions I: Polynomially Solvable and NP-Complete Cases. Networks 51, 178–189 (2008)
12. Levin, A., Paulusma, D., Woeginger, G.J.: The Computational Complexity of Graph Contractions II: Two Tough Polynomially Solvable Cases. Networks 52, 32–56 (2008)
13. Robertson, N., Seymour, P.D.: Graph Minors. XIII. The Disjoint Paths Problem. Journal of Combinatorial Theory, Series B 63, 65–110 (1995)

Dynamic Edit Distance Table under a General Weighted Cost Function

Heikki Hyyrö[1], Kazuyuki Narisawa[2,3], and Shunsuke Inenaga[4]

[1] Department of Computer Sciences, University of Tampere, Finland
heikki.hyyro@cs.uta.fi
[2] Department of Informatics, Kyushu University, Japan
[3] Japan Society for the Promotion of Science (JSPS)
k-nari@i.kyushu-u.ac.jp
[4] Graduate School of Information Sci. and Electrical Eng., Kyushu University, Japan
inenaga@c.csce.kyushu-u.ac.jp

1 Introduction

String comparison is a fundamental task in theoretical computer science, with applications in e.g., spelling correction and computational biology. *Edit distance* is a classic similarity measure between two given strings A and B. It is the minimum total cost for transforming A into B, or vice versa, using three types of edit operations: single-character insertions, deletions, and/or substitutions.

Landau et al. [1] introduced the problem of left incremental edit distance computation: Given a solution for the edit distance between A and B, the task is to compute a solution for the edit distance between A and B', where $B' = bB$. The alternative problem in which B and B' are interchanged is called the left decremental edit distance computation. Applications of left incremental/decremental edit distance computation include cyclic string comparison and computing approximate periods (see [1,2,3] for more).

Let m and n be the lengths of A and B, respectively. The basic dynamic programming method for the above problem requires $\Theta(mn)$ time per added/deleted character in front of B. For a unit edit cost function (the insertion, deletion, and substitution costs are all 1), Landau et al. [1] presented a fairly complicated $O(k)$-time algorithm, where k is an error threshold with $1 \leq k \leq \max\{m, n\}$. When k is not specified, then the algorithm takes $O(m+n)$ time. Other $O(m+n)$-time solutions for the unit cost function were presented in [2,3,4].

This paper deals with a more general, weighted edit cost function: we allow the edit cost function to have arbitrary non-negative integer costs. Schmidt [2] presented a complicated $O(n \log m)$ time solution per added/deleted character for a general cost function. In this paper, we present a simple $O(\min\{c(m+n), mn\})$-time algorithm for the same problem, where c is the maximum weight in the cost function. This translates into $O(m+n)$ time under constant weights. Our algorithm uses a *difference table*, a representation of a dynamic programming table proposed by Kim and Park [3]. We also show that the algorithm of Kim and Park is not easily applicable to the case of general weights.

J. van Leeuwen et al. (Eds.): SOFSEM 2010, LNCS 5901, pp. 515–527, 2010.

We report some preliminary experimental results which show advantages of our algorithm over a basic dynamic programming method for general edit cost functions and the Kim-Park algorithm for the unit cost function.

2 Preliminaries

Let Σ be a finite *alphabet*. An element of Σ is called a *character* and that of Σ^* is called a *string*. The empty string is denoted by ε. For any string $A = a_1 a_2 \cdots a_m$, let $A[i:j] = a_i \cdots a_j$ for $1 \leq i \leq j \leq m$. For convenience, let $A[i:j] = \varepsilon$ if $i > j$.

For any string $A = a_1 a_2 \cdots a_m$, we define the three editing operations:

1. Insert character b after position i of A, where $i = 0$ means inserting at front.
2. Delete character a_i from position i of A.
3. Substitute character b for character a_i at position i of A.

The above operations can be represented as pairs (ε, b), (a_i, ε), and (a_i, b), respectively. Each (x, y) has a positive cost function $\delta(x, y)$. That is, $\delta : (\{\varepsilon\} \times \Sigma) \cup (\Sigma \times \{\varepsilon\}) \cup (\Sigma \times \Sigma) \rightarrow \mathcal{N}$, where $\mathcal{N}$ denotes the set of non-negative integers. For any $a, b \in \Sigma$, we assume $\delta(a, b) = 0$ if $a = b$, and $\delta(a, b) > 0$ otherwise.

The *edit distance* of between strings A and B under cost function δ is the minimum total cost of editing operations under δ that transform A into B, or vice versa. Such an edit distance between A and B under δ is denoted by $ed_\delta(A, B)$.

The fundamental solution for $ed_\delta(A, B)$ is to compute a dynamic programming table D of size $(m + 1) \times (n + 1)$ s.t. $D[i, j] = ed_\delta(A[1 : i], B[1 : j])$ for $0 \leq i \leq m$ and $0 \leq j \leq m$, using the well-known recurrence (1) shown below.

$$\begin{aligned} D[i, 0] &= \textstyle\sum_{h=1}^{i} \ \delta(a_h, \varepsilon) \text{ for } 0 \leq i \leq m, \\ D[0, j] &= \textstyle\sum_{h=1}^{j} \ \delta(\varepsilon, b_h) \text{ for } 0 \leq j \leq n, \text{ and} \\ D[i, j] &= \min\{D[i, j-1] + \delta(\varepsilon, b_j), D[i-1, j] + \delta(a_i, \varepsilon), \\ &\qquad D[i-1, j-1] + \delta(a_i, b_j)\}, \text{ for } 1 \leq i \leq m \text{ and } 1 \leq j \leq n. \end{aligned} \tag{1}$$

As seen above, for a given D-table for A and $B[1 : j]$, we are able to compute $ed_\delta(A, B[1 : j + 1])$ and $ed_\delta(A, B[1 : j - 1])$ in $O(m)$ time. This paper deals with the symmetric problem of *left incremental (resp. decremental) edit distance computation*: Given a representation of $ed_\delta(A, B[j : n])$ for strings A and B, compute a representation of $ed_\delta(A, B[j - 1 : n])$ (resp. $ed_\delta(A, B[j + 1 : n])$).

3 The Kim-Park Algorithm

A *unit cost function* δ_1 is s.t. $\delta_1(\varepsilon, b) = 1$ for any $b \in \Sigma$, $\delta_1(a, \varepsilon) = 1$ for any $a \in \Sigma$, and $\delta_1(a, b) = 1$ for any $a \neq b$. The unit cost edit distance is known as the *Levenshtein edit distance* or *edit distance*. This section briefly recalls the algorithm of Kim and Park [3] that solves the problem in $O(m + n)$ time for δ_1.

3.1 Solution for the Unit Cost Function

Essentially the same techniques can be used to solve both the left incremental and decremental problems; as in [3], we concentrate on the decremental problem.

Let D denote the D-table for A and B, and D' denote the D-table for A and $B' = B[2:n]$. We find it convenient to use 1-based column indices with D'. Now column 1 acts as the left boundary column with values $D[i,1] = \sum_{h=1}^{i} \delta(a_h, \varepsilon)$, and columns $j = 2 \ldots n$ obey recurrence (1) in normal fashion. Now $D'[i,j] = ed_\delta(A[1:i], B[2:j])$ and cell (i,j) corresponds to a_i and b_j in both D and D'.

Kim and Park use a difference representation (the DR-table) of the D-table, where each position (i,j) has two fields such that $DR[i,j].U = D[i,j] - D[i-1,j]$ and $DR[i,j].L = D[i,j] - D[i,j-1]$. $DR[i,j].U$ is the difference to the upper neighbor and $DR[i,j].L$ is the difference to the left neighbor when row indices grow downwards and column indices towards right.

Let DR' denote the DR-table of strings A and B'. In what follows, we recall how the Kim-Park algorithm computes the DR'-table from the DR-table.

The Kim-Park algorithm is essentially based on the change table Ch, which is defined under our indexing convention[1] as $Ch[i,j] = D'[i,j] - D[i,j]$.

Lemma 1 ([3]). *For the unit cost function* δ_1*, each* $Ch[i,j]$ *is* -1, 0, *or* 1.

Lemma 2 ([3]). *For any* $0 \le i \le m$*, let* $f(i) = \min\{j \mid Ch[i,j] = -1\}$ *if such* j *exists, and let* $f(i) = n$ *otherwise. Then,* $Ch[i,j'] = -1$ *for* $f(i) \le j' < n$ *and* $f(i) \ge f(i-1)$ *for* $1 \le i \le m$*. Also, for any* $0 \le j \le n$*, let* $g(j) = \min\{i \mid Ch[i,j] = 1\}$ *if such* i *exists, and let* $g(j) = m+1$ *otherwise. Then,* $Ch[i',j] = 1$ *for* $g(j) \le i' \le m$ *and* $g(j) \ge g(j-1)$ *for* $1 \le j < n$.

$Ch[i,j]$ is said to be *affected* if $Ch[i-1,j-1]$, $Ch[i-1,j]$, and $Ch[i,j-1]$ are not of the same value. $DR'[i,j]$ is also said to be affected if $Ch[i,j]$ is affected.

Lemma 3 ([3]). *If* $DR'[i,j]$ *is not affected, then* $DR'[i,j] = DR[i,j]$*. If* $DR'[i,j]$ *is affected, then* $DR'[i,j].U = DR[i,j].U - Ch[i,j] + Ch[i-1,j]$ *and* $DR'[i,j].L = DR[i,j].L - Ch[i,j] + Ch[i,j-1]$.

By Lemmas 1 and 2, there are $O(m+n)$ affected entries in Ch, and these entries are categorized into two types: (-1)-boundaries and 1-boundaries. Consider the four neighbors $Ch[i-1,j-1]$, $Ch[i-1,j]$, $Ch[i,j-1]$ and $Ch[i,j]$. Among these, the upper-right entry $Ch[i-1,j]$ belongs to the (-1)-boundary if and only if $Ch[i-1,j] = -1$ and at least one of the other three entries is not -1. In similar fashion, the lower-left entry $Ch[i,j-1]$ belongs to the 1-boundary if and only if $Ch[i,j-1] = 1$ and at least one of the other three entries is not 1.

The Kim-Park algorithm scans the (-1)- and 1-boundaries of Ch and computes the affected entries in DR' using Lemma 3.

Theorem 1 ([3]). *The algorithm of Kim and Park [3] transforms DR to* DR' *in* $O(m+n)$ *time for* δ_1.

---

[1] [3] used 0-based indexing with D' and defined $Ch[i,j] = D'[i,j] - D[i,j+1]$.

D

		a	c	a	a	a	a	a
	0	5	10	15	20	25	30	35
a	1	0	5	10	15	20	25	30
b	2	1	5	10	15	20	25	30
b	3	2	6	10	15	20	25	30
b	4	3	7	11	15	20	25	30
b	5	4	8	12	16	20	25	30
c	6	5	4	9	14	19	24	29
a	7	6	5	4	9	14	19	24

D′

			c	a	a	a	a	a
		0	5	10	15	20	25	30
a		1	5	5	10	15	20	25
b		2	6	6	10	15	20	25
b		3	7	7	11	15	20	25
b		4	8	8	12	16	20	25
b		5	9	9	13	17	21	25
c		6	5	10	14	18	22	26
a		7	6	5	10	14	18	22

Ch

			c	a	a	a	a	a
		-5	-5	-5	-5	-5	-5	-5
a		1	0	-5	-5	-5	-5	-5
b		1	1	-4	-5	-5	-5	-5
b		1	1	-3	-4	-5	-5	-5
b		1	1	-3	-3	-4	-5	-5
b		1	1	-3	-3	-3	-4	-5
c		1	1	1	0	-1	-2	-3
a		1	1	1	1	0	-1	-2

Fig. 1. From left to right, D, D' and Ch tables for strings A = **abbbbca** and B = **acaaaaa**, with cost function $\delta(\varepsilon, b) = 5$ for any character b, $\delta(a, \varepsilon) = 1$ for any character a, and $\delta(a, b) = 5$ for any characters $a \neq b$

3.2 Exponential Lower Bound for a General Cost Function

As became evident in the preceding section, the primary principle of the Kim-Park algorithm could be frased as "trace the x-boundary in Ch for each possible boundary-type x". Here we consider how a direct application of this principle would to a general weighted function δ. An important fact is that now Lemma 1 does not hold. See Fig. 1 that illustrates D, D' and Ch for A = **abbbbca** and B = **acaaaaa**, with $\delta(\varepsilon, b) = 5$ for any $b \in \Sigma$, $\delta(a, \varepsilon) = 1$ for any $a \in \Sigma$, and $\delta(a, b) = 5$ for any $a \neq b$. The entries of the Ch-table have seven different values -5, -4, -3, -2, -1, 0, and 1.

Even if we leave aside the non-trivial question of how to define the possible boundary types under general costs, the feasibility of "tracing each possible x-boundary" seems to depend heavily on the number of different values in Ch.

It was shown in [5] that the number of different values in Ch is constant if each edit operation cost is a constant rational number. Let us now consider an integer cost function that may have an exponential edit cost w.r.t. the length of a given string. We may obtain the following negative result. The proof is omitted due to lack of space.

Theorem 2. *Let $A = a_1 a_2 \cdots a_m$ and $B = b_1 b_2 \cdots b_{m+1}$ be strings such that $a_i \neq a_{i'}$ for any $1 \leq i \neq i' \leq$, $b_j \neq b_{j'}$ for any $1 \leq j \neq j' \leq m+1$, and $a_i \neq b_j$ for any $1 \leq i \leq m$ and $1 \leq j \leq m+1$. Let $\delta(\varepsilon, \sigma) = \delta(\sigma, \varepsilon) = (m-1)2^m - 1$ for any $\sigma \in \Sigma$, $\delta(a_i, b_j) = 2^m$ if $i \neq j$, and $\delta(a_i, b_j) = 2^{i-1}$ if $i = j$. Then, Ch-tables under δ can have $\Omega(2^m)$ different values.*

Due to the above theorem, a natural extension of the Kim-Park algorithm might need to check if there is an x-boundary in the Ch-table for exponentially many different values x. Note e.g. from Fig. 1 that different boundaries do not all begin from column 1, and now the boundaries may also be non-contiguous, making their tracing more difficult. Also note the input strings may define which of the $\Omega(2^m)$ values actually appear within the $O(mn)$ entries of the Ch-table.

In part due to these difficulties, we propose in the next section an algorithm that discards the notion of tracing boundaries.

4 A Simple Algorithm for a General Cost Function

As became evident in the preceding discussion, the essential question in incremental/decremental edit distance computation is: Which entries in DR do we need to change in order to transform DR into DR'? The algorithm of Kim and Park finds such changed entries by traversing the affected entries of the Ch-table.

We ignore the Ch-table and concentrate only on the difference table DR (and its updated version DR'). Recurrence (1) showed how to compute the value $D[i,j]$ when the three neighboring values $D[i,j-1]$, $D[i-1,j]$ and $D[i-1,j-1]$ are known. Consider Fig. 2, where the values of $D[i,j-1]$, $D[i-1,j]$ and $D[i,j]$ are represented by using $D[i-1,j-i] = d$ as a base value. Now $DR[i-1,j].L = x$ and $DR[i,j-1].U = y$.

	$j-1$	j
$i-1$	d	$d+x$
i	$d+y$	$d+z$

Fig. 2. Illustration of computing $DR[i,j]$

Computing $DR[i,j]$ consists of computing $DR[i,j].U = d+z-(d+x) = z-x$ and $DR[i,j].L = d+z-(d+y) = z-y$. If we assume that $DR[i-1,j].L = x$ and $DR[i,j-1].U = y$ are already known, then the only missing value is z. Based on recurrence (1), the relationship between the values in Fig. 2 fulfills the condition $d+z = \min\{d+y+\delta(\varepsilon,b_j), d+x+\delta(a_i,\varepsilon), d+\delta(a_i,b_j)\}$. Since d appears in each choice within the min-clause, we may drop it from both sides. Now $z = \min\{y+\delta(\varepsilon,b_j), x+\delta(a_i,\varepsilon), \delta(a_i,b_j)\}$. This leads directly into the following recurrence (2) for the entry $DR[i,j]$.

$$\begin{aligned}
&DR[i,0].U = \delta(a_i,\varepsilon) \text{ for every } 1 \le i \le m,\\
&DR[0,j].L = \delta(\varepsilon,b_j) \text{ for every } 1 \le j \le n, \text{ and}\\
&DR[i,j].U = z - DR[i-1,j].L \text{ and } DR[i,j].L = z - DR[i,j-1].U, \text{where}\\
&z = \min\{DR[i-1,j].L + \delta(\varepsilon,b_j), DR[i,j-1].U + \delta(a_i,\varepsilon), \delta(a_i,b_j)\}, \text{ for}\\
&\quad \text{every } 1 \le i \le m \text{ and every } 1 \le j \le n.
\end{aligned} \tag{2}$$

To avoid references to the Ch-table, we use the following alternative to decide if $DR'[i,j]$ is affected, that is, if it is possible that $DR'[i,j] \ne DR[i,j]$. The next lemmas follows directly from recurrence (2).

Lemma 4. *For $1 \le i \le m$ and $1 \le j \le n$, the entry $DR'[i,j]$ is affected if and only if $DR'[i-1,j].L \ne DR[i-1,j].L$ or $DR'[i,j-1].U \ne DR[i,j-1].U$.*

Our algorithm for transforming DR into DR' uses Lemma 4 to keep track of which entries in DR may become different. All such affected entries are recomputed using recurrence (2).

The columns $j = 1 \ldots n$ of DR' are processed one column at a time in the order of increasing j. During the computation we maintain a $prev\Delta$-table as follows: When starting to process column j, the table $prev\Delta$ contains the row numbers i for which $DR'[i, j-1].U \neq DR[i, j-1].U$. These row numbers are recorded in increasing order.

The column $j = 1$ of DR is a special case. It is transformed directly into the first boundary column of DR' by setting $DR'[i, 1].U = \delta(a_i, \varepsilon)$ for $i = 1 \ldots m$. For simplicity we add each $i = 1 \ldots m$, into $prev\Delta$ even if $DR'[i, 1].U = DR[i, 1].U$.

Each column $j = 2 \ldots n$ is processed according to Lemma 4 that states that the value $DR'[i, j]$ needs to be computed (i.e. its value may change from $DR[i, j]$) only if $DR'[i, j-1].U \neq DR[i, j-1].U$ or $DR'[i-1, j].L \neq DR[i-1, j].L$.

The entries $DR'[i, j]$ are recomputed for all i that appear in $prev\Delta$, in the order of increasing row indices i. This handles all entries in column j where the first condition, $DR'[i, j-1].U \neq DR[i, j-1].U$, of Lemma 4 is true.

The second condition, $DR'[i-1, j].L \neq DR[i-1, j].L$, corresponds to recomputed and consequently changed values in the currently processed column j. This is easily checked during the computation as we proceed along increasing row indices i: Whenever we recompute the entry $DR'[i, j]$, that is, recompute $DR'[i, j].U$ and $DR'[i, j].L$, we also check whether $DR'[i, j].L \neq DR[i, j].L$. If this condition is true, then the next-row entry $DR'[i+1, j]$ is affected and will be recomputed next. This ensures that also all entries $DR'[i, j]$, for which $DR'[i-1, j].L \neq DR[i-1, j].L$ holds, will be recomputed in column j.

In order to prepare the table $prev\Delta$ for the next column $j+1$, we record each row index i where $DR'[i, j].U \neq DR[i, j].U$ into a second table $curr\Delta$. This is done whenever an entry $DR'[i, j]$ has been computed. When we later move from column j to column $j+1$, the roles of the tables $prev\Delta$ and $curr\Delta$ are interchanged. Hence the affected row indices recorded into $curr\Delta$ in column j will be read from $prev\Delta$ in column $j+1$, and the new affected row indices in column $j+1$ will be recorded to $curr\Delta$, which previously acted as $prev\Delta$ in column j and was holding the affected values for column $j-1$.

The above-described steps are implemented by Algorithm 1. Let us present the following clarifying comments on the pseudocode of the algorithm:

- In the pseudocode we do not use the separate notation DR' to refer to the transformed version of DR.
- In the pseudocode, the tables $prev\Delta$ and $curr\Delta$ are indexed starting from 1. The variables $prevIdx$ and $currIdx$, respectively, denote the current positions in these tables.
- The end of the table $prev\Delta$ is marked by inserting a sentinel value $m+1$ as the last value in the table. Also the loop on lines 1-2 does this (and instead leaves out the first row 1, as the computation in any case starts by using the row index $i = 1$).
- Lines 6-8 compute the updated values $DR'[i, j].L$ and $DR'[i, j].U$ into the variables $new.L$ and $new.U$ according to recurrence (2).
- Line 9 stores the old values $DR[i, j].L$ and $DR[i, j].U$ into the variables $old.L$ and $old.U$
- Lines 13-18 check the condition $DR'[i-1, j].L \neq DR[i-1, j].L$ of Lemma 4 in the following way: Line 15 increments the current row index i as if the

Algorithm 1. Generalized traversal of affected entries

```
1  for i ← 1 to m do
2      prevΔ[i] ← i + 1;  DR[i, 1].U ← δ(a_i, ε)
3  i ← 1;  j ← 1;  DR[0, j].L ← δ(ε, b_j);  currIdx ← 1;  prevIdx ← 1
4  while i ≤ m and j ≤ n do
5      while i ≤ m do
6          x ← DR[i − 1, j].L;  y ← DR[i, j − 1].U
7          z ← min{x + δ(a_i, ε), y + δ(ε, b_j), δ(a_i, b_j)}
8          new.L ← z − y;  new.U ← z − x
9          old.L ← DR[i, j].L;  old.U ← DR[i, j].U
10         DR[i, j].L ← new.L;  DR[i, j].U ← new.U
11         if old.U ≠ new.U then
12             currΔ[currIdx] ← i;  currIdx ← currIdx + 1
13         i ← i + 1
14         if old.L = new.L then
15             now = i
16             repeat
17                 i ← prevΔ[prevIdx];  prevIdx ← prevIdx + 1
18             until i ≥ now
19     currΔ[currIdx] ← m + 1
20     Interchange the roles of the tables currΔ and prevΔ
21     currIdx ← 1;  i ← prevΔ[1];  prevIdx ← 2;  j ← j + 1
```

condition would be true and $i+1$ would be the next row to process. Line 16 checks if this condition was not true. If it was not, the repeat-until reads still unused row indices from the *prev*Δ-table until either one which is at least $i+1$ is found (and it becomes the next row to process) or *prev*Δ becomes fully processed (sentinel $m+1$ was read).

- Line 19 adds the end sentinel $m+1$ to the table *curr*Δ.
- Line 20 corresponds in practice to e.g. swapping two pointers that point to the Δ-tables.
- Line 21 already reads the first row value $i = prev\Delta[1]$ for column $j+1$. Therefore *prevIdx* becomes 2.
- The main loop of line 4 stops either when line 21 sets $i = m+1$, which means that the *prev*Δ-table for the current column was empty, or when the last column n has been processed.

Let $\#_j$ denote the number of actually changed entries in column j. That is, $\#_j = |\{i \ : \ DR'[i,j] \neq DR[i,j]\}|$.

Theorem 3. *Algorithm 1 recomputes a total of* $\Theta(m)$ *entries in columns* $j = 1 \ldots 2$ *and a total of* $O(\sum_{j=2}^{n} \#_j)$ *entries in columns* $j = 3 \ldots n$.

Proof. The case for columns $j = 1 \ldots 2$ follows directly from how the m entries $DR'[i,j].U$ in column 1 are recomputed (i.e. reset) and how the *prev*Δ-table is initialized with $\Theta(m)$ row indices prior to processing column 2.

When the algorithm starts to process a column $j > 2$, the *prev*Δ-table contains $O(\#_{j-1})$ row indices (and one sentinel). Hence in column j at least these

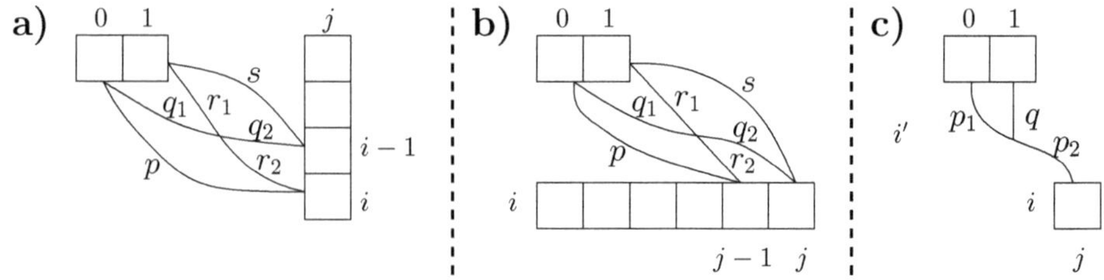

Fig. 3. Illustration of crossing paths in proof of Theorem 4

$O(\#_{j-1})$ entries will be recomputed. In addition to these, further entries $DR'[i,j]$ will be recomputed only if the entry $DR'[i-1,j]$ was recomputed and it became different than $DR[i-1,j]$. The number of such entries is at most $\#_j$. No other cells are recomputed in column j. Hence the total number of cells recomputed in any column $j > 2$ is at most $O(\#_{j-1}+\#_j)$. Therefore the total number of entries recomputed in columns $j = 3 \ldots n$ is $O(\sum_{j=3}^{n}(\#_{j-1} + \#_j)) = O(\sum_{j=2}^{n} \#_j)$. □

Theorem 3 states that Algorithm 1 makes the minimum possible work in columns $j > 2$, as clearly any algorithm that transforms DR into DR' must change at least $\#_j$ values in column j. The columns $j = 1$ and $j = 2$ possibly involve up to $\Theta(m)$ unnecessary work due to how the boundary column $j = 1$ and the $prev\Delta$-table are first initialized. Minor modifications and a further preprocessing stage would allow us to make the algorithm completely minimal, i.e. to recompute only $O(\#_1 + \#_2)$ entries in the first two columns. We omit this consideration for now, as one of the main goals of this paper is to propose an algorithm that is both general and practical. The current form of Algorithm 1 seems to fulfill this goal well. The pseudocode is compact but nevertheless already provides such a detailed description of the algorithm that it is very straight-forward to compose a working implementation in real code, even if one has little background knowledge. We believe that our Algorithm 1 is not only more general than the previous algorithm of Kim and Park; it also seems even simpler in terms of implementing and understanding all steps of the algorithm. These are valuable qualities in practice.

Corollary 1. *Algorithm 1 transforms DR into DR′ in $O(m+n)$ time under the unit cost function δ_1.*

Proof. It follows from Theorems 1 and 3 and the preceding discussion that the work is at most $O(m+n) + \Theta(m) = O(m+n)$. □

Theorem 4. *Let c be the highest weight in the used cost function δ, that is, $c = \max\{\delta(a,b) \ : \ a,b \in \Sigma \cup \{\varepsilon\}\}$. Then $\sum_{j=1}^{n} \#_j = O(c(m+n))$.*

Proof. We analyse the tables DR', DR and Ch in similar fashion as Schmidt in the proof of Theorem 6.1 in [2]. The basis is to consider table D as a weighted grid graph that has a horizontal edge with weight $\delta(\varepsilon, b_j)$ from $D[i, j-1]$ to $D[i, j]$ for $i = 0 \ldots m$ and $j = 1 \ldots n$, a vertical edge with weight $\delta(a_i, \varepsilon)$ from $D[i-1, j]$ to $D[i, j]$ for $i = 1 \ldots m$ and $j = 0 \ldots n$, and a diagonal edge with weight $\delta(a_i, b_j)$ for $i = 1 \ldots m$ and $j = 1 \ldots n$. Now the edit distance $D[i, j] = ed_\delta(A[1:i], B[1:j])$ is equal to the cost of the cheapest weighted path from $D[0, 0]$ to $D[i, j]$.

Let us consider the rows i in column j where $DR'[i, j].U \neq DR[i, j].U$. Since $D'[i, j] = D[i, j] + Ch[i, j]$, we have that $DR'[i, j].U = D'[i, j] - D'[i-1, j] = D[i, j] + Ch[i, j] - D[i-1, j] - Ch[i-1, j] = DR[i, j].U + Ch[i, j] - Ch[i-1, j]$. That is, $DR'[i, j].U \neq DR[i, j].U$ if and only if $Ch[i, j] \neq Ch[i-1, j]$.

Figure 3a depicts minimum cost paths corresponding to the distances $D[i, j] = p$, $D[i-1, j] = q_1 + q_2$, $D'[i, j] = r_1 + r_2$ and $D'[i-1, j] = s$. The path from $D[0, 0]$ to $D[i-1, j]$ must cross with the path from $D[0, 1]$ to $D[i, j]$. In Figure 3a, the crossing point divides these paths into the subpaths q_1, q_1, r_1 and r_2.

Each path and subpath has a minimal cost, and so the inequalities $p \leq q_1 + r_2$ and $s \leq r_1 + q_2$ hold. Hence $D[i, j] + D'[i-1, j] = p + s \leq q_1 + r_2 + r_1 + q_2 = D[i-1, j] + D'[i, j]$. This leads into the inequality $D'[i-1, j] - D[i-1, j] \leq D'[i, j] - D[i, j]$, that is, $Ch[i-1, j] \leq Ch[i, j]$. Since we deal with integers, $Ch[i, j] \neq Ch[i-1, j]$ iff $Ch[i, j] \geq Ch[i-1, j] + 1$. Note that the $Ch[i, j]$ values are non-decreasing with growing i, and the minimum increment is 1.

Now consider the possible range of values for $Ch[i, j]$ when $i \geq 1$ and $j \geq 1$. The value $D[i, j]$ can never be larger than the alternative of first going to $D[0, 1]$ along the edge with weight $\delta(\varepsilon, b_2)$ and then following the minimal path of cost $D'[i, j]$. That is, $Ch[i, j] \geq -\delta(\varepsilon, b_2) \geq c$, where c is the maximum weight in δ. On the other hand, the value $D'[i, j]$ can never be worse than the alternative of going directly down until the path corresponding to $D[i, j]$ is reached in some point $D[i', 1]$, and then following that path to the end. This is depicted in Figure 3c so that $D[i, j] = p_1 + p_2$ and q is the cost of the direct downward path from $D[0, 1]$ up to the point of crossing $D[i', 1]$. The paths (with costs) p_1 and q have the same cost $\sum_{h=1}^{i'-1} \delta(a_h, \varepsilon)$ up to row $i' - 1$. It is not difficult to show that $q + p_2 \leq p_1 + p_2 + \min\{\delta(\varepsilon, b_1), \delta(a_{i'}, b_1) - \delta(a_{i'}, \varepsilon)\}$, which means that $Ch[i, j] \leq \min\{\delta(\varepsilon, b_1), \delta(a_{i'}, b_1) - \delta(a_{i'}, \varepsilon)\} \leq c$.

Since $-c \leq Ch[i, j] \leq c$ and the Ch-values are non-decreasing with increments ≥ 1, column j may contain at most $O(c)$ different rows i where $Ch[i, j] \neq Ch[i-1, j]$, that is, at most $O(c)$ different rows i where $DR'[i, j].U \neq DR[i, j].U$.

In similar fashion we may show each row i contains at most $O(c)$ columns j where $DR'[i, j].L \neq DR[i, j].L$. As seen by comparing Figures 3a and 3b, the underlying cases are very similar. We omit further details due to lack of space.

The end result is that columns $j = 1 \ldots n$ contain $O(cn)$ points (i, j) where $DR'[i, j].U \neq DR[i, j].U$, and rows $i = 1 \ldots m$ contain $O(cm)$ points (i, j) where $DR'[i, j].L \neq DR[i, j].L$. Since an entry $DR'[i, j]$ is affected only in the preceding types of points, we may conclude that $\sum_{j=1}^{n} \#_j = O(c(m + n))$. □

Corollary 2. *Algorithm 1 transforms DR into DR′ in $O(\min\{c(m + n), mn\})$ time under an arbitrary cost function δ whose maximum weight is c, and in $O(m + n)$ time under a cost function δ with constant (but arbitrary) weights.*

Proof. The $O(mn)$ bound is due to the fact that Algorithm 1 recomputes each of the $O(mn)$ entries at most once. The other bounds follow from Theorems 3 and 4. □

5 Experiments

In all experiments of this section, we computed a representation of D for A and $B[j:n]$ for each $j = n, n-1, \ldots, 1$, where the length of both A and B was n. All the experiments were conducted on a CentOS Linux desktop computer with two 3GHz dual core Xeon processors and 16GB memory.

5.1 Random Data

First we performed some experiments to investigate the performance of our algorithm under various edit operation costs. The running times shown in this section are average times for 10 runs with randomly generated string pairs.

Figures 4a-4c show the running times of our algorithm for random texts of length 5000 with an alphabet of size 26.

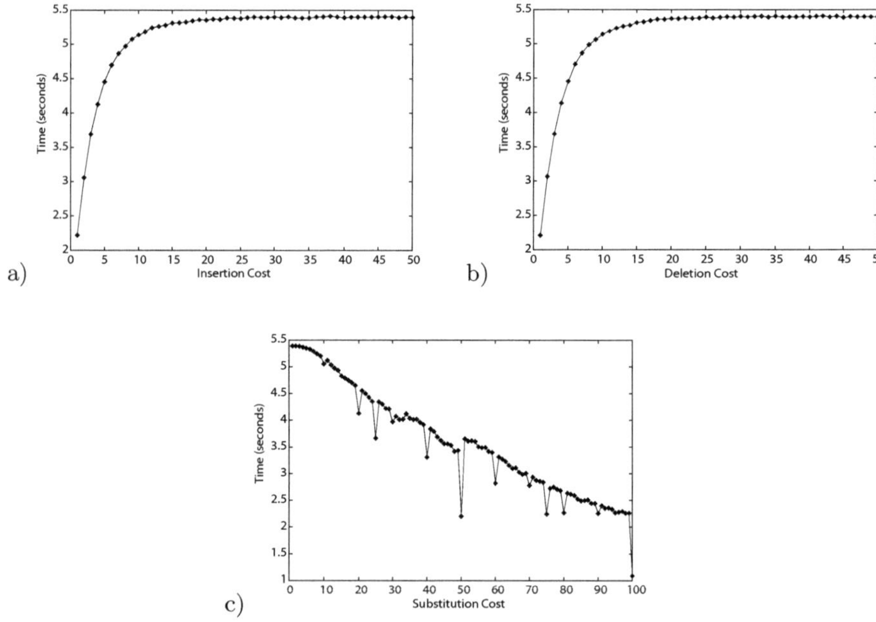

Fig. 4. Running times of our algorithm on random text data of length 5000 from an alphabet of size 26 with; a) variable insertion cost from 1 to 50 and fixed deletion and substitution costs 1, b) variable deletion cost from 1 to 50 and fixed insertion and substitution costs 1, c) variable substitution cost from 1 to 100 and fixed insertion and deletion costs 50.

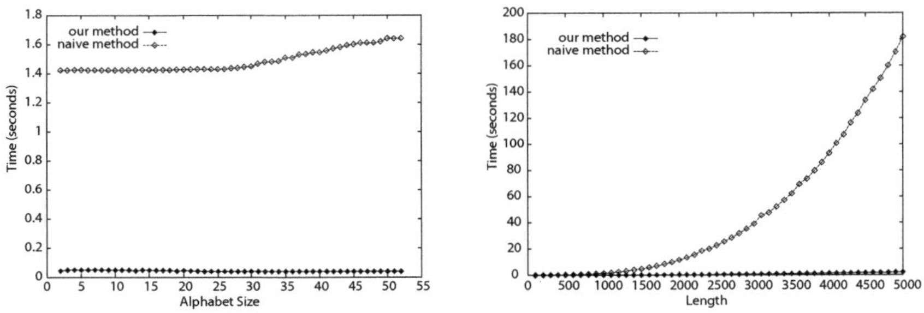

Fig. 5. Running times of our algorithm and the naive method on random text data with; (left) fixed length 1000 and variable alphabet sizes from 2 to 52, (right) fixed alphabet size 26 and variable lengths from 100 to 5000

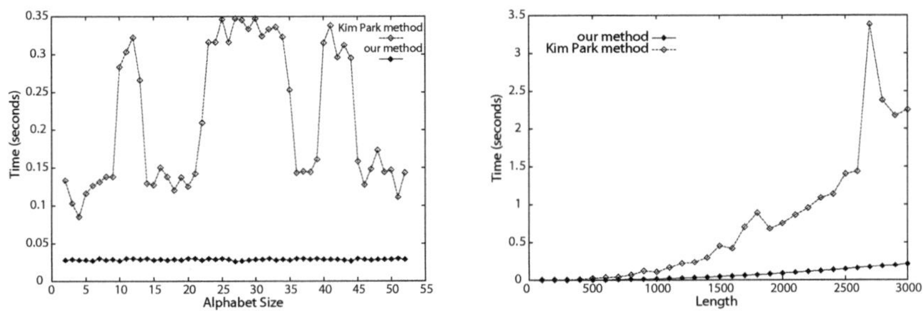

Fig. 6. Running times of our algorithm and the Kim and Park algorithm on random text data with; (left) fixed length 1000 and variable alphabet sizes from 2 to 52, (right) fixed alphabet size 26 and variable lengths from 100 to 3000

In the test of Fig. 4a, deletion and substitution costs were fixed to 1 and the insertion cost varied from 1 to 50. Fig. 4b is otherwise similar, but now the insertion and substitution costs were fixed to 1 and the deletion cost varied from 1 to 50. From these it is evident how our algorithm becomes slower as the insertion or deletion cost becomes larger.

Fig. 4c corresponds to a test where the insertion and deletion costs were fixed to 50 and the substitution cost varied from 1 to 100.

Next we performed experiments to compare running times of our algorithm with the naive method and the Kim-Park algorithm [3] on random text data, varying the alphabet size and string length as parameters. Ours and the Kim-Park algorithm compute DR-tables, while the naive method computes D-tables.

Fig. 5 shows running times of our algorithm and the naive method on random text data with; (left) fixed length 1000 and variable alphabet sizes from 2 to 52, (right) fixed alphabet size 26 and variable lengths from 100 to 5000. In these experiments, the insertion, deletion, and substitution costs for our algorithm and the naive method were randomly selected to be 137, 116 and 242, respectively.

Fig. 6 shows running times of our algorithm and the Kim-Park algorithm under the unit cost function on random text data with; (left) fixed length 1000 and variable alphabet sizes from 2 to 52, (right) fixed alphabet size 26 and variable lengths from 100 to 3000. The Kim-Park algorithm has more variance, probably due to the poor locality of its memory access patterns.

5.2 Corpora Data

In this section, we show our experimental results on data from two corpora: one consists of English texts from Reuters-21578 text categorization test collection[2], and the other of biological data from the canterbury corpus [6].

Table 1. Comparison of running times for the Reuters data (in seconds)

length	our method	naive method
1000	0.04	1.50
2000	0.27	12.0
3000	0.71	40.4
4000	1.36	97.1
5000	2.29	189

Table 2. Comparison of running times for the E.coli data (in seconds)

length	our method	naive method
1000	0.01	1.43
2000	0.09	11.5
3000	0.23	38.8
4000	0.43	92.8
5000	0.70	181

Table 3. Cost function for the E.coli data

δ	ε	A	C	G	T
ε	-	3	3	3	3
A	3	0	2	1	2
C	3	2	0	2	1
G	3	1	2	0	2
T	3	2	1	2	0

Table 1 compares the running times of our algorithm and the naive method when processing English text. In this experiment, we used the same randomly selected insertion, deletion, and substitution costs which are 137, 116 and 242, respectively. For each length $l = 1000, 2000, 3000, 4000, 5000$, we randomly selected 10 files of length around l and performed left incremental edit distance computation between each possible file pair within the selected similar-length files. The table shows the average time in seconds over all computations with the given length.
Table 2 shows a similar comparison when processing DNA sequences from "E.coli", the complete genome of the E. Coli bacterium of length 4638690. For each length $l = 1000, 2000, 3000, 4000, 5000$, we randomly picked 10 substrings of length l and performed left incremental edit distance computation between each equal-length substring pair. In this experiment we used the cost function shown in Table 3, which was proposed in [7] for weighted edit distance computation between DNA sequences.

The difference between the highest costs 242 and 3 in these two experiments seemed to result in the difference of running times of our algorithm, since our algorithm runs in $O(\min\{c(m+n), mn\})$ time, where c is the highest cost used.

[2] `http://kdd.ics.uci.edu/databases/reuters21578/reuters21578.html`

References

1. Landau, G.M., Myers, E.W., Schmidt, J.P.: Incremental String Comparison. SIAM J. Comp. 27(2), 557–582 (1998)
2. Schmidt, J.P.: All Highest Scoring Paths in Weighted Grid Graphs and Their Application in Finding All Approximate Repeats in Strings. SIAM J. Comp. 27(4), 972–992 (1998)
3. Kim, S.R., Park, K.: A Dynamic Edit Distance Table. J. Disc. Algo. 2, 302–312 (2004)
4. Hyyrö, H.: An Efficient Linear Space Algorithm for Consecutive Suffix Alignment under Edit Distance. In: Amir, A., Turpin, A., Moffat, A. (eds.) SPIRE 2008. LNCS, vol. 5280, pp. 155–163. Springer, Heidelberg (2008)
5. Masek, W.J., Paterson, M.: A Faster Algorithm Computing String Edit Distances. J. Comput. Syst. Sci. 20(1), 18–31 (1980)
6. Arnold, R., Bell, T.: A Corpus for the Evaluation of Lossless Compression Algorithms. In: Proc. DCC 1997, pp. 201–210 (1997), `http://corpus.canterbury.ac.nz/`
7. Kurtz, S.: Approximate String Searching under Weighted Edit Distance. In: Proc. 3rd South American Workshop on String Processing (WSP 1996), pp. 156–170 (1996)

How to Complete an Interactive Configuration Process?

Configuring as Shopping

Mikoláš Janota[1], Goetz Botterweck[2], Radu Grigore[3], and Joao Marques-Silva[3]

[1] Lero, University College Dublin, Ireland
[2] Lero, University of Limerick, Ireland
[3] University College Dublin, Ireland

Abstract. When configuring customizable software, it is useful to provide interactive tool-support that ensures that the configuration does not breach given constraints. But, when is a configuration complete and how can the tool help the user to complete it? We formalize this problem and relate it to concepts from non-monotonic reasoning well researched in Artificial Intelligence. The results are interesting for both practitioners and theoreticians. Practitioners will find a technique facilitating an interactive configuration process and experiments supporting feasibility of the approach. Theoreticians will find links between well-known formal concepts and a concrete practical application.

1 Introduction

Software Product Lines (SPLs) build on the assumption that when developing software-intensive systems it is advantageous to decide upfront which products to include in scope and then manage construction and reuse systematically [4].

This approach is suitable for families of products that share a significant amount of their user-visible or internal functionality. Parnas identified such *program families* as: ... *sets of programs whose common properties are so extensive that it is advantageous to study the common properties of the programs before analyzing individual members.* [20]

A key aspect of SPLs is that the scope of products is defined and described *explicitly* using models of various expressivity [14,1,23,10]. Conceptually, we can consider an SPL as a mapping from a *problem space* to a *solution space*. The problem space comprises requirements that members of the product line satisfy, and, the solution space comprises possible realizations, e.g., programs in C^{++}. These spaces are defined by some constraints, i.e., requirements or solutions violating the constraints are not within the respective space.

A specification for a new product is constructed from the requirements which must be matched to the constraints that define the scope of the product line. In effect, the purchaser picks a particular member of the problem space. Subsequently, software engineers are responsible for delivering a product, a member of the solution space, corresponding to the given specification.

J. van Leeuwen et al. (Eds.): SOFSEM 2010, LNCS 5901, pp. 528–539, 2010.

If the problem space is complex, picking one of its members is not trivial. Hence, we strive to support interactive configuration with *configurator* tools. Despite the fact that this has been researched extensively (see [17,8,1,24,11,9]), little attention has been paid to the completion of a configuration process. Namely, how shall we treat variables of the configuration model that have not been bound by the user at all? (This issue has been noted by Batory in [1, Section 4.2].)

This article studies this problem (Sect. 2.2) and designs an enhancement of a configurator that helps the user to get closer to finishing the configuration process by binding variability without making decisions for the user, i.e., it is aiming at not being overly smart. The article focuses mainly on this functionality for propositional configuration (Sect. 3) and it relates to research on Closed World Assumption (Sect. 3.4). The general, non-propositional, case is conceptualized relying on the notion of preference (Sect. 4).

2 Background and Motivation

Kang et al. developed a methodology *Feature Oriented Domain Analysis* (*FODA*), where *feature models* are used to carry out *domain analysis*—a systematic identification of variable and common parts of a family of systems [14]. For the purpose of this article, it is sufficient to consider a feature as "*a prominent or distinctive user-visible aspect, quality, or characteristic of a software system or system*" [14], and a product as a combination of its features. A *Software Product Line* is a system for developing products from a certain family captured as a set of feature combinations defined by a *feature model*.

The semantics of a feature model is typically defined with propositional logic. Each feature f is represented by a propositional variable v_f and a Boolean formula is constructed as a conjunction of formulæ representing the different modeling primitives. The satisfying assignments of the resulting formula define the set of possible feature combinations [23]. A popular notation is the *FODA notation* [14] with the primitives in Fig. 1a exemplified by Fig. 1b whose semantics is in Fig. 1c. The corresponding feature combinations, defining the problem space, are listed in Fig. 1d. The FODA notation has several extensions, e.g., *feature attributes* represent values such as price. For general attributes, Boolean logic is insufficient and the semantics is expressed as a Constraint Satisfaction Problem [2].

2.1 Configuration Process

In the interactive configuration process, the user specifies his requirements step-by-step, gradually shrinking the problem space (see Fig. 1e). Hence, this process can be seen as a step-wise refinement of the constraint defining the space [5,11]. How the problem space is refined in each step is called a *decision*.

A *configurator* is a tool that displays the model capturing the constraints, presents the user with possible (manual) decisions, and infers necessary (automatic) decisions. The tool discourages the user from making decisions inconsistent with the constraints, and, it suggests decisions that are necessary to satisfy

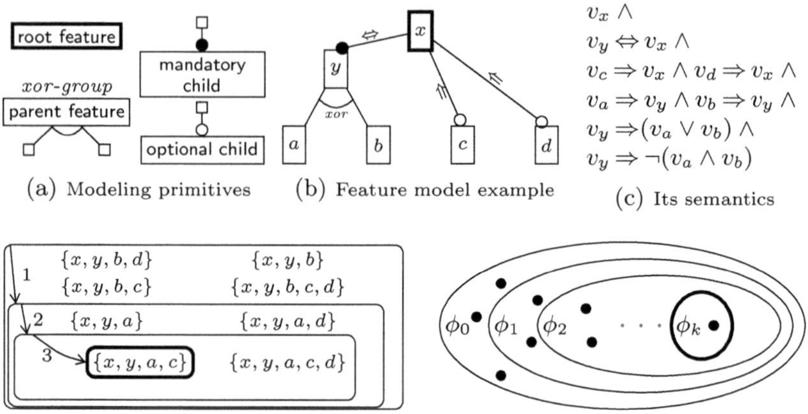

(a) Modeling primitives (b) Feature model example (c) Its semantics

(d) Example configuration of Fig. 1b (e) Configuration schematically

Fig. 1. FODA notation and Configuration Processes

the constraints. For convenience, configurators enable the user to *retract* previously made decisions; some even enable to temporarily violate the constraints but this is out of the scope of this article and gradual refinement will be assumed.

For illustration consider the feature model in Fig. 1b and the following steps (see Fig. 1d). (1) The user selects the feature a. This implicitly deselects b as a and b are in an xor-group and there are no feature configurations with both a and b. (2) The user selects the feature c, which has no further effects. (3) Finally, he deselects the feature d and the process is completed since exactly one feature combination is left, i.e., each feature is either in the product or not.

In summary, the input to the configurator is a constraint defining a large set of possibilities—the outermost ellipse in Fig. 1e. Gradually, this set is shrunk until exactly one possibility is left (assuming the user succeeded).

2.2 Completing a Configuration Process and the Shopping Principle

The concepts introduced in the previous sections are well known [8]. However, the configuration literature does not study the completion of a configuration process. As stated above, at the end of the process the decisions must determine exactly one feature combination (the innermost ellipse in Fig. 1e). So, how does the user achieve this? This article introduces the following classification.

***M** (Manual).* The user makes decisions up to the point when all considered variables have been bound, i.e., each variable has been assigned a value by the user or by a decision inferred by the configurator. The disadvantage of this approach is that the user needs to fill in every single detail, which is cumbersome especially if there are some parts of the problem that are not of a high relevance to the user. The only assistance the tool provides is the mechanism that infers new decisions or disables some decision. We will not discuss this case further.

***A** (Full blind automation).* A function automatically computes *some* values for all variables that do not have a value yet. The disadvantage of this option is that it takes all the control from the user as it is essentially making decisions for him.

A$^+$ *(Smart automation).* If we make some form of a priori, common sense assumptions, there is an approach somewhere between the options **M** and **A**. In the example above, the user had to *explicitly* deselect the optional feature d but would it be possible to instead say that all features not selected should be deselected? The motivation for this approach can be explained by an analogy with shopping for groceries (thus the *shopping principle*). The customer asks only for those items that he wants rather than saying for each item in the store whether he wants it or not. If some variables cannot be bound according to this principle, due to some dependencies, the tool will highlight them since it is possible that the user forgot to make a certain decision, e.g., we wouldn't want the tool to decide between features in an xor-group (a and b).

In some sense, the scenario $\mathbf{A}^+$ is a more careful version of scenario **A**. Both support the user to complete the configuration process. Scenario **A** binds **all** variables, whereas $\mathbf{A}^+$ only those for which this doesn't mean deciding something for the user. The following section investigates these scenarios in constraints defined as Boolean formulæ (recall that FODA produces Boolean formulæ).

3 Propositional Configuration

First, let us recall some basic terms from propositional logic. Let $\mathcal{V}$ be some finite set of variables. The propositional formulæ discussed from now on will be only on these variables. A *variable assignment* assigns either *true* or *false* to each considered variable. Often it is useful to think of a variable assignment as the set of variables that are assigned the value *true*, e.g., the variable assignment $x \mapsto \mathit{true}, y \mapsto \mathit{false}$ corresponds to the set $\{x\}$ in the set-based notation.

A *model* of a formula ϕ is such a variable assignment under which ϕ evaluates to *true*. We say that the formula ϕ is *satisfiable*, denoted as $\textsc{Sat}(\phi)$, if and only if ϕ has at least one model, e.g., the formula $x \vee y$ is satisfiable whereas the formula $x \wedge \neg x$ is not. We write $\phi \models \psi$ to denote that the formula ψ evaluates to *true* under all models of ϕ, e.g., it holds that $x \wedge y \models x$.

3.1 Propositional Configuration Process

In order to reason about the feature model and the user's requirements, the configurator translates them in some form of mathematical representation. In this section we assume that the model has already been translated into propositional logic (see Fig. 1c for illustration).

Definition 1. *A* propositional configuration process *for some finite set of variables $\mathcal{V}$ and a satisfiable propositional formula ϕ only on the variables from $\mathcal{V}$ is a sequence of propositional formulæ $\phi_0, \ldots, \phi_k$ such that $\phi_0 \stackrel{def}{=} \phi$, $\phi_{i+1} \stackrel{def}{=} \phi_i \wedge \xi_i$ for all $i \in 0 \ldots k-1$, and ϕ_k is satisfied by one variable assignment. The formulæ*

ξ_i are decisions made by the user or decisions inferred by the configurator. If ξ_i is of the form v for some variable $v \in \mathcal{V}$, then we say that the variable v has been assigned the value *true in step i; if ξ_i is of the form $\neg v$, we say that it has been* assigned the value *false in step i. Observe that $\phi_{i+1} \Rightarrow \phi_i$ for all $i \in 0 \ldots k-1$, i.e., the set of models is shrunk along the process.*

Example 1. Let $\phi_0 \stackrel{\text{def}}{=} (\neg u \vee \neg v) \wedge (x \Rightarrow y)$. The user sets u to *true* ($\phi_1 \stackrel{\text{def}}{=} \phi_0 \wedge u$); the configurator sets v to *false* as u and v are mutually exclusive ($\phi_2 \stackrel{\text{def}}{=} \phi_1 \wedge \neg v$). The user sets y to *false* ($\phi_3 \stackrel{\text{def}}{=} \phi_2 \wedge \neg y$); the configurator sets x to *false* ($\phi_4 \stackrel{\text{def}}{=} \phi_3 \wedge \neg x$). The process is finished as all variables were assigned a value.

The inference mechanism of the configurator typically inspects for all variables $v \in \mathcal{V}$ whether $\phi_l \models v$, in which case it sets v to *true*, and whether $\phi_l \models \neg v$, in which case it sets v to *false*. If a value has been inferred, the user is discouraged by the user interface to change it ("graying out"). This can be computed with the help of a SAT solver [9] or Binary Decision Diagrams (BDDs) [8].

3.2 Completing a Propositional Configuration Process

Let us look at the scenarios for completing a propositional configuration process. Earlier, we have identified two types of functions that the user may invoke at any step of the process: (**A**) a function that binds all the remaining variables; (**A**$^+$) a function that finds values for only some variables according to an a priori knowledge; we call this function a *shopping principle function*.

The case **A** is straightforward, finding a solution to the formula ϕ_i in step i is a satisfiability problem which can be solved by a call to a SAT solver or by a traversal of a BDD corresponding to ϕ_i (see [9,8] for further references).

The scenario **A**$^+$, however, is more intriguing. The a priori knowledge that we apply is the shopping principle (see Sect. 2.2), i.e., what has not been selected should be *false*. According to our experience and intuition (as well as other researchers [1, Section 4.2]), this is well in accord with human reasoning: the user has the impression that if a variable (a feature in a feature model) has not been selected, then it should be deselected once the process is over.

However, it is not possible to set all unassigned variables to *false* in all cases. For instance, in $u \vee v$ we cannot set both u and v to *false*—the user must choose which one should be *true*, and we do not want to make such decision for him (otherwise we would be in scenario **A**). Another way to see the problem is that setting u to *false* will *force* the variable v to be *true*, and vice-versa. If we consider the formula $x \Rightarrow (y \vee z)$, however, all the variables can be set to *false* at once and no further input from the user is necessary.

In summary, the objective is to maximize the set of variables that can be set to *false* without making any decisions for the user, i.e., variables that can be deselected safely. Upon a request, the configurator will set the safely-deselectable variables to *false* and highlight the rest as they need attention from the user.

3.3 Deselecting Safely

We start with an auxiliary definition that identifies sets of variables that can be deselected at once. This definition enables us to specify those variables that can be deselected safely; we call such variables dispensable variables (we kindly ask the reader to distinguish the terms deselectable and dispensable).

Definition 2 (Deselectable). *A set of variables* $X \subseteq \mathcal{V}$ *is* deselectable *w.r.t. the formula* ψ*, denoted as* $\mathcal{D}(\psi, X)$*, iff all variables in* X *can be set to false at once. Formally defined as* $\mathcal{D}(\psi, X) \stackrel{def}{=} \text{SAT}\left(\psi \wedge \bigwedge_{v \in X} \neg v\right)$*. Analogously, a single variable* $v \in \mathcal{V}$ *is* deselectable *w.r.t. the formula* ψ *iff it is a member of some deselectable set of variables, i.e.,* $\mathcal{D}(\psi, v) \stackrel{def}{=} \text{SAT}(\psi \wedge \neg v)$*.*

Definition 3 (Dispensable variables). *A variable* $v \in \mathcal{V}$ *is* dispensable *w.r.t. a formula* ψ *iff the following holds:* $(\forall X \subseteq \mathcal{V})\,(\mathcal{D}(\psi, X) \Rightarrow \mathcal{D}(\psi \wedge \neg v, X))$*.*

In plain English, a variable v is dispensable iff any deselectable set of variables X remains deselectable after v has been deselected (set to *false*). Intuitively, the deselection of v does not force selection of anything else, which follows the motivation that we will not be making decisions for the user. In light of the shopping principle (see Sect. 2.2), a customer can skip a grocery item only if skipping it does not require him to obtain some other items. The following examples illustrate the two definitions above.

Example 2. Let $\phi \stackrel{\text{def}}{=} (u \vee v) \wedge (x \Rightarrow y)$. Each of the variables is deselectable but only x and y are dispensable. The set $\{x, y\}$ is deselectable, while the set $\{u, v\}$ is not. The variable u is not dispensable as $\{v\}$ ceases to be deselectable when u is set to *false*; analogously for v. The variable x is dispensable since after x has been deselected, y can still be deselected and the variables u, v are independent of x's value. Analogously, if y is deselected, x can be deselected.

Observe that we treat *true* and *false* asymmetrically, deselecting y forces x to *false*, which doesn't collide with dispensability; deselecting u forces v to *true* and therefore u is *not* dispensable.

Example 3. Let ϕ be defined as in the previous example and the user is performing configuration on it. The user invokes the shopping principle function. As x and y are dispensable, both are deselected (set to *false*). The variables u and v are highlighted as they need attention. The user selects u, which results in the formula $\phi_1 \stackrel{\text{def}}{=} \phi \wedge u$. The variable v becomes dispensable and can be deselected automatically. The configuration process is finished as all variables have a value.

As we have established the term dispensable variable, we continue by studying its properties in order to be able to compute the set of dispensable variables and to gain more intuition about them.

Lemma 1. *Let* Υ_ϕ *denote the set of all dispensable variables of* ϕ*. For a satisfiable* ψ*, the dispensable variables can be deselected all at once, i.e.,* $\mathcal{D}(\psi, \Upsilon_\phi)$*.*

Proof. By induction on the cardinality of subsets of Υ_ψ. Let $\Upsilon_0 \stackrel{\text{def}}{=} \emptyset$, then $\mathcal{D}(\psi, \Upsilon_0)$ as ψ is satisfiable. Let $\Upsilon_i, \Upsilon_{i+1} \subseteq \Upsilon_\psi$ s.t. $\Upsilon_{i+1} = \Upsilon_i \cup \{x\}$, $|\Upsilon_i| = i$, and $|\Upsilon_{i+1}| = i + 1$. Since x is dispensable and $\mathcal{D}(\phi, \Upsilon_i)$, then $\mathcal{D}(\phi \wedge \neg x, \Upsilon_i)$, which is equivalent to $\mathcal{D}(\phi, \Upsilon_i \cup \{x\})$.

The following lemma reinforces that the definition of dispensable variables adheres to the principles we set out for it, i.e., it maximizes the number of deselected variables while not arbitrarily deciding between variables.

Lemma 2. *The set Υ_ϕ—the set of all dispensable variables of ϕ—is the intersection of all maximal sets of deselectable variables of ϕ.*

Proof (sketch). From definition of dispensability, any deselectable set remains deselectable after any dispensable variable is added to it, hence Υ_ϕ is a subset of any maximal deselectable set. Υ_ϕ is a maximal set with this property because for each deselectable set that contains at least one non-dispensable variable there is another deselectable set that does not contain this variable.

3.4 Dispensable Variables and Non-monotonic Reasoning

After defining the shopping principle in mathematical terms, the authors of this article realized that dispensable variables correspond to certain concepts from Artificial Intelligence as shown in this subsection.

The *Closed World Assumption (CWA)* is a term from logic programming and knowledge representation. Any inference that takes place builds on the assumption that if something has not been said to be *true* in a knowledge base, then it should be assumed *false*. Such reasoning is called *non-monotonic* as an increase in knowledge does not necessarily mean an increase in inferred facts. In terms of mathematical logic, CWA means adding negations of variables that should be assumed *false* in the reasoning process. Note that not all negateable variables ($\phi \nvDash v$) can be negated, e.g., for the formula $x \vee y$ both x and y are negateable but negating both of them would be inconsistent with the formula.

The literature offers several definitions of reasoning under Closed World Assumption [3,7]. A definition relevant to this article is the one of the *Generalized Closed World Assumption (GCWA)* introduced by Minker [19] (see [3, Def. 1]).

Definition 4. *The variable v is* free of negation *in the formula ϕ iff for any positive clause B for which $\phi \nvDash B$, it holds that $\phi \nvDash v \vee B$. The* closure *$C(\phi)$ of a formula ϕ is defined as $C(\phi) \stackrel{\text{def}}{=} \phi \cup \{\neg K \mid K \text{ is free for negation in } \phi\}$.*

It is not difficult to see that dispensable variables are those that are free of negation as shown by the following lemma.

Lemma 3. *Dispensable variables coincide with those that are free of negation.*

Proof. Observe that $\phi \nvDash \psi$ iff $\text{SAT}(\phi \wedge \neg\psi)$, then the definition above can be rewritten as: For $B' \stackrel{\text{def}}{=} \bigwedge_{v \in V_B} \neg v$ for some set of variables V_B for which $\text{SAT}(\phi \wedge B')$, it holds that $\text{SAT}(\phi \wedge \neg v \wedge B')$. According to the definition of $\mathcal{D}$, this is equivalent to $\mathcal{D}(\phi, V_B) \Rightarrow \mathcal{D}(\phi \wedge \neg v, V_B)$ (compare to Definition 3).

Table 1. Experimental Results

Name	Features	Clauses	Length	Done	Minimal models
tightvnc	21	22	5.5	5.5	1.0 ± 0.0
apl	27	41	12.2	11.9	1.0 ± 0.0
gg4	58	139	10.0	3.8	15.3 ± 22.6
berkeley	94	183	26.6	17.9	1.7 ± 1.1
violet	170	341	56.1	47.1	1.6 ± 0.9

Circumscription, in our case the *propositional circumscription*, is another important form of reasoning [18]. A circumscription of a propositional formula ϕ is a set of minimal models of ϕ. Where a model α of a formula ϕ is *minimal* iff ϕ has no model α' which would be a strict subset of α, e.g., the formula $x \vee y$ has the models $\{x\}, \{y\}, \{x, y\}$ where only $\{x\}$ and $\{y\}$ are minimal. We write $\phi \models_{\text{min}} \psi$ to denote that ψ holds in all minimal models of ϕ, e.g., $x \vee y \models_{\text{min}} \neg(x \wedge y)$.

The following lemma relates minimal models to dispensable variables (The proof of equivalence between minimal models and GCWA is found in [19]).

Lemma 4. *A variable v is dispensable iff it is false in all minimal models.*

Example 4. Let $\phi_0 \stackrel{\text{def}}{=} (u \vee v) \wedge (x \Rightarrow y)$. The minimal models of the formula ϕ_0 are $\{u\}$, $\{v\}$, hence $\phi_0 \models_{\text{min}} \neg x$ and $\phi_0 \models_{\text{min}} \neg y$. Then, if the user invokes the shopping principle function, x and y are deselected, i.e., $\phi_1 \stackrel{\text{def}}{=} \phi_0 \wedge \neg x \wedge \neg y$. And, the user is asked to resolve the competition between $u \vee v$, he selects u, resulting in the formula $\phi_2 \stackrel{\text{def}}{=} \phi_1 \wedge u$ with the models $\{u\}$ and $\{u, v\}$ where only the model $\{u\}$ is minimal hence v is set to *false* as dispensable. The configuration process is complete because u has the value *true* and the rest are dispensable.

3.5 Experimental Results

The previous section shows that dispensable variables can be found by enumerating minimal models. Since the circumscription problem is Π_2^P-complete [7] it is important to check if the computation is feasible in practice. We applied a simple evaluation procedure to five feature models[1]: For each feature model we simulated 1000 random manual configuration processes (scenario **M**). At each step we enumerated minimal models. (Algorithmic details can be found online [12].) We also counted how many times there was exactly one minimal model: At those steps the configuration process would have been completed if the user invoked the shopping principle function.

The results appear in Table 1. The column **Length** represents the number of user decisions required if the shopping principle function is not invoked; the column **Done** represents in how many steps an invocation of the shopping principle function completes the configuration; the column **Minimal models** shows that the exponential worst case tends not to occur in practice and therefore enumeration of all minimal models is feasible.

[1] From `http://fm.gsdlab.org/index.php?title=Model:SampleFeatureModels`

4 Beyond Boolean Constraints

The previous section investigated how to help a user with configuring propositional constraints. Motivated by the shopping principle, we were trying to set as many variables to *false* as possible. This can be alternatively seen as that the user **prefers** the undecided variables to be *false*.

This perspective helps us to generalize our approach to the case of non-propositional constraints under the assumption that there is some notion of preference between the solutions. First, let us establish the principles for preference that are assumed for this section. (1) It is a partial order on the set in question. (2) It is static in the sense that all users of the system agree on it, e.g., it is better to be healthy and rich than sick and poor. (3) If two elements are incomparable according to the ordering, the automated support shall not decide between them, instead the user shall be prompted to resolve it.

To be able to discuss these concepts precisely, we define them in mathematical terms. We start by a general definition of the problem to be configured, i.e., the initial input to the configurator, corresponding to the set of possibilities that the user can potentially reach—the outermost ellipse in Fig. 1e.

Definition 5 (Solution Domain). *A* Solution Domain (SD) *is a triple* $\langle \mathcal{V}, \mathcal{D}, \phi \rangle$ *where* $\mathcal{V}$ *is a set of variables* $\mathcal{V} = \{v_1, \ldots, v_n\}$, $\mathcal{D}$ *is a set of respective domains* $\mathcal{D} = \{D_1, \ldots, D_n\}$, *and the constraint* $\phi \subseteq D_1 \times \cdots \times D_n$ *is an n-ary relation on the domains (typically defined in terms of variables from* $\mathcal{V}$*).*

A variable assignment *is an n-tuple* $\langle c_1, \ldots, c_n \rangle$ *from the Cartesian product* $D_1 \times \cdots \times D_n$, *where the constant* c_i *determines the value of the variable* v_i *for* $i \in 1 \ldots n$. *For a constraint* ψ, *a variable assignment* α *is a* solution *iff it satisfies the constraint, i.e.,* $\alpha \in \psi$.

An Ordered Solution Domain (OSD) *is a quadruple* $\langle \mathcal{V}, \mathcal{D}, \phi, \prec \rangle$ *where* $\langle \mathcal{V}, \mathcal{D}, \phi \rangle$ *is an SD and* $\prec$ *is a partial order on* $D_1 \times \cdots \times D_n$. *For a constraint* ψ, *a solution* α *is* optimal *iff there is no solution* α' *of* ψ *s.t.* $\alpha' \neq \alpha$ *and* $\alpha' \prec \alpha$.

Recall that the user starts with a large set of potential solutions, gradually discards the undesired ones until only one solution is left. From a formal perspective, solution-discarding is carried out by strengthening the considered constraint, most typically by assigning a fixed value to some variable.

Definition 6 (Configuration Process). *Given a Solution Domain* $\langle \mathcal{V}, \mathcal{D}, \phi \rangle$, *an* interactive configuration process *is a sequence of constraints* $\phi_0, \ldots, \phi_k$ *such that* $\phi_0 \stackrel{def}{=} \phi$ *and* $|\phi_k| = 1$. *The constraint* ϕ_{j+1} *is defined as* $\phi_{j+1} \stackrel{def}{=} \phi_j \cap \xi_j$ *where the constraint* ξ_j *represents the decision in step* j *for* $j \in 0 \ldots k-1$. *If* ξ_j *is of the form* $v_i = c$ *for a variable* v_i *and a constant* $c \in D_i$, *we say that the variable* v_i *has been assigned the value* c *in step* j. *Observe that* $\phi_{j+1} \subseteq \phi_j$ *for* $j \in 0 \ldots k-1$ *and* $\phi_j \subseteq \phi$ *for* $j \in 0 \ldots k$.

A configurator in this process disables certain values or assigns them automatically. In particular, the configurator disallows selecting those values that are not part of any solution of the current constraint, i.e., in step l it disables all values

$c \in D_i$ of the variable v_i for which there is no solution of the constraint ϕ_l of the form $\langle c_1, \ldots, c, \ldots c_n \rangle$. If all values but one are disabled for the domain D_i, then the configurator automatically assigns this value to the variable v_i.

Now as we have established the concept for general configuration, let us assume that a user is configuring an Ordered Solution Domain (Definition 5) and we wish to help him with configuring variables that have lesser importance for him, similarly as we did with the shopping principle. The configuration proceeds as normal except that after the user configured those values he wanted, he invokes a function that tries to automatically configure the unbound variables using the given preference.

The assumption we make here is that the variables that were not given a value yet should be configured such that the result is optimal while preserving the constraints given by the user so far. Since the preference relation is a partial order, there may be multiple optimal solutions. As we do not want to make a choice for the user, we let him focus only on optimal solutions.

If non-optimal solutions shall be ruled out, the configurator identifies such values that never appear in any optimal solution to reduce the number of decisions that the user must focus on. Dually, the configurator identifies values that appear in all optimal solutions, the following definitions establish these concepts.

Definition 7 (Settled variables.). *For a constraint ψ and a variable v_i, the value $c \in D_i$ is* non-optimal *iff the variable v_i has the value c only in* non-optimal *solutions of ψ (or, v_i has a different value from c in all optimal solutions of ψ). A value c is* settled *iff v_i has the value c in all optimal solutions of ψ. A variable v_i is settled if there is a settled value of v_i.*

Observation 1. *For some constraint and the variable v_i, a value $c \in D_i$ is settled iff all values $c' \in D_i$ different from c are non-optimal.*

Example 5. Let $x, y, z \in \{0, 1\}$. Consider a constraint requiring that at least one of x,y,z is set to 1 (is selected). The preference relation expresses that we prefer lighter and cheaper solutions where x, y, and z contribute to the total weight by 1, 2, 3 and to the total price by 10, 5, and 20, respectively. Hence, the solutions satisfy $(x + y + z > 0)$, and $\langle x_1, y_1, z_1 \rangle \prec \langle x_2, y_2, z_2 \rangle$ iff $(10x_1 + 5y_1 + 20z_1 \leq 10x_2 + 5y_2 + 20z_2) \wedge (1x_1 + 2y_1 + 3z_1 \leq 1x_2 + 2y_2 + 3z_2)$. Any solution setting z to 1 is non-optimal as z is more expensive and heavier than both x and y, and hence the configurator sets z to 0 (it is settled). Choosing between x and y, however, needs to be left up to the user because x is lighter than y but more expensive than y.

Propositional configuration, studied in the previous section, is a special case of a Solution Domain configuration with the variable domains $\{\mathit{true}, \mathit{false}\}$. The following observation relates settled and dispensable variables (definitions 7, 3).

Observation 2. *For a Boolean formula understood as an OSD with the preference relation as the subset relation, a variable is settled iff it is dispensable or it is true in all models (solutions). Additionally, if each variable is settled, the invocation of the shopping principle function completes the configuration process.*

This final observation is an answer to the question in the title, i.e., configuration may be completed when all variables are settled. And, according to our experiments this happens frequently in practice (column **Done** in Table 1).

5 Related Work

Interactive configuration as understood in this article has been studied e.g., by Hadžić et al. [8], Batory [1], and Janota [9]. In an analogous approach Janota et al. [11] discuss the use of interactive configuration for feature model construction. The work of van der Meer et al. [24] is along the same lines but for unbounded spaces. Lottaz et al. [17] focus on configuration of non-discrete domains in civil engineering.

There is a large body of research on *product configuration* (see [22] for an overview), which typically is conceptualized rather as a programming paradigm than a human-interaction problem. Moreover, the notion rules are used instead of formulæ. Similarly as do we, Junker [13] applies preference in this context. We should note that preference in logic has been studied extensively, see [6].

The problem how to help the user to finish the configuration process was studied by Krebs et al. [16] who applied machine learning to identify a certain plan in the decisions of the user.

Circumscription has been studied extensively since the 80's [18,19,7]. Calculation of propositional circumscription was studied by Reiter and Kleer [21]; calculation of all minimal models by Kavvadias et al. and work referenced therein [15].

6 Summary

This article proposes a novel extension for configurators—the shopping principle function (Sect. 3.2). This function automates part of the decision-making but is not trying to be *too* smart: it does not make decisions between equally plausible options. The article mainly focuses on the propositional case, as software engineering models' semantics are typically propositional. The relation with GCWA, known from Artificial Intelligence, offers ways how to compute the shopping principle function (Sect. 3.4). Several experiments were carried out suggesting that the use of the shopping principle function is feasible and useful (Sect. 3.5). The general, non-propositional, case is studied at a conceptual level opening doors to further research (Sect. 4). The authors are planning to integrate this function into a configurator and carry out further experiments as future work.

Acknowledgment. This work is partially supported by Science Foundation Ireland under grant no. 03/CE2/I303_1 and the IST-2005-015905 MOBIUS project. The authors thank Don Batory and Fintan Farmichael for valuable feedback.

References

1. Batory, D.: Feature Models, Grammars, and Propositional Formulas. In: Obbink, H., Pohl, K. (eds.) SPLC 2005. LNCS, vol. 3714, pp. 7–20. Springer, Heidelberg (2005)
2. Benavides, D., Trinidad, P., Ruiz-Cortés, A.: Automated Reasoning on Feature Models. In: Pastor, Ó., Falcão e Cunha, J. (eds.) CAiSE 2005. LNCS, vol. 3520, pp. 491–503. Springer, Heidelberg (2005)

3. Cadoli, M., Lenzerini, M.: The Complexity of Closed World Reasoning and Circumscription. In: The Eighth National Conference on Artificial Intelligence (1990)
4. Clements, P., Northrop, L.: Software Product Lines: Practices and Patterns. Addison-Wesley, Reading (2002)
5. Czarnecki, K., Helsen, S., Eisenecker, U.: Staged Configuration Using Feature Models. In: Nord, R.L. (ed.) SPLC 2004. LNCS, vol. 3154, pp. 266–283. Springer, Heidelberg (2004)
6. Delgrande, J., Schaub, T., Tompits, H., Wang, K.: A Classification and Survey of Preference Handling Approaches in Nonmonotonic Reasoning. Computational Intelligence 20(2), 308–334 (2004)
7. Eiter, T., Gottlob, G.: Propositional Circumscription and Extended Closed World Reasoning Are Π_2^P-Complete. Theoretical Computer Science (1993)
8. Hadzic, T., Subbarayan, S., Jensen, R., Andersen, H., Møller, J., Hulgaard, H.: Fast Backtrack-Free Product Configuration Using a Precompiled Solution Space Representation. In: The International Conference on Economic, Technical and Organizational Aspects of Product Configuration Systems, DTU (2004)
9. Janota, M.: Do SAT Solvers Make Good Configurators? In: First Workshop on Analyses of Software Product Lines, ASPL (2008)
10. Janota, M., Kiniry, J.: Reasoning about Feature Models in High-Order Logic. In: SPLC (2007)
11. Janota, M., Kuzina, V., Wasowski, A.: Model Construction with External Constraints: An Interactive Journey from Semantics to Syntax. In: Czarnecki, K., Ober, I., Bruel, J.-M., Uhl, A., Völter, M. (eds.) MODELS 2008. LNCS, vol. 5301, pp. 431–445. Springer, Heidelberg (2008)
12. Janota, M., Marques-Silva, J., Grigore, R.: Algorithms for Finding Dispensable Variables, `http://arXiv.org/abs/0910.0013`
13. Junker, U.: Preference Programming for Configuration. In: Workshop on Configuration (2001)
14. Kang, K.C., Cohen, S.G., Hess, J.A., Novak, W.E., Peterson, A.S.: Feature-Oriented Domain Analysis (FODA), feasibility study. Technical Report, SEI, Carnegie Mellon University (1990)
15. Kavvadias, D.J., Sideri, M., Stavropoulos, E.C.: Generating All Maximal Models of a Boolean Expression. Information Processing Letters (2000)
16. Krebs, T., Wagner, T., Runte, W.: Recognizing User Intentions in Incremental Configuration Processes. In: Workshop on Configuration (2003)
17. Lottaz, C., Stalker, R., Smith, I.: Constraint Solving and Preference Activation for Interactive Design. AI EDAM 12(01), 13–27 (1998)
18. McCarthy, J.: Circumscription—a Form of Non-Monotonic Reasoning. Artificial Intelligence 13, 27–39 (1980)
19. Minker, J.: On Indefinite Databases and the Closed World Assumption. In: Loveland, D.W. (ed.) CADE 1982. LNCS, vol. 138. Springer, Heidelberg (1982)
20. Parnas, D.L.: On the Design and Development of Program Families. IEEE Transactions on Software Engineering (1976)
21. Reiter, R., de Kleer, J.: Foundations of Assumption-Based Truth Maintenance Systems: Preliminary Report. In: Proceedings of AAAI (1987)
22. Sabin, D., Weigel, R.: Product Configuration Frameworks-a Survey. IEEE Intelligent Systems 13(4), 42–49 (1998)
23. Schobbens, P.-Y., Heymans, P., Trigaux, J.-C.: Feature Diagrams: A Survey and a Formal Semantics. In: Requirements Engineering Conference, RE (2006)
24. van der Meer, E.R., Wasowski, A., Andersen, H.R.: Efficient Interactive Configuration of Unbounded Modular Systems. In: Symp. Applied Comput. (SAC) (2006)

Design Patterns Instantiation Based on Semantics and Model Transformations

Peter Kajsa and Ľubomír Majtás

Faculty of Informatics and Information Technologies, Slovak University of Technology,
Ilkovičova 3, Bratislava, 842 16, Slovakia
{kajsa,majtas}@fiit.stuba.sk

Abstract. Design patterns provide generalized and verified solutions of non-trivial design problems. The application of patterns improves the quality of software design considerably. This paper presents a method of design pattern application support in software projects. The method reduces problems found in traditional tools and contributes to design pattern instantiation at more levels of abstraction. The elaborated method is based on semantics defined via UML profile and transformations of models. Semantics defined via UML profile support specialization of pattern instances and model transformations support and automate the concretization of design pattern instances. The method supports the variation and customization of design patterns and also puts into practice ideas of model driven, iterative and incremental development of software systems. Moreover, the transformation of models is driven by models of design patterns. So the method is not limited only to design pattern support but also provides technique for the creation and addition of support of another custom model structures which are often created in models mechanically.

Keywords: Design patterns, UML profiles, MDA.

1 Introduction

Design patterns represent important part of developers' equipment in software design construction. Application of design patterns in software projects guides to creation of a modifiable, recursive and extensible software design [4]. Software development teams are capable to produce better software effectively thank to patterns application. Consequently, tool based support of design patterns application has great significance.

In general, when creating the instances of design patterns we can distinguish two different processes, which are depicted on the Figure 1. The first of these two processes is the specialization process of the general design pattern form. The goal of this process is to recast the general form of the design pattern to the single application specific form. The specialization process of the design pattern instantiation is achieved mainly by defining of associations between parts of design pattern instance and the rest of the application model, etc. Simply, it is integration of pattern instance and its parts into the domain specific context, in this case into the model of developing application. This process is difficult to automate, because it requires very specialized and detailed understanding of the domain context and the specific application

J. van Leeuwen et al. (Eds.): SOFSEM 2010, LNCS 5901, pp. 540–551, 2010.

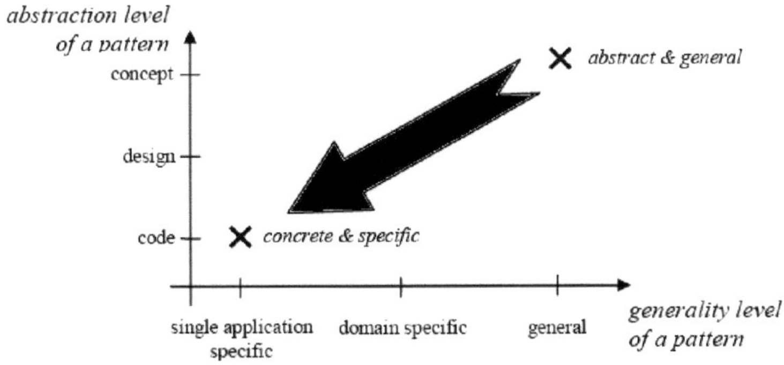

Fig. 1. Two processes of design pattern instantiation [5]

itself. This knowledge is only available to the developers and the domain experts associated with the design process. Despite this difficulty, it is possible to support and make this process much easier by providing an appropriate mechanism for the application of design patterns to the developer.

The second process of design pattern instantiation is the concretization process of the design pattern abstract form. The goal of this process is to recast abstract form of the design pattern into concrete form with all its parts, methods, attributes and associations, but only within the scope of the pattern instance and its participants, but not the rest of application model. The more parts that the structure of the pattern instance contains, the more concrete it becomes. The most concrete level of the design pattern instance is source code, because at this level of abstraction the pattern instance contains all parts from its structure.

It is important to remark that from the perspective of the MDA approach, the concretization process is included within transitions between computer independent, platform independent, platform specific models and source code level [3], [6].

The majority of activities in the concretization process depend on stable and fixed definition of the design pattern structure so that these activities are fairly routine. So that gives us a good initial assumption for automation of this process.

2 Problem Outline

Design patterns support in traditional CASE or other modeling tools is usually based on UML templates of each design pattern [1], [2] which are copied into the model when instances of design patterns are created. The support provided by these traditional tools lies only in the insertion of some UML template of chosen pattern into a model. In addition to such support, some CASE tools provide wizard dialogues with options to choose an appropriate configuration of design pattern instances. However, these dialogues are often long and tedious and so they are not very useful.

The most significant deficiencies of this traditional support of design patterns are demonstrated in an example of the Observer pattern instance creation in the CASE tool Borland Together Architect [7]. As can be noticed in the Figure 2, the instance of the Observer pattern created by this tool has not been recast from its general form into

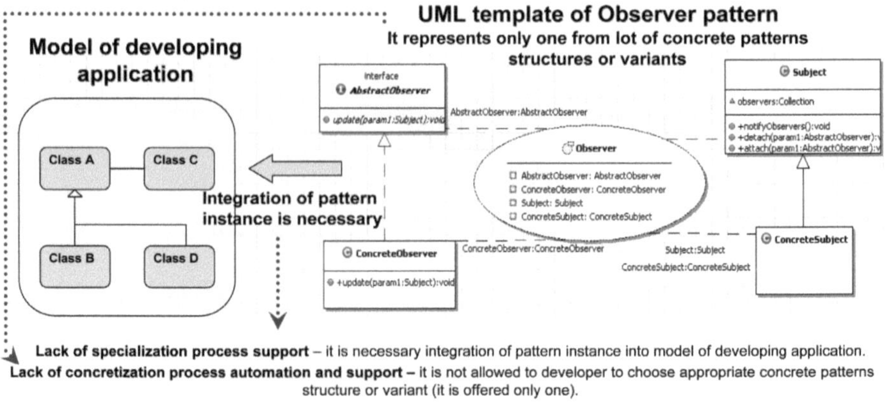

Fig. 2. Design pattern support in Borland Together Architect [7]

the application specific form. So it has not been integrated into the rest of developing application model, e.g. it lacks associations with the rest of the application model, the names of pattern parts are general, and so on. In consequence, there is absence of specialization process support.

Another observation concerning Figure 2 is the lack of automation and support of the concretization process. A developer is not allowed to choose appropriate variant or concrete structure of the design pattern. Only one generic form is offered to the developer for use in the concrete application realization. Any other adjustments needs to be performed by a developer manually without any tool based support. A summary of the deficiencies of traditional tools is as follows:

- design pattern support is usually based on UML templates for each pattern, which are then copied into the model with minimal possibilities for modification
- there is no support of specialization process - the recasting of the general form of the template of pattern into application specific form has to be done manually
- there is weak support of the concretization process – adjustments of concrete form of design patterns must be done manually
- there is no support of design pattern variations
- it is not possible to work with pattern instances at more levels of abstraction

3 Improvement Proposal

In order to eliminate the previously identified drawbacks, it is necessary to provide an appropriate mechanism of the application of required semantics into the application model. In consequence, tool would be able to understand the model of the application and recognize its parts. In other words, it would be possible to recognize relations and parts of design patterns that are present in the application model already. This mechanism has to support insertion of semantics directly on elements of application model and in this way support specialization process of design pattern instantiation.

Further it is necessary to automate concretization process by model transformation in a suitable way giving the possibility to choose appropriate configuration or variant of pattern instances. In addition, it would be useful to support the work with instances of design patterns at more levels of abstraction according to ideas of the MDA development process and in such way improve simultaneous application of both significant elements of software engineering and consider ideas of model driven, iterative and incremental development of software systems.

Proposal of this described process of design patterns instantiation process is presented below in the Figure 3.

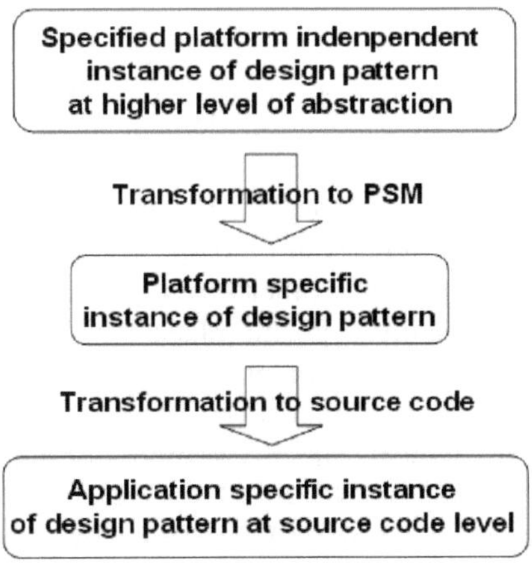

Fig. 3. Proposal of the design pattern instantiation process

It is important to remark, that the first transformation to platform specific models (PSM) is also necessary, because it is at this level that the first differences between instances of design patterns may occur. For example, some platforms allow multiple inheritances, other provides interfaces, etc.

4 Realization

Our approach to design pattern support is based on applying semantics into models provided by the UML profiles. UML profiles contain definitions of stereotypes, tagged values or meta-attributes of stereotypes, enumeration and constraints that could be applied directly to specific model elements, such as Classes, Attributes, Operations and so on [6]. So in this way it is possible to specify participants of design patterns and relations between them directly in the context of the application model. With such techniques we do not need to force the developer to explicitly mark the pattern participants. Our approach is to encourage him just to suggest the pattern instance occurrence while the rest of the instantiation process can be automated. For example, in the Figure 4 there is shown suggestion of the Observer pattern instance application via applying one stereotype <<Observes>> on desired association. From such

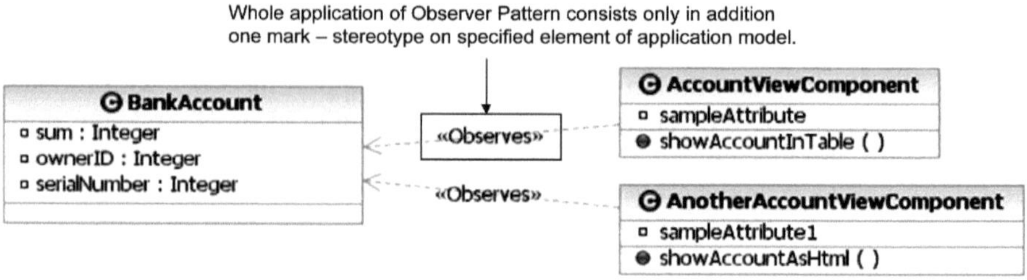

Fig. 4. An example of an application of the Observer pattern to a model. It represents specified platform independent instance and thus the most abstract form of the Observer pattern instance.

information the tool can recognize that the source element of the association should represent Concrete Observer, the destination element should be Concrete Subject, and other pattern participants need to be added to the model.

Consequently, the application of a desired pattern can usually consists only of applying one suggestion mark – stereotype onto specified model element by user, who only specifies instance of pattern. Any other activities will be subsequently completed by a tool via model transformations. In this phase developers do not have to bother themselves about the concrete details of pattern structure and they can comfortably work with pattern instances at its higher level of abstraction. The application of desired pattern is realized on elements of system model or context and thus specialization process is supported.

UML profiles provide suitable way to define semantics for each design pattern and allow applying this semantics directly to elements of a developing application model. The design of UML profile definition for Observer pattern is shown in Figure 5.

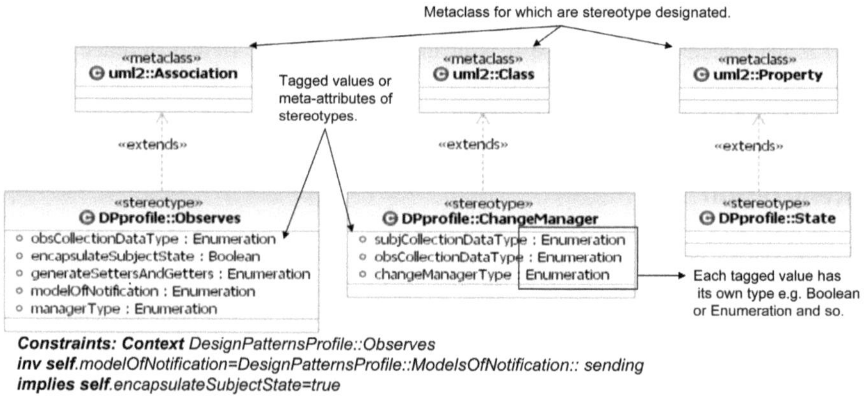

Fig. 5. Design of UML profile for Observer pattern

As it has been mentioned, the generation of the rest of the structure of a specified pattern instance (the concretization process) is realized by transformations of marked models to the lower levels of abstraction according to the proposal presented in Figure 3. We have considered two kinds of model transformations. In MDA terminology, the first is the transformation of a platform independent model to platform specific model and, the second is the transformation of platform specific model to source code.

Before each start of the model transformation it is allowed to set up desirable values of meta-attributes - tagged values of each applied stereotype. This simple way allows us to control or to adjust transformation process and its results. In other words, developer is allowed to choose appropriate concrete form or desired variant of pattern instance. Even it is possible to allow implementing particular parts of pattern instance via other pattern instance. Moreover, this step is optional, because default values of the tagged values have been set up.

Inconsistent configurations of values are handled with enumeration and OCL constraints defined in UML profile of design patterns and evaluated immediately during values setting (example of such constraint has been shown in Figure 5). UML profile also represents standard extension of UML meta-model and thus is compliant with majority of other UML tools [6].

Then concretization process is automated and supported as well as variations of design patterns. In the following section we will look closer on the process of design pattern instances creation.

4.1 Design Pattern Instances Creation in Action

In the previous text we have explained that the process of creating a concrete instance of a desired design pattern consists of three steps:

1. Application of desired design pattern – insertion of applicable stereotypes (marks) onto specified elements of the application model or context suggesting the pattern instance occurrence.
2. (Optional step) Choice of the adjustment of the concrete form or desired variant of the patter instance – set up desirable values of tagged values (meta-attributes) of appropriate stereotype.
3. Launching the appropriate model transformation to desired destination platform.

The whole process described above and its sample result is demonstrated in the Figure 6. Since two kinds of model transformations have been proposed, it is possible to perform the described steps on a resulting PSM model again (at lower level of abstraction). In this way it is possible to get to the lowest level of abstraction – source code. The only difference is that at the lower level of abstraction (PSM) in step 2 more implementation dependent choices (e.g. data types) are offered, with which a developer was not asked to bother himself at the previous PIM level. In this way, our approach has achieved support for processing pattern instances in three different levels of abstraction:

- Pattern suggestion level (for example model in the Figure 4)
- Design model level
- Source code level

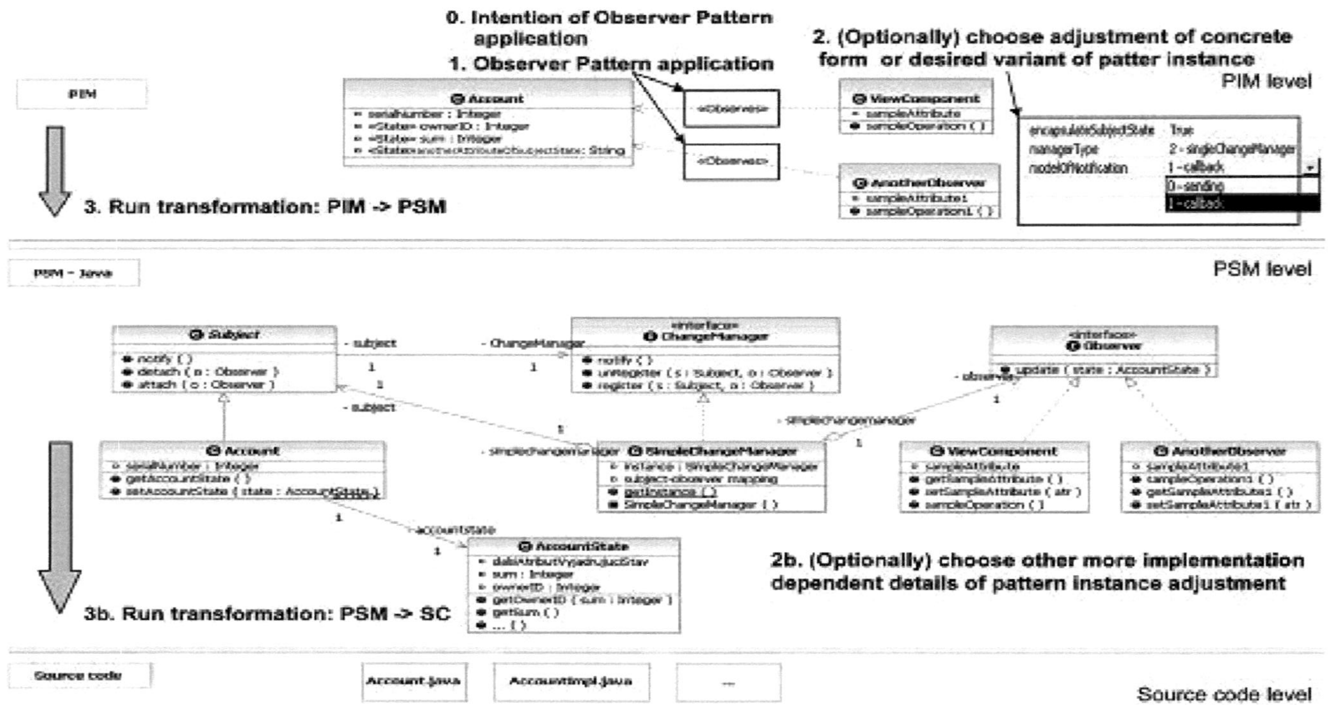

Fig. 6. Observer pattern instance creation in action. In the first step the developer specifies where and which design pattern instance he wants to apply via the insertion of semantics into the model. Next he specifies the variant of pattern instance and the way he wants its to generate via setting up the values of stereotype meta-attributes.. Subsequently, using this specification the transformation tool is capable properly generate the rest of pattern instance in desired form.

4.2 Tool Under the Hood

Transformations performed by the tool are driven by properly specified models of design patterns. These prepared models cover all pattern variants and possible modifications. Each element of these models is marked. There are two types of marks in pattern models. The first type of marks expresses the role of element in scope of pattern. On the basis of this type of marks the tool is capable of creating mappings between models. The second type of marks expresses the affiliation of the element to the variant of the pattern. On the basis of this type of marks the tool is capable of deciding which element should be generated into the model and in what form. For the second type of marks the following notation is defined:

```
[~]?StereotypeName::Meta-attributeName::value;
```

An element from pattern model is generated into the model only if the specified meta-attribute of the specified stereotype has set the specified value. These marks can be joined via ";"while the symbol "~" expresses negation. If an element has no mark, it will be always generated into the model. A sample section of the model of Observer pattern is exposed in the Figure 7.

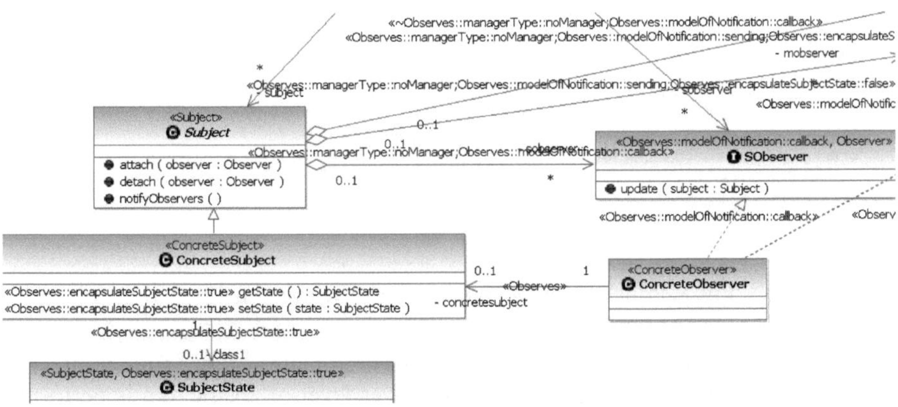

Fig. 7. Sample section of Observer pattern model by which is transformation driven

The whole process of the tool performance is captured in the Figure 8. The first action performed by the tool after starting the transformation is comparison of first type of marks in the prepared design pattern models with marks in the model of the application on which the transformation has been started. Based on this comparison the tool is capable of making a mapping between these marked models and consequently, to recognize which parts of the structure of the design pattern instance are in the model of developing application already presented and which are not.

For example, in Figures 4 and 6 in the previous sections we have shown the application of Observer pattern by applying one stereotype <<observes>> on the directed association. From such marked association, the tool can recognize that parts Concrete Observer and Concrete Subject of this Observer pattern instance have been presented in model already and it knows which elements (in this case classes) of application model represent these roles or parts.

Decisions about which variant of pattern and which elements from the pattern model need to be generated into the application model are based on the comparison of the second type marks in the pattern model with the values of the meta-attributes of stereotypes. These values are set up by the developer in the second step of the creation of pattern instance (see preceding sub-section and Figures 6 and 7).

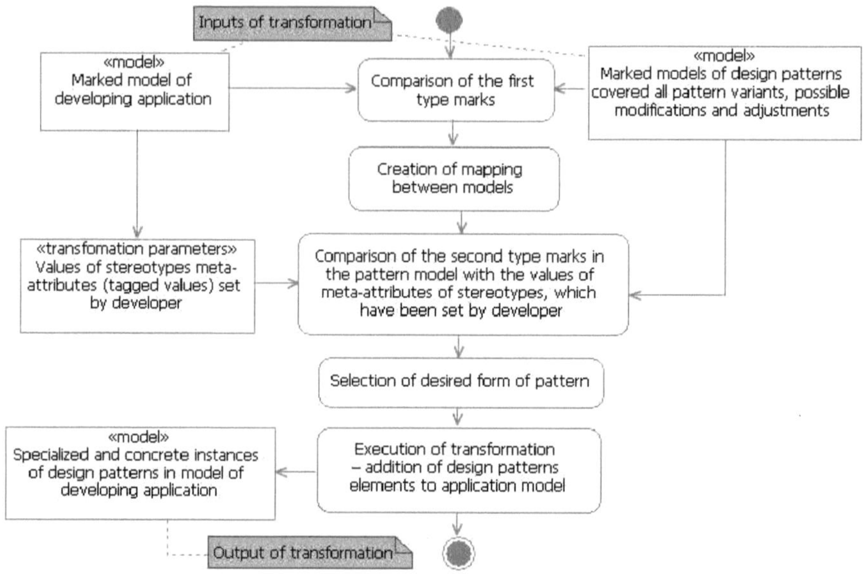

Fig. 8. Principles of tool functioning - tool under the hood

After decision-making and selection of the desired pattern form, final transformation from the pattern suggestion level to the lower level of abstraction is performed. Results of transformation are correctly specialized and concrete instances of patterns in chosen and desired form, as presented in Figure 6 in the previous sub-section.

Driving the model transformations by pattern models allows us to determine and to adjust results of transformations also by modifying the pattern models that drive the transformations. Marks in the models ensure, that tools is always capable create correct mappings betweens the model of application and the model by which is transformation driven and consequently decide which element should be generated into the model and in what form. So this way it is possible to model any custom structure and achieve support of its application into model.

4.3 Implementation

The presented method and the tool itself was implemented and verified in the form of an IBM Rational Software Modeler transformation plug-in. Till now the following features have been implemented:

- Semantics in the UML profile for the patterns Factory Method, Decorator, Observer and Mediator
- Transformation of the highest level of abstraction (PIM) to the lower level (PSM) and transformation of PSM to source code
- Transformation of PIM to the lower level model PSM is driven by pattern models.
- Models of design pattern covered all pattern variants and modifications which provide the basis upon which the transformational tool is driven
- Mechanism for adjustments of concrete form or desired variant of patter instance for the patterns Factory Method, Decorator, Observer and Mediator

5 Evaluation

The presented method and the implemented tool have been evaluated in several ways. The first evaluation was realized through experiments in which we have monitored the time of carrying out of an assigned task with and without usage of the tool. Also the count of generated and added source code lines has been observed. The tasks consisted of implementing specified instances of design patterns in specified form. Average results of the experiments on a group of five programmers and five master degree students of software engineering are summarized in the Table 1.

Table 1. Average results of executed experiments

Time with using the tool t1	Time without using the tool t2	Speed up t2/t1	Number of generated code lines Ng	Number of added code lines Nd	Improving coefficient (Ng / Nd) + 1
< 30 min	> 120 min	> 4	478	52	10,2

The quantity of the generated source code has been evaluated for each design pattern via metrics. Results of this evaluation are shown in Table 2.

Table 2. Quantity of generated source code

Design Pattern	LOC	NOA	NOC	NOCON	NOIS	NOM	NOO
Decorator pattern	223	9	6	7	11	103	22
Mediator pattern	212	6	6	7	9	50	15
Observer pattern	193	14	6	1	10	60	14

Results of experiments show a significant improvement gained by use of the method and tool in the area.

6 Related Work

There exist several approaches introducing their own tool based support for the pattern instantiation. El Boussaidi et. al. [11] present model transformations based on Eclipse EMF and JRule framework. Wang et. al. [12] provide similar functionality by

XSLT based transformations of the models stored in XMI-Light format. Both approaches can be considered as the single template driven while they are focusing most on the transformation process and do not set a space for the pattern customizations.

Another method was introduced by Ó Cinnéide et. al. [13]. They have presented a methodology for the creation of behavior-preserving design pattern transformations and applied this methodology to GoF design patterns. While Ó Cinnéide's approach is supposed to guide the developers to pattern employment in the phase of refactoring (based on source code analysis), Briand et. al. [8] are trying identify the spots for pattern instance in design phase (based on UML model analysis). They provide semi-automatic suggestion mechanism based on decision tree combining evaluation the automatic detection rules with user queries.

All the former approaches were focusing on the creation of pattern instances. The ones presented by Dong et. al. presume the presence of the pattern instances in the model. They are providing the support for the evolution of the existing pattern instances resulting from the application changes. The first one [9] implementation employs QVT based model transformations, the other one [10] does the some by the XSLT transformations over the model stored as XMI. However, both are working with the single configuration pattern template allowing only the changes in presence of hot spots participants. Other possible variabilities are omitted.

All of these approaches are based on strict forward participants generation - participants of all roles are created according the single template. Our approach emphasizes on collaboration between the developer and the CASE tool. We allow the developer specify via application of semantics into models, where to apply the instance of what pattern, and which variant and how he want to generate. On the basis of this specification and pattern model the transformation tool is capable of properly generating the rest of the pattern instance according to the desired form.

7 Conclusion

The presented approach focuses on application of the design patterns at higher levels of abstraction by allowing the developer to place pattern occurrence suggestions into the model that can be subsequently automatically processed by the tool into final pattern instance form. The approach splits details of concrete design pattern instantiation into two levels of abstraction. Following this approach, developers do not need to take care about concrete details of pattern structure and comfortably work with pattern instance at its higher level of abstraction. Further, the approach supports the specialization process and automates the concretization process of design pattern instances creation. A developer is allowed to decide which concrete form or desired variant of a pattern instance he wishes to generate into a model. So the approach supports variability of design patterns.

Moreover the method provides to developer further option to adjust result of transformation also via modification of design pattern models by which is the transformation driven. Developer is in this way capable to model any custom structure or create a new one and in this way achieve support for his custom needs. The method is not strictly oriented only to GoF design pattern support but represents also framework of creation and addition of support for another custom model structures which are often created in models mechanically.

Our approach is based on standard extension of UML meta-model and thus is compliant with majority of other UML tools and it is also considering ideas of model driven, iterative and incremental development process.

Acknowledgments. This work was partially supported by the Scientific Grant Agency of Republic of Slovakia, grant No. VEGA 1/0508/09 and by Slovak Research and Development Agency, grant No. APVV-0391-06 "Semantic Composition of Web and Grid Services".

References

1. Arlow, J., Neustadt, I.: Enterprise Patterns and MDA: Building Better Software with Archetype Patterns and UML. Addison-Wesley, Reading (2003)
2. France, R., Dae-kyoo, K., Ghosh, S.: A UML-Based Pattern Specification Technique. IEEE Transactions on Software Engineering, 193–206 (2004)
3. Frankel, D.: Model Driven Architecture: Applying MDA to Enterprise Computing. Wiley Publishing, Chichester (2003)
4. Gamma, E., Helm, R., Johnson, R., Vlissides, J.: Design Patterns, Elements of Reusable Object-Oriented Software. Addison-Wesley Professional Computing Series (1995)
5. Návrat, P., Bieliková, M., Smolárová, M.: A Technique for Modeling Design Patterns. In: Knowledge-Based Software Engineering - JCKBSE 1998, pp. 89–97. IOS Press, Amsterdam (1998)
6. Object Management Group: MDA, MOF, UML Specifications (accessed May 9th, 2009), `http://www.omg.org/`
7. Borland Software Corporation: Borland Together Architect. (accessed February 5th, 2009), `http://www.borland.com/together/`
8. Briand, L., Labiche, Y., Sauve, A.: Guiding the Application of Design Patterns Based on uml Models. In: ICSM 2006, Proceedings of the 22nd IEEE International Conference on Software Maintenance, Washington, DC, USA, pp. 234–243. IEEE Computer Society, Los Alamitos (2006)
9. Dong, J., Yang, S.: Qvt Based Model Transformation for Design Pattern Evolutions
10. Dong, J., Yang, S., Zhang, K.: A Model Transformation Approach for Design Pattern Evolutions. In: ECBS 2006: Proceedings of the 13th Annual IEEE International Symposium and Workshop on Engineering of Computer Based Systems, Washington, DC, USA, pp. 80–92. IEEE Computer Society, Los Alamitos (2006)
11. Boussaidi, G., Mili, H.: A Model-Driven Framework for Representing and Applying Design Patterns. In: COMPSAC 2007: Proceedings of the 31st Annual International Computer Software and Applications Conference, Washington, DC, USA, pp. 97–100. IEEE Computer Society, Los Alamitos (2007)
12. Wang, X.-B., Wu, Q.-Y., Wang, H.-M., Shi, D.-X.: Research and Implementation of Design Pattern-Oriented Model Transformation. In: ICCGI 2007: Proceedings of the International Multi-Conference on Computing in the Global Information Technology, Washington, DC, USA. IEEE Computer Society, Los Alamitos (2007)
13. Cinnéide, M., Nixon, P.: Automated Software Evolution Towards Design Patterns. In: IWPSE 2001: Proceedings of the 4th International Workshop on Principles of Software Evolution, pp. 162–165. ACM, New York (2001)

A Complete Symbolic Bisimulation for Full Applied Pi Calculus

Jia Liu[1,2,⋆] and Huimin Lin[1]

[1] State Key Laboratory of Computer Science
Institute of Software, Chinese Academy of Sciences
[2] Graduate University, Chinese Academy of Sciences
{jliu,lhm}@ios.ac.cn

Abstract. Symbolic characterizations of bisimilarities for the applied pi-calculus proposed so far are sound but incomplete, even restricted to the finite fragment of the calculus. In this paper we present a novel approach to symbolic semantics for the applied pi-calculus, leading to a notion of symbolic bisimulation which is both sound and complete with respect to the standard concrete bisimulation. Moreover, our approach accommodates recursions hence works for the full calculus.

1 Introduction

The applied pi-calculus [2] can be regarded as a generalization of the spi-calculus [3] in that it allows user-provided primitives for cryptographic operations. The calculus inherits the constructs for communication, concurrency and scope extrusion from the original pi-calculus [21]. It has a special mechanism for outputting compound messages which entails an auxiliary substitution construct of the form $\{M/x\}$, known as an "active substitution" that behaves like a floating "let" and serves to capture the partial environmental knowledge.

As in the standard operational semantics for the pi-calculus and value-passing CCS, in the applied pi-calculus an input may give rise to an infinite number of branches, which hinders the efforts to develop automated tools for the calculus. The standard approach is to develop symbolic theory which enables more amenable and more efficient automatic verification. *Symbolic semantics* have been developed smoothly for the value-passing CCS and many of its derivatives[15,9,18], in which all possible values offered by the environment are replaced by a *single* "symbolic variable". However it turns out that defining a symbolic semantics for the applied pi-calculus is unexpectedly technically difficult [13]. Despite various efforts from the community, up till now no complete symbolic semantics has been established for the applied pi-calculus, even when restricted to the finite fragment of the calculus, *i.e.* the fragment without recursions.

⋆ This work is supported by the National Natural Science Foundation of China (Grants No.60721061 and No.60833001) and the National High Technology Development Program of China (Grant No.2007AA01Z147).

J. van Leeuwen et al. (Eds.): SOFSEM 2010, LNCS 5901, pp. 552–563, 2010.

Symbolic bisimulations for value-passing CCS [15] and the pure pi-calculus [18,9] are indexed by boolean conditions to constrain the sets of values which symbolic variables may take. To achieve completeness, when comparing two processes for bisimilarity, it is necessary to "partition" the indexing condition into some sub-conditions in such a way that the two processes can simulate each other's transitions under each sub-condition. In the applied pi-calculus a symbolic bisimulation will be indexed by *constraints* each of which encompass a similar condition as well as *deducibilities*. The concept of deducibilities is by now widely used in modeling security protocols to represent all the messages that can be computed by intruders using a given set of messages [20,12,4,13]. As such deducibilities can not, and should not, be partitioned. In the previous work on symbolic bisimulation for the applied pi-calculus, not only conditions and deducibilities are entangled together in constraints, but also constraints and processes are mixed in transitions and bisimulations. This makes it impossible to partition indexing conditions, causing incompleteness.

To harness the difficulty we need to separate constraints from processes and conditions from deducibilities. To this end we extend the language for boolean expressions with two novel operators, $\sigma \blacktriangleright \Phi$, read "$\sigma$ guards Φ", and $\mathrm{H}n.\,\Phi$, read "hide n in Φ". In $\sigma \blacktriangleright \Phi$, the substitution σ represents (partial) environmental knowledge for the variables occurring in Φ. In $\mathrm{H}n.\,\Phi$ the name n is made local in Φ. With these operators we are able to make constraints completely independent of processes and to clearly separate conditions from deducibilities. As a result our notion of a symbolic bisimulation will be of the form $A \approx^{(\mathcal{D},\Phi)} B$, where $\mathcal{D}$ is a special set of deducibilities and Φ a condition formula, only the later is subject to partitioning when A and B are compared for bisimilarity. Besides, recursions were outside the scope of [13,14], due to difficulties arising from infinite name binders. Having hiding in formulas helps to keep track of the scope of names in constraints, which enables us to handle recursions smoothly with an "on-the-fly" approach.

The main contributions of the paper are twofold: (1) establishing the first sound and complete theory of symbolic bisimulation for the applied pi-calculus, and (2) our result covers recursions and is the first symbolic theory for the full applied pi-calculus.

Related work. Our work is inspired by [13,14] and the notion of "intermediate processes" used in this paper is taken from there. An ad hoc symbolic method relying on a notion of unification is proposed in [8] for the analysis of security protocols in a calculus akin to the applied pi-calculus. In [17,5] two variants of the applied pi-calculus, called the extended pi-calculi and psi-calculi respectively, are proposed aiming at being more amenable to technical treatments. Automated tools for security protocols in the context of the applied pi calculus are reported in [6,7]. A sound symbolic semantics for spi-calculus is introduced in [11]. Recently this semantics is revised to achieve completeness in [10], but their techniques are not applicable to the applied pi-calculus.

Due to space limitation proofs have been omitted from this extended abstract. They can be found in the full version of this paper [19].

2 Applied Pi-Calculus

2.1 Syntax

We assume two disjoint, infinite sets $\mathcal{N}$ and $\mathcal{V}$ of names and variables, respectively. A signature is a finite set of function symbols, such as f, h, each having a non-negative arity. Terms are defined by the grammar:

$$\begin{array}{lll} M, N ::= & a, b, c, \cdots, k, \cdots, m, n, \cdots, s & \text{name} \\ & x, y, z & \text{variable} \\ & f(M_1, \cdots, M_\ell) & \text{function application} \end{array}$$

We write $names(M)$ and $vars(M)$ for the sets of names and resp. variables in M. Let $atoms(M) = vars(M) \cup names(M)$. A *ground term* is a term containing no variable.

We rely on a sort system including a universal base sort and a channel sort. The sort system splits $\mathcal{N}$ and $\mathcal{V}$ respectively into channel names $\mathcal{N}_{ch}$ and base names $\mathcal{N}_b$, channel variables $\mathcal{V}_{ch}$ and base variables $\mathcal{V}_b$. Function symbols take arguments and produce results of the base sort only. We will use a, b, c as channel names, s, k as base names, and m, n as names of any sort. We use meta variables u, v, w to range over both names and variables. We abbreviate tuples $u_1, \cdots, u_\ell$ and $M_1, \cdots, M_\ell$ to $\widetilde{u}$ and $\widetilde{M}$ respectively.

Plain processes are constructed using the standard operators 0 (nil), | (parallel composition), νn (name restriction), if-then-else (conditional), $u(x)$ (input), $\overline{u}\langle N \rangle$ (output), and recursion. Extended processes are created by extending plain processes with active substitutions that float and apply to any process coming into contact with it. The grammar for plain processes and extended processes are given below:

$$\begin{array}{ll} P_r, Q_r, R_r ::= & \text{plain processes} \\ & 0 \\ & P_r \mid Q_r \\ & \nu n.P_r \\ & \text{if } M = N \text{ then } P_r \text{ then } Q_r \\ & u(x).P_r \\ & \overline{u}\langle N \rangle.P_r \\ & K\langle \widetilde{M} \rangle \end{array} \qquad \begin{array}{ll} A_r, B_r, C_r ::= & \text{extended processes} \\ & P_r \\ & A_r \mid B_r \\ & \nu n.A_r \\ & \nu x.A_r \\ & \{M/x\} \end{array}$$

As in the pi-calculus, $u(x)$, νn and νx are binding, which lead to the usual notions of bound and free names and variables. We shall use $fn(A_r)$, $bn(A_r)$, $fv(A_r)$, and $bv(A_r)$ to denote the sets of free names and bound names (resp. variables), of A_r. Let $fnv(A_r) = fn(A_r) \cup fv(A_r)$ and $bnv(A_r) = bn(A_r) \cup bv(A_r)$. We shall identify α-convertible processes. Capture of bound names and bound variables is avoided by implicit α-conversion.

To define recursive processes we use process constants, ranged over by K, each of which is associated with a declaration of the form $K(\widetilde{x}) \triangleq P_r$, where $fv(P_r) \subseteq \{\widetilde{x}\}$ and $fn(P_r) = \emptyset$.

Substitutions are sort-respecting partial mappings of finite domains. Substitutions of terms for variables, ranged over by σ, θ, are always required to be cycle-free. The domain and range of σ are denoted by $dom(\sigma)$ and $range(\sigma)$, respectively. We say σ is *idempotent* if $dom(\sigma) \cap vars(range(\sigma)) = \emptyset$. We write $vars(\sigma)$ and $names(\sigma)$ for the sets of variables and names occurring in σ, respectively. Also let $atoms(\sigma) = vars(\sigma) \cup names(\sigma)$. Let Z be an expression which may be a term, a process, or a substitution. The application of σ to Z is written in postfix notation, $Z\sigma$. Let $\{M_1/x_1, \cdots, M_n/x_n\}\sigma = \{M_1\sigma/x_1, \cdots, M_n\sigma/x_n\}$. The composition of substitutions is denoted $\sigma_1 \circ \sigma_2$, and $Z(\sigma_1 \circ \sigma_2) = (Z\sigma_2)\sigma_1$. σ^* is the result of composing with σ repeatedly until obtaining an idempotent substitution. We use $\sigma_1 \cup \sigma_2$ to denote the union when their domains are disjoint.

Due to technical reasons active substitutions are required to be defined on the base sort only, but this does not impose any restrictions on applications. In an extended process, active substitutions must be cycle-free and there is at most one substitution for each variable and exactly one when the variable is restricted. We say A_r is *closed* if every variable is either bound or defined by an active substitution. A *frame* is an extended process built up from 0 and active substitutions by parallel composition and restriction. The domain of frame ϕ, denoted by $dom(\phi)$, is the set of variables x for which ϕ contains a substitution $\{M/x\}$ not under νx. The frame of an extended process A_r, denoted by $\phi(A_r)$, is obtained by replacing every plain process embedded in A_r with 0. Note that $dom(A_r)$ is the same as $dom(\phi(A_r))$.

2.2 Semantics

A *context* is an extended process with a hole. An *evaluation context* is a context in which the hole is not under an input, an output or a conditional. A *term context* is a term with holes. Terms are equipped with an equational theory $=_E$ that is an equivalence relation closed under substitutions of terms for variables, one-to-one renamings and term contexts. We write $M \neq_E N$ for the negation of $M =_E N$. Structural equivalence $\equiv$ is the smallest equivalence relation on extended processes closed by evaluation contexts, α-conversion and such that:

$$A_r \equiv A_r \mid 0$$
$$A_r \mid B_r \equiv B_r \mid A_r$$
$$A_r \mid (B_r \mid C_r) \equiv (A_r \mid B_r) \mid C_r$$

$$\nu x.\{M/x\} \equiv 0 \qquad \nu n.0 \equiv 0$$
$$\{M/x\} \equiv \{N/x\} \text{ when } M =_E N \qquad \nu u.\nu v.A_r \equiv \nu v.\nu u.A_r$$
$$\{M/x\} \mid A_r \equiv \{M/x\} \mid A_r\{M/x\} \qquad A_r \mid \nu u.B_r \equiv \nu u.(A_r \mid B_r) \text{ when } u \notin fnv(A_r)$$

The labeled operational semantics is given in Fig. 1. To handle recursions, we take advantage of an internal transition to unfold them.[1] We denote by $\Longrightarrow$ the

[1] We have chosen to use recursions with $K\langle\widetilde{M}\rangle \xrightarrow{\tau} P_r\{\widetilde{M}/\widetilde{x}\}$ to avoid the technical difficulties arising from the structural equivalence rule $K\langle\widetilde{M}\rangle \equiv P_r\{\widetilde{M}/\widetilde{x}\}$ or $!P \equiv P \mid !P$. Our results will carry over if replication is used with this rule removed and replaced by $!P \xrightarrow{\tau} P \mid !P$ in the operational semantics.

$$\text{Then if } M = M \text{ then } P_r \text{ else } Q_r \xrightarrow{\tau} P_r \qquad \text{Else if } M = N \text{ then } P_r \text{ else } Q_r \xrightarrow{\tau} Q_r$$
$$\text{if } M, N \text{ are ground terms and } M \neq_E N$$

$$\text{Comm } \overline{a}\langle M\rangle.P_r \mid a(x).Q_r \xrightarrow{\tau} P_r \mid Q_r\{M/x\} \quad \text{Rec } K\langle\widetilde{M}\rangle \xrightarrow{\tau} P_r\{\widetilde{M}/\widetilde{x}\} \text{ where } K(\widetilde{x}) \triangleq P_r$$

$$\text{In } a(x).P_r \xrightarrow{a(M)} P_r\{M/x\} \qquad \text{Out-atom } \overline{a}\langle u\rangle.P_r \xrightarrow{\overline{a}\langle u\rangle} P_r \text{ where } u \in \mathcal{N}_{ch} \cup \mathcal{V}_b$$

$$\text{Open-atom } \frac{A_r \xrightarrow{\overline{a}\langle u\rangle} B_r \quad a \neq u}{\nu u.A_r \xrightarrow{\nu u.\overline{a}\langle u\rangle} B_r} \qquad \text{Scope } \frac{A_r \xrightarrow{\alpha} B_r \quad u \text{ does not occur in } \alpha}{\nu u.A_r \xrightarrow{\alpha} \nu u.B_r}$$

$$\text{Par } \frac{A_r \xrightarrow{\alpha} A'_r \quad bnv(\alpha) \cap fnv(B_r) = \emptyset}{A_r \mid B_r \xrightarrow{\alpha} A'_r \mid B_r} \qquad \text{Struct } \frac{A_r \equiv C_r \xrightarrow{\alpha} C'_r \equiv B_r}{A_r \xrightarrow{\alpha} B_r}$$

Fig. 1. The Operational Semantics

reflexive and transitive closure of $\xrightarrow{\tau}$, and write $\xRightarrow{\alpha}$ for $\Longrightarrow\xrightarrow{\alpha}\Longrightarrow$, and $\xRightarrow{\widehat{\alpha}}$ for $\xRightarrow{\alpha}$ if α is not τ and $\Longrightarrow$ otherwise.

We say two terms M and N are *equal in the frame* ϕ, written $(M = N)\phi$, iff $\phi \equiv \nu\widetilde{n}.\sigma$, $M\sigma =_E N\sigma$ and $\{\widetilde{n}\} \cap names(M, N) = \emptyset$ for some names $\widetilde{n}$ and substitution σ. The notion of *static equivalence* is introduced to ensure that two processes expose the same information to the environment. Static equivalence is decidable for a large class of equational theories [1].

Definition 1. *Two closed frames ϕ_1 and ϕ_2 are statically equivalent, written $\phi_1 \sim \phi_2$, if $dom(\phi_1) = dom(\phi_2)$, and for all terms M and N such that $vars(M, N) \subseteq dom(\phi_1)$ it holds $(M = N)\phi_1$ iff $(M = N)\phi_2$. Two closed extended processes A_r and B_r are statically equivalent, written $A_r \sim B_r$, when their frames are.*

Definition 2. Labeled bisimilarity ($\approx$) *is the largest symmetric relation $\mathcal{R}$ on closed extended processes such that $A_r \mathcal{R} B_r$ implies:*

1. $A_r \sim B_r$
2. *if $A_r \xrightarrow{\alpha} A'_r$ and $fv(\alpha) \subseteq dom(A_r)$ and $bn(\alpha) \cap fn(B_r) = \emptyset$, then $B_r \xRightarrow{\widehat{\alpha}} B'_r$ and $A'_r \, \mathcal{R} \, B'_r$ for some B'_r.*

2.3 Intermediate Representation

The *intermediate representation* was introduced in [13] as a means to circumvent the difficulties caused by structural equivalence for developing symbolic semantics. In the sequel we shall abbreviate "intermediate" to "inter.". The grammar of inter. processes is given below:

$$\begin{array}{llll}
P, Q, R := & \text{inter. plain processes} & F, G, H := & \text{inter. framed processes} \\
& 0 & & P \\
& P \mid Q & & \{M/x\} \\
& \text{if } M = N \text{ then } P \text{ else } Q & & F \mid G \\
& u(x).P & A, B, C := & \text{inter. extended processes} \\
& \overline{u}\langle M\rangle.P & & F \\
& K\langle\widetilde{M}\rangle & & \nu n.A
\end{array}$$

$$\Gamma(0) = 0 \qquad \Gamma(u(x).P_r) = \nu\tilde{n}.u(x).P \quad \text{where } \Gamma(P_r) = \nu\tilde{n}.P$$

$$\Gamma(K\langle\widetilde{M}\rangle) = K\langle\widetilde{M}\rangle \qquad \Gamma(\overline{u}\langle N\rangle.P_r) = \nu\tilde{n}.\overline{u}\langle N\rangle.P \quad \text{where } \Gamma(P_r) = \nu\tilde{n}.P$$

$$\Gamma(\text{if } M = N \text{ then } P_r \text{ else } Q_r) = \nu\tilde{n}.\nu\tilde{m}.\ \text{if } M = N \text{ then } P \text{ else } Q$$
$$\text{where } \Gamma(P_r) = \nu\tilde{n}.P,\ \Gamma(Q_r) = \nu\tilde{m}.Q$$

$$\Gamma(A_r \mid B_r) = \nu\tilde{n}.\nu\tilde{m}.(F \mid G)\varphi(F \mid G)^* \quad \text{where } \Gamma(A_r) = \nu\tilde{n}.F, \Gamma(B_r) = \nu\tilde{m}.G$$

$$\Gamma(\{M/x\}) = \{M/x\} \qquad \Gamma(\nu n.A_r) = \nu n.\Gamma(A_r) \qquad \Gamma(\nu x.A_r) = \Gamma(A_r)_{\backslash x}$$

where $\Gamma(A_r)_{\backslash x}$ is obtained by replacing $\{M/x\}$ in $\Gamma(A_r)$ with 0

Fig. 2. Transformation

Inter. processes are required to be *applied*, that is, each variable in $dom(A)$ occurs only once in A. Thus, for example, $\overline{a}\langle f(k)\rangle \mid \{f(k)/x\}$ is applied while $\overline{a}\langle x\rangle \mid \{f(k)/x\}$ is not. For an inter. framed process F, we write $\varphi(F)$ for the substitution obtained by taking the union of the active substitutions in F. As an example, $\varphi(\overline{a}\langle f(k)\rangle \mid \{k/x\} \mid \{h(k)/y\}) = \{k/x, h(k)/y\}$. An *inter. evaluation context* is an inter. extended process with a hole not under an input, an output or a conditional. We shall also identify α-convertible inter. processes.

The function Γ in Fig. 2 turns an extended processes into an inter. extended process("$\downarrow$" in [13]) where we assume bound names are pairwise-distinct and different from free names. It transforms an extended process into an inter. extended process by pulling all name binders to the top level, applying active substitutions and eliminating variable restrictions. For example, $\Gamma(\nu x.(\overline{a}\langle f(x)\rangle.\nu n.\overline{a}\langle n\rangle \mid \nu k.\{h(k)/x\})) = \nu n.\nu k.(\overline{a}\langle f(h(k))\rangle.\overline{a}\langle n\rangle \mid 0)$. For a recursion $K\langle\widetilde{M}\rangle$ it is feasible to work "on-the-fly" and keep $K\langle\widetilde{M}\rangle$ invariant under Γ. It can be shown that Γ preserves α-conversion.

The inter. processes are a selected subset of the original processes. It turns out that it is sufficient to build symbolic semantics on top of inter. processes only. Thus this representation behaves like some kind of "normal form" and indeed facilitates the development of a symbolic framework.

3 Constraints

Symbolic bisimulations for value-passing CCS [15] and original pi-calculus [18,9] are indexed by boolean conditions under which transitions can be fired, and to achieve completeness it is essential to partition the indexing boolean conditions when comparing processes for bisimilarity. In the applied pi-calculus a symbolic bisimulation will be indexed by constraints, each of which encompass a similar condition as well as *deducibilities*. The concept of deducibilities is by now widely used in modeling security protocols to represent all the messages that can be computed by intruders using a given set of messages [20,12,4,13]. In the previous work on symbolic bisimulation for the applied pi-calculus, not only conditions and deducibilities are entangled together in constraints, but constraints and processes are mixed in transitions and bisimulations. This makes it impossible to partition conditions, thus causing incompleteness.

In our framework constraints are separated from processes. Furthermore, a constraint is split into a "trail" of deducibilities and a formula, only the latter is subject to partitioning when two processes are compared for bisimilarity.

A *deducibility* takes the form $x : U$ where $x \in \mathcal{V}$, U is a finite subset of $\mathcal{N}_{ch} \cup \mathcal{V}_b$, and $x \notin U$. Let $names(U) = U \cap \mathcal{N}$ and $vars(U) = U \cap \mathcal{V}$. We say that a set of deducibilities is a *trail* if it can be ordered as $x_1 : U_1, \cdots, x_\ell : U_\ell$ satisfying the following conditions:

1. $x_1, \cdots, x_\ell$ are pairwise-distinct and do not appear in any U_j $(1 \le j \le \ell)$;
2. for each $1 \le i < \ell$, $names(U_i) \supseteq names(U_{i+1})$ and $vars(U_i) \subseteq vars(U_{i+1})$.

We shall use $\mathcal{D}, \mathcal{E}, \mathcal{F}$ to range over trails.

Let $\mathcal{E} = \{x_i : U_i \mid 1 \le i \le \ell\}$ be a trail. We write $dom(\mathcal{E})$ for the set $\{x_1, \cdots, x_\ell\}$ and $atoms(\mathcal{E})$ for the set $dom(\mathcal{E}) \cup \bigcup_{i=1}^{\ell} U_i$. We shall often abuse the notation by writing $fnv(\mathcal{E})$ for $atoms(\mathcal{E})$. A substitution θ *respects* $\mathcal{E}$ if

1. $dom(\theta) = dom(\mathcal{E})$, and
2. for any $1 \le i \le \ell$, $vars(x_i\theta) \subseteq U_i$ and $names(x_i\,\theta) \cap U_i = \emptyset$.

Given an inter. extended process $A = \nu\widetilde{n}.F$, we say $\mathcal{E}$ is *compatible with* A if

1. $dom(\mathcal{E}) \cap dom(A) = \emptyset$,
2. $vars(\bigcup_{i=1}^{\ell} U_i) \subseteq dom(A)$, $fv(A) \subseteq dom(A) \cup dom(\mathcal{E})$, and
3. for any $x_i : U_i$ and $y \in vars(U_i)$, $x_i \notin vars(y\varphi(F))$.

Our notion of a deducibility relies on a set of names and variables rather than a set of terms [20,4] or a frame [13]. By dropping the details, a collection of processes can share a common trail. In the above definition of trail, the sets U_i are in increasing order on variables while decreasing on names. It records the variables which can be used and names which can not be used by x_i. Intuitively $vars(U_i)$ can be understood as a snapshot of environmental knowledge at the time when x_i is input. Since the knowledge never decreases, the order of deducibilities on variables reflects a coarse-grained order of inputs recorded by timing information in [11,10].

Example 1. Let $A = \overline{x}_3\langle k\rangle \mid c(x) \mid \{f(x_1)/y\} \mid \{g(x_1,x_2)/z\}$, $\mathcal{D} = \{x_1 : \emptyset,\ x_2 : \{y\},\ x_3 : \{y,z\}\}$ and $\mathcal{E} = \{x_3 : \{c\},\ x_1 : \emptyset,\ x_2 : \{y\}\}$. Clearly both $\mathcal{D}$ and $\mathcal{E}$ are trails and compatible with A. Let $\theta = \{k/x_1,\ f(y)/x_2,\ c/x_3\}$. Then θ respects $\mathcal{D}$ but not $\mathcal{E}$, because $\mathcal{E}$ forbids x_3 to access c.

Formulas are specified by the following grammar:

$$\begin{array}{lcl}\Phi,\ \Psi & ::= & \text{H}n.\Phi \mid \Phi \wedge \Phi \mid \sigma \blacktriangleright \Phi_{atom} \mid \Phi_{atom} \\ \Phi_{atom} & ::= & true \mid M = N \mid M \neq N\end{array}$$

where σ is idempotent. We identify $\sigma \blacktriangleright \Phi_{atom}$ with Φ_{atom} when $dom(\sigma) = \emptyset$. We write $fn(\Phi)$ and $fv(\Phi)$ for the sets of free names and free variables of Φ, respectively. In particular,

$$\begin{array}{ll}fn(\text{H}n.\Phi) \triangleq fn(\Phi) \setminus \{n\} & fv(\text{H}n.\Phi) \triangleq fv(\Phi) \\ fn(\sigma \blacktriangleright \Phi) \triangleq names(\sigma) \cup fn(\Phi) & fv(\sigma \blacktriangleright \Phi) \triangleq vars(\sigma) \cup fv(\Phi)\end{array}$$

In H$n.\Phi$ the name n is binding, and we shall identify α-convertible formulas.

The satisfiability relation $\models$ between idempotent substitutions θ and formulas Φ are defined by induction on the structure of Φ:

$$\begin{array}{lll} \theta \models true & & \\ \theta \models M = N & if & M\theta =_E N\theta \\ \theta \models M \neq N & if & M\theta \neq_E N\theta \\ \theta \models \sigma \blacktriangleright \Phi & if & \theta\sigma \text{ is cycle-free and } (\theta\sigma)^* \models \Phi \\ \theta \models \Phi \wedge \Psi & if & \theta \models \Phi \text{ and } \theta \models \Psi \\ \theta \models \mathrm{H}n.\Phi & if & n \notin names(\theta) \text{ and } \theta \models \Phi \end{array}$$

In $\sigma \blacktriangleright \Phi$, σ represents the environmental knowledge accumulated so far to define some variables occurring in Φ, hence Φ should be evaluated with the application of σ. Having substitutions embedded in formulas echoes the fact that active substitutions are part of the syntax for the extended processes in applied pi-calculus. $\mathrm{H}n.\,\Phi$ hides n in Φ. In the original pi-calculus, a restricted name can never appear in any constraint since this private information cannot be accessed. In contrast, the applied pi-calculus provides a mechanism to indirectly access a datum which may contain restricted names. For example, by the rules in Fig. 1, we have $\nu k.\ (a(x).\ \text{if } x = k \text{ then } \bar{c} \text{ else } 0 \mid \{k/y\}) \xrightarrow{a(y)} \nu k.\ (\text{ if } y = k \text{ then } \bar{c} \text{ else } 0 \mid \{k/y\}) \equiv \nu k.\ (\text{ if } k = k \text{ then } \bar{c} \text{ else } 0 \mid \{k/y\}) \xrightarrow{\tau} \nu k.\ (\bar{c} \mid \{k/y\})$. To reflect this we equip every equality test on terms with its own "private" environmental knowledge, which relies on the introduction of hidden names in formulas. This makes it possible for formulas to "stand alone", without depending on processes, which significantly simplifies technical developments. In particular, α-conversion, which was forbidden in the symbolic semantics of [13,14], is allowed in our framework. Furthermore, introducing hidden names enables us to handle recursions smoothly, which is beyond the scope of any previous approach.

We call a pair $(\mathcal{D}, \Phi)$ a *constraint*, where $\mathcal{D}$ is a trail and Φ a formula. We denote by $\Omega(\mathcal{D}, \Phi)$ the set of substitutions that respect $\mathcal{D}$ and satisfy Φ. Note that "θ respects $\mathcal{D}$" if and only if $\theta \in \Omega(\mathcal{D}, true)$, and $\Omega(\mathcal{D}, \Phi) \subseteq \Omega(\mathcal{D}, true)$ for any Φ. We also observe that $\Omega(\mathcal{D}, \Phi \wedge \Psi) = \Omega(\mathcal{D}, \Phi) \cap \Omega(\mathcal{D}, \Psi)$. For a collection of formulas Σ, we use $\Omega(\mathcal{D}, \bigvee \Sigma)$ to refer to the set $\bigcup_{\Psi \in \Sigma} \Omega(\mathcal{D}, \Psi)$.

Definition 3. *A collection of formulas Σ is a* partition *of Φ under $\mathcal{D}$ if $\Omega(\mathcal{D}, \Phi) \subseteq \Omega(\mathcal{D}, \bigvee \Sigma)$.*

Example 2. Let $\Phi = \mathrm{H}m.\mathrm{H}s.(\{enc(m, s)/y\} \blacktriangleright (dec(x, s) = m))$ where *enc* and *dec* are encryption and decryption functions, respectively, with the equation $dec(enc(x, y), y) =_E x$. Clearly $\{enc(m, s)/x\} \models dec(x, s) = m$. From $\{y/x\}\{enc(m, s)/y\} = \{enc(m, s)/x\}$, we have $\{y/x\} \models \Phi$. Let $\mathcal{D} = \{x : \{y\}\}$. Then $\Omega(\mathcal{D}, \Phi) = \Omega(\mathcal{D}, x = y) = \{\, \{M/x\} \mid vars(M) \subseteq \{y\}, M =_E y \,\}$.

4 Symbolic Semantics

Symbolic structural equivalence $\equiv_s$ is the smallest equivalence relation on inter. extended processes which is closed by application of inter. evaluation contexts and α-conversion and satisfies:

assume $u, v \in \mathcal{N}_{ch} \cup \mathcal{V}_{ch}$

$$\text{Then}_s \quad \text{if } M = N \text{ then } P \text{ else } Q \xrightarrow{M=N,\,\tau} P$$

$$\text{Else}_s \quad \text{if } M = N \text{ then } P \text{ else } Q \xrightarrow{M\neq N,\,\tau} Q$$

$$\text{Comm}_s \quad \overline{u}\langle M\rangle.P \mid v(x).Q \xrightarrow{u=v,\,\tau} P \mid Q\{M/x\}$$

$$\text{In}_s \quad u(x).P \xrightarrow{true,\; u(x)} P \qquad\qquad \text{Outch}_s \quad \overline{u}\langle v\rangle.P \xrightarrow{true,\,\overline{u}\langle v\rangle} P$$

$$\text{Outt}_s \quad \overline{u}\langle M\rangle.P \xrightarrow{true,\,\nu x.\overline{u}\langle x\rangle} P \mid \{M/x\} \quad x \in \mathcal{V}_b,\ x \notin fv(\overline{u}\langle M\rangle.P)$$

$$\text{Rec}_s \quad K\langle\widetilde{M}\rangle \xrightarrow{true,\,\tau} \nu\widetilde{m}.P\{\widetilde{M}/\widetilde{x}\} \quad K(\widetilde{x}) \triangleq P_r,\ \Gamma(P_r) = \nu\widetilde{m}.P,\ \{\widetilde{m}\}\cap fn(\widetilde{M}) = \emptyset$$

$$\text{Par}_s \quad \frac{A \xrightarrow{\Psi,\,\alpha} \nu\widetilde{n}.F \quad bv(\alpha)\cap fv(B) = \{\widetilde{n}\}\cap fn(B) = \emptyset}{A \mid B \xrightarrow{\Phi,\,\alpha} \nu\widetilde{n}.(F \mid B)}$$

$$\Phi = \begin{cases} \Psi & \text{if } fv(\Psi) = \emptyset \\ (\sigma \cup \varphi(B)) \blacktriangleright \Psi_1 & \text{else if } \Psi = \sigma \blacktriangleright \Psi_1 \text{ and } dom(B)\cap dom(\sigma) = \emptyset \end{cases}$$

$$\text{Scope}_s \quad \frac{A \xrightarrow{\Psi,\,\alpha} A' \quad n \notin names(\alpha)}{\nu n.A \xrightarrow{\Phi,\,\alpha} \nu n.A'} \qquad \Phi = \begin{cases} \Psi & \text{if } n \notin fn(\Psi) \\ \mathrm{H}n.\Psi & \text{otherwise} \end{cases}$$

$$\text{Opench}_s \quad \frac{A \xrightarrow{\Phi,\,\overline{u}\langle c\rangle} A' \quad u\neq c,\ c\in\mathcal{N}_{ch}}{\nu c.A \xrightarrow{\Phi,\,\nu c.\overline{u}\langle c\rangle} A'} \qquad \text{Struct}_s \quad \frac{A \equiv_s B \xrightarrow{\Phi,\,\alpha} B' \equiv_s A'}{A \xrightarrow{\Phi,\,\alpha} A'}$$

Fig. 3. Symbolic Operational Semantics

$$A \equiv_s A \mid 0 \qquad A \mid B \equiv_s B \mid A \qquad A \mid (B \mid C) \equiv_s (A \mid B) \mid C$$

A *symbolic action* is either an internal action τ, an input action $u(x)$ with $u \in \mathcal{N}_{ch} \cup \mathcal{V}_{ch}$ and $x \in \mathcal{V}$, an output action $\overline{u}\langle v\rangle$ with $u, v \in \mathcal{N}_{ch} \cup \mathcal{V}_{ch}$, or an bound output action $\nu w.\overline{u}\langle w\rangle$ with $u \in \mathcal{N}_{ch} \cup \mathcal{V}_{ch}$ and $w \in \mathcal{N}_{ch} \cup \mathcal{V}_b$.

Symbolic transition relations $\xrightarrow{\Phi,\,\alpha}$, where Φ is a formula and α a symbolic action, are defined by the rules in Fig. 3.

In Scope$_s$, we hide the restricted name n in Ψ so that it will not be exposed to the environment. In Par$_s$, when A is put in parallel with B, some of the variables recorded in the formula Ψ will be subject to the active substitutions in B, therefore we extract these substitutions from B (using operator φ) and add them to Ψ so that the formula Φ contains necessary environmental knowledge.

Example 3. By Then$_s$, Par$_s$ and Scope$_s$, we have $\nu k.($ if $x = k$ then P else $Q \mid \{h(k)/y\}) \xrightarrow{\Phi,\,\tau} \nu k.(P \mid \{h(k)/y\})$ with $\Phi = \mathrm{H}k.(\{h(k)/y\} \blacktriangleright (x = k))$.

When unfolding a recursion $K\langle\widetilde{M}\rangle$, we transform P_r to $\Gamma(P_r)$ first. This causes a problem that the result of evolution of an inter. framed process may contain bound names. To obtain an inter. extended process, in Par$_s$ rule the parallel component is placed inside the restricted names before juxtaposing it.

Example 4. Let $K(x) \triangleq P_r$ with $P_r = x(z).\nu n.\overline{z}\langle h(n)\rangle.K\langle x\rangle$. Clearly $\Gamma(P_r) = \nu n.\, x(z).\overline{z}\langle h(n)\rangle.K\langle x\rangle$. By Rec$_s$ and Par$_s$, $K\langle a\rangle \xrightarrow{true,\,\tau} \nu n.\, a(z).\overline{z}\langle h(n)\rangle.K\langle a\rangle$ and $K\langle a\rangle \mid \overline{a}\langle c\rangle \xrightarrow{true,\,\tau} \nu n.\, (a(z).\overline{z}\langle h(n)\rangle.K\langle a\rangle \mid \overline{a}\langle c\rangle)$.

Suppose a trail $\mathcal{D} = \{\, x_i : U_i \mid 1 \leq i \leq \ell \,\}$ is compatible with A and $A \xrightarrow{\Phi,\alpha} A'$. Then we define

$$\mathcal{X}(\alpha, dom(A), \mathcal{D}) \triangleq \begin{cases} \mathcal{D} \cup \{x : dom(A)\} & \alpha \text{ is } u(x) \\ \{\, x_i : U_i \cup \{c\} \mid 1 \leq i \leq \ell \,\} & \alpha \text{ is } \nu c.\,\overline{u}\langle c\rangle \\ \mathcal{D} & \text{otherwise} \end{cases}$$

and we can show that $\mathcal{X}(\alpha, dom(A), \mathcal{D})$ is also a trail compatible with A'. Intuitively, function $\mathcal{X}$ updates the current trail so that the resulting trail will be compatible with the residual process after a transition. It records the current environmental knowledge on inputs and prevents the prior input variables from using the fresh names generated by bound outputs.

Example 5. Starting with an empty trail, we have

$$\begin{array}{llr} & \nu k.\nu c.\ (a(x).\overline{b}\langle c\rangle \mid \{h(k)/z\}) & \emptyset \\ \xrightarrow{true,a(x)} & \nu k.\nu c.\ (\overline{b}\langle c\rangle \mid \{h(k)/z\}) & \{x : \{z\}\} \\ \xrightarrow{true,\nu c.\overline{b}\langle c\rangle} & \nu k.\ \{h(k)/z\} & \{x : \{c, z\}\} \end{array}$$

The updated trails are shown on the right. When inputting x, the knowledge represented by z is available to x. The private channel name c are opened after the input of x, hence x cannot access c.

To compare the knowledge of two inter. processes, we define *symbolic static equivalence* similar to [13,4].

Definition 4. *Let $(\mathcal{D}, \Phi)$ be a constraint, $A = \nu\widetilde{n}_1.F_1$ and $B = \nu\widetilde{n}_2.F_2$ inter. extended processes. A and B are* symbolically statically equivalent *w.r.t. $(\mathcal{D}, \Phi)$, written $A \sim^{(\mathcal{D},\Phi)} B$ if*

1. *$\mathcal{D}$ is compatible with A and B,*
2. *$dom(A) = dom(B)$,*
3. *for some fresh variables $x, y \in \mathcal{V}_b$, then $\Omega(\mathcal{E}, \Phi \wedge \Phi_1) = \Omega(\mathcal{E}, \Phi \wedge \Phi_2)$ where $\mathcal{E} = \mathcal{D} \cup \{x : dom(A),\ y : dom(A)\,\}$ and $\Phi_i = \mathrm{H}\widetilde{n}_i.\,\varphi(F_i) \blacktriangleright (x = y),\ i = 1, 2$.*

Intuitively, $x = y$ can be understood as representing a set of concrete equality tests on terms like $M = N$. The above definition symbolically characterizes the idea that such equality tests will be satisfied simultaneously by the frames of the concrete processes corresponding to A and B.

The symbolic weak transition relations $\overset{\Phi,\,\gamma}{\Longrightarrow}$ (γ is α or ϵ) are defined thus:

$$\begin{array}{ll} A \overset{true,\,\epsilon}{\Longrightarrow} A & A \xrightarrow{\Phi,\,\alpha} B \text{ implies } A \overset{\Phi,\,\alpha}{\Longrightarrow} B \\ A \xrightarrow{\Phi,\,\tau} \overset{\Psi,\,\gamma}{\Longrightarrow} B \text{ implies } A \overset{\Phi\wedge\Psi,\,\gamma}{\Longrightarrow} B & A \overset{\Phi,\,\gamma}{\Longrightarrow} \xrightarrow{\Psi,\,\tau} B \text{ implies } A \overset{\Phi\wedge\Psi,\,\gamma}{\Longrightarrow} B \end{array}$$

We write $\overset{\Phi,\,\widehat{\alpha}}{\Longrightarrow}$ to mean $\overset{\Phi,\,\alpha}{\Longrightarrow}$ if α is not τ and $\overset{\Phi,\,\epsilon}{\Longrightarrow}$ otherwise. Let

$$[\alpha = \beta] \triangleq \begin{cases} u = v & \alpha = u(x), \beta = v(x) \\ & \quad \text{or } \alpha = \nu w.\overline{u}\langle w\rangle, \beta = \nu w.\overline{v}\langle w\rangle \\ (u = v) \wedge (w = w') & \alpha = \overline{u}\langle w\rangle,\ \beta = \overline{v}\langle w'\rangle \\ true & \alpha = \beta = \tau \end{cases}$$

We now proceed to define the notion of a symbolic bisimulation. In the definition below, we assume $x \in \mathcal{V}_{ch}$, $y \in \mathcal{V}_b$ and $c \in \mathcal{N}_{ch}$.

Definition 5. *A constraint indexed family of symmetric relations* $\mathcal{S} = \{S^{(\mathcal{D},\Phi)}\}$ *between inter. extended processes is a* symbolic bisimulation *if for any* $(A, B) \in S^{(\mathcal{D},\Phi)}$,

1. $A \sim^{(\mathcal{D},\Phi)} B$
2. *for some* $\Delta = \{x, y, c\}$ *and* $\Delta \cap fnv(A, B, \mathcal{D}, \Phi) = \emptyset$, *if* $A \xrightarrow{\Phi_1,\,\alpha} A'$ *and* $bnv(\alpha) \subset \Delta$, *let* $\mathcal{F} = \mathcal{X}(\alpha, dom(A), \mathcal{D})$, *then there is a partition* Σ *of* $\Phi \wedge \Phi_1$ *under* $\mathcal{F}$, *such that for any* $\Psi \in \Sigma$ *there are* Φ_2, β, B' *satisfying*
   (a) $B \stackrel{\Phi_2,\,\widehat{\beta}}{\Longrightarrow} B'$
   (b) $\Omega(\mathcal{F}, \Psi) \subseteq \Omega(\mathcal{F}, [\alpha = \beta] \wedge \Phi_2)$
   (c) $(A', B') \in S^{(\mathcal{F},\Psi)}$.

We write $A \approx^{(\mathcal{D},\Phi)} B$ if there is a symbolic bisimulation $\mathcal{S}$ such that $(A, B) \in S^{(\mathcal{D},\Phi)}$ and $S^{(\mathcal{D},\Phi)} \in \mathcal{S}$.

Now we state the main result of this paper:

Theorem 1. *Let* A_r *and* B_r *be two closed extended processes. Then* $A_r \approx B_r$ *iff* $\Gamma(A_r) \approx^{(\emptyset,\, true)} \Gamma(B_r)$.

Example 6. Let $A = \nu c.\, a(x).\, \overline{x}\langle c\rangle$ and $B = \nu c.\, a(x).$ if $x = a$ then $\overline{a}\langle c\rangle$ else $\overline{x}\langle c\rangle$. Clearly $A \approx B$. Let $B_1 = \nu c.$ if $x = a$ then $\overline{a}\langle c\rangle$ else $\overline{x}\langle c\rangle$. The following sets constitute a symbolic bisimulation (the symmetric pairs are omitted):

$$S^{(\emptyset,\, true)} = \{(A,\ B)\} \qquad S^{(\{x:\emptyset\},\, true)} = \{(\nu c.\, \overline{x}\langle c\rangle,\ B_1)\}$$
$$S^{(\{x:\emptyset\},\, x=a)} = \{(\nu c.\, \overline{x}\langle c\rangle,\ \nu c.\, \overline{a}\langle c\rangle)\} \qquad S^{(\{x:\emptyset\},\, x\neq a)} = \{(\nu c.\, \overline{x}\langle c\rangle,\ \nu c.\, \overline{x}\langle c\rangle)\}$$
$$S^{(\{x:\{c\}\},\, x=a)} = \{(0,\ 0)\} \qquad S^{(\{x:\{c\}\},\, x\neq a)} = \{(0,\ 0)\}.$$

Hence $A \approx^{(\emptyset,\, true)} B$.

This is a typical example which shows partitions of indexing conditions are necessary for symbolic bisimulations to be complete. Simple as they are, A and B are *not* symbolically equivalent according to any previous symbolic theory for the applied pi-calculus [13,14].

Observational equivalence has been shown to coincide with the labeled bisimilarity in [2]. Hence by transitivity, our symbolic bisimulation is fully abstract w.r.t observational equivalence.

5 Conclusion

We have presented a symbolic framework for the applied pi calculus in which a sound and complete notion of symbolic bisimulation is devised. This is achieved by a careful separation of condition formulas from deducibilities, and constraints from processes. Moreover, our framework accommodates recursions hence our result works for the full applied pi calculus. To the best of our knowledge, this is the first symbolic theory for the applied pi calculus which is both sound and complete and which allows recursion.

As future work we would like to formulate a symbolic style proof system for the applied pi calculus along the lines of [16,9,18].

References

1. Abadi, M., Cortier, V.: Deciding Knowledge in Security Protocols under Equational Theories. Theor. Comput. Sci. 367(1-2), 2–32 (2006)
2. Abadi, M., Fournet, C.: Mobile Values, New Names, and Secure Communication. In: POPL, pp. 104–115 (2001)
3. Abadi, M., Gordon, A.D.: A Calculus for Cryptographic Protocols: the spi Calculus. In: CCS 1997: Proceedings of the 4th ACM Conference on Computer and Communications Security, pp. 36–47. ACM, New York (1997)
4. Baudet, M.: Deciding Security of Protocols against Off-Line Quessing Attacks. In: CCS 2005: Proceedings of the 12th ACM Conference on Computer and Communications Security, pp. 16–25. ACM, New York (2005)
5. Bengtson, J., Johansson, M., Parrow, J., Victor, B.: Psi-Calculi: Mobile Processes, Nominal Data, and Logic. In: LICS 2009: Proceedings of the 2009 24th Annual IEEE Symposium on Logic In Computer Science, pp. 39–48 (2009)
6. Blanchet, B.: An Efficient Cryptographic Protocol Verifier Based on Prolog Rules. In: CSFW 2001: Proceedings of the 14th IEEE Workshop on Computer Security Foundations, p. 82 (2001)
7. Blanchet, B., Abadi, M., Fournet, C.: Automated Verification of Selected Equivalences for Security Protocols. In: LICS, pp. 331–340 (2005)
8. Boreale, M., Buscemi, M.: A Method for Symbolic Analysis of Security Protocols. Theor. Comput. Sci. 338(1-3), 393–425 (2005)
9. Boreale, M., De Nicola, R.: A Symbolic Semantics for the Pi-Calculus. Inf. Comput. 126(1), 34–52 (1996)
10. Borgström, J.: A Complete Symbolic Bisimilarity for an Extended spi Calculus. Electron. Notes Theor. Comput. Sci. 242(3) (2009)
11. Borgström, J., Briais, S., Nestmann, U.: Symbolic Bisimulation in the spi Calculus. In: Gardner, P., Yoshida, N. (eds.) CONCUR 2004. LNCS, vol. 3170, pp. 161–176. Springer, Heidelberg (2004)
12. Comon-Lundh, H., Shmatikov, V.: Intruder Deductions, Constraint Solving and Insecurity Decision in Presence of Exclusive or. In: LICS 2003: Proceedings of the 18th Annual IEEE Symposium on Logic in Computer Science, p. 271 (2003)
13. Delaune, S., Kremer, S., Ryan, M.D.: Symbolic Bisimulation for the Applied Pi Calculus. In: Arvind, V., Prasad, S. (eds.) FSTTCS 2007. LNCS, vol. 4855, pp. 133–145. Springer, Heidelberg (2007)
14. Delaune, S., Kremer, S., Ryan, M.D.: Symbolic Bisimulation for the Applied pi Calculus. Journal of Computer Security (to appear, 2009)
15. Hennessy, M., Lin, H.: Symbolic Bisimulations. Theor. Comput. Sci. 138(2), 353–389 (1995)
16. Hennessy, M., Lin, H.: Proof Systems for Message-Passing Process Algebras. Formal Asp. Comput. 8(4), 379–407 (1996)
17. Johansson, M., Parrow, J., Victor, B., Bengtson, J.: Extended Pi-Calculi. In: Aceto, L., Damgård, I., Goldberg, L.A., Halldórsson, M.M., Ingólfsdóttir, A., Walukiewicz, I. (eds.) ICALP 2008, Part II. LNCS, vol. 5126, pp. 87–98. Springer, Heidelberg (2008)
18. Lin, H.: Complete Inference Systems for Weak Bisimulation Equivalences in the Pi-Calculus. Inf. Comput. 180(1), 1–29 (2003)
19. Liu, J., Lin, H.: A Complete Symbolic Bisimulation for Full Applied pi Calculus (full version) (2009), `http://lcs.ios.ac.cn/~jliu`
20. Millen, J., Shmatikov, V.: Constraint Solving for Bounded-Process Cryptographic Protocol Analysis. In: CCS 2001: Proceedings of the 8th ACM Conference on Computer and Communications Security, pp. 166–175. ACM, New York (2001)
21. Milner, R.: Communicating and Mobile Systems: the pi Calculus. Cambridge University Press, Cambridge (1999)

OTwig: An Optimised Twig Pattern Matching Approach for XML Databases*

Jun Liu and Mark Roantree

Interoperable Systems Group, Dublin City University, Ireland
{jliu,mark.roantree}@computing.dcu.ie

Abstract. Twig based optimisation is one of the current approaches to improving XML query performance. It uses structural joins to find all pairs of elements in the XML documents satisfying the primitive structural relationships specified in the XML queries. They focus on parent-child and ancestor-descendant relationships. Efficient location of all joins is one of the core operations in XML query processing. In this paper, we propose a pattern matching algorithm called OTwig, which extends existing research on twig pattern matching. It demonstrates an improvement over existing pattern matching algorithms while also optimising memory usage.

Keywords: Twig pattern matching, xml query processing.

1 Introduction

As the usage of XML for data representation increases, the poor performance of XML queries becomes a greater problem. XML documents are represented in a tree-structured data model, and XML queries express patterns of selection predicates on multiple elements across the data tree. Efficient location of every occurrence of requested twig patterns in an XML database is a core operation for XML query processing. Early work adopted a relational technique to solve the structural relationships existing in the XML database to locate appropriate twig patterns. However, it has been shown [1,2] that using traditional RDBMS join algorithms is both costly and slow. Subsequent research concentrated on structural-join algorithms [2] and twig pattern matching algorithms [3,4,5,6,7] to address this problem for finding XML patterns. To the best of our acknowledge, *TwigList* [7] is the most efficient pattern matching algorithms for providing a fast pattern matching process.

1.1 Motivation and Contribution

The research presented in this paper is part of the FASTX project [8], the goal of which is to provide fast read and write queries for XML data sources. This aspect of the FASTX project improves on the algorithms presented in [7] (*TwigList*) to obtain better query performance.

* Funded by Enterprise Ireland Grant No. CFTD/07/201.

J. van Leeuwen et al. (Eds.): SOFSEM 2010, LNCS 5901, pp. 564–575, 2010.

In this paper, we present an bottom-up algorithm called *OTwig*, which extends the work in [7] (*TwigList*). The enhancement is achieved through the following points:

- Based on the bottom-up approach, we process nodes as they reside in their index streams, rather than creating an additional working stack as described in [7]. This allows us to enhance the query processing performance by avoiding pop and push operations performed on each node.
- Applying efficient *pruning rules* to reduce the total number of nodes to be processed, which further reduces the memory requirements. The reason for that is because we do not need to maintain nodes, which do not contribute themselves to any match result, in memory.

This paper is organised as follows: we first give an overview of the related work in §2. In §3, we discuss the background knowledge and notations. In §4, we discuss the existing *TwigList* algorithm followed by our *OTwig* algorithm. We provide a detailed experimental evaluation in §5 against the current fastest twig matching algorithm *TwigList*. We outline our conclusions in §6.

2 Related Work

Twig pattern matching over XML documents has been researched extensively due to its fast query processing speed. One of the first efforts resulted in the Multi-Predicate Merge Join algorithm (*MPMGJN*) [1], whose implementation is similar to the classical merge-join algorithm developed *RDBMS*. Their experiment demonstrates that *MPMGJN* is much faster than traditional approach. Later Al-Khalifa et al. [2] observed that *MPMGJN* fails to process the *parent-child* relationship efficiently as many unnecessary nodes are visited. Motivated by this, they proposed a binary structural-join algorithm called *StackTree*.

TwigStack was then proposed by [3] to reduce the intermediate results generated by the binary approach. Rather than locating matches for each binary path, *TwigStack* finds potential instances for every root-to-leaf paths. Before any instance can be determined as a potential element for a pattern match, it must be evaluated all the way to the leaf node so that it has at least one instance for each of its descendants. This step significantly reduces the amount of useless intermediate results generated by the algorithm. However, it achieves optimality for twig queries with ancestor-descendant relations only. It is not optimised as long as there are sibling relations or parent-child relationship exist. *TwigStackList* [5] extends *TwigStack* by reducing the size of intermediate results to be a subset of the size generated by *TwigStack*. *TwigStackList* utilises a "looks ahead" technique which caches some data in the main memory in advance to make it optimal when all *parent-child* relationships are under non-branching nodes.

According to *TwigStack*, Lu et al. [6] proposed a holistic algorithm called *TJFast*, which is based on a variation of *Dewey* encoding scheme represented by a tuple of *idPath* and *tagPath*. As stated by Gou et al. [9], although Dewey-based join algorithms typically read fewer nodes from index than PrePost-based join algorithms, the process of reading the *idPath* and *tagPath* of data nodes to derive their ancestors is essentially backward navigation, which might involve accessing large numbers of query-irrelevant nodes. Therefore, Dewey-based join might be less efficient than PrePost-based join algorithms when the XML data tree is deep or when ancestor query nodes are very selective.

Twig²Stack [4] and *TwigList* [7] are two other twig pattern match processing approaches, which mainly focus on reducing the merge cost spent in the second phase of *TwigStack* and *TJFast*. *Twig²Stack* avoids the step of producing intermediate results as it utilises a complicated hierarchical stack encoding structure for storing nodes. Each query node is assigned a stack and each hierarchical stack consists of an ordered sequence of stack tree (ST), where ST contains one or more elements. Although this approach bypasses the issues of producing large amount of intermediate results by encoding twig matches in a set of stacks, it has to randomly access the memory space many times. To our best knowledge *TwigList* [7] is the most up-to-date technique for twig pattern matching. It is claimed to be fast than both *Twig²Stack* and *TJFast*. *TwigList* simply maintains a list for each query node. These lists maintain the pattern matches for twig pattern query in a compact fashion. It finally enumerates elements in the lists to obtain the results of an n-ary tuples for a twig pattern query.

3 Background

In this section, we provide an background overview followed by a description of the numbering encoding scheme for XML trees, often referred to as *positional region encoding scheme*, which is used in [3,4,5,6,7] and in this paper as well.

3.1 Data Model and Notations

For an XML document D (e.g., *Figure 1a*), it can be modeled as a rooted, ordered and node-labeled tree, $\mathcal{T}$ (e.g., *Figure 1b*). Each XML node within $\mathcal{T}$ is represented as a node (u) and the edge between elements can be either parent-child relationship (P-C) or ancestor-descendant (A-D) relationship. We treat the label of an arbitrary node as a value that always belongs to a *type* (tag-name). Therefore, a given node in $\mathcal{T}$ with value x_i belongs to a type X (denoted $x_i \in X$). For instance, a_1 in *Figure 1b* is type of A. Furthermore, a twig pattern query can be treated as a fragment of the XPath expressions. It can be also represented to a tree-structured layout as shown in *Figure 1e*. A twig pattern query within this paper is denoted as $Q(V, E)$ (*abbr.* Q) where $V = \{V_1, V_2, \cdots, V_n\}$ is a set of query nodes representing the node type, e.g., in *Figure 1e*, $V = \{A, B, D, F\}$. E is a set of edges describing the relationships between V_i and V_{i+1}. For instance, E between type B and D can be either associated with an XPath axis operator // or /, represented as $B//D$ or B/D. We use the method `edge` to return the relationship between either two query nodes (types) or two elements, e.g., `edge`(B, D) returns relationship between two query nodes and `edge`(b_1, d_2), where $b_1 \in B$ and $d_2 \in D$, returns relationship between two elements. V_1 represents the root of Q.

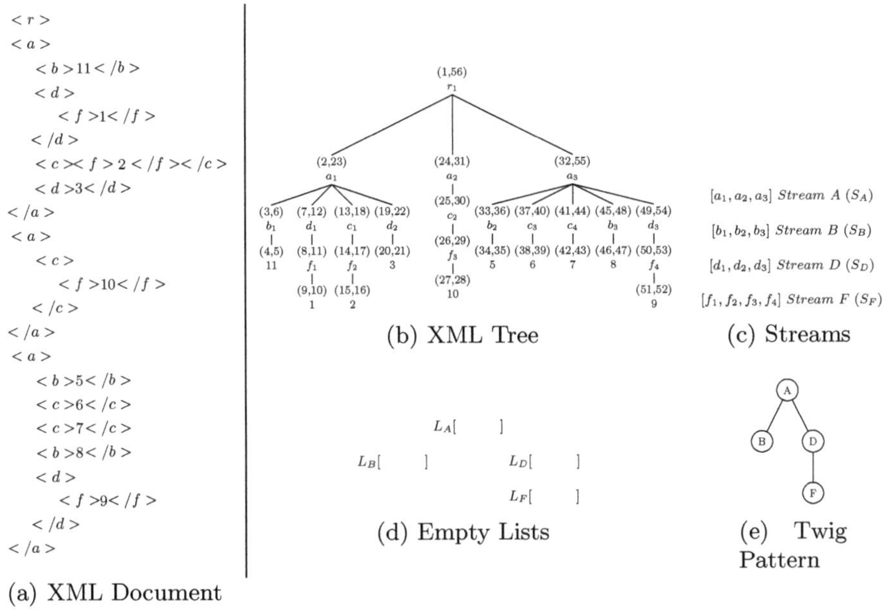

Fig. 1. XML Document and XML Tree

During twig pattern matching process, each query node V_i is associated with a pre-generated stream S_{V_i} (e.g., *Figure 1c*) containing all instances of V_i. The nodes within the streams are stored based on their *end* value (described in §3.2) sorted in ascending order. We use `front` to return the first node in S_{V_i}, denoted by $\texttt{front}(S_{V_i})$. Additionally, each query node V_i is also associated with a list L_{V_i} (e.g., *Figure 1d*). These lists are populated during evaluation with nodes that may potentially participate to a valid match. For instance, L_A in *Figure 1d* should contain A-typed nodes, a_i, where $a_i \in A$. The result of a twig pattern query $Q(V,E)$ is denoted by $tup^n(Q)$. $tup^n(Q)$ is a set of all n arity (n-ary) tuples. A single n-ary tuple is represented by $(v_1, v_2, \cdots, v_n)$ where $v_i \in V_i$ and $1 \leq i \leq n$. An illustration is shown in *Example 1*.

Example 1. Given that $Q(V,E) = //A[./B]//F$, where $V = \{A, B, F\}$, $E = \{/, //\}$, searching for Q over $\mathcal{T}$ (*Figure 1b*) will generate four 3-ary tuples. $tup^3(Q)) = \{(a_1, b_1, f_1), (a_1, b_1, f_2), (a_3, b_2, f_4), (a_3, b_3, f_4)\}$.

3.2 Logical Encoding Scheme

Indexing of XML data has been studied by many researchers [2,10,11,12,13]. However, many of the existing twig pattern matching algorithms adopt a positional region encoding scheme originally developed by [2]. It represents the position of a node u as a triple (*start*, *end*, *level*) based on the document order, where *start* and *end* can be generated by counting word numbers from the beginning of the document node until the start and the end of the element (e.g., the label above each node in *Figure 1b*). The region of u can be represented as $\texttt{reg}(u)$. *level* is the depth of u in $\mathcal{T}$ denoted by $\texttt{dep}(u)$. The structural relationship can be easily determined by this positional labeling scheme for *P-C* and *A-D* relationships.

Property 1 (Region Containment). Given two nodes u and v, the region of u is contained in the region of v iff $u.start > v.start$ and $u.end < v.end$, denoted by $\texttt{reg}(u) \subset \texttt{reg}(v)$.

Property 2 (Ancestor). Given two nodes u_i and u_{i+1}, $u_i \in \mathcal{T}$ and $u_{i+1} \in \mathcal{T}$. u_i is the ancestor of u_{i+1} iif $\texttt{reg}(u_{i+1}) \subset \texttt{reg}(u_i)$.

Property 3 (Parent). Given two nodes u_i and u_{i+1}, $u_i \in \mathcal{T}$ and $u_{i+1} \in \mathcal{T}$. u_i is the parent of u_{i+1} iif $\texttt{reg}(u_{i+1}) \subset \texttt{reg}(u_i)$ and $\texttt{dep}(u_i) + 1 = \texttt{dep}(u_{i+1})$.

4 Twig Pattern Matching

In this section, we give an overview of the *TwigList* algorithm followed by a detailed discussion of our *OTwig* algorithm.

4.1 TwigList Algorithm

The major difference between *TwigList* and previous works [3,4] is that previous require the maintenance of complicated hierarchical-stacks for nodes in a query tree Q (e.g., *Twig²Stack*), *TwigList* simply maintains a set of lists, L_{V_1}, L_{V_2}, $\cdots$, L_{V_n}. It minimises the cost of enumerating results compared to the previous works as the merging procedure of n joins is avoided.

Given an XML tree $\mathcal{T}$ (*Figure 1b*) and a twig pattern query $Q(V, E) = //A[.//B]//F$, where $V = \{A, B, F\}$, $A = \{a_1, a_2, a_3\}$, $F = \{f_1, f_2, f_3, f_4\}$ and $B = \{b_1, b_2, b_3\}$, *TwigList* reads nodes base on the ascending order of their *start* value. Therefore, it reads a_1, b_1, f_1, f_2, a_2, f_3, a_3, b_2, b_3 and f_4 in order. *TwigList* makes use of a working stack S to temporarily store the nodes. Before any node is added to a list (e.g., L_A, L_B in *Figure 1d*), it is pushed onto S. If either the context node is a descendant of the top node in S or there is no node

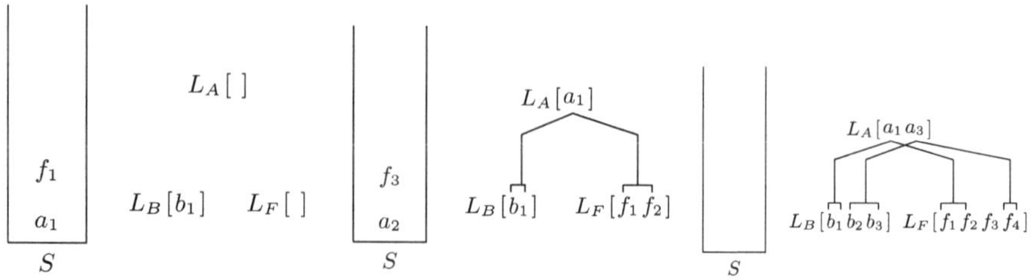

(a) After traversal to f_1 (b) After traversal to f_2 (c) End of evaluation

Fig. 2. TwigList Algorithm

in S at all, it is then pushed onto S. Otherwise, the top node of S is popped. *TwigList* continuously compares the context node to the top node on the stack until either an ancestor of the context node is found or there is no node left in S. In both of the situation, the context node is then pushed onto S. In this case, a_1 is the first node to be evaluated, therefore, it is pushed onto S directly with no further process. b_1 is a descendant of a_1, hence, it is also pushed onto S. f_1 is the next node being processed. As f_1 is not a descendant of the top node, b_1, in S. b_1 is popped out and appended to L_B (*Figure 2a*). f_1 is then pushed onto S as it is a descendant of a_1. Since f_2 is not descendant of f_1, f_1 is popped from S and appended to L_F. f_2 is then pushed onto S. a_2 is then retrieved. As a_2 is not a descendant of f_2 and a_1, f_2 and a_1 are popped out of S and appended to their corresponding lists, L_F and L_A respectively. a_1 then points to its descendants in L_B and L_F (*Figure 2b*). a_2 is then pushed onto S. The next node f_3 is pushed onto S as it is a descendant of a_2 (*Figure 2b*). Since a_3 is not the descendant of f_3 or a_2, both of them are popped from S. f_3 is appended to L_F as it is the leaf node, whereas a_2 is abandoned as it does not have any descendant in L_B and will not have any subsequent descendants because there is no further incoming node u that satisfies the condition of $\texttt{reg}(u) \subset \texttt{reg}(a_2)$. Next, a_3 is pushed onto S. b_2 is also pushed onto S since it is a descendant of a_3. b_3 is then pushed onto S as it is a descendant of b_2. Since f_4 is not the descendant of b_3 and b_2, b_3 and b_2 are popped out and appended to L_B. f_4 is then pushed onto S. All nodes in S are then popped and appended into their corresponding lists (*Figure 2c*) as f_4 is the last node. Each node in the list will have a start and end pointer which specifies the *interval* for its V_i-typed descendants. Eventually, *TwigList* merges all existing nodes and insert them into a set of 3-ary tuples. The result of Q would be $\{(a_1, b_1, f_1), (a_1, b_1, f_2), (a_3, b_2, f_4), (a_3, b_3, f_4)\}$.

The drawback of *TwigList* can be summarised into two parts: 1) every node has to be pushed onto a working stack first and popped out at a later stage. The *pop* and *push* operations performed on each node increase the processing steps during query evaluation. 2) *TwigList* maintains a large number of nodes in the lists which will not contribute themselves to any valid matches. This is because there is no way for *TwigList* to pre-determine whether an existing node within a list will have an ancestor in another list. e.g., f_3 in *Figure 2c* does not have an ancestor in L_A. We refine the *TwigList* algorithm based on these two drawbacks.

4.2 OTwig Algorithm

Our OTwig algorithm is a bottom-up approach that retrieves nodes based on their *end* position value. OTwig applies a set of pruning rules to evaluate nodes retrieved from $\mathcal{T}$ before they can be appended to their corresponding lists. This application avoids the extra processing steps caused by the push/pop operations, and also reduces the maintenance cost resulting from the storing nodes in the lists.

For a given twig pattern query $Q(V, E)$ and nodes u_A and u_B, where $V = \{A, B\}$, $u_A \in A$ and $u_B \in B$. One of the following situations may arise:

1) Suppose u_B is the current node being evaluated by *OTwig* and u_A is the first node in stream S_A.

Rule 1 (Pruning By Ancestor). *u_B is pruned from the result set iff $\texttt{reg}(u_B) \not\subseteq \texttt{reg}(u_A)$ when $\texttt{edge}(A,B)$ is ancestor-descendant relationship. If $\texttt{edge}(A,B)$ is parent-child relationship, then u_B is pruned iff $\texttt{reg}(u_B) \not\subseteq \texttt{reg}(u_A)$ or $\texttt{dep}(u_A) + 1 \mathrel{!}= \texttt{dep}(u_B)$.*

2) Suppose u_A is the current node being processed, u_B is the node that has already been evaluated before u_A, and it is the last node stored in L_B.

Rule 2 (Pruning By Descendant). *u_A is pruned iff $\texttt{reg}(u_B) \not\subseteq \texttt{reg}(u_A)$ when $\texttt{edge}(A,B)$ is ancestor-descendant relationship. If $\texttt{edge}(A,B)$ is parent-child relationship, then u_A is pruned iff $\texttt{reg}(u_B) \not\subseteq \texttt{reg}(u_A)$ or $\texttt{dep}(u_A) + 1 \mathrel{!}= \texttt{dep}(u_B)$.*

According to *Rule 1* and *Rule 2*, *OTwig* guarantees that before a node is added to a list, it should always have an ancestor (in S_{V_i}) and descendants (in L_{V_i}) exist. This step further reduces the memory requirements as invalid nodes are eliminated.

4.3 OTwig Algorithm by Example

In this section, we explain how *OTwig* works using the example of evaluating the twig pattern query $Q(V, E) = //A[.//B]//D//F$ (*Figure 1e*) over $\mathcal{T}$ (*Figure 1b*), where $V = \{A, B, D, F\}$. We use a set of streams to represent source data categorised by node *types* within Q (*Figure 1c*), $S_A = \{a_1, a_2, a_3\}$, $S_B = \{b_1, b_2, b_3\}$, $S_D = \{d_1, d_2, d_3\}$ and $S_F = \{f_1, f_2, f_3, f_4\}$. *OTwig* generates 4 empty lists at the start of processing, to maintain all potential matches for Q (*Figure 1d*). Each node will hold a set of *start* and *end* pointers which specify the node *interval* (interval between the node pointed by the *start* pointer and the *node* pointed by the end pointer) for its V_i-typed descendant, e.g., the *start* and *end* pointers of u_A, where $u_A \subseteq A$, to its B-typed descendant is denoted by ($start_B$, end_B). We first give a brief description of the major methods used in the algorithms. `SearchMatch` calls other methods for handling XML tree nodes and searching for

---

Algorithm 1. OTwig Algorithm

Require: $Q(V, E)$, where $V = \{V_1, V_2, \cdots, V_n\}$, $\mathcal{T}$;
Ensure: a set of n-ary tuples, $tup^n(Q)$;
let L_{V_1} be the root of Q, $L_{V_1}[start]$ and $L_{V_1}[end]$ are the start and end elements in L_{V_1};
let $L_{V_i}[start]$ and $L_{V_i}[end]$ be the start and end elements pointed by the elements in its parent list;
let *cur* be the cursor point to the current position in L_{V_i}, $start < cur < end$;
initialise list L_{V_i}, where $V_i \in V$
$tup^n(Q) = \text{SEARCHMATCH}(Q, \mathcal{T})$
return $tup^n(Q)$

```
7: procedure SearchMatch(Q, T)
8:     while (u_Vi ← GetNext(Q)) ≠ null do
9:         MoveToList(u_Vi, L_Vi);
10:        if V_i is root and reg(u_Vi) ⊄ reg(front(S_Vi)) then
11:            MergeResult( );
12:        end if
13:    end while
14:    if L_Vi is not empty then
15:        MergeResult( );
16:    end if
17: end procedure

18: procedure GetNext(Q)
19:     get u_Vi with smallest end in S_Vi;
20:     check if reg(u_Vi) ⊆ reg(front(S_Vk)), where V_k
  21: is ancestor of V_i within Q;
22: end procedure
```

Fig. 3. SearchMatch

```
23: procedure MoveToList(u_Vi, L_Vi)
24:     if u_V is a leaf node then
25:         add u_Vi into L_Vi;
26:     else
27:         for all V_j is descendant of V_i do
28:             check whether u_Vi has a valid
29:             descendant in L_Vj; ;
30:             if u_Vi has a valid descendant then
31:                 set u_Vi.start to the first element
32:                 that is a valid descendant of u_Vi in L_Vj;
33:                 set u_Vi.end to last element in L_Vj;
34:             end if
35:         end for
36:         if u_Vi is valid then
37:             add u_Vi into L_Vi;
38:         end if
39:     end if
40: end procedure
```

Fig. 4. MoveToList

potential matches. `GetNext` recursively retrieves nodes starting from the smallest *end* value from *streams*, and also validates whether a node that has been retrieved is valid or not (by *Rule 1*). `MoveToList` validates whether the context node has valid descendants in its descendant lists (by *Rule 2*) and appends valid ones to their corresponding list. `MergeResult` merges existing nodes within each list, and forms a set of n-ary tuples as the answer to a twig pattern query. (Due to space limitation, only part of the algorithm is shown in this paper, the rest can be found in our technical report [14]).

OTwig starts by creating a set of empty lists for maintaining valid nodes (*Line 4* in *Algorithm 1*). During query evaluation, *OTwig* reads nodes based on their *end* value in ascending order, b_1, f_1, d_1, f_2, d_2, a_1, f_3, a_2, b_2, b_3, f_4, d_3 and a_3. b_1 is the first node returned by `GetNext` as the smallest *end* value 5. It is then validated by `GetNext` at *Line 23* to check whether it has an A-typed ancestor in S_A. b_1 is valid as it has an ancestor a_1 in S_A, where $\texttt{reg}(a_1) \subset \texttt{reg}(b_1)$. b_1 is then appended to L_B (*Figure 5a*) by `MoveToList` at *Line 27* . f_1 is the next node returned by `GetNext` (*Line 8*). f_1 is appended to L_F as it has an ancestor d_1 in S_D (*Line 23*) as well as it is the leaf node (*Line 27*). The next node d_1 is checked by *Line 23* and *30*. It is then appended to L_B as it is a valid node. After that, the $start_F$ and end_F of d_1 point to its F-typed descendants in L_F. In this case, only f_1 exists in L_F, therefore, d_1's $start_F$ and end_F point to f_4 (*Line 33*) as shown in *Figure 5b*.

a_1 is the next node to be evaluated. Due to A being the root query node, therefore, a_1 is not required to be validated against its ancestor. However, a_1 is validated by the existing nodes within its B-typed and D-typed descendant lists. Since both L_B and L_D are not empty, and they both contain valid descendants of a_1 (e.g., b_1, d_1). Hence, a_1 is considered to be valid and appended into L_A with its ($start_B$, end_B) and ($start_D$, end_D) points to b_1 and d_1 respectively (*Figure 5c*). Thereafter a_1 is inserted to L_A. At this stage, *OTwig* will first check whether A is the root node of Q. It then compares a_1 to $\texttt{front}(S_A)$ if A is the root of Q (*Line 10*). Furthermore, if $\texttt{reg}(a_1) \not\subseteq \texttt{reg}(\texttt{front}(S_A))$, *OTwig* then merges the existing elements in the lists and generates a set of n-ary tuples. If $\texttt{reg}(a_1) \subset$

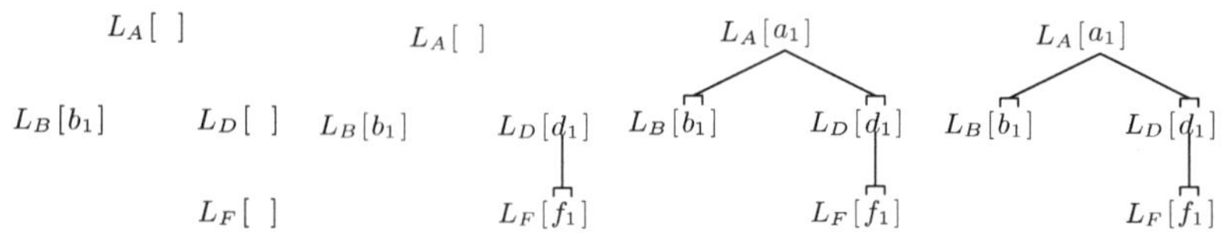

(a) After traverse to b_1 (b) After traverse to d_1 (c) After traverse to a_1 (d) After traverse to f_3

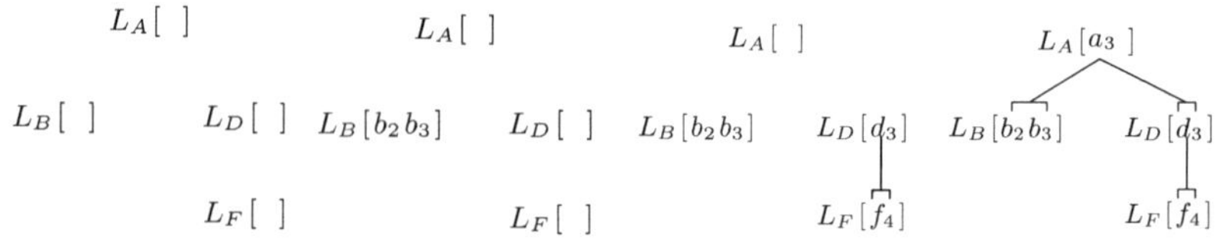

(e) After traverse to a_2 (f) After traverse to b_3 (g) After traverse to d_3 (h) After traverse to a_3

Fig. 5. OTwig Algorithm

`reg`(`front`(S_A)), *OTwig* will continue to process until the next A-typed node is reached. In this case, `reg`(a_1) $\nsubseteq$ `reg`(`front`(S_A)), therefore, (a_1, b_1, d_1, f_1) is generated. All lists are then cleared for further process. When f_3 is reached for processing, it is pruned (*Line 23*) as it does not have a valid ancestor in S_D. Therefore, it will not be appended into L_F as shown in *Figure 5d.* a_2 is the next node to be processed. a_2 is pruned as there is no descendant of a_2 existing in either L_B or L_D. b_2 and b_3 are processed after a_2. Due to B is the leaf node of Q and both of them have a valid ancestor a_3 in S_A, consequently, they are appended to L_B (*Figure 5f*). For the same reason, f_4 is also appended to L_F. d_3 is valid as it has a valid ancestor a_3 in S_A as well as a valid F-typed descendant f_4 in L_F. It is then appended in L_D, and both of its $start_F$ and end_F point to f_4 (*Figure 5g*).

Eventually, a_3 is about to be evaluated. Since A is the root of Q, therefore, a_3 is validated against its descendants only. As it has valid descendants of both B-typed and D-typed nodes, hence, it is appended into L_A (*Figure 5h*). `MergeResult` is then called to generate matches as there is no more node to be evaluated. Together with the previous tuple, the result of Q are a set of 4-ary tuples, $tup^4(Q) = \{(a_1, b_1, d_1, f_1), (a_3, b_2, d_3, f_4), (a_3, b_3, d_3, f_4)\}$.

5 Experimental Evaluation

In this section we first demonstrate the efficiency of the *OTwig* approach against *TwigList* by processing on three real and synthetic datasets DBLP (428MB), XMark (683MB) and PSD (568MB). The comparison is based on returning matches for each query and demonstrates our performance against similar approach. Then by applying a set of pruning rules, we demonstrate that while comparing to *TwigList*, we are also memory optimised by evaluating twig queries in main-memory. We implemented both our own *OTwig* and the *TwigList* pattern matching algorithms. All systems were implemented using Java JDK 6. Experiments ran on workstations with Intel Core2 Duo CPU 2.66GHz processor, 4GB main memory and Windows XP SP3 OS.

5.1 Performance

Figure 6 shows the processing time and memory usage spent on evaluating the queries listed in *Table 1* by both *OTwig* and *TwigList* algorithms. *OTwig* is considered to be both time and memory optimised according to the experimental result depicted below.

`DBLP Dataset` As shown in *Figure 6a*, *OTwig* outperforms *TwigList* for all queries. However, both performance and memory usage are very close, except for *DB4* and *DB5*, which requires relatively more memory space by *TwigList.* This is because the amount of nodes pruned by *OTwig* is larger than *TwigList*, especially for *DB5* and *DB6.* This is due to that *OTwig* prunes 35% and 65% nodes for *DB5* and *DB6*, however, *TwigList* only prunes very few nodes as shown in *Table 2.* Therefore, the memory required by *TwigList* is much higher.

`PSD Dataset` *OTwig* is optimised for both performance and memory usage (*Figure 6d* and *6c*). For query *PSD1*, the same amount of nodes are pruned by both *OTwig* and *TwigList.* However, *OTwig* is faster and requires far less memory. The main reason is because *OTwig* clears all lists after processing of each instance of the root node of the query. *OTwig* has a far higher pruning rate for the rest of the PSD queries this is the main reason why the performance for *PSD2* to *PSD6* by *TwigList* is much slower than *OTwig.*

`XMARK Dataset` For queries *XM1* and *XM2*, a similar amount of nodes are processed (see *Table 2*). *TwigList* requires almost identical time for both queries and *OTwig* is more efficient for both queries, especially *XM2.* This is because 77% of nodes are pruned. However, it spends approximately half of the time evaluating *XM1* comparing to *XM2.* Apart from pruning, it requires far less

Table 1. Twig Pattern Queries

DBLP Dataset
DB1: //dblp/inproceedings[./title]/author
DB2: //dblp/inproceedings[./cite][./title]/author
DB3: //article[./volume][./cite]/journal
DB4: //article[./mdate][./volume][./cite/label]/journal
DB5: //inproceedings[./key][./mdate][./author][./year][./url]/title
DB6: //article[./title][./author][./year][./ee]/key
Protein Sequence Database
PSD1: //ProteinEntry[./header[./accession]/created_date]/protein/name
PSD2: //ProteinEntry[./organism/source][./reference[.//year][.//month] //group]//gene
PSD3: //ProteinEntry[.//gene][.//label]/header/accession
PSD4: //ProteinEntry[./genetics[./label]/gene][./reference]/protein/name
PSD5: //ProteinEntry[./reference[./accinfo]//title]/classification
PSD6: //ProteinEntry[./classification/superfamily][./feature/description] /keywords
XMark Dataset
XM1: //item[location]/description//keyword
XM2: //person[.//address/zipcode]/profile/education
XM3: //item[location][.//mailbox/mail//emph]/description//keyword
XM4: //item[//location][.//mail//date]//payment
XM5: //person[./emailaddress][./phone]/profile[.//age]/education

Table 2. Data Pruning

Query	Total Nodes.	OTwig		TwigList		Matches
		Pruned	Rate	Pruned	Rate	
DB1	4082019	1272822	31%	1270976	31%	1595488
DB2	4254420	1923963	45%	1322555	31%	290144
DB3	1297362	502686	39%	21	0.000016%	47324
DB4	2376462	1170749	49%	81	0.000034%	13785
DB5	8093639	2853343	35%	8723	0.001%	1595475
DB6	6501573	4029283	62%	81	0.000012%	608053
PSD1	1948174	312506	16%	312506	16%	323043
PSD2	1169008	573758	49%	0	0%	2075
PSD3	1751474	395890	23%	312506	17.8%	709176
PSD4	1900571	864999	46%	396504	20.9%	4074
PSD5	1269229	230061	18%	0	0%	144505
PSD6	967704	271366	28%	40916	4.2%	207373
XM1	900871	394164	44%	180101	20%	136282
XM2	915971	708996	77%	0	0%	15859
XM3	1464611	848493	58%	316087	21.6%	86533
XM4	991628	499471	50%	102950	10.4%	104430
XM5	1012120	732783	72%	0	0%	7966

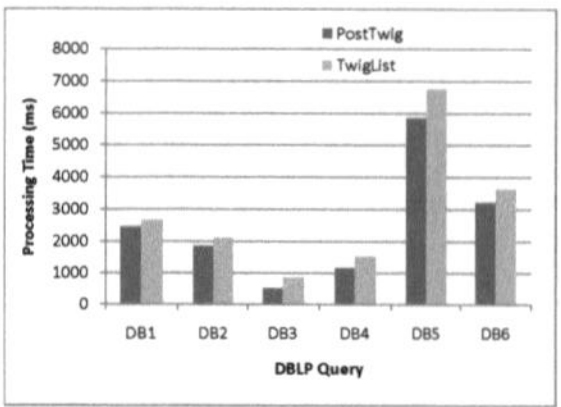

(a) DBLP Processing Time

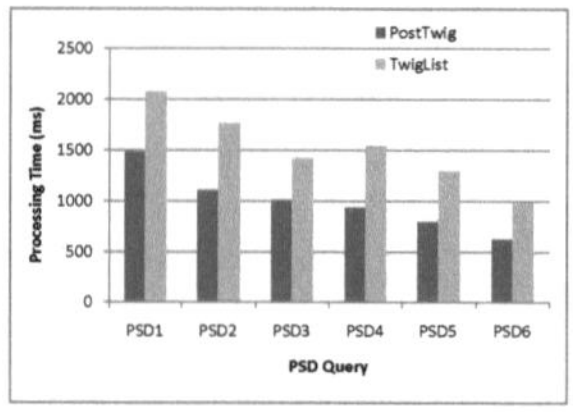

(b) PSD Processing Time

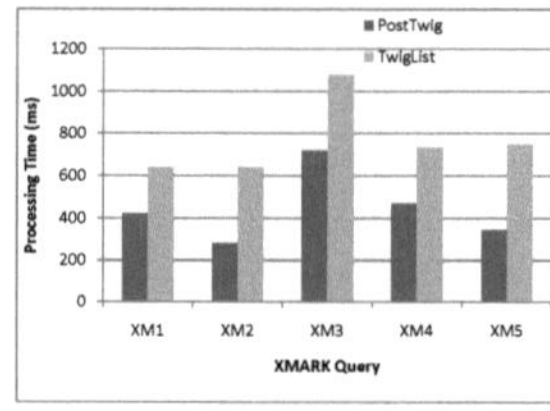

(c) XMARK Processing Time

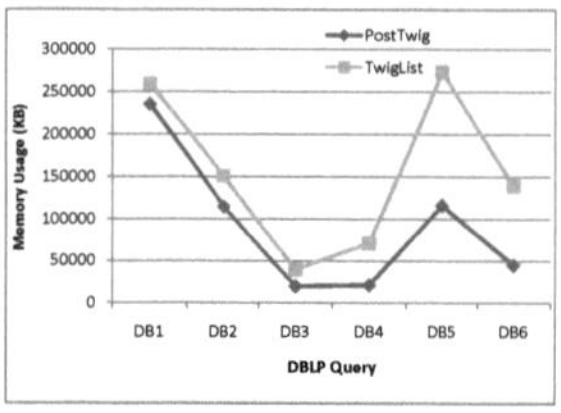

(d) DBLP Memory Usage

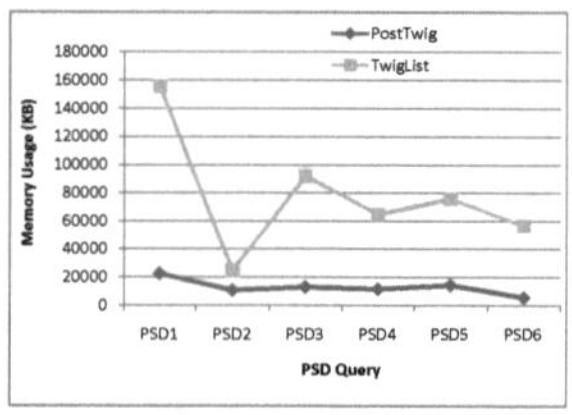

(e) PSD Memory Usage

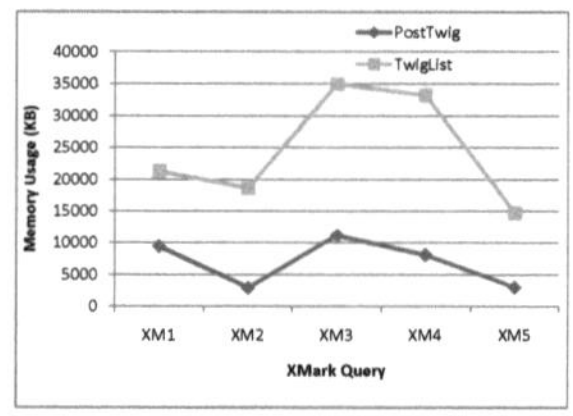

(f) XMARK Memory Usage

Fig. 6. Experimental Result Charts

joins than *XM1*, approximately 10%. As we can see from *Table 2*, a similar situation applies to *XM4* and *XM5*. By observation, query *XM3* in *Table 2* and *2*, 58% of the nodes have been pruned, therefore *OTwig* is both time and memory optimised when processing *XM3*.

6 Conclusions

With the need for managing and querying large XML datastores, comes the additional requirement for improving the poor query response times. One approach to improving query performance is twig pattern matching to quickly locate relevant matches in an XML document or database. In this paper, we make use of the traditional encoding scheme together with a query processing strategy utilising new pruning logic to reach new levels of performance. We employed traditional benchmarking databases and queries. *OTwig* is faster for all queries when compared against *TwigList*.

References

1. Zhang, C., Naughton, J., DeWitt, D., Luo, Q., Lohman, G.: On Supporting Containment Queries In Relational Database Management Systems. SIGMOD Rec., 425–436 (2001)
2. Al-khalifa, S., Patel, J.M.: Structural Joins: A Primitive for Efficient XML Query Pattern Matching. In: Proceedings of the 18th International Conference on Data Engineering. IEEE Computer Society, Los Alamitos (2002)

3. Bruno, N., Koudas, N., Srivastava, D.: Holistic Twig Joins: Optimal XML Pattern Matching. In: Proceedings of the 2002 ACM SIGMOD International Conference on Management of Data. ACM, New York (2002)
4. Chen, S., Li, H.G., Tatemura, J., Hsiung, W.P., Agrawal, D., Candan, K.S.: $Twig^2Stack$: Bottom-up Processing Of Generalized Tree Pattern Queries over XML Documents. In: Proceedings of the 32nd International Conference on Very Large Data Bases. ACM, New York (2006)
5. Lu, J., Chen, T., Ling, T.W.: Efficient Processing Of XML Twig Patterns With Parent Child Edges: A Look-Ahead Approach. In: Proceedings of the Thirteenth ACM International Conference on Information and Knowledge Management, pp. 533–542. ACM, New York (2004)
6. Lu, J., Chen, T., Ling, T.W.: TJFast: Effective Processing Of XML Twig Pattern Matching. In: WWW (Special Interest Tracks and Posters), pp. 1118–1119. ACM, New York (2005)
7. Qin, L., Yu, J.X., Ding, B.: Twiglist: Make Twig Pattern Matching Fast. In: Kotagiri, R., Radha Krishna, P., Mohania, M., Nantajeewarawat, E. (eds.) DASFAA 2007. LNCS, vol. 4443, pp. 850–862. Springer, Heidelberg (2007)
8. Marks, G., Roantree, M.: Pattern Based Processing of xpath Queries. In: IDEAS 2008: Proceedings of the 2008 International Symposium on Database Engineering Applications, pp. 179–188. ACM, New York (2008)
9. Gou, G., Chirkova, R.: Efficiently Querying Large XML Data Repositories: A Survey. IEEE Trans. on Knowl. and Data Eng., 1381–1403 (2007)
10. Wu, X., Lee, M.L., Hsu, W.: A Prime Number Labeling Scheme for Dynamic Ordered XML Trees. In: ICDE 2004: Proceedings of the 20th International Conference on Data Engineering, pp. 66–78. IEEE Computer Society, Los Alamitos (2004)
11. Wang, H., Park, S., Fan, W., Yu, P.S.: Vist: a Dynamic Index Method for Querying XML Data by Tree Structures. In: SIGMOD, pp. 110–121. ACM, New York (2003)
12. Rao, P., Moon, B.: Prix: Indexing and Querying XML Using Prufer Sequences. In: ICDE, pp. 288–300. IEEE Computer Society, Los Alamitos (2004)
13. Wang, H., Meng, X.: On the Sequencing of Tree Structures for XML Indexing. In: ICDE 2005, pp. 372–383. IEEE Computer Society, Los Alamitos (2005)
14. Liu, J.: Using OTwig to Boost XML Query Performance. TechReport, Dublin City University (November 2008)

Picture Recognizability with Automata Based on Wang Tiles*

Violetta Lonati[1] and Matteo Pradella[2]

[1] Dipartimento di Scienze dell'Informazione, Università degli Studi di Milano
Via Comelico 39/41, 20135 Milano, Italy
lonati@dsi.unimi.it
[2] IEIIT, Consiglio Nazionale delle Ricerche
Via Golgi 40, 20133 Milano, Italy
matteo.pradella@polimi.it

Abstract. We introduce a model of automaton for picture language recognition which is based on tiles and is called Wang automaton, since its description relies on the notation of Wang systems. Wang automata combine features of both online tessellation acceptors and 4-ways automata: as in online tessellation acceptors, computation assigns states to each picture position; as in 4-way automata, the input head visits the picture moving from one pixel to an adjacent one, according to some scanning strategy. We prove that Wang automata recognize the class REC, i.e. they are equivalent to tiling systems or online tessellation acceptors, and hence strictly more powerful than 4-way automata. We also consider a very natural notion of determinism for Wang automata, and study the resulting class, comparing it with other deterministic classes considered in the literature, like DREC and Snake-DREC.

Keywords: Picture languages, 2D languages, tiling systems, 4-way automata, online tessellation acceptors, Wang systems, determinism.

1 Introduction

Picture languages are a generalization of string languages to two dimensions: a picture is a two-dimensional array of elements from a finite alphabet. The literature on picture languages is quite rich of models, see e.g. [14,12,17,9,5,7,3,8]. Here we regard class REC, introduced in [12] with the aim to generalize to 2D the class of regular string languages. REC is a robust class that has various characterizations: for instance it is the class of picture languages that can be generated by *online tessellation automata* [13], *tiling systems* [11], or *Wang systems* [10].

In this paper we characterize REC by introducing a new model of 2D automata based on tiles. We call such model *Wang automaton*, since its description is based on the notation of Wang systems. Wang automata combine features of both online tessellation

* This work has been supported by the MIUR PRIN projects "Mathematical aspects and emerging applications of automata and formal languages", and "D-ASAP: Dependable Adaptable Software Architecture for Pervasive Computing".

J. van Leeuwen et al. (Eds.): SOFSEM 2010, LNCS 5901, pp. 576–587, 2010.

acceptors [13] and 4-ways automata [14]: as in online tessellation acceptors, computation assigns states to each input picture position; as in 4-way automata, the input head visits the input picture following a given *scanning strategy*, that is a method to visit its positions.

The choice of a suitable scanning strategy is a central issue in this context. In particular it has been considered recently in [2,6]. Here we introduce *polite* scanning strategies, that sort all positions in a picture, and visit each of them exactly once, in such a way that the next position to visit is always adjacent to the previous one, and depends only on this information: which neighboring positions have already been visited, and which direction we are moving from. Examples of such scanning strategies are those following the boustrophedonic order, spirals, and many others.

Differently from 4-way automata, Wang automata directed by polite scanning strategies visit each position exactly once; moreover, one can consider various polite scanning strategies, but next position cannot depend on the input symbol (in a sense, like traditional finite state automata on strings). However, we prove that this kind of automata are equivalent to tiling systems, thus they are strictly more powerful than 4-way automata [12].

An interesting aspect of this new model is the possibility to introduce quite naturally the notion of determinism, yielding class Scan-DREC, which is closed under complement and rotation. Determinism is a crucial concept in language theory, whereas in two dimensions it is far from being well understood. Tiling systems are implicitly nondeterministic: REC is not closed under complement, and the membership problem is NP-complete [15].

In the literature several notions of determinism for recognizable languages and automata have been proposed. For 4-way automata the definition of determinism is straightforward [14]. Online tessellation acceptors have a diagonal-based kind of determinism [13] and this notion is extended in [1], with the definition of a deterministic class we denote by Diag-DREC (the original name was DREC). In [16] we introduced the class Snake-DREC which is based on a boustrophedonic scanning strategy and proved that Snake-DREC properly extends Diag-DREC. Here we prove that Scan-DREC properly extends Snake-DREC (and hence Diag-DREC) and is closed under complement and rotation. Several questions concerning the relationship among these classes remain open and are proposed in the conclusions.

We cite also an interesting and radically different notion of determinism, proposed in [4], which is not based on prefixed scanning strategies. Such notion is built upon a definition of language recognized by a tiling system which is different from the usual one, e.g. of [12], so it is hard to compare it with other approaches. For instance, while it is decidable to check if a tiling system is deterministic in one of the senses presented before, at present we do not know anything about decidability for [4].

The paper is organized as follows. In Section 2 we recall some basic definitions and properties on two-dimensional languages, tiling systems, Wang systems, and determinism. In Section 3 we introduce polite scanning strategies and compare them with scanning strategies already studied in the literature. In Section 4 we present our model of Wang automaton and prove the main theorem characterizing REC as the class of picture languages recognized by Wang automata directed by polite scanning strategies. In

Section 5 we introduce the concept of determinism natural in this framework, and compare the corresponding class with Diag-DREC and Snake-DREC. In the last section we propose some open questions concerning determinism in 2D.

2 Preliminaries

The following definitions are taken and adapted from [12].

Let Σ be a finite alphabet. A two-dimensional array of elements of Σ is a *picture* over Σ. The set of all pictures over Σ is Σ^{++}. A picture language is a subset of Σ^{++}. If C denotes some kind of picture-accepting device, then $\mathcal{L}$(C) denotes the class of picture languages recognized by such devices.

For $n, m \geq 1$, $\Sigma^{n,m}$ denotes the set of pictures of size (n, m); $\# \notin \Sigma$ is used when needed as a *boundary symbol*; $\hat{p}$ refers to the bordered version of picture p. That is, for $p \in \Sigma^{n,m}$, it is

$$p = \begin{array}{|c|c|c|}\hline p(1,1) & \dots & p(1,m) \\ \hline \vdots & \ddots & \vdots \\ \hline p(n,1) & \dots & p(n,m) \\ \hline \end{array} \qquad \hat{p} = \begin{array}{|c|c|c|c|c|}\hline \# & \# & \dots & \# & \# \\ \hline \# & p(1,1) & \dots & p(1,m) & \# \\ \hline \vdots & \vdots & \ddots & \vdots & \vdots \\ \hline \# & p(n,1) & \dots & p(n,m) & \# \\ \hline \# & \# & \dots & \# & \# \\ \hline \end{array}.$$

A *pixel* is an element $p(i, j)$ of p. We call (i, j) the *position* in p of the pixel. We will sometimes use position (i, j) with i or j equal to 0, or $n + 1$, or $m + 1$ for referring to borders. We use the term *picture domain* (or domain for short) to refer to the set of possible positions in a generic picture of size (n, m), not considering borders, i.e. the set $n \times m = \{1, 2, \dots, n\} \times \{1, 2, \dots, m\}$. Each position has four *edges*, and an edge is identified by a pair of (vertically or horizontally) *adjacent* positions.

We will sometimes consider the 90° clockwise *rotation* of a picture p. E.g. if $p = \begin{array}{|c|c|}\hline a & b \\ \hline c & d \\ \hline \end{array}$, then $\begin{array}{|c|c|}\hline c & a \\ \hline d & b \\ \hline \end{array}$ is its rotation. Naturally, the same operation can be applied to languages, and classes of languages, too.

2.1 Tiling Systems

We call *tile* a square picture of size (2,2). We denote by $T(p)$ the set of all tiles contained in a picture p.

Let Σ be a finite alphabet. A (two-dimensional) language $L \subseteq \Sigma^{++}$ is *local* if there exists a finite set Θ of tiles over the alphabet $\Sigma \cup \{\#\}$ such that $L = \{p \in \Sigma^{++} \mid T(\hat{p}) \subseteq \Theta\}$. We will refer to such language as $L(\Theta)$.

Let $\pi : \Gamma \to \Sigma$ be a mapping between two alphabets. Given a picture $p \in \Gamma^{++}$, the *projection* of p by π is the picture $\pi(p) \in \Sigma^{++}$ such that $\pi(p)\ (i, j) = \pi(p(i, j))$ for every position (i, j). Analogously, the projection of a language $L \subseteq \Gamma^{++}$ by π is the set $\pi(L) = \{\pi(p) \mid p \in \Gamma^{++}\} \subseteq \Sigma^{++}$.

A *tiling system* (TS) is a 4-tuple $\tau = \langle \Sigma, \Gamma, \Theta, \pi \rangle$ where Σ and Γ are two finite alphabets, Θ is a finite set of tiles over the alphabet $\Gamma \cup \{\#\}$ and $\pi : \Gamma \to \Sigma$ is a projection. A picture language $L \subseteq \Sigma^{++}$ is *tiling recognizable* if there exists a tiling system

$\langle \Sigma, \Gamma, \Theta, \pi \rangle$ such that $L = \pi(L(\Theta))$. We say that τ generates L and denote by REC the class of picture languages that are tiling recognizable, i.e, REC $= \mathcal{L}(\mathrm{TS})$. Notice in particular that any local language is tiling recognizable.

Example 1. Consider the language L_{half} of pictures of size $(n, 2n)$ with the first row like $x \cdot \bar{x}$, where $\bar{x}$ is the reverse of x. We show that L_{half} is recognized by a tiling system. Let Γ be the set of letters of the form σ_ρ, with $\sigma, \rho \in \Sigma$. For each picture p in L_{half}, consider the picture $p' \in \Gamma^{++}$ where subscripts are used to connect each letter in x to the corresponding letter in $\bar{x}$, along nested paths following a ⊔-like form. Below there is an example of such pair of pictures p and p':

$$p = \begin{array}{|c|c|c|c|c|c|} \hline a & b & c & c & b & a \\ \hline b & b & a & c & b & a \\ \hline c & a & a & b & a & a \\ \hline \end{array}\,, \qquad p' = \begin{array}{|c|c|c|c|c|c|} \hline a_a & b_b & c_c & c_{c'} & b_b & a_a \\ \hline b_a & b_b & a_b & c_b & b_b & a_a \\ \hline c_a & a_a & a_a & b_a & a_a & a_a \\ \hline \end{array}\,.$$

One can show that the language of pictures p' is local, and hence L_{half} is in REC.

2.2 Wang Systems

In [10] a model equivalent to tiling systems but based on a variant of Wang tiles was introduced. A Wang tile is a unitary square with colored edges. Color represents *compatibility*: two tiles may be adjacent only if the color of the touching edges is the same. A *labeled Wang tile* is a Wang tile bearing also a *label*; a set of such tiles is called *Wang system*.

More formally, given a finite alphabet *Colrs* of colors, and a finite alphabet Σ of labels, a labeled Wang tile is a quintuple (n, s, e, w, x), with $n, s, e, w \in Colrs \cup \{\#\}$ (where, as usual, # is a color representing borders), and $x \in \Sigma$. Intuitively, n, s, e, w represent the colors respectively at the top, bottom, right, and left of the tile. For better readability, we represent the labeled Wang tile (n, s, e, w, x) as $\begin{array}{c} n \\ w\boxed{x}e \\ s \end{array}$.

Given $\Phi \subseteq Colrs^4 \times \Sigma$, a *Wang-tiled picture over* Φ is any picture in Φ^{++} such that adjacent pixels are compatible, also considering borders, as in the following example:

$$\begin{array}{|c|c|} \hline \begin{array}{c} \# \\ \#\boxed{a}4 \\ 1 \end{array} & \begin{array}{c} \# \\ 4\boxed{b}\# \\ 3 \end{array} \\ \hline \begin{array}{c} 1 \\ \#\boxed{b}2 \\ \# \end{array} & \begin{array}{c} 3 \\ 2\boxed{a}\# \\ \# \end{array} \\ \hline \end{array} \in \Phi^{2,2}.$$

The *label* of a Wang-tiled picture P over Φ is the picture over Σ having for pixels the labels of pixels of P. For instance, the label of the example above is $\begin{array}{|c|c|} \hline a & b \\ \hline b & a \\ \hline \end{array}$.

A Wang system ω is a triple $(Colrs, \Sigma, \Phi)$. The language generated by ω is the language over Σ of all labels of Wang-tiled pictures over Φ.

Example 2. A Wang system recognizing L_{half} can be defined using the same idea presented in Example 1. The resulting Wang-tiled pictures have the form

$$P = \begin{array}{|c|c|c|c|c|c|}\hline \begin{matrix}\#\\ \#\boxed{a}\cdot\\ a\end{matrix} & \begin{matrix}\#\\ \cdot\boxed{b}\cdot\\ b\end{matrix} & \begin{matrix}\#\\ \cdot\boxed{c}c\\ \cdot\end{matrix} & \begin{matrix}\#\\ c\boxed{c}\cdot\\ \cdot\end{matrix} & \begin{matrix}\#\\ \cdot\boxed{b}\cdot\\ b\end{matrix} & \begin{matrix}\#\\ \cdot\boxed{a}\#\\ a\end{matrix} \\ \hline \begin{matrix}a\\ \#\boxed{b}\cdot\\ a\end{matrix} & \begin{matrix}b\\ \cdot\boxed{b}b\\ \cdot\end{matrix} & \begin{matrix}\cdot\\ b\boxed{a}b\\ \cdot\end{matrix} & \begin{matrix}\cdot\\ b\boxed{c}b\\ \cdot\end{matrix} & \begin{matrix}b\\ b\boxed{b}\cdot\\ \cdot\end{matrix} & \begin{matrix}a\\ \cdot\boxed{a}\#\\ a\end{matrix} \\ \hline \begin{matrix}a\\ \#\boxed{c}a\\ \#\end{matrix} & \begin{matrix}\cdot\\ a\boxed{a}a\\ \#\end{matrix} & \begin{matrix}\cdot\\ a\boxed{a}a\\ \#\end{matrix} & \begin{matrix}\cdot\\ a\boxed{b}a\\ \#\end{matrix} & \begin{matrix}\cdot\\ a\boxed{a}a\\ \#\end{matrix} & \begin{matrix}a\\ a\boxed{a}\#\\ \#\end{matrix} \\ \hline \end{array} . \qquad (1)$$

2.3 Diagonal- and Snake-Deterministic Tiling Systems

Tiling systems are implicitly nondeterministic: REC is not closed under complement, and the membership problem is NP-complete [15]. Moreover, any notion of deterministic tiling systems seems to require some pre-established "scanning strategy" to read the picture, an important issue we deal with in the following section. Here we recall two notions of determinism recently introduced in the literature. They are both defined using the notation of tiling systems, but it is quite natural translate them from tiling systems to Wang systems.

Diagonal determinism [1] is inspired by the deterministic version of online tessellation acceptors [13], which are directed according to a corner-to-corner direction (namely, from top-left to bottom-right, or *tl2br*). Consider a scanning strategy that follows the tl2br direction: any position (x, y) is read only if all the positions that are above and to the left of (x, y) have already been read. An example of such scanning strategy is depicted in Figure 1(a). Roughly speaking, tl2br determinism means that, given a picture $p \in \Sigma^{++}$, its preimage $p' \in L(\Theta) \subseteq \Gamma^{++}$ can be build deterministically when scanning p with any such strategy: *tl2br-deterministic* tiling systems guarantee this condition (the formal definition can be found in [1]). They are proved to be equivalent to deterministic online tessellation acceptors.

Snake-determinism [16] is based on boustrophedonic scanning strategies. Given a tiling system $\tau = \langle \Sigma, \Gamma, \Theta, \pi \rangle$ and a picture $p \in \Sigma^{++}$, imagine to build one preimage $p' \in L(\Theta)$, $\pi(p') = p$, by scanning p as follows: start from the top-left corner, scan the first row of p rightwards, then scan the second row leftwards, and so on, as in Figure 1(b). This means that we scan odd rows rightwards and even row leftwards, assigning a symbol in Γ to each position. A tiling system is *snake-deterministic* if this choice is guaranteed unique (the formal definition can be found in [16]).

Diag-DREC (resp. Snake-DREC) is the family of languages such that one of their rotations is recognized by a *tl2br*-deterministic (resp. snake-deterministic) tiling system. Diag-DREC $\subset$ Snake-DREC $\subset$ REC with all proper inclusions.

3 Two-Dimensional Scanning Strategies

The notions of determinism in [1,16] are all based on some fixed and pre-established kinds of scanning strategy. This approach can be limiting, so we plan to define and consider here a wider range of possible strategies. We will start by introducing the central concept of *scanning strategy*, and then discussing the two related approaches of [2] and [6].

Definition 1. *A* scanning strategy *is a family*

$$\mu = \{\mu_{n \times m} : \{1, 2, \ldots\} \to n \times m\}_{n,m}$$

and $\mu_{m \times n}$ *is called the* scanning function over domain $n \times m$. *A scanning strategy is said to be* continuous *if* $\mu_{n \times m}(i + 1)$ *is adjacent to* $\mu_{n \times m}(i)$ *for every* n, m, i*; it is said to be* one-pass *if each scanning function* $\mu_{n \times m}$ *restricted to* $\{1, 2, \ldots, nm\}$ *is a bijection.*

Intuitively, a scanning strategy provides a method to visit positions in any picture domain: $\mu_{n \times m}(i)$ is the position visited in domain $n \times m$ at time i. One-pass strategies are those that visit each position in each domain exactly once.

Some one-pass scanning strategies are illustrated in Figure 1. Actually they are not fully defined: only the function $\mu_{3 \times 4}$ is depicted whereas the other functions should be defined analogously; each position c of domain 3×4 contains the number i such that $c = \mu_{3 \times 4}(i)$. The strategy (a) is not continuous and visits one row after the other, from left to right and from top to bottom; the other strategies are all continuous.

In the literature on 2D languages, two recent works considered the problem of defining scanning strategies for pictures, namely [2] and [6].

In [2] an automata model called *tiling automaton* is introduced, with the aim to define a general computational model for recognizable languages. This approach is centered upon the concept of scanning strategy itself, which directly depends on the size of the picture to be scanned. This definition is very general, and may exploit the size of the picture to perform "jumps", thus allowing complex behaviors. This freedom, together with the potential knowledge of the picture size, may be exploited to exceed REC (in practice, scanning strategies presented and used in [2] are simpler, and do not exhibit this issue). Consider e.g. the 1D non-regular language $x \cdot \bar{x}$, with $x \in \{a, b\}^+$ and $\bar{x}$ equal to the reverse of x: if we are able to jump back and forth, starting from the first character,

1	2	3	4
5	6	7	8
9	10	11	12

(a)

1	2	3	4
8	7	6	5
9	10	11	12

(b)

1	2	3	4
10	11	12	5
9	8	7	6

(c)

1	12	9	8
2	11	10	7
3	4	5	6

(d)

1	2	11	10
4	3	12	9
5	6	7	8

(e)

Fig. 1. Some one-pass scanning strategies: the number in each pixel denotes its scanning order. (a) is not continuous (b) has a boustrophedonic behavior, (c) has a spiral behavior, (d) draws nested ⊔-like paths, (e) combines the behavior of (b) in the first half of the picture and a counter-clockwise variant of (c) in the second one.

and then going to the last, then considering the second, the last-but-one and so on, we can easily define an accepting automaton.

The very recent work [6] is also based on the concept of scanning strategy. In it, the considered strategies are "continuous" (hence called "snakes", not to be confused with the homonym we used before), in the sense that the next considered position is adjacent to the current one. The actual definition of such strategies is not formally presented, as the authors preferred more qualitative considerations. This aspect could be source of some problems, since may admit different strategies depending on the picture size or shape (e.g. Peano-Hilbert curves are suitable only for square pictures). For example, if we consider unary languages, having different strategies which depends on the shape/size of the figure itself may be exploited to exceed REC also in this case.

In our opinion all these issues could be addressed by introducing a qualitative concept, that we will call of *blindness* of the strategy. We consider *blind* a strategy which proceeds locally, by scanning adjacent positions, and cannot "see" neither the picture content, nor its size: it can only "feel" a border and an already considered position, when it reaches it. Considering the strategies presented in Figure 1, (a) is not blind, since it uses the knowledge of picture's width, after reaching the end of a row, to "jump" back to the beginning of the next row. Analogously, (e) is not blind, since it exploits the knowledge of the width of picture, to change direction when reaching its half. We accept all the other presented strategies, as they only depend on local information: already considered positions, and borders.

In the following we try to capture this idea of blindness, by adding some constraints to the scanning strategies we consider. To this aim, we shall need some notations.

Given a position y, we use edges(y) to denote the set of 4 edges adjacent to y. *Dirs* is the set of directions {r, l, t, b}. For every position y, and $d \in Dirs$, the edge of y in direction d is denoted by $y|d$, and the position adjacent to y in direction d is denoted by $y \boxplus d$.

A *next-position function* is a partial function $\eta : 2^{Dirs} \times Dirs \to Dirs$ such that $\eta(D, d) = \perp$ if $d \notin D$. Informally, the meaning of η is that, for a given position, we have a set of already considered edges, given by the set D of directions, and d, the "last-considered" one. η is used to choose where to go next, i.e. the direction towards the position to visit next.

Now fix any next-position function η, any starting corner $c_s \in Corners = \{\text{tl}, \text{tr}, \text{br}, \text{bl}\}$ and any starting direction $d_s \in Dirs$. Then, for every picture domain $n \times m$, consider the following scanning function $\mu_{n\times m}$ over $n \times m$.

- The starting position is

$$\mu_{n\times m}(1) = \begin{cases} (1,1) & \text{if } c_s = \text{tl} \\ (1,m) & \text{if } c_s = \text{tr} \\ (n,1) & \text{if } c_s = \text{bl} \\ (n,m) & \text{if } c_s = \text{br} \end{cases}$$

  moreover we define E_1 as the set of outer edges (i.e. those adjacent to borders) of the picture domain $n \times m$, and we set $d_1 = d_s$.

- The inductive definition[1] of $\mu_{n\times m}(i+1)$ for $i \geq 1$ is given by:

$$D_i = \{d \in Dirs : \mu_{n\times m}(i)|d \in E_i\} \qquad E_{i+1} = E_i \cup \text{edges}(\mu_{n\times m}(i))$$

$$d_{i+1} = \eta(D_i, d_i) \qquad \mu_{n\times m}(i+1) = \mu_{n\times m}(i) \boxplus d_{i+1}$$

Notice that $\mu_{n\times m}(1)|d_1$ must be in E_1 for $\eta(D_1, d_1)$ to be defined.

We say that $\mu = \{\mu_{n\times m}\}_{n,m}$ is the scanning strategy *induced by* the triple $\langle \eta, c_s, d_s\rangle$.

Definition 2. *A scanning strategy is* blind *if it is induced by a triple $\langle \eta, c_s, d_s\rangle$, where η is a next-position function, c_s a starting corner, and d_s a starting direction.*

Notice that, in general, a blind scanning strategy is not one-pass. However, it is continuous and satisfies the other requirements we need. First, all scanning functions are defined by the same triple $\langle \eta, c_s, d_s\rangle$ for every picture domain; second, the next position to visit always depends only on this information: which neighboring positions have already been visited, and which direction we are moving from. This yields the following definition.

Definition 3. *A scanning strategy is called* polite *if it is blind and one-pass.*

4 Wang Automata

We are now able to formally introduce Wang automata and to show that they are equivalent to tiling systems.

Let *Colrs* be a set of *colors*. If the edges adjacent to a position are (partially or fully) colored, a coloring will be used to summarize their colors. Formally, we call *coloring* any partial function $\gamma : Dirs \rightarrow Colrs$. The set of directions where γ is defined is denoted by Δ_γ. If $\Delta_\gamma = Dirs$, then γ is called a *full* coloring. Given $\gamma_1, \gamma_2 \in Colrs$, we say that γ_2 extends γ_1 if $\gamma_2(d) = \gamma_1(d)$ for every $d \in \Delta_{\gamma_1}$.

Definition 4. *A μ-*directed Wang automaton *(μ-WA) is a tuple $\langle \Sigma, Colrs, \delta, \mu, F\rangle$ where:*

- *Σ is a finite input alphabet,*
- *Colrs is a finite set of colors, and C is the set of colorings over Colrs,*
- *F is a set of full colorings over Colrs,*
- *$\delta : \Sigma \times C \times Dirs \rightarrow 2^C$ is a partial function such that each coloring in $\delta(\sigma, \gamma, d)$ is full and extends γ,*
- *μ is a blind scanning strategy induced by some $\langle \eta, c_s, d_s\rangle$ such that $\delta(\sigma, \gamma, d) \neq \emptyset$ implies $\eta(\Delta_\gamma, d) \neq \perp$.*

A Wang automaton can be seen as having a head that visits a picture, by moving from a position to an adjacent one, and coloring at each step the edges of the position it is visiting (in a sense, the element of $C \times Dirs$ are the *states* of the automaton). For each

[1] In the definition, also d_i, D_i, and E_i depend on n and m. For better readability, this dependence is not explicit.

accepting computation, the automaton produces a Wang-tiled picture whose label is equal to the input picture. The movements of the head are lead by the scanning strategy μ, whereas the coloring operations the automaton performs are determined by a finite control formalized by function δ. Since the scanning strategy μ is blind, the automaton visits the picture positions independently of the input symbols, and only the choice of colors to assign to edges is nondeterministic.

More precisely, the behavior of a μ-directed Wang automaton over an input picture p can be described as follows. At the beginning, the head of the automaton points at the position in the starting corner c_s and the current direction is set to d_s. When the current direction is d, the head is pointing at position y, the pixel of p at position y is σ, and the colors of borders of y are summarized by γ, then let $d' = \eta(\Delta_\gamma, d)$ and $\gamma' \in \delta(\sigma, \gamma, d)$. Hence the automaton may execute this move: apply γ' to the borders of y, set the current direction to d', and move to the position $y \boxplus d'$. If no move is possible, the automaton halts. The input picture p is accepted if there is a computation such that the coloring of the final position is in F.

As illustrated in the following theorem, for nondeterministic Wang automata the choice of the scanning strategy (as long as it is polite) is not relevant from the point of view of the recognizing power of the device. In the next section we will show that this is no longer true when determinism is concerned.

Theorem 1. *For every polite scanning strategy μ, we have $\mathcal{L}(\mu\text{-}WA) = REC$.*

Proof. REC being generated by Wang systems [10], the result is proved if we show that, for every polite μ, μ-directed Wang automata are equivalent to Wang systems.

First let $A = \langle \Sigma, Colrs, \delta, \mu, F \rangle$ be a μ-WA recognizing a language L. Then, define the Wang system $\omega = (Colrs \times Dirs, \Sigma, \Phi)$ by setting, for every $\gamma' \in \delta(\sigma, \gamma, d)$ and $d' = \eta(\Delta_\gamma, d)$,

$$\begin{array}{c} (\gamma'(\mathrm{t}), a(\mathrm{t})) \\ (\gamma'(\mathrm{l}), a(\mathrm{l})) \boxed{\quad \sigma \quad} (\gamma'(\mathrm{r}), a(\mathrm{r})) \\ (\gamma'(\mathrm{b}), a(\mathrm{b})) \end{array} \in \Phi,$$

where $a(x)$ may represent current direction d or next direction d', i.e.

$$a(x) = \begin{cases} d' & \text{if } x = d' \\ d & \text{if } x = -d \\ \bot & \text{otherwise,} \end{cases} \qquad \text{where} \qquad -\mathrm{b} = \mathrm{t}, -\mathrm{t} = \mathrm{b}, -\mathrm{l} = \mathrm{r}, -\mathrm{r} = \mathrm{l}.$$

Together with their labels, these labeled Wang tiles carry two pieces of information: the colors assigned by the automaton and the path followed by the head of the automaton, corresponding to the scanning strategy μ. One can verify that each Wang-tiled picture over Φ corresponds to an accepting computation of the automaton. Hence, the language generated by ω is L.

Vice versa, let $\omega = (Colrs \times Dirs, \Sigma, \Phi)$ be a Wang system recognizing a language L. Then, take any polite scanning strategy μ, and define the μ-WA $A = \langle \Sigma, Colrs, \delta, \mu, F \rangle$ where F is the set of all full colorings over $Colrs$, and δ is defined only for those triples

(σ, γ, d) such that $\eta(\Delta_\gamma, d) \neq \perp$, and there exists some labeled Wang tile

$$\begin{array}{ccc} & c(\mathrm{t}) & \\ c(\mathrm{l}) & \boxed{\;\sigma\;} & c(\mathrm{r}) \\ & c(\mathrm{b}) & \end{array} \in \Phi \qquad \text{with} \qquad \gamma(x) = c(x) \text{ if } \gamma(x) \neq \perp .$$

In this case, also set $\delta(\sigma, \gamma, d) = \gamma'$ where $\gamma'(x) = c(x)$ for every direction x. One can prove that the language generated by A is L and this concludes the proof. □

5 Determinism in Wang Automata

In the framework of Wang automata, it is quite natural to introduce the concept of determinism:

Definition 5. *A μ-WA $\langle \Sigma, Colrs, \delta, \mu, F \rangle$ is deterministic if $\delta(\sigma, \gamma, d)$ has at most one element for every symbol $\sigma \in \Sigma$, coloring γ over Colrs, and direction d. Deterministic μ-WA are denoted by μ-DWA. The union of classes $\mathcal{L}(\mu\text{-DWA})$ over all polite μ is denoted by Scan-DREC.*

Example 3. Consider the language L_{half} presented in Example 1 and let $\sqcup$ be the scanning strategy that draws $\sqcup$-like paths, represented in Figure 1(d). Starting from the Wang system sketched in Example 2, one can define an equivalent $\sqcup$-DWA. Indeed, the Wang-tiled picture P in Equation (1) can be build deterministically from p by scanning it according to $\sqcup$.

Proposition 1. *For any polite μ, $\mathcal{L}(\mu\text{-DWA})$ is a boolean sub-class of REC.*

Proof (sketch). Given two μ-DWAs A_1 and A_2 recognizing two languages L_1 and L_2 respectively, one can reason as in [12, Theorem 7.4] to build a μ-DWA recognizing the intersection $L_1 \cap L_2$ (the set of colors will be the set of pairs (k_1, k_2) where each k_i is a color used by A_i).

The closure under complement is quite easy, too. Let $A = \langle \Sigma, Colrs, \delta, \mu, F \rangle$ be a μ-DWA recognizing L. We show how to build a deterministic Wang automaton recognizing the complement of L. First of all, modify δ so that any computation of A scans the whole input picture. For example, one can use a special color k to complete the computations that halt prematurely: for any coloring γ, let γ_k be the full coloring that extends γ with color k; then, whenever $\delta(\sigma, \gamma, d)$ is empty but $\eta(\Delta_\gamma, d) \neq \perp$, then set $\delta'(\sigma, \gamma, d) = \{\gamma_k\}$; also set $\delta(\sigma, \gamma, d) = \{\gamma_k\}$ if γ already assigns k to some edge. Finally, let γ be in F' if and only of it is not in F. One can verify that $\langle \Sigma, Colrs \cup \{k\}, \delta', \mu, F' \rangle$ is a μ-DWA accepting the complement of L.

The closure under union is a consequence of the previous properties. □

Corollary 1. *Scan-DREC is closed under complement and rotation.*

Proof (sketch). The closure under complement is a straightforward consequence of the previous proposition. The closure under rotation is quite obvious, since one could easily define the *rotation of a scanning strategy* (and consequently the *rotation of a μ-WA*) and this operation preserves determinism. □

In particular, if Ↄ is the spiral scanning strategy represented in Figure 1(c), one can prove the following lemma.

Lemma 1. *$\mathcal{L}$(Ↄ-DWA) is closed under rotation.*

Proof (sketch). Let Ↄ′ be the scanning strategy obtained as the 90° clockwise rotation of Ↄ. Then any Ↄ′-DWA can be simulated by a Ↄ-DWA as follows: propagate the symbols in the first row downwards and check them in the second spiral round; the rest of the computation is as before. □

Proposition 2. *Snake-DREC ⊂ Scan-DREC ⊂ REC.*

Proof (sketch). Let τ be a snake-deterministic tiling system. First, one can slightly modify the construction in [10, Proposition 12] in order to build a Wang system equivalent to τ preserving its snake-determinism. Then, one can apply the construction of Theorem 1 (second part) to build an equivalent μ-WA, where μ is the boustrophedonic scanning strategy represented in Figure 1(b). Such automaton can be proved to be μ-DWA, hence by applying rotations one gets Snake-DREC ⊆ Scan-DREC.

To prove that the inclusion is proper, consider the language L of square pictures of even size with the first row like $x \cdot \bar{x}$, where $\bar{x}$ is the reverse of x, and let L^R be its intersection with all its rotations. Then, one can prove L is in Snake-DREC; however, by counting reasons it is possible to prove that L^R is not in Snake-DREC. On the contrary, improving the reasoning of Example 3, one can prove that $\mathcal{L}$(Ↄ-DWA) contains L, hence it contains also L^R by Lemma 1.

The last inclusion is a consequence of the previous proposition, since REC is not closed under complement. □

6 Conclusion and Open Problems

In this paper we have introduced a new model of 2D automata that recognize class REC and hence are strictly more powerful than traditional 4-way automata. The deterministic version of such a model is very natural and satisfies some interesting properties: it defines a class of picture languages which is closed under complement and extends some relevant subclasses of REC already studied in the literature. We conclude by stating some open problems concerning determinism in 2D.

Is Scan-DREC closed under union or intersection? Notice that the argument in proof of Theorem 1 cannot be applied when we have to intersect languages that are recognized by DWAs directed according to different scanning strategies.

Which is the relation among Snake-DREC, $\mathcal{L}$(Ↄ-DWA) and $\mathcal{L}$(⊔-DWA)? We have some examples that distinguish these classes: for instance the language L^R used to prove Proposition 2 is in $\mathcal{L}$(Ↄ-DWA) but not in Snake-DREC. However we do not know whether these classes are included one in another.

Which is the relation between Scan-DREC and the class of languages recognized by deterministic 4-way automata? We know that the latter class is incomparable to both Diag-DREC and Snake-DREC. But the language that separates them and is not in Snake-DREC is again the one used to prove Proposition 2, which is in Scan-DREC.

References

1. Anselmo, M., Giammarresi, D., Madonia, M.: From Determinism to Non-Determinism in Recognizable Two-Dimensional Languages. In: Harju, T., Karhumäki, J., Lepistö, A. (eds.) DLT 2007. LNCS, vol. 4588, pp. 36–47. Springer, Heidelberg (2007)
2. Anselmo, M., Giammarresi, D., Madonia, M.: Tiling Automaton: A Computational Model for Recognizable Two-Dimensional Languages. In: Holub, J., Žďárek, J. (eds.) CIAA 2007. LNCS, vol. 4783, pp. 290–302. Springer, Heidelberg (2007)
3. Bertoni, A., Goldwurm, M., Lonati, V.: On the Complexity of Unary Tiling-Recognizable Picture Languages. Fundamenta Informaticae 91(2), 231–249 (2009)
4. Borchert, B., Reinhardt, K.: Deterministically and Sudoku-Deterministically Recognizable Picture Languages. In: Proc. LATA 2007 (2007)
5. Bozapalidis, S., Grammatikopoulou, A.: Recognizable Picture Series. Journal of Automata, Languages and Combinatorics 10(2/3), 159–183 (2005)
6. Brijder, R., Hoogeboom, H.J.: Perfectly Quilted Rectangular Snake Tilings. Theoretical Computer Science 410(16), 1486–1494 (2009)
7. Cherubini, A., Crespi Reghizzi, S., Pradella, M.: Regional Languages and Tiling: A Unifying Approach to Picture Grammars. In: Ochmański, E., Tyszkiewicz, J. (eds.) MFCS 2008. LNCS, vol. 5162, pp. 253–264. Springer, Heidelberg (2008)
8. Cherubini, A., Pradella, M.: Picture Languages: From Wang Tiles to 2D Grammars. In: Bozapalidis, S., Rahonis, G. (eds.) CAI 2009. LNCS, vol. 5725, pp. 13–46. Springer, Heidelberg (2009)
9. Crespi Reghizzi, S., Pradella, M.: Tile Rewriting Grammars and Picture Languages. Theoretical Computer Science 340(2), 257–272 (2005)
10. de Prophetis, L., Varricchio, S.: Recognizability of Rectangular Pictures by Wang Systems. Journal of Automata, Languages and Combinatorics 2(4), 269–288 (1997)
11. Giammarresi, D., Restivo, A.: Recognizable Picture Languages. International Journal Pattern Recognition and Artificial Intelligence 6(2-3), 241–256 (1992); Special Issue on Parallel Image Processing
12. Giammarresi, D., Restivo, A.: Two-Dimensional Languages. In: Salomaa, A., Rozenberg, G. (eds.) Handbook of Formal Languages, Beyond Words, vol. 3, pp. 215–267. Springer, Berlin (1997)
13. Inoue, K., Nakamura, A.: Some Properties of Two-Dimensional On-Line Tessellation Acceptors. Information Sciences 13, 95–121 (1977)
14. Inoue, K., Takanami, I.: A Survey of Two-Dimensional Automata Theory. Information Sciences 55(1-3), 99–121 (1991)
15. Lindgren, K., Moore, C., Nordahl, M.: Complexity of Two-Dimensional Patterns. Journal of Statistical Physics 91(5-6), 909–951 (1998)
16. Lonati, V., Pradella, M.: Snake-Deterministic Tiling Systems. In: Královič, R., Niwiński, D. (eds.) MFCS 2009. LNCS, vol. 5734, pp. 549–560. Springer, Heidelberg (2009)
17. Matz, O.: On Piecewise Testable, Starfree, and Recognizable Picture Languages. In: Nivat, M. (ed.) FOSSACS 1998. LNCS, vol. 1378, pp. 203–210. Springer, Heidelberg (1998)

Unilateral Orientation of Mixed Graphs

Tamara Mchedlidze and Antonios Symvonis

Dept. of Mathematics, National Technical University of Athens, Athens, Greece
{mchet,symvonis}@math.ntua.gr

Abstract. A digraph D is *unilateral* if for every pair x, y of its vertices there exists a directed path from x to y, or a directed path from y to x, or both. A mixed graph $M = (V, A, E)$ with arc-set A and edge-set E *accepts a unilateral orientation*, if its edges can be oriented so that the resulting digraph is unilateral. In this paper, we present the first linear-time recognition algorithm for unilaterally orientable mixed graphs. Based on this algorithm we derive a polynomial algorithm for testing whether a unilaterally orientable mixed graph has a *unique* unilateral orientation.

1 Introduction

A large body of literature has been devoted to the study of mixed graphs (see [1] and the references therein). A mixed graph is *strongly orientable* when its undirected edges can be oriented in such a way that the resulting directed graph is strongly connected, while, it is *unilaterally orientable* when its undirected edges can be oriented in such a way that for every pair of vertices x, y there exists a path from x to y, or from y to x, or both.

Several problems related to the strong orientation of mixed graphs have been studied. Among them are the problems of "recognition of strongly orientable mixed graphs" [2] and "determining whether a mixed graph admits a unique strong orientation" [3,5].

In this paper we answer the corresponding questions for unilateral orientations of mixed graphs, that is, firstly we develop a linear-time algorithm for recognizing whether a mixed graph is unilaterally orientable and, secondly, we provide a polynomial algorithm for testing whether a mixed graph accepts a unique unilateral orientation.

1.1 Basic Definitions

We mostly follow the terminology of [1]. A *graph* $G = (V, E)$ consists of a non-empty finite set V of elements called *vertices* and a finite set E of unordered pairs of vertices, called *edges*. A *directed graph* or *digraph* $D = (V, A)$ consists of a non-empty set of vertices V and a set A of ordered pairs of vertices called *arcs* (or directed edges). We say that in (di)graph G vertex y is *reachable* from vertex x if there is a (directed) path from vertex x to vertex y.

J. van Leeuwen et al. (Eds.): SOFSEM 2010, LNCS 5901, pp. 588–599, 2010.

A *mixed graph* $M = (V, A, E)$ contains both arcs (ordered pairs of vertices in A) and edges (unordered pairs of vertices in E). A *path in a mixed graph* is a sequence of edges and arcs in which consecutive elements (i.e., edges or arcs) are incident on the same vertex and all arcs are traversed in their forward direction. Note that, since a graph (digraph) is a mixed graph having only edges (resp. only arcs), any definition or property concerning mixed graphs also applies to graphs (resp. digraphs).

A *biorientation* of a mixed graph $M = (V, A, E)$ is obtained from M by replacing every edge $(x, y) \in E$ by either arc (x, y), or arc (y, x), or the pair of arcs (x, y) and (y, x). If every edge is replaced by a single arc, we speak of an *orientation* of a mixed graph M. The *complete biorientation* of a mixed graph $M = (V, A, E)$, denoted by $\overleftrightarrow{M}$, is a biorientation of M such that every edge $(x, y) \in E$ is replaced in $\overleftrightarrow{M}$ by the pair of arcs (x, y) and (y, x).

An *underlying graph* $UG(M)$ of a mixed graph $M = (V, A, E)$ is the unique undirected graph G resulting by "removing" the direction from each arc of M, i.e., by turning each arc of A into an edge. A mixed graph M is *connected* if $UG(M)$ is connected.

A digraph D is *strongly connected* (or, just *strong*) if, for every pair x, y of distinct vertices in D, x and y are mutually reachable from each other. A *strong component* of a digraph D is a maximal subdigraph of D which is strong. The *strong component digraph* $SC(D)$ of D is obtained by contracting strong components of D and by identifying any parallel arcs obtained during this process into a single arc. The digraph $SC(D)$ for any digraph D is acyclic as any cycle is fully contained within a single strongly connected component. A digraph D is *unilateral* if, for every pair x, y of vertices of D, either x is reachable from y or y is reachable from x (or both).

The definitions for the connectivity-related terms can be extended for the case of mixed graphs. A mixed graph M is *strongly connected* (or *strong*) if its complete biorientation $\overleftrightarrow{M}$ is strongly connected. A mixed graph M is *unilaterally connected* (or *unilateral*) if its complete biorientation $\overleftrightarrow{M}$ is unilateral.

A mixed graph M is *strongly (unilaterally) orientable* (or, equivalently, M *admits a strong (unilateral) orientation*) if there is an orientation of M which is strongly (resp. unilaterally) connected. A mixed graph M admits a *hamiltonian orientation*, if there is an orientation $\overrightarrow{M}$ of M which is hamiltonian. Note that a graph that admits a hamiltonian orientation also admits a unilateral orientation.

1.2 Problem Definition and Related Work

Given a mixed graph M, it is natural to examine whether M is strongly or unilaterally orientable. The mixed graph M_1 of Figure 1a, is strongly orientable as it is demonstarted by digraph D_1 (Fig. 1b). The directed graphs D_2 and D_3 (Fig. 1c and Fig. 1d) show two unilateral orientations of M, non of which is strong. Robbins [9] proved that an undirected graph is strongly orientable if

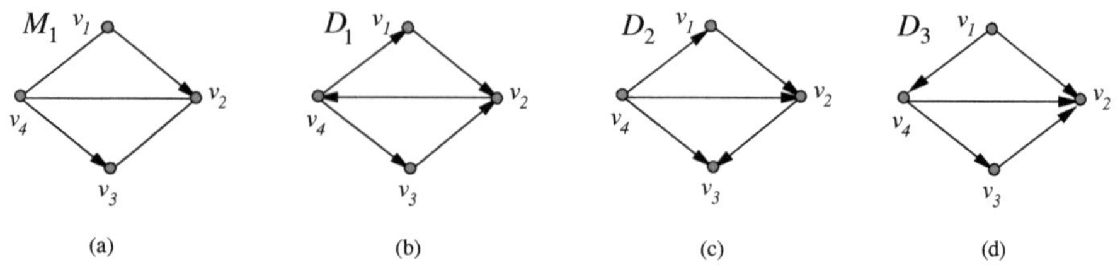

Fig. 1. (a) A mixed graph M_1. (b) A strong orientation of M_1. (c) & (d) Unilateral orientations of M_1 that are not strong, as there is no path from v_3 to v_1.

and only if it is connected and has no bridge[1]. Boesch and Tindel [2] generalized Robbins' result, showing that a mixed multigraph is strongly orientable if and only if it is strongly connected and has no bridges. Given that a digraph with n vertices and m arcs can be tested for strong connectivity and for being bridgeless in $O(m+n)$ time, the characterization given by Boesch and Tindel immediately leads to a polynomial time recognition algorithm of strongly orientable mixed graphs. Chung et al [4] presented an algorithm that computes a strong orientation of a mixed multigraph in linear time. Chartrand et al. [3] provided a characterization of unilaterally orientable graphs by showing that:

Theorem 1 (Chartrand et al., [3]). *A connected graph G has a unilateral orientation if and only if all of the bridges of G lie on a common path.*

As the unilateral orientation presents a different notion of connectivity, it is natural to ask wether a mixed graph admits a unilateral orientation. Even though unilateral orientation is a weaker notion of connectivity, not all mixed graphs admit a unilateral orientation. For example, the mixed graph M_2 in Fig. 2a does not admit a unilateral orientation since there is no directed path between vertices v_2 and v_3 in either direction. In this paper, we present a characterization of unilaterally orientable mixed graphs that leads to a linear-time recognition algorithm. Our characterization can be considered to be a generalization of Theorem 1 for mixed graphs.

Observe that not all mixed graphs admit more than one distinct orientation (strong or unilateral). For example, the mixed graph M_3 of Fig. 2b admits a unique unilateral orientation (given in Fig. 2c). Consider a mixed graph $M=(V,A,E)$ which has a *unique* strong (unilateral) orientation D. Then, we say that D is a *forced strong (resp. unilateral) orientation* for M.

Let $G=(V,E_1\cup E_2)$ be a graph, let A be an arc-set obtained from an orientation of the edges in E_1, and let $M=(V,A,E_2)$ be the resulting mixed graph. If M has a forced strong (unilateral) orientation then we say that A is a *forcing set* for a strong (resp. unilateral) orientation of G, or simply a *strong (resp. unilateral) forcing set.*

[1] An edge e of a connected mixed graph M is a *bridge* if $M\setminus\{e\}$ is not connected. A mixed graph containing no bridge is called *bridgeless.*

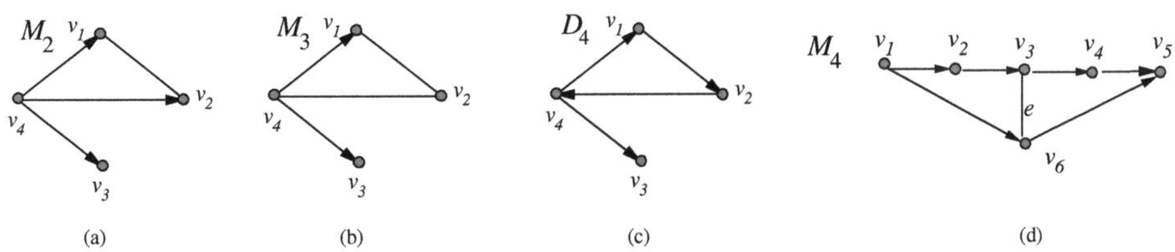

Fig. 2. (a) A mixed graph M_2 which does not admit any unilateral orientation. (b) A mixed graph M_3 which has a forced unilateral orientation. (c) The unique unilateral orientation of M_3. (d) A bridgeless unilateral mixed graph that does not admit a unilateral orientation.

The concept of forced strong (unilateral) orientation of graphs was first introduced by Chartrand et al [3] who defined the *forced strong (resp. unilateral) orientation number* of an undirected graph G to be the cardinality of the minimal forcing set for a strong (resp. unilateral) orientation of G. Strong orientations of graphs were later studied by Farzad et et al [5]. Forced unilateral orientations were studied by Pascovici [8]. In her work, she mentions that finding an efficient algorithm for calculating the forced unilateral orientation number of a graph is an open question which, to the best of our knowledge, has not been answered yet. In this paper, we partially resolve this question. Given a mixed graph $M = (V, A, E)$, we provide an algorithm which tests in polynomial time whether A is a forcing set for a unilateral orientation of M (i.e., it tests whether M has a unique unilateral orientation).

The paper is organized as follows: In Section 2 we develop a linear-time algorithm for recognizing whether a mixed graph accepts a unilateral orientation and, in the case it does, we produce such an orientation. In Section 3, we give a lemma which implies a polynomial algorithm for testing whether a mixed graph accepts a unique unilateral orientation. We conclude in Section 4.

2 Recognition of Unilaterally Orientable Mixed Graphs

2.1 Preliminaries

The following theorem, due to Boesch and Tindell, gives necessary and sufficient conditions for a mixed graph to have a strongly connected orientation.

Theorem 2 (Boesch and Tindell [2]). *A mixed multigraph M admits a strong orientation if and only if M is strong and the underlying multigraph of M is bridgeless.*

Note that, a corresponding theorem for unilaterally orientable graphs (i.e., *"a mixed multigraph M has a unilateral orientation if and only if M is unilateral and the underlying multigraph of M is bridgeless"*) does not hold. This is demonstrated by the mixed graph M_4 in Fig. 2d which is unilateral and bridgeless, but, it does not have a unilateral orientation. To see that, observe that if edge (v_3, v_6) is oriented towards v_6, then vertices v_4 and v_6 are not connected by a directed path in either direction, while, if edge (v_3, v_6) is directed towards v_3 then vertices v_2 and v_6 are not connected by a directed path in either direction.

Lemma 1 ([6], pp. 66). *Digraph D is unilateral if and only if D has a spanning directed walk*[2].

Lemma 2 ([3]). *A tree T admits a unilateral orientation if and only if T is a path.*

A vertex of a directed graph having in-degree (out-degree) equal to zero is referred to as a *source* (resp. *sink*). An *st-digraph* is a directed acyclic digraph having a single source (denoted by s) and a single sink (denoted by t).

Lemma 3 ([7]). *Let D be an st-digraph that does not have a hamiltonian path. Then, there exist two vertices in D that are not connected by a directed path in either direction.*

2.2 A Characterization for Unilaterally Orientable Mixed Graphs

Consider a mixed graph $M = (V, A, E)$ and let $V' \subseteq V$. The mixed subgraph of M *induced* by V', denoted by $M(V')$, is defined as $M(V') = (V', A', E')$ where, $A' = \{(u, v) \mid (u, v) \in A \text{ and } u,\ v \in V'\}$ and $E' = \{(u, v) \mid (u, v) \in E \text{ and } u,\ v \in V'\}$.

Let M be a mixed graph, let $D_i = (V_i, E_i)$, $1 \leq i \leq k$, be the strong components of the complete biorientation $\overleftrightarrow{M}$ of M. The *strong components* M_i, $1 \leq i \leq k$, of mixed graph M are defined as: $M_i = M(V_i)$, $1 \leq i \leq k$, that is, M_i is the mixed subgraph of M induced by V_i. Note that each M_i is strong since, by definition, D_i is its complete biorientation.

The *strong component digraph* of a mixed graph M, denoted by $SC(M)$, is obtained by contracting each strong component of M into a single vertex and by identifying all parallel arcs that are created during this process into a single arc. Fig. 3a shows a mixed graph having three strong components and Fig. 3b shows its corresponding strong component digraph. Note that the strong component digraph of any mixed graph is acyclic.

The next lemma gives the first necessary condition for a mixed graph M to have a unilateral orientation.

Lemma 4. *If a mixed graph M admits a unilateral orientation then its strong component digraph $SC(M)$ has a hamiltonian path.*

Proof. For the sake of contradiction, assume that $SC(M)$ has no hamiltonian path. Since $SC(M)$ is an acyclic digraph, it has at least one source and at least

---

[2] A *spanning directed walk* of a digraph is a directed path that visits all the vertices of the digraph, some possibly more than once.

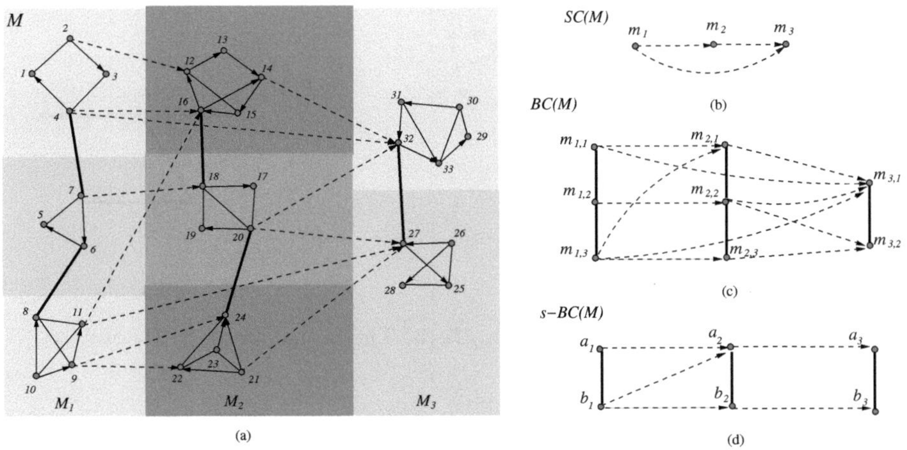

Fig. 3. (a) A mixed graph M. M_1, M_2 and M_3 are the three strong components of M. Dashed edges connect M_i with M_j, $i, j \in \{1, 2, 3\}$, $i \neq j$. The bold edges are the bridges of each M_i. (b) The strong component digraph $SC(M)$ of M. (c) The bridgeless-component mixed graph $BC(M)$ of M. (d) The simplified bridgeless-component mixed graph for mixed graph M, where the vertices a_i, b_i denote the endpoints of a bridge path $B(M_i)$.

one sink. If there are two or more sources (sinks) then it is clear that any two of the sources (sinks) are not connected by a directed path in either direction. If there is exactly one source and exactly one sink in $SC(M)$ then $SC(M)$ is an st-digraph and, by Lemma 3, there are two vertices of $SC(M)$ that are not connected by a directed path in either direction. So, in either case, we can identify two vertices of $SC(M)$, call them m_i and m_j, that are not connected by a directed path in either direction.

By the definition of the strong component digraph $SC(M)$, m_i and m_j correspond to contracted strong components of M. Let these strong components be M_i and M_j, respectively. Since m_i and m_j are not connected by a directed path in either direction, then for each vertex u of M_i and for each vertex v of M_j there is no directed path in the complete biorientation digraph $\overleftrightarrow{M}$ connecting u with v. Therefore, there is no path in the mixed graph M connecting u and v in either direction, and thus, there can be no orientation of M that creates a directed path connecting u with v in either direction. This is a clear contradiction of the assumption that M admits a unilateral orientation. □

Let $M = (V, A, E)$ be a strong mixed graph and $B \subseteq E$ be the bridges of M. Note that B might be empty. Then, all components of graph $M \setminus B$ are strong and bridgeless.

The *bridge graph* of a strong mixed graph M, denoted by $B(M)$, is obtained by contracting in M the vertices of each strong component of $M \setminus B$. Note that a bridge graph of any strong mixed graph is a tree. Fig. 4 shows a strong mixed graph and its bridge graph.

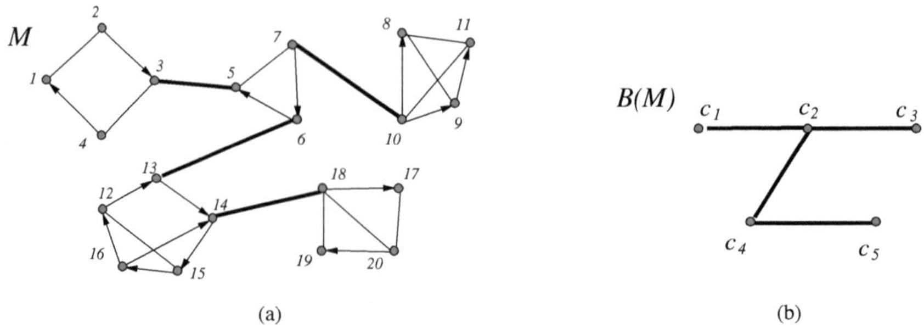

Fig. 4. (a) A strong mixed graph M. (b) The bridge graph $B(M)$ of M.

The following lemma gives the second necessary condition for the mixed graph to have a unilateral orientations.

Lemma 5. *If a mixed graph M admits a unilateral orientation then the bridge graph of each of its strong components is a path.*

Proof. Consider a unilateral orientation D of M. By Lemma 1, D has a spanning walk. This spanning walk of D induces an orientation of the bridges of M and, thus, an orientation of $B(M)$ which is unilateral. Recall that $B(M)$ is a tree. Then, by Lemma 2 we conclude that the bridge graph $B(M)$ of M is a path. □

Let $M = (V, A, E)$ be a mixed graph and let M_i, $1 \leq i \leq k$, be its strong components. Moreover, let B_i be the bridges of M_i, $1 \leq i \leq k$, and let $B = \bigcup_{i=1}^{i=k} B_i$. Then, the set of strong components of the mixed graph $M \setminus B$ is the union of the strong components of each $M_i \setminus B_i$, $1 \leq i \leq k$. The *bridgeless-component mixed graph* of a mixed graph M, denoted by $BC(M)$, is obtained by contracting in M the vertices of each strong component of $M \setminus B$ into a single vertex and by identifying any parallel arcs created during this process into a single arc. Fig. 3c shows the bridgeless-component mixed graph for the mixed graph of Fig. 3a. Note that the edge set of the bridgeless-component mixed graph $BC(M)$ is exactly set B. Moreover, $BC(M)$ can be considered to consist of a set of (undirected) trees (the bridge graph $B(M_i)$ of each strong component M_i of M) connected by arcs which do not create any cycle. Also observe that the strong component digraph $SC(M)$ of M can be obtained from $BC(M)$ by contracting all bridgeless components of M_i into a single vertex and by identifying all parallel edges created by this process into a single arc.

Observation 1. *Let M be a mixed graph. Then any orientation of $BC(M)$ is acyclic.*

Proof. It follows from the facts that (i) the strong component digraph $SC(M)$ is acyclic and (ii) the bridge graph $B(M')$ of any strong component M' of M is a tree. □

The following theorem provides a characterization of unilaterally orientable mixed graphs.

Theorem 3. *A mixed graph M admits a unilateral orientation if and only if the bridgeless-component mixed graph $BC(M)$ admits a hamiltonian orientation.*

Proof. ($\Rightarrow$) We assume that a mixed graph M admits a unilateral orientation and we show that $BC(M)$ admits a hamiltonian orientation. Consider a unilateral orientation of M. By Lemma 1, the unilateral orientation of M has a spanning walk. That spanning walk induces a spanning walk on $BC(M)$. Since any orientation of $BC(M)$ is acyclic (Observation 1) the induced spanning walk on $BC(M)$ is a hamiltonian path. Thus, $BC(M)$ admits a hamiltonian orientation.

($\Leftarrow$) We assume now that $BC(M)$ admits a hamiltonian orientation and we show that M admits a unilateral orientation. Recall that the vertices of $BC(M)$ correspond to the bridgeless strong components of M. By Theorem 2, it follows that each of these components admits a strong orientation. This strong orientation implies a spanning walk between any pair of vertices of the strong bridgeless component. The hamiltonian orientation of $BC(M)$ implies an orientation of the bridges of the strong components of M. The strong orientation of the strong and bridgeless components of M together with the orientation of the bridges of the strong components of M, result to orientation D of M.

The hamiltonian orientation of $BC(M)$ implies a hamiltonian path and, in turn, an ordering of the strong bridgeless components of M. Based on this ordering, we can easily construct a spanning walk on orientation D. Thus, based on Lemma 1, D is a unilateral orientation. We conclude that M admits a unilateral orientation. □

2.3 The Algorithm

Based on the the characterization of Section 2.2, Algorithm 1 decides whether a mixed graph that is given to its input is unilaterally orientable. In the first step of Algorithm 1, we construct the strong connected digraph $SC(M)$ of M. In order to do so, we have to compute the strongly connected components of the complete biorientation $\overleftrightarrow{M}$ of M. This can be easily accomplished in $O(V + A + E)$ time. In the second step of Algorithm 1, we test whether $SC(M)$ has a hamiltonian path. Note that since $SC(M)$ is an acyclic digraph, it has a hamiltonian path if and only if it has a unique topological ordering. This can be easily tested in linear time to the size of $SC(M)$. In the third step of Algorithm 1, we construct the bridge graph $BM(M_i)$ for each strong component M_i of M. Identifying all bridges can be trivially done by testing whether the removal of each individual edge disconnects the component. By using a depth-first-search based method, the identification of all bridges and the construction of all bridge graphs can be completed in $O(V + A + E)$ time. Testing whether each bridge graph is a path is trivial and can be completed in linear time to the size of the bridge graph.

By utilizing the already constructed bridge graphs of step 3 of the algorithm, we can construct the bridgeless-component mixed graph $BC(M)$ of M in time proportional to its size. Now, it remains to test whether $BC(M)$ is hamiltonian. Note that, since we have reached the fourth step of Algorithm 1, it holds that our graph satisfies two properties. Firstly, all of its bridge graphs are paths (thus, we refer to them as *bridge paths*) and, secondly, its strong component digraph $SC(M)$ is hamiltonian. We will exploit these properties in order to decide whether $BC(M)$ is hamiltonian in linear time.

Let M_i, $1 \leq i \leq k$, be the strong components of M and assume without loss of generality that they appear on the hamiltonian path of $SC(M)$ in this order. Firstly observe that in a hamiltonian path of $BC(M)$, if one exists, all vertices of the bridge path $B(M_i)$ are visited before the vertices of the bridge path $B(M_j)$, for all $i < j$. Since the graph $SC(M)$ is acyclic, if we leave component M_i before visiting all of its vertices there is no way to return to it and, thus, no hamiltonian path exists. Also observe that, in a hamiltonian path of $BC(M)$ each bridge path is traversed from one of its endpoint to the other and, thus, there are two possible orientation of the bridge path. As a consequence, the hamiltonian path of $BC(M)$, if any, only uses arcs which leave from the endpoints of a bridge path $B(M_i)$ and enter the endpoints of a bridge path $B(M_j)$, $i < j$. In addition, these arcs connect consecutive bridge paths. Thus, when testing whether the bridgeless-component mixed graph $BC(M)$ has a hamiltonian path, we can use a simplified leveled mixed graph, denoted by *s*-$BC(M)$, resulting by eliminating all vertices which are not endpoints of a bridge graph and all arcs that enter or leave them, as well as all arcs connecting vertices on non consecutive bridge pahts. Thus, each level of the graph is either an edge or a single vertex, and the levels which correspond to the strong components of M appear in the order of their corresponding strong component. Fig. 3d shows the simplified bridgeless-component mixed graph for mixed graph M, where the vertices a_i, b_i denote the endpoints of a bridge path $B(M_i)$.

We can decide whether the *s*-$BC(M)$ has a hamiltonian path by using a simple dynamic programming algorithm. Let p_i^a be a boolean variable which takes the value **true** if and only if there is a hamiltonian path that traverses all vertices of the first i levels of *s*-$BC(M)$ and terminates at vertex a_i, $1 \leq i \leq k$. Similarly we define p_i^b. It is easy to see that the following recursive relations hold:

$$\begin{aligned} &p_1^a = p_1^b = \textbf{true} \\ &p_i^a = \left(p_{i-1}^a = \textbf{true} \wedge \exists(a_{i-1}, b_i) \in A'\right) \vee \left(p_{i-1}^b = \textbf{true} \wedge \exists(b_{i-1}, b_i) \in A'\right) \\ &p_i^b = \left(p_{i-1}^b = \textbf{true} \wedge \exists(b_{i-1}, a_i) \in A'\right) \vee \left(p_{i-1}^a = \textbf{true} \wedge \exists(a_{i-1}, a_i) \in A'\right) \\ &(\text{for } 1 < i \leq k) \end{aligned}$$

Based on the above equations, we can decide whether there is a hamiltonian path in *s*-$BC(M)$ (and, as a consequence in $BC(M)$) in $O(k)$ time.

Observation 2. *The bridgeless-component mixed graph $BC(M)$ of a mixed graph M has exactly one hamiltonian path if and only if $p_i^a \oplus p_i^b =$ **true**, $1 \leq i \leq k$, where k is the number of strong components of M.*

We also note that, in the case where a unilateral orientation exists, we can compute one in linear time. This can be achieved by orienting the bridges of

Algorithm 1. UNILATERAL-ORIENTATION(M)

input : A Mixed graph $M = (V, A, E)$.
output : "YES" if M has a unilateral orientation, "NO" otherwise.

1. Construct the strong connected digraph $SC(M)$ of M.
   {*Denote the strong components of* $SC(M)$ *by* $M_1, \ldots, M_k$.}
2. **if** $SC(M)$ has no hamiltonian path **then return**("NO")
   else
3. For each strong component M_i of M, $1 \leq i \leq k$,
   Construct the bridge graph $B(M_i)$;
   if B_{M_i} is not a simple path **then return**("NO");
   { *All bridge graphs* B_{M_i} *are paths.* }
4. Construct the bridgeless-component mixed graph $BC(M)$ of M
5. **if** $BC(M)$ has no hamiltonian path **then return**("NO");
6. **return**("YES");

$BC(M)$ according to the hamiltonian path of $BC(M)$ and by using a strong orientation for each bridgeless strong component of the bridge graphs.

From the above description, we can state the following theorem:

Theorem 4. *Given a mixed graph* $M = (V, A, E)$ *, we can decide whether* M *admits a unilateral orientation in* $O(V+A+E)$ *time. Moreover, if* M *is unilaterally orientable, a unilateral orientation can be computed in* $O(V + A + E)$ *time.*

We also note that we can prove an additional characterization for unilaterally orientable mixed graphs that can be considered to be a counterpart of Theorem 1 given by Chartrand et al [3]. The proof of the following theorem is based on the properties of the strong component digraph $SC(M)$, and the bridgeless-component mixed graph $BC(M)$ for a mixed graph M.

Theorem 5. *A mixed graph admits a unilateral orientation if and only if all the bridges of its strong components lie on a common path.*

3 Recognition of Unilateral Forcing Sets

Let $M = (V, E, A)$ be a mixed graph. In this section we present a simple lemma stating whether M has a forced unilateral orientation or, equivalently, whether A is a unilateral forcing set for M. Based on this lemma and Algorithm 1, we infer a polynomial algorithm for testing whether A is a unilateral forcing set for M or, equivalently, G has a unique unilateral orientation.

Forced unilateral orientations were studied by Pascovici in [8], where she gave a general lower bound for the forced unilateral orientation number and showed that the unilateral orientation number of a graph G having edge connectivity 1 is equal to $m-n+2$, where m and n are the numbers of edges and vertices of G, respectively.

Lemma 6. *A mixed graph $M = (V, A, E)$ admits a unique unilateral orientation if and only if for each edge $e = (u, v) \in E$ either $(V, A \cup \{(u, v)\}, E \setminus \{(u, v)\})$ or $(V, A \cup \{(v, u)\}, E \setminus \{(u, v)\})$ has a unilateral orientation, but not both.*

Proof. ($\Rightarrow$) Let M admit a unique unilateral orientation and assume, for the sake of contradiction, that both $(V, A \cup \{(u, v)\}, E \setminus \{(u, v)\})$ and $(V, A \cup \{(v, u)\}, E \setminus \{(u, v)\})$ have a unilateral orientation. Then these unilateral orientations differ in at least one edge and hence are distinct. A clear contradiction. Otherwise, if we assume that neither $(V, A \cup \{(u, v)\}, E \setminus \{(u, v)\})$ nor $(V, A \cup \{(v, u)\}, E \setminus \{(u, v)\})$ has a unilateral orientation, then we have a contradiction again, as M was supposed to have at least one unilateral orientation.

($\Leftarrow$) Assume now that for *each* edge $e = (u, v) \in E$ either $(V, A \cup \{(u, v)\}, E \setminus \{(u, v)\})$ or $(V, A \cup \{(v, u)\}, E \setminus \{(u, v)\})$ has a unilateral orientation, but not both of them. It is clear that M has at least one unilateral orientation. Assume, for the sake of contradiction, that M has more than one unilateral orientations. Consider any two arbitrary unilateral orientations of M. As these orientations are distinct they differ in at least one edge, say $e' = (u', v') \in E$. So we conclude that both $(V, A \cup \{(u', v')\}, E \setminus \{e'\})$ and $(V, A \cup \{(v', u')\}, E \setminus \{e'\})$ have a unilateral orientation, a clear contradiction. □

Theorem 6. *Given a mixed graph $M = (V, A, E)$, we can decide whether A is a unilateral forcing set for M in $O(E(V + A + E))$ time.*

Proof. Follows directly from Theorem 4 and Lemma 6. □

4 Conclusion

For a mixed graph $M = (V, A, E)$, we presented a linear-time algorithm that recognizes whether M is unilaterally orientable, and in the case where it is, we also presented a characterization leading to a polynomial algorithm for determining whether A is a unilateral forcing set for M. Future research includes the study of the number of unilateral orientations of a mixed graph, as well as the complexity of the problem of finding a unilateral forcing set of minimum size.

References

1. Bang-Jensen, J., Gutin, G.: Digraphs: Theory, Algorithms and Applications. Springer, Heidelberg (2007)
2. Boesch, F., Tindell, R.: Robbins's Theorem for Mixed Multigraphs. American Mathematical Monthly 87(9), 716–719 (1980)
3. Chartrand, G., Harary, F., Schultz, M., Wall, C.E.: Forced Orientation Numbers of a Graph. Congressus Numerantium 100, 183–191 (1994)
4. Chung, F.R.K., Garey, M.R., Tarjan, R.E.: Strongly Connected Orientations of Mixed Multigraphs. Networks 15(4), 477–484 (1985)
5. Farzad, B., Mahdian, M., Mahmoodian, E.S., Saberi, A., Sadri, B.: Forced Orientation of Graphs. Bulletin of Iranian Mathematical Society 32(1), 79–89 (2006)
6. Harary, F., Norman, R.Z., Cartwright, D.: Structural Models: An Introduction to the Theory of Directed Graphs. Addison-Wesley, Reading (1965)

7. Mchedlidze, T., Symvonis, A.: Crossing-Optimal Acyclic Hamiltonian Path Completion and Its Application to Upward Topological Book Embeddings. In: Das, S., Uehara, R. (eds.) WALCOM 2009. LNCS, vol. 5431, pp. 250–261. Springer, Heidelberg (2009)
8. Pascovici, D.: On the Forced Unilateral Orientation Number of a Graph. Discrete Mathematics 187, 171–183 (1997)
9. Robbins, H.E.: A Theorem on Graphs, with an Application to a Problem of Traffic Control. American Mathematical Monthly 46, 218–283 (1939)

Maintaining XML Data Integrity in Programs
An Abstract Datatype Approach

Patrick Michel and Arnd Poetzsch-Heffter

University of Kaiserslautern, Germany
{p_michel,poetzsch}@cs.uni-kl.de

Abstract. In service-oriented loosely coupled distributed information systems, the format and semantics of the exchanged data become more and more important. We envisage that there will be an increasing number of general and domain-specific XML-based data formats for service-oriented computing. A typical example is a tax declaration form. If the schemas defining the formats specify structural and additional integrity constraints, we speak of constrained XML.

The paper describes a technique for an integration of constrained XML data into programming, which is able to handle integrity constraints. Our technique allows us to automatically check the correctness of programs manipulating constrained XML data. In our approach, constrained XML data is treated like an abstract data type with an interface of schema-specific procedures. Programs use these procedures to manipulate the XML data. The preconditions of the procedures guarantee that procedures maintain the constraints. Our approach allows us to automatically generate the preconditions and to simplify them to a minimal form. The technique is based on a path representation and logical embedding of XML data. The weakest precondition generation is implemented and exploits an SMT-solver for simplification.

1 Introduction

In service-oriented loosely coupled distributed information systems, the format and semantics of the exchanged data become more and more important. Having standardized data formats will simplify communication between different applications as well as among enterprises and clients. We envisage that there will be an increasing number of general and domain-specific complex data formats for service-oriented computing. Typical examples are formats for tax declaration or for negotiating insurance contracts. As XML has become a de facto standard to represent structured data, we assume that the formats are defined by XML schema languages.

We present a technique to improve programming support for constrained XML data where *constrained* means that the XML data satisfies a structural schema and *additional integrity constraints*. Our technique allows us to automatically check the correctness of programs manipulating constrained XML data. In particular,

J. van Leeuwen et al. (Eds.): SOFSEM 2010, LNCS 5901, pp. 600–611, 2010.

we guarantee that the XML data resulting from the manipulation satisfies the constraints. This is a first for integrity constraints, which are far more complex than structural constraints.

In our approach, constrained XML data is treated like an abstract data type with an interface of schema-specific procedures. These *interface procedures* can be used in a host programming language to manipulate the XML data. They hide the special aspects of structured XML data handling behind a host language API. The implementation of the interface procedures is kept separate from the host language and is tailored to the specific aspects of XML data handling. Domain experts develop the interface procedures together with the schema.

Implementing such an approach splits into a number of key challenges, which have to be tackled together. Both the schema language and the language for interface procedures have to be accessible by domain experts and feature explicit data specific primitives. To verify the correctness of interface procedures, their semantics have to be formally defined and they have to relate to the semantics of schemata. In realistic scenarios, however, correctness proofs cannot be created by domain experts, as this would require them to have extensive knowledge in formal methods. So to offer comprehensive support for the definition and *correct* usage of XML data with integrity constraints, it is necessary to maintain schemata as invariants automatically.

The contributions of this paper are the following:

- An abstract datatype approach for the integration of XML data with integrity constraints, which automatically guarantees that updates are indeed valid.
- A logical framework based on a path representation of XML data, which allows us to use the necessary automated analysis techniques.
- A pattern-based schema language with embedded integrity constraints, whose semantics can be completely expressed within the logical framework.
- An update language used to formulate the interface procedures of the datatypes, whose semantics can also be expressed within the framework.
- A direct application of the automated techniques first described in [7], which allow us to generate minimal preconditions that guarantee that the integrity constraints defined by the schema are maintained by procedures.

Related work. Support for constrained XML data has always been weak in programming languages. Low level APIs like DOM [10] and SAX [9] are cumbersome to use and offer no support to check or maintain schema constraints. Data binding approaches like JAXB [8] and language extensions like XJ [5] have eased the problem at least for basic structural constraints, yet they are unable to cope with integrity constraints. New languages like XDuce [6] have been developed to offer comprehensive support for sophisticated structural type systems. Such languages, however, do not integrate well into the existing languages and tools and suffer from being too specific. In the case of XDuce, the language excels at handling severe structural changes and transformations, which is not needed when working with a fixed schema. It also does not cover integrity constraints at all.

Gardner, et al. applied context logic [1] to an XML subset and a corresponding fragment of the DOM API [4]. Using their weakest precondition generation, they are able to analyze straight-line Java code. As an example they show how to prove structural schema invariants. Schema constraints are directly expressed in context logic, which makes them hard to read for common programmers. They do not define a higher level schema language and do not show how integrity constraints could be supported. Furthermore, there is currently no technique available to simplify preconditions. Their approach relies on manual proofs, rather than automated methods, which renders the technique inaccessible to domain experts.

In [7] we have presented an assertion language together with a technique to automatically generate preconditions for a core update language. These preconditions guarantee that integrity constraints are maintained. As the constraints can be complex, we developed a technique that allows us to simplify the preconditions to a minimal form. In particular, we do not want to check the full set of integrity constraints of the manipulated XML data at every call site. Many constraints are unaffected by an update and remain true, so they need not be checked over and over. Other affected constraints can be checked by a much smaller incremental check. By using this technique, we are able to present minimal preconditions to the programmer in a readable form, so he can prevent individual constraints from failing and knows how to react to the failure of others.

Overview. Section 2 describes our approach in more detail and gives an illustrating example. Section 3 introduces the formalization on which the rest of the paper is based. Section 4 and 5 define the schema and the update language, respectively. Section 6 concludes the paper.

2 XML Data as Abstract Datatype

We propose to view XML data as an abstract datatype and interface it with a target language by a set of *interface procedures*. To perform more complex tasks, programs can be written that use the interface procedures as primitive operations. In this way, the intricacies of the constraint handling are hidden from the programmer. The interface procedures are developed together with the schema by domain experts in a light-weight XML manipulation language which incorporates concepts for constrained data. We explain the manipulation language that we developed with a tiny usage scenario: Clients exchanging packets. Each packet has a packet header represented as constrained data. Here is the schema that a domain expert might develop for packet headers:

```
packetheader {
  capacity { INT [ sum(//kind/count) ≤ . ] } &
  kind * {
    count { INT [ . > 0 ] }
  }
}
```

A header consists of an integer expressing the `capacity` of the packet and a set of `kind` elements. A `kind` element records for each kind of item in the packet the count of items of that kind. Implicitly, the schema defines for each element an *identifier attribute*. If elements can occur with an arbitrary multiplicity, like the `kind` elements, all their identifiers have to be pairwise distinct. This implicit *uniqueness* constraint is enforced to make sure that elements are always structurally distinguishable. In addition, the above schema defines two integrity constraints: A `count` has always to be positive and the `capacity` of the packet has to be larger than the sum of the `counts`. These constraints are expressed by the *embedded* context rules enclosed in brackets. The dot refers to the element to which the context rule is attached.

For the manipulation of packet headers, the domain expert writes interface procedures. The following interface procedure adds `amount` items of kind `k` to an implicit packet header argument. If the amount is negative or zero, procedure `add` fails. Otherwise it creates a new element for items of kind `k` if necessary and increases the count:

```
add(ident k, int amount) {
  assume amount > 0;
  if not //kind[k] then
    new //kind[k];
    new //kind[k]/count;
    //kind[k]/count := 0
  fi
  //kind[k]/count := //kind[k]/count + amount
}
```

We are able to automatically generate weakest preconditions for such procedures and translate them to languages like Java. The example procedure `add` would result in a member method of a type `Packetheader` with the following signature:

```
// Precondition:
//   amount > 0                                  ( AssumptionException )
//   sum (//kind/count) + amount <= //capacity   ( CapacityException )
Packetheader add(Ident k, Integer amount) { ... }
```

In Java programs, the interface procedures are used to manipulate data of the schema type and realize more complex tasks. The `Ident` type is provided by the generated API and can be assumed to subsume at least all `Strings`. The exceptions raised by failing preconditions are generated as unchecked exceptions, as programmers should have the liberty to ignore them in contexts where they are sure they cannot arise. A Java method for packing a list of items and sending them to other clients could look like this:

```
void pack(List<Ident> items) {
  Packetheader cur = new Packetheader(42); // 42 is packet capacity
  for(Ident item : items) {
```

```
    try { cur.add(item, 1); }
    catch(CapacityException e) {
      sendPacket(cur);
      cur = new Packetheader(42).add(item, 1);
    }
  }
  sendPacket(cur);
}
```

The method creates new packets and fills them up with items. The programmer has to make sure that whenever he calls the add method, he can either guarantee the precondition or handle its failure. As the amount is set to the constant 1, the only thing that can possibly go wrong is that the packet is already full. In this case, the add method will abort *without changing anything* in the packet. The pack method then sends the full packet and creates a new one. Adding the item to the new packet will now never result in an exception, so the call is safe.

3 Paths and Documents

As usual in the domain of XML, we will refer to constrained XML data as *documents.* The basis of our approach is a path representation and logical embedding of such documents. Paths are an intuitive concept known to domain experts. At the same time, however, paths are the key to using automated methods to ensure schema correctness of manipulating procedures. We use paths to identify and give an identity to elements in a document. Documents can then easily be defined as sets of paths with attached values.

Example path: /packetheader/kind[k]/count

We present an enhanced version of the original formalization described in [7], which is in particular prepared to handle arbitrary values. The weakest precondition generation and simplification techniques described there easily extend to these changes.

Our formalization supports identifiers, strings, integers and the special complex value clx, which marks elements without value and inner elements of a document. There can be arbitrary many constants c and variables v of each value type and it is possible to cast values to the base types.

$$\begin{aligned}
\text{values } V &::= I \mid S \mid Z \mid \text{clx} \mid D(P) \\
\text{identifier } I &::= c_I \mid v_I \mid \text{null} \mid \text{cast}_I(V) \\
\text{strings } S &::= c_S \mid v_S \mid \text{cast}_S(V) \\
\text{integer } Z &::= 0 \mid 1 \mid v_Z \mid Z+Z \mid Z*Z \mid -Z \mid \text{cast}_Z(V) \\
&\mid \text{sum}(V^*) \mid \text{count}(V^*) \mid \text{rcount}(V, V^*)
\end{aligned}$$

Identifiers I and strings S are words over the alphabets Σ_I and Σ_S and we assume those words can be distinguished. Z represents the integer numbers with common arithmetic connectives. The constant null refers to the empty identifier. $D(P)$ denotes reading a value from document D at path P.

Paths represent the different elements in a document. The root path is denoted by root. Longer paths can be constructed by extending another path with a label, to select an element with that name, and an identifier, which separates this element from others with that name. Labels L are non-empty words on the alphabet Σ_L, like `packetheader` or `capacity` in the example.

$$\begin{aligned} \text{labels } L &::= c_L \\ \text{paths } P &::= \text{root} \mid P/L[I] \\ \text{documents } D &::= \text{blank} \mid D[P \rightarrow V] \mid D[P \rightarrow] \mid \$ \end{aligned}$$

The example path from above has the following formal representation:

Formal path: $\text{root}/\texttt{packetheader}_L[\text{null}]/\texttt{kind}_L[\texttt{k}_I]/\texttt{count}_L[\text{null}]$

A document consequently is a finite map from paths to values, where the blank document represents an initial document, which only contains the root path mapping to clx. We support local modifications in the form of adding (or replacing) a single path-value-pair and removing all pairs for a path and all its extensions. The dollar symbol is the only variable we use for documents. For example, the initial document with count of kind k set to zero is expressed with the following expression, in slightly abbreviated path syntax:

Example document: $\$\big[/\texttt{packetheader}/\texttt{kind}[\texttt{k}]/\texttt{count} \rightarrow 0\big]$

The sorts V^* and P^* represent value and path multisets and offer the usual singleton and union operations. We allow variables v_m on value multisets, have a constant named 'all', representing complete I, and can convert path multisets to value multisets by reading from the document using the syntax $D(P^*)$. Path multisets can also be created by extending all paths in another multiset with a label and an identifier from a value multiset, using the same syntax ./.[.] as for single paths.

$$\begin{aligned} \text{value multisets } V^* &::= V \mid V^* \cup V^* \mid D(P^*) \mid \text{all} \mid v_m \\ \text{path multisets } P^* &::= P \mid P^* \cup P^* \mid P^*/L[V^*] \end{aligned}$$

To sum up all the count elements in the example, we first create a path multiset representing all these elements and then read their values from the document. Within our schema, the expression sum(//kind/count) expands to:

Example: $\text{sum}\big(\$\big(\text{root}/\texttt{packetheader}_L[\text{null}]/\texttt{kind}_L[\text{all}]/\texttt{count}_L[\text{null}]\big)\big)$

4 Schema Language

In this section, we show by example how a schema language accessible by domain experts can look like. Any paradigm and feature, which can be translated into propositions on the terms of Section 3, can be supported.

We choose to combine the simplicity of a pattern-based approach in the spirit of abbreviated Relax NG [2,3] with a rule-based approach. The patterns define the structure of documents, while the rules define arbitrary integrity constraints. By embedding paths directly into the logic, integrity constraints can be understood and written by domain experts and read by programmers.

4.1 Syntax

We support a usual base of patterns, namely the empty pattern, groups, choice, element definitions and repetition of elements. The content of elements can be complex, a type or an enumeration (cf. pattern example in Section 2).

$$\begin{aligned} \text{pattern } Q &::= \epsilon \mid Q\&Q \mid Q|Q \mid L\{C\} \mid L*\{C\} \\ \text{content } C &::= Q \mid T \mid E \\ \text{enums } E &::= V \mid E|E \end{aligned}$$

Integrity constraints are defined in a rule-based approach, as propositions on paths and values. We support the normal boolean connectives, equality, integer comparisons and top level quantification over identifier variables. To formulate structural constraints and guards, we can also express that a path is contained in a document and that a value has a specific type.

$$\begin{aligned} \text{formulas } G &::= \forall v_I.G \mid F \\ F &::= \text{false} \mid F \wedge F \mid F \vee F \mid \neg F \\ &\mid \alpha = \alpha \mid Z < Z \mid P \in D \\ \text{types } T &::= \mathit{INT} \mid \mathit{ID} \mid \mathit{STR} \mid \mathit{CLX} \mid \text{typeOf}(V) \end{aligned}$$

4.2 Semantics

Patterns. The semantics of patterns are given in terms of the assertion language, i.e. patterns are completely translated into formulas. Each element definition in a pattern defines a set of paths using the same labels, but different identifiers. The existence of each of these paths is tied to that of other paths, like the parent path or non-optional children.

To formulate these dependencies, we define the *characterizing path* of an element definition. To compute the characterizing path of an element, the characterizing path of the next enclosing element definition is extended with the label of the element and the null identifier. For repeated elements, we choose a fresh variable as identifier instead, which is quantified in the context. If there is no next enclosing element definition, we extend the root path.

The characterizing paths for all element definitions of the example schema are the following:

$$\begin{array}{ll} /\texttt{packetheader} & /\texttt{packetheader}/\texttt{kind}[x] \\ /\texttt{packetheader}/\texttt{capacity} & /\texttt{packetheader}/\texttt{kind}[x]/\texttt{count} \end{array}$$

Using these paths, the relations defined by patterns can be expressed as propositions. For each element, for example, a proposition is created, which ensures the existence of its parent:

$$\forall x.\ /\texttt{packetheader}/\texttt{kind}[x]/\texttt{count} \in \$ \rightarrow /\texttt{packetheader}/\texttt{kind}[x] \in \$$$

Groups of elements exist if both patterns exist. For patterns combined in a choice, at least one of them has to exist. Both the empty pattern and a repeated element always exist, as the latter can also be an empty sequence.

Elements containing non-complex content, i.e. a datatype or enumeration of values, are translated into similar propositions. The typeOf function is used to guarantee that an assigned value has the appropriate type. Enumerations translate into a disjunction of equalities testing the different values.

$$\texttt{Example:}\ \forall x.\ \texttt{/packetheader/kind}[x]\texttt{/count} \in \$ \rightarrow \\ \text{typeOf}(\$(\texttt{/packetheader/kind}[x]\texttt{/count})) = \mathit{INT}$$

Propositions. The semantics of propositions are given in terms of the respective models of values, paths, multisets and documents, with respect to an interpretation of all variables, called *evaluation environment* E. We denote an evaluation in environment E with $[\![\cdot]\!]_E$. In order for the techniques of [7] to work and to facilitate static analysis, the semantics have to be carefully designed. Nevertheless, we are able to support the intuition behind the connectives.

Due to space limitations, we do not define them formally here and point out the important aspects instead. For simplicity of the logic, both the read function and all cast functions are defined as total, i.e. they return default values for invalid parameters. Section 4.4 explains how to deal with this behavior. The multiset operations sum and ./.[.], as well as .(.), are *selective* in the sense that they ignore values of the wrong type or paths which are not present in the document, respectively. This leads to much simpler specifications and allows us to use *infinite* path multisets to create *finite* value multisets by reading from documents.

4.3 Embedding Rules

We now extend the classical pattern-based structural schema language with the possibility to embed rules. A *rule* is a single proposition attached to an element definition. This approach has the following benefits:

- By tying rules to a structural schema, the paths in rules can be checked for validity, resulting in the detection of more errors at compile time.
- Paths in rules can use the usual convenience axes, like *parent* or *descendants*.
- The context of a rule is implicitly given by the location of the rule in the pattern, allowing us to use much shorter relative paths starting with the dot.

Rules can be embedded in any element definition, regardless if it is repeated or not, by enclosing it in brackets. Defining a rule at the top level is also possible, which means it has the root path as context. To support more navigational axes and relative paths, we extend the sort P^* as follows and introduce explicit conversions of singleton sets to paths using cast_P.

$$\begin{aligned} \text{paths } P &::= \text{root} \mid P/L[I] \mid \text{cast}_P(P^*) \\ \text{path multisets } P^* &::= \{P\} \mid P^* \cup P^* \mid P^*/L[V^*] \\ &\quad\mid\ . \mid P^*/.. \mid P^*/.L \mid P^*//L[V^*] \end{aligned}$$

The dot refers to the characterizing path of the enclosing element definition. The double dot can be used to navigate to a direct parent, whereas the single dot followed by a label jumps to the next parent of that name. A double slash refers to all possible descendants matching the supplied label.

To be able to use the new axes to select meaningful multisets and even single paths, the resulting path multisets have to be filtered with the paths defined in the structural schema. The set of all these paths is derived analogously to characterizing paths. The only difference is that instead of inserting a variable as identifier for repeated element definitions, we add an infinite number of paths, consisting of one version for each identifier.

With this set of paths, the semantics of the new constructs can be defined to work within the limits of the schema. Again, the formal definition of the new constructs leaves the scope of the paper, yet it is easily possible to capture the intuition behind them. Note that the reverse axes parent and ancestor both need to filter out duplicates, as they could otherwise produce an infinite number of duplicates of paths.

In order to further improve readability and conciseness of schema specifications, a concrete syntax for embedded rules will offer the following features:

- *Implicit casts* both on values and paths. In almost every case, the needed sort of an expression can be inferred from the context and a cast introduced accordingly.
- *Implicit document* both for reading values and domain checks. Schema constraints always refer to the document $, without any manipulations, which makes the $ obsolete. We can then neglect the parenthesis used for reading and the $\in$ symbol, as the context makes clear if a value or proposition is needed.
- *Implicit all and null.* Leaving out the brackets in a path step has the implicit meaning of 'all' for path multisets and 'null' for single paths.
- *Implicit root.* All paths start with root, either as unique path or singleton set, so in concrete syntax absolute paths just start with a slash.

4.4 Specification Errors

Although all operators are defined as total, there are several situations which should be considered specification errors and can in fact support the development of schemata immensely. Resulting empty sets, for instance, should be considered specification errors, as they most likely do not reflect the intention of the programmer, but reveal an inconsistency with the schema or just a simple typo. In particular it is undesirable that one of the following ever happens:

- A $\text{cast}_{I/S/Z}$ fails and returns the default value of that sort instead.
- A cast_P fails and returns the root path instead.
- A non-existent path is read from the document, resulting in the value clx.

All of these can easily be prevented by construction or treated as error by modifying the specification. In embedded rules, for example, it makes sense to automatically guard each document access using a unique path with a domain check for this path. The implied semantics is that a rule need only hold, if the paths used actually exist in the document in question. Especially the specification of rules in repeated elements benefits from this implicit assumption.

In procedures, it may be desirable to assert that no cast or document access fails, by extending the precondition of statements containing such terms with a guard for each. Value casts can be guarded using typeOf, unique document access with $\in$. We have defined the structural schema language in such a way, that all typeOf comparisons can be statically decided. A cast_P on a singleton path should be rejected if it is not statically decidable, which only happens in the context of choices or repeated elements and hints at bad programming practice.

Finally, it is possible to transform a formula such that failing casts and reads are treated as errors. This is done by case analysis and simply removing literals containing a failed cast or read access from their disjunction in conjunctive normal form. The underlying idea is that a literal containing a term raising an exception can no longer contribute to fulfilling a disjunction.

5 Procedures

We now define an exemplary core procedural update language, which can be used by domain experts to define the atomic manipulations necessary to use a schema. Analogous to the schema language defined in Section 4, any paradigm and feature can be supported, as long as the semantics of the language can be described in the logical framework of Section 3. In particular, all modifications have to translate to set $.[. \rightarrow .]$ or delete $.[. \rightarrow]$ operations.

The guiding principal for the core language is to provide the means to encapsulate alien aspects like paths from the host language and allow experts to build a toolset of atomic procedures to work with. At the same time, the language allows us to use automated methods to show the programmer the minimal conditions he has to ensure for an interface procedure to maintain the integrity constraints.

5.1 Syntax

Procedures have a name, a list of variables marked as parameters and a body containing a sequence of statements. A statement can create a new element, free an element or set the value of an existing one. It is possible to annotate assumptions and use conditionals for alternative control flows. Finally, variables for single values and value multisets can be declared and assigned.

$$\begin{array}{rl}
\text{procedures } R & ::= L\ (\ M\ )\ \{\ U\ \} \\
\text{parameters } M & ::= \mathbf{int}\ v_Z \mid \mathbf{str}\ v_S \mid \mathbf{ident}\ v_I \mid M, M \\
\text{sequences } U & ::= O \mid U; U \\
\text{statements } O & ::= \mathbf{new}\ P \mid \mathbf{free}\ P \mid P := V \\
& \quad \mid \mathbf{assume}\ G \mid \mathbf{if}\ F\ \mathbf{then}\ U\ \mathbf{else}\ U\ \mathbf{fi} \\
& \quad \mid v_Z = Z \mid v_S = S \mid v_I = I \mid v_m = V^*
\end{array}$$

Note that formulas in conditionals have to be quantifier-free. We do not support loops, as these would prevent *automated* weakest precondition generation.

5.2 Semantics

The operational semantics of procedures define how sequences of statements modify evaluation environments: $U, E \rightsquigarrow E'$. As there is only one document variable, we use the abbreviated notation $E[\![D]\!]_E$ instead of $E[\$ \mapsto [\![D]\!]_E]$.

$$\frac{U_a, E \rightsquigarrow E' \qquad U_b, E' \rightsquigarrow E''}{U_a; U_b, E \rightsquigarrow E''} \qquad \frac{[\![P/L[I] \notin \$]\!]_E \qquad [\![P \in \$]\!]_E}{\textbf{new } P/L[I], E \rightsquigarrow E[\![\$[P/L[I] \to \text{clx}]]\!]_E}$$

$$\frac{[\![P \in \$]\!]_E \qquad P \neq \text{root}}{\textbf{free } P, E \rightsquigarrow E[\![\$[P \to]]\!]_E} \qquad \frac{[\![P \in \$]\!]_E \qquad P \neq \text{root}}{P := V, E \rightsquigarrow E[\![\$[P \to V]]\!]_E}$$

$$\frac{[\![F]\!]_E \qquad U_t, E \rightsquigarrow E'}{\textbf{if } F \textbf{ then } U_t \textbf{ else } U_e \textbf{ fi}, E \rightsquigarrow E'} \qquad \frac{[\![\neg F]\!]_E \qquad U_e, E \rightsquigarrow E'}{\textbf{if } F \textbf{ then } U_t \textbf{ else } U_e \textbf{ fi}, E \rightsquigarrow E'}$$

$$\frac{[\![G]\!]_E}{\textbf{assume } G, E \rightsquigarrow E} \qquad \frac{}{v_m = V^*, E \rightsquigarrow E[v_m \mapsto [\![V^*]\!]_E]}$$

$$\frac{}{v_{I/S/Z} = I/S/Z, E \rightsquigarrow E[v_{I/S/Z} \mapsto [\![I/S/Z]\!]_E]}$$

The initial environment is constructed by binding the input document to \$, the parameter values to the declared parameter variables and default values to all other variables used in statements.

Note that although the formalization of documents permits arbitrary finite maps from paths to values, it is in practice desirable to only deal with documents which represent a tree. A document is a tree, if for every path it contains, it also contains all prefixes of that path. The presented update language is designed in such a way, that this property is maintained by all statements.

Weakest precondition generation for sequences and statements is defined as follows. The weakest preconditions for sequences and conditionals are as usual. We use the syntax $G_{[b/a]}$ to express that a is substituted by b in the formula G.

$$\begin{array}{lll}
\text{wp}\,(\textbf{new } P/L[I], & G) = G_{\left[\$[P/L[I] \to \text{clx}] / \$\right]} & \wedge P \in \$ \wedge P/L[I] \notin \$ \\
\text{wp}\,(\textbf{free } P, & G) = G_{\left[\$[P \to] / \$\right]} & \wedge P \in \$ \wedge P \neq \text{root} \\
\text{wp}\,(P := V, & G) = G_{\left[\$[P \to V] / \$\right]} & \wedge P \in \$ \wedge P \neq \text{root} \\
\text{wp}\,(\textbf{assume } G_a, & G) = G \wedge G_a & \\
\text{wp}\,(v_{I/S/Z} = I/S/Z, & G) = G_{\left[I/S/Z / v_{I/S/Z}\right]} & \\
\text{wp}\,(v_m = V^*, & G) = G_{\left[V^* / v_m\right]} &
\end{array}$$

The document manipulations of statements in procedures are directly expressed in the logical embedding. In [7] we have introduced the necessary rewriting rules to remove the two document manipulations from formulas. In most cases, these rules even reduce the size of formulas and lead to subsequent simplification. In this way, the weakest preconditions can indeed be checked on the prestate of procedures.

6 Conclusion

In this paper we presented a first approach to deal with XML data with *integrity constraints* from within common programming languages. Such XML data is seen as abstract datatype, exposing an interface of basic procedures for manipulation. Domain experts write structural schemata in a normal pattern-based approach, but can also embed sophisticated integrity constraints using paths. Using these paths, they also define the basic atomic manipulations associated with the schema as procedures. We are able to automatically translate and analyze procedures, forming a comprehensive approach to correctness.

The weakest preconditions of procedures are derived automatically and can also automatically be reduced to a minimal form. These preconditions guarantee that a procedure maintains the integrity constraints. The programmer using procedures is able to read the preconditions, guarantee them on calls or react to their failure. Procedures interface with the host language by using primitive types, especially identifiers.

All this is made possible by the underlying path-based formalization first presented in [7]. It allows specifications both to be easily accessible by domain experts and programmers and to be processed by automated tools. We have implemented a prototype system integrating an SMT-solver for simplification. In all example specifications, the system was able to derive the minimal precondition automatically.

References

1. Calcagno, C., Gardner, P., Zarfaty, U.: Context Logic and Tree Update. SIGPLAN Not. 40(1), 271–282 (2005)
2. Clark, J.: RELAX NG Compact Syntax (November 2002), `http://www.oasis-open.org/committees/relax-ng/compact-20021121.html`
3. Clark, J., Makoto, M.: RELAX NG Specification (December 2001), `http://www.oasis-open.org/committees/relax-ng/spec-20011203.html`
4. Gardner, P.A., Smith, G.D., Wheelhouse, M.J., Zarfaty, U.D.: Local Hoare Reasoning about DOM. In: PODS 2008: Proceedings of the Twenty-Seventh ACM SIGMOD-SIGACT-SIGART Symposium on Principles of Database Systems, pp. 261–270. ACM, New York (2008)
5. Harren, M., Raghavachari, M., Shmueli, O., Burke, M.G., Bordawekar, R., Pechtchanski, I., Sarkar, V.: XJ: Facilitating XML Processing in Java. In: WWW 2005: Proceedings of the 14th International Conference on World Wide Web, pp. 278–287. ACM, New York (2005)
6. Hosoya, H., Pierce, B.C.: XDuce: A Statically Typed XML Processing Language. ACM Trans. Internet Techn. 3(2), 117–148 (2003)
7. Michel, P., Poetzsch-Heffter, A.: Assertion Support for Manipulating Constrained Data-Centric XML. In: International Workshop on Programming Language Techniques for XML (PLAN-X 2009) (January 2009)
8. Microsystems, S.: Java Architecture for XML Binding (JAXB), `http://java.sun.com/developer/technicalArticles/WebServices/jaxb//`
9. Sourceforge. Simple API for XML (SAX),`http://www.saxproject.org/`
10. W3C. Document object model (DOM), `http://www.w3.org/DOM/`

Improving Classification Performance with Focus on the Complex Areas

Seyed Zeinolabedin Moussavi[1], Kambiz Zarei[1], and Reza Ebrahimpour[1,2]

[1] Departments of Electrical Engineering, Shahid Rajaee University, Tehran, Iran
Smoussavi@srttu.edu,
kambiz_zarei@yahoo.com
[2] School of Cognitive Sciences, Institute for Studies on Theoretical Physics and Mathematics, Niavaran, Tehran, Iran
ebrahimpour@ipm.ir

Abstract. In combining classifiers, effort is made to achieve higher accuracy in comparison with the base classifiers that form the ensemble. In this paper, we make modifications to the conventional decision template, DT, method, so that its classification performance is improved in experiments with Satimage, Image Segmentation and Soybean datasets. In our modified version, DT, an elegant strategy in classifier fusion, is used in the first stage of classification task, and in the second stage, the most misclassified classes are directed to a classifier that is specifically devoted to those classes. To identify the most misclassified classes, the confusion matrix of the output of the decision template stage is considered. Experimental results demonstrate the improved performance of the modified version by a 3% increase in the recognition rate for Satimage dataset in comparison with previously published results on Satimage dataset, a 10.57% increase in the recognition rate for Image Segmentation and 4.88% for Soybean dataset, in comparison with the conventional method.

Keywords: Combining classifier system, classifier fusion, classifier ensembles, decision template method.

1 Introduction

A combining classifiers system, composed of several simple classifiers or experts, is a possible way of solving a *complex problem* which might need a complicated network to be handled with [3,11,13]. Fig. 1 in the following page illustrates the general framework of a combining classifiers system.

There are two main strategies in combining classifiers: fusion and selection. In classifier fusion, it is supposed that each ensemble member is trained over the whole feature space, whereas in classifier selection, each member is assigned to learn a part of the feature space and are thereby considered as competitive rather than complementary [1,4,6]. This way, in the former strategy, the final decision is made considering the decisions of all members, while in the latter strategy, the final decision is made by aggregating the decisions of one or a few of experts [1,2].

J. van Leeuwen et al. (Eds.): SOFSEM 2010, LNCS 5901, pp. 612–626, 2010.

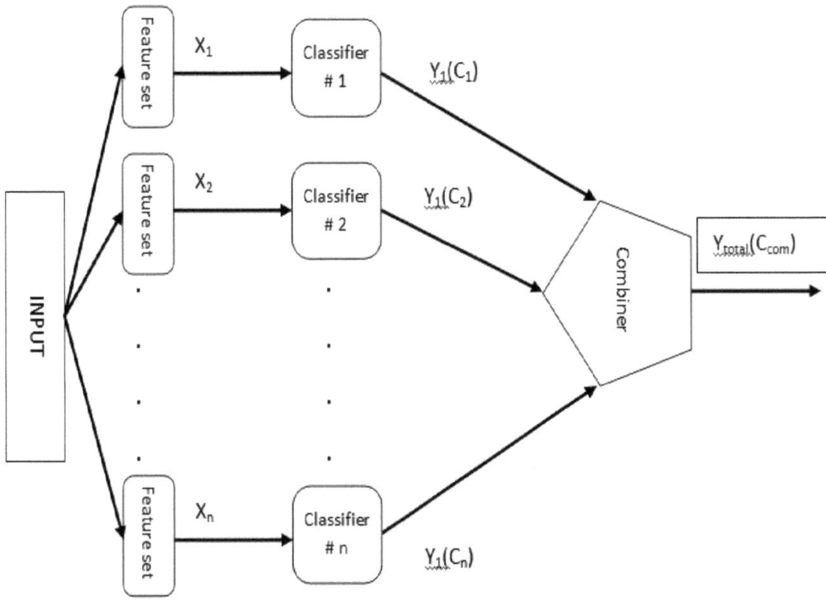

Fig. 1. General framework of a combining classifiers system

Our proposed method makes a modification to the decision template, DT, technique. In a multi-class classification problem, DT represents the decisions of a set of classifiers on each class. In other words, DT is formed according to the outputs of *all* classifiers on patterns of a particular class.

DTs have been compared with other techniques such as Naïve Bayes [5], behavior knowledge space, and Dempster Shafer aggregation [7,8,16] for combining classifiers and it has been shown that it outperforms those methods in terms of higher recognition rate and less computational complexity [1].

In our modified version of DT, we first try to find the classes that are mostly misclassified, hereafter referred to as "conflicting classes". This way, when DT realizes that an input sample belongs to one of the conflicting classes, it is then directed to a specific classifier that is trained to classify such classes. The point is that the specific classifier has to decide between a smaller number of classes in comparison with DT, therefore its classification is more accurate and reliable.

To find the conflicting classes we use the confusion matrices, *CMs*, of base classifiers. CM^j is a $K \times K$ matrix obtained from the output of classifier D_j with training set as its input. Each element of CM^j matrix, $cm^j_{k,s}$, expresses the number of input patterns whose true class label is *k*, but were incorrectly assigned to class S.

To label the patterns we use squared Euclidean distance to evaluate the similarity between the decision profile matrix, $DP(X)$, and each $DT_i, i = 1,2,\dots,K$. In the following we briefly describe *DP(X)*.

Let's consider $X \in \Re^n$ ($\Re^n$ is the initial feature space with n features), as a feature vector and $\{1,2,...,K\}$ the label set of K classes and *DP(X)*, the decision profile matrix for X in which, entries are *the intermediate features*. The classifier outputs can be organized in a decision profile matrix, *DP(X)* similar to the one shown below [1, 2]:

$$DP(X) = \begin{bmatrix} d_{11}(X) & \dots & d_{1j}(X) & \dots & d_{1k}(X) \\ \dots & & & & \dots \\ d_{i1}(X) & \dots & d_{ij}(X) & \dots & d_{ik}(X) \\ \dots & & & & \dots \\ d_{p1}(X) & \dots & d_{pj}(X) & \dots & d_{pk}(X) \end{bmatrix}$$

Where d_{pk}, for a given sample X, is the posterior probability that the pth classifier estimates that x belongs to the kth class.

Our experimental results support the proposed modified version of DT. We test our method on the Satimage dataset, known as a benchmark test for evaluating the performance of combining methodologies.

The remainder of this paper is organized as follows: Section 2 is devoted to the details of classifier fusion. Section 3 describes our proposed DT scheme. It is followed by experimental results in Section 4. Finally, section 5, concludes and summarizes the paper.

2 Classifier Combining Schemes

Combining schemes can be coarsely divided into the two categories of classifier selection and classifier fusion. In classifier selection one (or a number of) expert(s) are responsible for learning a part of the feature space; that is, each part of the feature space is assigned to one (or a number of) expert(s) to be learned. When a feature vector is presented to a system of this type, the output of the expert(s) responsible for that area of the feature space is given the highest credit.

In classifier fusion, all classifiers are equally trained over the whole feature space rather than part of it, and their outputs are fused to form the classification result of an input feature vector [5, 6]. The method that we use in this paper, DT, falls under the category of classifier fusion.

As the outputs of classifiers in the fusion type are to be combined, an important issue is the form of their outputs. Scaling the outputs of all classifiers into the interval of [0, 1] is a common way of having outputs that are effortlessly combinable [15].

The output vector of a classifier may be defined in one of the three types of Abstract level [12], Rank level [9] and Measurement level [8]. These levels are described in Table 1.

Table 1. The three type of classifier output. Refer to text for the description of symbols.

Type of Classifier Output	Definition
Abstract Level	$D_{ij}(X) \in \{0,1\},\ X \in \Re^n$
Rank Level	$D_{ij}(X) \in [0,1],\ X \in \Re^n$
Measurement Level [8]	$D_{ij}(X) \in Z,\ X \in \Re^n$

Considering $D = \{D_1, D_2, ..., D_p\}$ as the set of classifiers and $\Omega = \{W_1, W_2, ..., W_k\}$ as the label set of the classes, an input vector $X \in \Re^n$ to each classifier, returns a K-dimensional output vector (e.g. the ith classifier returns the vector as $D_i(X) = [d_{i1}(X) \quad d_{i2}(X) \quad ... \quad d_{ik}(X)]$), where $d_{ij}(X)$ is the degree of support given by classifier D_i to the decision that input vector *X* belongs to class j.

The output of a combining classifier system or in other words or the support for class i ($^{i}_{D}(X)$) given by the combining network based on the *DP(X)* can be obtained in two ways:

First, using some fusion methods like product, average, minimum, maximum and fuzzy integral. These methods use only the i th column of *DP(X)* for calculating the support for class W_i. Such methods are known as "class-conscious". The alternative approach is called "class-indifferent" in which all the elements of *DP(X)* is used to calculate the support for each class. In this approach, all elements of *DP(X)* as "intermediate feature space" are used to design the second (combining) stage. Methods such as "Decision template" and "Dempster-Shafer aggregation" fall in this group.

Note that 'class-conscious' methods use the context of *DP(X)* and only one column per class, and ignore the rest of information, while "class-indifferent" methods use all elements of DP(X) but do not use the context [1].

3 Proposed Method

3.1 Confusion Matrix

A common criterion to evaluate a classifier, D_j, is to form its confusion matrix, *CM*. Each column of the matrix represents samples in a predicted class, while each row represents the instances in an actual class. One benefit of a confusion matrix is that it is easy to see if the system is confusing two classes.

Classifier Precision, for class *i*, is defined as the proportion of the predicted positive cases that were correct and *Classifier Recall* as the proportion of positive cases that were correctly identified.

Example 1:
Consider a 3×3 $CM_{3\times3}$ shown below. We can calculate the PM (precision matrix) and RM (recall matrix) as so:

$$CM = \begin{bmatrix} 480 & 11 & 9 \\ 7 & 320 & 18 \\ 5 & 17 & 390 \end{bmatrix}$$

$$\Rightarrow PM = \begin{bmatrix} 0.96 & 0.02 & 0.02 \\ 0.02 & 0.92 & 0.05 \\ 0.01 & 0.04 & 0.94 \end{bmatrix}$$

$$\Rightarrow RM = \begin{bmatrix} 0.97 & 0.03 & 0.02 \\ 0.01 & 0.91 & 0.04 \\ 0.01 & 0.05 & 0.93 \end{bmatrix}$$

Note that the PM and RM are actually vectors for multi-class problems which we call them matrices. We can see from the above *CM* that the actual number of patterns for class W_1 is 480+11+9=500 and the total number of patterns labeled into class W_1 is 480+7+5=492.

Thus such a classifier assigned $\frac{11}{480+11+9} = 2.2\%$ of elements whose real class is W_1 to class W_2 and $\frac{18}{9+18+390} = 4.3\%$ of elements that actually belong to class W_2 is labeled as class W_3.

In brief, we can use the internal information available in rows and columns of confusion matrices, *CMs*, of base classifiers to improve the results (outputs) of a Multiple Classifier System (MCS). Another term which we can use to analyze a classifier behavior is its normalized *CM*. To calculate it, each and every element of the confusion matrix must be divided by the sum of all elements of the *CM*.

Following criterion can be obtained from *CM*:

- **Classifier precision for class W_i**

  It declares how much percent of the elements of W_i is labeled correctly by the classifier. To calculate this criterion, the diagonal elements of that particular class in the row must be divided by sum of the elements of that row:

$$Pi = \frac{Cii}{\sum_{k=1}^{k} Cik} \tag{1}$$

The classifier average precision for all classes is calculated like this:

$$Pav = \frac{\sum_{i=1}^{k} Pi}{K} \tag{2}$$

- **Classifier recall for class W_i**

  It states how much percent of the elements that are labeled by D_j into class W_i in truth belong to it. To calculate it, the diagonal element of W_i in the column must be divided by the sum of the elements of the column which the diagonal element is in (Eq. (3))

$$Ri = \frac{Cii}{\sum_{i=1}^{k} Cki} \tag{3}$$

3.2 Decision Templates

Decision templates, DTs , is a powerful tool for classifier fusion. Using outputs of all classifiers and comparing them with a characteristic template for each class, DT calculates the final support for each class [1] (therefore referred to as *characteristic template*).

Consider a set of labeled training data set, $X = \{X_1, X_2, ..., X_n\}$, $X \in \Re^n$ and apply them to the combining system $D = \{D_1, D_2, ..., D_p\}$. Based on the output vector of classifiers, DP matrices are calculated. DT_i can be obtained by averaging all DP matrices which belong to the elements of class W_i. The mathematical interpretation of DT is shown in Eq. (4) [10]:

$$\mathrm{dt}_i(\mathrm{k}, \mathrm{s}) = \frac{\sum_{j=1}^{N} \mathrm{Ind}(\mathrm{X}_j, \mathrm{i})\ \mathrm{d}_{ks}(\mathrm{X}_j)}{\sum_{j=1}^{N} \mathrm{Ind}(\mathrm{X}_j, \mathrm{i})} \tag{4}$$

$$K = 1,2,..., P \qquad S = 1,2,..., K$$

where $Ind\ (Z_j, i)$ is an index function which its value is 1 if X_j has crisp label i and 0 otherwise [10] and $d_{ks}\ X_j$ is the degree of support for W_j given by D_k to class W_s. So K decision templates (one per class) are calculated.

3.3 Decision Template Scheme

In our method we use confusion matrices of all classifiers, CM_i , i = 1,...,P. As mentioned before CMs express the classifier behavior and represent it in terms of classifier precision and recall criteria. Therefore, using the precision criterion, we can acquire which classes are mostly overlapped or in other words which classes' patterns are mostly misclassified. This way, we are able to develop a two-stage combining system with which we can better handle overlapped and non-overlapped classes. The basic idea is to feed the samples that are classified as one of the overlapped groups to the second stage classifier which is devoted to those classes. More details are given in the following.

In order to find the overlapped classes, we consider the CMs of each class that is obtained according to the output of each classifier with the training set as its input. When a test sample is given to the network, it is first checked whether it belongs to the overlapped or non-overlapped classes. If it is classified as a non-overlapped class, the result is considered as the final output, but in case it is categorized as a member of overlapped classes, it is directed to the second stage network for more accurate classification.

The second stage classifiers are those which are trained over the overlapped classes and therefore can classify them more effectively and accurately. To find whether a sample belongs to the first or second stage, we calculate its *DP* from the first stage and use a similarity measure to match it to DT_i, $i = 1,\ldots,K$ and this way, the support for each class, $\mu_i(X)$, is found. We use the squared Euclidean distance to measure the similarity between the obtained *DP (X)* and DT_i, $i = 1,\ldots,K$ (Eq. (5))

$$d_E = 1 - \frac{1}{P \times K} \sum_{i=1}^{P} \sum_{k=1}^{K} \left[DT_j(i,k) - d_{i,k}(X) \right]^2 = 1 - \frac{\left\| DT_j - DP \right\|^2}{P \times K} \tag{5}$$

Based on this similarity measure, among the calculated d_E for each class the minimum one determines the class label for sample X.

4 Experimental Results

In our experiments we use the Satimage dataset from the ELENA database, Image Segmentation dataset and Soybean dataset. The Satimage data was generated from Landset Multi-Spectral Scanner image data. It consists of 6435 pixels with 36 attributes (4 spectral bands 9 pixels in a 3x3 neighborhood) which are crisply classified into the six classes of red soil (23.82%), cotton crop (10.92%), grey soil (21.1%), damp grey soil (9.73%), soil with vegetation stubble (10.99%), and very damp grey soil (23.43%) and are presented in random order in the database [1]. Instances of Image Segmentation dataset (Vision Group, University of Massachusetts, 1990) were drawn randomly from a database of 7 outdoor images. The images were hand segmented to create a classification for every pixel. Each instance is a 3x3 region.

The Image Segmentation dataset consists of seven classes of brick face, sky, foliage, cement, window, path and grass. There are 210 samples for training data (30 instances per class for training data) and 2100 samples for test data (300 instances per class for test data) with 19 continuous features. In our version of Soybean dataset, there are 17 classes which we use only 14 of them without any missing value. These classes are diaporthe-stem-canker, charcoal-rot, rhizoctonia-root-rot, brown-stem-rot, powdery-mildew, downy-mildew, brown-spot, bacterial-blight, bacterial-pustule, purple-seed-stain, anthracnose, phyllosticta-leaf-spot, alternarialeaf-spot, frog-eye-leaf-spot. The folklore seems to be that the other four classes are unjustified by the data since they have so few examples or have missing value that is not appropriate for our experiment; In addition, there are 35 categorical attributes, some nominal and some ordered. Number of instances in this dataset is 307 which we duplicate it into 420 to have equal classes' distribution and take 310 samples for training and use the rest in the test phase.

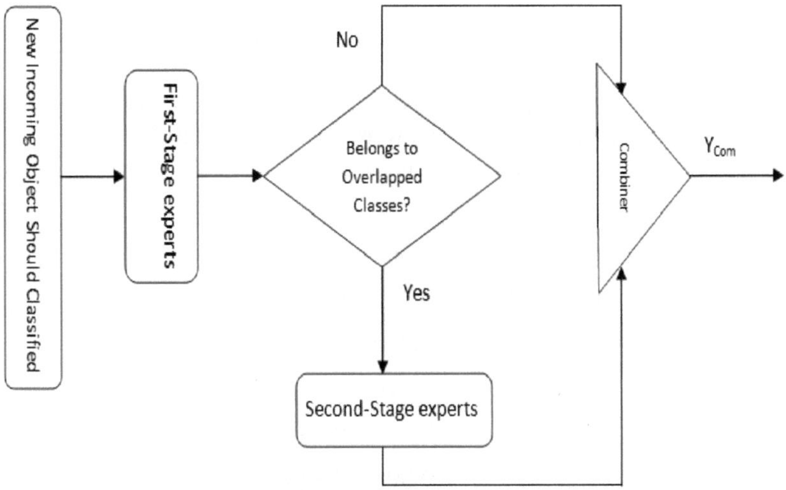

Fig. 2. Structure of proposed method

Table 2. (a) Description of the datasets used in the Experiments. (b) Number of Patterns used in the Experiments.

(a)

Dataset	#Classes	#Attributes
Satimage	6	36
Image Segmentation	7	19
Soybean	13	35

(b)

Dataset	#Patterns Train	Test Expert	Test MCS
Satimage	3000	1290	2145
Image Segmentation	210	1050	1050
Soybean	310	70	70

For the first stage of our proposed method, four individual classifiers were allocated and the approximate accuracy of 87.27% over Satimage dataset with the 3000-element training set; 66.57% over Image Segmentation dataset with 210–element training set and 83.45% over Soybean dataset with 310–element training set were obtained. The learning parameters, constant eta, were 0.051 for Satimage, 0.056 for Image Segmentation and 0.08 for Soybean and the training epochs were 200, 250 and 310, respectively. The rest of the dataset, the 3435 other elements in Satimage data, 2100 in Image Segmentation data and 140 in Soybean data, were used in the test phase (Table 2). The training and test sets were chosen randomly.

The normalized CMs for the first-stage classifiers, $CM_1,\ldots,CM_4$, on Satimage dataset are shown below:

$$CM_1 = \begin{bmatrix} 0.97 & 0 & 0.004 & 0.008 & 0.054 & 0 \\ 0 & 0.929 & 0 & 0 & 0.033 & 0 \\ 0.015 & 0 & 0.960 & 0.210 & 0.020 & 0.018 \\ 0 & 0.008 & 0.310 & 0.280 & 0 & 0.042 \\ 0.009 & 0.063 & 0 & 0.043 & 0.790 & 0.036 \\ 0 & 0 & 0.003 & 0.456 & 0.101 & 0.903 \end{bmatrix}$$

$$CM_2 = \begin{bmatrix} 0.977 & 0 & 0.011 & 0.009 & 0.047 & 0 \\ 0 & 0.968 & 0 & 0 & 0.033 & 0.003 \\ 0.120 & 0 & 0.941 & 0.140 & 0 & 0.021 \\ 0 & 0.007 & 0.043 & 0.333 & 0 & 0.048 \\ 0.009 & 0.023 & 0 & 0.052 & 0.831 & 0.030 \\ 0 & 0 & 0.004 & 0.465 & 0.087 & 0.897 \end{bmatrix}$$

$$CM_3 = \begin{bmatrix} 0.977 & 0 & 0.011 & 0.009 & 0.054 & 0 \\ 0 & 0.921 & 0 & 0 & 0.040 & 0 \\ 0.015 & 0 & 0.921 & 0.131 & 0.006 & 0.018 \\ 0 & 0.007 & 0.062 & 0.368 & 0.013 & 0.063 \\ 0.006 & 0.070 & 0 & 0.043 & 0.783 & 0.027 \\ 0 & 0 & 0.003 & 0.447 & 0.101 & 0.891 \end{bmatrix}$$

$$CM_4 = \begin{bmatrix} 0.975 & 0 & 0.004 & 0.008 & 0.067 & 0 \\ 0 & 0.952 & 0.004 & 0 & 0.033 & 0.003 \\ 0.015 & 0 & 0.937 & 0.140 & 0.006 & 0.015 \\ 0 & 0.008 & 0.041 & 0.377 & 0 & 0.045 \\ 0.009 & 0.039 & 0 & 0.052 & 0.790 & 0.027 \\ 0 & 0 & 0.007 & 0.421 & 0.101 & 0.909 \end{bmatrix}$$

the normalized CMs for the first-stage classifiers, $CM_1,\ldots,CM_4$, on Image Segmentation dataset are:

$$CM_1=\begin{bmatrix} 0 & 0 & 0 & 0 & 0 & 0 & 0 \\ 0 & 0.905 & 0 & 0.067 & 0 & 0 & 0 \\ 0 & 0 & 0.080 & 0 & 0 & 0 & 0 \\ 0.066 & 0.094 & 0.026 & 0.419 & 0.105 & 0.026 & 0 \\ 0.026 & 0 & 0.160 & 0 & 0.263 & 0 & 0 \\ 0.506 & 0 & 0.093 & 0.486 & 0.184 & 0.973 & 0.026 \\ 0.401 & 0 & 0.640 & 0.027 & 0.447 & 0 & 0.973 \end{bmatrix}$$

$$CM_2=\begin{bmatrix} 0 & 0 & 0 & 0.013 & 0 & 0 & 0 \\ 0 & 0.919 & 0 & 0.135 & 0 & 0 & 0 \\ 0 & 0 & 0.080 & 0 & 0 & 0 & 0 \\ 0.026 & 0.081 & 0.013 & 0.513 & 0 & 0 & 0 \\ 0 & 0 & 0.040 & 0 & 0.144 & 0 & 0 \\ 0.440 & 0 & 0.040 & 0.229 & 0.210 & 0.973 & 0 \\ 0.533 & 0 & 0.826 & 0.108 & 0.644 & 0.026 & 1.000 \end{bmatrix}$$

$$CM_3=\begin{bmatrix} 0.040 & 0 & 0 & 0.040 & 0 & 0 & 0 \\ 0 & 1.000 & 0 & 0.216 & 0 & 0 & 0 \\ 0 & 0 & 0.106 & 0 & 0 & 0 & 0 \\ 0.053 & 0 & 0.026 & 0.432 & 0 & 0 & 0 \\ 0 & 0 & 0.040 & 0 & 0.144 & 0 & 0 \\ 0.386 & 0 & 0.026 & 0.202 & 0.197 & 1.000 & 0 \\ 0.520 & 0 & 0.800 & 0.108 & 0.631 & 0 & 1.000 \end{bmatrix}$$

$$CM_4=\begin{bmatrix} 0.16 & 0 & 0.040 & 0.027 & 0.079 & 0.066 & 0 \\ 0 & 1.000 & 0 & 0.229 & 0 & 0 & 0 \\ 0 & 0 & 0.080 & 0.0 & 0 & 0 & 0 \\ 0.173 & 0 & 0.013 & 0.544 & 0.092 & 0.186 & 0 \\ 0.026 & 0 & 0.146 & 0.013 & 0.302 & 0 & 0 \\ 0.200 & 0 & 0.026 & 0.094 & 0.039 & 0.720 & 0 \\ 0.440 & 0 & 0.693 & 0.081 & 0.486 & 0.026 & 1.000 \end{bmatrix}$$

And finally, the normalized CMs for the first-stage classifiers, $CM_1,\ldots,CM_4$, on Soybean dataset are:

$$CM_1 = \begin{bmatrix}
1 & 0 & 0 & 0 & 0 & 0 & 0 & 0 & 0 & 0 & 0 & 0 & 0 & 0 \\
0 & 0.8 & 0 & 0 & 0 & 0 & 0 & 0 & 0 & 0 & 0 & 0 & 0 & 0 \\
0 & 0 & 1 & 0 & 0 & 0 & 0.2 & 0 & 0 & 0 & 0 & 0 & 0.2 & 0.2 \\
0 & 0 & 0 & 0.8 & 0 & 0 & 0.2 & 0 & 0 & 0 & 0 & 0 & 0 & 0.2 \\
0 & 0 & 0 & 0 & 1 & 0 & 0 & 0 & 0 & 0 & 0 & 0 & 0 & 0 \\
0 & 0 & 0 & 0 & 0 & 1 & 0 & 0 & 0 & 0 & 0 & 0 & 0 & 0 \\
0 & 0 & 0 & 0 & 0 & 0 & 0.4 & 0.2 & 0 & 0 & 0 & 0 & 0 & 0.2 \\
0 & 0.2 & 0 & 0 & 0 & 0 & 0 & 0.6 & 0 & 0 & 0 & 0 & 0 & 0 \\
0 & 0 & 0 & 0 & 0 & 0 & 0 & 0 & 0.8 & 0 & 0 & 0 & 0 & 0 \\
0 & 0 & 0 & 0 & 0 & 0 & 0 & 0 & 0 & 1 & 0 & 0 & 0 & 0 \\
0 & 0 & 0 & 0 & 0 & 0 & 0.2 & 0 & 0 & 0 & 0.6 & 0 & 0 & 0.2 \\
0 & 0 & 0 & 0.2 & 0 & 0 & 0 & 0.2 & 0.2 & 0 & 0.2 & 1 & 0.6 & 0 \\
0 & 0 & 0 & 0 & 0 & 0 & 0 & 0 & 0 & 0 & 0.2 & 0 & 0.2 & 0.2 \\
0 & 0 & 0 & 0.1 & 0 & 0 & 0.1 & 0 & 0 & 0 & 0 & 0 & 0.2 & 0.5
\end{bmatrix}$$

$$CM_2 = \begin{bmatrix}
1 & 0.2 & 0 & 0.2 & 0 & 0 & 0 & 0 & 0 & 0 & 0.2 & 0 & 0.2 & 0 \\
0 & 0.8 & 0 & 0 & 0 & 0 & 0 & 0 & 0 & 0 & 0 & 0 & 0 & 0 \\
0 & 0 & 1 & 0 & 0 & 0 & 0.2 & 0 & 0 & 0 & 0 & 0 & 0.2 & 0 \\
0 & 0 & 0 & 0.6 & 0 & 0 & 0 & 0 & 0 & 0 & 0 & 0 & 0 & 0.2 \\
0 & 0 & 0 & 0 & 0.8 & 0 & 0 & 0 & 0 & 0 & 0 & 0 & 0 & 0 \\
0 & 0 & 0 & 0 & 0 & 1 & 0 & 0 & 0 & 0 & 0 & 0 & 0 & 0.2 \\
0 & 0 & 0 & 0 & 0 & 0 & 0.2 & 0.2 & 0 & 0 & 0 & 0 & 0.2 & 0 \\
0 & 0 & 0 & 0 & 0 & 0 & 0 & 0.8 & 0 & 0 & 0 & 0 & 0 & 0 \\
0 & 0 & 0 & 0 & 0 & 0 & 0.2 & 0 & 1 & 0 & 0 & 0 & 0 & 0 \\
0 & 0 & 0 & 0 & 0.2 & 0 & 0.2 & 0 & 0 & 1 & 0 & 0 & 0 & 0 \\
0 & 0 & 0 & 0 & 0 & 0 & 0 & 0 & 0 & 0 & 0.8 & 0 & 0 & 0 \\
0 & 0 & 0 & 0.2 & 0 & 0 & 0.2 & 0 & 0 & 0 & 0 & 1 & 0 & 0 \\
0 & 0 & 0 & 0 & 0 & 0 & 0 & 0 & 0 & 0 & 0 & 0 & 0.2 & 0.4 \\
0 & 0 & 0 & 0.1 & 0 & 0 & 0 & 0 & 0 & 0 & 0 & 0 & 0.2 & 0.2
\end{bmatrix}$$

$$CM_3 = \begin{bmatrix}
1 & 0 & 0 & 0 & 0 & 0 & 0 & 0 & 0.2 & 0 & 0 & 0 & 0.2 & 0.2 \\
0 & 1 & 0 & 0 & 0 & 0 & 0 & 0 & 0 & 0 & 0 & 0 & 0 & 0 \\
0 & 0 & 1 & 0.2 & 0 & 0 & 0 & 0 & 0 & 0 & 0 & 0 & 0 & 0 \\
0 & 0 & 0 & 0.6 & 0 & 0 & 0.2 & 0 & 0 & 0 & 0 & 0 & 0 & 0.2 \\
0 & 0 & 0 & 0 & 1 & 0 & 0 & 0 & 0 & 0 & 0 & 0 & 0 & 0.2 \\
0 & 0 & 0 & 0 & 0 & 0.6 & 0 & 0 & 0 & 0 & 0 & 0 & 0 & 0 \\
0 & 0 & 0 & 0 & 0 & 0 & 0.4 & 0 & 0 & 0 & 0 & 0 & 0.2 & 0 \\
0 & 0 & 0 & 0 & 0 & 0 & 0 & 0.8 & 0 & 0 & 0 & 0 & 0.2 & 0 \\
0 & 0 & 0 & 0 & 0 & 0 & 0 & 0 & 0.8 & 0 & 0 & 0 & 0 & 0 \\
0 & 0 & 0 & 0 & 0 & 0 & 0.2 & 0 & 0 & 0.8 & 0 & 0 & 0 & 0 \\
0 & 0 & 0 & 0 & 0 & 0.2 & 0 & 0 & 0 & 0 & 1 & 0 & 0 & 0 \\
0 & 0 & 0 & 0 & 0 & 0 & 0 & 0 & 0 & 0 & 0 & 0.8 & 0 & 0 \\
0 & 0 & 0 & 0.2 & 0 & 0.2 & 0.2 & 0.2 & 0 & 0 & 0 & 0.2 & 0.4 & 0.4 \\
0 & 0 & 0 & 0 & 0 & 0 & 0 & 0 & 0 & 0.2 & 0 & 0 & 0 & 0
\end{bmatrix}$$

$$CM_4 = \begin{bmatrix} 1 & 0 & 0 & 0 & 0 & 0 & 0.2 & 0 & 0 & 0 & 0 & 0 & 0 & 0 \\ 0 & 1 & 0 & 0 & 0 & 0 & 0 & 0 & 0 & 0 & 0 & 0 & 0 & 0 \\ 0 & 0 & 0.8 & 0 & 0 & 0 & 0 & 0 & 0 & 0 & 0 & 0 & 0 & 0 \\ 0 & 0 & 0 & 0.8 & 0 & 0 & 0.2 & 0 & 0 & 0 & 0 & 0 & 0.2 & 0.2 \\ 0 & 0 & 0 & 0 & 1 & 0 & 0 & 0 & 0 & 0 & 0 & 0 & 0 & 0.2 \\ 0 & 0 & 0 & 0 & 0 & 1 & 0.2 & 0 & 0 & 0 & 0 & 0 & 0 & 0 \\ 0 & 0 & 0.2 & 0.2 & 0 & 0 & 0.2 & 0 & 0 & 0 & 0 & 0 & 0 & 0 \\ 0 & 0 & 0 & 0 & 0 & 0 & 0 & 0.8 & 0 & 0 & 0 & 0 & 0.2 & 0 \\ 0 & 0 & 0 & 0 & 0 & 0 & 0 & 0 & 0.8 & 0 & 0 & 0 & 0 & 0.2 \\ 0 & 0 & 0 & 0 & 0 & 0 & 0.2 & 0 & 0 & 1 & 0 & 0 & 0 & 0 \\ 0 & 0 & 0 & 0 & 0 & 0 & 0 & 0 & 0.2 & 0 & 0.8 & 0 & 0.2 & 0.2 \\ 0 & 0 & 0 & 0 & 0 & 0 & 0 & 0.2 & 0 & 0 & 0 & 0.8 & 0 & 0 \\ 0 & 0 & 0 & 0 & 0 & 0 & 0 & 0 & 0 & 0 & 0.2 & 0.2 & 0.4 & 0.2 \\ 0 & 0 & 0 & 0.1 & 0 & 0 & 0 & 0 & 0 & 0 & 0 & 0 & 0 & 0 \end{bmatrix}$$

Considering CMs we can observe the performance of each classifier. Apparently, on Satimage dataset, we observe that all classifiers have problems in recognizing patterns of class 4 and incorrectly classify them as class 6. on Image Segmentation dataset the problem is in recognizing between the patterns of classes 3 and 7 incorrectly classify them as class 7 and these two conflicting classes in Soybean dataset are 13 and 14 (Table 3).

Table 3. Conflicting classes' number in experimented datasets

Problem	Most Conflicting Classes
Satimage	4 and 6
Image Segmentation	3,5 and 7
Soybean	13 and 14

To decrease the error rate, we first find the most conflicting classes. The row and column number of *maximum non-diagonal value* of CM yields the label of those classes that the classifier has misclassified their samples. So, a second-stage MLP network is used, which actually consists of one single classifier and is trained over the classes with the most conflicting number of samples, or the conflicting classes; in this experiment there are 830 samples of classes 4 and 6 in Satimage dataset, 315 samples of classes 3, 5 and 7 in Image Segmentation dataset and 80 samples of classes 13 and 14 in Soybean dataset.

In Satimage dataset, classes 4 and 6 have 415 and 1036 samples, respectively. We take all 415 samples of class 4 and select 415 elements of the class 6 randomly and put them together to build the training set (note that taking all 1036 elements of class 6, causes the network to have a bias towards the particular class and therefore decrease the accuracy of classification). In Image Segmentation and Soybean number of patterns of those conflicting classes are equal.

Comparing our modified DT version with the classic scheme introduced in [1], we can experimentally achieve 3% increase in accuracy on Satimage dataset. The average test accuracy of DT in its conventional style is about 84.48%, whereas the average recognition rate of our model on Satimage data is 87.27%. The final normalized CM of our model on Satimage dataset is shown below:

$$CM_{MCS} = \begin{bmatrix} 0.966 & 0 & 0.004 & 0.009 & 0.066 & 0 \\ 0.001 & 0.919 & 0 & 0 & 0.012 & 0 \\ 0.021 & 0 & 0.926 & 0.170 & 0 & 0.014 \\ 0.001 & 0.016 & 0.060 & 0.720 & 0.029 & 0.201 \\ 0.007 & 0.064 & 0 & 0.014 & 0.795 & 0.019 \\ 0 & 0 & 0.008 & 0.085 & 0.095 & 0.764 \end{bmatrix}$$

The average test accuracy of DT in its conventional style on Image Segmentation dataset is about 56%, whereas the average recognition rate of our model is 66.57%. The final normalized CM of our model on Image Segmentation dataset is shown below:

$$CM_{MCS} = \begin{bmatrix} 0.019 & 0 & 0.020 & 0.053 & 0.013 & 0.033 & 0.006 \\ 0 & 0.993 & 0 & 0.106 & 0 & 0 & 0 \\ 0.291 & 0 & 0.745 & 0.073 & 0.308 & 0 & 0.026 \\ 0.066 & 0.007 & 0.020 & 0.440 & 0 & 0 & 0 \\ 0.178 & 0 & 0.167 & 0.033 & 0.550 & 0.013 & 0.006 \\ 0.443 & 0 & 0.047 & 0.294 & 0.127 & 0.953 & 0 \\ 0 & 0 & 0 & 0 & 0 & 0 & 0.959 \end{bmatrix}$$

And finally, the average test accuracy of DT in its conventional style on Soybean dataset is about 78.57%, whereas the average recognition rate of our model is 83.45%. The final normalized CM of our model on Image Segmentation dataset is shown below:

$$CM_{MCS} = \begin{bmatrix} 1 & 0 & 0 & 0 & 0 & 0 & 0.1 & 0 & 0 & 0 & 0 & 0 & 0.1 & 0 \\ 0 & 1 & 0 & 0 & 0 & 0 & 0 & 0 & 0 & 0 & 0 & 0 & 0 & 0 \\ 0 & 0 & 1 & 0 & 0 & 0 & 0 & 0 & 0 & 0 & 0 & 0 & 0 & 0 \\ 0 & 0 & 0 & 0.7 & 0 & 0 & 0.2 & 0 & 0 & 0 & 0 & 0 & 0.1 & 0.1 \\ 0 & 0 & 0 & 0 & 0.9 & 0 & 0 & 0 & 0 & 0 & 0 & 0 & 0.1 & 0 \\ 0 & 0 & 0 & 0 & 0 & 1 & 0 & 0 & 0 & 0 & 0 & 0 & 0 & 0 \\ 0 & 0 & 0 & 0 & 0 & 0 & 0.4 & 0 & 0 & 0 & 0 & 0 & 0 & 0.1 \\ 0 & 0 & 0 & 0 & 0 & 0 & 0 & 1 & 0 & 0 & 0 & 0 & 0 & 0 \\ 0 & 0 & 0 & 0 & 0 & 0 & 0 & 0 & 0.9 & 0 & 0 & 0 & 0 & 0 \\ 0 & 0 & 0 & 0 & 0 & 0 & 0 & 0 & 0 & 1 & 0 & 0 & 0 & 0 \\ 0 & 0 & 0 & 0 & 0 & 0 & 0 & 0 & 0 & 0 & 0.8 & 0 & 0 & 0 \\ 0 & 0 & 0 & 0 & 0 & 0 & 0.1 & 0 & 0 & 0 & 0 & 1 & 0 & 0 \\ 0 & 0 & 0 & 0.2 & 0.1 & 0 & 0.1 & 0 & 0.1 & 0 & 0.2 & 0 & 0.5 & 0.3 \\ 0 & 0 & 0 & 0.1 & 0 & 0 & 0.1 & 0 & 0 & 0 & 0 & 0 & 0.2 & 0.5 \end{bmatrix}$$

Note that we focused only on the greatest non-diagonal values of *CMs* for detecting the most misclassified classes in our method, but all non-diagonal values can be employed to have a more accurate viewpoint about the difficulty of each class in being classified. Furthermore, a larger sample size for training the second-stage classifier can be generated by duplicating samples of a particular class with fewer elements and put them randomly among those of other classes, so that a stronger and more accurate classification can be achieved for such classes. Additionally, a lot more can be done to measure the similarity between *DP(x)* and *DTs* by using other techniques instead of squared Euclidean distance.

5 Conclusion

In combining classifiers the goal is to achieve superior performance by dividing a complex task into a number of simple ones, and approach the whole solution by solving the simplified tasks.

In this paper we propose to improve the classification performance by finding the most misclassified classes in a dataset and devoting specific classifiers for such classes. In our proposed method, four MPL networks are trained on the training set, which are combined in a Decision Template framework. Considering the Decision Profiles of each classifier, two of the most conflicting classes were identified, and a network in the second stage was trained over these classes. This way, when a sample is classified as the conflicting classes, the decision of the second stage network is considered as the final output. The proposed method was tested on Satimage data of the ELENA dataset, on Image Segmentation dataset and on Soybean dataset, and an overall classification rates of 87.27% for Satimage, 66.57% for Image Segmentation and 83.45% for Soybean were achieved, which demonstrates a 3%, 10.57%, and 4.88% increase in comparison with the best of the state of the art methods on Satimage dataset, Image Segmentation dataset and Soybean dataset, respectively.

References

1. Kuncheva, L.I., Bezdek, J.C., Duin, R.P.W.: Decision Templates for Multiple Classifier Fusion: An Experimental Comparison. Pattern Recognition 34, 299–314 (2001)
2. Kuncheva, L.I.: Combining Classifiers by Clustering, Selection and Decision Templates. Pattern Recognition
3. Ghaderi, R.: Arranging Simple Neural Networks to Solve Complex Classification Problems. Ph.D. Thesis, Surrey University (2000)
4. Kuncheva, L.I.: Using Measures of Similarity and Inclusion for Multiple Classifier Fusion by Decision Templates. Fuzzy Sets and Systems 122, 401–407 (2001)
5. Xu, L., Krzyzak, A., Suen, C.Y.: Methods of Combining Multiple Classifiers and Their Application to Handwriting Recognition. IEEE Trans. System Man Cybernet 22, 418–435 (1992)
6. Ng, K.-C., Abramson, B.: Consensus Diagnosis: a Simulation Study. IEEE Trans. System Man Cybernet. 22, 916–928 (1992)
7. Rogova, G.: Combining the Results of Several Neural Network Classiffiers. Neural Networks 7, 777–781 (1994)

8. Lu, Y., Tan, C.L.: Combination of Multiple Classifiers Using Probabilistic Dictionary and Its Application to Postcode Recognition. Pattern Recognition 35, 2823–2832 (2002)
9. Cerisara, C., Fohr, D.: Multi-Band Automatic Speech Recognition. Computer Speech and Language 15(2), 151–174 (2001)
10. Kuncheva, L.I., Kounchev, R.K., Zlatev, R.Z.: Aggregation of Multiple Classification Decisions by Fuzzy Templates. In: Proceedings of the Third European Congress on Intelligent Technologies and Soft Computing, EUFIT 1995, Aachen, Germany, August 1995, pp. 1470–1474 (1995)
11. Jacobs, R.A., Jordan, M.I., Nowlan, S.E., Hinton, G.E.: Adaptive Mixture of Experts. Neural Comput. 3, 79–87 (1991)
12. Nabavi, S.H.: Thesis: Combining of Multiple Classifiers Based on Their Diversities (2005)
13. Ebrahimpour, R., Kabir, E., Esteky, H., Yousefi, M.R.: View-Independent Face Recognition with Mixture of Experts, accepted 2007. Neurocomputing 71, 1103–1107 (2008)
14. Haykin, S.: Neural Networks—A Comprehensive Foundation, 2nd edn. Prentice-Hall, Englewood Cliffs (1998)
15. Bezdek, J.C., Keller, J.M., Krishnapuram, R., Pal, N.R.: Fuzzy Models and Algorithm for Pattern Recognition and Image Processing. Kluwer Academic Publisher, Dordrecht (1999)
16. Woods, K., Kegelmeyer, W.P., Bowyer, K.: Combination of Multiple Classiffiers Using Local Accuracy Estimates. IEEE Trans. Pattern Anal. Mach. Intell. 19, 405–410 (1997)

CD-Systems of Restarting Automata Governed by Explicit Enable and Disable Conditions

Friedrich Otto

Fachbereich Elektrotechnik/Informatik, Universität Kassel
34109 Kassel, Germany
otto@theory.informatik.uni-kassel.de

Abstract. We introduce a new mode of operation for CD-systems of restarting automata by providing explicit enable and disable conditions in the form of regular constraints. We show that, for each CD-system $\mathcal{M}$ of restarting automata and each mode m of operation considered by Messerschmidt and Otto, there exists a CD-system $\mathcal{M}'$ of restarting automata of the same type as $\mathcal{M}$ that, working in the new mode ed, accepts the language $L_{\mathsf{m}}(\mathcal{M})$ that $\mathcal{M}$ accepts in mode m. Further, we will see that in mode ed, a locally deterministic CD-system of restarting automata of type $\mathsf{RR(W)(W)}$ can be simulated by a locally deterministic CD-system of restarting automata of the more restricted type $\mathsf{R(W)(W)}$.

Keywords: Restarting automaton, CD-system, modes of operation.

1 Introduction

The restarting automaton was introduced by Jančar et al. as a formal tool to model the *analysis by reduction*, which is a technique used in linguistics to analyze sentences of natural languages [3]. This technique consists in a stepwise simplification of a given sentence in such a way that the correctness or incorrectness of the sentence is not affected.

A (one-way) restarting automaton, RRWW-automaton for short, is a device M that consists of a finite-state control, a flexible tape containing a word delimited by sentinels, and a read/write window of a fixed size. This window is moved from left to right until the control decides (nondeterministically) that the content of the window should be rewritten by some *shorter* string. In fact, the new string may contain auxiliary symbols that do not belong to the input alphabet. After a rewrite, M can continue to move its window until it either halts and accepts, or halts and rejects, or restarts, that is, it places its window over the left end of the tape, and reenters the initial state. Thus, each computation of M can be described through a sequence of cycles (which each contain a single application of a rewrite) that is followed by a tail (which is the part of a computation that follows after the last restart step).

Many restricted types of restarting automata have been studied and put into correspondence to more classical classes of formal languages. For recent surveys see [8] and [9]. Also further extensions of the model have been considered. In

J. van Leeuwen et al. (Eds.): SOFSEM 2010, LNCS 5901, pp. 627–638, 2010.

particular, in [5] cooperating distributed systems (CD-systems) of restarting automata have been introduced, and it has been shown that CD-systems of restarting automata working in mode $= 1$ correspond to nonforgetting restarting automata [4,7]. Also some other modes of operation were introduced. In the $= j$ mode ($j \geq 2$) the active component automaton is required to execute exactly j cycles, while in the t mode the active component stays active until it cannot execute another cycle anymore. Hence, the former mode is *static*, as the number of cycles executed by the active component automaton is always the same, while the latter mode is *dynamic*, as the number of cycles executed by the active component automaton depends on the tape content and that component itself.

Here we introduce another dynamic mode of operation for CD-systems of restarting automata by associating explicit *enable* and *disable conditions* with each component automaton. These conditions are given as regular constraints. A component automaton can only become active if at that moment its enable condition is satisfied by the current tape content, and it stays active until its disable condition is satisfied by the (then modified) tape content. This is motivated by similar modes of operation considered for CD-grammar systems [1,2]. We study the expressive power of CD-systems of restarting automata working under this mode of operation, which we call ed *mode*. We will see that, for each CD-system $\mathcal{M}$ and each mode m of operation considered in [5], there exists a CD-system $\mathcal{M}'$ of restarting automata of the same type as $\mathcal{M}$ that, working in mode ed, accepts the language $L_{\mathsf{m}}(\mathcal{M})$ that $\mathcal{M}$ accepts in mode m. On the other hand, the mode ed computations of a CD-system of RR(W)(W)-automata can be simulated by mode $= 1$ computations of a modified CD-system of the same type of restarting automata, which proves that CD-systems of RR(W)(W)-automata working in mode $= 1$ and CD-systems of RR(W)(W)-automata working in mode ed have the same expressive power. Actually these results also extend to CD-systems of RR(W)(W)-automata that are locally or globally deterministic. Further, we will see that in mode ed, a locally deterministic CD-system of restarting automata of type RR(W)(W) can be simulated by a locally deterministic CD-system of restarting automata of the more restricted type R(W)(W). This is the first time that a non-monotone type of R-automaton without auxiliary symbols is shown to be as expressive as the corresponding type of RR-automaton.

This paper is structured as follows. In Section 2 we introduce CD-systems of restarting automata, in Section 3 we define the new mode of operation and compare it to the previously studied modes, and in Section 4 we establish the equivalence between locally deterministic CD-R(W)(W)-systems and locally deterministic CD-RR(W)(W)-systems working in mode ed. The paper closes with a number of open problems in Section 5.

2 Definitions

We first describe the types of restarting automata we will be dealing with. Then we restate the definition of a CD-system of restarting automata from [5].

A *one-way restarting automaton*, abbreviated as RRWW-*automaton*, is a one-tape machine that is described by an 8-tuple $M = (Q, \Sigma, \Gamma, \text{¢}, \$, q_0, k, \delta)$, where

Q is a finite set of states, Σ is a finite input alphabet, Γ is a finite tape alphabet containing Σ, the symbols $¢, \$ \notin \Gamma$ serve as markers for the left and right border of the work space, respectively, $q_0 \in Q$ is the initial state, $k \geq 1$ is the size of the *read/write window*, and δ is the *transition relation* that associates a finite set of *transition steps* to each pair (q, w) consisting of a state $q \in Q$ and a possible content w of the read/write window. There are four types of transition steps: *move-right steps*, *rewrite steps*, *restart steps*, and *accept steps*. However, the behaviour of M can be described more succinctly through a finite set of so-called *meta-instructions* (see below).

A *configuration* of M is described by a string $\alpha q \beta$, where $q \in Q$, and either $\alpha = \varepsilon$ (the empty word) and $\beta \in \{¢\} \cdot \Gamma^* \cdot \{\$\}$ or $\alpha \in \{¢\} \cdot \Gamma^*$ and $\beta \in \Gamma^* \cdot \{\$\}$; here q represents the current state, $\alpha\beta$ is the current content of the tape, and it is understood that the head scans the first k symbols of β or all of β when $|\beta| \leq k$. A *restarting configuration* is of the form $q_0¢w\$$, where $w \in \Gamma^*$; if $w \in \Sigma^*$, then $q_0¢w\$$ is an *initial configuration.*

A *rewriting meta-instruction* for M has the form $(E_1, u \to v, E_2)$, where E_1 and E_2 are regular expressions, and $u, v \in \Gamma^*$ are words satisfying $k \geq |u| > |v|$. To execute a cycle M chooses a meta-instruction of the form $(E_1, u \to v, E_2)$. On trying to execute this meta-instruction M will get stuck (and so reject) starting from the *restarting configuration* $q_0¢w\$$, if w does not admit a factorization of the form $w = w_1uw_2$ such that $¢w_1 \in L(E_1)$ and $w_2\$ \in L(E_2)$. On the other hand, if w does have factorizations of this form, then one such factorization is chosen nondeterministically, and $q_0¢w\$$ is transformed into the restarting configuration $q_0¢w_1vw_2\$$. This computation, which is called a *cycle*, is expressed as $w \vdash_M^c w_1vw_2$. In order to describe the tails of accepting computations we use *accepting meta-instructions* of the form (E_1, Accept), which simply accepts the strings from the regular language $L(E_1)$.

A computation of M now consists of a finite sequence of cycles that is followed by a tail computation. An input word $w \in \Sigma^*$ is *accepted* by M, if there is a computation of M which starts with the initial configuration $q_0¢w\$$, and which finishes by executing an accepting meta-instruction. By $L(M)$ we denote the language consisting of all words accepted by M.

We are also interested in various restricted types of restarting automata. They are obtained by combining two types of restrictions:

(a) Restrictions on the movement of the read/write window (expressed by the first part of the class name): RR- denotes no restriction, and R- means that each rewrite step is immediately followed by a restart.
(b) Restrictions on the rewrite-instructions (expressed by the second part of the class name): -WW denotes no restriction, -W means that no auxiliary symbols are available (that is, $\Gamma = \Sigma$), and -ε means that no auxiliary symbols are available and that each rewrite step is simply a deletion.

Obviously, a rewriting meta-instruction for an RWW-automaton has the form $(E_1, u \to v, \Gamma^* \cdot \$)$, which will be abbreviated as $(E_1, u \to v)$.

A *cooperating distributed system of* RRWW-*automata* (or a CD-RRWW-system for short) consists of a finite collection $\mathcal{M} := ((M_i, \sigma_i)_{i \in I}, I_0)$ of RRWW-automata $M_i = (Q_i, \Sigma, \Gamma_i, ¢, \$, q_0^{(i)}, k, \delta_i)$ $(i \in I)$, *successor relations* $\sigma_i \subseteq I$ $(i \in I)$, and a subset $I_0 \subseteq I$ of *initial indices.* Here it is required that $I_0 \neq \emptyset$, that $\sigma_i \neq \emptyset$ for all $i \in I$, and that $i \notin \sigma_i$ for all $i \in I$. Further, let $\mathrm{m} \in \{\mathsf{t}\} \cup \{= j, \leq j, \geq j \mid j \geq 1\}$ be the chosen *mode of operation.*

The computation of $\mathcal{M}$ in mode $= j$ ($\leq j$, $\geq j$) on an input word w proceeds as follows. First an index $i_0 \in I_0$ is chosen nondeterministically. Then the RRWW-automaton M_{i_0} starts the computation with the initial configuration $q_0^{(i_0)}¢w\$$, and executes j (at most j, at least j) cycles. Thereafter an index $i_1 \in \sigma_{i_0}$ is chosen nondeterministically, and M_{i_1} continues the computation by executing (at most, at least) j cycles. This continues until, for some $l \geq 0$, the machine M_{i_l} accepts. Should at some stage the chosen machine M_{i_l} be unable to execute the required number of cycles, then the computation fails.

In mode t the chosen automaton M_{i_l} continues with the computation until it either accepts, in which case $\mathcal{M}$ accepts, or until it can neither execute another cycle nor an accepting tail, in which case an automaton $M_{i_{l+1}}$ with $i_{l+1} \in \sigma_{i_l}$ takes over. Should this machine not be able to execute a cycle or an accepting tail, then the computation of $\mathcal{M}$ fails.

By $L_{\mathrm{m}}(\mathcal{M})$ we denote the language that the CD-RRWW-system $\mathcal{M}$ accepts in mode m. It consists of all words $w \in \Sigma^*$ that are accepted by $\mathcal{M}$ in mode m as described above. If X is any of the above types of restarting automata, then a CD-X-system is a CD-RRWW-system for which all component automata are of type X. By $\mathcal{L}_{\mathrm{m}}(\mathsf{CD\text{-}X})$ we denote the class of languages that are accepted by CD-X-systems working in mode m.

A CD-system $\mathcal{M} := ((M_i, \sigma_i)_{i \in I}, I_0)$ of restarting automata is called *locally deterministic* if M_i is a deterministic restarting automaton for each $i \in I$. As the successor system is chosen nondeterministically from among all systems M_j with $j \in \sigma_i$, computations of a locally deterministic CD-system of restarting automata are in general not completely deterministic. To avoid this remaining nondeterminism the following variant of determinism has been introduced. A CD-system $\mathcal{M} := ((M_i, \sigma_i)_{i \in I}, I_0)$ is called *globally deterministic* if I_0 is a singleton, if M_i is a deterministic restarting automaton for each $i \in I$, and if, for each $i \in I$, each restart operation of M_i is combined with an index from the set σ_i. Thus, when M_i finishes a part of a computation according to the actual mode of operation by executing the restart operation $\delta_i(q, u) = (\mathsf{Restart}, j)$, where $j \in \sigma_i$, then the component M_j takes over. In this way it is guaranteed that all computations of a globally deterministic CD-system are deterministic. However, for a component system M_i there can still be several possible successor systems. This is reminiscent of the way in which nonforgetting restarting automata (see, e.g., [7]) work. We use the prefixes det-local- and det-global- to denote locally, respectively globally, deterministic CD-systems. As shown in [6] the following inclusions hold for each type of restarting automaton $\mathsf{X} \in \{\mathsf{R}, \mathsf{RR}, \mathsf{RW}, \mathsf{RRW}, \mathsf{RWW}, \mathsf{RRWW}\}$:

$$\mathcal{L}(\mathsf{det\text{-}X}) \subseteq \mathcal{L}_{=1}(\mathsf{det\text{-}global\text{-}CD\text{-}X}) \subseteq \mathcal{L}_{=1}(\mathsf{det\text{-}local\text{-}CD\text{-}X}) \subseteq \mathcal{L}_{=1}(\mathsf{CD\text{-}X}).$$

3 A New Mode of Operation

Let $\mathcal{M} := ((M_i, \sigma_i)_{i\in I}, I_0)$ be a CD-system of restarting automata, and let $(S_i, T_i)_{i\in I}$ be a set of pairs of regular expressions. The system $\mathcal{M}$ is working in mode ed with *enable conditions* $(S_i)_{i\in I}$ and *disable conditions* $(T_i)_{i\in I}$, if a component automaton M_i chosen (be it as the initial component or as a successor component in the course of a computation) can become active only if the current tape content $¢w\$$ belongs to the language $L(S_i)$ – if not, then the current computation fails – and it stays active until it either accepts, rejects, or until the tape content $¢w'\$$ produced by the latest cycle of M_i belongs to the language $L(T_i)$. Thus, if M_i is chosen, and if the current tape content $¢w\$ \in L(S_i)$, then M_i executes a cycle, thereby transforming $¢w\$$ into $¢w'\$$. If $¢w'\$ \in L(T_i)$, then a system M_j with $j \in \sigma_i$ takes over, otherwise M_i executes another cycle. By $L_{\mathsf{ed}}(\mathcal{M})$ we denote the language consisting of all words $w \in \Sigma^*$ that the CD-system $\mathcal{M}$ accepts in mode ed, and by $\mathcal{L}_{\mathsf{ed}}(\mathsf{CD\text{-}X})$ we denote the class of languages that are accepted by CD-X-systems working in mode ed.

Example 1. Let $\mathcal{M} := ((M_i, \sigma_i)_{i\in I}, I_0)$ be the CD-R-system that is specified by $I := \{0, 1, 2\}$, $I_0 := \{0\}$, $\sigma_0 := \{1\}$, $\sigma_1 := \{2\}$, $\sigma_2 := \{0\}$, where the R-automata M_0, M_1, and M_2 are given through the following meta-instructions. Here $\Sigma_0 := \{a, b\}$ and $x, y \in \Sigma_0$:

$$\begin{aligned} M_0 : &(¢ \cdot ((\Sigma_0^2)^+ \cdot xy \cdot \#)^+ \cdot (\Sigma_0^2)^+, xy \cdot \$ \to x \cdot \$),\\ &(¢ \cdot (xy \cdot \#)^+ \cdot xy \cdot \$, \mathsf{Accept}),\\ M_1 : &(¢ \cdot ((\Sigma_0^2)^+ \cdot \Sigma_0 \cdot \#)^* \cdot (\Sigma_0^2)^+, xy \cdot \# \to x \cdot \#),\\ M_2 : &(¢ \cdot ((\Sigma_0^2)^+ \cdot \#)^* \cdot (\Sigma_0^2)^+, x \cdot \# \to \#),\\ &(¢ \cdot ((\Sigma_0^2)^+ \cdot \#)^+ \cdot (\Sigma_0^2)^+, x \cdot \$ \to \$). \end{aligned}$$

In [6] Proposition 13 it is shown that $L_{\mathsf{t}}(\mathcal{M})$ coincides with the *iterated copy language* $L_{\mathrm{copy}^*} := \{\, w(\#w)^n \mid w \in (\Sigma_0^2)^+, n \geq 1 \,\}$. Now we assign regular enable and disable constraints to the components of the system $\mathcal{M}$:

$$\begin{aligned} S_0 &:= ¢ \cdot ((\Sigma_0^2)^+ \cdot \#)^+ \cdot (\Sigma_0^2)^+ \cdot \$, & T_0 &:= ¢ \cdot ((\Sigma_0^2)^+ \cdot \#)^+ \cdot (\Sigma_0^2)^+ \cdot \Sigma_0 \cdot \$,\\ S_1 &:= T_0, & T_1 &:= ¢ \cdot ((\Sigma_0^2)^+ \cdot \Sigma_0 \cdot \#)^+ \cdot (\Sigma_0^2)^+ \cdot \Sigma_0 \cdot \$,\\ S_2 &:= T_1, & T_2 &:= S_0. \end{aligned}$$

Observe that $L_{\mathrm{copy}^*} \subseteq L(S_0)$ holds. Given an input word $w \in \Sigma^*$, $\mathcal{M}$ will reject immediately if $¢ \cdot w \cdot \$ \notin L(S_0)$; otherwise, w can be written as $w = w_0\#w_1\#\ldots\#w_n$ for some words $w_0, \ldots, w_n \in (\Sigma_0^2)^+$ and some integer $n \geq 1$. If all factors w_i are of length 2, and if they all coincide, then $w \in L_{\mathrm{copy}^*}$, and M_0 accepts in a tail computation. If all factors are of length at least 4, and if they all end with the same suffix xy of length 2, then M_0 executes the cycle

$$w = w_0\#w_1\#\ldots\#w_n \vdash^c_{M_0} w_0\#w_1\#\ldots\#z_n x =: x_1,$$

where $w_i = z_i xy$ for all $i = 0, \ldots, n$. In all remaining cases M_0 will reject, but then $w \notin L_{\mathrm{copy}^*}$ anyway.

So assume that M_0 executes the cycle above. As $¢\cdot x_1\cdot\$ \in L(T_0)$, M_0 terminates after this cycle, and M_1 takes over. As $S_1 = T_0$, the enable condition of M_1 is satisfied, and M_1 performs the following computation:

$$x_1 = w_0\#w_1\#\ldots\#z_nx \vdash^{c^*}_{M_1} z_0x\#z_1x\#\ldots\#z_nx =: x_2.$$

As $¢ \cdot x_2 \cdot \$ \in L(T_1)$, M_1 now terminates, and M_2 takes over, which is possible as $S_2 = T_1$ holds. Now M_2 performs the computation

$$x_2 = z_0x\#z_1x\#\ldots\#z_nx \vdash^{c^*}_{M_2} z_0\#z_1\#\ldots\#z_n =: x_3,$$

and as $¢ \cdot x_3 \cdot \$ \in L(T_2)$, M_2 then terminates. Now M_0 takes over again, and as $T_2 = S_0$, this is indeed possible. Inductively it follows that the input word x is accepted if and only if w belongs to the language L_{copy^*}, that is, $L_{\mathsf{ed}}(\mathcal{M}) = L_{\text{copy}^*}$ follows. Thus, using the given enable and disable conditions $\mathcal{M}$ accepts in mode ed the same language that it accepts in mode t.

Actually the above construction generalizes to arbitrary CD-systems of restarting automata.

Theorem 1. *Let* $\mathcal{M} := ((M_i, \sigma_i)_{i\in I}, I_0)$ *be a* CD-X-*system for any* $\mathsf{X} \in \{\mathsf{R}, \mathsf{RR}, \mathsf{RW}, \mathsf{RRW}, \mathsf{RWW}, \mathsf{RRWW}\}$. *Then there exists a collection of regular enable and disable conditions* $(S_i, T_i)_{i\in I}$ *such that, with respect to these conditions, the languages* $L_{\mathsf{ed}}(\mathcal{M})$ *and* $L_{\mathsf{t}}(\mathcal{M})$ *coincide.*

An analogous result can be established for the $= 1$ mode by choosing appropriate enable and disable conditions.

Theorem 2. *Let* $\mathcal{M} := ((M_i, \sigma_i)_{i\in I}, I_0)$ *be a* CD-X-*system for any* $\mathsf{X} \in \{\mathsf{R}, \mathsf{RR}, \mathsf{RW}, \mathsf{RRW}, \mathsf{RWW}, \mathsf{RRWW}\}$. *Then there exists a collection of regular enable and disable conditions* $(S_i, T_i)_{i\in I}$ *such that, with respect to these conditions, the languages* $L_{\mathsf{ed}}(\mathcal{M})$ *and* $L_{=1}(\mathcal{M})$ *coincide.*

Theorems 1 and 2 hold in particular also for CD-X-systems that are locally or globally deterministic.

A CD-system of restarting automata that is working in mode $= j$ for some $j \geq 2$ can also be simulated by a CD-system of restarting automata that is working in mode ed. However, the simulating system has j component automata for each component automaton of the system being simulated.

Theorem 3. *Let* $\mathcal{M} := ((M_i, \sigma_i)_{i\in I}, I_0)$ *be a* CD-X-*system for any* $\mathsf{X} \in \{\mathsf{R}, \mathsf{RR}, \mathsf{RW}, \mathsf{RRW}, \mathsf{RWW}, \mathsf{RRWW}\}$, *and let* $j \geq 2$. *Then there exists a* CD-X-*system* $\mathcal{M}' := ((M'_{(i,\mu)}, \sigma'_{(i,\mu)})_{(i,\mu)\in I\times\{1,\ldots,j\}}, I'_0)$ *and regular enable and disable conditions* $(S_{(i,\mu)}, T_{(i,\mu)})$, $(i,\mu) \in I \times \{1,\ldots,j\}$, *such that the languages* $L_{\mathsf{ed}}(\mathcal{M}')$ *and* $L_{=j}(\mathcal{M})$ *coincide. In addition, if* $\mathcal{M}$ *is globally deterministic or locally deterministic, then so is* $\mathcal{M}'$.

For nondeterministic CD-systems of restarting automata, Theorem 3 also extends to modes $\leq j$ and $\geq j$. Thus, the ed mode is sufficiently powerful to simulate all the other modes considered so far. On the other hand, it can be shown that the $= 1$ mode is as expressive as the ed mode.

Theorem 4. *Let* $\mathcal{M} := ((M_i, \sigma_i)_{i \in I}, I_0)$ *be a* CD-X-*system for any* $\mathsf{X} \in \{\mathsf{RR}, \mathsf{RRW}, \mathsf{RRWW}\}$, *and let* $(S_i, T_{i,})$, $i \in I$, *be a collection of regular enable and disable conditions for* $\mathcal{M}$. *Then there exists a* CD-X-*system* $\mathcal{M}' := ((M'_i, \sigma'_i)_{i \in I'}, I'_0)$ *such that the languages* $L_{=1}(\mathcal{M}')$ *and* $L_{\mathsf{ed}}(\mathcal{M})$ *coincide. In addition, if* $\mathcal{M}$ *is locally deterministic, then a locally deterministic system* $\mathcal{M}'$ *can be taken.*

Proof. Let $\mathcal{M} := ((M_i, \sigma_i)_{i \in I}, I_0)$ be a CD-X-system, and let $(S_i, T_{i,})$, $i \in I$, be a collection of regular enable and disable conditions for $\mathcal{M}$. Without loss of generality we can assume that $I = \{1, \ldots, n\}$.

We define a CD-X-system $\mathcal{M}' := ((M'_i, \sigma'_i)_{i \in I'}, I'_0)$ as follows. Each component M_i of $\mathcal{M}$ will be simulated by $n + 2$ components of $\mathcal{M}'$. In addition, we need three components for each initial component of $\mathcal{M}$. Accordingly, we take $I' := (I \times \{1, \ldots, n+2\}) \cup \{ (\hat{\imath}, j) \mid i \in I_0, 1 \leq j \leq 3 \}$. For each $i \in I$ and each $j \in \{1, \ldots, n+2\}$, $M'_{(i,j)}$ is a copy of M_i, and for each $i \in I_0$ and each $j \in \{1, 2, 3\}$, $M'_{(\hat{\imath},j)}$ is another copy of M_i. These copies are modified as follows:

- For $j = 1, \ldots, n$, component $M'_{(i,j)}$ verifies with each of its meta-instructions that the tape content $\cent w\$$ of the actual restarting configuration belongs to the regular set $L(S_i) \cap L(T_j)$, that is, that it satisfies the enable condition of component M_i and the disable condition of component M_j. In the affirmative, it just executes the current meta-instruction of M_i, but in the negative it halts and rejects.
- For $j = n+1, n+2$, component $M'_{(i,j)}$ verifies with each of its meta-instructions that the tape content $\cent w\$$ of the actual restarting configuration does not belong to the regular set $L(T_i)$, that is, that it does not satisfy the disable condition of component M_i. In the affirmative, it just executes the current meta-instruction of M_i, but in the negative it halts and rejects.
- For $i \in I_0$, component $M'_{(\hat{\imath},1)}$ verifies with each of its meta-instructions that the tape content $\cent w\$$ of the actual restarting configuration belongs to the regular set $L(S_i)$, that is, that it satisfies the enable condition of component M_i. Components $M'_{(\hat{\imath},2)}$ and $M'_{(\hat{\imath},3)}$ verify with each of their meta-instructions that the tape content $\cent w\$$ of the actual restarting configuration does not belong to the regular set $L(T_i)$, that is, that it does not satisfy the disable condition of component M_i.

For the initial indices of $\mathcal{M}'$ we take the set $I'_0 := \{ (\hat{\imath}, 1) \mid i \in I_0 \}$, and we define the successor relations as follows:

$$
\begin{array}{lll}
\sigma'_{(i,j)} & := \{(i, n+1)\} \cup \{ (l, i) \mid l \in \sigma_i \} & \text{for all } i \in I \text{ and all } 1 \leq j \leq n, \\
\sigma'_{(i,n+1)} & := \{(i, n+2)\} \cup \{ (l, i) \mid l \in \sigma_i \} & \text{for all } i \in I, \\
\sigma'_{(i,n+2)} & := \{(i, n+1)\} \cup \{ (l, i) \mid l \in \sigma_i \} & \text{for all } i \in I, \\
\sigma'_{(\hat{\imath},1)} & := \{(\hat{\imath}, 2)\} \cup \{ (l, i) \mid l \in \sigma_i \} & \text{for all } i \in I_0, \\
\sigma'_{(\hat{\imath},2)} & := \{(\hat{\imath}, 3)\} \cup \{ (l, i) \mid l \in \sigma_i \} & \text{for all } i \in I_0, \\
\sigma'_{(\hat{\imath},3)} & := \{(\hat{\imath}, 2)\} \cup \{ (l, i) \mid l \in \sigma_i \} & \text{for all } i \in I_0.
\end{array}
$$

Now, given an input $w \in \Sigma^*$, an index $i_0 \in I_0$ is chosen, and component M_{i_0} begins the computation of $\mathcal{M}$ on input w by executing a certain number of cycles. Actually, it is first checked whether $¢w\$$ belongs to the regular set $L(S_{i_0})$, and then M_{i_0} continues with the computation until it either terminates (accepting or non-accepting) or until the tape content $¢w_1\$$ obtained belongs to the regular set $L(T_{i_0})$. Then an index $i_1 \in \sigma_{i_0}$ is chosen, and component M_{i_1} continues with the computation, provided that the tape content belongs to the regular set $L(S_{i_1})$. This continues until the actual component terminates.

Now let us consider the possible mode $= 1$ computations of $\mathcal{M}'$ on input w. Here we can choose the initial component $M'_{(\hat{i}_0,1)}$. It verifies that the tape content belongs to the regular set $L(S_{i_0})$, and in the affirmative it executes the same cycle as M_{i_0}. Then $M'_{(\hat{i}_0,2)}$ becomes active. It checks that the current tape content does not belong to the regular set $L(T_{i_0})$, and in the affirmative it executes the same cycle as M_{i_0}. Thereafter $M'_{(\hat{i}_0,3)}$ becomes active. Thus, by alternating between the latter two components the computation of M_{i_0} described above is being simulated. At some stage the index $(i_1, i_0) \in \sigma'_{(\hat{i}_0,j)}$ $(j \in \{1,2,3\})$ is chosen, and component $M'_{(i_1,i_0)}$ continues with the computation. It verifies that the actual tape content belongs to the regular set $L(S_{i_1})$ as well as to the regular set $L(T_{i_0})$, which corresponds to the situation in the above computation of $\mathcal{M}$ when component M_{i_1} takes over from component M_{i_0}. If these constraints are met, then $M'_{(i_1,i_0)}$ executes the same cycle as M_{i_1}, and then $M'_{(i_1,n+1)}$ becomes active. It checks that the current tape content does not belong to the regular set $L(T_{i_1})$, and in the affirmative it executes the next cycle of M_{i_1}. It follows that in mode $= 1$, $\mathcal{M}'$ can simulate all mode ed computations of $\mathcal{M}$. Conversely, it can be shown that the mode $= 1$ computations of $\mathcal{M}'$ can only simulate mode ed computations of $\mathcal{M}$. It follows that $L_{=1}(\mathcal{M}') = L_{\mathsf{ed}}(\mathcal{M})$ holds. Further, $\mathcal{M}'$ is locally deterministic, if $\mathcal{M}$ is. □

Thus, we have the following consequences.

Corollary 1. *For all* $\mathsf{X} \in \{\mathsf{RR}, \mathsf{RRW}, \mathsf{RRWW}\}$,
$\mathcal{L}_{\mathsf{ed}}(\text{CD-X}) = \mathcal{L}_{=1}(\text{CD-X})$ *and* $\mathcal{L}_{\mathsf{ed}}(\text{det-local-CD-X}) = \mathcal{L}_{=1}(\text{det-local-CD-X})$.

For globally deterministic CD-RR(W)(W)-systems we have a corresponding result. However, for these systems we need a different technique for constructing the system $\mathcal{M}'$.

Theorem 5. *Let* $\mathcal{M} := ((M_i, \sigma_i)_{i \in I}, I_0)$ *be a globally deterministic* CD-X-*system for any* $\mathsf{X} \in \{\mathsf{RR}, \mathsf{RRW}, \mathsf{RRWW}\}$, *and let* $(S_i, T_{i,})$, $i \in I$, *be a collection of regular enable and disable conditions for* $\mathcal{M}$. *Then there exists a globally deterministic* CD-X-*system* $\mathcal{M}' := ((M'_i, \sigma'_i)_{i \in I'}, I'_0)$ *such that the languages* $L_{=1}(\mathcal{M}')$ *and* $L_{\mathsf{ed}}(\mathcal{M})$ *coincide.*

Proof. Let $\mathcal{M} := ((M_i, \sigma_i)_{i \in I}, i_0)$ be a globally deterministic CD-X-system, and let $(S_i, T_{i,})$, $i \in I$, be a collection of regular enable and disable conditions for $\mathcal{M}$. Again we can assume without loss of generality that $I = \{1, \ldots, n\}$.

We define a globally deterministic CD-X-system $\mathcal{M}' := ((M_i', \sigma_i')_{i \in I'}, i_0')$ as follows. Each component M_i of $\mathcal{M}$ will be simulated by three components of $\mathcal{M}'$. Accordingly, we take $I' := I \times \{1,2,3\}$, and take $i_0' := (i_0, 1)$. For each $i \in I$, the three components $M'_{(i,\mu)}$, $1 \leq \mu \leq 3$, are obtained as copies of M_i that are slightly modified as follows:

- $M'_{(i,1)}$ verifies with each of its meta-instructions that the tape content $¢w\$$ of the actual restarting configuration belongs to regular set $L(S_i)$. In addition, it checks with each of its rewriting meta-instructions whether the tape content $¢w_1vw_2\$$ produced by applying this meta-instruction belongs to the regular set $L(T_i)$. In the affirmative, the restart operation of this meta-instruction is associated to the index $(l,1)$, where $l \in \sigma_i$ is the index that is associated with the corresponding restart operation of M_i. In the negative, that is, if the resulting tape content does not yet meet the disable condition of M_i, the restart operation of this meta-instruction is associated to the index $(i,2)$.
- For $s \in \{2,3\}$, $M'_{(i,s)}$ checks with each of its rewriting meta-instructions whether the tape content $¢w_1vw_2\$$ produced by applying this meta-instruction belongs to the regular set $L(T_i)$. In the affirmative, the restart operation of this meta-instruction is associated to the index $(l,1)$, where $l \in \sigma_i$ is the index that is associated with the corresponding restart operation of M_i. In the negative the restart operation of this meta-instruction is associated to the index $(i, 5-s)$.

Thus, $\mathcal{M}'$ is indeed a globally deterministic CD-X-system. Further, it is easily seen that in mode $= 1$ it simulates the mode ed computations of $\mathcal{M}$. It follows that $L_{=1}(\mathcal{M}') = L_{\mathsf{ed}}(\mathcal{M})$ holds. □

Currently it remains open whether Theorems 4 and 5 extend to CD-R(W)(W)-systems. Thus, it is not known whether the inclusion $\mathcal{L}_{=1}(\text{CD-R(W)(W)}) \subseteq \mathcal{L}_{\mathsf{ed}}(\text{CD-R(W)(W)})$ of Theorem 2 is proper or not.

4 Locally Deterministic CD-R-Systems versus Locally Deterministic CD-RR-Systems

Here we compare the expressive power of locally deterministic CD-R(W)(W)-systems working in mode ed to that of locally deterministic CD-RR(W)(W)-systems working in mode ed. To this end we first study the information that a description by meta-instructions reveals on a deterministic RRWW-automaton.

Let $M = (Q, \Sigma, \Gamma, ¢, \$, q_0, k, \delta)$ be a deterministic RRWW-automaton, and let $I_0 = (E_0, \mathsf{Accept})$ and $I_i = (E_i, u_i \to v_i, E_i')$ $(1 \leq i \leq n)$ be a sequence of meta-instructions that describe the behaviour of M. Here we can assume without loss of generality that $|u_i| = k$ holds for all $i = 1, \ldots, n$. As M is deterministic, the above meta-instructions are used as follows. Assume that M is in the restarting configuration $q_0¢w\$$. Then M scans the tape from left to right until it detects the shortest prefix w_1 of w such that $w_1 = w_3u_i$ and $¢w_3 \in L(E_i)$ for some

$i \in \{1, \ldots, n\}$. It then rewrites u_i into v_i and checks whether the corresponding suffix w_2 of w belongs to the language $L(E'_i)$. At the same time it checks whether the original tape content $¢w\$$ belongs to the language $L(E_0)$. If the latter holds, then M halts and accepts; if $¢w\$ \notin L(E_0)$, but $w_2\$ \in L(E'_i)$, then M restarts in the restarting configuration $q_0¢w_3v_iw_2\$$. Finally, if $w_2\$ \in L(E'_i)$ does not hold, either, then M halts and rejects. If no prefix of the above form is found, then M halts and rejects as well, unless $¢w\$ \in L(E_0)$ holds, in which case M halts and accepts. Thus, we can replace each regular constraint E_i by a regular constraint F_i satisfying

$$L(F_i) = \{\, ¢w \in L(E_i) \mid \text{ No proper prefix of } ¢wu_i \text{ is in } \bigcup_{r=1}^{n} (L(E_r) \cdot u_r) \,\},$$

and the resulting meta-instructions $I'_i = (F_i, u_i \to v_i, E'_i)$ $(1 \le i \le n)$ will describe M together with I_0.

The new constraints have the following advantage. If $¢w\$ \in \bigcup_{i=1}^{n} (L(F_i) \cdot u_i \cdot L(E'_i))$, then there exist a unique index $i \in \{1, \ldots, n\}$ and a unique factorization $w = w_1u_iw_2$ such that $¢w_1 \in L(F_i)$ and $w_2\$ \in L(E'_i)$ hold. Thus, if it is known that $¢w\$ \in \bigcup_{i=1}^{n} (L(F_i) \cdot u_i \cdot L(E'_i))$ holds, then on detecting a prefix w_1 of w satisfying $¢w_1u_i \in L(F_i) \cdot u_i$, it is guaranteed that the corresponding suffix w_2 of w satisfies the condition $w_2\$ \in L(E'_i)$. Observe, however, that in general the intersection $L(E_0) \cap \bigcup_{i=1}^{n} (L(F_i) \cdot u_i \cdot L(E'_i))$ will not be empty, that is, some words are accepted by M in tail computations that have a prefix belonging to the language $L(F_i) \cdot u_i$ for some value of i. We now use this observation for establishing the following result on locally deterministic CD-R(W)(W)-systems working in mode ed.

Theorem 6
For all $\mathsf{X} \in \{\lambda, \mathsf{W}, \mathsf{WW}\}$, $\mathcal{L}_{\mathsf{ed}}(\text{det-local-CD-RRX}) \subseteq \mathcal{L}_{\mathsf{ed}}(\text{det-local-CD-RX})$.

Proof. Because of Corollary 1 it suffices to consider locally deterministic CD-RRX-systems that are working in mode $= 1$. So let $\mathcal{M} := ((M_i, \sigma_i)_{i \in I}, I_0)$ be a locally deterministic CD-RRX-system, and let $L = L_{=1}(\mathcal{M})$. Each component M_i can be described by a finite sequence of meta-instructions of the form $(I_{i,0}, I_{i,1}, \ldots, I_{i,n_i})$, where $I_{i,0} = (E_{i,0}, \mathsf{Accept})$ is an accepting meta-instruction, and $I_{i,j} = (E_{i,j}, u_{i,j} \to v_{i,j}, E'_{i,j})$ $(1 \le j \le n_i)$ are rewriting meta-instructions.

We now construct a locally deterministic CD-RX-system $\mathcal{M}'$ and enable and disable conditions such that $L_{\mathsf{ed}}(\mathcal{M}') = L$ holds. In this construction we will have two components $P_{(i,a)}$ and $P_{(i,c)}$ for each component M_i. Thus, we take $\mathcal{M}' := ((P_{(i,\mu)}, \sigma_{(i,\mu)})_{i \in I, \mu \in \{a,c\}}, I'_0)$, where

$$\sigma_{(i,a)} := \sigma_{(i,c)} := \{\, (j,a), (j,c) \mid j \in \sigma_i \,\} \text{ for all } i \in I,$$

and

$$I'_0 := \{\, (i,a), (i,c) \mid i \in I_0 \,\}.$$

For each index $i \in I$, the component $P_{(i,a)}$ is described by the accepting meta-instruction $I_{i,0}$. Its enable condition $S_{(i,a)}$ is simply the language $¢ \cdot \Gamma^* \cdot \$$, where Γ is the (combined) tape alphabet of the components of $\mathcal{M}$, and its disable condition $T_{(i,a)}$ is the same language. If this component is called during a computation of $\mathcal{M}'$, then the computation necessarily ends: either the tape content $¢w\$$ belongs to the regular language $L(E_{i,0})$ and $P_{(i,a)}$ accepts, or it does not belong to this language, and then $P_{(i,a)}$ rejects.

It remains to define the components $P_{(i,c)}$ and the enable and disable conditions $S_{(i,c)}$ and $T_{(i,c)}$ for all $i \in I$. Let $i \in I$, and let $j \in \{1, \ldots, n_i\}$. By $F_{i,j}$ we denote a regular expression for the language

$$L(F_{i,j}) = \{ ¢w \in L(E_{i,j}) \mid \text{No proper prefix of } ¢wu_{i,j} \text{ is in } \bigcup_{r=1}^{n_i}(L(E_{i,r}) \cdot u_{i,r}) \}.$$

We define $P_{(i,c)}$ by the meta-instructions $I'_{i,j} := (F_{i,j}, u_{i,j} \to v_{i,j})$ $(1 \leq j \leq n_i)$, and take

$$S_{(i,c)} := \bigcup_{j=1}^{n_i}(L(F_{i,j}) \cdot u_{i,j} \cdot L(E'_{i,j})), \text{ and } T_{(i,c)} := ¢ \cdot \Gamma^* \cdot \$.$$

If this component is called during a computation of $\mathcal{M}'$, and if $¢w\$$ is the corresponding restarting configuration, then the enable condition $S_{(i,c)}$ checks whether w admits a factorization of the form $w = w_1 u_{i,j} w_2$ for some index $j \in \{1, \ldots, n_i\}$ such that $¢w_1 \in L(F_{i,j})$ and $w_2\$ \in L(E'_{i,j})$. If such a factorization does not exist, then $P_{(i,c)}$ halts and rejects. However, we see from the discussion above that then none of the meta-instruction $I_{i,j}$ $(1 \leq j \leq n_i)$ of M_i is applicable, either. Otherwise, let $w_1 u_{i,j}$ be the shortest prefix of w to which a meta-instruction of M_i applies. Then $P_{(i,c)}$ executes exactly the same cycle that M_i would execute in this situation. From the disable condition $T_{(i,c)}$ we see that in mode ed the component $P_{(i,c)}$ will execute a single cycle only. It follows that $L_{\mathsf{ed}}(\mathcal{M}') = L_{=1}(\mathcal{M})$. □

Together with Corollary 1 and the trivial inclusion

$$\mathcal{L}_{\mathsf{ed}}(\text{det-local-CD-RX}) \subseteq \mathcal{L}_{\mathsf{ed}}(\text{det-local-CD-RRX})$$

this yields the following equalities.

Corollary 2. *For all* $\mathsf{X} \in \{\lambda, \mathsf{W}, \mathsf{WW}\}$,

$$\mathcal{L}_{\mathsf{ed}}(\text{det-local-CD-RX}) = \mathcal{L}_{\mathsf{ed}}(\text{det-local-CD-RRX}) = \mathcal{L}_{=1}(\text{det-local-CD-RRX}).$$

5 Concluding Remarks

It currently remains open whether Theorem 6 also holds for globally deterministic CD-systems. If $\mathcal{M}$ is a globally deterministic CD-RRWW-system, and if $¢w\$$ is the tape content at the beginning of a cycle in which component automaton M_i is active, then the suffix w_2 of a factorization $w = w_1 u_{i,j} w_2$, where $¢w_1 \in L(E_{i,j})$ for a meta-instruction $(E_{i,j}, u_{i,j} \to v_{i,j}, E'_{i,j})$ of M_i, may determine the corresponding successor component. However, the corresponding component automaton of a simulating globally deterministic CD-RWW-system will need to actually read this suffix in the corresponding cycle. Hence, the construction from the proof of Theorem 6 does not carry over to globally deterministic CD-systems. Further, it is open whether the corresponding result holds for nondeterministic CD-systems. Also the following questions and problems remain for future work:

1. Does Theorem 4 extend to CD-R-, CD-RW-, and CD-RWW-automata? If so, then together with Theorem 6 this would imply that also in mode = 1 locally deterministic CD-R(W)(W)-systems are as expressive as locally deterministic CD-RR(W)(W)-systems.
2. Does Theorem 4 extend to other modes of operation? Or is it possible to establish a proper separation result, at least for those types of restarting automata that have no auxiliary symbols?
3. Another topic for research is the question about the number of components that are needed to accept a certain language. From the proofs above it appears that less components may be needed in the ed mode of operation than in the = 1 mode of operation.

Acknowledgement. The author thanks Erzsébet Csuhaj-Varjú for a very interesting discussion on the enable/disable mode for CD grammar systems.

References

1. Csuhaj-Varjú, E., Dassow, J., Kelemen, J., Păun, G.: Grammar Systems. A Grammatical Approach to Distribution and Cooperation. Gordon and Breach, London (1994)
2. Dassow, J., Kelemen, J.: Cooperating/Distributed Grammar Systems: A Link between Formal Languages and Artificial Intelligence. Bulletin of the EATCS 45, 131–145 (1991)
3. Jančar, P., Mráz, F., Plátek, M., Vogel, J.: Restarting Automata. In: Reichel, H. (ed.) FCT 1995. LNCS, vol. 965, pp. 283–292. Springer, Heidelberg (1995)
4. Messerschmidt, H., Otto, F.: On Nonforgetting Restarting Automata that Are Deterministic and/or Monotone. In: Grigoriev, D., Harrison, J., Hirsch, E.A. (eds.) CSR 2006. LNCS, vol. 3967, pp. 247–258. Springer, Heidelberg (2006)
5. Messerschmidt, H., Otto, F.: Cooperating Distributed Systems of Restarting Automata. Int. J. Found. Comput. Sci. 18, 1333–1342 (2007)
6. Messerschmidt, H., Otto, F.: On Deterministic CD-Systems of Restarting Automata. Int. J. Found. Comput. Sci. 20, 185–209 (2009)
7. Messerschmidt, H., Stamer, H.: Restart-Automaten mit mehreren Restart-Zuständen. In: Bordihn, H. (ed.) Workshop Formale Methoden in der Linguistik und 14. Theorietag Automaten und Formale Sprachen. Proc., Institut für Informatik, pp. 111–116. Universität Potsdam (2004)
8. Otto, F.: Restarting Automata and Their Relations to the Chomsky Hierarchy. In: Ésik, Z., Fülöp, Z. (eds.) DLT 2003. LNCS, vol. 2710, pp. 55–74. Springer, Heidelberg (2003)
9. Otto, F.: Restarting Automata. In: Ésik, Z., Martin-Vide, C., Mitrana, V. (eds.) Recent Advances in Formal Languages and Applications. Studies in Computational Intelligence, vol. 25, pp. 269–303. Springer, Berlin (2006)

Source Code Rejuvenation Is Not Refactoring

Peter Pirkelbauer, Damian Dechev, and Bjarne Stroustrup

Department of Computer Science and Engineering
Texas A&M University
College Station, TX 77843-3112
{peter.pirkelbauer,dechev}@tamu.edu, bs@cse.tamu.edu

Abstract. Programmers rely on programming idioms, design patterns, and workaround techniques to make up for missing programming language support. Evolving languages often address frequently encountered problems by adding language and library support to subsequent releases. By using new features, programmers can express their intent more directly. As new concerns, such as parallelism or security, arise, early idioms and language facilities can become serious liabilities. Modern code sometimes benefits from optimization techniques not feasible for code that uses less expressive constructs. Manual source code migration is expensive, time-consuming, and prone to errors.

In this paper, we present the notion of *source code rejuvenation*, the automated migration of legacy code and very briefly mention the tools we use to achieve that. While *refactoring* improves structurally inadequate source code, source code rejuvenation leverages enhanced program language and library facilities by finding and replacing coding patterns that can be expressed through higher-level software abstractions. Raising the level of abstraction benefits software maintainability, security, and performance.

1 Introduction

Popular programming languages evolve over time. One driver of evolution is a desire to simplify the use of these languages in real life projects. For example, in the early 1970ies the C programming language was developed as a system programming language for the UNIX operating system on the PDP-11 [1]. With the proliferation of UNIX to other platforms, C evolved to reflect concerns such as portability and type safety. Later Stroustrup enhanced C with higher level abstractions to simplify the development of a distributed and modularized UNIX kernel [2]. Compared to C, ISO C++ [3] directly supports the program design with classes, dynamic dispatch, templates, exception handling, and more [2]. Abstraction mechanisms present in C++ can be compiled to efficient machine code on many architectures. This makes C++ suitable for software development of embedded systems, desktop computers, and mainframe architectures. C++'s proliferation and success is a constant source of ideas for enhancements and extensions. The ISO C++ standards committee has released a draft of the next revision of the C++ standard, commonly referred to as C++0x [4] [5]. C++0x will

J. van Leeuwen et al. (Eds.): SOFSEM 2010, LNCS 5901, pp. 639–650, 2010.

address a number of modeling problems (e.g., object initialization) by providing better language and library support. Until compiler and library implementations of C++0x become widely available, C++ programmers solve these problems through programming idioms and workaround techniques. These "solutions" are typically more involved than they would be in C++0x and can easily become another source of errors and maintenance problems.

This paper draws its examples from C++0x's proposed extensions to the language and its standardized libraries [6], but the topic is equally valid for other widely used and evolving languages, such as Python [7], C# [8], and Java [9]. For example, Java is currently undergoing its sixth major revision since its first release in 1995. Extensions under consideration for Java 7 include support for closures, null safe method invocations, extended catch clauses to catch and rethrow groups of exceptions, type inference for generics and others [10].
The contributions of this paper are:

- We define the term *source code rejuvenation* and delineate it from related fields.
- We demonstrate source code rejuvenation with examples that migrate code from C++03 to C++0x.

The rest of this paper is outlined as follows: In §2, we define the term source code rejuvenation. In §3, we demonstrate source code rejuvenation based on C++0x language features. In §4, we put our work in context to refactoring. In §5, we describe the tool we use to implement source code rejuvenation tools. In §6, we summarize.

2 What Is Source Code Rejuvenation?

Source code rejuvenation is a source-to-source transformation that replaces deprecated language features and idioms with modern code. Old code typically contains outdated idioms, elaborate and often complex coding patterns, deprecated language features (or data structures). The rejuvenated code is more concise, safer, and uses higher level abstractions. What we call outdated idioms (and patterns) are techniques often developed in response to the lack of direct language support. When programming languages and techniques evolve, these coding styles become legacy code, as programmers will express new code in terms of new language features. This leads to a mix of coding styles, which complicates a programmer's understanding of source code and can cause maintenance problems. Furthermore, the teaching and learning can be greatly simplified by eliminating outdated language features and idioms.

Source code rejuvenation is a *unidirectional process* that detects coding techniques expressed in terms of lower-level language and converts them into code using higher-level abstractions. High-level abstractions make information explicit to programmers and compilers that would otherwise remain buried in more involved code. We aim to automate many forms of code rejuvenation and to provide program assistance for cases where human intervention is necessary. In other words, our aim is nothing less than to reverse (some forms of) (software) entropy!

Preserving behavioral equivalence between code transformations is necessary to claim correctness. In the context of source code rejuvenation, a strict interpretation of behavior preservation would disallow meaningful transformations (e.g., see the initializer list example §3.1). We therefore argue that a valid source code rejuvenation preserves or improves a program's behavior. In addition, when a rejuvenation tool detects a potential problem but does not have sufficient information to gurantee a correct code transformation, it can point the programmer to potential trouble spots and suggest rejuvenation. For example, a tool can propose the use of the C++0x's array class instead of C style arrays. A C++0x array object passed as function argument does not decay to a pointer. The argument retains its size information, which allows a rejuvenation tool to suggest bounds checking of data accesses in functions that take arrays as parameters.

2.1 Applications

Source code rejuvenation is an enabling technology and tool support for source code rejuvenation leverages the new languages capabilities in several aspects:

Source Code Migration: Upgrading to the next iteration of a language can invalidate existing code. For example, a language can choose to improve static type safety by tightening the type checking rules. As result formerly valid code produces pesty error or warning messages. An example is Java's introduction of generics. Starting with Java 5 the compiler warns about the unparametrized use of Java's container classes.

Even with source code remaining valid, automated source code migration makes the transition to new language versions smoother. For example, programmers would not need to understand and maintain source files that use various workaround techniques instead of (later added) language constructs. For example, a project might use template based libraries (e.g., Standard Template Library (STL) [11], STAPL [12]) where some were developed for C++03 and others for C++0x. In such a situation, programmers are required to understand both.

Education: Integration with a smart IDE enables "live" suggestions that can replace workarounds/idioms with new language constructs, thereby educating programmers on how to better use available language and library constructs.

Optimization: The detection of workarounds and idioms can contribute a significant factor to both the development cost of a compiler and the runtime, as the detection and transformation requires time. Compiler vendors are often reluctant to add optimizations for every single scenario. The introduction of new language constructs can enable more and better optimizations (e.g., `const_expr` lets the compiler evaluate expressions at compile time [5]). Automated source code migration that performs a one-time source code transformation to utilize the new language support enables optimizations that might be forgone otherwise.

3 Case Studies

In this section, we demonstrate source code rejuvenation with examples taken from C++0x, namely initializer lists and concept extraction.

3.1 Initializer Lists

In current C++, the initialization of a container (or any other object) with an arbitrary number of different values is cumbersome. When needed, programmers deal with the problem by employing different initialization idioms.

Consider initializing a vector of **int** with three constant elements (e.g., 1, 2, 3). Techniques to achieve this include writing three consecutive push_back operations, and copying constants from an array of **int**. We can "initialize" through a series of push_back()s:

```
// using namespace std;
vector<int> vec;

// three consecutive push_backs
vec.push_back(1);
vec.push_back(2);
vec.push_back(3);
```

Alternatively, we can initialize an array and use that to initialize the vector:

```
// copying from an array
int a[] = {1, 2, 3};
vector<int> vec(a,a+sizeof(a)/sizeof(int));
```

These are just the two simplest examples of such workarounds observed in real code. Although the described initialization techniques look trivial, it is easy to accidentally write erroneous or non-optimal code. For example, in the first example the vector resizes its internal data structure whenever the allocated memory capacity is insufficient to store a new value; in some situations that may be a performance problem. The second example is simply a technique that people often get wrong (e.g. by using the wrong array type or by specifying the wrong size for the vector). Other workarounds tend to be longer, more complicated, and more-error prone. Rejuvenating the code to use C++0x's initializer list construction [13] automatically remedies this problem.

```
// rejuvenated source code in C++0x
vector<int> vec = {1, 2, 3};
```

In C++0x, the list of values (1, 2, 3) becomes an initializer list. Initializer list constructors take the list of values as argument and construct the initial object state. As a result, the rejuvenated source code is more concise – needs only one line of code (LOC) when compared to two and four LOC needed by the workaround techniques. The rejuvenated source code becomes more uniform: every workaround is replaced by the same construct. In this particular case, we gain the additional effect that the rejuvenated code code style is analogous to C style array initialization (compare the definition of the array a in the code snippet with the workaround examples). Thus, the reader does not have to wonder about the irregularities of C++98 initialization.

3.2 Partial Order of Templated Functions in a Generic Function Family

Current C++ supports generic programming with its template mechanism. Templates are a compile time mechanism that parametrize functions or classes over types. With current C++, the requirements that make the instantiation of template bodies succeed cannot be explicitly stated. To type check a template, the compiler needs to instantiate the template body with concrete types. Programmers have to look up the requirements in documentation or infer them from the template body. Attempts to instantiate templates with types that do not meet all requirements fail with often hard to comprehend error messages [14]. Concepts [14] [15] is a mechanism designed for C++0x to make these requirements explicit in source code. A concept constrains one or more template arguments and provides for the separation of template type checking from template instantiation.

Concept extraction: In [16], we discuss tool support for extracting syntactic concept requirements from templated source code. For example, consider the STL [11] function advance that is defined over input-iterator:

```
template <class Iter, class Dist>
void advance(Iter& iterator, Dist dist) {
  while (dist--) ++iterator;
}
```

Our tool extracts the following concept requirements:

```
concept AdvInputIter <typename Iter, typename Dist> {
  Dist::Dist(const Dist&); // to copy construct arguments
  void operator++(Iter&); // advance the iterator by one
  bool operator--(Dist&, int); // decrement the distance
}
```

Likewise, our tool extracts the following requirements from the advance implementations for bidirectional-iterators:

```
// for Bidirectional-Iterators
template <class Iter, class Dist>
void advance(Iter& iterator, Dist dist) {
  if (dist > 0)
    while (dist--) ++iterator;
  else
    while (dist++) --iterator;
}

concept AdvBidirectIter <typename Iter, typename Dist> {
  Dist::Dist(const Dist&);
  void operator++(Iter&); // move the iterator forward
  void operator--(Iter&); // move the iterator backward
  bool operator++(Dist&, int); // post-increment
  bool operator--(Dist&, int); // post-decrement
}
```

and random access-iterators:

```
// for RandomAccess−Iterators
template<class RandomAccessIterator, class Distance>
void advance(RandomAccessIterator& i, Distance n) {
  i += n;
}

concept AdvRandomAccessIter <typename Iter, typename Dist> {
  Dist::Dist(const Dist&);
  void operator+=(Iter&, Dist&); // constant time positioning operation
}
```

Callers of a generic function, such as the advance family, are required to incorporate the minimal concept requirements in its concept specification. Consider a function random_elem, that moves the iterator to a random position and returns the underlying value:

```
template <class Iter>
typename Iter::value_type random_elem(Iter iter, size_t maxdist) {
  advance(iter, rand(maxdist));
  return *iter;
}
```

The concept requirements on Iter depend on the minimal concept requirements of the generic function advance. From the concept requirements that were extracted for the advance family, the hierarchical concept relationship (or a base implementation) cannot be inferred. The sets of requirements extracted for input- and bidirectional-iterator can be ordered by inclusion. However, the set of requirements for randomaccess-iterator is disjoint from the other two sets. The minimal set of requirements cannot be automatically determined.

The lack of explicit information on the hierarchical order of templated function declarations is not only a problem for a concept extraction tool, but also for programmers. Without more information compilers cannot discern overloaded template functions for a given set of argument types. To overcome this problem, programmers have invented idioms, such as tag dispatching [17] and techniques that utilize the substitution failure is not an error mechanism [18]. This section of the paper demonstrates that a rejuvenation tool can recover the concept hierarchy by identifying the tag dispatching idiom in legacy code.

Tag dispatching: The tag dispatching idiom adds an unnamed non template parameter to the signature of each function-template in a generic function family (e.g., inputiterator_tag, bidirectional_iterator_tag, ...).

```
template<class InputIterator, class Distance>
void advance(InputIterator& iter, Distance dist, inputiterator_tag);

template<class RandomAccessIterator, class Distance>
void advance(RandomAccessIterator& iter, Distance dist, randomaccess_iterator_tag);
```

With the extra argument, the compiler can discriminate the tagged functions based on the non template argument dependent parameter type. A templated access function uses the class family iterator_traits [19] to construct an object of the proper tag type. An iterator tag is an associated type (i.e., iterator_category) of the actual iterator (or its iterator_traits).

```
template<class InputIterator, class Distance>
void advance(InputIterator& iter, Distance dist) {
  advance(i, dist, iterator_traits<InputIterator>::iterator_category());
}
```

Recovering structural information from tags: To distinguish tags from regular classes, we require parameters used as tags to possess the following properties.

- all template functions of a generic function family have unnamed parameter(s) at the same argument positions(s).
- the type tuple of tag parameters is unique for each function template within a generic function family.

In addition, we require that for each generic function family exist an access function that has the same number of non-tag arguments (and types). Tag classes are not allowed to have non-static members.

By identifying tag classes, our tool can deduce the refinement relationship of template functions from the inheritance relationship of the tag classes. Consider, the hierarchy of the iterator classes:

```
struct input_iterator_tag {};
struct forward_iterator_tag : input_iterator_tag {};
struct bidirectional_iterator_tag : forward_iterator_tag {};
struct randomaccess_tag : bidirectional_iterator_tag {};
```

By knowing that input_iterator is the base of the tag hierarchy, we can propagate the requirements of the corresponding template function advance to the requirements of its callers. For example, the requirements of function random_elem are:

```
concept RandomElem <typename Iter, typename Dist> {
  // requirements propagated from advance
  Dist::Dist(const Dist&); // to copy construct arguments
  void operator++(Iter&); // advance the iterator by one
  bool operator--(Dist&, int); // decrement the distance

  // additional requirements from random_elem
  Iter::Iter(const Iter&); // to copy construct arguments
}
```

4 Refactoring

The term refactoring is derived from the mathematical term "factoring" and refers to finding multiple occurrences of similar code and factoring it into a single reusable function, thereby simplifying code comprehension and future maintenance tasks [20]. The meaning of refactoring has evolved and broadened. In [21],

Opdyke and Johnson define refactoring as an automatic and behavior preserving code transformations that improves source code that was subject to gradual structural deterioration over its life time. Essentially, refactorings improve the design of existing code [22] [23].

Traditionally, refactoring techniques have been applied in the context of object-oriented software development. Automated refactoring simplifies modifications of a class, a class hierarchy, or several interacting classes [21]. More recently, refactoring techniques have been developed to support programs written in other programming styles (i.e., functional programming [24]).

Refactorings capture maintenance tasks that occur repeatedly. Opdyke [25] studied recurring design changes (e.g., component extraction, class (interface) unification). Refactoring is a computer assisted process that guarantees correctness, thereby enabling programmers to maintain and develop software more efficiently. In particular, evolutionary (or agile) software development methodologies [26], where rewriting and restructuring source code frequently is an inherent part of the development process of feature extensions, benefit from refactoring tools.

"Anti-patterns" [27] and "code smells" [22] are indicators of design deficiencies. Anti-patterns are initially structured solutions that turn out to be more troublesome than anticipated. Examples for anti-patterns include the use of exception-handling for normal control-flow transfer, ignoring exceptions and errors, magic strings, and classes that require their client-interaction occur in a particular sequence. Source code that is considered structurally inadequate is said to suffer from code smell. Examples for "code smell" include repeated similar code, long and confusing functions (or methods), overuse of type tests and type casts. The detection of code smell can be partially automated [28] and assists programmers in finding potentially troublesome source locations. Refactoring of anti-patterns and "code smells" to more structured solutions improves safety and maintainability.

Refactoring does not emphasize a particular goal or direction of source code modification – e.g., refactoring supports class generalization and class specification [25], refactoring can reorganize source code towards patterns and away from patterns (in case a pattern is unsuitable) [23].

Refactoring strictly preserves the observable behavior of the program. The term "observable behavior", however, is not well defined [20]. What observable behavior exactly requires (e.g., function call trace, performance, ...) remains unclear. Refactoring does not eliminate bugs, but can make bugs easier to spot and fix.

4.1 Source Code Rejuvenation and Refactoring

Table 1 summarizes characteristics of source code rejuvenation and refactoring. Both are examples of source code analysis and transformations that operate on the source level of applications. Refactoring is concerned to support software development with tools that simplify routine tasks, while source code rejuvenation is concerned with a one-time software migration. Both are examples of source

Table 1. Source Code Rejuvenation vs. Refactoring

	Source Code Rejuvenation	**Refactoring**
Transformation	Source-to-source	Source-to-source
Behavior preserving	Behavior *improving*	Behavior preserving
Directed	yes Raises the level of abstraction	no
Drivers	Language / library evolution	Feature extensions Design changes
Indicators	Workaround techniques / idioms	Bad smells Anti-patterns
Applications	One-time source code migration	Recurring maintenance tasks

code analysis and transformation. Source code rejuvenation gathers information that might be dispersed in the source of involved workaround techniques and makes the information explicit to compilers and programmers. Refactoring emphasizes the preservation of behavior, while source code rejuvenation allows for and encourages behavior improving modifications.

We might consider code rejuvenation a "subspecies" of refactoring (or vise versa), but that would miss an important point. The driving motivation or code rejuvenation is language and library evolution rather than the gradual improvement of design within a program. Once a rejuvenation tool has been configured, it can be applied to a wide range of programs with no other similarities than they were written in an earlier language dialect or style.

5 Tool Support for Source Code Rejuvenation

Source code evolution and modernization projects are an active branch of academic and industrial research. For our implementation of a source code rejuvenation tools, we utilize the Pivot source-to-source transformation framework [29]. The Pivot's internal program representation (IPR) allows for representing a superset of C++ including some programs written in the next generation of C++. IPR can be conceived as a fully typed abstract syntax tree. IPR represents C++ programs at a level that preserves most information present in the the source code. For example, IPR preserves uninstantiated template code. This allows us to analyse template and improve template definitions, for example, by deducing concepts or rejuvenating template function bodies.

We stress that the IPR is fully typed. Type information enables the implementation of source code rejuvenation that is type sensitive. Most of the potential rejuvenation analysis and transformations depend on type information. For example, concept extraction distinguishes operations that are template argument dependent from operations that are not. Likewise, the implementation to migrate source code to use initializer lists depends on whether the container type supports initializer-list constructors. This is the case for standard STL containers.

Related work includes systems for source code evolution and transformations. MoDisco [30], which is part of Eclipse, provides a model driven framework for source code modernization. The Design Maintenance System (DMS) [31] is an industrial project that provides a transformation framework. DMS supports the evolution of large scale software written in multiple languages. Stratego/XT [32] is a generic transformation framework that operates on an annotated term (ATerm) representation. Rose [33] provides a source-to-source translation framework for C++ and Fortran programs.

6 Conclusion

In this paper, we have discussed source code rejuvenation, a process that automates and assists source code changes to take advantage of improvements to programming languages and its libraries. We have supported our arguments with two specific examples from the migration from C++03 to C++0x.

We are aware that refactoring has been used to describe semantic preserving code transformations that migrate code to use new frameworks (e.g., Tip et al. [34], Tansey and Tilevich [35]). In this paper, we have demonstrated with examples that the difference between language evolution related code transformations and refactoring is subtle but important. We prefer and suggest the term "source code rejuvenation" for describing one-time and directed source code transformations that discover and eliminate outdated workaround techniques and idioms.

References

1. Ritchie, D.M.: The Development of the C Language. In: HOPL-II: The Second ACM SIGPLAN Conference on History of Programming Languages, New York, pp. 201–208. ACM, New York (1993)
2. Stroustrup, B.: The Design and Evolution of C++. ACM Press/Addison-Wesley Publishing Co. (1994)
3. ISO/IEC 14882 International Standard: Programming Languages: C++. American National Standards Institute (September 1998)
4. Stroustrup, B.: The Design of C++0x. C/C++ Users Journal (2005)
5. Becker, P.: Working Draft, Standard for Programming Language C++. Technical Report N2914 (June 2009)
6. Becker, P.: The C++ Standard Library Extensions: A Tutorial and Reference, 1st edn. Addison-Wesley Professional, Boston (2006)
7. van Rossum, G.: The Python Language Reference Manual. Network Theory Ltd., Paperback (September 2003)
8. ECMA: The C# Language Specification. Technical Report, ECMA (European Association for Standardizing Information and Communication Systems), Geneva, Switzerland (June 2006)
9. Arnold, K., Gosling, J., Holmes, D.: The Java Programming Language, 4th edn. Prentice Hall PTR, Englewood Cliffs (2005)
10. Miller, A.: `http://tech.puredanger.com/java7` (retrieved on July 6, 2009)

11. Austern, M.H.: Generic Programming and the STL: Using and Extending the C++ Standard Template Library. Addison-Wesley Longman Publishing Co., Inc., Boston (1998)
12. An, P., Jula, A., Rus, S., Saunders, S., Smith, T., Tanase, G., Thomas, N., Amato, N., Rauchwerger, L.: STAPL: A Standard Template Adaptive Parallel C++ Library. In: Dietz, H.G. (ed.) LCPC 2001. LNCS, vol. 2624, pp. 193–208. Springer, Heidelberg (2003)
13. Merrill, J., Vandevoorde, D.: Initializer Lists — Alternative Mechanism and Rationale. Technical Report N2640, JTC1/SC22/WG21 C++ Standards Committee (2008)
14. Gregor, D., Järvi, J., Siek, J., Stroustrup, B., Dos Reis, G., Lumsdaine, A.: Concepts: Linguistic Support for Generic Programming in C++. In: OOPSLA 2006: Proceedings of the 21st Annual ACM SIGPLAN Conference on Object-Oriented Programming Systems, Languages, and Applications, pp. 291–310. ACM Press, New York (2006)
15. Gregor, D., Stroustrup, B., Siek, J., Widman, J.: Proposed Wording for Concepts (Revision 4). Technical Report N2501, JTC1/SC22/WG21 C++ Standards Committee (February 2008)
16. Pirkelbauer, P., Dechev, D., Stroustrup, B.: Extracting Concepts from C++ Generic Functions. Technical Report, Dept. of Computer Science and Engineering, Texas A&M (October 2009)
17. Abrahams, D., Gurtovoy, A.: C++ Template Metaprogramming: Concepts, Tools, and Techniques from Boost and Beyond. C++ in Depth Series. Addison-Wesley Professional, Reading (2004)
18. Järvi, J., Willcock, J., Hinnant, H., Lumsdaine, A.: Function Overloading Based on Arbitrary Properties of Types. C/C++ Users Journal 21(6), 25–32 (2003)
19. Myers, N.C.: Traits: a New and Useful Template Technique. C++ Report (1995)
20. Mens, T., Tourwé, T.: A Survey of Software Refactoring. IEEE Trans. Softw. Eng. 30(2), 126–139 (2004)
21. Opdyke, W.F., Johnson, R.E.: Creating Abstract Superclasses by Refactoring. In: CSC 1993: Proceedings of the 1993 ACM Conference on Computer Science, pp. 66–73. ACM, New York (1993)
22. Fowler, M., Beck, K., Brant, J., Opdyke, W., Roberts, D.: Refactoring: Improving the Design of Existing Code. Addison-Wesley Longman Publishing Co., Inc., Boston (1999)
23. Kerievsky, J.: Refactoring to Patterns. Pearson Higher Education, London (2004)
24. Lämmel, R.: Towards Generic Refactoring. In: RULE 2002: Proceedings of the 2002 ACM SIGPLAN Workshop on Rule-Based Programming, pp. 15–28. ACM, New York (2002)
25. Opdyke, W.F.: Refactoring Object-Oriented Frameworks. PhD Thesis, University of Illinois at Urbana-Champaign, Champaign, IL, USA, UMI Order No. GAX93-05645 (1992)
26. Abrahamsson, P., Salo, O., Ronkainen, J.: Agile Software Development Methods: Review and Analysis. Technical Report, VTT Electronics (2002)
27. Brown, W.J., Malveau, R.C., McCormick III, H.W., Mowbray, T.J.: AntiPatterns: Refactoring Software, Architectures, and Projects in Crisis. John Wiley & Sons, Inc, New York (1998)
28. Parnin, C., Görg, C., Nnadi, O.: A Catalogue of Lightweight Visualizations to Support Code Smell Inspection. In: SoftVis 2008: Proceedings of the 4th ACM Symposium on Software Visualization, pp. 77–86. ACM, New York (2008)

29. Stroustrup, B., Dos Reis, G.: Supporting SELL for High-Performance Computing. In: Ayguadé, E., Baumgartner, G., Ramanujam, J., Sadayappan, P. (eds.) LCPC 2005. LNCS, vol. 4339, pp. 458–465. Springer, Heidelberg (2006)
30. Eclipse MoDisco Project, `http://www.eclipse.org/gmt/modisco/` (retrieved on September 20, 2009)
31. Baxter, I.D.: DMS: Program Transformations for Practical Scalable Software Evolution. In: IWPSE 2002: Proceedings of the International Workshop on Principles of Software Evolution, pp. 48–51. ACM, New York (2002)
32. Bravenboer, M., Kalleberg, K.T., Vermaas, R., Visser, E.: Stratego/XT 0.16: Components for Transformation Systems. In: PEPM 2006: Proceedings of the 2006 ACM SIGPLAN Symposium on Partial Evaluation and Semantics-Based Program Manipulation, pp. 95–99. ACM, New York (2006)
33. Quinlan, D., Schordan, M., Yi, Q., Supinski, B.R.d.: Semantic-Driven Parallelization of Loops Operating on User-Defined Containers. In: Rauchwerger, L. (ed.) LCPC 2003. LNCS, vol. 2958. Springer, Heidelberg (2004)
34. Balaban, I., Tip, F., Fuhrer, R.: Refactoring Support for Class Library Migration. In: OOPSLA 2005: Proceedings of the 20th Annual ACM SIGPLAN Conference on Object-Oriented Programming, Systems, Languages, and Applications, pp. 265–279. ACM, New York (2005)
35. Tansey, W., Tilevich, E.: Annotation Refactoring: Inferring Upgrade Transformations for Legacy Applications. In: OOPSLA 2008: Proceedings of the 23rd ACM SIGPLAN Conference on Object-Oriented Programming Systems Languages and Applications, vol. 43, pp. 295–312. ACM, New York (2008)

Empirical Evaluation of Strategies to Detect Logical Change Dependencies

Guenter Pirklbauer

Software Competence Center Hagenberg
Softwarepark 21, A-4232 Hagenberg, Austria
guenter.pirklbauer@scch.at

Abstract. Change impact analysis plays an immanent role in the maintenance and enhancement of software systems. There still exist many approaches to support change impact analysis. In the last years researchers try to utilize data in software repositories to gain findings for supporting miscellaneous aspects of software engineering, e.g. software evolution analysis or change impact analysis. In the context of change impact analysis, approaches (=strategies) try to detect logical dependencies among artifacts based on the version histories of files in the concurrent versioning system (e.g. CVS). They try to infer logical couplings of files (artifacts) based on co-changes (files which are frequently changed together). Based on these findings we want to contribute with the presentation of insights of deeper investigation of historical information in concurrent versioning systems in general. In this paper we have identified and described existing strategies to detect logical change couplings. These strategies will be illustrated by practical use cases. We have empirically evaluated these strategies based on versioning system repositories of two industrial projects. The analysis figures the absolute and relative contribution of dependency results per strategy. Furthermore we show overlappings of dependency results.

Keywords: Logical change dependencies, logical change couplings, change impact analysis, change prediction, mining software repositories.

1 Introduction

Change impact analysis (*identifying the potential consequences of a change, or estimated what needs to be modified to accomplish a change* [1]), is coined by approaches that try to exploit historical data in the versioning system [2,3,4,5,6]. These approaches have one thing in common: They try to detect logical change dependencies of artifacts based on co-changes in the versioning system. Logical change dependencies are relevant for change impact analysis and enlarge physical dependencies which are extracted by static code analysis. The basis of most of these approaches is the fact that files which are frequently changed together have dependencies to each other. "Changed together" in this context means, that files are in the same transaction of a unique commit of a developer. Transactions in versioning systems are the base of operations used by most approaches to detect

J. van Leeuwen et al. (Eds.): SOFSEM 2010, LNCS 5901, pp. 651–662, 2010.

logical change dependencies. Transactions represent *one* strategy to find logical change dependencies. A strategy in this sense is an algorithm or a rule that describes how to detect a specific kind of change dependency in the versioning system repositories. Fluri et al. attempt to discover patterns of change types using agglomerate hierarchical clustering [7]. The result of the work are low-level activities of developers.

The motivation of this research work is to support change impact analysis activities in software development and maintenance by the investigation of versioning system repositories in more detail. This will be performed by analyzing the check-in behavior of developers based on typical project scenarios and in consequence mining versioning system repositories under this aspect. Starting with the commonly used strategy to detect dependencies in the versioning system (see 3.1) we analyzed further strategies that contribute with additional dependencies which are relevant for change impact analysis. We have implemented these strategies to show results of empirical evaluation of two industrial projects.

The objective of this paper is to present strategies to detect logical change dependencies in versioning system repositories and to evaluate these strategies. Therefore the paper is structured as follows: Section 2 presents the study approach, Section 3 describes the investigation of strategies in industrial settings and Section 4 provides the results of the empirical evaluation and draws some conclusions, Section 5 outlines the related work in mining software repositories for change impact analysis and Section 6 summarizes the paper.

2 Study Approach

Our goal is to determine the quantities of results of each strategy by empirical research study. We analyze the contribution of each strategy in relation to the results of a transaction-based strategy (transaction-based strategy results serve as a basis). For this, we have investigated versioning system repositories (CVS and PVCS) of two industrial projects. We have implemented two components: (1) A parser which parses log files of versioning system repositories (supporting several log formats) and stores the data in database, and (2) a dependency detector which extracts dependencies from this database according to four strategies (see Section 3). Both are implemented as Java-RCP plug-ins. In the evaluation we show commons and differences of each result. Besides quantities of dependencies of each strategy we want to identify overlapping dependency quantities. Our results are confirmed by project staff regarding the correctness and plausibility of data.

As mentioned before we have analyzed versioning system repositories of two projects. The first is a Java-based ERP application to support processes in the building and construction industry which lasts over 3 years. The second is a COBOL- and 4GL-based application for a national insurance company that lasts for 8 years including maintenance and enhancement. Table 1 on page 653 holds some key-data of these projects.

Table 1. Key-Data of evaluated Projects

Measure	**Project 1**	**Project 2**
Number of Check-Ins	32.785	68.606
Number of Developers	12	66
Check-Ins / Developer [avg.]	2732	1039
Number of Transactions	4.291	32.728
Check-Ins / Transaction [avg.]	7,6	2,1
Number of Files	7.913	13.820
Check-Ins / File [avg.]	4,1	4,9
Number of Check-Ins with Change-ID [abs.]	15.093	4.809
Check-Ins with Change ID [rel.]	*46%*	*7%*
Change-ID-based Dependencies [rel.]	*55,6%*	*3,5%*

3 Strategies

As described in Section 2 the basis of our research are dependencies that result from implementing transaction-based strategy. This strategy is well established [2,3,4,5,6] and therefore often used to detect co-changes in versioning system, especially in CVS. In the case of CVS, the sliding time window technique is used to reconstruct transactions [8].

In the next Subsections the strategies will be described in detail. The *Transaction-based Strategy* [2,3,4,5,6] is well known in the community and therefore servers as a basis for three further strategies we have identified. The *Comment-based Strategy* is also part of the research of Zimmermann et al. [4]. *Change-ID-based Strategy* is integrated in the work of Zimmermann et al. [4], Sliwerski et al. [9], Robbes [10] and also implemented in Mylyn [11]. *Change-Hierarchy-based Strategy* is the fourth strategy we have found in the literature [12]. Additionally each strategy will be illustrated by practical use cases of daily project life. Furthermore, preconditions and limitations of strategies are analyzed.

3.1 Transaction-Based Strategy

This strategy is based on the project scenario on which developers check-in files which are changed together in the workspace. Based on the description of a bug, change request or an enhancement request, developers checkout all files which they believe that will change. Then implementation work will be done and afterwards all changed files will be checked in together. Together has the meaning of "in the same transaction".

Because of the fact that some versioning systems (e.g. CVS, PVCS) are not able to handle atomic transactions, the sliding time window approach [8] will be used to reconstruct transactions. Files in the same transaction will probably co-change in future. As mentioned before, a lot of approaches are using transactions to detect logical change dependencies in versioning systems.

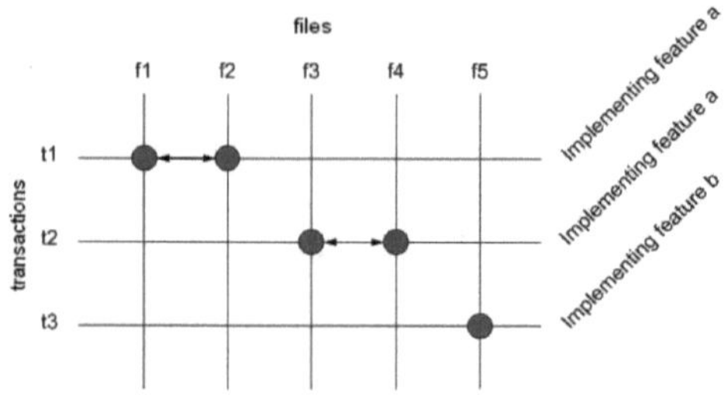

Fig. 1. Transaction-based Strategy

Preconditions and Limitations. The limitation of this strategy is, that changes that take several check-ins - and hence several transactions - can not be reconstructed. As can be seen in Figure 1 on page 654 the developer implemented feature *a* motivated by a change request. At first, he checked out file *f1*, and *f2*, implemented the feature and did the check-in with the comment "Implementing feature a (transaction *t1*). Afterwards he found out that he forgot to change file *f3* and *f4*. He checked out the files, finished implementing feature *a* and checked in with comment "Implementing feature a" (transaction *t2*). Here, two transactions (transaction *t1* with files *f1* and *f2* and transaction *t2* with file *f3* and *f4*) are done in the versioning system. Thus, the strategy is able to detect dependencies between files *f1, f2* and files *f3, f4*. But transaction *t1* and transaction *t2* belong together, because the same feature was implemented. Hence, co-changes between the files *f1*, *f2* and files *f3*, *f4* are still not detected. The next strategy is introduced to reconstruct this setting of co-changed files.

3.2 Comment-Based Strategy

To overcome the problem to interrelate transaction *t1* and *t2* we have introduced the comment-based strategy [13]. This strategy is able to detect dependencies between files in transaction *t1* and *t2* by checking if comments of transactions are corresponding. The central point of the strategy is the fact that developers tend to use the same comments for content-depending check-ins in the versioning system. Based on string-comparing or string matching the strategy is able to interrelate transaction *t1* and *t2*. As can be seen on the left hand side in Figure 2 on page 655, the comments of transaction *t1* and *t2* are matching by the comment "Implementing feature a". Therefore, dependencies between the files *f1*, *f2*, *f3* and *f4* can be stated.

Preconditions and Limitations. As can be seen on the right hand side in Figure 2 on page 655, the limit of this strategies will be reached if the developer will use a different comment in transaction *t2* than in transaction t1. Here, transaction *t2* has the comment "Supplementing Impl. of feature a", not the same comment of transaction *t1*. But the strategy is not able to interrelate transaction *t1* and *t2*, because it is based on a simple string-matching algorithm. To overcome this problem, the next strategy is introduced.

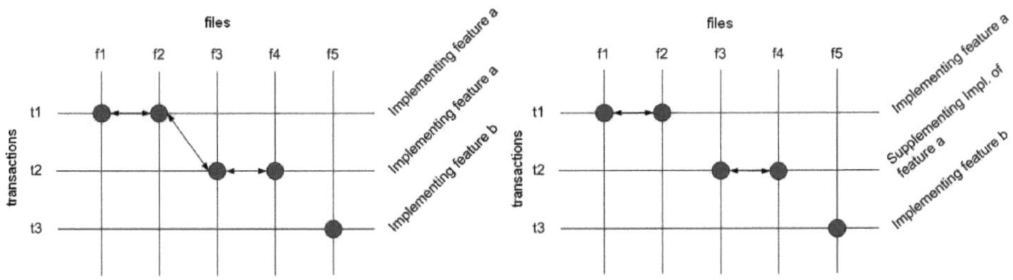

Fig. 2. Comment-based Strategy

3.3 Change-ID-Based Strategy

Here, the fix of a bug, change request or an enhancement needs several transactions in the versioning system of one ore more developers, typically over a time period of several days [13]. For example developer *d1* changes file *f1* and *f2* in an eclipse plug-in, does a check-in with the comment "Implementing feature a (Change *#123*)" in transaction *t1*. Afterwards he changes file *f3* and *f4* and does a check-in again in transaction *t2* with the comment "Supplementing Impl. of feature a (Change *#123*)".

Here developer *d1* uses an integrated task management system to interrelate change-sets in the workspace. As can be seen on the left hand side in Figure 3 on page 656, comments of check-ins are automatically enriched with IDs of related items in the mentioned repositories. As can be seen, comments of transaction *t1* and *t2* include the ID of the related change, in this case *#123*. So, afterwards, it is easy to reconstruct all related files in the context of a certain change. Furthermore, the URL of the change in the repository can be composed. The URL typically consists of the servername and the coded change-ID as one of the arguments.

After the implementation work of developer *d1* the version number of the plug-in has to be updated for delivery the software product to customers. This will be accomplished by developer *d2* that is responsible for preparing the software product for delivery. Developer *d2* also uses the integrated task management system. Therefore, developer *d2* changes file *f5* and does the check-in with the comment "Updating plug-in-properties (Change *#123*)" in transaction *t3*.

Here we can see the benefit of using integrated task management systems. But, generally, if comments of transactions are enriched by an unique change-ID, content-depending transactions and in succession content-depending dependencies between files can be determined. The strategy allows reconstructing dependencies independent of the actual comment, independent of time and independent of the developer who does the check-in.

Preconditions and Limitations. The precondition of this strategy is the importance of enriching the check-in comment with the related change-ID, which holds the context of the entire change. As can be seen on the left hand side in Figure 4 on page 656, several changes belong together if a main feature will be structured down in sub-features. This will be the case, if for example one change is to large to represent one task for one developer. Then the project manager, the software architect or the analyst breaks down the main change into several sub-changes. The criterion how to subdivide the main change maybe of technical or architectural reasons. In this case, the main change is structured into a change for the server-, client- and database-software (Change *#121*, Change *#122* and Change *#123*).

Figure 3 on page 656 (right hand side) shows check-ins according to the case described above. None of up to now presented strategies are able to detect dependencies between files in transactions *t1*, *t2* and *t3*. (There is no transaction with Change *#120*, because this change only holds together Change *#121*, Change *#122* and Change *#123*. Therefore Change *#120* has no relevant content for developers.)

In a nutshell, the essential point in implementing this strategy is to insert the change-ID in check-in.

3.4 Change-Hierarchy-Based Strategy

This strategy is very valuable to detect co-changes of files which are changed in the course of several (sub-) changes (check-ins marked with change-IDs) which belong to one top main change (see Figure 4 on page 656) [12]. Here, for the first

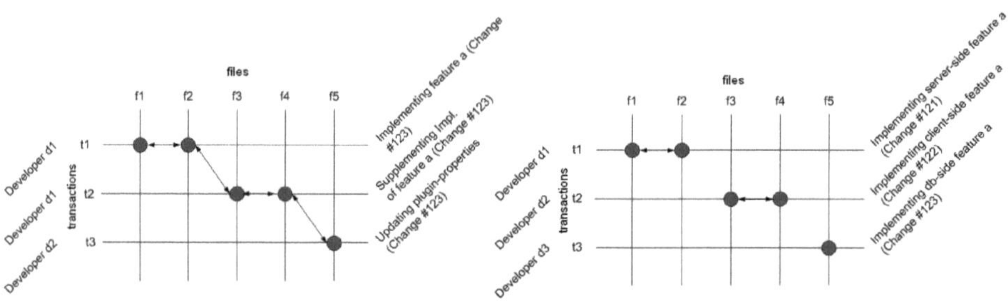

Fig. 3. Change-ID-based Strategy

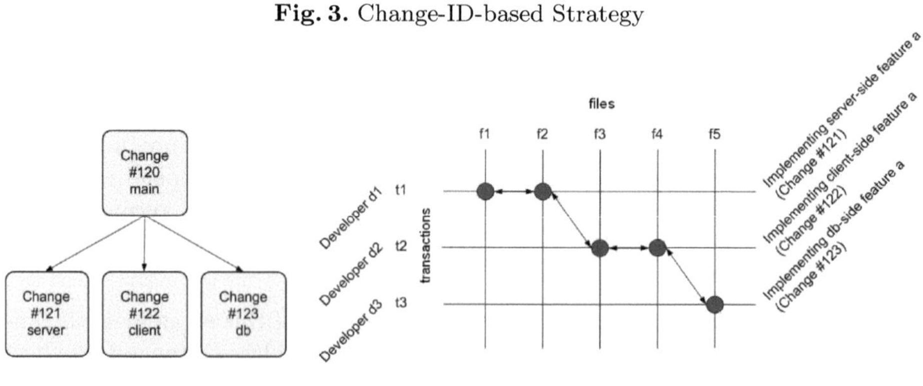

Fig. 4. Change-Hierarchy based Strateg

time we need additional data from outside the versioning system. In the case of Bugzilla, this kind of down-structuring of changes will be interrelated through "*depends on-*" and "*blocks-*" links. So, with extraction of linking-information this strategy is able to correspond logical related changes. Down-structuring of items in issue-, bug-tracking- or change management systems is a widespread approach in software engineering. Therefore, though additional data from these systems is needed, this strategy benefits by supporting change impact analysis with further dependencies.

Preconditions and Limitations. The most important precondition of this strategy is the fact that data from outside versioning system is needed to interrelate co-changes in files.

4 Results and Discussion

As mentioned in Section 2 the evaluation has the goal to show unique and overlappings of dependencies and interprets results. The results of the investigation are shown in Table 2 on page 657 and Table 3 on page 658.

In the next paragraphs we will explain each column to create understanding of data which will be discussed in Subsection 4.1 - 4.3. In the first column the dependency-types resulting from strategies are quoted. In our paper we define a dependency d as an interrelation between two check-ins $c1_x$ and $c2_y$ of file $f1$ and $f2$. This means, that file $f1$ and $f2$ can have more than one dependency based on available check-ins of file $f1$ ($c1_0 \ldots c1_n$) and $f2$ ($c2_0 \ldots c2_m$). The interrelation causes a change in file $f2$ if file $f1$ changes with a specific probability. The

Table 2. Results of Investigation of Project 1

					Overlapping			
Dependency Types	No. of Dep.	Unique No. of Dep. [abs]	Unique No. of Dep. [rel]	Unique-Ratio of Dep.	Trans.-based	Comment-based	Change-ID-based	Ch.-Hier.-based
Transaction-based	269.838	0	0%	0%	X	44,1%	55,9%	0,1%
Comment-based	196.184	77.102	39%	78,9%	60,7%	X	-	0,2%
Change-ID-based	658.791	506.670	77%	12%	22,9%	-	X	-
Ch.-Hier.-based	60.037	58.470	97%	9,1%	0,3%	-	2,6%	X
Total	**1.184.850**	**642.242**		**100%**				

Table 3. Results of Investigation of Project 2

					Overlapping			
Dependency Types	**No. of Dep.**	**Unique No. of Dep. [abs]**	**Unique No. of Dep. [rel]**	**Unique-Ratio of Dep.**	**Trans.-based**	**Comment-based**	**Change-ID-based**	**Ch.-Hier.-based**
Transaction-based	39.306	0	0%	0%	X	95,2%	4,8%	-
Comment-based	818.982	781.575	95%	96,4%	4,6%	X	-	-
Change-ID-based	30.935	29.036	94%	3,6%	6,1%	-	X	-
Total	**889.223**			**100%**				

quantity of probability is not considered in our investigation. A dependency d based on $c1_x$ and $c2_y$ can be detected by one or more than one strategy. If a dependency d is detected by more than one strategy, we label the dependency as overlapping.

In the second column you can see the absolute number of dependencies. In the last row of this column the total amount of dependencies is added up.

Column three and four (*Unique No. of Dep. [abs], Unique No. of Dep. [rel]*) hold the absolute and relative number of unique dependencies in relation to all identified dependencies per strategy. A dependency between file *f1* and *f2* is always based on two check-ins (check-in *c1* and *c2*). Now, a dependency is unique, if check-in *c1* and *c2* is unique between file *f1* and *f2*. In consequence, a dependency is not unique, if file *f1* and *f2* interrelate based on check-in *c1* and *c2* was identified by more than one strategy. In other words: A dependency is unique if it was detected by one strategy.

Column *Unique-Ratio of Dep.* cites the part of unique dependencies found with a certain strategy in relation to the sum of all unique dependencies which were found. In the last row of this column, the sum of all unique-ratios is of course 100%.

The following four columns describe the relatively overlapping quantities of dependencies per strategy. For example, transaction-based dependencies have a overlapping of 44% with comment-based dependencies. If fields hold an "-", no overlapping can be stated.

4.1 Distribution of Dependencies

Figure 5 on page 659 shows the distribution of dependency-types in Project 1 and Project 2. This illustration does not consider overlappings of dependencies, but only the number of dependencies found per strategy. We can see, that the majority of dependencies in Project 1 is detected by *Change-ID-based Strategy* with a quantity of 55,6% (658.791). In Project 2 this type of dependencies only scale 3,5% (30.935). The reason for this phenomenon will be discussed later.

In Project 1, dependencies detected by *Transaction-based Strategy* have a quantity of 22,8% (269.838). In Project 2 *Transaction-based Strategy* have a quantity of 4,4% (39.306). The tilt of quantities of transaction-based dependencies of Project 1 and Project 2 is caused by (1) the difference in check-ins per transaction on average and (2) the difference of contingent of check-ins with change-IDs (both see 1). Check-ins enriched with change-IDs in Project 1 represent a higher fraction than in Project 2. This results in a lower fraction of transaction-based dependencies. Comment-based dependencies scale 16,6% (196.184) in Project 1 and 92,1% (818.982) in Project 2. The reason for disparity again is based on the ratio of check-ins enriched by change-IDs. In our study, the implementation of *Comment-based Strategy* considers only check-ins with no change-ID added, because these dependencies will be covered completely by *Change-ID-based Strategy.* Change-hierarchy dependencies have a ratio of 5,1% (60.037) in Project 1. In Project 2 no change-hierarchy dependencies are available, because the tool for issue-, bug- and change-management changed several times during the project and therefore it was not possible to extract valuable information.

4.2 Unique and Overlapping Dependency Results

In Project 1, dependencies detected by *Transaction-based Strategy* which are unique have a quantity of 0%. They are covered completely by dependencies found by *Change-ID-based Strategy* (44,1%), *Comment-based Strategy* (55,9%) and *Change-Hierarchy-based Strategy* (0,1%). In Project 2, unique dependencies identified by *Transaction-based Strategy* also have a quantity of 0%. They are also covered completely by change-ID-based dependencies (4,8%) and comment-based dependencies (95,2%). The splitting of transaction-based dependencies is obvious, because check-ins in a certain transaction have at least the same

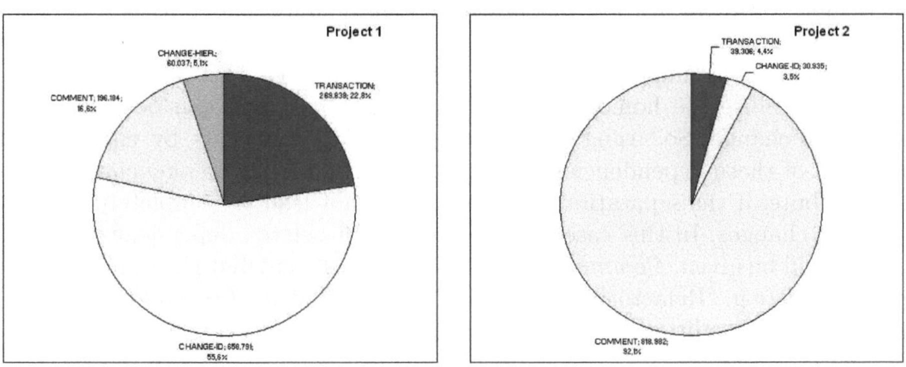

Fig. 5. Distribution of Dependency-Types in Project 1 and Project 2

comment and ideally a change-ID inserted in the comment. Change-hierarchy-dependencies (5,1% in Project 1, 0% in Project 2) are covered by transaction-based- (0,3%) and change-ID-based-dependencies (2,6%). The coverage rates are because check-ins in one transaction can include several change-IDs, if a developer implements more than one change simultaneously. If these change-IDs are related in the task management system, change-hierarchy-based strategy is able to detect additional but redundant dependencies. The majority of change-hierarchy-dependencies (97,1%) is unique and contribute well because of the direct relation to other changes established manually in Bugzilla.

4.3 Ratio of Check-ins with Change-ID and Change-ID-Based Dependencies

By analyzing the data of Project 1 and Project 2, the most important finding is the coherence between inserted change-IDs in comments of check-ins and number of dependencies found by *Change-ID-based Strategy*. If we look at Table 1 on page 653 (last two rows), we stated that in Project 1 a ratio of 46% of change-ID-enriched check-ins lead to a change-ID-based dependency ratio of 55,6%. In contrast, Project 2 has a ratio of 7% of change-ID-enriched check-ins and a change-ID-based dependency ratio of just 3,5%. Project 1 and Project 2 are very oppositional if we are looking at these measures. Change-ID-based dependencies are truthful in nature, because check-ins belonging to a change in the bug-tracking-, issue-tracking- or change management system are implicit content coherent. Therefore change-ID-based dependencies are high reliable dependencies for change impact analysis. I conclude, that in projects which have a majority of comments with change-IDs, Change-ID-based strategy will detect more dependencies. Here we can see the benefit of inserting change-IDs in comments of check-ins. Based on this finding, it advocates using tools that integrate the bug-tracking-, issue-tracking- or change management system with the versioning system and the IDE to get the relation of check-ins and changes automatically (change-IDs are inserted automatically in comments of check-ins). If developers have to insert change-IDs manually, they are lingered in their daily business and get demotivated. So introducing integrated task management tools contribute to support change impact analysis. So, overall, it can be stated that *Change-ID-based dependencies* implicate the most information in context of change impact analysis, because the homogeneity of commits is best and can be directly related to a change. So, using integrations like Mylyn benefits by enabling the detection of these dependencies. *Change-Hierarchy-based dependencies* are able to contribute, if the separation of changes does not lead to completely content-detached changes. In this case, no change impact related dependency between changes will be given. *Comment-based dependencies* contribute if comments with less content (e.g. “Refactoring”, “Merging”) are excluded. *Transaction-based dependencies* are traditionally and empirically evaluated in many case studies (see Section 5).

5 Related Work

In 2003 Harald C. Gall et al. [2] elaborated methods to analyze the evolution of software systems. The QCR-approach was used to learn about the evolution of a software system based on its (change) history. The approach comprises quantitative analysis, change sequence analysis and relation analysis to determine logical dependencies between different parts of a system. These logical couplings (dependencies) will be used to find architectural shortcomings in the software system.

Fluri et al. [3] use software evolution analysis tools [14] to extract historical data from CVS for change type pattern discovering. Here, the extraction of change dependencies is limited on sliding time window technique.

Zimmermann et al. [4] apply data mining techniques to find association rules to 1) suggest and predict likely changes, 2) prevent errors due to incomplete changes and 3) detect couplings undetectable by program analysis. The approach is able to compute rules based on transaction in the CVS. But, nevertheless, the basis of co-changes are transactions. They have not investigated additional strategies to find further logical change couplings in the CVS to broaden the data basis.

Kagdi et al. [5] combine single-version and evolutionary dependencies for estimating software changes. This approach is particular interesting, because they combine methods of dependency analysis and MSR-analysis. They hypothesize, that combining dependencies out of classical impact analysis approaches (e.g. dependency analysis) and out of mining software repositories will improve the support of software change prediction.

Zhou et al. [6] developed an approach to predict change couplings with a Bayesian network. One pillar of this framework is the extraction of historical CVS data. They also use the already elaborated tool EVOLIZER to retrieve modification reports from CVS using the sliding time window algorithm.

6 Summary

In this paper we presented strategies to detect logical change dependencies in common versioning systems. These dependencies contribute to avoid defects in implementing changes by supporting change impact analysis activities of analysts and developers. Based on transactions we have identified four strategies to investigate versioning system data in more detail to detect logical change dependencies. We have evaluated our findings in two industrial projects. Our next steps in research will be to integrate these strategies in an overall framework for change impact analysis as described in [15]. We aim to combine physical dependencies and logical dependencies to improve change impact analysis in the maintenance of software systems.

References

1. Arnold, R.S., Bohner, S.A.: Software Change Impact Analysis. IEEE Computer Society Press, Los Alamitos (1996)
2. Gall, H.C., Jazayeri, M., Krajewski, J.: CVS Release History Data for Detecting Logical Couplings. In: Proceedings of the International Workshop on Principles of Software Evolution, Helsinki, Finland, pp. 13–23. IEEE Computer Society Press, Los Alamitos (2003)
3. Fluri, B., Gall, H.C., Pinzger, M.: Fine-Grained Analysis of Change Couplings. In: Proceedings of the 5th International Workshop on Source Code Analysis and Manipulation, Budapest, Hungary, pp. 66–74. IEEE Computer Society Press, Los Alamitos (2005)
4. Zimmermann, T., Weißgerber, P., Diehl, S., Zeller, A.: Mining Version Histories to Guide Software Changes. IEEE Transaction on Software Engineering 31(6), 429–445 (2005); Student Member-Thomas Zimmermann and Member-Andreas Zeller
5. Kagdi, H., Maletic, J.I.: Combining Single-Version and Evolutionary Dependencies for Software-Change Prediction. In: MSR 2007: Proceedings of the Fourth International Workshop on Mining Software Repositories, Washington, DC, USA, , p. 17. IEEE Computer Society, Los Alamitos (2007)
6. Zhou, Y., Würsch, M., Giger, E., Gall, H.C.: A Bayesian Network Based Approach for Change Coupling Prediction. In: Proceedings of the 15th Working Conference on Reverse Engineering (WCRE). IEEE Computer Society Press, Los Alamitos (2008)
7. Fluri, B., Giger, E., Gall, H.C.: Discovering Patterns of Change Types. In: Proceedings of the 23rd International Conference on Automated Software Engineering. IEEE Computer Society, Los Alamitos (2008) (to appear) (short paper)
8. Fogel, K., O'Neill, M.: cvs2cl.pl: Cvs-Log-Message-to-Changelog Conversion Script (September 2002), `http://www.red-bean.com/cvs2cl/`
9. Sliwerski, J., Zimmermann, T., Zeller, A.: When Do Changes Induce Fixes? In: MSR 2005: Proceedings of the 2005 International Workshop on Mining Software Repositories, pp. 1–5. ACM Press, New York (2005)
10. Robbes, R.: Mining a Change-Based Software Repository. In: MSR 2007: Proceedings of the Fourth International Workshop on Mining Software Repositories, Washington, DC, USA, p. 15. IEEE Computer Society, Los Alamitos (2007)
11. Mylyn (2008), `http://www.eclipse.org/mylyn/`
12. Canfora, G., Cerulo, L.: Impact Analysis by Mining Software and Change Request Repositories. In: METRICS 2005: Proceedings of the 11th IEEE International Software Metrics Symposium (METRICS 2005), Washington, DC, USA, p. 29. IEEE Computer Society, Los Alamitos (2005)
13. Ying, A.T.T., Ng, R., Chu-Carroll, M.C.: Predicting Source Code Changes by Mining Change History. IEEE Trans. Softw. Eng. 30(9), 574–586 (2004); Member-Gail C. Murphy
14. Fluri, B., Wuersch, M., Pinzger, M., Gall, H.: Change Distilling: Tree Differencing for Fine-Grained Source Code Change Extraction. IEEE Trans. Softw. Eng. 33(11), 725–743 (2007)
15. Pirklbauer, G., Rappl, M.: A Novel Approach to Support Change Impact Analysis in the Maintenance of Software Systems. In: Cordeiro, J., Filipe, J. (eds.) ICEIS (1), pp. 453–456 (2008)

Efficient Testing of Equivalence of Words in a Free Idempotent Semigroup*

Jakub Radoszewski[1] and Wojciech Rytter[1,2]

[1] Department of Mathematics, Computer Science and Mechanics
University of Warsaw, Warsaw, Poland
{jrad,rytter}@mimuw.edu.pl
[2] Faculty of Mathematics and Informatics
Copernicus University, Toruń, Poland

Abstract. We present an automata–theoretic approach to a simple Burnside–type problem for semigroups. For two words of total length n over an alphabet Σ, we give an algorithm with time complexity $O(n \cdot |\Sigma|)$ and space complexity $O(n)$ which tests their equivalence under the idempotency relation $x^2 \approx x$. The algorithm verifies whether one word can be transformed to another one by repetitively replacing any factor x^2 by x or z by z^2. We show that the problem can be reduced to equivalence of acyclic deterministic automata of size $O(n \cdot |\Sigma|)$. An interesting feature of our algorithm is small space complexity — equivalence of introduced automata is checked in space $O(n)$, which is significantly less than the sizes of the automata. This is achieved by processing the acyclic automata layer by layer, each layer only of size $O(n)$, hence only small part of a large virtual automaton is kept in the memory.

Keywords: Burnside–type problem, finite automata, efficient algorithm.

1 Introduction

In this paper we study algorithmic aspects of some problems related to Burnside–type problems in semigroups. In 1902, Burnside [2] raised the following famous problem: "Is every group with a finite number of generators and satisfying an identical relation $x^r \approx 1$ finite?". Although the problem was solved negatively in 1968 by Adjan and Novikov [1], it has given birth to several related problems, including the Burnside problem for semigroups. The problem was first studied by Green and Rees, who proved [8] in 1952 that a finitely generated semigroup satisfying the identity $x^{r+1} \approx x$ is finite provided any finitely generated group satisfying the identity $x^r \approx 1$ is finite. In particular the free idempotent semigroup, i.e., satisfying the identity $x^2 \approx x$ is finite.

Although the theory of free Burnside semigroups was developed much slower than the corresponding theory for groups, tremendous progress was achieved in the former in the last 15 years — a summary of the known results can be found in

* Supported by grant N206 004 32/0806 of the Polish Ministry of Science and Higher Education.

J. van Leeuwen et al. (Eds.): SOFSEM 2010, LNCS 5901, pp. 663–671, 2010.

the excellent survey by do Lago and Simon [7]. In general, the semigroups satisfying $x^{r+s} \approx x^r$ for $r, s \geq 1$ are analyzed from different points of view: finiteness, regularity of languages corresponding to congruence classes of $\approx$, the structure of maximal subgroup of the semigroup and finally the *word problem*, in which it is investigated whether testing of $u \approx v$ is decidable. For $r \geq 3$ the word problem was proved to be decidable (due to the work of several authors [3,4,5,6,9,10,15]), for $r = 2$ the problem remains open (although for some cases effective algorithms were established, as in the recent paper [16]), finally for $r = 1$ the decidability of the word problem for groups implies decidability for semigroups [11].

To the best of our knowledge, the problem of efficient implementation of the algorithm for the word problem under idempotency relation ($r = 1$) has never been studied previously. For words $u, v \in \Sigma^*$ such that $|u|+|v| = n$, we design an algorithm with time complexity $O(n \cdot |\Sigma|)$ and memory complexity $O(n)$. Here we introduce an intuitive assumption that $|\Sigma| = O(n)$. This result is far better than a straightforward dynamic programming solution which yields $O(n^5)$ time complexity. Additionally, an interesting part of our result is that it combines methods from algebra, finite automata and algorithm analysis.

Let Σ be an arbitrary finite alphabet, $|\Sigma| = K$. Let Σ^* be the set of all words over the alphabet Σ and let $\Sigma^+ = \Sigma^* \setminus \{\epsilon\}$ where ϵ is the empty word. We introduce the *idempotency relation* $\sim_i$ in Σ^*

$$\forall_{x \in \Sigma^*} \quad xx \sim_i x$$

and denote by $\approx$ the congruence it generates. Then, the *free idempotent semigroup* (also called the free band) M generated by Σ is the set

$$M = \Sigma^* / \approx \ .$$

There also exists an alternative definition of M that is more relevant to our paper. We say that two words $u, v \in \Sigma^*$ are equivalent ($u \approx v$) if v can be derived from u, and vice versa, by a finite (possibly 0) number of applications of the rules:

- replace a factor x of u by its square xx, or
- replace a square factor xx by the word x.

Relation $\approx$ is an equivalence relation and the set of equivalence classes of this relation forms a semigroup (under concatenation) that is isomorphic to M.

Due to the Green–Rees theorem, the set M generated by any finite set Σ is also finite. The proof of the theorem [8,12,13,14] not only specifies its cardinality

$$\sum_{i=0}^{K} \binom{K}{i} \prod_{1 \leq j \leq i} (i - j + 1)^{2^j}$$

but also provides a recursive criterion for verification of equivalence of u and v under $\approx$ (see Theorem 1).

2 An Abstract Algorithm and Factor Automata

For $u = u_1 \dots u_k$, by $u[i..j]$ we denote a factor of u equal to $u_i \dots u_j$ (in particular $u[i] = u[i..i]$) and by $|u|$ we denote length of u, i.e. k. Words $u[1..i]$ are called prefixes of u, and words $u[i..k]$ suffixes of u.

Let $\mathrm{Alph}(u)$ be the set of all letters appearing in u. With each $u \in \Sigma^+$ we associate a (characteristic) quadruple

$$u \mathrel{\mathring{=}} (p, a, b, q), \quad \text{where:}$$

- $a, b \in \Sigma$, pa is a prefix and bq is a suffix of u;
- $\mathrm{Alph}(p) = \mathrm{Alph}(u) \setminus \{a\}$, and $\mathrm{Alph}(q) = \mathrm{Alph}(u) \setminus \{b\}$.

Example

$$\texttt{ababbbcbcbc} \mathrel{\mathring{=}} (\texttt{ababbb, c, a, bbbcbcbc})$$

Theorem 1 (equivalence criterion). [8]
Assume $u \mathrel{\mathring{=}} (p, a, b, q)$, $v \mathrel{\mathring{=}} (p', a', b', q')$. *Then,*

$$u \approx v \quad \textit{iff} \quad (\, p \approx p' \,\wedge\, a = a' \,\wedge\, b = b' \,\wedge\, q \approx q' \,).$$

The theorem implies correctness of the following abstract algorithm testing if $u \approx v$.

> **Algorithm TEST**(u, v)
> **if** $\mathrm{Alph}(u) \neq \mathrm{Alph}(v)$ **then return** *false*
> **if** $\mathrm{Alph}(u) = \emptyset$ **then return** *true*
> **let** $u \mathrel{\mathring{=}} (p, a, b, q)$, $v \mathrel{\mathring{=}} (p', a', b', q')$
> **if** $a \neq a' \vee b \neq b'$ **then return** *false*
> **return** $\mathrm{TEST}(p, p') \wedge \mathrm{TEST}(q, q')$

Let $\overline{\Sigma}$ be a disjoint copy of the alphabet Σ. For each letter $a \in \Sigma$ denote by $\overline{a}$ its copy. For words u, v with the same set of letters we define the *factor automaton* $A_{u,v}$ as follows:

- The set of input symbols is $\Sigma \cup \overline{\Sigma}$ and the set of states is the set of all factors of u and v.
- If x is a factor and $x \mathrel{\mathring{=}} (p, a, b, q)$ then we have two transitions

  $$x \xrightarrow{a} p, \quad x \xrightarrow{\overline{b}} q \,.$$

  Other transitions are undefined.
- There is only one accepting state: the empty word ϵ.

Observation 1. *From every state of* $A_{u,v}$ *there exists an accepting path.*

Recall that two states x, y of an automaton are called *equivalent* (notation: $x \sim y$) if the sets of labels of all accepting paths starting at x and at y are equal.

Lemma 1. $u \approx v$ *iff* u *and* v *are equivalent as states of the factor automaton* $A_{u,v}$.

Proof. We prove that for any two states x, y, $x \sim y$ iff $x \approx y$, by induction on $\min(|x|, |y|)$ (here we refer to x and y both as states of $A_{u,v}$ and as words from Σ^*).

The basis is very simple: if $x = \epsilon$ or $y = \epsilon$ then $x \sim y$ iff both x and y are accepting states $x = y = \epsilon$, what is equivalent to $x \approx y$.

If $|x|, |y| > 0$ then let

$$x \stackrel{\circ}{=} (p, a, b, q), \quad y \stackrel{\circ}{=} (p', a', b', q') .$$

In x there are transitions

$$x \xrightarrow{a} p, \quad x \xrightarrow{\overline{b}} q$$

whereas in y:

$$y \xrightarrow{a'} p', \quad y \xrightarrow{\overline{b'}} q' .$$

Assume that $x \sim y$. Due to Observation 1, there exists an accepting path starting from p, consequently there exists an accepting path from x starting with a transition with label a. Because $a \neq \overline{b'}$, this implies that $a = a'$ and $p \sim p'$. Similarly, there exists an accepting path starting from q, so $\overline{b} = \overline{b'}$ and $q \sim q'$. Thus we proved that

$$x \sim y \quad \Rightarrow \quad a = a',\ b = b',\ p \sim p',\ q \sim q' .$$

Conversely, let us observe that none of the states x, y is accepting. Therefore, by definition

$$a = a',\ b = b',\ p \sim p',\ q \sim q' \quad \Rightarrow \quad x \sim y .$$

Combining both implications, we obtain that $x \sim y$ iff $a = a'$, $b = b'$, $p \sim p'$, $q \sim q'$. Due to the inductive hypothesis, the last two conditions are equivalent to $p \approx p'$, $q \approx q'$. We conclude the proof applying the criterion from Theorem 1. □

We reduced equivalence of factors to equivalence of states in a deterministic automaton, however this does not give directly an efficient algorithm since the definition of the automaton is rather abstract.

3 Interval Automata: More Efficient Automata

We introduce interval automata as efficient implementation of factor automata. Because it is more convenient to deal with the same single word, we introduce the word $w = u\$v$, $|w| = n$, where \$ is a special delimiter that we add to Σ. From now on we deal only with the word w.

For a word w define the rank of an interval $[i..j]$ as $|\text{Alph}(w[i..j])|$. We say that an interval $[i..j]$ is *k–left* (for a fixed j) iff i is the smallest number such that $[i..j]$ is of rank k, similarly we define the *k–right* interval $[i..j]$ (for a fixed i) as the one for which j is the largest number such that $[i..j]$ is of rank k.

The k–left and k–right intervals are called *k–intervals*, and their set is denoted by $\mathcal{I}_k$ and called here the kth *layer*. Let $\mathcal{I}$ be the union of all $\mathcal{I}_k$'s.

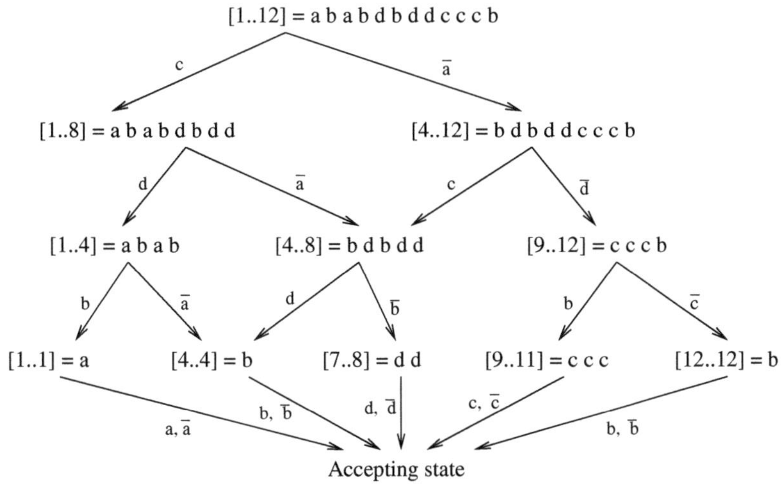

Fig. 1. The interval automaton of the word w = ababdbddcccb. For simplicity, the figure does not contain intervals from $\mathcal{I}$ that are not located on any path from $[1..12]$ to the accepting state $\emptyset$.

We define *interval automaton* $G(w)$ as follows. The set of states is $\mathcal{I}$ and the input alphabet is the same as for the factor automaton. If

$$x \stackrel{\circ}{=} (p, a, b, q), \quad \text{where} \quad x = w[i..j], \quad p = w[i..k], \quad q = w[l..j]$$

then we have two transitions

$$[i..j] \xrightarrow{a} [i..k], \quad [i..j] \xrightarrow{\overline{b}} [l..j] \ .$$

Other transitions are undefined. There is only one accepting state: the empty interval $\emptyset$ corresponding to the empty word ϵ.

Lemma 2. *Intervals corresponding to u and v within $w = u\$v$ are states of the interval automaton $G(w)$ and are equivalent iff their corresponding states are equivalent in the factor automaton $A_{u,v}$.*

Proof. Let us note that intervals corresponding to u and v are $|\text{Alph}(u)|$– and $|\text{Alph}(v)|$–intervals in w, therefore they appear in $G(w)$. Moreover, if states representing factors containing the \$ symbol are omitted, $G(w)$ is a subautomaton of $A_{u,v}$ and contains only the states that are "important" w.r.t. the algorithm of testing if $u \approx v$. In particular, since the defined transitions in $G(w)$ always lead to intervals from $\mathcal{I}$, all factors of w accessible from u and v are present in $G(w)$. □

The kth layer $\mathcal{I}_k$ will be represented by tables $LEFT_k$, $RIGHT_k$ where:
$LEFT_k[j] = i$ if $[i..j]$ is a k–left interval;
$RIGHT_k[i] = j$ if $[i..j]$ is a k–right interval;

if a corresponding k–left or k–right interval does not exist, $LEFT_k[j]$ and $RIGHT_k[i]$ are undefined.

Lemma 3

a) For each k we can compute in time and space $O(n)$ the set of intervals of rank k represented by the tables $LEFT_k$, $RIGHT_k$.

b) The interval automaton $G(w)$ can be constructed in $O(n \cdot |\Sigma|)$ time layer by layer, starting from layer 0 and finishing in layer K, in such a way that the construction of layer i requires only knowledge of layer $i-1$ and $O(n)$ additional storage.

Proof. To construct the table $RIGHT_k$ for a given $k \in \{0, 1, \ldots, K\}$ we use a sliding window algorithm (see the pseudocode of Compute_RIGHT1 and Fig. 2).

```
Algorithm Compute_RIGHT1(w, n, k)
    j ← 0
    Z ← ∅   (* a multiset *)
    for i = 1, 2, ..., n do
        if i > 1 then Z ← Z \ {w[i − 1]}
        while j < n and |Z ∪ {w[j + 1]}| ≤ k do
            j ← j + 1
            Z ← Z ∪ {w[j]}
        if |Z| = k  then RIGHT_k[i] ← j
```

In the ith step of the **for** loop of the algorithm we compute the *multiset* of characters

$$Z = \{w[i], w[i+1], \ldots, w[j]\} \quad \text{such that} \quad RIGHT_k[i] = j$$

using the observation that for each i, $RIGHT_k[i+1] \geq RIGHT_k[i]$.

If Z is implemented as a count array of size $K = O(n)$, it can be initialized in $O(n)$ time and all necessary operations on Z — inserting elements, deleting elements and computing the number $|Z|$ of *different* letters present in Z — can be performed in $O(1)$ time. The following pseudocode is an implementation of algorithm Compute_RIGHT1 using a count array.

```
Algorithm Compute_RIGHT2(w, n, k)
    Z : array[1..K] = (0, 0, ..., 0)
    size ← 0;  j ← 0
    for i = 1, 2, ..., n do
        if i > 1 then   (* performing the assignment "Z ← Z \ {w[i − 1]}" *)
            Z[w[i − 1]] ← Z[w[i − 1]] − 1
            if Z[w[i − 1]] = 0  then size ← size − 1
        while j < n and (Z[w[j + 1]] ≠ 0 or size < k) do
            j ← j + 1
            if Z[w[j]] = 0  then size ← size + 1
            Z[w[j]] ← Z[w[j]] + 1
        if size = k  then RIGHT_k[i] ← j
```

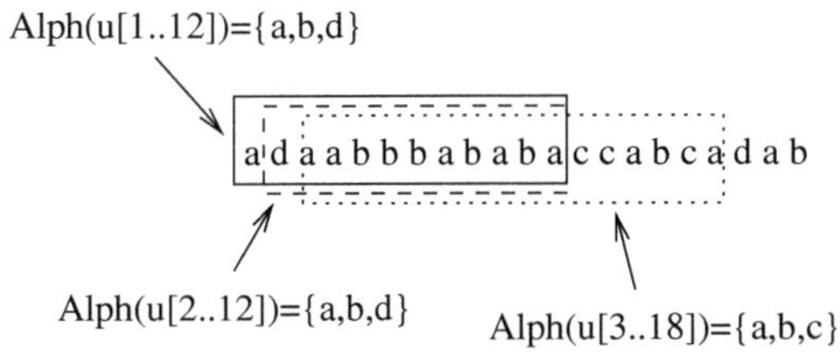

Fig. 2. Sliding window appearing during the computation of $RIGHT_3[1] = 12$, $RIGHT_3[2] = 12$ and $RIGHT_3[3] = 18$ for the word adaabbbababaccabcadab

The total number of steps of the **while** loop of the algorithm is $O(n)$, since in each step j increases by one. Thus, the total time and memory complexity of Compute_RIGHT2 is $O(n)$.

Computation of $LEFT_k$ can be performed analogically, what concludes the proof of point a).

Point b) follows from a), since transitions from interval $[i..j]$ in the interval automaton lead to intervals

$$[i..RIGHT_k[i]] \quad \text{and} \quad [LEFT_k[j]..j]$$

where $k+1 = |\text{Alph}(w[i..j])|$, and are labeled with letters

$$w[RIGHT_k[i]+1] \quad \text{and} \quad \overline{w[LEFT_k[j]-1]}$$

respectively. □

4 Testing Equivalence of States in $G(w)$

Our final goal is to design an algorithm for testing equivalence of states of the interval automaton $G(w)$. Let us first note that $G(w)$ also has the property mentioned in Observation 1.

Observation 2. *From every state of $G(w)$ there exists an accepting path.*

Lemma 4. *If x, y are states of $G(w)$ and $x \sim y$ then $x, y \in \mathcal{I}_k$ for some $k \in \{0, 1, \ldots, K\}$.*

Proof. Because $G(w)$ is acyclic, contains exactly one accepting state $\emptyset$ and all transitions from layer $\mathcal{I}_k$ for $k \geq 1$ lead to layer $\mathcal{I}_{k-1}$, it can be proved by simple induction that all accepting paths starting from $x \in \mathcal{I}_k$ are of length k. By Observation 2 there exists at least one such path for every x. This concludes that equivalent states of $G(w)$ cannot belong to different layers. □

We will label all states of $G(w)$ layer by layer in the order $k = 0, 1, \ldots, K$ in such a way that equivalent states from a single layer receive equal labels.

Lemma 5. *The following labeling ℓ:*

- $\ell(\emptyset) = 0$
- $\ell(x) = (\ell(p), a, b, \ell(q))$ *for every state* $x \in \mathcal{I}_k$ *such that transitions in* x *are labeled with letters* a *and* $\overline{b}$ *and lead to states* $p, q \in \mathcal{I}_{k-1}$ *resp.*

preserves the equivalence of states.

Proof. It is a consequence of the definition of $G(w)$ and Observation 2. □

Unfortunately, the labels assigned as in Lemma 5 can be quite large. However, we can keep them of constant size if we renumber the quadruples in each layer with integers of size $O(n)$. This is always possible since each layer of $G(w)$ contains at most $2n$ states. The renumbering can be performed by radix sort in $O(n)$ time and space per each layer by using arrays of size $O(n)$ and $K = O(n)$ for dimensions 1, 4 and 2, 3 of the quadruples resp.

Let us summarize the whole discussion. Due to Lemma 3, the interval automaton can be constructed layer by layer in $O(n)$ time and space per each layer. We have described an algorithm for labeling of states of $G(w)$ that preserves equivalence of states, executes in the same ordering of layers as the algorithm from Lemma 3 and has the same complexity. Due to Lemmas 1 and 2, this implies the following result.

Theorem 2 (Main result)
There exists an algorithm for checking whether $u \approx v$ *for two words of total length* n *in* $O(n \cdot |\Sigma|)$ *time and* $O(n)$ *space.*

5 Final Remarks

It can be observed that almost all labels of transitions in the automaton $G(w)$ can be removed without changing the output of the algorithm. More precisely, all labels from Σ apart from the transitions starting in layer 1 and all labels from $\overline{\Sigma}$ can be replaced by a special label $\# \notin \Sigma$, resulting in automaton $G'(w)$. It can be proved by a layer–by–layer induction that $u \sim v$ in $G'(w)$ iff $u \sim v$ in $G(w)$. Unfortunately, this does not lead to any improvement of the time complexity of the whole algorithm. We would like to thank Marcin Andrychowicz for showing us this observation.

We described a very efficient algorithm for testing if $u \approx v$ in a free idempotent semigroup. The remaining problem is to design an algorithm that transforms u to v replacing factors x^2 by x or z by z^2.

Lemma 6. *If* $u, v \in \Sigma^*$, $|u| + |v| = O(n)$ *and* $u \approx v$ *then there exists a sequence of "idempotent" transformations from* u *to* v *of length* $O(2^{|\Sigma|}n)$.

Proof. The proof of the Green–Rees theorem is constructive and the sequence of transformations it generates is of length $O(2^{|\Sigma|}n)$. □

The length of the sequence of steps from Lemma 6 is exponential in $|\Sigma|$. Thus the following open problems remain:

- Does there exist a polynomial time deterministic algorithm that always generates a sequence of transformations that is of polynomial length in terms of n and $|\Sigma|$?
- Does there exist such an algorithm for finding the *smallest* number of steps necessary to transform u to v?

References

1. Adjan, S.I.: The Burnside Problem and Identities in Groups. In: Ergebnisse der Mathematik und ihrer Grenzgebiete 95 [Results in Mathematics and Related Areas]. Translated from Russian by John Lennox and James Wiegold. Springer, Berlin (1979)
2. Burnside, W.: On an Unsettled Question in the Theory of Discontinuous Groups. Quart. J. Pure Appl. Math. 33, 230–238 (1902)
3. de Luca, A., Varricchio, S.: On Non-Counting Regular Classes. In: Paterson, M. (ed.) ICALP 1990. LNCS, vol. 443, pp. 74–87. Springer, Heidelberg (1990)
4. de Luca, A., Varricchio, S.: On Non-Counting Regular Classes. Theoret. Comput. Sci. 100, 67–104 (1992)
5. do Lago, A.P.: On the Burnside Semigroups $x^n = x^{n+m}$. In: Simon, I. (ed.) LATIN 1992. LNCS, vol. 583, pp. 329–343. Springer, Heidelberg (1992)
6. do Lago, A.P.: On the Burnside Semigroups $x^n = x^{n+m}$. Int. J. Algebra Comput. 6, 179–227 (1996)
7. do Lago, A.P., Simon, I.: Free Burnside Semigroups. Theoret. Informatics Appl. 35, 579–595 (2001)
8. Green, J.A., Rees, D.: On Semigroups in which $x^r = x$. Math. Proc. Camb. Phil. Soc. 48, 35–40 (1952)
9. Guba, V.S.: The Word Problem for the Relatively Free Semigroup Satisfying $t^m = t^{m+n}$ with $m \geq 3$. Int. J. Algebra Comput. 2, 335–348 (1993)
10. Guba, V.S.: The Word Problem for the Relatively Free Semigroup Satisfying $t^m = t^{m+n}$ with $m \geq 4$ or $m = 3, n = 1$. Int. J. Algebra Comput. 2, 125–140 (1993)
11. Kaďourek, J., Polák, L.: On Free Semigroups Satisfying $x^r = x$. Simon Stevin 64, 3–19 (1990)
12. Karhumaki, J.: Combinatorics on Words. Notes in pdf
13. Lallement, G.: Semigroups and Combinatorial Applications. J. Wiley and Sons, New York (1979)
14. Lothaire, M.: Combinatorics on Words. Addison-Wesley, Reading (1983)
15. McCammond, J.: The Solution to the Word Problem for the Relatively Free Semigroups Satisfying $t^a = t^{a+b}$ with $a \geq 6$. Int. J. Algebra Comput. 1, 1–32 (1991)
16. Plyushchenko, A.N., Shur, A.M.: Almost Overlap-Free Words and the Word Problem for the Free Burnside Semigroup Satisfying $x^2 = x^3$. In: Proc. of WORDS 2007 (2007)

An Amortized Search Tree Analysis for k-Leaf Spanning Tree

Daniel Raible and Henning Fernau

Univ.Trier, FB 4—Abteilung Informatik
54286 Trier, Germany
{raible,fernau}@informatik.uni-trier.de

Abstract. The problem of finding a spanning tree in an undirected graph with a maximum number of leaves is known to be $\mathcal{NP}$-hard. We present an algorithm which finds a spanning tree with at least k leaves in time $\mathcal{O}^*(3.4575^k)$ which improves the currently best algorithm. The estimation of the running time is done by using a non-standard measure. The present paper is one of the few examples that employ the Measure & Conquer paradigm of algorithm analysis, developed within the field of Exact Exponential-Time Algorithmics, within the area of Parameterized Algorithmics.

1 Introduction

In this paper we address with the following problem in graphs:

k-Leaf Spanning Tree
Given: An undirected graph $G(V, E)$, and the parameter k.
We ask: Is there a spanning tree for G with at least k leaves?

The problem has a notable applicability in the design of ad-hoc sensor networks [1,18]. In this area it might be referred to as Connected Dominating Set. A spanning tree with k leaves is equivalent to a connected dominating set with $n-k$ vertices. The k-leaf spanning tree problem already has been widely studied with regard to its approximability. Solis-Oba [17] obtained a 2-approximation running in polynomial time. In almost linear time Lu and Ravi [16] provided a 3-approximation. Bonsma and Zickfeld [3] could show that the problem is $\frac{3}{2}$-approximable when the input is restricted to cubic graphs.

Concerning parameterized algorithms, a sequence of papers culminated in the one of Kneis, Langer and Rossmanith [14]. This fairly simple branching algorithm achieves a running time of $\mathcal{O}^*(4^k)$[1]. Prior to this there were running time achievements by Bonsma *et al.* [2] of $\mathcal{O}^*(9.49^k)$, by Estivill-Castro *et al.* [8] of $\mathcal{O}^*(8.12^k)$ and by Bonsma and Zickfeld [4] of $\mathcal{O}^*(6.75^k)$. These bounds all have been obtained by using combinatorial arguments. The best kernelization result is due to [8] where they exhibited a kernel size of $3.75k$ (see [7] for a formal

[1] The $\mathcal{O}^*()$-notation suppresses polynomial factors in n.

J. van Leeuwen et al. (Eds.): SOFSEM 2010, LNCS 5901, pp. 672–684, 2010.

definition of *kernel*). There is also a directed version of the problem: Find an out-branching with k leaves. Here an out-branching in a directed graph is a tree in the underlying undirected graph. But the arcs are directed from the root to the leaves, which are the vertices of out-degree zero. The algorithm of Kneis, Langer and Rossmanith [14] solves also this problem in time $\mathcal{O}^*(4^k)$. Moreover, in Daligault *et al.* [6] an upper-bound of $\mathcal{O}^*(3.72^k)$ is stated. Koutis and Williams [15] could derive a randomized $\mathcal{O}^*(2^k)$-algorithm for the undirected version.

1.1 Our Framework: Parameterized Complexity

A *parameterized problem* P is a subset of $\Sigma^* \times \mathbb{N}$, where Σ is a fixed alphabet and $\mathbb{N}$ is the set of all non-negative integers. Therefore, each instance of the parameterized problem P is a pair (I, k), where the second component k is called the *parameter*. The language $L(P)$ is the set of all YES-instances of P. We say that the parameterized problem P is *fixed-parameter tractable* [7] if there is an algorithm that decides whether an input (I, k) is a member of $L(P)$ in time $f(k)|I|^c$, where c is a fixed constant and $f(k)$ is a function independent of the overall input length $|I|$.

1.2 Our Contributions

We developed the simple and elegant algorithm of [14] further. The running time improvement of $\mathcal{O}^*(3.4575^k)$ is due to two reasons: 1. We could improve the bottleneck case by new branching rules. 2. Due using amortized analysis, we were able to prove a tighter upper-bound on the running time. For this we use a non-standard measure which in its form is quite related to the measure & conquer-approach (M&C) in exact, non-parameterized algorithmics, see Fomin, Grandoni and Kratsch [12]. Notice however that there are only few examples for using M&C in parameterized algorithmics. In addition, we analyze our algorithm with respect to the number of vertices and obtain also small improvements for the Minimum Connected Dominating Set problem. This seems to be the first attempt to analyze the same algorithm both with respect to the standard parameter k and with respect to the number of vertices n. We mention that the approaches of [6, 9] is going to some extent into the same direction. The basic scheme of the algorithms is similar. Nevertheless, our running time shows that our results are different. Moreover, the first paper does not make use of M&C techniques and the second follows a non-parameterized route. Due to lack of space we refrain from giving all the proofs.

1.3 Terminology

We are considering undirected simple graphs $G(V, E)$ with vertex set V and edge set $E \subseteq \{\{u, v\} \mid u, v \in V\}$. An edge $\{x, y\}$ might also be abbreviated as $x\,y$. The *neighborhood* of a vertex $v \in V$ is $N_G(v) := \{u \mid \{u, v\} \in E\}$ and the *degree* of v is $d_G(v) = |N_G(v)|$. The *closed neighbor* is $N_G[v] = N_G(v) \cup \{v\}$. For some $V' \subseteq V$ let $N(V') := (\cup_{v \in V'} N(v)) \setminus V'$ and $E_{V'}(v) := \{\{u, v\} \in E \mid u \in V'\}$.

In case we have $V' = V$ or $E' = E$ we might suppress the subscript. $G[V']$ and $G[E']$ are the graphs induced on V' and E', respectively. An *edge cut set* is a subset $\hat{E} \subset E$ such that $G[E \setminus \hat{E}]$ is not connected. A *tree* is a subset of edges $T \subseteq E$ such that $G[T]$ is connected and cycle-free. A *spanning tree* is a tree such that $\bigcup_{e \in T} e = V$. A tree T' extends another tree T if $T \subseteq T'$. We will write $T' \succ T$. A *bridge* $e \in E$ leaves $G[E \setminus \{e\}]$ disconnected. For any $E' \subseteq E$ let $leaves(E') := |\{v \in V \mid d_{E'}(v) = 1\}|$ and $internal(E') := \{v \in V \mid d_V(v) = |E_V(v) \cap E'|\}$.

1.4 Overall Strategy

We address the following annotated version of our problem:

ROOTED k-LEAF SPANNING TREE
Given: An undirected graph $G(V, E)$ a root vertex $r \in V$, and the parameter k.
We ask: Is there a spanning tree T for G with $leaves(T) \geq k$ with $d_T(r) \geq 2$?

An algorithm solving this problem will also solve k-LEAF SPANNING TREE (with a polynomial delay) by considering every $v \in V$ as the root. All throughout the algorithm we will maintain a tree $T \subseteq E$ whose vertices are $V_T := \bigcup_{e \in T} e$. Let $\overline{V}_T := V \setminus V_T$. T will be seen as predetermined to be part of the solution. During the course of the algorithm, T will have two types of leaves. Namely, *leaf nodes (LN)* and *branching nodes (BN)*. The first mentioned will also appear as leaves in the solution. The latter ones can be leaves or internal vertices. Generally, we decide this by branching as far as reduction rules do not enforce exactly one possibility. *Internal nodes* (IN) are already determined to be non-leaves in T.

The algorithm will also produce a third kind of leaves: *floating leaves (FL)*. These are vertices from $\overline{V}_T$ which are already determined to be leaves, but are not attached to the tree T yet. If a vertex is neither a branching node nor a leaf node nor a floating leaf nor an internal node we call it *free*. We will refer to the different possible roles of a vertex by a labeling function $lab : V \to \{\text{IN}, \text{FL}, \text{BN}, \text{LN}, \text{free}\} := D$. A given tree T' defines a labeling $V_{T'} \to D$ to which we refer by $lab_{T'}$. Let $\text{IN}_{T'} := \{v \in V_{T'} \mid d_{T'}(v) \geq 2\}$, $\text{LN}_{T'} := \{v \in V_{T'} \mid d_{\overline{V}_{T'}}(v) = 0, d(v) = 1\}$ and $\text{BN}_{T'} = V_{T'} \setminus (\text{IN} \cup \text{LN})$. Then for any $ID \in D \setminus \{\text{FL}, \text{free}\}$ we have $ID_{T'} = lab^{-1}(ID)$. We always ensure that lab_T and lab are the same on V_T. The subscript might be suppressed if $T' = T$. If $T' \succ T$, then we assume that $\text{IN}_T \subseteq \text{IN}_{T'}$ and $\text{LN}_T \subseteq \text{LN}_{T'}$. So, the labels IN and LN remain once they are fixed. For the labels, we have the following possible transitions: FL $\to$ LN, BN $\to$ {LN, IN} and free $\to D \setminus \{\text{free}\}$. Subsequently, we assume $|V| > 4$.

1.5 Parameterized Measure and Conquer

We follow a more general approach of how to measure the running time in a parameter k than in the, say, traditional way where during the branching process usually recursive calls will be made with parameters $k' < k$. Our point of view is that we are given an initial budget k. During the execution of the algorithm this budget will be decremented due to obtained structural information. This structural information does not necessarily refer to the case that some objects are fixed to be in the future solution. It can comprise much more (i.e. degree-one vertices, four-cycles). We allow to count such structural information only fractional. Clearly, we have to show that the budget never increases on applying reduction rules and even decreases in case of recursive calls. But additionally once our budget has been consumed we must be able to give an appropriate answer in polynomial time. As in general we counted more than only future solution objects this might become a hard and tedious task. If we are able to fulfill all the recited conditions we can prove a running time of the form $\mathcal{O}^*(c^k)$.

2 Reduction Rules and Observations

2.1 Reduction Rules

We assume that reduction rule **(i)** is applied before **(i+1)**. The rules **(1)**-**(3)** also appeared in previous work [9].

(1) If there is an edge $e \in E \setminus T$ with $e \subseteq V_T$, then delete e.
(2) Every $v \in \mathrm{BN}$ with $d(v) = 1$ becomes a leaf node.
(3) Let $u \in \mathrm{BN}$. If the removal of $E_{\overline{V}_T}(u)$ in $G[V \setminus \mathrm{FL}]$ or $G[V]$ creates two components then u becomes internal.
(4) Let u, v be free and assume that there is a bridge $\{u, v\} \in E \setminus T$ in $G[V]$, where C_1, C_2 are the two components created by deleting $\{u, v\}$. If $|V(C_1)| > 1$ and $|V(C_2)| > 1$ then contract $\{u, v\}$. The new vertex is also free.
(5) Delete $\{u, v\} \in E$ if u and v are floating leaves.
(6) Delete $\{u, v\} \in E \setminus T$ if $d_V(u) = 2$ and $a)$ $d_V(v) = 2$, or $b)$ $v \in \mathrm{FL}$.
(7) Delete $\{u, v\}$ if $u \in \mathrm{BN}$ with $d(u) = 2$, $N_{\overline{V}_T}(u) = \{v\}$ and $d_{V_T}(v) \geq 2$, see Figure 1(a).
(8) If u, x_1, x_2 form a triangle, x_1 is free and $\{h\} = N(x_1) \setminus \{x_2, u\}$ such that $d(h) = 1$, see Figure 1(b). Then x_1 becomes a floating leaf and h will be deleted.
(9) Let $h \in \overline{V}_T$ be a free vertex such that $a)$ $N_{\overline{V}_T}(h) = \{q\}$ and $d(q) = 1$ or $b)$ $d_{\overline{V}_T}(h) = 0$, see Figure 1(c). Then h becomes a floating leaf and q is deleted in case $a)$.

Lemma 1. *The reduction rules are sound.*

Lemma 2. *Reduction rule* **(1)** *does not create bridges in* $E \setminus T$.

From now on we assume that G is reduced due to the given reduction rules.

2.2 Observations

If $N(internal(T)) \subseteq internal(T) \cup leaves(T)$, we call T an *inner-maximal* tree.

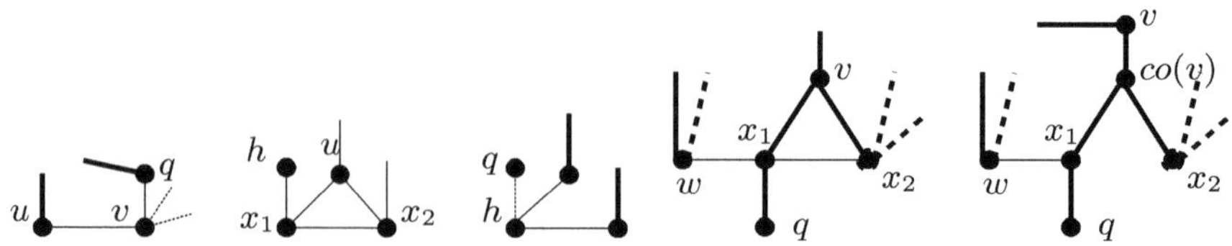

(a) RR7 (b) RR8 (c) RR9 (d) RR10 (e) RR10

Fig. 1. Bold edges are from T. Dotted edges may be present or not.

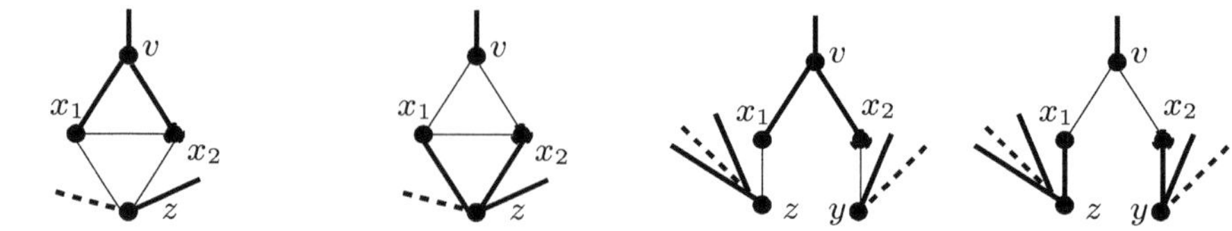

(a) Lemma 7.1 (b) Lemma 7.1 (c) Lemma 7.2 (d) Lemma 7.2

Fig. 2. Bold edges are from T. Dotted edges may be present or not.

Lemma 3 ([14] Lemma 4). *Let $v \in BN_T$ where T is a inner-maximal spanning tree. Then if there is a spanning tree $T' \succ T$ such that $v \in internal(T')$ there is also inner-maximal spanning tree $T'' \succeq T$ with $|leaves(T')| \leq |leaves(T'')|$.*

By the above lemma we can restrict our attention to inner-maximal spanning trees. And in fact the forthcoming algorithm will only construct such trees. Then for a $v \in internal(T)$ we have that $E_V(v) \subseteq T$ as by Lemma 3 we can assume that T is inner-maximal. Thus, in the very beginning we have $T = E_V(r)$.

Lemma 4. *Let $v \in BN_T$ and $N_{\overline{V}_T}(v) = \{u\}$. Then u is free and $d_{\overline{V}_T}(u) \geq 2$.*

Proof. Note that $d_V(v) = 2$. Moreover, $u \notin \text{IN} \cup \text{BN} \cup \text{FL}$ due to **(1)**, **(3)** and **(6.b)**. Thus, u is free. If $d_{\overline{V}_T}(u) = 0$ then **(9.b)** could be applied. If $d_{\overline{V}_T}(u) = 1$ then either we can apply **(3)** (if $\{u, v\}$ is a bridge) or **(6.a)** or **(7)** depending on whether $d_{V_T}(u) \geq 2$ or not. □

We are now going to define some function $co : \text{BN} \to V$. For $v \in \text{BN}$, let

$$co(v) = \begin{cases} v : d_{\overline{V}_T}(v) \geq 2 \\ u : N_{\overline{V}_T}(v) = \{u\} \end{cases}$$

Note that co is well defined as we have $d_{\overline{V}_T}(v) \geq 1$ (otherwise it becomes a leaf node **(2)**). Note that we have $d_{\overline{V}_T}(co(v)) \geq 2$. Either $d_{\overline{V}_T}(v) \geq 2$ or $d_{\overline{V}_T}(v) = 1$. In the latter case, $N_{\text{free}}(v) = N_{\overline{V}_T}(v) = \{u\}$, such that $d_{\overline{V}_T}(u) \geq 2$ by Lemma 4. This property will be used frequently.

Lemma 5 ([14] Lemma 5). *Let $v \in BN_T$ such that $N_{\overline{V}_T}(v) = \{u\}$. If there is no spanning tree $T' \succ T$ with k leaves and $lab_{T'}(v) = LN$, then there is also no spanning tree $T'' \succ T$ with k leaves, $lab_{T''}(v) = IN$ and $lab_{T''}(u) = LN$.*

Observe that for a vertex v with $co(v) \neq v$ once we set $lab(v) = \text{IN}$ then it is also valid to set $lab(co(v)) = \text{IN}$. By Lemma 5 we must only ensure that we also consider the possibility $lab(v) = \text{LN}$.

A Further Reduction Rule With the assertion of Lemma 4 we state another reduction rule:

(10) Let $w \in \text{BN}$ with $x_1 \in N_{\text{free}}(w)$ such that a degree one vertex q is attached to x_1, see Figure 1(d). Further, if *a*) there exists $v \in \text{BN}$ with $N_{\overline{V_T}}(v) = \{x_1, x_2\}$ and $\{x_1, x_2\} \in E$ or *b*) there exists $v \in \text{BN}$ with $co(v) \neq v$ and $N_{\overline{V_T}}(co(v)) = \{x_1, x_2\}$, see Figure 1(e), then set $lab(v) = \text{LN}$.

Lemma 6. *Rule* **(10)** *is sound.*

The next lemmas refer to the case where there is a $v \in \text{BN}_T$ with $d_{\overline{V_T}}(v) = 2$. In the following we use $\mathcal{N} := \{co(v), x_1, x_2\}$.

Lemma 7. *Let $T \subseteq E$ be a given tree such that $v \in BN_T$ and $N(co(v)) = \{x_1, x_2\}$. Let T', T^* be optimal spanning trees under the restrictions $T' \succ T$, $T^* \succ T$, $lab_{T'}(v) = LN$, $lab_{T^*}(v) = lab_{T^*}(co(v)) = IN$ and $lab_{T^*}(x_1) = lab_{T^*}(x_2) = LN$.*

1. *If there is a $z \in ((N(x_1) \cap N(x_2)) \setminus \{co(v)\})$, then $leaves(T') \geq leaves(T^*)$.*
2. *If $co(v) = v$, $y \in N(x_2) \setminus \{v\}$, $z \in N(x_1) \setminus \{v\}$ with $lab_{T^*}(z) = IN$, then $leaves(T') \geq leaves(T^*)$.*
3. *If $co(v) \neq v$ and if there is a $z \in ((N(x_1) \cup N(x_2)) \setminus \mathcal{N})$ with $lab_{T^*}(z) = IN$, then $leaves(T') \geq leaves(T^*)$.*

Proof

1. Firstly, suppose $co(v) = v$. Consider $T^+ := (T^* \setminus \{v\,x_1, v\,x_2\}) \cup \{z\,x_1, z\,x_2\}$, see Figures 2(a) and 2(b). We have $lab_{T^+}(v) = \text{LN}$ and z can be the only vertex besides v where $lab_{T^+}(z) \neq lab_{T^*}(z)$. Thus, z could be the only vertex with $lab_{T^+}(z) = \text{IN}$ and $lab_{T^*}(z) = \text{LN}$. Therefore, $leaves(T') \geq leaves(T^+) \geq leaves(T^*)$. Secondly, if $co(v) \neq v$ then consider $T^\# := (T^* \setminus \{v\,co(v), co(v)\,x_2\}) \cup \{z\,x_1, z\,x_2\}$ instead of T^+.
2. Consider $T^+ := (T^* \setminus \{v\,x_1, v\,x_2\}) \cup \{z\,x_1, y\,x_2\}$, see Figures 2(c) and 2(d). We have $lab_{T^+}(v) = \text{LN}$ and at most for y we could have $lab_{T^*}(y) = \text{LN}$ and $lab_{T^+}(y) = \text{IN}$. Hence, $leaves(T') \geq leaves(T^+) \geq leaves(T^*)$.
3. Consider $T^\# := (T^* \setminus \{v\,co(v)\}) \cup \{z\,x_1\}$. We have $lab_{T^\#}(v) = \text{LN}$ and therefore $leaves(T') \geq leaves(T^\#) \geq leaves(T^*)$. □

Lemma 8. *Let $T \subseteq E$ be a given tree such that $v \in BN_T$ and $N(co(v)) = \{x_1, x_2\}$. Let T', T^* be optimal spanning trees under the restrictions $T' \succ T$, $T^* \succ T$, $lab_{T'}(v) = LN$, $lab_{T^*}(v) = lab_{T^*}(co(v)) = IN$ and $lab_{T^*}(x_1) = LN$.*

1. *If $co(v) = v$, $\{x_1, x_2\} \in E$, $N(x_2) \setminus FL = \{v, x_1\}$ and if there is a $z \in N(x_1) \setminus \mathcal{N}$ with $lab_{T^*}(z) = IN$, then $leaves(T') \geq leaves(T^*)$.*
2. *If $co(v) \neq v$, $N(x_2) \setminus FL \subseteq \{co(v), x_1\}$ and if there is a $z \in N(x_1) \setminus \mathcal{N}$ with $lab_{T^*}(z) = IN$, then $leaves(T') \geq leaves(T^*)$.*

Algorithm 1. Description of the branching algorithm

Data: A graph $G = (V, E)$, k and a tree $T \subseteq E$.
Result: YES if there is a spanning tree with at least k leaves and NO otherwise.

```
if G[V \ FL] is not connected or BN = ∅ then
    return NO
else if κ ≤ 0 then
    return YES
else
    Apply the reduction rules exhaustively
    Choose a vertex v ∈ BN of maximum degree
    if d_{\overline{V_T}}(co(v)) ≥ 3 then
        ⟨v ∈ LN; v, co(v) ∈ IN⟩                                             (B1)
    else if N_{\overline{V_T}}(co(v)) = {x1, x2} then
        Choose v according to the following priorities:
        case ({x1, x2} ⊆ FL) or                                             (B2.a)
        (x1 free & d_{\overline{V_T}\N}(x1) = 0) or                         (B2.b)
        (x1 free & N_{\overline{V_T}\N}(x1) = {z} & (d_{\overline{V_T}\N}(z) ≤ 1 or z ∈ FL))   (B2.c)
            ⟨v ∈ LN; v, co(v) ∈ IN⟩                                         (B2)
        case x1 free, x2 ∈ FL or                                            (B3.a)
        x1, x2 free, N_{\overline{FL}}(x2) ⊆ {x1, co(v)} or                 (B3.b)
        x1, x2 free & d_{\overline{V_T}\N}(x2) = 1                          (B3.c)
            ⟨v ∈ LN; v, co(v) ∈ IN, x1 ∈ LN; v, co(v), x1, co(x1) ∈ IN⟩     (B3)
        case x1, x2 free & ∃z ∈ ⋂_{i=1,2} N_{\overline{FL}\N}(xi)
            ⟨v ∈ LN; v, co(v), x2, co(x2) ∈ IN, x1 ∈ LN; v, co(v), x1, co(x1) ∈ IN⟩
            (B4)
        otherwise
            ⟨v ∈ LN; v, co(v) ∈ IN, x1, x2 ∈ LN; v, co(v), x2, co(x2) ∈ IN, x1 ∈
            LN; v, co(v), x1, co(x1) ∈ IN⟩                                  (B5)
```

3. *If $lab_{T^*}(x_2) = IN$, $d_{T^*}(x_2) = 2$, $E_{\overline{V_T}}(co(v))$ is not a edge cut-set in G and if there is a $z \in N(x_1) \setminus \mathcal{N}$ with $lab_{T^*}(z) = IN$, then $leaves(T') \geq leaves(T^*)$.*

In [14] the bottleneck case was when branching on a vertex $v \in BN$ with at most two non-tree neighbors, that is $d_{\overline{V_T}}(v) \leq 2$. The last two lemmas deal with this case. If the bottleneck case also matches the conditions of Lemma 7 or 8 we either can skip some recursive call or decrease the yet to be defined measure by an extra amount. Otherwise we show that the branching behavior is more beneficial. This is a substantial ingredient for achieving a better running time upper bound.

3 The Algorithm

We are now ready to present Algorithm 1. We mention that if the answer YES is returned a k-leaf spanning tree can be constructed easily. This will be guaranteed by Lemma 9. For the sake of a short presentation of the different branchings, we introduce the following notation $\langle b_1; b_2; \ldots; b_n \rangle$ called a *branching*. Here the entries b_i are separated by a semicolon and stand for the different *parts of the branching*. They will express how the label of some vertices change. For example: $\langle v \in \text{LN}; v, co(v) \in \text{IN} \rangle$.This stands for a binary branching where in the first part we set $lab(v) = \text{LN}$ and in the second $lab(v) = lab(co(v)) = \text{IN}$. When we set $lab(v) = \text{IN}$ then we also set $T \leftarrow T \cup \{\{u,v\} \in E \mid u \notin V_T\}$. This is justified by Lemma 3. If we set $lab(v) = \text{LN}$, then we delete $\{\{u,v\} \in E \mid \{u,v\} \notin T\}$ as these edges will never appear in any solution. To derive an upper-bound on the running time for our algorithm, we use the measure

$$\kappa := k - \omega_f \cdot |\text{FL}| - \omega_b \cdot |\text{BN}| - |\text{LN}| \text{ with } \omega_b = 0.5130 \text{ and } \omega_f = 0.4117.$$

κ is defined by a tree T and a labeling (which both are to be built up by our algorithm). Thus, we use a subscript when we are referring to this, i.e., κ_T.

3.1 Correctness

In every branching of our algorithm, the possibility that $lab(v) = \text{LN}$ is considered. This recursive call must be possible as otherwise **(3)** would have been triggered before. Now consider the case $co(v) \neq v$. If the recursive call for $lab(v) = \text{LN}$ does not succeed, then we consider $lab(v) = \text{IN}$. Due to Lemma 5 we immediately can also set $lab(co(v)) = \text{IN}$. This fact is used throughout the branchings (B1)-(B5). Nonetheless, in the branchings (B1), (B2), (B3) and (B5) every possibility for v, x_1 and x_2 is considered in one part of the branching. (B4) is an exception to this as it does not consider the possibility that $lab(v) = \text{IN}$ and $lab(x_1) = lab(x_2) = \text{LN}$. Here we refer to Lemma 7.1, which states that a no worse solution can be found when we set $lab(v) = \text{LN}$.

When our algorithm returns YES, then T might still not be a spanning tree. We first have to attach all the floating leaves to T. It is possible that a branching node turns into a internal node and thus κ increases. The next important lemma shows if we take all the floating leaves and branching nodes into account then κ decreases.

Lemma 9. *If given a labeling our algorithm returns* YES, *a spanning tree* $\hat{T}$ *with* $leaves(\hat{T}) \geq k$ *can be constructed in polynomial time.*

Proof. Delete FL and compute a depth-first spanning tree DT for the remaining graph starting from T. Then attach the vertices from FL to one of its neighbors. This way we obtain a spanning tree $\hat{T} \succ T$. Let $\text{LBN} = \text{BN}_T \cap \text{LN}_{\hat{T}}$ and $\text{IBN} = \text{BN}_T \setminus \text{LBN}$. For $c \in \text{IBN}$ let T_c be the subtree rooted at c in $\hat{T}$. Clearly, $leaves(T_c) \geq 1$ (✱). Observe that every vertex $v \in \text{FL} \cup \text{LBN}$ now has weight zero. Thus, $\kappa_{\hat{T}}$ was decreased by $(1 - \omega_f)$ or $(1 - \omega_b)$, resp., with respect to κ_T due to making v a leaf node. Due to the next inequality we have $leaves(\hat{T}) \geq k$.

$$\begin{aligned} k - |\text{LN}_{\hat{T}}| = \kappa_{\hat{T}} &\leq \kappa_T - |\text{LBN}| \cdot (1 - \omega_b) + |\text{IBN}| \cdot \omega_b - |\text{FL}| \cdot (1 - \omega_f) \\ &\leq \kappa_T + |\text{IBN}| \cdot \omega_b - \sum\nolimits_{c \in \text{IBN}} leaves(T_c) \cdot (1 - \omega_f) \\ &\leq \kappa_T + |\text{IBN}| \cdot (\omega_b + \omega_f - 1) \leq \kappa_T \leq 0 \qquad \text{(by (✱))} \quad \square \end{aligned}$$

Next we consider the interaction of the reduction rules with the measure.

Lemma 10. *An exhaustive application of the reduction rules never increases κ.*

3.2 Run Time Analysis

In our algorithm the changes of κ are due to reduction rules or branching. In the first case Lemma 10 ensures that κ will never increase. In the second case we have reductions of κ of the following type. When a vertex $v \in \mathrm{BN}$ is made a leaf node (i.e., we set $lab(v) = \mathrm{LN}$) then κ will drop by an amount of $(1 - \omega_b)$. On the other hand when v becomes an internal node (i.e., we set $lab(v) = \mathrm{IN}$) then κ will increase by ω_b. This is due to v not becoming a leaf. Moreover, the free neighbors of v become branching nodes and the floating leaves become leaf nodes, due to Lemma 3. Therefore κ will be decreased by ω_b and $1 - \omega_f$, respectively. We point out that the weights ω_b and ω_f have to be chosen such that κ will not increase in any part of a branching of our algorithm.

Analyzing the Different Cases
(B1) Let $i := |N_{\overline{V}_T}(v) \cap \mathrm{FL}|$ and $j := |N_{\overline{V}_T} \cap \mathrm{free}|$. Note that $i + j \geq 3$. Then the branching vector is: $(1 - \omega_b, i \cdot (1 - \omega_f) + j \cdot \omega_b - \omega_b)$.

(B2) a) The branching vector is $(1 - \omega_b, 2 \cdot (1 - \omega_f) - \omega_b)$.
b) When we set $lab(v) = lab(co(v)) = \mathrm{IN}$ the vertex x_1 will become a leaf node due to **(1)**. The branching vector is $(1 - \omega_b, 1 + \min\{1 - \omega_f, \omega_b\} - \omega_b)$.
c) Firstly, suppose that $z \in FL$.

1. $d(z) = 1$:
   (a) $co(v) = v$: If $\{x_1, x_2\} \notin E$ then either **(9.a)** or **(3)** applies (depending whether $d_{V_T}(x_1) > 0$). If $\{x_1, x_2\} \in E$ then there is $z_1 \in N_{V_T}(x_1) \setminus \{v\}$ as otherwise **(8)** applies. But then **(10.a)** applies.
   (b) $co(v) \neq v$: If $d_{V_T}(x_1) = 0$ then either **(8)** or **(4)** applies (depending whether $\{x_1, x_2\} \in E$). If $d_{V_T}(x_1) > 0$ then **(10.b)** applies.
2. $d(z) \geq 2$: After setting $lab(v) = \mathrm{IN}$ and applying **(1)** exhaustively we have $d(x_1) = 2$ and $x_1, x_2 \in \mathrm{BN}$ afterwards. Observe that adding an edge to T does not create a bridge. The same holds for rule **(1)** (Lemma 2). Thus, rules **(3)** or **(4)** are not triggered before the rules with lower priority. As **(2)** and **(5)** do not change the local setting **(6.b)** will delete $\{x_1, z\}$, leading to a $(1 - \omega_b, 1 + \min\{1 - \omega_f, \omega_b\} - \omega_b)$ branch.

The case that $z \in \mathrm{free}$ can be seen by similar arguments.

Remark 1. From this point on, w.l.o.g., for a free vertex x_i, $i = 1, 2$, we have:

1. $d_{\overline{V}_T \setminus \mathcal{N}}(x_i) \geq 2$ or
2. $N_{\overline{V}_T \setminus \mathcal{N}}(x_i) = \{z_i\}$ such that $d_{\overline{V}_T \setminus \mathcal{N}}(z_i) \geq 2$ and $z_i \notin \mathrm{FL}$.

If $d_{\overline{V}_T \setminus \mathcal{N}}(x_i) = 0$ then (B2.b) would apply. If $d_{\overline{V}_T \setminus \mathcal{N}}(x_i) = 1$ and 2. would fail, then case (B2.c) applied.

Note that if 2. applies to x_i, then when we set $lab(v) = \mathrm{IN}$ we have that $co(x_i) = z_i$ after the application of the reduction rules. In this sense (with a slight abuse of notation) we set $co(x_i) = x_i$ if case 1. applies and $co(x_i) = z_i$ if case 2. applies.

(B3) If x_i is free let $fl_i := |(N(co(x_i)) \setminus \mathcal{N}) \cap \mathrm{FL}|$ and $fr_i := |(N(co(x_i)) \setminus \mathcal{N}) \cap \mathrm{free}|$. Due to Remark 1 we have $fl_i + fr_i \geq 2$.

a) Note that we must have that $S := N_{\overline{\mathrm{FL}}}(x_1) \setminus \mathcal{N} \neq \emptyset$ due to **(3)**. If $co(v) = v$, then also $N(x_i) \setminus \{v\} \neq \emptyset$ $(i = 1, 2)$ due to **(3)**. In the second part of the branch, every vertex in S can be assumed to be a leaf node in the solution. Otherwise, due to Lemmas 7.2 and 7.3, a solution, which is no worse, can be found in the first part of the branch when we set $lab(v) = \mathrm{LN}$. Hence, for $q \in S$ we get ω_f if $lab(q) = \mathrm{free}$ as we set $lab(q) = \mathrm{FL}$. If $lab(q) = \mathrm{BN}$, we set $lab(q) = \mathrm{LN}$ and receive $1 - \omega_b$. We have the following reduction in κ for the different parts of the branching.
$v \in \mathrm{LN}$: $1 - \omega_b$.
$v \in \mathrm{IN}, co(v) \in \mathrm{IN}, x_1 \in \mathrm{LN}$: $1 + fr_1 \cdot \omega_f + \max\{0, 1 - fr_1\} \cdot (1 - \omega_b) + 1 - \omega_f - \omega_b$
$v, co(v), x_1, co(x_1) \in \mathrm{IN}$: $1 - \omega_f + fl_1(1 - \omega_f) + fr_1 \cdot \omega_b - \omega_b$.

Remark 2. Note that from this point we have that x_1 and x_2 are free.

b) There is a $z_1 \in N_{\overline{\mathrm{FL}} \setminus \mathcal{N}}(x_1)$ (by **(3)**). If $co(v) = v$ then we must have $\{x_1, x_2\} \in E$ due to **(3)**. Thus, either Lemma 8.1 or 8.2 apply (depending whether $co(v) = v$ or not). Hence, analogously as in *a)* we obtain $\min\{\omega_f, 1 - \omega_b\}$ in addition from z_1 in the second part of the branch. Thus, we have the branching vector $(1 - \omega_b, 1 + fr_1 \cdot \omega_f + \max\{0, 1 - fr_1\} \cdot (1 - \omega_b) + \omega_b - \omega_b, \omega_b + fl_1(1 - \omega_f) + fr_1 \cdot \omega_b - \omega_b)$ (✧).

Remark 3. Observe that from now on there is always a vertex $z_i \in N_{\overline{\mathrm{FL}} \setminus \mathcal{N}}(x_i)$ $(i = 1, 2)$ due to the previous case.

c) Let z_1 be defined as above and $\tilde{T} \succ T$ be an optimal spanning tree such that $lab_{\tilde{T}}(v) = \mathrm{lab}_{\tilde{T}}(co(v)) = \mathrm{IN}$ and $lab_{\tilde{T}}(x_1) = \mathrm{LN}$. If $lab_{\tilde{T}}(x_2) = \mathrm{LN}$ then Lemmas 7.2 and 7.3 apply. This means in the branch setting $v, co(v) \in \mathrm{IN}$, $x_1 \in \mathrm{LN}$, we can assume that vertices in $(N(x_1 \cup N(x_2)) \setminus \mathcal{N}$ are leaves, i.e, we can adjoin them to FL or LN. This leads to an additional reduction of at least $\min\{\omega_f, 1 - \omega_b\}$. If $lab_{\tilde{T}}(x_2) = \mathrm{IN}$ then we must have $d_{\tilde{T}}(x_2) = 2$. Thus, Lemma 8.3 applies. This entails the same branch as in (✧).

(B4) Due to Lemma 7.1 a $(1 - \omega_b, 1 + fr_2 \cdot \omega_b + fl_2 \cdot (1 - \omega_f) - \omega_b, \omega_b + fr_1 \cdot \omega_b + fl_1 \cdot (1 - \omega_f) - \omega_b)$ branch can be derived.

(B5) In this case $\bigcap_{i=1,2} N_{\overline{\mathrm{FL}} \setminus \mathcal{N}}(x_i) = \emptyset$ is true as otherwise (B4) applies. This means for $i = 1, 2$ there are two different vertices $z_i \in N_{\overline{\mathrm{FL}} \setminus \mathcal{N}}(x_i)$. Due (B3.c) we have $d_{\overline{V_T} \setminus \mathcal{N}}(x_i) \geq 2$. Thus in the second part we additionally get $(fr_1 + fr_2) \cdot \omega_f$ due to Lemmas 7.2 and 7.3. If $fr_i = 0$ we get an amount of $1 - \omega_b$ by Remark 3.
$v \in \mathrm{LN}$: $1 - \omega_b$.
$v, co(v) \in \mathrm{IN}, x_1, x_2 \in \mathrm{LN}$: $2 + (fr_1 + fr_2) \cdot \omega_f + (\max\{0, 1 - fr_1\} + \max\{0, 1 - fr_2\}) \cdot (1 - \omega_b) - \omega_b$
$v, co(v), x_2, co(x_2) \in \mathrm{IN}, x_1 \in \mathrm{LN}$: $1 + fl_2 \cdot (1 - \omega_f) + fr_2 \cdot \omega_b - \omega_b$
$v, co(v), x_1, co(x_1) \in \mathrm{IN}$: $\omega_b + fl_1 \cdot (1 - \omega_f) + fr_1 \cdot \omega_b - \omega_b$.

We have calculated the branching number for every mentioned recursion such that $2 \leq fr_i + fl_1 \leq 5$, $i = 1, 2$, with respect to ω_b and ω_f. The branching number of any other recursion is upper-bounded by one of these. We mention the bottleneck cases which attain the given running time: Case *(B5)* such that $d_{\overline{V}_T \setminus \mathcal{N}}(x_i) = 2$ and *a)* $fl_1 = fl_2 = 0$, $fr_1 = fr_2 = 2$, *b)* $fr_1 = 2$, $fl_1 = 0$, $fr_2 = fl_2 = 1$; Compared to [6] case *(B5)* has been improved. We can find at least two vertices which are turned from free vertices to floating leaves or from branching nodes to leaf nodes. In [6] only one vertex with this property can be found in the worst case. Thus, due to the previous case analysis we can state our main result:

Theorem 1. k-LEAF SPANNING TREE *can be solved in time* $\mathcal{O}^*(3.4575^k)$.

4 Conclusions and Exact Exponential Time Analysis

Exponential Time Analysis. Fomin, Grandoni and Kratsch [13] gave an exact exponential-time algorithm with running time $\mathcal{O}^*(1.9407^n)$. Based on and re-analysing the parameterized algorithm of Kneis, Langer and Rossmanith [14], this was recently improved to $\mathcal{O}^*(1.8966^n)$, see [9]. We can show further (slight) improvements by re-analyzing our parameterized algorithm. We define a new measure:

$$\tau := n - \omega_f \cdot |\mathrm{FL}| - \omega_b \cdot |\mathrm{BN}| - |\mathrm{LN}| - |\mathrm{IN}| \text{ with } \omega_b = 0.272 \text{ and } \omega_f = 0.4721.$$

The remaining task is quite easy. We only have to adjust the branching vectors we derived with respect to κ to τ.

Theorem 2. MAXIMUM LEAF SPANNING TREE *can be solved in* $\mathcal{O}^*(1.89615^n)$.

Parameterized Measure & Conquer. Amortized search tree analysis, also known as *Measure & Conquer*, is a big issue in exact algorithmics. Although search trees play an important role in exact parameterized algorithmics, this kind of analysis has been rather seldomly applicable, the papers [5, 10, 11, 19] giving a hitherto complete list of exceptions. This paper contributes to this topic. Let us emphasize the difference to the, say, non-parameterized Measure & Conquer and to this case. Usually if a measure μ, which is used to derive an upper bound of the form $c^{|V|}$, is decreased to zero then we immediately have a solution. Almost all time this is quite clear because then the instance is polynomial-time solvable. Now if the parameterized measure κ is smaller than zero then in general a hard sub-instance remains. Also κ has been decreased due to producing floating leaves, which are not attached to the tree yet. Thus, it is crucial to have Lemma 9, which ensures that a k-leaf spanning tree can be indeed constructed. Beyond that, it is harder to show that no reduction rules ever increase κ. As vertices which have been counted already partly (e.g., because they belong to $\mathrm{FL} \cup \mathrm{BN}$) can be deleted, κ can even increase temporally. Concerning the traditional approach this is a straight-forward task and is hardly ever mentioned. It is a challenge to find further parameterized problems where this, say, parameterized M&C paradigm can be applied.

It is worth pointing out that our algorithm is quite explicit. This means that its statement to some extent lengthy but on the other hand easier to implement.

The algorithm does not use compact mathematical expressions which might lead to ambiguities in the implementation process.

References

1. Blum, J., Ding, M., Thaeler, A., Cheng, X.: Connected Dominating Set in Sensor Networks and MANETs. In: Handbook of Comb. Opt., vol. B, pp. 329–369. Springer, Heidelberg (2005)
2. Bonsma, P.S., Brueggemann, T., Woeginger, G.J.: A Faster FPT Algorithm for Finding Spanning Trees with Many Leaves. In: Rovan, B., Vojtáš, P. (eds.) MFCS 2003. LNCS, vol. 2747, pp. 259–268. Springer, Heidelberg (2003)
3. Bonsma, P.S., Zickfeld, F.: A 3/2-Approximation Algorithm for Finding Spanning Trees with Many Leaves in Cubic Graphs. In: Broersma, H., Erlebach, T., Friedetzky, T., Paulusma, D. (eds.) WG 2008. LNCS, vol. 5344, pp. 66–77. Springer, Heidelberg (2008)
4. Bonsma, P.S., Zickfeld, F.: Spanning Trees with Many Leaves in Graphs without Diamond and Blossoms. In: Laber, E.S., Bornstein, C., Nogueira, L.T., Faria, L. (eds.) LATIN 2008. LNCS, vol. 4957, pp. 531–543. Springer, Heidelberg (2008)
5. Chen, J., Kanj, I.A., Xia, G.: Labeled Search Trees and Amortized Analysis: Improved upper Bounds for NP-Hard Problems. In: Ibaraki, T., Katoh, N., Ono, H. (eds.) ISAAC 2003. LNCS, vol. 2906, pp. 148–157. Springer, Heidelberg (2003)
6. Daligault, J., Gutin, G., Kim, E.J., Yeo, A.: FPT Algorithms and Kernels for the Directed k-Leaf Problem. Journal of Computer and System Sciences (2009), http://dx.doi.org/10.1016/j.jcss.2009.06.005
7. Downey, R.G., Fellows, M.R.: Parameterized Complexity. Springer, Heidelberg (1999)
8. Estivill-Castro, V., Fellows, M.R., Langston, M.A., Rosamond, F.A.: FPT is P-Time Extremal Structure I. In: ACiD, pp. 1–41. King's College Publications, London (2005)
9. Fernau, H., Langer, A., Liedloff, M., Kneis, J.: An Exact Algorithm for the Maximum Leaf Spanning Tree Problem. In: Chen, J., Fomin, F.V. (eds.) IWPEC 2009. LNCS, vol. 5917, pp. 161–172. Springer, Heidelberg (2009)
10. Fernau, H., Raible, D.: Exact Algorithms for Maximum Acyclic Subgraph on a Superclass of Cubic Graphs. In: Nakano, S.-i., Rahman, M. S. (eds.) WALCOM 2008. LNCS, vol. 4921, pp. 144–156. Springer, Heidelberg (2008)
11. Fernau, H., Gaspers, S., Raible, D.: Exact and Parameterized Algorithms for Max Internal Spanning Tree. In: WG (to appear, 2009)
12. Fomin, F.V., Grandoni, F., Kratsch, D.: A Measure & Conquer Approach for the Analysis of Exact Algorithms. Journal of the ACM 56(5) (2009)
13. Fomin, F.V., Grandoni, F., Kratsch, D.: Solving Connected Dominating Set Faster than 2^n. Algorithmica 52(2), 153–166 (2008)
14. Kneis, J., Langer, A., Rossmanith, P.: A New Algorithm for Finding Trees with Many Leaves. In: Hong, S.-H., Nagamochi, H., Fukunaga, T. (eds.) ISAAC 2008. LNCS, vol. 5369, pp. 270–281. Springer, Heidelberg (2008)
15. Koutis, I., Williams, R.: Limits and Applications of Group Algebras for Parameterized Problems. In: Albers, S., et al. (eds.) ICALP 2009, Part I. LNCS, vol. 5555, pp. 653–664. Springer, Heidelberg (2009)
16. Lu, H.-I., Ravi, R.: Approximating Maximum Leaf Spanning Trees in Almost Linear Time. Journal of Algorithms 29, 132–141 (1998)

17. Solis-Oba, R.: 2-Approximation Algorithm for Finding a Spanning Tree with Maximum Number of Leaves. In: Bilardi, G., Pietracaprina, A., Italiano, G.F., Pucci, G. (eds.) ESA 1998. LNCS, vol. 1461, pp. 441–452. Springer, Heidelberg (1998)
18. Thai, M.T., Wang, F., Liu, D., Zhu, S., Du, D.-Z.: Connected Dominating Sets in Wireless Networks Different Transmission Ranges. IEEE Trans. Mobile Computing 6, 1–10 (2007)
19. Wahlström, M.: Algorithms, Measures and Upper Bounds for Satisfiability and Related Problems. PhD Thesis, Department of Computer and Information Science, Linköpings Universitet, Sweden (2007)

Approximate Structural Consistency

Michel de Rougemont and Adrien Vieilleribière

Université Paris II, & LRI CNRS
LRI, Bâtiment 490, 91400 Orsay, France
{mdr,vieille}@lri.fr

Abstract. We consider documents as words and trees on some alphabet Σ and study how to compare them with some regular schemas on an alphabet Σ'. Given an input document I, we decide if it may be transformed into a document J which is ε-close to some target schema T: we show that this approximate decision problem can be efficiently solved. In the simple case where the transformation is the identity, we describe an approximate algorithm which decides if I is close to a target regular schema (DTD). This property is testable, i.e. can be solved in time independent of the size of the input document, by just sampling I. In the general case, the *Structural Consistency* decides if there is a transducer $\mathcal{T}$ with at most m states such that I is ε-close to I' and his image $\mathcal{T}(I')$ is both close to T and of size comparable to the size of I. We show that Structural Consistency is also testable, i.e. can be solved by sampling I.

1 Introduction

Consider documents as large labeled, unranked, ordered trees with attributes [7], which need to be classified. We may want to transform them from some source schema S (regular language given by regular expression on word and DTD on trees), into a fixed target schema T. Data-Echange is a framework to address this problem. A *Data-Exchange setting* [3] is a triple $(S, T, \psi_{S,T})$ where $\psi_{S,T}$ a set of constraints. Given an input document I, the existence problem decides if there exists $J \in T$ such that $(I, J) \models \psi_{S,T}$. If we look for an algorithmic solution, we may want to decide if there is transducer $\mathcal{T}$ with m states, such that $J = \mathcal{T}(I)$ of size α-close to the size of I such that $(I, J) \models \psi_{S,T}$.

We study an approximate solution to this problem by allowing small errors on I and J. Property Testing [8,5] considers approximations of decision problems, and Testers for regular trees have been proposed [6,4] and extended to Data Exchange where predefined constraints are given by a fixed transducer $\mathcal{T}$ [2]. In this paper we extend the approach when $\mathcal{T}$ is unknown, and we approximately decide if there exists a $\mathcal{T}$ which satisfies the Data Exchange condition. Our goal is to show that the analysis of the statistics of schemas, transducers and documents lead to approximate algorithms whose complexity is independent of the size of the input structures.

Fix a source schema S, a target schema T, parameters ε (the precision), α (the ratio) and m (the number of states of a transducer $\mathcal{T}$), where $0 < \varepsilon \leq 1$

J. van Leeuwen et al. (Eds.): SOFSEM 2010, LNCS 5901, pp. 685–696, 2010.

and $0 < \alpha \leq 1$. An input I is a word w_n or an unranked ordered tree τ_n of size n following S.

Structural Consistency: Given a large input document I_n(word w_n or tree τ_n), decide if there is a transducer $\mathcal{T}$ with at most m states and an input I' ε-close to I, such that: $\alpha \cdot n \leq |\mathcal{T}(I')| \leq n/\alpha$ and $\mathcal{T}(I')$ is ε-close to T.

The transformed I' (word or tree) must satisfy two conditions: it must be of size proportional to n within a factor α, and ε-close to the schema T. A transducer which satisfies both conditions is called ε, α compatible. This problem captures the difficulties of Information Integration and Classification, as given target schemas $T_1, ..., T_k$ and an input document I, we can decide which schemas are ε, α compatible for I. For simplicity, we first consider words w_n where the techniques are simpler and generalize them to trees. Our main results are:

Theorem 1. Structural Consistency is testable on words.

Theorem 2. Structural Consistency is testable on unranked ordered trees.

We associate to a word w_n the statistics vector $\mathsf{ustat}_k(w_n)$, from which we can approximate any regular property [4]. In this paper we introduce a statistics matrix $\mathsf{ustat}_k(\tau_n))$, for an unranked ordered tree τ_n, from which we can similarly approximate any regular tree property. Regular schemas such as S and T are represented by unions of polytopes in the statistical space. A schema mapping μ is a mapping between some summits of a polytope H_S for S and some summits of H_T for T. A transducer $\mathcal{T}$ provides a linear transformation between the source and the target statistics and may be ε, α compatible for μ.

In section 2 we recall the basic notions on testers and the statistical embedding of [4] on words and trees. In section 3, we recall the basic results when the transformation is the identity, and in section 4 we study the Structural Consistency on words and trees.

2 Preliminaries

We consider classes of finite structures such as words and trees with possible attributes, and schemas are regular languages given by Tree-automata or DTDs. We approximate decision problems on such classes, given a distance between structures. We transform these structures with specific transducers.

Approximation. The *Edit distance with moves* between two structures I and I', written $\mathsf{dist}(I, I')$, is the minimal number of elementary operations on I to obtain I', divided by $max\{|I|, |I'|\}$. An *elementary operation* on a structure I is either an *insertion, a deletion* of a node or of an edge, a *modification* of a letter (tag) or of an attribute value, or a *move*. For trees, a move consists in moving an entire subtree of τ into another position; for words, it means moving a consecutive sequence of letter into another position. For simplicity, in this paper we transform structures ignoring attribute values. We say that two structures U_n, V_m (words or tress), whose domains are respectively of size n and m, are

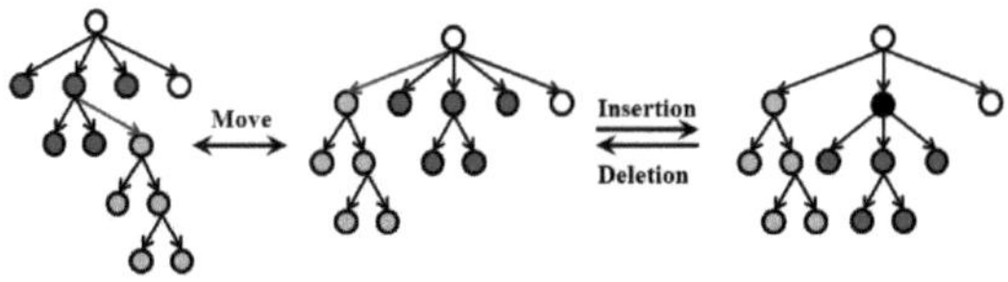

Fig. 1. Edit Distance with Moves: Elementary Operations

ε-close if their distance $\mathsf{dist}(U_n, V_m)$ is less than $\varepsilon \times \max\{n, m\}$. They are *ε-far* if they are not ε-close. We use a classical weak approximation:

Definition 1. *Let $\varepsilon \geq 0$ be a real. An ε-tester for a property P is a randomized algorithm A such that: (1) If I satisfies P, A always accepts; (2) If I is ε-far from P, then* $\Pr[A \text{ rejects}] \geq 2/3$.

A property is *testable* if for every sufficiently small $\varepsilon > 0$, there exists an ε-tester whose time complexity depends only on ε.

Statistical embedding on strings. For a finite alphabet Σ and a given ε, let $k = \frac{1}{\varepsilon}$. A word w of length n is embedded into a vector ustat_k of dimension $|\Sigma|^k$; $\mathsf{ustat}_k(w)[u] \stackrel{\text{def}}{=} \frac{\#u}{n-k+1}$ where $\#u$ is the number of occurrences of u (of length k) in w. This embedding is called a *k-gram* in statistics, and is related to [1] where the subwords of length k are called *shingles*.

Example 1. For $\Sigma = \{0, 1\}$, and $k = 2$, let w be the word 00011111. The statistic of w written in the lexicographical orderis $\mathsf{ustat}_2(w) = (2/7\ ,\ 1/7\ ,\ 0\ ,\ 4/7)$.

Statistical embedding on trees. We generalize k-grams on words to trees, using a matrix as in Figure 2. First, we transform an unranked tree with attributes into an extended binary tree[1], using the classical Rabin encoding[2] (Fig. 2.). In this encoding, paths of length k can be paths on the right successor, i.e. horizontal paths in τ, paths on the left successor, i.e. vertical paths in τ, or zigzags. There are 2^{k-1} types of paths, and for each type we keep the classical ustat_k vector. For paths of length k, we associate their type as a boolean vector of length $k-1$. We use 0 for the left branch and 1 for the right branch. For a tree τ, let $\mathsf{ustat}_k(\tau)$ be the matrix with 2^{k-1} columns and $|\Sigma|^k$ lines. In column 1, we have the densities of paths of type 0..0, i.e. vertical paths in the original unranked tree. The last column describes paths of type 1..1, i.e. horizontal paths in the original unranked tree, and all the columns enumerate the 2^{k-1} types. As the matrix is sparse we only enumerate some of the entries with their non zero probabilities.

Transformations. The transformations considered are simple top-down transductions which can be implemented by linear XSLT programs. A transducer in

[1] An *extended* 2-ranked tree is a binary tree with a left successor, or a right successor or both.

[2] First child relations in the unranked tree are represented by left successors in the Rabin encoding, and next sibling relations are represented by right successors.

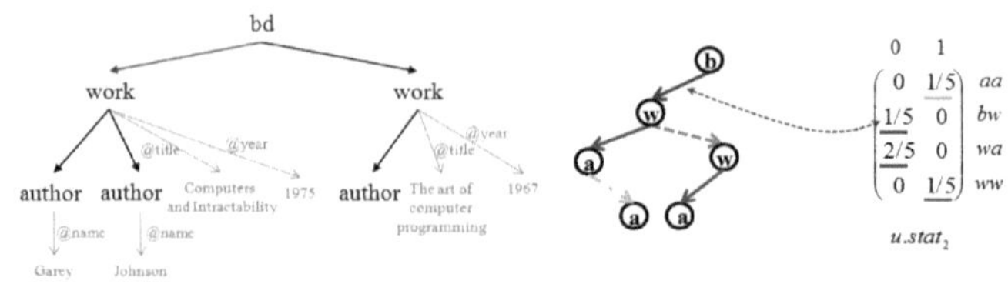

Fig. 2. A unranked tree with attributes, its Rabin encoding and its ustat_2 matrix null entries are not represented; the first line indicates the type of the column; "author" is abbreviated by a, "bd" by b, and "work" by w

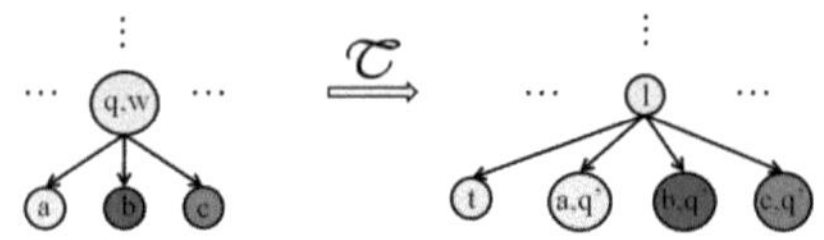

Fig. 3. Local transformation $(q, w) \rightarrow l(t, \underline{q'})$

state q transforms a letter of Σ_S (resp. a labeled node with attributes node, for trees) into a word (resp. a hedge, for trees) and continues the transformation top down, i.e. on the next letter (children, for trees) in another state q'. For instance, in state q, a transition on trees, denoted $(q, w) \rightarrow l(t, \underline{q'})$ transforms a node w into a node l with a first child τ and outputs the transformation of the children of w below l, on the right of τ, in state q'. This corresponds precisely to the linear restriction of a classical model of transduction of [7] and we restrict the study to deterministic transducers without λ transition.

3 Approximate Membership

This section recalls the basic membership testers for words and trees and gives a solution for Approximate Structural Consistency when the Transformation is the identity ($\mathcal{T} = id$). In all the following, let ε be fixed and $k = 1/\varepsilon$.

The Tester decides Approximate Membership (for words and trees) is based on the following property: if I is close to some schema T, I can be decomposed on simple loops, and then $\mathsf{ustat}_k(I)$ is ε-close to some polytope H_i^T of $H_T = \bigcup_i H_i^T$, i.e. ε-close to $H_i^T = \sum_{t_i \in C} \lambda_i \cdot t_i$, where $\sum_i \lambda_i = 1$, for some $C \subseteq \{t_1, ..., t_p\}$ of size at most d_T+1, where d_T is the dimension of the target vectors (Caratheodory theorem). Observe that for I large enough, I is ε-close to $I' = \Pi_{i \in C}(u_i)^{\lambda'_i.n}$ for $\lambda'_i = \frac{\lambda_i}{|u_i|}$, as λ_i reflects the density of loops u_i. In order to obtain I' from I, *moves* have been applied to regroup all identical loops and non loops have been deleted.

3.1 Word Case

The word embedding associates $\{\mathsf{ustat}_k(w) : w \in r\}$ to a regular expression r, a union of polytopes H in the same space, such that the distance (for the L_1 norm) between a vector and a union of polytopes is approximately $\mathsf{dist}(w, L(r))$, as shown in [4]. For a simple regular expression such as $(001)^*$, the polytope is a unique summit, the *base vector*, which by definition is $lim_{n\rightarrow\infty}\mathsf{ustat}((001)^n)$. For a more general regular expression, the polytope is the convex hull of the base vectors, associated with compatible *simple loops*, i.e. simple loops for which there is a run which follows them. Consider a word w as the input I, and its $\mathsf{ustat}_k(w)$ vector. The embedding associates with T a finite set H^T of polytopes H_i^T, with summits $t_1, ..., t_p$. Each geometrical summit t_i is associated with a set $U_i = \{u_i^j\}$ of loops u_i^j (j is an index), and all the u_i^j have the same ustat vectors, i.e. correspond to the same geometrical summit t_i. Some of these loops u_i^j may be decomposed as smaller loops: if ab is a loop for an automaton associated with a schema T, so is $abab$, ba, ... For $k = 2$, they all have the same statistics. A finite set of loops $\{u_i^j\}$ for $i = 1, \ldots, p$ is *compatible* if there is an input w which follows all these loops.

Example 2. Let $k = 2 = 1/\varepsilon$, $w = 000111$, $T = (001)^*.1^*$. For a lexicographic enumeration of the length 2 binary words, $\mathsf{ustat}_2(w) = (2/5, 1/5, 0, 2/5)$. Let $t = (1/3, 1/3, 1/3, 0)$ the base vector of the regular expression $(001)^*$, and similarly $t' = (0, 0, 0, 1)$ for 1^*. The polytope H associated with T is $\text{Convex} - \text{Hull}(t, t') = \{\lambda.t + (1-\lambda).t', \lambda \in [0, 1]\}$ and it approximates the set of $\mathsf{ustat}_2(w)$ when $w \in T$. The word w is at distance $1/6$ to T as it requires the removal of the first 0 to yield the corrected word $001.11 \in T$.

The $\mathsf{ustat}_k(w)$ vector can be approximated for the L_1 norm by taking N random samples to define the random variable $\widehat{\mathsf{ustat}_k(w)}$ which approximates $\mathsf{ustat}_k(w)$. These techniques yield the simple testers of [4] for Membership (w, r) between a word w and a regular expression r. Take $N \in O(\frac{|\Sigma|^{2/\varepsilon}.\ln|\Sigma|}{\varepsilon^3})$ samples, and let $\widehat{\mathsf{ustat}_k(w)}$ be the ustat_k of the samples. We compute the set of polytopes H associated with r in the same space and reject if the geometrical distance from the point $\widehat{\mathsf{ustat}_k(w)}$ to H is greater than ε. If w is in r then $\mathsf{ustat}_k(w)$ is close to H and the membership test accepts. On the other hand, if w is ε-far from the regular expression r, then the tester rejects with high probabilities. This shows that the approximate Membership is testable on words.

3.2 Tree Case

Sampling. The $\mathsf{ustat}_k(\tau)$ can be approximated, for the L_1 norm, by taking random samples as follows. Select with the uniform distribution a random node i of τ and let $\widehat{\mathsf{ustat}_k}(\tau)$ be the random matrix where we add each path of length $k-1$ from i as a unit in the corresponding position (type, labels). After N samples, we divide by the numbers of units. Observe that $\mathrm{E}(\widehat{\mathsf{ustat}_k}(\tau)) = \mathsf{ustat}_k(\tau)$, and that a Chernoff bound will determine $N = O(k^5 \cdot |2\Sigma|^{2k} \cdot \ln(\Sigma))$ with $k = 1/\varepsilon$, to insure that $|\mathsf{ustat}_k(\tau) - \widehat{\mathsf{ustat}_k}(\tau)| \leq \varepsilon$, with high probabilities.

DTD Embedding. We now generalize the notion of base loop from words to trees. We associate a set of *base loops* τ_i to a DTD T, i.e. a set of minimal

2-extended tree τ_i in a Rabin Encoding with a distinguished leaf *compatible* with the root of τ_i, i.e. with the same label and free successors to accept iterations. If the root of τ_i has one left successor, the distinguished element of τ_i has a free left successor, and similarly for the right successor or both successors. The base loop τ_i has at least two nodes and the distinguished element is underlined, for example $\tau_i = a(b, \underline{a})$ or $a(., \underline{a})$. We define $(\tau_i)^m$ as the m-th iteration of the tree τ_i on the distinguished element. Let τ_a be a *terminal tree* with a root labeled a associated with a DTD, in a Rabin Encoding, i.e. a valid subtree for the label a and no label occurs twice in a path. For each base loop τ_i, a *derived loop* from τ_i is a base loop τ_i where some terminal trees τ_a are connected to possible nodes a of τ_i. There are finitely many distinct terminal trees τ_a for each letter a. With each base loop and derived loop, we associate a *base matrix* $t_i = lim_{n\to\infty}\mathsf{ustat}_k((\tau_i)^n)$. The set of $\mathsf{ustat}_k(\tau)$ for $\tau \in T$ is a union of polytope H_i^T which is the Convex-Hull $(\tau_1^*, ..., \tau_l^*)$ of the base vectors of compatible base loops, restricted to some additional linear constraints. If $\mathsf{ustat}_k(\tau)$ is ε-close to H_i, then it is also close to $\sum_{s_i \in C} \lambda_i \cdot \tau_i^*$ where $C \subseteq \{\tau_1^*, \ldots, \tau_p^*\}$ of size at most $d_T + 1$, where d_T is the dimension of the vectors, i.e. $2^{k-1}. \mid \Sigma_T \mid$.

Example 3. Consider the DTD given by the rules: $\{root : a^*b;\ a : c.d;\ c : a.f\ +\ g;\ b : e^*\}$. The base loops are: $\tau_1 = a(., \underline{a})$, $\tau_2 = e(., \underline{e})$, $\tau_3 = a(c(\underline{a}(., f), d), .)$, as the "." indicates the absence of successor. A terminal tree for a is $\tau_a = a(c(g, d), .)$ and a terminal tree for c is $\tau_c = c(g, .)$. A derived loop from τ_1 is $\tau_4 = a(c(g, d), \underline{a})$. On the unranked trees, the base loops are equivalent to: $a*$, $e*$ and $a(c(\underline{a}(., f), d), .)*$. The base matrices for $k = 2$, with the notation of sparse matrices, are:

t_1	0	1
aa	0	1

,

t_2	0	1
ee	0	1

,

t_3	0	1
ac	1/4	0
af	0	1/4
ca	1/4	0
cd	0	1/4

and

t_4	0	1
aa	1/4	0
ac	0	1/4
cd	1/4	0
cf	0	1/4

for the derived loop t_4.

If τ is ε-close to the DTD, then $\mathsf{ustat}_k(\tau)$ is ε-close to

$$H = \left\{ \lambda_1 \cdot t_1 + \lambda_2 \cdot t_2 + \lambda_3 \cdot t_3 + \lambda_4 \cdot t_4 \mid \sum_i \lambda_i = 1 \right\}.$$

ε-Membership Tester

1. Sample τ (in a Rabin encoding) with $N \in O\left(\frac{|2\Sigma_S|^{2/\varepsilon}\ln(\Sigma_S)}{\varepsilon^5}\right)$ samples, and let $\widehat{\mathsf{ustat}_k(\tau)}$ be the estimation of $\mathsf{ustat}_k(\tau)$.
2. Enumerate all possible polytope H_T and Accept if one is ε-close to $\widehat{\mathsf{ustat}_k(\tau)}$, else Reject.

This shows that Membership is testable on unranked trees. The argument is similar to the case of words and the complexity is $O(1)$ for the size n of the tree τ but exponential in the size of the DTDs.

4 Approximate Structural Consistency

Fix a source schema S, a target schema T and parameters $k = 1/\varepsilon$ (the precision), α (the ratio) and m (the number of states of a transducer $\mathcal{T}$). Given an input (word or tree of size n) in S, we decide if there is a transducer $\mathcal{T}$ with m states, I' ε-close to I such that $\mathcal{T}(I')$ is ε-close to T and $\alpha \cdot n \leq |\mathcal{T}(I')| \leq n/\alpha$.

We approximate the k statistics of I by sampling, consider some possible *base mappings* or *schema mappings* μ between the summits of H_S and the summits of H_T, and some compatible 1-state transducer π associated with μ. The important observation is that we can enumerate all possible μ, π in time independent of n. We then decide if there are m input mappings $\pi_1, ..., \pi_m$ defining $\mathcal{T}$ such that I is ε-close to $I' = I'_1.I'_2, ..., I'_m$ such that $\mathcal{T}(I') = \pi_1(I'_1), ..., \pi_m(I'_m)$ and $\alpha \cdot n \leq |\mathcal{T}(I')| \leq n/\alpha$. The total number of operations is independent of n.

Sampling and decomposition. The embedding associates with S a finite set H^S of polytopes H_i^S, with summits $s_1, ..., s_p$. Each geometrical summit s_i is associated with a set U_i of base loops. $U_i = \{u_i^j\}$, and all u_i^j have the same ustat vectors, i.e. correspond to a summit s_i^j which coincide with the geometrical summit s_i. These loops cannot be decomposed as smaller loops, and are compatible, i.e. there is an input I which follows these loops. Similarly for T, we have a finite set of polytopes H_j^T with summits $t_1, ..., t_q$. Given an input I (word w_n or tree t_n) close to some schema S, we first take N samples as before, and $x = \widehat{\mathsf{ustat}_k(I)}$. We decompose x on a simplex for some polytope H_i^S of H_S, i.e. $\mathsf{ustat}_k(I)$ is ε-close to $\sum_{s_i \in C} \lambda_i \cdot s_i$, where $\sum_i \lambda_i = 1$, for some $C \subseteq \{s_1, ..., s_p\}$ of size at most $d_S + 1$, where d_S is the dimension of the source vectors. Observe that for large enough I, it is ε-close to $I' = \Pi_{i \in C}(u_i)^{\lambda'_i.n}$ for $\lambda'_i = \frac{\lambda_i}{|u_i|}$, as λ_i reflects the density of loops u_i. In order to obtain w' from w, some *moves* are applied to regroup all identical loops and non loops are deleted. In the decomposition, we can assume that each $\lambda_i > \frac{\varepsilon}{d_S} = c$. Otherwise we can find another input ε-close to I by deleting a few symbols and rounding the small coefficient to 0. The symbols are characters for the words and nodes for the trees.

Base mappings. Let $\{s_1..., s_p\}$ the set of summits of H_i^S, and $C \subseteq \{s_1, ..., s_p\}$ of size at most $d_S + 1$, where d_S is the dimension of the source vectors. If $\mathsf{ustat}_k(w)$ is ε-close to H_i, then it is also close to $\sum_{s_i \in C} \lambda_i \cdot s_i$ by Caratheodory's theorem, and the λ_i are larger than a fixed value c. Similarly let H_j^T be one of the polytopes associated with the schema T and let $D \subseteq \{t_1, ..., t_q\}$ of size at most $d_T + 1$, where d_T is the dimension of the target vectors.

Definition 2. *A (partial)* base mapping μ *between S and T is a partial function $H_i^S \rightarrow H_j^T$, only defined on some summits of the polytope, i.e. $\mu(s_i) = t_j$ for $s_i \in C$ and $t_j \in D$. A 1-state transducer π between S and T, is* compatible *with μ, if $\pi(u_i) = v_j$ if $\mu(s_i) = t_j$, $s_i = \mathsf{ustat}_k(u_i)$ and $t_j = \mathsf{ustat}_k(v_j)$.*

In the case of words, $\pi : \Sigma_S \rightarrow \Sigma_T^*$ and we talk about a π mapping. The domain of μ is C and the range is D. Each summit s_i corresponds to a base loop of the regular schema S, i.e. a minimal word u_i which can be iterated, and similarly each t_j corresponds to a base loop v_j for the regular schema T. Let $\alpha_i = \frac{|v_j|}{|u_i|}$ be the ratio between the length of the target loop and the source loop and $\lambda'_i = \frac{\lambda_i}{|u_i|}$. A μ-compatible mapping π is *(ε,α)-feasible for the decomposition $\sum_{i\in C}\lambda_i\cdot s_i$ on C* if there exists $w' = \Pi_{i\in C}(u_i)^{\lambda'_i.n}$, ε-close to w, such that $\alpha \leq \frac{\sum_{s_i\in C}\alpha_i.\lambda'_i}{\sum_{s_i\in C}\lambda'_i} \leq \frac{1}{\alpha}$.

4.1 Words

Notice that if $W = \pi(w')$ is the *source transformed by* π, then $\alpha.|w| \leq |W| \leq |w|/\alpha$. An (ε,α)-feasible μ-compatible mapping π yields directly a 1-state transducer.

Lemma 1. *If w is ε-close to S and there exists a μ-compatible mapping π which is (ε,α)-feasible, there exists an (ε,α)-feasible 1-state transducer $\mathcal{T}$ for w, S, T.*

Proof. If there is a μ-compatible mapping π, then $\mathsf{ustat}_k(w)$ is ε-close to $\sum_{s_i\in C}\lambda_i\cdot s_i$, where $\sum_i\lambda_i = 1$, for some $C\subseteq\{s_1,...,s_p\}$ of size at most d_S+1. Observe that for w large enough, w is ε-close to $w' = \Pi_{i\in C}(u_i)^{\lambda'_i.n}$, as λ_i is the density of loops u_i in w and the number of iteration of each loop is $\lambda'_i.n = \frac{\lambda_i}{|u_i|}.n$ after some rounding. If we erase all the letters of w which are not loops, and apply moves to regroup all identical loops, we obtain w' ε-close to w. Let $\mathcal{T}$ the 1-state transducer associated with π, with transitions $a/\pi(a)$ for $a\in\Sigma_S$. By definition, α_i is the expansion on loop u_i and the total expansion on w' is less than α. Because $\mathsf{ustat}_k(w') = \sum_{i\in C}\lambda_i\cdot s_i$, $W = \pi(w')$ is such that $\mathsf{ustat}_k(\pi(w') = \sum_{i\in C}\lambda_i\cdot\mu(s_i) = \sum_{j\in D}\lambda_j^T\cdot t_j$ where $\lambda_j^T = \sum_{i\in C,\mu(s_i)=t_j}\lambda_i$, hence $\pi(w')$ is ε close to T.

Example 4. Let $k = 2 = 1/\varepsilon$ and $S = (001)^*.(01)^*.1^*.(011)^*$ with $\Sigma_S = \{0,1\}$ as in the previous example, with summits $\{s_0,s_1,s_2,s_3\}$ associated with the simple loops $u_0 = (001), u_1 = (01), u_2 = 1, u_3 = (011)$ and $d_S = 2^2$. Let $T = (ab)^*.a^*.(aabc)^*$ with $\Sigma_T = \{a,b,c\}$, $d_T = 3^2$, and H_T be the polytope with summits $\{t_0,t_1,t_2\}$ associated with the simple loops $v_0 = ab$, $v_1 = a$ and $v_2 = aabc$. Let $w_1 = 0101111 = (01)^2.1^3 \in S$. Let $\mu(s_1) = t_0, \mu(s_2) = t_1$ and let $\pi(0) = b, \pi(1) = a$, which is μ-compatible as $\pi(u_1) = \pi(01) = ba$, $\pi(u_2) = \pi(1) = a$, and $\mathsf{ustat}_2(\pi(u_1)^*) = \mathsf{ustat}_2((ba)^*) = \mathsf{ustat}_2((ab)^*) = \mathsf{ustat}_2((v_0)^*)$ and $\mathsf{ustat}_2(\pi(u_2)^*) = \mathsf{ustat}_2((v_1)^*)$. In this case, the 1-state transducer $\mathcal{T}$ is such that $\mathcal{T}(0) = b$ and $\mathcal{T}(1) = b$, and $(0,1)$-feasible for w_1, i.e. $\alpha = 1$, and $\varepsilon = 0$. If we consider $w = 000111$, $1/6$-close to $w' = 00111 \in S$, $\mathcal{T}(w') = bbaaa$, at distance $2/5$ from T and $\alpha = 5/6$. Therefore $\mathcal{T}$ is $(2/5, 5/6)$-feasible for w.

We now generalize to transducers with m states and consider m distinct base mappings $\mu_1,...,\mu_m$, and μ-compatible mappings $\pi_1,...,\pi_m$ for the same H_i^S and H_j^T. We first describe a Verification Algorithm, which given $\pi_1,...,\pi_m$, C a subset of summits of H_i^S, D a subset of summits of H_j^T, such that $\mathsf{ustat}_k(w)$

is ε-close to $\sum_{s_i \in C} \lambda_i \cdot s_i$, where $\sum_i \lambda_i = 1$, decides if there is an (ε, α)-feasible transducer $\mathcal{T}$ with m states for w, C, D. We can find w' ε-close to w, such that $w' = \Pi_{i \in C}(u_i)^{\lambda'_i.n}$ for $\lambda'_i = \frac{\lambda_i}{|u_i|}$ and can also decompose w' into m components $w'_1, ..., w'_m$, i.e. $w'' = w'_1, ..., w'_m = (\Pi_{i \in C}(u_i)^{\lambda_i^{'1.n}})_1, ..., (\Pi_{i \in C}(u_i)^{\lambda_i^{'m.n}})_m$ such that $\sum_{j=1,...,m} \lambda_i^{'j} = \lambda'_i$. We divide each λ'_i into positive $\lambda_i^{'j}$ associated with the mapping π_j for $j = 1, ..., m$ and some of the $\lambda_i^{'j}$ are 0. Each π_j gives an expansion α_i^j for each loop u_i such that $s_i \in C$. The general expansion on u_i is $\alpha_i = \frac{\sum_{j=1,...,m} \lambda_i^{'j}.\alpha_i^j}{\lambda'_i}$ and the global expansion is $\alpha_g = \frac{\sum_{s_i \in C} \lambda'_i.\alpha_i}{\sum_{s_i \in C} \lambda'_i}$ which is either larger or smaller than 1. We can then write two Linear programs with positive variables $\{\lambda_i^{'j}, \alpha_i, \alpha_g\}$, whereas λ'_i, λ_i and α_i^j are constants, and $s_i \in C$, one for the case $\alpha_g \leq 1$ and the other for the case $\alpha_g \geq 1$:

Linear Programs $P(C, \lambda_i)$

$$Min\ (1 - \alpha_g) \geq 0 \text{ [case of } \alpha_g \leq 1]$$
$$Min\ (\alpha_g - 1) \geq 0 \text{ [case of } \alpha_g \geq 1]$$
$$\alpha_i = \frac{\sum_{j=1,...,m} \lambda_i^{'j}.\alpha_i^j}{\lambda'_i}, \ \alpha_g = \frac{\sum_{s_i \in C} \lambda'_i.\alpha_i}{\sum_{s_i \in C} \lambda'_i}, \quad \lambda'_i = \frac{\lambda_i.n}{|\ u_i\ |}, \ \sum_{j=1,...,m} \lambda_i^{'j} = \lambda'_i.$$

Let $\mathcal{T}_m$ be the transducer with m states operating on w'', ε-close to w, i.e. applying π_j on w'_j in state j, for $j = 1, ..., m$. We solve both linear systems and compare the parameter α_g to α to decide if the transducer $\mathcal{T}_m$ is (ε, α)-feasible.

Lemma 2. *If the solution of the linear programs P is such that $\alpha \leq \alpha_g \leq 1$ or $1 \leq \alpha_g \leq \frac{1}{\alpha}$, then $\mathcal{T}_m$ is (ε, α)-feasible for large enough inputs.*

Proof. Notice that w is ε-close to $w' = \Pi_{i \in C}(u_i)^{\lambda'_i}$ for $\lambda'_i = \frac{\lambda_i}{|u_i|}$ and to

$$w'' = w'_1, ..., w'_m = (\Pi_{i \in C}(u_i)^{\lambda_i^{'1}.n})_1, ..., (\Pi_{i \in C}(u_i)^{\lambda_i^{'m}}.n)_m \text{ such that} \sum_{j=1,...,m} \lambda_i^{'j} = \lambda'_i.$$

The solution of the linear program, if it exists, insures that the expansion factor is within α but may yield non integer values to the $\lambda_i^{'j}$. We round to the closest integer modifying slightly w'' into w''', which is still ε-close to w. By construction the image $\mathcal{T}_m(w''')$ is in T and the transducer $\mathcal{T}_m$ is (ε, α)-feasible.

Verification Algorithm $A(w, C, D, \pi_1, ..., \pi_m)$.

1. Decompose $\widehat{\mathsf{ustat}_k(w)}$ (which approximates $\mathsf{ustat}_k(w)$) ε-close to $\sum_{i \in C} \lambda_i \cdot s_i$, otherwise reject.
2. Solve the linear programs $P(C, \lambda_i)$.
3. If $\alpha \leq \alpha_g \leq 1$ or $1 \leq \frac{1}{\alpha_g} \leq \frac{1}{\alpha}$, accept else reject.

Tester for the Existence of an (ε, α)-feasible transducer: $TE(w, S, T, \varepsilon, \alpha, m)$.

1. Sample w with $N \in O(\frac{|\Sigma_S|^{2/\varepsilon} \cdot \ln|\Sigma_S|}{\varepsilon^3})$ samples, and let $\widehat{\mathsf{ustat}_k(w)}$ be the estimation of $\mathsf{ustat}_k(w)$.
2. Choose a possible polytope H_S, ε-close to $\widehat{\mathsf{ustat}_k(w)}$.
3. Enumerate all possible C, D, all possible base mappings μ, and all μ-feasible π. Accept if one $A(w, C, D, \pi_1, ..., \pi_m)$ accepts, else Reject.

Theorem 1. *If there exists an (ε, α)-feasible transducer with at most m states, then $TE(w, S, T, \varepsilon, \alpha, m)$ accepts. If w is ε-far from any w' such that there exists an (ε, α)-feasible transducer with at most m states, then $TE(w, S, T, \varepsilon, \alpha, m)$ rejects with high probabilities.*

Proof. If there exists an (ε, α)-feasible transducer for w, it must transform a simple loop of S into a simple loop of T. Otherwise if $w = (u_i)^j$, its image may be far from T. Therefore each state corresponds to some base mapping μ and to some μ-compatible mapping π. We generate all possible mappings for m states. Because each $\lambda_i > c$, the number of possible mappings π is independent of n, and only depends on ε and the dimensions. For the right choice, the Verification will accept and so will do the Tester TE. If w is ε-far from any w' for which there exists an (ε, α)-feasible transducer for w, then either $\mathsf{ustat}_k(w)$ is ε-far from any polytope H_S and this condition is detected with high probability from $\widehat{\mathsf{ustat}_k(w)}$, or $\mathsf{ustat}_k(w)$ is ε-close to a polytope H_S and to some $\sum_{i \in C} \lambda_i \cdot s_i$ but no mapping can map simple loops of s_i to simple loops of t_j. This last condition is detected as we analyze all possibilities.

4.2 Trees

Recall that we associate a union of polytopes to a DTD. Let $C \subseteq \{s_1, ..., s_p\}$ be a polytope described by its summits. To each summit s_i corresponds a set of base loops τ_i, i.e. extended binary trees (in a Rabin encoding) which can be iterated, with the same statistics. As in definition 2, a (partial) base mapping μ between two schemas S and T is a partial function $H_i^S \rightarrow H_j^T$, only defined on some summits of the polytopes, i.e. $\mu(s_i) = t_j$ for $s_i \in C$ and $t_j \in D$. A 1-state transducer π between S and T, is *compatible with* μ, if $\pi(\tau_i) = \tau_j$ if $\mu(s_i) = t_j$, $\mathsf{ustat}_k(\tau_i) = s_i$ and $\mathsf{ustat}_k(\tau_j) = t_j$. In this case π transforms trees. We follow an approach similar to the word case. We first estimate $\widehat{\mathsf{ustat}_k(\tau)}$ which approximates $\mathsf{ustat}_k(\tau)$. If τ is close to S, then $\mathsf{ustat}_k(\tau)$ has a decomposition on a polytope H^S, i.e. $\mathsf{ustat}_k(\tau)$ is close to $\sum_{i \in C} \lambda_i \cdot s_i$ for some summits C of H, where s_i are the base matrices. The tree τ is close to $\tau' = \Pi_{i \in C}(t_i)^{\lambda'_i.n}$ for n large enough, where each base or derived loop τ_i is iterated $\lambda'_i.n$ times after some rounding, as we regroup similar loops with moves and erase the other subtrees, for $\lambda'_i = \frac{\lambda_i}{|t_i|}$. For a given π, let $\alpha_i = \frac{|t_j^m|}{|t_i^l|}$ the ratio between the length of the target loop and the source loop. A μ-compatible mapping π is ε, α*-feasible* for the decomposition $\sum_{i \in C} \lambda_i \cdot s_i$ on C if there exists τ' ε-close to τ such that $\frac{\sum_{s_i \in C} \alpha_i . \lambda'_i}{\sum_{s_i \in C} \lambda'_i} \leq \alpha$ and $\alpha.|\tau| \leq |\pi(\tau')| \leq |\tau|/\alpha$.

Example 5. Consider the following source **S**, target **T** DTDs and $\epsilon = \frac{1}{2}$ fixed, i.e. $k = 2$.

S
```
<!ELEMENT bd (work*)>
<!ELEMENT work (author+)>
<!ATTLIST work title CDATA year CDATA>
<!ELEMENT author (EMPTY)>
<!ATTLIST author name  CDATA #REQUIRED>
```

T
```
<!ELEMENT bib (livre*,editeur)>
<!ELEMENT livre (titre, auteur+)>
<!ELEMENT auteur #PCDATA>
<!ELEMENT titre #PCDATA>
```

We use the standard abbreviations of the tags, where *bd* and *bib* are abbreviated by *b*. Let τ be a large tree of **S** and assume that sampling τ gives us a matrix: $\widehat{\mathsf{ustat}_2(\tau)}$. Let us explicit a $(1/2, 3/4)$-feasible one state transducer. The loops of the schema S are $\tau_1 = w(a, \underline{w})$ and $\tau_2 = a(., \underline{a})$. For $k = 2$, their statistical representation are s_1 and s_2. The schema **T** has two loops: $l(t(., a), \underline{l})$ and $a(., \underline{a})$, whose statistical representations are t'_1 and t'_2 :

$\widehat{\mathsf{ustat}_2(\tau)}$	0	1
aa	0	0.59
bw	0.01	0
wa	0.2	0
ww	0	0.2

,

s_1	0	1
wa	1/2	0
ww	0	1/2

,

s_2	0	1
aa	0	1

,

t'_1	0	1
ll	0	1/3
lt	1/3	0
ta	0	1/3

and

t'_2	0	1
aa	0	1

.

Take the base mapping $\mu(s_1) = t'_1$ and $\mu(s_2) = t'_2$. A possible admissible one state transducer π compatible with μ given below by the transition rules in a compact formalism : $(q, b) \to b(\underline{q}, .)$; $(q, w) \to l(t, \underline{q})$; $(q, a) \to a, \underline{q}$. Since the nodes 'bd', 'bib' and 'editeur' have a small impact on the statistics for big trees of **S** and **T**, only loops are considered. Decomposed over H_S, $\widehat{\mathsf{ustat}_2} \approx 0.6 \cdot s_1 + 0.4 \cdot s_2$. The distortion produced by the second rule is 3/2 and the third rule preserves size i.e. the total distortion is $0.6 \times \frac{3}{2} + 0.4 \times 1 = 1.3$ and it's inverse (≈ 0.76923) is higher that 3/4.

The generalization to transducers with m states is similar to the case of words. We consider m distinct base mappings $\mu_1, ..., \mu_m$, μ-compatible mappings $\pi_1, ...,$ π_m and decompose the tree τ into a forest with m components $\tau'_1, ..., \tau'_m$, i.e. $\tau'' = \tau'_1, ..., \tau'_m = (\Pi_{i \in C}(t_i)^{\lambda_i'^1})_1, ..., (\Pi_{i \in C}(\tau_i)^{\lambda_i'^m})_m$ such that $\sum_{j=1,...,m} \lambda_i'^j = \lambda'_i$. The forest τ'' is ε-close to τ, as we apply a limited number of moves. We use a linear program $P'(C, \lambda_i)$ to decide if we can find the $\lambda_i'^j$, and a verification algorithm $A'(t, S, T; C, \pi_1, ..., \pi_m)$, as in the case of words. We can use the same Verification algorithm and the Tester (TE') with $N \in O\left(\frac{|2\Sigma_S|^{2/\epsilon} \cdot \ln(|\Sigma_S|)}{\varepsilon^5}\right)$ samples. The number of possible C is bounded by the dimension $|\Sigma_S|^k \cdot 2^{k-1}$, and the number of possible μ is also bounded. We need to bound the number of possible π, as in the case of words by the following lemma:

Lemma 3. *If there exists an ε, α-feasible μ-compatible mapping π, then $|\pi(a)| \leq \frac{1}{c \cdot \alpha}$ for each letter $a \in \Sigma_S$.*

Proof. Recall that as in the case of words, the λ_i coefficients of the decomposition can be supposed greater than a constant $c < 1$. If the expansion $|\pi(a)|$ was larger than $\frac{1}{c \cdot \alpha}$, the global expansion would be larger than α.

We can finally state our main result:

Theorem 2. *If there exists an* (ε, α)*-feasible transducer with at most* m *states, then* $TE'(\tau, S, T, \varepsilon, \alpha, m)$ *accepts. If* τ *is* ε*-far from any* τ' *such that there exists an* (ε, α)*-feasible transducer with at most* m *states, then* $TE'(\tau, S, T, \varepsilon, \alpha, m)$ *rejects with high probabilities.*

5 Conclusion

The approximate embedding of trees and tree languages proposed in this paper gives an efficient solution to decide Approximate Structural Consistency, as the complexity of the algorithms only depends on the accuracy parameters. The methods are also robust to some noise ratio, as the statistics matrices are close on close inputs. We did not specify the exact complexity of the algorithms as a function of the size of the DTD and leave it as an open problem. Structural Consistency can also be applied to documents which do not have a schema, such as data words or streams but an input schema guarantees a much smaller number of potential mappings. General problems in formal languages and rewriting systems are often hard in their exact versions and approximate solutions are natural.

References

1. Broder, A.: On the Resemblance and Containment of Documents. In: SEQUENCES 1997: Proceedings of the Compression and Complexity of Sequences (1997)
2. de Rougemont, M., Vieilleribière, A.: Approximate Data Exchange. In: Schwentick, T., Suciu, D. (eds.) ICDT 2007. LNCS, vol. 4353, pp. 44–58. Springer, Heidelberg (2006)
3. Fagin, R., Kolaitis, P.G., Miller, R.J., Popa, L.: Data Exchange: Semantics and Query Answering. In: Calvanese, D., Lenzerini, M., Motwani, R. (eds.) ICDT 2003. LNCS, vol. 2572, pp. 207–224. Springer, Heidelberg (2002)
4. Fischer, E., Magniez, F., de Rougemont, M.: Approximate Satisfiability and Equivalence. In: IEEE Logic in Computer Science, pp. 421–430 (2006)
5. Goldreich, O., Goldwasser, S., Ron, D.: Property Testing and Its Connection to Learning and Approximation. Journal of the ACM 45(4), 653–750 (1998)
6. Magniez, F., de Rougemont, M.: Property Testing of Regular Tree Languages. In: Díaz, J., Karhumäki, J., Lepistö, A., Sannella, D. (eds.) ICALP 2004. LNCS, vol. 3142, pp. 932–944. Springer, Heidelberg (2004)
7. Martens, W., Neven, F.: Typechecking Top-Down Uniform Unranked Tree Transducers. In: International Conference on Database Theory, pp. 64–78 (2002)
8. Rubinfeld, R., Sudan, M.: Robust Characterizations of Polynomials with Applications to Program Testing. SIAM Journal on Computing 25(2), 23–32 (1996)

Comprehensive System for Systematic Case-Driven Software Reuse

Michał Śmiałek[1], Audris Kalnins[2], Elina Kalnina[2], Albert Ambroziewicz[1], Tomasz Straszak[1], and Katharina Wolter[3]

[1] Warsaw University of Technology, Poland
smialek@iem.pw.edu.pl
[2] IMCS University of Latvia, Latvia
audris.kalnins@lumii.lv
[3] HITeC e.V., University of Hamburg, Germany
kwolter@informatik.uni-hamburg.de

Abstract. Reuse of software artifacts (blueprints and code) is normally associated with organising a systematic reuse framework most often constructed for a specific problem domain. In this paper we present a system (language, tool, reuse process) where software reuse is based on building and retrieving of so-called software cases (large compound artifacts) that can be reused between domains. The system is opportunistic in that software cases result from usual (non-reuse oriented) activities where also semantic information is added. This information is used to support regular development but may serve later to retrieve software cases. Having this common semantic basis, we can organise a systematic cross-domain reuse process where application logic of one system can be reused for systems within different domains.

1 Introduction

1.1 Motivation

In 1967, McIllroy [1] has formulated a vision of global software reuse based on the production of "software integrated circuits". Despite many success stories it has to be admitted that this vision is still not fulfilled. The fundamental problem that did not find proper solution is the ability to cope with growing complexity of software systems and broadness of their problem domains. Thus, it is extremely difficult to find relevant assets for reuse and then apply them to the current problem at hand. The found solutions are usually very abstract (like generic design patterns) or specific to only a given problem domain ("domain-specific software ICs"). Reuse of generic solutions certainly helps in producing better systems but no significant productivity gains can be accomplished (considering the amount of work to find a generic solution and adapt to the current problem). Domain-specific approaches necessitate significant effort to conduct domain analysis and prepare assets for reuse. Thus, they are economically viable only for producing large families of similar systems (like e.g. cell phone software). Software development organisations

J. van Leeuwen et al. (Eds.): SOFSEM 2010, LNCS 5901, pp. 697–708, 2010.

that would like to adopt reuse processes face important barriers (see [2]). These barriers are associated with the complexity of reuse activities (preparing assets for reuse considering lack of proper tool support) and in resistance of developers and managers to undertake reuse activities "for the uncertain future".

As identified in a survey by Frakes and Kang [3], practically all approaches to software reuse are based on domain engineering. There, domain engineering is identified with software product lines (see below) and is declared as a key approach and research direction. The survey also stresses the importance of approaches to reuse pattern-based architectural frameworks with component technologies as technical enablers. Several important research directions have been identified: formal specification of architectures for automated construction of systems; broadening the scope of domains that can participate in the reuse process; behavioural contracts for components; reasoning support for component libraries; ability to predict variabilities in software assets needed by the re-users. The last research direction has been identified as a key point.

In this paper we present an approach to software reuse that follows most of the postulated directions and can be classified as a domain engineering approach. The main difference to the current trend of product lines is that we deliberately exclude variability and commonality analysis. Instead of preparing assets for reuse, we promote opportunistic reuse which is often neglected as ad-hoc and unorganised. In our approach we make this opportunistic reuse systematic and organise it around so-called *software cases*. Software cases are produced in a systematic process which is compatible with the most typical iterative approaches (either agile or formal). The process starts with writing use cases and is followed by architectural design and coding (repeated over iterations) where traces (detailed mappings) between these elements are generated automatically. Through following of this process, the software cases are prepared for reuse by adding semantic information to the requirements specifications. The effort of adding this information is relatively small and can be done even by unskilled people (domain experts). Reuse of software cases is accomplished by retrieving so-called *software case slices*. These slices can be extracted by determining similarity of sketched use cases for a new system with those stored in a reuse repository. By using this approach, a significant reduction of effort can be accomplished which is shown through a validation experiment. What is important, this reduction is possible even when the new system is built for a new problem domain.

1.2 Related Work

Our approach to case-driven reuse is based on use cases as basic indexes to software cases. Thus, we will relate our work to reuse approaches where requirements for the software systems are formulated with use cases. This research direction has been set in 1997 by introducing Reuse-Driven Software Engineering by Jacobson et al. [4]. In this approach, use cases drive both the software development and reuse process. Use cases are adorned with specific variability information. This variability analysis is supported with feature analysis as introduced in [5]. Use cases did trace to the other artifacts in the software process like design models and code. In contrast to our work, no tool support for automatic generation of traces existed as use cases were written in natural language.

The direction set in [4] is followed by many software product line approaches. Detailed guidelines for specifying use cases for system families have been given in [6]. An example notation for use case scenarios, modelling their variability and deriving specific scenarios is given in [7]. Another approach in the context of product line testing can be found in [8]. However, no real automation mechanisms for deriving and mapping design and code from use cases have been developed. A recent paper [9] shows an approach to automatic derivation of scenarios out of use case descriptions adorned with variability information.

In order to automate the transition from use cases to code, we need rigour in specifying use cases. A constrained language approach is introduced in [10] where the essential scenarios are treated as reusable elements of the application logic. This approach does not yet resolve the problem of automation as it simply suggests manual traceability to design. In [11], the scenarios are traced to code automatically through analysing test logs from a testing tool. Thus, scenarios are written in a test scenario language of the test tool. In [12] the approach to use-case based reuse is extended. The presented REUSER system compares structural information contained in sequence diagrams associated with use cases. By creating a partial sequence diagram one can find all similar diagrams and associated use case diagrams. Comparison is based on graph-matching technology. However, this approach is limited to structural comparison. No indication on similarity of problem domains is given. On the other hand, [13] uses semantic information from the WordNet terminology [14]. With this approach, similarity of problem domains for different use case models can be determined.

2 Scenarios for Case-Driven Software Reuse

The process of case-driven software reuse (CDSR) is designed to be compatible with typical software development methodologies. It assumes iterative development which is centred around use cases. Figure 1 illustrates the general activities of CDSR in the form of a UML activity diagram. It can be noted that for the purpose of this paper the process is simplified and does not include - for instance - testing and deployment. We now describe two typical scenarios where the difference is in retrieving legacy use cases (see highlighted action in Fig. 1).

In a basic - non reuse-oriented - scenario, the developers start a new project by sketching use cases. While writing initial use case descriptions, all the terms used are defined within a domain vocabulary associated with this new software case. Next, they plan for several iterations. Each of the iterations consists in developing a set of use cases. For each of the use cases, detailed scenarios are written. While writing scenarios, a complete domain vocabulary is constructed. This is done in a tooling environment which assures strict coherence between the vocabulary and the terms used in scenarios' text. After completing these detailed functional requirements, an automatic transformation generates the architectural blueprints of the system. Within this architectural framework, code

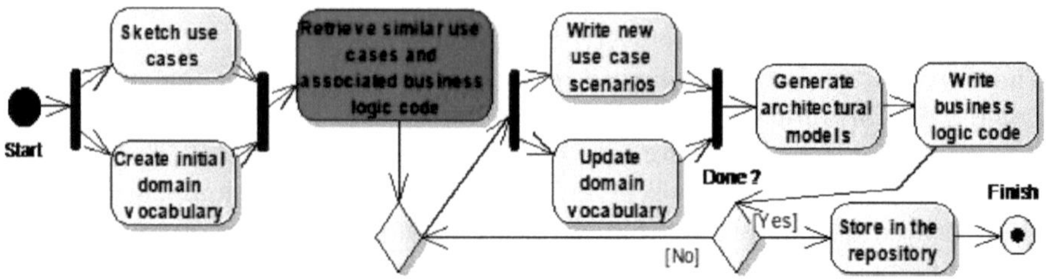

Fig. 1. Creation, storage and retrieval of software cases

is developed. The code for the application logic is taken directly from architectural sequence diagrams (interaction model). The code for the business logic is written manually for every generated business logic component and interface. This is repeated until the complete system is built. The final action is to store (copy) the created artifacts (requirements, architecture/design and code) without modifications to a repository.

The above scenario is compatible with "normal" software development using any of the available use case driven iterative methodologies. The main difference is in giving enough rigour to use cases to be able to perform automatic transformations to architecture. The result of the process is a so-called **software case** with its general structure presented in Figure 2. A software case can be defined as a combination of precisely mapped requirements, design (architecture) and code being the result of a specific project.

The use case model in a software case is structured so that all the terms used within use case descriptions are linked to a vocabulary which is central to all the use cases. To make the vocabulary comparable to the vocabularies of other software cases, it is linked to a global terminology. Thus, the resulting repository of software cases has a semantic backbone common to all the distinct software cases (see again Fig. 2).

The global terminology is used within the second scenario which contains the retrieval activity of Figure 1. In this scenario, after sketching the requirements (use cases and the related vocabulary), the developers run a query on the repository of past cases. The query tool uses similarity measures that compute semantic (WordNet based) and structural (graph based) distance between the newly sketched scenarios and the legacy complete scenarios. This is illustrated in Figure 3. When a matching use case is found within one of the stored software cases, all related design and code artifacts can be retrieved. In particular, the

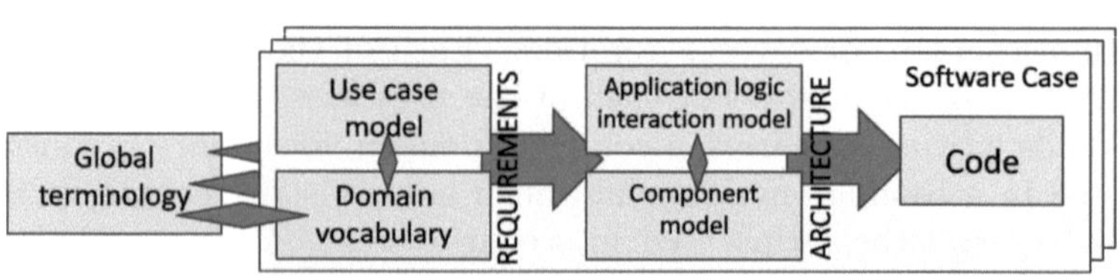

Fig. 2. General structure of a software case repository

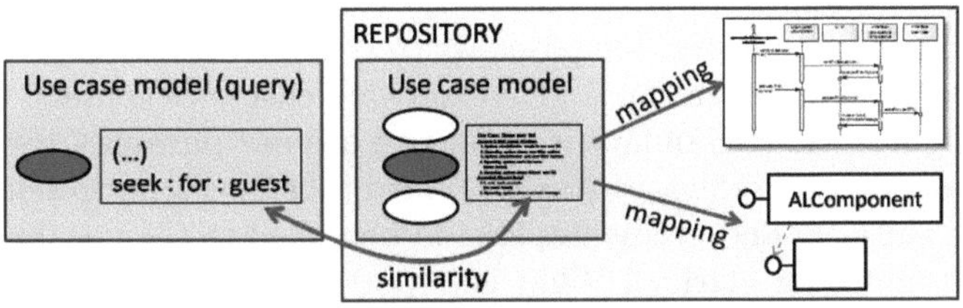

Fig. 3. General scheme for use case based retrieval of software artifact

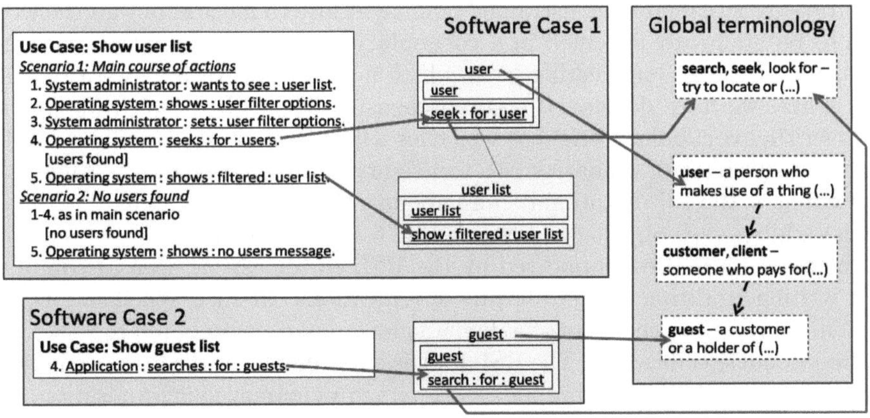

Fig. 4. RSL model example

retrieval engine shows the mapped interaction diagrams that define the application logic (user-system interactions) for the given use case and components that realise the business logic (data processing algorithms).

After finding relevant use cases, their contents (scenarios, see Fig. 4) together with the vocabularies and associated logic can be merged into the currently built software case. The rest of the process remains basically very similar to that without the retrieval step (the process is in fact presented as simplified to perform retrieval only once). Scenarios for other use cases are written and the vocabulary updated. Then, the architectural models are generated. It can be noted that now only some of the business logic components have to be written from scratch. These components that map from the legacy use cases are already written and necessitate only some adaptations. In the following sections we will give more technical details on the major steps of the above two scenarios.

3 Writing Semantically Rich Requirements

The key factor for the above described reuse process to become possible is a semantically rich use case language. We use the Requirements Specification Language as specified in [15] (see also [16]). The main characteristic of this language is that it offers a detailed syntax for use case scenarios. This syntax is based on writing simple subject+verb+object(s) sentences, and is presented in Figure 4 (see left). Moreover, scenarios written in RSL are composed of hyper-links to a vocabulary central for a given software case (see center). As it can be seen in the figure, the vocabulary is organised around phrases - like *seek : for : user* - that constitute predicates (verbs+objects) of the scenario sentences. Normally, all the subjects and predicates should be linked to the vocabulary (not all shown on the figure for clarity). What is important, all the phrases are grouped by the nouns which gives order to the vocabulary and is used for automatic transformation (see the next section).

It can be noted that the process of writing use cases is very rigourous. The scenarios are written in a constrained language close to natural but all the words need to be uniformly specified in a vocabulary. This poses a problem for traditional requirements engineering tools which normally operate on paragraphs of text. Thus, we have developed a comprehensive RSL editor which highly supports writing vocabulary-oriented scenarios which is illustrated in Figure 5. The developers write their scenarios (see top right) in a scenario editor. While writing sentences, the editor automatically updates the domain vocabulary with used words (adding verb-object phrases; see Fig. 5 bottom right).

The above activities, supported by the RSL editor can be seen as compliant with writing traditional requirements specifications. In such specifications, the vocabulary (often in the form of a domain class model) is prepared together with the functional specification. The RSL tool assures high level of coherence between these two major parts relieving the developers from manual synchronisation. This is in accordance with the approach proposed in [17], where the requirements specification resembles a wikipedia with extensive use of hyper-links.

In addition to the above activities which come from general software engineering practice, we introduce an extra activity of linking vocabulary entries with a

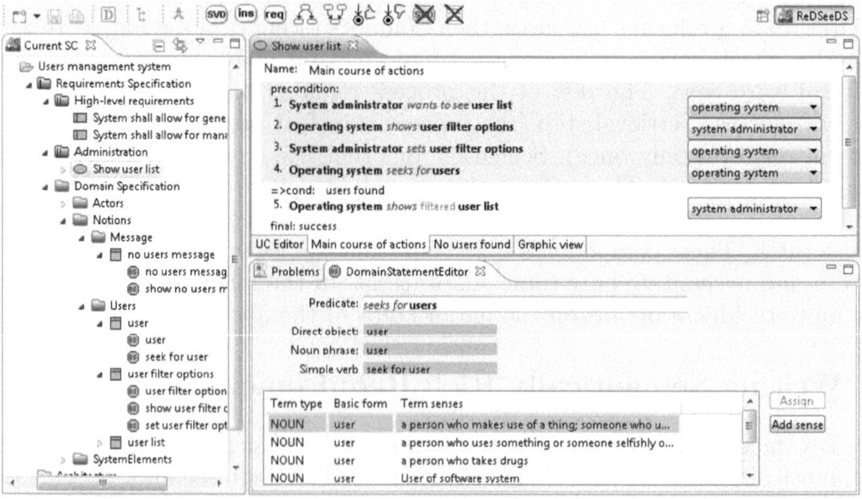

Fig. 5. The RSL editor

global terminology. This is illustrated in Fig. 4 (see right). Each of the words in the vocabulary (both the verbs and the nouns) has to be assigned to a WordNet element which is used as a global terminology for specifying senses of words. This again is highly supported by the RSL editor which offers all available senses of a given term (see Fig. 5, very bottom).

The above features of RSL can be used for transforming and mapping use case scenarios into architectural models and code. RSL was carefully designed to allow for generating very detailed component models with associated detailed application logic. Moreover, these generated components can be reused through comparing use case scenarios and retrieving traces from these scenarios to components. This will be explained in the following two sections.

4 Generating and Mapping Design from Requirements

The algorithms for transforming from requirements to design were implemented in the model transformation language MOLA[1] [18]. MOLA, as any other such language assumes that both the source and the target models are written in a meta-model based language. The RSL's meta-model is specified in [15]. The target models are expressed in UML with its meta-model defined in [19].

The target architectural model conforms to the requirements specification written in RSL by realising use case scenarios in a given logical architectural framework. Thus, two aspects need to be considered: static structure of the system and its dynamics in fulfilling the application logic (ie. use case scenarios). These two aspects are specified at component level for the architectural model and then refined up to implementation class level. The structure of the generated architecture depends on the chosen *architectural style*. The architectural style includes the definition of the system and model structure, the related set of design patterns and the general design principles that are applied. The selection of the most appropriate architecture style depends on non-functional requirements for the system but it is out of scope for this paper.

Here we will give an example of an architectural style conforming to a wide range of typical non-functional constraints. It is based on the most popular layered approach to architecting contemporary business systems. We assume *four layer* design with Presentation, Application Logic, Business Logic and Data Access layers. Another basic principle used, is *component based design* at all layers, with components comunicating through interfaces. In addition, several popular design patterns are used. First, the whole design is based on a simplified form of the MVC pattern, where no details of the view part are given. For each domain element a data transfer object for exchanging data flowing between layers and a data access object encapsulating persistence related operations is built. For the domain elements participating in business logic, corresponding business layer objects are created.

The above described architectural style provides clear guidelines as to what elements should be created in the target model of the transformation. Figure 6 il-

[1] http://mola.mii.lu.lv

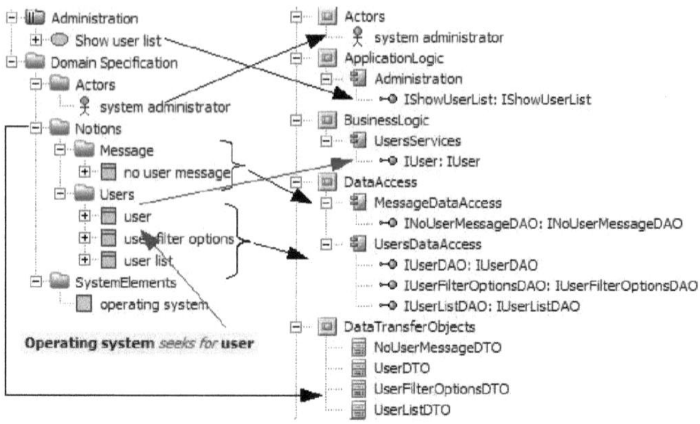

Fig. 6. Transformation of a vocabulary into a component structure

lustrates the correspondence between requirements and the obtained static structure on the example introduced previously (compare with Fig. 3).

The most non-trivial problem is to generate operations for all the interfaces. This can be done only using a thorough analysis of scenario sentences within each use case. During the analysis corresponding system behaviour is built and operations to relevant interfaces are added. The generation of messages and the corresponding operations depend upon the category (actor-to-system, system-to-actor, system-to-system) of the analysed sentence. Figure 7 illustrates the principles how the messages (and associated operations) are generated from the sentences and the receiving lifelines selected.

In order to support reuse, mapping links from requirements to architecture (and further to detailed design) are built by transformations. Rich mapping

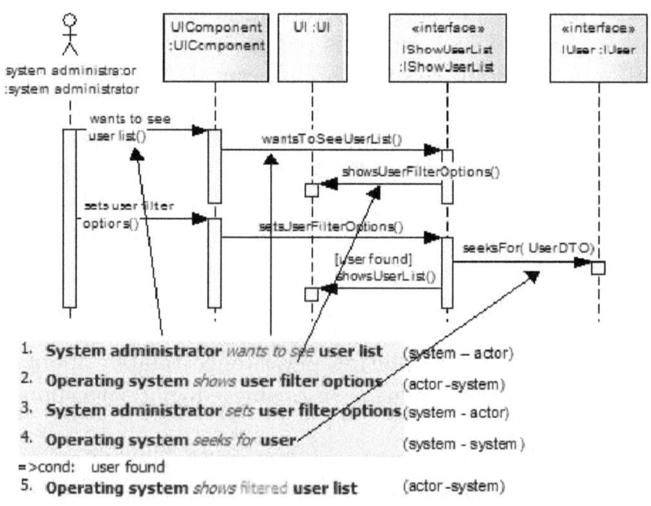

Fig. 7. Transformation of a scenario to a sequence diagram

links provide the basic prerequisite for traceability and software case slicing as described in the next section.

5 Reusing Software Cases

According to the second scenario described in section 2, the newly built use cases should be compared for similarity with use cases stored in the repository. The retrieval engine uses the initial sketch as a query. In the following we will use the example from Fig. 4. The query is based on the use case scenario from "Software Case 2". With this simple query we result with the engine showing the use case from "Software Case 1" as most relevant. This is shown in Figure 8 (bottom).

After determining the similarity we can browse through the found software cases and use cases. Moreover, we can determine *slices* which originate in the most similar use cases. The slice contains all the interfaces and components that are used within the interaction diagrams associated with the given use cases. This is illustrated in the upper part of Fig. 8.

When an appropriate slice is determined, we can retrieve all the elements contained therein. These retrieved elements are illustrated in Figures 9 and 10 (please compare with Fig 8). In the first figure we can see the possibility to reuse code based on the common application logic. We assume that the developers have reused the original use case scenarios. They have substituted the original notion "user" with the new notion "guest". This resulted in the transformation engine generating a new interaction diagram, leading to code that is depicted in the lower part of the figure. This can be also compared with the sequence diagram in Fig. 7. This new application logic code is ready to be used in the new system.

What is also available for reuse is the business logic code. This code is called from the application logic operations and performs certain data processing activities. In Fig. 9 calls to this code are highlighted and the code itself is presented in Fig. 10. The developers can follow the relationship between the generated application logic (Administration) and business logic (UsersServices) component.

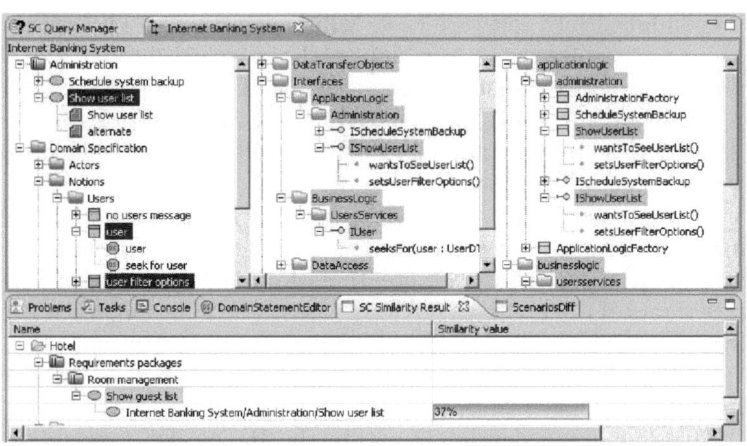

Fig. 8. The retrieval engine with visualisation of software case slices

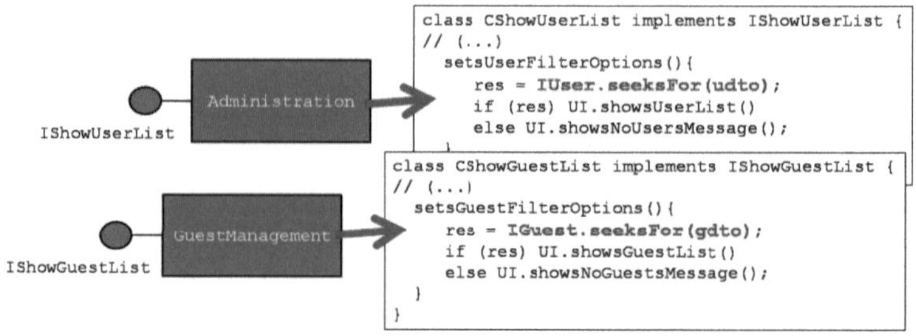

Fig. 9. Reuse of application logic through reusable transformations

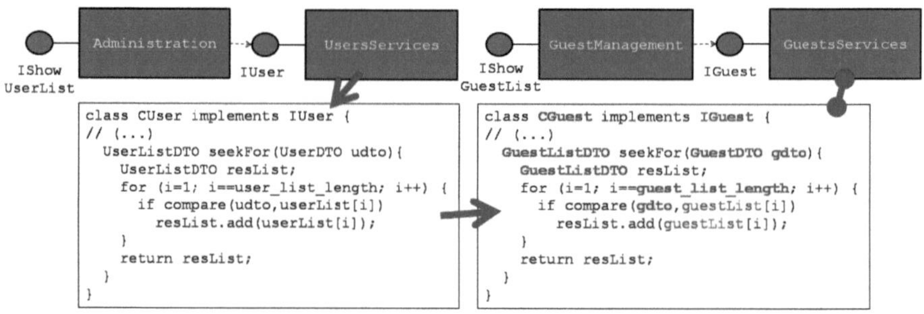

Fig. 10. Reuse of business logic through updating code

Analogous relationship is generated for the new system (see left in Fig. 10). What is not generated is the code of the operation. This code has to be taken from the old software case and reworked (see highlighted code in Fig. 10).

6 Conclusion and Evaluation Results

With the presented approach, the software artifacts produced within a software project are combined into software cases which drive reuse. The reuse environment contains many software cases which can be searched through and the most relevant for the problem at hand – retrieved. Unlike for typical software product line approaches, the effort of preparing a software case for reuse is highly reduced. What is also important, this effort pays off in the *current* project as it also enables automatic transformation to design.

The CDSR approach can be also used for building families of systems. A family is produced implicitly, and not explicitly as in product lines. This implicit "family construction" is performed through creation of consecutive software cases that constitute variants of the previous software cases. The following software cases of the family are added by finding the most similar one and adapting it to a slightly different problem at hand. Thus we can call this approach an "opportunistic product line".

The CDSR system was developed within the ReDSeeDS (www.redseeds.eu) project and consists of the RSL language, a comprehensive tool suite (ReDSeeDS

Engine) and the CDSR process description (ReDSeeDS Methodology). In order to confirm the validity of the CDSR system, these tools were used within a comprehensive validation cycle in the industrial context. The cycle was lead by Fraunhofer IESE with the participation of four industrial software development teams (see Acknowledgements). One of the teams had experience with a product line. The other teams had previously experienced only ad-hoc reuse. During the cycle, the following experimental validation activities were performed.

1. RSL training and case creation and retrieval training (two day tutorials).
2. Case creation. More than 20 software cases, with a total of over 300 use cases were created. The domains ranged from financial systems to rescue systems.
3. Case reuse. Four new software cases (over 80 use cases) were created through retrieving and reusing elements from the old cases. The domains for these new systems were significantly different than for the previous ones. Also, four other existing software cases were extended to create variants. Depending on the similarity of problem domains, the size of reuse ranged from single use cases and associated design/code to 90% of the whole software cases.
4. Acceptance and usage analysis, using the UTAUT method [20].

The qualitative analysis of supplied extensive questionnaires shows very promising results. The user attitude in four areas (effort expectancy, facilitating conditions, self efficacy, behavioural intention) is positive. In other four areas (like performance) it is neutral. This means that the users of the system (experienced software developers) believe that the approach would reduce their personal effort and has enough technical support (tools) to be effectively applied in real life. Moreover, the users show significant intention to use this technology in the future. On the other hand, the users do not expect that using the system influence the performance of their work. It has to be noted that the current results are obtained for the ReDSeeDS Engine prototype and not for a commercial and mature product. The users have raised several issues which can further improve the overall acceptance of the system and the CDSR approach. Detailed results of this study are available as a ReDSeeDS project report.

The above study showed applicability of CDSR to a broad range of problem domains. It was performed using the transformation algorithm presented in section 4. Also, other transformation algorithms can be used and are currently developed within ReDSeeDS. These algorithms capture the implications stemming from non-functional requirements. Obviously, the limitation of CDSR is that the transition from non-functional requirements to transformation algorithms is a manual process depending on experience of the transformation writers.

Acknowledgments. This work is partially funded by the EU: Requirements-Driven Software Development System (ReDSeeDS) (contract no. IST-2006-33596 under 6FP).

References

1. McIlroy, M.D.: Mass Produced Software Components. In: Naur, P., Randell, B., Buxton, J.N. (eds.) Software Engineering Concepts and Techniques, Proceedings of NATO Conference on Software Engineering, New York, pp. 88–98 (1969)

2. Sherif, K., Vinze, A.: Barriers to Adoption of Software Reuse. A Qualitative Study. Information and Management 41, 159–175 (2003)
3. Frakes, W.B., Kang, K.: Software Reuse Research: Status and Future. IEEE Transactions on Software Engineering 31(7), 529–536 (2005)
4. Jacobson, I., Griss, M., Jonsson, P.: Software Reuse: Architecture Process and Organization for Business Success. ACM Press, New York (1997)
5. Griss, M.L., Favaro, J., d' Alessandro, M.: Integrating Feature Modeling with the RSEB. In: Proc. 5th International Conference on Software Reuse, pp. 76–85 (1998)
6. Gomaa, H.: Designing Software Product Lines with UML: From Use Cases to Pattern-Based Software Architectures. Addison-Wesley, Reading (2004)
7. Bertolino, A., Fantechi, A., Gnesi, S., Lami, G.: Product Line Use Cases: Scenario-Based Specification and Testing of Requirements. In: Software Product Lines - Research Issues in Engineering and Management, pp. 425–445. Springer, Heidelberg (2006)
8. Kamsties, E., Pohl, K., Reis, S., Reuys, A.: Testing Variabilities in Use Case Models. In: van der Linden, F.J. (ed.) PFE 2003. LNCS, vol. 3014, pp. 6–18. Springer, Heidelberg (2004)
9. Choi, W.S., Kang, S., Choi, H., Baik, J.: Automated generation of product use case scenarios in product line development. In: 8th IEEE International Conference on Computer and Information Technology, CIT 2008, pp. 760–765 (2008)
10. Biddle, R., Noble, J., Tempero, E.: Supporting Reusable Use Cases. In: Gacek, C. (ed.) ICSR 2002. LNCS, vol. 2319, pp. 210–226. Springer, Heidelberg (2002)
11. Egyed, A., Grünbacher, P.: Supporting Software Understanding with Automated Requirements Traceability. International Journal of Software Engineering and Knowledge Engineering 15(5), 783–810 (2005)
12. Robinson, W.N., Woo, H.G.: Finding Reusable UML Sequence Diagrams Automatically. IEEE Software 21(5), 60–67 (2004)
13. Blok, M.C., Cybulski, J.L.: Reusing UML Specifications in a Constrained Application Domain. In: Proceedings of 1998 Asia Pacific Software Engineering Conference, pp. 196–202 (1998)
14. Fellbaum, C. (ed.): WordNet: An Electronic Lexical Database. MIT Press, Cambridge (1998)
15. Kaindl, H., Śmiałek, M., Svetinovic, D., Ambroziewicz, A., Bojarski, J., Nowakowski, W., Straszak, T., Schwarz, H., Bildhauer, D., Brogan, J.P., Mukasa, K.S., Wolter, K., Krebs, T.: Requirements Specification Language Definition. Project Deliverable D2.4.1, ReDSeeDS Project (2007), www.redseeds.eu
16. Śmiałek, M., Bojarski, J., Nowakowski, W., Ambroziewicz, A., Straszak, T.: Complementary Use Case Scenario Representations Based on Domain Vocabularies. In: Engels, G., Opdyke, B., Schmidt, D.C., Weil, F. (eds.) MODELS 2007. LNCS, vol. 4735, pp. 544–558. Springer, Heidelberg (2007)
17. Kaindl, H.: Using Hypertext for Semiformal Representation in Requirements Engineering Practice. The New Review of Hypermedia and Multimedia 2, 149–173 (1996)
18. Kalnins, A., Barzdins, J., Celms, E.: Model Transformation Language MOLA. In: Aßmann, U., Aksit, M., Rensink, A. (eds.) MDAFA 2003. LNCS, vol. 3599, pp. 62–76. Springer, Heidelberg (2005)
19. Object Management Group: Unified Modeling Language: Superstructure, version 2.1.1, formal/07-02-05 (2007)
20. Venkatesh, V., Smith, R.H., Morris, M.G., Davis, G.B., Davis, F.D.: User Acceptance of Information Technology: Toward a Unified View. MIS Quarterly 27, 425–478 (2003)

Comparison of Scoring and Order Approach in Description Logic $\mathcal{EL}(\mathcal{D})$

Veronika Vaneková[1] and Peter Vojtáš[2]

[1] Institute of Computer Science, Pavol Jozef Šafárik University
Košice, Slovakia
`veronika.vanekova@upjs.sk`
[2] Faculty of Mathematics and Physics, Charles University
Prague, Czech Republic
`peter.vojtas@mff.cuni.cz`

Abstract. In this paper we study scoring and order approach to concept interpretation in description logics. Only concepts are scored/ordered, roles remain crisp. The concepts in scoring description logic are fuzzified, while the concepts in order description logic are interpreted as preorders on the domain. These description logics are used for preferential user-dependent search of the best instances. In addition to the standard constructors we add top-k retrieval and aggregation of user preferences. We analyze the relationship between scoring and order concepts and we introduce a notion of order-preserving concept constructors.

1 Introduction

The main motivation of our research is a large amount of data available on the web. It is the effort of Semantic Web community to use ontologies and description logics (DLs) for expressing knowledge about this data. One of the approaches to tackle with this problem are fuzzy description logics (fuzzy ontologies). The connection of description logic and fuzzy set theory appears to be suitable for many areas of Soft Computing and Semantic Web.

One interesting application of fuzzy DLs is representation of user preferences. Users naturally express their preferences in a vague, imprecise way (e.g. "I want to buy a cheap and fast car"). It is possible to handle such vague requirements with fuzzy sets. Moreover, users often need only top-k best answers, ordered by their specific preferences. Therefore we use modified top-k algorithm [6] for user-dependent search of k best objects.

We explore a specific problem when the knowledge base has a simple structure but contains a large number of individuals. We choose the description logic traditionally called $\mathcal{EL}$ ([1,2]), which allows only concept conjunction and existential restrictions to define complex concepts. Then we add fuzzy concepts to be able to represent user preference. Thus an individual which belongs to a preferential concept `good_car` to degree 0.9 is preferred more than an individual with a membership degree 0.5. Fuzzy membership values are handled by a concrete domain $\mathcal{D}$ (inspired by [11], see also [8] chapter 6 for an introduction to concrete

J. van Leeuwen et al. (Eds.): SOFSEM 2010, LNCS 5901, pp. 709–720, 2010.

domains). This kind of fuzziness does not affect roles, so they remain crisp. We call the resulting DL a *scoring description logic*, s-$\mathcal{EL}(\mathcal{D})$.

The specific fuzzy membership value or score does not play any role in many applications - only the order implied by the fuzzy value matters. The actual score is hidden to user in some applications, e.g. Google search. Therefore we present another DL called *order DL* o-$\mathcal{EL}(\mathcal{D})$, where concepts are interpreted as preorders of instances, and roles remain crisp. Having such a DL enables us to combine a part of a knowledge base describing user preferences as a module with the rest of the knowledge base (i.e. using an ontology).

The two description logics defined in this paper have many similarities. We can define a corresponding order concept for every scoring concept. An important question is whether complex concepts also have this feature. The main contributions of this paper are results on connections of o-$\mathcal{EL}(\mathcal{D})$ to s-$\mathcal{EL}(\mathcal{D})$.

2 Description Logic s-$\mathcal{EL}(\mathcal{D})$ with Scoring Concepts and Aggregation

This section briefly recalls s-$\mathcal{EL}(\mathcal{D})$, first published in [4]. As any other DL, s-$\mathcal{EL}(\mathcal{D})$ describes its universe of discourse (domain) using *concepts* and *roles*. Concepts can be viewed as classes of individuals (objects), while roles can be viewed as binary predicates describing various relationships among individuals. See [8] for basic DL theory.

The description logic s-$\mathcal{EL}(\mathcal{D})$ is fuzzified, however, it differs from other fuzzy DLs. It is designed especially to represent user preferences and allow preferential top-k queries. The main difference is that we use *crisp roles* to describe relationships of objects from the domain and *fuzzy (scoring) concepts* to represent vague user preferences. Allowed constructors are top concept $\top$, conjunction $C \sqcap D$ and existential restriction $\exists R.C$. A DL knowledge base consists of a TBox with complex concept definitions $C \sqsubseteq D$ and $C \equiv D$ and an ABox with assertions about individuals (role assertions $(a, c) : R$ and concept assertions $\langle a : C, t\rangle$, where t is a truth value). We use a finite set of truth values $TV_n = \{\frac{i}{n} : i \in \{0, \dots, n\}\} \subset [0, 1]$.

Every interpretation $\mathcal{I}$ consist of a non-empty domain $\Delta^{\mathcal{I}}$ and an interpretation function $\bullet^{\mathcal{I}}$. Concepts are interpreted as fuzzy sets of elements from the domain (see Table 1, row 1), roles are interpreted as crisp relations $R^{\mathcal{I}} \subseteq \Delta^{\mathcal{I}} \times \Delta^{\mathcal{I}}$. Interpretations of complex concepts can be seen on Table 1, where A, C, D are concept names, R is a role, u is a concrete role and a, b are individuals.

An interpretation $\mathcal{I}$ is a model of TBox definition $C \sqsubseteq D$ iff $\forall x \in \Delta^{\mathcal{I}}$: $C^{\mathcal{I}}(x) \leq D^{\mathcal{I}}(x)$, definition $C \equiv D$, iff $\forall x \in \Delta^{\mathcal{I}} :\ C^{\mathcal{I}}(x) = D^{\mathcal{I}}(x)$, ABox concept assertion $\langle a : C, t\rangle$ iff $C^{\mathcal{I}}(a) \geq t$ and role assertions $(a, c) : R$ iff $(a, c) \in R^{\mathcal{I}}$.

The interpretation of existential quantifier $\exists R.C$ is similar to other fuzzy DLs (like $\sup\limits_{b \in \Delta^{\mathcal{I}}} \min\{R^{\mathcal{I}}(a, b), C^{\mathcal{I}}(b)\}$ in [11]), except that we use crisp roles, so the value of $R^{\mathcal{I}}(a, b)$ is always 0 or 1. Apart from standard $\mathcal{EL}$ constructors allowed in the TBox, we add concrete domain predicates P, aggregation $@_U$ and top-k constructor. They are described more closely throughout the rest of this section.

Table 1. Syntax and Semantics of $s\text{-}\mathcal{EL}(\mathcal{D})$

Syntax	Semantics
A	$A^{\mathcal{I}} : \Delta^{\mathcal{I}} \longrightarrow TV_n$
$\top$	$\top^{\mathcal{I}} : \Delta^{\mathcal{I}} \longrightarrow \{1\}$
$C \sqcap D$	$(C \sqcap D)^{\mathcal{I}}(a) = \min\{C^{\mathcal{I}}(a), D^{\mathcal{I}}(a)\}$
$\exists R.C$	$(\exists R.C)^{\mathcal{I}}(a) = \sup_{b \in \Delta^{\mathcal{I}}} \{C^{\mathcal{I}}(b) : (a,b) \in R^{\mathcal{I}}\}$
$\exists u.P$	$(\exists u.P)^{\mathcal{I}}(a) = \sup_{b \in \Delta^{\mathcal{D}}} \{P(b) : (a,b) \in u^{\mathcal{I}}\}$
top-k(C)	$\text{top-k}(C)^{\mathcal{I}}(a) = \begin{cases} C^{\mathcal{I}}(a), & \text{if } \lvert b \in \Delta^{\mathcal{I}} : C^{\mathcal{I}}(a) < C^{\mathcal{I}}(b) \rvert < k \\ 0, & \text{otherwise} \end{cases}$
$@_U(C_1, \ldots, C_m)$	$@_U(C_1, \ldots, C_m)^{\mathcal{I}}(a) = \frac{\sum_{i=1}^{m} w_i C^{\mathcal{I}}(a)}{\sum_{i=1}^{m} w_i}$

Example 1. Let the knowledge base contain data from the used car sales. We have a concept `car` and roles `has_horsepower`, `has_price`, `has_mileage`. Facts in the ABox are transfered from a (crisp) relational database, so the membership values of both individuals `Audi_A3` and `Mercedes_Benz_280` in the fuzzy concept `car` is equal to 1.

$\langle \texttt{Audi\_A3} : \texttt{car}, 1\rangle$
$(\texttt{Audi\_A3}, 7900) : \texttt{has\_price}$
$(\texttt{Audi\_A3}, 73572) : \texttt{has\_mileage}$
$(\texttt{Audi\_A3}, 110) : \texttt{has\_horsepower}$
$\langle \texttt{Mercedes\_Benz\_280} : \texttt{car}, 1\rangle$
$(\texttt{Mercedes\_Benz\_280}, 9100) : \texttt{has\_price}$
$(\texttt{Mercedes\_Benz\_280}, 127576) : \texttt{has\_mileage}$
$(\texttt{Mercedes\_Benz\_280}, 147) : \texttt{has\_horsepower}$

Different users may have different preferences to price, mileage and horsepower. Instead of exact preferences, we support vague concepts like `good_price`, `good_mileage`, `good_horsepower`. Interpretations of these concepts vary from user to user – for example, 20000 EUR is a good price for one user and unacceptable for another. Therefore all preference concepts will be user-specific (e.g. $\texttt{good\_price}_{U_1}$ for user U_1) and we represent them with concrete domain predicates [8].

We chose the concrete domain $\mathcal{D}$ originally defined in [11], because it contains basic trapezoidal predicates, sufficient to represent user preferences. It is defined as $\mathcal{D} = (\Delta^{\mathcal{D}}, Pred(\mathcal{D}))$, where the domain $\Delta^{\mathcal{D}} = \mathbb{R}$ and the set of predicates $Pred(\mathcal{D}) = \{lt_{a,b}(x), rt_{a,b}(x), trz_{a,b,c,d}(x), inv_{a,b,c,d}(x)\}$ contains monotone and trapezoidal fuzzy sets (unary fuzzy predicates). The interpretation of fuzzy predicates is fixed, handled by the concrete domain. Figure 1 shows $lt_{a,b}(x)$ (left trapezoidal membership function), $rt_{a,b}(x)$ (right trapezoidal), $trz_{a,b,c,d}(x)$ (trapezoidal) and $inv_{a,b,c,d}(x)$ (inverse trapezoidal) with one variable x and parameters a, b, c, d.

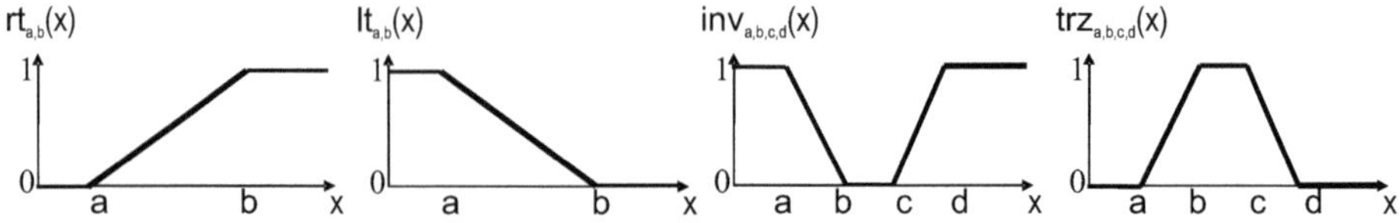

Fig. 1. Fuzzy membership functions of basic trapezoidal types

Fuzzy concrete domain $\mathcal{D}$ adds a concept constructor $\exists u.P$, where $P \in Pred^{\mathcal{D}}$ and u is a concrete role. This constructor generates a total preorder, because P has a fixed interpretation.

Example 2. We further extend the knowledge base stated above with preference concepts of user U_1.

$\texttt{good\_price}_{U_1} \equiv \exists(\texttt{has\_price}).lt_{7000,9000}$
$\texttt{good\_horsepower}_{U_1} \equiv \exists(\texttt{has\_horsepower}).rt_{100,150}$
$\texttt{good\_car}_{U_1} \equiv \texttt{car} \sqcap \texttt{good\_price} \sqcap \texttt{good\_horsepower}$

Then every model $\mathcal{I}$ of the knowledge base will satisfy the following:

$\langle \texttt{Audi\_A3} : \texttt{good\_price}_{U_1}, 0.55\rangle$
$\langle \texttt{Audi\_A3} : \texttt{good\_horsepower}_{U_1}, 0.2\rangle$
$\langle \texttt{Audi\_A3} : \texttt{good\_car}_{U_1}, 0.2\rangle$
$\langle \texttt{Mercedes\_Benz\_280} : \texttt{good\_price}_{U_1}, 0\rangle$
$\langle \texttt{Mercedes\_Benz\_280} : \texttt{good\_horsepower}_{U_1}, 0.94\rangle$
$\langle \texttt{Mercedes\_Benz\_280} : \texttt{good\_car}_{U_1}, 0\rangle$

Fuzzy conjunction is not always suitable to represent user preferences because it penalizes some objects that may be still interesting for the user. This is the case of the individual Mercedes_Benz_280, which has very good value of horsepower for user U_1, but the price is beyond preferred range. Instead of the conjunction, we can use aggregation to obtain overall preference value. Aggregation functions are m-ary fuzzy functions $@_U : TV_n^m \longrightarrow TV_n$, monotone in all arguments and such that $@_U(1,\ldots,1) = 1$ and $@_U(0,\ldots,0) = 0$. We do not require other properties such as being homogeneous, additive or Lipschitz continuous, though such functions can be more useful for the computation. Note that aggregations are a generalization of both fuzzy conjuctions and disjunctions. As such, unrestricted aggregations add too much expressive power to the language [10]. According to the paper [5], the instance problem for DLs with aggregation is polynomially decidable, provided that the subsumption of two aggregations can be decided in polynomial time.

If we use aggregation, the concept $\texttt{good\_car}_{U_1}$ from our example will be $@_{U_1}(\texttt{good\_price}_{U_1}, \texttt{good\_horsepower}_{U_1})$, where the aggregation is a weighted average $@_{U_1}(x,y) = \frac{x+2y}{3}$. Then the minimal model will be different:

$\langle \texttt{Audi\_A3} : \texttt{good\_car}, 0.32\rangle$
$\langle \texttt{Mercedes\_Benz\_280} : \texttt{good\_car}, 0.63\rangle$

Instead of standard reasoning tasks, we add a new task, *top-k retrieval*, to our description logic: for a given concept C, find k individuals with the greatest membership degrees. The value of top-k$(C)^{\mathcal{I}}(a)$ is equal to $C^{\mathcal{I}}(a)$ if a belongs to k best individuals from preference concept C (or it is preferred equally as k^{th} individual). Otherwise the value is set to 0. Note that according to the definition of top-k$(C)^{\mathcal{I}}(a)$ in Table 1, we return those elements for which the number of strictly greater elements is less than k, which includes the ties on the kth position. Thus the result can possibly include more than k individuals. The original top-k algorithm [7] is non-deterministic – instead of returning all ties on the kth position, it chooses some of them randomly and returns exactly k objects. We use this non-standard definition in order to make the top-k constructor deterministic.

Top-k algorithm [6] uses a preprocessing stage to generate lists of individuals ordered by role values. In the example above it would generate three ordered lists of individuals (for `has_price`, `has_mileage` and `has_horsepower`). The lists are traversed in specific order dependent on the particular fuzzy sets. The algorithm evaluates aggregation function on the fly and determines threshold value to find out if some other objects can have greater overall value than objects already processed. This algorithm has proved to be very efficient (see [6]).

3 Description Logic o-$\mathcal{EL}(\mathcal{D})$ with Concept Instance Ordering

Every preference concept defined in the previous section generates ordering of individuals according to the preference value. Conjunctions or aggregations are necessary to obtain overall order. This principle is similar to the decathlon rules: athletes compete in ten disciplines, each discipline is awarded with points according to scoring tables. All points are summed up to determine the final order. This is the case when all precise scores are important to determine the final score.

There are other cases when the score itself is not important. Recall another example from sport: in Formula 1, the first eight drivers gain points according to the point table (10, 8, 6, 5, 4, 3, 2, 1) regardless of their exact time, speed or headstart. The final order is also determined by summing up all points. A similar system is used in Tour de France, where riders can earn points at the end of each stage. The stages are divided into several types and each type has its own point table.

To return back to computer science, user preference is often represented as an order, partial or total. The partial order can be induced from user inputs like "object a is better than object b" or from sample set of objects rated by the user. Inductive learning of user preference from such rated set of objects means finding a linear extension of the partial order and thus be able to compare any pair of objects.

In this section we propose description logic o-$\mathcal{EL}(\mathcal{D})$ with concepts $C_{\leq}$ interpreted as non-strict preorders on the domain, $C_{\leq}^{\mathcal{J}}$. From a logical point of view, we interpret both concepts and roles as binary predicates. If $(a,b) \in C_{\leq}^{\mathcal{J}}$,

Table 2. Syntax and Semantics of $o\text{-}\mathcal{EL}(\mathcal{D})$

Syntax	Semantics
$A_{\leq}$	$A_{\leq}^{\mathcal{J}} \subseteq \Delta^{\mathcal{J}} \times \Delta^{\mathcal{J}}$
$\top_{\leq}$	$\Delta^{\mathcal{J}} \times \Delta^{\mathcal{J}}$
$C_{\leq} \sqcap D_{\leq}$	$\{(a_1, a_2) : (a_1, a_2) \in C_{\leq}^{\mathcal{J}} \wedge (a_1, a_2) \in D_{\leq}^{\mathcal{J}}\}$
$\exists R.C_{\leq}$	$\{(a_1, a_2) : \forall c_1\ (a_1, c_1) \in R^{\mathcal{J}}\ \exists c_2\ (a_2, c_2) \in R^{\mathcal{J}} : (c_1, c_2) \in C_{\leq}^{\mathcal{J}}\}$
$\exists u.P$	$\{(a_1, a_2) : \forall c_1\ (a_1, c_1) \in u^{\mathcal{J}}\ \exists c_2\ (a_2, c_2) \in u^{\mathcal{J}} : P(c_1) \leq P(c_2)\}$
$@_U(C_{\leq_1}, \ldots, C_{\leq_m})$	defined below
top-k(C)	defined below

then a belongs to the concept $C_{\leq}$ less than b (or equally). If $C_{\leq}$ is a concept representing user preference, we say that b is preferred to a. Complex concepts in $o\text{-}\mathcal{EL}(\mathcal{D})$ are constructed according to Table 2 (compare with Table 1). Lower-case letters denote individuals, except for u which denotes a concrete role. Two additional non-standard constructors (aggregation and top-k constructor) are defined in the subsequent text.

A preorder is a reflexive and transitive relation. We do not need the anti-symmetry condition (as is required for partial orders) because there can be two individuals that are not identical despite being equally preferred. We call such individuals *indiscernible* according to preference concept C. A preorder is *total*, if $\forall a, b \in \Delta^{\mathcal{J}} :\ (a, b) \in C_{\leq}^{\mathcal{J}} \vee (b, a) \in C_{\leq}^{\mathcal{J}}$ (one or both inequalities can hold).

We use the same concrete domain as in case of $s\text{-}\mathcal{EL}(\mathcal{D})$. Typical TBox definitions are $C_{\leq} \sqsubseteq D_{\leq}$ and $C_{\leq} \equiv D_{\leq}$. The ABox contains concept assertions $(a_1, a_2) : C_{\leq}$ and role assertions $(a, c) : R$. To distinguish the interpretations in $o\text{-}\mathcal{EL}(\mathcal{D})$ from $s\text{-}\mathcal{EL}(\mathcal{D})$, we denote the order-oriented interpretations as $\mathcal{J}$.

An interpretation $\mathcal{J}$ is a model of $C \sqsubseteq D$ iff $(a, b) \in C_{\leq}^{\mathcal{J}}$ implies $(a, b) \in D_{\leq}^{\mathcal{J}}$, and $C \equiv D$, iff $C^{\mathcal{J}} = D^{\mathcal{J}}$. $\mathcal{J}$ is a model of an ABox assertion $(a_1, a_2) : C_{\leq}$ iff $(a_1, a_2) : C_{\leq}^{\mathcal{J}}$. Role assertions are handled in the same way as in $s\text{-}\mathcal{EL}(\mathcal{D})$.

Top concept $\top_{\leq}$ is interpreted as a complete relation $\Delta^{\mathcal{J}} \times \Delta^{\mathcal{J}}$, where all individuals are equally preferred. Concept conjunction $C_{\leq} \sqcap D_{\leq}$ often produces partial preorder, even if $C_{\leq}$ and $D_{\leq}$ are total preorders. According to the *order-extension principle*, it is possible to extend $(C_{\leq} \sqcap D_{\leq})^{\mathcal{J}}$ to a total preorder. However, this extension does not have to be unique. Sometimes it is more convenient to use aggregation $@_U$ instead of concept conjunction, especially when we consider a conjunction of more than two concepts.

The semantics of $\exists R.C_{\leq}$ is chosen to be analogous with $s\text{-}\mathcal{EL}(\mathcal{D})$. Imagine that the individual a_1 is connected with c_1, c_2, c_3 (values of role R), while a_2 is connected with c_4, c_5, c_6. In the scoring case, we would simply take the supremum of $C^{\mathcal{I}}(c_1), C^{\mathcal{I}}(c_2), C^{\mathcal{I}}(c_3)$ as the fuzzy value of $\exists R.C^{\mathcal{I}}(a_1)$ and analoguously for $\exists R.C^{\mathcal{I}}(a_2)$. Then we just compare the suprema. To simulate the "supremum" in the ordering case, we must define that for every c_i connected with a_1 there exists a better c_j (with respect to the preference concept $C_{\leq}$) connected with a_2 via role R.

For every $@_U$ with arity m and for every m-tuple of order concepts $C_{\leq_j} \subseteq \Delta^{\mathcal{J}} \times \Delta^{\mathcal{J}}$ aggregation $@_U^{\mathcal{J}}(C_{\leq_1}, \ldots, C_{\leq_m}) \subseteq \Delta^{\mathcal{J}} \times \Delta^{\mathcal{J}}$ is a partial preorder. If $(a, b) \in C_{\leq_j}^{\mathcal{J}}$ for every $j = 1, \ldots, m$, then $(a, b) \in @_U^{\mathcal{J}}(C_{\leq_1}, \ldots, C_{\leq_m})$. We define aggregation similar to Formula 1 rules. First of all, it is necessary to define the *level* of instance a in the interpretation of concept C. It is the biggest possible length of a sequence such that the first element is a and every following element is strictly greater than its predecessor.

$$level(C, a, \mathcal{J}) = \max_{l \in \mathbf{N}}\{l : \exists b_1, \ldots, b_l \in \Delta^{\mathcal{J}}\ \forall i \in \{1, \ldots, l-1\}(b_i, b_{i+1}) \in C^{\mathcal{J}} \wedge (b_{i+1}, b_i) \notin C^{\mathcal{J}} \wedge b_1 = a\}$$

Next we define a *scoring table* for the aggregation, which is a finite strictly decreasing sequence $score_{@_U}(score_1, \ldots, score_m)$ like (10, 8, 6, 5, 4, 3, 2, 1). The differences bet ween adjacent elements are also decreasing, but not strictly. The pair (a, b) belongs to aggregation $@_U^{\mathcal{J}}(C_{\leq_1}, \ldots, C_{\leq_m})$ if

$$\sum_{j=1}^{m} score_{level(C_{\leq_j}, a, \mathcal{J})} \leq \sum_{j=1}^{m} score_{level(C_{\leq_j}, b, \mathcal{J})}.$$

This means that we find the level of individual a in every preference concept $C_{\leq_j}^{\mathcal{J}}$, then we determine the corresponding scores for these levels and sum up all the scores. If the individual b has better levels in the preference concepts $C_{\leq_j}^{\mathcal{J}}$ than individual a, it will also have a higher sum of all scores.

It is also straightforward to define top-k queries. Let $C_a = \{c \in \Delta^{\mathcal{J}} : (a, c) \in C_{\leq}^{\mathcal{J}} \wedge (c, a) \notin C_{\leq}^{\mathcal{J}}\}$ be a set of individuals strictly greater than a in ordering concept $C_{\leq}$. Then $(a, b) \in \text{top-k}(C_{\leq})^{\mathcal{J}}$, iff:

1. $(a, b) \in C_{\leq}^{\mathcal{J}}$ or
2. $|C_a| \geq k$

If $C_{\leq}$ was a total preorder, then top-k$(C_{\leq})$ will be also total. Top-k constructor preserves the original order of the first k individuals, including the ties. Note that the first k individuals often occupy less than k levels because some of them are ties. Concerning the ties on the last included level (not necessarilly the k-th level), we can either choose only some of them to fill up the needed amount of elements, or we can return them all. We choose the latter possibility, even if we end up with more than k elements in the result, because it makes our definition deterministic. If some element a has more than k strictly greater elements in $C_{\leq}^{\mathcal{J}}$, so that it is beyond the last included level (see condition 2), it is made lower or equal to all other elements, which moves it to the last level in top-k$(C_{\leq})^{\mathcal{J}}$.

Example 3. We transform the knowledge base from the previous section:

(`Audi_A3`, `Mercedes_Benz_280`) : `car`
(`Mercedes_Benz_280`, `Audi_A3`) : `car`
(`Audi_A3`, 7900) : `has_price`
(`Audi_A3`, 110) : `has_horsepower`
(`Mercedes_Benz_280`, 9100) : `has_price`

$(\texttt{Mercedes\_Benz\_280}, 147) : \texttt{has\_horsepower}$
$\texttt{good\_price}_{U_1} \equiv \exists(\texttt{has\_price}).lt_{7000,9000}$
$\texttt{good\_horsepower}_{U_1} \equiv \exists(\texttt{has\_horsepower}).rt_{100,150}$
$\texttt{good\_car}_{U_1} \equiv \texttt{car} \sqcap \texttt{good\_price}_{U_1} \sqcap \texttt{good\_horsepower}_{U_1}$

Every model $\mathcal{J}$ of the knowledge base will satisfy the following:

$(\texttt{Mercedes\_Benz\_280}, \texttt{Audi\_A3}) : \texttt{good\_price}_{U_1}$
$(\texttt{Audi\_A3}, \texttt{Mercedes\_Benz\_280}) : \texttt{good\_horsepower}_{U_1}$

The latter assertion is satisfied because $\forall c_1$ $(\texttt{Audi\_A3}, c_1) \in \texttt{has\_horsepower}^{\mathcal{J}}$ $\exists c_2 \in \Delta^{\mathcal{J}}$ $(\texttt{Mercedes\_Benz\_280}, c_2) \in \texttt{has\_horsepower}^{\mathcal{J}}$: $(c_1, c_2) \in rt^{\mathcal{J}}_{100,150}$. We have only one possibility $c_1 = 110$ and $c_2 = 147$ and moreover $(110, 147) \in rt^{\mathcal{J}}_{100,150}$.

Note that neither the tuple $(\texttt{Audi\_A3}, \texttt{Mercedes\_Benz\_280})$, nor the tuple $(\texttt{Mercedes\_Benz\_280}, \texttt{Audi\_A3})$ belongs to $\texttt{good\_car}^{\mathcal{J}}_{U_1}$ in every model $\mathcal{J}$. This is caused by the ambiguity in concept conjunctions (because the interpretation of the concept $\texttt{good\_car}_{U_1}$ is a partial preorder). This shows a necessity to use aggregations instead of concept conjunctions. Let us define the scoring table for aggregation $@_{U_1}$ as $(3, 2, 1)$ and the preferential concept $\texttt{good\_car}_{U_1}$ as $@_{U_1}(\texttt{good\_price}_{U_1}, \texttt{good\_horsepower}_{U_1})$. Individual $\texttt{Audi\_A3}$ has the first place in concept $\texttt{good\_horsepower}_{U_1}$, while $\texttt{Mercedes\_Benz\_280}$ is first in the concept $\texttt{good\_price}_{U_1}$. The result is that both individuals gain five points in total (three for the first place and two for the second place) and every interpretation must satisfy both:

$(\texttt{Mercedes\_Benz\_280}, \texttt{Audi\_A3}) : \texttt{good\_car}_{U_1}$
$(\texttt{Audi\_A3}, \texttt{Mercedes\_Benz\_280}) : \texttt{good\_car}_{U_1}$

4 Relationship between Scoring and Order Approach

Definitions for $s\text{-}\mathcal{EL}(\mathcal{D})$ and $o\text{-}\mathcal{EL}(\mathcal{D})$ are much similar, but the two logics are not equivalent. At the first sight, it is obvious that $o\text{-}\mathcal{EL}(\mathcal{D})$ drops exact membership degrees, thus it loses the ability to express some features of $s\text{-}\mathcal{EL}(\mathcal{D})$. If we have a "constant" fuzzy concept $C^{\mathcal{I}}(a) = w \in TV_n$ for every $a \in \Delta^{\mathcal{I}}$, the corresponding order concept in $o\text{-}\mathcal{EL}(\mathcal{D})$ will be $C^{\mathcal{J}}_{\leq} = \Delta^{\mathcal{J}} \times \Delta^{\mathcal{J}}$, regardless of the value w. Similarly, if $D^{\mathcal{I}}(a) \leq D^{\mathcal{I}}(b)$, the corresponding order concept contains the pair $(a, b) \in D^{\mathcal{J}}_{\leq}$, but we lose information about the difference $D^{\mathcal{I}}(b) - D^{\mathcal{I}}(a)$.

If we compare a scoring concept C with ordering concept $C_{\leq}$, we are concerned about the order of individuals. It is straightforward to define corresponding order-preserving concept $A_{\leq}$ for every primitive concept A and for any interpretation $A^{\mathcal{I}}$. We define $(a, b) \in A^{\mathcal{J}}_{\leq}$ iff $A^{\mathcal{I}}(a) \leq A^{\mathcal{I}}(b)$. Concept constructors should also preserve order of individuals. We start from a scoring concept A, transform it to a corresponding ordering concept $A_{\leq}$, use constructors (let us denote a generic constructor as $m(A)$, $m(A_{\leq})$) on both concepts and finally compare order of individuals in the results. If $m(A_{\leq})$ is a partial preorder, there are many possible total extensions.

Let $(a, b) \in A_{\leq}^{\mathcal{J}}$ iff $A^{\mathcal{I}}(a) \leq A^{\mathcal{I}}(b)$. Constructor $m(A)$ is *order-preserving* if there exists a linear extension $m(A_{\leq})'$ of $m(A_{\leq})$ such that $((a, b) \in m(A_{\leq})'^{\mathcal{J}}$ iff $m(A)^{\mathcal{I}}(a) \leq m(A)^{\mathcal{I}}(b))$. Note that the concrete domain $\mathcal{D}$ is already defined in such a way that $\exists u.P$ is order-preserving.

Lemma 1. *Existential quantification is order-preserving.*

Proof. Let $C_{\leq}$ be order-preserving concept for C. Let $(a_1, a_2) \in \exists R.C_{\leq}^{\mathcal{J}}$. According to the definition, $\forall c_1\ (a_1, c_1) \in R^{\mathcal{J}}\ \exists c_2\ (a_2, c_2) \in R^{\mathcal{J}} : (c_1, c_2) \in C_{\leq}^{\mathcal{J}}$. We know that the interpretation of roles is the same and C is order-preserving, thus $\forall c_1\ (a_1, c_1) \in R^{\mathcal{I}}\ \exists c_2\ (a_2, c_2) \in R^{\mathcal{I}} : C^{\mathcal{I}}(c_1) \leq C^{\mathcal{I}}(c_2)$. The same inequality holds for suprema: $\sup_{b \in \Delta^{\mathcal{I}}} \{C^{\mathcal{I}}(c_1) : (a_1, c_1) \in R^{\mathcal{I}}\} \leq \sup_{b \in \Delta^{\mathcal{I}}} \{C^{\mathcal{I}}(c_2) |\ (a_2, c_2) \in R^{\mathcal{I}}\}$ Therefore $(\exists R.C)^{\mathcal{I}}(a_1) \leq (\exists R.C)^{\mathcal{I}}(a_2)$.

For the reversed implication, suppose that $(\exists R.C)^{\mathcal{I}}(a_1) \leq (\exists R.C)^{\mathcal{I}}(a_2)$, and from the definition also $\sup_{b \in \Delta^{\mathcal{I}}} \{C^{\mathcal{I}}(c_1) : (a_1, c_1) \in R^{\mathcal{I}}\} \leq \sup_{b \in \Delta^{\mathcal{I}}} \{C^{\mathcal{I}}(c_2) : (a_2, c_2) \in R^{\mathcal{I}}\}$. Since the set of truth values is finite, the supremum must belong to the set. Towards the contradiction, suppose that $\exists c_1\ (a_1, c_1) \in R^{\mathcal{I}}\ \forall c_2\ (a_2, c_2) \in R^{\mathcal{I}} : C^{\mathcal{I}}(c_1) > C^{\mathcal{I}}(c_2)$. Then $C^{\mathcal{I}}(c_1)$ is upper bound of the set and it is greater than the maximum $C^{\mathcal{I}}(c_1) > \max_{b \in \Delta^{\mathcal{I}}} \{C^{\mathcal{I}}(c_2) : (a_2, c_2) \in R^{\mathcal{I}}\} \geq \max_{b \in \Delta^{\mathcal{I}}} \{C^{\mathcal{I}}(c_1) : (a_1, c_1) \in R^{\mathcal{I}}\} \geq C^{\mathcal{I}}(c_1)$, which is a contradiction. Thus $\forall c_1\ (a_1, c_1) \in R^{\mathcal{I}}\ \exists c_2\ (a_2, c_2) \in R^{\mathcal{I}} :\ C^{\mathcal{I}}(c_1) \leq C^{\mathcal{I}}(c_2)$. As C is order-preserving concept, we gain $(a_1, a_2) \in \exists R.C_{\leq}^{\mathcal{J}}$. □

Note that in case of fuzzy s-$\mathcal{EL}(\mathcal{D})$, we define $\sup \emptyset = 0$. In case of o-$\mathcal{EL}(\mathcal{D})$, if no individual is connected to a_1 with role R, then $(a_1, a_2) \in \exists R.C_{\leq}^{\mathcal{J}}$, so it yields correct inequalities for $0 \leq x$ and $0 \leq 0$.

Lemma 2. *Constructor top-k is order-preserving.*

Proof. Let us suppose that top-k$(C)^{\mathcal{I}}(a_1) \leq$ top-k$(C)^{\mathcal{I}}(a_2)$. Note that the condition $\left|c \in \Delta^{\mathcal{I}} : C^{\mathcal{I}}(a) < C^{\mathcal{I}}(c)\right| < k$ is equivalent to $|C_a| < k$ because C is order-preserving. Since top-k$(C)^{\mathcal{I}}(x)$ can be either 0 or $C^{\mathcal{I}}(x)$, we have three possibilities:

- *case 1)* top-k$(C)^{\mathcal{I}}(a_1) =$ top-k$(C)^{\mathcal{I}}(a_2) = 0$
- *case 2)* $0 =$ top-k$(C)^{\mathcal{I}}(a_1) \leq$ top-k$(C)^{\mathcal{I}}(a_2) = C^{\mathcal{I}}(a_2)$
- *case 3)* $C^{\mathcal{I}}(a_1) =$ top-k$(C)^{\mathcal{I}}(a_1) \leq$ top-k$(C)^{\mathcal{I}}(a_2) = C^{\mathcal{I}}(a_2)$

Case 1 and 2: From the definition and the equivalence of conditions above we have $|C_{a_1}| \geq k$. This is the condition 2 from the definition of top-k$(C_{\leq})$, and thus $(a_1, a_2) \in$ top-k$(C_{\leq})^{\mathcal{J}}$.

Case 3: $C^{\mathcal{I}}(a_1) \leq C^{\mathcal{I}}(a_2)$ means that $(a_1, a_2) \in C^{\mathcal{J}}$, which is the condition 1 from the definition of top-k$(C_{\leq})$, and thus also $(a_1, a_2) \in$ top-k$(C_{\leq})^{\mathcal{J}}$.

Now let $(a_1, a_2) \in \text{top-k}(C_{\leq})^{\mathcal{J}}$. This can be a consequence of the condition 1 or 2.

Let condition 2 hold – we know that $|C_{a_1}| \geq k$ and from the equivalence of conditions $\left|c \in \Delta^{\mathcal{I}} : C^{\mathcal{I}}(a_1) < C^{\mathcal{I}}(c)\right| \geq k$. From the definition of top-k(C) follows that top-k $(C)^{\mathcal{I}}(a_1) = 0$, so it will always be less or equal than top-k $(C)^{\mathcal{I}}(a_2)$.

Let condition 1 hold and let $|C_{a_1}| < k$ (otherwise we could apply the proof above). Because a_2 is greater than a_1 in preorder $C_{\leq}^{\mathcal{J}}$, the set of greater elements will also have cardinality less than k. Thus top-k$(C)^{\mathcal{I}}(a_1) = C^{\mathcal{I}}(a_1)$ and top-k$(C)^{\mathcal{I}}(a_2) = C^{\mathcal{I}}(a_2)$ and moreover $C^{\mathcal{I}}(a_1) \leq C^{\mathcal{I}}(a_2)$, which yields top-k$(C)^{\mathcal{I}}(a_1) \leq$ top-k$(C)^{\mathcal{I}}(a_2)$. □

Constructor $C_{\leq} \sqcap D_{\leq}$ produces partial preorders. Because of the minimum function in $(C \sqcap D)^{\mathcal{I}}$, we cannot model this constructor exactly in o-$\mathcal{EL}(\mathcal{D})$. There is no way of comparing elements without fuzzy degrees in two different preorders.

Lemma 3. *Concept conjunction is order-preserving.*

Proof. Let $(C \sqcap D)^{\mathcal{I}}(a_1) \leq (C \sqcap D)^{\mathcal{I}}(a_2)$. According to the definition of $C \sqcap D$, $\min\{C^{\mathcal{I}}(a_1), D^{\mathcal{I}}(a_1)\} \leq \min\{C^{\mathcal{I}}(a_2), D^{\mathcal{I}}(a_2)\}$. Let us suppose that $C^{\mathcal{I}}(a_1) = \min\{C^{\mathcal{I}}(a_1), D^{\mathcal{I}}(a_1)\}$ (the other case is analoguous). Then $C^{\mathcal{I}}(a_1)$ must be on the first place and we have six possibilities how to order all the values:

1. $C^{\mathcal{I}}(a_1) \leq D^{\mathcal{I}}(a_1) \leq C^{\mathcal{I}}(a_2) \leq D^{\mathcal{I}}(a_2)$
2. $C^{\mathcal{I}}(a_1) \leq C^{\mathcal{I}}(a_2) \leq D^{\mathcal{I}}(a_1) \leq D^{\mathcal{I}}(a_2)$
3. $C^{\mathcal{I}}(a_1) \leq C^{\mathcal{I}}(a_2) \leq D^{\mathcal{I}}(a_2) \leq D^{\mathcal{I}}(a_1)$
4. $C^{\mathcal{I}}(a_1) \leq D^{\mathcal{I}}(a_1) \leq D^{\mathcal{I}}(a_2) \leq C^{\mathcal{I}}(a_2)$
5. $C^{\mathcal{I}}(a_1) \leq D^{\mathcal{I}}(a_2) \leq D^{\mathcal{I}}(a_1) \leq C^{\mathcal{I}}(a_2)$
6. $C^{\mathcal{I}}(a_1) \leq D^{\mathcal{I}}(a_2) \leq C^{\mathcal{I}}(a_2) \leq D^{\mathcal{I}}(a_1)$

In cases 1, 2 or 4 we are done, because both $C^{\mathcal{I}}(a_1) \leq C^{\mathcal{I}}(a_2)$ and $\leq D^{\mathcal{I}}(a_1) \leq D^{\mathcal{I}}(a_2)$ hold and we have also $(a_1, a_2) \in (C_{\leq} \sqcap D_{\leq})^{\mathcal{J}}$. In cases 3, 5, 6 neither (a_1, a_2) nor (a_2, a_1) belong to $(C_{\leq} \sqcap D_{\leq})^{\mathcal{J}}$. We define the extension X to contain the tuple (a_1, a_2). All tuples added this way agree with order induced by $(C \sqcap D)^{\mathcal{I}}$. The extension X is a total preorder, so it must be reflexive, transitive and $\forall a, b \in \Delta^{\mathcal{J}} : ((a, b) \in X \vee (b, a) \in X)$. Because $(C \sqcap D)^{\mathcal{I}}$ is also a total preorder and all inequalities from $(C \sqcap D)^{\mathcal{I}}$ hold also in X, we only have to check whether X contains any extra tuples from $(C_{\leq} \sqcap D_{\leq})^{\mathcal{J}}$ that could be in conflict with $(C \sqcap D)^{\mathcal{I}}$.

Let $(a_1, a_2) \in (C_{\leq} \sqcap D_{\leq})^{\mathcal{J}}$. From the definition of concept conjunction, $(a_1, a_2) \in C_{\leq}^{\mathcal{J}} \wedge (a_1, a_2) \in D_{\leq}^{\mathcal{J}}$. Concepts C, D are order-preserving, hence $C^{\mathcal{I}}(a_1) \leq C^{\mathcal{I}}(a_2) \wedge D^{\mathcal{I}}(a_1) \leq D^{\mathcal{I}}(a_2)$. The same inequality holds for minimum, $\min\{C^{\mathcal{I}}(a_1), D^{\mathcal{I}}(a_1)\} \leq \min\{C^{\mathcal{I}}(a_2), D^{\mathcal{I}}(a_2)\}$, which means $(C \sqcap D)^{\mathcal{I}}(a_1) \leq (C \sqcap D)^{\mathcal{I}}(a_2)$. Thus X is a linear extension of $(C_{\leq} \sqcap D_{\leq})^{\mathcal{J}}$ and preserves ordering of $(C \sqcap D)^{\mathcal{I}}$. □

Note that aggregations are defined differently for o-$\mathcal{EL}(\mathcal{D})$ and s-$\mathcal{EL}(\mathcal{D})$, so we do not address their relationship here.

5 Related Work

There is a considerable effort concerning the connection of tractable description logics with top-k algorithm. Papers [9,16,17] use DL-Lite, a tractable DL with constructors $\exists R$, $\exists R^-$, $C_1 \sqcap C_2$, $\neg B$ and functional property axioms, together with top-k retrieval. Also DL $\mathcal{EL}$ is a subject of intensive research, in order to enhance the language without losing the tractability (see [3,14,15]).

The notion of instance ordering within description logics appeared in [12]. This paper defines crisp DL $\mathcal{ALCQ}(\mathcal{D})$ with special *ordering descriptions* that can be used to index and search a knowledge base. The paper [13] presents $\mathcal{ALC}_{fc}$, a fuzzy DL with *comparison concept constructors*, where it is possible to define e.g. a concept of very cheap cars (with fuzzy degree of "cheap" over some specified value), or cars that are more economy than strong. However, all of the mentioned papers use the classical (crisp or fuzzy) concept interpretation. To the best of our knowledge, there is no other work concerning interpreting concepts as preorders.

We already studied $\mathcal{EL}(\mathcal{D})$ with fuzzified concepts in [4]. We suggested the shift towards ordering approach, but the paper did not specify details of o-$\mathcal{EL}(\mathcal{D})$, nor the relationship between scoring and ordering description logic. In the paper [18], we proposed a basic reasoning algorithm for o-$\mathcal{EL}(\mathcal{D})$.

6 Conclusion

User preference is often represented as an order of objects. We show that it is possible to omit fuzzy scores (membership degrees) in description logics and to interpret concepts as preorders of the domain. We adopt the order-oriented approach for the standard concept constructors like existential restriction, concept conjunction and concrete domain predicates. We add extra constructors $@_U$ for aggregation and top-k for the retrieval of k best individuals from the concept. The resulting description logic is called o-$\mathcal{EL}(\mathcal{D})$. We show that the constructors in o-$\mathcal{EL}(\mathcal{D})$ preserve the order of individuals induced by fuzzy scores in s-$\mathcal{EL}(\mathcal{D})$. DL o-$\mathcal{EL}(\mathcal{D})$ is especially suited for user preference modelling, but it has also some limitations, e.g. it is difficult to adapt some classical reasoning problems to ordering case. As a part of our future research, we want to improve the reasoning algorithm for instance problem in o-$\mathcal{EL}(\mathcal{D})$ [18] and to devise a reasoning algorithm for subsumption of two order concepts.

References

1. Brandt, S.: Polynomial Time Reasoning in a Description Logic with Existential Restrictions, GCI Axioms, and - What else? In: Proceedings of the 16th Eureopean Conference on Artificial Intelligence, ECAI 2004, pp. 298–302. IOS Press, Amsterdam (2004)
2. Baader, F., Lutz, C., Suntisrivaraporn, B.: Is Tractable Reasoning in Extensions of the Description Logic EL Useful in Practice? In: Proceedings of the Methods for Modalities Workshop, M4M 2005 (2005)

3. Baader, F., Brandt, S., Lutz, C.: Pushing the $\mathcal{EL}$ Envelope Further. In: Proceedings of the Workshop on OWL: Experiences and Directions, OWLED 2008 (2008)
4. Vaneková, V., Vojtáš, P.: A Description Logic with Concept Instance Ordering and Top-k Restriction. In: Information Modelling and Knowledge Bases XX. Frontiers in Artificial Intelligence and Applications, vol. 190, pp. 139–153. IOS Press, Amsterdam (2009)
5. Vojtáš, P.: A Fuzzy EL Description Logic with Crisp Roles and Fuzzy Aggregation for Web Consulting. In: Information Processing and Management under Uncertainty (IPMU), pp. 1834–1841. Éditions EDK, Paris (2006)
6. Gurský, P., Vojtáš, P.: On Top-k Search with No Random Access Using Small Memory. In: Atzeni, P., Caplinskas, A., Jaakkola, H. (eds.) ADBIS 2008. LNCS, vol. 5207, pp. 97–111. Springer, Heidelberg (2008)
7. Fagin, R., Lotem, A., Naor, M.: Optimal Aggregation Algorithms for Middleware. In: PODS 2001: Proceedings of the Twentieth ACM SIGMOD-SIGACT-SIGART Symposium on Principles of Database Systems (2001); Journal of Computer and System Sciences 66(4), 614–656 (2001)
8. Baader, F., Calvanese, D., McGuinness, D.L., Nardi, D., Patel-Schneider, D.F. (eds.): Description Logic Handbook. Cambridge University Press, Cambridge (2002)
9. Straccia, U.: Towards Top-k Query Answering in Description Logics: the Case of DL-Lite. In: Fisher, M., van der Hoek, W., Konev, B., Lisitsa, A. (eds.) JELIA 2006. LNCS (LNAI), vol. 4160, pp. 439–451. Springer, Heidelberg (2006)
10. Baader, F., Sattler, U.: Description Logics with Aggregates and Concrete Domains. Information Systems 28(8), 979–1004 (2003)
11. Straccia, U.: Fuzzy $\mathcal{ALC}$ with Fuzzy Concrete Domains. In: Proceedings of the 2005 International Workshop on Description Logics (DL 2005), vol. 147, pp. 96–103. CEUR Workshop Proceedings (2005)
12. Pound, J., Stanchev, L., Toman, D., Weddell, G.E.: On Ordering and Indexing Metadata for the Semantic Web. In: Proceedings of the 21st International Workshop on Description Logics (DL-2008). CEUR Workshop Proceedings, vol. 353 (2008)
13. Kang, D., Xu, B., Lu, J., Li, Y.: Reasoning for Fuzzy Description Logic with Comparison Expressions. In: Proceedings of the 2006 International Workshop on Description Logics (DL 2006). CEUR Workshop Proceedings, vol. 189 (2006)
14. Stoilos, G., Stamou, G., Pan, J.Z.: Classifying Fuzzy Subsumption in Fuzzy-EL+. In: Proceedings of the 21st International Workshop on Description Logics (DL 2008). CEUR Workshop Proceedings, vol. 353 (2008)
15. Mailis, T., Stoilos, G., Simou, N., Stamou, G.: Tractable Reasoning Based on the Fuzzy EL++ Algorithm. In: Proceedings of the Fourth International Workshop on Uncertainty Reasoning for the Semantic Web (URSW 2008). CEUR Workshop Proceedings, vol. 423 (2008)
16. Straccia, U.: Answering Vague Queries in Fuzzy DL-Lite. In: Proceedings of the 11th International Conference on Information Processing and Management of Uncertainty in Knowledge-Based Systems (IPMU 2006), pp. 2238–2245 (2006)
17. Pan, J.Z., Stamou, G., Stoilos, G., Thomas, E., Taylor, S.: Scalable Querying Service over Fuzzy Ontologies. In: Proceedings of the 17th International World Wide Web Conference (WWW 2008), pp. 575–584. ACM, New York (2008)
18. Vaneková, V., Vojtáš, P.: Order-Oriented Reasoning in Description Logics. In: Proceedings of 6th Atlantic Web Intelligence Conference (AWIC 2009). Advances in Intelligent and Soft Computing, vol. 67. Springer, Heidelberg (to appear, 2010)

Homophily of Neighborhood in Graph Relational Classifier

Peter Vojtek and Mária Bieliková

Institute of Informatics and Software Engineering
Faculty of Informatics and Information Technologies
Slovak University of Technology
Ilkovičova 3, 842 16 Bratislava, Slovakia
{pvojtek,bielik}@fiit.stuba.sk

Abstract. Quality of collective inference relational graph classifier depends on a degree of homophily in a classified graph. If we increase homophily in the graph, the classifier would assign class-membership to the instances with reduced error rate. We propose to substitute traditionally used graph neighborhood method (based on direct neighborhood of vertex) with local graph ranking algorithm (activation spreading), which provides wider set of neighboring vertices and their weights. We demonstrate that our approach increases homophily in the graph by inferring optimal homophily distribution of a binary Simple Relational Classifier in an unweighted graph. We validate this ability also experimentally using the Social Network of the Slovak Companies dataset.

1 Introduction

Relational classifiers extend the attribute-based classifiers by adopting relations between classified instances, treating the dataset as a mathematical graph. For example, we can classify web pages according to their content only, however incorporating the content or class-membership of neighboring web pages[1] provides better results [1,2].

Methods which utilize the relations between classified instances are well suited for domains where instances have variable number of attributes (e.g., actors in a movie), attribute values are very sparsely distributed and inadequately correlate with classes, or instances have very few attributes but many relations (e.g., person in a social network identified by its nickname only but connected to many other people via friendship relation).

Univariate relational classifiers with collective inference [3,4] compose an interesting branch of classification methods where classified instances share only their class-membership between themselves via their relations (edges in a graph). The mechanism of final resolution of instance's class-membership is based on assumption of homophily – the classifier assumes that related (neighboring) instances are more likely to share similarities (e.g., the same class) as nonrelated instances [5].

[1] Neighboring web pages = connected via hyperlinks.

J. van Leeuwen et al. (Eds.): SOFSEM 2010, LNCS 5901, pp. 721–730, 2010.

This phenomenon is present in many graphs and mostly in social networks – people tend to group according to their race or ethnicity very strongly [6], and similarly it is with other person attributes (i.e., class-membership). Homophily is also induced in graphs where vertices are somewhat more abstract, like web pages or avatars, but generally they are created by humans and so they contain homophily tendencies.

In our work we analyze a Simple Relational Classifier [7] and discuss its dependency on homophily (Section 2). We draw the attention to the basic method of neighborhood acquisition applied in the Simple Relational Classifier and put it into contrast with a local graph ranking algorithm named spreading activation as an alternative in order to increase homophily. Next, we define how to measure homophily in a classified graph utilizing information entropy and we derive relationship between homophily and Simple Relational Classifier class assignment mechanism (Section 3). In Section 4 we provide an experimental evaluation that neighbors acquired via spreading activation outperform simple direct neighborhood in terms of homophily, using the Social Network of the Slovak Companies dataset. Section 5 contains related work and Section 6 concludes the paper and points out some issues requiring further work.

The goal of our work is to bring following contributions:

- we propose to use spreading activation as a better method to neighborhood acquisition in order to increase performance of the classifier,
- point out the close relation between classifier performance and dataset homophily,
- define how to measure the homophily in a classified graph,
- utilize homophily as a measure of classifier quality as an alternative to traditionally used supervised learning schema.

2 Neighborhood in Simple Relational Classifier

Simple Relational Classifier [7] estimates class-membership of the classified instance according to its neighborhood, exploiting a graph based data set $G = (V, E)$. If $p(c_m|v_k)$ is defined as a class-membership probability that vertex v_k belongs to class c_m then the Simple Relational Classifier assumes class-membership of v_k using Formula 1.

$$p(c_m|v_k) = \frac{1}{W} \sum_{v_j \in V_k | class(v_j)=c_m} w(v_k, v_j) \tag{1}$$

where V_k is the set of neighboring vertices of vertex v_k, $w(v_k, v_j)$ is a weight of the edge between vertices v_k and v_j, and $W = \sum_{v_j \in V_k} w(v_k, v_j)$ normalizes the result. The set of neighbors V_k contains all vertices directly connected to the classified vertex v_k via edges. If the class-membership consists of classes $c_m \in C$ (C is the set of all classes), the final class assigned to v_k is in Formula 2.

$$class(v_k) = argmax_{c_m}[p(c_m|v_k)] \tag{2}$$

Neighborhood Acquisition

In original Simple Relational Classifier as well as in other relational classifiers [2,8] neighborhood of a vertex v_k is designed as a set of vertices directly connected via edges, so that $V_k = \{v_j : v_j \in V, exists(e_{kj})\}$, where $exists(e_{kj})$ denotes an event that the graph contains an edge between vertices v_k and v_j.

Our hypothesis is that the neighborhood method should be more robust in order to absorb broader set of vertices along with weights indicating degree of vertex proximity. Due to this reason, we propose to adopt activation spreading algorithm [9,10], which is a local graph ranking method with following pseudocode[2]:

```
activate(energy E, vertex v_k) {
   energy(v_k) = energy(v_k) + E
   E' = E / |V_k|
   if (E' > T) {
      for each vertex v_j ∈ V_k {
         activate(E', v_j)
      }
   }
}
```

Activate is a recursive algorithm, its output is a set of vertices along with their weights (energy), indicating degree of affinity between v_k and ranked vertices. Minimum energy threshold T provides quick convergence of algorithm and $|V_k|$ is a number of neighboring vertices. Spreading activation assigns energy values to the vertices, not to the edges – in order to be consistent with (1) we establish $w(v_k, v_j)$ in Formula 3.

$$w(v_k, v_j) = \frac{energy(v_k)}{energy(v_j)} \tag{3}$$

Fig. 1(a) depicts example of a graph with unweighted edges. If we would classify v_1, then $V_1 = \{v_2, v_3, v_4\}$. However, if we adopt spreading activation (Fig. 1(b)), we get $V_1 = \{v_2, v_3, v_4, v_5, v_6\}$ along with weights indicating affinity between vertices, so that $w(v_1, v_2) = \frac{energy(v_1)}{energy(v_2)}$, $w(v_1, v_3) = \frac{energy(v_1)}{energy(v_3)}$, etc.

Discussion on alternative graph ranking methods is in Section 5.

3 Measuring Homophily

Evaluating the difference between original and proposed neighborhood acquisition method in terms of classifier error rate draws our attention to an observation that quality of Simple Relational Classifier class assignment depends on degree of

[2] In order to maintain simplicity and to be coherent with graph used in experimental evaluation, following algorithm is designed for unweighted graph, the original one can deal with weighted graphs.

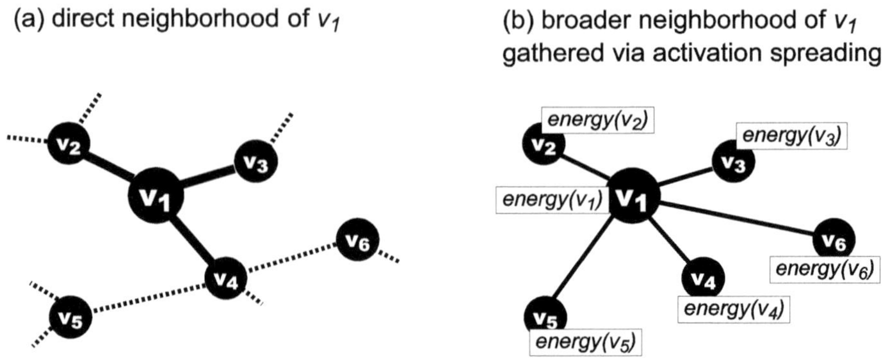

Fig. 1. Two methods of neighborhood acquisition

homophily in the classified graph. First we introduce homophily and its measure and then point out its relation to the Simple Relational Classifier.

Assumption of homophily is informally defined as following [6]:

> *Related instances are more likely to share same class as nonrelated instances.*

We can rewrite this sentence in terms of probability theory in following way:

$$p(exists(e_{kj})|class(v_k) = class(v_j)) > \\ > p(exists(e_{kj})|class(v_k) \neq class(v_j)) \quad (4)$$

where $class(v_k) \in C$ is class-membership of vertex v_k. We define the degree of homophily of vertex v_k as a measure based on class-membership distribution of its neighboring vertices by adopting information entropy:

$$homophily(v_k) = 1.0 + \sum_{c_m \in C} p(c_m|v_k) \log_{base} p(c_m|v_k) \quad (5)$$

This measure is designed to deal with unlimited number of classes and the homophily is in range $\langle 0, 1 \rangle$, so that 0 is the lowest homophily and 1.0 is the highest homophily.

If we consider binary classification with classes $C = \{c_+, c_-\}$, $base = 2$ and weights of all edges are set to 1.0 (i.e. unweighted graph), we gain following boundary states:

- the highest $homophily(v_k) = 1.0$ if all neighboring vertices are assigned to c_- or c_+ exclusively (Fig. 2(a));
- lowest $homophily(v_k) = 0.0$ occurs if 50% of neighboring vertices are assigned to class c_-, the rest belongs to c_+ (Fig. 2(b)).

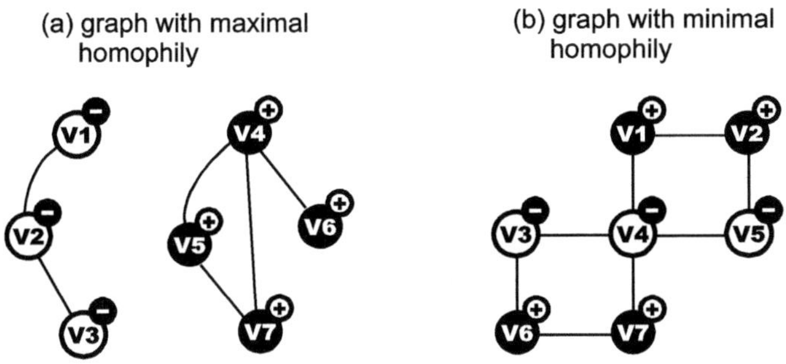

Fig. 2. Examples of homophily in a graph, each vertex in (a) has the same level of homophily (similarly (b))

If we include substitution $W = \sum_{v_j \in V_k} w(v_k, v_j)$ into (1) we can rewrite the general Simple Relational Classifier formula as following:

$$p(c_m|v_k) = \frac{\sum_{v_j \in V_k | class(v_j)=c_m} w(v_k, v_j)}{\sum_{v_j \in V_k} w(v_k, v_j)} = \frac{W_{k_{c_m}}}{W_k} \quad (6)$$

It is obvious that $W_k = \sum_{c_m \in C} W_{k_{c_m}}$.

Because our experiments are based on binary classification, with set of classes $C = \{c_+, c_-\}$, we get $W_k = W_{k_{c_+}} + W_{k_{c_-}}$. If we consider this adjustment within (2), in order to determine impact of various neighborhood acquisition methods we only need to observe the ratio $W_{k_{c_+}} : W_k$. If $\frac{W_{k_{c_+}}}{W_k} > 0.5$, classified vertex v_k is assigned to positive class, if $\frac{W_{k_{c_+}}}{W_k} < 0.5$ then $class(v_k) = c_-$, otherwise $class(v_k)$ is left unassigned.

4 Experimental Evaluation

If we return to our hypothesis presented Section 2, our goal is to compare basic direct neighborhood with neighbors acquired with spreading activation and determine how these two approaches influence homophily in a graph (which in turn influences classifier performance). With this knowledge we will be able to distinguish which neighborhood method should be included into Simple Relational Classifier with the aim to decrease its misclassification rate.

We employ dataset based on social network of Slovak Companies register (`http://foaf.sk/`) [11]. A bipartite graph consist of two vertex types, *Company* and *Person* and a relation between them (*is_ in*), which indicates that person P

plays a role in company C as a shareholder, director, etc. The dataset contains 350 000 persons, 168 000 companies and 460 000 edges between them. It is a typical social network with exponential distribution of vertex degree and graph component size.

Vertices in the graph hold several attributes – name, address, basic capital, scope of business activity, etc. A vertex class-membership is then derived from one of these attributes. We use class-membership named *is_ in_ Bratislava* which defines that $class(v_k) = c_+$ if person or company is located in the city Bratislava (capital city of Slovakia), otherwise $class(v_k) = c_-$. The distribution of $c_+ : c_-$ is 27 : 73.

In practice, such a classification task is useful for two reasons: derive (at least at the regional level) addresses of people and companies with unknown location and validate address of instances affected by noise of the data acquisition method[3].

In our experiment we put into contrast ratios from (6). The results are summarized in Fig. 3, x-axis represents the ratio of $\frac{W_{k_{c_+}}}{W_k}$ and y-axis is average vertex homophily, where vertices are grouped according to x-axis[4].

In Fig. 3 we compare three curves: the optimal homophily function (as defined in (5)) is put into contrast with the two observed homophily rates: basic neighborhood and spreading activation. We see that spreading activation fits optimal homophily much better than basic neighborhood. In terms of root mean square error (RMSE) we gain:

- *Company*: $RMSE_{basic\_neigh} = 0.360$ and $RMSE_{act\_spread} = 0.219$
- *Person*: $RMSE_{basic\_neigh} = 0.374$ and $RMSE_{act\_spread} = 0.222$

For a comparison a list of contingency table derived measures is in Table 1. We see that spreading activation clearly outperforms basic neighborhood in all measures except the recall of *Person* vertex type. Imbalance of recall is induced by imbalance between $c_+ : c_-$ ratio in the dataset, where c_- is assigned to 73% of vertices, but recall is computed on the subset of c_+ vertices.

There are more reasons why spreading activation outperforms basic neighborhood method and provides smoother and more robust homophily lapse. Consider a graph in Fig. 4. If we use basic neighborhood method, vertex v_1 is surrounded by vertices $V_1 = \{v_2, v_3\}$. This constellation implies very disadvantageous homophily; $class(v_2) = c_-$ and $class(v_3) = c_+$, so that $\frac{W_{1_{c_+}}}{W_1} = 0.5$ and $homophily(v_1) = 0.0$. However, if we consider neighborhood computed with spreading activation (starting with energy $E = 1.0$ and threshold $T = 0.15$), we get neighbors with weights as depicted in Fig. 4. If we compute homophily for this kind of neighborhood we get $\frac{W_{1_{c_+}}}{W_1} = 0.625$ and $homophily(v_1) = 0.045$.

[3] `http://foaf.sk/` dataset is gathered via wrapping the Slovak Companies register `http://orsr.sk/` administrated by the Ministry of Justice of the Slovak Republic.

[4] x-axis is sampled with $step = 0.1$, e.g., when a vertex v_k has three neighbors with positive class and one neighbor with negative class, $\frac{W_{k_{c_+}}}{W_k} = \frac{3}{4}$.

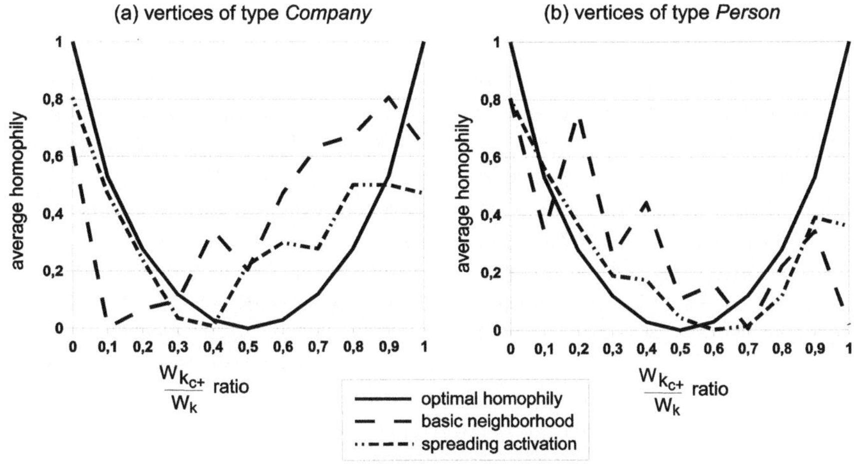

Fig. 3. Homophily comparison for basic neighborhood and spreading activation

Table 1. Contingency table derived measures

	Company		*Person*	
	basic neigh.	spread. act.	basic neigh.	spread. act.
recall [%]	85.8	90.8	71.0	56.8
precision [%]	18.2	59.5	24.3	89.1
f1 [%]	74.7	86.1	77.5	79.4
accuracy [%]	30.0	71.9	36.2	69.4
RMSE	0.360	0.219	0.374	0.222

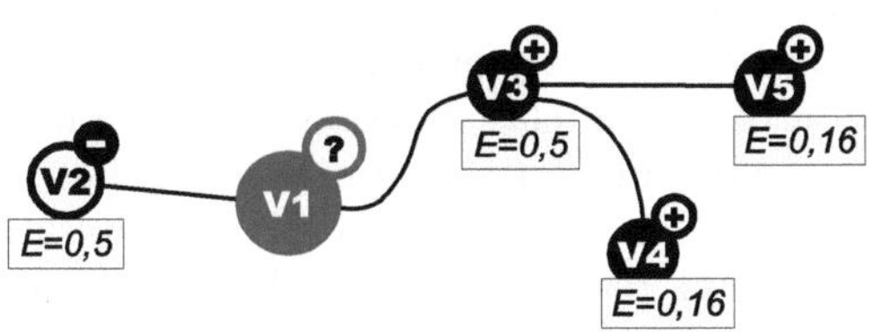

Fig. 4. Example of a graph with varying homophily according to the neighborhood acquisition method

The spreading activation energy was set to 300.0 in the experiment and threshold $T = 1.0$ so that the neighborhood usually contains between 10 and 100 vertices and the ranking converged very quickly. Increasing the energy or decreasing the threshold would provide us broader neighborhood of a vertex, however the computational time will heighten. Decreasing the activation energy should not be beneficial as then the energy would spread to direct neighbors only (the flow will be then stopped by the threshold limit), providing the same information about vertex' neighborhood as the basic method.

5 Related Work

Relational classifiers (also called 'collective') are new and a developing branch of predictive methods. Overview and *classification* of relational classifiers is available in [3,4]. More complex alternatives to Simple Relational Classifier are Iterative Reinforcement Categorization Algorithm [2] and Relational Ensemble Classifier [8], both capable to deal with more types of classified instances as well as handle more than one relation in a graph.

Graph ranking algorithms as spreading activation are well analyzed, mainly due to popularity of global ranking algorithms as PageRank and HITS in web search, an overview of these methods is in [10]. Spreading activation is a local ranking method similar to Random Walks with Restart [12]. We decided to employ spreading activation due to its simple understandability and effective runtime execution – we use the same method in real time on `http://foaf.sk` portal when searching for related people and companies, serving more than 500 000 page views per month.

There exist few proposals of alternative neighborhood acquisition methods to direct vertex neighborhood composed of directly connected vertices. Gallagher et al. [12] employs Random Walks with Restart method in order to improve classifier performance in graphs with weakly connected nodes, however without deeper homophily phenomenon analysis. An overview work by Jensen et al. [4] contains a neighborhood method concerning distance of neighboring objects but its impact on classifier performance is not provided.

Homophily in the task of classification is referenced in several works [5,12], using synonyms as 'auto-correlation' or 'local consistency'. A discussion of homophily measurement methods is in [13], however the degree of homophily is set-based (a homophily of chosen attribute in a set of vertices), while we are focused on homophily from a single vertex' point of view.

According to our contribution in previous sections we can refer to homophily as a quality metric of a relational classification. Classical measures as accuracy, recall, precision or F1 can be only derived from true and false positives/negatives from the contingency table, which subsequently requires the data set to be divided into a training and testing set, usually using some cross validation method [14]. Quality of relational classifiers evaluated via these contingency table measures is a subject of bias induced by relations between vertices in the training and the testing set [13,15]. On the other side, homophily explicitly requires these relations, being capable for relational classifier only (excluding attribute-based methods).

6 Conclusion and Further Work

We analyzed quality of class assignment in a relational classifier and its correlation with homophily in the classified data set represented as a graph. We proposed to adopt spreading activation as an alternative to traditionally used direct neighborhood in the classification of graph vertices using Simple Relational

Classifier. We demonstrated that to determine the positive impact of spreading activation on the misclassification rate it is sustainable to simply observe the homophily induced by this neighborhood method rather than set up an experiment with training and test set and calculate contingency table metrics, which acquits us from the bias induces by relational component in the dataset.

In further work we derive the relation between homophily and classifier quality of other relational classifiers, mainly Iterative Reinforcement Categorization Algorithm [2] and Relational Ensemble Classifier [8]. It is an interesting notice that Simple Relational Classifier is in fact a kind of Iterative Reinforcement Categorization method under specific conditions.

Acknowledgments. This work was partially supported by the Scientic Grant Agency of Slovak Republic, grant No. VG1/0508/09 and it is the partial result of the OPVaV - 2008/4.1/01 project ITMS 26240120005 implementation: SMART – Support of Center of Excellence for Smart Technologies, Systems and Services supported by the Research & Development Operational Programme funded by the ERDF.

References

1. Getoor, L., Segal, E., Taskar, B., Koller, D.: Probabilistic Models of Text and Link Structure for Hypertext Classification (2001)
2. Xue, G., Yu, Y., Shen, D., Yang, Q., Zeng, H., Chen, Z.: Reinforcing Web-Object Categorization through Interrelationships. Data Min. Knowl. Discov. 12(2-3), 229–248 (2006)
3. Macskassy, S.A., Provost, F.: Classification in Networked Data: A Toolkit and a Univariate Case Study. J. Mach. Learn. Res. 8, 935–983 (2007)
4. Jensen, D., Neville, J., Gallagher, B.: Why Collective Inference Improves Relational Classification. In: KDD 2004: Proceedings of the Tenth ACM SIGKDD International Conference on Knowledge Discovery and Data Mining, pp. 593–598. ACM Press, New York (2004)
5. Jackson, M.O.: Average Distance, Diameter, and Clustering in Social Networks with Homophily. In: Papadimitriou, C., Zhang, S. (eds.) WINE 2008. LNCS, vol. 5385, pp. 4–11. Springer, Heidelberg (2008)
6. Mcpherson, M., Lovin, L.S., Cook, J.M.: Birds of a Feather: Homophily in Social Networks. Annual Review of Sociology 27(1), 415–444 (2001)
7. Macskassy, S., Provost, F.: A Simple Relational Classifier. In: Workshop Multi-Relational Data Mining in conjunction with KDD 2003. ACM Press, New York (2003)
8. Preisach, C., Schmidt-Thieme, L.: Relational Ensemble Classification. In: ICDM 2006: Proceedings of the Sixth International Conference on Data Mining, Washington, DC, USA, pp. 499–509. IEEE Computer Society, Los Alamitos (2006)
9. Ceglowski, M., Coburn, A., Cuadrado, J.: Semantic Search of Unstructured Data Using Contextual Network Graphs (2003)
10. Suchal, J.: On Finding Power Method in Spreading Activation Search. In: Geffert, V., Karhumäki, J., Bertoni, A., Preneel, B., Návrat, P., Bieliková, M. (eds.) SOFSEM 2008. LNCS, vol. 4910, pp. 124–130. Springer, Heidelberg (2008)

11. Suchal, J., Vojtek, P.: Navigácia v sociálnej sieti obchodného registra SR. In: DATAKON, Srní, Czech Republic (2009) (in Slovak)
12. Gallagher, B., Tong, H., Eliassi-Rad, T., Faloutsos, C.: Using Ghost Edges for Classification in Sparsely Labeled Networks. In: KDD 2008: Proceeding of the 14th ACM SIGKDD International Conference on Knowledge Discovery and Data Mining, pp. 256–264. ACM, New York (2008)
13. Jensen, D., Neville, J.: Linkage and Autocorrelation Cause Feature Selection Bias in Relational Learning. In: ICML 2002: Proceedings of the Nineteenth International Conference on Machine Learning, pp. 259–266. Morgan Kaufmann Publishers Inc., San Francisco (2002)
14. Liu, B.: Web Data Mining: Exploring Hyperlinks, Contents, and Usage Data, pp. 55–115. Springer, Heidelberg (2006)
15. Korner, C., Wrobel, S.: Bias-Free Hypothesis Evaluation in Multirelational Domains. In: MRDM 2005: Proceedings of the 4th International Workshop on Multi-Relational Mining, pp. 33–38. ACM Press, New York (2005)

Multilanguage Debugger Architecture

Jan Vraný and Michal Píše*

Department of Computer Science and Engineering
Faculty of Electrical Engineering
Czech Technical University in Prague

Abstract. When debugging applications written in several programming languages, current debuggers usually fail to provide programmers with the same quality of user experience that is common for single-language application debugging. As a result, development of multilanguage applications tends to be more expensive both in terms of development and maintenance costs.

In this paper, we propose a flexible architecture that facilitates integration of multiple single-language debuggers into a single multilanguage debugger. In addition, we describe its proof-of-concept implementation that allows debugging of applications written in Smalltalk, XQuery and JavaScript.

1 Introduction

Nowadays, applications written in several programming languages are fairly common. For example, a frontend of a web application typically uses a template engine with limited scripting capabilities while business logic of the same application is implemented using a general purpose object-oriented language such as Java or C# and its persistence layer consists of a set of triggers and stored procedures written in a dialect of SQL.

The reasons for utilizing multiple languages within a single application vary:

- certain parts of the application logic can sometimes be better and more comprehensively expressed in a different language than the rest of it,
- it might be more efficient in terms of time and programmers' efforts to develop application components in different languages because of an already existing reusable codebase, libraries or suitable frameworks,
- a low-level language routines are often embedded into code written in a higher-level language to gain better performance and
- utilization of several languages in one application may simply be the only technologically viable option.

While from a broader perspective, multilanguage applications bring along many benefits, when considering the process of debugging itself, such applications are extremely difficult to deal with. The reason is simple: most debuggers are

* The authors would like to express many thanks to Roman Vaculín and anonymous reviewers for their helpful comments.

J. van Leeuwen et al. (Eds.): SOFSEM 2010, LNCS 5901, pp. 731–742, 2010.

single-language and even the few multilanguage ones usually support only a limited combination of programming languages.

Without truly multilanguage debuggers, developers are forced to debug multilanguage applications using single-language debuggers which, quite naturally, yields poor results. For instance, when debugging an application written both in Java and C without a suitable multilanguage debugger, developers may choose either to not use a debugger at all, use only a Java debugger, use only a C debugger or use both debuggers simultaneously—and none of these options is satisfactory enough.

Insufficiency of the first option is obvious, discussion of the three remaining options follows: using only a Java debugger provides developers with a fairly good grasp of what is going on in those parts of the application written in Java. However, apprehension of the behavior of the rest of the application is likely to be very limited—developers can inspect input parameters and return values of any Java-to-C method call but they are completely oblivious to all C-to-C calls.

On the other hand, when using only a C debugger, developers get a complete information about the execution of the whole application. However, they also get a complete information about the execution of the virtual machine (VM) in which the application is running (assuming the VM is written in C) and, unfortunately, that information is interleaved with the information about the execution of Java code. Given the complexity of contemporary VMs, any useful information about the behavior of Java code is therefore effectively lost.

The third option, running the application with both debuggers attached at the same time and using the Java debugger to debug only Java code and the C debugger to debug only C code, is probably the most productive one. Unfortunately, it is not productive enough because it forces developers to deal with two distinct user interfaces and combine information contained therein.

To summarize: using single-language debuggers to debug multilanguage applications results in developers knowing too little, too much or having the knowledge unsuitably partititoned. Therefore, a debugger that provides the same quality of user experience regardless of whether the application is single- or multilanguage is highly desirable.

The aim of this paper is to propose an architecture of such a debugger. Namely, its contributions are (i) description of a flexible architecture that facilitates integration of multiple single-language debuggers into a single multilanguage debugger and (ii) description of its proof-of-concept implementation that allows debugging of applications written in Smalltalk, XQuery and JavaScript.

The structure of this paper is the following: Sect. 2 provides the necessary background, Sect. 3 describes the proposed solution, Sect. 4 compares our solution with the related work and Sect. 5 concludes the paper.

2 Background

This section contains a brief description of types of execution runtimes, possible approaches to integration of multiple languages within one application and possible ways of implementing a source-level debugger.

2.1 Compiler and Execution Runtime

An implementation of a programming language usually consists of two parts: a compiler and a corresponding execution runtime. The role of the compiler is to transform the source code of an application into a representation which is understood by its respective execution runtime: a machine code, a byte code or an abstract syntax tree. In some cases, the runtime executes the source code directly, which eliminates the need for a compiler.

The role of the runtime is then to perform the computation by interpreting the intermediate program representation created by the compiler. Often, there is no need for execution runtime since the compiler generates machine code that runs on bare hardware. However, with the progression of VM technology and, at the same time, increasing complexity of standard libraries used in languages compiled into native code, the distinction between pure interpretation and direct machine code execution is getting more and more blurred. Also, from a hardware designer's point of view, even the machine code is interpreted by the underlying hardware.

2.2 Multilanguage Applications

There are three basic ways of mixing two languages in a single application:

- execution runtime of one of the languages is implemented using the other one,
- both languages share the same execution runtime and, consequently, the same intermediate program representation and
- each language has its own execution runtime.

Writing an execution runtime (interpreter) of one of the languages in the other one is usually employed to execute small pieces of code written in a specialized domain specific language[1] and is often based on the interpreter design pattern[2]. The advantage of this approach is that it is easy to implement, modify and extend. However, its performance tends to be poor. Method invocation across language boundaries is achieved by calling the interpreter with an identification of the called method supplied as its argument. In other words, the developer invokes the interpreter which in turn invokes the method written in the other language.

Runtime sharing is a way of language integration that is currently utilized quite often as it is very effective in terms of language implementors' efforts and usually provides good performance. However, it is suitable only for languages with fairly similar first-class abstractions. For example, it would probably be very difficult to use runtime sharing to integrate a prototype-based language with continuations and no notion of call stack with a language based on logic programming paradigm. Nevertheless, if this approach is suitable the integration of languages is almost seamless because the intermediate representation (compiled code) is the same.

Finally, the best efficiency and flexibility can be achieved by having both languages have their own execution runtimes. This approach requires for both runtimes to have some kind of support for invocation of methods written in other languages. In other words, the calling runtime must provide a mechanism of stepping out, converting all necessary data (e.g. parameters) and invoking the other runtime. At present, not all runtimes provide such a mechanism.

2.3 Debuggers

There exist two basic means of collecting data about program execution: code instrumentation and events emitted by the operating system, virtual machine or interpreter[3].

When using code instrumentation, the application's code is augmented to contain method calls that inform their recipient of the currently executed expression. The code may be instrumented statically—by the compiler or some kind of code instrumentation tool—or dynamically—when it is being loaded into the memory or even before it is executed for the first time[4].

The second approach differs from the first one in that the debugging events are emitted by the interpreter, virtual machine or operating system[5]. In other words, debugging-related instructions are part of the interpreter, virtual machine or operating system, not the application itself.

Both approaches share an important common trait: the primary means of communication is event-based.

3 Solution

This section contains a description of proposed solution: a flexible source-level debugger architecture that facilitates integration of multiple single-language debuggers into a single multilanguage debugger.

Its main idea is based on the following observation: when debugging code written in their respective languages, single-language debuggers provide a sensible information regardless of whether the application is single-language or multilanguage. In other words, validity of debugging events emitted by a single-language debugger depends solely on whether the code currently under execution has originally been written in a language for which the debugger has been designed.

3.1 Architecture

The architecture of the debugger consists of several components that communicate using event mechanism. Figure 1 shows its core components.

DebuggerAdapter. A core class that acts as a facade for underlying debugger and respective execution engine. It is used for both accessing the control flow structures such as contexts and variables and for controlling the execution of the program. There is one debugger adapter for each language.

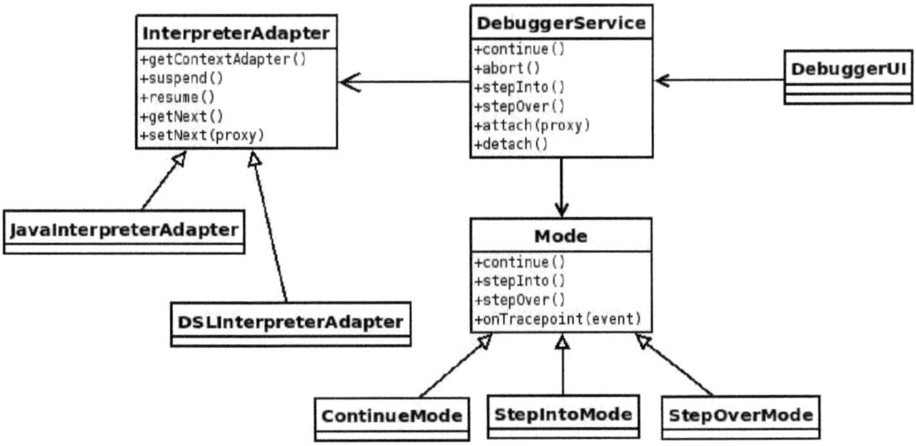

Fig. 1. Overall architecture of multilanguage debugger

ContextAdapter, VariableAdapter and InstructionAdapter. These are helper classes that provide uniform access to language's runtime internals.

DebuggerService. An instance of DebuggerService is responsible for performing debugging operations such as step-into or step-over. It is a mediator between debugger adapters and debugger's user interface.

DebuggerMode and its subclasses. These classes represent a mode of operation of the debugger.

DebuggerUI. The user interface of the debugger. It presents relevant information to the programmer and enables them to perform debugging operations.

3.2 Debugger Adapter

As we said before, the debugger adapter is a core class of whole system. It interfaces underlying execution engine in general way, no matter how it is implemented. More precisely, the debugger adapter (i) provides an uniform access to the current execution state, (ii) emits events whenever the execution state of the program changes and (iii) provides facilities for suspending/resuming the execution. Generally, there is one debugger adapter for every interpreter. In practice, debugger adapter implementations can be shared between several languages that are implemented in same way.

For example, the Perseus framework[10] provides a rich set of reusable classes for building language interpreters with integrated debugging facilities based on debuggable interpreter design pattern[6]. This framework also provides a debugger adapter implementation that can be used for adapters of all languages based on the framework.

Execution state model. The execution state modeled through set of adapters: a context adapter, a variable adapter and an instruction adapter. The adapter objects are used by the user interface to present the state to the programmer.

Context adapter. Context stack is model-led by context adapters. Each context adapter belongs to one activation record on interpreter's execution stack. The context adapter provides access to:

- name of the function or method that belongs to the context,
- source code of that function or method,
- context adapter of the sender (caller) context (as another instruction adapter),
- instruction being interpreted (as instruction adapter),
- set of variables that belongs to the context (as variable adapters).

The adapter also contains a reference to the debugger adapter it belongs to.

Instruction adapter. The instruction adapter represents an instruction being interpreted. It contains a line reference to the source code, which is used by the debugger to visually emphasize current position in the code. Although this object is called instruction adapter, it is generally not related to the interpreter's (or hardware processor's) program counter register. Here the instruction is just an abstraction of the smallest piece of code that is executed atomically by an interpreter. An instruction might be a single bytecode or an AST node, depending on interpreter's internal architecture.

Variable adapter. Variable adapters abstracts function arguments and local variables. It also enables the debugger read and modify variable's value.

Although presented set of adapters covers wide range of programming languages, it does not completely cover all possible languages. A new kinds of adapters and properties can be easily added using customized adapters.

Events Emitted by the Debugger Adapter. During a program execution the debugger adapter emits number of events. These events, called *announcements*, reflect changes in program's execution state such as entering or leaving a function, modifying a variable or the reach of a breakpoint. Announcements allows other objects such as debugger service to analyze interpreter's control flow an react whenever certain situation occurs. Figure 2 shows hierarchy of announcements.

Execution Control Facilities. During an interactive debugging session, the program execution is interlaced with debugging phase. In debugging phase, the program execution is temporarily suspended and programmers are given a chance to interactively explore and modify program state such as variable values. At the end of debugging phase, programmers might resume program execution by means of debugging operation or abort the execution at all.

To enable interactive debugging, the debugger adapter expose three methods with obvious meaning: *suspend*, *resume* and *abort*. Those method are used by the debugger service to drive the execution during an interactive debugging session.

3.3 Debugger Service

The debugger service implements the debugging operations such as step-into, step-over and continue. It acts as a model for debugger user interface. During

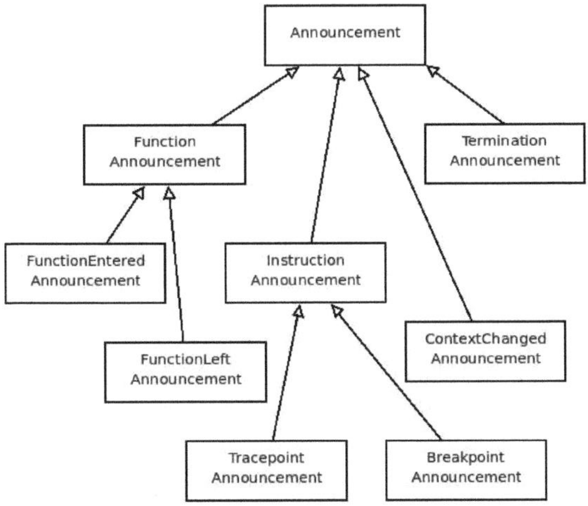

Fig. 2. Announcement class hierarchy

a debugging session the debugger service is *attached* to the debugger adapter. That means that the debugger service is registered to the adapter and receives emitted announcements:

```
DebuggerService>>attach: anDebuggerAdapter {
  adapter ← anDebuggerAdapter.
  adapter
    subscribe: TracepointAnnouncement
      send: #onTracepoint: to: self;
    subscribe: ContextAnnouncement
      send: #onContextChange: to: self;
}
```

At the end of debugging session the debugger service *detaches* from the debugger adapter:

```
DebuggerService>>detach {
  adapter unsubscribe: self.
}
```

For the more detailed description of the debugging service and debugging operation implementations please refer to [6].

3.4 Stacking Debugger Adapters

The basic idea of our unified debugger is following: in addition to to the execution stack, a stack of debugger adapters is maintained. Each debugger adapter corresponds to a bunch of activation records on the execution stack.

Debugger adapter stack must be maintained manually (i.e. programmer should include stack modification code into the code) whenever a program's control flow enters or leave a chunk of code in different language than the one currently being executed. Two functions are provided for managing interpreter adapter stack: *pushDebuggerAdapter:* and *popDebuggerAdapter*. When a new debugger adapter is pushed onto a stack, all debugger services that are attached to a current debugger adapter must attach a new debugger adapter:

```
DebugggerAdapter class>>
 pushDebuggerAdapter: newDebuggerAdapter {
  activeAdapter subscribers do:
    [:subscriber|
    subscriber detach.
    subscriber attach: newDebuggerAdapter].
  newInterpreter next: activeAdapter.
  activeAdapter ← newDebuggerAdapter
}
```

Similarly when the topmost adapter is to be removed, all attached debugging services must reattach the next one:

```
InterpreterAdapter class>>popDebuggerAdapter {
  activeAdapter subscribers do:
    [:subscriber|
    subscriber detach.
    subscriber attach: activeAdapter next].
  activeAdapter ← activeAdapter next
}
```

Manual management of debugger adapter stack is usually not difficult since calling foreign functions (that is routines implemented in another language) often requires some glue code.

Consider a following example of multi-language applications written in Smalltalk, XQuery and JavaScript. Smalltalk part of the application instantiates an XQuery interpreter and evaluates XQuery code:

```
|xqInterpreter |
xqInterpreter ← XQueryIntepreter new.
xqInterpreter evaluate: query
```

The `query` variable holds an XQuery code, that defines new function for computing combinatorial numbers:

```
import module namespace js = "http://sma...";
declare function combinatorial-number ( $n , $k ) {
  js:factorial( $n ) /
    ( js:factorial ( $k )
      * js:factorial ( $n - $k ) )
};

combinatorial-number ( 5 , 3 )
```

The XQuery code calls a function `js:factorial`, that is implemented in JavaScript:

```
function factorial ( a ) {
  if ( a == 0 ) {
    return 1;
  } else {
    return a * factorial ( a );
  }
}
```

Figure 3 shows execution and debugger adapter stack for the example above.

The method *evaluate:* in unified debugger-enabled XQueryInterpreter class is – on principle – implemented as follows:

```
XQueryInterpreter>>evaluate: query {
  | queryTree result |
  queryTree ← self parse: query.
  DebuggerAdapter pushDebuggerAdapter:
    (XQueryDebuggerAdapter on: self).
  result ← self visit: queryTree.
  InterpreterAdapter popDebuggerAdapter.
  ↑ result.
}
```

The XQuery interpreter supports number of primitives. Primitives are functions that are directly callable from within an XQuery code, but whose implementation is done in different language than XQuery. The XQueryInterpreter calls method *performJsPrimitive:withArguments:* to call primitive implemented in JavaScript:

```
XQueryInterpreter>>evaluateJsPrimitive: primName
 withArguments: args {
  | result |
  DebuggerAdapter pushDebuggerAdapter:
    (ByteCodeDebuggerAdapter on: self).
  result ← jsPrimitiveLibrary
    perform: primName withArguments: args.1
  DebuggerAdapter popDebuggerAdapter.
  ↑ result.
}
```

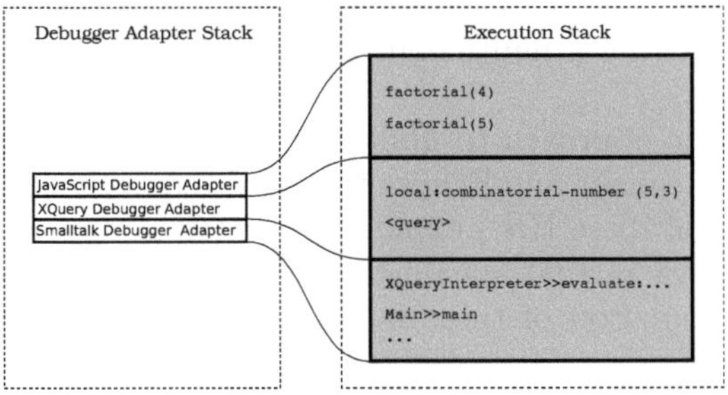

Fig. 3. Debugger adapter stack

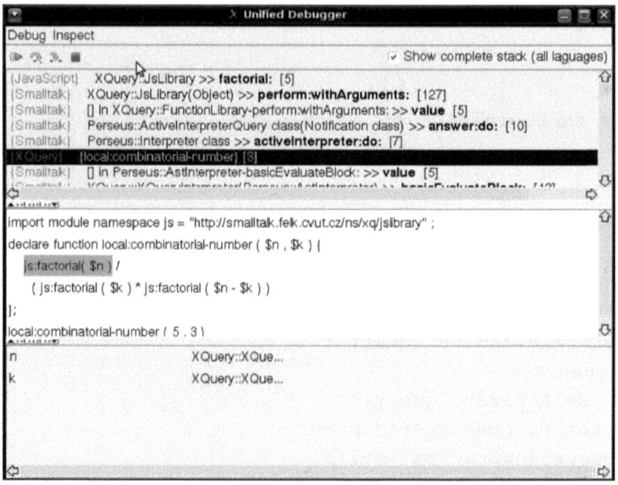

Fig. 4. Unified Debugger User Interface

The figure 4 shows a user interface for our unified debugger implementation. A user can explore the stack and resume the evaluation in both step-into and step-over manner.

4 Related Work

The authors of this paper have no intention to imply that this paper is the very first work in the field of multilanguage debuggers. Quite the contrary—there exists a number of multilanguage debuggers, however, majority of them is either proprietary or ad-hoc[7]. Obviously, proprietary solutions can not be commented upon or compared here.

Documented ad-hoc solutions, on the other hand, can. Our general opinion about them is this: although ad-hoc solutions surely solve the problem for a certain class of applications they are not a long-term remedy because the cost of writing an ad-hoc multilanguage debugger increases superlinearly with the number of supported languages. Conversely, the architecture proposed in this paper keeps the costs of writing a multilanguage debugger linear with the number of supported languages.

A more systematic approach to multilanguage debugger development is the one featured in NetBeans[8] and Eclipse[9] integrated development environments (IDEs). Developers of these IDEs exploit the fact that many modern languages run on top of the Java Virtual Machine (JVM) and that applications composed solely of some combination of these languages can be debugged by any JVM debugger.

This approach has a huge advantage: any language implemented on top of the JVM can be debugged by an already existing JVM debugger. In other words, the cost of implementing a multilanguage debugger that supports all JVM-based languages is the same as the cost of implementing a Java-only debugger. On the other hand, this approach implies the debugger is aware only of the JVM metamodel and can not accurately display information that goes beyond this metamodel—for example, it is completely oblivious to Python's dynamically added instance variables.

5 Conclusion and Future Work

Debugging of multiple-language applications is hard and current debuggers offer little help to alleviate the problem. The only debuggable multiple-language applications are those composed of languages compiled to the same runtime, e.g. applications composed of C and C++ code, applications composed of Java, JRuby and Jython code etc.

As a remedy, this paper proposed an architecture that is able to merge multiple single-language debuggers into a unified one capable of debugging multiple-language applications. The architecture introduces a new abstraction layer—the debugger adapter—which interfaces with underlying execution runtimes. Stack of debugger adapters then manages transition of control from one debugger adapter to another.

Validity of this architecture is based on two assumptions: (i) it is always possible to intercept a message invocation and (ii) it is always possible to tell the language of the method that is about to be invoked. The first assumption is always fulfilled as all real-world lanugages do have debuggers capable of emitting event on method dispatch. The second assumption is fulfillable easily: compilers of each language used in the application only need to generate a debug symbol (or an annotation) denoting the language of the currently compiled code.

We believe that the architecture is easily extensible to merge debug information from debuggers running in different processes. That makes it a good candidate for debugging of RPC-based applications as well as systems in which method invocation results in new process creation (such as shell scripts). In future, we also plan to integrate the unified debugger into an industry strength IDE such as NetBeans or Eclipse.

References

1. Mernik, M., Heering, J., Sloane, A.M.: When and How to Develop Domain-Specific Languages. ACM Comput. Surv. 37(4), 316–344 (2005)
2. Gamma, E., Helm, R., Johnson, R.E., Vlissides, J.M.: Design Patterns: Abstraction and Reuse of Object-Oriented Design. In: Nierstrasz, O. (ed.) ECOOP 1993. LNCS, vol. 707, pp. 406–431. Springer, Heidelberg (1993)
3. Lencevicius, R.: Advanced Debugging Methods. Kluwer Academic Publishers, Dordrecht (2000)
4. Hofer, C.: Implementing a Backward-in-Time Debugger. Master's Thesis (July 2006)

5. Wu, H., Gray, J., Roychoudhury, S., Mernik, M.: Weaving a Debugging Aspect into Domain-Specific Language Grammars. In: SAC 2005: Proceedings of the 2005 ACM Symposium on Applied Computing, pp. 1370–1374. ACM, New York (2005)
6. Vraný, J., Bergel, A.: The Debuggable Interpreter Design Pattern. In: Filipe, J., Shiskov, B. (eds.) ICSOFT 2007. CCIS, vol. 22. Springer, Heidelberg (2007)
7. Bothner, P.: A gcc-Based Java Implementation (1997)
8. NetBeans, `http://www.netbeans.org`
9. Eclipse, `http://eclipse.org`
10. The Perseus Framework, `http://smalltalk.felk.cvut.cz/projects/perseus`

Student Groups Modeling by Integrating Cluster Representation and Association Rules Mining

Danuta Zakrzewska

Institute of Computer Science Technical University of Lodz, Wolczanska 215, 90-924 Lodz, Poland
dzakrz@ics.p.lodz.pl

Abstract. Finding groups of students with similar preferences enables to adjust e-learning systems according to their needs. Building models for each group can help in suggesting teaching paths and materials according to member requirements. In the paper, it is proposed to connect a cluster representation, in the form of the likelihood matrix, and frequent patterns, for building models of student groups. Such approach enables to get the detailed knowledge of group members features. The research is focused on individual traits, which are dominant learning style dimensions. The accuracy of the proposed method is validated on the basis of tests done for different clusters of real and artificial data.

Keywords: Association rules, cluster representation, student models.

1 Introduction

In distance learning, educational software performance depends on the degree it is adjusted into students' requirements. Adaptation of the system into individual needs may be difficult, in the case of the big amount of students. Finding groups of learners with similar preferences and, then, personalizing the system in compliance with their needs, seems to be the good solution.

Students may be grouped in a supervise way by tutors or automatically by using clustering technique. The last method allows to consider multiple attributes simultaneously [1]. In that case the effectiveness of the process of the educational system adaptation depends not only on the quality of obtained clusters but also on the degree of the knowledge concerning their members' features. The model of each cluster of learners should be as much detailed as possible and should reflect the characteristics of the majority of them. Model accuracy should not depend on cluster shapes or sizes. The aim of the paper is to indicate the method, which will allow to discover patterns, representing the most popular attributes and their associations in clusters. It is proposed to integrate the cluster representation in the form of the likelihood matrix and frequent patterns, which occurred in the cluster. As cognitive traits characterizing students, there are considered individual learning style dimensions. The accuracy of the presented method is validated, by experiments, done for clusters of different structures and sizes.

J. van Leeuwen et al. (Eds.): SOFSEM 2010, LNCS 5901, pp. 743–754, 2010.

The paper is organized as follows. The related work is described in the next section. Then, the overview of the whole process of finding student group models is presented. In the following subsections of Section 3, all the phases of building group models are depicted, starting from learner models based on learning style dimensions, till the group model defined by using association rules and cluster representation. In Section 4 some experimental results are presented and discussed. Finally, concluding remarks and future research are outlined.

2 Related Work

In recent years many researchers examined possibilities of improving e-learning courses by using data mining methods. As the main goals of their applications there should be mentioned personalization of educational systems or recommendation possibilities. Most of investigations are focused on learner requirements identification. The broad review of areas of interactions between data mining and e-learning may be found in [2]. Many authors applied clustering for grouping students according to their behaviors, on the basis of pages they visited or historical navigational paths (see [3],[4] for example). Tang and McCalla [3] connected cluster analysis and collaborative filtering for the purpose of the recommender system, which enables to adapt the course content into personal needs. Association rule mining was used in many recommender systems (see [5],[6]). Shen et al. [7] connected student clustering according to their learning activities and finding sequential patterns. García et al. [8] combined association rule mining with collaborative filtering to build recommendations for teachers.

In the paper [9], it was presented different approach for grouping according to student preferences. Proposed there, intelligent e-learning system, was based on clustering methods, applied for learning styles data gathered by questionnaire surveys. That approach was farther investigated in [10]. Authors examined different techniques for students' learning styles investigations. Alfonseca et al. [11] used descriptive statistics for student grouping in collaborative learning. Xu et al. [12] built fuzzy models using learning activities and interaction history. Viola et al. [13] showed the efficiency of data-driven methods for pattern extractions.

3 Student Groups' Modeling

3.1 Overview of the Method

Groups created by cluster analysis are characterized by the similarity of all the attributes. But, for the purpose of an adaptation of the educational system, the label of each group should be known. A generative model of the cluster consisting of the mean, standard deviation and probability of sampling values does not take into account associations between attributes. Clustering by model-based methods, in turn, cannot be applied if attributes are correlated [14], what may take place for student learning style data [13].

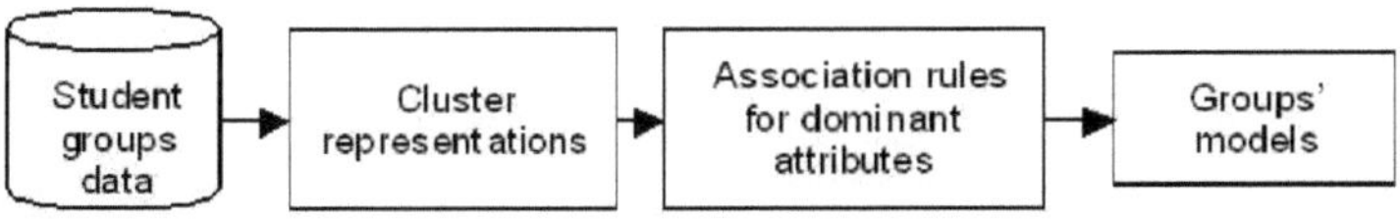

Fig. 1. Phases of group modeling

In the presented approach, it is assumed that students are grouped according to numeric attributes, which can be changed into nominal values, that represent students' characteristics. It is proposed to build group models in two steps. In the first one, the distributions of student features are found out and presented in the form of the matrix containing attribute likelihood. In the second phase association rules for dominant student features are discovered. The whole process is presented on Fig. 1. Obtained models present the rules for attribute values that are valid, for the majority of the students in the considered cluster. In the current study, it is assumed that students have already been assigned into clusters. Broad review of clustering techniques for student learning style data can be found in [10].

3.2 Student Models

Brusilovsky [15] recognized student dominant learning styles as user individual traits, which are stable and usually extracted by specially designed psychological tests, and that can be used for the purpose of web educational systems. The present study focuses on Felder & Silverman [18] model, which was often indicated as the most appropriate for the use in computer-based educational systems (see [16],[17]). The model is based on *Index of Learning Style* (ILS) questionnaire, developed by Felder & Soloman [19]. The ILS is a self-scoring questionnaire for assessing preferences on 4 dimensions of the Felder & Silverman model, from among excluding pairs: *active* vs. *reflective*, *sensing* vs. *intuitive*, *visual* vs. *verbal*, *sequential* vs. *global*. After selecting answers to 44 questions, learners obtain scores for the dimensions. The index has the form of the odd integer from the interval [-11,11], assigned for one of the dimensions from the pairs mentioned above. Each student, who filled ILS questionnaire, can be modeled by a vector SL of 4 integer attributes:

$$SL = (sl_1, sl_2, sl_3, sl_4) = (l_{\mathrm{ar}}, l_{\mathrm{si}}, l_{\mathrm{vv}}, l_{\mathrm{sg}}) \ , \quad (1)$$

where l_{ar} means scoring for *active* (if it has negative value) or *reflective* (if it is positive) learning style, and respectively $l_{\mathrm{si}}, l_{\mathrm{vv}}, l_{\mathrm{sg}}$ are points for all the other dimensions, with negative values in cases of *sensing*, *visual* or *sequential* learning styles, and positive values in cases of *intuitive*, *verbal* or *global* learning styles.

Score from the interval [-3,3] means that the student is fairly well balanced on the two dimensions of that scale. Values -5,-7 or 5,7 mean that student learns more easily in a teaching environment which favors the considered dimension;

values -9,-11 or 9,11 mean that learner has a very strong preference for one dimension of the scale and may have real difficulty learning in an environment which does not support that preference [19]. The above principles of Felder & Silverman model impose rules for changing SL into a vector SLN of nominal values. As scores from -11 to -5 (5 to 11) indicate the same favorite dimension, in our investigations nominal values will be limited to 3, as defined in (3)-(6).

$$SLN = (sln_1, sln_2, sln_3, sln_4) = (ln_{\mathrm{ar}}, ln_{\mathrm{si}}, ln_{\mathrm{vv}}, ln_{\mathrm{sg}}) \ , \tag{2}$$

where

$$ln_{\mathrm{ar}} = \begin{cases} a & l_{\mathrm{ar}} = -11, -9, -7, -5, \\ b & l_{\mathrm{ar}} = -3, -1, 1, 3, \\ r & l_{\mathrm{ar}} = 5, 7, 9, 11; \end{cases} \tag{3}$$

$$ln_{\mathrm{si}} = \begin{cases} s & l_{\mathrm{si}} = -11, -9, -7, -5, \\ b & l_{\mathrm{si}} = -3, -1, 1, 3, \\ i & l_{\mathrm{si}} = 5, 7, 9, 11; \end{cases} \tag{4}$$

$$ln_{\mathrm{vv}} = \begin{cases} vs & l_{\mathrm{vv}} = -11, -9, -7, -5, \\ b & l_{\mathrm{vv}} = -3, -1, 1, 3, \\ vr & l_{\mathrm{vv}} = 5, 7, 9, 11; \end{cases} \tag{5}$$

$$ln_{\mathrm{sg}} = \begin{cases} s & l_{\mathrm{sg}} = -11, -9, -7, -5, \\ b & l_{\mathrm{sg}} = -3, -1, 1, 3, \\ g & l_{\mathrm{sg}} = 5, 7, 9, 11. \end{cases} \tag{6}$$

3.3 Group Models

A generative cluster model may not represent the average student characteristics, in the case of learning style preferences. For example, the mean value for *active* and *reflective* students may indicate that all of them are balanced. Instead, we propose to use aggregate cluster profiles, based on nominal representations of learning style attributes and the number of their appearances. Each attribute value is associated with the support value which indicates its significance in the cluster (see Def. 1).

Definition 1. *Let CL be a cluster containing objects with SL data. As the cluster representation we will consider the matrix $CLR = [clr_{ij}]_{1 \le i \le 3, 1 \le j \le 4}$, where the columns represent attributes from SLN model and the rows nominal values of attributes. Each element of CLR is calculated as likelihood (relative frequency)P that students from CL are characterized by the certain attribute value from SLN model and is called the support for the respective SLN attribute value in CL.*

$$CLR = \begin{bmatrix} P(ln_{\mathrm{ar}} = a), \ P(ln_{\mathrm{si}} = s), \ P(ln_{\mathrm{vv}} = vs), \ P(ln_{\mathrm{sg}} = s) \\ P(ln_{\mathrm{ar}} = b), \ P(ln_{\mathrm{si}} = b), \ P(ln_{\mathrm{vv}} = b), \ P(ln_{\mathrm{sg}} = b) \\ P(ln_{\mathrm{ar}} = r), \ P(ln_{\mathrm{si}} = i), \ P(ln_{\mathrm{vv}} = vr), \ P(ln_{\mathrm{sg}} = g) \end{bmatrix} . \tag{7}$$

Let us consider that we got M groups of students after clustering process. To obtain cluster representations, the following steps are necessary:

[Input]: A set of M clusters CL_i, containing objects with SL data,
Step 1: For each cluster $CL_i, i = 1, 2, ...M$ count number of objects N_i,
Repeat Steps: 2,3,4 for each cluster $CL_i, i = 1, 2, ...M$:
Step 2: For each object from cluster CL_i change SL attribute values into nominal SLN according to (3),(4),(5),(6)
Step 3: Count number of each values of the attributes and calculate respective likelihood
Step 4: Build the matrix CLR_i
[Output]: Matrices CLR_i for clusters $CL_i, i = 1, 2, ...M$.

The cluster representation in the matrix form (Def. 1), allows to distinguish dominant characteristics of the student group, indicated by maximal values of the matrix columns. Those features can be considered as frequent items and can be used in the next step for building association rules. Such approach enables to use Apriori algorithm, which is based on the principle that " all nonempty subsets of a frequent itemset must also be frequent" [14]. The threshold of the required frequency, depends on the number of students from the cluster, characterized by the same dominant learning styles and should be determined according to tutors' criteria. Usually it is assumed to be not less than 50%.

The Apriori-type algorithm, implemented in Weka software [20], iteratively reduces the minimum support until it finds the required number of rules with the given minimum confidence. Application of that algorithm allows to limit the input parameters to the minimum confidence value (confidence of the rule $A \Rightarrow B$ is the likelihood that the itemset containing A holds also B). Having the required frequency threshold thr in the form of decimal fraction and likelihood from cluster representation matrix, the minimal required confidence value $conf(CLR)$ can be calculated by dividing the threshold value by its maximal element:

$$conf(CLR) = thr/max\{clr_{ij}, i = 1, 2, 3; j = 1..4\} \quad , \tag{8}$$

Confidence value, defined by (8), guarantees that discovered rules are valid for the majority (more than 50%)of students from the considered cluster. The respective algorithm may be presented as follows:

[Input]: The set of matrices CLR_i for each cluster $CL_i, i = 1, 2, ...M$; required threshold of the frequency in the form of decimal fraction,
Repeat Steps: 1,2,3,4 for each cluster $CL_i, i = 1, 2, ...M$:
Step 1: Choose the maximal value in the cluster representation CLR_i,
Step 2: Count required confidence value according to (8)
Step 3: Found association rules by Apriori type algorithm
Step 4: From among rules, choose the ones that contain dominant values of attributes of each column of CLR_i
[Output]: Set of rules for each cluster $CL_i, i = 1, 2, ...M$, their confidence and support values.

Obtained set of rules, together with their parameters may give the knowledge of majority student characteristics for each cluster, however the demanded model should also contain information from cluster representation matrix, presenting the distribution of all the learner preferences. Number of rules may be further limited by removing the ones containing balanced values of attributes, as balanced learners are not expected to require special attention concerning learning environments. That way the model consists of two parts: the first one indicating learning style preferences of the majority of students and the second one presenting associations between the dominant attributes.

As an example, consider the matrix cluster representation for 75 students:

$$\begin{bmatrix} 0.69, 0.52, 0.88, 0.12 \\ 0.31, 0.48, 0.12, 0.83 \\ 0, \quad 0, \quad 0, \quad 0.05 \end{bmatrix} \tag{9}$$

The required confidence value for $thr = 0.5$ according to (8) is equal to 0.568. The algorithm found 3 rules, with respective support and confidence:

$$\begin{aligned} &ln_{sg} = b \Rightarrow ln_{vv} = vs \ \text{supp:(0.72) conf:(0.87)} \\ &ln_{ar} = a \Rightarrow ln_{vv} = vs \ \text{supp:(0.57) conf:(0.83)} \\ &ln_{ar} = a \Rightarrow ln_{sg} = b \ \text{supp:(0.55) conf:(0.79).} \end{aligned}$$

After removing the rules containing balance values we obtain the association: $ln_{ar} = a \Rightarrow ln_{vv} = vs$. Additionally, taking into account maximal values of columns of (9)(without the second raw, which represents balanced students) we have the following model of cluster members:

$$\begin{aligned} &ln_{vv} = vs \ \text{supp: (0.88), or} \quad ln_{ar} = a \ \text{supp:(0.69), or} \\ &(ln_{ar} = a) \Rightarrow (ln_{vv} = vs) \ \text{supp: (0.57), or} \quad ln_{si} = s \ \text{supp: (0,52).} \end{aligned}$$

Finally, we may conclude that most of the students from the considered group are both *active* and *visual*, those who are not *visual* are *active* and reciprocally, the ones not *active* have to be *visual*. According to the last rule majority of students are *sensing*, but there are not associations between *sensing* and *visual* as well as between *sensing* and *active* learners, what means that, these students are mostly balanced according to other learning style dimensions. More exemplary models, built on different clusters, will be presented in Section 4.

The quality of an obtained model may be determined by two main criteria: its accuracy and its usefulness. The last factor should be examined in the context of pedagogical goals of the considered course and evaluated by tutors, who prepare the contents, teaching paths and learning materials. The accuracy of the model depends on the number of students, from the considered group, whose attributes do not fit into the rules from the model. Error of the model may be measured by likelihood that the rules are not valid for the cluster member and it is calculated by using support values of cluster representation matrix, as well as of respective association rules. If no rules are discovered, or the error is not acceptable, it may mean that most of students are balanced, the cluster is of bad quality or its members are characterized by only one learning style dimension. The first case takes place if there are no dominant learning styles in the cluster representation. The detailed analysis of obtained results may give more information about group members. We propose to consider separately the rules concerning learning style dimensions, which are not correlated. In the model presented in the example, the error should be calculated separately for the first three rules and for the last one. In the first case, if we take into account well known formula: $P(A \vee B) = P(A) + P(B) - P(A \wedge B)$, the error of the statement that students are *visual* or *active* is equal to 0, while the error that students are *sensing* is equal to 0.48, what is quite a big value.

4 Experiment Results and Discussion

The aim of the experiments was to evaluate the proposed method and to compare the results with models obtained by using only cluster representations. The tests were done for two different data sets: real of 194 Computer Science students, who filled ILS questionnaire and 100 artificially generated random odd integers from the interval [-11,11]. To obtain the most impartial results, data were gathered from students of different levels and years of studies, including part-time and evening courses. We consider clusters of disparate structures and sizes, built by application of different techniques, taking into account an influence of the choice of a threshold value. We consider clusters built by three well known algorithms, each representing different approach: statistical - EM, partitioning - K-means and hierarchical Farthest First Traversal (FFT) (see [14]). The quality of the obtained model should not depend on the applied clustering method, but as was shown in [21] clusters have completely different structure depending on the technique, which was used. In our experiments, data were divided, by each of the algorithms, into 5 clusters: the number, for which the clustering schemas occurred to be the optimal from the point of view of cluster qualities for K-means and FFT algorithm (see [21]). Application of 3 different techniques, on the two considered datasets, allows us to examine the performance of the method on 30 clusters that were expected to be of good qualities. As it may be easily noticed, the rules were not found for 46.7%(14) of all the clusters, in 13.3%(4) groups most learners were balanced, what may be also applied as the characteristic feature. One rule was generated in 23.3% (7), two - in 6.7% (2) and three in 10%(3) from all the clusters. From among those clusters, which cannot be described by any rule, it should be distinguished the ones with one dominant value in a cluster representation and respective small error value. There are 4 such cases with error less than 0.2 in the considered clusters. Finally, there were no models discovered for 33.3% (10) from among considered groups. The experiment results for considered cluster schemas and different data sets are shown in Tables 1- 6. For each cluster there are presented their sizes and models in the form of association rules valid for dominant learning styles and their errors, together with dominant SLN values from cluster representations. Errors contained in last columns of all the tables are counted as $1 - support(SLN)$ and represent the likelihood that learning style of cluster member is not equal

Table 1. Clusters built by EM algorithm (real data)

No	Quantity	Association rules	Error	Cluster represent.	Error
1	85	no rules		*visual*	0.11
2	18	*intuitive* $\wedge$ *global*	0.28	*intuitive*	0.17
		visual $\wedge$ *intuitive*	0.5	*global*	0.11
		visual $\wedge$ *global*	0.5	*visual*	0.39
3	21	*visual* $\wedge$ *sequential*	0.48	*sensing*	0
		visual $\wedge$ *sensing*	0.14	*visual*	0.14
		sequential $\wedge$ *sensing*	0.38	*sequential*	0.38
4	56	balanced		balanced	
5	14	*visual* $\wedge$ *active*	0	*visual*	0
		sensing $\wedge$ *active*	0.07	*active*	0
		visual $\wedge$ *sensing* $\wedge$ *active*	0.07	*sensing*	0.07

Table 2. Clusters built by K-means algorithm (real data)

No	Quantity	Association rules	Error	Cluster represent.	Error
1	50	*active* $\wedge$ *visual*	0.24	*active*	0.14
				visual	0.1
2	33	no rules		*visual*	0.3
				global	0.42
				intuitive	0.45
3	35	balanced		balanced	
4	30	balanced		balanced	
5	46	*sensing* $\wedge$ *visual*	0.5	*sensing*	0.41
				visual	0.13

Table 3. Clusters built by hierarchical (FFT) algorithm (real data)

No	Quantity	Association rules	Error	Cluster represent.	Error
1	117	no rules		*visual*	0.24
				sensing	0.47
2	8	no rules		*global*	0.13
3	28	no rules		*visual*	0.14
				global	0.43
4	16	balanced		balanced	
5	25	no rules		*active*	0.4

to SLN. In all the cases, operator $\Rightarrow$ was changed into $\wedge$ as the rules were valid for the both sides. Comparing the results for different groups, it may be noticed that the performance of proposed method differs depending on the cluster schema. Taking as the example statistical algorithm for the real data set

Table 4. Clusters built by EM algorithm (artificial data)

No	Quantity	Association rules	Error	Cluster represent.	Error
1	27	no rules		*visual*	0.3
				global	0.44
2	18	$intuitive \wedge sequential$	0.33	*intuitive*	0
				sequential	0.33
3	17	$sensing \wedge sequential$	0.41	*sensing*	0.41
		$verbal \wedge sequential$	0.47	*sequential*	0
				verbal	0.47
4	17	no rules		*active*	0
5	21	$global \wedge verbal$	0.33	*verbal*	0.19
				global	0.19
				sensing	0.48

Table 5. Clusters built by K-means algorithm (artificial data)

No	Quantity	Association rules	Error	Cluster represent.	Error
1	16	$sensing \wedge sequential$	0.38	*sequential*	0.06
		$verbal \wedge sequential$	0.44	*sensing*	0.31
				verbal	0.44
2	22	no rules		*visual*	0.27
				global	0.45
3	21	$global \wedge verbal$	0.43	*verbal*	0.24
				global	0.29
				sensing	0.33
4	25	no rules		*intuitive*	0.16
5	16	$reflective \wedge intuitive$	0.5	*reflective*	0.13
				intuitive	0.38
				visual	0.44
				global	0.44

(Table 1), students from all the clusters may be modeled, with error less than 0.3. This value may be even less after detailed analysis of the obtained rules. Contrarily, not too many rules can be built on clusters from schema obtained by hierarchical method (Table 3), however that technique was indicated as optimal in the case of 5 clusters for learning style data [21]. For artificially generated data, effects are worse, in each approach, there is at least one cluster without the rules, but the fact may be caused by the lower cluster quality for those data [21]. In the considered schemas, groups are of different sizes, what enables to compare the effects depending on the quantity of objects contained in each cluster. The biggest group includes 117 objects, while the smallest one 8. For that analysis, we divided clusters into 4 categories depending on their sizes:

Table 6. Rules for clusters built by hierarchical (FFT) algorithm (artificial data)

No	Quantity	Association rules	Error	Cluster represent.	Error
1	32	no rules		*sequential*	0.34
				intuitive	0.37
				verbal	0.47
2	23	no rules		*global*	0.26
				sensing	0.35
				verbal	0.39
3	22	no rules		*visual*	0.23
				global	0.37
				reflective	0.41
4	14	$active \wedge intuitive$	0.43	*sensing*	0.21
				active	0.36
				sequential	0.43
5	9	no rules		*active*	0.11
				intuitive	0.44
				global	0.44

1. Very small: less than 20 instances - 11 groups
2. Small: from 20 to 40 instances - 14 groups
3. Medium: from 40 to 60 instances - 3 groups
4. Big: more than 60 instances -2 groups

In the groups from the first category, rules were not found for one cluster of 9 students (see Table 6), in the second category -for 8 clusters (57%), in the third category rules are found for all the clusters; and in the last category, there is one cluster of visual students, and the second group (the biggest one) without the discovered rules. Concluding, there is no visible dependence between obtained effects and cluster sizes.

To have the full image of the performance of the algorithm, it should be examined, how including association rules may enhance the image of students in the group. Focusing on the clusters built by statistical method (see Table 1), we may respectively characterize groups as follows: *visual*, $(global \wedge intuitive) \vee visual$, $sensing \wedge (visual \vee sequential)$, balanced, $reflective \wedge intuitive \wedge active$. From among five characteristics, only two may be concluded from the cluster representation: the first and the fourth ones. The others were drawn from discovered association rules. If we take into account results from Table 2, in the first cluster students are *active* and *visual*, the characteristics that cannot be drawn from the cluster representation, the same concerns the last cluster, where half of students are *sensing* and *visual*.

The last part of the experiments focused on the choice of the threshold value. At the beginning it was assumed equal to 0.5, to guarantee that the rules are fulfilled for at least half of the students in each cluster. Investigations showed that the choice of higher value limited the number of obtained rules, however they were valid for more students. Diminishing of the threshold results in finding many rules but errors significantly increased. That approach may be applied, when tutors would like to divide clusters into subgroups of strong features.

5 Concluding Remarks

In the paper, it was considered integrating cluster representation and association rules for finding features of students, assigned into the same cluster according to their dominant learning style dimensions. The proposed method is based on learning style dimensions, however it can be easily implemented for any attributes, which characterize student preferences (like usability for example). Experiments done for real and artificial data sets showed that supplementing a cluster representation by association rules allows to give more complete image of student group characteristics. Test results indicated also that not all the cluster schemas, even of good quality, allow to build rules. It may mean that using association rules can help in evaluation of the semantic value of obtained clusters.

The proposed method can be used by educators, during the process of building teaching paths or preparing course materials as well as adjusting educational environments into student group preferences. Tutors, who know which of preferred learning style dimensions are associated in the cluster, will appropriately adapt the course. In the example, presented in Section 3.3 most of the students are *active*, *visual* or *sensing*, however only the first two features occur together and the fact should be taken into account during the teaching process.

Future research will consist in further improvements of the proposed method, by maximal possible automatization of the process of building models, taking into account assumed accuracy. It should be also examined, the performance of the considered technique, in a case of using 5 nominal attribute values instead of 3, distinguishing that way students, whose preferences for certain learning styles are not strong (see Section 3.2), what may give possibilities to ameliorate the process of tailoring contents into student needs. Automatization of that step together with the one of teaching material assignments should be also the subject of investigations in the near future.

References

1. Perera, D., Kay, J., Koprinska, I., Yacef, K., Zaïane, O.R.: Clustering and Sequential Pattern Mining of Online Collaborative Learning Data. IEEE T. Knowl. Data En. 21, 759–772 (2009)
2. Romero, C., Ventura, S.: Educational Data Mining: a Survey from 1995 to 2005. Expert Syst. Appl. 33, 135–146 (2007)
3. Tang, T., McCalla, G.: Smart Recommendation for an Evolving e-Learning System. International Journal on E-Learning 4, 105–129 (2005)
4. Talavera, L., Gaudioso, E.: Mining Student Data to Characterize Similar Behavior Groups in Unstructured Collaboration Spaces. In: Workshop on Artificial Intelligence in CSCL, 16th European Conference on Artificial Intelligence , pp. 17–23 (2004)

5. Wang, F.: On Using Data-Mining Technology for Browsing Log File Analysis in Asynchronous Learning Environment. In: Conference on Educational Multimedia, Hypermedia and Telecommunications, pp. 2005–2006 (2002)
6. Minaei-Bidgoli, B., Tan, P., Punch, W.: Mining Interesting Contrast Rules for a Web-Based Educational System. In: The Twenty-First International Conference on Machine Learning Applications, pp. 1–8 (2004)
7. Shen, R., Han, P., Yang, F., Yang, Q., Huang, J.: Data Mining and Case-Based Reasoning for Distance Learning. Journal of Distance Education Technologies 1, 46–58 (2003)
8. García, E., Romero, C., Ventura, S., de Castro, C.: An Architecture for Making Recommendations to Courseware Authors Using Association Rule Mining and Collaborative Filtering. Use Model. User-Adap. 19, 99–132 (2009)
9. Zakrzewska, D.: Cluster Analysis for Building Personalized e-Learning System. Pol. J. Environ. Stud. 16, 330–334 (2007)
10. Zakrzewska, D.: Cluster Analysis in Personalized e-Learning Systems. In: Nguyen, N.T., Szczerbicki, E. (eds.) Intelligent Systems for Knowledge Management. Studies in Computational Intelligence, vol. 252, pp. 229–250. Springer, Heidelberg (2009)
11. Alfonseca, E., Carro, R.M., Martin, E., Ortigosa, A., Paredes, P.: The Impact of Learning Styles on Student Grouping for Collaborative Learning: a Case Study. Use Model. User-Adap. 16, 377–401 (2006)
12. Xu, D., Wang, H., Su, K.: Intelligent Student Profiling with Fuzzy Models. In: HICSS 2002, Hawaii (2002)
13. Viola, S.R., Graf, S., Kinshuk, Leo, T.: Investigating Relationships within the Index of Learning Styles: a Data Driven Approach. Interactive Technology & Smart Education 4, 7–18 (2007)
14. Han, J., Kamber, M.: Data Mining. Concepts and Techniques, 2nd edn. Morgan Kaufmann Publishers, San Francisco (2006)
15. Brusilovsky, P.: Adaptive Hypermedia. Use Model. User-Adap. 11, 87–110 (2001)
16. Carver, C.A., Howard, R.A., Lane, W.D.: Addressing Different Learning Styles through Course Hypermedia. IEEE T. Educ. 42, 33–38 (1999)
17. Kuljis, J., Liu, F.: A Comparison of Learning Style Theories on the Suitability for Elearning. In: Proc. of IASTED Conference on Web Technologies, Applications, and Services, pp. 191–197. ACTA Press (2005)
18. Felder, R.M., Silverman, L.K.: Learning and Teaching Styles in Engineering Education. Eng. Educ. 78, 674–681 (1988)
19. ILS Questionnaire, `http://www.engr.ncsu.edu/learningstyles/ilsweb.html`
20. Witten, I.H., Frank, E.: Data Mining: Practical Machine Learning Tools and Techniques, 2nd edn. Morgan Kaufmann Publishers, San Francisco (2005)
21. Zakrzewska, D.: Validation of Cluster Analysis Techniques for Students' Grouping in Intelligent e-Learning Systems. In: Proc. of 14th International Congress of Cybernetics and Systems of WOSC, Wroclaw, Poland, pp. 893–901 (2008)

Finding and Certifying Loops*

Harald Zankl[1], Christian Sternagel[1], Dieter Hofbauer[2], and Aart Middeldorp[1]

[1] University of Innsbruck, Innsbruck, Austria
[2] Berufsakademie Nordhessen, Bad Wildungen, Germany

Abstract. The first part of this paper presents a new approach for automatically proving nontermination of string rewrite systems. We encode rewrite sequences as propositional formulas such that a loop can be extracted from a satisfying assignment. Alternatively, loops can be found by enumerating forward closures. In the second part we give a formalization of loops in the theorem prover Isabelle/HOL. Afterwards, we use Isabelle's code-generation facilities to certify loops. The integration of our approach in CeTA (a program for automatic certification of termination proofs) makes it the first tool capable of certifying nontermination.

Keywords: Rewriting, nontermination, certification.

1 Introduction

Proving termination of term rewrite systems is a challenging endeavor since it is undecidable in general. Nonetheless, there are many powerful algorithms that are able to automatically prove termination of a huge class of TRSs as witnessed by the international termination competition.[1] This event (where several termination tools compete on a large set of problems) evolved in 2004. Since then, it stimulated research and focused the efforts towards the automation of termination analysis. Surprisingly—compared to the vast amount of methods devoted to termination—only few techniques concerning nontermination are known and implemented. Nevertheless, checking for nontermination is especially useful for debugging programs, since concrete counterexamples are helpful for tracking down bugs. Most nontrivial approaches in that direction aim to find *looping* reductions and comprise ancestor graphs [28], narrowing [14], match-bounds [11,25], unfoldings [22], and transport systems [26]. The first automated approach [21] dealing with nonlooping nonterminating systems was presented during the 2008 edition of the termination competition.

The increasing complexity of proofs generated by termination tools makes certification of their output more and more important. Since 2007 a *certified* category is part of the termination competition. The participating tools have to generate proofs that can automatically be certified. Recent approaches for automatic certification of termination proofs are Coccinelle/CiME [6], CoLoR/Rainbow [4],

* This research is supported by FWF (Austrian Science Fund) project P18763.

[1] `http://termination-portal.org/wiki/Termination_Competition`

J. van Leeuwen et al. (Eds.): SOFSEM 2010, LNCS 5901, pp. 755–766, 2010.

and IsaFoR/CeTA [24]. The first two use Coq [3] as theorem prover. Coccinelle and CoLoR are Coq-libraries on rewriting whereas C*i*ME and Rainbow transform proof output of a termination tool into Coq-script using the respective library. Afterwards, Coq is used to certify the result. CeTA uses Isabelle/HOL (Isabelle for short) as theorem prover. IsaFoR (*Isa*belle *F*ormalization *o*f *R*ewriting) is an Isabelle-library on rewriting and CeTA (*Ce*rtified *T*ermination *A*nalysis) is a program that certifies a termination proof directly (without calling a theorem prover). It is generated from IsaFoR using Isabelle's code-generation facilities [16].

In Section 2 we recall term rewriting and in Section 3 we present two powerful methods to find loops for string rewriting. Afterwards, Sections 4 and 5 discuss our Isabelle formalization for IsaFoR and our check-functions for CeTA that are used to certify looping nontermination. An assessment of our contributions can be found in Section 6 before ideas for future work are addressed in Section 7.

Parts of Section 3 were first announced in two separate notes by the authors presented at the 9th and 10th International Workshop on Termination.

2 Preliminaries

We assume familiarity with term rewriting [2] in general and termination [29] in particular. A *signature* $\mathcal{F}$ is a set of function symbols with fixed arities. Let $\mathcal{V}$ denote an infinite set of variables disjoint from $\mathcal{F}$. Then $\mathcal{T}(\mathcal{F},\mathcal{V})$ forms the set of terms over the signature $\mathcal{F}$ using variables from $\mathcal{V}$. For a term $t \in \mathcal{T}(\mathcal{F},\mathcal{V})$ the *size* and *number of function symbols* of t is denoted by $|t|$ and $\|t\|$, respectively. If $t = f(\dots)$ then f is called the *root* of t. *Rewrite rules* are pairs of terms (l, r), usually written as $l \to r$, where l is not a variable and all variables of r appear in l. Function symbols that appear as roots of left-hand sides are called *defined*. A *term rewrite system* (TRS) is a finite set of rewrite rules. *Contexts* are terms over the signature $\mathcal{F} \cup \{\Box\}$ with exactly one occurrence of the fresh constant $\Box$ (called *hole*). The expression $C[t]$ denotes the result of replacing the hole in C by the term t. A *substitution* σ is a mapping from variables to terms and $t\sigma$ denotes the result of replacing the variables in t according to σ. Substitutions change only finitely many variables (thus written as $\{x_1/t_1, \dots, x_n/t_n\}$). The *rewrite relation* induced by a TRS $\mathcal{R}$ is a binary relation on terms denoted by $\to_\mathcal{R}$ with $s \to_\mathcal{R} t$ if and only if there exist a rewrite rule $l \to r \in \mathcal{R}$, a context C, and a substitution σ such that $s = C[l\sigma]$ and $t = C[r\sigma]$. The (reflexive and) transitive closure of $\to_\mathcal{R}$ is denoted by $(\to_\mathcal{R}^*)$ $\to_\mathcal{R}^+$. A TRS $\mathcal{R}$ is called *strongly normalizing* (SN) or *terminating* if $\to_\mathcal{R}^+$ is well-founded. A sequence $t_1 \to_\mathcal{R} \cdots \to_\mathcal{R} t_n \to_\mathcal{R} C[t_1\sigma]$ is called a *loop* of length n, written $([t_1, \dots, t_n], C, \sigma)$.

Next we recall the dependency pair framework [1,13,15,17]. The signature $\mathcal{F}$ is extended with *dependency pair symbols* $f^\sharp$ for every defined f, where $f^\sharp$ has the same arity as f, resulting in the signature $\mathcal{F}^\sharp$. In examples we write F for $f^\sharp$. If $l \to r \in \mathcal{R}$ and u is a subterm of r with defined root then the rule $l^\sharp \to u^\sharp$ is a *dependency pair* of $\mathcal{R}$. Here $l^\sharp$ and $u^\sharp$ are the results of replacing the roots of l and u by the corresponding dependency pair symbols. The set of dependency pairs of $\mathcal{R}$ is denoted by $\mathtt{DP}(\mathcal{R})$.

A *DP problem* is a pair of TRSs $(\mathcal{P},\mathcal{R})$ such that the roots of the rules in $\mathcal{P}$ do neither occur in $\mathcal{R}$ nor in proper subterms of the left- and right-hand sides of rules in $\mathcal{P}$. The problem is said to be *finite* if there is no infinite sequence of the shape $s_1 \to_{\mathcal{P}} t_1 \to_{\mathcal{R}}^{*} s_2 \to_{\mathcal{P}} t_2 \to_{\mathcal{R}}^{*} \cdots$. The main theorem underlying the dependency pair approach states that termination of a TRS $\mathcal{R}$ is equivalent to finiteness of the *initial* DP problem $(\mathsf{DP}(\mathcal{R}),\mathcal{R})$.

To prove finiteness of a DP problem, *DP processors* are employed. A DP processor is a function taking a DP problem as input while returning a set of DP problems or "no" as output. For proving termination they need to be *sound*, i.e, if all DP problems returned by a DP processor are finite then so is the original one. To ensure that a DP processor can be used to prove nontermination it must be *complete*, i.e., if one of the DP problems returned by the DP processor is not finite then the original DP problem is not finite. Hence if only complete DP processors are used and one returns "no" then the original TRS is nonterminating.

3 Finding Loops

A *string rewrite system* (SRS) is a TRS with unary function symbols only. Instead of $\mathsf{a}(\mathsf{b}(\mathsf{c}(x)))$ we write abc (i.e., the variable is implicit). For a string s we denote the i-th symbol ($1 \leqslant i \leqslant \|s\|$) in s by s_i, e.g., $\mathsf{abc}_2 = \mathsf{b}$.

Example 1. Consider the SRS $\mathcal{S} = \{\mathsf{ab} \to \mathsf{bbaa}\}$ which admits the looping reduction $\mathsf{abb} \to_{\mathcal{S}} \mathsf{bbaab} \to_{\mathcal{S}} \mathsf{bbabbaa}$ where the initial string abb is reached again after two rewrite steps wrapped in the context $C = \mathsf{bb}\square$ and instantiated by the substitution $\sigma = \{x/\mathsf{aa}\}$. Thus $\mathcal{S}$ admits the loop $([\mathsf{abb},\mathsf{bbaab}], C, \sigma)$ of length 2.

The main benefit of the dependency pair approach (for finding loops) is that leading contexts as in Example 1 are automatically removed by construction of the dependency pairs [14], and as a result a looping reduction in a DP problem $(\mathcal{P},\mathcal{R})$ takes the form $t \to_{\mathcal{P}\cup\mathcal{R}}^{+} t\sigma$. Our idea is to encode a looping rewrite sequence within the DP framework in SAT using a matrix of dimension $m \times n$ where $(0,0)$ denotes the top left entry and $(m-1,n-1)$ the bottom right one. Every row in the matrix corresponds to a string and the intended meaning is that there is a rewrite step from row i to row $i+1$. Nowadays many termination tools interface SAT solvers which makes our contribution little effort to implement.

Example 2. The SRS from Example 1 admits the dependency pairs $\mathsf{Ab} \to \mathsf{Aa}$ and $\mathsf{Ab} \to \mathsf{A}$. In a 3×5 matrix a looping reduction is possible. The entries marked with $\cdot$ indicate that any symbol might appear at these positions.

$$\begin{array}{ccccc} \mathsf{A} & \mathsf{b} & \mathsf{b} & \cdot & \cdot \\ \mathsf{A} & \mathsf{a} & \mathsf{b} & \cdot & \cdot \\ \mathsf{A} & \mathsf{b} & \mathsf{b} & \mathsf{a} & \mathsf{a} \end{array}$$

In the sequel we describe how to represent such matrices for a DP problem $(\mathcal{P},\mathcal{R})$ in propositional logic where the following variables are used:[2]

[2] The idea of encoding computation as propositional satisfiability goes back to [7]. Encoding cyclic structures in SAT originates from liveness properties in bounded model checking [5].

M_{ij}^a	symbol a occurs at position (i, j) of the matrix
$R_i^{l\to r}$	rule $l \to r$ is applied in row i of the matrix
$\mathbf{p}_i$	the position (= column) in row i where the rule is applied (in Example 2 we have $\mathbf{p}_0 = 0$ and $\mathbf{p}_1 = 1$)
$\mathbf{e}_i$	pointing to the last symbol of the i-th string (in the example $\mathbf{e}_0 = 2$, $\mathbf{e}_1 = 2$, and $\mathbf{e}_2 = 4$)

The variables $\mathbf{p}_i$ and $\mathbf{e}_i$ are not Boolean but represent natural numbers which are implemented as lists of Boolean variables encoding the actual value in binary. To distinguish them from proper propositional variables they are typeset in boldface. Furthermore, operations such as $>, \geqslant, =$, and $+$ are defined as usual for such SAT encodings (see, e.g., [10]).

Exactly one function symbol: To get exactly one function symbol at each matrix position, we ensure at least one symbol per entry and additionally ban multiple symbols at the same entry. Note that dependency pair symbols (those in $\mathcal{F}^\sharp \setminus \mathcal{F}$) can only appear at column 0 of each row. This is encoded as follows (where $X = \mathcal{F}$ if $j > 0$ and $X = \mathcal{F}^\sharp \setminus \mathcal{F}$ otherwise):

$$\alpha_{ij} = \left(\bigvee_{a\in X} M_{ij}^a \right) \wedge \bigwedge_{a\in X} \left(M_{ij}^a \to \bigwedge_{b\in X\setminus\{a\}} \neg M_{ij}^b \right)$$

Rule application: If a rule $l \to r$ applies in row i ($R_i^{l\to r}$), the rule must be applied correctly ($\mathsf{app}_i^{l\to r}$) and entries unaffected by the rule application must be copied from row i to row $i+1$ ($\mathsf{cp}_{ij}^{l\to r}$). The position of the rule application is fixed by $\mathbf{p}_i$ and satisfying $\mathsf{cp}_{ij}^{l\to r}$ ensures that only one rule is applied. Hence

$$\beta_i^{l\to r} = R_i^{l\to r} \to \left(\mathsf{app}_i^{l\to r} \wedge \bigwedge_{0\leqslant j<n} \mathsf{cp}_{ij}^{l\to r} \right)$$

where in case of $l \to r \in \mathcal{R}$ we set $\mathsf{app}_i^{l\to r}$ to

$$\bigwedge_{0\leqslant j<\|l\|} M_{i(\mathbf{p}_i+j)}^{l_{j+1}} \wedge \bigwedge_{0\leqslant j<\|r\|} M_{(i+1)(\mathbf{p}_i+j)}^{r_{j+1}} \wedge (\mathbf{e}_{i+1} + \|l\| = \mathbf{e}_i + \|r\|) \wedge (\mathbf{e}_i \geqslant \mathbf{p}_i + \|l\|)$$

and if $l \to r \in \mathcal{P}$ then $\mathbf{p}_i$ specializes to 0. The first (second) conjunct of $\mathsf{app}_i^{l\to r}$ expresses that l (r) matches the string encoded in the matrix at row i ($i+1$) at the abstract position $\mathbf{p}_i$. The last but one conjunct demands that the end pointer in line $i+1$ takes the value of $\mathbf{e}_i - \|l\| + \|r\|$. To ensure that the contracted redex fits the string in line i the last conjunct must be satisfied.

The formula for $\mathsf{cp}_{ij}^{l\to r}$ is defined as $\top$ if $j + \max\{\|l\|, \|r\|\} \geqslant n$ (these entries would be outside of the matrix), as

$$\left((j < \mathbf{p}_i) \wedge \bigwedge_{a\in X} (M_{ij}^a \leftrightarrow M_{(i+1)j}^a) \right) \vee \left((j \geqslant \mathbf{p}_i) \wedge \bigwedge_{a\in \mathcal{F}} (M_{i(j+\|l\|)}^a \leftrightarrow M_{(i+1)(j+\|r\|)}^a) \right)$$

(where $X = \mathcal{F}^\sharp \backslash \mathcal{F}$ if $j = 0$ and $X = \mathcal{F}$ otherwise) if $l \to r \in \mathcal{R}$, and if $l \to r \in \mathcal{P}$ then the encoding specializes to the second disjunct (since we know that $\mathbf{p}_i = 0$). All entries in the matrix before the position where the rule is applied are copied from row i to $i + 1$. The second disjunct copies the entries after $\mathbf{p}_i$ which are unaffected when applying the rule. The positions of these entries change if the applied rule is not length-preserving.

Initial string is reached again: To recognize a loop, the string in some row $i > 0$ has to match the one in row zero. Furthermore the end pointer for this row is not allowed to be smaller than the one of row zero.

$$\gamma = \bigvee_{0<i<m} \left(\bigwedge_{a \in \mathcal{F}^\sharp \backslash \mathcal{F}} (M^a_{00} \leftrightarrow M^a_{i0}) \;\wedge \bigwedge_{\substack{0<j<n \\ a \in \mathcal{F}}} (M^a_{0j} \leftrightarrow M^a_{ij}) \;\wedge\; (\mathbf{e}_i \geqslant \mathbf{e}_0) \right)$$

All together: For a DP problem $(\mathcal{P}, \mathcal{R})$ the formula $\mathsf{loop}^{m,n}_{\mathcal{P},\mathcal{R}}$ is defined as

$$\left(\bigwedge_{0 \leqslant i<m} (\bigwedge_{0 \leqslant j<n} \alpha_{ij}) \wedge (\mathbf{e}_i < n) \wedge \beta_i \right) \wedge \gamma$$

with $\beta_i = \bigvee_{l \to r \in \mathcal{P} \cup \mathcal{R}} R^{l \to r}_i \;\wedge\; \bigwedge_{l \to r \in \mathcal{P} \cup \mathcal{R}} \beta^{l \to r}_i$ which expresses that one rule has to apply in row i and that it is applied properly. The condition $\mathbf{e}_i < n$ ensures that all strings in the loop stay within the allowed matrix dimensions.

Different types of variables—concrete (M^a_{ij}) and abstract ones ($M^a_{i\mathbf{x}}$) where $\mathbf{x}$ is a list of propositional variables representing a natural number in binary—are used. The latter are needed when a rule is applied at the abstract position $\mathbf{p}_i$. By default, abstract variables $M^{\mathsf{a}}_{3[x_1,x_0]}$ and $M^{\mathsf{a}}_{3[y_1,y_0]}$ are different (since the variables differ) and hence may take different values. If the assignments for x_1 and y_1 as well as x_0 and y_0 are the same, we want to enforce that the variables take identical values. In the implementation we test for every such abstract variable whether it matches a concrete one and we identify them if that is the case in order to obtain consistent results: $\varphi_{\mathsf{cons}} = \bigwedge_{M^a_{i\mathbf{x}}} \bigwedge_{0 \leqslant j<n} \big((\mathbf{x} = j) \to (M^a_{ij} \leftrightarrow M^a_{i\mathbf{x}})\big)$. This allows to formulate the main theorem for encoding loops:

Theorem 1. *A DP problem $(\mathcal{P}, \mathcal{R})$ admits a loop of length at most m involving strings of size at most $n + 1$ if the formula $\mathsf{loop}^{m+1,n}_{\mathcal{P},\mathcal{R}} \wedge \varphi_{\mathsf{cons}}$ is satisfiable.* □

The previous theorem allows to implement a DP processor for nontermination.

Theorem 2 ([14, Theorem 26])**.** *The DP processor that maps a DP problem $(\mathcal{P}, \mathcal{R})$ to "no" if $(\mathcal{P}, \mathcal{R})$ loops and to $\{(\mathcal{P}, \mathcal{R})\}$ otherwise is sound and complete.* □

For our formalization the following lemma is essential (cf. Section 4).

Lemma 1. *If $\mathcal{P} \subseteq \mathtt{DP}(\mathcal{R})$ then any loop in the DP problem $(\mathcal{P}, \mathcal{R})$ can be transformed into a loop in $\mathcal{R}$.*

Proof. If $\mathcal{P} \subseteq \mathtt{DP}(\mathcal{R})$ then any sequence $t_1^\sharp \to_{\mathcal{P}\cup\mathcal{R}} t_2^\sharp \to_{\mathcal{P}\cup\mathcal{R}} t_3^\sharp \to_{\mathcal{P}\cup\mathcal{R}} \cdots$ can be transformed into a sequence $t_1 \to_{\mathcal{R}} C_1[t_2] \to_{\mathcal{R}} C_2[t_3] \to_{\mathcal{R}} \cdots$ involving only the original system by soundness of the dependency pair transformation [1]. □

The restriction $\mathcal{P} \subseteq \mathtt{DP}(\mathcal{R})$ does no harm since the initial DP problem $(\mathtt{DP}(\mathcal{R}),\mathcal{R})$ obviously satisfies it and all DP processors we employ only remove rules from $\mathcal{P}$.

The next corollary combines Theorem 1 and Lemma 1. Note that strings in the transformed loop might be of size larger than n due to additional contexts.

Corollary 1. *If* $\mathit{loop}^{m+1,n}_{\mathtt{DP}(\mathcal{R}),\mathcal{R}} \wedge \varphi_{\mathit{cons}}$ *is satisfiable then* $\mathcal{R}$ *admits a looping reduction of length at most* m. □

We state one nice property of the encoding from Theorem 1. Even for DP problems where all infinite *minimal* sequences are nonlooping our encoding may find looping nonminimal sequences [27, Example 5.5].

An alternative characterization of loops can be given in terms of *forward closures*. Define the set of *right forward closures* $\mathtt{RFC}(\mathcal{R})$ as the least set of reductions containing $\mathcal{R}$ (as a set of one-step reductions) and being closed under rewriting (if $(t_1,\ldots,t_n) \in \mathtt{RFC}(\mathcal{R})$ and $t_n \to_{\mathcal{R}} t_{n+1}$ then $(t_1,\ldots,t_n,t_{n+1}) \in \mathtt{RFC}(\mathcal{R})$) and under right extension (if $(t_1,\ldots,t_n) \in \mathtt{RFC}(\mathcal{R})$ and $t_n = sl_1$ for some $l_1 l_2 \to r \in \mathcal{R}$ with non-empty l_1 and l_2 then $(t_1 l_2,\ldots,t_n l_2, sr) \in \mathtt{RFC}(\mathcal{R})$). E.g., the loop in Example 1 is a right forward closure. By Theorem 9 from [12], $\mathcal{R}$ admits a loop if and only if there is a loop in $\mathtt{RFC}(\mathcal{R})$. Furthermore, if $\mathcal{R}$ admits a loop of length n then a loop of length at most n exists in $\mathtt{RFC}(\mathcal{R})$.

The set of *left forward closures* $\mathtt{LFC}(\mathcal{R})$ is defined symmetrically via *left extension*. By symmetry, either way we characterize loops of minimal length, but minimal length loops in $\mathtt{RFC}(\mathcal{R})$ and in $\mathtt{LFC}(\mathcal{R})$ can have quite different *widths*, where the *width* of a reduction is the size of the starting string. As a consequence, we will search for loops both in $\mathtt{RFC}(\mathcal{R})$ and in $\mathtt{LFC}(\mathcal{R})$.

4 Formalizing Loops

In the next two sections we assume some familiarity with Isabelle [20]. All lemmas and theorems within these sections have formally been proved in IsaFoR. Next we sketch how we formalized loops (for full rewriting). Figure 1 lists the most important function definitions and types. (Here we deviate from the syntax of IsaFoR, to increase readability, e.g., the application of a substitution would be $t \cdot \sigma$ rather than $t\sigma$.) A binary relation is a set of pairs. A loop is a triple consisting of a list of terms, a context, and a substitution. For a given relation $\mathcal{A}$, an element a is strongly normalizing (`SN_elt`) if there is no infinite sequence $\boldsymbol{s}$ such that $\boldsymbol{s}_0 = \mathsf{a}$ while for all i we have $(\boldsymbol{s}_i, \boldsymbol{s}_{i+1}) \in \mathcal{A}$. Strong normalization of a relation $\mathcal{A}$ (`SN`) holds if all elements of the domain are strongly normalizing with respect to $\mathcal{A}$. To guarantee that our definition of `SN` is suitable we proved an easy lemma stating equivalence to the built-in Isabelle notion of well-foundedness (`wf`), i.e., $\mathtt{SN}(\mathcal{A}) = \mathtt{wf}(\mathcal{A}^{-1})$. The rewrite relation $\to_{\mathcal{R}}$ induced by a TRS $\mathcal{R}$ is a binary relation on terms closed under contexts and substitutions. The function `rsteps`

```
types 'a brel      = "('a × 'a)set"
types ('f,'v)loop = "('f,'v)term list × ('f,'v)ctxt × ('f,'v)sub"
definition SN_elt where
 "SN_elt 𝒜 a ≡ ¬(∃s. s₀ = a ∧ (∀i. (sᵢ,sᵢ₊₁) ∈ 𝒜))"
definition SN where "SN(𝒜) ≡ ∀a. SN_elt 𝒜 a"
fun rsteps :: "('f,'v)term list ⇒ ('f,'v)term brel ⇒ bool"
where "rsteps [t] ℛ = True"
    | "rsteps (s#t#ts) ℛ = (s →ℛ t ∧ rsteps (t#ts) ℛ)"
fun is_loop :: "('f,'v)loop ⇒ ('f,'v)term brel ⇒ bool" where
 "is_loop (t#ts,C,σ) ℛ = rsteps (t#ts@[C[tσ]]) ℛ"
fun ith :: "('f,'v)loop ⇒ nat ⇒ ('f,'v)term" where
 "ith(t#ts,C,σ)ᵢ = (if i < length(t#ts)
   then (t#ts)!i
   else C[(ith(t#ts,C,σ)_{i-length(t#ts)})σ])"
```

Fig. 1. Basic definitions

checks for a list of terms if between two consecutive terms there is a rewrite step. Then the predicate `is_loop` is defined based on `rsteps`. The function `ith` returns for a loop $([t_1, \ldots, t_n], C, \sigma)$ and any $i > 0$ the i-th term in the sequence:

$$t_1 \to_{\mathcal{R}} \cdots \to_{\mathcal{R}} t_n \to_{\mathcal{R}} C[t_1\sigma] \to_{\mathcal{R}} \cdots \to_{\mathcal{R}} C[t_n\sigma] \to_{\mathcal{R}} C[C[t_1\sigma]\sigma] \to_{\mathcal{R}} \cdots$$

Using `ith` an infinite sequence s can be constructed, contradicting `SN_elt`. In IsaFoR, the main task was to prove the following lemma (which amounts to proving that rewriting is closed under contexts and substitutions).

Lemma 2. *If* `is_loop` ℓ $\mathcal{R}$ *then for all* i *we have* $\mathtt{ith}(\ell)_i \to_{\mathcal{R}} \mathtt{ith}(\ell)_{i+1}$. □

We obtain the main theorem for the abstract formalization:

Theorem 3. *If* `is_loop` ℓ $\mathcal{R}$ *then* $\to_{\mathcal{R}}$ *is not terminating.*

Proof. From `is_loop` ℓ $\mathcal{R}$ we get an infinite sequence s by defining $s_i = \mathtt{ith}(\ell)_i$. By Lemma 2 the sequence s satisfies $\forall i.\ s_i \to_{\mathcal{R}} s_{i+1}$. Hence, for the first term t of the loop ℓ we obtain $\neg$`SN_elt` $\to_{\mathcal{R}}$ t and thus by definition of `SN`, $\neg\mathtt{SN}(\to_{\mathcal{R}})$. □

5 Certifying Loops

This section aims at certification, i.e., an automatic check if a suspected loop indeed is a loop. For this task we use the code-generation [16] facilities of Isabelle which allow to generate verified code. We provide an implementation of the predicate `is_loop` from Section 4 by the check-function `check_loop` that tests if a list of terms, a context, and a substitution form a loop. First we state the main theorem for certifying loops:

Theorem 4. *If* `check_loop` ℓ $\mathcal{R}$ *then* $\to_{\mathtt{set}(\mathcal{R})}$ *is not terminating.* □

```
types ('f,'v)rule = "('f,'v)term × ('f,'v)term"
types ('f,'v)trsL = "('f,'v)rule list"
fun rewrites where
 "rewrites (s,t) C σ (l,r) ℛ = (s = C[lσ] ∧ t = C[rσ] ∧ (l,r) mem ℛ)"
fun rewrites_to
where "rewrites_to [(s,C,σ,rule)] t ℛ = rewrites (s,t) C σ rule ℛ"
    | "rewrites_to ((s,C,σ,rule)#(t,C',σ',rule')#xs) u ℛ = (
        rewrites (s,t) C σ rule ℛ ∧
        rewrites_to ((t,C',σ',rule')#xs) u ℛ)"
fun check_loop_d
where "check_loop_d [] _ _ _ = False"
    | "check_loop_d xs C σ ℛ = rewrites_to xs C[(fst(hd xs))σ] ℛ"
```

Fig. 2. Checking a loop with all details provided

This resembles Theorem 3, but on a *constructive* (executable) level. Here $\mathcal{R}$ is chosen as a list and `set` transforms a list into a set. The reason is that for lists executable code can be generated but for sets not. Before considering `check_loop` we focus on a simpler task, namely `check_loop_d` where more details of the loop are supplied. In the lemma below, the list xs contains the full information for every rewrite step $s \to_{\mathcal{R}} t$, i.e., the context C, the substitution σ, and the rewrite rule $l \to r$ such that $s = C[l\sigma] \to_{\mathcal{R}} C[r\sigma] = t$ (cf. Figure 2 for the definition of `check_loop_d` and the functions it relies on). Using `check_loop_d` no further information must be computed and certification of a candidate loop is already possible:

Lemma 3. *If* `check_loop_d` $xs\ C\ \sigma\ \mathcal{R}$ *then* $\to_{\mathtt{set}(\mathcal{R})}$ *is not terminating.*

Proof. The abstract formalization can be linked to the concrete implementation: If `rewrites_to` $xs\ t\ \mathcal{R}$ then `rsteps` (`map fst` xs@$[t]$) (`set`($\mathcal{R}$)). By unfolding the definitions of `check_loop_d` and `is_loop`, and using Theorem 3, the proof concludes. □

The main drawback of the function `check_loop_d` is that it requires all information about the rewrite steps. To the best of our knowledge not a single termination prover provides all these details. To make the certification of loops more appealing and user-friendly we turn our focus on the function `check_loop` again. Here for every rewrite step $s \to_{\mathcal{R}} t$ the context C, the substitution σ, and the rewrite rule $l \to r$ such that $s = C[l\sigma]$ and $t = C[r\sigma]$ are computed internally.

A function `get` $s\ t\ \mathcal{R}$ computes `Some`$(C, \sigma, (l, r))$ if there is a rewrite step from s to t involving C, σ, and $l \to r \in \mathcal{R}$. Hence `get` has to test for all rules $l \to r \in \mathcal{R}$ if for any context C in s there is a substitution σ satisfying $s = C[l\sigma]$ and $t = C[r\sigma]$.[3] To find this substitution we had to implement matching. With the help of `get` a function `get_list` returns the necessary information for a sequence of rewrite steps and `get_loop` computes all details for a looping reduction. Finally the function `check_loop` just calls `check_loop_d` on the output of `get_loop`.

[3] If $s \to_{\{l \to r\}} t$ and $s = C[l\sigma]$ then $t = C[r\sigma]$ holds for free by our definition of TRS. To handle systems that violate the variable condition we demand both conditions.

6 Experiments

The first part of this section evaluates the power of our approaches to find loops for SRSs. The second part focuses on certifying loops for SRSs and TRSs.

In our tests we considered the 1391 TRSs and 732 SRSs from the Termination Problems Data Base version 5.0 (TPDB). All tests have been performed on a server equipped with eight dual-core AMD Opteron® processors 885 running at a clock rate of 2.6 GHz and on 64 GB of main memory at a time limit of 60 s.

Finding Loops: We integrated the encoding from Section 3 into TTT2 [19] which was configured such that propositional formulas were solved by MiniSat [9] after a satisfiability-preserving transformation to CNF [23]. (Using the SMT solver Yices [8] as back-end produced slightly worse results.)

The implementation of the encoding differs from the presentation in Section 3 for reasons of readability. Our experiments showed that nontermination proving power can be slightly (i.e., a gain of about 10%) extended by addressing the following issues. Mutual exclusion of the M^a_{ij} variables can be expressed more concisely. After fixing an order on the variables, the property that at most one of the variables $x_1, \dots, x_n$ can be satisfied, is expressed by $x_i \rightarrow \neg x_{i+1} \wedge \cdots \wedge \neg x_n$ for all $1 \leqslant i < n$. Due to mutual exclusion of the M^a_{ij} variables, all bi-implications occurring in subformulas of $\mathsf{loop}^{m,n}_{\mathcal{P},\mathcal{R}}$ can safely be replaced by implications. The encoding contains the requirement $\mathbf{e}_{i+1} + \|l\| = \mathbf{e}_i + \|r\|$ where "=" could be weakened to "$\leqslant$". (This corresponds to cutting parts of the substitution.) However, due to the increased search space the more restrictive version performs better. To reduce the search space, fixing $\mathbf{p}_i < \min\{3 + i * \max_{l \to r \in \mathcal{R}} \{\|l\|, \|r\|\}, n\}$ applies rewrite rules close to the root in the first few rows.

Before applying the loop-finder, TTT2 uses termination methods like matrix interpretations [10] and bounds [18] to preprocess DP problems. Sometimes these methods suffice to prove termination and often they simplify DP problems. Heuristics for encoding loops try matrices of different dimensions ranging from 10×10 up to 25×25. Most successful proofs only take a few seconds.

As an alternative, an enumeration of looping forward closures (cf. Section 3) is implemented in KnockedForLoops (KFL), a tool developed by the third author. It is based on a simple brute force, breadth first search strategy. To overcome the problem with excessive memory consumption, we employ bounds on the width of forward closures, i.e., bounds on the number of extension steps. By a concurrent search both in $\mathsf{RFC}(\mathcal{R})$ and in $\mathsf{LFC}(\mathcal{R})$ with different width bounds, many long loops with small width can be exhibited. As a simple combinatorial optimization, we disregard reductions with a rewrite step to the left of the previous step in case these steps do not overlap (since those two steps would commute).

We compare our implementations with three powerful nontermination analyzers, namely the 2007 version of Matchbox [25] specialized to nontermination (enumerations of forward closures, reversing, transport systems), nonloop [21], and the 2008 edition of NTI [22]. Earlier versions of Matchbox and NTI participated in the *Standard SRS* category of the 2007 competition and nonloop did so in 2008. These tools were (apart from TTT2) the most powerful ones for

Table 1. Finding and certifying loops

	732 SRSs					1391 TRSs
tool	KFL /CeTA	Matchbox	nonloop	NTI	$\mathsf{T_TT_2}$ /CeTA	$\mathsf{T_TT_2}$ /CeTA
no	158 / 158	149	93	67	97 / 97	203 / 203
time	34853/ 6	35441	37855	39508	23039/ 3	25898/ 3
time (avg.)	2.45 /0.03	3.10	5.73	5.78	11.61/0.02	0.19 /0.01

nontermination in this division. The left part of Table 1[4] presents a comparison of the provers where the row labeled no shows the number of successfully found/certified nontermination proofs, time refers to the accumulated total time used by the tool in seconds and time (avg.) displays the average time needed for successfully finding/certifying a nontermination proof. The columns labeled CeTA are explained in the next subsection. We note that the algorithm underlying NTI performs much better for terms than for strings (cf. [22]) and that the main aim of nonloop is establishing nonlooping nontermination. In our experiments KFL subsumes Matchbox, NTI, and $\mathsf{T_TT_2}$. Only nonloop can disprove nine systems terminating which KFL misses. We anticipate that these systems are nonlooping nonterminating. Most remarkably, KFL finds a loop of length 80 and width 21 for the system Gebhardt/10 from TPDB, the termination status of which has been—at least to the authors' knowledge—open for several years.

Certifying Loops: Our contribution amounts to approximately 500 lines of Isabelle code that were added to IsaFoR (theory `Loop`). This includes the abstract formalization of loops and both approaches for certifying loops (the detailed one using `check_loop_d` and the user-friendly one based on `check_loop`). The key concept for certification presented here, is the code-generation mechanism of Isabelle (currently we export *verified* Haskell code). Thus the whole certifier consists of a bunch of automatically generated sources and a main file that just calls the check function on a given problem and proof. This paper refers to version 1.01 of CeTA the input format of which can be found at its website.[5] When calling CeTA, two arguments have to be supplied, namely the input problem and the proof attempt. The tool then tests if the specified proof attempt corresponds to a loop and terminates with exit code 0 in case of success and exit code 1 if the input could not be proved to be a loop.

Considering Table 1 again (this time only the columns CeTA) separate empirical data for certifying loops for 732 SRSs and 1391 TRSs is given.[6] For the columns labeled XXX/CeTA the tool XXX was used to find loops which CeTA then had to certify. The row labeled no indicates the number of successfully certified systems and time shows the accumulated time in seconds for certifying loops. The certifier was just called for the successfully found loops but still this number demonstrates

[4] Experiments are available from `http://cl-informatik.uibk.ac.at/ttt2/loops/`

[5] `http://cl-informatik.uibk.ac.at/software/ceta/`

[6] For completeness we mention how $\mathsf{T_TT_2}$ finds loops for TRSs: Apart from the approach proposed in [22] two trivial methods are employed (test for fresh variables on right-hand sides and test if a rule is self-embedding).

that the overhead for certification is negligible. This is remarkable, since the certifier has to compute for every two consecutive terms s and t in the loop a context C, a substitution σ, and a rewrite rule $l \to r \in \mathcal{R}$ such that indeed $s = C[l\sigma] \to_{\mathcal{R}} C[r\sigma] = t$. We conjecture that CeTA's efficiency is mainly due to code generation. (For a comparison in run time with other certifiers see [24].) CeTA could certify all 158 (97) SRSs and 203 TRSs nonterminating for which KFL ($\mathsf{T_TT_2}$) and $\mathsf{T_TT_2}$ provided a nontermination proof, respectively.

7 Conclusion and Future Work

This paper presents two methods for finding loops in SRSs. Since the encoding from Section 3 takes parameters for the length of looping sequences and the maximal size of strings occurring within the reduction it is especially suitable to find short(est) loops. This eases the task of debugging since the reason for nontermination is concisely represented. Our experiments revealed that detecting loops by enumerating forward closures is powerful. In the second part we formalized strong normalization in the theorem prover Isabelle and sketched how our contribution allows to generate verified code capable of certifying loops. The thereby generated check-function was incorporated into CeTA. Since CeTA is freely available our contribution allows any termination tool to certify its loop output.

Both contributions may be further investigated. One question concerning Section 3 is whether the encoding can be lifted from strings to terms. Concerning the formalization of loops one could try to incorporate the approach from [21] and also formalize nonlooping nontermination. It has to be clarified if from the output provided by nonloop the i-th term in a nonterminating sequence can be extracted easily. This issue will then make the task either easy or undoable.

Acknowledgments. We would like to thank René Thiemann for exploring the code-generation facilities of Isabelle and Johannes Waldmann for helpful comments and providing a version of Matchbox'07 specialized to nontermination.

References

1. Arts, T., Giesl, J.: Termination of Term Rewriting Using Dependency Pairs. TCS 236(1-2), 133–178 (2000)
2. Baader, F., Nipkow, T.: Term Rewriting and All That. Cambridge University Press, Cambridge (1998)
3. Bertot, Y., Castéran, P.: Interactive Theorem Proving and Program Development; Coq'Art: The Calculus of Inductive Constructions. In: Texts in Theoretical Computer Science. An EATCS Series (2004)
4. Blanqui, F., Delobel, W., Coupet-Grimal, S., Hinderer, S., Koprowski, A.: CoLoR, a Coq Library on Rewriting and Termination. In: WST, pp. 69–73 (2006)
5. Clarke, A., Biere, A., Raimi, R., Zhu, Y.: Bounded Model Checking Using Satisfiability Solving. FMSD 19(1), 7–34 (2001)
6. Contejean, E., Courtieu, P., Forest, J., Pons, O., Urbain, X.: Certification of Automated Termination Proofs. In: Konev, B., Wolter, F. (eds.) FroCos 2007. LNCS (LNAI), vol. 4720, pp. 148–162. Springer, Heidelberg (2007)

7. Cook, S.: The Complexity of Theorem-Proving Procedures. In: STOC, pp. 151–158 (1971)
8. Dutertre, B., de Moura, L.: A Fast Linear-Arithmetic Solver for DPLL(T). In: Ball, T., Jones, R.B. (eds.) CAV 2006. LNCS, vol. 4144, pp. 81–94. Springer, Heidelberg (2006)
9. Eén, N., Sörensson, N.: An Extensible SAT-solver. In: Giunchiglia, E., Tacchella, A. (eds.) SAT 2003. LNCS, vol. 2919, pp. 502–518. Springer, Heidelberg (2004)
10. Endrullis, J., Waldmann, J., Zantema, H.: Matrix Interpretations for Proving Termination of Term Rewriting. JAR 40(2-3), 195–220 (2008)
11. Geser, A., Hofbauer, D., Waldmann, J.: Termination Proofs for String Rewriting Systems via Inverse Match-Bounds. JAR 34(4), 365–385 (2005)
12. Geser, A., Zantema, H.: Non-Looping String Rewriting. TIA 33(3), 279–302 (1999)
13. Giesl, J., Thiemann, R., Schneider-Kamp, P.: The Dependency Pair Framework: Combining Techniques for Automated Termination Proofs. In: Baader, F., Voronkov, A. (eds.) LPAR 2004. LNCS (LNAI), vol. 3452, pp. 301–331. Springer, Heidelberg (2005)
14. Giesl, J., Thiemann, R., Schneider-Kamp, P.: Proving and Disproving Termination of Higher-Order Functions. In: Gramlich, B. (ed.) FroCos 2005. LNCS (LNAI), vol. 3717, pp. 216–231. Springer, Heidelberg (2005)
15. Giesl, J., Thiemann, R., Schneider-Kamp, P., Falke, S.: Mechanizing and Improving Dependency Pairs. JAR 37(3), 155–203 (2006)
16. Haftmann, F.: Code Generation from Specifications in Higher Order Logic. PhD Thesis, Technische Universität München (2009)
17. Hirokawa, N., Middeldorp, A.: Automating the Dependency Pair Method. I&C 199(1-2), 172–199 (2005)
18. Korp, M., Middeldorp, A.: Match-Bounds Revisited. I&C (2009), doi:10.1016/j.ic.2009.02.010
19. Korp, M., Sternagel, C., Zankl, H., Middeldorp, A.: Tyrolean Termination Tool 2. In: Treinen, R. (ed.) RTA 2009. LNCS, vol. 5595, pp. 295–304. Springer, Heidelberg (2009)
20. Nipkow, T., Paulson, L.C., Wenzel, M.: Isabelle/HOL. LNCS, vol. 2283. Springer, Heidelberg (2002)
21. Oppelt, M.: Automatische Erkennung von Ableitungsmustern in nichtterminierenden Wortersetzungssystemen. Master's Thesis, HTWK Leipzig, FH (2008)
22. Payet, É.: Loop Detection in Term Rewriting Using the Eliminating Unfoldings. TCS 403(2-3), 307–327 (2008)
23. Plaisted, D., Greenbaum, S.: A Structure-Preserving Clause Form Translation. JSC 2(3), 293–304 (1986)
24. Thiemann, R., Sternagel, C.: Certification of Termination Proofs Using CeTA. In: Berghofer, S., et al. (eds.) TPHOLs 2009. LNCS, vol. 5674, pp. 452–468. Springer, Heidelberg (2009)
25. Waldmann, J.: Matchbox: A Tool for Match-Bounded String Rewriting. In: van Oostrom, V. (ed.) RTA 2004. LNCS, vol. 3091, pp. 85–94. Springer, Heidelberg (2004)
26. Waldmann, J.: Compressed Loops, Draft (2007), `http://dfa.imn.htwk-leipzig.de/matchbox/methods/loop.pdf`
27. Zankl, H.: Lazy Termination Analysis. PhD Thesis, University of Innsbruck (2009)
28. Zantema, H.: Termination of String Rewriting Proved Automatically. JAR 34(2), 105–139 (2005)
29. Zantema, H.: Termination. In: TeReSe (ed.) Term Rewriting Systems. Cambridge Tracts in Theoretical Computer Science, vol. 55, pp. 181–259. Cambridge University Press, Cambridge (2003)

Vertex Ranking with Capacity

Ruben van der Zwaan*

Department of Quantitative Economics, Maastricht University
P.O. Box 616, 6200 MD Maastricht, The Netherlands
r.vanderzwaan@maastrichtuniversity.nl

Abstract. Vertex ranking has many practical applications, ranging from VLSI layout and sparse matrix factorization to parallel query processing and assembly of modular products.

Much research has been done on vertex ranking and related problems, polynomial time algorithms are known for a wide variety of graph classes as well as NP-hardness has been shown for other graph classes. In this paper we propose an extension to vertex ranking. Vertex ranking has many applications in computing a parallel schedule, but there is the assumption that the amount of parallel capacity is unbounded. Many applications do *have* restricted capacity, such as the number of processors or machines. Therefore we introduce *vertex ranking with capacity*.

In this paper we show that vertex ranking and vertex ranking with capacity do not have a polynomial sized kernel, unless all coNP-complete problems have distillation algorithms. Having to deal with the NP-hardness of both problems, we give, to our knowledge, the first $O^*(2^n)$ time exact algorithm for vertex ranking and use this for devising an $O^*(2.5875^n)$ time algorithm for vertex ranking with capacity. We also show that we can transform vertex rankings to vertex rankings with capacity, and use this for a polynomial time algorithm that transforms an $f(n)$-approximate vertex ranking to a vertex ranking with capacity of at most $f(n) + 1$ times the optimum size. Lastly, give an $\log(c)$ additive approximation for vertex ranking with capacity when restricted to trees and extend this to graphs of bounded treewidth.

1 Introduction

Vertex ranking has many practical applications, especially in the area of parallelization. Applications include VLSI layout [16], sparse matrix factorization [6,21], parallel query processing [11] and searching in partial orders [10]. Also, it can be applied to scheduling problems of assembly steps in manufacturing problems [4] and assembly of modular products [16,17,24,25]. Vertex ranking is equivalent to the minimum height elimination tree problem [4] and also known as *ordered coloring* [19] and *separation game* [22].

For a simple, undirected and connected graph $G = (V, E)$, a *vertex ranking* is a function $\varphi : V \rightarrow \mathbb{N}$ such that for any pair of vertices a and b for which

* The research was partly done while the author was at Utrecht University.

J. van Leeuwen et al. (Eds.): SOFSEM 2010, LNCS 5901, pp. 767–778, 2010.

$\varphi(a)$ equals $\varphi(b)$, on every path connecting a and b there is a vertex z with $\varphi(z) > \varphi(a)$. The size of the ranking $\varphi(G)$ is equal to the highest rank of all vertices. The *ranking number* $\chi_r(G)$ is the minimum size over all rankings of G.

Most applications described use vertex ranking to compute a parallel schedule. The parallel capacity is the amount of resources that can be used simultaneously. When using vertex ranking to model a problem, there is the assumption that the parallel capacity is very large, at least as large as the number of vertices. However, in many applications, such as multi-processor computing, parallel resources are restricted. Therefore we propose an extension of vertex ranking: *vertex ranking with capacity*. This variant allows a more natural and realistic representation of problems like parallel query processing and scheduling problems.

For a simple and undirected graph $G = (V, E)$ and a capacity $c \in \mathbb{N}$, a *capacity vertex ranking* is a vertex ranking such that no more than c vertices can be assigned the same rank. The size of the ranking $\varphi(G)$ is equal to the highest rank of all vertices. The *capacity ranking number* $\chi_r^c(G)$ is the minimum size over all rankings of G with capacity c.

Vertex ranking is the same as vertex ranking with capacity when the capacity is equal or larger than the number of vertices. From this it follows that vertex ranking with capacity is NP-complete when restricted to bipartite graphs or chordal graphs [4,12].

Kernelization is an useful technique in the design of fixed-parameter tractable algorithms. Fixed-parameter tractable is abbreviated as FPT. Having a kernel it is easy to develop a FPT algorithm, and polynomial sized kernels in general yield more efficient FPT algorithms and might serve as a preprocessing step in applications. Kernelization is a method to transform any given instance for a problem in polynomial time to an equivalent instance, with size and parameter bounded by a function in the parameter.

Our results. There are several ways to deal with the hardness of vertex ranking with capacity. We design in Section 4 an $O^*(2.5875^n)$ time and $O^*(2^n)$ space algorithm. This algorithm is based on a dynamic programming algorithm for vertex ranking, which we will show before. This is the first exact algorithm for vertex ranking as far as we know. We also show that there is an exact $O^*(9^n)$ time algorithm with only polynomial space to solve the vertex ranking problem.

There are quite a few graph classes for which vertex ranking can be solved in polynomial time [1,8,9,14,15,16,20,24]. To build upon this work, we detail a transformation in Section 5 from an input vertex ranking to a vertex ranking with capacity. This transformation is a $f(n) + 1$-approximation, if the input vertex ranking is $f(n)$-approximate where $f(n)$ is any function with parameter n.

We prove in Section 6 that there is an $\log(c)$ additive approximation for vertex ranking with capacity when restricted to trees. Further, this is generalized to graphs of bounded treewidth.

Related work. There are many polynomial time algorithms for vertex ranking for restricted graph classes such as interval graphs [1,8], permutation graphs [8], trees [16,24], d-trapezoid graphs, circular-arc graphs [9], star like graphs [14], block graphs [15] and asteroidal-triple free graphs [20]. There is an $O(\log^2 n)$-approximation algorithm for general graphs [6].

Vertex ranking is NP-complete for chordal graphs [12], bipartite and co-bipartite graphs [4]. Vertex Ranking is fixed parameter tractable [4], but note that this proof uses the graph minor theorem and is non-constructive. The proof does not state how to find all forbidden minors, and it might not be possible to obtain all forbidden minors [13]. Added to this problem, the hidden constants of the minor test algorithm are very large [2].

Vertex ranking is polynomial time solvable on graphs of bounded treewidth [18]. Unfortunately, the polynomials are very large. For example, for graphs of bounded treewidth 2, we can determine the vertex ranking number in $O(n^{20})$ time and for bounded treewidth 3 this increases sharply to $O(n^{40})$ time. There are other generalizations of vertex ranking, c-vertex ranking [18,26] and weighted vertex ranking [12].

2 Preliminaries

Let $\mathbb{N}$ be the set of natural numbers greater or equal to 1. We only consider simple, undirected graphs $G = (V, E)$. Let $d(v)$ be the degree of vertex v. We denote with n and m the number of vertices and edges, respectively. Let $|\varphi|$ be the size of a ranking φ.

The subgraph of $G = (V, E)$ induced by $S \subseteq V$ is denoted by $G[S]$. An induced subgraph $G[S]$ is a connected component if $G[S]$ is connected, and $G[S \cup v]$ is disconnected for any $v \in V \setminus S$. Let $P(V, s)$ denote the set of connected components in $G[V \setminus \{s\}]$. A *component independent set* is a set with at most one vertex from each connected component in a graph. We denote all component independent sets in a graph G with $\mathcal{I}(G)$. A *contracted* subgraph $G\{S\}$ of G is the graph obtained by contracting any edge that does not have both endpoints in S, until all edges have both endpoints in S.

Definition 1. *A* tree decomposition *of G is a pair (X, T), where T is a tree and X is a family of bags. The bags X_i are identified with the nodes of the tree. Every bag X_i contains a subset of V such that:*

(1) For each vertex $v \in V$, $\exists X_i \in X$ with $v \in X_i$.
(2) For each edge $\{u, v\} \in E$, $\exists X_i \in X$ with $u \in X_i$ and $v \in X_i$.
(3) For each vertex $v \in V$, the collection of bags containing v forms a connected subtree of T.

The *width* $w(X, T)$ of a tree decomposition (X, T) of G is equal to the size of its largest bag minus one. The *treewidth* $tw(G)$ of G is then the minimum width over all tree decompositions of G.

3 Kernelization

Kernelization is a technique for designing FPT algorithms, especially polynomial sized kernels are of interest for practical algorithms. In some sense kernelization is a formalized way of preprocessing with guarantees. No constructive FPT algorithm for vertex ranking is known yet. We observe that vertex ranking and vertex ranking with capacity do not have a kernel of size polynomial in the number of ranks, unless all coNP-complete problems have distillation algorithms [5].

Observation. Vertex ranking and vertex ranking with capacity do not have a polynomial sized kernel, unless all coNP-complete problems have distillation algorithms.

Proof. From [5, Lemma 7] we note that the complement of vertex ranking is compositional. In combination with the fact that a problem has a polynomial sized kernel if and only if its complement has a polynomial sized kernel, we conclude that vertex ranking has no polynomial sized kernel, unless all coNP-complete problems have distillation algorithms. Vertex ranking with capacity is a generalization of vertex ranking, so this result extends to vertex ranking with capacity. □

Although the existence of distillation algorithms for all coNP-complete problems is not (yet) related to any more well known complexity conjecture like P=NP, it gives some insight in the difficulty of the problem. Finding a polynomial sized kernel for vertex ranking now implies complexity theoretical consequences, and not only the existence of a more practical algorithm.

4 Exact Ranking of Graphs

In this section we give, to our knowledge, the first exact algorithm for vertex ranking. Our algorithm runs in $O(2^n 2^n)$ time and and requires $O(n2^n)$ space. We use this algorithm to construct an $O(n^2 2.5874^n)$ time and $O(n2^n)$ space algorithm to solve vertex ranking with capacity exactly. Also, an $O^*(9^n)$ time algorithm with polynomial space is presented.

We start with giving a recursive formula for the vertex ranking number for a given graph G.

Theorem 1. *Let $G = (V, E)$ be an undirected connected graph:*

$$\chi_r(G) = \begin{cases} 1 & \text{if } |G| = 1 \\ \min_{s \in V} \max_{S \in P(V,s)} \chi_r(G[S]) + 1 & \text{otherwise} \end{cases} \quad (1)$$

Proof. In every connected graph G and for every ranking φ of G, there is exactly *one* vertex with the highest rank. Since we try every possible vertex to have the highest rank in every connected subgraph, we try the optimal choice. Connected components are independent because there are no paths between vertices in different connected components. If a graph has several connected components, we can safely recurse on each component. □

Next, we turn the formula given in Theorem 1 into an algorithm. This algorithm serves as a basis for the algorithm for vertex ranking with capacity.

Theorem 2. *There is an $O(n^2 2^n)$ time and $O(n2^n)$ space algorithm for computing the optimal vertex ranking of a graph $G = (V, E)$ with n vertices.*

Proof. We use dynamic programming to solve the equation in Theorem 1. For every subset $S \subseteq V$ we store an entry with $\chi_r(S)$ as value in a table, that is computed from the bottom-up. For every subgraph $S \subseteq V$, $\chi_r(S)$ can be calculated using only the vertex ranking number of connected subgraphs $S' \subset S$. If for all subsets that are smaller than S the vertex ranking number is stored in the table, we can compute $\chi_r(S)$ in $O(n^2)$ time. For every vertex $s \in S$ we find all connected components $P(V, s)$. This clearly takes $O(n^2)$ time for all $s \in S$. Looking up an entry in our table can be done in $O(n)$ time. For all vertices $t \in V$ we can make an entry in the table $\chi_r(t) = 1$. There are at most 2^n connected subsets, and the algorithm will therefore take $O(n^2 2^n)$ time. The table has at most 2^n entries, and every entry takes at most $O(n)$ space, so the algorithm uses $O(n2^n)$ space. □

Unfortunately, although vertex ranking with capacity is similar to vertex ranking, vertex ranking with capacity has less desirable properties than vertex ranking has. Vertex ranking with capacity also has the property that at most one vertex has the highest rank in each connected subgraph. But in contrast to vertex ranking, we cannot recurse on connected components. Separate connected components still influence each other, since only a certain amount of vertices can be assigned the same rank.

For every subgraph there is one vertex of the highest rank in each connected component, and at most c vertices of any rank. Therefore, we can formulate the vertex ranking number with capacity as follows in Theorem 3. In Theorem 3 $\mathcal{I}(G)$ is the set containing all component independent sets of G, i.e. all sets of vertices such that there is at most one vertex of each connected component of G in this set.

Theorem 3. *Let $G = (V, E)$ be an undirected graph:*

$$\chi_r^c(G) = \begin{cases} 1 & \text{if } |V| = 1 \\ 1 + \min_{(|I| \leq c) \in \mathcal{I}(G)} \chi_r^c((G[V - I]) & \text{otherwise} \end{cases} \tag{2}$$

Proof. In every connected graph there is *one* vertex with the highest rank. Since we try every possible vertex as highest rank in every connected subgraph, we try the optimal one. Unlike Vertex Ranking, connected components are not independent. We cannot recurse on connected components.

We try all component independent sets of at most cardinality c in every subgraph. No vertices in the same connected component (induced by removing all higher ranking vertices) are assigned the same rank, and at most c vertices are assigned the same rank. □

Theorem 4. *There is an algorithm for a graph $G = (V, E)$ to calculate $\chi_r^c(G)$ in $O(n^2 2.5874^n)$ time and $O(n2^n)$ space.*

Proof. We use the same dynamic programming approach as in Theorem 1. Note that in $\mathcal{I}(G)$ we can ignore components of size one or two. If for any $I \in \mathcal{I}(G)$, $|I| < c$ then we can deterministically pick vertices from components of size two or one if there are no components of size two in G. Let $\mathcal{C}$ be all connected components in G larger than two.

We can bound $\mathcal{I}(V)$ with:

$$\mathcal{I}(V) \leq \binom{|\mathcal{C}|}{c} \prod_{C_i \in \mathcal{C}} |C_i|. \tag{3}$$

There are some extra bounds we will use later, $|\mathcal{C}| \leq \frac{|V|}{3}$ and $\sum_{C_i \in \mathcal{C}} |C_i| \leq |V|$. This allows us to bound the product of all component sizes:

$$\prod_{C_i \in \mathcal{C}} |C_i| \leq 3^{|V|/3}. \tag{4}$$

We now bound $\mathcal{I}(V)$:

$$\mathcal{I}(V) \leq \binom{|V|/3}{c} 3^{|V|/3} \leq \sum_{c=1}^{|V|/3} \binom{|V|/3}{c} 3^c = 4^{|V|/3}, \tag{5}$$

and

$$T(n) \leq \sum_{i=3}^{n} \binom{n}{i} 4^{i/3} = (\sqrt[3]{4} + 1)^n \leq 2.5875^n. \tag{6}$$

Deterministically picking vertices from components of size one and two takes at most $O(n^2)$ time. For each set of c vertices we pick, it takes $O(n^2)$ time to find the new connected components. From this follows that our algorithm runs in $O(n^2 2.5875^n)$ time. There are at most 2^n subgraphs, and every subgraph takes at most n space. □

The previous algorithms used exponential time and space. Because space is physically restricted by the machine the computation runs on but time is not, we present an exponential time but polynomial space algorithm. We show that vertex ranking and vertex ranking with capacity can both be solved exactly with polynomial space and $O^*(9^n)$ time. Although the base of the exponent is quite high, this is vastly better than a naive $O(n^n)$ time branch algorithm by trying all different ranks for each vertex.

Theorem 5. *For a given graph $G = (V, E)$ there is an algorithm that calculates $\chi_r(G)$ or $\chi_r^c(G)$ in $O^*(9^n)$ time and polynomial space.*

Proof. A ranking of a graph G with k ranks can also be described as a sequence of independent sets $I_1 ... I_k$, where I_j is the set with all vertices of rank j for all

$j \leq k$. For a graph G there are 3^n ways to split up the graph in three parts I_m, S_1 and S_2 such that $S_1 = \bigcup_{i<k} I_i$, $S_1 = \bigcup_{j>k} I_j$, $|S_1| < \frac{n}{2}$, $|S_2| < \frac{n}{2}$ and $I_,$ is an independent set in $G\{I_m \cup S_2\}$.

Vertices in S_1 will be ranked with ranks strictly smaller than any vertex in I_m and S_2. All vertices in S_2 will be ranked with strictly higher ranks than any vertex in I_m. All vertices in I_k will be ranked with the same rank, since I_m is an independent set in $G\{I_m \cup S_2\}$ there are no paths between vertices in I_m through vertices of lower rank. Since we recurse on $G\{S_2\}$ we know that if there is an path from two vertices in S_2 through smaller ranks in I_m or S_1, there is an edge in $G\{S_2\}$.

For a graph $G = (V, E)$ and I_m an independent set in $G\{I_m \cup S_2\}$ the following equation holds:

$$\chi_r(G) = \min_{(S_1, I_k, S_2) = V} \chi_r(G[S_1]) + \chi_r(G\{S_2\}) + 1. \tag{7}$$

To compute $\chi_r(G)$ for a graph G our algorithm works as follows, enumerate all different partitions of V in set S_1, I_m and S_2 such that I_m is an independent set in $G\{I_m \cup S_2\}$. We can compute in polynomial time in n if I_m is an independent set in $G\{I_m \cup S_2\}$ by checking if no vertex in I_m has a neighbor also from I_m in $G\{I_m \cup S_2\}$. Recurse on $G[S_1]$ and $G\{S_2\}$.

Let $T(n)$ denote the time needed to calculate $\chi_r(G)$ for a graph on n vertices and let $p(n)$ be the polynomial in n needed at each step. The recursion depth of the algorithm is at most $\lceil \log n \rceil$, because the number of vertices is at least halved every recursive call.

$$T(n) \leq 3^n \cdot 2 \cdot T\left(\frac{n}{2}\right) + 3^n \cdot p(n) \leq 2 \cdot \prod_{i=0}^{\log n+1} 3^{\frac{n}{2^i}} + \sum_{j=0}^{\log n+1} 3^{\frac{n}{2^j}} \cdot p\left(\frac{n}{2^j}\right) \tag{8}$$

$$2 \cdot \prod_{i=0}^{\log n+1} 3^{\frac{n}{2^i}} = 2 \cdot 3^{\sum_{i=0}^{\log n} \frac{n}{2^i}} \leq 2 \cdot 9^n, \sum_{j=0}^{\log n+1} 3^{\frac{n}{2^j}} \cdot p\left(\frac{n}{2^j}\right) \leq 2 \cdot 3^n \cdot p(n) \tag{9}$$

$$T(n) \leq 2 \cdot 9^n + 2 \cdot 3^n \cdot p(n) \tag{10}$$

The recursion depth of the algorithm is $O(\log n)$ and at most polynomial space is required for all graphs at any recursion depth. Therefore, the algorithm uses polynomial space. Our algorithm uses $O^*(9^n)$ time and polynomial space.

This algorithm can be easily extended to solve vertex ranking with capacity using the same running time and space. We just have to restrict the size of I_k, such that $|I_k| \leq c$, where c is the capacity. □

5 Approximation by Transformation

In this section we describe a transformation from a vertex ranking to a vertex ranking with capacity. The resulting vertex ranking with capacity of the transformation is at most $f(n)+1$ times the optimal capacity vertex ranking number if the input vertex ranking was a $f(n)$-approximation.

Lemma 1. *For any graph $G = (V, E)$ and an $f(n)$-approximate vertex ranking φ of G and any $c \in \mathbb{N}$, we give an algorithm that approximates $\chi_r^c(G)$ within a factor $f(n) + 1$.*

Proof. Consider any graph G and an $f(n)$-approximate ranking φ and the ranking ρ with capacity that we are constructing. We replace each rank r in φ by $\lceil a_r/c \rceil$ ranks in ρ, where a_r is the amount of vertices with rank r and c is the capacity.

The total number of ranks in ρ is equal to $\sum_{r\in\varphi} \lceil \frac{a_r}{c} \rceil \leq \sum_{r\in\varphi} \frac{a_r}{c} + 1 = \frac{n}{c} + |\varphi|$. In combination with $\frac{n}{c} \leq \chi_r^c$, $\chi_r(G) \leq \chi_r^c$ and $|\varphi| \leq f(n) \cdot \chi_r(G)$, it follows that $|\rho| \leq f(n) \cdot \chi_r(G) + \frac{n}{c} \leq (f(n) + 1) \cdot \chi_r^c$. □

Using this transformation there exists a 2-approximation for the capacity ranking number restricted to graphs for which a polynomial time algorithm is known, such as trees and interval graphs. Further, there is an $O(\log^2 n)$-approximation for general graphs by combining this transformation and the approximation algorithm by Bodlaender et al. [6].

6 Trees

It is interesting to see how vertex ranking with capacity works when restricted to trees. The analogues problem without capacity can be solved in linear time [24]. Simply transforming a ranking without capacity to one with capacity is not easy, as shown in Figure 1. This example shows that there might be a large difference in strategy to assign ranks to vertices between vertex ranking and vertex ranking with capacity.

First we prove that finding a ranking with capacity is easy if the graph consists of small connected components, secondly that every tree has a balanced vertex separator. This separator can easily be found in $O(n)$ time.

The following lemma is folklore.

Lemma 2. *Every tree $T = (V, E)$ has a balanced separator vertex x such that $T[V \setminus \{x\}]$ consists of connected components that are all smaller than $\lceil n/2 \rceil$.*

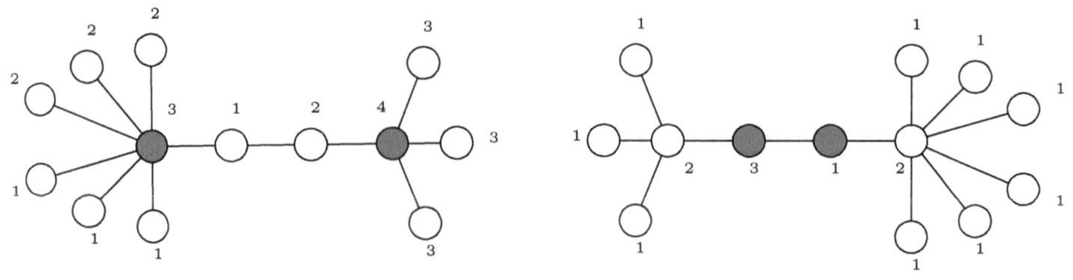

Fig. 1. An example where the optimal vertex ranking (right) differs significantly from the vertex ranking with capacity equal to four (left). In each case, one of the gray vertices has to be assigned the highest rank or the vertex ranking and vertex ranking with capacity are not minimum rankings.

Proof. Suppose such a vertex does not exist, but that y is the vertex of which the removal results in multiple components such that the largest is as small as possible. We denote the largest connected component in $T[V \setminus \{y\}]$ as C, and the rest as R. y has one adjacent vertex x in C. The removal of x would result in $C \setminus \{x\}$ and connected component $R \cup \{y\}$. $|C| > \lceil n/2 \rceil$ and $|R| < \lceil n/2 \rceil$ so $|R \cup \{y\}| \leq \lceil n/2 \rceil$ and if $C \setminus \{x\}$ consists of one connected component, it is one smaller than C. This is contradicting that the removal of y results in the smallest largest connected component. □

Lemma 3. *For every graph $G = (V, E)$ that consists of connected components that are all smaller than $\lceil n/c \rceil$, $\chi_r^c(G) = \lceil n/c \rceil$.*

Proof. Consider a graph $G = (V, E)$ that consists of connected components smaller than $\lceil n/c \rceil$. There must be at least c connected components for this to be true. Repeat the following procedure until the graph is empty: rank a vertex from each of the largest c connected components with the highest rank. Remove those vertices from the graph. The ranking is correct because every vertex in each connected component is assigned different ranks, and at most $\lceil n/c \rceil$ ranks are used. $\lceil n/c \rceil \leq \chi_r^c(G)$ and we have a ranking using $\lceil n/c \rceil$ ranks, so we can conclude that $\chi_r^c(G) = \lceil n/c \rceil$. □

Before we give an approximation algorithm and an algorithm for vertex ranking with capacity for any capacity, we show that $\chi_r^2(T)$ is easy to find and is just dependent on the number of vertices in T.

Lemma 4. *Given a connected tree $T = (V, E)$ on n vertices, then $\chi_r^2(T) = \lceil \frac{n-1}{2} \rceil + 1$.*

Proof. For any tree $T = (V, E)$ take the balanced separator vertex x, and assign it the highest rank. Since every connected component after the removal of x is smaller than $\lceil \frac{n}{2} \rceil$ we apply Lemma 3. $\lceil \frac{n-1}{2} \rceil + 1 \leq \chi_r^c(G)$ for connected graphs, and we have found a ranking using $\lceil \frac{n-1}{2} \rceil + 1$ ranks. There is only one vertex with the highest rank, and the remaining $n - 1$ vertices require at least $\lceil \frac{n-1}{c} \rceil$ different ranks, so $\chi_r^2(T) \geq \lceil \frac{n}{c} \rceil + 1$. We conclude that $\chi_r^2(G) = \lceil \frac{n-1}{2} \rceil + 1$ for every connected tree $T = (V, E)$. □

For capacities at least three it is not as easy as the case with capacity equal to two. However, we can also use the balanced vertex separators to find approximations.

Theorem 6. *For vertex ranking with capacity restricted to trees there is an $\log c$-additive approximation algorithm that runs in $O(n \log c)$ time.*

Proof. Consider a tree $G = (V, E)$ and we want to find a vertex ranking with c-capacity. We now recursively find balanced vertex separators until all connected components are smaller than $\lceil n/c \rceil$. This takes at most $\log c$ steps of taking the balanced vertex separator in each connected component. In each step no more than c balanced vertex separators are removed, and at step i rank the vertices removed at that step with $\lceil n/c \rceil + \log c - i$. In the situation that all connected components are smaller than $\lceil \frac{n}{c} \rceil$ we can apply Lemma 3. The connected components can be ranked with $\lceil \frac{n}{c} \rceil$ ranks. The balanced vertex separators are ranked with $\log c$ ranks. $\lceil n/c \rceil \leq \chi_r^r(G) < \lceil n/c \rceil + \log c$.

Finding this approximation can be implemented in $O(n \log c)$ time. Finding balanced vertex separators in each connected component costs at most $O(n)$ time at each step, and there are at most $\log c$ steps. □

Now we extend our approximation algorithm for trees to graphs of bounded treewidth. We assume that we are given a tree decomposition. For methods to find tree decompositions we refer to the overviews on treewidth by Hans Bodlaender [2,3].

Theorem 7. *Given a graph G and tree decomposition (X, T) of G with $w(X, T) \leq k$, there is an $((k+1) \cdot (1 + \frac{c \log c}{n}))$-approximation algorithm than runs in $O(n^2)$ time.*

Proof. Given a graph $G = (V, E)$ and a tree decomposition (X, T) with $w(X, T) \leq k$, we can use Theorem 6 to find a ranking φ of T such that $|\varphi| \leq \log c + \lceil \frac{n}{c} \rceil$. Every node $i \in T$ corresponds to a bag $X_i = \{x_1, ..., x_l\} \in X$. Let $o(X_i, v)$ be the index of v in bag X_i. The size of every bag X_i is at most $k+1$. Now we construct ranking γ for G. Basically we expand every ranking in T to $k+1$ ranks in γ. The rank of a vertex $v \in V$ is $\gamma(v) = \max_{X_i \ni v}(k+1)(\varphi(i)-1)+o(v)$. Ranking γ is correct because all vertices in every bag have different ranks and for all two vertices of the same rank, they are separated by a bag of higher rank in which all vertices have higher rank.

We use at most $k+1$ ranks per bag, so we used at most $k + 1 \cdot (\log c + \lceil \frac{n}{c} \rceil)$ ranks. We can now prove our approximation ratio, we know that $\lceil \frac{n}{c} \rceil \leq \chi_r^c(G)$, therefore $\lceil \frac{n}{c} \rceil \leq \chi_r^c(G) \leq \lceil \frac{n}{c} \rceil \cdot ((k+1) \cdot (1 + \frac{c \log c}{n}))$.

Obtaining φ from the tree decomposition takes at most $O(n \log c)$ time. For every vertex v we need to look at most $O(n)$ bags to determine $\gamma(v)$ therefore constructing γ from φ takes at most $O(n^2)$. □

Observe that when c is bounded by a constant our algorithm is an $O(k)$-approximation when n is sufficiently large.

7 Conclusions

We presented a new generalization of vertex ranking, a natural and practical generalization. Aside from introducing vertex ranking with capacity, we gave the first exact algorithm for vertex ranking of general graphs. For small graphs these algorithms seem more practical than even the $O(n^{40})$ time algorithm for graphs of bounded treewidth 3. The transformation from vertex ranking to vertex ranking with capacity provides a way to use the extensive work on vertex ranking. For trees we gave a $\log c$ additive approximation algorithm, and generalized this to an approximation algorithm for graphs of bounded treewidth.

Vertex ranking with capacity is fixed parameter tractable with the the capacity and amount of ranks as parameters, since $n \leq ck$, where c is the capacity and k the amount of ranks. Perhaps it is more useful to ask if the following variation is fixed parameter tractable. Given a graph $G = (V, E)$ and integer k, can G be ranked with $\lceil \frac{n}{c} \rceil + k$ ranks such that any rank is assigned to at most c vertices? Is vertex ranking with capacity NP-complete when the capacity is bounded by a constant? Is vertex ranking with capacity NP-complete when restricted to trees?

We gave a $O^*(2^n)$ time algorithm for vertex ranking of general graphs, is there a $O^*(c^n)$ time algorithm where $1 < c < 2$? Another interesting question is if there is a faster exact algorithm than $O^*(9^n)$ time with polynomial space. Lastly, we will mention the problem of finding an efficient FPT algorithm for vertex ranking. Basing this algorithm on current treewidth algorithms for vertex ranking or invoking Courcelle's theorem [7] seem to yield algorithms that have prohibitively large constants.

Recently, Makino et al. [23] introduced minimum ranking spanning trees. Minimum ranking spanning trees are spanning trees of which the edge or vertex ranking is minimal over all spanning trees of a graph. The result on vertex ranking with 2-capacity on trees implies that if we want to find a minimum vertex ranking spanning tree with 2-capacity, any spanning tree is such a tree. This could be useful for practical applications where the parallel capacity is limited to two. Is this an exception, or are there more vertex ranking problems that become 'easy' with a capacity constraint?

Acknowledgments. I thank Hans Bodlaender and Jesper Nederlof for the numerous discussions on the topic of vertex ranking. In particular, I am grateful to André Berger for proof reading and many suggestions for the presentation of this paper. Suggestions and comments of the reviewers greatly improved the quality of this paper. The original idea of vertex ranking with capacity is due to Hans Bodlaender.

References

1. Aspvall, B., Heggernes, P.: Finding Minimum Height Elimination Trees for Interval Graphs in Polynomial Time. BIT 34, 484–509 (1994)
2. Bodlaender, H.L.: A Tourist Quide through Treewidth. Acta Cybernetica 11, 1–23 (1993)
3. Bodlaender, H.L.: Discovering Treewidth. In: Vojtáš, P., Bieliková, M., Charron-Bost, B., Sýkora, O. (eds.) SOFSEM 2005. LNCS, vol. 3381, pp. 1–16. Springer, Heidelberg (2005)
4. Bodlaender, H.L., Deogun, J.S., Jansen, K., Kloks, T., Kratsch, D., Müller, H., Tuza, Z.: Rankings of Graphs. SIAM Journal on Discrete Mathematics 11, 168–181 (1998)
5. Bodlaender, H.L., Downey, R.G., Fellows, M.R., Hermelin, D.: On problems without polynomial kernels (Extended abstract). In: Aceto, L., Damgård, I., Goldberg, L.A., Halldórsson, M.M., Ingólfsdóttir, A., Walukiewicz, I. (eds.) ICALP 2008, Part I. LNCS, vol. 5125, pp. 563–574. Springer, Heidelberg (2008)

6. Bodlaender, H.L., Gilbert, J.R., Hafsteinsson, H., Kloks, T.: Approximating Treewidth, Pathwidth, Frontsize, and Minimum Elimination Tree Height. Journal of Algorithms 18, 238–255 (1995)
7. Courcelle, B.: Graph Rewriting: An Algebraic and Logic Approach. In: van Leeuwen, J. (ed.) Handbook of Theoretical Computer Science, pp. 194–242. Elsevier, Amsterdam (1990)
8. Deogun, J.S., Kloks, T., Kratsch, D., Müller, H.: On Vertex Ranking for Permutations and Other Graphs. Discrete Applied Mathematics 98, 39–63 (1993)
9. Deogun, J.S., Kloks, T., Kratsch, D., Müller, H.: On the Vertex Ranking Problem for Trapezoid, Circular-Arc and Other Graphs. Discrete Applied Mathematics 98, 39–63 (1999)
10. Dereniowski, D.: Edge Ranking and Searching in Partial Orders. Discrete Applied Mathematics 156(13), 2493–2500 (2008)
11. Dereniowski, D., Kubale, M.: Efficient Parallel Query Processing by Graph Ranking. Fundamenta Informaticae 69(3), 273–285 (2006)
12. Dereniowski, D., Nadolski, A.: Vertex Rankings of Chordal Graphs and Weighted Trees. Information Processing Letters 98, 96–100 (2006)
13. Friedman, H., Robertson, N., Seymour, P.D.: The Metamathematics of the Graph Minor Theorem. Contemporary Mathematics 65, 229–261 (1987)
14. Hsieh, S.: On Vertex Ranking of a Starlike Graph. Information Processing Letters 82(5), 131–135 (2002)
15. Hung, R.-W.: Optimal Vertex Ranking of Block Graphs. Information and Computation 206(11), 1288–1302 (2008)
16. Iyer, A.V., Ratliff, H.D., Vijayan, G.: Optimal Node Ranking of Trees. Information Processing Letters 28(12), 225–229 (1988)
17. Iyer, A.V., Ratliff, H.D., Vijayan, G.: Parallel Assembly of Modular Products an Analysis. Information Processing Letters 28(5), 225–229 (1988)
18. Kashem, M.A., Zhou, X., Nishizeki, T.: Algorithms for Generalized Vertex-Rankings of Partial k-Trees. Theoretical Computer Science 240, 407–427 (2000)
19. Katchalski, M., McCuaig, W., Seager, S.: Ordered Colourings. Discrete Mathematics 142(1-3), 141–154 (1995)
20. Kloks, T., Müller, H., Wong, C.K.: Vertex Ranking of Asteroid Triple-Free Graphs. Information Processing Letters 68, 201–206 (1998)
21. Liu, J.W.H.: The Role of Elimination Trees in Sparse Factorization. SIAM Journal on Matrix Analysis and Applications 11(1), 134–172 (1990)
22. Llewellyn, D.C., Tovey, C., Trick, M.: Local Optimization on Graphs. Discrete Appl. Math. 23(2), 157–178 (1989)
23. Makino, K., Uno, Y., Ibaraki, T.: Minimum Edge Ranking Spanning Trees. In: Kutyłowski, M., Wierzbicki, T., Pacholski, L. (eds.) MFCS 1999. LNCS, vol. 1672, pp. 398–409. Springer, Heidelberg (1999)
24. Schäffer, A.A.: Optimal Node Ranking of Trees in Linear Time. Information Processing Letters 33(2), 91–96 (1989)
25. de la Torre, P., Greenlaw, R., Schäffer, A.A.: Optimal Edge Ranking of Trees in Polynomial Time. Algorithmica 13, 592–618 (1995)
26. Zhou, X., Nagai, N., Nishizeki, T.: Generalized Vertex-Rankings of Trees. Information Processing Letters 56(6), 321–328 (1995)

Author Index

MIX
Papier aus verantwortungsvollen Quellen
Paper from responsible sources
FSC® C105338

If you have any concerns about our products,
you can contact us on
ProductSafety@springernature.com

In case Publisher is established outside the EU,
the EU authorized representative is:
Springer Nature Customer Service Center GmbH
Europaplatz 3, 69115 Heidelberg, Germany

Printed by Libri Plureos GmbH
in Hamburg, Germany